JAPANESE-ENGLISH DICTIONARY OF ACTIVE USAGE
Words and Their Nuances

和  英
表現辞典

松井恵美/M・リン・レックライン[共著]

TAISHUKAN

まえがき

この辞典の出版を思い立ったのは1979年，20年以上前であった。私の前著『英作文における日本人的誤り』（大修館書店）の最後に付録のように「誤りやすい語彙解説」を付けたところ，大修館書店の鵜沢敏明氏から，この語彙をもう少し増やしてちょっとした本を書かないかとのお話があった。「やります」と即座に答えたものの，これは思いのほかの大仕事になり，私の力不足で10年引きずり，原稿はなんとかできたが，その頃から世の中の出版事情が厳しくなり，ついに今日に至った。それでもこの仕事が日の目を見ることになったのは本当に有り難く，感無量である。

この仕事に取りかかった頃は，中高生向けの学習用の和英辞典は例文が堅く不自然であり，何とかもっと生きた英語を満載した辞典を作りたいと張り切ったものだった。しかし当時はどこの出版社も同じようなことを考え，辞典出版の準備を始めていたようだった。1980年代に入ると各出版社は競って新しい辞典を世に問い，和英辞典はぐんとレベルアップした。私が米国人の友人 Roecklein さんと２人だけで教員としての公務の合間に進める仕事なので，結果的には思わぬ時間を取られた。

私達が重点を置いたのは，まず第一に日本人がなかなか英語で言えない表現，したがって誤りを犯しやすい表現である。取り上げた項目は1312と多くはないが，日常的な表現に役立つ語句を精選している。第二に，類義語のニュアンスの違いを解説することに力を入れた。英語の類義語の意味の違いはネイティブ・スピーカーの Roecklein さんの直感に頼り，なおかつ*Collins COBUILD English Language Dictionary, The American Heritage Dictionary of the English Language, The Random House Dictionary of the English Language, Cambridge International Dictionary of English* 等で確かめて記述した。

和英辞典の編纂でまず行うべきことは，日本語の語義分類である。言葉は最初は生活に密着した物の呼称に始まり，徐々に比喩的・観念的なものを生み，その後にはさらに抽象的な意味が派生する。私なりにこのプロセスを念頭に置いて，実用的な表現を分類したつもりである。その過程で日本語についても新しい発見が種々に得られたが，スペースの関係上そこまで書くことはできなかった。日本語例文，およびその英訳文をどちらも自然な文にすることに努め，日本語では主語を言わないのが自然と思うときは，主語は（　）に入れた。訳文は意味が日英同じになるようにしたのであって，必ずしも直訳ではない。この対比は，日本語を勉強している英語圏の学習者にも役立つかと思う。

この仕事を始めて約20年の間，私の周囲におられた英米・カナダの先生方にはインフォーマントとしてお世話になった。共著者の Roecklein さんが米国人なので，スペリングも英語例文も米国英語が中心になっているが，英国の語彙語法も入れたいと思い，岐阜市立女子短期大学元講師の英国人 Eurwen Ann Takeda さんには全原稿に目を通していただき，かつご意見もいただいた。明徳女子短期大学の George Sawa 氏，岐阜聖徳学園大学の同僚だった Craig Volker, Jean Van Troyer, Curt Rulon の各先生にも英語の疑問点が出るたびに教えていただいた。また，柴田達子さんには英語のタイピングでお世話になり，野下理子さんには可愛い挿絵をいただいた。以上の方々に心から御礼申し上げる。

2003年 4 月

松井恵美

One of the wonders of human language is its creative quality. Except for a few greetings and set expressions for particular situations such as *Please pass the cucumbers* at the dinner table, almost everything people speak or write is new, created, original. One of the greatest 20th century researchers of language, the linguist Noam Chomsky, created a revolution in the study of language based on this insight. However, this creative quality of human language also makes learning a language difficult, even for babies, since there are always so many words, so many ways to say something, so many ways to fail at communicating your message.

The Japanese-English Dictionary of Active Usage is a **performance dictionary**. Each of its features is designed to help you increase and manage your personal vocabulary bank in order to make your speaking and writing performance in English better.

The central feature of this dictionary is a deep treatment of **so-called synonyms**. When you look up a word, in the ordinary dictionary, you often find a long list of words after it. The listed words look as if they all mean the same thing. But they do not; each word has a unique meaning and feeling. This dictionary gives you the **precise** meaning and feeling of each word in such a list, so that you can create more exact and more natual English communication.

Although words are not true synonyms of each other, they gather into word groups called **semantic fields**. All the words in one field are closely related to each other, like a family. Each language has many semantic fields. However, a particular word in one language will be included in a different semantic field than the same word in another language. In other words, although the Japanese word and English word for a particular thing may seem to have the same meaning, the words are often placed in different semantic fields and so they have different connections or relationships with other words, ideas and feelings. When you become aware of this, you will never again say ×*My school will open a speech contest* when you mean that your school will organize and manage the contest, because you will understand that in English, 'open' belongs in the same semantic field as 'begin' and 'start' and 'initiate,' not the field for 'plan and carry out,' 'hold' or 'organize'. Many notes in this dictionary help you develop a sense of English word connections by pointing out where English and Japanese place words in different semantic fields.

This dictionary also emphasizes **focus, tone and register**. Which is better, *They don't know what it is to be poor* or *They have never experienced poverty* or *They have no experience of poverty*? All three are grammatically correct; they all mean the same thing on the surface. But they are not the same. The best way to say or write something depends greatly on what is most important to you in the message (focus), what your feelings are about the message and the situation (tone), and when (occasion) and to whom you are speaking or writing (register). This dictionary will help you recognize and actively use these factors to create more exact, subtle communication.

The words and sentences chosen for this dictionary cover a very **wide variety of** topics and situations in truly natural language. Differences between **spoken and written language** are pointed out.

This dictionary contains **whole sentences**, not just individual words or phrases, that illustrate almost every important meaning and nuance. They are written in **up-to-date**, **straightforward language**. You will be understood by English users everywhere in the world.

Finally the appendices give you **quick access** to some basic material and save you time hunting in other books as you write.

This dictionary will most certainly improve your English expression by bringing you to greater mastery of English words and their many subtle nuances.

Many people helped to make this dictionary special. **Grateful thanks** in particular to John Williams and Michael Horne for enduring endless questions about British English and to Ingeborg Hopf for eagle-eyed proofreading and invaluable advice concerning the clarity of explanations to non-native English users.

April, 2003

M. Lynne Roecklein

この辞典の使い方

見出し語

私たち日本人が言いたくて英語にしにくい，また，間違いやすい1312語を取り上げ，五十音順に配列した。

矢印マーク

見出し語の後にある矢印マーク(→)は「〜を見よ」の意。

「いかに → どう，どんな」は，「どう」と「どんな」の項を見よ，の意。

語義

見出し語の語義は，原則としていちばん元になる意味をまず挙げ，それから派生した意味，さらに転じた観念的な意味の順に分類し，示した。さらにその下位区分は【　】で示した。

［例］はる(張る)

1.　たるみをなくす

【ロープ】

【テント・ネット】

2.　一面に覆う

【氷】

【根】

【水】

3.　その他

【腹】

【肩】

【平手で打つ】

枠囲み（冠詞の省略）

「医療」「音楽」「動物」などの見出し語では語彙を集めて掲げるのが目的であるから語彙のみを挙げ，------の枠で囲んで示した。この場合，スペースの節約のため，冠詞を省略し，とくに必要な場合に限り説明を加えた。

普通の見出し語の項目でも，《関連語》《類義語》は枠囲みにして名詞を列挙しているが，この場合も冠詞を省略した。

語義の示し方と記号

[ ]　直前の語句と交換できる語句を示す。[ ]で示す互換可能な語句の範囲が分かりにくい場合は，その開始部分に└ 印をつけて示した。

You can do as you please [like].

(You can do as you please. または You can do as you like. の意)

We sat └next to each other [side by side].

(We sat next to each other. または We sat side by side. の意)

(　)　1.　省略可能であることを示す。

He suggested that we (should) go to see her.

(He suggested that we go to see her. または He suggested that we should go to see her. の意)

2.　注記の中の英文に対する和訳，和文に対する英訳

3.　付加的説明

《 》　動詞の目的語が必要な場合，《a thing》《a person》などとして表示。

《米》　米国語法　　《英》　英国語法

米国式と英国式のつづりがあるときは，米国式を優先した。

〔 〕　ある表現が形式ばったものか日常語か，くだけた口語かといった区別を表すスピーチレベルは，〔 〕に入れて示した。

×　誤文であることを示す。

△　文法的には正しくても，慣用からみて避けたほうがよい文を示す。

○　誤文の訂正文であることを示す。

/　短い例文を列挙する場合，および[ ]内で異なる意味の語を並列する場合の区切り。

/ /　発音記号を示す。

スピーチレベルおよび含意

casual	格式ばらない，気楽な
cliche	言い古された表現
colloq.	口語の
common	ごく普通に使われる
conversational	会話体の
derogatory	けなし言葉の
euphemism	婉曲表現
exclamation	驚嘆，詠嘆の叫び

factive	事実を述べる形の(non-factiveと対比される)
familiar	親しい，くだけた表現の
fictional	虚構の，フィクションの
figurative	比喩的，観念的(physicalと対比される)
formal	格式ばった，堅い表現の(informalと対比される)
general	一般的な
informal	格式ばらない，くだけた表現の
intensive	強意の
ironical	反語的，皮肉の
literary	文章語の
negative	否定的な，よくない意味の
non-factive	抽象的，観念的表現の(事実を述べる形，factive ではないことを示す)
old-fashioned	古風な，古くさい
personal	個人的な
physical	実際に見たりさわったりできる(figurativeと対比される)
poetic	詩語の
polite	ていねいな，礼儀正しい表現の
praise	ほめ言葉
rare	あまり使われない
slang	俗語，スラング
slogan	スローガン
spoken	話し言葉の
standard	標準的な
stiff	堅くて不自然な
verbal	言葉の，言葉による
written	書き言葉の

以上に次のような度合(頻度)を表す語を組み合わせて表示することもある。

英語表示

very　たいへん，more　もっと，most　もっとも，terribly　ひどく
a bit　少し，somewhat　いくらか，rather　やや，slightly　少々
often　しばしば，occasionally　時たま

日本語表示

強(意味が強い)，弱(意味が弱い)

修辞的(レトリック，言葉を巧みに使い美しく表現するやり方の)

比喩的(たとえを使う表現の)

転義(言葉のもとの意味から派生的に別の意味に転じた)

あ

ああ

ah; oh

〈注〉 多くの場合 ah と oh は同じように使うが，oh の方が一般的で，どんな場合にも使われる。ah は主として快いときのみ。

1．喜び・驚きなどの種々の感情

ああ，うれしい。

Oh, I'm so glad.

Great! / Wonderful! / How nice!

ああ，よかった。（ほっとしたとき）

Thank God!

ああ，驚いた[驚くじゃないか]。

Oh [Ah], what a start you gave me!

Oh, you gave me a shock [surprise].

ああ，暑い。（暑いじゃないか）

Oh, it's hot, isn't it?

Isn't it hot?

Oh, it's so hot!

ああ，困った。（どうしよう）

Oh, no! / Oh my goodness! / Oh, dear! / How awful [terrible]! / Oh, what shall I do?

〈注〉 この場合は ah は使わない。

ああーっ。（すべって転んだり，びっくりしたときの叫び声）

Aaaa.

2．認知

ああ，ここ[そこ]にある。（情報が主となる）

Oh [Ah], here [there] it is.

ああ，あった。（満足がある）

(Oh) (I've) got it.

ああ，これ[ここ]だ。

(Ah) Here we go.

Here you are.

ああ，そのとおり。

That's it! / Right! / Of course.

ああ，わかった。（よくわかった）

Oh [Ah], I see.

ああ（半わかり，上の空）

Ah, Oh

〈注〉 Aha は次のような場合に使われる。

(1) 感情的な強い驚きを表す。

(2) 何かすでに話題になっていることについて理解したことを表す。

(3) 得意・納得を表す。

ああ，やっぱり(私の思ったとおり)。

Aha, I'm right.

あいさつ（挨拶）

名 **greeting(s)**　動 **greet; salute**

1．一般

毎朝全職員で挨拶をしてから仕事に取りかかる。

We greet [say hello to] everyone every morning and then get down to work.

ちょっとご挨拶に[顔を見に]寄った。

I dropped in just to say hello.

あの人は別れの挨拶もせずに[さよならも言わずに]行ってしまった。

She left without even saying good-bye.

彼は手を振って私に挨拶した。

He waved his hand in greeting.

【公式な大会などでの】 an address

開会の辞　an opening address

2．儀礼的挨拶

クリスマスおめでとう。よいお年をお迎えください。

I wish you a Merry Christmas and a Happy New Year!

Merry Christmas and Happy New Year!

Season's Greetings!

【お祝い】

大学合格おめでとうございます。

Congratulations on
{ passing the entrance exam.
{ being accepted into university.

ご卒業[ご結婚]おめでとうございます。

Congratulations on your graduation [wedding].

ご著書の出版おめでとうございます。

Congratulations on your book (which was just published).

新居完成おめでとうございます。

Congratulations on your new house.

赤ちゃんのお誕生おめでとうございます。

Congratulations on the birth of your baby.

【お悔やみ】

[口頭で]

お父様がお亡くなりになりましたそうでお悔やみ申し上げます。

I'm very sorry about your father's death.

I was sorry to hear about your father's death.

[手紙で]

父上の御逝去をお悔やみ申し上げます。

I'm very [truly] sorry about your father's death.

御尊父の御逝去をお悔やみ申し上げます。

Please accept my sincere regrets on the death of your father. 〔*formal*〕

You have my deepest regrets on the death of your father. 〔*formal*〕

3．日常的な挨拶

【人に会ったとき】

Good morning. (朝の挨拶)

Good afternoon. (午後の挨拶)

Good evening. (夕方の挨拶)

Hello. / Hullo. / Hi. 〔*informal*〕 (やあ)

【別れるとき】

Good-bye. / Bye.(親しい間で) / See you. / So long. / Bye-bye. (小児語)

【寝るとき】

Good night. / Sleep well. / Sweet dreams.

よくお眠り，虫に刺されないように。(子供に)

Night, night, sleep tight. Mind the bugs don't bite [Don't let the bedbugs bite].

【出かけるとき】

I'm going now; bye [so long].

〈注〉「行ってまいります」のような決まった言い方はないが，このように言うこともできる。その時の都合により，帰宅の予定などをつけ加えることもある。以下「行ってらっしゃい」「ただいま」についても同様に決まった言い方はない。

【送り出すとき】

行ってらっしゃい。今晩またね。

Bye. See you tonight [when you get back].

いい一日を。

Have a good [nice] day.

気をつけて。

Bye. Return safely.

【遠足などに行くとき】

楽しんでらっしゃい。

Bye. Have a great time.

あとでまたね。

See you when you get back.

【長い旅行に際して】

旅行を楽しんでらっしゃい。

Enjoy your trip!

【家に戻って】

帰ったよ。

Hello; I'm home.

うちはやっぱりいいね。

It's good to be home.

【帰った人を迎えて】

今日はどうだった。

Hello. How was your day?

Hello. Had a good day, (Nora)?

まぁよかったよ[無事だったよ]。

Yes, pretty good. / OK.

あまりよくなかったよ。

No, not so good.

【ひさしぶりに会って】

どうしていたの？

How have you been?

会えてうれしいよ。

It's nice to see you again.

ずいぶん会わなかったね。

It's been a long time.

Long time no see. 〔*slang*〕

I haven't seen you for ages.

【辞去するとき】

そろそろおいとましなければなりません。

I must be / I think [guess] I should be {off / leaving} now.

［別れ際に］

Good-bye. / Bye. / See you.

こんどは月曜にまたね。

See you next Monday.

【送るとき】

よく来てくださいました。また来てください。

Good-bye. Thanks for coming.

{Please come again. / Let's get together again soon.}

【紹介するとき】

〔*formal*〕スミス氏とジョーンズ氏を紹介

(Mr. Smith に)

Mr. Smith, this is Mr. Jones.

(Mr. Jones に)

Mr. Jones, this is Mr. Smith.

(Mr. Jones と Mr. Smith のあいさつ)

How do you do? It's nice to meet you.

〔*informal*〕メアリとスーザンを紹介

(Mary に) Mary, this is Susan.

(Mary と Susan のあいさつ)

Nice to meet you.

〈注〉 目上の人に先に話しかける。

【人を励ますとき】

(気軽に) がんばって!

Good luck.

〈注〉 日本人はすぐ挨拶として「がんばって」と言うが，欧米にはその習慣がないのでこれを言いすぎないように注意。

(就職や結婚する人に)うまくいきますように。

All the best.

【誘うとき】 Would you like to ...?

ドライブに行きませんか。

How about [What about] going for a drive [ride]?

Shall we [Let's] go for a drive?

【誘われたとき】

［受けるとき］

いいですねえ。

Thank you, I'd love to.

That's a good idea. / How nice!

OK. Sounds good to me. 〔*informal*〕

［断るとき］

残念だけど歯医者に行くんで。

I'm sorry, but I have to go to the dentist.

I'd love to, but I have to .... (How about going tomorrow instead?)

〈注〉 ただぶっきらぼうに断るのではなく，理由を言うか代案を提案することが多い。

【頼むとき】

お願いがあるんですが。

Can [May] I ask you a favor? ...

Will [Would] you do me a favor? ...

【頼まれたとき】

［承諾のとき］

ええ，いいですとも。

Yes, of course. / Certainly. / Sure. / OK.

［内容を確かめて］

ええ，何でしょうか。

Maybe, what is it?

ええ，事によりますけれど。

Maybe, it depends what it is.

【人に忠告，提案するとき】

…したらどうですか。

How about ...?

If I were you, I'd ....

Why don't you ...?

〈注〉 You had better .... は強すぎてなかば命令的になるので避ける方がよい。

【お礼を言うとき】

ありがとうございます。

Thank you. / Thanks. / Thank you very much. / Thanks a lot.

〈注〉 日本語ではお礼としても「すみませんでした」と言うが，英語でお礼を言うのに "I'm sorry." とは言わない。

【聞き返すとき】

［ていねいに］ Sorry? / Pardon?

［親しい人に］ What?

【お礼を言われたとき】

どういたしまして。

That's all right.
You're welcome.〔米〕/ Don't mention it.
Not at all. / Anytime. / Sure.〔*informal*〕
My pleasure.

【謝るとき】

本当にすみません。

Sorry.
I'm sorry.
I'm really [terribly, awfully] sorry.

【謝られたとき】

いいんです。

Don't mention it.
That's all right.
Never mind.（気にしないで）

【その他】

どうぞお先に。

After you.
Please go ahead.

〈注〉 冗談めかして Age before beauty. と言い，年上の人を先に通す。自分が美人ということになる。

【ほめられたとき】

〈注〉 服や持ち物はほめても顔や姿を無遠慮にほめたりしないこと。
何かの行為をほめられたら，Thank you, but … と大したことではないといった意味のことを言う。例えば It was easy. などと謙遜するのは，日本人と同じ心情である。

［親しい仲で］

「今日はきれいだね」「あら，ありがとう」。

"You look beautiful today." "Oh, do I? Thanks."

【食事での挨拶】

〈注〉 「いただきます」「ごちそうさま」に当る決り文句はない。皆が食べ始めたら食べ始めればよい。食事が終らないうちに席を立つときは Excuse me. ごちそうになって帰るときは，
Thank you for a wonderful { evening. / dinner.
これも決まり文句ではないので言い方は自由。

【避けたい言い方】

［May I …? Can I …? の返事］

△ Yes, you may.

〈注〉 きつく聞えるので Yes, you can. の方がよい。

あいじょう（愛情）

名 **(a) love; (an) affection**
愛情深い 形 **affectionate; warm-hearted; loving**

【愛情をもつ】 動 love; have [feel] affection (for)

シュバイツァーはアフリカ［アフリカ人］に大きな愛情をもっていた。

Schweitzer
{ loved Africa deeply.
had a great love for Africa.
felt a great affection for Africans.

〈注〉 上の3文の文意は同じである。love は一般的な語，強い愛情，男女間の恋愛感情も言う。affection は特定の人物や物に対する温かく穏やかな愛情，親の子に対する愛情などを表す。

【愛情を失う】 lose affection

彼は自分の子供たちに対してさえすっかり愛情を失っていた。

He has lost all affection for his own children.

彼の私に対する愛情はもう冷めてしまった。

His love for me is dead.

あいだ（間）

1. 空間

between; among

【二者の間】

私は父と母の間の席についた。

I took my seat between my parents.

その川は切り立った崖の間を流れ，やがて平野に出る。

The river flows for some time between high cliffs before coming to a plain.

【多数の間】

赤屋根の小さな家が白樺の間に散在している。

Some red-roofed cottages are scattered among white birches.

2．時間

in; for; during; between; while

〈注〉 in と for, during と while が混同されやすいので注意を要する。

I'll be back in a week's time.
（1週間のうちに帰る）
I'll have to work for a week.
（1週間ずっと働かねばならない）

上の2文が示すとおり，**in** とはある期間内に何事か（ここでは帰宅ということ）が起る場合に使われ，**for** は，ある期間内ある状態(ここでは労働)が持続する場合に使われる。

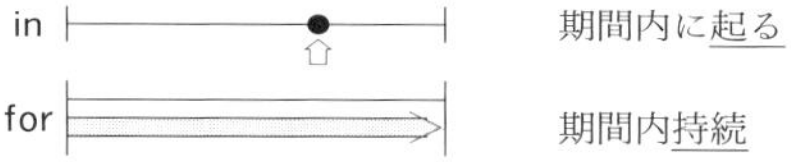

during は throughout the continuance of, in the course of の意で in, for どちらの意味にも通じる。ただし during は前置詞であるから，節を導くことはできず，反対に **while** は接続詞であるから節が続くべきで，名詞だけをとることはできない。

during my illness＝while I was ill（私の病気中）

【期間】 ［in, for, during, while の比較］

私たちは2週間にわたり英語の教育実習をやった。

We had two weeks' training in teaching English.

この2週間いろいろな体験をした。

In those two weeks I had various experiences.

この2週間たいへん忙しかった。

For those two weeks I was very busy.

この期間中は全体的に見て楽しかったと言える。

During the whole period I was happy on the whole.

この期間中，毎日のように男の子や女の子がおしゃべりにやってきた。

Every day during this period boys and girls came to chat with me.

そこで働いている間に教育実習にやってきたほかの実習生ともたくさん知り合いになって楽しかった。

While I was working there I met many students who had also come to do their teaching practice, and I was happy working with them.

【…時と…時の間】

事件は12時から1時の間に起った。

The event took place between 12 and 1 o'clock.

3．関係

between; among

事件は私たちの間で解決しよう。

［2人の間］
Let's settle the matter between ourselves.
［3人以上の間］
Let's settle the matter among ourselves.

2人の間の秘密にしておこう。

Keep it to yourself.
Keep it between you and me.

それはアナとベティの間だけの秘密だった。

It was a secret between Anna and Betty.

あいて（相手）

1．話し相手，生活の相棒，仲間

a companion

【話し相手】

（あの人は）話し相手を探しているようだ。

He seems to be seeking for a person to talk to [with].

【相談相手】

あの人には相談相手がいない。

He has no one to turn to for advice.

【お客の相手】

しばらくお客さまのお相手をしていただけませんか。

Could you keep the guest company for a while?

【伴侶】

彼女にかつての花のような美しさはないけれども，今でもよき人生の伴侶(話し相手)である。

Though she has lost her flowerlike charm, she is still a good companion.

2．競争や試合の相手

（競争の）**a rival;**（試合の）**an opponent**

【競争相手】

その２人は小学校以来の競争相手である。

The two boys have been rivals ever since their primary school days [years].

【試合の相手】

試合の相手はクラスの子であった。

My opponent in the match was my classmate.

I played (against) my classmate.

最終ゲームの相手はタイガースであった。

Our team played [met] the Tigers in the last game.

〈注〉 baseball や football のような big team sports では game と言うことが多い。soccer では match を使う。

【相手と激しく戦う】

１点を奪うために相手と激しく戦わねばならなかった。

We had to play hard against our opponents to score a goal.

3．結婚の相手

the man [**woman**] **whom** one **is to marry;** one's **fiancé**（男）; one's **fiancée**（女）; one's **marriage partner**

あう（会う，合う，遭う）

1．会う，出くわす

see; meet（会合で）; **come across**（ひょっこり）

【訪問】

今日の午後ある人が会いに来た。

A man came to see me this afternoon.

【待ち合せ】

どこで会おうか。

Where shall we meet?

【面識】

「あの人を知っていますか」「会ったことはありません」。

"Do you know him?" "No, I've never met him before."

〈注〉 この場合の meet は正式に紹介されて知り合いになることを意味する。

【出くわす】

30年間商売をやっていて変ったお客さんにもずいぶん出会いました。

During {the thirty years of my career / my thirty years} as a merchant I have come across some strange customers.

【公式会見】

会長は本日，来日中のクリントン前大統領とお会いになる。

The chairman will meet (with) ex-President Clinton, who is visiting Japan today.

【困難】

あの人もずいぶんつらい目にあっている。

She's gone through a lot of hardships.

（僕は）ひどい目にあったよ。

I had a horrible experience.

【雨】

彼は帰り道で夕立にあった。

He was caught in a shower on his way home.

【事故】

彼は交通事故にあった。

He was in a traffic accident.

2．一つになる，一致する

【合流】

藍川（あい）の地名は二つの川の「会う所」から来たものです。

Aikawa is called so because two rivers meet there.

【意見】

初めて意見が合いました。

For the first time we agreed [we had the same opinion].

父親は保守的で彼は革新的，あれでは意見が合わない。

His father is conservative and he's radical. They never agree.

【勘定】
勘定(収支と残金)が合っている。
The account balances and the cash (on hand) agrees.
どうしても勘定が合わない。
The figures just won't agree.
We can't { make the figures agree. / get the figures to agree.
【収支】
母がやりくりして何とか(赤字を出さず)収支が合っている。
Mother barely manages to make both ends meet.
〈注〉 計算などがやっとうまく合ったときの快哉。
合った！(パズルが解けたときもこう言う)
Got it! / Finally!
cf.「見つけた」の意味の「あった！」は
(I) Found it!
【答え】
君の答えは合っている。
Your answers are correct.
【時計】
時計は合っている。
The clock is correct [right].

3. 適合する
【型】
「試してみて[着てみて]ごらん」「ぴったり合うわ」。
"Try it on for size." "It's a good fit."
このコートは私にぴったり合う。
This coat fits me perfectly.
【色】
あのネクタイはあのスーツに合う。
That tie matches [goes well with] that suit.
【体質】
ここの気候は私の体に合わない。湿気がひどすぎる。
The climate here doesn't suit me [agree with me]. It's too damp.
こんな油っこい料理はあなたには合わないのではないかしら。
I'm afraid such greasy food won't agree with you.
【料理】
赤ワインは牛肉とよく合う。
Red wine goes well with beef.
【趣味】
あの絵は私の趣味に合う。
I like that picture.
〈注〉 That picture suits my taste. は正しい文だが I like ～ が一番普通の言い方。
×My taste suits that picture. は誤り。
ニューミュージックは私の趣味に合わない。
I don't like New Music.
New Music isn't to my taste.
【気が合う】
私たちは初めて会ったときからとても気が合ってしまった。
We got along well [excellently] from the moment we met.
We hit it off immediately. 〔*colloq.*〕

4. 引き合わない
この仕事は引き合わない。
This work just doesn't pay.

あお(青)

1. 色彩
blue
〈注〉 日本語では緑(green)も青葉, 青信号などで「あお」と呼ぶので注意。
青い目　blue eyes
青い海[空]　the blue sea [sky]
青葉 green leaves
【青信号】
信号が青になった。
The signal turned green.

2. 顔色・果実
【青くなる】
彼はその知らせに青くなった。
He { turned pale / blanched } at the news.

〈注〉 He looks pale. は「青い顔をしている」とも言えるが，普通は「顔色が悪い」と言う。

【未熟】

トマトは青いうちに市場に出される。

Tomatoes are picked and sent to market before they are properly ripe.

【青二才】

a young and inexperienced person

a greenhorn

〈注〉 green は口語で「未熟な」の意味がある。greenhorn は，もとは young animal，転じて inexperienced person。日本語の「口ばしの黄色い奴…」に似ている。

あか（赤）

1．色彩

red

《関連語》

ピンク pink / とき色 reddish pink / ぼたん色 pinkish red / 緋色 scarlet / 紅色 bright red / 真紅 crimson / つやのある深紅 ruby [vivid reddish orange] / えび茶色 maroon [purplish, deep red] / えんじ色 deep red, burgundy red [dark red] / 暗赤色 very dark red-brown color

2．日常の中の「赤」

【もみじ】

秋になるともみじの葉が赤くなる。

In autumn maple leaves turn red.

【激怒】

彼は怒りで真っ赤になった。

He {turned red / flushed} with anger.

【恥じらい】

彼女は恥ずかしくて顔を赤らめた。

She blushed with embarrassment.

3．「赤」の連想

血 blood，熱 heat，火 fire，危険 danger，共産主義 Communism，情熱 passion，怒り anger

〈注〉 スコットランドの農民詩人 Robert Burns の詩に次の一節がある。

My love's like a red, red rose
That's newly sprung in June.

私の恋人は 6 月の朝（あした）咲きいでた真紅のばらのよう。

あがる（上がる）→ あげる

1．上にあがる

go up; rise; soar

【凧】

大きな凧が空に揚がっている。

A big kite is soaring up in the sky.

【階段】

我々は暗い階段を上がっていった。

We went up the dark stairs.

【気温】

正午には気温は37°C以上に上がった。

At noon the temperature rose [went] past 37 degrees C.

【成績】

その子は成績が上がった。

The boy has progressed in his studies.

He had better grades this time.（今度は）

His school record improved.

【物価】

物価がかなり上がった。

Prices {have gone up / have risen} considerably.

野菜の値が上がった。

Vegetables have gone up.

バス代が来月 1 日から上がる。

The bus fares will {be raised / go up} on the 1st of next month.

【地位・月給】

月給が上がった。

He got a raise.

His salary has {gone up. / risen. / been raised.}

彼は格が上がって部長になった。

He was promoted to department head.

2．その他

【就学】

一番下の子が４月には小学校に上がる。

Our youngest child is going to enter primary school in April.

【終り】

雨が上がった。

It has { stopped raining. / cleared up.

（トランプで）私が一番先に上がった。

I came out first.

I won first place.

【平常心を失う】

あの子はいつも試験で上がってしまう。

She always gets nervous during examinations.

その子は舞台で観客を見たら上がってせりふを忘れてしまった。

The little boy suddenly got frightened by the audience and forgot his lines.

あきらめる（諦める）

1．断念する

give up《an idea, all hope》

彼を仲間に誘うのはもうあきらめた。

I have given up trying to persuade him to join us.

丸１年外国で生活することを考えたがもうあきらめた。

I have given up (on) the idea of spending a whole year abroad.

〈注〉 on が入ると強調された表現になる。ただし目的語が idea, thought などの場合にのみ使える。

彼はもう治らぬものと皆あきらめた。

They gave up all hope of his recovery.

2．仕方なく受け入れる

get over《one's loss》; **resign** one**self to**《fate》

【あきらめない】

母親は息子の死をあきらめきれないでいる。

The mother cannot get over the death of her son.

【運命とあきらめる】

すべて運命とあきらめて一言もぐちをこぼさなかった。

She resigned herself to her fate and never complained.

〈注〉 resign oneself to はもっと軽い意味でも使われる。

I resigned myself to having to take my mother shopping.（面倒だけれども仕方がないとあきらめてお母さんを買物に連れていった）

あきる（飽きる）

be tired; be bored

be sick of; have enough of

読書に飽きた。

I'm tired of reading.

I'm sick of reading.〔強〕

近頃のテレビドラマには飽きた。みんな同じようだもの。

TV dramas these days bore me [tire me out]; they're all the same.

人生に飽きた。

I'm sick of life.

雨はもううんざりだ。（あきあきした）

We've had enough of this rain.

長話に飽きた。

His long talk bored us.

話が長くてあきあきした。

We were all bored to death with [by] his long talk.

あきれる（呆れる）

（驚く）**be amazed;**（驚きあきれる）**be shocked;**（嫌気がさす）**be disgusted**

【無知に】

君のものを知らないのにはあきれた。

I'm amazed at your ignorance.

【ばかなのに】

あのばかさ加減にあきれた。

I'm shocked by [at] her foolishness.

【自分に】

我ながら物忘れのひどいのにあきれた。

I'm disgusted at [with, by] my poor memory.

【あきれた顔をして】 with an amazed look

〈注〉「あきれる」は驚き（amazement）に非難（disapproval）を加えた感情と言える。

あく（開く）・あける

1．開く，開ける

【ドア】

ドアがひとりでに開いた。

The door opened by itself.

彼は私にドアを開けてくれた。

He opened the door for me.

彼はドアを押し開けた。

He pushed open the door.

私が通りかかったとき，ドアは開けっぱなしになっていた。

The door was open when I passed by.

cf. 彼はちゃんとドアを閉めないでいった。

He left the door ajar.

【引き出し】

引き出しがかたくて開かない。

The drawer is stuck and won't open [come open].

【幕】

ベルが鳴って幕が開いた。

The bell rang and the curtain rose.

【鍵】

彼はポケットから鍵を取り出してドアの錠を開けた。

He took the key out of his pocket and unlocked the door.

【包み】

包みを開ける

open a parcel [package]

unpack one's baggage [suitcase]（大きい物を）

【ページ】

本の50ページを開けてください。

Please { open your books at [to] page 50. / turn to page 50.

【行間】

行と行の間をあけてください。

Leave a space between the lines.

【執務・営業】

うちの地方郵便局は８時45分から夕方５時まで開いている。

Our local post office is open from 8:45 to 5:00.

2．からにする，からである

【水】

彼女はバケツの水をあけた。

She emptied the bucket (of water).

She dumped the water out of the bucket.

She dumped out the water.

〈注〉前後関係でバケツの水とわかっていれば，第３の文のようにバケツの語を略すのが自然。

【空席】

この席あいていますか？

Is this seat vacant [free, empty]?

〈注〉「この席は人が来ます」は This seat is taken [occupied].

【座席の提供】

皆座席をつめて老婦人に席をあけた。

They moved up closer and made a seat [room] for the old lady.

若者が立って老婦人に席をあけた［譲った］。

A young man offered [gave up] his seat to the old lady.

【空室】

２階の１部屋があいている。

One room upstairs is vacant [open, available] now.

【引っ越し】

来月の末までに家をあけてください。

Please move out by the end of next month.

【留守】

彼はもう１か月も家をあけている。

He's been away from home nearly a month.

【不在】
今ちょっと席をあけています。
He isn't in [is out] just now.

3. 職場・ポスト

【空席】
9月になればあきができるだろう。
There'll be a vacancy [an opening] next September.
We'll need someone next September.

4. 用がない

【品物】
その本があいたら貸してください。
If you've finished / If you're done } with that book, could you lend it to me?

【体】
次の日曜はあいていますか。
Are you free next Sunday?

【手】
もし手があいていたら来て手伝ってください。
If you are free now, please come and help me.

あくせく

【あくせく働く】 work hard; work one's head [tail] off; work like a dog; work with one's nose to the grind-stone; slave away

【あくせく金もうけする】 be engrossed in moneymaking; think only about making money

【くだらぬことにあくせくする】
worry (oneself) { over / about } { trivial things / nothing }
be a fussbudget〔米〕; be a fusspot〔英〕

あげる（上げる，揚げる，挙げる）→ あがる

1. 上昇

raise; lift

【手】
右手を上げなさい。
Raise your right hand.
Put your right hand up.
彼は手を上げてタクシーを止めた。
He hailed a taxi.
彼は手を上げて静かにさせた。
He { raised his hand / motioned } for silence.

【凧】
子供たちが凧を揚げている。
Children are flying kites.

【荷物など】
スーツケースを2階の私の部屋に上げておいてください。
Please carry the suitcase upstairs into my room.
ここの本を一番上の棚に上げてください。
Put these books on the top shelf, please.

【運賃】
JR は運賃を10%上げることに決めた。
Japan Railways has decided to raise [increase] fares (by) 10 percent.

【給料】
会社側は給料を一律8%上げることに決めた。
The company decided to raise all salaries (by) 8 percent.
〈注〉「上がる（自動詞）rise」と「上げる（他動詞）raise」を混同しないように。

2. 敬意表現

【贈る】
お母さんの誕生日に何をあげようか。
What shall I give my mother for her birthday?

【申し出】
その手紙，私が出してあげましょうか。
Shall I post [mail] the letter for you?

3. 料理（油で揚げる）

fry

【少量の油で】
じゃがいもをバターでいためます。(料理本の記述)
Fry [Sauté] the potatoes in butter.
【たっぷりの油で】
じゃがいもをたっぷりの油で揚げます。(同上)
Deep fry the potatoes.

4．示す
mention; give
【例】
何か例をあげてください。
Please give me some examples.
【名前】
あの人の名前が例の贈収賄事件関係であげられていた。
His name was mentioned in connection with the bribery case.
【問題】
平安朝のすぐれた女流作家の名前を2名あげなさい。
Give the names of two eminent women writers in the Heian Period.

あこがれる（憧れる）

long for; long to be; yearn for; hunger for
〈注〉 long for が一番普通に使われる。yearn for は正式な表現であり，強い感情を表し「焦がれる」に近い。

1．志向
【名声に】
名声にあこがれる人もいる。
Some people long for fame.
【都会生活[田園]に】
田舎の若者は都会生活にあこがれ，都会の人は田園にあこがれる。
Young people in the country yearn for city life, while city people hunger for the countryside.
【歌手に】
私は子供のとき歌手にあこがれていた。
When I was a child I longed to be a singer.

2．夢中
【アイドルに】
あの子たちはジェームス・ディーンにあこがれている。
They idolize James Dean.

あじ（味）

(a) **taste;** (a) **flavor**（風味・においも含む）

1．味覚
どんな味ですか。
How does it taste?
What does it taste like?
【味覚表現】
蜂蜜は甘い。
Honey is sweet.
Honey tastes sweet.
Honey has a sweet taste.
これは味がよい。
This tastes good.
これはすっぱい。
This tastes sour.
緑茶は苦く出ることがある。
Green tea tastes bitter sometimes.

2．調味
味が濃い　strongly [highly] seasoned
味が淡い　lightly seasoned
【味をつける】 salt （塩味をつける）
肉と野菜に味つけをしなさい。
Add seasoning to the meat and vegetables.
あの人は野菜料理に塩を入れすぎる。
She always
{ salts the vegetables too much.
{ puts too much salt on the vegetables.
【味がしない】
病気のときは何を食べても味がしない。
Food has no flavor [loses its flavor] when

one is ill.

【味にうるさい】

あの人は味にうるさい。

He is particular about { his food. / what he eats.

3. 比喩的表現

【後味】

いやな後味が残った。

It left an unpleasant aftertaste.

〈注〉 本当の後味にも比喩的な後味にも使われる。

【経験】

あの人は貧乏の味を知らない。

He doesn't know what it is to be poor.

He has no experience of poverty.

【味わい】

このエピソードにはコメディの味わいがある[喜劇の味がきかせてある]。

This episode has a flavor of comedy.

ロマンスの味のある[香りの高い]物語

a story with a flavor of romance

あずかる(預かる)・あずける

1. 預かる

keep; look after

【犬を】

私が旅行をするときはあの人が犬を預かってくれる[あの人に犬を預けていく]。

She keeps my dog when I travel.

【子供を】

私の留守中は母が子供を預かってくれる[母に子供を預けてゆく]。

My mother looks after my children while I'm away.

【物を】

あの人が玄関の鍵を預かっている。

He has the key of the front door.

皆が留守の間彼が家を預かっている[留守番をしている]。

He looks after the house while they are away.

2. 預ける

leave 《a thing》 **with** 《a person》

【子供を】

その若夫婦は赤ちゃんをいつも祖父母に預けていた。

The young couple used to leave their baby with his grandparents.

(あの人の)子供たちは叔父さんに預けられている。

Her children are being looked after by their uncle.

3. 預金する

deposit; put money in a bank

お金を預けに銀行に行ってきたところだ。

I have been to the bank to deposit some money.

蓄えがあるなら銀行に預けておきなさい。

If you have any savings, put them in the bank.

4. 任せる〔*figurative*〕

【事件を】

この件は君に預ける。

I'll leave this with you. (1)

I'll leave this (up) to you. (2)

I'll turn this over to you. (3)

〈注〉 (1)は物を預ける場合，事件のような抽象物を預ける場合，どちらにでも使える。(2)(3)は事件のような抽象物にのみに使用。

あせる(焦る)

1. 急ぐ

あせらなくてもよい。まだ3日ある。

We don't need to hurry. We have three more days.

2. 気がはやる

be impatient to; be eager to

【競争】

我々は勝とうとあせった。

We were impatient to win.

彼は他の生徒たちとの間の遅れを取り戻そうとあせった。

He was eager to catch up with the other students.

【成功】

成功をあせってはいけない。

One must not be too eager for success.

【あせるな】

じっくりやれ。

Don't be in such a hurry.

Take your time.

Slow down.

気楽にやれ。

Take it easy.

Be patient.

Hold your horses. 〔*informal*〕

〈注〉「あせるな」「急がば回れ」に当ることわざ。

Haste makes waste.

あそぶ（遊ぶ）

【遊戯】play（子供の遊びについてのみ）

子供たちはままごとをして遊んでいる。

The children are playing at keeping house.

【楽しむ】enjoy

人々は皆遊んでいた。テレビを見たりトランプをしたり，おしゃべりをしたり。

They were all {enjoying themselves / having a good time}, some watching TV, some playing cards and others just talking.

【無為に過す】

大学の2年間というものただ遊んで暮した。

During my two years in college, I did nothing but {enjoy myself. / play around. / fool around.}

大学を卒業してから私は職探しをしようともせずにぶらぶら遊んで暮した。

Since I graduated from college, I have idled away my days without making efforts to find a job.

あの（男の）子たちは何もせずに遊びまわっている。

Those boys are just loafing (around).

今日は一日遊んでしまった［何も仕事ができなかった］。

I haven't got(ten) a thing done today.

〈注〉大人が遊ぶのは play とは言わない。play は play tennis, play chess, play the piano のようにスポーツ・ゲーム・楽器などについて使う。ぶらぶらすることを「遊ぶ」と言うが，その意味で play は使えない。

△I played during the vacation, so I have to do my homework now.

何もしなかったのなら

I've idled away my [the] days.

（毎日ぶらぶらしていた）

テレビを見たとか釣に行ったのなら具体的に何をしたかを述べる。

ex. We enjoyed ourselves watching TV.

We went fishing.

あたりまえ（当り前）→ とうぜん

natural; no wonder

【当然】

（それは）当り前だ。

Naturally. / Well, of course.

お父さんは週末の食事のしたくは当り前のこととしてやっている。

My father cooks weekend suppers as a matter of course.

あの人が怒るのも当り前だ。

It's no {wonder / surprise} she {should get / got} angry.

No wonder she got angry.

She has good [every] reason to be angry.

〈注〉このような場合，相づちとしてよく使われるのが "You can say that again!"（まったくそのとおり）。

あったりまえ！

Naturally!

息子を自慢に思うのも当り前だ。

He has a right [It's natural for him] to be proud of his son.

〈注〉He may well be proud ... という言い方もある

がやや古風である。

そんなことできて当り前さ。(相手を見下げた言い方)

Anyone can do that. What's so wonderful [surprising, great, fantastic] about it?

【普通の】 ordinary

「どんな子？」「そう，ごく当り前の女の子さ」。

"What is she like?" "Well, just an ordinary young girl."

当り前の女の人なら負けてしまうところだ。

An ordinary woman would have given in.

〈注〉 人について ordinary の意味で common は使わない。→ふつう

あたる（当る）→ あてる

1. ぶつかる

strike; hit

【石】

石が彼の頭に当った。

A stone struck [hit] him on the head.

【銃弾】

頭に銃弾が当り熊は倒れた。

The bear was shot in the head and fell.

【雨】

雨が窓に当ってぱらぱら音をたてている。

The rain is beating against the window.

【波】

岸の灰色の岩に波が当って砕けている。

The waves are breaking over the grey stones on the shore.

【風】

一晩中ヒューヒューと風当りがひどかった。

The wind has been whistling round the house all night.

【車】

車が塀に当った。

The car hit the wall.

【人】

あの人はむしゃくしゃするといつも私に当る。

She always lets out her frustration on me.

2. 入る

【日】

私の部屋はよく日が当って居心地がよい。

My room is sunny and very comfortable.

私の部屋はよく日が当る。

My room gets lots of sunshine.

3. ふれる，こすれる

touch; rub

【靴】

ブーツがきつくてつま先が当る。

These boots are too tight and pinch my toes.

新しい靴は小さすぎてかかとの後ろが当る。靴ずれができそうだ。

The new shoes are too small; they are rubbing against the back of my feet and I'm going to have blisters.

4. 的中・成功

的に当る hit the mark

【予言】prove right; come true（夢など）

あの人の予言が当った。

Her prophecy { proved right. / has come true. }

【答え】

当ったよ。

You've guessed right. / You hit it. / You hit the nail on the head.

【事業】

事業は当った。

The project worked [turned] out well.

その映画は大当りであった。

That movie made [was] a big hit.

【くじ】

彼はくじに当った。

He drew a winning number in the lottery.

579番が当り。

Five seventy-nine [579] is the lucky [winning] number.

〈注〉 The lot fell on me. は損なくじに当ること。貧乏くじを引くことである。「くじを引いて負けた」は We drew lots and I lost. と言う。

5．関係

【方向】

私たちの学校は公園の南に当る。

Our school is (located) south of the park.

【月日】

今年の10月10日は母の10年目の命日に当る。

This year October 10th happens to be the 10th aniversary of my mother's death.

【曜日】

今年はクリスマスが日曜日に当る。

This year Christmas falls on Sunday.

【人間関係】

元良博士は私の祖父に当る。

Dr. Motora is my grandfather.

【相当】

日本の参議院は英国の何に当りますか。

What in Britain corresponds to "Sangi-in" in Japan ?

1ドル[ユーロ]は約120[122]円に当る。

A {dollar / euro} {is worth / gets} about {120 / 122} yen.

6．中毒

昼食に食べたものにあたった。

Something I ate at lunch disagreed with me.

7．当番・指名

大晦日に当直が当った。

He happened to be on night duty on New Year's Eve.

スミス先生のフランス語で最初に訳が当った[当てられた]。

In Mr. Smith's French lesson I was asked [called on] to translate first.

あつい（暑い，熱い，厚い）

【暑い】 hot, warm;（蒸し暑い）humid, muggy

暑いですね。

It's hot, isn't it?

ああ暑い！「暑い」なんてものじゃない。焼けてしまいそう。

Hot isn't the word! It's baking [roasting, boiling]!

【熱い】 hot

コーヒーは熱いのがよい。

I like my coffee hot [hot coffee].

そんなにお熱いの[仲がいいの]！

Oh, is he that sweet on her?

【厚い】 thick; fat

厚い本　a thick book; a fat book

厚化粧をしている　wear thick makeup

あつまる(集まる)・あつめる

1．集まる

gather; assemble

【人】

火の周りに集まれ。

Gather round the fire.

シドニー・オリンピックに世界中から人が集まった。

Many people came to the Sydney Olympic Games from all over the world.

彼の家の前に人が集まっている。

There is a crowd of people in front of his house.

どこで集まろうか。

Where shall we meet?

ツアーの一行は4時に銅像の前で集まる。

The tour group will meet [assemble] at the statue at 4:00.

2．集める

gather; get [**bring, put**] **together; assemble; collect**

【人】

皆を集めてくれ。

Call them all together.

Summon them.

【収集】

彼は切手をたくさん集めている。

He has a large collection of stamps.

【金】

クラブハウス建設資金を集めなければならない。

We have to collect money to build our club house.

【寄付金】

They are asking for contributions. (募っている)

They are collecting donations [contributions]. (集めている)

3. 集中

【注目】

一般の注目が消費税に集まった。

Public attention centered [focused] on the consumption tax.

彼の新教育理論が一般の注目を集め始めた。

His new principle of education began to { attract public attention. / arouse interest. }

【同情】

人々のあつい同情が孤児たちに集まった。

Everyone feels great sympathy for the orphans.

あてる (当てる) → あたる

1. ふれる, ぶつける

【手を】

熱があるかどうか子供の額に手を当てた。

She put her hand on the child's forehead to see if he had a temperature [fever].

【耳に】

彼は受話器を耳に当てたが何も聞えなかった。

He picked up the phone but heard nothing.

【日に】

鉢植えは時には日に当てなければいけない。

Those potted plants should be { taken out / put } in the sun once in a while.

【車を】

彼は車を塀に当てて前の部分をへこませてしまった。

His car hit the wall and the front part was crushed.

車を車庫入れで当ててしまった。

The car { crashed into / hit } the garage.

I crashed into [hit] the garage with the car.

車は後ろから当てられた。

The car was hit from behind.

〈注〉 英語の hit は日本語の「当てる」と同様に, わざと当てる場合と成り行きで当ってしまう場合の両方を含む。crush は「つぶす, へこます」こと。crash はガチャンと大きな音で物が衝突したり, 落ちて壊れたりすること。

2. 的中

【くじ】

その子はくじで1等賞を当てた[が当った]。

The child won the first prize in the lottery.

【株】

彼は株(の売買)で当てた。

He's made a big killing in the stock market.

【興業】

あの映画で当てた。

That movie was [made] a big hit.

【推測】

あなたにいいものがあるの。この袋の中が何だか当ててごらん。

Here's a surprise for you. (Please) guess { what I have / what I've got / what's } in this bag.

3. 指名

彼はクラスで一番よくできるが, 僕はあまり当てないんだ。ほかの生徒たちにも考えさせたいから。

He's the cleverest one in his [the] class, but I don't call on him very often because I want the other students to think.

今日のフランス語はしっかり予習して出たので, 当てられるかとびくびくしないですんだ。

Today I attended French class well prepared, so I wasn't afraid of being asked to translate.

4. 充当

彼は余暇のすべてを勉強に当てている。

He spends all his spare time studying.

He gives all his spare time to his studies.

100万円が備品購入に割り当てられた。

One million yen was allotted for new equipment purchases.

あと（後）

1. 空間的

【後から】

その犬は主人の後から，どこにでもついて行った。

The dog followed his master wherever he went.

【後を】

後を見ずに without looking back

その子は兄の後を追ったが，じきに遅れて取り残された。

The child ran after his brother but soon dropped behind.

【後をつける】 track

警察は殺人犯の後をつけた。

The police tracked down the killer.

私は後をつけられているのに気づいた。

I noticed I was being shadowed.

【後ずさり】

彼女は草むらの中に蛇を見つけておびえて後ずさりした。

She drew back in fear when she saw a snake in the grass.

2. 時間的

【のちほど】

あとから行きます。

I'll come later.

あとでまた。

See you later.

彼は2，3日あとに会いに来た。

He came to see me a few days later [afterwards].

【後払い】

どうぞ持っていってください。お金はあとで結構です。

Please take them. You can pay later.

【復唱】

さあ皆さん私のあとについて言ってください。

Repeat after me, everybody.

【居残り】

あの人は一番遅く着いたので皆が帰ってもあとに残っていた。

She arrived last and so she
- stayed later [longer] than everyone else.
- remained behind after everyone else went home.

【先立つ】

彼は妻と赤ん坊をあとに残して若くして死んだ。

He died young, leaving his wife
- to bring up the baby alone.
- with a baby.

【あれからあと】

（私たちが）別れたあとどこへ行ったんだ？

Where did you go after we left each other?

3. 慣用

【結末】

あとのことを考えなさい。

Think of the consequences.

あとはどうなろうと知ったことではない。

I don't care what
- happens afterwards.
- comes of it.

そんなことをするとあとで困るよ。

If you do something like that, you'll have to
- pay for it afterwards.
- take the consequences.

【残り】

出発まであと1時間しかない。

Only an hour is left before we start.
There's only an hour left (to go) before we start.

あと100円で1000円になる。
One hundred yen more and it will be a thousand yen.

あと2人だけ座れます。
Only two more people can sit down.
There're only two more seats.

2人だけ部屋に入れてもらい，あとの人は外で待たされた。
Only two people were admitted into the room and the rest had to wait outside.

【後任】
彼のあとを探さなければならない。
We must find someone to take his place.

あの → この，その

1. あのう（呼びかけ）

【女性に】 Ma'am
【男性に】 Sir
【あのう，ちょっと】 Excuse me.
〈注〉 女性への呼びかけでは既婚・未婚の区別なく，ma'am と言う（miss とは言わない）。店員がお客に呼びかけるときなどに使う。

2. 話の途中

【口ごもるとき】 Say, ...; Umm, ...
【話題を持ち出す】 By the way, ...
〈注〉 by the way は話題を変えるときの言い方である。使いすぎないように。
【説明の言葉を探して】 Well [But], as I was saying ...
【相手の印象の訂正】
あのう，こうなんですが
Well, it's this way ... / Well, ...
【次の言葉を考えているとき】
あのう，ええと…来週水曜日はあいています。
Let me see ... ok, next Wednesday I'll be free.
あのう，…彼は明日は東京でしょう。
Let's see ... he'll be in Tokyo tomorrow.
【相手の言葉がよくわからないとき】
あのう，すみません。
Er, sorry.
あのう，もう一度言っていただけますか。
Er, sorry. Could you repeat it?
あのう，何て言われたのですか。
Er, what did you say [what was that]?
〈注〉 I beg your pardon. は礼儀正しいが古風にひびく。

あぶない（危ない）

【危険な】
その橋は危ない。
This bridge is dangerous.
その道は危ない。
That's a dangerous road (to take).
この川で泳ぐのは危ない。
This river is dangerous to swim in.

【警告】
危ない! (上に / 下に)気をつけろ！
Stop! Watch out (above / below)!
Watch it!
Danger (ahead)! (看板)
ほら，塀が危ない！
Look out! The wall!
彼の命が危ない！
His life is in danger!

【冒険】
危ないことはやめろ。
Don't run risks.
Don't take chances.
Don't court danger.〔強〕

【容態が悪い】
その病人は危ない。
The patient is very sick [in critical condition].

【不確実】
彼が約束を守るかどうか危ないもんだ。
I doubt that he'll keep his promise.

【危なく】
危なく忘れるところだった(君が思い出させ

てくれた)。

You reminded me just in time.

危なく列車に乗り遅れるところだった。

I nearly missed the train.

彼は危なく車にひかれるところだった。

He was almost hit by a car.

あぶら（油, 脂）

［総称］（獣脂・植物油・鉱物油） **oil;** 獣脂（固形） **fat;** 精製された豚脂 **lard;** グリース **grease;** 機械油 **machine oil**

【油が切れる】

［機械などの］ need oiling

この古いミシンは油がきれている。

This old sewing machine needs oiling.

［料理油］

油を切らしてしまった。

We've run short of oil.

【油でいためる［揚げる］】 fry → りょうり

【油をさす】 動 oil

彼は自転車に油をさしてもらった。

He had his bicycle oiled.

【油を売る】

あの人はまた(どこかで)油を売っているんだろう。

She may be lazying [loafing] around again.

【脂っこい食べ物】 greasy food

【脂がのる】

彼は仕事に脂がのってきた。

He has warmed up to his work.

あまい（甘い）

【味】 sweet

私は甘いものが好きです。

I am fond of sweet things.

I have a sweet tooth.

このケーキは甘すぎる。

This cake is [tastes] too sweet.

【しつけ】 → あまえ・あまえる・あまやかす

父親は彼に甘い。

His father { indulges him. / is easy on him. }

おばあさんの中には孫に甘すぎる人もいる。

Some grandmothers spoil their grandchildren.

〈注〉 spoil は「甘やかしてだめにする」の意。

あの先生は生徒に甘い。

He is lenient with his students.

〈注〉 逆に「厳しい」は strict。

【点数】

あの先生は点が甘い。

That teacher is a generous [an easy] marker.

【考え方】 →のんき

彼は人生を甘くみている。

He doesn't take life seriously enough.

彼は考え方が甘い。

His thinking is not realistic enough.

He's too easy-going [optimistic].

相手を甘くみるな。

Don't underestimate your opponent.

あまえ（甘え）・あまえる・あまやかす

1. 子供の甘え

子供を甘やかす　spoil a child

甘やかされる　be spoilt [spoiled]

甘やかされた子　a spoilt child

〈注〉 behave like a spoilt child だだっ子のように振舞う。

【甘えた仕草】

子供は私にすり寄って小さな手で私の首に抱きついた。

The small boy nestled against me and threw his little arms around my neck.

2. 大人の甘え

【親に】

私は母の愛情に慣れっこになり，甘えて母には何をしても許されるような気になっていた。

I got used to Mamma's love. I took her love for granted and felt I could behave quite willfully with impunity.

【社会に】
私は学生の身分に甘えていたが，これからは実社会に出て現実に直面しなければならない。

I have been treated as a student, one of that privileged class, but now I have to face the outside world.

【仕草】
（女性が男性に対し）色っぽく甘える

be coquettish / try to be cute

甘え声で相手の歓心を買おうとする

coo at / purr at

【ご親切に[お言葉に]甘えて】
〈注〉 かしこまった英語では I'll presume upon your kindness ... のような表現もあるが，古風であまり使われない。この日本語は相手の申し出を受け入れる場合の丁寧なお礼の挨拶に使われるのであるから，直訳しないで次のような表現で感謝の気持ちを表せばよい。

If you could ..., I'd really appreciate it [I'd be really grateful]. (そうしていただければ本当にありがたいのですが)

「ご親切に甘えて…させていただきました」とすでにすんだ事に対するお礼であれば

Thank you very much for ... / I really appreciate ... / I'm really grateful ...

とでも言えばよい。

3．甘えを戒める表現

【子供に】
甘えるんじゃない［まとわりつくんじゃない］。

Stop clinging. Go away!

［心情的甘えを戒める］

Don't act like a baby.

Don't be a baby.

Quit being such a baby.

Grow up!

Act your age!

【社会的に自立をすすめる】
本分を尽す　do one's duty

自分の行為には自分で責任をとる心構えでなければならない。

You should always be ready to take responsibility for what you do.

もう20歳だから就職して親から独立して生活したい。

Now that I'm twenty I'd like to get a job and live independent of my parents.

あまる（余る）→ のこる・のこす

1．残部

remain; be left (**over**)

いくつ[どれだけ]余っているか。

How many (of them) remain [are left (over)]?

旅費が1000円余った。

A thousand yen is left of [over from] the traveling allotment.

何も余っていない。

Nothing is left over.

There's nothing left over [remaining].

ごちそうの余った分でパーティーができる。

What's left (over) we can use for a party.

〈注〉 余りもの(食物の) left-overs

車を買ってもまだお金がたくさん余っている。

Even after buying a car, he has lots of money left.

2．余分

be too much (**many**)

一つ余っている。

There's one too many.

人間があり余っている国

an overcrowded [overpopulated] country

金が(あり)余っている。

He has more money than he can spend. (1)

He has enough money to spare. (2)

〈注〉 (1) 使いきれないほど金を持っている。
(2) 何かにお金を出す余裕がある。

3．算数（余る，余り）

10 − 4 = 6 （10から4を引いて6余る）

Ten minus four is [equals] six.

Four from ten is [leaves] six.

7 ÷ 3 = 2 … 1（7 を 3 で割って 2 と余り 1）

Seven divided by three equals two with {a remainder of one. / one remaining.}

あみもの（編み物）

knitting（2 本棒編み）; **crocheting**（かぎ針編み）

編む **knit, crochet** /krouʃéi/ ;

髪を編む **braid, plait**

ビルは青と白毛糸で自分のセーターを編んでいる。

Bill is knitting a blue and white sweater for himself.

ケイトは髪を三つ編みにしている。

Kate wore her hair in braids.

《関連語》

（2 本棒で）表編みをする　knit

裏編みをする　purl

ゴム編み　rib (ribbing)

ガーター（表編みのみ）

garter stitch (all knit stitches)

メリヤス（表編み 1 段裏編み 1 段）

stocking stitch (knit one row, purl one row)

編み目をつくる　cast [bind] on

編み目をとめる　cast [bind] off

編み目を増やす　increase the stitches

編み目を減らす　decrease the stitches

かぎ針編みをする　crochet

あやしい（怪しい）

1. 不審な

suspicious; doubtful; dubious

あやしげな 2 人の男を殺人現場の近くで見かけた。

I saw two suspicious(-looking) men near the scene of the murder.

I saw two men skulking near the scene.

〈注〉 skulk であやしい感じが出せる。

【うさんくさい】

あの男はどうもあやしい感じだ。

He's a dubious character.

【情事】

あの 2 人の仲はどうもあやしい。

I suspect there's something going on between the two.

2. あやふや

【記憶】

どうも記憶があやしいが。

I'm not sure if I remember right.

【言語】

ガイドがあやしい英語で説明した。

The guide tried to explain in his poor [broken, halting] English.

【出典など】

宇宙計画についてのその情報はあやしい。

That information about the space program is hard to believe.

〈注〉 ニュースがあやしいとき次のようにも言える。

It has been reported, though not so reliably, that ....

cf. 確かな筋の報道によれば…

Reliable sources have reported that ....

It is reported by reliable sources that ....

a reliable source とは言うが an unreliable source とはあまり言わない。

【…かどうか】

私たちの言っていることが本当にわかったかどうかあやしい。

It is doubtful whether he really understood what we were saying.

3. あやしむ

彼が本当のことを言っている[正直]かどうかあやしいものだ。

I doubt if he is telling the truth.
I suspect he is not telling the truth.
（おそらく真実を言っていない）

I doubt whether he is honest.
I wonder about his honesty.
（おそらく正直ではない）

〈注〉 ◆suspect は「くさいぞ」と疑いをかけること。

"I suspect" は "I think" に近く, doubt は「おや？」と疑念を抱くこと。"I doubt" は "I don't think" に近い。同じ心情を表現するのに反対の観点に立っていることに注意。

◆疑念を表す表現にも段階があり，次の表現の(1)から(3)にいくにしたがって強い疑念となる。

我々のチームが勝つかどうかあやしい。

(1) I wonder if our team can win.

(2) (a) It's doubtful if our team can win.
(b) I doubt that our team can win.

(3) I suspect our team cannot win.

(2)の2文は疑念の程度はほぼ同じだが，客観・主観の差がある。(a)は more people believe that ... の含み。(b)は「私はあやしいと思う」という個人の印象の形で述べている。

4. 悪化しそうな

【天候】

空模様があやしい。
It looks like rain.

あらい（荒い，粗い）

1. 荒い

【自然】

荒海　a rough sea

今日は波が荒い[海が荒れている]。
The sea is rough today.

【人】

彼は気性が荒い。
He is a man of violent temper.

彼は言葉づかいが荒い。
He uses rough language.

あの人は金づかいが荒い。
She spends her money recklessly.

彼は人使いが荒い。
He's a slave-driver.

彼は人使いが荒いので，皆いやがっていた。
They hated his slave-driving.

【動物】

この馬は気性がおとなしいが，あの馬は荒い。
This horse is tame but that one is wild.

2. 粗い（素材のきめなど）

【粉】coarse（↔ fine）

粗い粉[砂糖 / 雪]
coarse powder [sugar / snow]

【表面・きめ】rough（ざらざら）

きめの粗い木材
wood of rough grain（↔ fine grain）

This { is rough-grained. / has a rough grain.

この生地は織りが粗い。
This material is very loosely woven.（↔ tightly woven）

この布は手触りが粗い。
This cloth feels rough.（↔ smooth）

このネットは目が粗い。
This net has large holes.

【仕上げ】

粗い仕事[仕上げ]
rough workmanship [finish]

粗削りの板　a rough-planed board

〈注〉 plane とは，かんなをかけること。

粗く縫う[粗い縫い目で縫う]
sew pieces of cloth together using large [long] stitches

〈注〉 baste（しつけ，仮縫い）
tack（ちょっと布をおさえるため一針二針だけ縫って留める）

【芸術作品が】 unrefined,unpolished

これらの彫刻は粗けずりである。
These sculptures have an unpolished surface.

3. 大まか

粗筋　a rough outline; a summary

あらかた
for the most part; nearly; almost

〈注〉 almost は誤用が多い。「ほとんど」参照。

あらう（洗う）

1. 汚れを落す

wash

【顔・手・足】

食事の前に手を洗いなさい。
Wash your hands（clean）before meals.

【洗濯】
この材質は洗っても大丈夫。
This material washes well.
1週間雨つづきで洗い物がたまった。
Dirty clothes have [Washing has] piled up, because it's [it has] rained for a week.
それはもう1週間も着ているでしょう。そろそろ洗った方がいいよ。
You've been wearing that for a week. It could do with a wash.
このしみは洗っても取れないだろう。
This stain won't wash [come] out.
【すすぐ】rinse
このびんはもう洗ったの?
Have you rinsed these bottles yet?
【皿】do the dishes
皿洗いをしなければならない。
I have to do the dishes.
【髪】wash [shampoo] one's hair
【傷】clean [cleanse] a wound
【車】
父の車を洗って車庫の掃除をした。
I washed my father's car and cleaned the garage.
【床】
時には床を洗わなければならない。
I have to scrub the floor once in a while.

2. 調べる
inquire into; check
あいつがあやしい。経歴をあらってくれ。
He's suspicious. Check into his past.

あらそい(争い)・あらそう

1. 公的な争い
名 **a dispute** (about, concerning, over); **an argument; a quarrel**
動 **dispute; have a dispute; argue;** けんかする **quarrel**
【法廷で】
彼らは争点を法廷で争った。
They went to law to settle the point.
【財産を】
双方とも財産権を主張して争った。
They both claimed the property.

2. 不和
a conflict; strife; (**a**) **feud** (宿敵同士の長期の不和)
両家の争いがロメオとジュリエットの悲劇を生んだのだ。
A feud between two families caused the tragedy of Romeo and Juliet.

3. 競争
名 **a competition**
動 **compete** 《with a person for something》; **contend** 《with [against] a person for something》
彼らは1等賞を目指して争った。
They contended [competed] for the first prize.
彼らは先を争って1か所の戸口に殺到した。
They struggled with one another to get out of the one door.
乗物で先を争って席をとるようなことはしないよう親が子供に教えなければならない。
Parents should teach their children not to rush for a seat in buses and trains.

4. けんか
名 **a fight** (実力行使); **a quarrel** (口げんか)
動 **fight; quarrel**
あの夫婦は争いが絶えない。
That couple is always quarreling [fighting].

5. 慣用
1分を争う時だ。
There's not a moment to lose.
年は争えない。
Age will tell.

ありがたい・ありがとう

1. 儀礼的表現

…願えればありがたいのですが。

If you could (kindly) …,

{I should / I would} {be (very) appreciative. / appreciate it (very much).}

2. 感謝

【ありがとう】

Thank you very much.

Many thanks.

Thanks a lot.

【助かる】

天気がよくてありがたい。

We are lucky to have such fine weather.

Such good weather is a great boon.

年寄りには暖冬でありがたい。

Such a mild winter is (a) blessing [mercy] to us old people.

臨時収入がありがたかった。娘が結婚するので。

I was {glad to get the unexpected income / relieved to get the extra income} because my daughter is getting married soon.

〈注〉 I was relieved … の方は「やれやれ助かった」の感じがある。

私たちの国がどこの国とも戦争をしていないのはありがたいと思う。

I am grateful [happy] that our country is not at war anywhere (with anyone).

健康なのをありがたいと思いなさい。

You should appreciate [value, be grateful for] your health.

Be thankful [glad] that you are quite healthy.

【しめた！】

ありがたい！ 彼女がうんと言った。

Oh, I'm delighted! [Great! / Wonderful! / Thank God!] I've got her consent.

【ありがたみ】

自分に子供ができなければ親のありがたみはわからない。

You will [may, can] never know how much you owe your parents until you have a child of your own.

【ありがたいことに】

ありがたいことにバスは混んでいなかった。

I was glad the bus was not so crowded.

ありがたいことに夕方になって雨が上がった。

Luckily [Fortunately] the rain cleared up toward evening.

〈注〉 happily はこの場合しっくりしない。happy, fortunate, lucky については「さいわい」の項参照。

ある

1. 肯定・断定

〈注〉 「AはBである（だ）」に関しては「…だ」の項参照。

我輩は猫である。

I am a cat.

2. 存在

〈注〉 ある物の存在を述べるときは「（どこに）…がある。（There＋be＋初めて話題にのぼるもの（新情報）＋場所）」が一番基本的な形。

角に銀行がある。

There is a bank on [at] the corner.

劇場の正面に男女の大きな写真があった。

There was a large photograph of a man and (a) woman in front of the theater.

角には大きな3階建ての家があった。

On the corner was a big three-storied building.

〈注〉 上例のように［場所＋be＋新情報］の形もある。

3. 所在

〈注〉 ある物の「ありか」を述べるときは「…は（どこ）にある」。

あなたの腕時計は台所のテーブルの上にある。

Your watch is on the kitchen table.

【さがし物】
あっ，ここにあった[ある]。
(I) Found it!
Here it is! / Here we go! / Here you are!

4．所持・所有
お金はあるか。
Have you got some money?
あの子は音楽の才能がある。
She has a gift for music.
あの人はユーモアのセンスがある。
He has a sense of humor.

5．出来事・行事
試験はいつあるの？
When is the exam?
遠足は来週あります。
We'll have [There'll be] a school excursion next week.
昨夜火事[地震]があった。
There was a fire [an earthquake] last night.

6．売っている
スキージャケットはありますか。
Do you have [sell] ski jackets?

あるく（歩く）

walk

《**類義語**》
肩で風を切って歩く swagger / 大またにすたすた歩く stride / 気取って歩く strut / 小走りに歩く trot（子供など）; jog（ジョギング）/ よちよち歩く（幼児）toddle / とぼとぼ歩く trudge / ぶらぶら歩く stroll, amble / はってゆく crawl / つま先立ってそうっと歩く tiptoe / よろよろ歩く totter, stagger / 足を引きずって歩く limp
〈注〉 これらの語には along, through, by, away, off, about などの語が続くことが多い。

学校までは歩いてほんの５分です。
It's only five minutes, on foot from here to our school.
銀行は郵便局から歩いて10分のところです。
The bank's a 10 minute walk from the post office.
〈注〉 バスで（by bus），車で（by car）などと同様に，徒歩で（on foot）を応用して，I go to school on foot. などと書く人が多い。誤りではないが I walk to school. とか I walk home. で十分である。

アルバイト

〈注〉 英語では特にアルバイトに当る語はないので「どこそこで夏の間働いた」とか「パートタイムで働いた」のように書けばよい。
夏休みの前半はウエイトレスのアルバイトをした。
I worked as a waitress during the first half of the summer vacation.
夏休みや休日には宅配の小包配達のアルバイトをした。
In the summers and holidays he delivered parcels for a delivery service.
大勢が湖畔の行楽地でのアルバイトにありついた。
Many got a vacation job at a lake resort.
あの人はレジ係のアルバイトをみつけた。
She got a part-time job as a cashier.
〈注〉 part-time は full-time に対する語。夏休みなどの間だけのアルバイトは a holiday [vacation / summer time] job である。
パートタイムの記述の仕方は，形容詞として用いる場合は part-time，副詞として用いる場合も part-time が普通。
He has a part-time job / He worked part-time } in the post office.

あれ → それ・これ・あれ

あわせる（会わせる，合せる）

1．会わせる
彼はエイミーとビルを招待して２人を会わせた（２人が会う機会をつくった）。
He invited both Amy and Bill to give them a chance to get to know each other.

あの子のお父さんは僕をあの子に会わせてくれなかった。

Her father didn't allow me to see her.

2. 一つにする

put together

あの横綱は君たち３人を合せたより重い。

That yokozuna is heavier than you three put together.

幼い子供たちが小さな手を合せてお祈りをしていた。

The little children were saying their prayers with their tiny palms pressed together.

【加算】

数字を足してごらん。合せていくつ？

Add up the figures. How much do they come to [What is the total]?

合せて95。

It's ninety-five.

【収支】

収支を合せる

balance the budget（役所などで）

〈注〉 収入 revenue [income] と支出 expenses [outgo] をそれぞれ計算し，手持ちの残金と照合すること。

母がやりくりしてやっと（赤字を出さずに）帳じりを合せている。

Mother barely manages to make both ends meet.

【協力】

皆で力を合せたので仕事が早く片付いた。

Everyone cooperated and the work was finished quickly.

皆で声を合せて歌った。

People all sang in chorus.

3. 適合・照合

【服装】

あの人は茶のコートに合せてピンク色のスカーフをしていた。

She wore a pink scarf with her brown coat.

あの人は茶のコートに合せてピンクのスカーフを買った。

She bought a pink scarf to match her brown coat.

私はその服を自分の寸法に合せて縫い込んだ。

I took in the dress to fit me.

【時計】

私は目覚し時計を５時半に合せた。

I set the alarm clock for five-thirty.

君の時計をこの時計に合せておきなさい。

Set your watch by this clock.

【カメラ】

カメラのピントが合っていないんじゃない？

Is your camera out of focus?

【ラジオ】

ラジオをFMアイチに合せてください。

Tune the radio to FM AICHI.

【答え合せ】

黒板に正解を書きますから，各自で答え合せをしてください。

I'll write the correct answers on the blackboard. Check your papers yourselves.

【音楽に】

私たちは音楽に合せて踊った。

We danced to the music.

〈注〉 「ピアノに合せて歌った」を We sang to her piano accompaniment. と訳すと，伴奏が主で歌が従と焦点が逆になってしまう。日本語の「ピアノ…」は普通に言うことであるが，英訳すると奇異な印象の文になる。伴奏とは歌に合せて弾くもので，歌が伴奏に合せるのではないようだ。She accompanied us on the piano.

あわてる（慌てる）

1. 急ぐ

あわてて財布を忘れてしまった。

In my hurry I forgot to take my purse with me.

あわてるな。ゆっくりやれ。

Don't be so hasty. / Don't rush.（軽い注意）

Take it easy.（気楽にやれ）

2．ろうばい

遅れそうになってあわてて列車を間違えた。

I was so flustered at [by] being late I took the wrong train.

あわてないで！（真面目な忠告）

Don't get excited.

Keep cool.

Pull yourself together.

あの人は地震の最中もあわてなかった。

She kept [stayed] calm in the midst of the earthquake.

洪水のときあわてなかったので溺死した人はほとんどいなかった。

They kept their presence of mind during the flood, so few were drowned.

〈注〉「平常心を失う」ことを意味する表現には次のようなものがある。

be shocked [stunned]　はっと肝をつぶす。

be scared [frightened]　はっとこわくて体がすくむ（frightened はあがって頭がぼうっとしてしまうことも指す cf. stage fright）。

be alarmed（強い語）何か突然危険を感じて恐怖にぎょっとする。

be confused　まごつく。

be flustered　頭が混乱しぼうっとしてよく考えられなくなる。

be flurried　頭が混乱し，どうしたらよいかわからずうろたえる。

be in a panic; 動 panic（過去形 panicked）; lose one's head ; lose self-control　パニック状態になり，わけのわからぬめちゃくちゃな行動をする。

あわれな（哀れな）・あわれむ

1．哀れな

（無力で何もできない）**helpless;**（みじめな）**miserable;**（悲惨な）**wretched;**（痛ましい）**pathetic;**（いじらしい）**touching**

雨の中でぬれて震えている小犬がいかにも哀れで彼は家につれて帰った。

A puppy trembling in the rain touched him with pity and he took it home with him.

〈注〉「何と哀れな！」は「かわいそう」の項の「かわいそうに！」参照。

2．哀れむ

動 他 **pity; have [take] pity on**

私を哀れんでください。

Have pity on me.

3．もののあわれ

〈注〉日本古来の美意識であり英語にならないが，pathos が「そこはかとない悲しみ」を表す語であるからこれに近いと思われる。

源氏物語は恋物語の集成とも言うべきものだが根底にあるものは人生の無常とものののあわれである。

The Story of Genji is a collection of love stories, but the essence of it is the mutability and pathos of life.

あんしん（安心）→ しんぱい

1．安堵・ほっとする

be [feel] relieved（安心する［した］）

その事故で皆無事だったと知ってやれやれと安心した。

He was greatly relieved to know that no one was hurt in the accident.

無事と聞いて安心した。

He relaxed only when he heard they were all safe.

To my great relief I found out that they were all safe.

母子ともにもう安心だ［危機を脱した］。本当に安心しました。

Both the mother and the baby are out of danger; I'm really relieved.

【自信を持つ】

be [feel] reassured（安心する［した］）

彼は就職を決めてから少々不安だったが，友だちが賛成してくれて安心した。

He felt reassured about his job decision when his friend approved of it.

【心配するな】

安心なさい。

Be easy (about that).

Be at ease.

安心していなさいよ。

Don't worry.

安心してなさい，彼はきっと無事に帰ってくるから。

Rest assured, he will come back safe and sound.

〈注〉◆Please set your mind at ease [rest]. は正しい文だが古風である。
◆「安心させるように」「『大丈夫』と言うように」の意味で reassuringly 副 が使用できる。
彼女は僕に「安心なさい」と言うようにうなずいてにっこり笑いかけた。
She nodded and smiled at me reassuringly.

2. 平静・心配ないと思っている

安心している

feel confident（確信をもっている）

feel at ease（心配しない）

君の成功は間違いないと安心しているよ。

I feel confident of your success.

私は子供たちとはうまくいっていると安心している。

I feel easy about my relationship with my children.

そのことに関しては安心している。

I'm not a bit worried about that.

3. 安心感・こわくない

feel secure（安心だ）

あなたと一緒だと安心です。

I feel secure when you're with me.

全部戸締りをしないと安心できない。

Unless all the doors are locked he doesn't feel secure.

安心しろ，僕がついている。

Don't be afraid; I'm with you.（何かこわいことがあるとき）

【信頼できる】

安心して物事を任せられる[頼れる]人

a trustworthy [reliable] person

あの人なら安心だ。

We can trust him.

He can be trusted.

あんな

〈注〉「こんな，そんな，あんな」の相違については「それ・これ・あれ」参照。

あんな家に住みたい。

I'd like to live in a house like that.（家が目の前に見えていれば like this）

あんな働き者は見たことがない。

I have never seen such a hard worker.

あんなことは二度と言ってはならない。

Don't ever / Never } say that [this].

（今言ったのと同じ言葉を言うな）

Don't ever / Never } say { such a thing. / that sort of thing.

（いまの言葉およびそれに類することを言うな）

〈注〉「こんなこと」は such a thing を使うまでもなく that やthis だけで十分な場合が多い。

い

いい・よい

〈注〉「いい」は「よい」の口語形であり，「よい」よりもむしろ広く使われている。「いい」「よい」を一括して扱う。ただし主として「よい」が用いられる表現もあるので，それらについては「よい」の項にも収録する。

1. 上質・優良（評価）

【物】

いい品質の
　of good quality

これが一番いいワインです。
　This wine is of the highest quality.

このコートはものがいいのです。
　This coat is made of the finest fabric.

2. 人・能力

【頭がいい】

彼は頭のいい学生だ。
　He is a bright student.

〈注〉clever は「利口な，気のきいた」であり，bright は「頭のさえた」の意味である。smart は米語では「気のきいた，利発な」の意味で使われるが，英国では外見についてのみ用いる。

【腕がいい】

彼は腕のいい大工だ。
　He is {a very skilled / an excellent} carpenter.

【記憶力がいい】

彼は記憶力がいい［よい］。
　He has a good memory.

【物覚えがいい】

彼は物覚えがいい［よい］。
　He learns very quickly.

【物わかりがいい】

彼は物わかりがいい［よい］。
　He's a very understanding person.

【成績がいい】

彼は学校の成績がいい［よい］。
　He does well at school.
　His school record is very good.

【いい点】

彼はいい点を取った。
　He got a {high score. / good mark.}

3. 抽象物

【景気がいい】

彼の会社は景気がいい。
　His company is doing good business.

このところ景気がいい。
　Business is {going well. / brisk.}

【運がいい】

あの人は運がいい。
　He's lucky.

【いい金になる】

自分の土地を貸し駐車場にしていい金もうけをしている。
　He earns good money by letting cars park on his field.

【いい給料をとっている】

　He gets a good salary.
　He is well-paid.

【いい値(段)】

ずいぶんいい値段だね。
　That's pretty expensive, isn't it?

彼の家はいい値で売れた。
　He made a lot of money on the sale of his house.

〈注〉His house was sold ... と書き出す場合，for ¥50,000,000のように値段を入れるのが自然。

4. 善（事の善悪，道徳的判断）

【いい人】

　an honest person; a good [nice] person

【人がいい】

　a good-natured person

【いい本［話／行い］】

　a good book [story / deed]

【行儀のよい子】
a well-behaved boy [girl]
あの女の子は行儀がいい。
She has good manners.
【いい子】
ちょっと新聞もってきて。いい子だね。
Bring me the newspaper. That's a good boy [girl].

5. 快い，好ましい（感性的・感覚的判断）
【調子がいい（一般）】
いい調子でやってます。
I'm doing fine.
【調子がいい，気分がいい（体調）】
今朝は気分がいい。
I feel { well / better（前日よりよい）} this morning.
【気分がいい（快適）】
いい気分です。
I'm comfortable.
【病気】
「かぜはどうですか」「ありがとう。もうすっかりいいのです」。
"How's your cold?" "I'm all right now, thanks."
だいぶよくなりました。
I'm getting better, thanks.
【いい天気】
いい天気ですね。
It's a lovely [beautiful] day, isn't it?
The weather's pleasant today, isn't it?
【美観】
よい景色　beautiful scenery
景色のよい所　a scenic place
なんていい眺めでしょう。
What a beautiful view!
【音】
いい音楽　beautiful [lovely] music
あの人はいい声をしている。
She has a good [lovely, nice] voice.
【香り】
いいにおいがする。
It has a sweet [nice] smell.
このバラはいいにおいがする。
These roses are fragrant.
【味】
いい味だ。
This tastes [is] good.

6. 適切
【十分】
準備はよい。
Everything is ready.
出発準備はよい。
We are ready to start.
もういい（やめてくれ）。
That's enough.
もういいんだ（終った）。
It's all finished.
It's all right now.
【いい時】
君はちょうどいいときに来た。
You've come just at the right moment.
【都合】
いつがご都合がいいでしょうか。
When is it convenient for you?
【サイズ】
この服は私にちょうどいい。
This dress fits me perfectly.
【調和】
この服にはこのネクタイがいい。
This tie goes well with this suit.
〈注〉 dress はいわゆるワンピース，suit はスーツ，男性用なら背広のこと。
【有効】
自然食品は健康によい。
Natural food is good for health.
睡眠が一番いい薬だ。
Sleep is the best medicine.

7．是認

【それがいい】

そうだ，それだ。

That's it.

よろしい[その通り]。

That's right.（認める言い方）

【それでいい】

That will do.

That'll be enough.

That's good [enough].

【どちらでもいい】

Either is fine [good].

It doesn't matter.

〈注〉「解答は日本語でもよい」は ×Japanese is good. とは言わない。You can [may] answer in Japanese. が正しい。

8．選択

【どちら】

ビールとワインとどちらがいいですか。

Which {do you prefer / would you like} beer or wine?

ビールがいいです。

Beer please.

〈注〉◆Which do you like better, beer or wine? はどちらが好きか嗜好を尋ねる言い方で，食卓に着いてどちらにするか尋ねるのは上記の言い方である。

◆並と上とどちらにしましょうか。

Which shall we take, nami or jotoh?

並でいい。/ 上がいい。

Nami will do. / I prefer jotoh.

「それで我慢する」という意味の「それでいい」は That will do. であり，「その方がよい」と選択する意味合いは prefer で表す。

【いつ】

いつがご都合がいいでしょうか。

What time would suit you?

When will it be convenient for you?

いつがいい?

What's a good time (for you)?

【正しい選択】

青森行きはこの列車でいいでしょうか。

Is this the right train for Aomori?

9．希望

【未来】（…すると[しないと]いい）

明日は天気だといいが。

I hope it will be sunny tomorrow.

明日は雨が降らなければいいが。

I hope it won't rain tomorrow.

【現在・過去】（…だったらいい[よかった]のに）

もっと若かったらよかったのに。

I wish I were [was] younger.

もっと速く走れたらいいのに。

I wish I could run faster.

It'd be good to be able to run faster.

あの子にもっと優しくしてやればよかったと思った。

I wished I had been kinder to her.

10．当然（…していい頃だ）

東京を出発して1時間になる。そろそろ静岡に着いていい頃だ。

It's been an hour since we left Tokyo, so it's about time {to arrive at [in] / to get to} Shizuoka.

あと2か月で二十（はたち）になる。もうそろそろ親から独立していい頃だ。

You'll be twenty in two months. You should [ought to] be independent of your parents.

11．忠告・提案（…した方がいい → よい）

【忠告】

お父さんに話した方がいい。（強い言い方）

You had better tell your father about it.

だれにも話さない方がいいと思う。

I think we had better not tell anyone about it.

【提案】

ドライブに行くのなら，早く出かけた方がいい。

If you are going on a drive, I suggest you (should) start early.

〈注〉 you had better は命令のように強くひびくので

要注意。→「よい」の〈注〉参照。

12．許可

入ってもいいですか[いいかしら]。

Can [May] I come in?

Is it all right [OK] to come in?

いいですよ。

(Yes,) certainly. / Of course. / Yes, do.〔英〕/ Yes, do come in.

〈注〉 Yes, you may [can]. は正しい文だが You may は堅苦しい。you can はいばって聞えるので使わない方がよい。

まあいいさ[そのままにしておけ]。

OK, let it go (at that).

It's all right as it is.

Let it be.

OK, never mind.

たばこを吸ってもいいでしょうか。

Do [Would] you mind {if I smoke? / my smoking?} (あまり親しくない人に)

Is it all right if I smoke?（親しい間柄の人に）

明晩電話してもいいだろうか。

Is it all right to call you tomorrow evening?

いいかしら。いいかい。

(Is it) All right? / OK?（ごくくだけた形）

パンフレットを1冊いただいていいでしょうか。

Can [Could, May] I have a copy of this pamphlet?

いいきもち（いい気持ち）

1．快感

とてもいい気持ちです。

I'm feeling very good.

This is wonderful [nice].

How pleasant [nice]!

Just great!

【居心地のよい】 be comfortable, feel good

火の周りに座り，冷たい手や足先を暖めていい気持ちだった。

It felt good [comfortable] to sit round the fire warming our cold fingers and toes.

やっと腰を下ろし火に当って，いい気持ちになった。

We were comfortable at last, sitting around the fire.

「寒くありませんか」「いいえ，ここはとても気持ちがいいですよ」。

"Aren't you cold?" "No, it's very comfortable here."

〈注〉 comfortable は温度などが快適で居心地がよく，もう動きたくないような状態を言う。

【うっとり】

ジャズを聞いているといい気持ちになる。

Jazz music always transports me.

【いい気味】

二日酔で参ってるって。いい気味だ[自業自得だ]。

He had a bad hangover. It serves him right.

2．爽快

気持ちのいい風が吹いていた。

A pleasant wind was blowing.

午後の猛練習の後で涼しい風に当り，いい気持ちだった。

The cool wind felt [was] (wonderfully) refreshing after the hard training we had (had) all through the afternoon.

ふろに入り，皆いい気持ちになった(さっぱりした)。

We all felt refreshed after taking a bath.

〈注〉 pleasant は light, airy, cheerful で「爽快な感じを与える」という意味であるから「私はいい気持ちになった」のつもりで×I was pleasant. とは言えないので注意。

cf. He made an effort to be pleasant to them.
（彼は皆に気持ちよく接しようと努力した）

refresh は疲れた後，食べたりふろに入ったりして生気を取り戻すことであり，自分が主語で，いい気分になったのなら I felt refreshed. また主語がいいふろや冷たいおしぼりで，それが人を元気にさせたのなら They were refreshing. である。

いう（言う）→ はなす

〈注〉 発言の意味をもつ動詞 say, tell, talk, speak の区別については「はなす」の項参照。

1. …を言う

【物を言う】speak

あの人は内気で，よく知らない人の前では物が言えない。

She is too shy to speak {before / in front of} {people she doesn't know. / strangers.}

あの人はびっくりして物が言えなかった。

He was speechless with astonishment.

赤ちゃんは何か物を言い始めましたか。

Is the baby learning to talk [speak]?

【…のことを言う】talk about

何のことを言ってたの？

What were you talking about?

だれにもこのことは言わないで。

Don't tell anyone about it.

先日君の言っていた本はこれか。

Is this the book you mentioned the other day?

彼が君の新しいやり方のことを言っていたよ。

He referred to your new method (in his speech).

【どう[こう/そう]言う】say so

何て言っていた?

What did he say?

彼は自分でもそう言っていた。

He said so himself.

彼は何も言わなかった。

He didn't say anything.

何も言わないで!

Don't say anything!

2. …と言う

【名前】

人々は彼をビリー・ザ・キッドと言っている。

People call him Billy the Kid.

「この花は日本では何と言いますか」「椿と言います」。

"What do they call this flower in Japan?"

{"They call it / "It's called} "tsubaki"."

車で送ってくれたのは何と言う子だ。

What's the name of the boy who drove us home?

玄関にスミスさんという人が面会に来ていますが。

There's a Mr. Smith at the door who wants to see you.

3. 「…」と言う（発言引用の直接・間接話法）

〈注〉 いつでも喜んでお手伝いしますと彼女は言った。

She said, "I'm always willing to help you." (1)

She said that she was always willing to help me. (2)

ネイティブスピーカーによると(1)の直接話法は不自然で，ほとんどの場合(2)の間接話法をとるという。発言が特に面白い表現だったとき((3)の文のように）や口まねをする場合以外は小説の中の会話は別として，直接話法で発話を引用することはあまりないという。

［直接話法］子供たちが「おカネはあるかい」と言うところを「ネカはあるかい」と言うのを聞いておかしかった。 (3)

I was amused when I heard children say, "Have you any yenom?" instead of saying, "Have you any money?".

［間接話法］出張でパリに行くという手紙をもらった。 (4)

I got a letter from him saying that he would go to Paris on business.

［強調］あの人は絶対に（自分）一人で全部やったと言った。 (5)

She declared that she had done it all by herself.

【…してください[くれ]】ask to do

彼はドアを開けて入れてくれと言った。 (6)

He asked her to open the door and let him in.

【…しないでくれ】ask not to do

こわいからひとりっきりにしないでと言った。 (7)

She asked me not to leave her alone, as she was frightened.

【…しなさい[しろ]】tell to do

医者が1か月の休養をとれと言った。 (8)

The doctor told him to {take a month's rest. / rest for a month.

【…してはいけない[するな]】tell not to do

医者がたばこは吸うなと言った。 (9)

The doctor told him not to smoke.

【…してはどうか】suggest

みんなでピクニックに行ってはどうかと言った。 (10)

He suggested that they should all go on a picnic together.

〈注〉 日本人は第三者の発言をそのままの形で英作文・英会話の中に入れることが多く，不自然な印象を与える。これは，日本文の中では発言を引用する際，直接話法と間接話法の中間話法とも言うべき形をとるからではないか。上にあげた例文(3)〜(10)の日本文を見るとわかるが，引用されている発言が(3)を除き，直接発言そのもの(直接話法)か，発言の大意要約(間接話法)か判定がつきにくい。(8)(9)は要約(間接話法)と考えられる。(6)(7)はほとんどそのまま「 」をつけて直接の発話ととることもできる。このように日本語の話法は英語の間接話法のように客観的な要約ではなく，また発言そのものをそのまま移した形とも違う。日本語では発言に主格を示す語が表示されないことが多いので，このように中間的であいまいな形が可能になる。そのために日本人の書く英語には直接話法の使用が多くなるので注意が必要である。

4. オノマトペとの結合

【「あっ」と言う】

部屋の中に招じ入れられると(驚きと喜びで)あっと言った。

When she was shown into the room, she exclaimed in joy and astonishment.

あっと言う間に in the twinkling of an eye

【「きゃっ」と言う】

大きなヘビが目の前をはってゆくのを見てきゃっと言った。

She screamed at the sight of a big snake moving ahead of her.

【ぶつぶつ言う】

不平を言う complain

口ごもる mutter

【がみがみ言う】scold, nag

5. 慣用

【言うこと】what one says

あの人の言うことはわからない(思考パターンが違う)。

I can't understand what he says.

あの人の言っていることがわからない。(今言っていることが)

I can't understand what he is saying.

… ×understand his saying.

言うことを聞きなさい。

Be obedient.(従順)

Listen to me.(耳を貸しなさい)

言われた通りにしなさい。

Do as I tell you.

Do as you are told.

【言いたいこと】

what one wants to say(言い分)

君の言いたいことはそれだけか。

Is that all you want to say?

言いたいこと[言い分]があれば何でも言いなさい。

Say anything you want to.

君の言いたいこと(意味)はわかっている。

I know what you mean.

【…と言われている】

It is said that ….

They say that ….

【…と言うほどの】

趣味と言うほどのものはない。

I have no special hobby.

I have no hobby to speak of.

【…言[口]を言う】

小言を言う scold, nag, chide

泣き言を言う

complain (of), complain (that) …

たわ言を言う talk nonsense

つくり言を言う
　tell a made-up story
　tell a lie（意味が強い）
悪口を言う
　speak ill of a person
陰口を言う
　backbite
　speak ill of a person behind his back
【言いつける】
あんたのこと言いつけてやる。
　I'll tell on you.
【物を言う（有効である）】
物を言うのは本人の能力だ。
　It's one's real ability that tells.
【諺】
言うは易く，行うは難し。
　Easier said than done.

いえ（家）→ うち，かぞく

a house;（a）home

〈注〉 house は「家屋」を指し，home は「家庭」を指すと言われるが，今では home をhouse と同様に使う傾向が強い。

【建物・場所】
これが彼の住んでいる家[所]だ。
　This is where he lives.
〈注〉 この文に house や home という語は含まれていないが，これが一番普通の言い方である。
これがエマーソンの生れた家だ。
　This is the house in which Emerson was born.
家に帰ろう。
　Let's go home now.
1週間家をあけていた。（留守にしていた）
　He has been away for a week.
【住所】 one's place of residence〔*formal*〕
家はどこですか。
　Where do you live?

家　House

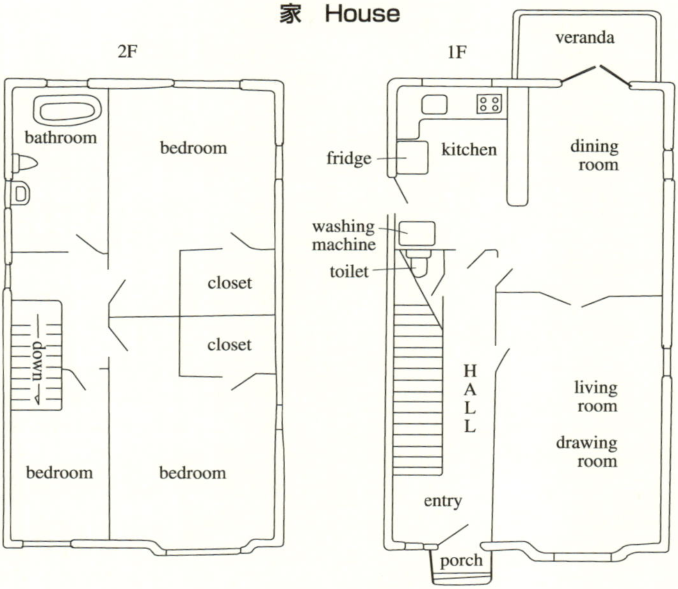

平面図　Floor Plan of the House

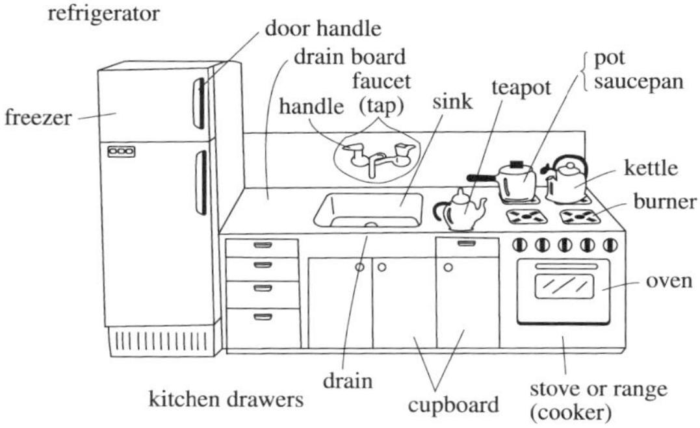

台所　Kitchen

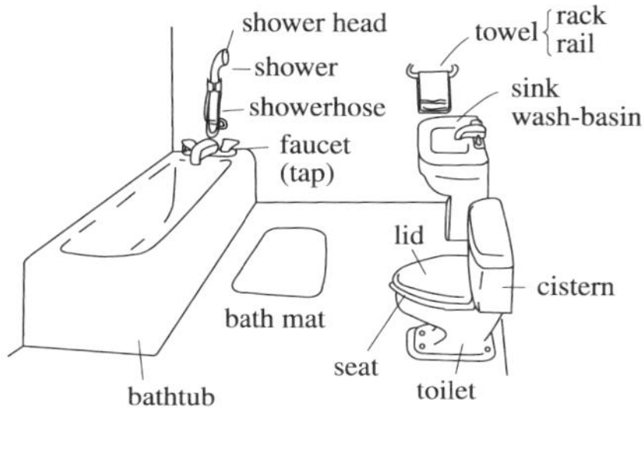

浴室　Bathroom

【家族・家系】

彼は貧しい家に生れた。

He was born poor.

あの人は良家の出です。

The girl {is of / comes from} a good family.

彼の家は代々学者の家だ。

For generations his family have been scholars.

彼の家は15世紀から続いている家だ。

His family line {goes back / can be traced back} to the 15th century.

いがい（以外）→ ほか

【除 外】**except (for); but; excluding; excepting**

進学するトムとビル以外は皆卒業後には就職を希望していた。

All of them wanted to get a job after graduation except Tom and Bill, who were to go up to college.

[－(Tom and Bill)＝excluding (Tom and Bill)]

〈注〉 except（除外）も besides（追加）も日本語では同じく「以外」と表現するためによく混同される。わかりやすいように(＋, －)の記号をつけてみた。

スペリングの誤りが少々ある以外は君のレポートはよく書けている。

Your report is all right except for a few spelling mistakes.

[－(a few spelling mistakes)＝if it were not for (...)]

〈注〉◆except とexcept for

except は not including; but（…を除いて）の意。

Everyone is ready except Jim.（ジムだけまだ用意ができていない）

except for は if it were not for, but for（…を除いてほかは）の意。

The beach was deserted except for a tall girl in a black bathing suit walking along the water's edge.（黒の海水着の背の高い少女が水際を歩いていることを除けば海岸は人気(ひとけ)がない）

そのために完全に deserted とは言えない。ただし except と except for は意味が接近しているのでどちらでも使える場合があり，区別なしに使うことが多い。

Except (for) these few, our students are studying hard.（この2, 3人の生徒（が怠けている）以外は皆一生懸命勉強しています）

「彼は妻以外の女性を愛した」は

×He loved a woman except his wife. は誤り。

He loved a woman other than his wife. としなければならない。

◆except /iksépt/と expect /ikspékt/の発音を混同しないよう注意。

【追加】besides; in addition to

トム以外にだれが進学しますか？

Who is to go up to college besides Tom? [＋(Tom)＝in addition to (Tom)]

彼はよい父親だ。それ以外でも完璧だが。

He's a good father besides being everything else.

【その他】other; other than; others; else (除外，追加どちらにも使われる)

トムとビルは進学，それ以外は就職希望だ。

Tom and Bill want to go up to college, but all the others want to get a job.

トム以外に進学希望者はあるか。

Is there anyone other than Tom who wants to go up to college?

(Tom wants to go up to college.) Who else wants to go up to college.

彼は詩人で学者で批評家だ。それ以外にもまだあるかな？

He is a poet, scholar and critic. What else is he?

いがい (意外) → おどろく

【意外な】

形 unexpected (意外な); unforeseen (予想できない，よくない結果を思わせる); unsuspected (気がついてよさそうなのに気づかなかった); surprising (思いがけない，驚きの感情が強い)

意外な出来事だった。

It was quite a surprise.

意外なことが起った。

Something unexpected happened.

【意外に(も)】

副 unexpectedly; to one's surprise; 予想に反して contrary to one's expectation; 予想以上に beyond one's expectations

彼女は意外にも数学の学年末試験にパスした。

Contrary to her expectation, she passed the math final.

彼の数学の学年末試験の点は意外によい点だった。

The score on his math final was far beyond his expectations.

意外に時間がかかった。

It took {more time / longer} than we (had) expected.

彼は意外に早く回復した。

He recovered faster than we (had) expected.

【意外だ】

彼が1等を取るとは意外だ。

We were all surprised that he got [should have gotten] the first prize.

cf. (意外にも) Quite unexpectedly [To our surprise] he got the first prize.

〈注〉「…するとは意外だった」は下記の通り。
We were surprised that
{he should get [have got(ten)] …〔*formal*〕 / he got …〔*informal*〕}

いかが → どう

いかす (生かす) → つかう

【活用する】

use, make the most [best use] of

英語を生かす仕事に就きたい。

I'd like to get a job in which I can {put my English to (practical) use. / use my knowledge of English.}

このところ女性にとって，大学での専門を生かす仕事に就くことは難しい。

Nowadays it is hard for women to get a job in which they can use {the knowledge they acquired / what they specialized in} in college.

【趣味を生かした生活】

〈注〉「趣味を生かす」を英語にすると抽象的で奇妙に聞えるので，次の例文のように趣味を具体的に述べた方がよい。

趣味と実益を兼ねて花を育てよう。

I will grow flowers for

both pleasure and profit.
pleasure and profit both.

私はバイオリンを生涯続けていきたい。

I'd like to continue practicing the violin all my life.

【最大限に活用】

彼は数学者になれば才能を十分に生かすことができる。

He can make the most of his talents by becoming a mathematician.

あの人は預金を株に注ぎ込んで，最大限に生かした。

She made the most [best use] of her savings by investing in stocks.

いかに → どう，どんな

〈注〉「いかに」は形式ばった表現で下記のような特殊な場合に限り使われるので，同義語として「どう」「どんな」の項参照。

【いかに…べきか】

何をいかに読むべきかを彼は教えてくれた。

He taught us what to read and how to read.

人生に絶望していたとき，生きる勇気を与え，いかに生きるべきかを教えてくれたのは聖書であった。

It was the Bible that gave me courage and taught me how to live when I was in despair about my life.

いかり（怒り）

anger; 激怒 **rage, fury**〔強〕; 憤慨 **indignation**

【慣用的な言い方】

怒らせる

make a person angry [furious]

put a person into a rage

怒りを抑える　control one's anger

怒りにまかせて　in a fit of anger [rage]

怒りを抑えかねて[怒りにまかせて]彼をぶってしまった。

I just couldn't control my anger, and I hit him.

I hit him in a fit of anger.

いきがい（生きがい）

something to live for

【生きがいがある[を見つける]】

よい人生を送るには何か生きがいを見つけることだ。

To live a good life, it is essential to find something to live for.

彼は何か生きがい[人生の目標]を持つことが必要だ。

He needs some purpose [aim, goal] in [for] his life.

私には何も生きがいがない。

I have nothing to live for.

【生きがいある人生】

私は生きがいある人生を送りたい。

I would like to lead a worthwhile [useful] life.

I'd like to live to some purpose.

生きがいになる[やりがいある]仕事

work / a job } worth { doing / making an effort for

×work worth living

いきる（生きる）

生きる　動自 **live**

生きている　**be alive; be living**

赤ん坊はたった3日間生きていただけだった。

The baby lived only for three days.

寝る前に見たときは魚は生きていた。

The fish was alive when I looked at it before going to bed.

〈注〉形容詞としての alive は be alive の形で補語としてのみ用いる。×an alive fish は誤りで，a living fish とするのが正しい。

生きている限り

as long as one lives; to the end of one's life; for the rest of one's life

80歳まで生きる　live to be eighty
生きて帰る　return alive
生き残る　survive; remain alive
全乗客中生き残ったのはわずか7名であった。
Only seven (out) of (all) the passengers survived.
生き返る　come to life; revive
生き物　a living creature [being / thing]
cf.　家畜（集合名詞）livestock (live- /láiv-/ は「生きている」の意の形容詞）

いく（行く）→ ゆく，こうつう

いくつ（幾つ）

1．年齢

いくつですか。
How old are you?
高校を卒業するといくつになりますか。
How old will you be when you {graduate from / finish} high school?
彼のお父さんが亡くなったのは彼がいくつのときでしたか。
How old was he when his father died?
いくつで小学校にあがるのですか。
At what age do children enter primary school?

2．数

【いくつあるか】
箱の中にいくつりんごがありますか。
How many apples are there in the box?
パーティーのためのオレンジはいくつありますか。
How many oranges do you have for the party?
いくつ欲しいのですか。
How many of these do you want?
あといくつ(りんごが)足りないのですか。
How many more (apples) do you want [need]?

【いくつか(の)】 some; several
〈注〉 **several**　3つ以上で many と言うには少ない数。
some　はっきりした量や数で言えない，また言う必要のない場合，漠然と「いくらか」，「いくつか」の意で使う。
a few　2，3の（場合によってはほとんど some と同義）。しかし There are a few apples on the table. と言うと Where are all the others?　のように「少ない」という気持ちがある。some には特にそれはなく，主観的な差である。ただし quite a few は「かなり多い」の意。
もういくつか欲しい。
I want several [some] more.
過去2，3年の間に世界史に残るような政治上の重大事件がいくつか起った。
During the past few years several politically important incidents have occurred which will be recorded in world history.

いくら（幾ら）

1．値段

これはいくら？
How much is this?
How much does it cost?
この指輪はいくら？
What's the price of this ring?
これでいくらになりますか。
How much {does it come to / are they} all together?
これはいくらでしたか。
How much was this?
How much did it cost?
How much did you pay for it?
時給いくら？
How much do they pay an hour?
妻の病気を治すためならいくらでも出します。
I would pay any price [give anything] to cure my wife's illness.

2．譲歩

【いくら…でも】

no matter how …; however …

いくら君が金持でもあの子の心は買えないよ。

No matter how / However } rich you are [may be], you cannot buy her heart with money.

いくら働いても借金が返せなかった。

No matter how / However } hard he worked, he could not pay back his debts.

いくら遅くとも10時までにはそこに着くはずだ。

They will get there by ten o'clock at the latest.

あの子はいくらほめてもほめ足りない。

You cannot praise her too much.

〈注〉 how, however は副詞であるから形容詞，副詞があとに続く。×however he worked hard は誤りである。however hard と続けねばならない。米国では no matter how の方が一般的になりつつある。英国では however も no matter how も同じように使われている。

いけない

1．禁止（…してはいけない）

授業中に私語してはいけない。

Don't talk in class.

You must not talk in class.

無断で部屋に入ってはいけません。

You cannot enter the room without permission.

「出かけていい？」「いけません。ガレージの掃除が先ですよ」。

"May I go out?"

"No, { you should clean the garage first." / not until you've cleaned the garage."

お母さんが川に泳ぎにいってはいけないと言った。

My mother told me not to go swimming in the river.

2．用心（…するといけない）

【遅れると…】

終電に乗り遅れるといけないからタクシーに乗った方がいい。

You should take a taxi so (that) you won't miss the last train home.

【冷えると…】

何か暖かい服を持っていきなさい。急に寒くなるといけないから。

Take warm clothes with you in case the weather turns [should turn] cold.

【忘れると…】

ちょっと電話番号を書くからね。忘れるといけないから。

I'll jot down your telephone number { so I won't forget it. / or (else) I might forget it.

【迷うと…】

暗くなってきたね。道に迷うといけないな，気をつけてね。

It's getting dark. { Don't get lost. / Be careful not to get lost.

〈注〉 文法で習う lest … should (…するといけないから) はあまりに時代遅れである。for fear … も日常の会話にはおおげさである。上記のような表現が自然。

3．必要（…しなくてはいけない）

have to

8時を過ぎた。もう出かけなくてはいけない。

It's past eight. I have to go now.

4．不満・同情表現

［挨拶として］

「ひどいかぜをひいてね」「そりゃいけないね」。

"I've caught a bad cold." "That's too bad."

〈注〉 「頭が痛い」"I have a headache." とだれかが言ったときの応答として，子供が相手なら「かわいそうに」"Oh, you poor thing." などと言うが，通常は「少し横になって休んだら」"Oh dear! Why don't you lie down for a while?" のような提案をする。

天気が悪くていけないね。(現在降っている)

What a pity that { it's raining. / it should rain. }

遠足の日に雨降りでいけなかったね。(後から述べる場合)

What a pity that it rained on the day of their picnic.

5. 非難

【悪い】

そんなやり方ではいけない。

That's wrong.

あなたがいけない。(ひどい非難)

You are wrong [at fault].

【絶望】

病人はもういけない。

The patient is getting worse; there's no hope he'll be cured.

【失敗】

彼は司法試験がまたいけなかった。

He failed the bar examination again.

【失望の叫び】

あっ, いけない。すっかり忘れていた。

Oh no! I've completely forgotten.

あっ, いけない。もう11時半, 終電に間に合わない。

Oh no! It's already eleven thirty. I won't be able to catch the last train home.

〈注〉 oh no は標準的, oh dear は上品な女性が言う。口語, 俗語ではほかにもいろいろある。

いけん(意見)

意見 **an opinion;** 見解 **a view;** 忠告 **advice;** 提言 **a suggestion;** 思いつき **an idea**

【意見を述べる】

give one's opinion (on, about)

〈注〉 意見の性質が忠告であれば give advice または 動 他 advise を使えばよい。「…したらどうか」のような言い方なら suggest 他 を使い, その意見は a suggestion である。

【意見がある】

何かご意見はありませんか(全員に向かって)。

Does anyone have an opinion?

ほかにご意見は?

Is there anyone who has something more to say?

Are there any other opinions?

(違ったご意見は)

Do any of you have different opinions?

(いい考えがないか)

Is there any suggestion?

Does anyone have a suggestion?

(だれか特定の人, 特にその道の権威などに発言を求めて) 何かコメントはございませんか。

Would you like to comment [say something]?

Would you like to speak about [to] this?

【意見を求める】

ask a person's opinion

【意見が合う[一致する]】

賛成する

agree with a person [person's opinion]

お別れ会を開くことに意見が一致した。

We all agreed to hold a farewell party.

【意見が合わない[違う]】 don't agree; disagree with a person [person's opinion]

その点で私は父と意見が合わない。

I disagree with my father on that point.

We have different opinions about it.

彼はほとんどいつでも同僚たちと意見が違う。

His opinion almost always differs from that of his colleagues.

最後まで意見の一致を見なかった。

We couldn't reach an agreement.

We failed to come to an agreement.

私と父とは意見が正反対だ。

My opinion is the opposite of my father's.

いごこち（居心地）→ いいきもち

いし（石）→ ちしつ

いし（意志・意思）→ こころ，つもり

意図　**will, an intention**

1．性格（意志の強弱）
彼は意志が強い。
He is a strong-willed man [a man of iron will].
He is strong-willed.
私は意志が弱い。
I am weak-willed.
I have a weak will.
I have no will power.
I am easily tempted.

2．決断（自分の意志）
私は自分の意志でそうしたのだ。
I did it of my own free will.
私は自分の意志に反してそうさせられた。
I was forced to do that.
私は仕事をやめる意志はない。
I have no intention of giving up my work.
〈注〉この形は慣用的な用法で，常に否定の意味合いで使われる。

3．意志の疎通
あの人たちは意志の疎通が悪い。
There's a lack of understanding between them.
あの人たちは意志が完全に通じ合っている。
They understand each other perfectly.

いじめる

《類義語》
pick on　口でちくちくいびる（意味的にはさほどきつくない）。
bully　子供の弱い者いじめ（主に腕力でだが，口でいじめる場合にも用いる。意味的には強い）。
push around　大人・子供について，主として口でいじめる。時には腕力による場合も含む。

1．腕力
小さい者をいじめるんじゃない。
Don't bully smaller kids [children].
あいつはいじめっ子だ。
He's a bully.
〈注〉口でいじめるのなら He picks on smaller children. とする。

2．口で
いじめないでよ。
Stop picking on me.
Don't pick on me.
がみがみ言わないで。
Stop nagging me.
そうつらく当らないで。（不当に批判されたり，用事を言いつけられたりした場合）
Don't be so hard on me.
〈注〉be hard on は天候や台風など自然が厳しい場合にも用いられる。
Cold weather is hard on old people.
（寒いのは老人にはきつい）
× ... bullies old people. とは言わない。

【からかい】　tease
兄さんはいつもボーイフレンドのことで私をいじめるの。
My brother {always teases me / is always hard on me} about my boyfriend.

いじょう（以上）

1．より上
over; more than; above; further; beyond; upwards of
1万円以上
［正確］from ten thousand yen up
［概算］more than ten thousand yen
〈注〉「1万円以上」は「1万円を含めて，それ以上」。

"more than ¥10,000" は「1万円より多額な金」で1万円を含めて考えないので厳密には同じではない。以下 "more than" と「以上」の相違を念頭において読んでいただきたい。ただし "more than one" は1より多いが通例単数扱いである。

私は1万円以上使った。（ずいぶん使った）

I spent even more than 10,000 yen.

I spent a whole 10,000 yen or more.

1マイル以上

a little more than a mile; just over a mile

6歳以上の子供

children (of) six (years) and up [over]

children from six years (up)

〈注〉 children over six years old はちょうど6歳を含まない。6歳半くらいから考える。

50円以上100円まで

from 50 (yen) to 100 yen

between 50 and 100 yen

台風の被害は予想以上であった。

The typhoon did [caused] much more damage than we expected.

There was much greater damage from the typhoon than we expected.

2. 上記の

以上の事実（公式文書に用いられる正式な言い方）

the above-mentioned facts

the facts mentioned [stated] above

以上のように（上述のように）

as (I) said before

as already mentioned

as (I've) already said [mentioned, stated]

〈注〉 I に適当な主語を入れる。

3. …からには

since; now that; so long as

やりかけた以上は最後までやり遂げるべきだ。

Once you've started, stay at it until you're finished.

親の世話になっている以上，モーターバイクを買う前に親に話すべきだ。

Since your parents support you, you should ask them before you buy a motorbike.

4. おしまい

以上 the end（作文などの終りにいちいち the end と書く必要はない）

以上です。

That's all.

〈注〉 以上で私の話を終ります。

… (*after a pause*) Thank you.（話を終えるときの挨拶としては，2～3秒の間をおいて清聴のお礼として Thank you. で締めくくる）

いたたまれない → はずかしい

恥ずかしくていたたまれない思いだった。

I was so embarrassed that I felt like running away.

人々の視線を感じていたたまれなかった。

I couldn't stand remaining there with all the people staring at me.

〈注〉 いたたまれない理由として，ただきまりが悪くて (embarrassed) 居心地が悪い (uncomfortable) こともあれば，実際に道徳的な間違いを犯し，恥じ入って (ashamed) いたたまれない場合もある。「恥ずかしい」の内容に注意。「穴があったら入りたい」に当る次のような言い方もある。

I could have crawled under the rug.（敷物の下）

I wish the floor had swallowed me.
I could have fallen through the floor.｝（床下）

I could have crawled into a hole.（穴）にもぐりたい。

いたみ（痛み）・いたい

《類義語》

pain 痛みを表す一般的な語。ache より強く，ここが痛いと指摘できる。

dull pain 鈍痛

sharp pain
bad pain
severe pain ｝きつい痛み ひどい痛み

throbbing pain ずきんずきんと脈打つ痛み

ache 持続的な鈍痛で，部位を特定しにくいもの。

headache(頭痛), toothache(歯痛), stomach-ache (胃痛)
smart ひりひり，ずきずきする痛み。
pang 激痛

1. 痛む，痛みがある

〈注〉「人」を主語にする言い方 "I have pain in my chest." と「痛む場所」を主語にする言い方 "My chest hurts." とがあるので注意。また，冠詞は a dull pain とか a bad pain のように特に形容詞がつくときは必要。

【人主語】 have [feel] pain

胸に痛みがある。
　I have (a) pain in my chest.

のどが痛い。
　I have a sore throat.

腰がひどく痛む。
　I have a bad pain in my back.

歯[頭]が痛い。
　I have a toothache [headache].

【場所主語】（この形が最も一般的）
　動 hurt; smart（ひりひり，ずきずきする）; ache（うずく）

足の切り傷が痛む。
　The cut on my leg hurts [smarts].

足[脚]が痛む。
　My leg hurts (me).

節々が痛む。
　My joints ache.

【it 主語】（動作などで痛む）
　be painful; 動 hurt, pain

呼吸をすると痛い。
　It's painful to breathe.
　It hurts when I breathe.

左腕が痛くて上がらない。
　I can't raise my left arm. It hurts me.
　It hurts to raise my left arm.

どこが痛むんですか。
　Where does it hurt?

2. その他

【痛いところ】

痛いところにボールが当った。
　The ball hit my sore spot.

【叫び】

あいたっ！
　Ouch!

ああ痛い！
　Oh, it hurts!
　Oh, it's awful!

【痛みが止まる[始まる]】

痛みが止まった。
　The pain stopped.

また痛み出した。
　The pain started (up) again.

この薬で痛みが止まるだろう。
　This medicine will { stop [kill] / reduce(和らげる) } the pain.

痛み止め　a painkiller

いちばん（一番）

1. 第一番

the first; number one (No.1); the first place

私が一番に到着した。
　I got [arrived] there first.
　I was the first to arrive.

その人たちは一番[始発]列車で出発した。
　They took the first train in [of] the morning.

2. 最優秀

ジョンは一番だ。
　John is the best student.
　John is first in his class.

数学ではスーザンが一番だ。
　Susan leads [is first in] the class in mathematics.

期末試験ではケンが一番だった。
　Ken came out { on top / first [at the top] } in the final exams.

一番は370点だった。

The highest {points were / score was} 370.

The best student [candidate] got 370 points.（在学生[受験生]の）

3．最上級

一番下の娘

the [our, their] youngest daughter

一番の問題は金だ。

The biggest problem is money.

Money is the biggest problem.

一番残念なのは…

What I regret most is that ....

メアリの一番好きな科目は音楽だ。

Mary likes music best (of all her subjects at school).

【遠近】

一番近いバス停　the nearest bus stop

一番手前の列の赤い帽子の女の子

the girl with a red cap standing in the line [queue] nearest us

【内外】

一番内側[外側]の部分

the innermost [outermost] part

【上下】

本棚の一番上[下]段で右の方の青い本

the blue book on the top [bottom] shelf on the right

【方角】

日本で一番北の港

the northernmost port in Japan

いっしょうけんめい（一生懸命）

1．全力

彼は朝から晩まで一生懸命働いた。

He worked hard from morning till night.

ひどいかぜで数学の授業を２回休んだので，追いつくために一生懸命勉強しなければならなかった。

He missed two math classes because of the flu and had to study hard to catch up.

僕は一生懸命走りに走った。

I ran all out.〔*colloq.*〕

I ran with all my might.

I ran as fast as {I could. / possible.}

2．夢中

子供たちは粘土細工に一生懸命だった。

The children are absorbed in (their) clay modeling.

彼は一生懸命命がけで逃げた。

He ran for his life.

いっしょに（一緒に）

1．共に

【いる】

一緒にいる　be with

一緒に住む　live with

一緒の部屋に住む

share a room with

私たちは祖父母と一緒に暮している。

We live with our grandparents.

私たちは（座って）一緒にテレビを見ていた。

We sat together watching TV.

【行く，来る】

go [come] (along) with; go [come] together

さあ一緒に行こう。

Let's go along [too].

〈注〉　×Let's come [go together] with me [us]. は誤り。let's のus の中に you も me [us] も含まれている。

次の日曜日にハイキングに行くんですが一緒にいらっしゃいませんか。

We are planning to go on a hike next Sunday. Would [Won't] you {join us? / come along?}

【連れて】

私は妹も一緒に連れていった。

I took my little sister along with me.

ねえ，一緒に連れてって！
Please let me go with you!
【一緒になる】join
ビルは仙台からだから，明日の夕方我々と一緒になる予定だ。
Bill is coming from Sendai, so he'll join us tomorrow evening.
【その他】
さあみんなで一緒に歌いましょうよ。
Let's all sing together.（勧誘）
（さあ歌って，）はい一緒に。
(Let's sing.) All together!（指示）

2．混同
【物について】一緒にする mix
これをほかの書類と一緒にしないでくれ。
Don't mix up these papers with the others.
Set them aside.（別にしておいてくれ）
【比喩的に】
あいつと一緒にしないでくれ。（人間が違うのだから）
Don't compare me to him.
Don't think I'm the same as him.
I'm not him.

いっち（一致）

1．合意
私と彼の意見が一致した。
I agreed with him.
我々は新しい日程に関し意見の一致をみた。
We agreed on [about] the new schedule.
我々は提案を受け入れることで意見が一致した。
We agreed to accept the proposal.
提案は満場一致で採択された。
The proposal was accepted unanimously.
だれが行くかについて意見が一致しなかった。
We could not agree on who should go.
Our opinions differed.（意見が分かれた）
〈注〉 **agree の用法**（×We are agree. は誤り）
不定詞をとる We agreed to go.
that 節をとる We agreed that he should go.
種々の前置詞については次のようになる。
agree on [about]（論議の題目に）
agree to（提案・行動に）
agree with（意見・考えに）
agree with（人の言うことに）

2．その他
【共通】
我々は趣味が一致する。
We have tastes in common.
我々は2人ともクラシック音楽が好きという点で一致している。
We both have a taste for classical music.
【矛盾】
理論と実践はしばしば一致しないものだ。
Theory and practice do not necessarily [always] go together.
彼は言行が一致しない。
His behavior { is at odds with / contradicts / does not agree with } his words.
His words and actions are usually inconsistent.
His words and actions have [show] no consistency.
His actions are rarely consistent with his words.
【協力】
全員一致協力のおかげで仕事は早く片付いた。
Everyone cooperated and the job was finished quickly.
あのグループはなかなか一致しなかった[まとまらなかった]。
The group lacked unity.

いっぱい（一杯）

1．充満
〈注〉「…が…でいっぱい」は be filled with, be full of のどちらでもよいが，この二つの形を混同し

た ×be full with, ×be filled of, は誤り。

そこはスキーヤーでいっぱいだった。

The place was { full of / filled with / crowded with } skiers.

水差しには水がいっぱい入っていた。

The pitcher was { full of / filled with } water.

【器】

コップ1杯の水　a cup of water

バケツ1杯の水　a bucketful of water

本のいっぱい入った箱

a box { packed with / full of } books

【腹】

おなかがいっぱいだ。

I'm full.

【胸】

胸がいっぱいだった。

My heart was full.

胸がいっぱいで何も言えなかった。

I was overcome with emotion and could not speak a word.

【思い出】

この場所には思い出がいっぱいある。

I have so many memories about [connected with] this place.

2. 多数

【人で】

午後11時過ぎなのに通りは人でいっぱいだった。

The street was crowded although it was past eleven p.m.

彼の家の前にいっぱい人が押しかけていた。

There was a crowd in front of his house.

3. 慣用句

一杯食わす　play a trick on a person

一杯機嫌で　feeling high [tipsy]

〈注〉 feeling mellow はいい気分になったところ。feeling sozzled というと千鳥足でもうろうとなっていること。

いつまでも

〈注〉 日本語の「いつまでも」は時間的に区切りをつけず漠然と「ずっと長く」の気持ちである。英語でも forever と言うことがあるが，as long as you like（お好きなだけ），all my life（生きている限り）のようにもう少し具体的に表現するのが普通のようである。人間は「いつまでも」生きられるものではないから。

1. 一生

いつまでも忘れません。

I'll never forget you { all my life. / as long as I live.

I'll remember you forever.

2. ずっと長く

【長すぎる】

いつまでも子供のつもりではいけない。

You're old enough to stop [quit] being a child.

本をいつまでもお借りしていてすみません。

I'm sorry I'm keeping your book so long.

【名残りを惜しんで】

列車がトンネルに消えるまで，彼女はいつまでも手を振っていた。

She waved until the train disappeared into the tunnel.

【好きなだけ】

どうぞいつまでもここにいらしてください。

Please stay here as long as you like.

【儀礼的挨拶】

いつまでもお元気で。

Good luck!

Take care.

〈注〉 この場合，「いつまでも」は無理に訳さない方がよい。友人や親しい人に別れ際の挨拶としては

I'm glad we met.

It was nice seeing you.

Good luck!

また，米国では Take care (of yourself). ともよく言う。

いと（意図）→ つもり，こころ

an intention

彼の意図がわからない。

I cannot figure out his intentions.

His intentions are not clear.

I wonder what he is aiming at.

〈注〉 もっとくだけた口語表現「いったいどんなつもりだろうか」となると What's he up to?

彼に面倒を起す意図はない。

He has no intention of making trouble.

いとしい（愛しい）→ かわいい

いなか（田舎）

1．田舎

the country (cities, town に対して); **the countryside;** 田園 **rural district**(s); 地方 **local area**(s)

あの人たちは田舎に住んでいる

They live in the country.

【田舎の生活】

近頃都会の人たちは田舎の生活にあこがれている。

City people yearn for rural life nowadays.

田舎の生活には田舎の厳しさがある。

Rural life has its hardships, too.

【田舎の景色】

半世紀前の日本の田舎は，きっと信じがたいほど美しかっただろう。

The countryside in Japan must have been incredibly beautiful half a century ago.

【田舎の人】

a country person（1人），country people, rural people

〈注〉 rural（田舎の）に対する語は urban（都会の）。

あいつは田舎者だ，とはけなす言い方だ。

"He's very countrified" is derogatory.

〈注〉 「田舎者」という言い方は軽蔑的であるが，unsophisticated（洗練されていない，自然な，素朴な）はよい意味でも使われる。ruralは「のどかな」といったよい意味もあり，一般に中立的な立場で使われる安全な語である。rustic は「あか抜けしない，粗野な」の意味に使われることが多いが，「純朴な」というよい意味もある。「田舎風」に対する評価の多様性が表れていると言える。

【田舎の出身】

彼は田舎の出身に違いない。(やや中傷する響きがある)

He must've {been born on / come from} {a / the} farm.

【すごい田舎】

きのうすごい田舎に行ってきた。

We went to
{a wonderful rustic place yesterday. (1)
a terribly rustic place yesterday. (2)}

〈注〉 (1)田舎を美しいと評価している。
(2)田舎は不便で野暮だと軽蔑している。

2．故郷

one's **home;** one's **hometown**

【田舎は…だ】

「どちらの出身ですか」「田舎は四国です」。

"Where are you from?" "I'm from Shikoku."

【田舎へ帰る】

正月を田舎で過そうと人々が帰省する。

People go home [back to their hometowns] to spend the New Year holiday with their folks.

〈注〉 欧米では正月休みはない。クリスマスとその翌日(Boxing Day〔英〕)および元日が休みになるだけである。holiday は3日あるからといって holidays と複数にしなくてよい。

いのる（祈る）

【神仏に】

pray; say a prayer（お祈りをする）

人々は記念日には集まって世界平和を祈った。

People gathered on the memorial day and prayed for {the peace of / peace in} the world.

出発前に神に加護を祈った。

Before starting he prayed to the gods to

protect him from danger.

〈注〉 God はキリスト教の神。gods と小文字で複数にすれば異教の神々を指す。日本なら神道の神々のこと。

【儀礼的挨拶】

ご成功を祈ります。

I wish you success.

Good luck!

お幸せを祈ります。

We all wish you happiness [good luck].

いばる（威張る）

1. 態度

【いばって歩く】**swagger**

彼は父親が金持で顔役だということで，肩で風切っていばって歩いている。

He swaggers because his father is a wealthy and influential man.

【いばっている】

彼は気取っている［もったいぶっている］。

He {gives himself / puts on} airs.

彼は自分が偉いと思っている。

He thinks himself a somebody.

He thinks he's something [(a) somebody].

He's stuck-up.〔*colloq.*〕

【いばるな】

頭がいいと思っていばるな。(傲慢な態度をとるな)

Don't be arrogant [haughty] just because you are clever.

2. 豪語

自慢する **boast;** ホラを吹く **brag**

成功してもいばるな。

Don't brag [boast] about your success.

彼はいばる癖がある。

He's always boasting.

3. 圧力をかける

彼はいばりすぎる［いばりちらす］。

He throws his weight around too much.

〈注〉 be proud は心に誇りを持つことで悪い意味ではない。be haughty, be arrogant は他を見下した尊大な態度をとることであるからよくない意味である。さらに無礼な態度をとるのが be insolent, 口に出していばるのが boast。ただし boast にはほとんど have と同じ意味の用法もある。

ex. Tokyo can boast of several skyscrapers.
(東京には天をつくような高層建築がある)

いふく（衣服）

衣服一般　**clothes**(常に複数形); 衣類の総称 **clothing**(集合名詞); (ある時代，ある地方独特の)服装　**costume;** 女性のスーツ，男性の背広　**suit;** 婦人・子供のワンピース(衣服の総称ではない)　**dress;** 特定の目的のための服装　**〜wear**(複合語として使う; ex. skiwear)

正装　full dress

制服　uniform

喪服　mourning clothes

注文服　custom-ordered [order-made] clothes

既製服　ready-made clothes

正装でご来場ください。(オペラの初日など)

Please come in full dress.

〈注〉 男性はモーニング (a morning coat)，タキシード (a tuxedo)，女性はすその長いフォーマル (a long formal)，カクテルドレス (a cocktail dress)。

彼女は喪服を着ている。

She's in mourning.

彼女はたくさん服を持っている。

She has a lot of clothes.

〈注〉 貴族や映画スターなどのように服をたくさん持っている場合，She has a large wardrobe. のような言い方もあるが，一般に使うには時代遅れの表現である。

《関連語》

●生地・素材　material

繊維 fabric

綿 cotton, 絹 silk, 毛 wool, 麻 linen

合成繊維 synthetic fabric

アクリル acrylic, ナイロン nylon

ポリエステル polyester, レーヨン rayon

アセテート acetate

反物 yard goods (ヤール単位で小売りされる

衣服　Items of Clothing

hat
scarf
overcoat
shawl
skirt
sweater
(jumper)
shoes
cap
coat
pants
(trousers)
boots
undershirt
(vest)
socks
briefs / underpants
slip
bra
panties
panty hose
(tights)
jacket
blouse
tie
dress
suit
(女)
suit
(男)
bathrobe
(dressing gown)
night
gown
pajamas
suitjacket
suitskirt
suitcoat
suitpants

布；その小売店は yard goods store)
●縫製・裁縫
型紙を置く　pin the pattern
裁断する　cut the material
端を切りそろえる　trim，縫う　sew
手縫い　sew by hand，端かがり　hem
縫い目　seam，とじ合せる　seam
しつけをかける　baste
ミシンで縫う　sew by machine, machine sew
ボタンをつける　sew on a button
アイロン　iron
アイロンをかける　iron, press
●洗濯　wash
洗濯機　washing machine
洗剤　soap
合成洗剤　(synthetic) detergent
脱水機　spin drier，乾燥機　drier
〈注〉脱水する dehydrate, 脱水機 dehydrator のような語があるが，これは主として工業用のものを指し，家庭の機械には使わない。
洗濯物　washing
洗濯物を(ロープに)干す
hang out [up] the clothes {to dry. / on the clothes line.}
peg out the clothes〔英〕(peg で挟んで干す)
洗濯ばさみ　clothes pins [pegs]
洗濯物を取り込む
bring the washing in
take the clothes off the line
クリーニング屋　laundry, cleaner's
クリーニング屋に出す
send clothes to the laundry [wash]
ドライクリーニング　dry cleaning
●衣服のタイプ
【頭部用】
帽子　hat (縁つき)，cap (縁なし)
【首】
スカーフ　scarf, scarves
ショール　shawl，ネクタイ　tie
【服】
コート　coat, jacket
オーバー　overcoat
セーター　sweater; jumper〔英〕
スーツ　suit，ワンピース　dress
シャツ　shirt，ブラウス　blouse
ズボン　pants, trousers，スカート　skirt
パジャマ　pajamas
ガウン　dressing gown, robe, nightgown
【足】
靴　shoes，ブーツ　boots
【下着】 undergarments
ランニングシャツ　undershirt; vest〔英〕
スリップ　slip
ブラジャー　brassiere, bra
パンツ　briefs
パンティ　underpants, panties
パンティストッキング　panty hose, tights
靴下　socks

いみ（意味）

名 **a meaning; a sense; significance**
意味する　動他 **mean; signify**

1．内容

【…という意味である】
この文中の "boast" は "have" の意味で使われている。
Here "boast" means "have".
【…の意味は？】
「さすが」とはどんな意味ですか。
What does the word "sasuga" mean?
UFO とはどんな意味ですか。
What does UFO stand for? (UFO という表記について何の略語か尋ねる；UFO＝unidentified flying object)
cf. What's a UFO? (UFO って何？)
【それはどういう意味ですか】
意味をとる
understand; interpret
意味を取り違える
misunderstand
どういう意味[つもり]？(なじる調子，言外の意味を聞く)
How do you mean that?
What do you mean by that? (はっきりわか

らなくて説明を求めるときにも使える）
君の言うことの意味がわからない。
I can't understand you [what you say].
意味がわからなかった。
I could not catch [get, understand] the meaning.
彼女は私の言ったことの意味を取り違えた。
She misunderstood what I said.

2．意義

【人生の意味】
the meaning of life; the significance of life
【意味がない】
そんなことをしても意味がない［無意味だ］。
There's no point [significance, meaning, sense] in doing that.

3．その他

【ある意味で】
ある意味でそれは本当だ。
That's [It's] true in { a way. / a sense. }
【含意】
意味を含む　imply
含まれた意味
an implication; a connotation
"naive" という語は「単細胞な」，「ばかな」という意味を含むことがある。
The word "naive" sometimes implies simple-mindedness.
"sophisticated（洗練された，不自然な）" という形容詞は，文の前後関係でよい意味にも悪い意味にもなり得る。
The adjective "sophisticated" has either positive or negative connotations according to the context.
〈注〉 connotation とは denotation（明示的意味）に対する語で，その語の持つ連想，感じ，色合などを包含した言外の意味を指す。
【意味ありげな】 meaningful
彼は意味ありげな目つきで私を見た。
He gave me a meaningful [significant] look.
【意味深長な】 knowing
彼は意味深な笑い方をした。
He smiled knowingly.
意味がはっきりしない。
That's too ambiguous.
【…な意味（で）】
一般的な［広い］意味で
in a general [broad] sense
大ざっぱな意味で
in a loose sense
厳密な意味で
in a strict sense
文字［字義］通りの意味　literal meaning
隠れた意味　hidden [latent] meaning

いやしい（卑しい）→ きたない

いやな（嫌な）

〈注〉 「いや」にも「気が進まない」「うんざりする」「むかつく」「まっぴらだ」等々意味の差，強さの段階があるので，その情況に合う語を選ばねばならない。また，人を主語にするか，物を中心に述べるかにより形容詞を選ばねばならないことにも注意。
ex. He's disgusted at it.（彼はそれにうんざりしている）
It's really disgusting.（それは全くうんざりだ）

1．事物中心

【不快な】 unpleasant; nasty; disagreeable
【好ましくない】 undesirable
【ありがたくない】 unwelcome
【むっとするような】 offensive
【忌わしい】 hateful; loathsome; abominable
【強い嫌悪】 odious; disgusting; revolting
いやな［うんざりする］仕事
an irksome [a bothersome, a tedious] task
いやな客　an unwelcome guest
いやなやつ
a disagreeable fellow（不快）
a disgusting fellow（強い嫌悪）

いやな場所　a horrible place
いやな天気
　nasty [terrible] weather; vile weather
いやなにおい
　a bad [an offensive] smell
　a repulsive smell（強い意味）

2．人主語

【不快感を持つ】
　displeased; disgusted; offended
【気が進まない】［形］　reluctant; unwilling
　［動］［他］　don't like＜dislike＜hate＜detest
【主観的表現】
来る日も来る日もあんな退屈な仕事をするなんていやになった。
　I'm tired of doing such an irksome job day after day.
あんなやつが世の中でうまくやって幅をきかすなんてまったくいやになる。
　I feel disgusted seeing [to see] such fellows rising in the world.
世の中（生きるの）がいやになった。
　I'm sick of life.
あんなやつ見るのもいやだ。
　I hate the very [mere] sight of him.
いやならいいのだ。
　You don't have to, if you don't want to.
私はいやだ。
　I don't like it.
　I don't want to ...（意思表明）
　I won't, I tell you.（拒んで）
いや（だよ）！
　Oh, no!
いや（だねえ）！
　Ugh!
　How awful!
いや（やめて）！
　Don't do that, I tell you! / Stop it!（いたずらされたり，からかわれたとき）
【客観的表現】
彼はそれをするのをいやがっている。
　He's not happy about doing that.
　He's reluctant to do that. / He's unwilling to do that.
　He hates to do that.
〈注〉下へ行くほど意味が強くなる。
彼はいやな顔をした。
　He looked { displeased [annoyed].
　　　　　　 offended [hurt].（むっとした）
　He frowned [scowled].（顔をしかめた）

いらい（以来）

〈注〉since を使うことが多いので since の種々の用法の例をあげる。
あれ以来彼女に会っていない。
　I haven't seen her（ever）since.（副詞として）
昨年の夏以来彼女に会っていない。
　I haven't seen her since last summer.（前置詞として）
東京に来て以来彼女に会っていない。
　I haven't seen her since I came to Tokyo.（接続詞として）
日本に来て以来10年になる。
　It's [It's been] ten years since I came to Japan.
〈注〉since には上記の例のように副詞，前置詞，接続詞としての用法がある。また，since は「…から」と起点（過去の一時点，何月何日，1980年，上京したとき，等々）を示すが，「10年前から」は for the past [last] ten years; these ten years と言うのが普通で，since ten years ago は正しい用法として認められていない。
「私はここに10年(以)来住んでいる」は
　I have been here for the past [last] ten years.
　I came here ten years ago.
が普通の言い方である。

いらいらする → おこる

be [get] nervous [irritated, impatient]
be provoked（むしゃくしゃして何かに当りたくなる）
［動］いらいらさせる　**irritate; get on one's nerves; fret**
眠ろうとすると頭の周りで蚊がぶんぶんうる

さくて，いつもいらいらする。

Mosquitoes buzzing about my head as I try to sleep always irritate me.

隣の赤ん坊の泣き声でいらいらする。

The crying of {the baby next door / the next door neighbor's baby} gets on my nerves.

クラブの会合に人がそろわないといつもいらいらして，遅刻した者は着いた途端にしかられる。

They always get irritated when someone is late for the club meeting and scold him when he finally comes.

会合に人がそろわないといらいらして，遅刻者が到着するとほっとする。

They always get nervous when someone is late for the meeting and feel relieved when he finally comes.

〈注〉 上記の例文で対照させてあるように irritated には腹立たしさがあるが，nervous には怒りはない。「はらはらする」に近い。impatient は何か早くやりたくて「いらいら」することである。

いりょう（医療）

medical treatment（治療）; **medical care**（医療活動）; **medicine**（医学）

医療費　medical bill

医療保険　medical insurance

《関連語》

診察　medical examination

症状　symptoms → びょうき

容態　the condition of a patient

診断　diagnosis

動 診断する　diagnose; make a [the] correct [wrong] diagnosis

肺癌と診断する　diagnose《a case as》cancer of the lungs

応急手当　first aid

救急車　ambulance

救急病院　hospital with an emergency ward [emergency facilities]

治療　treatment

注射　injection, shot

静脈注射　intravenous injection

点滴　drip infusion, intravenous drip

投薬，処方　prescription

検査する　check on《someone》for disease [condition]

検査を受ける　be examined; have a test [be tested] for《disease》

尿検査　urinalysis

血液検査　blood test

レントゲン写真　X-ray

(肺の)レントゲン写真をとる

have（one's chest）X-rayed

心電図　electrocardiogram; EKG

心電図をとる　take an electrocardiogram;（とってもらう）have an electrocardiogram taken [done]

血圧　blood pressure

血圧を計る　take [measure] one's blood pressure

(血圧が)上は130下は80

130/80（one（hundred）thirty over eighty）

胃カメラ　gastrocamera

内視鏡　endoscope

CTスキャン　computerized axial tomography; CAT; CAT scan

MRI　magnetic resonance imaging

手術　operation, surgery

輸血　blood transfusion

輸血をする

（与える）give blood to someone

（もらう）have [be given] a blood transfusion

麻酔　anesthesia [anaesthesia]

局部麻酔　local anesthesia

全身麻酔　general anesthesia

麻酔医　anesthetist, anaesthesiologist

全身麻酔で手術を行う

perform an operation under {a general anesthetic / general anesthesia}

人工呼吸　artificial respiration

人工呼吸を行う　do [try] artificial respiration

人工心肺　heart-lung machine

人工腎臓　dialyzer; dialyser〔英〕
透析　dialysis　透析する　dialyze
放射線療法　radiotherapy; X-ray therapy
流産　miscarriage
人工妊娠中絶　abortion
リハビリ　rehabilitation
臓器移植　organ transplant
生体肝移植　liver transplant from a living donor
脳死　brain death; 形 brain dead
安楽死　euthanasia, mercy killing

いる（…している）→ している

〈注〉「…している」の意味の英語の表現は次の形をとる。
(1) 状態を表す動詞(知っている know; 住んでいる live など)
(2) be＋形容詞(句)(眠っているbe asleep; 働いている be at work など)
(3) 動詞の進行形(歌っている be singing; 勉強している be studying など)

私たちは愛し合っている。
We love each other.
私は彼をよく知っている。
I know him very well.
〈注〉×I'm knowing のように進行形にしない。
彼らは同じ町に住んでいる。
They live [are living] in the same town.
赤ちゃんはよく眠っている。
The baby is { sleeping well. / fast asleep.
弟は長良高校に行っている。
My brother goes to Nagara High School.
（進行形にしない）
彼女は今日新しいスーツを着ている。
She's wearing a new suit today.
彼は新しいネクタイをしていた。
He wore a new tie.
〈注〉あの人はめがねをかけている。（常に）
She wears glasses.
cf. She's wearing glasses.（今かけている）
She wore new glasses.（新しいめがねをかけていた）
※She was wearing new glasses.（新しいめがねをかけていた）
wear は状態を表す動詞であるが，状況を目に見えるように描写するときは上の※の例のように進行形にしてよい。

いる(居る)・いた・いない → ある

〈注〉英語では animate（生物）, inanimate（無生物）による「いる」「ある」の区別をしない。存在そのものを紹介する There is … 構文と既知の者（物）の居場所（ありか）を示す文の違いについては「ある」の項参照。

1．存在の提示

exist; be; remain（残存）

【存在】
一時期恐竜が地球上のどこにでもいたときがあった。
Dinosaurs existed almost all over the earth at one time.
今や象は地球上ほんの2, 3か所にいるだけだ。
Elephants remain [exist] in only a few places now.
半世紀前まではこのあたりにもオオカミがいたそうだ。
They say { wolves lived / there were wolves living } in this region half a century ago.
叔父さん叔母さんのところは子供が5人いる。
My aunt and uncle have five children.

【(ある場所)に(誰々)がいる】
There is [are] …
パーティには男の子5人と女の子4人が来ていた。
There were five boys and four girls at the party.

【飼う】
あの家には大きなすごい犬がいる。
They have [There is] a big fierce dog in that house.

【居合せる】
事故が起ったとき駅にはたくさんの人がい

た。

There were many people at the station when the accident occurred.

【所在】

どこにいるの?

Where are you?

ここにいるよ。

I'm here.

トムは駅にいた。

Tom was at the station.

トムが駅にいるのを見た。

I saw Tom at the station.

【在宅】

日曜日と月曜日は家にいます。

I stay [am] at home on Sunday and Monday.

一日中家にいた。

I stayed [was] at home all day.

【足留め】

迎えにゆくまでそこにいなさい。

Stay [Remain] where you are till I come for you.

【滞在】

いま叔父の家にいます。

I'm staying at my uncle's now. (一時的に)

I live with my uncle. (長期間)

【居所】

マクドナルドさん一家は今カリフォルニアにいる。

The Macdonalds { are now in California. / live in California now. }

2. いない

【絶滅】

もうこの国にオオカミはいない。

There are no more wolves in this country.

【不在】

大講堂にはだれもいなかった。

There was nobody in the big hall. (単なる描写)

Nobody was in the big hall. (人がいることを期待しているような場合)

彼女に会いに行ったが買物に出て家にいなかった。

When I went to see her she was out shopping.

彼らには子供がいない。

They have no children.

【失跡】

家に帰ってみたら犬がいなくなっていた。

When I got home I found my dog was missing.

【その他】

君がいなくてさびしいよ。

I miss you awfully.

君がいなくてはつまらない。

It won't be fun without you.

いる(要る)・いらない → ひつよう

1. 必要

〈注〉「…が要る」を英訳する際,まず人主語の構文にするか,物中心の構文にするかを決めねばならない。次にまとめると

{ 人主語+need (I need ...) / 物・事主語+be necessary (it is necessary ...) }

「私はこんな物は要らない」は

×I'm not necessary these things.

I don't need these things.

These things are not needed [necessary].

【要る】

金が最低50万円は要る。

We need 500,000 yen at least.

【要らない】

そんなにたくさん荷物は要らない。ほんの2,3日泊るだけだから。

We won't need so many things.

We're { staying only / only going to stay } for a few days.

そんな物は旅行に要らないよ。

These things are unnecessary [not necessary] for the trip.

2. 役に立つ (置いておきたい)

〈注〉「要る」は「必要とする」から転じて,手元に置いておきたいことを意味する場合もあり,その

場合は want が当てはまる。まだ必要だと考えるなら need も使える。

この雑誌はみんな要るのか。

Do you want to keep all these magazines?

要る物と要らない物を分類しよう。

Let's sort out what we want [need] from [and] what we don't.

この中から要らない分を取り出してください。

Will you sort out
{ the papers to be thrown away?
{ useless things?

いれる（入れる）

〈注〉「入れる」で日本人の頭にすぐ浮ぶのは enter であるが，enter は「入る」であり，他動詞としては enter a room, enter high school のように使い，「入れる」の意味では enter a name on a list（記入する，書き入れる）ぐらいである。次のように使うことはできない。

×Please enter sugar in my tea.
×He entered them into his room.
×She was entered in hospital in town.

1．入れ物・家などに

let [put, take, bring, get] a thing in

【入室】

入れてください。

Let me in please.（cf. 出してください。Let me out.）

ドアを開けて部屋に入れてくれた。

He opened the door and admitted us into the room.（面接の場合などの硬い表現）

彼女は彼を裏口から入れてくれた。

She let [brought, got] him into the house by the back door.

【取り込む】

暗くなるので洗濯物を入れた。

She took [brought] her washing in as it was getting dark.

窓を開けていい空気を入れてください。

Please open the window and let some fresh air in.

【突っ込む】

両手をポケットに入れる

put one's hands in one's pockets

彼は両手をポケットに入れて突っ立っていた。

He stood there with both hands in his pockets.

【注入・挿入】

フロッピーディスクをコンピュータに入れた。

I put [inserted] the diskette into the computer.

やかんに水を入れて。

Put water in the kettle.

〈注〉put the kettle on と言えば，水を入れてやかんを火にかけ，湯を沸かすことになる。

英国人は通常，紅茶にはミルクを入れる。

English people usually drink tea with milk.

もう少し砂糖を入れてください。

Please put some more sugar into my tea.

Please add some more sugar to this.

【収納】

彼は車の車庫入れをいつも慎重にやる。

He is always careful { when he puts / in putting } his car into the garage.

ガイドは洞窟の中に5人ずつ客を入れた。

The guides admitted five people at a time into the cave.

このホールには2000人入れられる。

This hall { will hold [take] / holds [admits〔*formal*〕] } 2,000 people.

2．入学・入院・入社

息子を寄宿学校に入れた。

He sent his son to a boarding school.

あの大学では毎年1000人以上の新入生を受け入れる。

That university takes [admits] more than one thousand（new）students every year.

あの子を町の病院に入れた。

They {sent her to / put her in} the hospital in town.

木曜日に彼女を病院に入れた。

She was admitted to the hospital on Thursday.

クラブに入れてください。

Let me join the club.

営業に大卒２名を入れた。

They hired two college graduates in the sales department.

3．含めて

子供も入れて15人だった。

There were fifteen in all including the children.

私たちを入れずに15人だった。

There were fifteen people {not counting us. / besides us.}

乗車賃を入れて１万2000円かかった。

The cost was 12,000 yen including the railroad tickets.

4．慣用表現

お茶を入れましょうか。

Would you like some tea?

コーヒーを入れてくださいませんか。

Would you make some coffee for me?

電気あんかのスイッチを入れてください。

Turn on the foot-warmer please.

新知事は教育に力を入れることを約束した（教育の重要性を強調し，その改善に最善をつくすことを約束した）。

The new governor emphasized the importance of education and promised to do his utmost to improve the situation.

いろ（色）

色 名 **color; hue**（色合い）

色をつける 動 **color; paint**（絵の具で）; 染める **dye**

色あせる 動 **fade**

色づく **turn yellow [red]**（秋の木の葉）

【色が白い】

fair（complexioned）

〈注〉 欧米人に関して fair と言えば金髪碧眼色白，要するに色素が全体に薄い容貌のことになる。

【色が黒い】

dark（complexioned）（生れつきの小麦色の肌）

【日焼け】

be [get] sunburnt（日焼けで炎症を起している）

be tan（日焼けして肌が黒褐色になった）

彼は真っ黒に日焼けしていた。

He was tanned [very tan].

He was tan from the sun.

【顔色が青い】

pale

【慣用表現】

色っぽい　sexy, coquettish

色男　a dandy

色めがね　colored glasses, sunglasses

色めがねで見る　have a prejudice against

〈注〉 色に関する注意としては顔色に関する慣用的な表現や，「青」が blue と green を含めた表現であることに注意。「信号が青になってから…」は when the lights turn green であり， blue ではない。

《色と感情の対応の例》

black / purple : rage（激怒）

white / black : frustration（胸のむしゃくしゃ）

white: terror（恐怖）

yellow: {fear（恐怖） / cowardice（卑怯）}

green: envy（羨望，嫉妬）

いんしょう（印象）

名 **impression;** 動 **impress**（印象を与える）

【第一印象】

彼女の第一印象によると，そこは静かで活気がない所ということだった。

Her first impression of the place was that it was quiet and dull.

私は第一印象で彼に好感を持った。

My first impression of him was favorable [good].

He impressed me favorably on our first meeting.

【印象を受ける】

私はあの人が幸せではないという印象を受けた。

I got the [an] impression that she is not happy.

【印象を与える】

彼らは訪問客にできるだけよい印象を与えようと努力した。

They tried to give the visitors as good an impression as possible.

【印象的な】

その日は晴天で，列車が三島駅を過ぎるあたりの富士山は美しく印象的だった。

It was a nice day and the beauty of Mt. Fuji {impressed me / was impressive} as I went past Mishima on the train.

〈注〉 動詞の impress は普通「よい印象」を与える場合に使う。I was deeply impressed は「すっかり感心してしまった」の意。何に感心したかは "by" its beauty のようにする。

一方，名詞のimpression はよい印象にも悪い印象にも使われる。

いんよう（引用）

quotation; citation; excerpt; extract（抜粋）

【引用符】 quotation marks

【二重引用符】 double quotes

【引用する】

quote 論文・スピーチなどで自分の論点を権威づけたり，例証するために他の本や文から原文の一部をそのまま取り出すこと。この場合は " " で囲み出典を示すのが普通である。

彼は音の効果で雰囲気をつくり出す好例としてエドガー・アラン・ポーの『アッシャー家の崩壊』から一部を引用した。

He quoted a passage from Edgar Allan Poe's *The Fall of the House of Usher* to illustrate the effect of sound in creating atmosphere.

cite quote と同じく他の本や文から言葉を引くことを表すが，原文から引用する場合もあるし，要約して述べることもある。法律などで先例をあげる場合にも cite を用いる。

彼は隠喩の例としてハムレットから 2, 3 行引用した。

He cited a few lines from *Hamlet* as an example of metaphor.

彼はジュネーブ協定を引用し，その政策を痛烈に非難した。

He cited the Geneva Convention and condemned the policy.

〈注〉 上の文は According to the Geneva Convention it is forbidden to ...（ジュネーブ協定によれば…は禁止されている）のように彼が書いたまたは言ったことの要約である。

extract 他の本や文から一部を取り出すこと。extract では取り出した文そのものが興味の中心，論議の対象となる。前述の quote や cite と異なる点は，自分の論の援用として用いるのではないことである。原文をそのまま取り出すこともあれば，要点をまとめて述べることもある。また extract は動詞としてだけでなく，名詞として用いることが多い。

彼らは経済の動向に関する情報を国連経済統計年鑑から引用した。

They extracted information about trade flow from the *UN Yearbook of Economic Statistics.*

この本にはエマーソンの主要なエッセイのすべてからの抜粋が集められている。

This book contains extracts from all Emerson's major essays.

〈注〉 抜粋であることを示すときは extract from を用い，from に続く語は作品名でも作家名でもよい。

ex. an extract from { a play of Shakespeare / Shakespeare / *Romeo and Juliet* }

rofer to 言及する，ふれる。ある作品や論文の名称または著者の名前をあげる。本文の一部を引用する cite, extract とは区別される。

う

うえ（上）

1．位置

〈注〉 位置関係を示す前置詞のうち「上」に当るものをあげる。卓上・机上のように上に接して置くのは on であり，上方にあるのは above，全体を覆うように上にあるのは over である。

私たちは山の頂上に立ち，上空には雲一つない青空が広がっていた。

We stood on the top of the mountain with the blue sky above [over] us without [and not] a speck of cloud.

《反対の意味の前置詞》

on ↔ off
above ↔ below
over ↔ under

2．順位

【年上】

彼は私より二つ上だ。

He is two years older than I.

これが一番上の兄です。

This is my oldest brother.

【身長】

高校のときはクラスで身長が上から3番目だった。

I was the third tallest in my high school class.

【成績】

(高校のときの)成績はクラスで上から3番だった。

I was the third from the top (in my high school class).

I was in [had] the third place academically.

3．上下関係

【地位】

彼の方が地位が上だ。

He is above me in rank.

〈注〉 欧米では日本のように上下関係にうるさくないので，上司とか先輩などとあまり言わない。「長」であれば boss〔*informal*〕と言う。

彼は人の上に立つ器ではない。

He lacks leadership.

【上級】

彼は上のクラスにいたが，病気で進級できなかったので今は僕と一緒のクラスにいる。

Originally he was ahead of me, but because of an illness he couldn't move up, so now he's in my class.

彼は上の学校に行きたかったのだ。

He wished to enter [go to] college [high school].

〈注〉 英語では「上の学校」などと言わずに，具体的に高校とか大学などの学校の種類を述べればよい。school of higher grade とすると程度の高い学校のように受け取られる。

4．おまけに

【その上】

あの子のボーイフレンドは親切でハンサムなうえに頭もよい。

Her boy friend is
- clever besides being kind and handsome.
- kind, handsome, and (more than that) clever too.
- not only kind and handsome but also clever.

彼はビジネスマンだったが，その上音楽家でもあった。

He was a businessman, and a musician too [as well].

5．成績・技量の優位

英語は広瀬が一番だが，数学では石田の方が上だ。

Hirose is the best in English no doubt, but Ishida is better in mathematics.

ゴルフの腕は山田の方が課長より上だ。

Yamada is { better at golf / a better golfer } than our boss.

Oh, my! I've forgotten all about it!
Oh, it slipped my mind completely.

うかつ・うっかり

〈注〉「うかつ」は十分な気配り・警戒を怠ること。「うっかり」はもっと軽い意味で，ぼんやりして気づかないこと。この二つは意味に差があるが重複する部分もあるので一括して扱う。

【怠慢】

私もまったくうかつだった。あの男を一度も疑ったことがなかったのだから。

I never once suspected [questioned] his truthfulness. It was quite stupid of me.

私もまったくうっかりしていた［うかつだった］。あの人が家を離れひとりぼっちでどんなに心細い思いをしているか気がつかなかったんだから。

How thoughtless of me not to have noticed how helpless and lonely she must have felt away from home!

【不注意】

これは機密文書だ。うかつに［うっかり］その辺に出しっぱなしにしないように。

These are confidential papers. Don't leave them lying about.

うかつに物を言うな。

Think twice before [Be careful when] you speak.

うっかりして乗り越してしまった。

I was so absentminded that I missed my station.

うっかり口をすべらして秘密を漏らしてしまった。

I let slip her big secret.

In an unguarded moment he let it out.

（上の文よりも重要な秘密を漏らした感じ）

私はまったくうっかり者で，財布をどこにでも置きっぱなしにしてしまう。

I'm always so careless I leave my purse (lying about) everywhere.

あっ! うっかりしていた。すっかり忘れていた。

うかぶ（浮かぶ）・うく

1．空間・水上

浮かぶ，浮く　**float (on the water, in the air)**

【雲】

白い雲が空に浮かんでいる。

White clouds are floating in the sky.

【物】

船員が海に何か浮かんでいるのを見つけた。

The sailors found something floating in [on] the sea.

【体】

こわがらないで，息を吸いこんで体を楽にしてごらん。浮きますよ。

Don't be afraid of sinking [going under]. If you take a deep breath and relax, you will float.

2．浮き上がる

アザラシは長時間水中に潜っていられる。ほんのときたま息をしに浮き上がってくるだけですむのだ。

Seals can stay underwater for a long time, coming up for air only once in a while.

あぶくを見てごらん。すっと浮き上がってきてはすぐ消えてしまう。

Watch the bubbles; they rise to the surface and soon disappear.

大きな白い船が霧の中から浮かび上がってきた。

A large white ship loomed out of the fog.

3．心に

come across [**into**] one's **mind; flit into** one's **mind; occur to**

【考え】

いい考えが浮かんだ。

A good idea came [occurred] to me.

I had a good idea.

I had a brainwave. 〔英 *colloq.*〕

【思い】

結局，完全な失敗に終るかもしれない。そんな思いがふと心に浮かんだ。

It occurred to me that it might be a total failure after all.

【言葉】

母の言葉がふと心に浮かんだ。「正直に生きるんだよ」と別れ際に母は言ったっけ。

My mother's words came to mind [me] just then. "Be honest," she had said when we parted.

4．慣用

【表情】

彼に気がつくと彼女の顔に晴れやかな微笑が浮かんだ。

She smiled happily as she recognized him.

A happy smile of recognition spread over her face.

彼女は目に涙を浮かべて，行かないでと彼に懇願した。

She entreated him with tears in her eyes not to leave.

【浮き上がる】

彼の提案は浮き上がってしまった。

His proposal was left pending.

No decision was made about his suggestion.

【浮かす】

弁当を持って行こう。昼食代が浮かせるよ[浮くよ]。

Let's bring {lunch boxes / our lunches} and save money.

【浮かぬ顔】

何をそんな浮かぬ顔をしているんだ。

Why do you look so glum?

うかる（受かる）→ うける

【入試】

彼女は慶応大学に受かった。

She passed the entrance exam for Keio University.

彼女は慶応と早稲田に受かったが東大はだめだった。

She passed the Keio and Waseda University entrance exams but failed Tokyo University's.

うけもち（受け持ち）→ たんとう・たんにん

1．担任

【先生】

このクラスは阿倍先生の受け持ちだ。

This is Mr. Abe's class.

Our homeroom [form 〔英〕] teacher is Mr. Abe.

阿倍先生がこのクラスの受け持ちだ[を受け持っている]。

Mr. Abe is {in charge of / responsible for} this class.

阿倍先生はこの学校で英語を受け持っている。

Mr. Abe teaches English at this school.

各先生とも週12時間の授業を受け持っている。

Each teacher is assigned 12 hours a week.

【生徒】

彼女は私の受け持ちの生徒です。

She's my pupil [in my class].

2．担当区域

受け持ち区域を巡回する（警官）

make one's rounds / walk one's beat

このセールスマンは中部地区の受け持ちだ。

This salesman covers [is responsible for] the Chubu district.

うける（受ける）

1．得る

湯川博士は1949年にノーベル物理学賞を受けた。

Dr. Yukawa won the Nobel prize for

physics in 1949.

彼は殊勲章を受けた。

He was awarded [given] the D. S. O.（Distinguished Service Order）[D. S. M.（Distinguished Service Medal）].

彼は先週運転免許を受け取った。（もらった）

He got a [his] { driver's license〔米〕 / driving licence〔英〕 } last week.

〈注〉 He passed his driving test last week.（試験に受かった）

彼が医師免許を受けたのは半世紀も前のことだ。

The doctor got his（medical）certification half a century ago.

2. 受諾・応答

【申し出】

あなたの申し出をお受けします。

I（will）accept [take] your offer.

I'll take you up on that.〔*colloq.*〕

【電話】

私の留守中に彼が電話したそうだが，だれが電話を受けたのか。

He says he called [phoned] me when I was out [gone]. Who answered（the phone）[Who took the call]?

私の留守中にだれかあの人からの電話を受けなかったか。

Did anyone take a call from him while I was out [gone]?（be out は短時間，be gone は長時間の留守の意）

3. 受験・受診

【試験】

来春は医師国家試験を受けなければならない。

Next spring I'll have to take [sit（for）〔英〕] the national medical examination.

【診察】

是非一刻も早く専門医の診察を受けた方がいい。

I think you had really better { go to / go to see / go and see } a specialist as soon as possible.

【手術】

彼は盲腸炎の手術を受けた。

He had { an operation for appendicitis. / an appendectomy. }

He was operated on for appendicitis.

〈注〉 undergo an operation は，特に医師・患者にとってつらい大手術だというような場合に使い，普通は have でよい。

4. 被害など

【災害】

先日の台風で九州は大きな被害を受けた。

There was damage in Kyushu from the last typhoon.

Kyushu suffered from the last typhoon.

Kyushu got [was] hit by the last typhoon.〔*informal*〕

【衝撃】

政府が都市の道路拡張事業への援助を打ち切ったことにより，地方自治体は大打撃を受けた。

Local governments got [received, suffered] quite a blow when the central government cancelled all payments to cities for road expansion.

【酷評】

彼の処女作は酷評を受けたが，第2作は好評だった。

His first novel was severely criticized, but his second one was { well received. / received favorably. }

5. 好まれる

映画「E.T.」は若い人たちにたいへん受けた。

E.T. was a tremendous hit [a great success] among young people.

6．される

私はあの人たちの結婚式への招待を受けた。

I was invited to their wedding.

〈注〉「…を受ける」と「…される」がほとんど同義になる日本語表現があるので，よく使われるものを下にあげる。

招待を受ける / 招待される	be invited
歓迎を受ける / 歓迎される	be welcomed
処罰を受ける / 処罰される	be punished
補助を受ける / 補助される	be subsidized
援助を受ける / 援助される	be aided
許可を受ける / 許可される	be permitted
支払いを受ける / 支払われる	be paid

上記のように英語では動詞の受動形がこの「受ける」の意を表す。

うごく（動く）・うごかす

1．動作・移動

㊫㊣㊥ **move**

【身動き】

動くな。（ギャングが脅して）

Don't move (a step).

列車が動き出した。

The train began to move.

ほんの少し車を動かしてくださいませんか。

Will you move your car just a bit?

荷車が泥にはまってしまって，いくら押してもびくとも動かなかった。

We tried to push the cart out of the mud, but it wouldn't { move at all. / budge an inch. }

彼は何か言いたげに唇を動かした。

He moved his lips trying to say something.

この歯は動く。（ぐらぐらする）

This tooth is loose.

【行動】

彼にはすぐに動いてくれる部下がたくさんいる。

He has many men { under him. / who work for him. }

【移転】

彼は1，2か月のうちに動くだろう。

He'll move out in a month or two.

2．運転

㊫㊣ **work; run; go;** ㊥㊣ **operate**

その機械は24時間動いています。

That machine is working [going, running] 24 hours a day.

時計が止まってしまった。どうやって動かしたらいいの?

The clock has stopped. How can I set [get] it going again?

このエレベーターは動いていない。

This elevator is not working.

3．動揺・感動

彼の雄弁に動かされ，人々は皆飢饉救援基金に寄付金を出した。

His eloquence moved everyone, and so they donated money to the famine relief fund.

あの子は周囲の人の言葉ですぐ動かされる。

She is easily influenced by the people around her.

4．動かぬ，動かせない

【事実】

動かぬ事実　an established fact

【証拠】

動かぬ証拠

positive [incontestable] proof

incontrovertible evidence

【決心】

彼の決心は動か(せ)ない。

His resolve can't be shaken.

We can't make him change his mind.

【計画】

その計画は動かせない。

We can't change the schedule.

うすい（薄い）

1．厚さ

thin（固体）

薄い紙[材質] thin paper [material]

薄い本　a thin book

薄い｛唇　thin lips
　　　髪　thin hair｝

パンを薄く切ってください。

Cut the bread into thin slices, / Slice the bread thin, } please.

セーターのひじが薄くなった。

This sweater has worn thin at the elbow.

2．濃度・密度（気体・液体）

薄い空気　thin air

薄い牛乳　watery milk

薄いお茶　weak tea

【薄くする】

このお茶[コーヒー]は濃すぎる。もう少し薄くしてください。

This tea [coffee] is too strong. Please make it a bit weaker.

3．光・色

夜明けの薄明り

faint light of dawn

この画家は薄い[淡い]色を好んで使う。

This painter uses pale [pastel] colors.

壁は薄い青に塗ってあった。

The walls were painted light blue.

印刷が薄くて読めない。

The print was too faint to read.

4．程度

【望み】

もはや手掛りが見つかる望みは薄い。

There is little hope that
{ we can still find clues. / any clues still remain [exist]. }

【関心】

あの人は政治には関心が薄い。

She has little interest in politics.

【もうけ】

もうけは薄い。

The profit margin is narrow.

The profit is small.

うそ（嘘）

名 **a lie**

動 自 **lie**（うそをつく）

〈注〉 lie は悪意のある「うそ」のことであるから，日本語の「うそ」のつもりで軽い意味で使うことはできない。「うそをついている」と決めつけるのではないときは，「本当ではない」It isn't true. であるとか「からかっているんでしょう」You're kidding. のような言い方をする。

うそをつくのは悪いことです。

It's bad [wrong] to tell lies.

〈注〉 「うそをつくこと」のように一般的な言い方をするときは，tell lies と複数にする方が一般的である。

見えすいたうそ

an obvious [a transparent] lie

うそ八百を並べる

tell a pack of lies

うわさはうそだった。

The rumor [story] proved false.

It proved (to be) only a rumor.

うそでしょう！　信じられない！（驚きを表すとき）

It isn't true, is it?

It can't be true!

I don't believe it!

【感嘆の言葉】

うそッ！　Really?

〈注〉 驚きの叫びの「うそッ！」「ウッソー！」は「ほんと?」の裏返しであるから Really？ となる。Do you mean that?（本気でそのつもり？）とか You must be kidding me.（からかっているんでしょう）の意味である。You must be lying. とか That's a lie. などと言うと，たいへん強くひびいて相手を怒らせてしまう。

うたがう（疑う）・うたがい → あやしい

1．嫌疑

名 **suspicion;** 動 **suspect**

【犯罪】

彼は詐欺の疑いで警察に調べられた。

He was examined by the police on suspicion of fraud.

彼は文書偽造の疑いをかけられた。

He was suspected of forgery.

彼にはアリバイがないので疑わしい。

He is under suspicion because he has no alibi.

【伝染病】

彼はコレラの疑いで，ただちに隔離された。

He was quarantined at once as a suspected case of cholera.

2．疑念

名動 **doubt**

【疑わしい】

それは少々疑わしい。

That is rather doubtful.

彼が成功するかどうか疑わしい。

It is doubtful if he will succeed.

I doubt that [if] he will succeed.

【疑わない】

彼の成功を疑わない。

I'm sure he will succeed.

He will surely succeed.

Undoubtedly he will succeed.

〈注〉◆I don't doubt that he will succeed. は文法的に正しいが，内容が単純なのに文体がおおげさで不自然である。内容が複雑であればこの形も使える。

ex. I don't doubt that it's a very difficult job to mediate in international disagreements. (国際間の意見調整の仲介をするのはたいへん困難な仕事に相違ない)

◆doubt の使い方として，「…かどうか疑う」という肯定文では I doubt if [whether, that] he's telling the truth. のように接続詞は if, whether または that を使い，「…であることを疑わない[疑うか?]」のような否定文・疑問文では，接続詞に that を使うのが普通のようである。

【わが目を疑う】

私はわが目を疑った。

I could not believe my eyes.

It was unbelievable.

3．不信

【疑い深い】

形 懐疑的な　skeptical; sceptical〔英〕

逆境でいじめられて育ったためにその子は疑い深くなってしまった。(人間不信に陥った)

Adversity and ill-treatment made the boy distrustful.

〈注〉 doubt と suspect は疑い方が逆になるので注意。(「あやしい」〈注〉参照)

He is innocent. ということに疑念を持っている場合，下のようになる。下にいくほど疑いが強くなり，suspect はたいへん強い疑いを表す。

It is doubtful that he is really innocent.

I doubt if he is really innocent.

I suspect that he is not innocent.

懐疑論者　a skeptic; a sceptic〔英〕

【疑いを持っている】

形 suspicious（あやしい）

彼女は彼の意図を疑っている。

She is suspicious of his intentions.

彼は疑わしい[何かあやしい]人物だ。

He's a suspicious character.

（＝People have suspicions about him.)

うち（内）

1．内

inside（↔ outside)

内はまっ暗だ。

It was dark inside.

この浴室は，必要な場合は外からでも鍵が開けられるが，たいていの浴室は内からしか鍵の開閉ができない。

This bathroom door can be unlocked from the outside if necessary; most bathrooms, however, have only
{ inside locks.
{ locks that operate from (the) inside.

彼はまた部屋にこもって，内から鍵をかけてしまった。

He's locked himself in [into] his room again.

2．間

【時間】

2, 3 日のうちにできあがるだろう。

It will be completed in a few days.
赤ちゃんが眠っているうちに家の仕事をしなくてはならない。
I have to do housework while the baby is sleeping.
夜が明けない［暗くならない］うちに出発した。
He started before dawn [dark].
【範囲内】
5人の子供のうち末の子が一番利口だ。
His youngest is the cleverest [most clever] of his five children.
Of (all) his five children the youngest is the cleverest [most clever].

うち（家）

1. 家
うちに帰る　go home
うちに居る
be at home; be home; be in
私のうちは駅の近くだ。
My house is near the station.

2. 我が家
うちは4人家族だ。
There are four people in my family.
My family consists of four people.
We are a family of four.
うちは金持ではない。
We are not rich.
うちの人　one's family（家族）
one's husband（夫）

3. 家の職業　→ しごと，しょくぎょう
うちは公務員だ。→ やくにん・かんりょう
My father [husband]
is a {government / public} {official.（高位の役人） / employee.} / civil servant.
works for the government [city].
うちは八百屋だ。
My father runs a greengrocer's shop.
うちは農家だ。
We are farmers.
I come from farming stock [people].
〈注〉「うちは八百屋だ」のつもりで ×My house is greengrocer. などと書かないこと。baker, greengrocer, butcher などは皆その職業に従事する人のことで，日本語の「パン屋」「八百屋」「肉屋」のように店を指す言葉ではない。「…屋の人」を指すのである。

4. 家庭
うちの仕事
household affairs（家庭生活に関する諸々の仕事）
housework（掃除・洗濯・料理のような毎日お決まりの仕事）

うつ（打つ・撃つ）

1. たたく，ぶつ
hit; strike（強く打つ）; **slap**（ぴしゃりと打つ）; **beat**（**the drum**）（どんどんたたく，力をこめて打つ）
【ほお】
ほおを打つ
hit [strike, smack, slap] one on the cheek
【波】
波が岸壁を打っている。
The waves were slapping against the dock.
【雨】
雨が窓を打っている。
The rain was striking [beating〔強〕] against the window.
【時計】
時計が12時を打った。
The clock struck twelve.
【くぎを打つ】 hit nails
この木片にくぎを打ったら割れてしまう。
If you put [drive] nails into this piece of wood, it will split.

【野球】
トムが2回にホームランを打った。
Tom hit a home run [homer] in the second inning.

2．撃つ
shoot
彼は飛んでいる鳥を撃つことができた。
He could shoot birds even while they were flying.

3．感動
【心を打つ】be (deeply) moved
彼の話に心を打たれた。
She was deeply moved by his story.
心を打つ話だった。
It was a very moving story.
〈注〉 be deeply moved はおおげさな表現であるから使いすぎないように。

4．その他
【手を打つ】
政府は政府自体を改革するため何か手を打つべきだ。
The government has to take some measures to reform itself.
【電報】
彼のところは電話がないから電報を打たなくてはならない。
You'll have to send him a telegram because he hasn't got a phone.

うつくしい(美しい) → きれいな・きれいに

うったえる(訴える) → さいばん

1．訴訟・告発
【訴える】
prosecute [sue]《a person》for《an offense》（民事訴訟には sue を使う）
bring (a) suit against a person
charge a person with a crime
accuse a person of a crime（広義）
そのパン屋は土地の境界線不法侵害で隣の人を訴えた。
The baker sued his neighbor for boundary encroachment.
【訴えられる】
be prosecuted [indicted] for
be accused of（広義）
彼は殺人の罪で訴えられた。
He was prosecuted for murder.
彼は詐欺罪で訴えられた。
He was charged with fraud.
彼は収賄罪で訴えられた。
He was accused of taking bribes.
彼は学生のストライキを扇動したかどで訴えられた。
He was accused of agitating the students to strike.

2．苦痛などを
彼はひどい頭痛を訴えている。
He's complaining of a bad headache.

3．働きかける，動かす
【行動】
彼は道に立ち，通行人に難民救済の募金への協力を訴えた[難民問題の深刻さを訴えた]。
He stood in the street
{ making appeals to the passers-by for donations for the refugees.
exhorting passers-by about the seriousness of the refugee problem.
【共感】
彼の作品の人間味が今日の若者にも訴える。
The humanity in his works appeals to the young people of today.
【目に】
テレビは直接視覚に訴えるのでその影響がたいへん大きい。
The influence of TV is very great because it appeals directly to the eye.

4．頼る

武力に訴える

resort to arms; use arms

腕力に訴える

resort to violence; use force

うっとり

うっとりする[心を奪われる]

be enchanted; be enraptured

私はあまりの美しさにうっとりと[心を奪われて]半時間ほども景色に見とれていました。

I was enchanted [captivated, awed] by the beauty and stood looking at the scenery for half an hour.

〈注〉 I was awed.（畏敬の念に打たれた）

うつる（移る）・うつす

1．引っ越す

動自他 **move**

あの人たちは大阪に移った。

They moved to Osaka.

来週私たちは新しい家に移る。

We are moving to [into] a new house next week.

彼は事務所を５階に移した。

He moved his office to the fifth floor.

2．興味・話題など

私たちのおしゃべりはいつか深刻な住宅事情に移っていった。

{Our conversation / We} {drifted / shifted} to the difficulty of having a house of our own.

彼の興味は徐々に天文学に移っていった。

His interest gradually shifted to astronomy.

3．伝染

君に私のかぜをうつさないように注意しなければ。

I have to be careful not to give you my cold.

あの人は夫からインフルエンザをうつされた。

She caught the flu from her husband.

ジフテリアはうつりやすい病気だ。

Diphtheria is an infectious [a contagious] disease.

〈注〉 形 contagious は接触伝染する（transmitted by contact）。

うつる（映る，写る）・うつす

1．反映

古い城が湖に映っている。

The old castle is reflected {in the lake. / on the water.}

湖は古城の影を映している。

The lake [water] reflects the old castle.

鏡に自分の姿を映してみた。

She looked at herself in the mirror.

2．写真 →とる

【写す】

彼は旅行でたくさんの写真を写してきた。

He took hundreds of photographs on his trip.

彼は子供たちが砂浜で遊んでいるところを写真に写した。

He photographed his little children playing on the beach.

みんないらっしゃい。写真を写してもらいましょう。

Come here, girls. Let's have our photo taken.

【写っている[いない]】

あの人はこの写真に写っている[いない]。

He's [He isn't] in this picture.

この写真には，彼の家族がそろって甲府の彼の旧家の前に並んで写っている。

In this picture {his whole family can be [is] seen / you [we] see his whole family} standing in front of his old house in Kofu.

この写真はよく写っている。
This picture came out well.（ピンぼけでない）
君がよく写っているよ。
This is a good picture of you.
〈注〉「誰々が何々している写真」という場合，たとえば「父がゴルフをしている写真」を ×the picture that my father is playing golf のように同格接続詞 that で結んだり，×the picture which my father is playing golf のように関係代名詞で直接結んだりすることはできない。
the picture in which my father is playing golf のように which の前に in を入れるか，the picture of my father playing golf と of を使って書くこともできる。

3．映写・撮影

【テレビ】
昨夜，田中さんがテレビに写っていたよ。
I saw Mr. Tanaka / Mr. Tanaka was } on television last night.
スライドを写す　project a slide
ビデオを写す　show a video
【撮影する】
record a video; 動 videotape
人が綱渡りをしているところをビデオに撮りました。
We videotaped a man walking on a tightrope.
cf. 映画を撮る　film a movie

4．筆写

私はその詩をノートに書き写した。
I copied the poem in [into] my notebook.

うまい・うまく

1．美味

delicious; good
【うまい!】
(It's) good [delicious]!
〈注〉日本人は delicious を使いすぎる。普通は good でよい。
It tastes good [great]!
【うまそう!】
Looks yummy!（子供の言葉。yum, yum とも言う）
【うまそうな】
tempting; appetizing（be 動詞の補語としても使える）
delicious-looking（名詞を直接形容する場合のみ; ex. a delicious-looking pie）
【うまい料理】
このレストランは(料理が)うまい。
They serve delicious food in this restaurant.
【うまくない】
このレストランは(料理が)うまくない。
The food in this restaurant { isn't very delicious. / doesn't taste good.
〈注〉Food ... isn't good. とすると，「悪くなっている(spoiled)」の意味にとられるおそれがある。

2．上手

【ピアノ】
あの人はたいへんピアノがうまい。
She is very good at playing the piano.
She plays the piano very well.
【テニス】
あの人はテニスがうまい。
She's a good tennis player.
【外国語】
彼はフランス語がうまい。
He speaks French well.
He is a good speaker of French.
彼はドイツ語よりフランス語の方がうまい。
He is more at home in [with] French than in [with] German.
【料理】
彼は料理がうまい。
He's a very good cook.
【文章】
彼はうまい文章を書く。
He is a very good writer.
【字】
あの人は字がうまい。

She writes a good hand.（古い言い方）
She has good handwriting [penmanship].
【うまいぞーッ(称賛)】
Very good! / Excellent! / Great! / Well done! / Bravo!〔*colloq.*〕

3．慣用
【話】
話がうますぎる。
That is too good to be true.
【口】
あいつは口がうまいから乗せられないようにしなさい。
Don't be deceived by that man. He says clever things.
【考え】
それはうまい考えだ。
That's a good [bright] idea.

4．うまく
【首尾よく】
新しいお仕事がうまくいくといいですね。
I hope you will be successful in your new business.
何もかもうまくいっている。
Everything is going well [fine, great, wonderfully, beautifully].
彼は新しい方法を取り入れたが，それがたいへんうまくいった。
He adopted the new method. It worked fine [wonderfully, very well].
うまくいけば…
If things go well ...
If we [you] are lucky ...
彼は今のところうまくやっている。
He is getting along well [fine] at present.
【うまくいかない】
これではうまくいかないと思う。
I am afraid this won't work.
何もかもうまくいかない。
Things are against me.
Everything has gone wrong.（うまくいかなかった）
二人はうまくいっていない。
They aren't getting along well.
二人の結婚生活はうまくいかなかった。
Their marriage { ended in failure. / failed.

うまれる（生れる）

1．出生する
【人間】
彼は1950年４月３日に東京で生れた。
He was born in Tokyo on April 3, 1950.
一姫二太郎が生れた。
First came a girl and then [next] came a boy.
彼女に赤ちゃんが生れるんだって。
She's going to have a baby.
彼女の赤ちゃんは来月生れる予定だ。
Her [Their] baby is due next month.
長子が生れた直後，あの人は病気になった。
She fell sick immediately after the birth of her first baby.
その子は小さな妹(赤ちゃん)にやきもちを焼いて，母親に赤ちゃんなんか生れない方がよかったとやんちゃを言った。
The little girl was jealous of her baby sister and told her mother that it would have been better if she hadn't had a baby.
〈注〉 私の祖母は10人も子供を生んだ。
My grandmother had ten children.
受動態で（a baby）was born は普通だが，能動態で bear [bore] a baby とはあまり言わない。have a baby でよい。
【動物】
うちの猫にまた子猫が生れた。
Our cat had kittens again.
うちの鶏は毎日卵を産む。
Our hen lays an egg every day.
【生れた土地】
どこ[どちら]のお生れですか。
Where do you come from?
Where are you from?

2. 比喩的用法

小泉新内閣が生れた。

The new Koizumi Cabinet has been chosen.

この前のオリンピックでは水泳で三つの世界記録が生れた。

Three new world records in swimming were set in the last Olympics.

うめる(埋める)・うまる・うもれる

1. 埋没

埋める　動他 **bury**

埋まる，埋もれる　**be buried**

【地中に】

言い伝えによれば，この島のどこかに海賊が宝物を埋めた[宝物が埋まっている]ということだ。

People say {the pirates buried the treasure / the treasure is buried} somewhere on this island.

【水道管】

水道管を埋める[埋設する]

lay water pipes

その人たちは新しい住宅地に水道管の埋設をしている。

Those men are laying water pipes for the new housing estate.

どの辺に水道管が埋まっているでしょうか。

Where are the water pipes?

【雪に】

小道は雪に埋もれていた。

The lane was buried in snow.

2. 補充

【空所を】

空所を埋める　fill (in) the blanks

すき間を埋める　stop [fill (up)] a gap

次の空所を適当な前置詞で埋めなさい。

Fill (in) the blanks with appropriate prepositions.

天皇の60歳の誕生日に，天皇を一目見てお祝いしようと集まった群衆が皇居前広場を埋めつくした。

The crowd filled the Imperial Plaza to see the Emperor and to celebrate his 60th birthday.

埋め立て地

reclaimed land / a landfill area〔米〕

【比喩的用法】

空席を埋める

fill a vacant post

(欠損の)穴埋めをする

make up for; cover the loss

欠損の穴埋めをできるだけ早くしておかねばならないよ。

Our shop must make up the loss as soon as possible.

彼は生涯世に埋もれたままであった。

He remained in obscurity all his life.

うら（裏）

the reverse [other] side; the back; the wrong side (↔the right side)

1. 物の裏

封筒の裏　the back of an envelope

本の裏表紙　the back cover

テープの裏面

{the reverse [other] side / side two} of a tape

衣服の裏　lining

足の裏，靴底　the sole

【裏返す，裏返し】

(書類)　turn over the paper

(ページ)　turn the page

ポケットを裏返しにする

turn one's pockets inside out

シャツを裏返しに着る

wear a shirt {wrong side out / inside out}

【裏打ちをする】 動他 line

毛皮の裏のついた手袋　fur-lined gloves

このコートには絹の裏がつけてある。

This coat { has a silk lining. / is lined with silk. }

2. 位置の裏

裏口　the back door

裏の小川

a little stream at the back of our house

裏通り　a back street

3. 比喩的用法

【野球】

9回の裏に3点入れた。

They scored three runs in the second [bottom] half of the ninth inning.

【隠れた部分】

裏の意味　the hidden meaning

裏話　a story behind a story

【裏工作】

だれかが裏で糸を操っている。

Somebody is pulling (the) strings.

舞台裏で何かが行われている。

Something is going on { behind the scenes. / backstage. }

うらやましい・うらやむ

うらやましい　㊒ **envious**

うらやむ　動他 **envy**

うらやましいなあ!

How I envy you!

彼の成功をうらやましく思う。

I envy (him) his success.

僕は君の成功をうらやましいとは思わない。

I am not envious of your success.

私はあの人の幸運をうらやんだ。

I felt a little jealous of her good luck.

〈注〉 羨望を表す表現を以下にあげる。

へえ，いいアルバイトが見つかっていいなあ。

Gee, how lucky you are to have such a good part-time job! (I wish I had ... の形より軽い表現)

あの子のような新しい服があったらよかったのに。

I wish I had a new dress like hers.

ああ，僕が彼に代りたいよ。

I'd really like to be in his shoes. 〔*informal*〕

ああ，男の子だったらよかったのに。

I wish I were a boy.

私はあの2人に対する羨望でいっぱいになった。(つくづくうらやましいと思った)

I was full of envy for those two.

【うらやましそうに】

with an envious look; enviously

うる (売る)

sell; deal in 《goods》**; offer** 《articles》 **for sale; put** 《articles》 **on sale**

1. 販売する

【何を，どこで】

あの店では何を売っているんですか。

What do they sell at that store?

スーパーでは日用品は何でも売っている。

In supermarkets { they sell / you can get } nearly everything you need for daily life.

(それなら)どのデパートでも売っている。

You can buy [get] one at any department store.

【いくらで】

これはいくらで売るのか。(値踏み・駆引き)

What will you { sell this for? / take for this? }

How much will you { sell this for? / take for this? }

How much do you want?

お米は1キロいくらで売りますか。

How much does a kilo of rice cost?

彼は辞書を1000円で売ってくれた。

He sold me his dictionary for 1,000 yen.

米は1キロ1000円で売っている。

Rice is sold at [for] 1,000 yen a kilo.

この種のアルバムは600円で売っている。

This type of photo album {sells for / costs} ¥600.

この服はみな１着5000円(で売ります)。

These dresses are 5,000 yen each [apiece].

このメロンは２個で1500円，１個なら800円。

These melons are 1,500 yen for two or 800 yen for one.

2．安売り・売れ行きなど

安売り　sale

定価で売る　sell at a fixed [set] price

特売[売出し]中

The sales are on.（TV ad.）

There's a sale at Daimaru.

棚ざらえ a clearance sale

【安売り】

20%引きで売る

take 20% off the price

give a 20% discount

半値で売る

sell a thing for [at] half price

reduce the price by half

食品や日用品はスーパーが安い[安く売っている]。

Food and household goods are cheap in supermarkets.

彼はすぐに引っ越さなければならないので，車の値を下げて売りに出している。

He's selling the car cheap because he must move soon.

【よく売れる】

小型車がこのところよく売れる。

{Small types of cars / Small-type cars} sell well these days.

〈注〉 車が主語でも are sold としないで sell を使う。

【元値を切って売る】 sell at a loss

残品を元値を切って売りさばいた。

They sold what was left over {at a loss. / below cost.}

【大もうけ】

〈注〉 不当に高い金を請求することを overcharge という。

あのホテルで食事をしたらぼられた。

They overcharged for food at that hotel.

連中は輸入品を売って大もうけしている。

They make a lot of money on imported goods.

【売り切れ】

ぶどうパンは売り切れです。

Raisin buns are sold out today.

There are no raisin buns left today.

We're sold out of raisin buns.

うるさい → やかましい

1．音がやかましい

その子たちは授業中たいへんうるさい。

Those boys are very noisy in class.

(その)音がうるさくてやりきれない。

I can't stand [bear] the noise.

テレビがうるさい。

The TV is too loud [noisy].

【うるさく】

うるさい！（相手を黙らせるために）

Be quiet! / That's enough! / Shut up!（強い）

2．わずらわしい

蚊が一晩中ブンブンうるさかった。

Mosquitoes kept bothering [annoying] me all night.

うるさいねえ！（邪魔しないでくれと撃退する）

{Stop bothering me! / Don't bother me!}（うるさくしないでくれ）

Don't interrupt me!（邪魔しないでくれ）

Leave me alone!（ほっといてくれ）

Get [Go] away!（あっちへ行け）

そのくらいの子供は何を見ても聞いてもなぜなぜとうるさく質問して親を困らせる。

Children at that stage are inquisitive and pester their parents with whys.

【うるさいもの】a nuisance; a bother

子供はただうるさいものだと思っている人もいる。

To some people children are a nuisance [nuisances, a bother].

〈注〉 a nuisance が最も一般的。

3. うるさい，気難しい → やかましい

【金】

彼は金のことにうるさい。

He's fussy about money.

【時間】

彼は時間にうるさい。

He's particular about time.

【食べ物・着る物】

あの人は食べる[着る]物にかなりうるさい。

She's rather particular [fussy] about what she eats [wears].

うれしい → よろこび・よろこぶ

【挨拶】

お目にかかれてうれしいです。

I'm glad [delighted, pleased, happy] to meet you.

〈注〉 Nice to meet you. (It's nice …の略) とも言える。

【喜び】

運転免許がとれてうれしい。

I'm so happy I got my driver's license.

いい知らせを聞いてうれしい。

I'm glad [pleased] to hear the good news.

家のローンがやっと終ってうれしい。

I'm delighted the house is finally paid for.

うれしいわ，こんないい物をいただいて。

I'm delighted with this gift.

【有頂天】

まったくうれしいよ，優勝したなんて。

How good that we have won!

本当にうれしいよ。

I'm positively elated.

あまりうれしくて２時間ほど寝つけなかった。

I lay awake for two hours unable to get over my happiness.

——Margaret Drabble, *The Millstone*

【感嘆の言葉】

わーうれしい。

Great! / Wonderful! / Fantastic!

【うれしそう】

〈注〉 自分以外の人について言う。→よろこび・よろこぶ

彼はマリーに会えてうれしそうだった[喜んでいた]。

He looked [was] happy to see Mary.

うん（運）

〈注〉 luckily 幸運の偶然性を強調している。
fortunately, happily 幸運を受ける本人の幸せを中心に考えた言い方。

【運が良い[悪い]】

今までのところ試験運が良かった［悪かった］。

I have been lucky [unlucky] in exams up till now.

こんないい家族に恵まれて君は運がいいよ。

You are fortunate to have such a fine [wonderful] family.

なんて運がいいんだ。

What a stroke of good luck!

How lucky [fortunate] you are!

【運良く[悪く]】

幸運にも好天に恵まれた。

Fortunately [Luckily] the weather was good.

運悪く天候はよくなかった。

Unfortunately [Unluckily] the weather was not good.

【運が向く】

僕にも運が向いてきた。

I'm finally in luck.

Luck has finally come my way.

【運が尽きる】

僕の運も尽きてきた。

My luck has run out.

I'm down on my luck now.

【運が良ければ】

運が良ければ，僕の英語連語の研究も完成するだろう。（完成できればと思っている）

With luck, I hope to complete my research on English collocations soon.

【運を天に任せる】

運を天に任せなさい。

Leave your fate to Heaven.

うんざり → あきる，いやな，たいくつ

〈注〉 ほかの感情を表す形容詞と同様，人間主語の場合とうんざりの対象を中心にする場合で英語の形が変化することに注意。

1．人間が主語のとき

be bored（飽きる）; **be sick of** [**be fed up with**]（食傷する）

be disgusted（嫌悪）

あの人の自慢話[ぐち]を聞かされるのはうんざりだ。

I'm fed up with his boasting [complaining].

〈注〉 仕事に(with my job)うんざり，悪天候(the bad weather）にうんざり等々にも使える。

まったくうんざりだ。

I'm bored to death.

あの人の長話にはいつもうんざりする。

I always get sick of listening to her endless talking.

彼のお説教は[あなたのかんしゃくは] もううんざりだ。

I've had enough of { his preaching. / your tantrums. }

考えてもうんざりするよ。

The very idea of it makes me sick.

あの人のおべんちゃらにはうんざりする。

I am disgusted with her flattery.

2．対象中心

boring; irksome（あきあきする）; **disgusting**（いやな）

単純でうんざりするような仕事

a simple and boring [irksome] task

うんてん（運転）→ じどうしゃ

1．機械

【運転する】

［人主語］operate a machine

【運転開始】

［人主語］start a machine

［機械主語］start operating; go into operation

【運転中】

［機械主語］be in motion

【フル運転】

running [operating] at full speed [in full swing]

年末になると印刷所の機械は昼夜兼行でフル運転だ。

At the end of the year they operate the printing machine day and night. (1)

Toward the end of the year printing machines are running [operating] at full speed. (2)

〈注〉 operate は(1)では他動詞，(2)では自動詞である。

2．交通機関

【列車】

運転する　run a train

鉄道は夏期特別列車を運転する。

The railroad runs [operates] special trains during summer.

【中止・開始】

台風のため新幹線は2時間以上運転が中止されていたが，10分以内には運転が再開されるだろう。

Because of the typhoon the Shinkansen has been stopped [halted] for more than two hours, but it will start in ten minutes.

ストライキで20本の列車が運転中止となった。

Twenty trains were canceled because of the strike.

【自動車・バスなど】

運転する　drive a car [bus]

静岡・焼津間にはバスが運行している。

A bus runs / There is bus service } between Shizuoka and Yaizu.

バスは10分間隔で運転している。

A bus leaves [runs] every ten minutes.

エレベーター運転中。

The elevator is working.

試運転　trial run

酔っ払い運転

drunken driving; 動 drive when drunk

彼は酔っ払い運転で警察につかまった。

He was arrested for drunken driving.

〈注〉 飲酒運転は公式には driving while intoxicated と言い，DWI と略されることがある。

居眠り運転をする

fall asleep { while driving / at the wheel

【運転免許】

運転免許をとる

get a driver's license [driving licence〔英〕]

うんどう（運動）

1．物理的

motion; movement

上下運動　an up and down motion

回転運動　a rotary motion

運動エネルギー　kinetic energy

2．身体的

exercise; sports

もう少し運動をするようにしなさい。

You should do [get] more exercise.

適度の運動をしなさい。

Take moderate exercise.

彼は運動不足だ。

He needs more exercise.

英国人は野外の運動が好きだ。

English people love outdoor sports.

運動場　a playground

運動靴　sport(s) shoes

運動会　a sports meet　→うんどうかい

3．政治的，社会的

movement(政治的，社会的); **campaign**(特定の目的のために行われる組織的活動); **drive**（募金運動など）; **activity**（活動）

市民運動，草の根運動

a grass roots movement

学生運動　the student movement

学生運動員　student activists

労働運動員　labor activists

消費者運動員　consumer activists

【反対運動】

多数の学生がその法案の反対運動に参加した。

Many students joined the campaign against the bill.

【核廃絶運動】

Non-Nuclear [Anti-Nuclear] Movement; Campaign for Nuclear Disarmament（CND と略す）

世界的に核兵器廃絶運動が行われている。

There's a world-wide movement for the abolition of nuclear weapons.

【選挙運動】

目下(…選挙に向けて)選挙運動中だ。

There are election campaigns going on at present.

【募金・救済運動】

その人たちは目下精力的に難民救済運動を繰り広げている。

They are carrying on a vigorous campaign for the relief of the refugees.

数人の女優・俳優のグループが内戦にあえぐアフリカの人々に毛布を送る運動を始めた。

A group of actors and actresses launched a campaign to get blankets for civil war victims in Africa.

学校では今，水泳プールのための募金運動が行われている。

There's a drive on at the school to collect money for a swimming pool.

【労働運動】

労働運動は目的のためしばしば過激な戦術[駆引き]を使ってきた。

Labor movements have sometimes used violent tactics.

【消費者保護運動，不買運動】

消費者保護運動では不買運動[ボイコット]のような行動をたびたびとってきた。

Such actions as boycotts have often been used in the consumer protection movement.

うんどうかい（運動会）

an athletic meet(ing); a sports meet; a sports day

私たちの学校の運動会は次の日曜日に行われる。

The athletic meet(ing) of our school / Our school's athletic meet(ing) will be held next Sunday.

今日はうちの運動会です。

Today's our sports day.

(うちの学校の)運動会は雨が降れば延期になる。

Our school sports meet will be {put off / rescheduled} if it rains.

【学内競技会】

intramural athletics; intramurals

【学校対抗競技会】

大学対抗フットボール試合

an intercollegiate football match

全国バスケットボールトーナメント

All-Japan Basketball Tournament

中部地区高校剣道大会

Chubu Regional High School Kendo Meet

え

え（絵）

a picture; a painting（着色画）; **drawing**（鉛筆画など）; 挿絵　**an illustration;** 版画　**a print;** 写生画　**a sketch**

絵をかく　draw [paint] pictures
挿絵入りの雑誌　an illustrated magazine
絵のような景色　a picturesque view

【…が…している絵】
彼女は，ロメオとジュリエットがバルコニーで互いに呼び合っている場面の絵をかいた。
She painted the balcony scene in which Romeo and Juliet are calling to each other.

〈注〉◆「…が…している絵」の直訳のつもりで ×She painted the picture that [which] Romeo and Juliet are calling ... とするのは誤りである。in which（その絵の中で…）としてつなげればよい。
◆paint と draw
絵のなかで paint（絵の具）でかいた（paint した）ものが paintings である。
water-color paintings 水彩画；oil paintings 油絵；鉛筆・ペン・クレヨンなど線でかいた（draw した）絵が drawings。
He drew the picture in charcoal.
（木炭画をかいた）
The child drew a horse with his crayons.
（クレヨンで馬の絵をかいた）

えいが（映画）

movies〔米〕; **films**〔英〕
（総称）**the screen; the movies**〔米〕; **the cinema**〔英〕

《関連語》
テレビ映画　TV movies; TV films / ミュージカル　musical / ドキュメンタリー　documentary film / 歴史もの・時代劇　historical film [movie] / 戦争もの　war film [movie] / SF　science fiction film / 恐怖映画　horror film / カウボーイもの　cowboy film / 西部劇　western / ロマンス　romance / 漫画・アニメ　animated cartoon, animation

1．製作

【製作者】 a producer
【監督】 a director
【助監督】 an assistant director
【シナリオ】 a scenario; a screen play
〈注〉 scenario は全体の筋書の意味。日本で言うシナリオはむしろ細部まで詳しく説明する意の screen play が合致する。その台本（script）作家はscreen writer; TV screenwriter。

【映画俳優】
a（movie, film）actor（男）[actress（女）]
映画スター　a（movie, film）star

【主演俳優[女優]】 a leading actor [actress]
主演する　star in ～; play [take] the leading part [role] in ～
…でチャーリー・チャプリンが主演している。
Charlie Chaplin is the leading actor in ...
チャーリー・チャプリンが主演している映画
a picture [film] { starring Charlie Chaplin / in which Chaplin stars }

【共演者】 a co-star
共演する（させる）　co-star
【わき役】 a supporting role [actor, actress]
【端役】 a bit player
【エキストラ】 an extra
【スタジオ】 a studio
【ロケ】 location
【字幕スーパー】
superimposed dialogue; subtitles
【吹き替え】 dubbing（せりふの吹き替え）
吹き替えした映画　a dubbed movie
【クランクイン[アップ]】
撮影開始　crank in
撮影終了　crank up

2．上映

screening
【映画館】 a movie theater; a cinema〔英〕
【映画ファン】 a moviegoer〔米〕

【入場料】admission (fee)
【予約席】a reserved seat
【上映中】
～劇場で「風と共に去りぬ」を上映している。
Gone with the Wind is now playing at ～.
～で上映中の映画
a picture now running [showing, playing] at ～
【上映時間】
この映画は上映時間が3時間だ。
This film runs [lasts] (for) three hours.
【ロードショー】a road show
〈注〉 road show〔米〕とは，(1)地方巡業，(2)一般封切り前に行う映画の独占興業，ロードショーのこと。

えいきょう（影響）

名 **influence**（他に及ぼす力）; **(an) effect**（効果）; **(a) consequence**（結果）

1．影響する
動 **influence; have an influence [an effect] on; affect**

2．影響を受ける
be influenced [affected] by
【自然】
北陸の大雪の影響でダイヤがひどく乱れている。
The heavy snow in Hokuriku has greatly disrupted the railway schedule.
【人】
私が医者になったのは高校時代の1人の先生の影響であった。
It was one of my high school teachers who [that] influenced me to become a doctor.
あの人は周囲の人の影響を受けやすい。
She is susceptible to the influence of those around her.
【思想】
禅との出会いが私の人生観に影響を与えた。
My encounter with Zen greatly influenced my idea of life.

3．悪影響を与える
do harm; be injurious to; have a bad effect on
冷夏が作物に悪影響を与えた。
The cold weather (in summer) affected the crops.
こんなテレビ番組は子供たちに悪影響を与える。
These TV programs will have a bad effect on children.

えいご（英語）

English; the English language
【アメリカ英語】American English
【和製英語】Japanese English
【英語国民】English-speaking people
【英語がわかる】understand [know] English
【英語が話せる】
can speak English (well)
be a good speaker of English
英語がもっと上手に話せたらいいのに。
I wish I could speak English better.
【英語ができる】
［学校で］
He is good at English.
He did well in English.（よくできた）
［達者だ］
He has a good command of English.
［よい英語だ］ He speaks good English.
［力がある］ He's proficient in English.
【英語の力をつける】
彼はだいぶ英語の力がついた。（上達した）
His English has improved a lot.
彼は英語の力をつけようと努力している。
He's trying hard to improve his English.
英語は苦手だ。
I'm poor [not good] at English.
【英語を和訳する】
translate from English into Japanese

translate the passage into Japanese
英語では「花」を何と言いますか。
What is 'hana' in English?

《関連語》
標準的英語 standard English / 形式ばった英語 formal English / 文語 literary English / くだけた英語 informal English / 口語 colloquial English / 俗語 slang / よい英語 good English

[その表現は]	[That expression is]
かたい	stiff
ぎこちない	stilted
聞き苦しい	awkward
おかしい	strange
めったに使わない	rare
古風だ	old-fashioned
陳腐だ	clichéd

えいよう（栄養）

名 **nourishment; nutrition**
栄養学 dietetics
栄養価 nutritional value
栄養士 a dietician
【栄養がある】 形 nourishing; nutritious
この食物は栄養がある。
This food is nourishing [nutritious].
【栄養のない】
形 not nourishing; not nutritious
【栄養不良の】
この子は栄養不良だ。
This child is undernourished.
この子は栄養失調だ。
This child suffers from malnutrition.
【栄養過多】
この頃は栄養をとりすぎる子がいる。
Some children are overweight nowadays.

ええ，ええーッ！

1．肯定
「あなた大丈夫?」「ええ大丈夫よ」。
"Are you all right?" "Yes, I'm fine."
「寒くありません？」「ええ寒くありません」。
"Aren't you cold?" "No, I'm just fine."
〈注〉「はい」「いいえ」が必ずしも英語で Yes, No にならないのと同じく，「ええ」は必ずしも Yes ではない。
【強め】
ええ，もちろんですとも。
Why yes! / Of course! / Oh, yes! / Certainly!

2．ショック
ええーッ！ Aaaa!
何だって。
What! What did you say?
まさか。
Really! / Impossible!
いやだあ。
Oh, no!

3．ためらい →あの
ええと（そのう）uh, er
Well ... let me see ...(考えながら話すとき)

えらい（偉い）

1．卓越
great（偉大な）; **famous; distinguished** 〔*formal*〕(有名な); **excellent; superior**（すぐれた）; **admirable**（感心な）
【すぐれた，有名な】
その後彼は偉い学者になった。
Later he became a distinguished scholar.
〈注〉great は業績に，famous は知名度に関した言葉。もっと形式ばった言い方には distinguished（卓越して高名な）もある。
【地位の高い】
ケンは市役所ではかなり偉くなっている。
Ken has risen to a rather high position in the city office.
私は今のままでよい。別に偉くなりたいと思わない。
I am happy as I am. I don't want to be a

somebody.
市の偉い様　city authorities
【いばる】
彼はいつも偉そうな顔をしている。
He always acts big.〔*colloq.*〕
【感心な】
そこがあの人の偉いところだ。
That's what she's really admirable for.
【感嘆の言葉】
えらいッ！
Great! / Excellent! / Capital!
Well done!（よくできた）

2．たいへんな
serious; grave
えらいことになるぞ。
This will lead to grave consequences.
えらいことになった！
That it should have come to this!〔*literary*〕
〈注〉 苦痛のうめきとしては Oh no!
【えらい騒ぎ】 a big fuss
【えらい目にあった】
I had an awful experience.

えらぶ（選ぶ）

1．選択
choose（一般的な語）; **select**（慎重に選び出す）
あの子の誕生日プレゼントに美しいネックレスを選んだ。
I chose a pretty necklace for her birthday present.
我々はビルを主将に選んだ。
We chose Bill to be our captain.
彼らは若者向けの本のベストテンを選んだ。
They selected the best ten books for young people.

2．好む
prefer（必ずしも現実に手に入れるのではなく，気持ちのうえで選ぶ；より好む）
私なら軽音楽の方を選ぶ。
I prefer light music.

3．選挙
vote for（投票する）; **elect**（投票によって選出する）
私は今度の選挙では佐藤氏を選んだ。
I voted for Mr. Sato in this election.
人々は彼を大統領に選んだ。
They elected him president.
〈注〉 president, mayor のような役職の場合は冠詞なしでよい。

えんそく（遠足）

名 **an excursion; an outing**
a picnic（弁当持ち）; **a hike**（徒歩）
【遠足に行く】
ハイキングに行く
go for [on] a picnic [picnics]
go on a day's outing
go on a hike [on an excursion, hiking]
遠足で動物園へ行く。
We'll go on a class trip to the zoo.
We'll go to the zoo for a class trip.
【遠足で】 at the [a] picnic(s)
〈注〉 picnic は可算名詞で，単数なら冠詞を，複数なら s をつける。
遠足では煮炊きは許されなかった。
We weren't allowed to cook our food at the picnic.
私たちは子供たちを遠足に連れて行った。かわいそうに「遠足なんて初めて」という子供もいた。
We took the kids on picnics. Some of these poor kids had never been on a picnic.
山へ行く　go to the mountains
キャンプに行く　go camping

えんちょう（延長）

1．空間
extend; lengthen（長くする）

地下鉄が豊田まで延長された。

The subway was extended as far as Toyota.

もう少しコードを延長しないと届かない。

The cord is too short. We need an extension cord.

2. 時間

extend; prolong; lengthen

国会は3日間延長された。

The Diet session was prolonged [extended, lengthened] for three days.

彼は滞米期間の1年延長を考えている。

He is thinking of extending his stay in the U.S. for one year.

He is applying for a one-year extension of his stay in the U.S. (申請している)

〈注〉 extend が一般的。prolong は時間的に状況をのばすこと。

えんりょ（遠慮）

1. 控えめ

【遠慮がちな[に]】

控えめな[に] reserved(ly); 謙虚な[に] modest(ly); はにかみがちな[に] shy(ly); ためらいがちな[に] hesitating(ly)

私の若い頃は女の子はもっとはにかんで遠慮がちだったものだ。

When I was young, girls were more shy and reserved.

【遠慮のない】

控えない unreserved; 率直な frank; 自由な free; 遠慮なく without reserve, frankly, freely

私は彼の新しい小説について遠慮のない意見を言わせてもらった。

I gave my frank [honest] criticism of his new novel.

もし私にできることがあれば遠慮なくそう言ってください。

If there's anything I can do for you, do tell me.

遠慮しないで先生に質問しなさい。

Don't hesitate to ask your teacher.

遠慮はいりません。皆いい人ばかりですから。

Make yourself at home. People here are all very friendly.

遠慮なく訪ねてください［遊びに来てください］。

Please {feel free / don't hesitate} to call on me.

遠慮なくいつでも僕の車を使ってください。

Please use my car whenever you want.

2. ためらう，やめる

【遠慮をする】

ためらう hesitate; …しないでおく refrain from; 断る decline《an offer》

彼らはドライブに行こうと私たちを誘ってくれたが遠慮した。邪魔しない方がいいと思ったので。

They invited me to go driving with them, but I declined

because {I thought they would rather be left alone with each other. / I thought it better not to intrude.}

車内での喫煙はご遠慮ください。(掲示)

Kindly [Please] refrain from smoking in the car.

お

おいしい → うまい・うまく

形 **good; nice; delicious**

【おいしい，おいしくない】

おいしい！（感嘆）

(It's) Good [Delicious]!

(It) Tastes great [good]!

食べてごらんよ。本当においしいよ。

Do try this one. It's [It tastes] very good.

これ，おいしくないよ。

This isn't good.

何かおいしいものある？

Is there anything good to eat?

【おいしそう】

形 delicious-looking; tempting; appetizing

わっ，おいしそう！

Looks yummy! / Yum, yum.（幼児語）

台所からおいしそうなにおいがしてる。

There's an appetizing smell [aroma] coming from the kitchen.

おいしそうだ。

It smells [looks] really good!

〈注〉 日本人は delicious を一つ覚えで使いすぎる。食事の時その場で delicious とほめるのはよいが，文章表現には工夫が必要である。例えば The food was wonderful [very good]. のように言ってもよい。おいしさの度合いは

good＜very good＜delicious [wonderful]

おうえん（応援）

1．援助

【応援する】

aid; help; assist; support; back up; go to a person's help [aid]

私たちがこのアパートに引っ越すとき，大学の友達が応援に来てくれた。

When we moved into this apartment, my college friends helped us.

僕たちが応援しているんだから元気を出して。

We are {supporting you. / backing you up.} Don't feel discouraged.

【応援を求める】ask for someone's help

2．競技で

【応援する】cheer; root for〔米 *colloq.*〕

私たちは皆慶応大学のチームを応援した。

We all {cheered (for) / rooted for} the Keio University team.

【応援団】cheering squad; cheerleaders

【応援団長】the captain of the cheerleaders

応援(団)がやかましくて頭がおかしくなる。

Cheering fans drive me crazy.

【応援歌】a cheer; a supporter's song〔英〕

〈注〉 バスケットボールの試合など，ごく普通の応援の掛け声

〔米〕 Go team go.
Go team go.
Go, go,
Go team go.
We're number one.
We're number one.
We're the champs.
We're the champs.

〔英〕上記のような決まった掛け声はないが，フットボールの試合の時など，チームの名前を呼んだり We are the champions! と叫んだりする。

3．選挙などの応援

【応援演説】campaign speech

【応援演説をする】speak in support of a candidate

私は佐藤氏の応援演説を頼まれた。

I have been asked to make a (campaign) speech for Mr. Sato.

おうじる（応じる）

1．答える，反応する

【問いに】

彼はそんな個人的な質問には応じられないと言った。

He said he wouldn't answer such personal questions.

【招きに】

私は彼に戻って来るように手招きしたが，彼は応じなかった。

I signaled him to come back but he didn't respond.

諸大学からの招請にも応ずることなく，詩人は田舎に引きこもり詩を書き続けた。

Several universities requested [asked] the poet to join their staff, but he declined all such invitations and stayed [went on living] in the countryside writing poems.

He declined all job offers from famous universities and ....

【要望に】

「皆様のご希望に応じてバンドは何でも演奏いたします」。

"The band will play any music the audience requests."

会社側はいつでも労働者側の要求に応じる姿勢をとっていた。

The company was ready to comply with the workers' demands.

我々は諸君の要望に応じるべく全力を尽すものである。

We'll do all we can to meet [grant, fulfill] your request.

【応募】

病弱な老人介護のボランティアの呼びかけに100名以上の人が応じた。

More than one hundred people volunteered to help infirm old people.

奨学基金設置のための寄付に多くの卒業生が応じた。

Many graduates offered to donate money to a scholarship fund.

2. 見合う

【収入に】

我々は収入に応じた生活をしなければならない。

We should live according to our means.

We should adjust our life style to our income.

【年齢・能力に】

子供たちに年齢・能力に応じた仕事を受け持たせなさい。

Give the children chores according to their age and abilities.

【仕事量に】

労働者は仕事の出来高[能率]に応じて賃金が支払われた。

The workers were paid
{ piece rate [by the piece].
{ according to their efficiency.

おうふく（往復）

【交通】

往復にどれくらい時間がかかりますか。

How long does it take to go there and back?

東京・大阪の往復にどれくらいお金がかかりますか。

How much is
{ the return [round-trip] fare from Tokyo to Osaka?
{ it from Tokyo to Osaka and back?

学校への往復の道で英単語を覚えたものだ。

I used to memorize English words on my way to and from school.

往復切符　a round-trip ticket〔米〕
　　　　　a return ticket〔英〕

【郵便】

往復葉書　a reply-postcard; a return postcard

〈注〉 欧米には往復葉書はないので，是非返事の必要な場合は自分のあて名を書き，切手を貼った封筒 (a self-addressed stamped envelope;［略］SASE) を封入して送る。

おえる（終える）・おわる

終る㊍㊒ **end; finish; come to an end**

終える動他 **finish; get through; put an end to; bring to an end; graduate from**《school》

1. 完了

仕事が終った。

I'm through with [I've finished] my work.

宿題は終った[終えた]の？

Have you finished your homework?

宿題を終えて[が終って]子供は遊びに行った。

After finishing [Having finished] his homework the child went out to play.

4年間の学業を終えて中学校理科の教員免許状を取得した。

He finished (a four year course at) university and got [received] his certificate in teaching secondary school science.

学生生活が終る[を終える]のがさびしい。

I'll be sad [unhappy] to finish student life.

2. 時の経過

早く試験が終ればよい。

I wish the exams were over [done].

夏休みも終った。

The summer vacation is over.

〈注〉「終った」と日本語は過去でも，今終ったばかりならば is over で，was over とはしない。

3. 終了

会議は6時に終った。

The meeting ended [was closed, broke up] at six o'clock.

家のローンが終ってほっとした。

I'm glad the house is finally paid for.

今日はこれで終ります。

That's all [So much] for today.

おおいに(大いに) → たいへん,とても・とっても

〈注〉「大いに」「たいへん」というと greatly を使いがちだが，このような強めの表現には程度・場合により異なった副詞が使われる。

very; much; very much

very 形容詞・副詞を強める。
ex. very happy; very fast

much 過去分詞形の形容詞並びに比較級の形容詞・副詞を強める。ただし，近頃は I'm much interested ... の代りに very interested の形が普通になってきた。

〈注〉◆much, very much は述語動詞を修飾できるが，慣用的に他の副詞と結びつく動詞もある。位置に注意。
◆Thank you very much. から類推してか，very much を文の最後にとってつけたように付け加えることが多いので注意。「カラオケがやかましくて大いに迷惑している」は
×We are annoyed very much
○We are very much annoyed
by the loud noise of *karaoke*.

【他の副詞】 highly; widely; badly; hard

大いに結構

be highly welcome

大いに異なる

widely different

大いに窮乏して[傷ついて]いる

be badly in need [hurt, injured]

大いに勉強する[働く / やってみる]

study [work / try] hard

〈注〉次のような言い方もある。
大いに結構じゃないか。
That's not half bad. = It's very good.
大いに助かった。
It was a great help.

おおきい(大きい)

big 数量・規模の大きさを表し，large より口語的で改まった文にはあまり使われない。また big は事の「重大」の意味にも使われる。

large 主に面積・容積の大きさを表す。また a large number のように数の多さにも使われる。

1. 量・かさ・サイズ〔*physical*〕

大きい石　a big [large] stone

大きい家　a big [large] house

大きい都市　a big [large] city
大きくなったね。わからなかったよ。
You've grown so much [so big, a lot]. I didn't recognize you.

2．無形物〔*figurative*〕
【重大】
大きな間違い　a great mistake
大きな問題　a serious [grave] problem
大きなニュース　big news
大きな地震　a severe earthquake
【音】
もっと大きな声で。聞えません。
Louder please [Speak up]. I can't hear you.
もっと音を大きくして。(ラジオなど)
Please turn up the volume.
【態度】
あいつは態度が大きい。
He's arrogant [haughty].
あんなやつが大きな顔をしている(幅をきかせている)のが腹立たしい。
I feel annoyed to see a man like him having influence around here.
大きな顔をするな。
Don't be [act] so cocky.
Don't put on (such) airs.
Don't try to look so important.
〈注〉 同じ気持ちで Who do you think you are？ のようにも言う。
彼はいつでも大きな口をきく。
He's always boasting [talking big].
気が大きくなる　feel rich
〈注〉 feel rich は食事などをおごるのに相手に気をつかわせないために次のように使ったりする。
I feel rich tonight, so let me treat you to dinner.
(今日は気分がいいからおごらせてください)

おかしい

1．滑稽
funny; (面白い) **amusing**
何がそんなにおかしいの？
What's so funny?
What's making you laugh (so)? (笑っている人に)
あの人はおかしなことばかり言うの。
He always says funny things.
あの子が大人ぶって老婦人のような気取った話し方をするのがおかしかった。
We were amused / It was amusing } to hear the child speak like a prim old lady.

2．不審な，変な　→へんな
【不思議】
おかしいな。どこへ行ったんだろう。
It's really strange. Where has it gone?
おかしなことに，急に元気になった。
Strangely [Curiously, Oddly enough], I suddenly felt strong.
【奇妙】
あのおじいさんはおかしな人だ。
He's a strange old man.
【不調】
体がおかしい。
Something's wrong with me.
今日は君，何だかおかしいよ。
You aren't your usual self today.
【あやしい】
あいつの行動はちょっとおかしい。
His behavior is a bit suspicious.

3．狂った　→へんな
【頭が】
彼は少々頭がおかしいんじゃないか。
He's a little off, don't you think?
〈注〉 「頭が変だ」を意味する表現はこの他にも多い。
He's gone crazy [mad]. は一般的な言い方。
He's got a screw missing. 〔*slang*〕
(ネジが１本はずれてる)
He's not playing with a full deck of cards. 〔*cliché*〕
(「トランプのカードがそろっていない」から)
以上すべて「頭がおかしい」(crazy, mad, strange, weird) の意。

4. 腐った

このミルクおかしいよ。(not fresh の意)

This milk's { a bit off. / gone off. }

おきに → ごとに

おきる(起きる)・おこす

〈注〉「起きる」は下に分類してあるように「目を覚ます」「起床する」の両方の意味に使われるので注意。

1. 目を覚ます

【起きる】 動自 wake up

【起される】 be awakened

変な音で起された。(起きてしまった)

I was awakened by a strange sound.

【起す】 動他 wake; awaken

忘れずに5時に起してね。

Be sure to / Don't fail to } wake me (up) at five.

ジョンは8時になったので，とうとうスーを起した。スーは7時半に起きるつもりだと知っていたので。

John finally woke Sue at 8:00 because he knew that she had wanted to wake at 7:30.

【起きている】 be awake

兄ちゃんはとなりに寝ているので，起きていれば気配でわかる。眠っている時と何か違うのだ。

My brother's bed is beside mine so that I can feel when he is awake because it is different from when he is asleep.

——W. Saroyan, *Our Friends the Mice*

2. 起床する

【起きる】 動自 get up; rise; get out of bed (寝床から出る)

寒い朝は起きるのがつらい。

It is hard for us to get out of bed on cold mornings.

あの人はもうベッドの上に起きられる。

Now she can sit up in bed.

【起す】

彼はベッドの上に体を起した。

He sat up in bed.

彼女は彼の体をベッドの上に起してやった。

She helped him sit up in bed.

彼は子供を起してやった。(立たせた)

He helped the child to his feet.

【起きている】 stay up

私たちは一晩中起きて議論をしていた。

We stayed up all night arguing.

おきわすれる(置き忘れる) → わすれる

leave

財布を台所のテーブルの上に置き忘れてきた。

I left my purse on the kitchen table.

傘を列車の中に置き忘れたに違いない。

I must have left my umbrella in the train.

〈注〉 When he moved this time, he left lots of books behind. (彼は今回の引越しでは本をたくさん置いてきた)

意図的に置いてくるのは leave, うっかりして置き去りにするのも leave である。前後関係やイントネーション，表情などでどちらかわかる。

おくる(送る，贈る)

1. 物を send

【郵送】

彼はアメリカから美しいクリスマスカードを送ってくれた。

He sent me a beautiful Christmas card from America.

【発送】

陶器製品を南米に(船便で)送っている。

They ship earthenware products to South America.

【急送】

部品は至急航空便でお送りします。

We will send the parts by air.

【贈与】
彼の両親は毎月彼に金を送っている。
His parents send him money every month.
彼が去るとき，記念に小さな本を贈った。
When he was leaving,
{ we made him a small present of a book / we gave him a book } as a token of our friendship.

2．人を
【見送り】
そこまでお送りしましょう。
I'll go part of the way with you.
子供たちは村はずれの橋のところまで彼を送って来た。
The children followed him as far as the bridge at the boundary of the village to see him off.
The children saw him off as far as the bridge at the boundary of the village.
私たちは皆で駅まで彼を見送りに行った。
We all went to the station to see him off.
【送り届ける】
車で家までお送りします[送ってあげるよ]。
I'll take you home (in my car).
I'll drive you home.
I'll see you home.
〈注〉「連れて行く」の意味の時は send は使えない。
【護送】
犯人は刑務所に送られた。
The criminal was sent to prison.

3．日々を
彼は子供時代をニュージーランドの小さな町で送った。
He spent his childhood in a small town in New Zealand.
彼は今自分の生れた村で静かな日々を送っている。
He is now leading a quiet life in the village where he was born.

おこない(行い) → こうい

an action;（行動）**a deed;**（振舞い）**conduct; behavior**
【よい行い】
a good deed（老人を助けるといった特定［1回限り］の行い）
good conduct（いつも行いがよいこと）
【親切な行い】an act of kindness
【行いを改める】
行いを改めないと君は人生を誤ることになる。
You should try to mend your ways; otherwise you'll be a failure in life.
行いを改めないと(心を入れ替えないと)君自身だけでなく家族までだめにしてしまうだろう。
You'll ruin yourself and your family if you don't reform yourself.
【行いを慎む】
行いを慎みなさい。
You should be careful in your conduct.
〈注〉慣用的表現の英訳
「ご出発の日にいいお天気になりましたね。あなたの日頃の行いがいいから」。
"It's ideal weather for your flight. You must have God's blessing because of your good conduct."

おこなう(行う)

1．行事
【運動会】
運動会は次の月曜日に行う[行われる]。
The athletic meet will { be held / take place } next Monday.
【修学旅行】
修学旅行は6月1日から5日まで行われる。
The school trip will be from the 1st to the 5th of June.
【委員会】
第3回の委員会は今月20日に行われる。
The committee will hold [have] its third

meeting on the 20th of this month.

〈注〉 日本語の「委員会」は委員を集合的に body としてとらえた意味と，委員たちの会 meeting の意味と両方に用いられるが，committee は body であり，その会合は meeting であることに注意。

【試験】

学年末試験は2月末に行われる。

(The) Final exams will be given at the end of February.

【選挙】

先月総選挙が行われた。

There was a general election last month.

【正月行事】

この神社では正月行事は旧暦によって執り行われる。

At this shrine
{ the traditional New Year rites are observed
{ they observe the traditional New Year rites
according to the lunar calendar.

2．式

【結婚式】

結婚式はウィリアムズ神父によって執り行われた。

The wedding was conducted by Father Williams.

Father Williams conducted the wedding ceremony.

【卒業式】

卒業式は3月10日に行われる。

The graduation ceremony will be held on the 10th of March.

3．実施

【改革】

政府は来年度より改革案により万事執り行う［改革案を実施する］。

The government will put the reform bill into action from the next fiscal year.

おこる（怒る）

get angry; get mad at;（かんかんに怒る）**get furious;**（堪忍袋の緒が切れる）**lose patience; lose** one's **temper**

《類義語》

〈注〉「怒らせる」意の他動詞およびそれらの動詞の受身形の憤慨の意味をもつ語彙を弱いものから強度のものへと列挙する。

annoy; be annoyed

彼はバスが2，3分遅れてもすぐ怒り出す。

He is always annoyed when the bus is late even by two or three minutes. (Why don't they run on time! と舌打ちする感じ)

私は彼のジルに対する仕打ちに改めて憤りを覚えた。

I began to feel annoyed with him once more for what he had done to Gill.

——M. Drabble, *The Millstone*

vex; be vexed

提出物が遅れるといつも怒る先生がいます。

One of our teachers is always vexed with us when we don't hand in our papers on time.

あの数学の問題にはまったく頭に来て(畜生！と)鉛筆を投げてしまった。

I became so vexed at that math problem I threw my pencil across the room.

〈注〉 米国では irritate の方が多く使われる。

irritate; be irritated（いらいらする）

映画の間中たばこの煙にいらいらして，まったくたばこを彼の手からたたき落してやりたいほどだった。

I got so irritated at his smoking during the movie, (that) I wanted to knock the cigarette out of his hand.

拡声器をつけたトラックが来るとやかましくていらいらするという人もいる。

Some people find sound trucks irritating [annoying].

〈注〉 annoyed と irritated はどちらも不安の意を含み，後者の方が程度が強い。ここでは怒らせた側に怒らせる意図があったかなかったかは問題外であるが，次の provoke, offend は意図的に怒らせる場合を含み，be provoked [offended] では怒る原因にかなり重点が置かれている。

provoke; be provoked

〈注〉 be provoked は怒った結果何らかの行動に出る含みがある。

隣のステレオがあんまりいつまでもやかましいので，とうとうたまりかねて「止めてくれ」と怒鳴り込んだ。

My neighbor kept on playing his stereo loudly until finally I was provoked [irritated] enough to knock at his door and tell him to turn it off.

子供が5, 6人で犬を棒切れでつついて怒らせて遊んでいた。

Several children were provoking a dog by poking sticks at it.

offend; be offended

〈注〉 offend はプライド，道徳，礼儀などを損なったり，それに反したことをして怒らせることであり，be offended は「むっとする，気に障る，憤慨する」の意。

朝の7時半に電話をかけてくるなんてと彼女は腹を立てた。

She was offended by his telephoning her at 7:30 a. m..

腹におさまらないことがあっても，仕返しをしようなんて気になるなよ。

Even if you are offended, don't be provoked to retaliate.

くだらないことが気に障る人もある。たとえば「ハロー」と挨拶しないで「ハーイ」と言ったとか何とかで。

Some people are offended by very small things, for instance, being greeted by "Hi" instead of "Hello".

〈注〉 be impatient, be confused, be upset は平静を失った状態であり，怒りに近いが必ずしも怒りを含まない。

【怒っている】（状態）

be angry [mad, furious, annoyed]

何を怒っているの？

Why are you angry?

What are you angry at?

まだ彼のこと怒っているの？

Are you still angry at [with] him?

彼は怒って，ドアをバタンと閉めて出て行った。

He walked out angrily, slamming the door (to).

【怒る】（状態の変化）

get angry [mad, furious, annoyed, etc.]

lose patience; lose one's temper

父はその知らせを聞いてかんかんに怒った。

My father got furious at the news.

スキー教室の先生は若い子が受講中にぺちゃくちゃおしゃべりするのでついに怒り出した。

The ski instructor began losing patience with the teenagers when they kept talking to each other during the lessons.

【怒らせる】

make someone angry [mad, furious]; annoy; vex; irritate; provoke; offend

私を怒らせたいのか。

Do you want to make me angry?

あの人はすぐ怒るから刺激しないように[怒らせないように]しなさい。

He is easily offended. Please be careful not to provoke him.

【怒られる】 be scolded

トムは塀に落書して怒られた。

Tom was scolded [spanked] for scribbling on the wall.

〈注〉 scold は口でしかること。spank は罰としてお尻をたたくこと。

（そんなことすると）怒られるぞ。

You'll catch [get] it. 〔*slang*〕

〈注〉 「父親に怒られた」He was scolded by his father. のような文は，特に主語に重点を置くのでなければ His father scolded him. とした方が自然である。また「怒られる」は行為を示し，be angry は感情であるから，「怒られた」は ×He was got angry by his father. のような言い方はできない。

【怒りっぽい】 touchy; be easily offended

疲れると怒りっぽくなる。

We tend to {get touchy / be irritable} when we are tired.

おこる(起こる)・おきる・おこす

1. 起る，起きる

【偶発・自然災害など】

take place; happen; occur

〈注〉 偶発には上記のどの語も使えるが，思いがけない感じが強いのは happen, 次いで occur であり，take place は前もってわかっているときにも使える。

いつまた地震が起るかわからない。

Another earthquake may take place [happen, occur] at any time.

チリ地震の影響で日本の東海岸に津波が起った。

The earthquake in Chile caused a tidal {wave which struck / wave at [on]} the eastern coast of Japan.

ひどい雪崩が起った。

There was a terrible avalanche.

A terrible avalanche occurred.

私の夢ではよく不思議なことが起る。

Sometimes strange things happen [take place, occur] in my dreams.

【人為的事件など】 occur; take place; break out（戦争）; originate（起源）

一瞬の不注意から交通事故が起る。

Momentary carelessness may cause a traffic accident.

今日の新聞にスペインで暴動が起ったと書いてある。

Today's paper reports that a riot broke out [occurred] in Spain.

まず18世紀のヨーロッパに起った民主化の波は19世紀の間に着々と大きな運動に育っていった。

The movement for democratization which originated in 18th century Europe continued to develop through the 19th century.

ストレスから胃病が起ることがよくある。

Stomach diseases are often caused by stress.

2. 起す

㊍㊐ **cause; cause something to happen**

気圧の違いが風を起すということがわかっている。(気圧の違いから風が起る)

We know that differences in atmospheric pressure cause winds.

〈注〉 1.の「起る」の英語例文は「地震が津波を起す」「不注意が事故を引き起す」「ストレスが病を起す」と日本語訳をつければ「起す」の例文としても通用することになる。

【争い・面倒】

彼はいつでも面倒を起す。

He's a troublemaker.

He always causes difficulties to others.

新しい法律はいろいろと論争を引き起した。

The new law caused much controversy.

これも戦争を引き起した原因の一つだ。

This is one of the causes of the war.

おさえる（押える，抑える）

1. 押えつける

hold down

犬を押えていてください。

Please keep your dog away from me.

戸を開けて押えています。

I'll hold the door open.

その人はわき腹を押えて倒れた。

The man held [clutched] his side and fell down.

はしごをしっかり押えていてください。

Please hold the ladder steady.

救急手当ではまず出血を押えることだ。

"Stop bleeding" is the number one rule of first aid.

2. 抑止する

hold down; restrain

【感情を】

彼女は気持ちを抑えることができなかった。

She couldn't restrain her feelings [contain herself].

私は涙を抑える[こらえる]ことができなかっ

た。

I couldn't keep back my tears.

彼女はこみ上げてくる笑いを抑えようと必死であった。

She desperately tried to stifle a laugh.

【力で】

現在その国の政府が直面する最大の課題はインフレ［物価の上昇］を抑えることである［の抑止である］。

The greatest problem for the present government of that country is how to control inflation [hold down prices].

その会社は組合に抑えられている。

The company is {controlled by / under the thumb of} the union.

3．捕える

警察は犯人［泥棒］を現行犯で取押えた。

The police arrested the culprit at the scene of the crime.（犯人を）

The police caught the robber red-handed.（泥棒を）

おさめる（納める，治める）・おさまる

1．収納する，落ち着く

奈良時代からの皇室の宝物が数多く正倉院に納められている。

Many Royal treasures that date back to the Nara Period are kept [housed] in the Shoso-in.

彼は本が多すぎて新しい部屋の三つの書架に納まらない。

{He has too many books for / His books won't fit in} the three bookcases in the new room.

私たちに１部ずつ配ってから彼は残りのパンフレットを書類かばんに納めた。

After giving each of us a copy, he put the rest of the pamphlets back into his briefcase.

【納入】

月末までに税金［家賃／授業料］を納めなければならない。

We must pay our taxes [the rent / the school fees] by the end of this month.

【納品】

わが社は大手スーパー数社に品物を納めている。

Our company supplies goods to several big supermarkets.

【入居】

彼は新居に納まった。

He's now settled in his new house.

彼は新しい職場［役職］に納まった。

He's now settled in his new job [position].

2．鎮静する，解決する

【統治】

以前は殿様が領地を治めていた。

In former days feudal lords ruled over the land.

【鎮静】

暴動はまもなく治まり，平和と秩序が戻った。

The riot was soon put down, and peace and order returned.

双方ともくたびれてしまってけんかは治まった。

Both parties got tired of their quarrel and so it ended.

彼は両家の争いを治めるべく最大の努力をした。

He did his best to settle the conflict between the two families.

風が治まった。

The wind has gone down [fallen, dropped, died].

台風は夕方には治まった。

The typhoon subsided toward evening.

彼の怒りも徐々に治まった。

His anger gradually left him.

痛みが不思議に治まった。

The pain has miraculously gone.

それでは彼(の気持ち)が治まらない。

He won't be satisfied with that.

3．得る

【勝利】

グラフとの最終戦でヒンギスが勝利を収めた。

Hingis won in the final match against Graf.

【利益】

あの会社は織物輸出で莫大な利益を収めた。

That company has made huge profits on its exported fabrics.

おしい（惜しい）→ もったいない

1．捨てがたい（事前）

【金】

私は買わない。金が惜しいよ。

I wouldn't buy it. It's like throwing money away.

【時間】

時間が惜しいよ。(時間の無駄だ)

It would merely be a loss [waste] of time.

1時間でも時間が惜しい。

I grudge even an hour.

【命】

まだ命が惜しいよ。

I don't want to die yet.

命が惜しければ医者の言いつけを守りなさい。

If you want to live, do as the doctors told you.

〈注〉 追いはぎ（a highwayman）の言う「命が惜しければ金を出せ」は Your money or your life. である。

【衣服など】

子供たちに着られなくなった服なのだが，まだ丈夫で捨てるのは惜しい。

The children have outgrown these clothes but they are still too good to
{ throw away.
{ be thrown away.

2．残念（事後）

【惜しいことをした】

いいチャンスを逃がして，君，惜しいことしたね。

(It's) Too bad that you missed that good chance.

【惜しい人】

惜しい人を亡くした。

His death is a great loss to us.

【惜しいところ，惜しくも】

惜しいところで負けた。(勝てるところだったのに)

It was a game we could have won.

It's a shame we lost when we were so close to winning.

【惜しいことに】

彼は正直で賢くて思慮深いが，惜しいことにユーモアのセンスがない。

He's honest, intelligent and thoughtful; he lacks only a sense of humor.

おしえる（教える）

〈注〉 「教える」と言うとすぐ teach が頭に浮ぶようだが，内容によって下記のように使い分けねばならない。先生（teacher）が教えるのが teach である。

1．学芸

【学校】

彼は高校で教えている。

He is a high school teacher.

He teaches at Nagara High School.（長良高校で）

【学科】

彼はニューヨークの高校で英語を教えている。

He teaches }
He is teaching }
He is a teacher of }
English at a high school in New York.

〈注〉 「高校[小学校，中学校]で教えている」という場合の冠詞は，単に「高校［小学校，中学校]の教員である」の意味ならばなくてかまわない。特定の学校を念頭に浮かべているのなら冠詞をつける。ニューヨークのある高校なら a high school in New York と不定冠詞をつける。～町の町立で1校しかなくて相手にもそれとわかる高校なら the high school とするか校名をそのまま言えばよい。

【個人的】

母は私に編み物や裁縫を教えてくれた。

My mother taught me how to knit and sew.

私は個人的に高校生に数学を教えている。

I teach mathematics privately to some high school students.

I give private lessons in mathematics to some high school students.

〈注〉 塾のようなものは英米にはないので，上記の文は日本の状況を知らない者にはわからない。個人教授もあまりないそうである。日本の事情に詳しい人には juku とか cram school と言えばわかる。

【芸事】

彼女は子供にピアノを教えている。

She {teaches piano / gives piano lessons} to children.

2．情報

【道を】

どこか一番近いバス停に行く道を教えてくださいませんか。

Can [Could] you tell me the way to the nearest bus stop?

〈注〉 Will you show me the way to … ? とか I'll show you …. と言うときは一緒に「ついていって教えてくれ」とか「連れていってあげる」ことになる。また地図を持ってきて地図の上で指で示す場合も考えられる。道を「教える」の「教える」は teach とは言わない。

【予約など】

何かの都合で空席ができるようなことがあったら教えてください。

Please {let me know / inform me} if by any chance there is a vacancy.

3．注意喚起

(出発の)時間になったら教えてください。

{Tell me / Call me / Let me know} when it is time to start.

4．しつけ

トムはおしっこを教えるようになった。

Now Tom says [tells me] when he wants to go to the toilet.

子供にはまず善悪の区別をしっかり教えておかなければならない。

Children should be taught first of all what is right and what is wrong.

おしゃべり

名 話　**a chat;** 多弁な人　**a talkative person;** うわさ好き　**a gossip**

形 **talkative**

しゃべる 動自 **talk; speak**

おしゃべりする　動自 **chat; have a chat; gossip**(うわさ話をする)

【歓談】

きのうは昔のクラスメートに会ってしばらくおしゃべりをした。

I met an old classmate yesterday and chatted with her for a while.

【私語】

授業中におしゃべりをしてはいけない。

Don't talk in class.

【うわさ話】

あの人に言わないで[しゃべらないで]。あの人はおしゃべりだから。

Don't tell her. She's a gossip.

【多弁】

あの人はおしゃべりだ。

She chatters non-stop.（子供など）

She goes on and on.

〈注〉 a talker は「おしゃべり」のこと。speaker は話者，講演者で，a great speaker と言えば「話し上手（eloquent）」の意味になる。

おせん（汚染） → こうがい(公害)

おそらく → だろう

probably; perhaps; maybe

おそらく気がつかないだろう。

Probably he will not notice.

おそらくだめだろう。

Most probably he will not succeed.（成功しない）

I dare say it will come to nought.（無駄骨になる）

〈注〉◆「おそらく」は否定的な内容と結びつきやすいので，「残念ながらだめだろう」という気持ちであれば I'm afraid it will not . . . のような形でもよい。

◆probably, maybe, possibly による可能性の程度の表現（下にいくほど弱くなる）

Probably he will succeed.（たいてい，たぶん成功）

Maybe [Perhaps] he will succeed.（成功するかもね）

Possibly he will succeed.（もしかしたら成功するかもね）

Probably he will not succeed.（おそらくだめ）

He cannot possibly succeed.（絶対だめ）

◆possibility による程度の表現（合格の可能性は下にいくほど弱い）

There's a strong possibility that he'll pass.

There's a possibility that he'll pass.

There's a small [faint, slim] possibility that he'll pass.

There's only a faint possibility that he'll pass.

There's no possibility that he'll pass.

おそろしい(恐ろしい) → こわい・こわがる

1. 恐怖

〈注〉「恐怖感をもつ」意味では「こわい・こわがる」参照。

【主観】

まあ恐ろしい！（事故の話などを聞いて）

How terrible [awful]!

Oh no!

恐ろしい目にあった。

I had a horrible experience.

【客観】

あれは恐ろしい男だ。

He's {a horrible / an awful} man.

都会は恐ろしい所だと信じ込んでいる人がいる。

Some people believe that big cities are dangerous and horrible places to live in.

2. 強意

〈注〉強意語（intensive）としては「すごい，ひどい」参照。

けさはおそろしく早く目が覚めた。

I woke up unusually [incredibly] early this morning.

山口はおそろしく頭がいい。

Yamaguchi is very [really, incredibly] clever.

彼はおそろしく近眼だ。

He is dreadfully [terribly] near-sighted.

彼はおそろしく怒りっぽい。

He's awfully [terribly] touchy.

トラックがおそろしいスピードで走って来た。

A truck came along at a terrible [an incredible] speed.

おそわる（教わる）

be taught; learn; けいこに通う **take lessons**

【学ぶ】

私は祖父から多くのことを教わった。

I have learned a great deal from my grandfather.

【やり方】

私はごく小さいときに泳ぎを教わった。

I was taught how to swim when I was very little.

【指示】

その子はピアノの小曲を先生に教わった通り忠実に弾いた。

The child played the piano piece, faithfully following his teacher's instructions.

私は教わった通り，まず1番のバスに乗り，それから3番目のバス停で降りて5番のバスに乗り換えた。

I took the Number 1 bus and then changed at the third stop for the Number 5 bus, just as I had been told.

【おけいこ】

私はあの先生にピアノ[フランス語]を教わっている。

I am taking piano lessons from him.

He's teaching me French.（語学の場合はこの形が普通）

おたがいに（お互いに）

each other; one another

〈注〉「お互いに励まし合った」「互いに顔を見合せた」など日本語では「お互いに」をよく使うので，その直訳として each other がよく使われる。しかし each other はAがBに働きかけ，同時にBがAに働きかける場合，すなわち文法的に言えば each other が他動詞（または前置詞）の目的語になる場合にのみ用いられるので，「お互いに体に気をつけましょう」のようにあなたはあなたの体に，私は私の体に気をつけるのでは相手に働きかけることにならない。そんな場合に each other は使えないのである。したがって each other は単独に副詞句としては使えない。

お互いに体に気をつけよう。
×Let's take care of our health each other.
お互いにがんばろう。（勉強の場合）
×Let's study hard each other.
Let's each study hard.

each other は不要。Let's は Let us であるから Let's の中に「私」も「あなた」も含まれる。

私たちは互いに積もる話をした。
×We talked each other.

この talk は自動詞であるから talked with each other と前置詞 with が必要である。

私たちは互いに励まし合った。

We encouraged each other.（他動詞の目的語）

私たちは互いに顔を見つめた。

We looked at each other.（前置詞の目的語）

〈注〉 each other は二者の間，one another は三者以上の間という区別は今日ではないようである。どちらを使ってもよい。違いがあるとすれば，一般的な記述には one another を使い，特定の人に関してはeach other を使うという傾向であるとのこと。

——Michael Swan, *Practical English Usage*

おだやかな（穏やかな）→ おとなしい

1. 自然

calm; mild

【天候】

この辺は気候が穏やかです。

The climate here is very mild.

【海】

今夜は海が穏やかです。

The sea is calm tonight.

2. 人

【穏やかな人】a gentle person

私の母はだれにでも穏やかな微笑で接する人だ。

My mother has a gentle smile for everyone.

【穏やかに】

彼は穏やかに，それは多少事実と違うのではないかとたしなめた。

He gently protested that it wasn't exactly true.

彼は穏やかな口調で私に話しかけてきた。

He spoke to me
{ in a gentle and quiet tone.
{ gently and quietly.

おちつく（落ち着く）

1. 落ち着いている（状態）

【気持ち】be composed; be calm; be poised

何事が起ってもあの人は落ち着いている。

Whatever happens
{ she's composed.
{ she never loses her presence of mind.
{ she remains poised.

議論しているうちに私はかっかしてきたが，彼は最後まで落ち着いていた。

While arguing I got excited, but he was calm [composed] to the end.

【性格】calm

加藤さんは落ち着いた性格の人だ。

Mr. Kato is calm by nature.

【生活】be settled

あの人たちも新居に落ち着いて何とかうまくやっている。

Now they're settled (in) in their new place and they're getting along well with each other.

2．落ち着く (状態の変化)

【気持ち】become composed; compose oneself; regain one's presence of mind; calm down

まあ落ち着きなさいよ。

Calm yourself. Don't get so excited.

【生活】settle down

私たちもニューヨークに落ち着きました。

We've settled in New York.

(=... moved to New York permanently.)

赤ちゃんが生れてからジムも落ち着いた。

After the baby was born Jim settled down.

3．落ち着かない

【気持ち】be nervous; feel uneasy

結果が発表になるまで彼は落ち着かないだろう。

He will be nervous until the result is announced.

午後に来客があると思うと落ち着かなくて何も手につかない。

I can't settle down to do anything because we are expecting a visitor this afternoon.

オフィスが変ってまだ落ち着きません。

I still {feel uneasy / don't feel at home} in my new office.

【性向】restless

彼はいつも落ち着きがない。

He is always restless [fidgeting].

おちる(落ちる)・おとす

1．落下する

落ちる ㊍㊖ **fall**

落す ㊍㊕ **drop; let** 《a thing》 **fall**

大きな雨粒がぽつぽつ落ちてきた。

Big raindrops started to fall.

雪が屋根[軒]からどさっと落ちた。

The snow on the roof [eaves] fell off with a thud.

水道の蛇口をしっかり締めてね。ぽたぽた落ちている。

Turn the tap [faucet] off. It's dripping.

あそこのあの木に雷が落ちたのだ。

That big tree you see over there was hit [struck] by lightning.

落さないようにね。壊れるから。

Don't {drop it. / let it fall.} It will break.

2．転落する

【落ちる】

乗客を満載したバスが飛騨川に落ちた。

A bus full of passengers fell into the Hida River.

飛行機が福井市の近くの山中に落ちた。

A plane crashed in the mountains near Fukui City.

子供が木から[屋根から]落ちて足の骨を折った。

The child fell from [off] the tree [the roof] and broke his leg.

【沈下】

日が落ちると急に寒くなる。

When the sun sets it suddenly gets cold.

3．紛失する，脱落する

家に帰る途中どこかで新しい財布を落した。

I dropped [lost] my new wallet somewhere on my way home.

子供が道路に100円玉の落ちているのを見つけた。

The child found a 100-yen coin on the street.

何か落ちていないかリストをもう一度チェックしてみてください。

Check the list and see if
- anything's been left out.
- everything is included.
- everything's been done.

書類をコピーしていて1ページ落してしまった。

He has dropped [left out] a page in copying the document.

20ページばかり落ちている[抜けている]。

Some twenty pages are missing.

4. 洗い落す

靴の泥をまず落してから家にお入り。

Get [Wash] the mud off your boots before coming in.

僕はベンジンでペンキを落そうとした。

I tried to remove the paint with benzene.

私は染みを落そうとした。

I tried to wash the stains off.

この染みはなかなか落ちない。

This stain wouldn't
- wash off [out].
- come out.

5. 学業

【落第】

彼は東大を落ちた。

He failed
- the Todai entrance exam.
- Todai.

僕は数学を落した[落された]。

I failed math(s) [the math(s) exam].

I flunked math. 〔米俗〕

〈注〉 maths〔英〕; math〔米〕

安藤先生に数学で[筆記試験で]落された。

Mr. Ando failed me in math(s) [on the basis of the written test].

【成績の低下】

彼は今学期成績が落ちた。

He got poor marks this term.

His marks have dropped [gone down].

His grades have fallen [gone down].

彼は1番から15番に落ちた。

He's fallen [gone down] from 1st to 15th place in his class.

彼は10番も落ちた。

He fell [went down] ten places.

6. 低下する

彼は力を落している。

He's disheartened.

気[力]を落さないで。

Don't lose heart. Cheer up.

彼は声を落して，これはだれにも言うなと言った。

He lowered his voice and told me not to tell anyone.

彼女は膝の上に持った小さな包みに目を落した。

She looked down at the small parcel she was holding on her lap.

【社会的評価】

彼は家の名を落した[汚した]。

He disgraced his family name.

He is a disgrace to his family.

彼はそのスキャンダルで評判を落した。

He has lost his reputation because of the scandal.

彼は人気が落ちた。

He has lost his popularity.

このところ彼女の人気は落ちてきている。

Her popularity has fallen off [decreased] recently.

【速度】

向かい風になると速度が急速に落ちる。

Speed drops off rapidly when you are running against the wind.

危険箇所に近づくにつれて列車は速度を落した。

The train slowed down as it approached the

dangerous spot.

7. 質・品質・量など

テレビ番組製作者は，大衆の悪趣味に媚びてレベルを落すべきではない。

TV producers and directors shouldn't lower the level to cater to people's vulgar tastes.

この 2, 3 年，生徒の質が落ちてきている。

The quality of students has been declining the last few years.

こちらの真珠はそちらのより質が落ちる。

These pearls are inferior to those [aren't as good as those].

こちらのソックスは値段は安いが，品質があちらのものより落ちる。

These socks are cheaper than those but the material isn't as good.

我々は品物の質を落さないよう努力しています。

We are trying to keep up the quality of our products.

ここ 2, 3 年，生産高が落ちている。

Production has fallen these few years.

売り上げが落ちた。

Our sales have dropped off [fallen, decreased].

風が落ちた。(静まった)

The wind has { gone down. / dropped. }

8. ある状態になる

彼女は深い眠りに落ちていった。

She fell into a deep sleep.

おと（音）

a sound;（雑音，騒音）**a noise**

昨夜は変な音で目が覚めた。

I was awakened by a strange noise [sound] last night.

そんな大きな音をたてるな。

Don't make so much noise.

ラジオの音が大きすぎる。もう少し小さくしなさい。

The radio is { too noisy. / too loud. / making too much noise. }

Turn it down.

【音がする，聞える】

外で変な音がする。

I can hear a strange noise [sound] outside.

あの音が聞えますか。

Can you hear that noise [sound]?

〈注〉「音がする[した]，聞える[えた]」には I [You, We ...] hear [heard] を使うとよい。

教会の鐘の音[だれかの足音]が聞える。

I hear the church-bells [footsteps].

【オノマトペ】

〈注〉ドシン，カチン等々の音については「擬声語・擬態語」の項参照。

玄関の戸がバタンと閉まる音がした。

I heard the front door bang shut.

だれかがドアをたたく音がした。

I heard someone knocking at the door.

バサリと物の落ちる音がした。

I heard something fall on the floor with a thud [go thud on the floor].

おどす（脅す）・おどかす

threaten; menace（脅迫的表情・身振りで）**;**
blackmail（ゆする）

彼らは動いたら撃つぞと彼を脅した。

They threatened to shoot him if he moved.

その男の子は気味の悪い幽霊話を聞かせて弟を脅かした。

The boy scared his little brother by telling eerie ghost stories.

彼は脅すようなすごい目つきでその子をじろりと見た。

He glared at the child with a menacing expression.

〈注〉「脅すような身振り」は menacing gesture である。He's a menace. というのは，He's dangerous. の意。

近所の不良が僕を脅したんだ。「もしビデオレコーダーを盗み出して来なければ，お前がたばこを吸っているっておやじに言いつけるぞ」って。

The neighborhood bully said he would tell my father that I smoke unless I stole a video recorder for him.

〈注〉 上の文のような行為が blackmail（「ばらす」と言って脅すこと，恐喝）であり，また動詞として He blackmailed me. のようにも使える。ただし子供たちの行為は普通 blackmail と言わない。

おとな（大人）

an adult; a grown-up （person）

彼は成人に達した。

He has {attained / arrived at / reached} adulthood. 〔*formal*〕

He has come of age.

彼は大人になった。

He has become an adult.

彼はりりしい若者になった。

He has grown up to be a handsome young man.

もう大人だ。行きたかったら行かせてやれ。

Let him go if he wishes. He's now grown up.

大人になったら何になりたいの？

What do you want to be when you grow up?

大人になって世の中[大人の世界]に出て数々の困難に対処しなければならないとき，事の軽重を見極めるバランス感覚が私たちの助けになるだろう。

A sense of proportion helps us to deal with the many problems we face when starting out in adult life.

——Kirkup, *Mother Goose's Britain*

おとなしい

おだやかな **gentle; mild; good-tempered**
従順な **obedient; submissive**
無口な **quiet; reticent;** 素直な **docile;**
控えめな **modest;** 動物が飼いならされた **tame**（↔ wild 野生の）

おとなしい人

a {gentle [mild, good-tempered] / quiet / modest} person

おとなしい[反抗的でない]子

an obedient child

おとなしそうな人

a mild-looking person

彼はおとなしそうだ。

He looks gentle.

おとなしくしておいで。（子供に向かって）

Be a good boy [girl].

赤ん坊は教会でお説教の間中おとなしかった。

The baby was quiet during the sermon.

子供たちはおとなしくテレビを見ていた。

The children were quietly watching TV.

〈注〉 子供はテレビを見ているときはおとなしい。
Children are quiet when they are watching TV.

おとなしくしなさい。（しかる口調）

Be quiet.

教室ではおとなしく[行儀よく]しなさい。

Behave yourself in the classroom.

おどろく（驚く） → びっくり

《類義語》

wonder at いったいどうしたのかしら，と不思議に思う，軽い驚き。

be surprised {at《a thing》/ that ...} もっとも一般的。意外なことに驚く。

be taken by surprise 不意打ちを食わされる。

be astonished びっくりする。startle より持続的な反応。

be astounded 驚きで何も手につかなくなる，呆然とする。

be amazed at 驚嘆（とまどうほどの驚き）。be surprised は普通の言い方なのに対して，be amazed は驚きを強調するために口語では非常によく使われる。be amazing も great や fantastic とともに「すごい」の意味でよく使われる。
marvel at 賛嘆〔*literary*〕。形 marvelous は「すごい，すばらしい」の意でよく使われる。
be startled あっと驚く。(はっとする) 瞬間的かつ身体的な反応。
give 《one》 **a start** (あっと驚かす) の言い方もある。
be stunned by 気が遠くなるほどの驚き。
be shocked 衝撃，(何か悪い事に) ショックを受ける。
be flabbergasted おおげさに「びっくり仰天」の意味で，口語で非常によく使われる。
be frightened ぎょっとする，びっくりして上がってしまう。
be scared お化けを見たようなこわい驚き。
be appalled 恐怖の驚き。
be alarmed 身の危険を感じておののく。
be disconcerted ろうばいする，面くらう。
〈注〉 上にあげた語のほとんどが be 〜ed の形であるが，もとの動詞は「驚かす」の意味の他動詞で，形を〜ing にすれば主語の性質を述べる形容詞，即ち「驚くべき」の意となる。〜ed の形と〜ing の形を混同しないように。
人が《物・事》に驚いた。
[人] be 〜ed at [by] [物・事]
[物・事] be 〜ing
彼女の腕前には驚いている。
I'm amazed at her skill.
Her skill is really amazing.
×I'm amazing at her skill.
「驚くべき」は上述の surprising; astonishing のほかに admirable; marvelous; wonderful などがある。

彼が物を知らないのには驚いた。
I'm really surprised
{ at his ignorance.
{ that he doesn't know anything.
His ignorance is really surprising.
その子の物覚えがよいのに驚いた。
I'm amazed that the child is so quick to learn.
突然音がしてはっと驚いた。
The sudden noise startled me [gave me a start].
彼があの子と結婚すると聞いてまったく驚いた [びっくり仰天した]。
I was absolutely flabbergasted when I heard he was going to marry that girl.
彼がどうやってお父さんを説得したのかしらと驚いた。
I was amazed that he managed to persuade his father.
人々は皆ソロモンの知恵に驚嘆した。
All the people marveled at Solomon's wisdom. 〔*literary*〕
この絵皿は技術の粋を集めた驚嘆すべき出来ばえのものである。
This plate is a wonder [marvel] of workmanship.
技のすぐれているのに驚嘆した。
I am filled with admiration at her skill.
〈注〉 be filled with admiration は陳腐な表現であるから使いすぎないこと。

おなじ (同じ)

the same as [that]; (類似) **be similar to; be alike**
〈注〉 same は the same と常に the を伴う (口語や商業英語では the を伴わないことがある)。副詞用法でも the same である。the same の次に as と続くが，as は前置詞，接続詞どちらの用法でもよい。また as と同様 that も用いられる (同種の場合は as, 同一物の場合は that を使うという区別は今はない)。

1. 同一

彼は私と同じ大学の出身です。
He graduated from the same college as I did.
ジキル博士とハイド氏は同じ人物と判明した。
Dr. Jekyll and Mr. Hyde turned out to be the same person.
きのう聞いたのと同じ歌だ。
It is the same song that [as] I heard yesterday.

私がそこに到着したのと同じ(その)日に彼はそこを離れている。

He left the place on the very same day (that) I arrived there.

2. 同型，同類

彼は君と同じ時計を持っている。

He has the same watch as yours [you have].

日本人にはハネムーンでよく同じような服装をしたカップルがいる。

Japanese honeymoon couples often dress alike [like each other].

あの双生児の姉妹はよく似ていてどっちがどっちかわからない。

The twin sisters look just alike. We can't tell {them apart. / which is which.}

〈注〉 identical twins (一卵性双生児)

3. 類似

姉と私は服を共通にしている。2人とも背丈もサイズもだいたい同じだから。

My sister and I share our clothes because we are about the same height and size.

彼はうちの弟と年がほとんど同じです。

He is about {the same age as / as old as} my brother.

あの人たちは考え方が私たちと同じではない。

They do not think the same way as we do.

わが国の若者についても同じことが言える。

The same is true of the young people in our country.

私(について)も同じです。

It is the same with me.

(どちらにしても)私にとっては同じことだ。

That makes no difference to me.

It is all the same to me.

毎日毎日，同じような日が過ぎていった。

Each day was the same as the one before it.

Each day was similar to the day before it.

〈注〉 the same は「まったく同じ」，similar は「よく似た」の意。

どの歌を聞いても皆同じよう[似たり寄ったり]だった。

The songs all sounded alike.

おぼえる（覚える）・おぼえている

1. 習得する

learn

あの子は小学校に入る前に九九［読み書き］を覚えた。

He learned {the multiplication tables / to read and write} before he entered primary school.

車の運転を覚えたい。

I'd like to learn how to drive a car.

2. 記憶する

memorize; learn by heart

入試に合格するためには5000語以上の英単語を覚えなければならないという学校がある。

Students in some schools have to memorize more than five thousand English words in order to pass entrance examinations.

3. 覚えている (状態)

［人主語］ **remember; don't forget; keep**《a thing》**in mind**

〈注〉 物・事主語では対象を live in one's memory と表現することもできる。→おもいで

私はいつでもあなたのお力になりたいと思っていることを覚えていてください。

Remember [Don't forget] that I'm always ready and willing to help you.

私が生れた小さなかわいい家を今でも覚えています。

I remember the pretty little house where I was born.

そんなこと言ったのを全然覚えていない。

I don't remember saying anything of the sort.

4．感じる
彼は胸に痛みを覚えた。

He felt {some pain in his chest. / a slight ache {by / near} his heart.}

〈注〉 ache は持続的で，この場合は心臓周辺の鈍痛・不快感を指す。

良心の呵責を覚えた。

He had a guilty conscience.

He felt the pangs of conscience.〔*literary*〕

おもいがけない（思いがけない）

形 **unexpected**

思いがけないことが起った。

Something unexpected happened.

ベティ，思いがけないお客様[こと，贈り物]ですよ。

Betty, here's a surprise for you.

彼女は今日，思いがけない贈り物をもらった。

She got a surprise present today.

母さんが今夜は思いがけないごちそうを作ってくれた。

Mom fixed us a surprise meal tonight.

だれだかわかりますか。思いがけない方ですよ。

Can you guess who it is? Someone you least expect.

【思いがけなく】

私のいとこが思いがけなく訪ねて来た。

My cousin visited me quite unexpectedly.

I had a surprise visit from my cousin.

おもいだす（思い出す）

［人主語］**remember; recall; recollect**

［物・事主語］**remind**《a person》**of; take [carry] back to; put back in**

私は母の声を今もありありと思い出す。

I still remember the very sound of my mother's voice.

【…すると思い出す】

あの絵を見るといつも子供時代を思い出す。

That picture always reminds me of my childhood.

あのＣＤを聞くと高校時代を思い出す。

That CD {takes me back to my high school days. / puts me back in high school.}

春になってライラックが薫ってくると，いつも子供のときの家を思い出す。

The smell of the lilacs in spring never fails to carry me back to my childhood home.

私はあの絵が好きだ。あれを見ると父があんな風景が大好きだったことを思い出すから。

I like that painting because it reminds me of my father's love for such scenes.

おもいで（思い出）

名 **memories; recollections; reminiscences**（具体的な追憶を表すときは通常複数形）

【思い出がある】

大学に入学したての最初の１週間にはなつかしい［楽しい / 悲しい / いやな］思い出がある。

I have sweet [happy / sad / unpleasant] memories of that first week in university.

〈注〉 have a good memory は「よい思い出」ではなく「記憶力がよい」の意味である。

思い出の中にはにおいによって呼び覚されるものが多いと彼は言う。

He says many of his memories are awakened by smells.

私は屋根裏部屋を探険するのが大好きだ。いつでも過ぎし日々の思い出の数々がいっぱい詰っているから。

I love poking around in attics, which are always full of reminders of days long gone.

【思い出を忘れない】

この楽しかった日々の思い出は決して忘れない。（一生忘れない）

I'll never forget these happy days.

The memory of these happy days will last

all through my life.

These happy days will stay in my memory as long as I live.

〈注〉「この思い出はいつまでも忘れない」のつもりで I'll never forget ... forever. と書くひとが多いが，forever は「永久に，永遠に」という意味なので，ここで使うのはおおげさであるし，never と重複する。remember forever は使える。

【よい思い出になった】

それはよい思い出になった[よい思い出の一つである]。

It is one of my dearest memories.

〈注〉「この夏休みはよい思い出をつくりたい」「それはきっとよい思い出になるだろう」のような発想は欧米人にはないようで英語になりにくい。×It will make [become] a good memory. のような文はまず a memory がおかしい。「記憶」は無冠詞で memory であり，「思い出」は小さなことがいっぱい詰っているから複数で memories である。次に memories は過去に関するものなのに，will が未来を示す語で，「時」の混線で非論理的に響く。また何かをするのは今やりたいからやるのであり，それを後から懐しむことはあっても，後から懐しむために何かをするのではないだろう。

しかし何事もやがて過去となり，思い出の領域に押し流されてゆくのを惜しむ心に洋の東西の別はないわけで，「別れるときにもらった物が思い出のよすがとなるだろう」は次のように表現できる。

Perhaps that will become a remembrance [keepsake].

お別れのとき交換した写真が2人の友情の記念[思い出の写真]となりました。

The pictures we exchanged then have become tokens of our friendship.

次に文学作品の中の「思い出」の部分を引用する。

My first memories are fragmentary and isolated and contemporaneous, as though one remembered some first moments of the Seven Days.

——W. B. Yeats, *The Memoirs*

(私の最初の思い出は断片的で脈絡がなく，しかも同時期のことのように思われる。まるで天地創造の7日間の最初の瞬間を思い出すようである)

おもいやり（思いやり）

【思いやりがある】

be considerate (of); be thoughtful (of)

〈注〉「思いやり」から「優しさ」が出ると be kind となり，「思いやり」で心が通い合うと「共感を覚え」て be sympathetic (to); sympathize with となる。

彼は思いやりがある。(他人の気持ちに思いやりがある)

He is thoughtful towards others.

He is considerate of other people's feelings.

あの人は弱い人や貧しい人を思いやる心があつい。

She is very sympathetic to the weak and the poor.

【思いやりがない】

be inconsiderate; be thoughtless; be cold; be unsympathetic

彼は思いやりがない。(他人の気持ちを思いやる気持ちがまるきりない)

He is inconsiderate.

He has no consideration at all for other people's feelings.

〈注〉◆「思いやり」に感謝する言い方

It is very kind [considerate, thoughtful] of you to say so.

I appreciate your kindness [thoughtfulness].

〈参考〉「相互の思いやりが世界をつなぐ」

——ホノルル市長のメッセージより(1984)

We begin by caring about one another. This simple concern for others can spread outward from our own families to our communities, cities, provinces, countries and across the entire world.

(私たちはまず身近な者同士で思いやることから始める。この何でもない思いやりが我々の家庭から住んでいる地域社会へ，市へ，地方へ，国へと広がっていき，遂に全世界をつなぐのだ)

おもう（思う）

〈注〉「思う」は次に示すように多くの場合に用いられ，また判断「AはBだ」を柔らかく言うために「AはBだと思う」のようにも頻用される。「思う」と言えば think が使われることが多く，また誤用も多い。まず think の正しい用法を覚えるとともに think 以外の動詞も活用できるようにすることが望ましい。

1．心に思う

【考え】

思っていることを言いなさい。

Say what you think.

どう思いますか。

What do you think?

こんなふうに思います。

This is what I think.

【予想】

思った通り

just as I thought

思ったほど…でない

not as ... as I thought

本当になるなんて夢にも思わなかった。

I never dreamed that it would [could] come true.

【想像】

パリにいると思ってごらん。

Imagine yourself in Paris.

2．「…」と思う

「AはBだ」と思う。

I think that A is B.

「Aは正しい」と思う。

I think that A is right.

「Aは私の恩人だ」と思っている。

I consider A (to be) my benefactor.

【誤認】「…」と思う（間違える）

双子の兄を彼だと思った。

I mistook his twin brother for him.

【確信】「絶対に…」と思う

絶対にジキル博士はハイド氏だと思う。

I believe [am convinced] that Dr. Jekyll is Mr. Hyde.

【推量】「…だろう」と思う

Aは来るだろうと思う。

I suppose that A will come.

【予想】

まさかAが試験に落ちるとは思わなかった。

I never dreamed that A would fail the exam.

彼の病気は治らないのではないかと思う。

I'm afraid he will not get over his illness.

【心づもり】「…しよう」と思う

旅行に行こうと思っている。

I intend to go on a trip.（意志表明）

I'm planning to go on a trip.（既に計画中）

【希望】「…したい」と思う

旅行に行きたいと思う。

I want to go on a trip.

I'd like to go on a trip.

【願望】「…するとよい」と思う

明日天気になるとよいと思う。

I hope it will be fine tomorrow.

行かれたらいいのにと思う。（仮定）

I wish I could go.

私もそこにいたらよかったと思う。（仮定）

I wish I had been there.

【感情表現】

うれしく思う

I'm glad .... →うれしい

いやだと思う

I don't like ....

さびしく思う

I miss .... →さびしい

犬と遊べなくてさびしく思うだろう。

I'll miss playing with my dog.

【疑念】「…かしら」と思う，「どうか？」と思う

Aは本当にBかしらと思う。

I wonder if A is really B. (Perhaps A is not B. 違うかもしれない)

I doubt if A is really B. (Probably A is not B. たぶん違うんだ)

AはBではないらしい［違うらしい］と思う。

I suspect (that) A is not really B. (I'm nearly certain that A is not B. きっと違う)

3．「…(名詞)」を思う

【考え】

(そんなこと)思ってもみてごらん。

Just think of it!

そのことを今思っています。

I'm thinking about it.

【愛情】

子を思う親心　parents' love for children
【恋】
ひそかにAを思う　love A secretly
【偲ぶ】(なつかしむ)
故国を思う　long for his homeland
昔を思う　long for the bygone days
〈注〉◆think の用法

think (動自)	**of**	Just think of it.
	about	I'm thinking about it.
think (動他)	**that**	I think that it is likely.
	(that 省略)	I don't think it is likely.
think O+C (不完全動他)		I don't think it likely. (正しい用法だが，I don't think it is likely. の方が一般的な表現)

◆「…したいと思う」は直訳で，×I think I want としないこと。
×I think I want to go abroad this summer.
I want to .... / I'd like to .... だけでよい。
◆「どう思いますか」は What do you think?
×How do you think? は誤り。
感想を尋ねるのなら
How do you {like it? / feel about it?} でよい。

おもかげ（面影）

顔かたち《a person's》**face** [**looks**]
生き写し　**image; picture**
跡形　**trace; vestige; shadow**
〈注〉「面影」に当る英語の名詞を直訳的に当てはめると不自然な文になるので注意。
【人】
息子には若くして亡くなった夫の面影がある。
My son always reminds me of my husband, who died young.
あの人には昔の侍の面影がある。
There is something about him which reminds me of a samurai.
彼にはまだ昔の面影がある[もう昔の面影は何もない]。
He {still has something / has nothing} of his former self.
彼はもう年をとって昔の面影はまるでない。
He has grown old and is not what he used to be.
【場所】
行ってみたら何もかも変ってしまい，昔の面影が何もなくてがっかりした。
I was very much disappointed to find that the whole place had been utterly changed.

おもしろい（面白い）

〈注〉◆「面白い」に当る英語で日本人の頭にまず浮かぶのは interesting だが，「面白い」は interesting と同一ではない。類義語を検討し適切な語を選択すること。
◆他の「気持ちを表す形容詞」と同様，人間中心の表現と事物中心の表現とで形容詞を使い分けなければならない。
この本は面白い。
[人間中心]
I enjoyed this book very much.　(a)
I was interested in this book.　(b)
[事物中心]
This book was very interesting.　(c)
×I'm interesting in this book.　(d)
上の文(b)と(c)は interested と interesting の用法を対照したものであるが，(c)の形の方が使用頻度が高い。

《類義語》
[～ing形…事物中心 / ～ed形…人間中心]
fun〔米〕普通にスポーツやゲームの面白さに使う。
It's fun. / It's a lot of fun.
exciting / excited　胸のわくわくする面白さ。
diverting / diverted　気晴らしになる。
entertaining / entertained　人を楽しませる(軽い娯楽)。
merry; jolly　愉快な。
amusing / amused　面白おかしく笑いを誘う。
comic(al)　滑稽な。
funny　滑稽な，奇妙な。
queer; odd; curious; strange　奇妙な。
interesting / interested　知的興味をそそる。
thrilling / thrilled　ぞくぞくする。

今夜は面白かった。

We had a great [very good] time this evening.

すごく面白い試合だった。9回の裏でホームランで勝ったんだ。

It was a very exciting game. / We were all excited. } We won with a home run in the latter half of the 9th inning.

旅行記にはたいへん面白い[愉快な]ものがよくある。

Travelogues [Travel accounts] are often highly entertaining.

サリーがお人形さんをしかっているのがとても面白いの。ママそっくりな声色でやっているんです。

It's amusing / I was amused } to hear Sally scolding her dolly. { She's / She was } talking just like her Mommy.

〈注〉 It's amusing ...「…が面白い」は一般的。I was amused ... は「…が面白かった」と経験を述べているので She was と過去形で続ける。

僕たちはカヌーで急流下りをした。まったく，ぞくぞくはらはらで面白かった。

We shot down the rapids in a canoe. It was very thrilling. [I found it very thrilling.]

【面白くない】

あの先生の講義は面白くない[退屈だ]。

His lecture is dull [boring].

この本はちっとも面白くない。

This book is not interesting at all.

君が一緒に行かなければ面白くない[楽しくない]。

We shall have no fun unless you go with us.

It'll be no fun without you.

ニューミュージックは僕には面白くない。

New Music doesn't appeal to me.

I'm not interested in New Music.

彼女は仲間はずれにされて面白くなかった。

She felt hurt because she was left (out) in the cold.

おもわず（思わず）→ しらずしらず

〈注〉 「思わず」を和英辞書で引くと，involuntarily; unconsciously; unintentionally などの副詞が出ているが，文意に添うかどうか考え，下の例文などを参考に文を作ることが望ましい。

口頭試問で上がって，思わずみんな忘れてしまった。

In the oral exam I was so frightened I forgot all I'd learned.

〈注〉 忘れるのは自分の意志と無関係であるから，unconsciously（無意識に），involuntarily（思わず知らず，心ならずも），unawares（知らないうちに）などは上の文と合わない。何も副詞をつけなくてもよい。

成功の知らせに思わず「万歳！」と叫んだ。

When I got the news of success, I cried "Hurrah" in spite of myself.

思わず彼の弁護をしてしまった。

I began to speak in his defense before I knew it.

思わずうとうとしたらしい。

It seems I fell into a doze unawares.

サイレンの音に思わず外に飛び出した。

Hearing the siren I instinctively rushed out of doors.

おやつ

【おやつ】

snacks { 軽食 (light lunch) / 間食 (food eaten outside of meals) }

〈注〉◆軽食の例

サンドイッチ sandwiches / ホットドッグ hotdogs / ハンバーガー hamburgers / ドーナツ doughnuts

◆間食の例

ポテトチップス potato chips / ピーナッツ peanuts / ヨーグルト yogurt / 干しブドウ raisins / クッキー cookies

【デザート】 dessert

アイスクリーム ice cream

ゼリー jello〔米〕; jelly〔英〕

シャーベット　sherbet
プディング　pudding
ケーキ　cake
【果物】fruit　→くだもの
fruits〔米〕 各種の果物の意味で複数形にすることができる。

およぶ（及ぶ）

1．達する

【空間】動自 spread; extend
動他 include; cover

アレクサンダー大王の領地ははるか中東にまで及んでいた。

The empire of Alexander the Great extended far into Asia.

もしも核戦争が始まったら，地球全土に被害が及ぶだろう。

If a nuclear war breaks [should break] out,
{ the whole world will [would] be affected.
{ the effects will [would] extend over the whole earth.

【時間】

会議は深夜に及んだ。

The session lasted far into the night.

この期に及んでそんなことを言うとはどういうつもりだ。

What do you mean by saying something like that at this stage of the proceedings?

(話がはずみ)話題は生命の化学的合成の可能性にまで及んだ。

It happened that our conversation turned to the possibility of creating life out of chemicals.

【数量】

犠牲者は約1000名に及んだ。

The casualties rose to some 1000 people.

火事による被害額は5000万円に及ぶ。

The damage caused by the fire } amounted
(The) Fire damage } to fifty million yen.

2．及ばない

【かなわない】

僕は君には及ばない。

I'm no match for you.

数学で彼に及ぶ者はいない。

No one can match him in mathematics.

役者として彼は彼の父に及ばない。

As an actor he does not come up to his father.

【…するには及ばない】

大丈夫です。心配するには及びません。

It's all right. You need not worry about it.

彼は帰って来た。心配するには及ばなかった。

He came back. We need not have worried about him.

【及ばずながら】

及ばずながらできるだけのことは致します。

I'll do what I can.

おりる（下りる，降りる）・おろす

1．下りる，降りる（自動詞）

【高い所から】

動自（上から）come [go] down; descend;（階段を）come [go] downstairs

山岳隊は北壁のルートで山を下り始めた。

The team began to go down [descend] the mountain by the northern route.

ティムはシャツのボタンをかけながら，２階から駆け下りて来た。

Tim came running downstairs buttoning his shirt.

【乗物から】

get off the bus [train, airplane]
get out of
{ the taxi [car]
{ the bus（混んだり，せまくて出にくい感じ）

彼は名古屋で降りる。

He gets off [out] at Nagoya.

次の停留所で降りたい[降ろしてください]。

I want to get out [off] at the next stop.

【その他】
幕が降りた。
　The curtain fell.
初霜は11月の初めに降りる。
　Frost comes in early November.
許可が下りた。
　I got the permission.
(勝負などを)降りる　give up

2．下ろす，降ろす（他動詞）
【高い所から】 get [take] a thing down; put [set] a thing down（地上などに）; pull down（引っ張り下ろす）
棚から古いアルバムを下ろし，ほこりを払った。
　He took down an old album from the shelf and dusted it.
彼はかばんを地面に下ろしてポケットの中を探し始めた。
　He put his bag down on the ground and began searching his pockets.
ブラインド[日よけ]を下ろしてください。
　Pull down the blind, please.
やかんを火から下ろして。
　Please take the kettle off the fire.
【乗物から】 let《a person》off
東山で降ろしてください。
　Let me off at Higashiyama stop, please.
次で降ろしてください。
　Drop me at the next stop.
　Next stop please!
(運転手さん)ここで降ろしてください。
　(Driver,) Let me out here, please.
数人の男がトラックから荷物を降ろしていた。
　Some men were unloading the truck.
【その他】
新しい紅茶茶わん(ティーカップ)をそのパーティーのときに下ろした。
　We first used the new teacups at our party.
おニューの背広を下ろした。
　I put on my new suit for the first time.
グラタン用にチーズをおろした。
　I grated cheese for the gratin.
枝を下ろす
　cut off branches; prune a tree
根を下ろす　take root
銀行預金から５万円おろす
　withdraw 50,000 yen from one's bank account

おわりに（終りに）

in conclusion;（講演の結び）**to conclude**（one's **speech**）
リサイタルの終りに彼女のヒット曲「北の宿」を歌った。
　To conclude her recital she sang
　Her last song in the recital was
　"At the Hotel in the North Country", one of her most popular numbers.
終りに(臨んで)(エッセイやスピーチの締めくくり)
　In conclusion, I would like to …
〈注〉 文章で「終りに」の意味で last, at last, at the last を使っているのをよく見かけるが適切ではない。
　日本の手紙文には締めくくりの決り文句があるが，英文手紙では無理にそれを直訳しない方がよい。→てがみ
　「終りになったが大事なこととして…」の意味で last but not least は慣用的な言い方で，スピーチの終りに述べられることがある。

おわる（終る）→ おえる・おわる

おん（恩）

【恩を受ける】
ホワイト氏には恩を受けた。
　I am greatly indebted to Mr. White.
　cf. I owe Mr. White what I am now.（私の今日あるのはホワイト氏のおかげです）
あの方のご恩は決して忘れない。
　I will never forget her kindness.
【恩を返す】

いつかご恩返しをしなければならない。
I must repay [return] her kindness some day.
【恩知らず】an ungrateful fellow
【恩師】a former teacher
【恩人】a benefactor
あなたは私の命の恩人です。
I owe you my life.

おんがく（音楽）

music; 旋律 **melody**
形 **musical**

《関連語》

1．種類

【クラシック】classical music
ソナタ sonata / 協奏曲 concerto / 狂詩曲 rhapsody / 夜想曲 nocturne / 小夜曲 serenade / 幻想曲 fantasia / 序曲 overture / 前奏曲 prelude / 第1［2］楽章 the first [second] movement / 終楽章 finale /fináːli/
【ポピュラー・ミュージック】popular music
ジャズ jazz / ブルース blues / スウィング swing / ソウル soul music / ラテン Latin / ボサノヴァ bossa nova / タンゴ tango / マンボ mambo / ボレロ bolero / ロックンロール rock and roll
【フォークミュージック】folk music
フォークソング folk song / バラッド ballad / 子守唄 lullaby
【宗教音楽】religious (sacred) music
讃美歌 hymn / 黒人霊歌 negro spiritual / オラトリオ oratorio
【音楽家】musician
作曲家 composer / 作詞家 song writer / 編曲者 arranger / 指揮者 conductor / オーケストラ団員 orchestra member

2．演奏　performance
コンサート concert / リサイタル recital / ソロ solo / オーケストラ orchestra / 室内楽 chamber music / コーラス chorus / 伴奏 accompaniment / アンコール encore
【楽団】
管弦楽団 symphony orchestra / 室内楽団 chamber music group / 吹奏楽団 brass band / (弦楽)四重奏団 (string) quartet / 五重奏団 quintet / 合唱(奏)団 ensemble / 合唱団 chorus / 聖歌隊 choir / ジャズバンド jazzband
【演奏者】performers of music
ピアニスト pianist / ヴァイオリニスト violinist / チェリスト cellist / オルガニスト organist / ギタリスト guitarist
【声楽】
歌手 singer / 声楽家 vocalist / ソプラノ soprano / メゾソプラノ mezzo-soprano / アルト alto / テナー tenor / バリトン baritone / バス bass

3．楽器 musical instruments
【鍵盤】keyboard instruments
ピアノ piano / アコーディオン accordion / オルガン organ / パイプオルガン pipe organ / ハープシコード harpsichord / クラビコード clavichord
【弦】strings
バイオリン violin / ビオラ viola / チェロ cello / コントラバス contrabass / ギター guitar / マンドリン mandolin / ハープ harp / リュート lute / シタール sitar
【管】woodwinds; brass winds
トランペット trumpet / フルート flute / クラリネット clarinet / ピッコロ piccolo / バスーン bassoon / ホルン horn / トロンボーン trombone / サクソフォーン saxophone / ハーモニカ harmonica
【打】percussion
ドラム drum / シンバル cymbals / タンバリン tambourine / カスタネット castanets / トライアングル triangle / ゴング gong / チャイム chimes / シロホン xylophone / マリンバ marimba / ビブラホン vibraphone

4．その他の音楽用語 musical terminology
旋律 melody / リズム rhythm / テンポ tempo / ビート beat / 音階 scale / オクターブ octave / 全音階 diatonic scale / 半音階 chromatic scale

長音階 major scale

{ドレミファソラシ　ハ長調
do re mi fa sol la ti [si] C major
C D E F G A B

短音階 minor scale / ハ短調 C minor / 音符 (musical) note / 休符 (musical) rest

楽譜 (総称) music; (1枚) a sheet of music; (総譜) a score

(1) 五線 staff, stave
(2) 縦線 barline
(3) 小節 bar, measure
　第1小節 the first measure, measure 1
(4) 拍子記号 time signature
　3/4拍子 three-four time
(5) ト音記号 G clef, treble clef
　ヘ音記号 F clef, bass clef
(6) シャープ sharp (♯; 半音高く)
　フラット flat (♭; 半音低く)
　ナチュラル natural (♮; 元に戻す)

【音符】 2分音符 (𝅗𝅥) half note; minim
　4分音符 (♩) quarter note; crochet
　付点4分音符 (♩.) quarter dot note
　8分音符 (♪) eighth note; quaver
　16分音符 (𝅘𝅥𝅯) semi-quaver

5. オーディオ

エフエム FM (=frequency modulation)
エイエム AM (=amplitude modulation)
ハイファイ high-fidelity, ステレオ stereo
レコーディング recording
マイクロフォン microphone
ヘッドフォン headphones
スピーカー speaker
アンプ amplifier, イコライザー equalizer
レシーバー[チューナー] receiver [tuner]
レコードプレーヤー record player
ターンテーブル turntable
ピックアップ [アーム] (the) pick-up [arm]
針 needle
45回転レコード a 45 [45 r. p. m.] record
LPレコード an LP [long playing] record
テープデッキ[テープレコーダー] tape deck [tape recorder, cassette recorder]
オープンリール open reel
カセット(テープ) cassette
シーディー CD (=compact disc)
シーディープレーヤー CD player [CD deck]
レーザーディスク laser disc
レーザーディスクプレーヤー laser disc player

6. 有名作曲家 popular composers

(生誕が19世紀まで；生年順)

バッハ Bach /bάːk/, Johann Sebastian (1685-1750)
モーツァルト Mozart, Wolfgang Amadeus (1756-91)
ベートーベン Beethoven, Ludwig van (1770-1827)
ウェーバー Weber, Carl Maria von (1786-1826)
マイヤーベーア Meyerbeer, Giacomo (1791-1864)
シューベルト Schubert, Franz (1797-1828)
ショパン Chopin, Frédéric (1810-49)
シューマン Schumann, Robert (1810-56)
リスト Liszt, Franz (1811-86)
ワーグナー Wagner, Richard (1813-83)
ヴェルディ Verdi, Giuseppe (1813-1901)
オッフェンバック Offenbach, Jacques (1819-80)
ブルックナー Bruckner, Anton (1824-96)
シュトラウス(ヨハン) Strauss, Johann (1825-99)
ブラームス Brahms, Johannes (1833-97)
サンサーンス Saint-Saëns, Charles-Camille (1835-1921)
ビゼー Bizet, Georges (1838-75)
チャイコフスキー Tchaikovsky, Pyotr Ilyich (1840-93)
ドボルザーク Dvořák, Antonin (1841-1904)
グリーグ Grieg, Edvard (1843-1907)
リムスキーコルサコフ Rimsky-Korsakov, Ni-

kolay Andreyvich (1844–1908)
マーラー　Mahler, Gustav (1860–1911)
ドビュッシー　Debussy, Claude Achille (1862–1918)
シュトラウス(リヒャルト) Strauss, Richard (1864–1949)
ラベル　Ravel, Maurice (1875–1937)
ストラビンスキー　Stravinsky, Igor Fyodorovich (1882–1971)

か

が

1．格

【主格】

天気がよい。

It's a nice day. / The weather is good.

頭が痛い。

My head aches. / I have a headache.

【存在】

山の上に城がある。

There is a castle on the mountain.

〈注〉 城は山の上にある。(所在)

The castle is on the mountain.

【…は…が】

ウサギは耳が長い。

A rabbit has long ears.

彼は足が速い。

He walks fast.

彼女は色が白い[黒い]。

She is fair [dark] (skinned).

彼は耳が遠い。

He is hard of hearing.

二つの壺は形が似ている。

The two pots are shaped almost alike [almost the same shape].

あの人は虫が好かない。

Somehow I don't like him.

【選択】

君が悪い。(強い言い方)

It's your fault. / You are to blame.

私が行きます。

I will go.

【対格・対象】

水が飲みたい。

I want some water.

ピアノが習いたい。

I want to take piano lessons.

2．論理

【しかし】

僕は行きたいが行かれない。

I'd like to go, but I can't.

彼は80歳を越えているが，いたって元気だ。

Although he is over eighty he is still very healthy.

【比較】

長男はおとなしいが，次男坊は騒々しい。

The eldest son is a quiet boy, while the second one is boisterous.

【そして】

私もその映画を見たが，とても面白かった。

I saw that movie too, and it was very interesting.

彼には息子が3人いるが，今はみな成人して都会に出ている。

He has three sons, who are all grown up now and live in the city.

かい（貝）

貝 **a shellfish;** 貝殻 **a shell**

《関連語》

アコヤガイ pearl oyster / アサリ short-neck clam / アワビ abalone / カキ oyster / サザエ turban shell, turbo / ハマグリ hard clam / ホタテガイ scallop / ホラガイ trumpet shell, conch, triton

かい（階）

〈注〉 階の呼び方は英米で違うので注意。floor は建物の内側から，story は外側から見た呼称。

	[英国]	[米国]
1階	the ground floor	the first floor [story]
2階	the first floor	the second floor [story]
3階	the second floor	the third floor [story]
地下1階	the first basement	英米共通
地下2階	the second basement	英米共通

3階建ての建物 a three-story building

3階に住む

live on the third〔米〕[second〔英〕] floor

何階建てですか。

How many floors does it have?
How many stories high is this building?
12階建てです。
It has twelve stories.
There are twelve stories.
事務所は10階にあります。
The office is on the tenth floor.
【一戸建ての場合】
彼女は２階にいる。
She's upstairs.
彼女は２階から降りて来た。
She came downstairs.

かいがん（海岸）

（一般的）**the seashore;**（行楽地としての）海岸 **the seaside;** 渚 **the beach;** 沿岸 **the coast**
【浜辺】
子供たちがバケツやシャベルを持って海岸で遊んでいた。
Children were playing on the beach [in the sand] with buckets and spades.
彼女は海岸[海辺]の小さな美しい町に住んでいた。
She lived in a small, beautiful town by the seashore.
彼は海岸に小さな別荘を持っていた。
He had a small villa
{ on the beach
in a seaside town.
on the coast.
【西海岸】
ロサンゼルスは西海岸の最大の都市である。
Los Angeles is the biggest city on the West Coast.

かいぎ（会議）

1. 会合
a meeting; an assembly; a gathering;（公式の）**a conference; a convention; a congress**

《類義語》
conference 最も普通に使われる。規模の大きい公式な会議。学問研究，その他の問題についての情報交換・討論の場となる。
ex. 2002年 JALT 第27回語学教育国際会議
JALT '02: The 27th Annual International Conference on Language Teaching/Learning
congress 大規模で重要な大会，いくつかの会の合同大会。
ex. 米国議会 the Congress
医学会 a medical congress
convention 総会行事，すなわち役員改選，予算，事業等の議事を中心にした学会，宗教，政治上の代表者協議会・大会。
ex. TESOL 第６回総会
TESOL Sixth Annual Convention
日本英文学会年次大会
The Annual Convention of the English Literary Society of Japan
〈注〉研究発表だけの会は convention と呼ばない。
meeting 一般的な会合，通常小規模。非公式，個人的な会にも使われる。

2. 開会
【会議を開く】（個人的な）have a meeting
【開催する】
（公的な）hold a meeting [conference]
【会議を招集する】
convene a meeting [council]〔*formal*〕
日本化学会は年次大会を福岡で開催する。
The Japan Chemical Society will hold [have] their annual conference at Fukuoka.
衆議院予算委員会は次の木曜日に会合[委員会]を開く。
The Diet Financial Committee will meet [convene] next Thursday.
衆議院予算委員長は次の木曜日３時に会議を召集した。
The chairman of the Diet Financial Com-

mittee convened a meeting for next Thursday at 3:00.

〈注〉◆ convene = call《a meeting》
国際法審議会は本日開催された。
The Council on International Law was convened today.
◆日本語では会議，委員会などは団体の名称にもなるし，その団体の会合の意味にもなる。
ex. 財務委員会 (the) Financial Committee; meetings of the Financial Committee

3. 審議

【会議にかける，議案を提出する】
submit《a plan, a proposal》to the conference〔*formal*〕
予算の修正案が衆議院財務委員会に提出される。
The revision of the budget will be submitted to the Diet Financial Committee.
案件［計画 / 問題 / 提案 / 決議案］を会議にかける
bring a matter [plan / problem / proposal / resolution] before the conference

【会議中】
前田氏は会議中です。
Mr. Maeda is in conference now.
執行部会は会議中です。
The Executive Committee is in session now.
(討論中の意味にも会期中の意味にもとれる)

《関連語》
会議室
(学生用) assembly room / (公式会議用) conference room / (会社) board room
議事 agenda
会議録，議事録
中部支部月例会の議事録 (詳細なもの)
the minutes of the monthly meetings of Chubu Chapter
大学英語教育学会会報 (議事録・会報・論文集)
the proceedings of the JACET conference

かいけつする (解決する)

㊍㊎ **settle; solve; resolve**

大気汚染の問題を解決するのは容易ではない。
It will not be easy
{ to solve the problem of / to work out effective measures against } air pollution.
我々は国際紛争の平和的解決を図らねばならない。
We must try to settle [resolve] international conflicts peacefully.

【解決策】 a solution

【未解決】
新幹線の騒音問題は未解決である。
The Shinkansen noise problem has not been
{ solved yet. (1) / resolved yet. (2) }
新幹線訴訟は未解決である。
The Shinkansen court case has not been settled yet.
誘拐事件はまだ解決されていない。
The kidnapping case has not been solved yet.

〈注〉 同じ「解決」でも settle, resolve は紛争 (dispute, disagreement) の決着をつけること，solve はわからなかった部分をはっきりさせることである。上の(1)では騒音を防ぐ手だてを見つけることを，(2)では補償問題などの解決を意味する。

かいしゃ (会社)

〈注〉 「会社」は企業の意味のほかに office の意味に使われることに注意。

1. 企業

a company; a corporation; a firm; 商社 **a concern**

【会社社主】 an owner

【重役】 a director(経営管理を行う); 役員 an executive(業務執行をする)

【重役会】
a board of directors (経営の意思決定機関)

a board of executives（執行役員会）

〈注〉 これらは社長(president)の上に位する。

【社長】a president; a managing director〔英〕

〈注〉 米国では最高の権限をもつトップを CEO (Chief Executive Officer) と呼び，president より実権をもつ。日本の代表取締役に当る。英国ではこれに相当するのが managing director である場合が多い。

【副社長】vice-president

【部長】 vice-president in charge of ...

部課長

director [manager, chief, head] of a department [division]

(経理)係長

supervisor 《of the accounting office》

〈注〉 日本の係長，課長，部長に相当するきまった英語はない。また英・米でも呼び方が異なる。

【会社員】an employee of a company; a company employee

事務員，書記 a clerk

文書係 a file clerk [filing clerk]; a claims clerk （保険会社の保険金請求書類を処理する係）

記録係 a records clerk

会計係 an accountant

秘書 a secretary

受付，応接係 a receptionist

派遣社員 a worker sent from a temporary employment agency

契約社員 a contract worker

私は会社員だ。

I work in the office.（役職でない場合）

ビルはアメリカの大手化学薬品会社で働いている。

Bill works for a large American chemical corporation.

〈注〉 欧米ではただ「会社員」というのではなく仕事の内容もともに述べることが多い。日本では配置転換があると仕事が変るが，欧米では入社の時からある特定の職種のポストに採用する。システムが違うので日本の会社の事情を英訳するときは説明が必要である。「会社員である」は次のように具体的な形をとることが多い。

加藤さんは大会社の技師です。

Mr. Kato is an engineer at [in] a big company.

私は百貨店で事務職に就いている。

I'm an office worker at the department store. （役職のない一般事務）

〈注〉 an office worker [a general office worker] とは単純な事務をしている事務員。

【その他】

年功序列 seniority system

能力主義 merit-based (pay) system

2. 事務所

an office

名古屋の会社まで通勤にまる1時間かかる。

It takes me a whole hour to reach my office in Nagoya.

かいだん（階段）

(a flight of) stairs; a staircase; a stairway; 段 **steps**

らせん階段 **a winding staircase**

階段式観覧席の段 **tier(s)** /tíər(z)/

1. 動詞との結合

【上る，下りる】

彼は階段を上って[下りて]行った。

He went up [down] the stairs.

彼は階上に[階下に]行った。

He went upstairs [downstairs]. (→かい(階))

【踏みはずす】

私は階段を踏みはずした。

I slipped [missed my footing] on the stairs.

2. 場所の指示と階段

入口の階段を上ってすぐの部屋

the room nearest (to) the top of the entrance staircase

階段を上った[下りた]所で待っています。

I'll be waiting for you at the {top [bottom] / head [foot]} of the steps.

地下室に通じる階段
the stairway [stairs] (leading) down to the cellar

《関連語》
階段の手すり　banister; (壁に取り付けた物) railing
(階段中間の)踊り場　landing
正面[裏の]階段　the front [back] stairs
階段を2段ずつ飛び上がる
take the steps [stairs] two at a time
〈注〉 go up two flights of stairs は，ひと続きになった階段(上下階と踊り場との間)を二つ上ること。それで1階から2階に達することになる。

かう（飼う）

1．ペット

家では犬1匹，亀1匹と小鳥を2羽飼っている。
We have [We've got] a dog, a turtle and two birds.
〈注〉 I have [I've got] a dog, ... とも言える。

2．飼育する（職業・生業として飼育する）

keep; raise
家では鶏と豚を飼っている。
We raise chickens and pigs.（養鶏・養豚業）
あそこの家では乳牛を飼っている。
They keep cows.

【飼い主】
所有者　the owner（金銭的価値を考える）
主人　the master（主従関係，親愛の情がある）
飼い主は誰だ。(馬)　Who owns this horse?
(犬)　Whose dog is this?

かえす（返す）・かえる

1．返す

repay 《money》; **repay** 《a person》; **return** 《a thing to a person》; **return** 《money to a person》; **bring back** 《a thing》; **send back** 《a thing》

【金を】
貸した金を返してください。
Please return the money I lent you.
彼はいったん貸したら返してくれない。
He never pays me back.

【物を】
先日貸した本を返してください。
Please return [give back] the book I lent you the other day.
そこの本をみんな，もとのところに返してください。
Put all those books back where they were [belong].
車を5時までに返してもらえますか。
Can you bring the car back by five?

【返品する】
店の人が壊れたガラス食器を3ケースも返して[返品して]きた。
The storemen sent back three cases of broken glassware.

2．返る

〈注〉 「返す」を受け身にすると「返る」の意味になる。
【金が】　be paid back
【金・物が】　be returned

かえる（変える）→ かわる

かえる（帰る）

1．帰宅する

go home; go back (**home**)（出先を中心にして考えるとき）
come home; come back (**home**)（家を中心にして考えるとき）
return home（どちらでもよい）
〈注〉 home は副詞なので，go（自動詞）に続けて to my home としなくてよい。
彼は7時頃に帰って来る。
He comes home around seven o'clock.
すぐに帰って来るよ。
I'll be back soon.

【帰国する】
日本に帰る
go [come] back to Japan; return to Japan

2. 去る
動自他 **leave;** 動自 **start**
暗くならないうちに彼は帰って行った。
He left for home before it was dark.
私は帰途についた。
I left (the place) for home.
I started for home.
山本さんは10分ほど前に帰られました。
Mr. Yamamoto left (the office) some ten minutes ago.（今はもういない）
もうそろそろ帰らなくては。
I think I must be going now.（辞去）
（小学生などに）はい，席にお帰り。
Get to your desk.
Go back to your seat.

3. 到着する
get home; arrive home
彼は夜の11時頃に帰って来た。
He arrived [got] home about eleven at night.
彼は帰って来たとき，ひどく疲れた様子だった。
He looked exhausted [terribly tired] when he got home.

かお（顔）

face; 顔つき **a look; a countenance**
目鼻立ち **features;** 表情 **expression**

1. 顔かたち
【美醜】
いい顔をしている。
She's beautiful [pretty].
He's handsome [good-looking].
あの子は顔が良くない。
She's not at all attractive.（ugly はひどすぎるので避ける）
彼ははっきりした顔立ちをしている。
He has clear-cut features.
【顔色】
彼女は顔を赤らめた。
She blushed.
彼の顔は真っ赤になった。
He turned red.
彼はその知らせを聞いて顔が青ざめた。
He paled [turned pale] at the news.
彼女は顔色がよい。
She has a good complexion.
顔色が悪いですよ。
You look pale.

2. 動詞との結合
【顔を見る】
私の顔を見て。
Look at me.
2人は顔を見合せた。
They looked at each other.
彼の顔を見るのもいやだ。
I don't even like to see him.
I cannot bear (even) the sight of him.
彼は私の顔を見れば小言を言う。
Every time he sees me he
{ begins preaching to me about my faults.
{ starts grumbling about what I do.
彼らは顔を合せればすぐけんかを始める。
The moment they meet each other they begin quarreling.
きまり悪くて彼に顔が合せられない。
I'm too embarrassed to see him.
【顔を知る】
彼の顔は知っている。
I know him (only) by sight.
知らない顔がパーティーに来ていた。
Someone I didn't know was at the party.
〈注〉 このあたりで見ない顔を a stranger とも言う。
【顔を覚えている】
彼の顔はよく覚えている。
I remember him very well.

彼はパーティーで一度私に会ったことがあると言うが，私は彼の顔を覚えていなかった。

He said he met me once at a party, but I couldn't remember him.

【顔がわかる】

彼は年をとりすぎて，息子の顔もわからなかった。

He was too old to recognize his own son.

3. 顔つき

【知らん顔】

（道で会ったとき）彼は知らん顔をした。

He pretended not to recognize me [ignored me].

彼は弟が困っているのに知らん顔をしている。

He is quite unconcerned about his brother's problem.（無関心）

【何食わぬ顔】

皆に大迷惑をかけているのに，彼は何食わぬ顔をしてやって来た。

Although he knew he was the cause of all the trouble, he came in
{ as if nothing had happened.
looking innocent.

【いやな顔】

彼女はいやな顔をした［眉をしかめた］。

She frowned.

彼女は不満そうな［むっとした］顔をした。

She looked displeased [annoyed].

【つまらない顔をする】 pull a long face

何でそんなつまらなそうな顔をしているの。

Why are you pulling such a long face?

【顔に出す】

彼は感情を顔に出さなかった。

He showed no emotion at all.

He remained poker-faced.（無表情）

His face didn't betray his anger.（怒りを顔に出さない）

4. 慣用表現

【大きな顔をする】

大きな顔をするな。

Don't act so important.

Who do you think you are?（自分を何様だと思っているんだ）

【顔を立てる】 save one's face

【顔をつぶす】

disgrace oneself; lose one's face

【顔がきく，顔役である】

彼はこの辺では顔役だ。

In this neighborhood he is a big man.〔*colloq.*〕

He is an influential [important] person in this neighborhood.

【顔が広い】

彼は顔が広い。

He knows a lot of people.

He has many connections.

【顔で】

テッドはお父さんの顔で就職した。

Ted used his father's influence to get a job [himself a job].

【顔合せ】

明日新役員の顔合せがある。

The new members of the board will meet tomorrow.

【顔を出す】

彼はたまに顔を出す。

He turns [shows] up once in a while.

かがく（化学）

chemistry

《関連語》
化学反応　chemical reaction
化学式　chemical formula
化学実験　chemical experiment
化合物　compound / 混合物　mixture / 有機物の　organic / 無機物の　inorganic / 酸　acid / アルカリ　alkali / 塩　salt / 塩基　base / 溶解する　dissolve / 水溶液　(water) solution / 水溶性の　water-soluble / 濃度　concentration / 飽和　saturation

一酸化炭素　CO（carbon monoxide）
二酸化炭素［炭酸ガス］　CO_2（carbon dioxide）
二酸化窒素　NO_2（nitrogen dioxide）
塩化水素　HCl（hydrogen chloride）
青酸カリ　KCN（potassium cyanide）
アンモニア　NH_3（ammonia）
シアン化物　cyanide
アセチレン　C_2H_2（acetylene）
ベンゼン環　benzene ring
元素　elements
亜鉛　Zn (zinc) / アルミニウム　Al (aluminum) / 硫黄　S (sulfur) / ウラン　U (uranium) / 塩素　Cl (chlorine) / カドミウム　Cd (cadmium) / カリウム　K (potassium) / カルシウム　Ca (calcium) / 金　Au (gold) / 銀　Ag (silver) / ケイ素　Si (silicon) / コバルト　Co (cobalt) / 酸素　O (oxygen) / 水銀　Hg (mercury) / 水素　H (hydrogen) / スズ　Sn (tin) / タングステン　W (tungsten) / 炭素　C (carbon) / チタン　Ti (titanium) / 窒素　N (nitrogen) / 鉄　Fe (iron) / 銅　Cu (copper) / ナトリウム　Na (sodium) / 鉛　Pb (lead) / ネオン　Ne (neon) / 白金　Pt (platinum) / バリウム　Ba (barium) / ヒ素　As (arsenic) / フッ素　F (fluorine) / プルトニウム　Pu (plutonium) / ヘリウム　He (helium) / マグネシウム　Mg (magnesium) / ヨウ素　I (iodine) / ラジウム　Ra (radium) / ラドン　Rn (radon) / リチウム　Li (lithium) / リン　P (phosphorus)

かかり（係）

【係の人】　a person in charge
この仕事はだれが係ですか。
Who is in charge of this project?
私の係ではない［係が違います］。
This is not { my responsibility. / in my department. / handled here. }
詳細は…係に尋ねてください。
For further information, contact the person in charge of the … department.

【係長】 supervisor　→かいしゃ
〈注〉「何々係」の係に当る語は英語にないようだ。ただし次のような係を示す語がある。
会計係　an accountant
受付係　a receptionist
出納係　a cashier
銀行の窓口　a bank teller
文書係，書記　a clerk

かきとめ（書留）→ ゆうびん

【書留郵便［小包］】
a registered letter [package]
【書留で送る，書留にする】
手紙を書留で送った。
I sent { a registered letter. / a letter by registered post [mail]. }
この手紙を書留にしたいのですが。
I want to have [get] this letter registered.

かくご（覚悟）→ ようい（用意）

1．心の用意

【覚悟している】
これから先苦労することは覚悟している。
I am ready to face the difficulties (lying) ahead.
【覚悟ができている】
どんなことを聞いても大丈夫。覚悟ができています。
I am (well) prepared to hear anything.
【覚悟ができていない】
彼の死はあまりに急だった。彼女には最悪の場合の覚悟ができていなかった。
His death was so sudden. She was not prepared for the worst.

2．決心

【覚悟である】
私はたとえどんなに長くかかっても，仕事をやり遂げる覚悟だ。
I'm determined to accomplish my work no matter how long it takes.

がくし（学資）

school expenses

1．動詞との結合

【学資を出す】

学資は全面的に親が出している［に頼っている］。

I depend wholly on my parents for my school expenses.

阿部氏が彼の学資を出すと言ってくれた。

Mr. Abe offered to pay for his education.

【学資を稼ぐ】

彼は学校が終ってからガソリンスタンドで働いて学資を稼いだ。

After school he worked at a gas [petrol] station { to pay for his education. / to earn his school expenses.

彼は自力で学資を稼いで大学を出た。

He worked his way through college.

【学資が足りない】

彼は学資が足りなくなって学校を中退した。

He had to leave [give up] school half way { because he didn't have the money. / for lack of money.

He didn't have enough money to finish school.

2．授業料

〈注〉 英国では教育は無料であるので「…料，…費」のような言葉は不必要。以下は米国の語彙である。

《関連語》

授業料　tuition (fee)

実習費　lab fees; breakage fee（フラスコ・試験管などの消耗品費）

自治会費　student government fee [dues]

書籍代　book fee; money to buy books

生活費［下宿代］ room and board

受験料　application fee

入学金　registration payment

かくじつ（確実）

1．確かな

【確実である】

彼が勝つのは確実だ。

It is certain that he will win.

He is sure to win.

He will certainly [surely] win.

〈注〉 It is sure that … は口語で実際に使うようであるが，日本語の「確実」は堅い表現であるから，もう少し堅い It is certain that … が無難。主観的に自分の確信を述べるのは I'm sure that … が普通である。

【当選確実】

彼は当選確実である。

He has a good chance of winning.（選挙前の予測）

Victory is assured.〔*formal*〕（開票の結果，当確）

X氏は市長選で当確だ。

Mr. X is a shoo-in for mayor in the election.〔*colloq.*〕

〈注〉 「当確」に当る英語は，口語では He's gone over the top. とか He has it in the bag. などと言う。He has more than enough [votes] to win. は標準的な言い方。

2．安全な

【確実な商売】

a sound business（経済的側面から健全な）

【確実な会社】 a reliable firm

〈注〉 reliable は「信頼できる」の意であるから「客扱いが丁寧で堅実な」ことを指す。

3．信頼できる

【確実な情報】（新聞用語）

reliable information; information obtained from a reliable source

【確実な証拠】 indisputable evidence

かくしん（確信）→ おもう，しんじる

かげ（陰，影）

1．日陰

shade

私たちは日陰でひと休みした。

We rested in the shade.

大きな木がその家を陰にしている。

The big tree shades the house.

１歩左によけてください。ここが陰になりますので。

Move [Step] a little to the left. You're blocking the [my] light.

2．影法師・姿

a shadow; a silhouette

古城の影が湖面に映っていた。

The shadow of the old castle fell on the lake.

The old castle was reflected in the lake water.

(日が傾いて)彼女の先を行く彼女の影は長くのびて，頭のあたりは道端のキンポウゲの花にとどいていた。

Her long shadow was walking ahead of her with its head in the buttercups on the roadside.

ほんの一瞬鳥の影が月面をよぎった。

For a second, a bird was silhouetted against the moon.

憂いの影が彼の顔をよぎった。

A shadow of worry flitted over his face.

3．物陰

彼女は建物の陰に立っていた。

She stood behind the building.

人の陰口をきくな。

Don't speak ill of people behind their backs.

かけい（家計）

予算 **family budget;** 家計費 **housekeeping costs;** 生活費 **living expenses;** 財政状況 **family finances**

【生活費】

家計が豊かだ。

We are well off.

家計が苦しい。

We are badly off.

Our finances are in bad shape.

We have a hard time making both ends meet.

家計がピンチだ。

We can't afford to live these days.

We are hard up.

家計を10%切り詰める

cut (my) living expenses by ten percent

家計が赤字だ。

Our finances are in the red.

We can't { make both ends meet. / stay within our budget. }

{ We went / We're } over our (household) budget.

We've spent

{ more (money) than we have [can cover]. / too much (money). }

〈注〉 Our budget is in the red. とすると赤字予算を組むことになるので誤りである。We are broke. と言えばピンチどころか無一文。

cf. I'm in the red this month.

The government is in the red.

どちらも結果として赤字になったことを指す。

【倹約する】

㊍㊀ economize

cut down on one's living costs

家計[生活費]を切り詰めねばならない。

We should

{ try to cut down on our living costs. / tighten our belts. }

〈注〉 家計の節約に関連して参考文をあげる。

旅行費用[光熱費]を節約しなければならない。

We have to save on our traveling expenses [to economize on electricity and fuel].

かける(掛ける,架ける,懸ける)・かかる

1. 支えとめる

【かける】

彼は額をかけた。

He hung the picture.

彼女はコートをハンガーにかけた。

She hung her coat on a hanger.

あの子はめがねをかけている。

She wears glasses.

あの子は真珠のネックレスをかけている[している]。

She { is wearing a pearl necklace. / has a pearl necklace on. }

【立てかける】

屋根にはしごをかける

stand [put] a ladder against the roof edge

【渡しかける】

市は海峡をつなぐ橋をかけることを計画中だ。

The city is planning to build a bridge over [across] the strait.

【上にのせる】

いすに腰かける　sit on a chair

やかんを火にかける

put a kettle on (the fire)

【かかる】

若い婦人の肖像画が壁にかかっていた。

A portrait of a young lady was hung [hanging] on the wall.

There was a portrait of a young lady on the wall.

白いコートがハンガーにかかっていた。

A white coat was hanging on a hanger.

私のドレスがくぎにひっかかった[私はドレスをくぎにひっかけた]。

My dress (was) caught on a nail.

川に古い木の橋がかかっている。

There's an old wooden bridge acoss [over] the river.

大きな魚がかかった。

They caught a big fish.

年とったキツネがわなにかかった。

An old fox was caught in the trap.

There was an old fox in the trap. (かかっていた)

【転義】

私のことを心にかけてくださってありがとう。

Thank you very much for { thinking / worrying / feeling concerned } about me.

そのことが死ぬまで彼の心にかかっていた。

That was on his mind till he died.

彼は息子に望みをかけていた。

He expected a great deal of his son.

2. 留める

【かける】

鍵をかける　lock the door

ボタンをかける

button one's coat (↔ unbutton)

ホックをかける

fasten a hook (↔ unfasten); ㊍㊉ hook

彼女は小包にひもをかけた。

She tied the parcel with string.

彼女は古雑誌をまとめてひもをかけた[ひもでしばった]。

She tied the old magazines together.

飛行機で旅行するとき，スーツケースにバンドをかけておくのはいい思いつきだ。

It's a good idea to bind a suitcase with a strap when you fly.

【かかる】

ドアの鍵がかかっている。

The door is locked.

3. 機能させる

【かける】

ラジオをかける　turn on the radio

レコード[テープ / CD]をかける

play a record [tape / CD]

エンジンをかける　start the engine

ブレーキをかける

step on [hit(急ブレーキ)] the brake; 動 brake

〈注〉 step on it〔英〕= speed up (速度を出せ)と言う場合の it は accelerator を指す。

電話をかける

call [phone] a person; ring up a person〔英〕; make a telephone call

わなをかける

set the trap (↔ release)

目覚しをかける

set the alarm clock (↔ turn off)

【かかっている】

早くして！もうエンジンがかかっているのよ。

Hurry up! The car's started [The engine's going].

部屋は明るく暖かく，ラジオ[ステレオ]で優しい音楽がかかっていた。

The room was light and warm, and the radio [stereo] was playing soft [mood] music.

4. 処理する

【(機械に)かける】

はかりにかける　weigh

この絹のブラウスは洗濯機にかけないでください。

Please don't put this silk blouse in the washer.

【(道具を)かける】

シャツにアイロンをかける　iron a shirt

コートにブラシをかける　brush a coat

じゅうたんに掃除機をかける

run the vacuum over } the carpet
vacuum

5. 取り扱う

【かける】

議案[提案]を会議にかける

submit a proposal at a meeting

新しい法案を国会にかける

submit a new bill to [in] the Diet

事件を裁判にかける

take a case to court; 動 sue

【かかる】

かかりつけの医者　one's family doctor

医者にかかる

see a doctor

私は医者にかかっている。

I'm seeing a doctor [taking medicine].

6. 覆う，接触する，降下する

【かける】

テーブルクロスをかけてください。

Put the table cloth on the table.

寒くありませんか。もう１枚毛布をかけましょうか。

Aren't you cold? Shall I put another blanket on [over] you?

イチゴに砂糖をかける

put sugar on [over] the strawberries

ソースを少々かけて召し上がってください。

Please put a bit of [some] sauce on it.

葉のほこりを洗い流すため水をかけてやる

pour water on the leaves to wash the dust off

〈注〉 野菜畑に水をやる
water the vegetable garden

(人に)はねをかける

splash water on a person

車が私にはねをかけていった。

The car splashed me. (故意ではない)

彼は妹に水をはねかけた。

He splashed water on his sister. (偶然とも故意ともとれる)

He splashed his sister with water. (故意に)

【かかる】

風に乱れた髪が彼女の頬にかかっていた。

A strand of hair was blown across her face.

髪が彼女の額にかかっていた。

Hair was hanging down over her forehead.

山のてっぺんに雲がかかっていた。

The mountain top was covered with clouds.

町全体に霧がかかっていた。

The whole town lay in mist.

はねがかかった。

I got [was] splashed.（故意ではない）

7．転義

(人に)重圧をかける

put pressure on

苦労[心配]をかける

cause a person much anxiety

ご面倒[迷惑]をおかけしてすみません。

I'm sorry I've given you so much trouble.

あなたにご迷惑をかけたくないのです。

I don't want to bother you.

彼は若いとき肺結核にかかった。

He had TB when he was young.

運転に気をつけろと親がやかましいんだ。もし事故でも起したら親に責任がかかるからね。

My parents always tell me to be careful in driving because they'll {have to take the responsibility / be responsible} if I have an accident.

【税金・保険をかける】

税金をかける

impose a tax on; 動 tax

車に保険をかける

insure a car

私たちの少しばかりの貯金に税金をかけないでほしい。

We hope the government won't tax our small savings.

外国から宝石類を持ち込むと税金がかかる。

You have to pay duty [a tax] on jewelry which you bring in from abroad.

彼は家に保険をかけた。

He took out an insurance policy on his house.

【時間をかける】

spend a lot of time (in) ...

彼はその絵を完成するのにまる1年をかけた。

He spent a whole year completing that picture.

【時間がかかる】

It takes a lot of time to ...

あの絵が完成するにはまる1年かかった。

It took a whole year to complete that picture.

この本を完成するのに10年以上かかった。

It took us more than ten years to write this book.

駅までどのくらいかかりましたか。

How long did it take to get to the station?

彼がよくなるまで1，2か月はかかるだろう。

He won't be well for a month or two.

【手間をかける】

手間のかかる仕事　a troublesome job

彼女は料理に手間をかけることをいとわない。

She devotes a lot of time and effort to cooking.

She doesn't mind going to a lot of trouble cooking.

【金をかける】 spend a lot of money on《clothes, skiing》

彼は持ち金全部をかけてあの豪勢な庭園を造った。

He spent all his money (in) doing that gorgeous garden.

【金がかかる】 It costs a lot of money to ...

いくら(お金が)かかりましたか。

How much [What] did it cost (you)?

1万円かかりました。

It cost (me) ten thousand yen.

費用の負担はすべて彼にかかってきた。

He must pay [take care of] all the expenses.

8．その他

【掛け算】

3×4＝12

Three times four equals [is] twelve.

【かけ合せる(交配する)】
スピッツとテリヤをかけ合す
cross a spitz with a terrier

かさなる(重なる)・かさねる

1. 積み上げる

【重ねる】

pile up　きちんと重ならなくてもよい。りんごのような形の物でも pile up と言える。

stack　きちんと重ねる。本や新聞のように平らで重ねやすい物をそろえて重ねる。

put [**lay**] 《one thing》 **on top of** [**upon**] 《another》 上に積む

床を掃いて本や書類を机の上にきちんと重ねたら，部屋がだいぶさっぱりした。
We swept the floor and stacked books and papers on the desk; then the room looked much better.

本が机の上にきちんと重ねてあった[重なっていた]。
The books were piled up neatly on the desk.

うちの本棚の背の低いのを2つ重ねて置けるだけのスペースがあった。
There was enough room [space] to stack two of our low bookshelves
{ one on top of the other.
{ on top of each other.

食器棚の上の段にお皿をきちんと重ねてしまってください。
Stack the dishes neatly on the upper shelf in the cupboard.

お皿がきちんと重ねられて[重なって]いて何もかも清潔に見えた。
The dishes were stacked neatly and everything looked clean.

子供たちがきゃあきゃあ笑い転げながら折り重なって倒れた。
The children fell one on top of the other, shrieking with laughter.

ちょっと寒気がしたので下着を2枚重ねて着てます。
I'm wearing two undershirts because I had a chill.

玉ねぎとトマトを薄切りにして肉の上に重ね，ホイルで覆ってください。
Put the onions and tomatoes in layers on top of the meat and cover with foil.

【転義】
私の研究は彼の研究と重なる部分もある。
Part of my research overlaps with his.

次の祝日は日曜日と重なる。
The next national holiday will fall on a Sunday.

2. 繰り返す

【不幸】
災害が重なって起った。まず地震，次に飢饉，それから大火であった。
There was a series of disasters; first an earthquake, next a famine and then a great fire.

悪いことは重なるものだ。
Misfortune never comes singly.
Misfortunes come in succession.

【苦労】
彼は多くの苦労を重ねてきたのだ。
He's gone through many hardships.

【罪】
彼は次々と罪を重ね，最後は獄死した。
He committed one crime after another and finally died in jail.

【失敗】
彼女は失敗して一からやり直し，失敗してはまたやり直しを重ねてついに新型プラスチックの合成に成功した。
She finally succeeded in synthesizing a new plastic after many false starts.

【試行錯誤】
試行錯誤の積み重ねが科学の発見の一部なのだ。
Trial and error is a part of scientific discovery.

〈注〉 上のような抽象的な一般論に trial and error は

ふさわしい。多くの試行錯誤を表すには much trial and error とする。(×many trials and errors)

【寝不足】

慢性的寝不足が重なって彼女はとうとう病気になった。

She became ill from chronic [cumulative] lack of sleep.

【版】

あの本は5版を重ねた。

That book has {gone through / had} five editions.

かし（菓子）

cake ケーキ; **confectionery** ［集合的］; **sweets, candy** キャンディー

《関連語》
菓子屋[店] confectionery / ホットケーキ hotcake; pancake; griddlecake / ワッフル waffle / ドーナツ doughnut / パイ pie / マフィン muffin / パウンドケーキ pound-cake / カステラ sponge cake / シュークリーム cream puff / エクレア éclair / プリン custard (pudding) / ゼリー jello〔米〕; jelly〔英〕 / イチゴショートケーキ strawberry shortcake / クッキー cookie〔米〕/ ビスケット biscuit〔英〕/ クラッカー cracker / ポテトチップス potato chips / チョコレート chocolate / キャンディー candy (棒付き飴 lollipop [sucker〔米〕]; キャラメル caramel) / チューインガム (chewing) gum

かじ（家事）→ うち（家）

housekeeping (tasks) (家庭生活に関するもろもろの仕事);

housework (掃除・洗濯・料理のような日常的な手仕事)

1. 家事をする

do household tasks; do housework

彼女は昼まで家事をして，それから3時間はものを書く仕事をする。

She does housework until noon, then writes for three hours.

2. 家事に慣れる

【家事がうまくなる】

私はやっと家事に慣れた[うまく仕事をさばけるようになった]。

I've learned at last to {do housework / keep house} efficiently.

〈注〉 米国で She keeps house well. と言えば，いつも家が片付いていてきちんと整理されている状態を指す。ただし英国では housekeeper とは職業で，お金を払って雇うものであるから，主婦などについて keep house well のような表現はあまりしない。

かす（貸す）

1. 無償で他人に利用させる

lend; loan〔米〕(金または移動可能な物を)

君のペンを貸してくださいませんか。

Will you lend me your pen?

彼は1万円貸してくれと言った。

He asked me {to lend him 10,000 yen. / for a loan of 10,000 yen.}

傘を貸していただけませんか。

Will you loan me your umbrella?

〈注〉 lend は有料，無料のどちらにも使われる。loan は〔米〕口語で lend の意に使われるが，lend を好む人もある。名詞 loan は借入，借入金で利子付き貸し付け金(ローン)の意味もある。

2. 使用料，利子をとって貸す

let〔英〕; **rent (out)**〔米〕; **hire (out)**〔英〕; **lease**

ボートは1時間いくらで貸している。

We rent a boat by the hour.

駅前でレンタカーを貸し出している。

They {rent (out)〔米〕 / hire (out)〔英〕} cars in front of the station.

この家は家賃10万円で貸します。

This house lets for
The rent for this house is } 100,000 yen a month.

彼は夏の別荘を安く貸している。

He rents his summer house cheaply.

彼は自分の土地の一部を市に貸している。

He rents out a part of his land to the city.

彼は仕事で家を留守にする1年の間，家を他人に貸したいと考えている。

He's planning to lease his apartment for a year while he's away on business.

3．転義

【知恵を】

知恵を借していただけますか。

Could you give me some advice?

【手を】

手を貸してほしいのです。

I'd like you to help me.

【耳を】

あの人たちは私の言うことに耳を貸そうとしない。

They wouldn't listen to me.

かぜ（風）

wind; そよ風 **a breeze;** 一陣の風 **a gust of wind;** 疾風 **a gale**
台風 **a typhoon**
ハリケーン **a hurricane**

1．動詞との結合

【風が吹く】

風が吹いている。

The wind is blowing.

【風がひどく[強く]なる】

風がだんだん強く[ひどく]なってきた。

The wind is { rising. / blowing harder. / getting worse.

風がだんだん弱くなってきた。

The wind is { falling. / dying down. / getting better.

【風がやむ】

風がやんだ。

The wind has died [stopped].

〈注〉 一般的に風と言うときは the wind とする。強い風，一陣の風のように種類を言うときは a gale, a gust of wind のように数えられる名詞として扱う。

2．方向

風が南に吹いている。

The wind is blowing to the south.

〈注〉 マザーグースの中に "The north wind does blow." とあり，またイソップ寓話の中に北風が旅人のマントを脱がせようとする話があるように，北風は寒い風であるが，英国では "When the east wind roared over the fenlands..." (J. Hilton, *Good-bye Mr. Chips*) とあるように東風も寒い冬の風である。

3．その他

【風のひどい日】 a windy day

【風のない日】 a windless [calm] day

今日は全然風がない。

There's no wind [not a breath of air] today.

【向かい風】

向かい風にはばまれながら彼は進んだ。

He trod forward into [against] the wind.

【追い風】

追い風に送られて船は快走した。

The ships sailed fast before the wind.

【風通し】

私の部屋は風通しがよい。

My room is airy.

【風を入れる】

窓を開けて風を入れなさい[通しなさい]。

Open the window to let in some fresh air.

かぜ（風邪）→ びょうき

1．風邪の表現

【風邪をひく】 catch (a) cold

〈注〉 catch (a) cold 中の冠詞 a はつけることもつけないこともあるが，a slight cold, a bad cold のように限定の意味をもつ形容詞がつくときは a が必要。
take (a) cold は古い表現で，現在ではあまり使わない。

【風邪をひいている】

have a cold

have caught (a) cold

〈注〉 「(風邪をひいて)寒けがする」は get a chill。「骨の髄まで冷え込んだ」は get [be] chilled to the bone と言う。

【風邪をうつされた】

主人の風邪をうつされた。

I've caught my husband's cold.

【風邪で寝込んでいる】

彼はひどい風邪で寝込んでいる。

He has been laid up [in bed] with a bad cold.

2. インフルエンザ

(the) flu; influenza

〈注〉 正確には influenza だが，a bad cold との見分けは難しい。

風邪をひきそうだ。

I'm afraid I'm getting [catching] the flu.

I feel the flu coming (on).

I'm coming down with the flu.

かぞく（家族）

family

うちは5人家族です。

My family consists of five members.

There are five persons [people] in my family.

私の家は5人家族，父と母[両親]と兄と姉と私です。

There are five people in my family — my father and mother [my parents], my brother, my sister and I.

〈注〉 father と mother は一つの単位と考え，冠詞や人称代名詞の所有格をはじめに一つつければよい。brother や sister は elder, younger などの区別をする必要はない。I は最後にまわす。

【親戚関係】

彼は父方の親戚です。

He is related to me on my father's side.

【家系】

うちの家系は15世紀までさかのぼれる[15世紀から続く家である]。

My family line can be traced (back) [goes back] to the 15th century.

彼の家は音楽家の家系だ。

Musical ability runs in his family.

【一員】 a member of the family

彼はまるで家族の(一員の)ようなものだ。

He's like one of the family.

【規模】

大[小]家族　a large [small] family

彼は大家族をかかえている。

He has a large family.

彼の家は家族が多い。

His family is a large one.

〈注〉 この場合×He has many families. としてはいけない。

【家族旅行】 a family trip

【家族手当】

a family allowance; a dependent's [dependant's] allowance (扶養控除の対象者がいるとき)

〈注〉 英国では子供がいると child benefit (児童手当)がもらえる。

【安否を尋ねる】

ご家族は皆さんお元気ですか。

How is [are] your family?

〈注〉 family を一つの単位として見るときは is と単数扱い。また Are they healthy? の意味で家族のひとりひとりを念頭に浮かべながら言うのであれば，are と複数扱いになる。

《関連語》

		[愛称]
両親	parents	
父	father	Daddy; Dad; Papa
母	mother	Mommy; Mom; Mum
祖父母	grandparents	
祖父	grandfather	Grandpa
祖母	grandmother	Grandma; Granny

〈注〉 以下 one's child; a child のように使われるが冠詞等は省略する。
子 child (pl. children)
息子 son; 娘 daughter
孫 grandchild (pl. grandchildren)
孫息子 grandson; 孫娘 granddaughter
伯[叔]父 uncle; 伯[叔]母 aunt
甥 nephew; 姪 niece
いとこ cousin; 親類[戚] relative
義父 father-in-law; 義母 mother-in-law
義理の息子 son-in-law
義理の娘 daughter-in-law
義兄[弟] brother-in-law
義姉[妹] sister-in-law
赤ん坊 baby; 男の子 boy; 女の子 girl

ガソリン

gasoline; gas〔米〕**, petrol**〔英〕

ガソリンスタンド
a filling [gas, petrol] station
a self-service station (セルフサービスの)

ガソリンが切れそうになってきた。セルフサービスのガソリンスタンドがないか気をつけて見ていてね。
We're running out of gas, so let's watch for a self-service station.

かた (方) → やりかた

1. 方法

【水泳】
泳ぎ方 how to swim
僕は6歳のときに泳ぎ方を教わった。
I learned (how) to swim when I was six.
〈注〉 learn to ... と learn how to ... は同じように使われる。

【楽器】
ギターの弾き方
how to play the guitar

【料理】
パンの作り方
how to make bread

2. …ぶり

【歩き方】
彼の歩き方 his way of walking

【話し方】
彼の話し方 his way [manner] of speaking

【笑い方】
彼はいやな笑い方をした。
He laughed in a way [manner] I didn't much like.

3. やり方

【議事進行】
議長の議事の進め方が上手なので，いつも妥当な結論が出る。
The chairman's way of handling meetings usually results in very fair decisions.

【教授法】
彼は独自の教え方を持っている。
He has his own way [method] of teaching.

《類義語》
way 最も一般的な語。
manner 個人的な癖などを含む。
method 論理的かつ細部にわたる方法論。

かた (型)

名 **form; shape; size; type; style; fashion; cut; model; make**
鋳型 **mold, mould**〔英〕; 型紙 **pattern**

1. タイプ

【この型】
この型の冷蔵庫は維持費が少なくてすむので有名だ。
This make of refrigerator is noted for its low operating cost.

【新型】
これが最新型の皿洗い機です。
This is the newest type of dishwasher.

【2000年型】 a 2000 model
2000年型キャデラック
a 2000 Cadillac

【流行の型】
流行のスタイルの服装をしている。

She is always { in fashion. / fashionably dressed.

She always has [dresses in] the latest fashion.

彼女の靴は流行の型のものだ。

Her shoes are stylish [modish].

〈注〉（流行に左右されない）基本的なスタイルの服装をしている場合は次のように言う。
Her clothes are always in a classic cut.

【大型・小型】 the larger [smaller] size
小型カメラ　a miniature camera

2．形　→かたち
L字型　L-shaped
S字型　S-shaped
卵型だ。

It's egg-shaped.

【型がくずれる】
get [go] out of shape; lose its shape
このセーターはもう型がくずれてしまった。

This sweater has already { gone [got(ten)] out of shape. / lost its shape.

帽子は型がくずれやすい。

Hats often go out of [lose their] shape quickly.

3．伝統
set form; convention
【型にはまった】 stereotyped; conventional
【型にはまらない】 unconventional
【型やぶりの】
flouting tradition [convention]（flout＝軽べつする）

かたい（堅い，固い）・かたく

1．堅い
【感触】
hard（かんかん）; **stiff**（こちこち）; **tough**
堅い材質　some hard material（↔soft）
堅いカラー　a stiff collar（↔soft）
堅い結び目　a tight knot（↔loose）
堅い肉　tough meat（↔tender）
【感覚】
堅い決心　firm resolution
堅い人
a trustworthy person（まじめな人，良心的で信頼できる人）
堅い職業[仕事]
secure [steady, regular] job [work];（確実で立派な仕事）respectable work
彼は頭が堅い。

He's obstinate [stubborn, hard-headed].

〈注〉「頭が堅い」と言うと conservative が頭に浮かぶが，急進的であって頑固な人もいる。

【形式ばった】
堅い文
a stiff sentence（ぎこちない）
a formal expression（紋切り型）
【儀礼】
堅いことは抜きにしよう。

Let's do without formalities.

2．固く
【断固】
正しい者が最後に勝つと私は固く信じている。（信念）

I firmly believe [am confident] that the just will win in the end.

【禁止】
（そこでは）動物にえさを与えることは固く禁じられている。

It is strictly forbidden to give the animals any food.

【辞退】
その人たちはお金を受け取ることを固く辞退［固辞］した。

They firmly refused to take the money.

〈注〉 hard は「かたい」であるが，「かたく」は hardly ではない。

【ぎこちない】（固くなる）
彼女は多勢の人の前だったので固くなってし

まった。

She got nervous in the presence of so many people.

固くならないでください[気楽にしてください]。

Please make yourself at home [ease].

Please relax.

かたち（形）

shape

《関連語》

1. 線

まっすぐな straight / 直線 straight line / 垂直な vertical, perpendicular / 垂直線 vertical line / 水平な horizontal / 水平線 horizontal line / 平行の parallel / 平行線 parallel lines / 直角の at right angles, right angled / 直角 right angle / 鋭角 acute angle / 鈍角 obtuse angle / 曲線 curve / カーブした curved / ジグザグの zigzag / 波状の wavy / 曲った crooked / ねじれた線 crooked line / 弧を描いた arched / U字形の U-shaped / L字形の L-shaped

2. 平面

三角形 triangle / 三角形の triangular / 正三角形 equilateral triangle / 正方形 square / 四角形 square / 長方形 a rectangle / 長方形の rectangular; oblong（横長の）/ 菱形の diamond-shaped / カイト形の kite-shaped / 五角形 pentagon / 五角形の pentagonal; five-sided / 六角形 hexagon / 六角形の hexagonal, six-sided / 八角形 octagon / 八角形の octagonal, eight-sided / 円 circle / 直径 diameter / 半径 radius / 円の circular / 半円 half circle, semicircle / 楕円 oval, ellipse / 半月形(の) crescent / 卵形の egg-shaped / ベル形の bell-shaped, bell-like / ハート形の heart-shaped / そら豆形の kidney-shaped / 西洋ナシ形の pear-shaped / 8の字形の in [shaped like] a figure eight / 凸面の concave / 凹面の convex / S字形の S-shaped

〈注〉「…のような形」と言うとき，-shaped，または look(s) like ... を使うとよい。

3. 立体

立方体[立方形] cube

立方体の[さいころ形の] cubic

〈注〉箱のサイズ「縦20cm 横15cm 厚さ 5 cm」は，20×15×5 (cm)のように書き，20 by 15 by 5 と言う。米国では inch を使う。

三角錐（すい） pyramid / ピラミッド形の pyramidal / 円錐 cone / 円錐の cone-shaped, conic / 円柱，円筒 cylinder / 円柱の，円筒の cylindrical / 球 sphere / 球の spherical, round / らせんの spiral

〈注〉平面でも立体でも -shaped, look(s) like ... で表現できる。

かたる（語る）→ はなす（話す）

かつ（勝つ）

win; 勝ち誇る **triumph over**

征服する **conquer**

負かす **overcome; defeat; beat**

1. 戦い

有名な関が原の戦いでは徳川方が(豊臣方に)勝った。

The Tokugawa side won the famous battle of Sekigahara.

The Tokugawa side was victorious over (those on) the Toyotomi side.

【試合】

早稲田が慶応に 2 対 0 で勝った。

Waseda won against [defeated, beat] Keio (by) 2-0.

〈注〉 2-0 は two to nil〔英〕, two to zero〔米〕と読む。

【議論】

議論ではだれも彼に勝てなかった。

No one could get the better of him in an argument.

No one could defeat him in an argument.

2．慣用表現

【勝ち目】

彼ならサンプラスとやって勝ち目がある。

He has a chance against Sampras.

彼ではサンプラスにあまり勝ち目がない。

He has little chance against Sampras.

彼では絶対にサンプラスに勝ち目がない。

He can never defeat [beat] Sampras now.

He has absolutely no chance against Sampras.

がっか（学科）

subject

1．小学校　elementary [primary] school

国語

読みかた　reading;　書きかた　writing;　文法　grammar（英米ではすべてを含めて English）;　初歩の書きかた　spelling

算数　arithmetic

〈注〉 基本的学習「読み，書き，そろばん」に当る reading, writing, arithmetic は “the three R’s” と呼ばれる。

理科　science

社会　social studies（歴史 history，地理 geography）

音楽　music

美術　art

体育　P. E.（physical education）

P. T.（physical training）

体操　gymnastics;　球技　ball games

2．中等学校　secondary school

［米国］	［英国］
国語　English	
文学 literature; 弁論 public speaking; 作文 composition; ジャーナリズム journalism	English language English literature
外国語　foreign languages	
フランス語 French; スペイン語 Spanish; ドイツ語 German; 日本語 Japanese; 中国語 Chinese	French; German; Spanish; イタリア語 Italian; ロシア語 Russian; ラテン語 Latin; ギリシャ語 Greek
数学　mathematics [math]	maths
算数 arithmetic; 代数 algebra; 幾何 geometry; 三角法 trigonometry; 立体幾何 solid geometry; 微積分 calculus	米国と同じ
理科　science	
化学 chemistry; 地質学 geology; 物理 physics; 生物 biology; 生態学 ecology	chemistry; physics biology
社会　social studies	
歴史 history; 社会学 sociology; 経済 economics; 心理学 psychology; 公民 civics; 地理 geography	history; geography （economics; sociology は規模の大きな学校または 6 年生のみ）
美術　fine arts	
音楽 music; 演劇 drama, theater 美術 art（映画 cinema のある学校もある）	music; art （drama は規模の大きな学校のみ）
家庭　home economics	domestic science

家計 budgeting and finance	
料理 cooking; 裁縫 sewing	sewing
技術 industrial arts	
機械製図 mechanical drawing	
木工 woodworking; 金属細工 metalworking	woodworking; metalworking
自動車 auto mechanics	(規模の大きな学校ではほかにもある)
実務 business course	
簿記 bookkeeping, accounting; 速記 shorthand	(英国では行われない)
コンピュータ computer operations	

※学制については「きょういく」の教育制度参照。

がっかりする → ざんねん

be disappointed (in, at, with); be discouraged; be disheartened

1. 失望する

be disappointed (be disappointed が最も多く使われるので,前置詞の使い分けを記す)

be disappointed { at (原因・理由・行為) / in (人) / with (物)

【at】

君が怠け者なのには［君の返事を聞いて］がっかりした。

I was disappointed at your laziness [your reply].

【in】

息子[君]にはまったくがっかりした。

I was disappointed in my son [you].

【with】

新しい家[試験の結果]にがっかりした。

I was disappointed with my new house [the result of the exam].

My new house [The result of the exam] disappointed me.

〈注〉 at, with については上述の用法が標準的であるが, by も使われる場合がある。

【to】

行ってみたら留守でがっかりした。

I was disappointed to find him not at home.

2. 落胆する

be discouraged

彼はパートの給料があまりに安いのでがっかりした。

He was discouraged because his part-time job paid so little.

彼は欲しい本が見つからなくてがっかりした。

He was discouraged { not to have found / at not finding } the book he wanted.

彼女は自分自身にがっかりして沈んでいる。

She was discouraged with herself.

〈注〉 She was disappointed in [with] herself. は何か事件があって，我ながら情けなくてがっかりしていること。discouraged の方はもっと長続きのする気持ちで，何かについてというのではなく何となく意気のあがらないこと。上の３つの例文は be disappointed でも言えるが disappointed はそのときの一時的な気持ち，discouraged の方が長く続く気持ちという違いが出てくるのである。

かっき (活気)

【活気がある】 lively; full of life; energetic

１年生の方が２年生より活気がある。

The first year students are more lively than the second year ones.

春はすべての生物が活気に満ちている。

Every living thing is full of life in spring.

【活気がない】 dull; washed-out

月曜日はみな憂うつな顔をして活気がない。

On Mondays they look blue and dull.

〈注〉 文章の中の描写や思い出などが眼前に見えるように「生き生きしている」の意味の vivid には，「(色が)鮮やかな赤」(vivid red) とか，「(人柄が)快活な」(animated)，「元気な」(lively)の意味もあるが，a vivid personality のように名詞を直接修飾する時にしか使えない。×He is vivid. とは言えない。上の lively とか full of life を使ったほうがよい。

かっこう（格好）

a shape; a form; appearance

1. かたち

【格好の良い】

格好の良いコート　a well-cut coat

あの子は口元の格好が良い。

She has a well-shaped mouth.

【格好の悪い】

格好の悪い[変な格好の]　ill-shaped

僕のコートは格好が変になった[型がくずれた]。

My coat has got(ten) out of [lost its] shape.

2. 慣用表現

【格好をつける】 put on airs

【格好の良い，かっこいい】

smart; trendy; fashionable

彼はいつもかっこいい服装をしている。

He's always dressed in style [stylishly].

【変な格好】

そんな古風な服着て変な格好だよ。

You look funny in that old-fashioned dress.

【こんな格好】

こんな格好では人前に出られないわ。ちょっと着替えてくるからね。

I'm not fit to be seen, so let me change my clothes first.

こんな格好ですみません。

Please excuse my dirty clothes.（ペンキ塗りなどしていて汚れた服のままのとき）

I'm sorry I'm not dressed.（パジャマのまま人前に出たときなど）

【格好が悪い，困る】 be embarrassed

あんなに皆にお別れ会をしてもらって，今さら都合でもう1年いることになりましたなんて格好悪くて言えない。

After all those farewell parties for me, {I don't know how / I'm embarrassed} to say I'm going to stay one more year.

がっこう（学校）→ きょういく，だいがく

school

㊩ **scholastic; academic**（大学以上）

学校教育　education in (the) school(s)

学校嫌い　a school hater

cf. 落ちこぼれ a school dropout

学校給食　school lunch

学校生活　school life

学校時代　school days [years]

専門学校　a technical college

職業訓練学校　a vocational school

【学校へ行く】

どこの学校に行っているの？

What [Which] school do you go to?

姉さんは高校に行っている。

My sister goes to high school.

〈注〉 授業の場としての school は無冠詞でよい。

【学校へやる】

彼は息子を東京の学校にやった。

He sent his son to school in Tokyo.

【学校が始まる】

学校は9時に始まる。

School begins [starts] at nine.

(大学の講義など)

Class begins [starts] at nine.

【学校が終る】

学校はだいたい午後3時頃に終る。

School is over about three in the afternoon.

学年が終って夏休みになった。

School is out for the summer.

終った！

School's out! / We're out!

【卒業する】

finish school; graduate from school

【学校を出て働く】

僕は高校を出たら働く。

I'll get a job after I finish high school.

【学校をさぼる】

(小・中・高の場合)

play [be] truant from school

(大学の場合)

cut a class

《関連語》

年間行事予定　school calendar

時間割　class schedule, class timetable

学年　[the] school year, [the] academic year

〈注〉 欧米の学校は9月に始まって6月に終り，7，8月が夏休みである。

学期　2期制　semester (fall semester, spring semester)〔米〕

term (autumn term, spring term)

3期制　term (autumn term, winter term, spring term)

休暇　vacation〔米〕

holiday(s)〔英〕

学年　(小・中・高) the 1st [2nd / 3rd] year[小学校 grade〔米〕]

…年生　(小学) 1［2…6］年生 a first [second … sixth] grader〔米〕

〈注〉 学校によっては8年生 eighth grader まである。

中学2年生になった。

I'm now in the second year of junior high school.

I'm now { a second-year junior high school student. / an eighth grader.

学童　children [schoolchildren] (小・中学生)

生徒　pupils (教え子の感じ)

学生　students (高校生，大学生 (〔英〕では大学生のみ)

high school students (高校生)

university [college] students (大学生)

何年何組　3の1　Class One of the third grade または three one

4のG　4 G(英国ではアルファベットでクラスを呼ぶことが多い)

担任　one's homeroom teacher〔米〕; one's class teacher; the teacher in charge of a class; a class advisor (高校)

授業する　teach《a class / English》

勉強する　study

学習する　learn (習い覚える)

宿題　homework; assignments〔米〕

テスト　test; exam

点　points, marks

物理で80［0］点をとった。

I got 80 points [zero] in physics.

成績　one's { school record / marks / grades〔米〕

彼の成績が上がった［下がった］。

His grades improved [fell].

標準偏差 / **偏差値** } standard deviation

課外活動　extracurricular activities

クラブ　club(s)

修学旅行　school trip [excursion]

遠足　school picnic

文化祭　annual school festival〔米〕

運動会　athletic meet(ing); sports day〔英〕

落ちこぼれ　動 drop out; 名 dropout

青少年の非行化　juvenile delinquency

校内暴力　violence in schools

卒業　graduation; 動 graduate (from)

〈注〉 secondary school までは finish を使い，graduate は大学のみ〔英〕に使う。

卒業式

graduation ceremony

commencement (ceremony)〔米〕

がっしゅく（合宿）

〈注〉 外国の学校には日本の学校の「合宿」に当るものはあまりないようだが，一般的には intensive training session でよい。

1. スポーツ系

うちのクラブでは夏の合宿をやった。

My club held a summer camp for training.

バレーボール部は箱根で合宿をした。

Our volleyball club had an intensive training session at Hakone.

テニス部は学校の体育館で１週間の合宿をすることにしている。

We tennis club members are to have a week of intensive training, during which we will spend the nights in our school gym.

2. 文化系

ESS は例年の夏合宿を蓼科で行った。

Our ESS club held its yearly summer session at Tateshina.

3. 実習を伴う研修会

workshop（講義 lecture 及び実習 practice や活動 activities などをする）

英語の先生たちが夏期研修会を行った。

Our English teachers held a summer workshop.

彼は自閉症の研修会に参加した。

He attended a workshop on autism.

かてい（家庭）→ うち（家）

かてい（過程）

a process

1. 道筋

…の過程をたどる[通る]

go through ⌊the process of [the stages of] …

すべての文明は生成，発展，成熟，衰退の過程をたどることを世界の歴史が示している。

World history shows that every civilization has gone through the stages [process] of growth, development, maturity, and decline.

2. 中途

そのプラスチックの生産過程で産出される有害物質が論議の的になっている。

The toxic substance [material] produced during {the production of the plastic / the manufacturing process} is at the center of the controversy.

The core of the controversy is the toxic substance produced during the production of the plastic.

〈注〉「生産される過程」のつもりで×the process which they are manufactured のように書くことはできない。なお process は「全体の過程」を指し，stage は全体の過程のうちの，「その時々の段階」を示す。

かなう（適う，叶う）

1. 適合する

【めがねにかなう】

［対象が主語］suit one's taste

［人主語］be pleased with

どうやら彼の娘の婚約者は彼のめがねにかなったようだ。

He seemed pleased with his daughter's fiancé.

【目的にかなう】

新しいプランの方が我々の目的にかなっている。

The new plan serves our purpose better.

【法の精神にかなう】

そんなのは憲法の精神にかなっていない[反する]。

That's ⌊against [contrary to] the spirit of the Constitution.

2. 実現する

［事主語］**be fulfilled; be realized; come true**

［人主語］**have** one's **wishes realized**

【夢が叶う】

長年の夢がやっと叶いました。

My dream has finally come true.

【願いが叶う】

願いが叶えられました。

My prayer was answered.
おじさんがハワイ行きの航空券を贈ってくれて，私の望みを叶えてくれました。
My uncle gave me a plane ticket to Hawaii and made my dream come true.

3．対抗できる
【かなわない】 be no match for
数学で彼にかなう者はいない。
He has no equal in mathematics.
社交性という点で，僕はとても彼にはかなわない。
I'm no match for him in sociability.
【閉口する】
まったくやかましくてかなわない。
I can't stand that noise.
暑くてかなわない。
It's unbearably hot.
I can't stand this heat.

かなしい(悲しい)・かなしみ・かなしむ

悲しい 形 **sad; sorrowful;** 悲しみを誘う **pathetic; plaintive**
悲しみ **sorrow; sadness;** 深い悲しみ **grief;** 哀悼 **mourning**
【悲しい話[事件]】
a sad [pathetic] story [event]
【悲しい，悲しんでいる】
be [feel] sad; be unhappy about
深く悲しむ be full of sorrow; grieve; be (deeply) grieved; be deep in grief; lament (over)
【悲嘆に暮れる】
彼は彼女を失って悲嘆に暮れた。
He was overcome [overwhelmed] {by sorrow [grief] / with sorrow} at her loss.
【悲しそう】 look sad [sorrowful]
優勝したのにあの子は悲しそうであった。
Although she won the first prize, she looked sad.
【悲しそうに】
彼は悲しそうに荒れ果てた寺を眺めた。
He looked sadly at the ruined temple.
〈注〉 look sad は主語の人物が悲しそうであることで sad は補語。look sadly《at something》は主語の人物が何かを見る見方が悲しげであることで sadly は副詞。したがって「彼女が悲しそうに見えた［だった］」を×She looked sadly. とするのは誤り。正しくは She looked sad.

かね（金）・きんせん → かけい，こづかい

1．収入
income
【収入を得る】
金を稼ぐ earn money
【給料】 pay
月給 salary
日給 a day wage
時給 an hourly wage
時［日］給である be paid by the hour [day]
〈注〉 雇用の形態により次のように言う。
正社員 a full-time worker
パートタイマー a part-timer
（長期契約の） permanent
（短期契約の） temporary
日雇い労働者 a day laborer
【貯金】 save《a certain sum of money》

2．支出
expenditure（高額の支出）〔*formal*〕
【費用】 expenses
旅行費用 traveling expenses
【…代・…料金】 fare
バス［タクシー］代［料金］ bus [taxi] fare
飛行機代 air fare
【…料】 charge（サービスに対する料金）
サービス料 service charges
ホテルの料金 hotel charges
器具取付け工事費 installation charge
【…費・料金・会費】 fee（医師・弁護士などに支払う料金；学会・スポーツクラブなどの会費）

【…代】
rate（使用量に対してかけられる料金）
ガス代　gas rate
郵便代　postage rate
電話代　telephone rate
【支払う[使う]】
pay [spend]《～ yen》for《something》
【買う】
buy《something》for ～ yen
buy《someone》《something》
いくらしましたか。
How much was it?
How much did it cost (you)?
How much did you pay for it?

3．貸借　→かす，かりる
【貸す】 lend（物または金を貸す）
彼は1万円[辞書]を貸してくれた。
He lent me { 10,000 yen. / his dictionary.
【借りる】 borrow（物または金を借りる）
トムは兄さんから金[辞書]を借りた。
Tom borrowed { money from his brother. / his brother's dictionary.
【分割払い】
月賦　monthly payments
分割払いで結構です。
You can pay monthly [on a monthly basis].
月賦で払っている。
I'm making monthly payments.
車のような大きな買物は普通何らかの形で分割払いにする。
Expensive items such as cars are usually bought on some kind of installment plan.
【ローン】
家のローン　mortgage; house loan
車のローン　car loan
〈注〉 家具，電化製品などの分割払いは installment という。
【送金】
為替　money order
振替　account transfer
銀行自動引き落し
automatic deduction (from a bank account)
小切手[チェック]を送る
send a check [cheque] to a person
英国での国際会議申し込みに50ポンドを為替で送金する
send fifty pounds by international money order to register for a conference in England

かのうせい（可能性）

possibility; chance
【可能性がある】
あの人たちの見たものは蜃気楼だったという可能性も十分ある[ということも十分考えられる]。
It is quite possible that what they saw was a mirage.
その計画は十分成功の可能性がある。
There is a good possibility [chance] that the project will succeed.
【可能性を検討】
彼らは今(その計画の)可能性を検討中だ。
They are now making a feasibility study.
【可能性は五分五分】
可能性[成功率]は五分五分[50%]である。
The odds are fifty-fifty.〔*colloq.*〕
There is a 50% [fifty-fifty] chance of success.
The possibility of success is fifty percent.
【可能性がない】
彼の成功の可能性はまずない。
There is no { possibility [chance] that he will succeed. / hope for (his) success.
〈注〉 possibility による表現の程度については「おそらく」を参照。

かぶしき（株式）

株　a stock〔米〕; a share〔英〕
株券　a stock certificate

株式市場　the stock market
株主　a stockholder, a shareholder

《関連語》
株式公開　offering of stock to the public;（公債などの発行）public flotation
未公開株　preflotation shares [stocks]
店頭売買株　over-the-counter stocks
株の配当　(stock) dividend
株主総会　stockholders' meeting; general meeting of stockholders; annual meeting of stockholders（年1回の場合）
証券　securities, security certificates
証券取引所　stock exchange
東京証券取引所　the Tokyo Stock Exchange
株式相場　stock quotations
株価　stock prices
株式市況　stock market situation
株価暴落　crash, tumble, collapse
ダウ平均　the Dow-Jones average
国債　government bond
社債　corporation bond
中期国債ファンド　medium-term government securities fund

かまわない（構わない）・かまう

1. 関心がない，気にしない

【他人の評】
人が何と言っても別にかまわない。
I don't care what others (might) say.

【無関心】
あの子はあまり身なりをかまわない。
She doesn't care much about her appearance.

彼は食べる物は別に何でもかまわない。
He isn't particular about what he eats.

2. 干渉，世話

【干渉しない】
かまわないでくれ[放っておいてくれ]。
Leave [Let] me alone.

そんなことにかまっていられない。
I can't be bothered with such things.

【気づかい】
どうぞおかまいなく。これで結構ですから[至極快適です]。
Please don't worry about me. I'm quite comfortable.

どうぞおかまいなく。電話番号がわかりますから自分で(電話は)かけられます。
Please don't {go to any trouble. / trouble yourself.}
As I have his phone number, I can call him myself.

【世話をする】
彼女が今になって悔んでいるのは，息子が母親の愛情を一番必要としていたときに，忙しすぎて十分かまってやれなかったことだ。
Now she regrets she hadn't had enough time to be with her son when he most needed her.

彼女はひとり息子をかまいすぎる。
She always makes a fuss over [of] her only son.

3. 許可を得る，差し支えない

【容認】
たばこを吸ってもかまいませんか。
Do you mind {my smoking? / if I smoke?}

ええ，かまいませんとも。
No, not at all.

別にかまいません。
I don't mind.

〈注〉◆mind とは「いやだと思う」ことであるから，日本語では「ええ，かまいません」であるが，英語では No, I don't mind. と No にしなければならない。なお，たばこを吸ってもらいたくないときは，次のように言えばよい。
Well, I'd rather you wouldn't.
◆何かしてもよいかと尋ねられたときの応答
「ええ[いや]かまいません。本当にいいんです」
No, I don't mind. / It's quite all right.（相手の心の負担を軽くする言い方）

赤ちゃんをお連れになってもかまいませんよ。

It's quite all right to [if you] bring your baby with you.
もしいやなら，いやでかまいませんよ。
You don't have to if you don't want to.
もし忙しければ，来られなくてもかまいませんよ。
You don't have to come if you are busy.
【都合】
私はいつでもかまいません。
Any time is fine with me.
5時で，かまいません。
Five o'clock will be all right.（結構です）
鉛筆でもかまいません。
A pencil will do.

4．いじめる
猫をかまうんじゃないよ。引っかかれるよ。
Don't tease the cat. It will scratch you.
僕はいつも妹を「おさるさん」と呼んではかまった［からかった］ものだ。
I would always tease my little sister by calling her "Little monkey".

かよう（通う）

1．通勤・通学
【通う】 **go [come] to; commute to**〔米〕（かなりの距離の通勤・通学）
〈注〉 視点を学校［会社］に置けば come（来る）となり，視点をそれ以外に置けば go（行く）となる。常に話者がどこで話しているのか注意。
通学する　go [come] to school
通勤する
go / commute〔米〕 } to the [one's] office
【交通機関】
学校には何で通っているの？
How do you come [go] to school?
電車とバスで通っています。
I come [go] to school by train and bus.
歩いて通っています。
I walk to school.
〈注〉 by bus に対応する on foot を使って I come to school on foot. は正しい文だが，I walk to school. で十分である。
お仕事にはどうやって通っておられますか。
How do you go [come] to work?
電車とバスで通っています。
I take the train and the bus.
行きも帰りもバスで通っています。
I use the bus both to and from work.
【所要時間】
会社［役所］に通うのに1時間以上かかる。
It takes more than an hour to get to the [my] office.
【…から通う】
結婚した姉の所から通っています。学校から歩いてほんの10分ほどです。
I live with my married sister, who lives about ten minutes' walk from school.
【通い】
若い社員はほとんど社員寮に入っていますが，下宿して通う方がよければそれでも結構です。
Most of the young workers live in the company { residence, / apartment building, / dormitory〔米〕, } but you can live elsewhere if you want.
〈注〉 apartment は台所付き。dormitory, dorm〔米〕は普通は大学の寮。
通いのお手伝い［メイド］
a helper [maid]; a cleaning lady
〈注〉 helper は通いが普通で，住み込みならば a live-in helper [maid] のように言う。maid は上流家庭のお手伝いの感じ。

2．往復便
go to and from《a place》; **run between**《A and B》
その島と本州の間を毎日船が通っている。
Steamers run [go] daily between the island and Honshu.
21世紀には地球と月を往復するロケット便が通うようになるだろう。
In the 21st century rocket service will be

available between the moon and the Earth.

名古屋，浜松間はバスが通っている。

Bus service is available / Buses run } between Nagoya and Hamamatsu.

…から

1. 人

【…からもらう】 get [receive] 《a letter, money》 from 《a person》

【…から聞く】

ビルから君のことを聞いた。

I heard about you from Bill.

〈注〉 I heard of you at the business meeting. のhear of はうわさを聞くこと。

だれから聞いたの？

Who told you?

Who said that?

【…から習う】

私は彼からそれを習った。

I learned it from him.

【…から独立する】

親から独立したいと思う。

I'd like to be independent of my parents.

【…からもらう】

だれからお金をもらったの？

Who gave you the money?

【…から始める】

まず君から始めなさい。

You go first.

You start [begin]. (ゲームなど)

【…から選ばれる】

10人の応募者の中から彼女が１人だけ選ばれた。

She alone was chosen out of ten applicants.

2. 場所

【起点】

東京から大阪まで　from Tokyo to Osaka

25ページから始める

begin from [at, with] page 25

窓から見る

look out (of) the window

開いている窓から入る[出る]

get in [out] through the open window

裏口から部屋に入る

enter [come into] the room through [by] the back door

【落下】

木[窓]から落ちる

fall from [out of] a tree [window]

屋根から落ちる

fall off the roof

がけから落ちる

fall over [off] a cliff

高い建物のてっぺんから飛び降りる

jump from the top of a tall building

車から降りる　get out of a car

【方向】

後ろ[下]からのぞく

peep from behind [under]

カーテンの後ろからのぞく

peep from behind the curtain

エーゲ海から風が吹く。

The wind is blowing from the Aegean Sea.

火は彼の家から出た。

The fire started in his house.

3. 時間

【…時[…日]から】

朝から晩まで

from morning till [to] night

３時から５時まで

from three to five

午前の授業は９時から始まる。

Morning classes begin at nine.

(×begin from)

夏休みは７月12日から始まる。

The summer vacation begins on { the 12th of July. / July 12.

３時からはひまです。

I'll be free from three o'clock.

願書の受付は2月1日からです。

Applications will be accepted from [starting] Feb. 1.

2年生のときから岐阜高校にかわった。

I changed to Gifu High School (when I was) in my second year.

【いつから】

いつから日本にいらっしゃいますか。

How long have you been in Japan?

いつからピアノを習っていますか。

When did you begin learning the piano?

【…してから】

［未来］

仕事が全部片づいてからお茶にしましょう。

We shall have tea after everything's finished [when we finish everything].

私たち子供が皆学校に出かけてしまってから，母さんは家の掃除にかかります。

My mother starts cleaning the house after we children have left for school [leave for school].

〈注〉 上記の文のように「…してから」が未来のことで，しかも習慣を表すときに時制について迷うが，上記のように現在完了か，または単に現在でよい。同義「…が…したら」の「た」に引きずられて過去形にしてはならない。(×My mother starts ... after we children left ...)

［過去］

母が亡くなってから10年になります。

(1) It is [It's] already } ten years } since
(2) It's already been
(3) Ten years have already passed
my mother died.

(4) My mother has been dead ten years already.

〈注〉 上記のどの文も普通に使われる。(3)はやや堅い。(1)は is をはっきり残している方が強い調子。(2)の It's は It has の短縮形。(4)は日本人の発想とは異質であるが普通の言い方である。

【…日前から】

10日前から彼女は病気で休んでいます。

She has been absent from school (for) ten days.

〈注〉 10日前は×before ten days とは言わない。また，論理的にはよさそうな since ten days ago も正用法と認められていない。上記例文のように「ここ10日間」としてとらえる。

4．原因

必要から　from [out of] necessity

好奇心から　out of curiosity

羨望から　through [out of] envy

不注意から　through (one's) carelessness

5．根拠

外見からすると

judging from [by] one's appearance

【経験から】

私の経験からあなたにお勧め［お話し］しているのです。

I'm saying this {to you / for your sake [benefit]} from [based on] my own experience.

私は自分の経験から両親が不和であることが子供にとってどんなにつらいか知っている。

I know from my own experience how hard it is for children when their parents do not get along well.

【…からの引用】

これは聖書からの引用です。

This is a quotation from the Bible.

6．理由　→ …だから

7．材料・原料

ぶどう酒はぶどうから作る。

Wine is made from grapes.

水は水素と酸素から成る。

Water consists of hydrogen and oxygen.

8．範囲

【…から…まで】

お値段はサイズにより500円から1000円まであります。

The price varies from 500 to 1000 yen {according to / depending on} the size.

10歳から上の子はチームに入れます。

Children of ten and above can join the team.

子供から大人まで楽しめる映画です。

Both children and adults can enjoy this film.

家事手伝い募集，年齢30歳から50歳まで，１日５時間勤務（広告文）

home helper wanted, 30–50, 5 hrs a day

医療は70歳から無料です。

Medical care is free from the age of 70.

9．慣用表現

【…からには】

私たちが来たからにはもう何も心配はいりません。万事うまくゆきます。

Now that we have come to help you, feel assured that everything will {go well. / be all right.}

からい（辛い）

1．ひりひり辛い

hot; コショウのきいた **peppery;** 舌がぴりぴりする，鼻をつく **pungent**〔*formal*〕

夏はカレーのような辛い食物がいい。

I like a hot food like curry in summer.

2．塩辛い

salty

辛い塩魚［ハム］ heavily cured fish [ham]

この料理はちょっと［とても］塩辛い。

The dish is⌊a bit [much] too salty.

あの人の味つけは塩辛い。

She uses a lot of salt⌊in her cooking [when she cooks].

3．厳しい

【点がからい】 be strict [severe] in marking

安藤先生は答案［レポート］の点が辛い。

Mr. Ando is a strict marker.

Mr. Ando {is strict in marking papers. / marks papers strictly. / grades papers severely.}

からだ（体）→ p.149の図

かりる（借りる）

1．貸してもらう

borrow; use

【金または移動可能な物を】

ちょっと辞書をお借りしてもいいですか。

May I borrow your dictionary?

私は彼から１万円借りた。

I borrowed 10,000 yen from him.

【移動できない物を】

電話をお借りしてもいいですか。

May I use your telephone?

〈注〉 この場合 borrow は使えない。use を使う。

2．使用料を払って借りる

rent〔米〕**; hire**〔英〕**; lease**

駅前で自転車を借りられますよ。

You can {rent〔米〕 / hire〔英〕} a bicycle in front of the station.

昨年の夏は白馬に別荘を借りました。

Last summer I rented a summer house in Hakuba.

庭のある家を借りたいものです。

I'd like to rent a house with a garden.

今年は小さなすてきな夏別荘を借りたい。

This year I'd like to lease a neat little summer house.

	貸す	借りる
傘・本など 金	lend loan〔主に米〕	borrow
ボート・自転車・車・部屋・家・別荘・土地	rent（out） hire（out） let lease	rent hire lease

〈注〉 上記は「貸す・借りる」にあたる英語の表である。見てわかるとおり rent, hire, lease は「貸す」にも「借りる」にも使われる。どちらの意味かは文脈から判断しなければならない。
また，let, lend (lend の過去 lent)，rent の l, r の発音を正確にして意味の取り違いがおこらないように注意。

かわいい

形 **cute; dear; darling; precious**

かわいがる　love; be fond of; be attached to

〈注〉 日本語の「かわいい」を英語に訳す場合は，客観的立場（その者が「愛らしい」性質を持っている）か，主観的立場（自分または主語の人物がその者に愛情を持っている）のいずれかに訳し分けなければならない。

1．客観的立場

【子供】（見た目にかわいい）

あそこの赤ちゃんは本当にかわいい。

Their baby is just the cutest little thing.

隣の子はとてもかわいい子だった。

The child next door was darling [very cute].

〈注〉 口語の「かわいこちゃん」にあたる表現をいくつか挙げる。
She's a little doll. / She's all suger and spice.
She's a real sweetie. / Isn't he cute as a bug's ear?
What a cuddly baby! / He's the apple of her eye.

【その他】

かわいい服　a darling dress

かわいい家　a darling house

かわいい犬　a cute dog

2．主観的立場

【いとし子】

私は我が子がかわいい。

I love my children.（宝と慈しんでいる）

〈注〉 客観叙述では My children are my most precious treasures. They are very precious to me.

おばあさんは私をとてもかわいがってくれる。

My grandmother { loves me a lot. / is very fond of me. / feels attached to me. }

おばあさんは幼い孫がかわいくてしかることができない。（何でも言いなりになっている）

My grandmother is so fond of her little grandchild that { she never scolds her. / she can never refuse her anything. }

【描写】

母親は息子を愛情をこめて抱きしめた。

The mother { hugged her son affectionately. / gave her son an affectionate hug. }

【恋愛感情】

彼はガールフレンドがかわいくてならない。

He's absolutely attached to his girl friend.

He really [actually, absolutely] dotes on her.

He holds her very dear.（首ったけである）

〈注〉 客観叙述では She is very dear to him.

【その他】

彼は生徒たちをかわいいと思った。

He felt attached to the pupils.

He thought the pupils were cute [lovely].

彼はその子をかわいく思った。

He felt fond of the child.

かわいそう

1．客観叙述

【かわいそうな話】　a sad story; a sob story（哀れな身の上話など）

【かわいそうに思う】　be sorry for（一般的）; 憐む　pity; feel pity for; take pity on; have mercy on

浦島太郎は亀を捕えたが，かわいそうに思って逃がしてやった。

Urashima Taro caught a turtle, but feeling sorry for it, let it go.

私はその貧しい，小さな子が本当にかわいそうだと思った。

I felt really sorry for the poor little child.

体 body

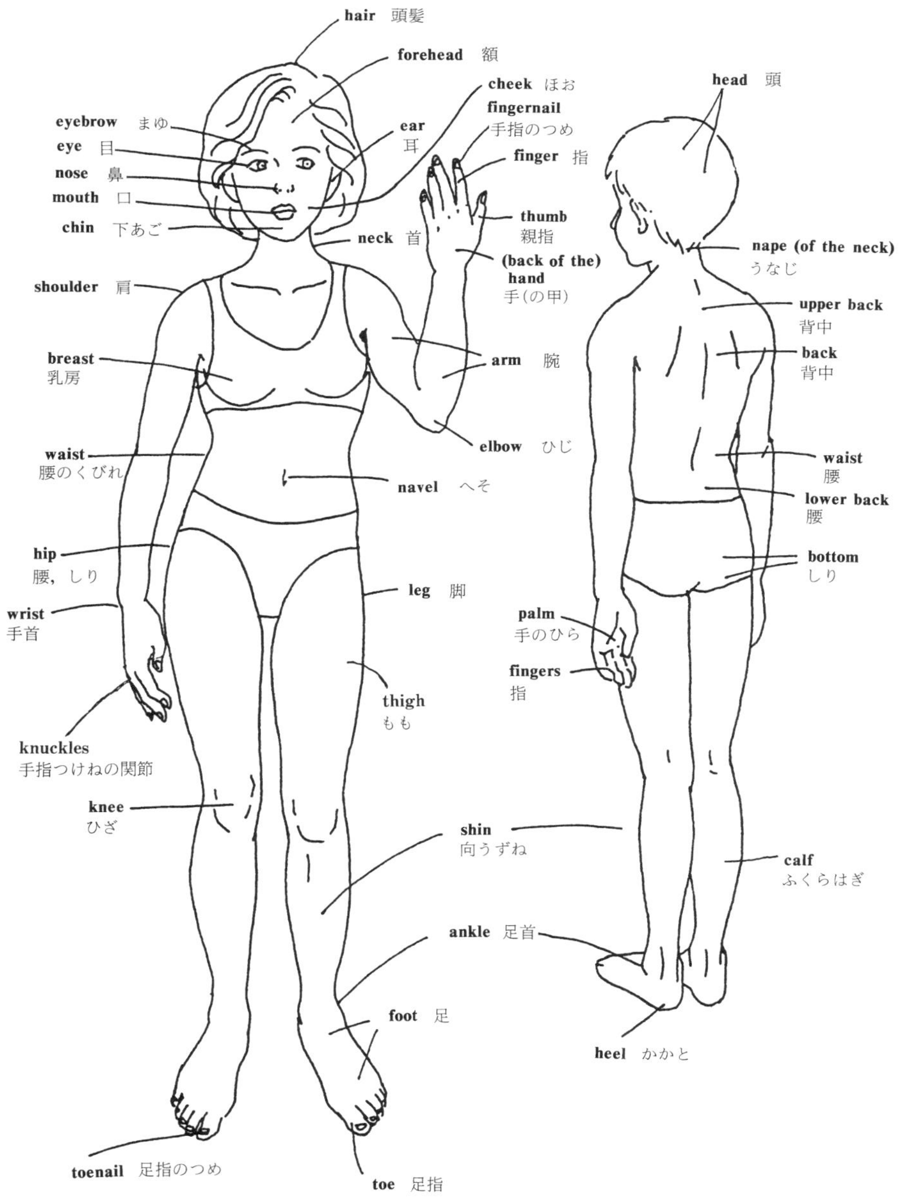

hair 頭髪
forehead 額
cheek ほお
fingernail
手指のつめ
eyebrow まゆ
eye 目
nose 鼻
mouth 口
chin 下あご
ear
耳
finger 指
thumb
親指
neck 首
(back of the)
hand
手(の甲)
head 頭
nape (of the neck)
うなじ
shoulder 肩
upper back
背中
breast
乳房
arm 腕
back
背中
elbow ひじ
waist
腰のくびれ
navel へそ
waist
腰
lower back
腰
hip
腰，しり
bottom
しり
leg 脚
wrist
手首
palm
手のひら
fingers
指
thigh
もも
knuckles
手指つけねの関節
knee
ひざ
shin
向うずね
calf
ふくらはぎ
ankle 足首
foot 足
heel かかと
toenail 足指のつめ
toe 足指

お酒を飲んで憂さ晴らしをしている人たちを見ると，ちょっとかわいそうっていう気もする。

I feel a bit sorry for people who get drunk to forget their frustrations.

かわいそうですよ。祝日の連休に宿題なんか出さないでください。

Take [Have] pity on us. Don't give any homework over the festival week.

2．主観叙述

【かわいそうに！】

（ごく軽く） Oh, dear! / What a pity!

（やや強く） Poor《Tommy》! / Poor man [woman]! / Poor boy [girl]! / Poor thing!（動物などに対して）

〈注〉 日本語で感想としてもらす「かわいそうに」は英語では形＋名の形で表現する。副詞のつもりでPoorly! などとしないように。また「かわいそう」の意味の poor は名詞を直接形容する用法に限る。cf. Tommy is poor.（トミーは貧乏だ）

なんてかわいそうなのだろう。生れつき目が見えないなんて。

How sad [awful] that the boy was born blind!

【かわいそうなことをした】

かわいそうなことに，ほんの 2，3 日で死んでしまいました。

Poor little thing, it died a few days later.

トミーを１日中ひとりぼっちで留守番させるなんて，本当にかわいそうなことをしました。

It was terribly heartless of me to have left poor Tommy alone in the house all day.

〈注〉 文化的相違で欧米，特にゲルマン系の人は小犬・捨て猫の類に「かわいそう（He took pity on the poor puppy.）」などとするのはあまりに月並みで好まない。また本気で助ける気もなくただ「かわいそう」と言うのはごまかしの感傷であると反発を受けることもある。

かわせ（為替）→ ゆうびん

1．郵便為替

a money order〔米〕; **a postal money order; a postal order**〔英〕

電報為替 a telegraph(ic) transfer

為替振出人 the sender; the payer

為替受取人 the receiver; the payee

郵便為替を組む

have a money order issued

get a money order

郵便為替で１万円送る

send 10,000 yen by money order

send a money order for 10,000 yen to a person [a company]（人・会社に）

郵便為替を現金に換える

have a money order cashed

2．相場

為替相場

the exchange rate; the rate of exchange

今日の為替レートは１ドル120円です。

The exchange rate for today is 120 yen to the dollar.

外国為替 foreign exchange

ドル［円］為替相場 dollar [yen] exchange

かわる（変る）・かえる

〈注〉 自動詞と他動詞の区別に注意。

1．変る

動自 **change; be changed; turn into; be turned into**

【人が】

彼はすっかり人が変ってしまった。

He is quite another man now.

結婚したからといって，彼が変るかどうかあやしいものだ［変わるとは思われない］。

It is doubtful that he will be changed [turned into a reasonable man] just because he's married.

【変らない】

彼はちっとも変っていない。（昔のままだ）

He is exactly what he used to be.

彼は相変らず若い。

He is as young as ever.

【気が】

私，気が変ったわ。

I've changed my mind.

【考えが】

彼の考えは決して変らない。

His opinions never change.

【顔色が】

伝言を見て彼女の顔色が変った。

She turned pale when she saw the message.

【家が】

（新居に引っ越す） move into a new house

【変態】

毛虫が美しいチョウに変るなんて思えない。

I can't imagine those ugly caterpillers will turn into beautiful butterflies.

2．変える・替える

動 他 **change; turn**《something》**into; exchange**

【人を】

戦争体験が彼を変えてしまった。

His war experience changed him.

【血相を】

彼は怒りで血相を変えた。（真っ赤になった）

He turned red with anger.

【計画を】

計画を変えましょうよ。

Let's change our plans.

【仕事を】

なぜ仕事を変えたのですか。

Why did you change your job?

【着替える】

ちょっと待ってください。着替えてきますから。

Wait a moment. I'll go and change my clothes.

【席を】

私と席を替えていただけませんか。

Will you exchange seats with me?

【模様替え】

彼はたまに部屋の模様替えをして気分を変えるのが好きです。

He likes to rearrange the furniture to change the mood of his room once in a while.

【両替】

どこで円をドルに替えたらいいでしょうか。

Where can we exchange yen for dollars?

かんがえる（考える）→ おもう

1．思考する

自分で考えろ。

Think for yourself.

英語で考えろ。

Think in English.

よく考えて物を言え。

Think well [carefully] before you speak.

彼はひとりでじっと考えていた。

He sat alone deep in thought.

2．…と考える

【判断】

私はAはBだと考える。

I think (that) A is B.

あいつの様子から見てエイブの仕業とは考えられない。

I judge from [by] his appearance that Abe is not the offender.

His appearance { tells me / makes me think } that Abe is not the offender.

【意見】

私は新しく規則を制定すべきだと考える。

I am of the opinion that new regulations should [could, might] be established.

3．…を考える

【…のことを考える】

そのことをよく考えた方がよい。

We had better think carefully about that matter.

老後のことを考えておくべきだ。
We should provide for our old age.
お父さんの言われたことをよく考えなさい。
Think over what your father (has) said.
自分のしたことを考えなさい。
Reflect upon [Consider] what you have done.

【…を考える】
他人の気持ちを考えなければならない。
We should think of other people's feelings.
We should be considerate of other people's feelings.
あの人の家庭の事情を考えなければならない。
We ought to consider her family circumstances.
最悪の事態を考えておきなさい。
Be prepared for the worst.
彼は新しい方法を考え出した。
He has thought up a new method.
彼は新しい機械を考え出した。(発明した)
He has invented a new machine.

かんかく (感覚)

(a) sense; (a) sensation
方向感覚　a sense of direction
平衡感覚　a sense of balance

1. 五感
five senses

【視覚】 sight
ぼんやり(見える) 形 vague, dim, shadowy
はっきり(見える) 形 clear
生き生きして(見える) 形 lively, vivid
光り輝く　bright
まばゆい　dazzling
派手な色　gay colors

【聴覚】 hearing
音楽的な　musical
調和している　harmonious
不協和音の　discordant, in discord
静かな優しい声　a soft, quiet voice
心をなごます声　a soothing voice
大きなやかましい声　a loud and noisy voice

【臭覚】 smell
におい 名 odor; scent
よい香り(の)
名 aroma; fragrance
形 fragrant, sweet, good smelling
動 smell sweet
いやなにおい　bad smell, offensive smell
ぷんぷんいやなにおいがする 動 stink

【味覚】 taste
おいしい　good, delicious
まずい　not good, bad, terrible
塩辛い　salty
甘い　sweet
酸っぱい　sour
苦い　bitter
辛い　hot

【触覚】 touch
なめらかな　smooth
やわらかな　soft
ざらざらの　rough
かたい　hard

2. 皮膚感覚・体感
熱[暑]い　hot
温[暖]かい　warm
ぬるい　lukewarm
蒸し暑い　humid, muggy, close
冷めた，冷えた，涼しい　cool
冷え冷えした　chilly
冷たい，寒い　cold
氷のように冷たい　icy
鼻がむずむずする。
My nose tickles.
背中がむずむずする。
I feel my back itch.
My back itches.
足の指がかゆい。
My toes itch.
体中がかゆい。

I itch all over.
やめて。くすぐらないで。
Stop! Don't tickle me.
くすぐったくて死にそうである
be tickled to death（腹を抱えて笑うの意味もある）
ちくちくする(痛み)　prick; prickle; tingle
足がしびれて感覚がなくなった。
My foot went {to sleep. / numb.}
しびれが切れて足がちくちくする。
My foot feels like pins and needles.
痛む　ache; be painful
快い[さわやかな] pleasant　→いいきもち
[居心地よい] comfortable

かんかん → ぎせいご・ぎたいご

1．日差し

太陽がかんかん照りつけていた。
The sun was blazing [blistering, glaring] (hot).
日照り続きで池の底がかんかんに干上がった。
The pond dried up completely because of the long drought.

2．怒り

【かんかんになる】
彼はかんかんに怒ってしまった。
He got furiously angry.
He flew into a rage.
彼女の人を見下げたような言葉に，彼はかんかんに怒ってしまった。
He got furious at her arrogant remark.

3．音

鐘の音　ding-dong
カンカンとくぎを打つ音　hammering sound

かんきゃく（観客）

[集合的] **an audience;** [個別的] **a spectator**
観客が多い[少ない]
have a large [small] audience
歌舞伎では観客席から役者に大声で呼びかけて励ます慣習がある。
In Kabuki it is a tradition for certain people in the audience to shout out encouragement to the actors.

《類義語》
audience　[集合名詞]音楽会の聴衆，演劇の観客，講演会の聴衆。
spectator　スポーツなどの見物人。火事や事故のやじ馬も指す。
onlooker　偶然その場に居合せて見ているやじ馬。
bystander　偶然その場に居合せた人。
viewer　テレビ視聴者，映画の客など。(個人) cf. audience
observer　（研究で）観察・観測を行う人。発言権はあるが議決権をもたないで会議に列席を許されている人。

かんけい（関係）

relationship; relation
関係がある　**be related to**

1．因果関係

経済専門家によれば需要と供給の関係が物の価格を決めるそうだ。
The relation between supply and demand determines prices, economists say.
低気圧と天候の変化とはどんな関係になっていますか。
How is low atmospheric pressure related to a change of [in] weather?
光と植物の生育との関係はどうですか。
What's the relationship between light and vegetation?
彼が貧しい環境に育ったことと，彼が異常に金銭に執着することは無関係ではないはずだ。

His childhood poverty must have something to do with his excessive love of money.

【関係がない】

ハンセン病は遺伝とは関係がない。

Hansen's disease is not hereditary.

血液型と性格との関係は科学的には認められていない。

It is not scientifically accepted that blood types have anything to do with one's temperament.

2. 人間関係

【血縁】

「あの方とはどういうご関係ですか」「私は彼の伯母です」。

"How are you related to him?" "I'm his aunt."

【交際上】

君は彼とはどういう関係ですか。

How are you connected with him?

What's your connection with him?

彼は NTV と何か関係がある。

He has some connection with NTV.

同情がいつか愛に変り二人は性的関係をもつようになった。

Sympathy developed into love and their relationship became a sexual one.

【関係を尋ねるほかの言い方】

彼とはどういう知り合いですか。

How do you know him?

あれはだれですか。

Who's he?

彼は友だちの友だちさ。

He's ⌊my friend's friend [a friend of a friend].

昨夜パーティーで一緒にいた人はどういう人ですか。

Who was that boy you were with at the party last night?

ちょっと知ってる人さ。

Oh, (just) somebody I know.

〈注〉 この答え just somebody I know ははっきり言いたくないときの答え。

3. 利害・関心

an interest; concern

君には関係ないことだ。

Well, you don't need to be concerned about it.

It's none of your business. (失礼な言い方)

私にはそんな事関係ない[関心がない]。

I'm not interested in that.

I have no interest in that.

4. 関与

【関係する】

参加する　participate in; take part in

巻き込まれる　be [get] involved in

〈注〉 「関係する」は漠然としているので，英語では関係の仕方まで具体的に言う方が自然。
ex. He's a shareholder in that business. (彼はあの会社では株主になっている)

彼は贈収賄事件に関係して辞職しなければならなくなった。

He had to leave his post, because he got involved in a bribery case.

私はそのことには関係ない。

I have nothing to do with that affair.

I'm not involved in that business.

5. その他

【関係を断つ】 break (with)

その2国は外交関係を断った。

Those two countries broke off diplomatic relations.

【…関係の会社】

彼は電気器具[コンピュータ]関係の会社に勤めている。

He works for a company dealing in ⌊electric appliances [computers].

【関係なく】 irrespective of

成人なら年齢性別に関係なくクラブに入会できる。

Any adult can join the club ⌊irrespective [regardless] of age or sex.

【関係者】

the persons [parties] concerned; (参加者) a participant; (利害関係者) an interested party

【関係書類】

the documents relating to the case

【関係法規】 the related laws and regulations

【関係当局】 the authorities (concerned)

かんげき(感激)

【感激する】

be deeply moved [affected, touched] by

感動している be carried away with emotion

感銘を受ける be deeply impressed

【感激の涙を流す】 be moved to tears

彼自身あんなに忙しいのに引越しの手伝いを申し出てくれて,彼女は感激した。

She was deeply appreciative of his offer to help her move when he was already so busy.

『風と共に去りぬ』は多くの人を感激させた[感動させた]。

Gone With the Wind moved many people to tears.

〈注〉 be moved to tears も be carried away ... も「感動」に限らず,怒りや無念の思いにかっとして我を忘れたり,涙を流す場合にも用いられる。

かんこう(観光)

sightseeing

【観光をする,観光に行く】

go sightseeing; see the sights; visit

彼らは京都に観光に行った。

They went to Kyoto for sightseeing.

彼は仕事と観光を兼ねて来ていた。

He was there for business and sightseeing.

私達は朝は会議を行い,午後は観光に行った。

We had meetings in the morning and {went [did] sightseeing / saw the sights} in the afternoon.

〈注〉 They went to Kyoto to do the sights. という言い方もあるが,時代おくれの表現である。わざと皮肉をこめて使うことはある。

観光客 a sightseer; a visitor; a tourist

観光団 a tourist [sightseeing] party [group]

観光事業 the tourist industry [trade]

観光地 a (tourist) resort

ガイドのついた観光旅行

a guided tour of (Kyoto)

観光ガイド a tour guide

市内観光 a city tour

半日コース[1日コース]の観光

a half-day [day] tour

かんじ(感じ)

1. 感覚

feeling; sense; 触覚 **touch; feel**

【触覚】

すべすべ[ざらざら]した感じだった。

It felt smooth [rough].

ビロードのような感じだった。

It felt like velvet.

指が凍えて感じがなかった。(無感覚)

My fingers were numb with cold.

【気持ち】

何かおかしい感じがした。

I had a feeling that something was wrong.

泣きたい感じだった。

I felt like crying.

また学生時代に戻った感じだ。

I feel as if I were [am] a student again.

2. 印象

【…という感じを与える】

impress [strike] 《a person》 as ...

どんな感じの人でしたか。

How did she impress [strike] you?

彼女は感じが良かった[悪かった]。

She gave me a good [bad] impression.

I liked [didn't like] her.

【(人が)感じの良い】 形 likable, pleasant

3．効果・気分
effect
【感じが出る】
雪がなくてはクリスマスの感じが出ない。
It doesn't feel like Christmas without snow.
【感じを出す】
電灯をやめてろうそくをつけてクリスマスの感じを出した。
We lit candles instead of turning on the lights to create a Christmas atmosphere.

かんしゅう（慣習）→ しゅうかん

名 **a custom; convention; tradition**
【慣習的な】 形 traditional; conventional
我々は慣習的な考え方から抜け出せない。
We cannot get rid of conventional ideas.
日本では儀礼的祝い事の席で酒を出すのが慣習である。
It's customary [traditional] in Japan to serve sake on ceremonial occasions.
それら辺地の山村では，古い慣習がかなり残っている。
Many old customs are still observed [kept] in those remote mountain villages.

がんしょ（願書）→ にゅうし

【用紙】 an application form
【願書提出（する）】 application; 動 apply
数校の大学に願書を出した。
I applied for admission to several universities.
【願書を送る】 send in the application
【願書の受付】
願書は２月１日より受け付けます。
Applications will be accepted from the 1st of February.

かんじょう（感情）

〈注〉 日本語と英語は１対１で意味が対応するものではない。また文脈により同じ語でもニュアンスが変化する。ここにリストアップした日英両語の表現はごく大ざっぱに文脈と無関係に対応させたものである。ここにあるほとんどの語は本書の中に例文と共に示されており，特に＊印の語は項目として取り上げてあるのでそれぞれの項目を参照されたい。

1．快・不快
【快】
*うれしい / *喜ぶ / *楽しい・楽しむ — be delighted / be happy [glad] / enjoy
*元気である / *朗らかである / *明朗である / 快活である — be cheerful / be lively

【不快】
*苦しい　feel pain
*つらい　have a hard life
*悩む　be troubled
*憂鬱である　be depressed
*悲しむ　be sad
悲嘆に暮れる　be deep in sorrow
不機嫌である　be sulky / be cross

【満足】
満足である　be content
幸せである　be happy
*いい気持ちである　be comfortable

不満である　be discontented
不幸せ［惨め］である
be unhappy [miserable]
*迷惑である　be disturbed [bothered]

2. 好み・興味

*好き, *気に入る / 大事に思う　like, be pleased
*面白い / 興味深い　be curious, be interested

【共感・愛情】
愛する / *かわいいと思う　like, love, cherish
仲良しである / *親しい仲である　be friends with
共感[同情]する　sympathize with
哀れみをもつ / いたわりをもつ / *かわいそうと思う　be kind to / be considerate to / be sorry for
尊敬する　be full of respect / respect
うらやましい　be envious
*ありがたい　be thankful / be grateful
すまない　be sorry [apologetic]
謝る　apologize
*許す, 我慢する　forgive
譲り合う　make mutual concessions

【自意識】
*自信をもつ / 誇りに思う　be proud

嫌い　dislike
憎む, 憎らしい　hate
面白くない, *退屈である　be bored

失恋する　be broken-hearted
敵対する　be hostile
批判的である　be critical
反発する　be repelled

*ばかにする　sneer at
軽蔑する　despise; disdain
妬む(ねた), 妬く(や)　be jealous
憤慨する　be indignant [offended]
*怒る　be angry
激怒する　be furious
恨む　be resentful; resent

【自意識】
*恥ずかしい / *困る　be embarrassed
*恥じる　be ashamed
恥をかく　be put to shame
取り乱す　be upset
*傷つく　be hurt

3. 安心・不安・恐怖

*平気[平静]である　be calm / have peace
*安心する / *ほっとする / 気がゆるむ　be relieved / be [feel] at home
*安心[安堵]　㊔ relief

*不安である　be uneasy
*心配である　be anxious
*焦る, *あがる　be nervous
落ち着かない　be uncomfortable
緊張する　be tense [strained]
*驚く / *あわてる　be surprised / be astonished [alarmed〔強〕]

【恐れ・恐怖】
*恐ろしいと思う　fear
*こわい　be afraid

*ぞっとする　be terrified [horrified]
ショックを受ける　be shocked
やりきれない　can't bear [stand]
必死である　be desperate

4. 夢・希望

*願う，望む　hope; wish
*夢見る　have a dream
*…したい，(…して)*欲しい
wish to; hope to; want to; would like to
期待する　look forward to＋名
(期待 名 expectation)
*がんばる　do one's best
熱中する，*張り切る　be enthusiastic about
*本気である　be in earnest
決心している　be determined to
絶望する { be in despair / have no hope
失望している　be disappointed
失意の中にある　be bitterly disappointed
*くよくよする　worry
幻滅している　be disillusioned
*残念である　be (very) sorry
*後悔している { regret / be full of regret / be remorseful
*面倒臭い { won't be bothered / feel lazy
なげやりである　be careless

5. 感動

*感激する　be moved [impressed]
美しい，すばらしい
be beautiful, be wonderful
*夢中である，熱中する　be engrossed
*あこがれる　be full of yearning [longing]
*懐かしい } long to＋動
*恋しい } long for＋名
*忘れられない(→わすれる)　never forget
無感動である　be cool
無関心である { be indifferent / be unconcerned
すねる　have a critical attitude
無常観　名 mutability
*むなしい　形 vain (むなしさ 名 vanity)
*あきらめ　名 resignation to fate

かんしん(感心)

【感心な】 admirable; commendable
感心，感心！
Well done! (よくやった)
Great! / Wonderful! (すごい)
Fantastic! / Marvellous! / Splendid! (すばらしい)
【感心する】 賛嘆する admire; be impressed; (良くも悪くも) wonder at
ニューヨークに着いて，建物が高いのと人が多いのに感心した。
Arriving in New York, I marvelled at the tall buildings and crowded streets.
あの人の辛抱強さに感心する。
I admire him for his patience.
あの人の演奏[演技]には感心しました。
We were impressed by her performance.
【感心しない】 think it isn't good to ...; don't approve
朝食抜きで学校に駆けつけるのは感心しない。
I think it isn't good to rush to school without having breakfast.
あなたが着る物にお金を使いすぎるのは感心しない。

I don't approve of your spending so much money on clothes.

かんする(関する)・かんして → ついて

1. …について (特に強調しない場合)

about; on

彼は安楽死の問題に関して(研究)発表する[彼の論文は安楽死の問題に関するものだ]。

He will read a paper / The paper he will read is / His paper is } { about / on } the euthanasia problem.

私はそれに関して何も知らない。

I know nothing about it.

私はそれに関して何も言うことはない。

I have nothing to say about that.

非武装問題に関しては様々な意見がある。

Opinions about [concerning] disarmament differ.

2. 強調・注意喚起 (新しいトピックとして持ち出す場合など)

regarding; in regard to; as regards 〔*formal*〕; **as for**

【…に関しては】

この問題に関しては目下のところ適当な解決策がないと思われる。

I don't think there's any good solution to this problem at present.

ジムに関しては卒業以来何も消息を聞いていない。

As for [In regard to] Jim, I've heard nothing of him since graduation.

【…に関するかぎり】

as far as … is concerned

私に関するかぎり，何も問題はありません。

There's really no problem as far as I'm concerned.

かんそう (感想)

impression(s); **what** one **thinks of** something

【感想を求める】

新しいスピルバーグ映画のご感想は？

What do you think of [What are your impressions of] the new Spielberg film?

女性のニューファッションのご感想は？

How do the new women's fashions strike you?

日本料理のご感想は？

How do you like Japanese cooking?

〈注〉 「どうですか」と感想を求める言い方として What do you think? が正しく，×How do you think？は誤りである。次の2つの形も正しい。
○How do you feel about …?
○How do you like …?

かんどう (感動) → かんげき，かんしん

がんばる (頑張る)

〈注〉 「がんばろう」「がんばって」は激励の決り文句であり，それに Let's do our best. とか Do your best. をあてはめると欧米人には奇妙に聞えるようである。日本人はやたらに do one's best を使うと言われる。

【何か仕事にとりかかるとき】

さあがんばろう！ (英語の決り文句はない)

Okay. (Time to start.)

Here we go!

1. 激励

(テストなどに出かけるとき) がんばって。

Give it all you've got.

Good luck!

がんばっておいで[大丈夫だよ]。

Do your best. (I'm sure you'll do fine.)

「明日の数学のテストはもうだめだ」「がんばれよ，大丈夫だよ。この前のテストだって80点もとれたじゃないか」。

"I can't possibly pass the math test tomorrow." "Come on, you can do it. Last time you got 80 points."

がんばれ。世の中はいいこともあるさ。へこ

たれるな。

Cheer up! The world's not all bad. Don't let things get you down.

（何をぐずぐずしているか）がんばれ。

Pull your socks up!

【競技観戦のときなど】

（もう少しだぞ）がんばれ。

Keep at it just a little longer!

Stay with it! / Hold out!

Stick with [to] it! / Never say die!

Go on! / Come on! / Don't give up!

（元気を出せ）がんばれ。

Show'em. / Get in there! / Fight, fight! / Buck up!

2．努力する

exert oneself; do one's **best; work hard**

がんばれよ。

Do your best.

Give it all you've got.

きのうの夜のゲームでうちのサッカーチームは技を出しつくして本当にがんばった。

Our soccer team exerted all their cleverness last night.

あまりがんばるなよ。(サボっている者に皮肉に言うこともある)

Don't exert yourself too [so] much.

Don't work so hard.

3．言い張る

persist in; insist on

（意見を）**stick to** one's **own opinion**

彼はどうしても…だとがんばる。

He persists in his opinion that ....

彼はその土地・建物は生得権で自分の物だとがんばった。

He insisted that the estate was his by birthright.

かんべんする（勘弁する）→ ゆるす

1．許す

【過去の過失について】

勘弁してください。私が悪うございました。

Please forgive me. I was wrong.

〈注〉 本当に謝罪するときも使えるし，Excuse me. の代りに軽い意味で使うこともある。
ex. I'm late, please forgive me.

【現在または未来について】

勘弁してくださいよ。

Don't be so [too] hard on me.（お手やわらかに）

【放免】

もう勘弁してやりなさいよ。彼もこりたろうから，放免してやりなさい。

That will be enough. He'll never do that again, so let him go.

2．我慢する

彼のこと勘弁してやってください。(もうしばらくの我慢だから)

Please bear with him just for a while.

〈注〉 bear with はしばらく我慢するときに使う。

もう勘弁できない。

I can't {put up with / take / stand} it any longer.

This is more than I can bear.

かんぼう（願望）→ きぼう，ねがう・ねがい

a desire; a wish

【願望をかなえる】

長い間の彼の願望がかなえられた。

What he had {dreamed of / wished for / worked for} so long finally came true.

かんりょう（官僚）→ やくにん

き

き（木）

a tree; 灌木 **a bush; a shrub;** 木材 **wood** 形 **woody; wooden**

〈注〉 日本語では灌木も木の一種であるが英語では bush, shrub と, tree とははっきり区別されている。

常緑樹　名 an evergreen
常緑の　形 evergreen
針葉樹　a conifer
広葉樹　a broad-leaved tree
落葉性の　形 deciduous
幹　a trunk;　枝　a branch
小枝　a twig;　根　roots
つる植物　a vine（ブドウ，フジなど）
まきひげ，つる　tendrils; runners

《関連語》
アカシア acacia / イチイ yew / イチョウ ginkgo tree / 梅 plum tree / エゾマツ spruce / カシ oak / 樺 birch / カラマツ larch / クルミ(の木) walnut tree / 栗(の木) chestnut tree / 月桂樹 laurel / 桜 cherry tree / ジンチョウゲ daphne / 杉 Japanese cedar / ツタ ivy / ツツジ azalea / 椿 camellia / ナシ(の木) pear tree / ニレ elm / ネコヤナギ pussy willow / ハシバミ hazel / ヒイラギ holly / ヒマラヤスギ cedar / ブドウ(の木) grape vine / 藤 wisteria / ブナ beech / ポプラ poplar, aspen / 松 pine (tree) / 桃(の木) peach tree / モミ fir (tree) / モミジ maple (tree) / ライラック lilac / リンゴ(の木) apple tree

き（気）　→ きにいる，きをつける

1. 気質

【気が強い】（自己主張が強い）

頑固な　terribly strong-minded, stubborn〔*negative*〕
自信満々な　confident, self-assured, over-confident〔*negative*〕, too self-assured〔*negative*〕
負けず嫌いな　competitive〔時に *negative*〕
攻撃的な　aggressive（口で攻撃または攻撃的行動に出る）
こわいものなしの　brave（ほめ言葉）; bold, daring〔時に *negative*〕; foolhardy〔*negative*〕
外向的な　outgoing

【気が弱い】

意志薄弱　weak-willed, indecisive, hesitant

〈注〉◆wishy-washy（人の言うままにふらふらして自己の信念のないこと〔*very negative*〕）
◆weak-minded には頭の弱いという意味があるので,「気の弱い」には weak またはweak-willed の方がよい。また「私は気が弱い」は会話で “I have a weak character.” と言うことがあるが，この表現には「道徳的に弱い，わいろや麻薬に誘惑されやすい」の意味がある。

強く押せない
　not assertive, passive, faint-hearted

【気が小さい】

心配性な　nervous
小事にこだわる　fussy

〈注〉 似ているが fidgety はせこせこ動きまわること。

批判がこわい
　faint-hearted, cowardly〔*negative*〕
引っ込み思案の　timid; shy（はにかみやの）

【気が大きい】

気が大きくなる（気質というより一時的な状態）
　become light-hearted
　feel generous about spending money

【気前のよい】 generous

おおらかな，心の広い　broad-minded

〈注〉 文の内容により選択し，その語がほめ言葉か，けなし言葉かは文化的相違もあるので気をつけなければならない。「気が強い」は日本語ではだいたいけなし言葉だが，上記の形容詞は必ずしも悪い意味ではない。「気が強い」と批判的に言うには too self-assured, over-confident のようにする。

【気が若い】 be young in spirit [mind]

【気が早い】

向う見ずな，早とちりの　rash

【気が短い】quick-tempered, short-tempered

【気がつく】 →きづく・きがつく

心配りが行き届く　attentive

人の気持ちがわかる　considerate

【気がきく】

状況に応じて気転のきく　tactful

2．状況

【気が合う】be congenial; get along (well)

ジムとはとても気が合う。

Jim and I really { get along (well). / hit it off.〔米 *colloq.*〕 }

We really enjoy { each other's company. / being with each other. }

【気が合わない】

ビルとはあまり気が合わない。

I don't get along very well with Bill.

２人は気が合わなかった。

The two didn't hit it off (well).〔米 *colloq.*〕

ジムとは合せられるが，フランクとはどうも気が合わない。

I can get along with Jim, but not with Frank.

【気が置けない】

あの人なら気が置けない。

I feel { comfortable [at home] / at ease } with him.

〈注〉 feel at ease は先生や相談相手など目上の人で，普通一緒にいると固くなりがちな人について，「誰々は気が置けない」と言うときに使用する。

【気を許す】be off one's guard

【気を許さない】be on one's guard

【気を回す】

気を回さないで[変な風にとらないで]ください。

Don't { get the wrong idea. / get me wrong. / take it that way. }

3．好き嫌い

【気に入る】 →きにいる

like, be pleased (with)

【気が向く】

feel like ...ing; feel inclined to do ...

【…してやりたい気がする】 →…したい・したがる

have a good mind to do ...

【気が乗らない】be half-hearted, be not keen on, can't get very enthusiastic about

私はその計画には気が乗らない。

I'm not keen on the project.

【気が進まない】be not willing

〈注〉 前後関係によっては I'm not willing ... は拒絶の意志表示にもなるので注意。

4．心配り

【気をきかす】use one's head

【気を使う】be sensible enough (not) to ...

〈注〉 use one's brains は状況判断を的確にして対応することで，"Use your brains." と命令形で言うと「頭を使え，気をきかせろ」(気がきかないね，との批判)になる。

【気のきいた】

(スピーチなど) witty; (言葉が) clever

【気のきいた服装の】smartly dressed

〈注〉 smart は英国では外見についてのみ使う。米国では a smart student (頭の良い学生); a smart answer [idea, solution, policy] など intelligent の意味に使われる。clever は英国では「ずるがしこい」といった悪い意味になることがある。子供に a clever boy と言うのは「利口な子」のことで悪い意味はないが，大人については clever を避け an intelligent person と言う方がよい。

5．心労

【気が張る[張りつめる]】 →きんちょう

be [feel] tense, be on edge

〈注〉「気が張る」は「気楽」の逆であるから，be ill at ease という状態も含む。

【気が気でない】

nervous; 緊張して落着かない　jittery

〈注〉 be strained は The conversation was strained. (緊張したやりとりがなされた)のように使う。I was strained. とは言わず，I was [felt] tense. とする。

【気になる】
［事主語］ be on one's mind
［人主語］ be preoccupied〔強〕
be somewhat worried〔弱〕
彼はまもなく始まる試験が気になっていた。
The approaching exam was on his mind.
He was somewhat worried about the approaching exam.
彼は受験のことが気になって，旅行に行っても楽しめなかった。
He was too preoccupied with the coming exam to enjoy the trip.
【気にする】be concerned about
彼は健康を気にしている。
He is concerned about his health.
【気がもめる，気をもむ，気が気でない】
worry about; be worried about; be anxious about
【気が引ける】not have the nerve to
気が引けて彼にはとても尋ねられない。
I don't have the nerve [courage] to ask him.
【気がねする】
（遠慮） be afraid of giving trouble
（心配） be afraid of offending by acting too freely
（緊張） feel ill at ease with a person
彼は上司に気がねしてそのことは黙っていた。
He was afraid of giving trouble to his supervisor, so he said nothing about it.
だれにも気がねはいりません。楽にしてください。
Please make yourself at home. You don't have to worry about anything here.
気がねはいりません。いつでも遊びに来てください。
Don't hesitate [Please feel free] to drop in whenever you like.

6．不興

【気に障る】
［事主語］ get on one's nerves, annoy, irritate, offend
［人主語］ be irritated, be annoyed
【気を悪くする】
［事・行為者主語］ hurt one's feelings, offend
［受動・被害者主語］ be hurt, be offended
〈注〉 be offended は憤慨の気持ち。be hurt には悲しみがある。

7．忘我

【気を取られる】
集中する keep one's mind on, concentrate on; 没頭する，面白くて夢中になる be absorbed in; 目的をもって一心不乱である be intent on
バックハンドの練習に気をとられて6時間もテニスをしていた。
They were so intent on improving their backhand that they played tennis for six hours.
【気をそらす】
one's attention is attracted by ...
【気が散る】be distracted from one's work, can't concentrate on one's work

8．落胆

【気を落す】
失望する be disappointed
くじける be disheartened, be discouraged, be dejected（気落ちした状態，原因不明の場合もある）
【気が滅入る】be depressed
【気がふさぐ】
be down in the dumps〔*colloq.*〕
be moping around〔*colloq.*〕（主として他人について言う表現）
〈注〉 be blue は古い表現。ただし，blue Monday（憂うつな月曜日）は今も使われる。be disappointed は何かをしようとしてうまくいかず，がっかりしていることで，行動を意識した語。be depressed, be disheartened, be dejected などはもっと状況を中心にした語である。

9．意識

【気が遠くなる，気を失う】

faint; lose consciousness

【気が違う】 go [become] mad [insane]

10．慣用表現

【気の持ちよう】

それは[何事も]気の持ちようです。

It depends on how you think of it.

Everything depends on how you look at it.

【気のせい】

それは君の気のせいだよ。

It's only your imagination.

(私の)気のせいかもしれないが，ジムがバスに乗るのを見たと思う。

It may be only [just] my imagination, but I think I saw Jim get on the bus.

【気がつく】 発見する →わかる

きえる（消える）→ けす

1．火・灯

火が消えたような

cheerless and deserted（活気のない）

火[火事]はすぐに消えた。

The fire was soon [quickly] put out.

窓の明りは一つ一つ消えていった。

The lights in the windows went out one by one.

2．視覚

disappear; vanish; fade（away）; go out of sight

【姿が】

男の子は私のそばを通り抜け角を曲って姿を消した。

The boy walked past me and disappeared round the corner.

あの子の姿はまもなく群衆の中に飲み込まれて消えてしまった。

We lost sight of her soon in the crowd.

【雪が】

大通りの雪は消えてしまった。

The snow on the main road has thawed [melted（away）]

【露が】

朝日に当ると露は消える。

Dew drops vanish in the morning sun.

【星が】

夜が明けかかると星は消える。

The stars fade toward(s) dawn.

【傷跡が】

切り傷の跡はほとんど消えてしまった。

Hardly any scar remained from the gash.

【筆跡などが】

石に刻まれた字がほとんど消えてしまった。

The inscription has worn away.

【跡形もなく】

（最後の痕跡まで）跡形もなく消えてしまった。

Even the last trace has been effaced.

3．聴覚

die away; go out of earshot [hearing]

その音はしだいに消えていった。

The sound gradually died away.

騒々しい楽隊の音はやがて消え去り，再び静寂が戻った。

The noisy bands passed out of earshot, and silence returned.

4．気持ち

いつか彼の怒りも消えた。

His anger gradually { died down. / left him. }

きおく（記憶）→ おもいだす，おもいで

名（a）**memory;**（a）**recollection**

【記憶する】

動 memorize, learn（a thing）by heart

試験に受かりたければ5000語記憶しなければならないという。

They say you have to memorize 5000 words

if you want to pass the examination.

彼は出かける前に旅行ルートを記憶にたたきこんだ。

He memorized the route before starting his trip.

【記憶がいい[悪い]】

君は記憶がいい[悪い]ね。

You have a good [poor] memory.

【記憶力】

(我々の)記憶力は年とともに衰える。

Our memory declines with age.

【記憶にある[ない]】

おばあさんとこの道を歩いた記憶がある。

I remember walking with my grandmother along this street.

私が３歳の時亡くなった姉のことはほとんど記憶にない。

I can hardly remember (anything about) my sister who died when I was three.

【記憶に新しい】

それはまだ記憶に新しい。

It is still fresh [vivid] in my memory.

I can still remember it vividly [clearly].

【記憶に頼る】 trust to [rely on] one's memory

【記憶が正しければ】

If my memory is correct [right], ...

If I remember rightly, ...

【コンピュータの記憶装置】

記憶装置　memory, storage

外部記憶装置　external storage (ハードディスクなど)

内部記憶装置　internal storage (RAM など)

きかい (機会)

opportunity　「機会」を表す一般的な語。

男女雇用機会均等法

the Equal Employment Opportunity Law

chance　偶然に与えられた機会。chance と opportunity は多くの場合同じように使われる。

occasion　何かをするのにふさわしい好機。「この機会に」on this occasion などのように使う。

【機会がある】

ビルにはほかの若者同様，勉学の機会があった。

Bill had the same opportunity [chance] to study as most young people.

【機会がない】

テッドはビルのような勉学の機会がなかった。

Ted { didn't have / hadn't 〔英〕 } the same opportunity [chance] to study as Bill did [had 〔英〕].

テッドは家庭の事情で勉学の機会がなかった。

Ted had no opportunity [chance] to study due to family reasons.

私は彼のすぐそばに住んでいるのに彼になかなか会う機会がない。

I have had no chance [opportunity] to see him although I live quite near him.

【機会を失う[逃す]】

学校の友だちはみな修学旅行で北海道に行っているのに，私は母の病気のために機会を逃してしまった。

My classmates are now on their school trip in Hokkaido. I've missed [lost] this chance because of my mother's illness.

【またの機会に】

またの機会に行ければいいでしょう。

You can go { some other time. / at the next opportunity. }

【できるだけ早い機会に】

できるだけ早い機会に彼に会いに行きましょう。

We'll go to see him
{ as soon as possible. / at the earliest possible { opportunity. / time. } }

【機会があれば】

機会があればフランスに行きたいと思う。

I'll go to France { when I / if I can } find an opportunity.

I'd like to go to France if I have a [the] chance.

ジョンは機会さえあれば山登りに出かける。

John goes mountain climbing
{ at every opportunity.
whenever he can.
whenever he has the opportunity.
whenever he gets the chance. }

【機会をつくる】

私がみんなで集まるような機会をつくりましょう。

I'll plan [arrange] a meeting to get us all together.

彼女にもう少し世の中を見る機会をつくってやらなくては。

You should give her more opportunities [opportunity] to go out and see the world.

【いい機会】

お互いに知り合ういい機会だ。

It's a good opportunity [chance] to get to know each other.

こういう仕事のひまなときは棚卸しをする[在庫目録をつくる]いい機会だ。

This slack period would be a good occasion to take inventory.

【この機会に】

この機会を借りまして皆様のご協力に深く御礼申し上げます。

On this occasion I'd like to thank all of you for your cooperation.

こんな機会はまたとない。(絶好のチャンスだ)

You'll never have
{ { an opportunity / a chance } like this again.
another chance [opportunity] like this. }

There will never be a chance like this again.

No better chance [opportunity] will ever come to us.

〈注〉 上記 chance を使う場合は「逃したらたいへん」という感じが強く，opportunity を使う場合は「これこそ絶好の機会」という点が強調される。

きがつく(気がつく) → きづく

きかん (期間)

a period; a term; duration

【短[長]期間】 a short [long] period (of time)

【期間中】 during the period

1. 契約

【有効期間】 the term of validity

この切符の有効期間[期限]は7日間だ。

This ticket is valid for seven days.

このクーポンの有効期間は今月中だ。(今月のうちに使用しなければならない)

The coupons must be used [redeemed] within this month.

〈注〉 valid は「サービスを受けられる」という意味。賞品を受け取る(お年玉年賀はがきなど)ことができるという意味では redeem を使う。
The coupons must be redeemed within this month. (クーポンの賞品引替えは今月中)
available は「入手できる」の意味で，The ticket is available for seven days. (7日間に限り切符発売)のように使う。

【賃貸借期間】 the period of leasing

私たちはアパートを期間3か月の契約で借りた。

We rented an apartment on a three-month lease.

The term of the lease is three months.

〈注〉 a term of the lease とすると，賃借の「条件」の意味にもとれる。

【償還期間】

the period of repayment (of loans)

〈注〉 loans はお金にかかわることであるから repay と言えるが，lease は契約のことであるから ×The lease is repaid. とは言わない。

【期限が切れる[過ぎる]】

この切符は通用期間を過ぎている。

This ticket has [is] expired.

(契約)期間が切れた。

The term has expired.

支払い期限が過ぎてしまった。

This is overdue.

2. 行事

大売出しの期間中は半額にてご奉仕します。

During the sale all goods will be sold at half price [at a 50% discount].

ききめ (効き目) → こうか

きぎょう (企業) → かいしゃ

1. 会社

an enterprise; a company; a corporation

【中小企業】a minor [small] firm

【大企業】

a large / a vast / a giant { enterprise 企業体 / company 会社一般 / corporation 法人 }

a big business

〈注〉 big business (冠詞のない形) は大企業のもつ力, 善かれ悪しかれその影響力なども含めた見方をもつ語。

複合企業 conglomerate (多くの子会社を抱えた大企業)

多国籍企業 multinational corporation

XY 有限会社

XY Inc.〔米〕(incorporated の略)

XY Co., Ltd.〔英〕(company limited の略)

2. 商工業

【企業化する】industrialize

〈注〉 commercialize も企業化し商業ベースに乗せることであるが, 品質を落し金もうけ主義に走るような連想を伴うので, 文中の前後関係がはっきりしていないと悪い意味にとられやすい。またよく使われる慣用表現に to go commercial がある。これはそれまで趣味でやっていたものを商売にすること。

果実収穫機の発達のおかげで果樹栽培の企業化が達成された。

The development of fruit-picking machines has allowed the industrialization of fruit-growing.

クリスマスはこのところすっかり商業化されてしまった。

Christmas is now terribly commercialized.

きく (聞く)・きこえる

1. 耳にする

hear

彼女がショパンを弾いているのを一度聞いたことがある。

I heard her play Chopin once.

ブラックバードが鳴いているのが聞えた。

I heard blackbirds singing.

ラジオなんか聴きながら宿題ができるわけがない。

How can you do your homework with the radio playing?

(人から)ジョーンズさんは近々日本を去られると聞いた。

I heard that Mr. Jones is leaving Japan soon.

【聞かされる】

その辺の島でたくさんの人が餓死したと, よく父に聞かされた。

My father used to tell me that many people had starved to death on those islands.

私は久々に彼に会ってそのことを聞かされた[聞いた]。

I met him after a long time and was told about it.

〈注〉 「聞いた」も「聞かされた」も後者にやや迷惑感があるだけで大差はない。うっかり受身にして ×I was heard. などとしないように。be heard は次の場合は使えるが意味が違う。

He was heard to murmur. (彼が何か小声でぶつぶつ言うのが聞えた)

「聞えた」のであって「聞かされた」のではない。

I was told that ... は第三者から私が改まってはっきりと聞かされる場合。 They told me that ... はもっと気軽に聞かされる場合。I heard that ...; I learned (from him) that ... は「…と聞いた」の

意。

【消息を】hear of

私はあれ以来彼のことは聞いたことがない。

I have never heard of him since.

2. 傾聴する

listen

私の話をよく聞いてください。

Please listen to me carefully.

私は一度コンサートで彼女のショパンをじっくり聞いた。

I once listened to her play Chopin at a concert.

大学であの先生の講義を聞きました。

I took his class at college.

3. 尋ねる

ask

私は彼女に(万事)うまくいっているかと聞いた。

I asked her if everything was going all right.

彼は私に銀行への道を聞いた。

He asked me the way to the bank.

〈注〉「尋ねる」の意味での「聞く」だから,「道を聞かれた」を ×I was heard the way … としては間違い。I was asked … または,尋ねた人を主語に He asked me … とする。

4. 受け入れる,従う

【言うことを】

彼の言うことを聞いて朝早く出発した。

I followed his suggestion and started early.

【願いを】

父さんはとうとう私の願いを聞いて小遣いを値上げしてくれた。

My father was at last persuaded to increase my pocket money.

5. 聞かない

【言い張る】

みんなでそれは危険だと止めたのに,彼はどうしてもひとりで行くと言って聞かない。

We all say it will be dangerous, but he still {insists on / persists in} going alone.

【反抗】

その子は親の言うことを聞かなかった。

The boy didn't obey [listen to] his parents.

6. 聞える

このあたりは静かで,どこか遠くの村の教会の鐘の音が聞える。

The neighborhood is very quiet and the church bells can be heard ringing from some distant village.

ここではいろいろな小鳥の鳴き声が聞える。

We can hear so many birds here.

〈注〉 hear は意識的に聞こうとしなくても耳に入ってくる意味も含めて一般に聞くこと。上の例文の場合は日本語の「聞える」に当る。listen は聞こうとして耳を傾けること。

He likes listening to birds. (彼は鳥の声を聞くのが好きだ)

I heard her play Chopin. (偶然聞いたのかも知れない)

I listened to her play Chopin. (じっと傾聴した)

I went to Rubinstein's concert to hear him play Chopin. (ルービンシュタインのショパンを聞きに行った)

この場合,コンサートにわざわざ行ったのだから「傾聴した」とするのが当然だが,普通 hear を使う。

【ひびく】

能動態で書いてごらん。そう,その方が自然に聞える。

Write the sentence in active voice. Ah, that's better. That sounds more natural.

きく(効く)

have an effect; be effective; do 《a person》 **good; work**

1. 効能

この錠剤はかぜに効く。

These pills are good for colds.

【よく効く】
この薬はたいへんよく[驚くほど]効く。
This medicine is very effective.
The medicine works {like magic [a charm]. / wonders.}

【効かない】
この薬は私にはいっこうに効かない[効かなかった]。
This drug didn't do (me) any good.
This drug didn't help me at all.
The drugs were useless.

2. 本来の働き

【ブレーキが】
ブレーキがきかなかった。
The brake didn't work.
The brake failed.

【手足が】
彼は事故で両足[手]がきかなくなった。
He lost the use of both (his) legs [hands] because of the accident.

【左きき】a left-handed person; a left-hander

【味】
このスープは塩味がきいている。
This soup is salty.

3. できる，できない

【修理が】
彼の車は修理がきかないほど壊れた。
His car was damaged beyond repair.

【洗濯が】
この布は洗濯がきく[きかない]。
This material washes [doesn't wash] well.

【融通がきかない】inflexible; rigid

4. 悪影響が出る

tell on

【過労が】
彼はこのところすごく怒りっぽい。過労はきくからね。
He's been quite short-tempered recently. Overwork tells upon [on] a person.

【酷使】
ひどい乗り方をすれば車にきいてくる。(ついには乗りつぶしてしまう)
Hard driving {tells on / wears down} a car eventually.

【無理が】
彼も年だから無理がきかない。
He's too old to {push [exert] himself. / work so hard.}

きげん（機嫌）→ きぶん

1. 気分

【機嫌が良い】
be in good spirits [humor]
be in a good mood

【機嫌が悪い】
be in bad humor
be in a bad mood [an ugly mood]
be cross [sulky]

【機嫌をとる】
be anxious [eager] to please

【機嫌を損じる[損なう]】
offend《a person》
hurt a person's feelings

〈注〉「機嫌が悪い」は，be in bad temper よりは上の言い方の方が一般的。be in a temper は怒っていること。また，bad-tempered となるとそのときの気分ではなく，性質に関する形容詞で「性質が良くない」ことである。

彼のご機嫌はどうでしたか。
What was his frame of mind?

2. 挨拶

ご機嫌はいかがですか。
How are you?

きず（傷）・きずつく・きずつける → けが

1. 身体の傷

an injury（事故などの）; **a wound**（戦傷など）; 切り傷 **a cut;** 打撲傷 **a bruise**

《類義語》
be [get] injured　やや形式ばった語。事故(スポーツ・自動車事故)などでけがをする。病院で手当を受けねばならないけがの場合。
be wounded　戦争などで故意に傷つけられる場合。
be [get] hurt　広く一般的に使われる。injured と同じ程度かもっと軽い場合にも用いられ，精神的痛手を受ける意味にも用いられる。また hurt は，It hurts (me). のように「痛む」意にも使われる。

【けが】
彼はけがをした。
He was [got] injured.
He was [got] hurt.
〈注〉「傷」をもっと具体的にすると，
He fell down some steps (階段から足を踏みはずし)
and bruised his leg. (打撲傷を負った)
sprained his ankle. (ねんざした)
broke his leg. (骨折した)
was all black and blue. (青あざだらけになった)

彼は足にけがをした。
His leg was [got] injured.
His leg was hurt.
His leg was wounded.
〈注〉He wounded his leg. は「故意に傷つけた」の意味にもとれるがまれである。
He injured his leg.
He hurt his leg. (自分で何か不注意で足にけがをした)
〈注〉「彼はプライドを傷つけられた」は His pride was hurt. であって，×He was hurt his pride. とは言えない。hurt は give のように二重目的語をとることができないからである。(cf. He was given some money.)

【傷跡】a scar
男は左頬に切り傷の跡があった。
The man had a scar on his left cheek.

2．欠点
a fault; a defect; a flaw
あの子は頭がよくて，かわいくて，ただ背の低いのが玉にきずだ。
She's intelligent and pretty; her only flaw is that she's too short.

3．品物の傷
a flaw; ひび **a crack; a bruise** (果物の); しみ **a stain**
【傷をつける】
だめにする　動 mar, ruin, spoil
(家名などに)disgrace, bring disgrace upon
彼は家名を傷つけた。
He brought disgrace upon [on] his family.

ぎせいご(擬声語)・ぎたいご(擬態語)

1．人間に関する音・声
【笑い】
にこにこ，にっこりする　smile 名動
にやり，にたりと笑う　grin 名動
くすくす笑う　giggle 動名 (主に子供や女性)
ウフフと笑う　chuckle 動名 (男性)
ハッハと笑う　laugh 動名
【泣く】
一般的，また声を上げて泣く　cry 動名
しくしく泣く(すすり上げる)　sob 動名
(赤ん坊などが)ギャーギャー泣く　scream 動名
むずかる　fret 動
【うなり声】うーんとうなる　groan 動名
【呼吸】
はあはあ言う　gasp 動名
ぜいぜい[ひーひー]言う　wheeze 動名
【不平】
ぶつぶつ[ぶうぶう]言う　complain 動
【叱責】
がみがみ言う　nag at《a person》
【たたく音】
ピシャリとたたく　slap 動名
ドンドンとたたく　bang, thump 動名
トントン[ポン]とたたく　tap 動名
【走り過ぎる音】

ヒューッと走り過ぎる
whiz past ... 動, fizz 名動
【動作】
のろのろ[ゆっくり]と　slowly
きびきびと　briskly
こそこそと　sneakily; sneak 動
そわそわと　nervously
いそいそと(出かける)
happily; lightheartedly; cheerfully
【跳躍】
ぴょんぴょん(と跳ぶ)　leap, jump 動名
【醜態】
ぐでんぐでんに酔う　be dead drunk
よたよた[よろよろ]歩く(千鳥足)
wobble, reel, stagger
walk with an unsteady gait
【ふらふらする】
頭がふらふらする。
My head is swimming.
I feel dizzy.
【ふらふらする】
(決断できない) waver
【うきうき[いそいそ]する】
be cheerful; be in high spirits
家に帰るかと思うと心がうきうきした。
I felt elated as I started for home.
【わくわくする】be excited (over, with)
初めてのデートでわくわくしていた。
She was excited {because it was / over} her first date.
【しんみり】
その夜は夜ふけまでしんみりと語り合った。
We had a heart to heart talk till the small hours of the morning.
彼の物語にしんみりと聞き入った。
We quietly listened to his story, which was very moving.
【かんかんになる】
その知らせを聞いて彼はかんかんに怒った。
He got furious at the news.
【いらいらする】
彼にはいつもいらいらさせられる。
He always irritates us.
〈注〉 英語で本当に感じを出したいなら，その場その場でふさわしい音をつくって表現することが望ましい。
ex. "Bam, bam, he hit the table."
"Boom [Bam]. Away he went, ..."
【肉体的痛み】
ちくちく，ちくりと痛む prick, prickle 名動
しくしく，ひりひり痛む smart 名動
きりきりした
{痛み　nagging ache / 胃痛　a stabbing stomach pain}
がんがんする頭痛　a splitting headache

2．事物の音
【時計】
チクタク　tick-tock
【乗物】
ガタガタ走る　rattle along
蒸気機関車がシュッシュッポッポとあえぎながら走り続けた。
A puffing locomotive slowly chugged along.
【鈴】
リンリンなる　ting-a-ling
【電話】
リンリン　ring 名動
【鐘】(日本の鐘(gong)のように低音ではない)
ディン，ドン　ding-dong, ding-dong
カラン，カラン　clang, clang
【どさっ】
彼はナップサックをどさっと降した。
He threw down his knapsack with a thud.
【ガシャン，カチャン】a crash (粉砕する音)
【ブーン】
a boom (砲弾などが飛ぶ音，倒れる音)
【カチン】a clatter (硬いものが触れ合う音)
【カタカタ】
台所で食器がカタカタと触れ合う音が聞えた。
I heard the clatter of dishes in the kitchen.

【ガタガタ】rattle 名動
【バタン，ガタン】bang 名動
ドアがバタンと閉った。
The door slammed shut with a bang.
彼はバタンとドアを閉めた。
He banged the door shut.

3．自然界の音

【ぽたぽた】
レインコートから水がぽたぽたしたたり落ちていた。
Water was dripping from his raincoat.
【ちょろちょろ】
ビールを冷やすために水をちょろちょろ出しておきなさい。
Keep the water trickling to cool the beer.
【さらさら】
家の前には小川がさらさら流れていた。
There was a little stream murmuring in front of the house.
【ごうごう】
川は渦を巻いてごうごうと流れた。
The turbulent river made a great roaring sound.
【しとしと】
雨がしとしと降っていた。
It was raining gently.
【ぴかり，ドンゴロゴロ，ザアザア】
急にあたりが暗くなり，ぴかっと稲妻が走り，ドンゴロゴロと雷鳴が続き，次の瞬間ザーッと雨が降ってきた。
It got suddenly dark, lightning flashed, thunder clapped and the next moment the rain came pouring down.
遠くで雷がゴロゴロいっている。
There's thunder rolling in the distance.
【そよそよ】
風がそよそよ吹いていた。
There was a gentle breeze.
【ざわざわ】
松にざわざわ[ごうごう]と風が鳴った。
The wind rustled [whistled] among the pines.
【さっ】
一陣の風がさっと吹きわたった。
There was a gust of wind.
〈注〉 音を表した言葉は echoic words と呼ぶ。
【ぽとり，ぽとん】（落下音）
熟柿がぽとんと落ちた。
A ripe persimmon fell with a plop [thud, thump].
【光】
ぼおっと光る　gleam
ぼおっと輝く　glow
きらきら輝く　twinkle
ぎらぎら光る　glare
ぱっと光る　flash

4．動物の鳴き声

〈注〉 動物には，犬，猫に示すようにいろいろな鳴き方があるがここでは代表的な鳴き声のみ記す。
【犬の仲間・オオカミ・コヨーテ】
ワンワン鳴く
bark, yap（けたたましくほえる）
キャンキャン鳴く　yelp, yip
ワォーとうなる　bay, howl, wail, yowl
ウーとうなる　snarl, growl
くんくん鳴く　whine
【猫】
ニャーと鳴く　mew, mewl, meow〔米〕
ギャオギャオ　hiss, squall
アオーアワー　caterwaul（発情期の声）
ゴロゴロのどを鳴らす　purr
【牛】
モーと鳴く　moo, low
子牛[子馬]が鼻を鳴らす；大声で鳴く
bawl /bɔ́ːl/
【馬】
ヒヒンと鳴く　neigh, nicker, whinny
鼻をならす　snort
【豚】
ブウブウと鳴く　grunt, oink
鼻を鳴らす snort
【鳥】

小鳥がさえずっている。
Birds are singing.
チッチッと鳴く　twitter
チュンチュンと鳴く　chirp, cheep
【ニワトリ】
雌鶏がコッコッコッと鳴く　cluck, cackle
雄鶏がコケコッコと鳴く　crow
〈注〉 擬音として鳴き声を cock-a-doodle-do と表現することもある。
【その他の動物の鳴き声】
ロバ　bray; 羊　bleat
ネズミ　squeak; ライオン・トラ　roar
熊　growl; 象　trumpet
ハト　coo; カラス　caw
アヒル　quack; 七面鳥　gobble
ガチョウ　quack, gobble, hiss
ガン　honk; フクロウ　hoot
〈注〉 小鳥がさえずるのは上述以外にもその声に似せた warble, pipe, whistle, trill, squawk などが用いられる。また，動物でも鳥でも高い鋭い声で鳴くのは scream, screech などが使われる。
ミツバチ，ハエ　buzz; コオロギ　chirp
カエル　croak

きだて（気立て）→ せいしつ・せいかく

【気立てがいい】
good-natured; good-tempered
【気立てが優しい】
哀れみ深い　tender-hearted; soft-hearted（「甘い」に近い）; 親切な　warm-hearted; kind-hearted

きたない（汚い）

1．不潔な

dirty（↔clean）
ほこりっぽい　**dusty**
ひどく不潔な　**filthy**（↔spotless）
きたないシャツ[手]
a dirty shirt [hand]
〈注〉 dirty は本当に汚いこと。それほどでないが人前に出るのがはばかられる程度の服装ならば not clean でよい。

その人は汚い[みすぼらしい]身なりをしていた。
The man was shabbily dressed.

2．散らかっている

messy（↔neat）
【部屋】
台所も居間も汚かった。
The kitchen and the living room looked [were] dirty and disorderly.
【ゴミで】
こんなに美しい観光地がゴミで汚らしくなってるなんてまったくひどい。
What a pity those scenic places { had trash everywhere! / were strewn with trash!〔*literary*〕}

3．卑しい

mean; foul; 公正を欠く **unfair; stingy**（金銭的に）**; nasty**
【お金に】
彼は金に汚い。
He is { nasty in [over] money matters. / mean with money. }
He's stingy.
【汚い手】
そいつは汚い手だ。（卑劣な手段）
That was a dirty [mean, nasty] trick.
政治家はよく汚い手を使うと非難される。
Politicians are often accused of (using) dirty tricks.
ビリーは汚い手で勝った。
Billy won by foul play.

4．下手な

【字が汚い】
あの人は字が汚くて[下手で]よく読めない。
His (hand) writing [penmanship] is so bad it's almost illegible.
〈注〉 「字」のつもりで letters とすると「手紙」の意味にとられる。

ぎちょう（議長）→ しかい

きちんと → ちゃんと

1．人柄

彼女はきちんとした老婦人だ。

She is a prim old lady.

あれはきちんとした若者だ。服装も言葉づかいもきちんとしている。

He's a proper young man. He's neatly dressed and talks politely.

あいつはきちんとしたやつだ。

He's all right. 〔*colloq.*〕

2．状態

【清潔】

彼はいつもきちんとした服装をしている。

He is always neatly dressed.

【適切】

式に出る時はきちんとした服装で行かねばならない。

When you attend ceremonies, you should be suitably dressed.

【整然とする】

tidy; put to rights; straighten up

部屋はいつもきちんとしておきなさい。

Keep your room in good order.

部屋をきちんと片付けなさい。

Tidy (up) your room. / Put your room to rights. / Pick your room up. / Straighten (up) your room. / Put everything away.

〈注〉 Things were not {in their places. / where they usually are [were].}

きちんと片付いていない。(物がいつもの場所に収まっていない)

3．行動

【時間】

彼はいつもきちんと(約束の)時間に来る。

He always comes on time.

彼はきちんと(約束の)時間に到着した。

He got there right on time.

彼はきちんと１時ぴったりに現れた。

He appeared at one o'clock sharp [at exactly one o'clock, right at one (o'clock), at one on the dot].

【期日】

彼は家賃を毎月きちんと期日までに納めている。

He pays the rent regularly and on time.

【計算】

うちの子は足し算がちゃんとできるようになった。

My boy has learned {to do sums / to add} accurately.

彼の計算がきちんとできていなかったばかりに小切手帳の収支が合わなかった。

His checkbook didn't balance simply because he hadn't added accurately [correctly].

4．その他

【念入りに】

部屋をきちんと掃除しなさい。

Clean your room thoroughly.

本を全部きちんと片付けなさい。

Put all your books away.

靴をきちんと磨きなさい。

Polish your boots carefully.

〈注〉 「きちんとした」はほめ言葉であるが，scrupulous は几帳面すぎて堅苦しいイメージがあり，たいていの場合悪い意味で使われる。

Such a scrupulous person is hard to live with.
(あんな几帳面な人と一緒に住んだら息が詰る)

きづく（気づく）

1．気づく

財布を開けてみて，お金がなくなっていることに気づいた。

When I opened my purse, I found [noticed] all my money was gone.

まもなく私はそばに若い女の子が立っている

のに気づいた。

Soon I {became conscious [aware] of / noticed} a young girl standing beside me.

彼は本能的に危険[異変]に気づいた。

He instinctively sensed {danger. / that something was wrong.}

2. 気づかない

だれも彼が出て行くのに気づかなかった。

No one noticed him go out [leave].

彼はだれにも気づかれずに出て行った。

He went out {without anyone noticing. / unnoticed. / without being noticed.}

【動作と状態】

彼は私に気づかないで通り過ぎて行った。

He passed by without noticing me.

彼は私に気づいていなかった。(状態)

He wasn't aware of me.

【心に】

彼は妻が，ひどく孤独な日々を送っていたなどとは打ち明けられるまで全然気づいていなかった。

He didn't realize that she had been leading a terribly lonely life until she told him.

【意識】

まだ夢うつつであったが，彼が私のベッドのそばにいることはおぼろ気に気づいていた。

Although half asleep, I was dimly {aware of / conscious of} his presence by [at] my bedside.

きっと

1. 未来に関する確実性

形 **sure; certain;** 副 **surely; certainly**

〈注〉 だいたい交換可能であるが，certain はより客観的，sure はより主観的。

彼はきっと来る。

Undoubtedly he'll come.

He's sure to come.

I'm sure he'll come.

He'll surely come.

彼は次の列車できっと来る。

It is certain [definite] that he'll arrive on the next train.

〈注〉 sure の用法に He's sure of his success. (＝He's sure he'll succeed.) の形もあるが，堅いのであまり使われない。It is sure (that) ... の形は口語で実際に使われているが不可とする人が多い。It is certain that ... はやや形式ばった言い方だが無難。

【きっと…してくれ】

明日きっと来てくれ。

Be sure to come tomorrow.

〈注〉 上記のような依頼に答える言い方の「きっと…します」「まかしといて」などは次のように言う。I'll be sure to. / Depend on it. / Count on it. You can depend [count] on it [me]. / Sure.

きっと6時に起して。

{Don't forget / Be sure} to wake me up at six.

〈注〉 Never fail to wake me up at six. / Wake me up at six without fail. などは英国で使われるが，古いと感じる人が多い。上述の表現などを使うのが無難。

きっと[ぜひ]来てくださいね。

Please come to see us by all means.

明日はきっと伺います。

I'll definitely come to see you tomorrow.

〈注〉 英国では「きっと来てください」といった招きには by all means を使うが，「きっと行きます」と確約するのには使わない。米語でも主として招きに使い，その他は上述の例文のような表現が普通。

2. 過去についての推測

彼女は昔はきっと美人だったろう。

She must have been a beauty in her day.

だれもうちから迎えに来ていないのを見てきっとがっかりしただろう。

He must have been disappointed when he saw no one at the airport to welcome him home.

きにいる（気に入る）→ き

［人主語］**be pleased with; be happy with; like**
［対象，物主語］**please; satisfy**

1．気に入る
今あなたのセーターを編んでいるの。気に入ってもらえるといいんだけど。
I'm now knitting a sweater for you. I hope you'll {like it. / be pleased with it.}
彼は新しい家が気に入っているようだ。
He seems to {like / be pleased with} his new house.
新しい計画は皆の気に入った。
The new plan satisfied everybody.
みんなが気に入るというわけにはなかなかいかない。
It is hard to please [suit, satisfy] everybody.

2．気に入らない
彼は新任の助手があまり気に入っていない。事務処理がてきぱきできないのだ。
He's not very happy [pleased] with his new assistant; she's not good enough at office management.
お前の成績[成果]は気に入らない。(不満だ)
I'm not at all pleased [satisfied] with your result.

3．好きになる →すき
彼はその踊り子がひとめで気に入ってしまい，公演のたびに見に行った。
He took a liking to the dancer and attended every performance.
彼はその絵がすっかり気に入ってしまった。
That picture caught [took, struck] his fancy.

4．お気に入りの
これは私のお気に入りだ[これが一番気に入っている]。
This is {my favorite. / the one I like best.}
This suits me best [the most].（衣服・絵画・色・ヘアスタイルなどの好みに関して）
赤がお気に入りの色だ。
Red appeals to me.
I like red.

きのどく（気の毒）→ かわいそう

1．客観的叙述
【気の毒に思う】 feel sorry for
彼は気の毒に思って老人にいくらか金をやった。
He gave the old man some money out of compassion [sympathy].
Feeling sorry for the old man, he gave him some money.
【気の毒にも】
気の毒なことにその人は全財産を失ってしまった。
The wretched man lost all his property.
【気の毒だ】
また引っ越しとは気の毒だな。
It's a pity they have to move again.
〈注〉 It's a pity … は軽い気持ちである。

2．主観的叙述
【直接相手に】
お気の毒に！
I'm sorry about that.
〈注〉 I'm sorry.（お気の毒に）がもっとも一般的な同情を表す表現である。ただし，I'm sorry for you. は皮肉にひびくことがあるので for you はつけない方がよい。
まあ，お気の毒に！(軽く相手を慰める)
Too bad!
What a pity!
That's too bad!
(cf. Oh, you poor thing.〔英〕子供などに)
本当にお気の毒でしたね[いけませんでしたね]。

It must have been awful [terrible, trying] for you.

How awful [terrible, unfortunate]!

【第三者に関して】

全財産をなくすなんてまったくお気の毒な。

How awful (that) he's lost all his property!

奥さんを亡くしてなんてお気の毒なんでしょう。

Wasn't it sad [dreadful] that he lost his wife?

気の毒に，ウィリアムはまた騒々しい大都会に帰って行くのね。

Poor William, going back to the din and bustle of the big city.

きびしい（厳しい）

《類義語》

severe　決められたことを厳格に守り，妥協を許さない。

stern　情け容赦せず断固としている。

strict　規律などを厳正忠実に守る。

austere　感情を表に出さずに冷たく厳しい。

harsh　とげとげしく手厳しい。

rigid　堅くて融通がきかない。

rigorous　厳格で妥協せず苛酷である。

1. 人に対して

【厳しい先生】a strict teacher

彼は教室では厳しいが，いったん教室を出ると親しみやすい先生だった。

He was strict [rigorous] in class but outside class he was quite friendly.

【厳しい人】

私の祖父は自分の子供たちには厳しかったが，孫の私たちには厳しくなかった。

My grandfather was harsh [severe] with his children but not so with us grandchildren.

子供たちをそんなに厳しく罰しないで。

Don't punish the children so harshly [severely].

そんなにあの人に厳しくしないで。

Don't be so harsh on [with] him.

先生は生徒の書く文章に関しては厳しかった。

He was very exacting about the students' writing.

先生は点[評価]が厳しかった。（辛かった）

He was strict [severe] about [in] marking.

2. 規則が

あの学校は規則が厳しい。

That school has strict regulations.

新しい校長が来てから規則が厳しくなった。

The regulations have been tightened up since the new head was appointed.

3. その他

厳しい人柄　a rigid personality

厳しい顔　a stern face

厳しい罰　a stiff penalty

厳しい現実[人生]

stern [harsh] reality [an austere life]

厳しい暑さ[寒さ / 冬]

intense heat [severe cold / a hard winter]

きふ（寄付）

名 **contribution; donation; endowment; subscription**

動 **contribute; donate; subscribe; endow**

【寄付する】

共同募金に寄付する

contribute to the community chest

cf. contribute food for the homeless（ホームレスに食糧を提供する）

赤十字に寄付をする

donate money to the Red Cross

同窓会基金に寄付をする

subscribe to the alumni fund

〈注〉 subscribe とは書類の下に署名して寄付の申し込みをすること，寄付の約束をすること。

【寄付を募る】

make [take up] a subscription

raise money from《companies》

【寄付を求める】ask for a contribution

視覚障害児救済のためにライトハウスあてに10ドルの善意のご寄付をよろしくお願いいたします。

We're appealing to you to send a voluntary contribution of $10 to the Light House to help visually handicapped children.

【寄付を集める】collect contributions

【寄付者】a donor; contributor

《類義語》

subscription　寄付の申し込み，雑誌などの購読予約。

contribution　寄付一般。

donation　慈善事業や非営利的事業への寄付。

endowment　公共施設・個人への基金の寄贈。

きぶん(気分) → かんじ, きげん, きもち

1．体調

今朝は気分はいかがですか。

How are you [How do you feel] this morning?

気分はいい方だ。

I feel { rather [pretty] good. / better.

気分はあまり良くない。

I don't feel so well.

I don't feel very good.

気分が悪い[吐き気がする]。

I feel sick.

2．気持ち

気分は上々だ。

I feel great [fine].

【気分を損ねる】

hurt one's feelings; ［受動］be hurt

私たちは彼女の気分を損ねてしまった。

We've hurt her feelings.

あの子は気分を害してしまった。

She's hurt.

【…な気分】

私は泣きたい気分だ。

I feel like crying.

3．ムード

【…な気分】

歌でも歌いたい気分だ。

I feel like singing.

パーティーの[料理をしたい]気分だ。

I'm in a party(ing) [cooking] mood.

桜の咲いているあいだは，町中がお祭り気分だった。

The whole town was in a festive mood while the cherry blossoms were in bloom.

【気分を出す，気分が出る】

明りを消してろうそくつけて，ロマンチックな気分を出そう。

Let's have candles instead of lights to create a romantic atmosphere.

雪がなくちゃクリスマスの気分が出ない。

It's not like Christmas without any snow.

It doesn't feel like Christmas when there's no snow.

4．気まぐれ

【気分屋】a whimsical person

彼女はどうも気分屋だ。

She tends to be moody.

【気分転換】

気分転換に散歩に行くといい。

Why don't you take a break and go for a walk?

たまには気分転換に映画でも見るといい。

You should go to the movies for a change.

【気分が変る】

彼の気分が変るまで待ちなさい。

Wait till he's in a different frame of mind.

彼女はその時その時でくるくる気分が変る。

She changes according to the mood of the moment.

【気分にならない】

彼女は冗談なんか言う気分ではない。

She's in no mood { for joking. / to joke. }

She doesn't feel like joking.

【いい気分】

彼がいい気分になっている［ご機嫌がいい］，今のうちに頼んでごらん。

Ask him now, while he's in a { good mood. / happy frame of mind. }

cf. Don't ask him now, he's in a strange frame of mind.（今頼むのはまずいよ，御機嫌がよくないから）

きぼう（希望）

a hope; a desire; a wish; 大きな望み **an ambition**

1．望ましい見込み

【希望を持つ，希望する】

彼の父は，自分と同様に彼も法律家になるよう希望している。

His father hopes he'll be a lawyer like himself.

「大きな希望を持つこと」こそ私が若者に期待することだ。

"To have ambition" is what I expect of young people.

【希望通り】

息子の卒業までは万事彼の希望通りにいったかに見えた。

Everything seemed to go as he wished [wanted, hoped] until his son's graduation.

【希望に反して】

彼の希望に反して［とは逆に］彼の息子は突然俳優になると宣言した。

Contrary to his hopes [wishes] his son suddenly declared that he would become an actor.

事は彼の希望通りにはいかなかった。

It did not turn out as he had hoped [wished].

2．夢

【希望に燃える】

彼の前に横たわるあらゆる可能性を思って，彼の心は希望に燃えていた。

His heart was full of hope as he thought of the thousands of possibilities that lay before him.

【希望を実現する】

彼はついに希望を実現した。

He at last realized his hopes.

His wishes at last came true.

【希望を失う】

彼はすべての希望を失った。

All his hopes were gone.

【…の希望がない】

それはまったく実現の希望がない。

It's completely [utterly] hopeless.

〈注〉 hope は実現の可能性の感じられることについての希望。wish は難しいと感じつつもこうありたいとの思い。desire は形式ばった語で強い希望を表す。以下，hope, wish の使い方を比較する。

I { hope { to be / (that) I'll be } / wish { to be / (that) I'd be } } better at English.

（英語が上手に { なりたい / なれたらなあ } と思う）

I { hope (that) he'll / wish (that) he'd } try once more.

（彼がもう一度やって { みるといい / みればいいのに } と思う）

△I wish him to try once more. は正しい文だが，堅い表現なので上述の方がよい。

3．選択

【希望の】

彼は自分の希望の大学に受かった。

He passed the entrance examination for the university he wished to enter.

うちの10代の息子は幸いにも希望の大学に入れた。

Our teen-age son happily has been admitted to the college of his choice.

彼は希望の大手商社に入社できた。

He was able to get a job in the big trading company he had wanted to work for.
彼はずっと希望していた東海オーケストラに入ることができた。
He was accepted into the Tokai Orchestra, which { he has always wanted to be in. / he had been hoping to join. }

【希望で】
彼は彼女の希望[都合]でデートを延期した。
He put off the date at her desire.

【希望的観測】
それは希望的観測にすぎない。
That's just wishful thinking.

きまりがわるい(決りが悪い) → はずかしい

きまる（決まる） → きめる

きみがわるい(気味が悪い) →ぞっとする,こわい

1．無気味なもの

気味の悪い光景　a weird scene
気味の悪い微笑　an eerie smile
気味の悪い物語　a creepy [scary] story

2．無気味なものに対する反応

［事物主語］**be scary; be frightening**
動 **scare, frighten**
［人主語］**be scared; be frightened**
夜，墓地のそばを通るのは気味が悪い。
{ I am scared / It scares me / It's scary } to pass by the graveyard at night.

3．いやな予感

このところ変に暖かい日が続く。地震でもありそうで気味が悪い。
It has been unusually [unnaturally] hot these days. I feel nervous [uneasy], as if there's going to be an earthquake or something.

ぎむ（義務）

obligation; duty; responsibility

1．義務である（法律的）

【義務教育】compulsory education
中学は義務教育である。
Junior high school (education) is obligatory [compulsory, required].
親たる者は子供にきちんとした教育を受けさせる義務がある。
It is { a duty [an obligation] of parents / the parents' responsibility } to give their children a good education.

【納税の義務】
obligation to pay taxes
すべての国民に納税の義務がある。
All adult citizens are obliged to pay taxes.

【兵役の義務】
韓国ではすべての男子は18歳で兵役につく義務がある。
In the Republic of Korea all men are liable to military service at 18.
身体障害者は兵役につく義務が免ぜられる。
The handicapped are exempt from military service.
日本では今は兵役の義務はない。
In Japan now we have no military service.

【選挙の義務】
１票を投ずることは我々の権利であると同時に義務でもある。
Voting is our duty [obligation] as well as our right.

2．義務がある，義務を果す（道徳的・社会的）

【義務がある】
have an obligation [a duty]
我々には住みよい自然環境を後世の人々に伝えてゆく義務がある。
We surely have an obligation to pass on a habitable natural environment to future generations.

【義務を果す】

fulfill [meet] one's obligations（親・子・医師などとしての役割上の義務を果す。人に対する義務を果す）

do one's duties（一般的に義務を果す。具体的な任務を果す）

〈注〉 ex. duties of policemen [firemen, guards, doctors, nurses etc.]

obligation よりも duties の方が具体的任務が思い浮かぶ語である。on duty が「任務中である，当番である」の意であることからもわかるように，警官や守衛などの任務は duties がぴったりする。ただし duty という観念はもともと道徳的なものであるから一般的・抽象的にも用いられる。

【義務感がない】

彼には義務感がない。

He {has no / is lacking in a} sense of duty.

〈注〉 He has no sense of responsibility.（彼には責任感がない）

責任感と義務感はほとんど同じだが，duty と responsibility の意味は表と裏である。

【義務はない】

私には彼を助ける義務はない[彼を助けなければならない義理はない]。

I have [am under] no obligation to help him.

彼を助けるのは私の義務ではない。

He's not my responsibility.

It's not my responsibility to help him.

《類義語》

duty 道義感からくる絶えず心にかかる義務感および任務。

obligation 契約書などに明記された義務の条項(いつまでに何をするなど)のように特定された義務。

responsibility ある任務を引き受けた，または引き受けなければならないことを決意する内面的態度。

きめる（決める） → けっしん

1．決定・決断

〈注〉「決める」は人が主語であるから能動態。「決る」は事が主語であるから受動態になる。

【決める】

［人主語］decide, settle, fix, determine, make up one's mind; 合意する agree upon; come to an agreement

【決る】

［事主語］be decided, be settled, be fixed, be determined; 合意する be agreed upon

【決心する】

私は学費を稼ぐためパートで働くことに決めた。

I have decided to work part-time to earn my school expenses.

【決定する】

君の成功不成功は君の努力で決る。

Your success depends on your effort.

【議決する】

だれか動議を支持する者があればその件について討議し，最後に投票によって決める。(票決する)

If someone seconds a motion, they discuss it and finally determine the outcome by vote.

【募金を】

我々は彼を助けるため金を集めることに決めた[決った]。

We have decided [It has been decided] to collect some money to help him.

【日取りを】

彼女の結婚式は11月3日に決った。

Her wedding ceremony was {arranged / fixed〔米〕} for November 3rd.

【賃上げが】

賃上げが決った。

The wage increase has been determined [settled, agreed upon, decided (upon)].

【就職が】→しゅうしょく

彼の就職が決った[彼は就職を決めた]。

He has settled [decided] on《a certain company》.（会社の名をあげるのが普通）

He has found a position.

It's now clear [certain]
He knows now
} where he will work.

〈注〉 It has been decided where he will work. は正しい文だが，人まかせにしているように聞える。能動態の方が好ましい。

卒業後の就職先をまだ決めていない[がまだ決っていない]。

I haven't decided where I will work after graduation.

【条件が】

条件がまだ決っていない。

The terms are not yet agreed upon.

〈注〉 「重大なことを決める」には decide upon [on] が使われる。

He must { decide on his / settle on a } career.

(進路を決めなければならない)

2. 習慣

【…することに決めている】

make it a rule to do; make a point of … ～ing; … always《do so》

私は3時にお茶を飲むことに決めている。

I make a point of having tea at three.

I always have tea at three.

彼は毎晩ビールは2本までと決めている。

He limits himself to two bottles of beer a day.

〈注〉 make it a rule to do … は正しいが使いすぎるきらいがある。I always … が一番普通。

3. 確実・必然

【…に決っている】

be sure to; surely; certainly

彼が勝つに決っている。

He will surely [certainly] win.

He is sure [certain] to win.

〈注〉 sure, surely は主観的。certain は話者の主観以外に客観的データに基づいており，やや形式ばった語。definitely は確信100%。

あんな気立ての良い子はいない。あの子はきっと幸せになるに決っているわ。

Such a good-natured girl! I'm sure [certain] she'll be happy.

【決っていない】

何もまだ決っていない。

Nothing is certain [definite] yet.

【一定の】

彼女は決った収入がない。

She has no regular income.

きもち（気持ち）→ かんじ，きぶん

[名] **a feeling [feelings]; a sentiment; sensation**

〈注〉 気持ちを表現するには動詞 feel を活用するとよい。

1. 心地

【気持ちがいい】→いいきもち

気持ちいい風　a pleasant wind

気持ちがいい。

I feel great [fine].

猫が彼女の膝の上で気持ちよさそうだ。

The cat looks comfortable [cozy] on her lap.

〈注〉 pleasant は爽快であること，comfortable は居心地のいいこと。なお pleasant は「人にいい感じを与える」ことであるから，「私は気持ちがいい」を ×I am pleasant. とはしないこと。

気持ちが悪い。

I feel sick.（吐き気がする）

気持ちがよくない。

I don't feel very well [good].

2. 気分・心境

【気分】

人の気持ちを悪くするようなことは言ってはいけない。

Don't say anything that would hurt other people's feelings.

そんなこと人に話す気持ちにはなれない。

I am in no mood to talk to anyone about it.

泣きたい気持ちだった[気がした]。

I felt like crying.

【心境】

それが今の私の気持ちだ。

That is how I feel now.
だれも話し相手がいないときの(さびしい)気持ちが私にはわかる。
I know how it feels when one has no one to talk to.
貧乏がどんなものか私にはその気持ちがわかる。
I know what it feels like [it is] to be poor.

3．その他
【気持ちのいい人】
an agreeable [a pleasant] person
〈注〉 She has a pleasant smile for everyone.（だれにもにこにこと気持ちよく接する）
【気持ちよく】willingly, readily
彼はその会合でスピーチをすることを気持ちよく承諾してくれた。
He quite willingly consented to giving a short speech at the meeting.
父が私たちの結婚を気持ちよく許してくれるなんて思ってもみなかった。
We didn't expect that my father would approve of our marriage without making any difficulties.
【気持ちが悪い，気味が悪い】creepy
あの人，気持ちが悪いわ。（ぞっとする）
That man gives me the creeps.

きゃく（客）

1．訪問客
a visitor; a caller; a guest
【来客】
今日の午後来客がある。
We'll have a visitor this afternoon.
【泊り客】
今，泊り客があるの，１週間ほどだけど。
We have guests staying with us for a week.
〈注〉 2～3日の泊り客なら visitor でも guest でもよい。長い泊り客は普通 guest と言う。caller は短時間の訪問者。

2．招待客・特別の客
a guest; 主賓 **a guest of honor**
私たちは土曜日の夜，夕食に５人お客様をお呼びしました。
We've invited five dinner guests for Saturday night.
【客に呼ぶ】
メアリさんをお呼びして，うちでおもてなしすることにしている。
There'll be / We're giving [having] } a party for Mary at our house.
スミス夫妻をお客様としてお呼びする。
We're going to invite Mr. & Mrs. Smith.
〈注〉 文に書くときは，we や I を主語とせず間接的な書き方が好まれる。
Mr. & Mrs. Smith will be invited.

3．その他の客
商店の顧客　a customer
宿屋の客
a lodger; a paying guest〔英〕（a guest にはホテルの顧客の意味もある）
観光客
people visiting the town; sightseers
役者の(ひいき)客　a patron
劇や音楽会の客　the audience（集合的に）
乗客（電車・船・飛行機の）　a passenger
タクシーの客　a fare; a passenger
通勤客　commuters
弁護士，広告業者，旅行業者などの客
a client（長い付き合いのお得意関係）
【呼びかけ】
お客さん！
（女性に）Ma'am! / Madam!
（男性に）Sir! / Excuse me, Sir!
〈注〉 「おい，兄ちゃん」Hey, buddy!〔*colloq.*〕

ぎゃく（逆）

reverse; the opposite
【逆に】on [to] the contrary

【逆の方向に】
in [to] the opposite [reverse] direction

1．逆になる

風が逆方向から吹く[風向きが逆だ]。
The wind is blowing the wrong way.
我々の予想とは完全に逆の[正反対の]結果が出た。
The outcome was completely contrary to our expectations.〔*formal*〕
〈注〉 口語では We didn't expect that at all. でよい。
(彼を)あんまりせっつくのも逆効果になるだろう。
It will have the opposite effect if you urge him.
If you urge him, that'll make things [the matter] worse.
逆もまた真なり。
The reverse [opposite] is also true.

2．逆にする

順序を逆にする
reverse the order
上下を逆にする
turn upside down
表裏を逆にする　turn inside out
逆からやってごらん。
{Do it / Turn it} the {other way (a)round. / opposite way.}
1から20まで数えて，次に逆に20から1まで数えてごらん。
Count from one to twenty and then backwards to one.
シャツを前後逆[後ろ前]に着る
wear one's shirt {back to front / turned around / the wrong way round}
靴を左右逆にはく
wear shoes on the wrong feet
違うよ，(それは)話が逆だよ。
No, it's just the opposite.

キャリア

career

1．キャリアがある

彼女には技術者としての長いキャリアがある。
She was a technician for a very long time.
〈注〉 She had a long career as … は形式ばった表現であるし，外交官またはそれに類する高官の仕事を思わせる。

2．キャリアを持つ

私の夢は結婚しても続けられるキャリアを持つことだ。
My dream is to have a career {in which I can continue / which I can follow} after marriage.
〈注〉 ×I want to have a career which can work after marriage. (career が働くのではない)
career は次のように定義される。
1)特に専門的訓練を受け，生涯にわたって携わる仕事・職業。
He sought a career as a lawyer. (彼は法律家［弁護士］として身を立てようとした)
2)経歴(の中のある時期)。
She spent most of her career as a teacher in London. (彼女は生涯の大部分をロンドンで教師をして過した)
またこの英文は次のようにもとれる。
(彼女はその教師生活のほとんどをロンドンで過した)

きゅう（急）

1．時間

【緊急】
急な用事だ。
It's urgent business.
緊急に処理しなければならない。
This requires immediate attention.
【非常】
急の場合に備える
provide for an emergency

【突然】
彼の死は急だったので驚いた。
His sudden death surprised us.
階下の物音で急に目が覚めた。
Suddenly I was awakened by a noise downstairs.
急にいい考えが頭に浮かんだ。
All of a sudden I got an idea.
前方に猫を見つけ，急ブレーキをかけた。
Seeing a cat ahead of me I braked suddenly.

2. 空間

【急な坂】
彼の家は急な坂の上にあった。
His house was at the top of a steep slope.
【急カーブ】
その道路は急カーブが多い。
The road is full of sharp curves.
【急流】
川は前夜の雨で流れが急であった。
The river was running fast / The current was rapid } after the overnight rain.
〈注〉 running high とすれば，川が増水して流れが急なこと。

3. 慣用表現

【急を聞いて駆けつける】
父の病の急変を聞いて私たちは病院に駆けつけた。
Hearing that our father's illness had taken a sudden turn for the worse we all hurried to the hospital.
【急を救う】
会社がまさに倒産寸前というとき，彼が来て急場を救った。
He came to the rescue when the company was on the point of bankruptcy.
〈注〉 came to the rescue は急を聞いて救助に駆けつけることであるが，同時に救助に成功した含みがある。もし失敗したのなら，They attempted to rescue the company. などと言う。

【急を告げる】
2国関係はまさに風雲急を告げる状態になってきた。
The relations between the two countries are becoming more and more tense.

きゅうか（休暇）

vacation〔米〕; **holiday**〔英〕
【1か月の休暇をとる】
take a month's vacation [holiday]
【休暇で…へ行く】
休暇でスペインへ（3週間ほど）行く。
I'm going on holiday to Spain.〔英〕
I'm going to Spain for three weeks / I'm spending three weeks in Spain } for [on] vacation.〔米〕
（夏期）休暇はどこへ行きますか。
Where are you going for the vacation〔米〕 [your holidays〔英〕]?
【クリスマス休暇】
the (Christmas) holiday(s)
（子供たちは）クリスマス休暇で帰省している。
They're staying at home for the holidays.
The children came home for Christmas [the (Christmas) holidays].
【イースター休暇】(the) Easter holiday; (the) Easter weekend (Good Friday から Easter Monday まで)
イースター休みはどうしますか。
What are you going to do over Easter [the Easter weekend]?
〈注〉 holiday は1日だから a holiday，2日以上続くから holidays となるのではなく，慣用的に用法が決っている。
【有給休暇】
a vacation（有給なのは当然だから特に paid ～とは言わなくてよい）
paid personal holidays〔米〕(個人的な用件のための有給休暇)
paid leave　有給休暇
cf. sick leave（病欠）

僕の父は年20日有給休暇がとれる。

My father gets 20 days of paid vacation a year.

【有給休暇をとる】

take (a day) off

be on vacation [holiday]

明日は有休をとる。

I'll take tomorrow off.

I'll be off tomorrow.

来週は有休をとる。

I think I'll take {next week off.（1週間）/ a day off next week.（1日）}

I'm going on holiday next week.（どこかへ出かける）

あの人は今週有休をとって休んでいる。

He's {on vacation [holiday] / off} this week.

《関連語》

学校生活にかかわる休暇

欧米の学年は9月に始まり6月または7月初めに終る。

米国

【夏】 summer vacation

小・中・高　約6週間。学区により差がある。2期制・3期制・4期制がある。学年始めはふつう first Monday (Labor Day) の次の Tuesday in September

大　6月半ばから8月末まで休み(その間 summer school などがある)

【冬】 the Christmas holidays [vacation]

小・中・高　クリスマス・正月にかけて10日前後。Christman Eve, Christmas Day, New Year's Day を含み，クリスマス直前から元日の直後まで

大　12月半ばから約1か月

【春】 spring holiday [break]

Easter Break（復活祭休み）

Plam Sunday(シュロの聖日；Easter 直前の日曜日)から Easter までの1週間を Holy Week という。平日は小中高は休みではないが，Good Friday(キリスト受難日)は半日休み，土日(この日曜日を Easter Sunday という)はもともと休み。大学で spring break のある場合は Easter の前か後に1週間程度。

英国

【夏】 the (summer) holidays

小・中高　6週間またはそれ以上

大　約2か月(5月末か6月～8月末)

【冬】 the Christmas holidays

小・中高　12月半ばから約2週間

大　12月半ばから約1か月

{Christmas Eve / Christmas Day / Boxing Day (クリスマス後の贈り物の日) / New Year's Day} を含む

【春】 the Easter holiday(s)

小・中高　the Easter Weekend を含む2週間

大　Easter に関係なく1か月

〈注〉 欧米の大学教師には「サバティカル」(sabbatical) といって数年に1度，研究のための休暇 (study leave) が1年間与えられる所が多い。

きゅうがく（休学）

【休学する】

(1年間学校を)休学する

have (a year's) leave of absence (from school)

彼は家庭の事情で1年間休学しなければならない。

He will have to {stay out of / leave} school for a year for family reasons.

彼は家計を助けるため1年間休学して働かなければならなかった。

He had to drop out of school for a year so that he could get a full-time job to help his family.

あの子は病気で1年以上休学している。

She has been gone from [out of] school for

more than a year because of illness.

あの子は1年間の休学を願い出た[許可された]。

She asked for [got] a year's official leave of absence.

うちのクラスの学生が2人ＮＧＯの海外派遣協力隊に参加するため1年間休学します。

Two students in my class have taken a year's leave of absence to work overseas in an NGO project [program].

〈注〉 absent oneself from school は堅すぎる表現である。休学して学費を稼いで復学するというやり方は米国ではしばしばあるが，教育がすべて無料の英国ではこの考え方はない。

きゅうけい（休憩）→ やすむ・やすみ

名 **a rest; a break**

1. 休憩する

動 **rest; take [have] a rest**

少し[10分間]休憩しましょう。

Let's take [have] { a short rest. / a ten minute break.

2. 休憩時間

小学校　**recess**〔米〕; **playtime**

(職場の)休憩時間　a coffee break

幕間の休憩時間(芝居・コンサート)

an intermission; an interval; a fifteen minutes' [minute] interval（15分の）

コンサートでは全演奏のちょうど半ばの頃に10分から15分の休憩時間をとるのが普通だ。

In a concert there is usually a ten to fifteen minute intermission in about the middle (of a concert).

会合などの休憩時間　a break

法廷の休憩時間

a recess; 休憩する 動 recess

きゅうじつ(休日)→ ねんちゅうぎょうじ

きゅうじん（求人）→ しゅうしょく

今年は求人が多い[少ない]。

This year there are many [few] job vacancies [openings, offers, opportunities].

【会社側の出す条件】

（労働時間，賃金など）

terms of employment

【応募者の必要条件】

（学歴，資格，特技など）　requirements

【求人広告】

a position-wanted ad [a help-wanted ad]〔米〕

a situation-vacant advertisement [a position-available ad]〔英〕

今日は技術系の求人広告がたくさん出ていた。

Today there were many ads for positions [jobs] available in the engineering area.

きゅうりょう（給料）

pay　給料を指す一般的な語。もらう側からの呼称。

salary　官公庁・会社の月給・固定給。欧米では年俸で考えることが多い。

wages　主として労務者の賃金・時給。今日では労働組合などで「給料一般」の意にも使う。

〈注〉 fee は医師・歯科医・弁護士などに支払われる金。commission はセールスマンなどに支払われる歩合給。

給料日　(a) payday

給料取り　a salaried worker; a wage earner

給料総額　gross

手取り　net

〈注〉◆a wage earner には「一家の生活の担い手」の意味もある。

「彼は月給取りだ」は次のように言える。

He gets a salary.

He's paid on a salary basis.

◆給料の支給方法を問題にしているのでなければ，「うちの父はサラリーマンだ」のように言うより，具体的に職種（ex. an executive; an accountant; an engineer; a salesman）を述べるのが普通。

【給料をもらう】
get one's salary [wages, pay]
【給料は…円/給料を…円もらう】
彼は月給30万円だ[30万円もらっている]。
He is paid 300,000 yen a month.
His monthly salary is 300,000 yen.
彼は年間500万円(の給料を)もらっている。
He earns 5,000,000 yen a year.
【給料がよい[少ない]】
彼は給料がよい。
He's well paid.
私は給料が少ない[悪い]。
I don't earn much.
My salary is small [low].
【(少ない給料で)やりくりする】
そんな給料でどうやって生活をやりくりしているの？
How do you manage to live on such a small [meager] salary?
【賃上げ】 a raise〔米〕, a rise〔英〕
彼らは賃上げ要求をした。
They demanded a raise (in their wages).
彼らは5パーセントの賃上げとなった。
They had a 5 percent pay raise.
【給料が上がる】
近頃彼は給料が上がった[昇給になった]。
He got a raise〔米〕[rise〔英〕] recently.
【賃上げスト】
労働者は賃上げストをやった。
The workers went on strike for higher wages.

きょういく(教育)

education; instruction; teaching; schooling; 動 **educate; train**
形 **educational; instructive; scholastic**
義務教育　compulsory education
初等教育　primary education
教育制度　educational systems

《関連語》
試験制度　system of examinations
男女共学　形 coeducational; 名 coeducation
職業教育　vocational education
通信講座　correspondence course
6-3-3制　6-3-3 plan
定時制高校
high school equivalency program
high school equivalency classes
学習指導要領　course of study (published by Ministry of Education, Culture, Sports, Science and Technology as a guide to [for] making a curriculum)
教科課程[カリキュラム]　curriculum
指導[ガイダンス]　guidance
相談員[カウンセラー]
counselor〔米〕; counsellor〔英〕
指導教官　academic counselor; academic advisor; tutor〔英〕
PTA　Parent-Teacher Association
教育委員会　Board of Education
日教組　Japan Teachers' Union
義務教育　compulsory education
ex. Elementary and junior high school education is compulsory in Japan.
学童[生徒]　children, students
教員　teacher
教授　professor
准教授　associate professor
助教授　assistant professor
講師　lecturer; instructor
part-time lecturer (非常勤)
part-time instructor (非常勤)
〈注〉 学部教授陣は faculty members と言う。
校長
headmaster [headmistress]〔英〕
principal〔米〕
学長　president; rector
学部長　dean
学生部長　dean of student affairs
学校　→がっこう
大学　→だいがく

〈注〉 英国，米国ともに，学校によりいろいろで，ここにあげたのは標準的な一例。

米国・英国の教育制度
(**American / British Educational Systems**)

<table>
<tr><th>age</th><th colspan="2">米国</th><th colspan="2">英国</th></tr>
<tr><td>3</td><td colspan="2" rowspan="3">nursery school
pre-school
kindergarten</td><td colspan="2" rowspan="3">nursery (school)</td></tr>
<tr><td>4</td></tr>
<tr><td>5</td></tr>
<tr><td>6</td><td rowspan="6">elementary school (1st～6th grade)</td><td rowspan="8">grade school (1st～8th grade)</td><td>infant school</td><td rowspan="6">primary school</td></tr>
<tr><td>7</td><td rowspan="5">junior school</td></tr>
<tr><td>8</td></tr>
<tr><td>9</td></tr>
<tr><td>10</td></tr>
<tr><td>11</td></tr>
<tr><td>12</td><td rowspan="3">junior high school*</td><td colspan="2" rowspan="4">grammar school
comprehensive school
secondary modern school</td></tr>
<tr><td>13</td></tr>
<tr><td>14</td><td rowspan="4">high school</td></tr>
<tr><td>15</td><td rowspan="3">senior high school*</td></tr>
<tr><td>16</td><td colspan="2" rowspan="2">sixth form(大学進学コース)</td></tr>
<tr><td>17</td></tr>
<tr><td rowspan="3">18</td><td colspan="2">community college
2-year college</td><td colspan="2" rowspan="2">university: 3 years
(languages: 4 years)
(medicine: 6 years)</td></tr>
<tr><td colspan="2">college (4 years)
university
(medicine: 6 years)</td></tr>
<tr><td colspan="2">graduate school
M. A. / M. S. program:
1 or 2 years
Ph.D. [Doctoral] program:
3 years ＋</td><td colspan="2">postgraduate school
M. A. / M. S(c). course:
1 or 2 years
Ph.D. course: 年限制限は10年間まで</td></tr>
</table>

[米国] *を合せた junior-senior high school(6年制ハイスクール)もある。義務教育は6～17, 18歳の12年間。

[英国] 上記の例は公立学校。私立学校には pre-preparatory school (5～7歳), preparatory school (7～13歳), public school (13～18歳)と independent school (5～18歳)がある。義務教育 (compulsory education)は5～16歳の11年間。university は普通3年間であるが, 日本のように一律ではない。

きょういんめんきょ(教員免許)→ めんきょ

a teacher's certificate〔米〕; **a teaching certificate**〔英〕

彼には教員免許がある。

He has a teacher's certificate.

〈注〉 実際に教員になっている人については, He's a qualified teacher. (彼は資格を持った先生だ) が普通の言い方。

ぎょうぎ（行儀）

manners; etiquette

あの子は行儀がよい[悪い]。

She has good [no] manners.

行儀をよくしなさい。

Try to behave yourself.

行儀を知らないの［行儀はどうなっているの］?

Haven't you got any manners?

Have you no manners?

Where are your manners?

Mind your manners!

〈注〉 Behave yourself. (行儀よくしなさい) の behave の名詞形 behavior は行儀だけでなく, 広く「行い」のこと。manners や etiquette は世の中の慣習となっている行儀作法のことである。

きょうし(教師) → きょういく, せんせい

a teacher; an instructor

小学校の教師

a primary school teacher

an elementary school teacher〔米〕

a teacher in an elementary school

中学[高校]の教師

a junior [senior] high school teacher

英語の教師

a teacher of English; an English teacher

体育の教師

a sports teacher

a physical education teacher

家庭教師

a (private) tutor; a private teacher

〈注〉 governess は, 昔, 金持ちの上流階級の子女の教育のために雇われた女性のことで, 今日の学生アルバイトとは違う。

【教師をする】teach; teach school (〔米〕小学校の教師をする)

日本に来る前は郷里の町で小学校の英語の教師をしていた。

Before coming to Japan I taught English [was an English teacher] at a primary school in my hometown.

ぎょうじ（行事）→ ねんちゅうぎょうじ

an event; a function

【年中行事】annual events

お盆は主要な伝統的年中行事の一つだ。

Obon is one of the traditional events of the year.

【学校行事】school events

【行事予定】

the schedule of school activities

school calendar

ＰＴＡ後援の全校ピクニックはうちの学校の大きな行事の一つだ。

The PTA-sponsored school picnic is one of the year's big functions [events] at our school.

【諸行事】

この部屋は結婚式やその他の行事に使用できる。

This room can be hired for weddings and other functions.

〈注〉 an event は一般的に大きな出来事・行事。a function は公式行事。一定の型にそって行われる大きな行事。政府の行う外交上の夕食会のほか, 宴会, 結婚式, 葬式など。

きょうそう（競争）

(**a**) **competition; a contest; rivalry**

形 **competitive**

動 **compete with**《a person》**for**

競争入札　a competitive bid

自由競争市場　a free competitive market

生存競争　the struggle for existence [survival]
【競争する】
compete with [against]《a person》for《a prize》in《a race, trade》
【激しい競争】
(a) keen [fierce, severe] competition（テニスの試合など）
a tight race（選挙戦・競馬・オートレースなど）
〈注〉 a fierce competition は食うか食われるかのぎりぎりの熾烈な競争。時には違反もやりかねない，なりふりかまわない激しいもの。
a severe competition は激烈でレベルが高いために難しく激しい競争。
21世紀には世界の貿易競争はもっともっと激しくなるだろう。
World trade will become [be] much more competitive in the 21st century.
ナショナルリーグのペナントレースは激しい競争だ。
Competition [The race] for the National League Pennant is very tight.
【競争試験】
a competitive examination
【競争相手】 an opponent
【競争心】
a competitive spirit, a fighting spirit
【競争率】
the rate of success, the success rate, the failure rate
入試の競争率は 4 倍であった。
The rate of success was one out of four.
Only one in four was accepted.
Only one fourth of the applicants were admitted.

きょうたん（驚嘆）→ おどろく

きょうみ（興味）→ おもしろい

(an) **interest**
興味ある ㊎ **interesting; of interest**
【興味がある】［人主語］be interested
私は民俗学にたいへん興味がある［を持っている］。
I'm very [much, keenly] interested in folklore.
民俗学は多くの人類学者の興味を強く引きつけた。
Folklore deeply interests many anthropologists.
彼は焼き物作りにたいへん興味を持っている。
He is greatly interested in pottery.
【興味がない】
私はスポーツには興味がない。
I have no interest in sports.
Sports don't interest me.
【興味をかきたてる】 arouse [awaken, stimulate, stir up] interest
科学は人間の周囲にある物についての興味から発達した。
Science developed from human curiosity about the things that surrounded them.

きょうよう（教養）

culture; liberal education
【教養をつける】
enrich one's mind with knowledge
【教養をつけること】self-enrichment
【教養のある人】
a cultured person
a man [woman] of refinement
彼はなかなか教養がある。（幅広い知識）
He seems to have had a broad education.
彼の姉たちは中産階級できちんとしていて，いかにも教養のある感じの人だった。
His sisters were middle-class, respectable and apparently cultured.
〈注〉 「教養を高める」のような言い方は漠然としているので，その内容を具体的に述べる方がよい。
【大学の教養学部】（学士号を与える学部）
faculty of letters〔米〕[arts〔英〕, liberal arts

〔米〕]

【一般教養科目】arts and sciences

arts { fine arts（美術・音楽・彫刻など） humanities（ギリシア・ラテン語学[文学]など） } 人文科学
natural sciences　自然科学
social sciences　社会科学

きょうり(郷里)・こきょう(故郷) → しゅっしん

one's **home town** 自分の子供時代を過し郷里として愛着をもっている町。

one's **birthplace** 自分の生れた土地。そこで育って愛着があれば故郷となる。

one's **ancestral home** 先祖代々住んでいた土地。地方の名家の出身者に当てはまる。

one's **home** 今住んでいる所。しかし今の住所に愛着がもてず，自分が育ち父母や親戚の住む土地を home と感ずれば，その土地が故郷 home になる。

正月休みにはたくさんの人が郷里に帰り身内の人々と正月を過します。

Many people go back to their home town to spend the New Year holiday with their folks.

郷里はどちらですか。

Where ⌊do you come [are you] from?

〈注〉「田舎，出身地」の意味で native country は適切ではない。one's native city [town, village] あるいは area とすべきである。

彼は10年ぶりに郷里に帰省した。

He came home after ten years' absence.

【故郷】　one's old home

長崎は私の第二の故郷だ。

Nagasaki is my second home.

ぎょうれつ（行列）

1. 進行する行列

荘重な行列　procession

葬列　a funeral procession

ショーの行列　parade

仮装行列　a fancy parade, a masquerade

復活祭の行列(イースターパレード)

Easter parade

以前は聖ジョージ祭にボーイスカウトがパレードをやったものだ。

On St. George's Day the Scouts had a parade.

名古屋祭りの呼び物は信長行列だ。

The main event of the Nagoya Festival is the Nobunaga Parade.

【行進】　march

cf. 大集会　rally; 政治集会　a political rally; 学生大会 the students' rally

非核武装を訴える行列[行進]

a CND march［CND＝Campaign for Nuclear Disarmament］

2. 停止している行列

line; queue〔英〕

行列に割り込む

break [cut, horn〔米俗〕] into the line; skip [jump] the queue; push in

劇場の前には切符を買おうと人々が長い行列をつくっていた。

There was a long line [queue] (of people) in front of the theater to buy tickets.

3. 数学

行列　matrix（pl. matrices）

きょか（許可）→ ゆるす

1. 許すこと

名 **permission; a permit**

【許可する】動 permit; allow

【許可を得る，許可される】

私は今日の午後は有給休暇の許可をもらっている。

I have ⌊a paid holiday [official permission to be absent] this afternoon.

〈注〉"Can I be excused?" は子供が授業中トイレに行きたくなって許可を求めるときなどに使う。

デモ隊の人たちはやっと上野公園での集会の許可を得た。

The marchers finally {received / got} {a permit / permission} to rally in Ueno Park.

【許可を与える】

東京都公園課はやっと上野公園での集会の許可を与えた。

The Tokyo Park Commission finally granted [gave] the marchers permission to rally in Ueno Park.

【許可が下りる】

私の父が4か月も前に申請した建築許可がきのうやっと下りた。これで家の増築工事が始められる。

Yesterday my father got the building permit for which he had applied almost four months ago, and now work can begin on our house addition.

【許可せず】

この病棟では面会は許可しない[許可されていない]。

Visiting the patients in this ward is not permitted [allowed].（禁止）

喫煙は許可されていない。

Smoking not permitted.（禁煙）

2. 免許

licence〔英〕; **license**〔米〕

彼女が託児所経営の許可をとって，もうそろそろ5年になる。

She has been authorised [licensed] to operate a (children's) day-care center for some five years now.

3. 承認

approval; admission; leave

【許可する】動 approve; admit; give leave to

志願者1000人の中から300名だけが入学を許可された。

There were 1000 applicants, but only 300 students have been admitted to the school.

私の奨学金貸与が許可になって両親は喜んでいる。

My student loan application was approved, so my parents are happy.

テニスの試合に出るのに学生部長が欠席の許可をくれると思うか。

Do you suppose {the dean will let us / we can get permission to} miss class to attend the tennis tournament?

きょくたん（極端）

【極端な】形 **extreme;** 行き過ぎの **excessive;** 思い切った **radical**

【極端に】副 **extremely; excessively; to excess [an extreme]; too far; radically**

1. 行動

【極端に走る】go too far

そんな極端なことしなくても[そこまでやらなくても]よかったのに。

You needn't have gone to such lengths.

それはちょっと極端[やりすぎ]だよ。

That is going a bit [rather] too far.

君は極端から極端に走る。

You go from one extreme to another.

2. 性格

【極端に[な]】

あの人は極端なきれい好きだ。

She has a mania for cleanliness.

子供の健康を心配するといっても，彼はちょっと極端だ。だって子供たちは特に弱いわけでもないのだから。

He worries excessively about his children's health, for they {are no more sickly / get sick no more often} than the average child.

3．非常手段
我々がもっと上手に水の節減をすれば水の割当給水制のような極端な手段[非常手段]はとらずにすむだろう。
If we conserve water more carefully, perhaps such an extreme measure as water rationing will become unnecessary.
中国は人口増加を抑止するために極端な方法をとった。
China has taken radical steps to control its population growth.
極端な改革
radical [fundamental] change（憲法改正など）
〈注〉 極端を意味する語に ultra-(超…)がある。
ultra-modern 超モダン
ultrahigh frequency（UHF）極超短波
ultranationalist　超国家主義者，国粋主義者

ぎょっとする → おどろく

start; be startled; be frightened
私たちは物音にぎょっとした。家の中には私たちのほかにだれもいないと思っていたものだから。
We started at the noise because we had thought we were all alone in the house.
あの変な人が私たちのグループに突然割り込んで来たときにはまったくぎょっとした。
We got a great scare [fright] when that strange person suddenly burst into our group.

きらきらする → ぎせいご・ぎたいご

glitter 動 きらきら輝く(金属・宝石などの輝き)
glisten 動 きらりと光る(反射光の感じ)
glow 動 白熱[赤熱]する
glimmer 動 ちらちら光る(かすかなきらめき，夜明けの光，ろうそくの光)
gleam 動 かすかに光る(闇の中にぼうっと輝く光)
twinkle 動 星などがきらきら光る
sparkle 動 火花のように明るく輝く(目の輝き・宝石・炭酸飲料などを連想)

きらく（気楽）→ のんき

形 **easy; care-free; comfortable**（のんびり）; **easygoing; lighthearted**
気楽な仕事　an easy job; a soft job
気楽に暮す
lead a comfortable and easy life
気楽にしてください。
Please { make yourself at home. / relax. }
気楽に考えなさい。
Take it easy.
気楽に遊びに来てください。
Please { stop by / drop in / call on me } whenever you wish.
〈注〉 Please feel free to call on me. はやや形式ばった表現なので上の方が普通。

きりつめる(切り詰める)→ かけい，けんやく

cut down; reduce; economize
【生活を】
今年は去年より生活を切り詰めなくてはならない。
This year we { can't spend so much money as we did / have to economize much more than / have to spend even less than we did } last year.
彼はずいぶん生活を切り詰めている。
He lives on a very strict budget.
His living expenses are low.
彼はローン返済のため生活を切り詰めなければならない。
He has to { cut back (on) / cut down / reduce } his living costs to pay off [back] his loan.

〈注〉 We have to be careful about money.
We have to watch the budget.
これらも「切り詰める」の意味に使える。

【費用を】
交通費以外の旅行費用は1人1日7000円に切り詰めよう。
Let's limit our non-transportation expenses on the trip to 7,000 yen a day per person, shall we?

きる（切る）・きれる

1. 切る

【ナイフで切る】
cut; 薄切りにする slice; ぶつ切りにする chop; 切り刻む chop into small pieces; hash; mince

【はさみで切る】
爪を切る cut; clip; 大ばさみで羊毛・植木・生け垣などを切る clip; trim; 切符を切る punch

【散髪】
今日は午後に髪を切りに行ってくる。
I'll go to town this afternoon to have a haircut [my hair cut].

【のこぎりで切る】saw

【なたで切る】chop

【斧で切り倒す】cut down; fell

【水を切る】（皿などの） drain the dishes
ほうきの水をしゅっと切る
swish the broom through the air (to remove some water)
（船などが）水を切って走る
cut one's way through the waves

【スイッチを切る】
（ラジオ・電灯の） turn off the radio [light]

【ハンドルを切る】
彼は対向車を避けようと急ハンドルを切ってガードレールにぶつかった。
He swerved to avoid the on-coming car and hit the guard-rail.

【トランプを切る】shuffle

【電話を切る】hang up; ring off
彼女は電話を切った。
She hung up [rang off].
（電話を）切らないでください。（そのままでお待ちください）
Please hold the line.

【下回る】
寄付金は100万円を少し切った。
The donations came to just under one million yen.
目玉商品とは客を店に引きつけるために元値を切ってまで格安に売り出す商品のことです。
A loss-leader is an item sold at a loss in order to attract customers into a store.

2. 切れる

【鋭利な】
よく切れる［切れない］ナイフ
a sharp [dull] knife
このナイフはよく切れる［切れない］。
This knife cuts well [is blunt, dull].
うちのマネージャーは頭が切れる。
Our manager is sharp.

【切断】
ロープが切れた。
The rope broke.
糸が（ぷつりと）切れた。
The thread snapped.

【磨耗】
すり切れる wear out; become threadbare

【尽きる】
ガソリンが切れそうだ。
We're running low on { gas〔米〕. / petrol〔英〕.
The gas is low.（比喩的に「精魂尽き果てた」の意にも使える）
油が切れそうだ。
The oil is low.
砂糖が切れた［を切らした］。
We have run out of sugar.

【商品が切れる】
青のブラウスが切れている［を切らしてい

る]。

The store was out of blouses in blue.

The store didn't have any blue blouses left.

The store had sold out of blue blouses.

【息が切れる】 be out of breath

ずっと走って来たので，着いたときには息切れがした。

I was out of breath when I arrived because I ran all the way.

彼は息を切らして駆け込んで来た。

He rushed in breathless.

【期限などが切れる】

時間切れだ。

Time is up.

契約に明記された期限が切れた。

The time limit specified [stated] in the contract has been reached.

彼の学校との契約が切れた。

His contract with the school has expired.

私のパスポートは次の9月末で切れる。

My passport will expire at the end of next September.

雑誌の予約購読料が次号で切れます。

Your subscription to the magazine will expire with the next number.

このクレジットカードは有効期限が切れている。

This credit card is already past the expiration date.

〈注〉 契約 contract，協定 agreement が有効期限を過ぎると expire（終了）するが，期限・期日が expire するのではない。

【返却期限】

私が図書館から借りている本はみんな今週末で返却期限が切れる[の返却期限は今週末だ]。

My library books are all due (back) at the end of this week.

〈注〉 My rent is due the 1st of each month.（私の家賃は毎月1日に納めることになっている）

きる（着る）・きている

1. 動作（服を身につける）

【着る】 put on 《a shirt》**; get dressed**

トミーはパジャマをひとりで着られると得意だ。

Now Tommy is very proud because he can put on his pajamas〔米〕[pyjamas〔英〕] all by himself.

さあ早く服を着ておいで。

Hurry up and get dressed!

【着てみる】 try on

このコートを着てごらんなさい。…どう，体に合いますか。

Try on this coat .... Does it fit nicely?

〈注〉 「ぴったり合う」は It's a good fit.

【着せる】 ㊍ ㊓ dress

2. 状態（服を身につけている）

【着ている】 wear; have on; be dressed in

彼は学校が休みのときでもいつも高校の制服を着ている。

He always wears his high school uniform even { when there's no school. / on non-school days. }

彼女はいつもグリーン(の服)を着ている。

She always wears green.

〈注〉 「いつも着ている」と習慣の意を表す場合は，現在形 wear を用いる。一方，目の前で「人が…を着ている」と言うときは He is wearing などと進行形にする。過去形のときも wore は「いつも着ていた」の意。目の前に見えた情景を描くときは He was wearing などを使う。She's putting on a nice dress. とすると「身じたくの最中」の意味になる。

【着ていた】

彼女はすてきなピンクのドレスを着てとてもかわいかった。

She was wearing [dressed in] a nice pink dress and looked pretty.

【着て出かけた】

彼女はよそ行きを着て出かけた。

She went out in her Sunday best.

【着てみたら似合う】
新しい服を着てみたら彼女にとてもよく似合う。
Her new dress looks very nice on her.
【着られなくなる】(子供が成長して)
うちの娘はもうここにある服は着られなくなった。
My daughter has outgrown these clothes.
【着方】
現代は年代によって着るものもその着方も異なる[まちまちだ]。
In recent times each generation has its own types of clothes and ways of dressing.
【着られる】(長持ちする)
ウールは何年でも着られる。
Wool lasts [wears] for years and years.
〈注〉 なお,「着る」の意味の put on, wear, have on は身につける意味の「かぶる,つける,はめる,はく」などすべてに用いられる。
【着るものがない】
(パーティーなどへ行くのに)着るものがないわ。
I have nothing proper to wear [go in].
I don't have a thing to wear! 〔*colloq.*〕

3. 慣用・転義
【罪を着る】 take the blame on oneself
【着物】 →いふく

きれいな・きれいに

1. 美しい
beautiful; pretty; lovely
きれいな子[娘] a cute girl; a pretty girl
きれいな女の人 a nice looking woman
きれいに飾る
decorate; make beautiful
きれいに着飾る[きれいな服を着る]
dress up
彼女はきれいにお化粧している。
She looks beautiful when she wears make-up.
She is beautiful [lovely] with that make-up.
Her make-up looks good [is attractive].
彼女はきれいな字を書く。
She writes neatly.

2. 清潔な
clean; clear; 心のきれいな **be pure in heart;** きちんとした **tidy; neat;** 公正な **fair**《play》; **a clean**《fight》
【きれいにする[しておく]】keep clean
公園はいつもきれいにしておこう。
Let's always keep the parks neat and clean.
【きれいにする,片付ける】
片付けて部屋をきれいにしなさい。
Put your things in order.
Tidy up your room.
【きれい好き】
彼女はきれい好きだ。
She is a (very) clean person.
彼女は異常にきれい好きだ。(潔癖)
She has a mania for cleanliness.
【心のきれいな】be pure; be innocent 〔*rather clichéd*〕; 良心に恥じるところがない have a clear conscience

3. 全部
【きれいに】**entirely; completely; wholly**
【きれいに忘れる】
私ったらきれいに忘れてたわ。
I have completely [entirely] forgotten it.
【きれいに食べる】
彼は何もかもきれいに食べてしまった。
He ate everything up.
He licked the plate clean. 〔*colloq.*〕
【きれいに(支)払う】
彼はついに借金をきれいに払ってしまった。
He has at last paid up [off] all his debts.

ぎろん(議論)

1. 討議
a discussion 結論を求めるため冷静に話し合って解明してゆく。

【討議する】discuss《something》; have a discussion《about something》

我々は長時間その問題について討議した。

We discussed this matter for a long time.

【討議中】

その問題は目下討議中です。

The problem is under discussion.

2．討論

a debate　公式の debate は公開の場で，一定のルールに従いある問題について賛否双方の立場から冷静に問題を掘り下げ，論を尽すこと。非公式の debate は discussion に近い。

【討論する】have a debate; ㊠ ㊀ debate

我々は人口(抑制)問題について討論をしているところだ。

We are having a discussion [a debate] about population control.

【討論に付す】(議事として持ち出す)

外国貿易を討論に付す

bring up the subject of foreign trade for discussion

【国会討論】

国会で税制改正案の討論が行われた。

The Diet { (1) debated [argued] / (2) argued about } the tax reform bill.

〈注〉 (1)は理路整然と冷静に討論が進められたことを意味する。(2)はその討論が対立し，多分に感情的になったことを意味する。なお，論争する意味では argue about と自動詞だが，他動詞の argue は「(理性的に)主張する」(support, speak for or against)の意で，次のように使われる。

argue innocence (無実を主張する)

argue that ... (…と主張する)

3．主張・議論

【主張する】

人口増加は厳しく抑制すべきだと中のひとりが主張した。

One of them argued [One person's argument was] that population growth must be severely controlled.

【議論】**an argument**　対立・緊張があり，熱が入ってしばしば感情的になり，相手を説得しようとするもの。

【議論する】㊠㊂ argue about《something》; have an argument

〈注〉 argument は感情的とは限らないが，動詞 argue about は常に感情的なものを含む。

我々はその問題について白熱した議論を交わした。

We had a heated argument about that matter.

委員会は現行の入試制度の是非について真剣に議論を戦わせた。

The committee seriously argued about the validity of the present examination system.

The committee vigorously argued whether the present examination system was a desirable one.

科学者たちは人道的見地からの遺伝子組み換え[遺伝子工学]の是非について議論を戦わせた。

The scientists argued about the morality [moral implication] of gene alteration [genetic engineering].

【議論になる】

そのことで議論になった。

We started an argument about [over] it.

【議論に勝つ[負ける]】

win [lose] an argument about [over]《something》

【大いに議論すべき…】

その問題は大いに議論すべきだ。

The problem should be { open to argument [debate, discussion] / debatable [arguable] }

【議論の余地がない】

be beyond dispute [argument]

【議論好き】

彼は議論好きだ。

He likes to argue.

He's argumentative.

4. 論争

dispute　理性よりも現実に根差し，口論に近くなることもある。argument に近い。

controversy　口頭以外に誌上論争も含む。広範な問題に関して長期にわたるもの。

【論争する】

dispute the problem (cf. dispute that ... は「異議を唱える」の意)

have (a) dispute about

be engaged in controversy (論争中である)

我々はそのことで論争をした。

We had (a) dispute about it.

【論争がある】

人口(抑制)問題についてはしばしば論争がある[議論される]。

They frequently { have arguments / argue [dispute] } about population control.

新しい道路の建設に関してはかなりの論争があった。

There was a great deal of controversy [argument] about the construction of the new highway.

5. その他

【協議事項，議事日程表】 an agenda

議事目録をつくる

make [draw up] an agenda

次の審議事項は予算だ。

The next item on the agenda is the budget.

議事が盛りだくさんで会議は5時間続いた。

The agenda was very long and the meeting lasted for five hours.

きをつける(気をつける) → ちゅういする

1. 用心する

【食べ物に】

旅行するときは食べ物に気をつけなければならない。

When you travel, you should be careful of what you eat.

【体に】

体に気をつけてください。

Take care of your health.

かぜをひかないように気をつけて。

Take care { not to catch (a) cold. / that you don't catch (a) cold. }

【事故に】

階段で転ばないよう気をつけてください。

Mind you don't fall down the stairs.

Be careful on the stairs.

ここは危ないから足元に気をつけてください。

This place is a little dangerous.

Please watch your step here.

迷子にならないように気をつけて。

[子供に]

Mind [Be careful] you don't get lost.

[保護者に]

Take care the child doesn't get lost.

〈注〉　英米人は，特に注意を要する場合のみ注意し，日本人のように挨拶として「気をつけて」と言うことはない。ただし，アメリカ人は別れ際に Take care. とよく言う。

2. 警戒する

彼に気をつけろ。危険人物だ。

Keep an eye on him, because he's dangerous.

車に気をつけなさい。(子供に)

Look out for cars. / Be careful of cars.

気をつけろ！

Watch out!

3. 注意を集中する　→きく・きこえる

先生のおっしゃることを気をつけて聞きなさい。

Listen to what your teacher says.

年上の人の言われることを気をつけて聞きなさい。経験者の話だから。

You should pay attention to what older people say because they are more experienced.

〈注〉「あの人の話には気をつけろ」は pay attention ではなくて guard against になる。前後関係や語調で判断しなければならない。

4．配慮する →ちゅういする

彼らが生活に不自由なんかしないように私が気をつけてやります。

I'll see (to it) that they will never want for anything.

だれにも触られない[だれも触らない]ように気をつけてください。

See / Watch / See to it } that no one touches this.

きんきょう（近況）

information about personal state of things

近頃どうだい？（近況をたずねる言い方）

How are things [How's everything] (with you)?

How's the world treating you (these days)?

How have you been?

近況をお知らせください。

Let me know { how you're getting along. / how things are with you. / how you've been.

ぎんこう（銀行）

1．銀行の種類

【世界銀行】 the International Bank for Reconstruction and Development; 略 IBRD

【中央銀行】 the central bank

［日本］日本銀行 the Bank of Japan

［米国］連邦準備理事会[銀行] the Federal Reserve Board [Bank] (略 FRB)

［英国］イングランド銀行 the Bank of England

【市中銀行】 a commercial bank

【その他】

信託銀行 a trust bank

信用金庫 a credit union; a credit association

貯蓄貸付組合〔米〕

a savings and loan association; 略 S&L

2．銀行業務

【営業時間】 banking hours

【預金】

普通預金 an ordinary deposit

当座預金 a current account

定期預金 a fixed deposit, time deposit (略 T / D)

20万円をＳ銀行で定期預金にした。

I put two hundred thousand yen in S Bank [in a fixed deposit account [on fixed deposit].

【支払い】

現金 cash

小銭 coins; change

札 a bill; a banknote

小切手 a check〔米〕; a cheque〔英〕

手形 a bill of exchange

銀行手形 a bank draft

外貨 foreign currency

外国為替 foreign exchange

トラベラーズチェック

a traveler's check; a traveller's cheque

為替レート exchange rate

【口座，振り込み】

口座 a bank account

口座を作る open an account

お金[小切手]を振り込む

deposit money [checks] in an account

お金を引き出す

withdraw [draw out] money from an account

口座を閉じる

close an account

ほかの口座に振り込む

transfer money to (a person's) account

給料は銀行振り込みだ。

My salary is [paid automatically into [automatically deposited in] the bank.

ほとんどの銀行は自動振込みができる。
Most banks offer automatic deposit options.
私の口座に5万円振り込まれた。
Fifty thousand yen has been paid into my account.
キャッシュカード
a cash card; an ATM card
クレジットカード　a credit card
キャッシュカード[クレジットカード]を作る
make out an application for a cash card [credit card]; apply for a cash card [credit card]
自動預金支払機
ATM (automatic teller machine)
預金通帳　a bankbook; a passbook
預け入れ伝票　a deposit slip
引き出し伝票　a withdrawal slip
【貸付】 a loan
〈注〉 貸している金も借りている金も loan と言う。
元金　(the) principal
利子　(the) interest
【利率】
預金利率　the interest rate
貸出利率　(the) loan rate
【従業員】
頭取　the president;　支配人　a manager
支店　a branch office
支店長　a branch manager
銀行員　a bank clerk; a bank teller〔米〕
貸出係　a loan officer

きんし（禁止）→ きょか，ていし

きんじょ（近所）→ ちかい・ちかく，となり

名 **neighborhood**
【近所に】 in this [my] neighborhood; near [around] here; nearby; close by; hard by
【近所の人】
a neighbor; people in the neighborhood
【近所の子】 the neighborhood children
〈注〉 neighbor は隣近所。neighborhood はもう少し広く，近所数軒を含む地域。向う三軒両隣は close neighbors，文字通りのお隣さんは next-door neighbors と言う。
【近所の店】 a nearby shop
【近所にある】
私の家は駅の近所です。
My house
{ is not far from the station.
{ is / is located } near [close to] the station.
【近所に来る】
近所にいらっしゃったらどうぞお立ち寄りください。
Please drop in if [when] you come this way.
【近所に住む】
彼はすぐ近所に住んでいる。
He lives { quite close to me. / right nearby. / just around the corner.
【近所迷惑】
いつもあんな大きな音でラジオをかけて，まったく近所迷惑だ。
That loud radio is an annoyance to the neighborhood.

きんちょう（緊張）

名 **strain; tension**
【緊張する】 become tense [strained]
【緊張している】 be tense [strained]
[人が] 男の子たちは緊張している。
The boys are tense.
最初の日，私たちはすっかり緊張してしまった。
The first day we were all strained and nervous.
[情勢が] アイルランド情勢は緊張している。
Things are very strained with Ireland.
2国間の関係が緊張した。
The relations between the two countries have become tense.
【緊張した顔】
a tense and nervous look

【緊張をほぐす】
私たちの緊張をほぐそうと彼女はにっこり笑いかけてくれた。
She smiled kindly to make us relax [feel at ease].
【緊張を緩和する】
relieve [relax, ease] the tension
フランスの首相が世界情勢の緊張緩和のためにサミットの開催を提案した。
The French Premier suggested a summit meeting to relieve world tensions.
【緊張を欠く，たるんでいる】
be careless [inattentive]
not pay enough attention to
私たちは仕事に慣れてくると緊張がゆるんで小さなミスをするようになりやすい。
As we get used to our job we tend to become careless and make small mistakes.

きんぱつ（金髪）

名 形 **blond**
あのすてきな金髪の女の子はナンシーの姉さんよ。
The girl with the beautiful blond hair is Nancy's sister.
〈注〉 次の文は文法的には正しいが奇妙にひびく。
The girl who has the beautiful blond hair ....

きんむ（勤務）

service; work; duty
【勤務している】
あの人は{この会社に / IOC に}勤務している。
He works {in this company [office]. / for IOC.}
【勤務先】
the company [office] where one works
one's workplace
【勤務時間】 working hours
1日8時間勤務(する)
work [have] an eight-hour day
【勤務中】
あの人は今，勤務中だ。
He is now on duty.
〈注〉 on duty は公務員・警察官・警備員など市民にサービスをする職種について使う言葉。教員などは He's teaching now. で，当直のような場合のほかは on duty とは言わない。
勤務中はたばこは吸ってはいけないことになっている。
We are not allowed to smoke while on duty.
【…勤務】
彼は名古屋支店勤務となった。
He was appointed to the Nagoya branch office.
【勤務条件】 conditions [terms] of work [a job]
【勤務成績】
one's (performance, work) evaluation
【勤務評定】 an evaluation system

く

くい(悔い)・くやむ → こうかい

名 動 **regret**

〈注〉「悔い」は「悔いのない生活［青春，人生］」「後から悔いのないように」「悔いの残らないように」などのように使われるが，without regret と訳すのは誤り。悔いとは後から心に浮かぶものであるからこう言えない。

【悔いのないように】

悔いのないようにがんばろう。

I'll do my best so that I will not regret what I have done [my actions] afterwards.

悔いのない人生を送りたい。

I'll try to live in such a way that I won't {have any regrets. / regret the way I've lived.}

I don't want to regret the way I've lived.

〈注〉「悔いのないように」はごく当り前の「決り文句」であるが，日本人が作文などでこれを使いすぎるのは変に響くようだ。後悔をしようと思って怠けることはあり得ない。わかり切ったことを書いているように聞えるのだろう。とにかく使いすぎない方がよい。

【悔いる】

［人主語］repent; be repentant

【悔やまれる】

青春をあんな風に浪費したことが悔やまれる［を悔いている］。

I regret having wasted my youth in such a way.

〈注〉◆「前非を深く悔い…」のように深刻なのは repent, be repentant for ... であるが，これらの語には宗教的な響きがある。日常的表現には適さない。

◆regret は「残念に思う」「悔いる，悔やむ」に当るが，日本語の「悔いる，悔やむ」は自分が原因で起ったことについて残念に思い自分を責めることである。次の文の regret は「残念に思う」の意だが「悔いる」の意ではない。

He regrets that he can't come.
（彼は行かれなくて残念だと言っています）

【お悔やみ】

お父上のご逝去をお悔やみ申し上げます。

Many [My] regrets on the death of your father.

〈注〉 I regret to inform you that ... は何か不幸を相手に伝えるときの正式の表現。

くうかん（空間）

space; room

【空間がある】

トランクにはまだまだ空間がある［何でも入れられる］。

There is enough room [space] in the trunk for everything.

空間のない大都市では駐車のスペースが限られている。

Parking space in big cities is very limited.

大都会では生活空間が少ない。

Living space is scarce in huge cities.

【空間と時間】

死がやがて時間と空間の制約から我々を解き放ってくれるだろう。

Death will bear us away from the world of time and space.〔*literary*〕

くうそう（空想）

a day dream; an idle fancy

【空想家】 a(day) dreamer; a woolgatherer; a visionary 夢想家

【空想物語】

fantasy 実在しない空想の世界の不思議な，時にグロテスクな物語。

fiction 実話に対する語。想像上の人物・事件を扱う物語。小説も含む。

そんなの空想物語さ。

That's a mere fiction.（つくり話）

That's utterly unrealistic.（現実離れしている）

【空想科学小説】 SF（Science Fiction）

【空想する】

私は若い頃よく空想にふけったものだ。

I used to daydream a lot when I was young.
その子は，自分が宇宙飛行士となって宇宙服に身をかため，宇宙の旅を無事終えてスペースシャトルから出てくる，そんな姿を空想しては楽しんでいる。
The boy likes to imagine himself dressed in a space suit coming out of a space shuttle after a successful flight.

【空想にすぎない】
(それは)空想にすぎない。
It's a mere fancy.
うん，ちょっと空想にふけっているだけ。
I'm just dreaming.

くさい（臭い）

動自 **smell bad; stink**
動他 **smell**《something》
くさいにおい 名 **bad smell; stench**

1. …くさい

この部屋はたばこくさい。
This room smells of tobacco.
彼は酒くさい。
He smells of *sake*.
何か生ぐさいにおいがしませんか。
Can't [Don't] you smell something fishy?
何か焦げるにおいがする。
I smell something burning.
生ごみ入れの缶は夏になるとくさい。
The garbage cans stink in summer.
彼は息がくさい。
He has bad [foul] breath.
〈注〉 foul は bad よりも強意的。

2. 怪しい，疑わしい

suspicious; fishy
くさいぞ[悪だくみのにおいがする]。
I smell a rat.
cf. I smell trouble brewing [coming].
(面倒なことが起りそうだ)
〈注〉 (1)［くさい］Someone's deceiving us [doing something dishonest].
(2)［いやな予感］Something {was done / has been done} that will create a problem.
(1)と(2)はたいへん近い表現だが，(1)は上の例文と同じく悪だくみのにおいがすることを意味し，(2)は問題が起こりそうな予感がすることで必ずしも不正が行われていることを意味しない。
あいつはうさんくさい。
He's suspicious-looking.
He arouses suspicion.
世間はあの男がくさいと思っている。
They suspect〔強〕) / They are suspicious of } that man.

【くさい芝居】
何てくさい芝居だ。
What a hammy performance!
〈注〉 ham it up 演技がオーバーで見るに耐えないこと。

くさる（腐る）

1. 物の腐敗

《類義語》
go bad 一般的に用いられる。青少年が不良化することにも用いる。
decay 細菌などで徐々に腐る。
rot 有機物が腐る。
be spoiled [spoilt] 食物が悪くなる。子供がわがままになるの意にも用いる。

【食物】
暑いと食物がすぐ腐る。
Food goes bad in hot weather.
この肉はくさい。腐ってしまった。
This meat stinks. {It's spoilt. / It has gone off [bad].}
停電で冷蔵庫の中の物が腐ってしまう。
Because the power isn't on, things in the fridge [refrigerator] will go bad.
〈注〉 パンなどは古く固くなると stale，さらにかびが生えると moldy (〔英〕mouldy)。炭酸飲料，ビールなどの気が抜けることは go flat。バターや油脂類の古く油くさくなったのは rancid と言う。

【木材】

木の柱が腐って建物全体が倒壊寸前である。

The wooden pillars are rotten and the whole structure is about to { fall down. / crumble. }

2. 人間の堕落・落胆

【堕落】

彼らは芯まで腐っている。

They are rotten to the core.

They are corrupt.

〈注〉 rotten と corrupt は重なる部分もあるが次のような相違がある。

rotten 道徳心喪失の状態を指す。主として人柄・行為について「醜悪な，不快な」。

ex. rotten man, rotten job, rotten movie

corrupt 汚職など計画的・知的犯罪を犯すような堕落ぶり。政治・ビジネスについて「不正な，後ろ暗い」。

【落胆】

彼は仕事が見つからなくてくさっている。

He's depressed,
He's disheartened,
He's (down) in the dumps, 〔*colloq.*〕
} because he couldn't get a job.

ぐず・ぐずぐず

1. 性格

【不決断】

ぐずは大嫌いだ。(ぐずな男には耐えられない)

I can't bear an irresolute man.

【のろま】

あれはぐずで仕事がのろい。

He is very slow to do his work.

2. 行動

ぐずぐずするな。

Stop [Quit] wasting time!

Don't waste time!

Waste no time! / Be quick!

Hurry up! / Don't delay!

何をぐずぐずしているんだ。

What are you so long about?

What's taking you so long?

What's the [your] problem?

ぐずぐずしているひまはない。

There's no time to lose [waste].

3. 文句

ぐずぐず言うな。

Don't grumble [complain].

Stop grumbling.

Do as you are told. (親が子に対して)

Shut up! I don't want to hear about it any more. (おだまり，もう聞きたくない)

くすり (薬)

medicine; medication; drug (drug は一般的に使われる語。ただし殺虫剤，麻薬の意味にも使われる)

1. 薬の形状 (Forms of Medicine)

錠剤 a pill; a tablet
カプセル a capsule
粉薬 powder
水薬 liquid
} ～を飲む take ～

ぬり薬

(頭髪用) lotion
(油性) ointment
salve /sæv/
} 傷に～をつける apply ～ to a wound

2. 薬屋

店 a pharmacy, a drugstore 〔米〕
a chemist's 〔英〕

店主 a pharmacist, a druggist 〔米〕
a chemist 〔英〕

《関連語》

1. 家庭常備薬 (Home Medicines)

【内服薬】

かぜ薬 cold remedy [medicine]

鎮痛・解熱剤 aspirin, non-aspirin painkiller / せき止め　cough syrup / のどあめ，トローチ　medicated drop;［医学用語］troche; throat lozenge

胃腸薬

消化剤　indigestion relievers / 制酸剤　antacids / 便秘薬　laxatives

【外用薬】

包帯　bandage / ばんそう膏　adhesive plaster, band-aid（商品名）/ 筋肉痛はり薬　(medicated) plaster / 氷のう　ice pack / 消毒薬　antiseptic; antiseptic ointment / 点眼薬　eye drops / 点鼻薬　nose drops; nose spray

〈注〉 英米は医薬分業で，医師の処方箋 (prescription) を持って薬局に行って薬を買う。上記のような簡単な薬は家庭に備えておく。

2．処方薬（Prescription Medicines）

抗生物質　antibiotics / 抗アレルギー薬　allergy medicines /（強い）鎮痛剤　(strong) painkillers / 精神安定剤　tranquilizers / 抗鬱剤　antidepressants

3．医薬外薬剤（Non-Medical Chemicals）

消毒・滅菌剤　disinfectant / 毒性物質　toxic substances（medicine とは言わない）/ 防かび剤　fungicide / 除草剤　herbicide; weedkiller / 殺虫剤　pesticide

くせ（癖）→ しゅうかん・かんしゅう

a habit; a way

1．…の癖がある

【気質上の】

彼はくだらないことで大騒ぎする癖がある。

He has a habit of making a fuss about nothing.

He tends to make a fuss about [over] trivial things.

【身振り・しぐさ】

彼はいらいらすると指で机をトントンたたく癖がある。

He has a habit of tapping on the desk with his fingers when impatient.

彼はてれると頭をかく癖がある。

He has a habit [trick] of scratching his head when embarrassed.

〈注〉 trick は奇妙な癖に用いられる。上の文では habit がより一般的。

彼は話し方に独特の癖がある。

He has a peculiar way of speaking.

2．…の癖がつく

彼は喫煙の癖がついてしまった。

He got into the habit of smoking.

私は夜ふかしの癖がついてしまった。

I have {picked up / fallen into} the habit of {staying up late. / keeping late hours.}

〈注〉 fall into ... は悪い癖がついたと思うとき使う。

【癖をつける】

子供には小さいうちによい癖［生活習慣］をつけてやりたいと思う。

I'd like my children to form good living habits when they are still very young.

子供を甘やかすな。（癖をつけるな）

Don't spoil [indulge] your children.

【癖を直す】

一度ついた癖はなかなか直せない。

It is difficult to get rid of one's bad habits.

くたくた → つかれる

1．人主語

【くたくたに疲れる】

その晩，私はくたくたにくたびれて正体なく眠った。（英語では丸太のように）

I was {dead tired / exhausted} and slept like a log that night.

一日中庭仕事で彼はくたくたに疲れた。

He is utterly worn out from working in the garden all day.

〈注〉 口語では wash out, drain などが使われる。utterly は意味を強めている。

2. 物主語

彼のオーバーはくたくただ[だいぶくたびれている]。

His overcoat is completely worn-out.

くだもの（果物）

fruit

〈注〉 fruit は果物一般を指すときは集合名詞。食品として考えるときは物質名詞で無冠詞・単数形。いろいろな種類を念頭においた場合は〔米〕普通名詞・単数で冠詞をつけて a fruit，または複数形で fruits のように使う。

【果物一般】

カリフォルニアの土壌は果物の栽培に適している。

The soil of California is fit for growing fruit.

【食品】

私は甘いお菓子はあまり好きでないが果物は好きだ。

I don't care for sweets but I like fruit.

病院の前に大きな果物屋がある。

There's a big fruit shop in front of the hospital.

【種類】

今は季節の果物各種，ブドウ，梨，それに出はじめの柿やリンゴなどが出そろっている。

Now we have all the fruits of the season—grapes, pears, early persimmons and apples.

【果物に関するイディオム】

He must be bananas.（＝crazy）
He went bananas.
（あいつは頭がおかしい）

They drove him bananas.（とうとういかれてしまった）

He's nutty (as a fruitcake).（あいつは頭がおかしい）

〔米〕It's a lemon.（＝defective）（それは欠陥商品だ）

〈注〉 この場合の lemon は調子が悪くてどこかいつも具合の悪い機械，カメラなどについて言う。

《関連語》
リンゴ apple / 西洋梨 pear / 桃 peach / アンズ apricot / バナナ banana / パイナップル pineapple / ミカン mandarin orange / オレンジ orange / レモン lemon / グレープフルーツ grapefruit / ブドウ grapes / ザクロ pomegranate

くだらない（下らない）→ つまらない

ばかばかしい **foolish; silly**

名 **rubbish; nonsense**

無益な **useless; worthless**

ささいな **trivial**

テレビにはずいぶんとくだらない番組がある。

There are a lot of silly TV programs.

この本はくだらない。

This book's rubbish.

【くだらないこと】

くだらないことを言うな。

Don't talk such rubbish [nonsense].

くだらないことを気にするな。

Don't {worry / get worried} about {nothing. / trivial things. / trivialities. / such minor [small] things.}

2人はくだらないことでけんかを始めた。

They started fighting about [over] nothing.

【まったくくだらない！】

Nonsense! / How absurd! / Rubbish! / Ridiculous!

くばる（配る）

1. 分配する

【新聞】

少年は毎朝自転車で新聞を配っていた。

Every morning the boy delivered newspapers by bicycle.

【印刷物】
プリントを配ります。
I'm going to give you a handout.
今，プリントを配りました。
I've given out the handouts.
〈注〉◆配って歩くのならば give でよい。
前列の人に渡して取りまわしてもらうのなら，
Here are the handouts. Each of you, take one please.（プリントあげます。１部とってください）
このほかの表現としては次のような言い方がある。

Pass them { back.（後ろにまわして）
along [across, up].（方向により表現が変る）
around.（円形に座っている場合）}

◆a handout は何枚とじてあっても単数でよい。特に説明するなら，a two-page handout（２枚１組），また，ひとつは gist（論文の要旨），もうひとつは exercise（練習問題）のように２種類であればhandouts と複数にする。

若い男の人が２人で校門の所でちらしを配っているのを見た。
I saw two young men at the school gate distributing [handing out] handbills.

【食べ物】
食事を配る　serve（up）the food
ウエディングケーキは普通食事の終ったところで切ってお客様ひとりひとりに配られる。
The wedding cake is usually cut and served to each guest at the end of the dinner.

【贈答品】
日本では引っ越しをするとご近所に何かお近づきのしるしを配る習慣がある。
In Japan it is customary for people coming to live in a new place to take [give, distribute〔*formal*〕] small presents to their neighbors.

【トランプ】
トランプを配る　deal（out）cards

２．気配り

彼女は気配りがよく行き届く。
She's considerate and attentive.
外交官は気配りの行き届く人でなくてはならない。
Diplomats have to have tact.
〈注〉 have tact とか be tactful とは，人間関係をスムーズにして緊張を和らげ，人を不愉快にさせない能力を持っていることを言う。intellectual, analytical ability であり skill（知的，分析的な技能）であるが，同時に personality（個人の資質）の一部のようになり得る。be considerate とは他人の気持ちになることができることで，これも personality と考えられる。「気配り」は tact と consideration の中間。

くべつ（区別）

名 **distinction**

【区別する】 distinguish
ＡとＢを区別する
tell [know] A from B; distinguish A from B; draw a line between A and B

【公私の区別をする】
公私の区別をはっきりつけなければならない。
You have to { distinguish clearly / draw a sharp line } between public and private affairs.

【正邪の区別をする】
子供にはまず第一に善悪の区別を教えなければならない。
Children should first of all be taught the distinction [difference] between right and wrong.
かわいそうにその子は良いことと悪いことの区別もできない。
The poor boy { doesn't know / can't tell [distinguish] } right from wrong.

【にせ物を区別する】
私には天然真珠か養殖真珠か区別できない。
I cannot tell real [natural] pearls from artificial [cultured] ones.

【区別なしに】
あの学校は18歳以上ならば男女・人種の区別なしに受け入れる[入学できる]。

That school admits anyone over eighteen
- without regard to sex or race.
- without discrimination by race or sex.
- irrespective of sex or race.

くみ（組）

a group; a class; a team; ２人組 **a pair**

1．学校関係

a class

【同じ組の子】 a classmate

彼女はうちの組の子だ。

She's in my class.

私たちは去年同じ組だった。

We were classmates last year.

【組の担任(の先生)】

the teacher in charge of my [our] class; my [our] homeroom teacher

【３年１組】

3.1; three one; Class 1 [one] of the 3rd grade

〈注〉「１組」を the first class と言うと能力別クラスのように聞える。A組，B組のようにアルファベットで組名をつけることもあるが「３年B組」は 3B; three B と言う。

【クラス会】 a class meeting

2．グループ

２人ずつ組になってスケートをしている。

They are skating two by two [in pairs].

彼は子供たちを５人ずつの組に分けた。

He divided the children into groups of five.

3．セット

このカップは６個で１組になっている。

These cups come six to a set.

このティーポットはこちらのカップと組になっております。セットでお売りしています。

This teapot goes with these cups. They are sold as a set.

くむ（組む）

1．組み立てる

本箱を組み立てる

assemble a bookcase

活字を組む

set (up) type（コンピュータで）

大工さんたちは家の骨組みをせっせと組み立てている。

Carpenters were busy putting up [making] the frame of the house.

彼らは足場を組んでいるところだ。

They are now putting up the scaffolding.

【予算】

政府は今，来年度の予算を組むのに忙しい。

The Government is now busy drawing up the budget for the new fiscal year.

2．交差させる

彼は腕を組んで聞き入っていた。

He listened with his arms folded.

彼女は腰かけて足を組んでたばこを吸っていた。

She sat smoking with her legs crossed.

その若い男女は腕を組んで歩いていた。

The young couple walked arm in arm.

スクラムを組め。

Form a scrummage.

3．協力する

【チーム】

僕はビルと組んで河井兄弟と対戦した。

Bill and I played against the Kawai brothers.

その試合ではビルと組んだ。

Bill was my partner in the match.

僕はテッド，ジョン，ビル，エイミーと組んでいる。

Ted, John, Bill and Amy are in my group.

バレーボールチームを組むにはもう２人足りない。

Two more people are needed / We need two more people } to { form / set up } a volleyball team.

看護婦数人，麻酔医１人，外科医１人か２人がチームを組んで治療に当っている。

Several nurses, an anesthetist, and one or two surgeons work as a team.

【事業】

彼は叔父と組んで事業を始めるところだ。

He's starting a business in conjunction [together] with his uncle.

二つの会社が組んで特殊なセラミックス開発に挑んでいる。

Two companies are cooperating to develop some special ceramics.

くむ（汲む，酌む）

1．液体をすくい取る

池から水をバケツ１杯くんできてくださいませんか。

Will you fetch a bucket of water from the pond?

私たちは流れまで下りてゆき，冷たい水を手の平にくんで飲んだ。

We went down to the stream, scooped the cool water into our hands and drank.

ジョニー，水を１杯くんできてね。

Johnny, bring me a glass of water, please.

僕は井戸にまわって冷たい水を水差しにくみ，老人のところに持って行った。

I went around to the well and poured some cool water into a pitcher and took it to the old man.

私はやかんに水をくみ，ガスにかけた。

I filled the kettle with water and put [set] it on the gas.

井戸から水をくみ上げるには普通ポンプを使う。

A pump is usually used in drawing water from a well.

2．考慮する

明らかに彼は上司をかばうために偽証をしたのだった。裁判官はその間の事情をくんで［情状酌量して］禁固２年に減刑した。

It was clear that he had given false evidence to cover up for his boss. Taking that into consideration, the judges gave him a reduced sentence of two years.

彼女の気持ちをくんで，彼らは少年をあまり厳しく罰しなかった。

Taking her feelings into consideration, they didn't punish the boy so severely.

〈注〉 take《something》into consideration はよく使われるが，次のような文では「ふところ具合を考えて」ぐらいの意になる。

Taking my budget into consideration [Considering my budget], I think I won't join the trip this year.

くやしい（悔しい）→ おこる

［事柄が］ **annoying; frustrating; mortifying**

［人がくやしく思う］ **annoyed; frustrated; mortified**

【くやしい】

彼の娘さんが私を悪く言っているなんてすごくくやしい。

I was terribly irked to hear that his daughter had spoken ill of me.

彼女の皮肉たっぷりな言葉に何とかやり返したいと彼はくやしがっている。

He was vexed about how to respond to her sarcastic remark.

ジムは負けず嫌いなのでゲームに負けるといつもくやしがった。

Jim was very competitive and always felt mortified [annoyed, angry] when he lost a game. （普通なら disappointed 程度である）

【しゃくに障る】

テッドは利口すぎてどうも苦手だ。私たちはよく一緒に仕事をするが，どういうものか人は彼がやったのだと思うらしい。くやしいよ[しゃくに障るよ]，まったく。

Ted is too clever for me. We often work together but somehow people think he did it. I'm always frustrated.

トムは遅刻ばかりしていていっこうに勉強しているようには見えないのに，試験になるといい点をとる。まったくくやしいよ[しゃくに障る]。

Tom is always late and doesn't seem to be working hard, but in exams he gets good marks. It's really annoying.

くやしいけど[しゃくだけど]彼にはとうていかなわない。

Though I hate to admit it, I'm not his equal.

Though it's annoying [frustrating], I have to admit that he's far better than I.

【くやしいときの叫び】

How exasperating [annoying, irritating, frustrating]!

〈注〉 くやしいときの表現には Damn it! / Hell! など数かぎりなくある。

ずるーい。

That's not fair!

よくも汚い手を使ったな。

What a dirty trick!

How devious!

〈注〉◆「くやしい」は英語にするなら

feel { angry and frustrated / annoyed and angry with some feeling of defeat or rivalry }

《something is》 annoying and mortifying

とでも言おうか。この感情は競争意識からくるもので，日本人はこの意識が強いと言う人もいる。

次の文は典型的な「くやしい」状況。

A mother who believes her son will triumph over his rival(s) and win the prize feels mortified and angry when he loses.（息子が賞をとると信じていた母親，競争相手に賞をもってゆかれ腹立たしいやらくやしいやら）

◆「しゃくに障る」は「くやしい」より表面的で一時的な感情。

彼はまったくしゃくに障る。

He really gets on my nerves.

しゃくに障る言葉[態度]

{ a provoking / an irritating } remark [attitude]

◆相手にくやしい思いをさせる表現には次のようなものがある。

{ prick / pop } somebody's { balloon / bubble }（得意の鼻をくじく）

put someone on the spot（窮地に追い込む）

be put on the spot（窮地に追い込まれる〔米 *slang*〕）では，たとえば知ったかぶりをしたすぐ後で何か聞かれて，それを知らなくて返答に窮したような状況。当の本人はやりこめられたくやしさを味わう。

くやみ（悔やみ）→あいさつ

くやむ（悔やむ）→くい・くやむ

くよくよする

1．こだわる

【くよくよする】 worry about

くよくよするな。（激励）

Don't worry.

Don't take it too seriously.

くよくよして眠れないなんてことないように。

Don't lose any sleep over it.

くだらないことにくよくよするな。

Don't worry about such a trivial thing.

〈注〉 Take it easy. も似た表現だが，Relax.（気楽にしろ）に近い。

2．あきらめ

【くよくよしても仕方ない】

覆水盆に帰らず。

It's no use crying over spilt milk.

過ぎたことにくよくよしても始まらない。

No one gets anywhere looking backward.

過ぎたことは過ぎたこと。

What's done is done.

過去なんか放っておけ。

Let the past take care of itself.

気にしなさんな。明日という日がある[またチャンスがある / 捨てたもんじゃないよ]。

Never mind.
{ Tomorrow's another day. [There's always tomorrow.]
You'll have another chance.
It's not so bad.

クラブ

a club

【クラブ活動】 正課外の活動 extracurricular activities; club activities

【クラブに入る】 join a club

彼は ESS クラブに入ろうかと思っている。

He's thinking of joining the ESS (club).

彼はコーラスクラブに入った。

He joined the chorus club.

【クラブに属する】 belong to a club

彼は演劇クラブに属している[入っている]。

He belongs to the drama club.

〈注〉 **join** と**belong to**

join は「入る」行為を表し，したがって入る前は will join と未来形，入ってしまったら joined と過去形(または完了形 have [has] joined)を使う。belong to は「～に属している」という状態を表し，He belongs to ... と現在形もあり得る。belong to を「入る」の意味に，また join を「入っている」の意味によく誤用するので注意。

join ← become a member
belong to ← be a member

【クラブが盛んである】 (具体的に述べるのがよい)

うちのクラブは部員も多いし活発に活動をしている。

Our club has many members and they are all very active.

【クラブで忙しい】

我々はクラブで忙しい。

We are busy with club activities.

【クラブで合宿する】 →がっしゅく

【クラブがある】

今日はクラブがある。

I have a club meeting today.
I have some club activities today.
There'll be some club activities today.

〈注〉◆「クラブは楽しい」は ×The club is happy. とは言えない。私たちが楽しいのであって，漠然と楽しいとか辛いと表現せず，具体的に状況を述べる方が自然である。たとえば次のように始める。

I like the club because ...
I'm happy when ...
I [We] enjoy myself [ourselves] { when ... / because ...
The club is a happy one. (雰囲気がよい)
The club is enjoyable because ...
I find it pleasant to { be in the club because ... / be with club members ...

◆米国の大学には chorus, drama, debate, film などのクラブはあるが運動系はクラブではなく対外試合用に大学のチームがある。日本の大学ほどクラブが重視されておらず，参加しない者も多いといわれる。大学によっては fraternity, sorority と呼ばれるクラブのようなものがあるが，これらは学究的または社交的な集まりで日本のクラブとは違う。

英国の大学にも日本の大学のクラブに当るものはないが，オーケストラや合唱隊などはあり，She belongs to the orchestra. とか She's a member of the school choir. のように言う。運動系のチームはあり，He belongs to the football team. とか He plays cricket.のように言う。

くらべる (比べる) → ひかく

compare A **and** B**; compare** A **with** (**to**) B**; make a comparison between** A **and** B

【比べると】

アフリカ中部の夏と比べれば日本の夏は暑すぎるなんて文句は言えないと思う。

Comparing summer in Japan with that of Central Africa, we feel we shouldn't complain that it is too hot.

日本の夏はアフリカ中部(の夏)と比べれば楽なものだ。

Summer in Japan is tame compared with { the one / that } in Central Africa.

〈注〉◆**compared** と **comparing**

主語 (最初の例文なら we) が何かと何かを比較しているのなら comparing, また compare の意味上の主語 (同 summer in Japan) が比較される側であれば compared を使う。~ing の形は能動，~ed は受動の原則を考えればよくわかる。

◆次の「比べて」は必ずしも compare を使わなくても表現できる。

【比較級】

ギリシャ語はラテン語と比べてずっと難しい。

Greek is more difficult to learn than Latin.

メアリはベスと比べてずっと頭がいい。

Mary is far cleverer than Beth.

【最上級】

彼はクラスでほかの生徒とは比べものにならない，一番頭の切れる生徒だった。

He was by far the most brilliant student in his class.

彼女は私なんかと比べものにならない。

She's much much better than I. (技量を比べている)

I'm no match for her. (競争を念頭においた言い方)

〈注〉 比較表現に関する注意事項は「ひかく」の項に述べている。次にあげる例文の下線部は脱落しやすいので注意。

学校時代と比べてあんな長い夏休みはとれない。

I cannot have such a long vacation as <u>we had while at</u> school.

今の生徒たちは僕たちの中学時代と比べておとなしい。

The boys are docile compared with <u>those I knew in</u> my high school days.

くる（来る）

〈注〉 現在いる場所や自分の家の場所を中心として，こちらに向かって来るのが come である。ただし，相手の立場を尊重して「そちらへ行きます」の意で “I'll come.” のように言うこともできる。「来る」「来た」は come のほかに be やその他の動詞でも表現できる。

1. 空間的

【到着】

バスは10分ごとに来る。

The bus comes every ten minutes.

さあ，動物園に来ましたよ。

Here we are at the zoo.

あっ，タクシーが来た。

Here comes the taxi.

車が玄関に来ている。

The car is (ready) at the door.

玄関にだれか来た。

There's someone at the door.

今頃何しに来たの？

What brings you here now?

【出身】

どこから来たんですか。

Where are you from?

オハイオから来ました。

I'm from Ohio.

【入手】

手紙が来ましたよ。

Here's a letter for you.

うちからちっとも手紙が来ない。

I haven't heard from home for a long time.

今日は何も手紙が来なかった。

We didn't get any letters today.

今日は郵便が何も来ていない。

There's no mail today.

There's nothing in the mail.

No mail came today. （来なかった）

朝刊は来ましたか。

Have you got the morning paper?

【襲来】

今日の午後，台風が九州にやって来る（だろう）。

The typhoon will hit Kyushu this afternoon.

【伝来】

仏教はインドで興り，6世紀に日本に伝来した。

Buddhism, which originated in India, was introduced into Japan in the sixth century.

2. 時間的

誕生日が来たら17歳になる。

I'll be seventeen on [at] my next birthday.

もうすぐ夏休みが来る。

Summer vacation will { come soon. / soon be here. }

We'll have {a holiday〔英〕/ summer vacation} soon.

今年は春の来るのが遅い。

Spring is late this year.

3. 原因

あなたの病気は過労からきたものだ。

Your illness comes from overwork.

文化の違いや言語の障壁からくる誤解というものがある。

There are misunderstandings caused by cultural differences and language barriers.

偏見は無知からくるものだ。

Prejudice comes from ignorance.

4. 動詞＋来る

〈注〉「持って来る，取って来る，行って来る」など，「来る」は多くの動詞に続けて使われるが，それぞれに別の英語表現が対応する。come には関係ない。

【往復】

持って来る bring（↔ take 持って行く）

取って来る get, pick up, fetch

車を取って来なければならない。

I have to go and get my car.

帰り道にクリーニング店に寄って洗濯物を取って来た。

She picked up the laundry on her way home.

ボールを取っておいで。

Go and fetch the ball.

〈注〉fetch は米国では犬にしか使わないそうであるが，英国では犬に限らない。

駅まで彼女を送りに行って来たところだ。

I've been to the station to see her off.

ちょうど旅行から帰って来たところだ。

I've just returned from a trip.

【開始】

雨が降ってきた。

It's begun to rain.

It has begun to rain.

日に日に暑くなってきた。

It's getting hotter day by day.

自分の町の歴史がだんだん面白くなってきた。

I'm getting interested in the history of our town.

くるしい（苦しい）・くるしむ

1. 肉体的

痛みに苦しむ

feel pain, be in pain, suffer

苦しいよ。

I feel awful [terrible].

彼女はのどの渇きに苦しんだ。

She was beset〔*literary*〕[tormented, plagued] by thirst.

彼は激しい痛みに苦しんだ。

He was tortured [racked] with pain.

呼吸が苦しい。（走ったあと）

I am short [out] of breath.

彼は喘(ぜん)息の発作が起きると呼吸がひどく苦しくなる。

When he has a fit (of asthma), he can hardly breathe [has great difficulty (in) breathing].

2. 精神的 →くろう

苦しい言い訳　a poor [weak] excuse

生活が苦しい　be badly off

彼は苦しい立場に立たされていた。

He was in {a difficult / an awkward} position [situation].

彼は経済的に苦しい立場になった[ピンチになった]。

He felt caught [trapped, stuck] in money problems.

その当時，農民は重税に苦しんでいた。

Those days peasants suffered under heavy taxes.

その年は人々は干ばつに苦しんだ。

People suffered from drought that year.

くろう（苦労）

【苦労する】

仕事を持っていたので3人の子供を育てるにはずいぶん苦労した。

Because I had a job {it was difficult for me to bring / I had a difficult time bringing} up my three children.

あの頃はお金には苦労した。

In those days we were pressed for money.

【苦労を共にする】

彼は長年，苦労を共にした妻を失った。

He lost his wife, who'd shared many troubles with him.

【苦労して】

彼はさんざん苦労してやっと老人組合結成にこぎつけた。

After a lot of effort he succeeded in organizing the old people's union.

これは苦労して手にした金だ。むだ遣いをしないでくれ。

This is hard-earned money. Don't waste it.

彼は苦労して働きながら大学を卒業した。

He worked his way through college.

【苦労をかける】

ご苦労をおかけしてすみませんでした。

I'm sorry {to have put you to / I've given you} so much trouble.

私は母に苦労をかけっぱなしだった。

I was a constant source of anxiety for [to] my mother.

【苦労のない】

彼女は苦労知らずに育った。

She was brought up free from care.

彼女は苦労知らずの生活をしている。

She's leading an easy life.

【苦労が報われる】

彼の苦労は報われた。

His efforts were {not wasted. / rewarded.}

【慣用表現】

彼女は苦労性である。

She worries about everything.

She's a worrywart.

彼女は苦労やつれしていた。

She looked careworn.

〈注〉 hardships は本当に深刻な艱難(かんなん)辛苦を指すので，普通の文に使うと大げさに響く。

け

けいかく（計画）

名 **a plan**

【計画する[を立てる]】

動 他 plan; make a plan

彼らは北海道行きを計画している。

They are planning to go to Hokkaido.

次年度の始まる半年前に，その年度の行事予定を計画します。

We make the plan for the next year six months beforehand [ahead of time].

今月末までに旅行計画を作成し，教育委員会に提出せねばならない。

We have to work out the schedule of the trip and hand it (in) to the school board by the end of this month.

市当局は5か年計画に基づいて事業計画を立てる。

The city plans its projects five years at a time [in five-year cycles].

実現できないような計画を立てるな。

Don't make impracticable [unworkable] plans.

【計画中】

まだ計画中[の段階]だ。

It is { in the planning stage. / being planned. / under consideration.

The planning is under way.

【計画を実行する】 carry out the [a] plan

計画を立てたら最後までやり通しなさい。

If you make a plan, try to carry it through.

計画通りうまくいった[いかなかった]。

The plan worked well [did not work out].

【計画の中止】

彼らの仲間の1人が病気になって計画は中止せざるを得なくなった。

They had to give up the plan because one of the members became [fell] ill.

計画は中止となった。

The program was cancelled.（公的行事・事業の場合）

【慣用表現】

5か年計画[長期計画]で

on a five-year [a long-range] plan

計画的犯罪

a premeditated crime

計画的に…する

do《something》deliberately

《類義語》

plan　一般的に広く使われる。それだけ漠然とした語でもある。

program　計画から実施・完成までを考えに入れた語。

project　大規模で壮大な計画。具体的でしばしば実験的。実施に重点を置いた語。

ex. reforestation project　造林計画
birth control project　産児制限計画

campaign　団体・組織などが社会的な目的をもって一般に呼びかけて行う運動。寄付金募集を伴う場合が多い。各自が役割をもって目的に立ち向かう。

けいき（景気） → けいざい

けいけん（経験）

名 **an experience**

経験する　動 **experience**

【経験がある[ない]】

have an [no] experience

彼はその方面では豊かな経験がある。

He has a lot of experience in that.

私は看護婦の経験がある。

I once worked as a nurse.

彼は教職の経験がなかった。

He had no { experience (in) teaching. / teaching experience.

1年以上の経験のある人を求めている。

We want a person with more than one year's experience.

【経験を問わない】

お手伝いさん求む。経験を問わず。

Help wanted. Experience not necessary.（広告）

【経験を生かす】

私は自分の経験を生かせる仕事に就きたい。

I'd like to get a job in which I can use [make use of] my experience.

〈注〉 上の文は正しいが，経験を具体的に述べることがさらに望ましい。

【いい経験になった】

それはいい経験になった[その経験から多くを学んだ]。

The experience taught me a lesson [great deal].

I learned much from the experience.

失敗はいい経験になった。

The failure was a good experience.

〈注〉「いい経験になった」は次のようにも言える。

It was a good experience.

I had a good experience.

The experience {was good for me. / did me good.}（ためになった）

【今まで経験した中で…】

この冬は今まで経験したことのない[今まで経験した中で一番の]寒さだ。

This winter has been one of the coldest I have ever been through.

【経験から】

私はそのことを経験から知っている。

I know it from experience.

経験して学ぶのが一番だ。本を読んだり人に指図されたりするよりも。

It is best to learn by experience, not by reading nor by directions of others.

〈注〉

learn {from experience 自分の経験をもとにして何かを学ぶ。 / by experience 直接体験するという方法で何かを身につける。}

【経験がなければ】

これは経験してみなければなかなかわからない。

It takes experience to understand this.

【楽しい[苦しい，忘れられない]経験】

a pleasant [a bitter, an unforgettable] experience

それは私にはまったく新しい経験だった。

It was quite a new experience for me.

【経験のある】 形 experienced

経験豊かな先生

an experienced teacher

〈注〉 experience が一般的な経験を意味するときは抽象名詞で数えられない。

我々は経験で物事を学ぶ。

We learn by experience.

一方，experience が個々の体験を指すときには数えることができ，It was a new experience./I had a bitter experience. と冠詞が必要。

次の文の experience の冠詞の有無に注意。

Joining the international camp was a good experience, because it gave me experience in getting along with different kinds of people.（国際キャンプに参加したことはいい経験になった。いろいろな人たちと付き合うという経験をすることができたから）

けいこ（稽古） → れんしゅう

名（a）**practice**

けいこする 動 **practice**〔米〕; **practise**〔英〕

【楽器】

彼女は5歳のときピアノのけいこを始めた。

She began [started] piano lessons when she was five.

She began to go for piano lessons when she was five.

【茶・華】

お茶[お華]のけいこをする[に行く]

have [take] lessons in tea ceremony [flower arrangement]

【舞踊】

踊りのけいこに行く

take dancing lessons

〈注〉 take lessons in の次には flower arrangement のように名詞がくるのが普通で，in ～ing の形はあまり使われない。

【柔道】
僕は高校で柔道(のけいこ)をやった。

I {received [got] training / was trained} in judo in high school.

【練習】
彼女は今ピアノのけいこをしている。

She's now practicing [practising] the piano.

もう少しけいこをすれば上手になるだろう。

You'll be a good player with [after] a little more practice.

僕はこのところけいこ不足だ。

I'm out of practice lately.

【演劇】
演技のけいこ　a rehearsal
演技のけいこをする　動 rehearse
舞台げいこ　a stage rehearsal

〈注〉 take lessons は先生があって習うこと，practice は自分１人で反復練習すること。スポーツは種類により practice も have training（トレーニングをする）も使う。

けいこう（傾向）

名 **a tendency; a trend;**（個人の）**(an) inclination**

傾向がある　動 **tend**

《類義語》
tendency　統計的なまたは個々の人の指向・傾向。
trend　個人でなく社会全体の風潮・動向。ある時代・国における風潮・思潮。時代とともに変化する流行，ファッションなどにも使える。
trend of thought（思潮）
the latest trends in women's clothes（女性服の最新の流行）
inclination　個人の好み。tendency ほど強くない傾向。

1．社会的な動向

【景気回復】
景気は改善の傾向にある。

Business is showing signs of improvement.（傾向が見える）
Business is improving.（回復してきた）

銀行が金利を下げると，そのあと景気回復の傾向が出るものだ。

{Business tends / Business usually shows a tendency} to improve after banks lower their interest rates.

【人口増加】
この地域の人口は増加の傾向にある。

The population of this area is increasing.

〈注〉 The population ... shows a tendency to increase. は不自然。

【麻薬常用】
若者の間に麻薬常用の傾向が広がってきている。

Among young people there is a growing tendency toward drug taking.

【暴力】
校内暴力は低年齢化の傾向にある。

Violence is tending to occur in the lower schools rather than in the upper ones.

【結婚年齢】
10年前と比べると，男女とも結婚年齢が2，3年遅れる傾向がある。

There is a tendency [trend] for both men and women to remain unmarried two or three years longer than they did ten years ago.

〈注〉 この場合の「傾向」は tendency でも trend でもよいが，tendency は個々の人々の指向を，trend は常に移りゆく現象としてのその時代の風潮を意味している。

2．性向

老人は保守的に，若者は急進的になる傾向がある。

Older people tend to be conservative and young people radical.

彼女は何にでもすぐ感心する傾向がある。

She is easily impressed.

彼は物事を深刻に考えすぎる傾向がある。

He tends to take things too seriously.

彼女は何でもおおげさに言う傾向がある。

She has a tendency to exaggerate things.

彼は難しいことは逃げてしまう傾向がある。

He is inclined to avoid confrontation.

cf. His inclination to ... is ... のような構文もつくれる。

〈注〉「…の傾向がある」と言いたいとき，次のように同格の that 節で tendency を修飾するのは誤り。

×There is a tendency that young people squander money.(若者はお金を浪費する傾向がある)

次のように for ... to の形にするのが正しい。

There is a tendency for young people to squander money.

けいこく（警告）

名 (a) warning

動 warn; give warning to

【警告する】

外出するなという警告が出た。囚人が1人脱獄したというのだ。

They warned us not to go out because there was a report that a criminal had escaped from prison.

【警告される】

彼は勉強をしないと単位を落すと先生から警告された。

He got a warning from his professor that he would fail his course unless he worked harder.

こんな悪天候に山に登るなと森林監視員に警告された。

The ranger warned me not to climb the mountain in such bad weather.

医者に過労を避けるよう警告された。

The doctor warned me against overworking [not to overwork].

〈注〉だれが警告するかに重点が置かれていない場合，特に警告される側が me「私」であれば，日本語では「された」と受動態にするのが一般的。一方，英語では能動態が自然である。

けいざい（経済）

名 **economy; economics**

1．経済一般

【景気】

インフレ(ーション) inflation

デフレ(ーション) deflation

不況　depression

景気の後退　recession

あの会社は景気がいい。

That company is doing well.

景気はどうだね。

How's business?

このところ景気がよくない。

Recently business hasn't been good.

その国の経済は10年間の繁栄のあと今や下降しつつある。

The economic condition of that country is declining now after ten years of prosperity. (cf. 景気が回復しつつある be improving; be recovering)

【好況】

経済は好況[景気は上々]である。

The economic conditions are good.

ファッション産業は目下好況である。

The fashion industry is now prosperous.

【黒字[赤字]である】 be in the black [red]

そのコンサートは，主催者側の発表によれば入場料収入により収支は黒字とのことである。

According to the organizer, the balance of accounts showed that admission fees had put the concert in the black.

2．国際経済

世界経済　(the) world economy

国際経済　the international economy

欧州連合　European Union (略 EU)

欧州議会　the Council of Europe

経済協力開発機構

Organization for Economic Cooperation

and Development (略 OECD)
東南アジア諸国連合(アセアン)
Association of Southeast Asian Nations (略 ASEAN)
石油化学工業を発展させるために外国資本の投入を求めている。
They are seeking foreign capital [investment] to develop their petrochemical industry.

3. 流通・産業

【通貨】 currency
a dollar; a cent〔米〕
a pound; a penny (pl. pence)〔英〕
金本位制　gold standard
【資本】 capital
基金　a fund
投資　an investment
原価　the (prime) cost(生産にかかった費用)
元金　the principal
値段　a price
費用, 出費　expenses(生産費および雑費を合計した経費)
料金　(a) charge (サービスに対する支払い)
【産業】 an industry
第一次[二次/三次]産業
a primary [secondary / tertiary] industry
コンビナート　an industrial complex [park]
国民総生産
Gross National Product (略 GNP)
国内総生産
Gross Domestic Product (略 GDP)
独占禁止法
Anti-Monopoly Law (of Japan)
公正取引委員会
Fair Trade Commission (of Japan)
〈注〉 独禁法, 公取委ともに (of Japan) を (Japan's) … としてもよい。

4. クレジット, ローン

クレジットカード　a credit card
クレジットで　on credit
リボルビングチャージ revolving charge
月賦で　(→げっぷ)
by [in] installments; on installment
頭金, 手付金　down payment
家のローン
mortgage; house purchasing loan
家のローンを支払う
pay back the [one's] mortgage
【その他】
家計費　(→かけい)
予算　family budget
支出　household expenses
小遣い　(→こづかい)
pocket money; spending money〔米〕; an allowance
倹約する　(→けんやく)
economize on; cut down on
貯金する　(→ぎんこう)
save (money)

《関連語》
財政　finance / 経済学　economics / 経済学者 economist / 経済事情　the state of the economy / 経済状況　economic [financial] conditions / 経済同盟　economic league [union, alliance] / 経済圏　economic bloc / 経済危機 economic crisis / 経済引締め　economic crunch / 経済恐慌　economic panic / 経済の行き詰まり　an economic deadlock / 経済協力 economic cooperation / 経済援助計画　an economic aid program / 自由経済　free economy / 統制経済　controlled economy / 資本主義 capitalism (cf. 社会主義 socialism)

けいさつ (警察)

police
警察庁　National Police Agency
警視庁　Metropolitan Police Department
警察署　a police station

警官　a policeman; an officer
特殊(勤務)警察　special forces [police]〔米〕
私服警官
　a plainclothes police(man) [officer]
刑事　a detective
警察機動隊　riot police [squad]

《関連語》
1. 捜査・逮捕
逮捕　arrest / 逮捕状　arrest warrant / 拘置　custody; detention / 拘置所　detention house / 刑務所　prison; gaol /dʒéil/〔英〕; jail〔米〕/ 独房　cell / 厳重取締り　clampdown / 一斉検挙　roundup / 捜査　investigation / 捜査網　dragnet / 非常線　cordon / 家宅捜査令状　search warrant / 手錠　handcuffs / 指紋　fingerprints
逮捕する　arrest / 拘置する　hold [keep] in custody; detain; confine / 厳重に取締る　clamp down on《gangs》/ 捜査網を張る　spread [drop] a dragnet / 捜査網にかかる　be caught in the police dragnet / 非常線を張る　form a cordon / 取り調べる　examine; investigate《a case》
過失致死で逮捕される
　be arrested on the charge of inflicting bodily injury resulting in death
彼は収賄容疑で逮捕された。
　He was arrested on (the) suspicion of having accepted a bribe.

2. 犯罪
犯罪　crime; felony (重罪); offense, misdemeanor (軽犯罪) / 犯罪者　criminal; felon; offender / 共犯者　accomplice / 強盗　robbery; burglary (押し込み);［人］robber; burglar (押し込み) / 窃盗　theft;［人］thief / すり　pickpocketing;［人］pickpocket / ひったくり　purse snatching;［人］purse snatcher / 不法侵入　forcible entry / 暴行　assault (法律用語); mugging (背後から襲って首を絞めること) / 誘拐　abduction; kidnapping / 誘拐犯　abducter; kidnapper / 人質　hostage / 身の代金　ransom / 不法監禁　illegal detention / 脅喝　threat / ゆすり　blackmail;［人］a blackmailer / 強姦　rape / 売春　prostitution / 売春婦　prostitute / 放火　arson / 殺人　murder; homicide; manslaughter / 殺人者　murderer / 殺人未遂　attempted murder / 重傷害(罪)　grievous bodily harm / 過失致死　unintentional manslaughter [murder] / 業務上過失致死　professional negligence resulting in death / 過失傷害　accidental [unintentional] injury / ひき逃げ(運転手)　hit-and-run (driver) / 酔っ払い運転　drunken driving / 無謀運転　reckless [dangerous] driving / 暗黒街　underworld; gangland / ギャング［総称］gang;［個人］gangster / 賄賂　bribe / 贈賄［収賄］行為　bribery / 横領　embezzlement / 汚職　corruption; graft / 詐欺　fraud; swindle / 詐欺師　swindler / 偽金造り　counterfeit;［人］a counterfeiter / 密輸　smuggling / 密輸業者　smuggler / 容疑　suspicion / 容疑者　suspect / 身元　identity / 少年非行　juvenile delinquency
横領する　embezzle / 詐欺をはたらく　swindle / 密輸する　smuggle

けいひ（経費）

expenditure; expense(s); cost(s)
an outlay

【経費がかかる】
　require a lot of money; be expensive
この企画は経費がかなりかかる。
　This project involves [requires, will cost] a lot of money.
　This program is too expensive.（かかりすぎる）
　I'm afraid the project will cost too much.（かかりすぎる）

【経費をかける】
市当局は莫大な経費をかけて市内全小学校に水泳プールを建設した。
　The city built a swimming pool at every elementary school at great expense.
軍備に莫大な経費をかけることは多くの貧し

い国の貧困をさらに増大させることにつながる。

Heavy expenditure for [on] arms makes / Heavy arms expenditures make poverty even greater in many poor countries.

【…の経費は】

新しい学校建設には見積り額で約3億円の経費がかかる。

The cost of the new school is estimated at [to be] 300 million yen.

The estimated cost of the new school is 300 millon yen.

【経費を削減する】

我々は可能な限り経費を削減しなければならない[経費節減をはからなければならない]。

We have to {decrease costs / cut down on expenses} as much as possible.

けが（怪我）

けが　**injury**

けがをする　**be injured;** 戦いで傷を負う **be wounded; be [get] hurt**

ティムがきのう野球をしていてけがをしたことを聞きましたか。

Did you hear that Tim {got hurt / was injured} during the baseball game yesterday?

【ひどいけが】

帰り道で彼は車にはねられてひどいけがをした。

On his way home he was hit by a car and was badly hurt [injured].

【軽いけが】

その事故で母親は亡くなったが子供は頭に軽いけがをしただけで助かった。

The mother was killed in the accident, but the child escaped with only (a) slight injury to his head.

【…にけがをする】

けがをしないように気をつけてよ。

Be careful not to {hurt yourself. / get hurt.

彼は自転車に乗っていて転び，足にけがをした。

He fell while riding his bicycle and injured [hurt] his leg.

〈注〉 他人については単に hurt his leg のように言うが，自分のことであればもっと具体的にけがの程度・部位を話すのが普通。以下に表現例を示す。

ex. scraped my leg on the road（すりむいた）
sprained my ankle（足をねんざした）
cut my leg（何かで切って血が出た）
hit my knee hard（膝をひどく打った）

けしき（景色）

(a) **scene**　ある一つの場所の景色。scenes と複数にもできる。

scenery　ある地方の全体的景観。

(a) **landscape**　田園・遠望など一目で眺めた風景。

a view　眺め(見る人が中心)。

松島は景色が美しいので有名である。

Matsushima is noted for its scenic beauty.

この窓からこのあたりの田園風景が一望のもとに見えます。

From this window you can {get / have} a {very good / grand / commanding} view of the whole countryside.

まったく景色が台なしだわ。(目ざわりな建物などについて)

It is an eye-sore.

It is a blot on the landscape.

〈注〉 景色・風景・光景の説明をする場合「…が～する景色」の直訳を試みてはならない。

かもめが波とたわむれる景色[風景]はいかにも平和であった。

×The scenery that the seagulls were flying over the white breakers was very peaceful.

scenery はこのように同格接続詞 that でつなげることはできない。次のように工夫する。

It was really a peaceful scene with the seagulls flying over the white breakers.

It made me (feel) very peaceful to watch the seagulls flying over the white breakers.

10年ぶりの再会に母親と息子が抱き合う光景は感動的であった。

○It was really touching to see the man embracing his old mother after ten years' separation.

×The scene that the man embraced his old mother after ten years' separation was very touching.

光景・風景の説明は次のように of 〜ing で表すこともできる。

Seeing the seagulls flying … made me very peaceful.

The scene [sight] of the man embracing … was very touching.

また，sight, scene を使わずに上の例のように to watch [see] … 〜ing でも表せる。

げしゅく（下宿）

【下宿屋】

（食事付き）a boarding house;（食事なし）a lodging house;（食事なしで外食して泊るだけ）a rooming house;（台所付きの部屋）a student hostel

家主のおばさん［おじさん］

the [our] landlady [landlord]

下宿人（食事なし）a roomer; a lodger〔英〕

（食事付き）a boarder

【借りている部屋】

a room (rooms); lodgings〔英〕(大学生の下宿。1部屋に限らない); a bedsit〔英〕(1部屋で bedroom と sitting room 兼用); a flat〔英〕; an apartment〔米〕(いわゆる1DK, 2DK式のもの)

【下宿する】

room and board　食事付き下宿

私は今川通りに下宿している。

I {have a room [an apartment] / took lodgings〔英〕} on Imagawa Street.

私はBさんの所に下宿している。

I live with the B's.

彼は姉さんの所から通っている。

He is {rooming [lodging] / boarding（食事付き）} at his elder sister's.

【下宿代】部屋代　rent

君のところ（食事付きの）下宿代はいくらですか。

How much {do you pay for / is} your room (and board)?

【寮】 dormitory〔米〕; hall〔英〕

彼は去年は自宅から通学していたが，今年は大学の近くの素人下宿に部屋を借りた。

Last year he lived at home, but this year he is boarding with a family near the campus.

彼は今度の所はだいぶ気に入っていて，卒業するまで山田さんの所にいると言っている。

He likes his new place very much, so he says he will live at the Yamada's until he finishes college.

先日手紙を書いてから部屋を引っ越した。大学の近くにいい部屋が見つかったのだ。

I've moved since last writing. I've found a nice room near my college.

しかし，ここは外食なのでお金がかかる。個人の家に下宿するより寮の方が経済的だ。

But here I have to dine out, which costs me a lot. It's more economical to live in a dorm [dormitory] than live in a private home.

次の学期には寮に入れそうだ。しかしどうも相部屋ということになりそうだ。

Next semester I'll be able to move into the dormitory, though I'm afraid I'll have to share a room with another student.

けす（消す）→ きえる

【火・灯】

火を消すのに1時間以上かかった。

It took more than an hour to extinguish〔*formal*〕[put out] the fire.

寝る前に電灯を消しなさい。

Turn out [off] the light before you go to bed.

まず第一にガスを消さなければならない。

The first thing you should do is (to) turn off the gas.

彼はろうそくの火を吹き消してから眠った。

He blew out the candle and went to sleep.

【ラジオ・テレビ】

テレビ[ラジオ]を消しなさい。

Switch [Turn] off the television [radio].

【姿】

あっと叫ぶ間もなく，すりは人込みに姿を消した。

Before I could shout, the pickpocket disappeared in the crowd.

【消失】

彼の声は吹きすさぶ風の音にかき消された。

His voice was drowned in the howling wind.

【除去】

高橋先生はいつも黒板に何か書かれると私たちが写す暇もなく消してしまわれた。

Prof. Takahashi used to erase what he had written on the blackboard before we had time to { write it down. / copy it. }

壁の落書を消しなさい。

Wipe the scribblings off the wall.

間違った言葉は赤線で消しなさい。

Strike [Cross] out the wrong words with red.

ピクニック参加者名簿で彼の名前が消してある。

I see he's (been) crossed off the picnic list.

〈注〉 リストで名前が消してあるのはこの場合 He won't be going. の意味ととれるが，参加者名簿で来た人をチェックするために線を引くこともある。

このスプレーは冷蔵庫のいやなにおいを消す。

This spray will { take away / remove } the bad smell in the { ice box. / fridge. }

けちな → きたない

【物惜しみ】stingy; miserly; tight-fisted; close-fisted /klóusfístid/

【欲張り】 greedy; grasping

【心の狭い】 narrow-minded

けちなやつ　a stingy fellow; a miser

けちなこと言うな。

Don't be stingy.

【卑劣な】base; nasty; mean

あいつはけちな手で私をごまかした。

He used a mean trick on me.

【つまらない，みすぼらしい】

poor; shabby

けちな贈物　a cheap present

けちなウサギ小屋

a shabby [miserable] rabbit hutch

【慣用表現】

あいつは僕らのすることにいちいちけちをつける。

He finds fault with whatever we do.

けっか（結果）

1. 総合的結果

【成功】

手術の結果，彼女は視力を回復した。

The operation succeeded and { she regained her sight. / her eyesight was restored. }

彼はリハビリの結果歩けるようになった。

He was able to walk again { as a result of rehabilitation. / after physical therapy. }

彼の成功は長年にわたる努力の結果である。

His success was { due to / the result of }

his long { years' / years of } hard work.

【妥協】

交渉の結果，妥協点に達した。

The negotiation resulted in a compromise.
（双方歩み寄りということになった）

【合意】

5日間にわたる討論の結果，ついに双方に満足のゆく結論に達した。

After five days of discussion, they finally reached [came to] a conclusion satisfactory to both parties.

【不成功】

センター試験は入試制度の上で，期待した結果を得られなかった。

The Center Test has not had the desired effect on the entrance examination system.

結果はただ混乱と非能率である。

The result is simply chaos and inefficiency.

結果は失敗であった。

The result was failure.

It turned out to be a failure.

It failed.

【その他】

どんな結果になるかわからない。

There is no knowing { the results. / how this will go [come out, turn out].

2. 結果としてのスコア・データ・決定

【試験】

試験の結果がわかりしだいお知らせください。

Please let me know the { exam results / results of the exam } as soon as you know.

〈注〉 親しい仲ならば「きっと知らせてよ…」Be sure to let me know ... とも言える。

【実験】

彼らの実験の結果は「メディカル・ニュース」3月号に載っている。

Their experimental results were published in the March issue of *Medical News*.

【検査】

検査をしたが期待した結果は得られなかった。

The test did not bring about the desired results.

血液検査の結果が出た。

I got the result of the blood test.

【審査】

審査結果は10分以内に発表されます。

The results will be announced in ten minutes.

【選挙】

選挙の結果はどうだった？

How did the election go [come out, turn out]?

選挙の結果は今夜11時までにはわかるだろう。

The election results will be known by eleven o'clock tonight.

【試合】

結果はどうだ？

How has it turned out?

What is the result?

（結果は）2対0です。

(The score is) 2-0.

〈注〉 2-0の読み方は two-(to-)zero; two nil〔英〕。

《類義語》

effect すぐ見える結果。効果・ききめ。

ex. 原因と結果 cause and effect

その薬は期待したほどきかなかった。

The medicine did not have the desired effect.

result 最も一般的な語。ある行動や原因の結果。総合的・全体的帰結を指すこともある。

outcome 目的のための行動の結果。

検査［調査／討論］の結果（出てきたもの）は…

The outcome of the test [survey / argument] was ...

たとえば「水質検査の結果ペーハー(pH)が高すぎた」とか，「放射能が検出された」には

outcome が使われる。
consequence　当初，予期・予測しなかった結果。
◆result, outcome, consequence は同じように使われることもある。
　次の例文はこの3語の使い方の例である。
When insect killer was sprayed in the park the result was that many caterpillars and other irritating insects died, which was the desired outcome [effect] of course. However, bees also died, and as a consequence [result] many new flowers and bushes couldn't grow because they weren't pollinated. Another consequence was that many birds couldn't get enough insects to eat. The outcome [final result] of all this was widespread destruction of the ecological balance in the area of the park.
(公園で殺虫剤をまいたら害虫は死んだが，蜜蜂まで死んで花は受粉が行われず実をつけられなくなった。また虫が減って鳥の餌がなくなった。かくして自然環境のバランスが失われた)

けっこう（結構）

1．よい
fine; nice; lovely
【よい】
結構な贈物をありがとうございます。
　Thank you for the lovely [nice] gift.
【反語的用法】
貧しい人のために募金するのは結構なことだけど…
　It's all very well to gather money to help the poor, but ....
〈注〉 英語のこの表現も but と続くのが普通で，批判的な内容が後に続く。
【満足】
僕は今の給料で結構だ。
　I'm satisfied with my salary.
　I make enough money (to meet my needs).
「コーヒーですか，紅茶ですか」「水で結構です」。
　"Coffee or tea?" "Just water, please."
「短すぎるかしら」「いや(それで)結構」。
　"Is this too short?"　"Oh no, that will do."
「鉛筆で書いていいでしょうか」「どちらでも結構」。
　"May I write in pencil?" "Either will do [be all right]."
お支払いはいつでも結構です。
　You may [can] pay whenever you like.

2．かなり
もうこの車は10年走っているがまだ結構いける。
　I've been driving this car for ten years and it still runs very well.
このワインは結構いける。
　This wine is pretty good.

3．拒絶
「もう少しいかが」「ありがとう，でももう結構です。十分いただきました」。
　"How about some more?" "Oh, no more, thanks. I've had enough."

《類義語》
be content　(1)精神的のみならず肉体的充足感。すてきなディナーの後や，友だちとお茶を飲んでくつろいでいるときの充足感など。(2)仕事の進み具合に対する満足感。
　ex. I'm content with their progress in English.
　　(彼らの英語が着々と上達して満足だ)
　I'm content with the way { it is progressing. / the work is going. }
　　(仕事の進捗状況に満足だ)
　ただし，content はやや古い感じの表現。
be satisfactory　まあまあ結構，合格である。It will do. の心境。
　［対象主語で使用］
　ex. Their progress in English is satisfactory.
　　(彼らは英語が着実にうまくなってきているね)
be satisfied　結構(That's OK.)の心境。

［人主語で使用］
ex. I'm satisfied with their progress in English.
（彼らが英語がうまくなって結構だ）
〈注〉 be satisfied の方が be satisfactory より満足感が強い。satisfied をpleased にすればもっと強い。

けっこん（結婚）

1．結婚する

marry《a person》; **get married**《to a person》《date》

あの２人はずいぶん若くして結婚した。
The couple married very young.

【だれと】

兄は芸術家と結婚した。
My brother married an artist.

私はビルと結婚します。
I'm going to marry Bill.

性格の違った者同士が結婚することもあるのだ。
People sometimes marry people very different from themselves.

【いつ】

姉さんは来月結婚する。
My sister will get married next month.

彼は先月［2003年に］結婚した。
He got married last month [in 2003].

私はこの日曜日に結婚します。
I'm getting married this Sunday.

私たちは結婚して10年になる。
We've been married for ten years.

2．結婚している

【配偶者がある】be married《to a person》

兄は芸術家と結婚している。
My brother is married to an artist.
（現在も夫婦である）

彼女は結婚している。
She is married.（既婚である）

3．結婚していない

single; not married; unmarried

彼はまだ結婚していない。
He {isn't / hasn't / hasn't got(ten)} married yet.
He is still single.

4．結婚させる

㊐㊎ **marry**

娘を結婚させる
marry one's daughter to《a man》

ウィリアムズ神父が２人を結婚させた［の司式で２人は結婚した］。
Father Williams married them.

5．その他

〈注〉◆上の例文が示すようにmarry（動 自）は「結婚する」という行為を表し，また他動詞として使われるときは「…と」と結婚相手も併せて述べるのが普通。get married は結婚するという行為に重点があり，to ... と相手を言うこともあるが，言わなくてもよい。結婚する日・時を伴うことが多い。他動詞 marry にはまた，「結婚させる」の用法もある。be married は既婚の状態，すなわち配偶者がいることで，その配偶者の名前も併せて述べれば「その人と結婚し，今も夫婦である」の意になる。

◆marry 用法のまとめ
I'll marry for love.（恋愛結婚したい）
I'm going to marry Jim.（結婚相手を決めた）
I'll get married (to Jim) next Sunday.（日取りが決まった）
I'm getting married this Sunday.（もうすぐ）
Father McDonald married us.（式を挙げた）
We are now married.（これで夫婦だ）
We've been married for ten years.（結婚して10年たった）

【プロポーズ】

結婚を申し込む
propose to《a person》

結婚を断られる
be refused [rejected〔強〕]

彼はベスに結婚を申し込んだが断られた。
He proposed to Beth but was refused.

【結婚相手】

私の結婚相手
the man [woman] whom I will [want to] marry;［婚約者］fiancé(男); fiancée(女)

「メアリが婚約したって」「相手はだれ？」

"Mary's engaged." "Who is she going to marry?"

【結婚式】marriage (ceremony); wedding

結婚式を挙げる

hold [have] a wedding [a marriage ceremony]

披露宴　wedding reception [dinner]

結婚式への招待　wedding invitation

メアリの結婚式は次の日曜日の午前10時からで，その後1時から披露宴がある。

Mary's wedding [marriage (ceremony)] will be at 10:00 a.m. next Sunday, and after that there will be a reception from 1:00 p.m.

【結婚祝い】

おめでとう。

Congratulations!

Best Wishes!

贈物　a wedding present [gift]

《関連語》

恋愛結婚　a love marriage

見合い結婚　an arranged marriage

仲人

a go-between; matchmaker（実質的仲人）

【婚約】engagement

婚約する　get engaged

婚約している　be engaged

婚約指輪　an engagement ring

新婚旅行　honeymoon

新婚ほやほやのカップル　newly weds

【離婚】名 divorce

離婚する　動 divorce; get a divorce;［状態］be divorced

協議離婚　no-fault divorce

彼は妻と協議離婚をした。

He divorced his wife by agreement.

サリーはテッドと別れた。

Sally got a divorce from Ted.

2人は別れた。

They have been divorced.

離婚届を出す（日本のやり方）

turn in the form (at the City Hall) stating our intention to divorce

〈注〉アメリカは州により異なるが，まずとる手続きは書類で離婚の意思を表示すること（file for divorce）。あとはそれぞれの場合による。

離婚訴訟を起す　sue for divorce

前夫　ex-husband; 前妻　ex-wife

【未婚の】

独身の　single

未婚の母

an unmarried mother; an unwed mother

けっしん（決心）

名 **(a) decision; (a) determination; (a) resolution**

【決心する】

decide; make up one's mind

強く決意する resolve

私は早起きする決心をした。

I made up my mind to get up early.

彼はお父さんの会社で働く決心をした。

He decided to work at [in, for] his father's company.

私はきちんと予習して授業に出る決心をした。

I've resolved to attend classes well prepared.

【決心している，決意を固めている】

be determined; have made up one's mind

彼は危険を覚悟で行く決意を固めている。

He is determined / He has made up his mind } to go although it is dangerous.

〈注〉◆decide, resolve, determine について

decide がいちばん普通に使われる。resolve はもっと強い決意を表し，determine はそのままでは形式ばった語で「決める」「判断を下す」ことであり，決意を表すときは be determined to となる。この形はごく普通に使われ，特に危険や何らかの困難に立ち向かう強い決意を表す。

◆「決心・決意」は自分の心に関することであり，客観的な事を対象にすると「決定」となるが，英語では同じ decide, determine, また settle などが使われる。→きまる，きめる

けってん（欠点）

名（性格上の）**a fault;**（主として物につい

ての欠陥） **a defect;** 弱点 **a weakness, weak points ; a flaw**

1．人について

私の欠点の一つはそそっかしいことだ。

One of my faults [weak points] is carelessness.

教員としての彼の欠点[弱点]は学生時代に優等生すぎたことだ。

His weakness as a teacher is that he was always too good [excellent] a student.

2．物・事について

この論文は推論の進め方，まとめ方にいくつかの欠点がある。

This paper has several flaws [faults] in its organization.

この映画はキャスト[俳優の人選]に重大な欠陥がある。（ひどいミスキャストである）

This movie has serious faults [flaws] in casting.

彼の提案の欠点は，どこの国もそのように多額の金を開発銀行に拠出することを喜ばないだろうということだ。

The weakness [weak point] in his proposal [argument] is that no nation will be willing to contribute so much money to the development bank.

新型エンジンは性能抜群であるが，欠点は燃費が悪いことだ。

The new engine is highly efficient but it uses too much gas.

〈注〉 have a weakness for は時として「…に目がない」の意味に使われる。すなわち，weakness＝special fondness（大好物）で次のように使う。
She has a weakness for ice cream.（彼女はアイスクリームには目がない）

3．動詞との結合

【欠点をさがす】

君はいつも他人の欠点をさがしている[あらさがしをしている]。

You are always finding fault with others.

【欠点を発見する】

調査官は原子力発電所の構造に重大な欠陥を発見した。

The investigators found some serious defects in the construction of the nuclear power plant.

【欠点を直す】 correct one's faults

私は欠点がありすぎてどこから直したらいいかわからない。

I have so many faults that I don't know where to start (in) correcting them.

げっぷ（月賦）

an installment; an instalment〔英〕

月賦による買物（分割払い）

installment buying

月賦による買い方（分割払いの方法）

an installment plan; an installment system

【月賦で】

in installments; on the installment plan

冷蔵庫は月賦で買う人が多い。

Many people buy their refrigerator on the installment plan.

車を買うにはローンを使う人が多い。

Many people use [get] a car loan to finance their cars.

私はテレビを月賦で買った。

I bought the TV set
- on installment.
- by [in] monthly installments.
- on 24-month installment.（24回分割払い）

〈注〉 英国では分割払いを口語で HP（＝hire purchase）とも言う。ex. They bought it on HP. また，buy on the never-never〔*slang*〕などとも言う。

【月賦にする】

月賦[毎月の分割払い]にするよう手続きすることもできます。

We can arrange
for you to pay in installments. 〔*most common*〕
for you to buy it on installment.
for (you to make) installment payments.

【月賦を払う】
私は来年の夏まで１万円ずつテレビの月賦を払わなければならない。
I have to pay 10,000 yen a [per] month on [for] the TV (set) until next summer.

【月賦が終る】
うれしいなあ，車の月賦がやっと終った。
I'm glad the car is finally paid for.

【家のローン】mortgage
家を買うにはローンを使うのが普通だ。
A mortgage is usually used to purchase [finance] a house.
Houses are usually bought on mortgage.
私の家は20年(間の)ローンで買った[家のローンは20年間だ]。
I have a 20-year mortgage for [on] the house.
The mortgage on the house is for 20 years.
My house is mortgaged for 20 years.

げんいん（原因）

原因 (a) **cause**; 理由 (a) **reason**

【原因は…である】
けんかの原因は何だ。
What are they quarreling about? 〔*very common*〕
What has caused this quarrel?
What led to their quarrel?
Why are they quarreling?
〈注〉 上の日本文の訳として頭に浮かぶのは What is the cause of this quarrel? である。これは文法的に正しいが，いかにも名詞化が過ぎて堅い印象を与える。上掲の文の方が自然。
彼の病気は過労が原因だ。
His {sickness / illness} {arises from / is the result of} overwork. 〔*formal*〕
It's overwork that {caused his sickness. / made him sick.}
He's sick because {of overworking. / he overworks.}

【原因不明】
彼の死因は不明だ。
The cause of [reason for] his death is unknown.
He died of unknown causes. (公式発表)

【…の原因】
フランス革命の原因
causes of [reasons for] the French Revolution

【原因と結果】cause and effect
〈注〉◆原因(cause)の類義語には，reason(理由)，origin(発端)，factor(要因)などがある。cause, reason は意味が近いがそれぞれ日本語の原因，理由に当ると考えればよい。
パニックを起す原因[理由]は何もない。
There is no {cause for / reason for} panic.
◆原因を尋ねる言い方
"Have you heard that Peter died last night?"
"No. (驚きのやりとりがあり，その後) What did he die of?"
"(He died of) A heart attack."
(cf. 事故なら Peter was killed ... を使い，尋ねる方も No ... how? と尋ねる)

けんかい（見解）→ いけん

an opinion; a view
〈注〉 **opinion** 具体的，実際的なことに関して私はこう思うという個人的な意見。
view 広い視野に立ち，政治，人生，生死などのような問題についての個人独自のものの見方，見解。

【見解の相違】
disagreement, difference of opinion
それは見解の相違である。
That's a matter of opinion.
(立場が違うので仕方がない)

【見解を異にする】disagree
その点で我々は見解を異にする。

We disagree on that point.

【見解が分かれる】

我々とその人たちとの見解が分かれた。

We hold one view and they hold another.

【見解が面白い】

彼の工業に関する見解はユニークかつ興味深い。

His views on industry are unique and interesting.

【政府見解を発表する】 announce the government view on 《a matter》

げんき（元気）

1．健康

元気ですか。

How are you?

元気です。

I'm fine.

お元気で。（別れの挨拶）

Good-bye.

Have a good [safe] journey.（遠くへ発つ人に）

Good-bye. Take care.〔米〕

〈注〉 英国人でもしばらく会いそうもない人や旅に出る人などには言う。

Good luck!

So long.（親しい人に）

彼女はすっかり元気になった。

She's completely well now.

彼[彼女]は元気だ。

He's [She's] in good shape.（男女どちらにも使える）

元気なうちに方々に旅行に行きたい。

I'd like to travel to many places before I'm too old and weak.

70過ぎても彼はまだまだ元気だった。

In his seventies he was still vigorous [energetic].

2．生気・活力

子供たちは元気がいい。

The children are full of life [vitality, energy, vigor, pep〔*colloq.*〕].

子供たちは元気よく旅行[遠足]に出かけた。

The children started on their trip in high spirits.

彼は元気がない。

He looks [seems to be] depressed [blue, down-hearted].

He's in low spirits.

きょうは何か元気が出ない。

I'm feeling low today.

I feel down today.

I feel a bit out of sorts today.

元気を出せ。

Cheer up!（激励）

コーヒー1杯飲んだら，元気が出ますよ[になりますよ]。

A cup of coffee will { cheer you. / revive you. / perk you up. }

You'll feel better if you have a cup of coffee.

【元気づける】

ますます励ます　encourage

慰め安心させる　comfort; reassure

もう一度やり直せばいいと言って，彼は私を元気づけてくれた。

He encouraged me saying that I can try again.

彼女は私を元気づけるようににっこり笑った。

She smiled at me reassuringly.

けんきゅう（研究）

名 (a) **study;** (a) **research**

研究する　動 **study; make a study** (**of**); **do research** (**in, on**)

【研究者】　a student

研究員　a researcher（理科系・社会学系など）; a scholar（文科系に多く使われる。数学者や特に偉大な科学者を scholar と呼ぶことがある）

【研究室】 a study; an office（大学の文科系）
実験室 a laboratory
大学院生などの共同研究室
a seminar room, a common room〔米〕
〈注〉 a common room は英国では学生寮（student hall; hall of residence）の中の共同で使う部屋のことで研究室ではない。

【研究所】
a research institute（特に自然科学・社会科学の研究所）
laboratory（広義；実験を伴う研究所）

【研究論文】
a paper《on a subject》（学術論文のみ）

【研究熱心】
彼女はとても研究熱心だ。
She { is dedicated to (her) research. / has a passion for (her) research. }
She is { engrossed [absorbed] in her research. / all wrapped up in her studies. }

【…を専門に研究する】
be a researcher in ... ; be a ... researcher; one's speciality is ...
彼は水力学を専門に研究している。
He is { a researcher in hydrodynamics. / a hydrodynamics researcher. }
His field [speciality] is hydrodynamics.
〈注〉 He studies chemistry. はよいが ×His study is ... のように書かないこと。

【研究助成金を出す】
政府は校内暴力の要因の研究に助成金を出すことにした。
The government funded a study on [of] the factors causing school violence.

【研究の余地】
その現象はさらに研究の余地がある。
We'll have to investigate the phenomenon further.
委員会は農産物増産対策をまとめて報告したが，その問題はなお研究の余地がある。
The commission reported on measures to increase agricultural production, but it requires further study [investigation].
〈注〉 特に学問的研究であれば research または study を使うが，調査研究では investigation を使う。生物学者，考古学者などの実地調査は fieldwork と言う。

【研究資料】 research materials
研究データ research data

げんじつ（現実）

実情 **realities; reality**（観念的）
〈注〉 actuality は「現実，今ある状態」を指すが，あまり使われない。reality は哲学的にはすべての現象の根源にある「実在」を指す。実人生の「現実」を指すときは可算名詞で realities と複数にすることが多い。

【厳しい現実】
(大人の)社会に出たならば，厳しい現実に直面せねばならない。
You have to face the stern realities of life after going into the adult world.
今や新しい世紀を迎え，新しい現実に直面するだろう。がんばって，死にはしないから。
You're seeing the new century with its new realities. Pull your socks up, it won't kill you!
現実は君が考えているより厳しい[ように甘くはない]。
The realities are harsher than you think.

【理想と現実】 the ideal and the real（哲学的なとらえ方）
理想と現実の差に彼は幻滅を感じた。
The discrepancy between his ideal and the reality disenchanted him.
「一つの世界」の理想に厳しい現実がいつも立ちはだかる。
Stubborn realities continue to challenge our ideal of a unified world.

【現実的】
もっと現実的になれよ。君は夢ばかり見ている。
Be realistic [practical]. You're always dreaming.
今の若者は我々の頃より現実的だ。

Young people these days are more realistic [pragmatic] than we were at their [the same] age.

けんせつてき（建設的）

constructive

それは建設的な意見[考え/提案]だ。

That's a constructive idea [thought / proposal].

批評はただのあら捜しであってはならない。建設的でなければならない。

Criticism should not be mere faultfinding. It ought to be constructive.

それについて建設的に話し合おう。

Let's talk about it constructively.

けんぶつ（見物）→ かんこう

名 **sightseeing; a visit**

見物する **see;** 観光する **see the sights; go sightseeing**

【見物人】

観光客　a sightseer （→ かんきゃく）

観客　a spectator（スポーツ）; the audience; a member of the audience（芝居）

傍観者　an onlooker（事件・火事など）

【見物に行く】

芝居見物に行く

go to the theater [a play]

会合が終ってからみんなで見物に出かけた。

After the meeting we all went
{sightseeing by bus.（バスで）
{out to see the sights of the town.（町へ）

けんやく（倹約）→ かけい, けいざい, せつやく

名 **economy**

倹約する **economize**《on something》（→きりつめる）

私たちは生活費を倹約した。

We tried to
{reduce our household expenses.
{cut down on our living costs.

光熱費を倹約しなければならない。

We have to economize on electricity and gas.

叔母さんはものすごく倹約することがあるかと思うとそうでもないこともある。

My aunt is extremely thrifty in some ways but not in others.（平気で無駄にする）

こ

こいしい（恋しい）→ なつかしい

家が恋しい

I'm homesick.

I miss home.

父母が恋しい。

I miss my parents (back home).

I want to be back home with my parents.

30年たっても私の祖父母は故国のことを恋しく思っていた。

Even thirty years later, my grandparents {had a longing / longed} for their old {country. / homeland.}

〈注〉 long for は強い感情なので，むやみに使うとおかしい。

こうい（行為）

an act; 行動 (an) **action;** 行動，業績 **a deed;**

(総合的に見た)行い **conduct;**

(ある時の)行い **behavior**

親切な行為　an act of kindness

彼の勇敢な行為は新聞に報じられた。

{His bravery / His brave act [deed]} was reported in the newspaper.

パーティーでの彼の行為にあいそがつきた。

I was disgusted with [by] his behavior at the party.

彼は不正行為で処罰された。

He was punished for cheating.

君は自分の行為を恥じるべきだ。

You should be ashamed of yourself [your behavior].

《類義語》

act　短時間に行われる一つの行為。

ex. an act of kindness [mercy / courage / desperation / love] 親切な[情け深い/勇敢な/自暴自棄な/愛の]行い

action　ある時間継続する一つ以上の行為を集合的に見た語。ある目的をもった行動。

ex. I'm ashamed of my actions yesterday. (私はきのうの私の行動を恥ずかしく思う)

The townspeople took action against a company which had polluted their area. (町民はその地域を汚染した会社を相手に立ち上がった)

She is certainly a woman of action. (彼女はたしかに行動の人だ)

deed　完結した行為の質に重点が置かれ，良くも悪くもかなり注目を集めるような行為。

ex. an irrevocable deed (取り返しのつかない行為); a deed of daring (大胆な行為)

conduct　個人の習慣的日常的行いを総合的に，社会的基準から見た言い方。

ex. Conduct is judged according to principles of ethics. (行いとは道徳的基準によって判断されるものだ)

behavior　対人的行為。特にある場面におけるその人の振舞い。

ex. His behavior at the party was childish. (パーティーでの彼の振舞いは子供っぽいとしか言えない)

こうい（好意）

1．善意

good will; kindness; friendliness

【好意から】

out of good will; out of kindness

あなたが好意からしてくださったことです。(うまくいかなかったからといって)そんなに恐縮しないでください。

You did it {out of kindness. / with good intentions.} Don't feel bad about it (although it went wrong).

【好意を持つ[示す]，好意的である】

be friendly; be sympathetic

村の人たちは新しく来た人に好意的であっ

た。

The villagers were friendly to the newcomer.

2. 好き

【好意を持つ】 like; love

最初からお互いに好意を持った。

They liked each other {immediately. / (right) from the beginning.}

They hit it off well from the start. 〔*colloq.*〕

自分でも知らないうちに好意を持っていた。

He had begun to love her before he knew it.

こうえん（講演）→ はなし

an address; a speech; a talk; a lecture

《類義語》

address 式辞・開会の辞のように公式なもの。原稿を作って話をする場合が多い。

speech 一般的な語。テーブルスピーチ，演説も含む。

talk 一般的な語。くだけた，思いつくままといった話。

lecture 公式の場や学問的な演題についてのまとまった講演，講義。

【講演をする】

give a lecture [a speech, an address]

スミス先生は世界経済の今後の見通しについて講演をされた。

Professor Smith gave a lecture on the outlook for the world economy.

きのう彼女は婦人グループに青少年非行について講演をした。

Yesterday she {spoke to / gave an address to / addressed} a ladies' group on the problem of juvenile delinquency.

【講演を頼まれる】

彼女は来月の PTA の会合で講演を頼まれている。

She has been invited to deliver [give] a lecture [speech] to the PTA gathering next month.

【講演の内容を尋ねる】

演題は何でしたか。

What was his speech [lecture] about?

内容はどんなことでしたか。

What did he say in his speech [lecture]?

【講演者】 a speaker

【講演料】 a speaker's fee

こうか（効果）→ きく（効く）

名 **(an) effect;** 効果的な **effective**

【薬効など】

効果てきめんだ。

The effect was marvelous.

The medicine worked at once.

この薬はさっぱり効果［ききめ］がない。

This medicine doesn't work at all.

新しい薬はこの種の病気には効果がない。

The new medicine has no effect on this kind of illness.

セールスマンはそのローションが皮膚に与える様々な効果を述べたてた。

The salesman recounted the various effects of the lotion on our skin.

【その他】

いくらしかっても言い聞かせてもその子には全然効果がない。

All the scoldings and lectures have utterly no effect on the boy.

もう少し効果的にやりなさい。

Do it {in a more effective way. / more effectively.}

こうかい（後悔）→ くい・くやむ

名 **repentance; regret**

後悔する 動 **repent (of); regret; be sorry for**

私は子供に厳しくしすぎたと後悔している。

I regret that I have been so severe on my children.

後できっと後悔するよ。
　You'll be sorry for it.

【後悔しないように】

後悔のない生き方をしたい。
　I'll try to live so that I won't regret { my actions. / what I've done. }

後悔しないように，精一杯がんばりなさい。
　Try to do your best so that you won't have any regrets.

〈注〉◆×without regret は「これから先，後悔しないように」の意味には使えない。
◆regret は feel sorry (残念に思う) と同義。repent はもう少し深刻で，悔い改めること。remorse 名 は自責の念である。remorse も深刻で，過ちによって引き起された痛切な苦しみを伴う悔恨の意味。

こうがい (公害)

(**environmental**) **pollution** (環境汚染); **public hazard**

産業公害 industrial pollution
騒音公害 noise pollution
情報公害 information pollution
視覚公害 visual pollution (看板など)

【公害病】 a pollution disease
公害病患者　a patient with a pollution disease; a pollution victim

《関連語》
【環境汚染】 environmental pollution
大気汚染　air pollution
水質汚染　water pollution
【環境破壊】 environmental destruction
【汚染物質】 pollutants
流出石油　oil slicks / 排気ガス　exhaust; gases; fumes / 産業廃棄物　industrial waste / 工場廃液　industrial effluent / スモッグ　smog / オキシダント　oxidant / ダイオキシン　dioxin / 赤潮　red tide / ヘドロ　sludge
【食品関係】
食品添加物　food additive
防腐剤　preservative
着色料　artificial coloring
【対策】
公害防止法　anti-pollution law
公害対策　anti-pollution measure
公害防止措置　anti-pollution device
【その他】
水銀汚染　mercury contamination [pollution] / カドミウム中毒　cadmium poisoning / 悪臭　offensive smell / ごみ捨て場　garbage dump / 廃棄物処理場　waste treatment plant / 廃液処理　liquid waste treatment / 汚水処理場　sewage treatment plant
環境省　Ministry of the Environment
　[米国]環境保護庁 the Environmental Protection Agency
生態学　ecology
環境権　environmental quality rights
日照権　right to sunlight

こうがい (郊外)

郊外に[の]　**in the suburbs** 《of a big city》; **on the outskirts** 《of a big city》

郊外は広々として静かなので皆住みたがるが，通勤時間がかかるのが難点だ。
　People like living in (the) suburbs because there's more open space and less noise, but one disadvantage is that it usually takes pretty long to get to work.

東京の郊外の都市化はこのところやや伸び悩んでいる。
　Greater Tokyo is expanding a little less quickly these days.

〈注〉 a suburb は one of the suburbs のことで，普通に「郊外」と言うときは the suburbs とする。

《関連語》
Greater Tokyo　東京都心と周囲の郊外を含めた呼称。
metropolitan area　市の中心，人口密度の高い地域。はっきりとした区画を指すのではない。
the greater metropolitan area　metropolitan area の周囲まで含む地域。the city proper と suburbs との区別ははっきりしていない。
inner city　市の中心部で，古く老朽化のイメージがある地域。
city center　市の中心。ビジネス街の中心地。
bedroom city [**town**]　ベッドタウン。
satellite town [**city**]　衛星都市。

ごうかく（合格）→ にゅうし

こうぎ（講義）→ こうえん

[名] **a lecture**
集中講義　an intensive course
連続講義　a series of lectures
【講義をする】
安倍教授はエリザベス朝英詩について講義をした。
Professor Abe lectured [gave a lecture] on Elizabethan poetry.
〈注〉 a lecture とすると１回限りの講義になる。
【講義がある】
あの先生の講義は毎週月曜日にある。
We have his class every Monday.
美術史の講義は毎週月曜日にある。
We have a lecture on art history every Monday.
【講義に出る】
私は彼の講義にはきちんと出ている。
I attend his class regularly.
【講義形式の授業】
君のとっている授業は皆，講義形式ですか。
Are all your classes lecture courses?

こうぎょう（工業）→ さんぎょう

[名] **industry; manufacturing;**
[総称]（**the**）**industries; industry**
[形] **industrial**
重[軽]工業　heavy [light] industry
主要工業　chief [main] industries
日本工業規格
Japan Industrial Standards（[略] JIS）
工業化　industrialization
工業大学　a technical college; an institute of technology

こうけい（光景）→ けしき

こうこう（高校）→ がっこう

【高等学校】　a(n upper) secondary school; a (senior) high school
〈注〉 米国では（senior）high school で問題はないが，英国では小学校（primary school）の次は secondary school（いろいろ種類あり）で，すぐに university につながる。学制については「きょういく」の項を参照。
【高校時代】
高校時代に
when [while] I was in [at]（high）school;
during my（high）school years [days];
in [at] high school
〈注〉◆ days はややセンチメンタルに響く。
◆「高校時代に」は in my high school days と訳されることが多い。誤りではないが上記，特に最初にあげた表現が普通。また，中学・高校を特に区別しないで at [in] school と言うのが簡単。
高校時代は楽しかった。
I enjoyed my high school life.
I was happy in [at] high school.
〈注〉 文は簡潔である方がよい。次の(1)はやや冗長であり，(2)のようにまとめられる。
(1) When I was in high school, I enjoyed my school life.
(2) I enjoyed my high school life.
【高校の】
高校の友人
my high school friend
a friend from high school
高校の成績
my high school grades〔米〕
my school marks〔英〕
成績表
a school record;（大学の）a transcript〔米〕

こうさい（交際）

〈注〉 「交際」にぴったり対応する英語はない。
【交際仲間】

人はその交際相手を見ればどんな人間か判断できる。

You can tell a man by the company he keeps.

【交際する】

戦前の日本では女子は男子と交際することも許されていなかった。

In prewar Japan girls were not allowed to associate with boys.

〈注〉「交際する」を意味する keep company with は前後関係により「恋仲である」ことを婉曲に言うのに使われることがある。

【交際がある[ない]】

彼女はいろいろな有名政治家と交際がある。

She knows a lot of famous statesmen.

彼の名前は知っているが交際はない。

I know only his name. I don't know him personally.

彼女は交際が広い。

She has a large circle of acquaintances.

【交際中である，交際を断つ】

あの人たちは今交際中だ。結婚ということになるかどうか。

They are dating. I wonder if they'll marry (or not).

あのことがあってから彼との交際を断った。

I broke off with him after the incident.

【交際好き】

彼女は交際好きだ。

She { is sociable.（社交的な） / { is fond of company. / likes company. }（にぎやか好きな） / is outgoing.（外向性の） }

こうし（講師）→ こうえん，だいがく

こうつう（交通）

交通量，交通状況　**traffic**

輸送　**transportation**

1．交通一般

【交通の便】

交通の便をよくする

improve the transportation system

この場所は交通の便がいい。

This place is { conveniently / inconveniently（悪い） } situated [located].

そこへ行くための交通の便がない。

No transportation is available to that place.

There is no transportation to that place.

【交通量】

この通りは交通量が多い。

There is a lot of traffic on this street.

This street is busy.

この場所は交通量が多い。

(The) traffic is heavy here.

この通りは年々交通量が増えるだろう。

This road will have more traffic every year.

【交通渋滞】 traffic congestion; a traffic jam; a traffic tie-up

道路は多くの場所で渋滞していた。

The traffic was { tied up / held up, / brought to a standstill } in many places.

【渋滞緩和】

渋滞緩和のために新しいバイパスが建設されている。

A new bypass is being constructed to relieve traffic congestion.

【不通，通行止め】

豪雪のためその村への交通が途絶した。

Because of the heavy snow the village was isolated [cut off].

村へのバスは運行されていないし，ほかにそこへ行く手だてもない。

The bus to the village isn't running, and we have no other means to get there.

バス路線が不通になっている。

The bus route is blocked.

バスの運行が停止されている。
The bus service has been stopped.
山崩れで道路が不通になっている。
A landslide has blocked (off) the road.
豪雪のため目下のところ，その村への交通は途絶えている。
Because of the heavy snow there is no {access / means of access} to the village at present.
救援を必要としているのに洪水被災地域への交通手段は何もない。
Despite the need, all means of access to the flooded area are closed.
〈注〉 access は「接近」「近づきやすいこと」から「交通の便」の意味になる。
名神自動車道は雪のため関ヶ原〜米原間が通行止めになっている。
The Meishin Highway has been closed between Sekigahara and Maibara because of snow.

【交通事故】 a traffic accident →じどうしゃ
その(交通)事故で 2 名死亡，3 名が重傷を負った。
Two people were killed and three badly injured in that traffic accident.
〈注〉 事故死にはしばしば be killed が使われる。

【交通規則】
一般的ルール traffic rules
駐車などの規則 traffic regulations
交通法規 traffic laws

【交通違反】
violations of traffic rules [regulations, laws]
速度違反 speeding
駐車違反 illegal parking

【交通信号】
a traffic light; a signal [stop] light

【交通標識】 a traffic sign

【交通整理をする】
control [regulate] traffic

【交通安全週間】
交通安全週間なので警官が交通量の多い通りに出て交通整理をしている。
Policemen are out on crowded streets directing traffic because this is Traffic Safety Week.

【交通手段】
車[バス，電車，飛行機]で
by car [bus, train, air]
車で通学[通勤]する
drive to school [one's office / work]
歩いて通学[通勤]する
walk to school [the office / work]

【通勤】
通勤者 a commuter
通勤列車 a commuter train〔米〕; a season-ticket train〔英〕
定期乗車券
a commuter ticket〔米〕; a season ticket〔英〕
通勤する commute (長距離の場合)
何で通勤していますか。
How do you commute to [come to, go to] your office [work]?

【交通費】
汽車賃[バス代 / 航空運賃]
(the) train [bus / air] fare

【切符】
片道切符 a one-way ticket〔米〕; a single ticket〔英〕
往復切符 a round-trip ticket〔米〕; a return ticket〔英〕
入場券 a platform ticket

【交通標識】
止まれ Stop
通行止め Closed to Traffic
行き止まり No Outlet; No Through Road
進入禁止 No Entry
左[右]側通行 Keep Left [Right]
一方通行 One Way
左[右]折禁止 No Left [Right] Turn
Uターン禁止 No U-turn
(他車に) 先を譲れ Yield
この先道路工事中
Road Construction Ahead

この先交通信号あり　Signal Ahead
この先151号に合流
　Junction Highway 151 Ahead
駐車禁止　No Parking; No Waiting
車両[自転車／歩行者]専用
　Cars [Bicycles / Pedestrians] Only
危険！　Danger!

2. 交通機関

【交通機関】
　means of transportation; transportation
山岳地帯への交通機関がここ10年の間に大幅に発達した[ぐっと良くなった]。
　Transportation into the mountains has been greatly improved in the last ten years.

【列車・電車】
超特急　a superexpress train
急行　an express train
特急　a limited express train
普通　a local train
(松本行き)直通
　a non-stop train (for Matsumoto)
新幹線
　a [the] Hikari [Kodama / Nozomi] Super Express　ひかり[こだま/のぞみ]; the Shinkansen; the Bullet Train (弾丸列車の意)
東海道新幹線　the New Tokaido Line
客車　a passenger train
窓側の席　a window seat
通路側の席　an aisle seat
通路　an aisle
指定席　a reserved seat
自由席　a free seat; a non-reserved seat
食堂車　a dining car
ビュッフェ　a buffet car
寝台車　a sleeper
貨物列車　a freight (train)

【乗り換える】
山手線に乗り換える
　change [transfer] to the Yamanote Line
長野行きに乗り換える
　change trains [cars] for Nagano
家から学校まで3度乗り換えしなければならない。
　I have to change buses [trains] three times to get to school from my house.
東海道線で米原まで行き北陸線の金沢行きに乗り換え，舞鶴で降りて駅前から市営の3番バスに乗ってください。
　Take the Tokaido Line as far as Maibara and change to the Hokuriku Line bound for Kanazawa, then get off at Maizuru and take [get] the No. 3 city bus from [in front of] the station.

【途中下車】　a stopover

【列車の発着】
列車がホームに入ってきた。
　The train was coming into the station.
列車はもうホームに入っていた。
　The train was already {at the platform. / in.}
列車は定刻に発車した。
　The train left [started] right [just] on time.
列車が動き出した。
　The train began to move.
列車が速度を増した。
　The train gathered speed.
列車が速度を落した。
　The train began to slow down.
この列車は時速100キロで走る。
　This train goes 100 kilometers {an / per} hour.

【市電・地下鉄】
市電　a streetcar〔米〕; a tram (car)〔英〕
地下鉄　the underground; a subway; the Tube (ロンドンの地下鉄); the Metro (パリの地下鉄)

【駅】
駅員　a station agent; a railway man
改札係　a ticket puncher; a ticket collector
ホーム係　a platform man
出札係　a ticket agent〔米〕; a booking clerk〔英〕

車掌　a conductor
ホーム　a platform
駅の案内所
an information window [office]
切符売場
a ticket window [counter]
自動切符販売機
a ticket vending machine
改札口　a ticket barrier; a wicket
入口　an entrance
出口　an exit
手荷物取扱所
a baggage office〔米〕; a luggage office

【バス】
路線バス　a bus
観光バス　a sightseeing bus; a tour bus
遠距離バス
a long-distance bus; a coach〔英〕
〈注〉今はワンマンバスが普通なので特に呼称はなく bus でよい。特に区別して言いたいときは「ワンマンバス」は pay-as-you-enter, 車掌のいるバスは a bus with a conductor と言えばよい。
運転手　a driver
車掌　a conductor
善光寺に行くにはどのバスに乗ったらいいでしょうか。
Which bus should I take {to get [go] to / for} Zenkoji?
どこで降りればいいでしょうか。
Where should we get off?
善光寺はいくつ目ですか。
How many stops are there before Zenkoji?
(そこまでいくつバス停があるか)
お降りの方はボタンを押してください。
Please push the button to get off at the next stop.
ここで降ろしてください。
Drop me here, please.
バスは15分おきに発車する。
The bus leaves every 15 minutes.

【タクシー】 a cab; a taxi
タクシー運転手　a taxi [cab] driver
タクシー料金　the taxi [cab] fare
基本料金　the minimum fare
メーター　a taxi meter

【バイク，自転車】
バイク　a motorcycle; a motorbike〔英〕; a (motor) scooter (座席の低いもの)
自転車　a bicycle; a bike
〈注〉bike は自転車のことでバイクのことではない。

【飛行機】 an airplane; an (aero)plane〔英〕
ジェット機　a jet
旅客機　a passenger plane
貨物輸送機　a cargo plane
乗務員　the crew
操縦士　a pilot
機長　the captain (flight crew の長)
副操縦士　the copilot
パーサー　the purser (cabin crew の長)
スチュワード　a steward } a flight attendant
スチュワーデス　a stewardess } a flight attendant
整備員　an air mechanic; a flight engineer
地上勤務員　ground crew〔米〕[staff〔英〕]
タラップ　landing steps; mobile stairs
搭乗橋　a boarding bridge; a jetway
空港　an airport
航空管制塔　a control tower
航空管制官　an air traffic controller
滑走路　a runway
空港ビル　an airport building [terminal]
送迎デッキ　an observation deck
空港バス　a limousine; an airport bus
離陸予定時間
Estimated Time of Departure (略 ETD)
離陸　(a) takeoff; 離陸する　take off
到着予定時間
Estimated Time of Arrival (略 ETA)
着陸　(a) landing; 着陸する　land
不時着　a forced landing
不時着する　make a forced landing
搭乗時間　(the) boarding time
搭乗券　a boarding card [pass]

切符の予約　a reservation
直行便　a non-stop [direct] flight
時差ボケ　jet lag
その便は直行便ではない。
The flight's not a direct one.
この飛行機はX経由Y行きだ。
This flight goes to Y via X.
あの飛行機は途中XとYに止まる。
That flight stops at X and Y.
この飛行機はニューヨークまでに1度止まる。
The flight stops once before we get to New York.（直行便ではない）

【船】
大洋航路の客船　an ocean liner
タンカー　an oil-tanker
フェリー　a ferry(boat)
漁船　a fishing boat
トロール船　a (fishing) trawler
ホバークラフト　a hovercraft
モーターボート　a motorboat
ヨット　a yacht
救命ボート　a lifeboat

こうどう（行動）→ こうい（行為）

an action; behavior（振舞い）; **what one does**
自分の行動に責任を持たねばならない。
I have to take responsibility for what I do.
理論には行動が伴わねばならない。
Theory and practice should go hand in hand.
あの人は言うことと行動がちぐはぐだ。
He says one thing and does another.

こうとうしもん（口頭試問）→ にゅうし

【大学の学期試験の】
(an) oral examination
この学期は二つも口頭試問があるんだ。一つは臨床心理学実験で，もう一つはスペイン語だ。
I'll have [I'm having] two oral examinations this semester, one for my clinical psychology laboratory and one in Spanish.

【面接】　interview
〈注〉　面接テストは日本式の言い方。

【大学院論文提出時の】
(an) oral defense of a thesis（修士(MA)，博士(Ph.D.)論文について）
(an) oral defense of a dissertation（博士論文について）
次の木曜日は論文の口頭試問だ。
I'll defend my thesis next Thursday.
I'll have my oral defense next Thursday.

こうはい（後輩）→ せんぱい・こうはい

こうほ（候補）

候補者　**a candidate; a nominee**（指名・推薦された人）

【立候補する】
加藤氏は市長選に立候補している。
Mr. Kato is running for
{ mayor.（市長）
{ Congress.（国会議員）
{ the Presidency.（会長，米国大統領）

【候補に立てる】
民主党は先の選挙で2人の候補者を立てた。
The Democratic Party of Japan ran [put up] two candidates in the last election.

【候補者になる】
彼はノーベル賞の候補に上がっている。
He has been nominated for a Nobel prize.
彼は芥川賞の候補に上がっている。
He is { an Akutagawa prize nominee.
{ a nominee for the Akutagawa prize.

【公認[非公認]候補】
an official [unofficial] candidate
彼は自民党の公認候補だ。
He's the LDP's official [the official LDP] candidate.

こうむいん（公務員）→ やくにん

a civil servant; a government employee; a civil service worker〔米〕; 責任ある地位の役人 **a public official, a government official**

私の父は公務員だ。

My father is { a civil servant. / a government employee.

僕は公務員になりたい。

I'd like to work { in civil service. / for the government.

〈注〉 civil [public] service は英国では慈善事業のように聞えるので government employee を用いる。

公務員を退職する

quit [leave, retire from〔*formal*〕] public life

こうやく（公約）

election promises; campaign pledges

公約する **promise; pledge**〔強〕

選挙戦中，彼は身障者，老人の福祉を推進すると公約した。

When running for election, he promised to promote the welfare of senior citizens and the disabled.

【公約を守る】

市会議員たちがみんな公約を守ってくれたらこの市ももっと住みやすくなるのだが。

If all the members of the city council carried out [kept] their election promises, the city would certainly be a far better place to live in.

こうらく（行楽）

【行楽地】a holiday resort

【行楽客】

vacationers〔米〕; holidaymakers〔英〕

【行楽シーズン】the vacation season〔米〕

〈注〉 英国では夏が行楽シーズンであるが別に呼び名はない。

【絶好の行楽日和】

a perfect [an ideal] day for a picnic [drive]

こうり（小売）

【小売商人】

a retail [small] merchant

【小売店を経営する】

own [run] a retail store [outlet]

ピータースさんはちょっとした小売店をやっている。

Mr. Peters runs [has, owns] a small retail business.

【小売価格で】at retail price

【小売する】(buy wholesale and) sell retail

この品物は1ダース1000円で小売します。

These articles retail [are retailed] at a [one] thousand yen a dozen.

その冷蔵庫は小売価格20万円です。

That refrigerator costs two hundred thousand yen retail.

〈注〉 store, shop, merchant などは，特に卸し(wholesale)と間違えるおそれがなければ，何も言わないでも小売の意味になる。一方 cost は小売値(retail cost) でいくら，卸値 (wholesale cost) でいくらと特定することが多い。

ex. This shirt costs 850 yen wholesale.（このシャツは卸値で850円です）

彼は文房具の小売店をやっている。

He is a stationer.

He has a small stationery shop.

こうりょ（考慮）

名 **consideration;** 考慮して **in consideration of**

動 **consider; weigh**《the significance [benefits] of》

【考慮する】

若年であることを考慮して不起訴処分に決定した。

Considering his youth, they decided to drop the case.

The case was dropped in consideration of his youth.〔*formal*〕

これらの事情を考慮しなければならない[考慮に入れなければならない]。

Such factors must [need to] be considered.

【考慮中】

目下考慮中である。

It is now { being considered. / under consideration. }

議会は米の政府買上げ制度についてなおも考慮中である。

The Diet hasn't finished thinking over the rice support system.

【考慮の余地】

その問題はまだ考慮の余地がある。

We shouldn't drop the matter yet.

We need to consider the matter further.

〈注〉 consider のかわりに think over でもよい。

こきゅう（呼吸）

breath; breathing; respiration

【呼吸が荒い】

彼女は呼吸が荒かった。

She was short of breath.（息を切らす）

She was panting.（あえぐ）

【深く呼吸する】 breathe deeply

【呼吸困難】

病人は呼吸困難を起していた。

The patient had difficulty (in) breathing.

【呼吸器】respiratory organs; [総称] respiratory system

呼吸器疾患 a respiratory disease

人工呼吸 artificial respiration

【こつ】

どうも呼吸がつかめない。

I haven't got the knack of it.

【息】

2人は初めから呼吸が合っていた。

The two { hit it off / got along well } from the very beginning.

こきょう(故郷) → きょうり・こきょう

こくさい（国際）

国際的な international

国際人

a cosmopolitan person; a cosmopolitan

国際情勢 the international situation

国際事情 international affairs

国際法 international law

国際交流 international exchange

国際的団体 an international body

国際的大女優

an actress of international fame

an internationally famous actress

【国際的に】internationally

あの女優は国際的に有名だ。

That actress is internationally famous.

【国際関係】

首相のヨーロッパ訪問で国際関係が好転するだろう。

The Premier's visit to Europe will improve international relations.

【国際感覚】

あの人たちは国際感覚を持っている。

They are internationally minded persons.

【国際電話】

カナダに国際電話をかける

make an overseas phone call to Canada

こくさいれんごう（国際連合）

The United Nations（㊕ **UN**）

国連総会 The UN General Assembly

議長 the president (of the UN)

事務総長 the secretary-general (of the UN)

常任理事国 a permanent member

安全保障理事会

the Security Council（㊕ UNSC）

国連決議 UN resolutions

国連安全保障理事会決議第660号

UN Security Council Resolution 660

国連憲章 the Charter of the United Nations

国連加盟国 a member of the United Nations

国連事務局 the United Nations Secretariat

国連職員　International Civil [Public] Servant
国連教育科学文化機関
　United Nations Educational, Scientific and Cultural Organization (略 UNESCO)
国連難民高等弁務官
　United Nations High Commissioner for Refugees (略 UNHCR)
世界食糧計画
　World Food Programme (略 WFP)
国連環境計画　United Nations Environment Programme (略 UNEP)
国際通貨基金
　International Monetary Fund (略 IMF)
世界貿易機構
　World Trade Organization (略 WTO)
国連児童基金　United Nations Children's Fund (略 UNICEF)
平和維持活動　Peace-Keeping Operations (略 PKO)
世界保健機構
　World Health Organization (略 WHO)

ここ

1. 空間

ここ　here
ここから　from here
ここにある。
　Here it is.
ここにおいで。
　Come (here).
ここは暖かい。
　It's warm here.
ここはどこですか。
　Where are we now?
ここは岐阜だ。
　We're in Gifu. (上の問いに対する答え)
　This is Gifu. (一般的)
　We're now going through Gifu. (車で通過するとき)
〈注〉「さあ，岐阜についた」といった感じで，Here's Gifu. と言うことがある。
ここだけの話にしておこう。
　Let's keep this between [among] ourselves.
今日はここまで。(授業の終りなど)
　That's all [it] for today.
　That's [This is] enough for today.

2. 時間

【ここ 2, 3 日】
ここ 2, 3 日涼しかった。
　It has been cool for the last few days.
【ここ 2, 3 週間】
ここ 2, 3 週間彼女に会っていない。
　I haven't seen her for the last few weeks.
【ここまで】
ここまではしっかりやっている。
　He has done well so far.
【ここのところ】(今のところ)
　for now / for the present / for the time being
【ここ当分は】　for some time

ごご (午後) → ごぜん

afternoon; 略 **P.M.; PM; p.m.; pm**
【午後に】 in the afternoon
午後には雨になった。
　It started to rain in the afternoon.
今日の午後はおひまですか。
　Are you free this afternoon?
ガレージの掃除に午後いっぱいかかってしまった。
　It took me all [the whole] afternoon to clean out the garage.
【…日の午後】
災害の起ったのは土曜の午後[3月3日の午後4時]だった。
　The disaster happened on
　　{ Saturday afternoon.
　　{ March 3rd at four in the afternoon.
【午後…時】
ショーは午後6時から始まる。

The show will begin at six [6 p.m.].

〈注〉 午前か午後か間違うおそれがなければ特に言わなくてもよい。プログラムなどに書くときは数字で 6 pm; 6 p.m. のように書く。
「午後に」は in the afternoon であるが，曜日を付け加えると，たとえば on Saturday の影響で on Saturday afternoon と on をつける。なお，「午後 6 時」は 6 p.m. で×p.m. 6 は英語としては誤りである。

【午後の】afternoon（形容詞的用法）

彼は午後の授業[会議]は嫌いだ。

He doesn't like afternoon classes [meetings].

こごと（小言）

名 叱ること **a scolding;** 非難 **a reproach;** 説教 **preaching**

動 **scold; reproach; preach;** 不平を言う **complain**

【小言を言う】

彼はいつもぶつぶつ小言を言っている。

He's always grumbling [complaining] about one thing or another.

【小言を食う】

遅刻すると小言を食うぞ。

You'll be scolded if you are late.

〈注〉◆「お目玉を食うぞ，怒られるぞ」を You'll catch it.〔*slang*〕と言う。
◆小言は親や主人が下の者にぶつぶつ言うことであるが complain, grumble そのものには，その含みがない。文脈の中で上の者が下の者の落度を grumble, complain する場合が小言になる。

こころ（心）

1. 意志・理性

mind

【心にある，思っている】

私は心に思っていることがある。

I have something on my mind.

【心ならずも】

彼は心ならずも行く[帰る]ことになった。

He had to go though he didn't want to.

He was forced to go.

【心に留める】→ちゅういする

pay attention to, listen to

彼は私に彼女と付き合うなと言ったが，私はまだ若くて彼の言ったことなど心に留めなかった。

He warned me to avoid her company, but I was too young to listen [pay atttention] to what he (had) said.

彼は母親の言うことなど心に留めなかった。

He didn't care what his mother said.

2. 情

heart

【心の優しい】gentle-hearted; tender-hearted

〈注〉 She is tender at heart. は「外見はこわいが心は優しい」という意味を含んでいる。

【心温まる話】a heart-warming story

【心に残る】

動 impress; 形 impressive

あの人たちのあけっぴろげな友情が何よりも心に残った。

Their open friendliness impressed me more than anything else.

【心を打つ】→かんげき

【心から】

from the bottom of one's heart; 情をこめて heartily; 真心をこめて sincerely

心からあなたのご成功を祈ります。

I sincerely hope you will succeed.

あの人たちは心から我々を歓迎してくれた。

They welcomed us heartily.

いろいろご助力いただき心からお礼申し上げます。

I thank you for your help from the bottom of my heart.

3. 慣用表現

【心強い】

あの人がリーダーをしてくれる限り心強い。

I feel confident as long as she's our leader.

【心細い】

外国で病気になると心細いものだ。特にお金が十分ないときは。

When we get sick in a foreign country we feel helpless and lonely, especially if we haven't [don't have] enough money.

【心当り】

あの人がいったいどこにいるのか[行ってしまったのか]全然心当りがない。

I have no idea where { she might be. / she's gone. }

ああ,ちょうどよさそうな[その仕事にうってつけの]人の心当りがある。

Ah, I have someone in mind who is just right for the job.

こしょう(故障)

【故障する】go wrong; get out of order; be broken; break (down)

【故障している】something is wrong with ...

私のヘアドライヤーは故障している。

My hair dryer has broken.

うちの事務所のコンピュータは故障している。

Our office computer { is out of order. / has broken down. }

このラジカセはどこか故障している。

{ There's something the matter / Something is wrong } with this cassette recorder with a radio.

車が故障した。

My car's broken down.

車のエンジンが故障した。

My car [I] had engine trouble.

車の電気系統が故障している。

The electrical system in my car doesn't work.

〈注〉 out of order は機械などの故障に使う。また「故障中」の掲示にも"Out of Order"を使う。

この機械は故障してうまく動かない。

This machine isn't working well [right].

【故障車】a disabled car (台風・火事などでボロボロになった車)

車が故障してしまった。エンジンがなかなかかからない。

Something's wrong with my car. It won't start easily.

〈注〉◆Something's wrong with ... は機械・器具の故障に限らず「おかしい」という意味で広く使われる。

Something's wrong with

{ the idea. (その考え方はどこかおかしい) / my stomach. (胃の調子がおかしい) }

◆故障した場合,具体的に状態を述べるのが普通である。

時計が止まってしまった。

My watch has stopped.

テレビが故障した。

We can't get

{ any picture on the TV. (画面が映らない) / any sound from the TV. (音が出ない) }

こぜに(小銭)

small money; change

【小銭にする,くずす】

この札をくずしていただけますか。

Can you break this for me?

これをくずしていただけますか。

Can you change this, please?

Can I have change (for this), please?

これを10円玉にしていただけますか。

Could I have 10 yen coins for this?

小銭で[ダイムとクオーターで]おつりをください。

Could I please have the change in small coins [dimes and quarters]?

小銭の持ち合せがないんです。

I have no change with me.

〈注〉[米国の硬貨] 次の種類がある。

1 cent, 10 cents [a dime], 25 cents [a quarter], 1 dollar

[英国の硬貨] 次の種類がある。

1p, 2p, 5p, 10p, 20p, 50p, 1 pound, 2 pounds

p は penny(単数), pence(複数) の略だが,普通,単数・複数の区別なしに /piː/ と発音されている。

£1.20 の読み方 one pound twenty (p, pence)

ごぜん(午前) → ごご

morning; 略 **A.M.; AM; a.m.; am**

【午前中】in the morning; before noon
午前中は授業がない。
I have no classes in the morning.
午前中に雨が上がった。
The rain stopped before noon.
明日の午前中に電話してください。
Call me tomorow morning.
彼らは月曜の午前中にホノルルに到着する。
They will arrive at [in] Honolulu on Monday morning.
【午前…時】
授業は午前10時に始まる。
The class will begin at 10 in the morning.
我々は東京を午前10時の列車で発った。
We left Tokyo by the 10 a.m. train.
〈注〉◆「午前に」は in the morning であるが，「月曜の午前」は on Mondayの影響で on Monday morning と前置詞は on になる。なお，「午前10時」は 10 a. m. であって a. m. 10 は英語としては誤り。
◆「いつもの習慣」については次のような言い方もできる。
午前は会社，午後は家で仕事をする。
He works mornings at the office and afternoons at home.
午前は授業に出て，午後は図書館で勉強する。
Mornings I take classes and I spend afternoons in the library.

こたえ（答え）・こたえる

1．答え
名 返答 **an answer; a reply;**
応答 **a response;** 解答 **an answer**
【返答】
まだ彼から答え[返事]をもらっていない。
We haven't got his answer [reply] yet.
【はっきりした答え】
彼はまだはっきり答え[返事]をくれない。
He hasn't given me any definite answer yet.
【応答】
私は彼の部屋のドアをノックしたが何も答えがなかった。
I knocked at [on] his door, but there was no response.
【解答】
これが正しい答えです。
This is the correct answer.
僕はまだ数学の問題の答えが出ない。
I haven't solved the math problem yet.

2．答える
動 **answer; give an answer (to)**
【返答をする】
私の問いにどうか答えてください。
Please answer my question.
君はまだ私の問いに答えていないよ。
You haven't answered my question yet.
彼の答えはイエス[ノー]だった。
He {said / answered} {yes [no]. / he would [he couldn't].}
彼は今回は必ず成功する自信があると答えた。
He {answered / replied} that he was quite confident of his success this time.
〈注〉 answer は一般的な語だが，reply は形式ばった語なので，パーティーへの招待に対する返事やビジネス上の返事などに使われる。また，answer は他動詞であるが，reply は that 節が続くとき以外は自動詞で reply to a question と to が必要。
ex. He replied to [answered] the examiner's questions slowly and thoughtfully. (彼は試験官の問いにゆっくりと慎重に答えた)

3．応える
【応じる】
歓呼に応える
respond to the cheers
期待に応える
live up to one's expectations
彼は人々の歓呼に手を振って応えた。
He waved to the cheering crowd.
彼は父親の期待に応え(られ)なかった。
He never lived up to his father's expectations.

4．身にしみる
私も年なので寒さがこたえる。

As I am getting old the cold bothers me.

手術してからどうも本調子に戻らず寒さがこたえる。

Since the operation I haven't been feeling as strong as I used to and the cold is hard to bear.

〈注〉 tell on は徐々に影響が現れるときに使う。

ex. Hunger is telling on me. (空腹がこたえてきた)

Age is telling on me. (私も年だなあ)

彼の言葉はこたえた。

His words [criticism] { struck home. / hit (me) hard. }

ごちそう (ご馳走)

【豪勢な食事】

たいへんなごちそうだった。

It was a wonderful dinner.

A wonderful dinner was served.

There were all sorts of good things to eat. (山海の珍味)

【おごり】

姉がアイスクリームをごちそうして[おごって]くれた。

My sister { treated me to ice cream. / bought me ice cream. }

ごちそうさま，おいしかったわ。

Thanks for the treat. It was delicious [wonderful]!

私がごちそうするわ[私におごらせて]。

Be my guest.

It's my treat.

It's on me.

私にごちそうさせてください。

You'll be my guest. 〔*rather formal*〕

〈注〉 英語で「ごちそうさま」に当る挨拶はない。しかし食事に招待されたとき It was good [delicious]. のようにほめたり，Thank you for a wonderful dinner. のようにお礼を言うとよい。その後，辞去するときの挨拶の例として次のような言い方がある。

Thank you [Thanks] for inviting me.

I had a wonderful [lovely] time.

I really enjoyed myself.

こっかい (国会) → せいじ

立法府 **the legislature**

［日本］ **the (National) Diet**

衆議院 the House of Representatives

衆議院議員

a member of the House of Representatives

参議院 the House of Councilors

参議院議員 a councilor

国会議事堂 the Diet Building

［米国］ **Congress**

上院 the Senate

上院議員 a senator

下院 the House of Representatives

下院議員 a representaive

国会議事堂 the Capitol

［英国］ **Parliament**

上院 the House of Lords

上院議員 a member of the House of Lords

下院 the House of Commons

下院議員 a member of Parliament; 略 MP

国会議事堂 the Houses of Parliament

【召集する，解散する】

国会を召集[解散]する

convene [dissolve] the Diet

国会は開会[閉会]中である。

The Diet is now in [out of] session.

総理は行政改革に必要な法案を通すために，9月初めに臨時国会召集を考えていると語った。

The Prime Minister said he was thinking of convening an extraordinary Diet session in early September in order to have [get] the necessary administrative reform bills passed.

こづかい (小遣い)

《類義語》

pocket money 〔英〕子供に定期的に与える小遣い。大人の場合はほんの少額の小遣い。spend-

ing money [spence〔*colloq.*〕] とも言う。
spending money　少額の小遣い。〔米〕大人の小遣い。〔英〕pocket money と同じ。
an allowance　〔米〕子供に定期的に与える小遣い。〔英〕下記〈注〉参照。
extra money　臨時に与える小遣い。臨時収入。へそくり。

(子供に)小遣いをやる
give a child a little money for his own use
父は私に月3000円小遣いをくれる。
My father gives me
{ an allowance of 3000 yen a month.〔米〕
{ 3000 yen a month as pocket money.〔英〕
〈注〉 allowance は米国では小遣いだが，英国では16歳以上の未成年者などに与えるまとまった金や遺産から定期的に一定額もらう金などで，仕送り(routine expenses; a support payment〔米〕)のことになる。allowance はまた政府や企業の出す手当などの意味にもなる。
ex. family allowance (家族手当)
小遣いが足りなくなった。
I have run out of pocket money.
My pocket money is gone.
小遣いの前借りしたいんだけど。
May I have an advance on my allowance?〔米〕
小遣いの範囲内でやっていかなければいけないよ。
I think you ought to budget your money better.
これだけあげるが，今月はもうこれでおしまいだよ。
I'll give you this, but it's the last (time) this month.

こづつみ（小包）

小包　**a package**〔米〕; **a parcel**〔英〕
小荷物(郵便局の) a parcel
手荷物　luggage; baggage〔米〕
【小包を送る】
郵便でクリスマスの小包を送りました。今年はクリスマスに帰省できそうもないので。
I sent you a Christmas present (by parcel post) because this year I'll not be able to come home for Christmas.
今朝小包を送り出してきた。
I mailed [sent out] some parcels [packages] this morning.
【小包を書留で送る】
send a package [parcel] by registered mail〔米〕 [post〔英〕]
【航空便[船便]小包を出す】
send a parcel by airmail [seamail]
【貨物】 freight (cargo)
貨物運搬専用の車両　freight train
貨物運搬専用の航空機　cargo plane
貨物運搬専用の船
freighter; cargo ship [boat]
〈注〉 荷物を扱う場所としては airport(空港), seaport(港), trucking terminal(トラックの終点), train terminal(列車の終点), container terminal(コンテナーの終点)などがある。

こと（事）

1. 文の名詞化

【…したこと】
彼はひどく酔っ払って昨夜自分のやったことを覚えていない。
He was so drunk he doesn't remember what he did last night.
私が言ったことを忘れてしまったの？
Have you forgotten what I told you?
あの人の考えていることは難しくてわからない。
It's difficult to understand what he is thinking.
何か月も家をあけていたので留守中に起ったことは知らない。
I've been away for months, so I don't know what's happened at home during my absence.

《出来事を示す類義語》
incident　ちょっとした出来事。偶発的または付随的な小事件。

旅行中の出来事　incidents on a journey

accident　不慮の出来事，事故。うれしいことについては使わない。

ひどい交通事故　a terrific traffic accident

event　比較的重要な出来事。年中行事，競技や試合のことも言う。

1年間の主な出来事の一つ

one of the major events of the year

occurrence　一般的な語。

日常の出来事　daily occurrences

世にも不思議な出来事

a most mysterious { occurrence / incident 〔*formal*〕 }

happening　偶発的な事件。

地方の出来事　local happenings

奇妙な出来事

a strange { happening 〔*informal*〕 / occurrence / incident 〔*formal*〕 }

experience　経験，体験。出来事に自分もかかわると，経験，体験となる。

私はたいへん面白いことを体験した。

I had a very interesting experience.

【…であるということ，…したということ】

彼の息子が結婚した(という)ことを知らなかった。

She didn't know that his son was married.

そんなことを決めるのにはまだ若すぎるってことを忘れないで。

Remember that you are still too young to decide a thing like that.

殺人現場にいたということで，彼が犯人だということにはならない。

The fact that he was present at the site of the murder does not mean he is guilty.

【やりたいこと】

困ったことに，彼はやりたいことが何かわからない。

The trouble is he doesn't know what he wants to do.

【考えるべきこと】

ガールフレンド以外にも考えるべきことがたくさんある。

There are many other things you should think about besides your girlfriend.

〈注〉　やりたいことがたくさんある。

There are a lot of things I want to do.

するべきことがたくさんある。

I have a lot of things to do.

上記2例の表現を混同してはいけない。

×I have a lot of things to want to do.

なぜいけないのか（【…すること】の〈注〉参照）

(1) things I want to do（やりたいと思っていること）「いる」は現在の事実を述べる形(factive）である。

(2) things to do（やるべきこと）
ex. food to eat（食べるべき食物）
の「べき」は方向を示すもので事実を述べる形ではない(non-factive)。不定詞の心はちょうど矢印(→)のようなもので「方向」を示す。

(1)(2)を組み合わせた例

×things to want to do（×やりたいと思うべきこと）は考え方として現実にありそうもない内容になる。

【…すること】

人を教えることは習うことより難しい。

To teach is more difficult than to learn.

見ることは信じることだ。

To see is to believe.

Seeing is believing.

〈注〉　日本語では factive(事実に立脚した叙述。ex. 彼はよく働く), non-factive(事実に立脚しない叙述。ex. よく働く約束)の語形上の区別がないので，その区別を認識していない。一方英語では下に示すように non-factive の場合は不定詞句が用いられ，節にする場合は should, would, could などの助動詞が必要である。

彼がよく働くことは皆知っている。

Everybody knows he { is a hard worker. / works hard. }

〔*factive*〕

彼はよく働くことを約束した。

He promised { to work hard. / he would work hard. }

〔*non-factive*〕

次の誤文例は fact と non-fact を混同したものである。

変らないことが一つある。

There was one thing
{ ×not to change. / ○that hadn't changed. }

私の弱点はものを知らないことだ。

My weakness is
{ ×to be ignorant.
{ ○ ignorance.

○ I am ignorant.　That's my weakness.

2．単一の「こと」

matter; affair; business; thing; something

このこと　this

そのこと，あのこと　that

何のこと　what

このことは秘密よ。

This is a secret.

〈注〉 This thing is ... とはしない。

何のことを話してるの？

What are you talking about?

私のことを話していたでしょう。

You were { talking / saying something } about me, weren't you?

例のマイクの転勤のことですが，考え直してもらえないでしょうか。

This business of Mike's transfer. Can't you think it over again?

金のことがかかわっているのでややこしい。

It's a bit difficult because it involves money.

彼にはいいこと[悪いこと]があった。

Something good [bad] happened to him.

それは感心しない(ことだ)な。

That is something I can never approve of.

これは大事なことだ。

This is { very important. / a very important thing. / something very important.

3．限定語＋こと

【出来事】 →できごと

【本当のこと】 a fact

それは本当のことですよ。

That's true.

【困ったこと，もめごと】 a problem

【すべきこと】 duty; a duty

すべきことをしているだけです。

I do this because it's my duty.

【くだらないこと，無意味なこと】 nonsense

くだらないことをしゃべるな。

Don't talk rubbish [rot, nonsense].

4．慣用表現

【…することにしている】

私は1日に2マイルは歩くことにしている。

It's my habit to walk two miles a day.

私は昼，たいてい「すかいらあく」で食事することにしている。

I usually [generally] have lunch at Skylark.

【…することになっている】

一行は今日の午後，総理大臣に会うことになっている。

They are to meet the Prime Minister this afternoon.

彼は来月結婚することになっている。

He's { going to get / getting } married next month.

【…だということだ】

They say .... / People say .... / It is said ....

この土地は数百年前は海の底だったということだ。

{ They say / People say / It is said } that this place was under the sea centuries ago.

【…ことがある[ない]】 →とき(時の表現)

〈注〉 「…したことがあるか」「…したことがある[ない]」を単純過去形で表すか現在完了形で表すかは文脈による。

彼が笑うのを(それ以来)見たことがない。

I never saw him smile.(1)

I have never seen him smile (since then).(2)

〈注〉 (1) [単純過去] すべて過去のこととして述べている。たとえば子供の頃，近所にこわいおじさんがいて「私は彼の笑顔を見たことがない」というとき。

(2) [現在完了] その状態が現在にまで及んでいることとして述べている。たとえば知人の家に不幸があって，「それ以来私は彼が笑うのを見たことがない」というとき。

【…ことがあるか】

［現在にまで及ぶ］

パンダを見たことがありますか。

Have you ever seen a panda?

［具体的に述べる］

ええ，上野動物園で。

Yes, I have, at Ueno Zoo.

ええ，よく上野動物園にカンカンを見に行きました。

Yes, I have often gone [been] to Ueno Zoo to see Kankan.

［何か付け加える］

いいえ，まだです。でも行ってみたいわ。

No, I haven't [I never have]. I'd like to, though.

［過去の一時期］

中国滞在中パンダを見たことがありましたか。

Did you see a panda while you were in China?

ロンドン滞在中にケンジントン公園に行ったことがありますか。

Did you (ever) visit Kensington Gardens while you were in London?

ええ，もちろん。日曜の午後なんか子供たちを連れてよく行きました。

Yes, I certainly did. I often took my children there on Sunday afternoons.

いいえ，行ったことがないのです。忙しかったので。

No, I never did. I was always busy.

〈注〉 ever の誤用について

「富士山を見たことがありますか」Have you ever seen Mt. Fuji?の類推で「見たことがあります」を×I have ever seen Mt. Fuji. としてはいけない。

次にこの問いの答えの例を示す。何回も見たのなら完了形，1回見ただけなら単純過去形を使う。

I have often seen Mt. Fuji on my way to and from Tokyo. (東京への行き帰りの車窓でたびたび見た)

I saw Mt. Fuji last summer when I went to Japan. (昨年の夏，日本に行ったときに見た)

こどく（孤独）

名 **solitude**

孤独な 形 **solitary**

【孤独を愛す】

その詩人は世俗的な人々との交わりよりも孤独を愛した。

The poet preferred solitude to the company of worldly people.

【孤独な生涯】

その詩人は世間から離れ，孤独な生涯を送った。

The poet lived a lonely life isolated from the world.

ことし（今年）

this year

【展望】

今年は学生生活最後の年だ。

This will be the last year of my school life.

大学へ行っている子供への仕送りが今年でやっと終りになる。

This will be the last year that I have to support a child in college.

今年は卒論で忙しくなる。

I'll be busy this year because I have to
{ complete [finish] my thesis.
{ get my thesis done.

〈注〉 This year will be busy. とも言える。

論文をまとめるのに今年いっぱいはかかる。

It will take the rest of the [this] year to finish [complete] my thesis.

今年中には新居に移れるだろうと思っている。

I hope we will be able to move into our new house by the end of this [the] year.

【現状】

今年の夏はいつになく涼しい。

This is an unusually cool summer.

It has been unusually cool this summer.

This summer has been unusually cool. (今までのところを振り返る)

ごとに（毎に）

2日ごとに［1日おきに］
 every other day; every second day
3日ごとに［2日おきに］ every third day
3日に1度　once every three days
一雨ごとに暖かくなる。
 It gets [It's getting] warmer with every rainfall.

【ダイヤの説明のしかた】

［9:00　9:30　10:00　10:30　…］
バスは9時の始発から30分おきに出発する。
 The bus leaves every 30 minutes starting at 9:00

〈注〉　ある時刻から20分おき，15分おきに出発する意の例文を次に示す。
 The bus leaves every 20 minutes starting from [at, on] the hour.
 9：00　9：15　9：30　9：45
 The bus leaves every 15 minutes [quarter hour], starting from [at, on] the hour.

【会う】

彼は会う人ごとに孫の自慢話をする。
 He boasts of his grandson to everyone he meets.
彼女は会うごとに［たびに］美しくなっている。
 Every time I see her she looks [is] more beautiful than before.

ことば（言葉）

1．言語

language ことば，言語; **a language**（ある1つの言語）
自国の言葉　《one's》native language; a native [mother] tongue
お国言葉　a dialect（郷里の方言）
聞き慣れない言葉で
 in a strange language

2．表現

「自由」という言葉
 the word [term] "freedom"
「ほっておく」という言葉
 the phrase "to let him alone"
「とらぬ狸の皮算用」という言葉
 the proverb "Don't count your chickens before they are hatched"
彼の言葉が忘れられない。
 I cannot forget { his words. / his remark. / what he said. }

〈注〉　words は一般的，remark は簡潔な感想などを指す。

お別れの言葉
 a farewell speech [address〔*formal*〕]
感謝の気持ちは言葉では表せない。
 I have no words to express my gratitude.

〈注〉　say に ing を付けた saying は「ことわざ，言いならわし」の意であるから「言った言葉」の意味には使えない。
 ×I cannot forget his saying.
 ただし，次のような使い方はある。
 うちの母のおはこ
 my mother's favorite saying

【言葉づかい】

言葉づかいから見ると彼は教養のある人らしい。
 Judging from the way he speaks, I think he's probably a well-educated person.
 He speaks like an educated person.
言葉づかいに気をつけなさい。
 Be careful of the way you speak.
 You must be careful in your speech.
言葉づかいがぞんざいだ。
 He is rough-spoken.（荒々しい）
 He uses a lot of vulgar language [words].（下品な）

3．言葉の選択

word choice
言葉を選ぶ
 pick [choose] one's words
うまい言葉が見つからない。
 I can't find the right { words. / way to put it. }

I don't know how to put it.
〈注〉「うまく表現できている」は well-put (↔ badly-put), well-expressed でよい。

ことわる（断る）

1. 申し出・誘いなどを拒む

decline; refuse; say no

せっかくですが，お断りしなければなりません。

I'm afraid I'll have to decline your offer.

彼女を私たちの旅行に誘ったが断ってきた。

She {turned down / declined} our invitation to join the trip.

彼は金は受け取れないと断った。

He refused to accept the money.

ホテルはいっぱいで断られた。

The hotel was full and we were turned away.

【頼み事】

彼は機嫌が悪いから今頼んでも断られますよ。

He's in a bad mood. If you ask him now, he'll {refuse. / say no.}

【求職】

その求人に応募したが断られた。

He applied for the job but he {didn't get it. / wasn't accepted.}

2. 約束の取り消し

cancel

ホテル(の予約)を断ってください。

Please cancel the hotel (reservation).

新しいお手伝いさんはちっとも働かないので断った。

We fired the new home helper because she was lazy.

3. 許可を求める

私たちと一緒に来ることをお母さんに断ってきましたか。

Did you tell your mother that you are [were] coming with us?

〈注〉 時制の一致の規則から，まだ行っていないのならば are，もう行ってしまったのならば were を使う。

出かける前に彼に断ってきた方がいいよ。

You should ask his permission before you start.

断りなしに部屋に入ってはいけない。

Don't enter the room without permission.

4. 掲示

【お断り】

駐車お断り　No Parking

未成年者の入場お断り

Minors [Those under age] will not be admitted.

来る2月26日(月)より3月2日(土)まで店内改装のため休業致します。ご迷惑をおかけ致しますが今後も何卒お引立の程お願い申し上げます。

Notice to our customers [patrons]

This store will be closed from Monday February 26 for renovation. It will be reopened Saturday March 3.

Sorry for the inconvenience.

We thank you for your continued patronage.

〈注〉 上記のお知らせは商店の場合で，事務所であればあて名は to our clients，医院であれば to patients とする。だいたいの順序は閉店のお知らせ(notice of closing)，理由(reason)，開店日(reopening day)，お詫び(apology)，お礼(thanks , appreciation) が普通。

この

this(すぐ目の前にある，手で触れられるようなもの)

cf. その，あの (やや離れた所にあり，指させるようなもの)

【この間】

ついこの間，松田さんに会いました。

I met Mr. Matsuda a few days ago.

この間[先日]，私たちは彼の事務所に訪ねて行った。

The other day we visited him in [at] his office.

ついこの間まで，あの人は病気だった。

He has been sick until quite recently [lately].

〈注〉「この間はありがとう[失礼しました]」など，儀礼として前に会ったときの礼を言う習慣は欧米にはない。特別なことがあれば，"Thank you for all you did to help me find a job."（就職のことですっかりお世話になりありがとうございました）のように具体的に述べ，何のお礼を言っているのかわかるように言う。

【この頃】（最近）→さいきん

この頃，この辺は物騒だ。

The neighborhood is unsafe these days.

この頃[このところ]，夜眠れない。

I {haven't been able to / can't} sleep {these days. / lately.}

このところ，あの人に会っていない。

I haven't seen her lately [recently].

〈注〉recently は近い過去を表すので，過去形または現在完了形と共に使う。現在形と共に使う場合は recently ではなく these days を用いる。「この頃の若い者」the young people of today のような言い方もある。

【この辺】

この辺はたいへん静かだ。

It is very quiet {in {these parts. / this neighborhood.} / here.}

この辺(の地理)はよくわからない。

I'm a stranger around here.

I don't know this area [part of the city].

【この前】

この前会ったときは元気そうだった。

Last time I saw her she looked quite well.

この前からちっとも変らないね。

You haven't changed a bit (since we met last).

彼女はこの前と全然変らず[相変らず]若々しく美しい。

She looks just as young and beautiful as before [ever].

【このまま】

このまま[そのまま]にしておきなさい。

Leave it as it is.

Leave them as they are.

Leave it alone.

このままにしておくわけにはいかない。

We cannot leave things {as they are (now). / like this.}

Something must be done.

(一生懸命働いてくれたのだから)このままというわけにはいかない。

He must not go unrewarded.

このごろ（この頃）→さいきん

このみ（好み）→しゅみ

1．嗜好・趣味

【好みが良い】

彼女は服の好みが良い。

She has good taste in clothes.（センスがある）

彼女は服の好みが良くない。

She has no [poor] taste in clothes.（センスがない）

【好みに合わない】

私の趣味じゃない。

This {doesn't suit / is not to} my taste.

Well, I don't like it [this, that].

【好みが難しい[うるさい]】

彼女は服の好みが難しい[着る物にうるさい]。

She is particular about what she wears.

2．選択

お好みしだいです。(選り取り見どり)

You can take whichever you like.
You can take your choice.

ごぶさた（ご無沙汰）

〈注〉 しばらくぶりに人に会ったり，手紙を書くとき，「ご無沙汰致しました[致しております]」のようにわびるのは日本の習慣的儀礼で，欧米では本当に便りをしなくてすまなかったと思う場合にだけ言えばよい。

ご無沙汰して申し訳ありませんでした。

I'm sorry I haven't
{ written you for so long.（手紙）
{ called you for a long time.（電話）

〈注〉 親しい人にひさしぶりに手紙を書くのであれば，次のように書くこともできる。
You may be surprised to hear from me after such a long silence.

ご無沙汰しました[おひさしぶりですね]。

It's been a long time (since we met each other last), hasn't it?

〈注〉 そのあとに It's nice [good] to see you again. などと続ける。

こまる（困る）

1. 当惑する

be embarrassed

子供たちに「赤ちゃんはどこから来たの」と聞かれて困った。

I was embarrassed when my children asked me where their new baby came from.

（ひとに見られたくなくて）彼女は困って，「人が来ます」と小声で言った。

She whispered, embarrassed, "People are coming."

2. 困惑する

be in trouble　ごたごたがあって困っている。

get into trouble　ごたごたに巻き込まれる。

have trouble (with)　手こずる，…に困る。

be troubled

(1) 対処の仕方に困る

訪問販売員にずっと困っていたが，とうとううまく断る妙案を考えついた。

I used to feel rather troubled by door to door salesmen, but I finally found a great way to get rid of them.

(2) 悩んでいる

両親はこのところ沈んだ顔をしている。何かひどく悩んでいるにちがいない。

My parents look depressed these days; they must be awfully troubled about something.

悩める青年　a troubled youth（内面的な悩みを思わせる）

〈注〉 be troubled はかなり深刻だが troublesome は軽く「面倒くさい」の意。

be confused　まごつく。

be perplexed　困惑する。

be puzzled　困惑する。

地下鉄はいくつも出口があって，どっちに行っていいやら困ってしまった。

There were so many exits in the underground I was confused [perplexed / puzzled] about which way to go.

〈注〉 単に … I didn't know which way to go. でもよい。

be bewildered　当惑する，ろうばいする

〈注〉 知的な意味の困惑。何かわからなくて困る。

be at a loss　途方に暮れる。かなり強い意味なので使いすぎない方がよい。ただし，「言葉に窮す」be at a loss for words はよく使われる。

be at one's **wits' end**　途方に暮れる，お手あげである。

be upset　広く使われる。気が動転し，冷静に考えられなくなる。感情的な言葉。

親切で言ってくれるのだから悪いと思うけど，彼の持って来てくれた就職の話，気が進まないんだ。困っているんだよ。

He meant it kindly. I don't want to disappoint him, but I don't really like the job he's offering. I don't know what to do.

彼に質問されたのがあまりに突然だったので，何と答えたらよいか困ってしまった。

His question was so abrupt
{I was at a loss for an answer.
{I didn't know what to say.

(食事の後)勘定を払おうと財布を開けたら，お金が入っていなかった。まったく困ってしまった。

When I opened my purse to pay the bill, I found that I had no money. I was
{really shocked.
{mortified. (ひどく恥ずかしい思いをした)

彼は息子の素行がどうもよくないので困って[心を痛めて]いる。

He's worried about his son, who's gone somewhat delinquent.

〈注〉 be horrified は「困る」よりも強い表現であるが，似たような心情なのでここで取り上げる。
He was horrified when he heard that his bank has gone bankrupt. (彼の銀行が破産したと聞いて彼はひどいショックを受けた)

3. 困難

have difficulty; I have difficulty ～ing; it's difficult; It's difficult for me to ...

〈注〉 be in {a fix 〔*colloq.*〕 / a dilemma} (実際的)
うっかり同じ日時に二つのアポをとってしまったとか，パーティーに着て行く服を出してみたら汚れていたとかの小さなことについて使う。

彼は今や従業員に支払う給料にも困っている。

Now he has difficulty even paying his employees.

いったい息子が何を考えているのかわからなくて困る。

It's difficult to know what my son is thinking about.

レポートは明日までなのにまだできていなくて困っている。

I'm in a fix because my paper is due tomorrow and I haven't finished it yet.

同じ時間にうっかり二つの約束をしてしまって困っている。

I'm in a fix because I made two appointments for the same time.

彼女は不眠症[便秘]で困っている。

She suffers from insomnia [constipation].

彼はリューマチで困って[難儀して]いる。

He's suffering from rheumatism.

〈注〉 be afflicted with は古い表現であるが，使うとすればひどい苦しみ，不当な扱いなどに苦しむときに使う。

4. 迷惑・被害

be bothered by; be annoyed at

隣の犬がよくほえるので，やかましくて困っている。

He's bothered by his neighbor's dog barking all the time.

彼は隣のステレオの音が大きすぎてやかましくて困って[腹を立てて]いる。

He's annoyed with his neighbor for playing his stereo too loudly.

5. 貧窮

be hard up; be badly off

彼は金に困っている。

He's hard up.

He's badly off.

〈注〉 for money は言わなくともわかる。
ただし，hard up for ideas [time / friends] (考えが浮かばない[時間がない / 友達がいない])のようにも使える。

6. 慣用表現

困ったことには金がかかりすぎる。

The trouble is (that) it will cost too much money.

さらに困ったことには[悪いことには]…

to make things worse ...

what was worse ...

ごみ → きたない

《類義語》
refuse /réfjuːz/　ごみ全体を指す一般的な語。
trash　紙くず，ごみ〔米〕。
litter　特に公共の場所に散らかっている紙くず・空き缶の類。散らかった状態は be littered。
garbage　台所の生ごみ。
dirt　ちり，ほこり (dust)
junk　〔*informal*〕粗大ごみ
粗大ごみ集収日　junk day
rubbish　ごみ。捨てられたもの。主に〔英〕でごく普通に使われる。ごみ箱の内容物は rubbish または refuse。
scrap　金属を再利用のために細かくしたもの。
scraps　野菜・果物の皮や切れ端など，腐敗させて自然に還元される性質のごみ。
rubble　建物を壊した後や地震の後のコンクリートの破片などを rubble and debris と言う。
debris　洪水で寄せられた木片などのごみ。事故現場に散乱した破片など。

【ごみを掃く】
床の掃除をしなさい。
Sweep the floor.

【ごみを散らかす】 litter (up)
こんな景勝地がごみで汚されてまったく情けない。
What a pity those scenic places were all littered up (with trash).

【ごみを投げ捨てる】
ごみをどこでもかまわず捨てるんじゃない。ごみ箱に入れなさい。
Don't {throw away trash / litter} anywhere.
Put it in the wastebasket [dustbin].

【ごみ入れ】
a waste(paper) basket
a wastepaper bin〔英〕
〈注〉 上記は紙くず用でこぎれいな物もある。または公共の場所のくず入れも言う。
列車のごみ入れ
trash container [bin]
(工場・事業所などの)大型ごみ入れ
trash bin
〈注〉 trash〔米〕は紙くずのみでなく，空き缶・空き瓶・プラスチック・布・生ごみなども指す。

【台所の生ごみ入れ】
家の勝手口などに置かれるふた付きのもの
a trash [garbage] can, a dustbin〔英〕
〈注〉 ごみ入れもかごであれば basket，金属製なら can (英国では bin) とよび，container (入れ物) はすべての場合に使える。

【ごみ置き場】
junkyard　粗大ごみ・廃車などを集積し，再利用できる物を分類したりする場所。

【ごみ捨て場】
the dump; the refuse pit
〈注〉◆埋め立てる目的で捨てる場所は the landfill (area) と言う。
cf. My house is built on a landfill. (私の家は埋め立て地に建っている)
◆dump は動詞では「ごみなどをあける[捨てる]」の意味。

【ごみ収集】
ごみトラック　a garbage truck; a dustbin lorry〔英〕
ごみ集め　waste removal; refuse collection
ごみ収集人
a refuse collector; a dustbin man

【ごみ再生場】 recycling station
再生用ごみ入れ　recycling bins
再生できるごみ　recyclables

こら

1. いたずらをやめさせる
こら，やめろ。
Stop it!
Cut it out!
Don't do that!
こら，何をやっているんだ。
What's going on here?
Hey, what are you doing?

2. 静かにさせる
しーっ！　Shh! / Hush!

こら，静かに！

Be quiet! / Pipe down!

こら，黙りなさい！

Shut up! / Close your mouth!

これ → この，それ・これ・あれ

this;（複数）**these**

ころ（頃）

1．およその時間

【…頃】

３時頃　about [around] three（o'clock）

明日[来年]の今頃

about this time tomorrow [next year]

月末頃

toward [about, around] the end of this [the] month

【頃合】

桜の頃

the cherry-blossom season [time]

…する頃

It is about time for … to …

もうあの人たちが駅に到着する頃だ。

It's about time for them to arrive at the station.

君の仕事が終る頃には戻って来る。

I'll come back by the time you finish your work.

彼らは今頃はもうハワイでハネムーンを楽しんでいる頃だ。

I guess by this time they are in Hawaii enjoying their honeymoon.

2．回想年月

【若い頃】　when I was young

【あの頃】　those days

あの頃はまだ若くて何か大きなことをやろうと燃えていた。

I was young and full of ambition in those days.

こわい（怖い）・こわがる

〈注〉「こわい」は「かわいい」などと同様，主観・客観双方にまたがる表現である。何かを自分が「こわい，恐ろしい」と思う（主観）のか，何か物事が「こわい，恐ろしい」性質を持っている（客観）のか，英語では区別しなければならない。

×I am horrible the earthquake.

[主観・人主語] be afraid（of）; be frightened [scared]（of）; be terrified（of）

[客観・対象主語] be terrible [awful, fearful] be eerie [scary, uncanny]（無気味）

1．厳格な

【こわい先生】　a strict teacher

田中先生はこわい。

Mr. Tanaka is strict.

I'm afraid of Mr. Tanaka.（主観）

うちの先生は怒るとすごくこわい。

Our teacher is really frightening when he gets angry.

2．恐怖

【直接修飾】

こわい犬　a fearful dog

〈注〉fearful は causing fear（こわがらせる），feeling fear（こわがる）の両方の意味があるので客観構文にも主観構文にも使われる。

The future doesn't seem fearful to me. / I am not fearful about my future.（これから先のことは別にこわいとは思わない）

私はこわい話が好きだ。

I love scary stories.

私はこわい夢を見た。

I had a nightmare [very bad dream].

【述部修飾】

その子は暗闇がこわい[暗闇をこわがる]。

The child { has some fear / is afraid } of the dark.

私はこわくて眠れなかった。

I was so scared I couldn't sleep.

私はこわくない。

I'm not afraid [frightened, scared].

僕にはこわいものはない。
I fear nothing.

【感嘆の叫び】
ああ，こわかった！
You scare me!
Don't frighten me!

【強度の恐怖】 be horrified; be terrified
彼女はその光景にこわさで足がすくんだ。
She stood terrified [horrified] at the sight.

〈注〉 horrify, terrify はともに強い恐怖心を起させる意の他動詞。be horrified は「恐怖＋強い嫌悪」を感じる，be terrified は身に危険を感じて戦慄する感じである。in a panic はぎょっとして思考力を失った状態。

3．危険な
冬山はこわい。
The mountains are dangerous in winter.

《類義語》
terror ある程度持続する激しい恐怖。身に危険を感じて体が凍るような恐怖。
horror 激しい嫌悪感を伴う強い恐怖。
fright 突然ぎょっとする恐怖。
panic 根拠もなく理由もないのに襲われる強い恐怖。理性のコントロールのきかないもの。

こわす（壊す）・こわれる

1．物・機械
壊す **break (down); smash [crush] into bits**
壊れる **break; be broken; collapse**
壊れている **be out of order; be broken**

【ガラス・陶器】
落さないように注意してね。壊れるから。
Be careful not to let it fall. It will break.
壊れ物注意。
"Fragile—Handle with Care."

【機械】
この機械は壊れている。
This machine { has got [gotten] out of order. / is broken.

【車】
車が壊れた。エンジンがかからない。
My car's broken down. The ignition isn't working.
事故で車が壊された。
The car was damaged in the accident.

【その他】
彼は使い方が荒っぽいのでワープロを壊してしまった。
He ruined the word processor by [with] his clumsy handling.
ラジオ[テレビ]が壊れてしまった。
The radio [TV] is broken. It isn't working (right).
お前がテレビを壊した。
You broke the TV.
腕時計が壊れた。
My watch has stopped.（止まってしまった）
Something has gone wrong with this watch. It doesn't work.（故障して動かない）
波が砂の城を壊した。
The waves collapsed [broke down] the sandcastle.
波で砂の城が壊れた。
The sandcastle collapsed [broke down] in the waves.

2．無形のもの
ruin; spoil

【体を】
彼は過労で体を壊した。
He injured [ruined] his health by overwork.
His health was ruined by overwork.
彼はよく腹[胃]を壊す。
He often has stomach trouble.

【景色を】
あの不格好な建物がせっかくの景色を壊している。
That ugly building spoils the beauty of the scenery.

【楽しみを】
つまらないことに腹を立てて，彼は僕らの楽しみを壊してしまった。

He has completely spoiled our fun by being angry at trivial things.

【夢を】

子供たちの夢を壊さないでおきましょう。サンタクロースを信じさせておきましょう。

Don't destroy [take away] children's dreams. Let them believe in Santa Claus.

こんな → そんな，あんな

こんなん(困難)→ むずかしい，めんどう

[名] **difficulty; hardship**

[形] **difficult; hard**

それは困難な仕事だ。

It's { a tough [hard] job. / difficult work.

私は今，困難な立場にいる。→こまる

I am now in a difficult [awkward, embarrassing] position.

【困難にあう】

30年間商売を続けてきて，ずいぶん困難にも出くわした。

During the thirty years of my career as a merchant, I have met (with) lots of hardships [difficulties].

政府は今大きな困難に直面している。

The government is encountering [facing] great difficulties these days.

【困難を克服】

英雄と呼ばれる人のほとんどが彼らの直面した困難を克服した人々だ。

Almost all heroes overcame the difficulties that they met.

さ

さ（差）→ ちがう・ちがい

1. 違い

二者の間には大きな差がある[何も差はない]。

There is {a great / no} difference between the two.

2人の給料には大差がある。

The two persons' salaries are very different.

【気温・寒暑の差】

夏の初めは日によって気温の差が甚だしい。

In early summer the temperature varies a lot.

【貧富の差】

インドでは貧富の差が激しい。

In India the lives of the rich and the poor are vastly different.

【世代間の差】 generation gap

【見解の差】

彼らの見解にはかなりの差がある。

There's a huge gap between their views.

【点差】

我々は1点差で勝った。

We won the match by one point.

【票差】

市長選挙で松田氏は対立候補にわずか500票の差で勝った。

In the mayoral election Mr. Matsuda defeated his opponent by (a margin of) only 500 votes.

〈注〉 margin は「余裕，票差」の意。

2. 差別

差別 discrimination; 人種差別 racial discrimination; 男女(性)差別 sexual discrimination

(男女を)差別する discriminate between《men and women》

今でもかなりの会社で男女間に給料の差があることからみても，男女差別はちょっとやそっとではなくならないだろう。

The difference between men's and women's salaries still found in many companies shows that sex discrimination will not be abolished so soon.

さあ

さあ来い。

Come on!（挑戦を促す言い方）

〈注〉 教室で Anyone?（誰か(わかる人は)？）と言ってもだれも手を上げないときなどにも使える。

さあ始めよう[行こう]。

Now [OK], let's begin [let's go].

さあ仕事を始めよう。

OK, let's get to work.

さあどうかね。

Well, I don't know.

さあ駅に着きましたよ。

Here we are at the station.

さいがい（災害）

(a) **calamity,** (a) **disaster;** 大災害 (a) **catastrophe**

【自然災害】

地震 an earthquake; 余震 an aftershock

震源地 a seismic /sáizmik/ center

地震帯 a seismic area

マグニチュード magnitude

(トルコ地震は) マグニチュード7.4を記録した。

The Turkey earthquake registered 7.4 on the Richter scale.

There was a big earthquake with a magnitude of 7.4 (on the Richter scale).

亀裂 a crack

津波 a tidal wave; a tsunami

活火山 an active volcano

噴火　an eruption
溶岩　lava; 火山灰　volcanic ash(es)
台風　a typhoon; ハリケーン　a hurricane
台風の目　the eye (of a typhoon [hurricane])
暴風雪　a blizzard
なだれ　an avalanche
落雷　a lightning strike
山火事　a forest fire
竜巻　a tornado
集中豪雨　a local downpour
長時間の豪雨　a torrential rain
鉄砲水　a flash flood
地滑り　a landslide
洪水　a flood; 浸水　flooding
床上1メートルまで浸水して家が水浸しになった。
　The houses were flooded a meter above the floorboards.

【人為的災害】
火事　a fire; 全焼する　be burned down
爆発　an explosion
交通事故　a traffic accident (→ じどうしゃ)
衝突　a collision
列車事故　a railway accident
脱線　(a) derailment
転覆(する)　overturn
海難事故　a disaster at sea
難破　a shipwreck
航空機事故　a plane crash (墜落)
列車が大宮駅近くで転覆した。
　A train overturned near Omiya station.

【被災者】
死傷者　casualties
犠牲者　a victim
重傷　(a) serious injury
重傷者　a severely injured person
行方不明である　be lost; be missing
3名は救出されたが，5名が死亡し3名はまだ行方不明である。
　Three people were rescued, but five were found dead and three are still missing.

さいきん（最近）

1. 近頃

君は[あいつは／仕事は]最近どうだい？
　How have you been [How is he / How's business] these days?
彼の仕事は最近景気がいい[悪い]よ。
　His business seems to be {thriving / doing badly} these days.
最近彼を見ない[から音汰沙がない]。
　I haven't seen him [heard from him] lately [recently].
最近彼に会ったか。
　Have you seen him lately?
最近彼に会ったのはいつですか。
　When did you see him last?
このあたりは最近急に開けた。
　This part of the city has been developed (only) recently.

【最近まで】
最近までこの辺はほんの田舎だった。
　Until quite recently this part of the city was still undeveloped.
最近までここには古い田舎家があった。
　There was an old farm house here until just recently.

2. 当世の

最近[近頃]の若い者は行儀を知らない。
　The young people of today don't know how to behave.

3. このところの

最近［この］10年間で急激に車の数が増えた。
　The number of cars has rapidly increased in the last ten years.
〈注〉 recently, lately は近い過去を示すので現在形ではなく，過去，現在完了とともに用いる。現在時制では these days, nowadays などを用いる。lately は英国では疑問文・否定文に用いる傾向があるが，米国では次のように用いる。
　I had several accidents recently [lately].

（このところ5, 6回も事故を起してしまった）
How have you been these days [lately]?
（近頃どんな調子ですか）
I haven't seen him lately.
（このところ彼を見かけない）

さいしょ（最初）→ だいいち, はじめ

ざいせい（財政）→ けいざい

㊔ **finance;** ㊒ **financial;** ㊓ **financially**

財政投融資計画 a government investment and loan(s) program

市の財政は健全である。

The city is financially sound.

The city's finances are sound [in good shape].

彼はこの会社の財政に通じている。

He {knows a lot about / is knowledgeable about} the finances of this company.

【赤字財政】

deficit financing; red-ink〔*colloq.*〕

政府は財政赤字である。

The government is (running) in the red.

この会社は今財政的に困っている。

This firm is now in financial difficulties.

現内閣は財政再建に全力をあげている。

The present Cabinet is concentrating on the reform [reconstruction] of national finances.

さいのう（才能）

(a) **talent; a gift;** (an) **aptitude**

彼女には音楽の才能がある。

She has a gift [talent] for music.

彼には語学の才能がある。

He has a talent [a gift, an aptitude] for languages.

語学の才能がない

have no aptitude for languages

彼女はすばらしい演劇の才能を発揮した。

She displayed her outstanding dramatic talents.

私は娘に演劇の才能を伸ばしてほしい。

I'd like my daughter to cultivate her talent for [ability in] dramatics.

《類義語》

talent　生れつきの, 主に芸術的な才能。またその人の持つ特殊な能力。

He has a talent for setting people at ease.（彼は人の緊張をほぐし気楽にさせる不思議な才能を持っている）

gift　天賦の才, 驚異的な才能。

ability　何かを成し得る力, 生得または後天的修練で得た力も含む。

capability　何かを成し得る力（しばしば複数）。潜在能力に焦点。

She has great capability as a singer.（彼女は歌手として大成する素質をもっている）

ただし形容詞 capable は「能力がある」のほかに「やりかねない」の意にも使われる。

She is capable of any crime.（彼女はどんな犯罪でもおかしかねない）

capacity　先天的, 後天的双方を含む潜在能力。物に関しては収容能力・容量の意。

aptitude　適性。生得または修得したもの。

faculty　(1)生得または修得した特殊な才能。(2)人間独得の精神的能力, 哲学などで用いられる用語で, 日常はあまり使われない。

faculty of reason（理性をもつ能力があること）

さいばん（裁判）→ じけん

(a) **jurisdiction; a court;** 個々の裁判 **a trial**

1. 裁判所

最高裁判所　the Supreme Court

最高裁判所長官

the Chief Justice of the Supreme Court

最高裁判所判事　a Supreme Court Justice

高等裁判所　a high court

上訴裁判所　an appellate court

地方裁判所　a district court
家庭裁判所　a family court
少年裁判所　a juvenile court
簡易裁判所　a summary court
〈注〉 federal court〔米〕連邦裁判所; state court 州裁判所
刑事裁判所　a criminal court
民事裁判所　a civil court [traffic court, small claims court]
遺言検証の裁判所
　a probate court（civil court の一部）
裁判官
　a judge;［全体］the bench
　a magistrate（〔米〕下級裁判所判事,〔英〕軽犯罪を扱う治安判事）
裁判長　the chief justice; the presiding judge
〈注〉 上訴裁判所（an appellate court）では複数の裁判官が当り, 裁判長は the chief justice, 他の裁判官は an associate justice と呼ぶ。
検察庁　Public Prosecutor's Office
検察官　a public prosecutor
地方検察官　a district prosecutor
陪審員　a jury;［全体］the jury〔米〕

2．訴訟

【民事事件】 a non-criminal case
訴訟を起す　file a suit; sue
ＡがＢをＣのかどで提訴した。
　A took B to court for C.
　A brought a case against B for C.
　A sued B for C.
損害賠償訴訟　a damage suit
離婚訴訟　a divorce suit
離婚訴訟を起す
　file a divorce suit; file for divorce
告訴を取り下げる　withdraw the complaint
【刑事事件】 a criminal case
刑事　a police detective
送検する
　refer the case to the prosecutor's office
告発する
　charge; accuse; indict /indáit/〔米〕
起訴する
　charge《a person》with《a crime》
　accuse《a person》of《a crime》
　prosecute [indict]《a person》for《a crime》
起訴される
　be charged with; be accused of
　be prosecuted [indicted〔米〕] for
彼は詐欺で告発された。
　He was charged with fraud.
彼は収賄で告発された。
　He was accused of taking bribes.
彼は殺人罪で起訴された。
　He was prosecuted [indicted] for murder.
〈注〉◆prosecute は多くの場合司法用語であるが, accuse, charge は日常的に人を非難する意味にも使われる。米国では陪審員の評決で有罪・無罪が決められる。
◆訴訟の手続き
arrested（検挙）
the trial {
charged [indicted]（告発）
prosecuted（訴追）—defended（弁護）
（verdict passed by the jury（陪審の評決）〔米〕）
if judged guilty, sentenced by the judge（判事の判決）
}

【その他の訴訟用語】
不起訴とする　drop a case
取調べ　an examination; an investigation
拘留　detention; custody
保釈　bail
予審　a preliminary hearing
公判　a trial
原告(民事)
　a plaintiff; a complainant〔*formal*〕
被告　the accused; a defendant
罪状を認める　plead guilty
罪状を否認する　plead not guilty [innocent]
証人(目撃者)　a witness
証拠　evidence
証言　testimony
有利な証言をする
　testify for [on behalf of]《a person》
不利な証言をする
　testify against《a person》

尋問　questioning
反対尋問　(a) cross-examination
弁護士
a lawyer; an attorney〔米〕; a defense counsel; a defense lawyer
弁護する　plead
最終弁論
the final [concluding] argument by the defense attorney
供述者　an affidavit
調書　the record of questioning; the court record

3. 判決

a sentence; a decision; a verdict
判決文　a verdict
判決を下す
sentence《a person》to《five years》
控訴を棄却する
reject [dismiss] an appeal
控訴を差し戻す
refer the appealed case back to the lower court
控訴を取り下げる　withdraw the appeal
判決を支持する　uphold the decision
無罪とする　acquit
無罪放免　acquittal
地方裁判所は彼に禁固５年の判決を下した。
The District Court sentenced him to five years imprisonment.
裁判官はその名誉毀損事件に無罪の判決を下した。
The judge delivered a judgement of 'not guilty' in the libel case.
裁判官はその被告に有利な[不利な]判決を下した。
The judge decided in favor of [against] the accused.
控訴する
appeal to a higher court
bring the case to the court of appeals
最高裁は大阪地裁の判決を支持した。
The Supreme Court upheld the decision of the Osaka District Court.

4. 刑

punishment
罰金　fine
禁固　imprisonment without labor
懲役　imprisonment with hard labor
死刑　death sentence
執行猶予　probation
執行猶予で　on probation
執行猶予５年
a 5-year suspended sentence
a suspended sentence of 5 years
恩赦　amnesty

さいふ（財布）・ハンドバッグ

〈注〉 英米で呼び方が異なるので注意。
彼は妻の誕生日プレゼントに財布の底をはたいた。
He spent all the money he had on his wife's birthday present.
奥さんが財布のひもを握っている。
His wife holds [controls] the purse strings.
彼女はめったに財布のひもをゆるめない。
She rarely loosens the purse strings.
She keeps the purse strings tight.

《類義語》
wallet　男性用の革製二つ折り平型の札入れ。〔米〕billfold とも呼ばれる。
woman's billfold [wallet]　〔米〕女性用札入れ。
purse　〔米〕ハンドバッグ;〔英〕(通例) 女性用の財布。
handbag; bag　ハンドバッグ。
pocketbook　札入れ;〔米〕ハンドバッグ (purse)。肩ひものない小型, 中型のもの
credit card purse　クレジットカードや名刺を入れる。
briefcase　書類入れ。平型・中型のもの。attaché case, executive case とも呼ばれる。
coin purse　〔米〕小銭入れ。

財布・ハンドバック

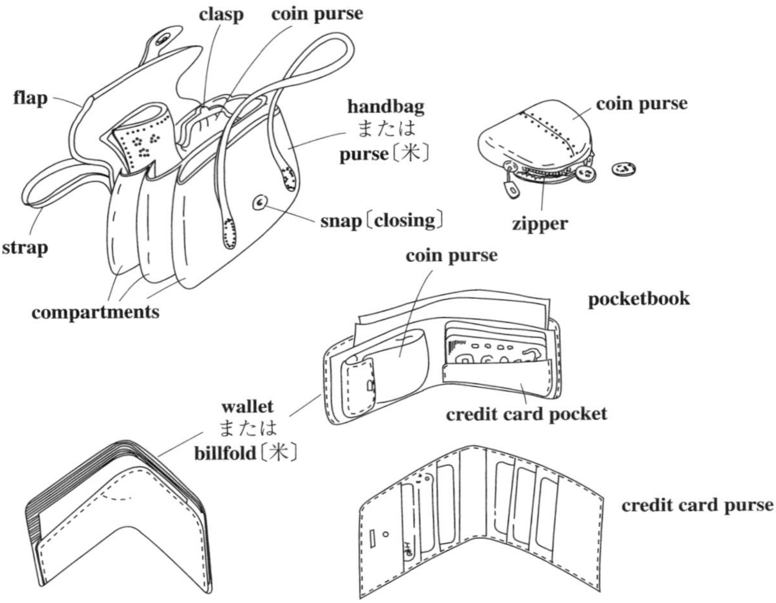

さいよう（採用）

1. 取り上げる

採用する　**adopt**

教育委員会は新しい教授法の採用を決定した。

The Board of Education has decided to adopt a new method of teaching.

この教科書は全国的に採用されている。

This textbook has been adopted throughout the country.

2. 雇用

採用試験　an employment examination

採用条件

employment [job〔*informal*〕] qualifications

採用申し込み

an application for employment

さらに5名の技術者を採用した。

They employed [hired, took on] five more engineers.

Five more engineers were employed.

〈注〉 英語では能動態が好まれる。しかし次の例は she に焦点があてられているので受動態。

彼女はサンタイムズのレポーターとして採用された。

She was employed [hired, taken on] as a reporter on the *Sun-Times*.

〈注〉 employ は hire, take on よりやや堅い語である。

さいわい（幸い）

形 **happy; fortunate; lucky**

幸いに(も)　**fortunately; luckily; by good luck**

幸いけがはたいしたことはなかった。

Fortunately his injury was not serious.

Luckily he wasn't seriously injured.

幸いその事故ではだれもけがをしなかった。

No one was injured in the accident, fortunately.

事故が起きたときその場にいなかったのは幸いだった。

It's lucky [fortunate] that I wasn't there when it happened.

I'm glad that I wasn't there when it happened.

〈注〉◆happy は fortunate, lucky と区別しなければならない。happy は幸せな状況，喜ばしく満足した状況であるから，人が主語となる。× It's happy that ... とは言えない。

◆fortunate, lucky は幸運の意味で同じように使われるが，副詞の fortunately はやや形式ばった語で，起った事柄の結末についての感想に使われる。一方 luckily は偶然性を強調するといった，重点の置き所に微妙な差がある。どちらがよいか迷う場合は luckily を使う方が無難。

ex. Why wasn't he injured seriously? Luck.
(なぜひどいけがをしないですんだのだろう。運がよかったのさ)

次のように言ってもよい。

He wasn't injured seriously. He was fortunate.

【慣用表現】

これでお役に立てば幸いです。

I shall be happy if this can help you. 〔*formal*〕

〈注〉 happy が「幸い」の英訳として使われるのは，上記慣用のみ。通常「幸せ」が happy に当る。happily は次のような場合に使う。

a happily married couple (仲むつまじい夫婦)
The child went off happily to buy ice cream.
(うれしそうにアイスクリームを買いに行った)
They smiled happily.
(うれしそうににっこり笑った)

要するに happily は動作の修飾語(副詞)としては使えるが，文章全体にかかる副詞としては使われない。一方 luckily, fortunately は文章全体にかかる副詞である。

「幸い」は文章全体にかかる修飾語であるから，happily は使わない。happily と luckily, fortunately の混同はよくある誤りである。

さがす（探す）

look for; search

1．手さぐりで探す

feel for; grope

ポケットに手を突っ込んで切符を探した。

I searched [felt inside] my pocket for the ticket.

〈注〉 search は時間をかけ，なかなか見つからないような場合。

暗闇のなか手さぐりでスイッチを探した。

I groped for the switch in the dark.

2．見て探す

財布[ハンドバッグ]を探している。

I'm looking for my purse.

彼はアパートを探している。

He is looking [hunting] for an apartment.

私たちは家中探したが書類は見つからなかった。

We searched all over the house for the document but couldn't find it.

泥棒は部屋中ひっくり返して金を探した。

The thief ransacked the room for money.

彼は財布を探しに，それまで立ち寄った所を一つ一つ訪ねて歩いた。

He went back to the places he had been trying to find his wallet.

このスラックスに合うジャケットを探さなければならない。

I have to find a jacket to match these slacks.

人々は我も我もと金を探しにカリフォルニアに集まった。

People flocked to California in search of gold.

〈注〉 look for, search はほとんど同義に使われるが，look for の原義は見て探すことであるから，目を使わずにポケットの中を手でさぐって探す場合には使わない。

3．求人

赤十字病院で看護師を探している。

Nurses are wanted at the Red Cross Hospital.

さかな（魚）

魚　**a fish**
魚介類　**seafood**

《関連語》
【海水魚】 saltwater fish
アジ horse mackerel / アナゴ Japanese conger eel / アンコウ goosefish / イトマキエイ manta ray / イワシ sardine / ウツボ moray eel / ウナギ eel / エイ ray / カサゴ scorpion fish / カタクチイワシ Japanese anchovy / カツオ bonito, skipjack / カレイ flatfish, flounder, plaice / カワハギ triggerfish / キンメダイ alfonsin / クロダイ black sea bream / コノシロ gizzard shad / サケ salmon / サバ mackerel / サメ shark / サワラ Spanish mackerel / サンマ saury / シタビラメ sole / シラウオ icefish / スズキ sea bass / タイ sea bream / タチウオ hairtail / タラ Pacific cod / チョウザメ sturgeon（卵はキャビア caviar）/ トビウオ flying fish / トラフグ ocellate puffer / ニシン Pacific herring（薫製ニシン kipper）/ ハモ conger pike / ヒラメ flatfish, halibut, fluke, turbot / ブリ yellow tail / ホッケ Atka mackerel / マカジキ Pacific marlin / マグロ tuna / マンボウ ocean sunfish / ムロアジ mackerel scad / メカジキ swordfish
【淡水魚】 freshwater fish
アユ ayu / イワナ char / ウグイ common dace / コイ carp / ドジョウ loach / ナマズ catfish / ニジマス rainbow trout / フナ crucian carp / ワカサギ pond smelt
【イカ・エビ・カニなど】
イセエビ Japanese spiny lobster / ウニ sea urchin / クルマエビ kuruma prawn, Japanese shrimp / ケガニ horsehair crab / コウイカ cuttlefish / シャコ mantis shrimp / スルメイカ short-finned squid / ズワイガニ snow [queen] crab / タラバガニ king crab / タコ octopus / ホタルイカ firefly squid / ヤリイカ arrow squid / ロブスター lobster

さからう（逆らう）→ はんかん

1．意志に

どうして君は先生たちに逆らうのだ。
Why do you defy your teachers?

その年齢の子供たちは親によく逆らうものだ。
Children of that age tend to disobey their parents.

彼らは親（の希望）に逆らって結婚した。
They married against their parents' wishes.

2．時流に

時流に逆らうと苦労をしますよ。
You'll have a hard time if you
{ go against the times [wind].
{ swim against the stream [tide, current].

さき（先）→ まえ

1．先端

point; tip

鉛筆の先　the tip [point] of a pencil
指先　a finger tip

あの人は口先だけで何もやりはしない。
He never really carries out what he promises. That's only lip service.

〈注〉 口先だけで体を動かさないことを lip service と言う。

2．目的の場所

【行き先】 one's destination

あなたの行き先を教えてください。
Let me know where you will be [are going].

あの人は朝早く出かけたが行き先は知らない。
He left early in the morning but I don't know where he has gone.

【勤め先】 one's place of work

勤務先のオフィス　one's office

勤め先の人たちはいい人たちだ。
The people where I work are friendly.

【連絡先】
連絡先を教えてください。
Tell me where I can get in touch with you.

3. 空間
ahead; beyond
この先100メートル道路工事中。
Road (under) construction 100 meters ahead.
この先の十字路を右に曲ってください。
A little further ahead is a junction. Turn (to the) right there.
彼女の家は3軒先の家です。
Her house is three doors down [up].
この通りの中ほどに温室がありますが，そこから3軒先が彼女の家です。
There's a green house halfway down the street. Her house is three doors further on.
（ここから）2駅先で降ります。
I get off {two stations / at the second stop} from here.
関ヶ原から先は豪雪のため不通です。
Because of (the) heavy snow, traffic is tied up beyond Sekigahara.

4. 時間
先の総理大臣 the former Prime Minister
〈注〉「前」「元」また「故」など日本語でもいろいろあるが，英語の言い方を記す。
元総理細川氏 Mr. Hosokawa, (the) former Prime Minister（存命）
元総理故大平氏 the late Prime Minister, Mr. Ohira
〜年前の総理村山氏 Mr. Murayama,(who was) Prime Minister 〜 years ago
ずっと前に亡くなった人はもう歴史上の人物であるから，the late をつけなくてよい。
先にふれた事件（書類上）
the incident mentioned above
the above-mentioned incident
先にも申し上げた通り…（口頭）
as I said before ...
【前もって】
先[前]払いでお願いします。
Please pay in advance.
cf. 着払い C. O. D. [Cash on Delivery]
私はその件について先に知っていた。
I already knew that.
【これから先】 from now on; in [the] future
【10年先】 ten years from now; in ten years
10年先，世界はどうなっているだろう。
What will the world be like in [after〔米〕] ten years?
【将来】
君はまだまだ先が長い。
You have {the whole future / a lifetime [your whole life]} {ahead of / before} you.
私の命は先が長くない。
I won't live much longer.
I don't have long to live.
我々は先が見えない。
We had little foresight.
（このままでは）あの子の先が思いやられる。
The way he is, I feel uneasy how he will turn out.
What will become of him?
先のことはわからない。
It is difficult to know what will happen next.
【仕事】
この商売は先の見込みがないと思う。
I think this business has no future.
The future of this business is bleak.
この仕事は先の見込みがある[ない]。
This job has {a good [promising] / no [little]} future.
This job shows (no) promise.
【子供】
この子供は先が楽しみだ[見込みがある]。
This child {is promising. / shows promise. / will go far.〔*colloq.*〕}
〈注〉 be promising は人間，特に子供について使う。

【貿易】
（世界貿易）の先の見通しは明るい[暗い]。
The future looks bright [dark] for world trade.
The outlook is bright [dark].
【続き】
これから先は任せる。
I will leave the rest to you. 〔*formal*〕
【物語】
その先はどうなるの[なったの]？
What happens [happened] next?
その子はこの先どうなるの？
What will happen to the boy?

5．順位
【真っ先に】
宿題を真っ先にしなさい。
Do your homework first thing.
彼の名前が真っ先に出ている。
His name { heads the list. / is at the head [top] of the list.
彼がまず先に来た。
He came first.
あの人は私より先に来た。
She came (here) earlier than I.
She got here before me.
【先に立って】
彼が先に立って歩いた。
He led the way.
彼が先に立ってまず１万円を寄付した。
He took the lead and donated 10,000 yen.
先立つものはまず金だ。
The question of money is the most important (one).
【優先】
社会福祉を防衛より先にしろ。
Place [Put] public welfare before defense.
どうぞお先に。
After you.
Please go ahead [first].（戸口で先を譲るとき）
Please go on ahead. I'll come later.（後から行きます）
〈注〉 年配の人に冗談に Age before beauty. と言ったりする。「お年の方お先に，美人の私はおあとから」の意。

さすが

1．期待どおりの
さすがビルだ！
That's our Bill!
あいつ，さすがじゃないか。
Isn't that just like him?
さすが東大出だけあって本当に教養がある。
He's a truly well-educated person, as a Tokyo University graduate so often is.
「(歌が)うまいもんだなあ」「イタリア出身さ」「さすがだなあ！」。
"What wonderful singers!" "They're from Italy." "Oh, no wonder!"
さすが大チャンピオンだ。若い挑戦者をやっつけた。
The Grand Champion won against the young challenger, as expected.
As might be expected, the Grand Champion beat the young challenger.

2．あれほどの
さすがの勇者もライオンが20メートル先に現れたときはひるんだ。
Brave as he was, he was daunted when he saw a lion only twenty meters ahead [away from him].
しっかり者で鳴らしたあの女性も会社の倒産にはさすがにすっかり参っていた。
That usually stout-hearted woman looked really discouraged when her company went bankrupt.

させる・させられる

【(さ)せられる】
〈注〉 日本語では他動詞と使役の区別があいまいであるために，「(さ)せる」(使役)「(さ)せられる」(使役の受身）が「(ら)れる」（受身）と，音および意味内容の近似から混同されることがあり，次のような誤文が書かれることがあるので注意を要する。

泣かされた。

×I was cried.

△I was made to cry.

○He often made me cry.

歌を歌わされた。

×I was sung a song.

△I was made to sing.

○They made me sing.

○They urged me to sing.

【使役】

強いて…させる

make《a person》《do》

force《a person》to《do》(強い強制)

彼らは子供たちに1日8時間も勉強させた。

They made their children study eight hours a day.

子供たちは1日8時間も勉強させられた。

Their children were made [forced] to study eight hours a day.

【許可】

(さ)せる

allow《a person》to《do》

let《a person》《do》

彼は息子に海外留学をさせた。

He allowed his son to study abroad.

He let his son study abroad.

彼は海外留学をさせてもらった。

He was allowed to study abroad.

彼は自分の釣りざおを使わせてくれた。

He allowed me to use [let me use] his fishing rod.

私は彼の釣りざおを使わせてもらった。

I was allowed to use his fishing rod.

もう一度やらせてください。

Let me try again [once more].

Give me one more [another] chance.

彼女には私のような苦労をさせたくない。

I would never let her suffer as much as I did.

子供たちに私と同じように愉快な学校生活を過させてやりたい。

I'd like to have my children enjoy their school life as much as I did.

【依頼】

彼らはポーターにスーツケースを2階に運ばせた。

They {asked [told] the porter to carry / had the porter carry} their suitcases upstairs.

彼らはスーツケースを2階に運ばせた。

They had [got] the suitcases carried upstairs.

【させる，してもらう，される】

He had [got] his hair cut.

髪を切らせた。(1)

髪を切ってもらった。(2)

髪を切られてしまった。(3)

〈注〉 上の英文の意味は要するに，彼が自分の手ではなく第三者の手で散髪したことであるが，日本語ではそれを三つの場合にわけ，それぞれ異なった言い方で表現する。

自分の意志で {(1)(2)は自分から散髪を希望した場合の言い方。 / (1)は「切ってくれ」と頼んで切らせた。 / (2)は「切ってください」と頼んで切ってもらった。}

意志に反して {(3)は自分は髪を切りたくなかったのに切られてしまった。}

ざつだん(雑談) → しゃべる

さびしい(寂しい，淋しい)

1. 場所

remote; desolate; deserted; out of the way

その人たちは一番近い家でさえ6マイルも離れているというさびしい所に住んでいた。

They lived in the remotest area with the nearest neighbor six miles away.

僕らは全旅程の中でも一番さびしい場所で，それも夕暮れ時にガス欠になってしまった。

We ran out of gas at nightfall in the most deserted place of the whole trip.

2. 心情［人主語］

feel lonely [lonesome]; feel forlorn

さびしい生活を送る　lead a lonely life
さびしく死ぬ　die forlorn
〈注〉 forlorn はひどい孤独感に苦しんでいる状態。
(誰かが)いなくてさびしい
miss《someone》
事務所の新入りの女の子が昼食を一緒に食べる仲間はいないかとさびしい気持ちでまわりを見回した。
The new office girl looked about for a lunch companion, feeling very lonely.
あなたがいなくなるとさびしいわ。
I'll miss you when you are gone.
親というものは子供がどんなに大きくなっても，そばにいないとさびしいと思うもののようだ。
Parents always seem to miss their children no matter how old their children are.
彼はまったく思いもよらなかったのだ。…彼の妻が新しい知人，新しい音楽や絵画などに焦がれて，どうしようもなくさびしい思いをしていたなんて。
He hadn't the remotest notion that … she was desperately lonely, pining for new people and new music and pictures and so on.
——Katherine Mansfield, *Marriage à la Mode*
〈注〉 **lonely, lonesome, alone**
lonely は人にも物にも場所にも使える。lonesome は人の心情についてのみに使え意味が強い。
alone は状態として「ひとり」であることで，心情とは直接関係がない。日本語の「独り」と異なり，be alone with a personとなると「2人きり」の意になり，We are alone. と複数で「だれもほかの人がいない」ことになる。
At last I'm alone with you.
(やっと2人きりになれた)

3. 物足りない
壁のところがさびしいから絵でもかけよう。
The wall looks bare, so let's hang a picture on it.
この絵は何かさびしい。
Something is missing in this picture.

サボる
〈注〉 フランス語 sabotage(怠業)から来た言葉。

1. 仕事を怠ける
君は家の仕事をいつもサボってばかりいる。
You hardly ever do your household chores.
彼はサボっていて仕事の期限になかなか間に合わない。
He's lazy about getting things done on time.
自分の仕事をサボるんじゃない。
Don't be negligent about your work.
彼はいつもサボってぶらぶらしている。
He's always loafing around.

2. 授業に出ない
彼はきのう学校をサボった。
He cut school yesterday.
He played truant [hooky] from school.
彼はきのう，午後の授業をサボって映画を見に行った。
He cut [skipped] classes yesterday afternoon and went to see a movie.
〈注〉 小・中学校で授業をサボることを play [be] truant [hooky〔米〕], 大学などで授業を受けず，ほかの場所にいるのが cut classes。

さます(覚す)・さめる → おきる・おこす

1. 眠りから
【目を覚す, 目が覚める】
㊍㊎ **wake up**
〈注〉 自動詞として awake, awaken もあるが，wake が最も一般的。
㊍㊐ **awaken, wake** の受動形
be awakened [woken up / waked up〔米〕]
しーっ！ 赤ちゃんが目を覚す。
Hush! The baby will wake up.
真夜中に突然変な音で目が覚めた。
I was suddenly {woken [waked] up / awakened} at midnight by a strange sound.
夜中に何度も目を覚した。

I woke up several times during the night.

I was up and down all night. 〔*colloq.*〕

朝までずっと目を覚したままだった。

I lay awake all night.

〈注〉 普通に目が覚めるのは wake, 何かの力で目を覚ますのは be awakened, 目覚めている状態は be awake である。 動 awake は古風で，比喩的に「心の目が覚める」の意味で使われる傾向がある。
Please wake me at 8:00. は普通だが，日本語では「目を覚す」ではなく「起す」と言う。

2. 酔いから

冷たい水で顔でも洗って酔いを覚しなさい。

Wash your face in cold water to make yourself sober [sober yourself up].

酔いは覚めている。

I am sober.

彼はまだ酔いが覚めていない。

He isn't sober yet.

He's still drunk.

3. 迷いから

失敗してやっと目が覚めた。

Failure has brought me to my senses.

彼はまだ目が覚めない［夢ばかり追っている］。

He has not yet awakened to reality.

サラリーマン → しょくぎょう

a white-collar worker; a salaried worker

〈注〉「Aは農家，Bは商売，Cはサラリーマンだ」のようによく言うが，英語にするときはもっと具体的に職業を言う方がよい。

公務員，役人

a civil servant; a government employee;（高い地位にある公務員）a public official

会社員

a company employee; an office worker（公務員でも会社員でも平(ひら)でオフィスで働く人）

部長，課長

the chief [head, director] of a department [section, division]

社長

the president; the head of a firm [company]

さる（去る）→ しゅっぱつ

1. 場所

go away from《a place》; **leave**《a place》 **for**《another place》; **start from**《a place》 **for**《another place》

彼はこの前の日曜日に日本を去り香港に向かった［成田から香港に向かった］。

He left Japan [from Narita] last Sunday for Hongkong.

〈注〉 leave は他動詞であるから leave Narita が正しいと思いがちだが，成田に住んでいたのならこれでよい。しかし東京在住であったり日本にしばらく滞在して成田空港から出国したのであれば left Tokyo [Japan] であり，特に成田からと言いたければ from Narita を加える。

2. 職場

彼は職場を去った。（→やめる・やむ）

He { retired (at sixty). ……(1)
resigned (from the army). ……(2)
quit his job (and went to live in New Zealand). ……(3) }

〈注〉 (1) retire 退職する，退職して悠々と暮すイメージで，定年退職や女性の結婚退職などに用いられる。
(2) resign 辞職する，仕事をやめる。特に正式に届けて辞任する。
(3) quit one's job〔口語〕やめる，give up [leave] work の意。

3. 消え去る

危険は去った。

The danger { has passed. / is gone. }

痛みが去った。

The pain is gone.

される → れる

〈注〉「される」は日本語の動詞のタイプにより使役の受身を表すときがある。意味内容を考えて混同しないよう注意。また，英語の受身形が作れるのは他動詞に限ることも併せて注意。

1．受身

滅ぼされる　be destroyed

起される　be awakened

2．使役受身（「せられる」の短縮形）

教室の後ろに立たされた。

I was told [made, forced] to stand at the back of the classroom.

×I was stood …

漱石の作品を夏休みに読まされた。

We were told to read some works of Soseki during the summer vacation.

×We were read some works of Soseki …

〈注〉 上の2例では was [were] told としたが，これは「立っていろ」「読め」と言われたことで実際に命令に従ったことは意味しないため，厳密には使役にはならない。しかし be made, be forced とすると「意に反して」の気持ちが強くなりすぎるので，前記の記述に前後の文で足りないところは補うくらいが妥当である。

いじめっこに泣かされた。

They bullied me until I cried.

×I was cried …

おじいさんにはいつも苦労話を聞かされたものだ。

Our grandfather used to tell us that they had lived through many many difficulties.

×We were heard that …

彼女は気がついていないが，実はいつも彼に踊らされて[操られて]いるんだ。

Though she doesn't realize it, she always dances to his tune.

×She is danced …

さわる（触る，障る）

1．ふれる

feel; touch

ショーケースの中の展示品に触らないでください。

Don't touch the articles exhibited in the showcase.

肩に触らないで！　ひりひりするんだ。

Don't touch my shoulder, it's very sore.

〈注〉「肩に触る」

touch { me on the shoulder (1) / my shoulder (2) }

(1)も(2)も「肩に触る」であるが，(2)は何かが肩に触ることを述べている。(1)の方にはやさしい気持ち，なぐさめる気持ちなどの感情が含まれるか，または「私がそばにいます」とか「ひさしぶりじゃないか」など，場面によってメッセージがある場合の言い方である。

これ[この材質]は手触りがいい。

This material feels nice.

これ[この材質]は肌触りがよい。

This material feels good against my skin.

2．障る

夕食に食べた魚がおなかに障った。

The fish I ate at dinner disagreed with me.

飲みすぎると体に障りますよ。

Drinking too much will affect your health.

飲みすぎると翌日の仕事に障りますよ。

Drinking too much will affect your work the next day.

彼の笑い方が気に障る。

His way of laughing { irks me. / irritates me. / annoys me. / gets on my nerves. }

さんぎょう（産業）

industry; 形 **industrial**

第一次産業　(a) primary industry

農業　agriculture; 林業　forestry; 水産業　fishery

第二次産業　(a) secondary industry

鉱業　a [the] mining industry; 製造業　a [the] manufacturing industry (→こうぎょう); 建設業　a [the] construction industry

第三次産業　(a) tertiary industry

流通産業　the retail industry; 情報通信業　the information and communication indus-

try; サービス業　a [the] service industry など
基幹産業　(a) basic industry
主要産業　a major industry
地場産業　(a) local industry
軍需産業　a [the] weapons industry
エネルギー産業　(an [the]) energy industry
自動車産業　the car [auto〔米〕] industry
ハイテク産業　(a) high-tech industry
映画産業　the film industry
観光産業　(a [the]) tourist industry
レジャー産業　(a) leisure industry
産業廃棄物　industrial waste
産業別労働組合　an industrial union
国内の産業を奨励する
　encourage domestic industries

《関連語》
生産者　manufacturer; producer
生産量　production; output
生産性　productivity
国内総生産　gross domestic product (略 GDP)
国民１人当り生産高
　gross national product (略 GNP)
大量生産　mass production
設備投資　capital investment
省力化　labor-saving
オートメーション　automation
工業用ロボット　industrial robot
ベルトコンベア　conveyor belt
流れ作業　assembly line
商品化する　put a product into production
規格品　standard product; approved product [model]
規格に合格する　meet [satisfy] / be up to } a standard
不合格品　(factory) reject; rejects
欠陥商品　defective product
日本工業規格
　the Japan Industrial Standard (略 JIS)
製造物責任法(PL法)　Product Liability Law
生産原価　production cost
原価計算をする　calculate the cost
原価見積り　(cost) estimate
鉄鋼業　steel industry
造船業　shipbuilding industry
石油化学工業　petrochemical industry
　ナイロン nylon / ビニール vinyl(一般に plasticと呼ばれる) / 塩化ビニール vinyl chloride / ポリエステル polyester / プラスチック plastic (総称; かたいものも vinyl のようなやわらかいものも含む) / 発泡スチロール styrene foam; polystyrene

さんせいする (賛成する)

1. 同意する

agree with《a person, a person's opinion》(意見が一致する); **agree to**《a person's proposal》(提案に賛成する)

私はあなたに大賛成である。
　I quite agree with you [your opinion].
　I'm all for it.〔*informal*〕

【賛成しない】
　disagree with《a person's opinion》
僕はあなたに賛成できない。
　I don't agree with you.
この点ではあなたに賛成できない。
　I can't quite agree with you on this point.

2. 賛同する

approve of《a plan》

両親とも僕たちの結婚に賛成している。
　My parents { consented to [approved] (1) / approved of (2) } our marriage.
〈注〉 (1)は正式に承認すること, (2)は感情的に好ましく思っていること。

3. 討論・裁決

support《a bill》(支持する)

委員の大多数が法案に賛成であった。
　Most of the committee members supported the bill.
動議に賛成[反対]である
　be for [against] the motion

賛成の方はご起立願います。
　All in favour, please stand (up).

【賛成多数】

賛成多数と認めます。
　I see that the ayes have it.

３分の２以上の賛成を得る
　receive a two-thirds majority

投票の結果，賛成12票，反対８票でした。
　The result of the voting was 12 for and 8 against the bill.

賛成の演説をする
　{make a speech / speak} {in support of / for [in favour of]} the motion

ざんねん（残念）

残念に思う **be sorry;** がっかりする **be disappointed** (**at, in**); 残念に思う **regret**

そりゃ，残念だ。
　That's too bad. / Oh, I'm sorry.

【未来】

残念だけど行かれません。
　I'm sorry I can't go with you.

【過去の事実に今の思い】

行かれなかったことが残念だ。
　I'm sorry I couldn't go with you.

【過去の思い】

行かれなくて残念に思った。
　I was sorry I couldn't go with you.
　×It was sorry for me that …

休みの間中天気が悪くて残念だった。
　It was a shame the weather was so bad during the vacation.

【現在】

あなたが一緒に来られなくて残念だわ。
　It's a pity you can't come with us.

彼は結局来ないらしい。残念だ。
　He isn't coming after all. I'm disappointed.

氏がかくも早く当地を去られるとは誠に残念に存じます。
　We regret that he {should have to / has to} leave us so soon.〔*formal*〕

残念ながら会合には欠席させていただきます。
　I regret to say that I can't attend the meeting.〔*formal*〕

…したいんですけれど，残念ながらだめみたい。
　I'd love to but I'm afraid I can't …

残念ながら彼女は自分で願っているほどきれいではない。
　Unfortunately she isn't so [as] pretty as she would like (to be).

〈注〉 to my regret, to my disappointment などは堅い表現で，くだけた文には合わない。It is regrettable that … も会話体ではない。It's a pity, It's a shame (that) は会話で使えるがかなり強い表現で，軽い意味で「残念」というときには使わない。

さんぱい（参拝）→ ねんちゅうぎょうじ

【参拝する】 visit

元旦にはたくさんの人が明治神宮に参拝する。
　A great number of people visit the Meiji Shrine on New Year's Day.

【参拝客】

神社は参拝客で大混雑であった。
　The shrine was {very crowded. / full of people.}

〈注〉 参拝客は worshippers と訳されることが多いが，worshippers は本当の意味の信者のことで欧米でもあまり使われない。

し

し（死）→ しぬ

し（詩）

一編の詩 **a poem; poetry**（集合的）; 韻文 **(a) verse**

詩を作る　compose [write] a poem

詩を鑑賞する　appreciate poetry

【詩にうたう】

「序曲」という詩でワーズワースは子供時代への郷愁をうたっている。

In the poem "Prelude", Wordsworth wrote of his nostalgia for his childhood.

〈注〉 もともと poetry は詩の「うたごころ」の面から, verse は韻文という形の面から呼ぶ言い方であるが, それほど厳格に区別されているわけではない。軽い詩（light poetry）はよく verse と呼ばれる。しかし次のような批評も可能である。

These lines are written in verse but are unworthy to be called poetry.（これらの詩行は韻文で書かれてはいるが詩とはとても呼べない）

じ（字）→ もじ

しあい（試合）

a game; a match; competition

勝ち抜き試合 **a tournament**

第1試合　the first game; the first round

1. 試合＋動詞

試合に出る

take part [play] in a match [game]

明日フットボールの試合がある。

There'll be a football game [match] tomorrow.

私たちは明日フットボールの試合をする。

We'll have a football game [match] tomorrow.

私たちは試合に勝った[負けた]。

We've won [lost] (the game).

テレビで試合を見るつもりだ。

I'm going to watch [see] the game on TV.

雨で試合が中止になった。

The game was called off [cancelled] because of (the) rain.

テニスの試合を申し込む

challenge a team to a tennis competition 〔*formal*〕

試合をしませんか。（誘い）

Let's have a game of badminton.（バドミントン）

How about a game of badminton?

Let's play tennis.（テニス）

2. スコア

【同点】

試合は4対4の同点だった。

The game was four all.

【引き分け】

試合は引き分けに終った。

The game ended in a draw.

【圧勝・完敗】

試合は10対0で終った。

The game ended with a score of 10-0.

〈注〉 10-0の読み方は ten (to) zero [nil, naught, nothing]。

彼らは10対0で圧勝[完敗]した。

They won an overwhelming victory with / They were completely defeated by } a score of 10-0.

しかい（司会）

1. 会議

司会をする[議長をする]

act as a chairman [chairperson]

take the chair

chair [conduct, preside at 〔*formal*〕] a meeting

cf. preside over [be head of] the city council（市の議長職にある）

市の交通安全会議はジョン・スミス議長のもとに今年１回目の会合を行った。

The city's Traffic Safety Board, under the chairmanship of John Smith, held its first meeting of the year.

彼は会議の司会がうまい。

He is good at chairing [conducting] meetings.

He is an excellent chairman.（名議長だ）

スミス氏が議長［司会］で委員会（の議事）はスムーズに進んだ。

The committee made fast progress under the chairmanship of Mr. Smith.

2．式

司式者　master of ceremonies（卒業式・成人式など）

儀式を行なう牧師［僧侶／判事］

an officiating minister [priest / judge]

パネルディスカッションの司会者

a panel leader

ウィリアムズ神父の司式で式は執り行われた。

The ceremony was conducted by Father Williams.

Father Williams officiated at the ceremony.

3．ラジオ・テレビなど

司会者　master of ceremonies

〈注〉 宴会などの場合にかぎり MC と省略できる。正式な式の司会は MC と言わない。

【司会する】 emcee

彼はテレビの子供向けショー番組の司会をやっている。

He emcees children's TV shows.

〈注〉 a radio announcer, a news announcer（今は a newscaster の方が多く使われる）などが司会することもある。また talk show の司会者は a host とも呼ばれる。テレビのインタビュー番組「徹子の部屋」の黒柳さんは interviewer。

しかく（資格）

1．法的資格

a qualification; a certification（資格の認証）

彼は高校の理科教員の資格を持っている［がある］。

He is qualified [certified] to teach
{ science in [at] high school.
{ high school science.

彼は事務弁護士［法務官］の資格を持っている。

He is { qualified [certified] as a solicitor.
{ a qualified solicitor.

彼は弁護士の資格を取った。

He got a lawyer's license.

彼は法律事務を取扱う資格を取った。

He obtained his qualification to practise law.

【選挙権】（→せんきょ）

the franchise; voting rights; right to vote

彼女はまだ選挙する資格がない。

She hasn't got the right to vote yet.

2．要件

会員（など）の資格　requirements [qualifications] for membership

とやかく指図する資格は私にはない。

I have no right to give you orders.

【入学資格】 entrance requirements; requirements for admission

本学入学資格の最低要件は高校卒業者であることである。

The minimum academic requirement for admission to the university is senior high school graduation.

3．能力

【資格がある】

彼は優秀な言語学者と呼ばれる資格がある。

He is fully qualified to be called an expert linguist.

【資格がない】do not deserve
彼には学者と呼ばれる資格はない。
He does not deserve to be called a scholar.
私にはとても先生の助手をやらせていただく資格はありません。
I'm not qualified to be your assistant.
〈注〉 日本語では目上の人に「あなた」「君」のような代名詞は使わず役職名かその人の名前を言うが，英語では you でよい。

じかく（自覚）

【責任[任務]を自覚する】
become aware [conscious] of one's responsibility [duty]
ドライバーがほかのドライバーに気を配るのは当然で，その責任の自覚がなければならない。たとえば方向指示ライトをきちんと出す注意を怠らないことなどである。
Car drivers should be aware of their responsibility to consider other drivers; for example, they should be careful to use directional lights.
〈注〉 I think we young people should be aware [conscious] of our responsibility to be the driving force of the future world.（我々若者はこれからの世の中を担っていく者としての自覚が必要だ）
この文は文として誤りはないが，内容はわかり切ったことであり，欧米人には陳腐・平凡の印象を与える。
【自己の能力を自覚する】
realize one's own strength [ability]
【自己の価値を自覚する】
awake [be awakened] to one's own worth
cf. self-awakening（自我の目覚め）
あの人は自分の欠点を自覚していない。
She is not aware of her own defects.
【自覚症状】
初期の癌では（患者に）自覚症状がないのが普通だ。
In the early stages of cancer most patients are unaware of any symptom of the illness.

しかた → やりかた

しかたない（仕方ない）・しかたなく

1．やむを得ない

【しかたない】
I can't help it.
It can't be helped.
There's no help for it.
何と言われてもしかたがない。
I know we deserve their criticism.
【しかたなかった】
I couldn't help it.
It couldn't be helped.
It was unavoidable.
言いつけに従うよりしかたなかった。
I had no alternative [choice] but to obey his orders.
あきらめるよりほかしかたがなかった。
There was nothing for it but to give up.
I had to give up.
I was forced to give up.〔強〕

2．無益

すんだことはしかたがない。
What is done cannot be undone.
It's no use crying over spilt milk.
彼は絶対行かないと言っているんだから待っていてもしかたがない。
There's no use waiting for him since he is determined not to come.

3．我慢できない

眠くてしかたない。
Oh, I'm terribly sleepy.
子供がどたばたうるさくてしかたがない。
I can hardly stand the noise those children make.
息子のことが心配でしかたがない。
I cannot help feeling uneasy about my son.
【…したくてしかたがない】
be dying {for [to do]《something》

水が飲みたくて飲みたくてしかたがなかった。

I was dying for a glass of water.

私も一緒に行きたくてしかたがなかった。

I was dying to go with them.

4. しかたなく

〈注〉「しかたなく」を unavoidably, inevitably のような1語の副詞で表現するのは無理である。

ドアが閉まっているのでしかたなく引き返した。

As the door was locked, I had to turn away.

子供が泣いてぐずるのでしかたなく買ってやった。

The child howled for it and I couldn't but buy it for him.

しがん(志願) → にゅうし

1. 入学志願

志願する

apply for {admission to / enrollment in} a school

志願[応募]者　an applicant

〈注〉 applicant は応募者, すなわち志願票を出す人の意。

2. ボランティア志願

介護ボランティアを志願する

volunteer to nurse the sick and the old

災害援助ボランティアを志願する

volunteer to do disaster relief

3. 従軍志願

【志願する】 volunteer (for military service)

従軍看護婦を志願する

volunteer one's services as a nurse

〈注〉 volunteer はこのほかにも種々のサービス, 物の提供の意にも使われる。

volunteer {《one's》 home for a party / 《one's》 ideas [advice]}

じかん(時間) → とき

1. 時間の単位

一瞬　a moment

1秒　a second

1分　a minute=60 seconds

1時間　an hour=60 minutes

1日　a day=24 hours

1週間　a week=7 days

1か月　a month=28, 29, 30, or 31 days

1年　a year=12 months

四季　four seasons (spring, summer, autumn [fall〔米〕], winter)

2. 時間表現

今何時ですか。

What time is it?

9時です。

It's nine o'clock.

9時10分前です。

It's ten to nine.

9時5分過ぎです。

It's five past nine [nine-oh-five].

9時15分過ぎです。

It's quarter past nine [nine fifteen].

9時30分[半]です。

It's nine thirty. / It's half past nine.

9時45分です。

It's (a) quarter to [of] ten [nine forty-five].

【時刻】

…時頃に来てください。

Please come to see me

{ (at) around [about] seven in the evening. (7時頃に)
in the morning [afternoon]. (午前［午後］に)
in the evening [at night]. (夕方［夜］に) }

【日・曜日】

赤ん坊は…日に生れた。

The baby was born

on Sunday.（日曜日に）
on the third of June.（６月３日に）
last night.（昨夜）
yesterday.（きのう）
ten days ago.（10日前に）

【月・年】

彼に会ったのは…のことだ。

I met him { last summer.（昨年夏に） / in January.（１月に） / in 1970.（1970年に） }

【期間内】

彼は…くらいで戻ってくるだろう。

He will come back
{ in a few days.（2,3日中に） / in a week [a month / a year].（１週間［１月/１年］以内に） }

彼はそこに2,3日間滞在する予定だ。

He will stay there for a few days.

しげき（刺激）

名（抽象的）**stimulation;** 興奮 **excitement;** 激励 **encouragement;** 刺激するもの **a stimulus**（*pl.* stimuli）; **an impetus; a spur; an incentive**

刺激する 動 **stimulate; excite; irritate**

刺激性の 形 stimulating; ぴりっとする pungent

1．感覚

目［口］を刺激する　irritate the eyes [mouth]

舌を刺激する　sting the tongue

アンモニアの臭いが鼻を刺激する。

The smell of ammonia goes right up my nose.

2．興奮

若者は刺激を求めるので麻薬に走りやすい。

Because young people seek excitement, they can easily begin to use drugs.

【扇情的】

刺激的な見出しや写真を満載した雑誌が多すぎる。

There are too many magazines full of sensational headlines and pictures.

3．生活の変化

我々の毎日の生活には刺激がない。

Our everyday life is too dull [monotonous].

都会の生活にはいろいろと刺激が多い。

City life is full of
{ excitement.（うわべの面白さ） / stimulation.（深く動かすもの） }

4．励み

ジョンがコンテストで１等賞をとった。ほかの生徒のいい刺激になるだろう。

John got the first prize in the contest. It will { encourage / be a good stimulus [incentive] to } the other boys.

5．怒らす

あまり彼の感情を刺激するようなことを言わないで。

Don't say anything that will
{ irritate him. / get on his nerves. }

彼を刺激しないでくださいよ。また何かやらかすといけないから。

Don't provoke him to do anything rash.

しけん（試験）→ きょういく

1．学力テスト

an examination; an exam; 簡単な試験 **a quiz;** 小試験 **a test**

先週英国史［英語］の試験があった。

We had { a test in English history / an English examination } last week.

学年末試験は２月15日から28日までである。

The final [semester] exams will be (held) from the 15th to the 28th of February.

【試験をする】 give an examination [a test]
安倍先生は来週ドイツ語の試験をすると言った。
Mr. Abe announced
{ a test in German next week.
{ that he would give us a test next week.

【試験を受ける】 take [sit (for)] an exam
彼は早稲田(の入学試験)を受ける。
He is going to take the entrance examination of Waseda University.
彼は試験でカンニングをした。
He cheated in the exam.
〈注〉 ×cunning とは言わない。

【試験に合格する[不合格になる]】
試験に合格する
pass [succeed in] an examination
試験に不合格になる
fail an examination
彼は高得点[満点]で試験に合格した。
He passed the examination with a high [perfect] score.
4月4日, 5日両日行われた医師国家試験の受験者は8000人を超え, その中の75パーセントが合格した。
Of more than 8,000 candidates who took [sat for] the national examination for doctor certification on the 4th and the 5th of April, 75 percent of them passed [succeeded in passing].

【試験勉強】
この問題は試験に出そうだ[この前の試験に出た]。
This question will probably be asked in the exam [was asked in the last exam].
私は試験問題の山をかけた。
I guessed [anticipated] what the questions were going to be.
I zeroed in on the questions.
〈注〉 zero in on〔米 *colloq.*〕「…に銃の照準を合せる」の意より。
彼は試験のため猛勉強をしている。
He's really grinding〔米〕[swotting〔英〕] for the exam.
彼は入試のために英単語や熟語を詰め込んでいる。
He's cramming English words and idioms for the entrance exam.
試験の範囲は教科書の10ページから40ページまでだ。
The examination will cover [be on, be over] the material from page 10 to page 40 in the textbook.

《関連語》
国家試験 state [a national] examination
資格試験 qualifying examination
検定試験 certification examination
入学試験 entrance examination (for a school [a university])
人物試験 character [personality] test
面接試験 personal interview
筆記試験 written examination
口頭試問 oral examination
学力[実力]試験 achievement test
適性検査 aptitude test
模擬試験 mock [practice, trial] examination
〈注〉 前後関係から内容がはっきりしていれば a trial run とも言われる。

【学校】
期末[中間]試験 term [midterm] examination
最終試験(大学など)
the final examinations; the finals
(大学院)卒業時の総合試験
(MA) comprehensive(s)〔米〕

【就職】
採用[入社]試験 employment examination
公務員試験 the civil service examination

【その他】
試験科目 examination subjects; subjects of an examination
化学も試験科目に入っていた。
Chemistry was one of my examination subjects.
試験官 examiner
試験地獄 examination hell; the ordeal of taking the entrance examination

試験会場　examination room [hall]
試験問題
examination problem（作図・計算など）
examination question（質問形式）
test question
試験用紙　examination papers
試験方法　method of examination
試験検定料
examination fee
the fee for an examination

2．実験

an experiment; a test; a trial

【試験的な】 experimental
新しい方法はまだ試験的段階である。
The new method is as yet in its experimental stage.

【試験的に】 experimentally; on trial
新薬は試験的に使用することを許可された。
The experimental drug has been approved for trial use.
我々は新型ドリルを試験的に使っている。
We are using the new drilling machine which we have on trial.
私たちはコンピュータを1か月ほど借りて試験的に[試しに]使ってみている。
We've got a computer for a month on trial.
彼は新車の試乗をしてみた。
He tried out a new car.

【試験をする[行う]】
test; make a trial [an experiment, a test]
最終的な試験をする
put《a thing》to the test
新車のテストをする
test a new model
このエンジンは大気汚染に対する厳しい安全基準試験を通った。
This engine passed the strict anti-pollution tests.
試験の結果,燃料噴射系は優秀である[には欠陥がある]ことがわかった。
The fuel injection system proved [excellent [defective] on trial.

《関連語》
試験方法　testing procedures
試験済みの　passed
その車はすでに2003年の車検済みである[のステッカーが貼ってある]。
The car
{has passed its 2003 safety inspection.
has its 2003 inspection sticker already.
試験的作品[試作品]
test models（大きな機械）
（test）samples（小さい物）
性能試験　performance test
試験場[所]
laboratory; experimental station
農業試験場
agricultural experimental station
水産試験場　fisheries experimental station
林業試験場　forestry experimental station
試験飛行　test flight
試験飛行士[テストパイロット]　test pilot

じけん（事件）→ こと

1．出来事

出来事 **what happened;** 小さな事件 **an incident, a happening;** 大きな事件 **an event;** 事柄 **a matter, an affair;** 事故 **an accident**
恋愛事件　a love affair
社会的事件　a social event
人類史上特筆すべき事件
prominent events in the history of humankind
例の幽霊事件を覚えていますか。
Remember the ghost incident?
これは今年の10大事件の一つだ。
This is one of the ten outstanding events of this year.

2．刑事事件・民事事件

a case

【当事者】
事件を起す　start some trouble

贈収賄事件に関係する
be [get] involved in a bribery case
事件を弁護士に依頼する
turn a case over to a lawyer
彼は事件のもみ消しをはかった。
He tried to hush up the matter.
cf. 事件はもみ消された。
The incident has been covered up.

【警察】
事件を担当する
handle the case
事件はなお捜査中である。
The police are still working on the case.
事件は解決した。
The case has been solved.
事件は解決されていない。
The case hasn't been solved yet.
その事件は複雑でついに迷宮入りとなった。
The case is so complicated, {it has been given up. / the police have given up trying to solve it.}

《関連語》
【民事事件】 civil (law) case
訴訟　law suit
重婚　bigamy; 離婚　divorce
横領　embezzlement
契約の不履行　breach of contract
男女[人種]差別事件　discrimination case
人権問題事件　human rights case
【刑事事件】 criminal case (→けいさつ，さいばん)
軽犯罪事件　misdemeanor
cf. 重罪　felony (殺人 murder; 放火 arson; 強姦 rape など)
詐欺事件　fraud case
汚職事件　graft case; corruption case
贈収賄事件　bribery case
傷害事件　bodily harm case
殺人事件　murder case
ひき逃げ事件　hit and run case
事件目撃者　witness
〈注〉 犯罪名は例えば fraud (詐欺), murder (殺人) であり，それが警察が捜査をはじめたり裁判にかかった場合に～ caseと呼ばれる。

じこ（事故）→ こと，じけん

an accident
交通事故　a traffic accident
飛行機事故(墜落事故)
an air [a plane] accident; an air crash
列車事故　a train [a railroad] accident
水の事故(水死)　drownings
交通事故防止運動
a safety-first campaign
交通事故死　a traffic death
〈注〉「事故で死ぬ」は die in an accident とは言わず，be killed in an accident と受け身にする方が普通。
この前の日曜日に二つの水の事故があった。
There were two drownings last Sunday.
2年前ここで大きな列車事故があり，その事故で15人が死亡，50人以上が重軽傷を負った。
{There was a big railroad accident / A big railroad accident occurred} on [at] this spot two years ago; fifteen people were killed and more than fifty were injured.
彼は自宅に帰る途中で事故にあった。
He had an accident on his way home.
この村は1年間無事故だった。
There have been no traffic accidents in this village for a whole year.
万事事故もなく運んでよかった。
I'm glad everything has {turned out / gone} well.

じこく（時刻）

(a) **time; an hour**
【こんな時刻に】 at this time of day
こんな時刻にすみません。緊急な用事ができたものですから。
Sorry to {wake you so early (早すぎる場合) / call you so late (遅すぎる場合)} but I have something urgent to tell you.
【時刻表】 a train schedule

しごと（仕事）

《類義語》

work　仕事を表す一般的な語。意味も用途も広い。work は動詞「働く」としても使われるので，名詞としても働いているイメージがある。不可算名詞であるから ×a work, many works とは言えない。

job　賃仕事，手間仕事，ちょっとしたお使い。口語では仕事・職業の意味で一番普通に使われる語。(cf. job hunting 職探し)

employment　堅い語で，すべての職業に共通して用いられる。

occupation　職業，人が生計のため従事する仕事。

profession　専門知識を必要とする職業（doctors, nurses, teachers, lawyers, ministers, priests, artists など）。

career　「生涯の経歴」を念頭においた職業。相当に打ち込んでいる含みがある。

business　営利を目的とする職業。商品の製造販売，サービス業を含む。

trade　「交易・商売」以外に，特別の訓練と修練を必要とする職人仕事の意味に使われる。

task　単純だが手間のかかる仕事。職業としてではなく，一時的に従事する仕事，課せられた仕事，ちょっとした仕事。多少古風な語。

〈注〉 duty も仕事であるが，「やらねばならない」と努めてする仕事を指す。

undertaking　手間のかかる仕事，骨の折れる仕事（子供たちを大学にやること，住宅のためのお金の工面，学位論文を書くことなど）。

labor　肉体的，精神的に厳しい仕事。

vocation, calling　職業であるが，神より賜った「天職」の意味もある上品な語。

mission　布教活動のような「使命」としての仕事。

1．職業

【いい仕事】

ほら，君にちょうどいい仕事があるよ。

　Here's just the right job for you.

彼からいい仕事の話があった。

　I've got a good job offer from him.

掲示板[新聞]にいい仕事の口が出ている。

　There's a good job notice { on the announcement board. / in the newspaper. }

今のところ仕事がない[失業中だ]。

　I'm now ⌊out of work [unemployed].

　I don't have any job now.

　I'm not working.

【仕事を探す・見つける】

　look [hunt] for ⌊work [a job]

　seek ⌊work [employment]〔*formal*〕

彼は自分に向いたいい仕事を見つけた。

　He found ⌊a job [work] that would suit him.

叔父さんが僕の仕事を見つけてくれた。

　My uncle found me a job.

【仕事を引き受ける】 accept [take] a job

彼女はデータ管理の部署[営業部／会計課]に回された。

　She was assigned to the data management section [the sales department / the accounting section].

【仕事は…だ】

彼の仕事はアナウンサーです。

　He is an announcer.

彼の仕事は弁護士だ。

　He is a lawyer.

私たちはＸＹ会社の社員だ［ＸＹ会社勤務だ］。

　We work for XY Company.

【仕事をやめる，退職する】（→やめる）

　leave《one's》job; give up work; quit《one's》job; resign from the company [(from) the post]; retire(定年退職でやめる)

2．労働

【一日の仕事】 a day's work

今日一日の仕事を終えた。(しっかり働いた)

　I've done a good day's work.

毎日の仕事

　《one's》daily routine（朝起きてから寝るまでのおきまりの日常）

　《one's》daily work（仕事に関することの

み）

家の仕事　housework; household chores

一生の仕事　《one's》lifework

苦しい仕事　hard work; a hard job

〈注〉 work は不可算名詞，job は可算名詞。

【仕事がある［ない］】

今日はたくさん仕事がある。

I have a lot of things to do today.

I've got a lot of work.

これからまだひと仕事ある。

We've got a long way to go yet.

仕事がない。（することがない）

I have nothing to do.

【仕事をする［やめる］】

週44時間仕事をする。

We work 44 hours a week.（自分について）

The workweek is 44 hours.（労働者一般について）

仕事に行く　go to work

仕事を始める

begin to work

start { to work / working

set { to work / about《one's》work

〈注〉 begin [start] work と言うときは通常「始業」（例えば 8：30より）を意味する。実際に行動を開始するのは begin [start] to work [working] である。

仕事をやめる

stop; quit（for the day）（その日の仕事を）

ちょうど今日の仕事を終えたところだ。

I have just finished my work for the day.

【仕事を休む】

have [take] { a holiday / a vacation（1週間以上休む）

have [take] a day off（1日休む）

take time off from《one's》work（数時間または午前，午後のような形で休みをとる）

set [lay] aside《one's》work（席を立つ，電話に出る。すぐ戻る含みがある）

〈注〉「産休をとる」は take maternity leave。「病休をとる」は take sick leave。

【仕事が】

彼は仕事が速い［遅い］。

He is a fast [slow] worker.

彼は仕事がていねい［ぞんざい］である。

His work is neat [sloppy].

彼は仕事がよくできる。

He is an able worker.〔*formal*〕（推薦書（job recommendations）などでの書き方）

彼はコンピュータのプログラムをやっているがなかなか仕事がよくできる。

He programs computers and he's very good at it.

彼女は仕事がたいへんよくできるようになった。

She's got much better at her work.

【仕事で】

一日の仕事でくたびれていた。

I was tired from the day's work.（原因）

仕事で大阪へ行った。

I went to Osaka on business.（目的）

【仕事をくびになる】

be fired; be laid off

〈注〉 be fired は雇主の気に入らずくびになることだが，be laid off の場合も雇われている者にとっては職を失う点で同じであるから広義では be fired に含まれるだろう。

be laid off は会社が不景気のために人員整理でやめさせられること。景気が回復すれば復職ということもある（be temporarily laid off 一時的に解雇される）。

しじ（支持）

support

支持する　動 support

NHK の世論調査によれば回答者の58.5パーセントが新政府を支持している。

In a NHK public opinion poll, 58.5 percent of the respondents support the new government.

私は新首相を全面的に支持する。

I'm all for the new premier.〔*colloq.*〕

【支持を受ける】

彼の政策は全国民の支持を受けている。
The whole nation supports his program.
彼女は世論の支持を受けている。
She has the backing of public opinion.
【支持者】
彼女は労働階級に相当数の支持者を獲得した。
She gained considerable support from the working class.
彼は新人候補者渡辺氏を支持する演説をした。
He made a speech in support of Mr. Watanabe, the new candidate.

しじ（指示）

instructions; directions
指示する 動 **instruct; direct**
課長[係長]の指示に従う
follow the section chief's instructions
指示を待つ
wait for instructions from《a person》
外務省は当地の日本大使以下全員に即刻大使館を閉鎖して帰国するよう指示した。
The Ministry of Foreign Affairs directed [instructed] all the Japanese Embassy staff there to close the office and return home as soon as possible.
次に何をしたらよいか指示してください。
Please tell me what to do next.

じじつ（事実）

1．真実

a fact; (a) truth; (a) reality
確固たる事実
an undeniable fact; an established fact
事実を認める admit (the fact)
事実を否定する deny (the fact)
…という事実を否定できない
It cannot be denied that …
There is no denying (the fact) that …
(夢が)現実となる
come true
事実を調査する
investigate
〈注〉 inquire into the facts はどちらかというと使い古され，今はあまり使われない表現である。口語では dig out the facts などともいう。
私が何も知らなかったのは事実だ。
The fact [truth] is that I didn't know anything about it.
彼がもらい子だという事実は養父母の死後明らかにされた。
The fact that he was an adopted child was disclosed after the death of his foster parents.
〈注〉◆The circumstances of his birth were disclosed …(彼の出生に関する事実は…)のように書くこともできる。
◆the fact that … のように同格 that 節で修飾できる名詞は「情報・考え・確かさ」などを表す特定の名詞に限られる。巻末付録の that リスト参照。
そのうわさは事実に基づいている。
The rumor is based on fact.
そのうわさは事実に反している。
That rumor is inconsistent with the facts.
The facts are otherwise.
革命当時，この場所に金が埋められたとかいう話は事実無根である。
There are [We have] no grounds for believing / We have no reason to believe } that gold might have been buried here at the time of the revolution.
だれかが故意に事実を曲げたに違いない。
Someone must have deliberately twisted [perverted] the truth.

2．強調

actually; really
私は事実ＵＦＯがビルの上を飛んで行くのを見たんだ。
I actually [really] did see the UFO flying over the building.

僕は人生で成功したとは言えない。事実人生の敗者さ。

I have not been very successful in life; {as a matter of fact, / in fact,} I am a failure.

じじょう（事情）→ わけ

circumstances; conditions; the situation; the state of affairs

1. 理由

何か事情があるにちがいない。

There must be some unknown reasons.

彼は何か事情があって来られなかったんだろう。

Something must have prevented him from coming.

やむを得ない事情で

for (some) unavoidable reasons

彼は家庭の事情で退学した。

He left school {for family reasons. / because of family circumstances.}

〈注〉 経済上の事情は economic reasons [circumstances]。

2. 実情

住宅事情　the housing situation

食糧事情　the food situation

こういう事情だから取りやめなければならない。

Under these circumstances we'll have to give up our plan.

〈注〉 under these circumstances は通常これから先の見通しについて述べる文の中で使われる。すなわち，「こんな事情では［事態が変らなければ］…だろう」といった場合に用いる。同じ意味では，such being the case という言い方もあるが，多少形式ばった言い方で話し言葉ではない。

私達は事情が許すかぎりこの仕事は続ける。

We'll go on with this work for as long as possible.

〈注〉 as far as circumstances allow という言い方もあるが，形式ばった言い方で話し言葉ではない。

ここ日本では事情が違う。

Things [Matters] are different here in Japan.

10年前は事情が違った。

Ten years ago things were different (than they are now).

アメリカの事情に明るい［通じている］。

have a very good knowledge of things American

cf. 私はアメリカの事情はよく知らない。

I don't know much about things American.

〈注〉 things American は文章語。普通のくだけた言い方 American things との違いは，前者がアメリカの生活習慣や伝統のような抽象物も含むのに対し，後者は物のみを指す傾向があることである。

中国の事情に明るい［中国通である］

be (well-)informed [knowledgeable] about Chinese affairs

じしん（自信）

self-confidence; confidence in《oneself》

【自信を持つ】 have confidence in《oneself》

【自信がある】 be confident of《one's》ability

彼はたいへん自信がある［たいへんな自信家だ］。

He has great confidence [faith] in himself.

彼は今度の小説は今まで書いた中で一番の出来だと自信を持っている。

He is confident that his new novel is the best he has ever written.

今度は合格する自信がある。

I feel confident that I will pass the exam this time.

試験に合格する自信がない。

I am not sure that I will pass the exam.

彼に賭事をやめさせる自信があるのか。

Are you confident [sure] you can persuade him to give up gambling?

【自信満々】

彼は自信満々だ。

He is full of confidence.

【自信過剰】

彼は自信過剰だ。

He is overly confident.

【自信をなくす】

lose confidence in oneself [one's (own) ability]

【自信を取り戻す】

regain [recover, get back] confidence in oneself [one's (own) ability]

【自信を持って】 with confidence

若い警官は十代の子の自転車マナー改善のための提案を自信を持ってとうとうと話した。

The young policeman spoke with confidence about his proposal for improving teenage bicycle habits.

しずかな（静かな）・しずめる（鎮める）

（音のない状態） **silent;**（静かな音） **quiet**

（動きのない状態） still

（心情・態度） calm; serene; peaceful; gentle

〈注〉 silent は無音，quiet は音がしても静かな音であるから，a quiet voice はよいが，a silent voice とは言えない。a quiet day [night, place] などとは言える。比喩的に a quiet boy [mind] とも言う。

1．静寂な

静かに！

Be quiet! / Be silent!（おしゃべりをやめて）

Shut up!（黙れ）

Hush!（しっ！）

Keep still!（still は「じっとしている」）

Sit still and be quiet!

静かな夜だった。

The night was very still [quiet, silent].

子供たちは静かにしていた［おとなしくしていた］。

The children kept quiet [still].

cf. 彼はびっくりして言葉が出なかった。

He was dumbstruck [struck dumb].

大講堂［聴衆］はしいんと静まりかえった。

The big hall became [fell] quiet.

A deep [profound] silence fell upon [over]
{ the big hall.
{ the audience.

〈注〉◆A dead silence fell ... とすると恐怖のため息をのんでいる感じになる。

◆Hushed silence reigned over the big hall. は古風でおおげさに響くが，文としては正しい。

嵐の前の静けさ

the lull [quiet] before the storm

山の静けさを破って教会の鐘が鳴り響いた。

The church bell rang through the stillness [quiet] of the mountain air.

2．穏やかな

quiet; calm; peaceful

海は鏡のように静かだった。

The sea was as calm as the surface of a mirror.

〈注〉 英米で as calm as a pond〔*cliché*〕と言う。

静かに眠らせてやりなさい。

Don't disturb her while she's sleeping.

〈注〉 RIP（Rest in peace）「静かに眠れ」は墓碑などに書く言葉。

彼は故郷信州の大町に帰り，静かな生活を送った。

He retired to Omachi in Shinshu, where he led a quiet life.

3．鎮［静］める

警官が来て騒ぎを鎮めた。

The policeman came and
{ calmed things [people] down.
{ got things under control.

【心を静める】

calm down（怒り，いら立ちなどを静める）

collect oneself（心を落ち着かせる）

compose oneself（何か言ったりしたりする前に心を落ち着かせる）〔*rather formal*〕

pull oneself together（しゃんとする）

〈注〉 Pull yourself together!（しゃんとしなさい）と命令形で使われることが多い。

恐怖［怒り］を静める

calm one's fears [rage]

【痛みを鎮める】

reduce the pain; soothe the pain〔*literary*〕

しそこなう（仕損なう） → しっぱい

した（下）

1. 位置

under; below; beneath

満開の桜の下でお茶の会をやった。

We had a tea party under [beneath] blossoming cherry trees.

（飛行機から）下には山や川が朝日に輝いていた。

(From our plane) We saw hills and rivers below, bright in the morning sun.

うちの子猫はこの石の下に埋められている。

Our kitten is buried under [beneath] this stone.

彼はスーツケースを下に下ろした。

He set his suitcase down.

枕の下からウイスキーの小瓶を出し，彼はほくそ笑んだ。

He produced a small bottle of whisky from under his pillow and grinned.

おばかさんが親方の所へ行き，家は上から下の順で作るのか下から上に作るのかを尋ねた。

One of the little morons went to his boss and asked if they should start building the house from the top down or from the bottom up.

【下部】

洪水で家（の下の方）は１メートルも水につかった。

The houses were flooded one meter deep.

その絵の右下に署名がしてある。

There's a signature at the bottom right-hand corner of the picture.

「ボブはどこにいるの」「下でお母さんと話してるよ」。

"Where's Bob?" "He's downstairs talking to Mother〔英〕[mother〔米〕]."

〈注〉 家族同士の会話ならば冠詞なしで Mother または mother。家族以外の人が話しているのなら to his mother とする。

その建物の下の階は日が当らない。

The lower floors [part] of the building don't [doesn't] get any sun.

【内側】

どうぞ心配なさらないで。ちっとも寒くありません。（コートの）下にベストとセーターを着込んでいますから。

Please don't worry. I'm not a bit cold. I'm wearing a vest and a sweater under my coat [underneath].

あの白のナイロンのドレスは下が透けて見える。

You can see through that white nylon dress.

2. 順位

【年・級】

（小・中学校の）下のクラスの子

the children in the lower grade

ケイトは私より二つ年下だ。

Kate is two years younger than I.

マイクが一番下の子で，ビルは下から２番目だ。

Mike is his youngest child and Bill is his second youngest.

彼女は学校で２年下だった。

She was two years behind me at school.

【地位】

私は加藤さんの下で働いている。

I work { under [for] Mr. Kato. / in Mr. Kato's department. }

【成績】

彼の成績は平均より下だ。

His grades are below average.

3. その他

彼は明日の授業の下調べをしている。

He's now preparing for tomorrow's classes.

【下見】
私たちはそこを下見しておいた方がよい。
We'd better go and have a look at the place beforehand.
【下書き】
論文の下書きがやっとできたところだ。
I've just finished a very rough draft of the thesis.
【(さび止めなどの)下塗りをする】
put on an undercoat [undercoating]
〈注〉 同じペンキを塗り重ねるときは，初めが first [under] coat，二度塗りは second coat，一番上は塗り重ね回数により second [third] coat または topcoat，また違った塗料を塗り重ねるときの塗料は，下塗りは primer，上塗りは topcoat。
【下心】
あいつがばかに愛想がいいのは何か下心があるんじゃないか。
It's strange (that) that nasty man should be so agreeable! I suspect he has something at the back of his mind.
【下回る】
今年の調査では，あの県の児童は体力的に全国平均を下回った。
The physical strength of the children in that prefecture fell below the national average this year.
今年の夏の平均気温は昨年を下回りそうだ。
It seems that this summer's average temperature will {fall below / be lower than} last year's.

…したい・…したがる

1. 意志

intend to do; be going to do
私は家族を連れて行きたいと思っている。
I intend to take my family with me.

2. 希望の表明

…したい
I would [should] like to … (現在の希望)
I'd like to … 〔*colloq. most common*〕
I want to [I wanna … 〔米〕〔*colloq.*〕]
I wish to …
いつかそのうちヨーロッパに行きたい。
I want to go to Europe sometime.
もし行けたらいつかヨーロッパに行きたいものだ。
I wish I could go to Europe sometime.
いつかナポリ湾の絵を描いてみたい。
Someday I hope to paint the Bay of Naples.
泣きたい[逃げ出したい]気がする
feel like crying [running away]

《**I wish** と **I hope** の比較》
【同義】未来への希望を表す。下の表現は一種のきまり文句である。
クリスマスおめでとう。
I wish you a Merry Christmas.
あなたの新しい仕事がうまくいきますように。
{I hope you'll be successful / I wish you success} in your new job.
【ニュアンスの相違】
(1) I wish it wouldn't rain. (天気予報は明日雨だというが)「降らないといいのに」
I hope it won't rain. (予報は関係なく)「天気だといいですね」
(2) I wish you liked them. (好き嫌いの多い子に「ニンジンおいしいよ，食べてごらん」と勧めるときなど。You don't like them. が背後にある)
I hope you'll like it. (贈物をするときなど)「気に入ると思うよ」「気に入るといいのですが」
(3) I hope [wish] to get home before it rains.
hope は，「降らないうちに帰れるだろうか，帰れるといいが」の含みがある。
wish は，「雨が降りそう，早く帰りたいのに」(だれかにつかまってなかなか帰れずいらいらしている，または「早く帰してください」といういら立ちが感じられる)
以上を要約すると，hope は単に「こうなればよいが」という思いを表すのに対して，wish は何か障害になる条件があるにもかかわらず「そうなってほしい」という思いを表す。

なお，仮定法で wish には次の用法がある。
・現在の事実に反する仮定

I wish { I were a boy.（男の子だったらなあ）
I could go with you.（一緒に行けたらなあ）}

・過去の事実に反する仮定
I wish I could have gone with them.
（一緒に行っていたらよかったのに）

【希望表明のいろいろ】
I hope は上の例で見たように遠慮がちな希望を表しているが，ほかにも次のような表現がある。

feel inclined to《do》（どちらかというと…したい気がする）
feel like《doing》（…したい気持ちだ）
have a mind to《do》（…したい）
have a good [great] mind to《do》（…してやりたい；意志がはっきりしている。普通腹を立てているとき）
have half a mind to《do》（…しようかと思っている）
care to《do》（否定形・疑問形に限る）
「…したくない」I don't care to《do》
「…したいか」Do you care to《do》?

3. 強い希望

be anxious to《do》; **be eager to**《do》
be dying to《do》〔*colloq.*〕

早くその映画が見たい。
I'm eager to see the movie.

早くあなたの赤ちゃんが見たくてたまらない。
I'm dying [I can hardly wait] to see your baby.

彼らは早く結果を知りたがっている。
They are anxious to know the result.

〈注〉 anxious には eager（…したい）の意味と worried（心配している）の意味とがあるので，紛らわしい場合は使わない方がよい。

子供たちはあなたにとても会いたがっている。
The children can hardly wait to see you.

〈注〉 一人称主語の I'm longing to see you. はおおげさ。

4. したくない

今日は何もしたくない。
I don't { want to do / feel like doing } anything today.

彼女は今日は何もしたくない気分だ。
She doesn't care to do anything today.

〈注〉 There is nothing I would care to do. はきざで上品ぶって聞える。

5. 慣用表現

したい放題する
do as《one》likes [pleases]

食べたい放題食べる
eat《one's》fill

彼女はしたいようにする。
She does everything her own way.
She would do things in her own way.
（強い意志を表す would は強勢をおいて発音）

しだい（次第）

1. 順序

order; program

式次第　order of the ceremony

2. 直ちに

immediately; as soon as

朝食が済みしだい行きます。
I'll come as soon as I finish breakfast.

天気になりしだい出発しよう。
Let's leave as soon as the weather improves.

飛行機がとれしだい行きます。
I will take the first flight available.

3. …によって決る

depend on

【努力】
成功するもしないも努力しだいだ。
Your success depends on your efforts.
You make your own success.

【選択・決断】
どちらにするかは君しだいだ。
It's up to you to decide.
我が家はすべて父親しだいだ。
Our father controls our life.
彼は何でもかみさんしだい[の言いなり]だ。
He is tied to his wife's apron strings.
お値段は品質しだいでいろいろです。
The price varies with the quality.
【金しだい】
すべてこの世は金しだい。
Money rules the world.
Money makes the world go around [round].
【注文しだい】
ご注文しだいでいかようにも調整いたします。
We can have it custom-made.
We can have it done
{ according to your specifications.
{ any way you wish.

4. 事情
circumstances; the state of things; the case
ことの次第はこうだ。
This is how it happened.
It happened this way.
これが事の次第です。(事情説明を先にして)
These are, in brief, the facts.
こんな次第だから彼にはあまり期待はできない。
Given this state of affairs, }
Such being the case, } 〔*formal*〕
I don't think we can expect much from him.

5. 段々に
gradually
彼はしだいに健康と体力を回復した。
Gradually he recovered his health and strength.
10月が近づき,しだいに日が短くなってきた。
October was coming and the days were getting shorter and shorter.

じだい (時代)

a period; an epoch; an age; the times

1. 人生のひと区切り
【子供時代に】 in my childhood
【中学・高校時代に】
during my junior and senior high school years; at school; When I was in high school, ...〔話し言葉として *most common*〕
〈注〉 英国では小学校なら at primary school。at school と言えば secondary school のことになる。
高校時代の成績はどうでしたか。
What kind of grades did you make [get] in your senior high school years?
What marks did you get at school?
【…の時代】
父母の時代　in my parents' day
会社勤めの時代は自分のための時間はほとんど持てなかった。
When I was a company employee I hardly had any time for myself.

2. 歴史上の区切り
明治時代　the Meiji Era [Period]
エリザベス時代　the Elizabethan Age
〈注〉 歴史上の時代呼称としてはこの形だが,その頃をさすのはもっと自由で,例えば during Elizabethan times のようにも言える。
原子力時代　the atomic age
核の時代　the age of nuclear power
〈注〉 the nuclear powers と複数にすると「核兵器保有国」のことになる。
宇宙時代
the space age
these days of space travel [exploration]

3. 慣用表現
時代の要請に応える
meet the demands of the time(s)

〈注〉「時代」の意味の times は単数で time としてもよい。以下「時代遅れ」の項も同じ。

同時代人(である)

one's contemporary

be contemporary with …

若者たちは国の次の時代を担わなければならない。

The younger generation must be responsible for the future of the country.

時代遅れの

out of date; old-fashioned

時代遅れにならないように

to keep up with the times

not to fall behind the times

時代に先駆ける

go [be] ahead of the times

be in advance of the times

時代が変った。

Times have changed.

時代精神　the spirit of the age

時代思潮　the trend of the times

時代錯誤　(an) anachronism

(…に)新時代を画す

mark a new epoch (in …)

【…という時代】

…という時代もあった。

There was a time [were times] when …

車はすべて電気自動車という時代も来るだろう。

The time will come when people will use only electric cars.

The future will see us using only electric cars.

したく(支度，仕度)

preparations; 手はず　**arrangements**

【したくする】[人主語]

動他　make [prepare] dinner 食事を作る

動自　prepare for a trip 旅行のしたくをする

make arrangements 手配する，手はずを調える

get《things》ready

食事のしたくをする

make breakfast

get the dinner ready

【したくができる】[物主語]

食事のしたくができました。

Dinner is ready.

〈注〉 I got the dinner ready. / I made the dinner myself. は夕食を自分で作ったの意。I got ready for dinner. は晩餐会のために着替えや化粧をしたこと。

パーティーのしたくができた。

Everything is ready for the party.

〈注〉 party のため，手はず(arrangements お客・業者との連絡や注文)をととのえ，準備(preparations 料理，飾りつけ，テーブルセッティング)をして，万事でき上り ready となる。

【身じたくをする】

(外出の) したくをする

dress《oneself》(up); get dressed

〈注〉 dress up はパーティー用ドレスなどのすてきな服を着ること。get ready to go out はふだん着を外出用の服に着替えること。

登山や探険隊の装備

(an) outfit and equipment (テニスなどスポーツについても使える)

旅行のしたくをする

get ready to travel [for the trip]

したこと → すること

したことがある → こと

したしい(親しい) → ともだち

いい友達　a good friend

親しい友達　a close friend

一番親しい友達《one's》best friend

〈注〉 an intimate friend と言うと，時として友情以上の(性的な)意味が含まれることがある。使わない方が無難。

仲が良い　be friends with

彼は私に親しげに話しかけてきた。

He spoke to me in a friendly manner.

あの人たちは親しい[親密な]間柄だ。

They are very close.

〈注〉◆They are on friendly terms with each other. は何か仲の悪そうな事情があるのに友好的だということ。また町内会長と on friendly terms になっておくと何かと都合がよいといったような使い方をするので特に親密な間柄を意味しない。

◆friend と friendly について

a friend＝a person whom one knows, likes and trusts（よく知っていて，好きでまた信頼している人）

friendly＝favorably disposed; not antagonistic; warm（好意的である；敵対関係でない；あたたかい関係）

親しくなる

become friends; make friends with; meet people

〈注〉「旅行してたくさんの人と親しくなった」というような場合，旅で会ってすぐ別れた程度ならば meet people でよい。

ex. I met a lot of people on my trip.

make friends with は子供たちが仲良しになるときに使う。

じち（自治）

autonomy; the right of self-government

自治(団)体　a self-governing body

地方自治　local autonomy

地方自治体　local government

自治に関する政府機関

［日本］総務省　Ministry of Public Management, Home Affairs, Posts and Telecommunications

［英国］the Ministry of Housing and Local Government

【大学の自治会】

学生自治会

a student government [council]

a student union〔英〕

自治会代議員会

student council; student representatives

自治会実行委員会[執行部]　executives

自治会役員

officers of student government

会長　president; 副会長 vice president

書記　secretary; 会計 treasurer

〈注〉〔米〕では student union はorganization（団体としての生協），building（生協会館）どちらの意味にも使う。これは自治会ではない。

学生自治会の呼称は大学ごとに多少相違があるようである。

しっかり

1．物事の堅固な状態

【建造物】

しっかりした建物だ。

This building is well-built.

【結び目】

しっかり結んでくれ。

Tie the rope tightly.

【戸締り】

しっかり戸締りがしてあった。

The doors were shut fast.

戸締りをしっかりしなさい。

Be sure { to lock the doors. / the doors are locked.

2．人について

【体格】

彼はしっかりした体格だ。

He is solidly built.

【足取り】

彼の足取りはまだしっかりしている。

His steps are still steady.

【声】

彼はしっかりした声で話した。

He spoke in a steady [firm] voice.（↔ a feeble voice）

【頭脳】

90すぎなのに彼はまだ頭はしっかりしている。

He isn't senile / His mind is clear } though he is over ninety.

【人柄】
彼はしっかりした人物だ。
He is a reliable [trustworthy] man [person].
彼の奥さんはしっかりしている。
His wife is a self-reliant [stout-hearted, strong, staunch] person.
(子供が)しっかりしている
independent (独立心がある)
mature (年のわりに分別がある)
しっかりしろ。
Cheer up! (落胆している人に)
Take heart!
Never say die!
Don't give in [up].
Take courage.
Pull yourself together.
Pull your socks up. (だらしのない人に)
〈注〉 映画などで瀕死の人を抱き起し「しっかりしろ」と叫ぶ場面があるが，英米の人ならばその人の名前を叫び，金切り声をあげ，Oh no! とか God help us! などと叫ぶ。特に決った言い方はない。

じっかん (実感)

【実感する】
1か月病院勤めをしてみて，健康のありがたさをつくづく実感した。
I realized after (my experience of) working at a hospital for a month that to be healthy is really a blessing.
【実感がある[ない]】
本当に賞をもらったなんて実感ありますか。
Can you believe that you have really won the prize?
本当だなんて実感がありません。
It can't be true. (事件・報道など)
It still doesn't seem real.
I just can't make myself believe it.
【実感をこめて】
彼は実感をこめて経験談を話した。
He {told his story / spoke of his experience} with feeling.

しつけ (躾)

discipline; training; upbringing
行儀作法 **manners**
【しつけをする】
子供は小さいうちにきちんとしつけをしなければいけない。そうしないと子供をだめにしてしまう。
Children need discipline even when they are young because otherwise they grow up spoiled.
彼女の母はしつけの厳しい人だった。
Her mother was very strict.
ジョンソン兄弟はきちんとしつけられた人たちだった。
The Johnson brothers [boys] {were all well-behaved youngsters. / had good manners.}
〈注〉 He had (a) good upbringing. は「良家の子」という感じ。
子供は親のしつけしだいだ。
Children are what their parents make them.
しつけを厳しくしないと子供をだめにする。(かわいい子には旅をさせよ)
Spare the rod and spoil the child.
【用便のしつけ】toilet-training

じつげん (実現)

【実現する】
[人主語] realize〔*formal*〕; 実行する carry out
[事主語] come true
私たちの願いは実現するかもしれない。
Our wish may come true.
僕らの夢が実現する[される]よう努力しよう。
Let's try to make our dream come true.
彼の野望はまず実現しない[されない]だろう。
His ambition is not likely to be realized.
その計画は実現不可能だ。
It's impossible to carry out that plan.

じっけん（実験）→ しけん

しつこい

1．人について

persistent　（いつまでもやめない）

【勧誘】

保険外交員がまったくしつこいんだ。

The insurance salesman was very persistent.

彼が仲間に入れ入れとしつこくてね。

He is always after me to join their party.

【ねだる】

その子はおばあさんに自転車を買ってくれとしつこくねだった。

The child wouldn't stop pestering his grandmother to buy him a bicycle.

【質問】

彼女はしつこく僕に質問を浴びせた。

She wouldn't stop asking me questions.

彼女は何につけてもなぜなぜとしつこい。

She is too inquisitive about everything.

【要求】

彼はしつこく借金の返済を迫った。

He was importunate in his demand for the debt repayment.〔*formal*〕

He plagued [pestered] me about my debt repayment.

2．その他

【病気】

しつこい病気　a stubborn [persistent] illness

今度のかぜはまったくしつこい。

My cold { sure hangs on. / is certainly persistent. }

【食べ物】 heavy; cloying

今夜はしつこい物は食べたくない。

{ I don't want to / I wouldn't like to } have anything heavy [rich, greasy] tonight.

【色彩】

けばけばしい

gaudy, showy, loud

じっこう（実行）→ じつげん

実行　**practice**

実行する　**carry out; put into practice**

実行力のある

can get things done

have executive ability [talent]

実行委員会

an executive committee

an organizing committee

実行委員

an executive committee member

an organizing committee member

【考え】

彼女はもうじき彼女の「段差のない家」のアイデアを実行に移す機会に恵まれそうだ。

She's going to have a chance to carry out her idea of a barrier-free house soon.

【計画】

私は自分のプランをできるだけ早く実行に移したい。

I'd like to carry out my plan as soon as possible.

この計画は実行不可能だ。

This plan is { unworkable. / impractical. / infeasible.〔*formal*〕 }

This plan will not work.

上院委員会の提案は実行不可能だ。

The plan suggested by the Senate committee can [could] never be executed.

警官隊は救出作戦を実行できなかった。

The police squad couldn't execute their rescue plan.

【制度】

政府は次の6月までに週休2日制を実行に移したい[実施したい]と言っている。

The government says it wants to put the five-day workweek into effect by next June.

【約束】

約束を実行する[守る]

keep《one's》promise

【契約】

契約を実行する　fulfill a contract

〈注〉「実行に移す」の意味の put into practice が使えるのは次のような語を目的語とする場合である。

put {a policy / a code / a decision / a resolution / a belief} into practice

「法律が実施された」は That law went into effect. のように言う。

【言葉と実行】

彼は口だけで実行が伴っていない。

He is all talk and no action.

言うだけでなく実行せよ。

Practice what you preach.

じっしゃかい（実社会）→ しゃかい

the world; the real [adult] world

じっと

1. 動かずに

【じっとしている】

彼はじっとしていた。

He {was / sat / remained} motionless.

じっとしていなさい。

Stand still. / Sit still. / Keep still.

そのままじっとしていてください。(写真撮影のとき)

Hold it, please.

【じっとしていられない】

心配でじっとしていられなかった。

Nervousness made me restless.

子供はちょっとの間もじっとしていられない。

Children cannot stay still even a moment.

あまりにいい天気なので家の中にじっとしていられなかった。

The weather was too good [nice] for me to stay indoors.

2. 集中する

【じっと見る】

彼女の目は隅に立っている背の高い人にじっと注がれていた[じっと見つめていた]。

Her eyes were fixed on a tall man standing at the corner.

彼女はその絵を見つめて長い間じっと立っていた。

She stood gazing at the picture for a long time.

〈注〉 gaze は感心してじっと見ること。stare は驚いたりあきれたりしてじろじろ見ること。

【じっと聞く】

その子は男の人の言っていることをじっと聞いているようだった。

The boy seemed to listen very attentively to what the man was saying.

【じっと考え込む】

彼はじっと考え込んでいた。

He was lost in thought.

3. 我慢する

【じっとこらえる】

彼はじっと痛み[悲しみ]をこらえていた。

He bore {the pain patiently. / the sadness stoically.}

しっぱい（失敗）

(a) **failure;** へま **a blunder; a miss;** 誤り **an error**

失敗する

[人主語] **fail (in); fail to** 《do》**; be unsuccessful in**

[事主語] **fail; be [prove, turn out] a failure; go wrong**

【試験】

彼は試験に失敗した。

He failed the exam.

【事業】

彼の事業は失敗した。
His business failed.

【計画】
彼の計画はすべて失敗した。
All his schemes have gone wrong.
大学祭にロックバンドを呼ぶ計画は失敗した。
We failed to get a rock band for our college festival.

【運動】
市で推進していた空き缶預り金制度は失敗に終った。
The city's campaign to have empty cans returned for deposit {turned out (to be) a failure. / ended in failure.}

【人生計画】
彼の結婚は失敗だった。
His marriage was a failure.
彼は芸術家[実業家]としては失敗であった。
He is a failure as an artist [a businessman].

【ことわざ】
失敗は成功のもと。
Every failure is a stepping stone to success.
You learn from your mistakes.

している → いる

1. 動作進行中

ほら，子供たちが野球をしている。
Look, (the) children are playing baseball over there.
母さんは夕食の用意をしている。
Mother is cooking dinner.
弟は今，夏期講習に行っています。
My brother is attending a summer course right now.

2. 状態

あの女の子はかわいい目をしている。
The girl has charming eyes.
うちの父は教員をしている[教員である]。
My father is a teacher.
cf. 彼は名古屋高校で英語を教えている。
He is teaching English at Nagoya High School.
〈注〉 状態動詞 (know, like, love など)では進行形は作れない。
ex. ×I am knowing your father.
僕は山田さんを知っている。
I know Mr. Yamada.
僕は君を愛している。
I love you.
彼は入院している。
He is now in (the) hospital.
cf. 彼は明日入院することになっている。(これから入る)
He is entering hospital tomorrow.
彼の息子はアメリカに行っている。
His son is now in the U.S.
His son has gone to the U.S.
〈注〉 His son is going to the U.S. は「行くことになっている[これから行く]」の意味。

してもらう → させる・させられる

荷物を駅まで運ばせました[運んでもらいました]。
I had my baggage carried to the station.
ヘンリー夫人に荷物を空港まで運んでいただきました。(丁寧)
Mrs. Henly kindly took our baggage to the airport.
〈注〉 目的地に持って行くのが take (to), 運ぶプロセスが carry だが，同じように使える場合もある。

しどう (指導)

指導する (上に立つ) **take the lead; lead; be a leader**
コーチする **coach**

1. 指導的立場

指導者 a leader
市立博物館建設については彼は指導的立場にあった。

He played a leading part [role] in establishing the city museum.

危機に際して彼は指導力を発揮した。

He displayed leadership during the time of crisis.

2. 研究・クラブなどの指導

学校の指導教官

a student adviser; an adviser

卒論の指導教官　a thesis adviser

カー先生が彼の研究指導に当っている。

Professor Carr supervises (him in) his research work.

浅野先生が指導している。

Mr. Asano directs their studies.

そのクラスはたいへんいい先生の指導を受けている。

The class is taught by a very good teacher.

私たちは英語は田中先生の指導を受けている。

We study English under Mr. Tanaka.

Mr. Tanaka is our English teacher.

【クラブなど】

小川先生は少年水泳教室で指導をしている。

Mr. Ogawa coaches boys' swimming [the boys' swimming club].

クラブなどの指導者　a coach; an adviser

じどうしゃ（自動車）

an automobile; a car

1. 車種

セダン　sedan / クーペ　coupe / コンバーチブル　convertible / オフロード車　off-road vehicle / ジープ　jeep / バン　van; small lorry〔英〕/ トラック　truck; lorry〔英〕/ キャンピングカー　camper; camping car / バス　bus / スポーツカー　sports car / ステーションワゴン　station wagon〔米〕, estate car〔英〕/ ハッチバック　liftback; hatchback〔米〕, fastback〔英〕/ 4WD　four-wheel drive vehicle / 低公害車　ecologically friendly car / 電気自動車　electric car

【サイズ】

大型車　a full-sized car / 中型・標準車　standard / 小型車　compact

2. 外部

【シャシー】 chassis

サスペンション　suspension (system) / ショックアブソーバー　shock absorber / 消音器　muffler; silencer〔英〕/ 排気管　exhaust (pipe); dual exhaust / スカート　skirt / 燃料パイプ　gas pipe / キャップ　gas cap / ホイール[車輪]　wheels; (wheel) rim / ハブ[ホイール]キャップ　hub cap / タイヤ　tire; tyre〔英〕/ スペアタイヤ　spare tire / ジャッキ　the jack / 泥よけ　mudguard; mudflap; tireflap / ブレーキ　brakes; (全体) braking system

【車体】 the body

トランク　trunk; boot〔英〕; luggage compartment / ナンバープレート　license plate〔米〕, number-plate〔英〕/ フェンダー　fender; wing〔英〕/ (前/後)バンパー　(front / rear) bumper / ラジエーターグリル　radiator grill / (前/後)ドア　(front / rear) door; [ドア付属部] ハンドル　door handle / ラッチ　door latch / ロック　door lock / ハッチバックのドア　tailgate [hatch] (door) / フロントガラス　windshield〔米〕, windscreen〔英〕/ ワイパー　windshield [windscreen] wiper [washer]; (後部窓用) rear window washer [wiper] / スポイラー　spoiler / ドアミラー　side mirror〔米〕; right [left] (wing) mirror / アンテナ　antenna / サンルーフ　sunroof / ルーフ　roof

【ライト】 external lights

(フロント)ヘッドライト　headlight; headlamp〔英〕/ ハイ[ロー]ビーム　high [low] beam / フォグランプ　fog lamp [light] / バッキングライト　backup [backing] light / (前／後)ブレーキライト　(front / rear) brake light / 方向指示ライト　turn signal [indicator]; directional light / パーキングライト　parking light / テールランプ　tail lamp; taillight / ハザードフラッシャー　emergency [hazard〔英〕] flasher

自動車　automobile

roof
rear-view mirror
windshield [windscreen]
windshield wiper
side windows
mirror [side [wing] mirror]
antenna
hood [bonnet]
headlight
bumper
door handle
door
fender
hub cap
tire
[tyre]
license plate
[number-plate]

roof
rear window
trunk [boot]
tailpipe
[exhaust pipe]
brake light
directional light
[turn indicator]
tail light
license plate
[number-plate]
mudguard

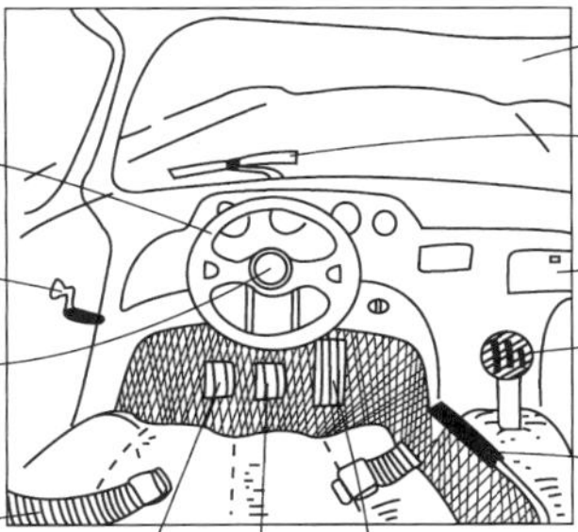
windshield
[windscreen]
wiper
steering
wheel
dashboard [front panel]
window handle [winder]
glove compartment
gear { shift
lever
horn
handbrake
seat belt
clutch
brake
accelerator [gas pedal] 〔米〕
pedal

【ボンネット内】 under the hood [bonnet]
エンジン engine (block) / ラジエータ(管) radiator (hose) / ファンベルト fan belt / バッテリー battery / オルタネータ alternator / ディストリビュータ distributor / ジェネレーター generator / スパークプラグ spark plug / エアフィルター air filter / キャブレター carburetor; carburettor〔英〕/ ウィンドーウォッシャーのリザーブタンク windshield-washer reservoir

3. 内部
前の席 front seats / 運転席 driver's seat / 助手席 passenger seat / 後部席 rear seats / 後部棚 rear shelf / アームレスト arm rests / つかまり handholds; handbars / ヘッドレスト head rest / シートベルト seat belt / エアバッグ air bag / 窓開閉ハンドル window handle [control (buttons) (電動)] / ドアロック door lock / ルームライト overhead [courtesy] light / サイドポケット side pocket / (備え付け)缶ホルダー (built-in) can holder / (備え付け)小銭入れ (built-in) coin holder / 日よけ sun visor; sun screen / バックミラー rear view mirror
【機器】 mechanical parts
温度調節機構 temperature control system / ヒーター heater / ファン fan / 空調器 air conditioner / 換気孔 (air) vents [blowers] / 霜取り defroster / 霜取りの熱線 defroster coil [wire] / (運転)ハンドル steering wheel / ロック lock / 警笛, クラクション horn / 点火装置 ignition (switch); starter〔英〕/ ギアレバー gear [shift] stick [arm, lever] / フロアシフト floor shift / コラムシフト column shift / 非常点滅灯スイッチ emergency flasher switch / トランスミッション, 変速機 transmission / 方向指示のレバー turn signal [indicator] lever / クルーズコントロール (自動定速走行装置) cruise control / クラッチ clutch (pedal) (マニュアル車のみ) / ブレーキ(ペダル) brake (pedal) / サイドブレーキ parking [hand, emergency] brake / アクセル gas pedal; accelerator

【ギアの名前】
[マニュアル] manual transmission
ファースト first [low] / セコンド second / サード third / フォース fourth / リバース reverse / ニュートラル neutral
[オートマチック] automatic transmission
【ギアの表示】
D_1(ロー low) drive one / D_2(セカンド) drive two / R(リバース) reverse / N(ニュートラル) neutral / P(パーキング) park [parking]
【制御装置】controls
ダッシュボード dashboard / コンソール console / スピードメータ (速度計) speedometer / オドメータ (積算距離計) odometer〔米〕, mileometer〔英〕/ トリップメータ, 区間距離計 trip meter〔米〕/ タコメータ (回転速度計) tachometer; revolution counter〔英〕/ 燃料計 fuel [gas] gauge / 残量警告灯 warning light / オルタネータ alternator [ampere] gauge / 油温計 (oil) temperature gauge / 警告灯 warning lights (計器の異常を知らせる)
(ラジオなどの)音量調節ボタン sound system control button [switch] / 温度調節ボタン temperature control button [switch] / 霜取りスイッチ defroster control button [switch] / ライトの調節 light controls
【その他付属品】
灰皿 ashtray / ライター cigarette lighter / 小物入 glove compartment / ラジオ radio / ステレオ (car) stereo / 時計 clock / 外気取り入れ口 fresh air inlet [intake] / カーナビ(経路誘導システム) car navigation system

4. その他
修理工場 garage / ガソリンスタンド filling station〔米〕; gas station〔米〕; petrol station〔英〕; service station / ガソリン gas〔米〕, petrol〔英〕/ 洗車 car wash / 機械調整 tune up / エンジン分解修理, オーバーホール overhaul / 自動車学校 driving school / 運転免許(証) driver's license〔米〕, driving licence〔英〕
【道路・交通】
幹線道路 highway / 高速道路 expressway〔米〕, motorway〔英〕/ インターチェンジ

interchange / 交通信号 traffic light / 停止信号 stop signal / 安全地帯 island; safety zone / 横断歩道 crosswalk; zebra crossing〔英〕/ 舗道 sidewalk; pavement〔英〕/ 一方通行 one-way street / Uターン禁止 no U-turn / 行き止まり dead end / 駐車禁止 no parking / 駐車場 parking lot〔米〕, car park〔英〕; (家の駐車場) car port / パーキングメーター parking meter / 交通巡査 traffic police officer; traffic warden〔英〕/ 駐車違反 parking violation / 駐車違反の通知書 parking (violation) ticket / 速度違反 speeding; 動 speed / 乱暴な運転 dangerous [reckless] driving; 動 drive recklessly / 飲酒運転 drunken driving

【事故】

(車輪が)滑る skid / 当て逃げ hit and run / 正面衝突 head-on collision / 追突 rear-end collision / 泥にはまる be stuck in mud / じゅずつなぎの渋滞 bumper-to-bumper traffic / むち打ち症 whiplash injury

タイヤがパンクする

blow out; have a flat tire [tyre]

〈注〉 blow out は急にパンとパンクすること。

(彼の車の)タイヤがパンクした。

He [His car] had a flat tire.

The tire blew out [went flat].

しぬ(死ぬ)

死 名 **death;** 死ぬ 動 **die; be killed**

[婉曲語法]

逝ってしまった passed away

彼岸にいってしまった

have gone / passed over } to the other side

(死んでしまって)もういない

be no longer with us

神の御手の中にいる be in God's hands

1. 命を失う

【病気[飢え, 心臓発作]で】

die of a disease [hunger, a broken heart]

彼のお母さんは心臓発作で死んだ。

His mother died of a heart attack.

【けががもとで】

die from wounds

彼のお父さんは頭のけががもとで死んだ。

His father died from [of] head injuries.

【交通事故・戦争などで】 be killed

彼の息子は交通事故で死んだ。

His son was killed [lost his life] in a traffic accident.

彼の息子は2人とも戦争で死んだ。

Both his sons were killed { in the war. (戦争で) / in action. (戦闘中に) }

【死んで…年になる】

彼の祖父母[彼ら]が死んでもう何年にもなる。

His grandparents have been dead for many years now.

It's been many years since they died.

They died [passed away] many years ago.

【死んでしまった】

彼が家に着いたとき母親はもう死んでしまっていた。

His mother had already died by the time he arrived home.

彼はもう死んだ。(生きていない)

He's dead.

〈注〉 die と be dead が混同されることが多い。die は生きていた者が死ぬことであり, be dead は死んでしまっている状態を示す。

「ジムのお母さんはジムが生れてすぐに亡くなった」のつもりで次の文は誤文。○の文のようにする。

×Jim's mother was dead after Jim was born.

○Jim's mother died just after Jim was born.

【死なれる】

奥さんに死なれて彼はがっかりしている。

His wife's death deeply depressed him.

〈注〉 日本語では被害の受動「死なれる, 泣かれる」などがあるが, 英語では自動詞を受動態にはできない。die は自動詞である。

×He was died by his wife.

【死んだ人】

死没者 the deceased〔*formal*〕

戦死者　the war dead
故大平氏　the late Mr. Ohira

2．比喩的表現
それではせっかくのアイデアが死んでしまう。
No, no, that will kill the idea!
この文は死んでいる。
There's no life in this writing.
パーティーが死んでるよ。だれか景気をつけてくれないか！
This party is dead. Somebody, put some life back into the party!

じめん（地面）→ とち

the ground; 土地 **the land; a lot**（建築用）; **a plot**

1．土地
広い土地　a large tract of land（開発・売買の対象となる）
土地を借りる　lease the land
彼は広い土地を持っている。
He owns a lot of land.

2．地表
彼は地面にひざまずいて神の許しを請うた。
He fell to the ground on his knees and prayed for God's forgiveness.
雪が1メートルも地面に積った。
The snow was one meter deep.

しゃかい（社会）

society; the world; the community
実社会（家庭や学校に対して）**the outside world; the real [adult] world; society**
社会科　social studies（中学校・高校）
社会学　social science; sociology
社会に出る（大人の仲間入りをする）
go out into the real world
enter the adult world
社会人として順調にスタートする
have a good start in life
成人して初めて社会に出て行く
go out into the world (to start work); build our own life; join the working world; start out in adult life; enter the business world for the first time

《関連語》
社会人　a member of society / 上流社会　the upper class / 中流社会　the middle class / 下層社会　the lower class; the working class〔英〕/ 封建社会　feudal society / 文明社会　civilized society / 文明　civilization / 社会の風潮　the current [social] trend / 社会的地位　one's social status [rank] / 社会問題　social problem / 社会主義　socialism / 社会主義者　socialist / 社会主義的な　socialistic / 社会民主党　the Social Democratic Party / 社会福祉　social welfare / 福祉国家　welfare state / 社会保障　social security / 社会事業　social work / 社会運動　social movement

しゃかいほしょう（社会保障）→ほけん

social security
社会保障制度
social security system; Social Security〔米〕, welfare state〔英〕

《関連語》
健康保険（制度）　health insurance (system)
National Health Insurance (略 NHI)
National Health Service (略 NHS)　〔英〕
Blue Cross/Blue Shield（〔米〕民間の非営利的健康保険組合）
失業保険　unemployment insurance
失業給付金　government-paid unemployment benefits
公的年金制度　public pension plan
年金　pension; annuity
老齢年金　old-age pension
障害年金　disability pension
保険掛金　contribution〔英〕（社会保険掛金）; premium（商業保険金の意が原義）

自己負担　individual payment
（保険の適用を）受けている　be covered by
ex. I'm covered by health insurance.（健康保険に入っている［保険診療が受けられる］）

しゃくにさわる（癪に障る）→ くやしい

しゃちょう（社長）→ かいしゃ

the president of a company; the head; the boss〔*slang*〕（社長・課長・主任など自分の上に立つ人）

社長になる　be appointed [elected] president (of ...)（任命・選挙）

しゃべる　→ はなす

talk; 雑談する **talk casually; have a talk; chat; have a chat**

〈注〉 chat はおしゃべり，うわさ話を連想させる軽い感じの語である。

村の居酒屋は一日の仕事を終えて人々が集まり，ビール1杯飲みながらおしゃべりを楽しむ所だ。

The village pub is a place where people gather after a day's work and enjoy talking over a glass of beer.

あの人はもう30分以上も電話でしゃべっている。

She's been talking (on the phone) for more than 30 minutes.

私たちは徒歩通学で，帰り道などみんなでよくしゃべったものだ。

We used to walk home together chatting all the way.

〈注〉 say, tell, talk, speak などの区別については「はなす」の項参照。

じゃま（邪魔）

邪魔する　**disturb; interrupt;** 干渉する **interfere with; get in the way of;** 邪魔になる　**be in**《one's》**way**

邪魔もの　名 **an obstacle; a hindrance;** 厄介者 **a nuisance**（→やっかい）

1. 中断

人が話をしているとき，邪魔してはいけない。

You should not interrupt
{ when people are talking.
{ people who are talking.

邪魔しないでくれ。ひとりにしておいてくれ。

Don't disturb me. Let [Leave] me alone.

今日は邪魔されたくないからだれにも会わないよ。

I don't want to be interrupted, so I won't see anyone today.

基地周辺の学校ではジェット機騒音で，しょっちゅう授業が邪魔されていた。

Jet noise greatly disturbed the schools near the base.

2. やっかい・重荷

私は彼女の幸せの邪魔になっていたのではないでしょうか。

I'm afraid I have been an obstacle to [hindered] her happiness.

お邪魔ではないでしょうね。

I hope I'm not intruding.

Are you sure I won't be a bother?

（手伝うつもりだろうが）かえって邪魔になるよ。

You are more of a hindrance than a help.

お前なんか邪魔だ。（けんかで）

You are not wanted [unwelcome] here.

3. 妨害

あの人たちは我々の計画の邪魔をしようとした。

They tried to ruin [spoil] our plans.

〈注〉 もし，ほかの計画を推すために邪魔をしたのなら次のように言える。
They tried to counter our plans.

邪魔しないでくれ。

Don't try to stop me.（やらせてくれ）

Don't interfere with me.（干渉しないでくれ）

Don't stand in the way. / Get out of my way.（どいてくれ）

大きな建物が邪魔になって何も見えない。

That tall building blocks our view.

We cannot see anything because of that tall building.

4．丁寧な表現

【訪問】

そのうちお邪魔します。

I'll call on you one of these days.

長い間お邪魔しましてすみません。

I'm afraid I've taken up a lot [too much] of your time.

【忙しい人に話しかける】

（用件を切り出す前に）お仕事中お邪魔してすみませんが，ちょっとよろしいでしょうか。

Excuse me for interrupting [disturbing] you, but could I speak to you for a moment? 〔*formal*〕（目上の人に）

I'm sorry to disturb you, but ....

（用件がすんでから）どうもお邪魔しました。

Excuse me for { interrupting [disturbing] you. / having interrupted you. 〔*formal*〕 }

しゅうかん（習慣）→ かんしゅう

1．社会的しきたり

名 (a) **custom;** (a) **tradition; a convention; a practice**

形 **customary; traditional**（伝統的な）

一般に人を訪問するときは手みやげを持って行く習慣がある。

It is customary for people to take a [some] present when visiting [they visit] people.

そこでは魔よけのために戸口に蹄鉄を打ちつける習慣がまだ守られている。

They still keep the custom of fixing a horseshoe on the threshold to drive away evil spirits.

イギリス人はクリスマスに戸外でキャロルを歌ってまわる習慣がある。

English people have a tradition of outdoor caroling at Christmas time.

めまぐるしく変っていく世の中で古い習慣はどんどん姿を消していく。

Old conventions are fast disappearing in this changing world.

日本では何か人に面倒をかけたときは，自分に落度があまりなくてもすみませんと言うのがごく当り前の習慣である。

It is the accepted practice in Japan to apologize for causing trouble regardless of the actual degree of one's responsibility.

〈注〉 次の文は customary を使った例文である。

It is customary to sound out public opinion before launching a new product.（新製品を売り出す前に一般消費者の反応を試すのはごく常套的なやり方だ）

2．個人的な習慣・癖

habit

【習慣にする】

［人主語］usually do

【習慣である】

［事主語］be customary

彼は朝食を食べながら朝刊を読むのが習慣だ。

It's his habit to read the morning paper during breakfast.

He usually reads the morning paper while eating breakfast.

彼女は寝る前にワインをグラス１杯飲むのが習慣だ。

She has the [a] habit of drinking a glass of wine before going to bed.

【習慣をつける】

青少年にとってよい生活習慣を身につけるの

は大切なことだ。

It is important for the young to form good daily habits.

彼は夜ふかしの習慣がついてしまった。

He got into the habit of staying up late.

一度喫煙の習慣がついたらやめるのはたいへんだ。

Once you get into the habit of smoking, it is very difficult to stop.

〈注〉「…の習慣」と説明を加える形として，custom, habit とも of ～ing の形をとるのが普通。

《類義語》

habit 個人の身についた習慣・癖。

custom 社会的なしきたりおよび個人の習慣。

tradition 歴史的に受け継がれてきたやり方・伝統。

convention 伝統的に受け継がれてきた社会的しきたり。

じゅうきょ（住居）

【家】

自分の家《one's》house / 借家 rented house / アパート(いわゆるマンション) apartment〔米〕; flat〔英〕/ 家賃 rent / 敷金 deposit, 敷金を払う pay [put down] a deposit / 家賃の前払い advance rent deposit / 保証金 security deposit; security money / 下宿 room, rooms, apartment（主として〔英〕); rooming house（泊まるだけ); lodging house（泊まるだけ); boarding house（食事付き）/ 寄宿舎 dormitory〔米〕, hall〔英〕/［建物］5階建ての建物 a five-story building; 1階 the first floor〔米〕, the ground floor〔英〕; 2階 the second floor〔米〕, the first floor〔英〕

【垣根】 fence

生け垣 hedge / 塀 wall

【諸空間】

玄関 porch / ベランダ veranda(h) / バルコニー balcony / 玄関の間 hall; foyer（大きな家の場合）/ 応接間 front room / 居間，リビング living room; sitting room〔英〕(広い家ではこのほかに家族がくつろぐ family room〔米〕などがある）/ 台所 kitchen / 食堂兼台所 dining kitchen [DK] / 浴室 bathroom（トイレと兼用の bathroom もある）/ トイレ toilet (room); lavatory cf. 公共トイレ restroom; washroom; john〔米 *slang*〕; loo〔英 *slang*〕/（大きい家の)洗濯室 laundry [utility] room / 娯楽室 rec room; rumpus room / 屋根裏部屋 attic / 寝室 bedroom; master bedroom（最上の寝室）/ 子供部屋 nursery / 押し入れ，物入れ closet;（大型）walk-in closet

【冷暖房】 air conditioning

扇風機 electric fan / クーラー air cooler / 冷暖房機 air conditioner / ガス[石油／電気]ストーブ gas [kerosene / electric] heater [stove] / セントラルヒーティング central heating (system)

【掃除】 cleaning

掃く sweep / ほうき broom / モップ mop / 床ブラシ scrub brush / 掃除機 vacuum / たわし scraping [steel wool] pad / ぞうきん dustcloth

【寝具】（→しんぐ）

［総称］ bedding; bedclothes

シーツ類 bed linen / ベッド bed / ベッドをきちんとする make a bed / ベッドメイキング bedmaking

［敷きぶとん］

マットレス mattress / 薄い敷きぶとん mattress pad / シーツ，下に敷くシーツ bottom sheet / 掛毛布にあてるシーツ top sheet

［掛けぶとん］

毛布 blanket / 薄いふとん quilt; comforter; continental quilt（やや厚いもの）/ 羽毛ぶとん feather bed / ベッドカバー counterpane; bedspread; bedcover / 枕 pillow / 枕カバー pillowcase; pillowslip / 長枕 bolster（通常この上に枕を置く）

じゅうじつ（充実）

充実した 形 **full; rich**

充実させる 動 **enrich; complete; fill up**

私は充実した人生を送りたい。

I'll try to lead a full life.

あの頃2，3年は生活が充実し幸福だった。
My life was full and happy during those few years.
この夏休みは充実していた［私は充実した夏休みを送った］。
I made the most of my summer vacation.
この本は内容が充実している。
This book is very substantial.
〈注〉「充実している」は具体性に欠けるのでどのように充実しているのか具体的説明を加えることが望ましい。英米ではそれが普通である。

じゅうしょ（住所）

an address;《one's》**address**
現住所　《one's》（present） address
住所不明　address unknown
住所不定である
have no fixed place of residence
あなたの住所はどこですか。
What's your address?
Where do you live?
May I have your address?
〈注〉×Where's your address? は誤り。
あなたの住所氏名を書いてください。
Write your name and address here.
私は彼女の住所を知っている。
I know where she lives [her address].
〈注〉Where do you live? や I know where she lives. は何丁目何番地までは求めない場合も含む。それに対し，May I have your address? では正確な住所を求めている。
彼はあの人の住所を知っている。
He has her address.
住所不定ジョー・スミス（新聞記事などで）
Joe Smith of no fixed place of residence
【住所変更】
住所が変ったら知らせてください。
Let me know if you change your address [move].
【住所録】
an address book（個人用）
a directory（会社や組織の名簿）

〈注〉◆現住所に対し本籍は法律用語で one's permanent [ancestral, family] domicile という。
◆住所の表記が日本語の逆であることは周知のとおり。
Taro Fujiyama
12-34, Higashiyama-Motomachi,
Chikusaku, Nagoya City, 567-0123 JAPAN

しゅうしょく（就職）

〈注〉「就職か進学か」とか「…に就職する」などの「就職」と，「就職が決った」「就職が決らない」の就職とは意味にずれがある。「就職」を辞書で引いて getting a job と出ていても，「就職が決らない」は ×My getting a job is not decided yet. ではおかしい。意味によって使い分けが必要である。

1．就職する

就職する **get a job; find employment [work, a job];**（公式文書）**obtain a position**〔*very formal*〕
私は卒業後，就職するつもりです。
I plan to {get a job / work / go to work} after graduation.
学生の大多数が卒業後就職する。
A large number of our students go to work after graduation.

2．求職・求人の表現

【就職先を探す】
今就職先を探している。
I'm looking for a job [work].
職探しを始めなければ。
I have to start job hunting.
英語の使える職場に就職したい。
I want to get a job in which knowledge of English is necessary.
I want to work at an office [I want a job] in which I must [can] use English.
〈注〉次の文は誤り。
×I want to get a job which [where] is necessary for English.
【就職口】
掲示板に就職口［求人］がいくつか出ている。

There are some job offers on the bulletin board.
いい所から2，3就職の口がかかっている。
I have a couple of good offers.
もうじき(仕事の)空きができる。
There'll be an opening soon.
今のところ(仕事の)空きはない。
There's no vacancy [opening] at present.
座ったきりの仕事はしたくない。
I don't like desk [sedentary〔*formal*〕] work.

【就職難】

このところ就職口が少ない。
Jobs are scarce these days.
今は就職がたいへん難しい。
It is terribly hard to get a job today.

〈注〉「父が就職の世話をしてくれる」
My father will
{ find me a good position.〔*formal*〕
{ get me a good job.

3．就職へのステップ

【応募】

就職の応募をする
apply for a job [a position〔*formal*〕]
…に就職応募の書類を出すことにした。
I decided to apply
{ to Tokyo Bank [Fuji Company].
{ for the civil service.（公務員）
{ for a teaching position.（教員）
(就職)応募者が多すぎる。
There are too many applicants.

【試験】

就職試験
an examination for employment
an employment examination
就職面接　an interview

〈注〉英米では学科試験はなく面接のみ。

私はサン社の(就職)試験を受けた。
I took an [the] examination for Sun Company.
就職試験に合格する
be chosen [selected]（by ...）
就職試験に不合格になる
be rejected（by ...）
私は東京銀行の入社試験に通った[落ちた]。
I passed [failed] the Tokyo Bank examination.
就職が決った。
I've decided where I will work.
彼は…に就職が決った。
He has decided on Toyo Company.
He has { found a position in〔*formal*〕 / got a job with [in] } a trading company.
He has found a teaching position.
He decided to take the job offered by Sakura High School.
私はまだ就職が決らない。
I haven't decided where I'll work yet.
私のやりたいような仕事が見つからない。
I haven't found a job I'd like to take.
私は(…に)就職をだいたい決めた。
I have nearly decided
{ which job I will take.
{ where I shall work.
I have almost decided [settled] on Sun Company.

〈注〉◆×I almost settled Sun Company. は誤り。
◆日本語では「就職が決った」と客観的表現をするのが普通だが，It has been decided where I will work. とすると他人が決めたような印象になり欧米人には奇妙に聞える。また「彼女のお父さんがいい仕事を見つけてくれた」Her father found her a good job. も自主性がないような印象をもたれかねない。「就職が決った」は次のような具体的表現にするのが普通。
I'll be working for Toyota.
Toyota { made（me）a job offer / offered me a job } and I took it.
また，もし数社間で選択したのなら次のように説明を加える。
Toyota made（me）the best offer ...

私は就職に役立つ科目を勉強します。
I will study those subjects which are needed to get a job.

しゅうせい（習性）

動物[犬／鳥]の習性 **animal [dog / bird] behavior**

〈注〉 人間について言えば habit(習慣)だが,「動物としての人間」の習性は human behavior と言う。

X大学Y教授のグループは鯨の習性を研究中である。

Prof. Y of X University and his students are researching whale behavior.

結局人間の習性も他の動物と似たようなところがある。

Human behavior turns out to be often the same as animal behavior.

じゅうたく（住宅）→ じゅうきょ

じゅぎょう（授業）

a class; class work;（school）lessons

教えること **teaching**

1. 講義一般

【授業がある】

午前には4時限授業がある。

We have four classes in the morning.

【授業がない】

午後は授業がない。

We have no class in the afternoon.

明日は授業がない。

We have a holiday tomorrow.

There'll be no school tomorrow.

We'll have no school tomorrow.

【授業をする】

授業をしなければならない。

I have to teach（my class).

【授業を受ける】

木曜日に安藤先生の授業を受けている。

I go to [take] Mr. Ando's class on Thursdays.

山本先生の米国史の授業を受けている。

I take American history from Mr. Yamamoto.

高校では化学の授業を受けていた[化学をとっていた]。

I took [had]（classes [lessons] in）chemistry in high school.

〈注〉 授業の意味の lesson は主として英国, class は英米とも使う。

【授業をサボる】 cut《one's》classes（ある時限, 授業をサボる); play truant [hooky〔米〕]（小・中学校など始業から終業まで校内にいなければならない学校をずる休みする）

2. 時間割

【授業が始まる】

何時に授業が始まるのですか。

What time do classes begin?

〈注〉 小学校は school begins [starts] …。高校, 大学は classes begin, 中学はどちらも使える。

あっ, 授業が始まるわ。

Oh, it's time for class.

【授業時間】

授業時間は8時半から3時半までです。

School hours are from 8:30 to 3:30.

School begins at 8:30 and ends at 3:30.

〈注〉 The school day runs from … to … ともいう。

授業は90分やって10分休む。

Classes last for 90 minutes with a 10-minute break between them.

2時限目は何の授業ですか。

What class do you have in the second hour [period]?

【授業中】

安藤先生は授業中です。

Mr. Ando is teaching his class now.

生徒は今授業中[数学の授業中]です。

The students are now in class [in math].

授業中おしゃべりしてはいけない。

No talking in class [during the lesson].

【授業終了】

授業は3時で終る。

School finishes [ends, is over] at three.

今日はこれでおしまい。

Class is { over / finished } for today.

So much [That's all] for today.

3. 学科

ドイツ語の授業はありますか。

Is German taught at your school?

英語の授業は週3時間だけだ。

We have only three hours of English [English classes] a week.

【授業料】 tuition

授業料の安い大学

a college with low tuition

英国では授業料は無料だ。(パブリックスクール以外)

English schools are free (except for public schools).

〈注〉 英国では大学の授業料 tuition は学生の親が裕福な場合以外は国が支払う。親に規準額以上の収入がある場合はその額に応じて親が一部負担する。

授業料以外に払わなければならないのは実習費に材料費でしょ，それから健康保険料，自治会費，コンピュータ情報使用料とおまけにばかにならない本代！

Besides the tuition fee, there's a laboratory fee and a materials fee, a health insurance fee, a student government fee, a computer resources fee, plus all the books!

しゅくじつ（祝日）→ねんちゅうぎょうじ

しゅくだい（宿題）

1. 学業の課題

homework; an assignment 〔米〕

宿題帳[練習帳]

a workbook; an exercise book

休暇中の宿題

a holiday task; vacation homework; a holiday theme（作文）

【宿題を出す】 give the students homework

ベイカー先生はすごく宿題を出す。

Mr. Baker gives us lots of homework [assignments].

毎週化学の宿題がある。

We have homework [an assignment] in chemistry every week.

【宿題をする】

今宿題をしているところだ。

He is now doing his homework.

今数学の宿題をしているところだ。

He is working on his math(s) homework now.

〈注〉 mathematics（数学）は略して math〔米〕; maths〔英〕ともいう。

彼は宿題を終えた。

He has finished his homework.

【宿題を見てやる】

僕は弟の宿題を見てやった。

I helped my brother with his homework.

《類義語》

homework (1) 宿題一般。特に学生・生徒の課題。家でするのであるから授業の復習，予習も含む。

(2) (1)の意味から発展して，学生以外の政治家，ビジネスマンなどの資料集め，会議などに備えての勉強なども homework と言う。これは自発的にやることが多い。

assignment 〔米〕与えられた課題。homework の一種で同義に用いられ，簡単な練習問題でも assignment と言える。

小学校低学年はまだ普通 assignment という語を知らないので homework を使う。

〈注〉 homework は不可算名詞であるから複数にできない。ただし，近年可算名詞化しつつあるようだ。assignment は可算名詞であるから an assignment, assignments とする。

「たくさんの宿題」は

a lot of [lots of] homework

a lot of [lots of] / many } assignments

×many homeworks

2. 懸案

宿題[懸案]である **be pending**

減税問題は今だに宿題になっている。
The question of a tax reduction is still pending.
当座の宿題にする[問題を先送りする]
shelve [table] a problem
leave a problem { for the time being / for [to] the future }

しゅくはく (宿泊)→ とまる，げしゅく

宿泊する **put up at an inn; stay at a hotel**
宿泊所 an inn; a hotel; ペンション a pension; 寮 a dormitory [dorm]〔米〕; a hall (of residence)〔英〕
宿泊客 a guest
宿泊料
hotel charges (ホテル側から見て); hotel rate; hotel expenses (客の側から見て)
宿泊料を支払う
pay a hotel bill
(pay the bill and) check out
宿泊料金はいくらですか。
What are your room rates?
シングル[ツイン/ダブル]でいくらですか。
How much is a single [twin / double]?
What is your rate for a single [twin / double]?

《関連表現》
宴会場を借りるといくらですか。
What are your rates for banquet facilities?
会議室はいくらですか。
What are your rates for meeting room facilities?

宿泊代はいくら払いましたか。
How much was the hotel?
How much did you pay for the hotel?
スキーシーズンには民宿に宿泊できる。
During the ski season private homes { take in / put up } skiers.

じゅけん (受験) → しけん，にゅうし

受験する **take an examination**
彼は来春の受験準備をしている。
He's studying [preparing] for next spring's entrance exams.
受験生
a student preparing for entrance exams
an examinee (試験場での呼称)
受験資格
qualifications for an entrance examination
受験科目 (→にゅうし)
the subjects of examination
《one's》 examination subjects
受験番号
a seat [registration] number; an examinee's number; a number
受験票 an admission ticket
受験料 an examination fee
受験参考書 a preparation [practice] book
〈注〉 米国では入試用ではなく各種資格試験，実力試験の受験参考書がある。英国の上級学力試験 (A-level) は各地方にそれぞれ教育委員会 (board) があり，課題，出題，採点も別々にやる。教育委員会により難易の差があることが問題になっている。この場合の「受験する」は sit for A-levels with the York Board (ヨークでAレベルを受験する)。

しゅちょう (主張)

名 **an assertion;** 権利の主張 **a claim;** 論点 **the point;** 持論《one's》**opinion**
主張する 動 **assert; maintain; claim;** 強調する **emphasize;** 言い張る **insist (on, that ...)**

《類義語》
assert 確かに…だと断言する。
彼は彼女を弁護する権利があると主張した。
He asserted his right to defend her.
彼は彼女が真実を語っていると主張した。
He asserted that she was telling the truth.
maintain 反論に対して主張し続ける。
彼女は男女同権を主張している。
She maintains that men and women have

equal rights.

insist　多くの反対に対して強力に主張する。

彼は彼女が絶対に無実だと主張した。

He insisted { on her innocence. / that she was innocent.

〈注〉 insist は強い言葉であり，I insist you should go. などと言えば命令になる。I suggest と言うのが普通。

claim　権利などを主張する。

彼はその物件に関し財産権を主張した。

He claimed that he had rights to the property.

cf. He claimed the property last week. とすると，主張したのみならず何らかの法的行動を起したことを意味する。

emphasize, stress　強調する。

彼は教育が重要であると主張[強調]した。

He emphasized [stressed] the importance of education.

advocate　唱導する。

彼は産児制限を主張している。

He advocates birth control.

stand firm　がんとして譲らない。

【主張を通す[曲げない]】

彼は最後まで主張を通した[曲げなかった]。

He defended his point to the end.

He held to his opinion.

大半の人は最初反対したが，彼の主張はついに通った。

Most people were at first against it, but his point was finally carried.

彼は子供たちのテレビ視聴時間を制限すべきだと主張して譲らなかった。

He stood firm on limited TV time for the children.

【主張を曲げる，妥協する】compromise

彼は主張を曲げるくらいなら死んだ方がましだと思った。

He thought he would rather die than compromise.

【自己主張】

彼は自己主張が強い。

He is strongly assertive.

しゅつえん（出演）

an appearance on stage

【舞台[テレビ]に出演する】appear on the stage [television（冠詞なし）]; act, perform（演ずる）; sing on television（テレビに出演して歌う）

彼女は３歳で初舞台を踏んだ[映画に初出演した]。

She made her { debut / first appearance } { on the stage / in film(s) } at the age of three.

彼女はコマ劇場［テレビ番組］に出演中です。

She's now { on stage at the Koma Theater. / on TV.

彼は今はテレビに出演しているが，もとは映画俳優[歌手]だった。

He's now on TV but he used to be a movie actor [a singer].

【出演映画】

彼女の出演映画

a movie [film] she appears in

【出演料】 acting fee

しゅっしん（出身）

1. 出身地

どちらのご出身ですか。

Where { are you from? / do you come from?

どちらの州のご出身ですか。

Which state are you from?

カリフォルニア州(出身)です。

I come [am] from California.

英国はどちらのご出身ですか。

Which part of England do you come from?

2. 出身校

彼はどこの大学の出身ですか。

Which university [college] did he graduate from?

慶応大学の出身です。

He { graduated from / is a graduate of } Keio University.

しゅっせき（出席）

出席する　**attend**〔*formal*〕; **go [come] to**

各国の大使が夫人同伴でパーティーに出席した。

Ambassadors from many countries attended the party with their wives.

彼女はボーイフレンドとパーティーに出席した。

She went to the party with her boyfriend.

この間の月曜日は学校に出席しましたか。

Did you go [come] to school last Monday?

〈注〉 attend は他動詞，自動詞として用いられるが，「出席する」の意味では他動詞が普通。attend to《one's health》は「気をつける」の意。またこの語は堅い語であるから，学校に出席したことを普通に述べるのには go [come] to school でよい。

【出席している】 be present at; be at

たくさんの人がパーティーに出席していた。

There were many people at the party.

【出席しない［欠席する］】

be absent from; not go to

stay away from（わざと）

佐藤先生，僕来週の先生の授業に出席できないんです［欠席しなければならないんです］。

Mr. Sato, (I'm afraid) I won't be able to come to your class next week.

出席していないのは女子が5人だ［女子が5人欠席だ］。

Five girls are absent today.

【出席率が良い［悪い］】

彼はなかなか出席率が良い。

He has a good attendance record.

彼女は出席率が悪い。

Her attendance record is bad [poor].

【出席したり欠席したり】

attend [go, be present] irregularly

【出席をとる】 take (the) roll, call (the) roll

【出席簿】 an attendance book [sheet]; a roll book [sheet]; a register

【出席者】 those present

〈注〉 英国では小学校，中学校では出席をとる。名前を呼ばれたら，"Here(, sir)." または "Present." と答える。また自分の番号を1番から順に自分で言う方式もあるようだ。米国でも名前を呼ばれたら "Here." または "Present." と手をあげて答える。

しゅっぱつ（出発）

出発　名　**departure**

出発する　動　**leave; start; set out**

彼らは世界旅行に出発した。

They set out on a tour around the world.

彼は今朝，高山へ出発しました。

He started for Takayama this morning.

彼は9時発の高山行きで出発した。

He took the 9:00 a.m. train for Takayama.

彼は昨夜，日本を出発した。

He left Japan last night.

〈注〉◆leave は他動詞で，去ってゆく国や市を目的語とするが，「成田空港から」と乗物の出発点を言うときには from をつける。He left from Narita.

◆start（自動詞）の用法は次の通り。

He started {
on Monday [in the morning, at noon, etc.].
by the 7:00 train [bus, etc.].
for Hokkaido [HongKong, etc.].
from Ueno [Tokyo Station, etc.].
}

（どの町［国］を発ったのかは普通文脈で明白）

しゅっぱん（出版）

出版物　**publications;** 発行，刊行　**publication;** 出版（業）　**the press;** ジャーナリズム　**journalism**

出版する　publish

【刊行サイクル】

日刊　**daily;** 週刊　**weekly;** 隔週刊　**biweekly;** 月刊　**monthly;** 隔月刊　**bimonthly;** 季刊　**quarterly;** 年刊　**yearly**

《関連語》

1．新聞

newspaper

【記事】

一大ニュース　big news / ホットニュース　hot news〔*slang*〕/ スクープ　scoop〔*slang*〕/ 見出し　headline / 一面トップ見出し　front page headline / 全段抜き大見出し　banner headline / 日曜特集版　Sunday features / 記事　article / 社説　editorial / 評　review / 書評　book review / 短評　comment / コラム　column / …ページ　… page (ex. sports page; children's page; society page) / 漫画　cartoon / 時事漫画　political cartoon / 漫画ページ　comics / (数)コマ漫画　comic strip; cartoon strip / 広報・公告　official notice / 死亡記事　obituary; death notice / 広告　advertisement; ad / 求人広告　wanted ads; job ads

【新聞社】

新聞社(建物)　newspaper office / 新聞記者　journalist; newsman〔米〕; pressman〔英〕/ 編集者　editor / 編集長　editor-in-chief / 編集補佐　subeditor / 整理部員　copyreader / 報道員, リポーター　reporter / スポーツ[社会部]記者　sports [society] reporter / 通信員　correspondent / 特派員　special correspondent / 常時寄稿家　columnist / 寄稿家　contributor / かけ出し記者　cub reporter

2. 通信社

news agencies

(ex. 共同 Kyodo; ロイター Reuter)

3. その他

発行部数　circulation / (新聞)購読[購読料]　subscription / 販売所　newsagent's; newspaper agency / 配達人　newsboy; newspaper girl

朝日新聞をとっている。

I take the Asahi.

I subscribe to the Asahi.

4. 定期刊行物

periodical

学会専門誌　journal (ex. 『生化学学会誌』 *Journal of Biochemistry*) / (一般)雑誌　magazine / 週刊誌　weekly (magazine) / 読者層の広い雑誌　widely-read magazine / ティーン向け[女性向け/男性向け]雑誌　teen's [women's / men's] magazine / 専門誌 (料理, 園芸, 手芸など)　special interest magazine (cooking, gardening, handicraft など) / 漫画雑誌　comics / 特集号　special number [issue] / バックナンバー　back number / 雑誌記者　magazine writer

しゅみ (趣味)

1. 好み

taste

【趣味が良い】

彼は服の趣味が良い。

He has good taste in clothes.

He dresses well.

あの子のドレスは趣味が良い。

Her dress is in good taste.

部屋は趣味良くまとめてあった。

The room is tastefully furnished.

【趣味が悪い】

あの子のドレスは趣味が悪い。

Her dress is in bad taste.

【悪趣味】

人と話をするときにやたら外国語を交えるのは悪趣味だ。

It is bad taste to use too many foreign words in your conversation.

〈注〉 It's bad taste. はかなりきつい言い方。次の表現は下の方ほどきつく聞える。

「あまりいい趣味じゃない」→「悪趣味」

It's rather poor taste. / It's not in the best taste.

That's not (in) such [very] good taste.

It's rather bad taste.

【上品な趣味の】 refined; elegant

【下品な趣味の】 vulgar; loud

【趣味に合う[合わない]】

壁にかけてあるあの絵は私の趣味にぴったりだ。

The picture on the wall suits my taste.

いわゆる「クラシック」は僕の趣味に合わない。

The so-called "classical" music is not to my taste.

2. 興味

taste; interest; liking

彼女は音楽に趣味がある。

She has a taste for music.

〈注〉 She likes music. よりもっと関心が深い意になる。have no taste for (＝dislike) は「嫌いである」。

僕は詩の趣味はない。

I have no taste for poetry.

I don't like poetry.

僕はあまりスポーツの趣味はない。

I have little [no] interest in sports.

3. 道楽

hobby; interests

私の趣味はいろんな国の人形を集めること[野球をすること]だ。

My hobby is
{ collecting dolls from various countries.
{ playing baseball.

〈注〉 「野球などを見物する」(watching baseball and other sports) はhobby ではなくて pastime(気晴らし)と言う。

【趣味を尋ねる】

趣味はなんですか。

What are your interests and hobbies?

What do you do in your spare time?

切手集めと庭いじりです。

Well, I collect stamps and I garden as hobbies.

趣味というほどのものはない。

I have no hobbies to speak of.

彼は多趣味だ。

He's a person with many interests.

趣味の園芸　gardening for pleasure

趣味として…を始める

take up ...

2年前に書道を始めました。

I took up calligraphy two years ago.

〈注〉 「趣味に生きる」とか「趣味を生かした生活」のような言い方をそのまま英語にすると抽象的で奇妙に聞こえるので，具体的に述べた方がよい。

I will grow flowers for both pleasure and profit.
(趣味と実益を兼ねて花造りでもしたい)

Being able to perform the tea ceremony will help enrich my life in many ways.
(お茶をやっていることで，いろいろと人生が豊かになると思う)

じゅんしん（純真）

innocent; naive; pure; 誠実　**sincere**

ジムは純真だ。

Jim is a good person.

Jim is sincere and trustful.

〈注〉 日本人は「純真だ」ということをよく言うが，欧米ではその行動を述べて純真であることを聞き手や読者に悟らせる方が普通。そこで上記2つの文は具体例を併せて述べるとよい。

あんなみごとな宝石類がどうやら盗品だと気がつかないとは，洋子も純真と言おうか足りないと言おうか。

It was naive of Yoko not to realize that such beautiful jewelry must have been stolen goods.

子供は純真そうに見えるだけだ。

Children only look innocent.

〈注〉◆「ナイーブ」は日本語では良い意味であるが，英語ではほめ言葉ではなく，You are a naive person. と言えば You are a fool. ということになる。原義は純真の意であり，かつてはほめ言葉であった。

◆pure は純潔 (chastity) を思わせる語でまた聖者のような清らかさ以外には使えない。△He has a pure heart. は不自然。世俗のけがれを知らないことは欧米ではほめ言葉にならない。

◆「純真」に含まれる要素は，次のような形容詞で表される。

guileless　狡猾なところがなく，まっすぐな。
ingenuous　率直な，天真爛漫な。
natural　自然体の。

じゅんび（準備）→ したく，ようい

準備をする **prepare for; arrange; get ready for**

1. 行事

準備委員会

planning committee

展覧会の準備中である。

They are preparing for the exhibition.

The preparations for the exhibition are progressing [moving along].

私たちが会合の準備をした。

We have made the arrangements for the meeting.

私たちは旅行の準備で忙しい。

We are busy getting ready for our trip.

2．食事など

母は夕食の準備[用意]があるので家にいる。

My mother is staying home to cook [make] dinner.

子供たちは朝食のテーブルの準備を手伝った。

The children helped their mother lay the table for breakfast.

〈注〉 伝統的日本食の食膳の準備は「お膳立て」と言うが，欧米では「お皿を並べましょうか」Shall I set the table? と言う。

食事の準備ができました。

Dinner is ready.

3．受験（→じゅけん）

高校最後の年は大学受験の準備をしなければならなかった。

When I was in the final year at school, I had to prepare for the college entrance examinations.

受験準備[試験勉強]に忙しかった。

I was busy studying for the examinations.

4．その他

準備運動　warm-up exercises

旅行の準備はすっかりできている。荷物もお金もビザもみんな準備できた。

I'm ready for the trip. I have all my luggage, money and visas.

いざというときの準備をしておきなさい。

Save money for a rainy day [an emergency].

老後の準備をしておきなさい。

Save money for your old age.

しょう（賞）→とる

じょう（情）

名 **a feeling; an emotion; a sentiment;**
愛情 **affection; love**
情熱 **passion**

情にもろい　tender-hearted

情のこもった　tender; very kind

情のこもった手紙

a very kind and thoughtful letter

親の情　parental affection

父[母]の情　paternal [maternal] love

親子の情

affection between parent and child

彼女は情が厚い[深い]。

She is warm-hearted [affectionate].

彼は情がない[不人情だ]。

He's { hard-hearted [cold -hearted]. / heartless [unfeeling].

国にはそれぞれ異なった慣習があるが，人情はどこも同じだ。親子の情愛にも変りはない。

Every country has its own way of doing things, but human nature is universal; parents love their children and children their parents.

〈注〉 sentimental や emotional は欧米では通常マイナスのイメージを持つ。「情が厚い」のつもりで使ってはいけない。

しょうかい（紹介）

名 **an introduction;** 推薦 **a recommendation**

動 紹介する **introduce;** 推薦する **recommend**

1．人・仕事

【引き合せ】

山田花子さんをご紹介します。

May I introduce Miss Hanako Yamada?（目上の人には丁寧な言い方「紹介してもよろしいでしょうか」の形をとる）

ジョンソン先生に紹介してください(ませんか)。

Please introduce me to Dr. Johnson.

【専門家を】

いい病院[医者/歯医者/家政婦]を紹介してください。

Please { recommend / let me know if there is } a good hospital [doctor / dentist / housekeeper].

〈注〉 「推薦する」の意味で introduce を使うのは誤り。人と人を引き合せるときのみ introduce を使う。

【仕事】

この秘書の仕事は彼の紹介です。

I got my job as a secretary through [because of] his recommendation.

彼の紹介で今の仕事につきました。

He recommended me for this job.

【職業紹介所】

an employment office (公的役所)

an employment agency [a placement agency] (民間の会社)

career counselling

placement service (大学などの職業紹介業務)

2. 方法・説

【学問】

元良博士は明治の初年にジョンズ・ホプキンス大学で心理学を学び，初めて心理学を日本に紹介した。

Dr. Motora studied psychology at Johns Hopkins in the early years of Meiji and { first introduced it / was the first to introduce it } to Japan.

【方法】

そのシンポジウムで加藤氏は新しい金属接合の方法を紹介した。

At the symposium Mr. Kato introduced [explained] a new method of bonding metals.

しょうがつ(正月) →ねんちゅうぎょうじ

元日 **New Year's Day**

〈注〉 欧米では元旦が休日なだけで2日からは平常通り仕事をするので，日本の「正月」に当る祝い事はない。日本の習慣を知っている人には *Shogatsu* でわかるが，知らない人には the first three days of January は the New Year holidays で休みだと説明しなくてはならない。

日本では1月の最初の3日間は正月休みです。人々はその間に神社に参拝して一家の健康と幸福を祈ります。

In Japan we have the New Year holidays for the first three days of January, during which people visit Shinto shrines and pray for the health and well-being of their family.

しょうぎょう (商業) → しょうばい

commerce 商品の交換・流通

trade 商品の仕入れ・販売

cf. (外国)貿易 foreign commerce [trade] (between countries)

(国内)商業 domestic commerce [trade] (within a country)

business 一般的な語。知的専門職および農業・漁業以外のすべての収益を目的とする事業を指す。

商業地区 the business section; downtown

商業都市 a commercial city

商業学校 a school of commerce

商業英語 business English

商業[営利]主義 commercialism

商業化する commercialize

オリンピックもこのところすっかり商業化されてしまった。

The Olympics have been completely commercialized these days.

商業に従事している be engaged in business

〈注〉 上の表現は抽象的で幅広く，小さな店の店主，店員もデパートの buyer についても言えるので，もっと具体的に言うのが普通である (ex. be engaged in sales 営業担当である)。

【商業の中心】the center of commerce
大阪は商業の中心である。
Osaka is a center of commerce [trade].

じょうきょう（状況）

circumstances; conditions; the situation
目下の状況[状態]では…
in [given] the present circumstances [situation] … / under the present conditions … / with the present state of affairs [things] … / as things stand now …
現在の経済状況では私の事業も欠損がどんどんひどくなっていく。
With the present state of the economy my business is rapidly losing money.
現在の国際[経済]情勢ではサミット(会談)にもあまり期待できない。
Given the present international [trade] situation, we can't expect much from summits.
経済情勢が悪化した[好転した]。
The economic conditions grew worse [better].
多くの人が教育の現状を憂慮している。
The situation of education today concerns [worries] many people.
平和をめぐる世界の状況は楽観を許さない。
The world situation in regard to peace is not very hopeful.
それは状況しだいです。
That depends.
〈注〉 situation, the state of things は全体的，包括的情勢，状況。circumstances は全体を構成するいろいろな事情。condition は個別的状態。conditions と複数にすると comprehensive（全体的）な状態。

しょうきょくてき(消極的) → せっきょくてき

passive (↔ active); 控え目な **reserved;** 無口な **taciturn, reticent;** 内向的な **introverted**
私は生来性格が消極的だ。
I am by nature timid and passive.
このクラスはどうも活気がなくて消極的だ。
This class is dull and somehow lacks life [lacking in life].
〈注〉 性格について日本語で「控え目な」は多くの場合ほめ言葉であり英語の reserved（控え目な）も悪い意味はない。「消極的な」と英語の passive はけなし言葉として使われることが多い。reticent（無口な），introverted（内向的な）もしばしばけなし言葉。negative（否定的な）は建設的・協調的なところのない好ましくない性格を言い，ひどいけなし言葉である。

じょうけい（情景）→ けしき

a scene; a sight
昨夜テレビで「上高地」という番組を見た。私は30年前そこに住んでいたことがあるので本当にどの情景も懐かしかった。
I saw a TV program "Kamikôchi" last night. Every scene I saw was really nostalgic because I lived there for some time thirty years ago.
【…が～している情景】
父と子がたこ揚げをしている情景がほほえましかった。
It was heartwarming to see father and son trying to fly a kite together.
The sight [scene] of father and son trying to fly a kite together was really heartwarming. (特定の父と子であれば the father and son)
〈注〉 同格接続詞 that で説明部分を結びつけてはいけない。
×the scene that father and son were trying to …

しょうけん（証券）→ かぶしき

じょうけん（条件）

conditions; terms; 要件 **requirements**

1. 交渉・折衝上の条件

【…の条件で】on the condition that …
条件つきで

with some reservations ; conditionally
…に条件をつける[つけない]

make / impose { conditions / no conditions } on …

無条件で　unconditionally
(…に)無条件降伏をする
surrender unconditionally (to …)
条件を受け入れる
accept the condition(s)
私は申し入れを受け入れたが，一つだけ条件をつけた—それは私は自由に…してもよいということだ。
I accepted his proposal on one condition: I would be free to …
彼は(身分は)現在の地位に留まれるという条件でそれを承諾した。
He consented on the condition that he could remain in his present position.

2. 必要条件
入学[入所]のための条件
admission requirements
会員になるための条件
requirements for membership
条件に合う
meet the requirements [conditions]

3. その他
【協定】
契約の条件
the terms of the contract; contract terms
【現況】
労働条件　working conditions
条件反射　conditioned reflex [response]

じょうしき (常識)

1. 人並の知識
common knowledge; what everybody knows
そんなことは常識さ。
Everybody knows that.
だれにでも基本的人権がある。それは今や常識である。
Everybody has fundamental human rights; that's now common knowledge.
この世界ではそのやり方が常識になっている。
That's common practice in this world.
車に保険をかけるのは常識だ。
It's (a) common practice to get a car insured.
It's considered routine to get a car insured.

2. 人並の思慮分別
common sense
ご心配なさることはありませんよ。お嬢さんは賢いし，それに常識もおありですから。
You don't need to worry about her. She's intelligent and has common sense as well.
常識のある人なら，こんな親切な申し出に，あんなにぶっきらぼうな断り方はしない。
Anyone with good sense would not decline that offer so bluntly, especially such a kind one.
あんたは非常識だ。

You { lack / have no } common sense.

【適正・妥当】
そんな値段は常識的ではない[非常識だ]。
I don't think the price is reasonable.
I think the price is preposterous.

3. 平凡
commonplace
彼は会誌に「若者への言葉」といったような随筆を頼まれたが，(彼は)ごく常識的なことしか考えつかないからといって断った。
They asked him to write about "Ethics for Young People" for their magazine, but he declined saying that he could think of nothing but commonplace ideas to offer them.

じょうたい（状態）→ じょうきょう

じょうたつ（上達）

上達する［人主語］ **progress in; make (much) progress in; improve in**
［事主語］ **improve; become better**

彼は英語がどんどん上達した。
He has made rapid progress in English.

彼の英語は急速に上達した。
His English has improved quickly.

君はずいぶん英語が上達したね。
Your English {has become / is} much better now.

彼女はピアノが一向に上達しない。
She (still) can't play the piano (very) well.
She hasn't made much progress in playing the piano.

文章は書く練習をしているうちに上達するものだ。
You can improve your writing by practising.

しょうち（承知）

1. 知っている
know; be aware of

ご承知のように校内暴力はこのところ治まっているようです。
As you probably know, school violence seems to be decreasing [declining] these days.

彼はたばこが健康に有害なことなど百も承知だ。
He {knows full well / is well aware} that smoking is bad for his health.

【承知の上で】
knowing ... ; deliberately; on purpose

彼女の宝石類がまがい物だと承知の上だったが，彼は気の毒に思って買ってやった。
Knowing (that) her jewelry was sham, he bought it anyway out of pity.

彼は給料のよくないことは承知の上でその仕事についた。
He took a low-paying job deliberately [on purpose].

2. 同意する
agree (to); consent (to)

私たちと行かないかと誘ったら，彼はすぐ承知した。
We all asked him to come with us, and {he at once agreed. / he said yes on the spot. / he quite readily consented.}

彼はしぶしぶ承知した。
He reluctantly consented [complied].

【承知しました】
All right. / Sure! / Fine. / OK. 〔*colloq.*〕/ Yes, I'd love to. / Yes, that would be great [very nice / lovely].

3. 許可する
let; allow

【承知しない】
彼の父は彼の外国留学をどうしても承知しない。
His father would not {let him / allow him to} study abroad.

彼の父はそれについてはほかの人が何と言おうと承知しなかった。
His father was [set] against it whatever other people said.

【承知させる】
prevail upon; persuade《a person》to do

彼は外国留学をとうとう父親に承知させた。
He at last persuaded his father to let him study abroad.

【承知しないぞ】
また今度そんなことしたら承知しないぞ。
You'll be sorry (for it) if you do that again.

しょうとつ（衝突）

1．乗物

a collision; a crash

【正面衝突】

乗用車とトラックの正面衝突

a head-on collision between a car and a truck

【二重衝突】

a three-way crash [collision]

a collision involving three vehicles

【玉突き衝突】

a pile-up; a chain-reaction traffic accident

【ひどい衝突】

a bad accident; a horrible collision; a crack-up〔米〕, a smash-up〔英〕

衝突事故のため，信越線は5時間も不通になっていた。

The Shinetsu Line was closed [was stopped] for five hours because of a collision.

先月はひどい列車衝突事故があった。

There was a horrible rail accident last month.

バスがトラックと角の所で(出会い頭に)衝突した。

A bus collided with a lorry at the corner.

車が塀に衝突した。

The car ran [crashed] into a wall.

〈注〉 He ran his car into a wall. とすると故意にまたは酔っ払ってぶつけたことになる。

船が霧の中で岩に衝突した[岩礁に打ちつけられた]。

The ship was dashed against the rocks in the fog.

〈注〉◆dash は自動詞用法もあるが，受動態にする方が普通。

◆「衝突する」には smash, ram が使われることもある。

A car smashed [crashed / rammed] into a wall.

「正面衝突」は head-on collision; frontal crash。「(後ろからの)追突」は rear-end collision,「(後ろから)追突する」は ram from behind。「横からの衝突」は side collision,「横から衝突する」は ram into the side of ... 。

2．比喩的用法

【意見の衝突】

彼は上司と意見が衝突した。

He disagreed with his boss.

【けんか】

彼は父親とひどく衝突した[口論した]。

He fell out with his father.

〈注〉 fall out はひどい衝突[けんか]をすること。

【感情の衝突】

2人の間に何か感情の上の衝突があった。

There was some emotional clash between the two.

〈注〉 clash は何か事件があったことを意味する。反目の状態であれば disparity, antagonism を使う。

【利害の衝突】

彼らの利害が衝突した。

Their interests conflicted.

会社側と組合の利害が衝突した。

There was a conflict between the company executives and the workers union.

しょうにん（承認）

1．容認する

承認する　**recognize**

【政治】

米国はクロアチアの独立を承認した。

The U.S. recognized the independence of Croatia.

政府は中華人民共和国を正式に承認した。

The government gave diplomatic recognition to the People's Republic of China.

【法律上】

彼は法的に相続人として承認された。

He was legally recognized as an heir.

2．許可する

承認する　**approve**

委員会は予算案を承認した。

The committee approved the budget.

しょうばい(商売) →しょうぎょう, みせ

【商い】

(広義の)商売 **business; commerce; (a) trade**

商売人 a merchant

商売敵 a business rival; a competitor

商売をはじめる go into business

本屋をはじめる start a bookstore

彼は中古車の商売をしている。

He deals in used cars.

商売が繁盛している。

Business [Trade] is brisk at present.

【職業】 occupation

商売替えをする change one's occupation

〈注〉「勤め先をかえる」は change one's job。

《関連語》

卸問屋

wholesale store (↔ retail store 小売店)

〈注〉普通 store と言えば小売店のことである。

仕入れて小売りする

buy wholesale and sell retail

卸売[小売]価格で

at wholesale [retail] prices

これは卸で1キロ1000円だ。

These are 1,000 yen a kilo wholesale.

この冷蔵庫は小売価格20万円だ。

This refrigerator costs 200,000 yen retail.

じょうひん(上品)

上品な 形 **elegant; refined** (↔ vulgar 下品な); **graceful** (主として動作について)

〈注〉**refined** 都会的に洗練されていること。悪くとれば「ぶっている」ことになる。

graceful 自然な気品があり美しいこと。主として動作についての言葉。

genteel 古風な語で, 時に皮肉[反語的]に使われる。

【上品な人】

上品な婦人 an elegant lady

物腰, 物言いの上品な婦人

a lady with refined manners and speech

上品な顔立ちの紳士

a gentleman with a noble face

彼女には持って生れた上品さがある。

She has (a) natural grace.

彼女は上品な服装をしている。

She is elegantly [tastefully] dressed.

彼女はお上品ぶっている。

She gives herself airs [airs and graces〔英〕].

〈注〉 refinedは趣味, お菓子などについても使える。

しょくぎょう(職業) → しごと

《関連語》

【サラリーマン】

white-collar worker; office worker

公務員

government official (高官)

civil servant (一般)

地方公務員

local government { officer (上級) / worker (一般) / clerk (事務官) }

警察官 policeman; police officer

自衛官 Self-Defence Force officer

郵便局員 mail clerk

郵便配達人

mailman〔米〕; letter carrier〔米〕

postman〔英〕

消防士 fireman; fire fighter

会社員 company employee (→かいしゃ)

役職, 管理職 executive

社長 president of ...

受付係 receptionist

秘書 secretary

総務係 supervisor; manager

技官 laboratory technician

プログラマー programmer

会計係 accountant

人事係 personnel manager

書記 clerk

記録係 records clerk

文書係 filing clerk

請求書係 billing clerk

〜会社社員である work at 〜

〈注〉「私は会社員[公務員]だ」といった漠然とした言い方をせず，具体的に上述のような職種または職場を言うのが普通。
I am a researcher in a company.
（会社で研究員をしている）
I work at [for] Mitsukoshi.（三越に勤めている）
My mother works at a post office.
（私の母は郵便局に勤めている）

【専門職】 professionals
教員　teacher
小学校教員
elementary [primary] school teacher
中学校教員　junior high school teacher
高校教員　high school teacher
大学教授　university [college] professor
大学准教授　associate professor〔米〕
大学助教授　assistant professor
大学講師　instructor〔米〕, lecturer〔英〕（専任）; [part-time] lecturer（非常勤）
（地位を言いたくないとき）
I'm on the teaching staff at ～ University.
医師　physician;（medical）doctor
看護師　nurse
薬剤師
pharmacist; druggist〔米〕, chemist〔英〕
歯科医　dentist
獣医　veterinarian; vet
弁護士　lawyer; attorney（at law）〔米〕
事務弁護士　solicitor〔英〕
法廷弁護士　barrister〔英〕
税理士　tax accountant
僧侶　Buddhist priest
尼僧　nun
神官　Shinto priest
牧師　clergyman; minister

【生産関係】（→かいしゃ）
農業従事者　farmer
漁業従事者　fisherman
技術者　engineer
工場労働者　factory worker
流れ作業従事者　assembly-line worker
（鉱業　→the mining industry）
鉱夫　miner
土建業従事者　construction worker
職人　craftsman; artisan; skilled workers
大工　carpenter
れんが職人　bricklayer
配管工　plumber
電気屋　electrician

【商業】（→みせ，や）
スーパー[デパート]に勤務する
work in [at] a supermarket [department store]; work for《Jusco》（店の名を言うときは for が使える）
肉屋[パン屋 / 八百屋]をやっている
be a butcher [baker / greengrocer]
have a butcher [bakery / greengrocery] shop
菓子屋をやっている
have a confectionary shop
果物屋をやっている
have a fruit shop
〈注〉「みせ」および「や」の項に列挙してある職業，店の種類を上述の文型にあてはめて言えばよい。
彼女は婦人服店をやっている。
She has a boutique [dress shop].

【サービス業】（→ぎんこう，こうつう）
金融　（→ぎんこう）
銀行　bank
銀行員　bank clerk; bank teller
支配人　manager
出納係　cashier〔英〕
証券会社　stock brokerage firm; securities firm
保険会社　insurance company
不動産業者　realtor; real estate agent
株式仲買人　stockbroker
理容師　barber
美容師　hairdresser
ホテル　hotel
支配人　manager
副支配人　assistant manager
フロント係　desk clerk
ボーイ　doorman
荷物運びのボーイ　bellman; bellhop〔*colloq.*〕
メイド　hotel maid; room maid
レストラン　restaurant
店主　owner
店長　manager

コック　cook
ウエイター / ウエイトレス　} table attendant
交通機関　(→こうつう)
JR勤務者　JR employee
運転者　driver
バス[タクシー]の運転手　bus [taxi] driver
列車の運転手　train engineer [driver]
電車の運転手　motorman
車掌(列車・バスの)　conductor [conductress]; (列車の) guard〔英〕
飛行機のパイロット　pilot
パーサー　purser
機内サービス係
cabin attendant; flight attendant

【芸術・娯楽】

作家　writer; author
科学記事ライター　science writer
詩人　poet
随筆家　essayist
劇作家　dramatist
画家　painter
彫刻家　sculptor
写真家
professional cameraman [photographer]
音楽家　musician
作曲家　composer
指揮者　conductor
演奏家　player (ex. Koto player)
〈注〉楽器+ist で演奏家の意になる。
ex. pianist; violinist
声楽家　singer ex. opera singer; *enka* singer; jazz singer
ミュージシャン　musician ex. rock musician
ダンサー　dancer
俳優　actor
女優　actress

【職業安定所[職安]】

job information center
employment security office〔英〕
ex. 連邦職業安定所ミズーリ支所
Federal Job Information Center, Missouri Division of Employment

しょくじ (食事)

a meal; meals

朝食　breakfast
昼食[軽食]　lunch
夕食[軽食]　supper
正餐　dinner
〈注〉Sunday dinner は昼食を指す。

食事をする[食べる]
have breakfast [lunch, dinner, etc.]

おいしい。
It's good.
It tastes good [wonderful].

おいしくない。
It doesn't taste very [so] good.

まずい[ひどい]。
It's terrible [horrible].

もっといかがですか。
Would you like some more [another helping]?

ご自由にお取りください。
Please help yourself.

もう少しいただけますか。
Can [Could] I have some more, please?

十分いただきました[もう結構です]。
No thank you. I've had enough.
I've had enough. (I'm full,) thank you.
It tastes wonderful [very good], but I've had enough. (家庭の晩餐会などで勧められて断るとき)

〈注〉「いただきます」「ごちそうさま」に当る英語の決り文句はない。皆が食べ始めたら食べ始めてよい。おいしければ It's good. とほめ，料理の作り方 (recipe) などを尋ねることもある。
食事をごちそうになって帰るときも決り文句はないが，Thank you for a wonderful evening [dinner]. と言ってもよい。
まだほかの客がテーブルについているときに席をはずす場合は次のように言う。
[子供] May I (please) be excused?
[大人] Excuse me(, please). (中座する理由を付け加える)
ただし，トイレに行くときなどは黙って行く。戻ってきたときも何も言わなくてよい。

しょくひん（食品）

食物　(a) **food; foods**〔米〕(食物一般では単数，各種食品の意味では複数形を使う)

《関連語》
【野菜】vegetable　(→やさい)
【肉】meat
牛肉　beef / 子牛肉　veal / 豚肉　pork / ハム　ham / ベーコン　bacon / 羊肉　mutton / 子羊肉　lamb / 馬肉　horse meat / 鶏肉　chicken / ハト　squab / キジ　pheasant / 七面鳥　turkey / アヒル　duck / ウサギ　rabbit / ソーセージ　sausage
【シーフード】seafood
魚　fish　(→さかな)
タイ　sea bream / マグロ　tuna(fish) / サケ　salmon / サバ　mackerel / イワシ　sardine / タラ　cod(fish) / ニシン　herring / マス　trout / ウナギ　eel
【甲殻類】the crustacean, shellfish
イセエビ　lobster / クルマエビ　prawn / 小エビ　shrimp / カニ　crab / カキ　oyster / ハマグリ　clam
【穀類】grains, cereals
米　rice / 小麦　wheat〔米〕, corn〔英〕/ トウモロコシ　corn〔米〕, maize〔英〕/ 大麦　barley / そば　buckwheat / あわ　millet
【自然食品】natural foods
無農薬野菜　organic [organically grown] vegetables
【加工食品】processed foods
缶詰　canned food〔米〕, tinned food〔英〕/ 冷凍食品　frozen food / インスタント食品　instant food / インスタントスープ　instant soup / 調理済み食品　precooked foods (半調理品を含む); cooked foods ready for serving / 総菜屋，調理済み食品店　delicatessen

しょくぶつ（植物）

a plant;［集合的］**vegetation;** (a) **vegetable** (動物・鉱物に対して); 植物相 **flora**
植物学　botany
植物学者　a botanist
植物園　a botanical garden

《関連語》
高山植物　alpine plants / 熱帯植物　tropical plants / 亜熱帯植物　subtropical plants / 海洋植物　marine plants / 水生植物　aquatic plants / 一年生植物　annual plants / 多年生植物　perennial plants / 球根植物　bulbous plants (球根 bulb) / 観葉植物　foliage plants / 薬用植物　herbs / 園芸植物　garden plants
【木】　(→き)
森　forest / 林　woods; woodland / 木　tree / 葉　leaf (pl. leaves); [総称]foliage / 幹　trunk / 枝　branch / 大枝 bough / 小枝 twig / 根　roots / 下生え　undergrowth / やぶ　underbrush / 灌木[茂み]　bush
【草・花】　plants　(→はな)
草　grass / 雑草　weeds / 花　flower / (木の)花　blossom / つぼみ　bud / 茎　stalk / 柄　stem / 花びら　petal / めしべ　pistil / おしべ　stamen / 蜜　nectar / (バラなどの)とげ　thorn
【実】［総称］**fruit**
小粒で水分の多い実　berry　(→み) / 穀物　grain / 堅果 nut
【種】　seed
【苗木】　seedling
剪定(せんてい)　cutting / さし木(の切り枝)　slip

じょげん（助言）→ ちゅういする

名 **advice; a suggestion**
〈注〉 advice は不可算名詞である。×an advice は誤り。

【助言する】 advise; counsel; suggest; give《a person》advice (かなりまじめな助言); give《a person》a practical suggestion (「こうしたらどうか」といった軽い気持ちの助言)
【助言を求める】
ask《a person》for advice
ask《a person's》advice
ask for a suggestion　(実際には What do you suggest? と尋ねること)

【助言を入れる】
follow [take]《a person's》advice
【助言を入れない】
not listen to《a person's》advice
【助言者】a counselor (カウンセラー)

しょっき (食器)

tableware

《関連語》
金属食器 cutlery / 銀食器 silverware / ナイフ knife (pl. knives) / 切り盛り用大ナイフ carving knife / パン切りナイフ bread knife / ステーキナイフ steak knife / 魚用ナイフ fish knife / 果物ナイフ fruit knife / バターナイフ butter knife / さじ spoon / ティースプーン teaspoon / テーブルスプーン tablespoon / フォーク fork / 切り盛り用大フォーク carving fork / はし chopsticks / 皿(大皿) platter / (とり皿)plate / (皿一般)dish / 深皿, ボウル bowl / カップ cup; mug / ソーサー saucer / コップ glass

しらずしらず(知らず知らず)→おもわず

〈注〉日本語では「思わず」が瞬間的なのに対して, 「知らず知らず」は時間の経過を思わせる表現である。「知らず知らず」「思わず」のつもりで unconsciously, unknowingly, involuntarily (無意識に) などを使っても内容に合わない場合があるので, それぞれの副詞のもとの意味をよく考えて使うこと。

知らず知らず, いつしか彼女に引かれていった。
I began to love her before I knew it.
知らず知らずのうちに彼をかばう側にまわっていった。
I found [realized] (that) I was speaking in favor of him {before I knew it. / unawares.}

しりあい (知り合い)

an acquaintance (friends ほど親しくない)

彼は古くからの知り合いだ。
He's an old acquaintance of mine.
彼とは最近知り合いになった。
I met him for the first time recently.
(あなた方)お知り合いですか。
Do you know each other?
(紹介しようとして)お知り合いですか。
Have you met (Mr. Yamada) (before)?
山田さんとお知り合いでしょうか。
Do you know Mr. Yamada?

《類義語》
fellow worker, coworker 工場などで労働に携わる人の仲間 (親しさの度合いは関係ない)
colleague 同僚
officemate オフィス仲間
classmate 同級生
someone I know 知っている人
friend 友人 →ともだち

【知り合いの度合】
彼とは知り合いだ。(個人的知人, 付き合っている)
I know him.
名前は知っている[顔は知っている]。(有名人など, 付き合いはない場合)
I know {the name. / who he is.}
I can recognize him.
彼のことは知っている。(以前付き合っていたが今どうしているかは知らない)
I used to know him.
(少し/よく)知っていた。1970年代頃知っていた。(過去の事実を述べている。ずっと以前付き合っていた)
I knew him (a little / well). I knew him back in the seventies.

しりつ (市立, 私立)

1. 市立

市立の **city**[形容詞的]; **municipal; civic**
名古屋市立大学
Nagoya City University

岐阜市立図書館
Gifu City [Municipal] Library
うちの大学は市立です。
Our college is { municipal. / run by the city.

2．私立
私立の　**private**
東京には有名私立大学がたくさんある。
There are many famous private universities and colleges in Tokyo.
おかしなことに英国のパブリック・スクールは公立でなく私立なのだ。
Although it may sound strange, English public schools are private (institutions).

しる（知る）・しらせる

come to know; get to know 〔*colloq.*〕**; find out; learn; get acquainted; be informed about**

【知っている（状態）】　know
〈注〉　×I am knowing などとは言わない。
know about [of]（聞いたことがある）
be informed of（知らされている）(cf. inform《someone》of《something》)
be aware of《something》（わかっている）
be acquainted with《a person, fact, place》
be familiar with《the idea, field, issue》（よく知っている）
彼は5か国語を知っている。
He knows five foreign languages.
相対性理論を知っていますか。
Do you know the theory of relativity? (＝understand it?)
Do you know of the theory of relativity? (＝heard of it?)
いい病院を知っていらっしゃいますか[教えてください]。
Do you know (of) a good hospital? (＝Please recommend ...)
〈注〉　know は本当にどんな人[もの]か知っていること。know of は人に聞いて評判で知っていること。
ex. Do you know Prof. Smith?（スミス先生を知ってますか）
No, I don't know him (personally) but I know of him.（いいえ，個人的な知り合いではありません。でもお名前は知っています）
動物や鳥は我々人間より先に危険を知る[察知する]。
Animals and birds sense danger before we do.
彼はロンドンは隅から隅まで知っている。
He is thoroughly acquainted with London.
He knows London like the back of his hand.
【私の知るかぎりでは】 as far as I know
【知らない間に】（→しらずしらず）
自分でも知らない間に彼を好きになっていた。
I was beginning to love him (1)before I knew it [without knowing it].
知らぬ間に弟が(僕の)一番好きなカセットテープを3本も大学に持って行ってしまった。
(2)Without my knowledge my brother took three of my favorite cassette tapes back to university with him.
〈注〉　上の文の(1)は「いったいいつの間に」という驚きを表し，(2)は「ひと言言ってくれればよかったのに」の含みがある。
知っているふりをする
pretend to know
知らないふりをする
pretend not to know; pretend ignorance
何も知らないふりをした。
I pretended I didn't know anything about it
（道で会っても）彼は知らんぷり［知らん顔］をして，さっさと角を曲って行ってしまった。
He pretended not to recognize me and strode off around the corner.
お前の知ったことじゃない[余計なお世話だ]。
That's really none of your business.（荒っぽい言い方）

【知らない】

〈注〉 何か尋ねられたときの答えとして，ぶっきらぼうに I don't know. と言いがちであるが，次のような段階がある。

I {don't know anything / know nothing} about it.（全然知らない）

I don't know much about it.（よく知らない）

I know very little about it.（ほとんど知らない）

I'm not familiar with those technical terms.（専門用語はよくわからない）

I don't know enough about haiku poetry to give a lecture.（俳句のことは人に話せるほどよくは知らない）

私はそれを知らなかった。

I {didn't know / wasn't aware of} it.

【知らせる】

let《a person》know

tell《a person》

inform《a person》of《a matter》

report《something》to《a person》

make《a matter》known to《a person》

できるだけ早く結果を知らせてください。

Please let me know the result as soon as possible.

だれにも知らせないで，秘密だから。

Don't tell anyone. It's a secret.

犬がいなくなったんだ。警察には届けたんだがまだ何も知らせがない。

My dog has been lost. I reported it to the police, but there's no news of him yet.

〈注〉◆know は「知っている」ことで，「知る」は come to know または話し言葉で get to know。ただし，多少あいまいなところがあり，例えば「いつ選挙の結果を知ることができるか」は，

When can we know the election results?

と言えるが，find out や get が自然。(→わかる)

◆「知った，わかった」は could know ではなく，realized, understood とすべきである。

母が入院して初めて母の仕事のたいへんさを知った[がわかった]。

My mother was in hospital and I {×could know / realized [understood]} how hard she usually works.

しんがく（進学）

中学[高校 / 大学]に進学する

enter [go on to] junior high school [high school / college, university]

〈注〉 「…に」を抜かしてただ「進学」という言葉は英語にはないので学校の種類を特定する。

【進学希望】

中学生の大部分は進学希望である。

Most [The majority of] junior high school students [pupils] want to go on to high school.

〈注〉 米国では大学入試（university placement test）に進学適性検査（aptitude test）を使っている。数学・国語運用力，論理的思考力（mathematical and verbal handling abilities, reasoning）をテストするのである。就職にも job placement test という適性検査がある。

じんかく（人格）→ せいしつ・せいかく

1．品性

character

【人格者】

彼は立派な人格者だ。

He is a man of fine [honorable] character.

〈注〉 He has character. は個性が強いということ。また He's a real character.（＝He's eccentric, not like everybody else.）は，変り者の意だが必ずしも悪い意味ではない。

【人格形成】

名 character formation [shaping]

動 人格を形成する build [form] character

人の人格は20歳までに形成される。

One's character is built [formed] before the age of twenty.

生後2, 3年は人格形成にきわめて重要である。

The first few years of life are vital for character formation.

2．人権

【人格を尊重する】

respect《a person》

have respect for《a person》

〈注〉 この respect は権利を尊重する意味で，「尊敬する」とは違う。日本語の「人格」もここでは基本的人権をもった一個の人間の意味で，人柄の意味ではない。character は道徳的見地から見た人間の性質。なお類義語については「せいしつ」参照。

しんぐ（寝具）

bedding

【ベッドカバー】

bedcover, bedspread, coverlet

【枕】 pillow

枕掛け　pillowcase, pillowslip

【掛けぶとん】 quilt（薄い刺し子にした掛けぶとん）

down quilt　羽毛ぶとん

eiderdown quilt　アイダーダウン(アイダーダック eider duck の羽毛を詰めたふとん)

patchwork quilt　パッチワークの美しいふとん。

comforter　掛けぶとん; ベッドカバー〔米〕

futon　日本の掛けぶとんのイメージ，タイプはいろいろ。

【毛布】 blanket

夏の毛布　summer blanket（薄手のもの）

冬の毛布　winter blanket（厚手のもの）

電気毛布　electric blanket

【シーツ】 sheets

top sheet / bottom sheet ｝毛布と敷きぶとんの間に敷く

〈注〉 上下のシーツはその上の毛布と共にマットレスの下に折りこみ，人はその間に入って寝る）

contour sheet(＝fitted sheet)　マットレスにすっぽりかぶせるように縫ったシーツ。

【敷きぶとん】 mattress

mattress pad　マットレスの上に置く厚手の木綿のキルトのパッド。

mattress　マットレス

bed　ベッド

【寝具に関する表現】

〈注〉 欧米では周知のようにベッドで寝るので，ふとんを「あげたり，敷いたり」する代りに make a bed, bedmaking をする。

ふとんを敷く　lay out the bed

ふとんをたたむ

(fold up and) put away the bed

ふとんを整える　straighten the bed

ふとんを掛けて寝る

get under a quilt [blanket]

get under the covers

毛布[ふとん]を引っ張り上げる

pull a blanket [quilt] up (over)《oneself》

put a blanket [quilt] on《oneself》

毛布[ふとん]を掛けなおす

put a blanket [quilt] back on《a person》

毛布をちゃんと掛けて寝なさい。

Pull up your blanket.

Put a blanket on [over] yourself.

母さんが毛布を掛けてくれた。

Mother ｛ put a blanket over me. / covered me with a blanket.

子供たちがちゃんとふとんを掛けているかどうか寝る前に見てきてください。

Before going to bed, check to see that the children are covered.

私は毛布も掛けずに寝た。

I slept without a blanket.

あの人はふとんを 2 枚掛けていてまだ寒いと言った。

She was using two quilts, yet she said she was cold.

おばあさんは子供をきっちりと毛布でくるんでやった。

Grandmother tucked the child in.

しんじつ（真実）→ ほんとう

しんじる（信じる）・しんこう（信仰）

1．本当だと思う

君の言うことを信じる。

I believe you.

彼の言葉を信じる。

I believe what he says.

彼の言うことは全然信じない。

I don't believe a word [anything] he says.

彼の無実を信じている。

I believe { in his innocence. / that he's innocent.

良いと信じることをやりなさい。

Do what you believe is right.

幽霊(の存在)を信じている。

I believe in ghosts.

君の成功を信じている[確信している]。

I'm sure you'll succeed.

教育こそ社会にとって最重要課題であると信じる。

I'm convinced that education is the most essential social need.

〈注〉 be sure [be convinced] of your success の形は堅い語で今はあまり使われない。

2. 信用する

【人】

私は君を信じている。(人間として君を信じる)

I believe in you. / I trust you.

彼女は夫を信じている。(夫は立派な人間だと信じている)

She trusts her husband.

【方法】

彼は新教授法を信じこんでいる。

He believes in the new teaching method.

3. 信仰する

私はキリスト教を信じて[信仰して]いる。

I'm a Christian. / I believe in God.

私は無信仰だ。

I am a nonbeliever.

I don't believe in God.

私の祖父は観音様を信仰している。

My grandfather believes in *Kannon-sama*.

半世紀ほど前は日本人のほとんどが仏教を信じていた。

Half a century ago, most Japanese were Buddhists.

【信仰】 faith, belief

無信仰の　unbelieving

信仰のない人　a nonbeliever; an unbeliever; an atheist (無神論者); an agnostic (不可知論者)

信仰の自由

freedom of religion, religious liberty

信仰生活を送る(キリスト教)

lead a Christian life [a devout Christian life]

信仰の厚いクリスチャン

a devout [committed] Christian

私は大学時代に信仰を失った。

I lost my faith during my college years.

4. 慣用句

信じられない!

Incredible! / Unbelievable! / I can't believe it.

しんせつ (親切)

親切な　**kind; warm-hearted; friendly; good; obliging**

親切な行為　a kindness, an act of kindness

親切から　out of kindness

ハワードさん一家にお願いしましょう。本当に親切な人たちだから。

I'll ask the Howards. They are very obliging [generous] people.

村人は皆気さくで親切だった。

The villagers were all friendly and kind.

【親切に感謝する言い方】

本当にご親切にありがとう。

Thank you very much (for your kindness).

I really appreciate your help.

It's very good [kind] of you (indeed).

アメリカ滞在中ずっと親切にしていただきました。

You have been very kind all through my stay here in America.

しんねん（信念）

(a) belief; (a) faith; (a) conviction

彼は正義がついには勝つという信念を持っている。

He { firmly believes / has a firm conviction 〔*literary*〕 } that the just will win in the end.

【信念に従う】

彼は信念に従っているのだ。

He acts according to his convictions.

He does what he believes right.

妻は自分の信念に従って人生を生きた。

My wife lived her life according to her beliefs and principles.

しんねん（新年）→ねんちゅうぎょうじ

a [the] new year

新年おめでとう

(A) Happy New Year!

I wish you a Happy New Year.

〈注〉 ×Happy New Year's Day.
a new year は新しい，これからの1年のことで正月数日間のことではない。

除夜の鐘とともに旧年を送り新年を迎え入れる

ring out the Old Year and ring in the New (Year)

新年を祝う

celebrate the new year

〈注〉 「新年はどうでしたか」は，How did you spend the New Year holiday(s) [New Year's]?

新年宴会　a New Year's party

しんぱい（心配）

1. 気がかり

名　**worry; anxiety; trouble; difficulty; cares**

心配する 動　**worry (about); be [feel] worried; feel concerned; feel anxious [uneasy] (about); feel nervous**

子供が大人になっても心配しすぎる親がいる。

Some parents are too worried [worry too much] about their grown-up children.

彼は試験の結果を心配している。

He's worried [anxious] about the result of the examination.

アパートに犬だけおいておくのは心配だ。

It worries me to leave my dog alone in the apartment.

あの人の将来が心配だ。

I am concerned about his future.

【心配するな】

Don't worry. (気を遣うな)

Never mind. (気にするな，何でもない)

Relax. (気楽にやれ)

私のことは心配しないで。

Don't worry about me.

〈注〉△Never mind about me. とは言わない。

心配することではない。

It's nothing to worry about.

この病気に関しては心配はいりません。

There's nothing to worry about regarding this illness.

【心配をかける】

受験勉強中は親にさんざん心配をかけた。

During the years I was studying for exams, I was always causing my parents worry.

【謝罪】

ご心配をおかけしてすみませんでした。

I'm sorry I made you worry.

ご心配をかけるつもりはなかったのです。

I didn't mean to make you worry.

【心配の種・心配事】

それだけが彼の心配の種だった。

That was the only source of his anxiety.

彼にはいろいろ心配事があるらしい。

He seems to have many troubles [worries].

There is something on his mind which troubles [worries] him very much. (心配事がある)

He had many troubles [worries] on his mind. (心配事があった)

金銭上の心配事
money troubles [worries]
家庭の心配事　family problems
【心配そうに】
anxiously; with a worried air [look]
彼女は眠っている子を心配そうに見た。
She looked at the sleeping child anxiously.

2. 配慮・世話
就職について彼はいろいろ心配してくれた。
He tried hard to find me a good job.
彼は心配して金銭的援助まで申し出てくれた。
He even offered me financial help.
こんなすてきな物をいただいて…ご心配かけてすみませんでした。本当にありがとうございます。
You must have gone to [through] / It must have been } a lot of trouble to find this. Thank you very much.
〈注〉 心配してもらったお礼として「ご心配おかけしてすみませんでした」と言うが，お礼の気持ちを表すのは Thank you. であって I'm sorry. ではない。日本人はわびる気持ちとお礼の気持ちが裏表の関係になっていて，そのために外国人に Japanese people apologize too much. という印象を与えるようである。これも文化の相違である。

《類義語》
fear　恐怖。
trouble　やっかいなこと，気苦労。
worry　気苦労。くよくよと不安で心が休まらないこと。
care　心にのしかかる気苦労。
anxiety　災いなどを恐れる不安。
concern　何ものかに関心を持ち，または責任感を持つことから来る不安。
uneasiness　不安（doubt＋worry）。
suspense　先行きがわからないために落ちつかず，気をもむこと。
nervousness　くよくよ，いらいら気をもむこと。

しんゆう（親友）→ ともだち

a good [**close, great**] **friend;** 一番の親友《one's》**best friend**
【親友になる】
become great [very good] friends with …
私たちは大の親友になった。
We became great friends.
〈注〉◆「A とB が親友になった」は次のように二通りの言い方がある。
A became great friends with B.
A and B became great friends.
◆one's best friend(s) は1人か2人で一番の親友。great friend, close friend は大の仲良し。その次にくるのが good friend。
a good friend を表す米語には，男性語で打ちとけた感じをもつ pal, buddy, chum がある。英国ではこの3語はあまり使われず mate が使われる。

しんよう(信用)・しんらい → しんじる・しんこう

名 **trust; confidence; credit;** 信頼 **reliance**
信用する 動 **trust; confide in; believe in; rely on**
信用される[がある]　be trusted [relied on]
信用がある[を得る]
have [win]《a person's》confidence
信用[信頼]できる　形 trustworthy, reliable
信用のある　reputable
信用[信頼]できる友人
a trustworthy [reliable] friend
信用[信頼]できる社員
a trustworthy employee
信用のある宝石店　a reputable jeweller's
ボスは彼を信用[信頼]している。
The boss trusts him.
係長は一番若い係員を信頼するようになった。彼が面倒なケースをうまく処理したからだ。
The supervisor came to trust the youngest worker because he handled a difficult case very well.

彼女の先生は彼女の的確な判断力を信頼している。

Her teacher {trusts / is confident of} her good judgment.

彼はボスに信用がある[信頼されている]。

He is trusted by his boss.

ジョージは真っ正直なのでボスの一番の信用[信頼]を得た。(ボスの信頼が一番厚かった)

George won [had] the boss's greatest trust because he was thoroughly honest.

彼女は信用できない。

She cannot be trusted.

あれは信用できる男ではない。

He is not the sort of man to be trusted.

彼は彼女の言葉を信用した。

He took her word for it.

信頼できる筋の情報

information from a reliable source

〈注〉 ニュースの出所を明らかにしたくないときに使われる。

未公表であるが信頼できる筋によれば，大統領は次期選挙には出馬しない模様だ。

It is not yet (officially) announced, but according to a reliable source the President will not run in the next election.

じんるい（人類）

humankind; the human race

人類愛　love for humanity

人類学　anthropology

エジソンの発明は人類に大きな貢献をもたらした。

Edison's inventions contributed a great deal to humankind.

軍拡競争は人類の存続そのものをおびやかすものだ。

The armament race endangers the existence of the whole human race.

す

ず（図）

図画　a picture; a drawing
挿絵，図解　an illustration
略図　a sketch
地図　a map
海図，図表　a chart
天気図　a weather chart

【論文記事のグラフ類】

図　a figure
第１図　Fig.1; Figure One
線[棒]グラフ　a line [bar] graph
円グラフ　a pie chart
図形　a diagram

図１は実験装置の図である。
　Fig.1 is a diagram of the experimental apparatus.

第１図のグラフは人口の増加を示す。
　The graph in Fig.1 shows the increase in population.

【設計図をかく】

実験室の設計図をかく
　draw a plan of a laboratory

図をかいて説明しましょう。
　I'll explain by
　　{ drawing a sketch [map].
　　{ making a sketch [chart, map].
　I'll illustrate with a diagram.

【絵画】

壁には玉堂の花蝶図─２羽の蝶が花にたわむれる図─がかかっていた。
　On the wall was Gyokudo's Kachozu ─ a fine painting of a pair of butterflies fluttering among flowers.

〈注〉　×a fine painting which butterflies are fluttering のようには言えない。ただし，in which とすれば文法的には正しくなる。

【慣用表現】

彼は彼女が優しいので図に乗った。
　He took advantage of her generosity [kindness].〔*standard*〕
　He presumed upon her kindness.〔*formal*〕

すいせん（推薦）

［名］**recommendation**

…に推薦する　**recommend**《a person; a thing》(**as, for**)

全員が彼女を会長[会員]に推薦した。
　They all recommended her for the presidency [membership].

私は山田さんを調整係に推薦します。
　I recommend Miss Yamada as a coordinator. (as＝in the capacity of)

〈注〉　「信頼できる人物として推薦する」は I recommend ... because ... is a reliable person. のようにする。

何か推薦していただけるような本はありませんか。
　Are there any books you would like to recommend?

先生がこの辞書を推薦された。
　Our teacher recommended this dictionary (to us).

〈注〉　recommend は「これがいいよ」とすすめることで次のような場合にも使える。
　They recommended bay leaves for getting rid of cockroaches.(ゴキブリ撃退には月桂樹の葉がよく効くとすすめた)

【推薦で】

加藤氏の推薦のおかげで今の仕事につけた。
　I got my present position through Mr. Kato's recommendation.

【候補に推薦する】 nominate (for, as)

自民党は大物２名を今回の選挙に候補として推薦した。
　The Liberal Democratic Party nominated two high-ranking members as candidates in this election.

すいみん（睡眠）→ ねむる・ねる

名 **sleep**

睡眠をとる　**sleep**

どのくらい睡眠(時間)をとっていますか。

How many {hours' sleep do you get / hours do you sleep} a night?

昨夜は十分睡眠をとった[よく眠った]。

I had a good sleep last night [night's sleep].

【睡眠が必要】

子供は8時間以上の睡眠が必要だ。

Children need more than eight hours' sleep.

【睡眠中である】 be sleeping

睡眠中は邪魔しないでくれ。

Don't disturb me while I'm sleeping.

Don't disturb.（ホテルのドアに掛ける札）

【睡眠を減らす】

睡眠(時間)を減らさなければならない。

I had to cut down on {sleep. / my sleeping hours.}

【睡眠不足】

今日は睡眠不足だ。

I haven't slept enough.

I slept badly [poorly] last night.（昨夜は眠れなかった）

このところ睡眠不足だ。

I haven't been getting enough sleep.

彼は過労と睡眠不足でやせてしまった。

He has lost weight from overwork and lack of sleep.

【睡眠薬】 sleeping pills

すう（吸う）

1．気体を

breathe in; inhale

【息】

声楽家は息を深く吸うように訓練されている。

Singers are taught to inhale [breathe in] deeply.

【たばこ】

私はたばこを吸わない。

I don't smoke.

彼は相当たばこを吸う［ヘビースモーカーだ］。

He is a heavy smoker.

たばこを吸ってもかまいませんか。

Would you mind {my smoking? / if I smoke?}

ええ，どうぞ。

No, not at all.

いやあ，実のところ[悪いけど]嫌いなんです。

Yes, I would actually.

I'd rather you wouldn't.（やめてくだされぱありがたいです）

2．液体を

すする **sip;** 吸い上げる **suck;** 飲む **drink**

彼女は注文したソーダをおちおち飲む気もしなくて，すすっただけだった。

She only sipped at her soda, being too uneasy to want to drink it.

子供は音をたててレモネードをストローで吸い上げた。

The child noisily drank up her lemonade through the straw.

赤ちゃんが親指を吸っている。

The baby is sucking its thumb.

【含む，吸い取る】 absorb; soak up

この材質は水をよく吸う。

This material absorbs [soaks up] water well.

雨水を吸って花の種が急にふくらんだ。

Soaked by the rain, the flower seeds have suddenly swollen.

すうがく（数学）

mathematics; math〔米〕**; maths**〔英〕

《関連語》

1．数

number

整数　integer / 自然数　natural number / 正の整数　positive　integer / 負の整数　negative integer / 偶数　even number / 奇数　odd number / 素数　prime number / 分数　fraction / 分母　denominator / 分子　numerator

〈注〉 分数の読み方

$\frac{a}{b}$ = a over b = a/b = a by b

1/2 = one half

3/2 = three halves; one and a half

小数　decimal / 小数部分　decimal part / 小数点　decimal point / 循環小数　recurring decimal / 四捨五入　rounding off [up(五入) / down(四捨)] / 有理数　rational number / 無理数　irrational number / 実数　real number / 複素数　complex number / 虚数　imaginary number / 集合　set / 符号　sign / 複号　double sign / 絶対値　absolute value / 根号　the radical (sign)

2. 算数
arithmetic

計算　computation / 約分, 通分　reduce to the least common denominator / 四則　four fundamental operations of arithmetic / 加法(足し算) addition / 減法(引き算) subtraction / 乗法(掛け算) multiplication / 除法(割り算) division / 倍数　multiple / 最小公倍数　the least [lowest] common denominator〔米〕[multiple〔英〕] / 約数　divisor / 最大公約数　the greatest common divisor〔米〕[measure〔英〕] / 和　sum / 差　difference / 積　product / 商　quotient / 比　ratio

3. 図形
figure; shape

幾何　geometry / 平面幾何学　plane geometry / 立体幾何学　solid geometry / 平面図形　plane figure / 点　point / 線　line / 直線　straight line / 線分　line segment / 接線　tangent / 平面　plane / 曲線　curve / 距離　distance / 辺 (多角形の) side; (立体の) edge / 角　angle / 頂点　vertex / 三角形　triangle / 二等辺三角形　isosceles triangle / 正三角形　equilateral triangle / 直角三角形　right(-angled) triangle / 四辺形　quadrilateral / 四角形　quadrangle / 正方形　square / 平行四辺形　parallelogram / 平行　parallelism / 平行な　parallel / 台形　trapezoid / ひし形　rhombus / 多角形　polygon / 正多角形　regular polygon / 円　circle / 円周率　pi(π) / 円周　circumference / 中心　center / 弧　arc / 弦　chord / 直径　diameter / 半径　radius / 弓形　segment / 楕円　ellipse / 放物線　parabola / 双曲線　hyperbola / 軌跡　locus / 作図　construction / 垂直な　perpendicular / 垂線　perpendicular line / 合同　congruence; 形 congruent / 相似形　similar figure; 形 similar / 拡大　extension / 縮小　reduction / 立体図形　solid figure / 立方体　cube / 球　sphere / 球面　spherical surface

4. 代数
algebra

等式　equality / 恒等式　identity / 不等式　inequality / 方程式　equation / 1次方程式　linear equation / 2次方程式　quadratic equation / n次方程式　n-th equation / 解　solution / 重解　equal root / 項　term / 係数　coefficient / 根　root / 平方根　square root / 立方根　cubic root / n乗根　n-th root / 2乗　square / 3乗　cube / 冪(べき), 累乗　power / bのn乗　b^n; b to the n-th power / 10^5　ten to the fifth power

Xの2乗[3乗]はY。

The square [cube] of X is Y.

Xの平方[立方]はY。

X squared [cubed] equals Y.

分数方程式　fractional equation / 多項式(=整式) polynomial / 連立方程式　simultaneous equations / 関数　function / 1次関数　linear function / 2次関数　quadratic function / 変数　variable / 変域　domain / 最大　maximum / 最小　minimum / 零　zero / 無限大　infinity / グラフ　graph / 正比例　proportion / 反比例　inverse proportion / 因数分解　factorization / 因数分解する　factor / スカラー　scalar / ベクトル　vector / 行列　matrix / 逆行列　inverse matrix / 写像　mapping / 1次写像　linear mapping / 1次変換　linear transformation / 内積　inner product

5．解析

analysis

微積分学　calculus／微分法　differentiation／微分学　differential calculus／積分法　integration／積分学　integral calculus／微分方程式　differential equation／不定積分　indefinite integral／定積分　definite integral／対数　logarithm／対数関数　logarithmic function／指数関数　exponential function／三角関数　trigonometric function／級数　series／数列　sequence of numbers／極大　local(ly) maximum／極小　local(ly) minimum

6．統計

statistics

確率　probability／有効数字　significant figure／近似値　approximation; approximate value／誤差　error／誤差関数　error function／順列　permutation／組合せ　combination／度数　frequency／度数分布　frequency distribution／平均(値)　mean (value)／標準偏差　standard deviation／分散　variance／相関係数　correlation coefficient

7．その他

公式　formula／定理　theorem／証明　proof／定理を証明する　prove the theorem／定義　definition／公理　axiom／必要十分条件　necessary and sufficient condition

すがた（姿）

1．姿・形

form; figure

〈注〉 form, figure は形のことであり，姿はもっと広い意味範囲をもつので，自分の言いたいことをよく考えることが必要である。

彼女はすらりとして姿[スタイル]がよい。

She's slim.

〈注〉 She has a slender [slim] figure. と言ってもよいが She's slim. で十分。

彼ののっぽの姿が(角を曲って)見えなくなった。

His tall figure vanished round the corner.

We watched his tall figure disappear.

今も彼の姿がありありと目に浮かぶ。

I can still recall his image vividly.

この子の晴れ姿を一目お父さんに見せたかった。

I wish our father could be here to see her (so beautifully dressed).

〈注〉 (　)の部分は前後関係で明らかであれば省略可能。

×I wish to let our father see her figure which is dressed ... このような直訳は誤り。

帰ってみると彼の姿はもう見えなかった。

When I came back, he was gone.

朝もやの中を立ち去って行く彼女の後ろ姿がさびしげであった。

I watched her walk away into the morning mist, which impressed me as something pathetic.

2．出現・変身・逃避

【姿を現す】 appear; turn up; show up

彼女は思いがけないときに姿を現した。

She showed up at an unexpected moment.

彼女はカーテンの後ろから姿を現した。

She appeared from behind the curtain.

【姿を消す】 disappear; vanish

(姿が)見えなくなる　go out of sight

【姿を見ない】

このところ彼は姿を見せない。

We haven't seen him around lately.

We have seen nothing of him lately.

【姿を隠す，隠れる】

hide《oneself》behind《something》

【姿を変える】 disguise《oneself》

男優が女の姿で現れた。

The actor appeared {in the guise of / disguised as} a woman.

3．様子

新著で彼女は18世紀の貴族生活の真の姿を浮き彫りにしようとしている。

In her new book she tries to give the true picture of the life of the aristocracy in the 18th century.
これが日本のありのままの姿だ。
Here [This] is Japan as it really is.
〈注〉 … as she really is のように国名を女性代名詞で表すのは古風になった。現在は it が普通。
こんな姿では人前に出られません。まず着替えさせてください。
I'm not fit to be seen, so let me change my clothes first.
〈注〉 I'm in no condition [state, shape] to see people. は精神的にも肉体的にも人に会える状態ではないという意味。

すき（好き）

好きである **like; love; be fond of**
〈注〉 love は「何か大好きである」の意味で女性がよく使う。また，恋愛感情の意味でも使われる。
水泳が好きだ。
I like swimming.
彼は動物が好きだ。
He's fond of animals.
【大好き】
音楽が大好きだ。
I love music.
彼女はロックが大好きだ。
She has a passion for rock music.
彼女はダンスが大好きだ。
She loves dancing [to dance].
彼はトランプがすごく好きだ。
He's extremely fond of playing cards.
【恋愛】
ジムはケイトが好きだ。
Jim loves Kate.
cf. 彼はあの子に首ったけだ。
He dotes on her.
【好きでない】
スポーツは好きじゃない。
I don't like sports.
寿司はあまり好きでない。
I don't much care for sushi.
〈注〉◆care for は上例のような否定文，または Would you care for sushi? のように疑問文で使う。
◆I like to swim. は「水泳が好き」という事実を述べている。I would [I'd] like to swim. は「泳ぎたい」という気持ちを述べている。
【好きになる】 come to like [love]; become [grow] fond of; take a fancy to; 恋をする fall in love (with)
好きな人 《a person》 whom 《one》 loves; a lover; a boyfriend; a girlfriend; a significant other
【好きな～】
好きなこと what 《one》 likes
好きな歌手 《one's》 favorite singers
好きな食べ物 《one's》 favorite food
好きなことをしなさい。
Do whatever [anything] you like.
好きな方を取りなさい。
Take whichever you like.
好きなときに来なさい。
Come whenever [any time] you like.
好きな所に行きなさい。
Go wherever you like.
【好き嫌い】 《one's》 likes and dislikes
彼は好き嫌いが激しい。
He has many likes and dislikes.
人には好き好きがあるさ。
There is no accounting for taste.
Everyone has their own taste.
To each his own.
彼はみんなに好かれる。
Everyone likes him.
彼はどうも虫が好かない。
There's something about him that puts me off.
モダンアートはどうも好きになれない。
I have something against modern art.

…すぎ（…過ぎ）→ すぎる・すごす

1. 時
past; after
【時刻】

4時15分過ぎだ。

It's {15 minutes / (a) quarter} {past / after} four.

It's four fifteen.

もう正午過ぎだ。

It's past noon already.

1時過ぎだ。

It's after [past] 1:00 [one (o'clock)].

7時過ぎにもう一度お電話します。

I'll call again after seven (o'clock).

彼らは夜の12時も過ぎて2時，3時まで話し続けた。

They talked past midnight and into the early [small] hours of the morning.

〈注〉 昼の12時は noon, 夜の12時は midnight。

【定刻】

列車は定刻10分過ぎに到着した。

The train arrived ten minutes behind time [late].

【日時】

20日過ぎにまた電話してください。

Please call again sometime after the 20th.

2. 年齢

over; past

60歳過ぎの人　a man past [over] sixty

彼はもう60過ぎだ。

He is over [past] sixty now.

3. 過度

too

食べすぎ，飲みすぎに注意しなければいけない。

You should be careful not to eat and drink too much.

働きすぎないように。

Don't work too hard.

Don't overwork.

ひとりで外に出すには彼は小さすぎる。

He is too young to go out alone.

着くのが少々早[遅]すぎた。

I arrived a little too early [late].

1000円もらいすぎです。

This is a thousand yen too much.

3冊多いです。

There are three books too many.

実験のクラスで生徒が10人多すぎた。

There were ten students {too many / over the limit} in the lab class.

〈注〉 too many の反対「少なすぎる」は too few。

すぎる（過ぎる）・すごす

1. 時

過ぎる 動 自 **pass;** 過す 動 他 **spend**

時が過ぎてゆく。

Time passes.

1週間が過ぎた。

A week passed.

日本に来て5年が過ぎた。

{It's (been) five years / Five years have passed} since I came to Japan.

〈注〉 次のように書くのは誤り。

×It's passed five years since ...

【時を過す】

東京で1週間過した。

I spent a week in Tokyo.

休暇はどうして過しましたか。

How did you spend your vacation?

〈注〉 ×How did you spend in your vacation?

いかがお過しですか。(手紙文)

How are you getting along?

飲んだり，しゃべったり愉快に過した。

We had a good time talking and drinking.

休暇を楽しく過した。

We had a nice vacation.

あの頃は無駄にぶらぶら時を過していた。

(In) Those days I just idled away my time.

〈注〉 **pass** と **spend** pass は何となく過す，spend は何かをして時間をつかうときに使う。

Time passes. [時主語]

People {spend 《time ～ing.》 / pass 《a night at a hotel.》} [人主語]

過ぎてしまったことにくよくよするな。(過去のこと)

Don't brood about something that's over and done with.

2. 空間・通過

㊍㊀ **pass; pass by; go past** 《a shop》

【通り過ぎる】

彼女は考えごとをしていて自分の家の前を通り過ぎてしまった。

Deep in thought, she passed [went past] her own house.

列車は長いトンネルを通り過ぎて高山に着いた。

The train passed through a long tunnel and arrived at Takayama.

毎朝駅に行く途中彼は，きれいな女の子の働いている花屋の前を通り過ぎるのだった。

Every morning on his way to the station he passed a flowershop where a pretty girl worked.

その子はキャンディーが大好きだったが，決然とキャンディーショップの前を通り過ぎた。

The little boy loved candy, but he resolutely passed by the candy shop.

3. 過度

【度をこす】

僕は酒を過してしまった。

I drank too much.

皆で子供の頃の話などしていてつい興に乗って冗談が過ぎて弟を怒らせてしまった。

We were all sitting around telling stories about our childhood, and I went too far and made my brother angry.

すぐに

1. 時間

即刻 **at once; immediately; right away**

(一刻の猶予もなく)ただちに **instantly; in an instant [a second, a moment]**

東京に着いたらすぐに電話をください。

Call [Phone] me as soon as you arrive in Tokyo.

彼を見たらすぐわかった。

I knew him the instant [moment] I saw him.

すぐ行くよ。(4, 5分以内)

I'm coming { in a minute [a moment, a second]. / in no time [right away].

〈注〉 in the twinkling of an eye〔*literary*〕; in a jiffy〔*Informal*〕のような言い方もある。

この薬はすぐに効く。

This medicine works at once [immediately, right away].

〈注〉 薬は instantly には効かない。

【まもなく】 soon; before long

すぐに4時だ。

It's nearly four o'clock.

すぐに晴れる。

It will clear up before long.

すぐに帰ります。

I'll be back soon [in a little bit].

I shan't be long.〔英〕

すぐに試験だ。

The examination is close at hand.

すぐにクリスマスだ。

Christmas is just around the corner.

もうすぐ40歳です。

I'll be forty before long.

I'm almost [close to] forty.

2. 容易に

easily; readily

彼はすぐに怒る。

He is easily [readily] offended.

彼女はちょっとしたことですぐに泣く。

She cries at the least provocation.

彼女はすぐに船に酔う。

She gets seasick easily [quickly]. (たちまち)

これはすぐに壊れるから取り扱いに気をつけて。

This will break easily, so be careful (in) handling it.
この問題はすぐに解ける。
This can be solved without difficulty.
【すぐに役立つ】 very useful; practical
この旅行案内書はすぐに役に立ちますよ。
This travel guide will be very useful.
【すぐに食べられる】 ready to eat
今すぐ食べられるものないかしら。
Is there anything I can eat now?
What is there to eat?
冷蔵庫の中にすぐに食べられるようにして食事３日分を入れてあるよ。
There're meals for three days in the refrigerator.
スーパーに行くとすぐに食べられる食品がますます多くなっている。
There are more and more ready-to-eat foods in the supermarket.
〈注〉 ready-to-eat foods は調理済み食品。

3. 空間
彼女は私のすぐ近くに住んでいる。
She lives nearby [close by, near me].
うちはここから歩いてすぐのところです。
My house is within easy walking distance of here.
私は男の人がすぐ目の前で車にはねられるのを見た。
I saw a car hit a man right before my eyes.
彼の小さな妹が彼のすぐ後からぴったりくっついてやって来た。
His little sister followed close behind him.

すごい（凄い）

1. ひどい，怖い
dreadful; horrible; 無気味な **ghastly; grim**
すごい光景
a ghastly [horrible] scene; a dreadful sight
彼はすごい目つきで私を見た。
He glared at me.
何かすごいにおいがする。
It smells awful in here.

2. 並はずれた
卓越した **amazing; wonderful**
すごい美人 a knock-out beauty 〔*slang*〕
彼はすご腕の持ち主だ。
He's a man of amazing ability.
すごい！
Fantastic！/ Superb！/ Incredible！/ Ohhhh ...！/ Amazing！
〔*colloq.*〕 Whew！/ Oh, boy！/ Man！
〔*slang*〕 Wow！/ Groovy！/ Out of sight！
〈注〉 このほかにも多くの言い方がある。俗語の場合は流行があり，次々と新しいものに変っていく。
【過度の】 awful, terrible
すごいスピードで
at tremendous [terrible] speed
列車はすごい込みようだった。
The train was terribly [awfully] crowded.

すこしも（少しも）→ ちっとも

ずっと

1. 継続 ［進行形・完了形を使うことが多い］
all the while (時間的)**; all the way** (空間的)
それでは私に会いたくてここまでずっと歩いて来たってわけか。
I see. You've walked all this way just to see me!
私はずっと１時間も彼を待っている。
I've been waiting an hour for him.
私は明日はずっと家にいる。
I'll be home all day tomorrow.
I'll be free all day tomorrow.（ひまだ）
ブラウン氏はずっと病気だ。
Mr. Brown has been ill [sick] for a long time.
彼女はずっと独身を通した。

She never married all her life.

【ずっと～(動詞)づめ】

大阪からずっと立ちづめだった。

I was standing all the way from Osaka.

朝早くからずっと働きづめだ。

She has been working from early this morning.

あの人はその間ずっとしゃべりづめだった。

She kept talking all the while.

〈注〉 all the while は上のように副詞句として使う用法のほかに節を導くこともできる。

All the while I was packing my things, he stood there smoking.（私が荷造りをしている間ずっと彼は立ったままそばでたばこを吸っていた）

2．程度

【時】

ずっと昔（昔話の出だし）

once upon a time; many years ago; quite a long time ago

ずっと後

many years later [afterwards]

long afterward(s)

私の生れるずっと前に祖父は亡くなった。

Grandfather died long before I was born.

(それから)ずっと後になって彼に会った。

I met him many years { after that (incident). / afterward(s). / later. }

【空間】

人波の中ずっと向うにその男の姿を認めた。

I spotted the man far off [away] in the crowd.

これをずっと行くと市の中心部に出ます。

{ If you go straight on you'll come / This road leads } to the center of the city.

道の両側は何マイルもずっととうもろこし畑だった。

On both sides of the road corn fields stretched for miles.

【比較】

彼はずっとよくなった。

He is getting much better.

彼はみんなが考えているよりずっと元気です。

He is { far healthier / healthier by far } than everyone believes.

この方があちらよりずっといい。

This one is much [far] better than that.

すなお（素直）→ おとなしい

〈注〉 単純に英訳できない語である。文化を背景にした価値感の相違があるので，それぞれの場合を考えて訳し分けねばならない。

1．子供の場合

素直な子[よい子]

an obedient child; a good child

2．中・高校生から若い人の場合

〈注〉 10代から21, 22歳ぐらいの者を大人が批評する言葉として。

トム[ケイト]は素直な子だ。

Tom is a nice boy.

Kate is a nice girl.

ジムは素直で扱いやすかった。

Jim wasn't troublesome; in fact he was easy to deal with.

〈注〉 docile（おとなしい)は反論や口答え（arguing back）をしないことで，しばしばよくない意味。日本との文化的相違である。

3．成人の場合

彼は人の意見を素直に聞く。

He is ready to listen to others' advice.

4．その他

素直に白状しろ。(容疑者を責める言い方)

Tell us [Say] frankly what you have done.

彼の文体は素直でわかりやすい。

His style is natural and easy to understand.

すばらしい（素晴らしい）

wonderful; marvelous

〈注〉（上より下が，また右にいくほど度合いが強い）
great; wonderful; excellent;
glorious; magnificent; splendid; superb

1．目に見える美しさ

すばらしい天気
glorious weather, a beautiful day
すばらしい眺望
a magnificent [splendid, superb, lovely] view
すばらしい演技　a superb performance
すばらしい美人　（→すごい）
a great [stunning] beauty
ルイーズはすばらしく美人だ。
Louise is strikingly beautiful.

2．すぐれている，立派な

すばらしい考え
a splendid [great, wonderful, superb] idea
すばらしい成功
a dazzling [glorious] success
すばらしい業績
a brilliant achievement

3．その他

彼はすばらしく英語ができる。
His English is wonderful [excellent].
He speaks wonderful [excellent] English.
すばらしい！　（→すごい）
That's great [super, wonderful, superb]!
That's simply marvelous!
How fantastic!

すべきこと → すること

すべて

all; every; whole

〈注〉 all は全体をひっくるめてみんな，全部。every はひとつひとつみんな。all が可算名詞を伴うときは複数にして動詞も複数一致。every は常に単数扱い。whole は全体をひっくるめ，丸ごとの感じであり，前後関係で単数・複数が決る。

【人はすべて】
人はすべて幸福を追求する権利をもっている。
Everyone has the right to seek happiness.
人はすべて食べることが好きだ。
Everybody likes to eat.
町中の人はすべて寝入ったところだった。
The whole town [Everyone in the town] was asleep.
〈注〉「すべての人」の意味では all (the) people よりも everyone の方が普通に使われる。前者の方が speech の style（演説調）で，All people everywhere fear war.（すべての人が戦争を恐れている）のように使われる。

【全面的に】
すべて私の責任である。
I { am wholly [entirely, solely] / alone am } responsible for this.
すべて君の決断にかかっている。
It depends entirely on your decision.
費用はすべて会社が持った。
The company paid for everything.

【あらゆる】
この計画の方がすべての点でまさっている。
This plan is better in all respects.

【すべてである】
金がすべての世の中だ。
In this world money is all [everything].
彼女には１人息子がすべてであった。
Her only son was everything to her.

【すべてをささげる】
give everything《one》has for《something》
彼はがん制圧に彼の持つものすべてをささげた。
He gave everything he had for the conquest of cancer.
彼は戦後，故郷の町の再建にすべてをささげた。
He devoted [gave] himself entirely to the

reconstruction of his home town after the war.

〈注〉 all, every が否定表現と結びつくと部分否定になるので注意。

He doesn't know everything about it.（すべてを知っているわけではない）

cf. He knows nothing.（何も知らない）

スポーツ

a sport; sports

スポーツをする　play sports

スポーツマン　a sportsman; an athlete

スポーツマンシップ　sportsmanship

スポーツマンタイプ　athletic type

スポーツ医学　sports medicine

スポーツウェア　sportswear

スポーツカー　a sports car

スポーツセンター　a sports center

スポーツドリンク　isotonic drink

スポーツニュース　sports news

スポーツ用品　sporting goods〔米〕, sports equipment〔英〕

スポーツ欄　a sports page; sports section

ウインタースポーツ　winter sports

屋外スポーツ　outdoor sports

室内スポーツ　indoor sports

プロスポーツ　professional sports

スポーティーな服装で　in sporty clothes

好きなスポーツは何ですか。

What sport do you like best?

何かスポーツをしていますか。

What sports do you ⌊enjoy doing [play]?

テレビでスポーツを見るのが好きだ。

I like to watch sports on TV.

《関連語》

1. 競技大会

オリンピック　the Olympics

オリンピック冬季競技大会　the Winter (Olympic) Games; the Winter Olympics

国際オリンピック委員会　International Olympics Committee(IOC)

日本オリンピック委員会　Japan Olympics Committee(JOC)

オリンピック憲章　the Olympics Charter

パラリンピック　the Paralympics

ユニバーシアード(国際学生スポーツ大会)　the Universiade

国民体育大会(国体)　the National Athletic Meet

2. 運動種目

【陸上競技】track and field

トラック競技　track

短距離走　short distance race

長距離走　long distance race

リレー　relay (race)

フィールド競技　field

走り幅跳び　broad (or long) jump

走り高飛び　high jump

三段飛び　triple jump

棒高飛び　pole vault

砲丸投げ　shot put

円盤投げ　discus throw

やり投げ　javelin throw

ハンマー投げ　hammer throw

ハードル競走　hurdle race

マラソン　marathon

駅伝競走

long-distance road relay race; Ekiden

【水泳】water sports

自由形　freestyle

平泳ぎ　breaststroke

バタフライ　butterfly

背泳ぎ　backstroke

クロール　the crawl (swimming stroke)

メドレーリレー　medley relay

水球　water polo

シンクロナイズド・スイミング　synchronized swimming

飛び込み　diving

【体操】

体操競技　gymnastics

新体操　rhythmic gymnastics

【球技】

野球　baseball(→やきゅう)

オールスターゲーム　an All-Star game

日本シリーズ　the Japan Series
大リーグ　Major League
ドラフト制　draft system
ゴルフ　golf
マスターズ　The Masters Tournament
グランドスラム　grand slam
パー　par
バーディ　birdie
ホールインワン　hole-in-one
キャディー　caddy
グリーン　green
サッカー　soccer
国際サッカー連盟　Federation Internationale de Football Association (FIFA)
ワールドカップ　the World Cup (soccer)
フォワード　forward
ミッドフィルダー　midfielder
ディフェンダー　defender
ゴールキーパー　goalkeeper
ペナルティー・キック　penalty kick
コーナー・キック　corner kick
ラグビー　rugby
アメリカン・フットボール　(American) football
スーパーボール　Super Bowl
テニス　tennis
グランドスラム　grand slam
ウインブルドン選手権大会　Wimbledon Championship
デビスカップ　Davis Cup
シングルス　singles
ダブルス　doubles
卓球　table tennis [pingpong]
バスケットボール　basketball
バレーボール　volleyball
ソフトボール　softball
バドミントン　badminton
ハンドボール　handball
ボウリング　bowling
ホッケー　(field) hockey
ラケットボール　racquetball
スカッシュ　squash

【格闘技・武道】
相撲　sumo
柔道　judo
剣道　kendo
弓道　Japanese archery
ボクシング　boxing
レスリング　wrestling
フェンシング　fencing
空手　karate
太極拳　Chinese Shadow boxing

【マリンスポーツ】 water sports
サーフィン　surfing
ボードセーリング　board sailing
スキューバダイビング　scuba diving

【ウインタースポーツ】 winter sports
スキー　skiing
アルペンスキー　alpine skiing
ダウンヒル(滑降競技)　downhill skiing
スラローム(回転競技)　slalom skiing
クロスカントリー　crosscountry skiing
モーグル　moguls
ジャンプ競技　ski jumping
スケート　(ice) skating
スピードスケート　speed skating
フィギュアスケート　figure skating
アイスダンス　ice dancing
アイスホッケー　(ice) hockey
リュージュ　luge sledding
ボブスレー　bobsledding
スノーボード　snowboarding

3. 運動競技関係語彙

【試合】
game　1打，1点で競う試合
set　一定の得点で勝負をきめる試合
match　対抗試合
tournament　勝ち抜き試合

【審判】
umpire　(野球・テニスなど)
referee　(ボクシング・サッカーなど)
judge　(フィギュアスケートなど)

【競技場】 stadium; sports arena
トラック　track
フィールド　field
グランド　sports ground
リンク　links

コート　court (grass court, clay court)
ゴルフコース　golf course
リング　ring
ジム　gym (gymnasium の略)
【関連表現】
勝つ　win (→かつ)
負ける　lose; be defeated (→まける・まかす)
新記録を作る　set [establish] a new record
自己ベスト　one's personal best
世界記録を破る　break the world record
優勝する　win the championship; win the gold medal in …
雨のため試合が中止になった。
The game was called off because of the rain.

すまい（住まい）→ じゅうきょ

すます（済ます）・すむ

1. 完了する

すます［人主語］**finish; be [get] through; get finished; be finished**
すむ［事主語］**end; come to an end; be over**

宿題をすませましたか[はすみましたか]。
Have you done [finished] your homework?
Are you through [finished, done] with your homework?〔米〕

すまして[すんで]からドライブに行こう。
Let's go for a drive after
{ we've finished.
 we're finished.〔米〕
 we're through.〔米〕

勘定はすましたよ[すんだよ]。
I have paid my bill.

何もかも無事にすますことができて[すんで]本当によかった。
I'm so glad everything has gone well [smoothly].

試験がすんだ。
The examination is over.

その本すんだら貸してくださいませんか。
Could you lend me the book
{ after [when] you are done with it?〔米〕
 after you've finished with it?〔英〕

昼食はすみましたか。
Have you eaten [had, finished] lunch yet?

2. 解決する

みんなすんだことだ。
That's all over and done with.

すんだことは仕方がない。
What's done is done.
What's done cannot be undone.

これで気がすんだ？
Are you satisfied?

金ではすまない。
Money cannot settle the problem.

このままではすまされない[何かしなければならない]。
Something should be done about it.

この問題はこのままではすまされない。いっそ真正面からぶつかってみてはどうだ。
This problem won't go away, so you might as well face it and do something about it.

雨が降れば行かないですむ。
If it's raining I don't have to go.

3. 間に合せる

【簡略】
朝食は紅茶とシリアルだけですませた。
I had only cereal and a cup of tea for breakfast.

【代用する】
バターを切らしたのでマーガリンですました。
I'd run out of butter, so I made do with margarine.

【省略する】
いつも朝食抜きですましたものだ。
I used to do [go] without breakfast.

【間に合せる】
1か月7万円ですましている。
I can just manage to get by on 70,000 yen a

month.

1か月10万円以内ですましている。

I can {get along / manage} on less than 100,000 yen a month.

彼女は車なしで何とかすましている。

She can do [manage, get along, get by] without a car.

〈注〉 can do は余裕が感じられる。manage, get along は何とかやること。get by はもっと厳しく努力をしたことが感じられる。

【すまされない】

昨今はクレジットカードなしではすまされない。

We cannot live [do] without credit cards nowadays.

その言葉は冗談ではすまされない。

What you have just said is too cynical to laugh away as a joke.

4. 軽くすむ

ほんのかすり傷ですんだ。

Luckily he got by [escaped] with only a few scratches [slight bruises].

彼は罰金ですんだ。

He was let off [got off] with a fine.

所得税を払わないですむ。

I can get out of paying income tax.

5. 感謝・陳謝

【感謝】

(ご多忙の中を)すみません。

Thank you for coming.

【陳謝】

お待たせしてすみません。

I'm sorry I've kept you waiting.

【呼びかけ】

すみません。郵便局はどう行ったらいいんでしょうか。

Excuse me, but can [will] you tell me the way to the post office please?

〈注〉 感謝の意味で I'm sorry. と言ってはおかしい。

する

1. 行動する

do

どうするつもり？

What are you going to do?

好きなようにしなさい。

Do as you like.

【do＋名詞】

買い物をする

do《one's, the》shopping; shop; go shopping

いつもどこで買い物するの？

Where do you do your shopping?

私が料理をして妹が洗濯をする。

I do the cooking and my sister does the washing.

皿洗いをする　do the dishes

〈注〉 日本語の「する」は行為を表す基本的な動詞で「勉強する」「野球をする」のように名詞に付け加えて動詞の働きをするが, do をそれと同じに考えてはいけない。「勉強する」は ×do study ではなくて1語の動詞 study,「野球をする」は ×do baseball ではなくて play baseball である。しかし「宿題をする」は do one's homework でよい。

【do 以外の動詞＋名詞】

トランプをしよう。

Let's play cards.

彼らは野球をしている。

They are playing baseball.

彼は柔道をしている。

He practices judo.

危いことをするな。

Don't take a risk.

【動詞のみ】

返事をする　answer

旅行をする　travel; go traveling

ダンスをする　dance

勉強をする　study

料理をする　cook; do the cooking

子守りをする　babysit; do babysitting

結婚をする　marry; get married

〈注〉 幸せな結婚をしたい。

×I wish to do a happy marriage.

○I wish [hope] to have a happy marriage.

2. 処理する

do with

その金をどうするつもりか。

What are you going to do with the money?

3. 変える，つくる

民衆は彼をスウェーデン王にした。

They crowned him King of Sweden.

彼らは私を部長にした。

They made me captain of the team.

彼を味方[仲間]にしよう。

Let's get him on our side.

彼は息子を医者にしたかった。

He wanted his son to be [become] a doctor.

彼は妻をきっと幸福にすると言った。

He said he would do his best to make his wife happy.

小切手を現金にしてください。

Please cash this check.

1000円札を小銭［100円硬貨］にしていただけますか。

Can you give me change [100 yen coins] for this (1000 yen note)?

4. 従事する

【職業】

店員をする　be a salesclerk (at a book store)

アルバイトをする(スーパーで/ウェイトレスとして)

work part-time (at a supermarket / as a waitress)

本屋をする　have [run] a bookstore

〈注〉 ×My father is doing a bookstore. とは言わない。

弁護士をする　practice [practise] law

教員をする　be a teacher; teach

通訳をする

be an interpreter; interpret; do interpreting

家庭教師をする

be a tutor; do tutoring; tutor

5. 病気にかかる

彼は病気をして退職を余儀なくされた。

He became [got] ill [sick] and had to retire.

彼女は5歳のときはしかをした。

She had measles when she was five.

〈注〉 「はしか」に限らず病気を「した」は，do を使うことはない。×My children did measles.

6. 値段

この時計はいくらしたの？

How much was this watch?

それは3万5000円もした。

It cost me a whole 35,000 yen.

7. 時の経過

彼は2，3日するとだいぶよくなった。

He began to improve [get better] in a few days.

3，4年もするとあの人も立派な調理師になるでしょう。

He will be a fine cook in three years or so.

8. 感覚

【声[音]がする】

となりの部屋から女の人の声[変な音]がした。

I heard a woman's voice [a strange sound] from [in] the next room.

【においがする】

階下からカレーのにおいがしてきた。

I smelled curry downstairs.

【気がする】

何かいいことがありそうな気がした。

I felt something good would happen.

9. その他

男は逃げようとした。

The man tried to run [get] away.

彼はおぼれる子を助けようとして川に飛び込んだ。

He jumped into the river to save the drowning boy.

すること

【…すること】

早起きすることは健康によい。

To get [Getting] up early is good for health.

【…したこと】

今朝あなたが早起きしたことは知っています。

I know that you got up early this morning.

〈注〉 上の例「…したこと」は事実を述べる形。それに対して「…すること」は一般化・抽象化された観念を述べる形である。

【すべきこと】 →こと

私のすべきこと

what I should do; my job; my duty

〈注〉 このmy job は職業の意味ではない。duty は道徳的義務感を感じさせる語。

私のすべきこと[私は何をすべきか]がわからない。

I don't know what I should do.

〈注〉 目の前の現実的な仕事についても，またもっと大きな社会的道徳的な任務についての決断の場合にも使える表現。

cf. I don't know what to do.（どうしたらいいかわからない）

この表現は「決断」がつかず困惑している場合や手持ち無沙汰で困っている場合にも使える。what to do と What I should do はたいへん近いが，この二つの表現の混同で×I don't know what I do と書くのは誤り。

せ

せい → ため

1. 原因

【…のせいで】 because of; due to

暑さのせいで皆不機嫌で怒りっぽかった。

They were sullen and irritable because of the heat.

過労のせいですよ。

You're overworking [working too hard].

〈注〉「病気になった」「体がだるい」といった前後関係から明らかなのが普通なので，Your illness comes from overwork. などとすると不自然になる。

そりゃ，気のせいですよ。

You're imagining things.

It's all in your mind [head].〔*colloq.*〕

2. 責任（→せきにん）

【…のせい】

列車に乗り遅れたのはお前のせいだ。

It's {because of you / your fault} that we missed the train.

〈注〉It's all your fault.（みんなお前のせいだ）はひどく責める言い方である。fault は誤っているということで道徳に通じる考え方を含む語。一方 mistake は不正確なこと。

だれのせいでもない。私が悪いのだ。

No, no one else is to blame! I am the one (who is) responsible (for that).

【人のせいにする】

自分が悪いのに人のせいにするんじゃない。

Don't blame others when you are at fault (yourself).

Don't put [lay] the blame on someone else for your own mistake.

It's your fault. Don't blame others.

彼はいつも何かあると人のせいにする。

He always shifts his responsibility onto others.

事故は彼のせい[責任]だ。方向指示のサインを出すべきだったのだから。

{The accident was his fault / He caused the accident / He was responsible for the accident} because he should have had his directional light on.

せいかく（性格）→ せいしつ・せいかく

せいかつ（生活）

生活 **life;** 生活する **live; get along**

生計 **livelihood;** 生計を立てる **make a living [livelihood]; support**《oneself》(**on**)

都会生活 town life

田園生活 country life

簡素[ぜいたく]な生活

plain [luxurious] living

日常生活 daily life

家庭生活 home [family] life

学生生活 school [college] life

社会生活 social life

独身[結婚]生活 single [married] life

【生活のため】

大部分の人が生活のために働かねばならない。

Most people must work for a living.

【生活している[生計を立てている]】

彼は魚を売って生活している。

He makes a [his] living by selling fish.

彼らは年金で生活している。

They are living on a pension.

【生活必需品】 daily necessities (of life)

【生活費】

cost of living; 家計費 living expenses

昨年は生活費の上昇はわずかであった。

The cost of living rose only a little last year.

彼らの生活費は1か月最低20万円は必要だ。

They need at least 200,000 yen a month to

cover living expenses.

【生活[暮しむき]が安定する】

彼は今,生活が安定している[安定した収入を得ている]。

He now has a good job and a stable income.

【裕福な生活をする】 live in comfort

【幸福な[みじめな]生活】

a happy [miserable] life

このところ私は幸福な生活をしています。

My life has been quite happy lately.

【生活に困る】 be very badly off; be very poor

交通事故で大けがをしてから，彼は生活にも困っている。

After being badly injured in a traffic accident, he was unable to make a living. 〔*written*〕

両親とも失業して家族は生活に困っている。

Now that both parents are unemployed, the family is very badly off.

【その日暮しの生活をする】

live from hand to mouth

never know where the next meal is coming from

《関連表現》

【一日の生活】

目覚める

wake (up)

お母さんは明るくなるとすぐ目を覚す。

My mother wakes up as soon as it gets light.

目覚しが鳴って目を覚した。

The alarm woke me (up).

起す　wake

お母さん，きっと7時に起してね。

Mum, {will you / be sure to} {call / wake} me at seven?

〈注〉 Will you ... ? の方がていねい。be sure は強く念を押す言い方。

起きる(床を出る) get up; get out of bed

〈注〉 wake は目覚める(自動詞)，目覚めさせる・起こす(他動詞)の両用法がある。

目覚める wake up と起き出す get out of bed は別のことであり，寝る go to bed と眠りにつく fall asleep も別のことである。

ex. On weekdays I have to get up at six, but on Sundays, I don't have to get up right away when I wake up. (ふだんの日は6時に起きなければならないが日曜日は目が覚めてもすぐに起きなくてもいい)

服を着る　get dressed

(着ている状態は be dressed)

〈注〉 dress (oneself) は子供の場合か，特別丹念に身じたくするときのみ使う。

顔を洗う　wash one's face

歯をみがく　brush one's teeth

髪をとかす　comb [brush] one's hair

髪を整える　do one's hair

ひげをそる　shave

化粧をする　put on one's make-up

朝食[昼食]をとる

have breakfast [lunch]

夕食をとる

have dinner [supper (軽い夕食)]

仕事に[学校へ]行く

go to work [school]

歩いて[自転車で / 車で]仕事に[学校へ]行く

walk [bicycle / ride] to work [school]

家を出る　leave home

会社[学校]へ着く　reach the office [school]

通勤する　commute (between Yokohama and Tokyo); commute from home to office

帰る，帰宅する　come home; return home

買い物に行く　go shopping

宿題をする　do one's homework

テレビを見る　watch TV

遊ぶ　play (子供)

ふざける　fool around〔*informal*〕

おしゃべりをする　talk to《a person》

CDをかける[聞く]

play [listen to] compact disc

トランプ[ゲーム]をする

play cards [a game]

入浴する　have [take] a bath

床につく　go to bed

眠りにつく　go to sleep; fall asleep

眠る　sleep

ぐっすり眠っている

be fast asleep ; be sleeping well

せいこう（成功）

成功 **success** （↔ failure）; 成就 **accomplishment;** 業績 **achievement;** 繁栄 **prosperity**
成功する **succeed in; be successful in;** 出世する **get on in life [in the world]; rise [succeed] in the world**

［人主語］
彼は事業に成功した。
He {succeeded / was successful} in business.
彼は成功者だ。彼は彼の会社の社長にまで出世した。
He was a success. He rose all the way to president of his company.
彼はエレクトロニクスの分野では成功者だった。
He was a great success in the electronics world.
彼は芸術家としては成功したが，父親としては失格だった。
He was a success as an artist but a failure as a father.
彼は舞台俳優としては大成功を収めたが，ハリウッド(映画)ではだめだった。
He was a great success in the theater, though he'd failed in Hollywood.

［事主語］
会社全体としてはまあ成功したと言える。
The company as a whole was successful.
彼の事業［彼女のコンサート］は大成功だった。
His business [Her concert] was a great success.

【成功しない】
実験が成功しなかった。
The experiment did not turn out well.

【成功させる】
彼はその事業を大成功させた。
He led the project to great success.
創業者松下幸之助は松下電器産業を国際的に名の通った会社として成功させた。
Matsushita Konosuke, founder of Matsushita Electric Industrial Co., has led it to international success and fame.

【成功する見込みがある［ない］】
この仕事で成功する見込みは十分ある［まずない］。
{He has a good [no] chance / There is every [no] chance} of {succeeding / success} in this business.

【成功を祈る】
Good luck!
I wish you success.

〈注〉 success は He was a great success. のように「成功者」の意にも使われる。この場合は可算名詞 a success と冠詞が必要。He was a great success at last Saturday's party. は「大喝采を浴びた」という程度の意。
　また，動詞 succeed は「成功する」の意のときは自動詞で succeed in《something》の形をとる。succeed to《a throne》(王位を継承する) と to をとるときや，他動詞として succeeded his father as King of Sweden (スウェーデン王として父の後を継いだ) のように使われる場合は「後継者となる」「後を継ぐ」の意となる。

せいじ（政治）

政治 **politics;** 統治，政府 **government;** 行政 **administration**
政治家 **a politician**

1．政治

【三権分立】 the division of the three powers
立法　legislature; 形 legislative
行政　the executive
司法　the judiciary; 形 judicial
【政府】 government
中央政府
national government （↔ local government）
【内閣】 a cabinet; the Cabinet
内閣総理大臣　Prime Minister
内閣府　Prime Minister's Office
内閣官房長官　Chief Cabinet Secretary
【閣僚】 cabinet ministers

【省庁】
省　ministry; 大臣　minister
庁　agency; 長官　director general
総務省[大臣]
Ministry [Minister] of Public Management, Home Affairs, Posts and Telecommunications
法務省[大臣]　Ministry [Minister] of Justice
外務省[大臣]　Ministry [Minister] of Foreign Affairs
財務省[大臣]　Ministry [Minister] of Finance
文部科学省[大臣]　Ministry [Minister] of Education, Culture, Sports, Science and Technology
厚生労働省[大臣]　Ministry [Minister] of Health, Labor and Welfare
農林水産省[大臣]　Ministry [Minister] of Agriculture, Forestry and Fisheries
経済産業省[大臣]　Ministry [Minister] of the Economy, Trade and Industry
国土交通省[大臣]　Ministry [Minister] of Land, Infrastructure and Transport
環境省[大臣]　Ministry [Minister] of the Environment
防衛庁(長官)　(Director General of the) Defense Agency
〈注〉◆大臣の呼称として「～相」という言い方があるが英語でも簡単な言い方がある。たとえば法相 Justice Minister, 環境相 Environment Minister のように省名のあとに Minister を付ける言い方である。外相は Foreign Minister。
◆国務大臣（～担当）は State Minister (for ～), Minister of State (in charge of ～)。
男女共同参画担当大臣　Minister of State (Gender Equality)
国家公安委員長　Chairman of the National Public Safety Commission
防災担当大臣　Minister of State for Disaster Management
沖縄及び北方対策担当大臣　Minister of State for Okinawa and Northern Territories Affairs
科学技術政策担当大臣　Minister of State for Science and Technology Policy
経済財政政策担当大臣　Minister of State for Economic and Fiscal Policy
規制改革担当大臣　Minister of State for Regulatory Reform
金融担当大臣　Minister for Financial Service
内閣法制局長官　Director General of the Cabinet Legislation Bureau
安全保障会議　Security Council of Japan
人事院　National Personnel Authority
組閣する　form [organize] a cabinet
総辞職する　resign en masse; 名 mass resignation; blanket resignation〔米〕
【政党】political party
与党　the ruling party; the party in power
野党　the opposition party
保守党　the conservative party
革新党　the reformist party
急進派　the radical wing of the party
右派　the right wing
左派　the left wing
自由民主党
the Liberal Democratic Party (略 LDP)
公明党　Komeito
民主党
the Democratic Party of Japan (略 DPJ)
社会民主党
the Social Democratic Party (略 SDP)
日本共産党
the Japanese Communist Party (略 JCP)
党首　the party leader（欧米では党により呼称が異なる）
党員　party members
…派　the ... faction
【議会】national assembly
[日本]
国会　the Diet
衆議院　the House of Representatives
衆議院議員　member of the House of Representatives, Representative
参議院　the House of Councilors
参議院議員　member of the House of Councilors, Councilor
国会議員　Dietman; Dietwoman; Diet member
衆議院議長　the Speaker
参議院議長　the President
[米国]
国会　Congress

上院　the Senate
上院議員　Senator
下院　the House of Representatives
下院議員　Representive; member of the House; Congressman [Congresswoman]（上院議員を指すこともある）
上院議長　President of the Senate（副大統領が兼ねる）
下院議長　Speaker of the House
臨時議長　President Pro-Tem of the Senate
［英国］
国会　Parliament
上院　House of Lords [Upper House]
下院　House of Commons [Lower House]
上院［下院］議員　member of Parliament
議長　President of the House of Commons [Lords]
【国会】
会期　session
本会議　plenary session
通常国会　ordinary [regular] session
特別国会　special session
臨時国会　extraordinary session
施政方針演説
policy statement [speech]
基本政策演説
keynote address [speech]（党大会などで行う）
議事日程　agenda
法案　draft; bill
政府は法案を国会に提出する。
The government will present [submit] the bill to the Diet.
修正案　draft amendment
予算案　budget
臨時予算案が次の国会に提出されるだろう。
An extraordinary budget will be {introduced in / proposed in} the next session of the Diet.
動議　motion; 緊急動議　emergency motion
質問　question; formal questioning
答弁　answer
小泉首相は野党質問の答弁に立った。
Prime Minister Koizumi took the floor to answer the opposition's questions.
財務長官は上院財務委員会で証言した。
The Secretary of the Treasury testified before the Senate Finance Committee.〔米〕
審議する　debate [take up] a bill
信任票　vote of confidence
不信任票　vote of no-confidence
決定票（賛否同数の場合，議長などが投ずる）
casting vote
採決する　vote; vote for
過半数　majority
可決される，通過する
pass; be passed; be carried
法案は下院を通過した。
The bill passed the Lower House.
否決される　be rejected
廃案となる，流れる　die
動議は150対120で否決［可決］された。（数字は大きい方を先にする）
The motion was rejected [passed] by a vote of 150 to 120.
税制の法案は上院で廃案となった。
The tax bill died on the Senate [Upper House] floor.
選挙（→せんきょ）
国勢調査　census
国勢調査を行う
conduct [take] a national census
世論調査　a public opinion poll
世論調査をする　take an opinion poll
【地方政治】
知事　governor
市長　mayor
県議会　prefectural assembly
cf. state legislature〔米〕州議会
県議会議員
a member of the prefectural assembly
市議会　city council
市議会議員
a member of the city council
a city councilor
自治　autonomy
【役人】（→やくにん）
高官　government official
公衆衛生の技官・警官などの上位の者

public official
一般の役人　civil servant

2．国際関係

大国　big power
超大国　superpower
先進国　advanced country
発展途上国　developing country
第三世界　the Third World
第三世界の国　third-world country

【主義・理念】

帝国主義　imperialism
国家主義　nationalism
社会主義　socialism
共産主義　communism
ファシズム　fascism
ナチズム　Nazism
民主主義　(idea of) democracy

【国際連合と国際機構】

国際連合，国連　the United Nations（略 UN）
国連憲章　the United Nations Charter
国連総会
the United Nations General Assembly
国連安全保障理事会
the United Nations Security Council
北大西洋条約機構
North Atlantic Treaty Organization（略 NATO）
欧州連合　European Union（略 EU）
アフリカ統一機構
Organization of African Unity（略 OAU）
アラブ連盟　Arab League
石油輸出国機構
Organization of Petroleum Exporting Countries（略 OPEC）
東南アジア諸国連合
Association of South-East Asian Nations（略 ASEAN）
米州機構
Organization of American States（略 OAS）
世界貿易機関
World Trade Organization（略 WTO）
世界保健機構
World Health Organization（略 WHO）
経済協力開発機構
Organization for Economic Cooperation and Development（略 OECD）
アムネスティ・インターナショナル
Amnesty International
赤十字国際委員会
International Committee of the Red Cross（略 ICRC）
ユネスコ
United Nations Educational, Scientific and Cultural Organization（略 UNESCO）
ユニセフ
United Nations Children's Fund（略 UNICEF）

【外交】 diplomacy

外務大臣
［日本］　Foreign Minister
［米国］　the Secretary of State（国務長官）
［英国］　Foreign Secretary（外務大臣）
大使　ambassador
大使館　embassy
領事　consul
総領事　consul general
領事館　consulate
使節　envoy
外交官　diplomat
折衝　negotiations
事前折衝　negotiation spadework
事前協議　prior consultation
行き詰り　deadlock
決裂　breakdown
外交関係正常化
normalization of diplomatic relations
外交関係断絶
breaking off [severing] of diplomatic relations
首脳会談　summit talk [conference]
ブッシュ大統領とブレア首相の首脳会談が行われた。
A summit (conference) was held between President Bush and Prime Minister Blair.
共同声明　joint communiqué [statement]（communiqué はフランス語）
発表する　release《a message, communiqué》
親書　personal message

覚え書き　memorandum
協定　agreement; accord（拘束力が強い）
【条約】 treaty; pact
作成する　draw up
調印する　sign
批准する　ratify
締結する　conclude
遵守する　observe
破る　violate
破棄する　renounce; abrogate
平和条約　peace treaty
不可侵条約　non-aggression treaty
安全保障条約　security treaty
日米安全保障条約
the US-Japan Security Treaty
核拡散防止条約
Nuclear Non-proliferation Treaty（略 NPT）
【同盟】
同盟　alliance
非同盟　non-alignment
同盟国　ally
非同盟国，中立国
non-aligned country [nation]
【地域紛争】 regional conflicts
国境　national border [boundary]
領土　territory
民族主義　nationalism（国ではなく民族の団結意識であるが，通常 nationalism と呼ぶ）
難民　refugees
ボートピープル　boatpeople

3. 軍事

【戦い】
戦争　war
宣戦布告する
declare war on [against]《a country》
革命　revolution
反乱　rebellion
内戦　civil war
テロリズム・テロ　terrorism
中立地帯　neutral zone
非武装地帯　demilitarized zone（略 DMZ）
勝利　victory
敗北　defeat
降伏　surrender
【軍隊】
陸軍　army
海軍　navy
空軍　air force
アメリカ海軍　the US Navy
部隊　squad; corps
徴兵(制度)　draft (system)
軍隊に入る　enlist in the army
志願兵(制度)　volunteer (system)
兵役を志願する
volunteer for military service
【軍備】
武器　arms
通常兵器　conventional arms
ミサイル　missile
空対空　air-to-air
空対地　air-to-ground
地対地　ground-to-ground
地対空　surface-to-air
核兵器　nuclear weapons [arms]
核弾頭　nuclear warhead
大陸間弾道弾
intercontinental ballistic missile（略 ICBM）
原爆　atomic bomb, A-bomb
水爆　hydrogen bomb [H-bomb]
中性子爆弾　neutron bomb
原子力潜水艦　nuclear submarine
戦闘爆撃機　fighter-bomber
航空母艦　aircraft carrier
【和平】 making peace
休戦　truce
停戦　ceasefire
停戦地帯　cease-fire zone
交渉　negotiation
譲歩　concession
妥協　compromise
和平協議　peace talks [conferences]
和平申し込み　peace offers
(一方的)武装解除　(unilateral) disarmament
紛争解決　conflict resolution
対外援助　foreign aid
経済[軍事]援助　economic [military] aid

せいしつ(性質)・せいかく(性格)

《類義語》

nature　生れつきの性質・気質。

personality　個人の人柄。種々の特性を総合したもの(他人に与える印象が中心)。

disposition　性向。いつも身につけているムード的なもの。「明るい」とか「あけっぴろげである」など。

traits　特性。

temperament　生れつきの性向。

character　性格。しばしば「正直」とか「勇気がある」など，道徳的見地から見た性格。

〈注〉 character の語義

◆主体が人なら，character は道徳的な意味の性格を言う。

ex. have a good character（立派な人である）

cf. He's a character.（=an eccentric person）（あの人は変り者だ）は例外的な慣用表現。

◆主体が「人」でないときは character はそのものの特質（essence; distinctive, major characteristics）を意味する。

◆小説では作中人物をcharacter と呼び，人物の性格描写を characterization と言う。

characteristics　特色。

make-up　体質と性質。

ex. the make-up of an athlete（スポーツマンタイプ）

attribute　(人または物について)属性，本来そなえている性質。

ex. Compassion is one of the attributes of humankind.（あわれみの心は人間に備わった性質だ）

quality　質，物の性質(一般的な語)。

〈注〉 人に関しては tenderness（やさしさ）なども quality である。物の「品質」も quality。

property　物の性質。

ex. One property of steel is its hardness.（鋼鉄の一つの特性は硬いことだ）

the chemical properties of alcohol（アルコールの化学的性質）

1. 総合的判断

【人柄・性質・性格】

彼は性格が良い。

He's a kind [nice] person.

〈注〉 a nice person とは率直で思いやりがあり，一緒にいて心のなごむような人。

【気立て・気性・人が良い】

彼女は気立てが良い。

She's good-natured.

〈注〉◆気立ての良さは kind, generous, amiable, agreeable, big-hearted を含む。「いいやつ」「付き合いやすい人」の意味では，good-natured, easy to get along with とも言える。

◆have a sweet temper は「育てやすい赤ちゃん」について言う以外には使われない。

【強い，弱い】

強い性格の人

a person with an aggressive personality [character]

〈注〉 aggressive（攻撃的）であることを道徳的価値観から良いとか悪いとか見るならば character を使い，ただ単にその人のもって生れた性質として受け取るならば personality を使う。ただし，その相違に無関心で同じように使う人もいる。

彼は強い性格だ。

He has a strong personality.（自信・指導力があり弁もたつ）

He has a strong character.（自己の価値観に基づき主義主張を貫く）

次の2文は negative にひびく。

He has an aggressive personality [character].

He's a person with an aggressive character [personality].（彼は攻撃的な性格だ）

次の文は強い性格の女性を描いている。

She was going to be an exciting woman, strong in all her feelings, intelligent, reflective.

——Joyce Cary, *Growing-up*

（痛快な女性，喜怒哀楽が強く，聡明で思慮深い女性になるだろう）

短気も強い性格と言えるかもしれない。

彼は短気な人だ。

He's a quick-tempered person.

弱い性格　a weak character

【明るい性質[性格]】

彼は明るい性格だ。

He has a cheerful, open disposition.

おばあさんは陽気な性質の人だった。

My grandmother was a cheerful person [had a bright personality].

〈注〉 character か personality か，3人のアメリカ人

に分類してもらった。かなり overlap していることもわかる。

honest　正直な	character（教育により身につけた性格）	
generous　寛容な		
perverse　ひねくれた，強精な		personality（もって生れた気質）
kind-hearted　親切な		
good-natured　気立てのよい		
cheerful　明朗な		
hot-tempered　短気な，怒りっぽい		
sweet-tempered　気のよい		
natural　自然な		

2．個別的・描写的判断

やさしい性格[人柄]の

be kind-hearted; warm-hearted; humane; tender-hearted; compassionate; always sympathetic

【おとなしい性質・性格の】

彼はおとなしい性質の人だ。

He's a gentle person.

【激しい性格・気性の】 have a fiery temper

【荒々しい気性の】 have a violent temper

【まっすぐな気性の】 be upright and honest

【素直な性質[人柄]の】（→すなお）

be natural and frank

【性格が似ている】

母とケイトは性格が似ているが私は全然違う。

My mother and Kate are alike [similar] but I'm quite different from them.（前後の文から外見か性格かを判断する）

【性格が違う】

彼は私とは性格が違う。

He's quite a different person from me.

ジョンとビルは正反対の性格だ。

John and Bill have exactly opposite personalities.

【性格が合わない】

私たちは性格が合わない。

We are incompatible (by nature).

He and I don't get along.（彼と私は）

【性格的欠陥】

a flaw [defect] in one's character [personality]

〈注〉 defect の方が flaw より大きな欠点。

【性格が変る[変らない]】

彼はすっかり性格[人]が変った。

He's completely changed.

He was a changed person after that.

彼の生れつきの性質は何ともならない。

He can't help his own nature.

【日本人の性格】

the character of the Japanese people

【性格描写(小説などの)】

characterization; character description

主人公の性格が巧みに描写されている。

The hero is characterized well.

主人公の性格が18ページにはっきり書かれている。

The author has characterized the hero very well on page 18.

頼まれたらいやと言えない性格[性質]なので，くたびれていたが手伝いに行った。

I cannot refuse when I'm asked, so I went to help him although I was tired.

彼女は勝ち気な[負けるのがきらいな]性格なのでそれをやらざるをえなかった[やってのけた]。

She doesn't like to be outdone by other people, and this characteristic [trait] of hers forced her to do it.

〈注〉 上の例文のように「性格」に限定的な説明のつく場合に ×my character that I cannot refuse ... とか ×She has a character that she doesn't like to be outdone ... のように直訳を that でつなげるわけにはいかない。このような場合には内容を分解して2文に分けるとよい。

【金属の性質】

the properties of this metal

【事の性質】

事の性質上慎重に考慮しなければならない。

From the very nature of the matter, we should give it very careful consideration.

事件の性質上捜査は慎重をきわめた。

The nature of the case compelled the police to investigate very cautiously.

せいじつ（誠実）

誠実な　sincere and honest
誠実に　with sincerity
XY は私が現在まで教えさせてもらった多くの学生の中でも最も誠実な者の一人です。
Miss XY is one of the most honest and sincere students whom I have ever had the privilege of teaching.

せいしん（精神）

精神　**spirit**（↔ body, matter）; 知力 **mind;** 意志 **will**
精神的な　**spiritual**（↔ material）; **mental**（↔ physical）; 道徳的な **moral**

【心を打ち込む】
devote oneself to
do something with (all) one's heart and soul
go all out for something〔*colloq.*〕

【精神を集中する】
concentrate one's attention on something

【精神に異常をきたす】→き（気）
彼は精神に異常をきたした。
He's mentally ill.
He has gone insane [mad, crazy〔*informal*〕].
He is out of his mind.〔*informal*〕
〈注〉　婉曲に次のように言う。
Something is wrong [There's something wrong] in his head.「彼はちょっとおかしいのではないか」といった感じ。

【精神的にまいる】
彼は精神的にすっかりまいってしまった。
He has had a mental breakdown.
〈注〉　have a mental breakdown とはただ「まいる」よりひどく，通常の生活に耐えられない状態のこと。

【健全な精神】
健全な肉体に健全な精神が宿る。
A sound mind in a sound body.

【総合失調症(精神分裂病)】
schizophrenia;（患者）a schizophrenic

【精神的打撃】 a shock; a mental blow

【精神衛生】 mental hygiene; mental health
精神衛生に悪い。
It's frustrating.

【精神修養】 self-discipline; character training
精神修養のために　to improve oneself
〈注〉　米国では学校教育で時事問題（social issue of the times）をとりあげ，討論を通して考え方の指導(values training)をする。

【精神主義者】 an idealist

【精神障害児】
an educationally disadvantaged child

【…の精神】
憲法の精神　the spirit of the Constitution
時代精神　the spirit of the times
批判精神　critical spirit [mind]
〈注〉「精神」の同義語である「魂」は spirit と soul にまたがる語。ただし soul は肉体は滅びても滅びない不滅の魂を意味し宗教的含みを持つ。

せいじん（成人）

成人　**an adult**（一般的な語。また法律上の成人）;（子供に対して）**a grown-up person; a grownup**
成人する　**grow into** [**become**] **a man** [**woman**]; 成人に達する **come of age**

【成人した娘[息子]】
one's grown-up daughter [son]

【成人の日】
Adult(s') Day; Coming-of-Age-Day

【成人式】
Adult Day Ceremony

【成人向け映画[雑誌]】
a film [magazine] for adults
an adult film [magazine]
a pornographic film [magazine]

【成人教育】 adult education

【成人病】
生活習慣病　lifestyle disease
〈注〉　lifestyle and degenerative disease が正式だが，次のように説明してもよい。
diseases which begin in [at] middle age, such as cancer, hypertension, diabetes, etc.（中年からかかりやすい病気，がん・高血圧症・糖尿病などの総称）

せいせき（成績）

1．学業

【学校の成績】 one's school record [marks]

高校の成績

one's high school performance

one's record in high school

【成績表】 one's school report; a report card

成績証明書　a (school) transcript

【試験の成績】

the results of an examination [test scores]

試験成績を発表する。

announce the results of the examination

【成績が良い[悪い]】

理科の成績が良い[悪い]

{get / make} {good / bad} {grades / marks} in science

〈注〉 get はとった成績（結果）に中心があり，make は努力してとった含みがある。

彼女はたいへん成績がいい。

She does very well at school.

Her grades are excellent.

成績はどうだね。

How are you getting along in school?

How are things at school?

〈注〉 How are your studies coming along?　のように studies を使うのは大学の専門課程に入ってからのレベルである。

【成績が上がる[下がる]】

彼は成績が上がった[下がった]。

His marks [grades]

{improved [went up, got better]. / fell [dropped, got worse].}

彼は今学期は生物の成績が上がった［下がった］。

He got a better [worse] grade in biology this term.

もっといい成績をとるようにしなさい。

Try to get better marks.

〈注〉 米国の大学では成績表記の grades は A（優），B（良），C（並），D（可）および F（不可）を使う。全教科の成績の平均を grade point average という。

彼の成績は上の部である。

He is in the top [upper] third of his class academically.

彼の成績は中の部である。

His grades are average.

He is average academically.

彼の成績は平均で優の下[良の上]であった。

His college grade average was A-minus [B-plus].

彼の高校の成績は平均良の上であった。

He had a B-plus grade average in [at] high school.

彼は優秀な成績で大学を卒業した。

He graduated from university with honors.

彼の高校時代の成績は優秀でした。

He had very good high school marks [grades].

〈注〉 英米の大学では優秀な生徒は honors course（優等生コース）をとり，卒業すれば優等学位，B. A. Hons (Bachelor of Arts Honors) を取得する。

2．スポーツ

【…勝…敗の成績】

貴乃花は13勝２敗の成績であった。

Takanohana

{has 13 wins and [against] 2 losses. / has a 13-2 record.〔米〕(13-2 は thirteen to two と読む)}

中日は15勝２敗の好成績であった。

Chunichi has won fifteen games and lost only two.

【…対…で勝つ】

我々は５対１で勝った。

We won the game (by a score of) 5-1.

3．事業

【成績が良い，好成績をあげる】

彼は仕事で好成績をあげている。

He is doing fairly well in his job [his business].

彼の会社は過去３年間好成績をあげている。

During the past three years

{ his company has done very well.
  his company has done [had] a lot of business.

〈注〉 do well の反対は do poorly（業績不振）。

セールスキャンペーンは好成績をおさめた。

The sales campaign had [gave] good results.

マイクロソフト社は Windows98 で大いに業績をあげた。

Microsoft Company made large profits on Windows 98.

本年の農産物の生産高はこの10年間で最高の成績であった。

The agricultural output this year was the highest in the past ten years.

ぜいたく（贅沢）

〈注〉 「ぜいたくな」は「豪勢な」を原義とし，それを非難する「浪費的な」の意味と，「身分不相応な」の意味がある。場面に応じ英語を使い分けなければならない。

1．豪勢な

luxurious

ぜいたくに暮す live in luxury; live in an expensive style; live expensively

【ぜいたくに育つ】

彼女はぜいたくざんまいに育った。

She was brought up
{ with a silver spoon in her mouth.
  in (the lap of) luxury.

【ぜいたくにもてなす】

彼女はぜいたくにもてなすのが好きだ。

She likes to entertain lavishly.

2．浪費的な

extravagant（非難の意を含む）

あの人は着る物にぜいたくをしている。

She is extravagant about clothes.

She spends an awful lot of money on clothes.

彼は食べ物にぜいたくを言う[やかましい]。

He is very [awfully, rather] particular about the kind of food he eats.

ぜいたくにはきりがない。

There are no bounds to our desires.

We're never happy with what we have.

3．身分不相応な

彼はぜいたくだ。

He asks for too much.

He expects too much.

ぜいたくを言うな

Don't ask for too much.

Don't expect so much.

Be content with what you have.

せいちょう（成長）→ せいじん

1．成育

成長 **growth**

成長する **grow**

子供はどんどん成長する。

Children grow up quickly.

太郎は立派な若者に成長した。

Taro grew up [into [to be] a fine young man.

親というものは子供の立派な成長を願うものだ。

Parents wish their children to grow up strong and healthy.

成長した息子（→せいじん）

《one's》 grown-up son

【成長するにつれて】

彼は成長するにつれて並々ならぬ音楽の才能を見せ始めた。

As he grew older he began to show an unusual talent for music.

2．経済

【経済成長】 economic growth

【成長率】 the rate of growth

【成長産業】 a growth industry

【成長株】 a growth stock

（人について） a promising youth; a youth with a bright future;（芸術・スポーツ・芸能

の世界で）an ascending star

せいと（生徒）

［小学校］ **a（school）child; a（school）boy; a（school）girl;** ［中学校］ **a pupil; a student**〔米〕; ［高校］ **a（high school）student**〔米〕

〈注〉 米国は日本と同様に小・中・高・大の学制であり，普通 high school 以上の生徒を students と呼ぶ。英国には小学校の次は中・高を合せた種々の secondary schools がある。生徒は pupils（やや古風）または（school）boys [girls] と呼び，students と呼ぶのは大学生以上である。なお，students は大人の「研究者」の意味にも使われる。

大学生 a university [college] student

個人教授の生徒 a pupil

〈注〉 米国では pupil は小・中学校の生徒よりむしろ個人的な弟子の意に多く使われるが，それもいつも pupil と呼ぶとはかぎらない。

…学校の生徒です。

I go to … school.

〈注〉 I am a student at … school. より上の表現の方が普通。

全校生徒（集合的に）

the whole school; all the school; all the students

担任の生徒

a pupil [boy, girl]
- under [in]《one's》charge
- in《one's》class（クラス担任の場合）

《one's》pupil

《one's》student〔米〕

生徒会 a student council

生徒大会 a students' meeting

せきにん（責任）

〈注〉 仕事の始めから終りまで，またその結果に至るまでかかわることを意味する。次の(1)(2)に分けて考えられる。
(1) 引き受けた仕事を遂行する責任（duty，obligation）
(2) 仕事が不成功に終った場合の引責（blame を引き受けること）

1．責務

【責任がある，責任者である】

be responsible for; be in charge of

彼は宴会の料理調達の責任者である。

He's responsible for arranging the catering for the banquet.

彼は今，営業部の責任者である。

He's now in charge of the sales department.

〈注〉 be responsible for も be responsible for the damage のように目的語が結果を表すときは(2)の引責の意となる。

【責任を引き受ける，責任者となる】

take（on）the responsibility

彼女は学校のバザーの責任者になることを引き受けた。

She agreed to take on the responsibility of managing the school fair.

彼はクラブの部長のような責任のある地位にはつきたくなかった。

He didn't want to take on the club presidency because of the responsibilities（which）that involved.

【…の責任である】

万事スムーズに運ぶように取り仕切るのは君の責任だ。（すべては君にかかっている）

It's up to you to see that everything goes all right.

【責任感がある】

彼は責任感が強い。（性格の特徴として）

He has a strong sense of responsibility.

He's a responsible person.

彼は自分の責任を自覚している。

He's aware of his responsibility.

【責任を果す】

do《one's》duty; meet《one's》obligation

2．引責

【責任をとる［負う］】

take [accept] the blame

彼は事故の責任をとった。

He took the blame for the accident.

子供が他人に物的損害を与えたときは親が責

任をとって弁償するのが常識となっている。

Parents are generally expected to take financial responsibility for any property damage their children may do.

隣の庭の修復代金は親父が払ってくれたけど，実は僕の責任なんだ。僕が酔っ払って車を乗り入れてしまったのだ。

My father paid for the damage to our neighbor's garden even though I was the one who was responsible for it because I drove my car over it when I was drunk.

船長は事故の責任をとって自らの命を絶ってしまった。

The ship captain committed suicide to show that he was taking responsibility for the accident.

3. 自己責任

【自分に責任を持つ】

人は自分自身に責任を持つべきだ。

One should be responsible for oneself.

〈注〉 上の文は「自分の言動すべてに責任を持つべきだ」ということ。よく似た表現だが One should take care of oneself. は「他人に頼らず自立せよ」という意味になる。「行動に責任を持つべきだ」は We should be responsible for [take responsibility for] what we do [our own actions].

【自分の責任で】

彼は自分の責任で決断を下した。(上司の指令を仰がず)

He made the decision on his own responsibility.

【言葉に責任を持つ】

我々は自分の言葉に責任を持たねばならない。

We should be true to our words.

Do what you say you will do.

Your actions should be consistent with your words.

【無責任，責任のがれ】

もう少し気をつけてくれなきゃ無責任だよ。

You should have been more responsible.

You must [should, ought to] act responsibly.（お説教のニュアンス）

無責任だ

be irresponsible（強くひびく）

have no sense of responsibility

責任のがれをする（→せい）

evade [avoid, escape] responsibility（他人のせいにする＝lay the blame on others）

せっかく（折角）

〈注〉 「せっかく」には人の好意や努力を尊重し，それを「無にしたくない」という思いが背後にある。これにぴったり対応する英語はないので，その文脈の中で合うように訳し分けねばならない。

1. 苦労して・待望

【苦労】

せっかく骨折ったのに失敗したとは気の毒なことだ。

Too bad that he failed {after / despite} such great effort.

せっかくこんなにたくさんのデータを集めてくださったのだから大いに活用しましょう。

Since you {made the effort / went to the trouble} to gather so much data, let's make good use of it.

【待望】

せっかくの遠足が雨でだめになった。

Bad weather spoiled the picnic everyone was looking forward to.

せっかくのチャンスを逃した。

I've missed a rare chance.

2. わざわざ

せっかく用意したのだから天気が良くても悪くても行こう。

Let's go rain or shine, since we've got everything ready.

昔の友人を訪ねてせっかく大阪から出て来たのに，もうそこに住んでいなかった。

I came all the way from Osaka just to see an old friend of mine, but he wasn't living

there any more.
せっかく見に来てくれたのに赤ちゃんは眠っていた。
She came specially to see the baby, but it was sleeping.

3. 親切にも
せっかくのご提案ですのでやらせていただきます。
I'll do that. I appreciate your suggestion.
【せっかくですが】
せっかくのご招待ですが実は先約がございまして残念ながらうかがえないのです。(儀礼的に誘いを断る)
Many thanks for your invitation. But I'm afraid I won't be able to come because I'm already engaged that evening.
〈注〉 But I regret I'm already engaged … とも言えるが古風である。
せっかくですがうかがえません。友人に会う約束をしてしまったので。
I'm sorry, but I can't come because I have promised to meet my friend.

せっきょくてき(積極的)

1. 人について
active (↔ passive)
【積極的な人】(次のように具体的に言うのが普通)
積極的な学生[教員/クラブ会員/地域住民/社会人]
an active student [teacher / club member / community member / society member]

2. 態度・意見
positive (↔ negative); **constructive**
積極的に振舞うべきだ。
You must take a positive attitude.
積極的な意見[提案]
a positive [constructive] idea [suggestion, proposal]
〈注〉 positive opinion と言うと何かに賛意を表す意見の意味になる。
積極的な経営戦略　a positive policy
〈注〉 たとえば，会社の財政再建のために社員の給料凍結のようなその場しのぎでなく，新しい市場開拓の努力をするといったこと。
【積極的な援助】
県は市の会議場建設計画に積極的な援助を惜しまなかった。
The prefecture gave willing assistance to the city project to build a convention center.
The prefecture willingly helped the city (to) build a convention center.

せっする(接する)

1. 接触する
come into contact with (触れる)
【文化に接する】
日本が西洋文化に接してまだやっと1世紀だ。
It is only a century since Japan came into contact with European culture.
〈注〉 ×Japan touched European culture only a century ago. は誤り。touch の正しい用法は次の通り。
be in touch
ex. I'll be in touch. (私が連絡します)
He's in touch with several scientists. (彼は数人の科学者と連携をとって仕事をしている)
touch on
ex. The essay touched on several related topics. (その論文はいくつかの関連のあるトピックにも触れている)
【接線】 a tangent (line)

2. 隣接する
【境を接する】
うちは病院と境を接している[の隣である]。
My house is next to the hospital.
幼稚園は小さな公園と境を接している。
The kindergarten is located next to a small park.
運動場の一方は川の堤防に接している。
The playground borders the river bank.
〈注〉 be adjacent to the park とか adjoins the park の

ような言い方もあるが堅い表現である。

3．応対する

【人と接する】

彼女はレポーターなのでいろいろなタイプの人と接する機会がある。

As she is a reporter, she meets all types of people.

彼は毎日たくさんの来客と接している。

He has a lot of visitors every day.

彼女は政治家と接する機会が多い。

She has many opportunities to {be / come in contact} with politicians.

4．受け取る

【知らせに接する】

彼はそのニュースに接し驚いた。

He was surprised at the news.

彼の急死の報に接しショックを受けた。

I was shocked to hear of his sudden death.

【吉報に接して】

彼女はその吉報に接し非常に喜んだ。

She was {very glad / delighted} to get the good news.

ぜったいに（絶対に）

1．主張・確信

【絶対に…である［ない］】

それは絶対に間違っている。

That's definitely wrong.

〈注〉 You are definitely wrong. と言うと非常に強く，けんか腰になるので注意。

【絶対に必要】

君が行くことが絶対に必要だ。

It's absolutely necessary for you to go.

【絶対に不可能】

これ以上経費を節約することは絶対に不可能だ。

It's absolutely impossible to cut down the expenses any further.

【絶対反対】

彼は絶対反対と言っている。

He's dead against it.

私は新しい企画に絶対反対だ。

I am positively against the new project.

【絶対すてき】

絶対すてきだわ。

It's absolutely fascinating.

【確信】

彼は絶対無事に帰る。

He will surely come back safe.

彼らは協力しなければ絶対に成功しない。

They will never succeed unless they cooperate.

彼はやると言ったら絶対にやる。

He always {keeps his word. / carries out his promises.}

私は絶対にうそは言わない。

I would never tell a lie.

私は絶対にうそは言ってない。

I swear I'm not telling a lie.

〈注〉 子供の間の誓いの言葉
I'm not telling a lie — cross my heart.
"Cross my heart and hope to die."
は「指切りげんまん」に当る。

彼は絶対にその男を見たと言う。

He swore that he had seen the man.

絶対に彼はまだ生きていると思う。

{I believe / I'm absolutely sure} that he is still alive.

2．決意・命令

【絶対にやり遂げる】

絶対に仕事をやり遂げる決心だ。

I'm determined to complete my work.

【絶対にやめる】

賭事には今後絶対手を出しません。

I will never gamble again.

【命令】

絶対に勝て！

You must win!

It's absolutely imperative that you（should）

win.
絶対に秘密を漏らすな。
Do not betray the secret to anybody [under any circumstances [whatever happens].
絶対に来るんだよ。
Be sure to come.
絶対会いに来て[遊びに来て]。(誘い)
By all means come to see me. (＝You're very welcome to come.)
あの展覧会を絶対見に行きなさいよ。
By all means / Be sure to } go and see that exhibition.
〈注〉◆by all means は上の例文のような誘いの場合に「ぜひ」の意味で，また「傘を貸していただける？」Can I borrow your umbrella? に対する答え「どうぞ，いいですよ」Certainly. の意で使われる。しかし「決意」の意味の「絶対に」として英国では使われず，米国の用法でも（例えば I'll go by all means.）古風になっているので，ほかの表現を使う方がよい。
◆absolutely を×I'll go [win] absolutely.（絶対に行く[勝つ]）のように使うのはおかしい。I'll absolutely go [win]. と語順を変えるか I'm determined to go (win). とする。「絶対にそう思う」は△I think so absolutely. ではなく，I'm absolutely sure ... としなくてはならない。このように absolutely は文全体を強めるのではなく，通常形容詞を強める副詞として使われる（ex. absolutely impossible, absolutely quiet）。また形容詞の absolute は形容詞的意味を担う名詞と結合する（ex. absolute silence, absolute absurdity）
◆「絶対に…ない」と言うときは，△I'll not tell anyone absolutely. ではなくて，I'll absolutely not tell ... または I absolutely will not tell ... とする。また，I'll never tell ... のようにも言える。

3. 慣用表現

【絶対多数】
絶対多数で
by an absolute majority
絶対多数を得る
get [win by] an absolute majority
【絶対安静】
病人は絶対安静にしていなくてはならない。
The patient must be kept absolutely quiet.

せつび（設備）

【宿泊設備】
ヒルトンホテルは500人の宿泊設備をもつ。
The Hilton Hotel { has accommodations for / accommodates } 500 people.
【宿泊施設】
その市にはあらゆる値段の宿泊施設がある。
You can find accommodations in every price range in that city.
その村にはドライブインが数軒あるが宿泊施設は一つもない。
There are some drive-ins in that village but not a single inn with sleeping facilities.
【病院】
あの病院は1000人入院させる[1000床の]設備がある。
That hospital has 1000 beds.
【運動設備】 athletic facilities（フィールド fields, プール pools, コート courts, トレーニングルーム workout rooms などを含む）
グリーンセンターにはスポーツやピクニック用の設備がある。
The Green Center has sport and picnic facilities.
岐阜スポーツグランドには，ネットゲーム，フィールドゲーム，弓道，水泳のできる設備がある。
The Gifu Sports Ground has facilities for net games, field games, archery and swimming.
【設備が良い】
そのホテルは設備が良い。
The hotel has good facilities.（具体的にはレストラン restaurants, バー bars, プール a swimming pool などがあること）
新しい寮は電気機器も設置され衛生にも気くばりが行き届いた設備のよい寮だ。
The new dormitory is provided with electric appliances as well as excellent arrangements for cleanliness.

【会議用の施設】
そのホテルは会議用の設備[施設]が整っている。
The hotel has convention facilities.
〈注〉 具体的には会議室 meeting rooms, ビデオ設備 video equipment, コピー，ファックス，伝言伝達など secretarial service（秘書的サービス）のあること。
【防火設備】 fire-prevention equipment
〈注〉 具体的には防火扉 fire doors, 煙探知器 smoke alarms, 家庭用消火器 home fire extinguishers, ホース hoses, ガスマスク gas-masks など。
【冷暖房設備】
そのアパートは冷暖房設備が完備している。
The apartment has a perfect air conditioning system.
彼の部屋には暖房設備がない。
His room has no heating system.
【衛生設備】
市当局は飲食店にかなり厳格な衛生設備設置を義務づけている[衛生基準を設けている]。
The city demands high sanitary standards in all restaurants.
【教育設備】
その学校は教育設備が良い[悪い]。
The school is well [poorly] equipped.
【コンピュータ】
あの高校は最近コンピュータ室を設備[設置]した。
That high school has recently set up [installed] a computer room.
【機械設備】
うちの病院は CAT スキャナを設置したところだ。
Our hospital has just installed a CAT scanner.
【炊事用設備】
その部屋には電話と炊事用設備がある。
The room has a telephone and cooking facilities.
【設備費】
防火設備設置には300万円近くかかった。
The fire prevention equipment cost nearly three million yen.
【設備投資】
会社は設備投資として1000万円をつぎ込んだ。
The company invested ten million yen in plant and equipment.

《類義語》
accommodation 宿泊施設(a place to stay)。
〈注〉◆hotel rooms は accommodation, 場合によっては facility とも考えられる。
◆動 accommodate とは必要なものを用立てるの意。
facilities 運動・娯楽・会議・医療・教育設備；実験設備(使用・利用できる設備)。
交通運輸機関 transportation facilities
〈注〉 動 facilitate は容易にする，楽にするの意。
equipment スポーツ器具・道具・教育機器(視聴覚教材など)。集合名詞である。
〈注〉 動 equip は(設備などを)備えつけること。equipped とは道具がそろっていること。
設備のよいスポーツ施設［研究所／教室／台所］well-equipped sports facilities [labs / classrooms / kitchen]
electrical appliances 家庭の電気機器など。
〈注〉 動 apply は当てる，つける，適用する，応用する。

せつやく（節約）→ けんやく

節約 **economy; (a) saving; thrift** 〔*formal*〕
節約する **save; economize on; cut down on**
【経費】
経費を節約しなければならない。
We have to cut down on expenses.
政府は経費節約のため強力な施策をとるといっている。
The government says it will take strong measures to reduce public spending.
【旅費】
旅費を節約しよう。
Let's save on our traveling expenses.

【光熱費】
私たちは光熱費をもっと節約できる。
We could economize on electricity and gas.
商店主たちは電気の節約のため，閉店時間の１時間繰り上げを協定した。
The shopkeepers agreed to close (their stores) an hour earlier to economize on electricity.
【時間】
君たち二人が一緒に来てくれれば時間の節約になる。
If you two come together, that will save (us) time.
【水】
節水 Save Water.（掲示）

ぜひ（是非）

1．善悪

【事の是非】
お前も事の是非[善悪]はわかっていい年頃だ。
You are old enough to know what is right and what is wrong.
彼は事の是非[善悪]がわからないようだ。
He seems unable to distinguish between right and wrong.
【是非を論じる】
委員会は現行入試制度の是非を真剣に議論した。
The committee seriously argued about the validity of the present examination system.
科学者たちは人道的立場からの遺伝子組み換えの是非について議論をした。
The scientists argued about the morality [moral implications] of gene alteration [altering genes].
〈注〉 argue about は賛否両論（pros and cons）入り乱れて議論すること。argue for は賛成演説をすること。
ex. argue for more vacation（休暇を延長するように主張する）
本日の国会の主要議題は減税の是非であった。
The main topic in the Diet today was whether {to lower taxes. / taxes should be lowered.}

2．必ず（→ぜったいに）

【ぜひ…したい】
できたらぜひ彼に会いたい。（切望）
I really want to visit him if it's at all possible.
何が何でもぜひ彼に会いに行きたい。
{I will definitely / I definitely want to} go and see him, come rain or shine.
ぜひ早くあなたにお会いしたい。（会いたくてたまらない）
I'm impatient to see you.
【ぜひ…してほしい】
彼はぜひあなたに訪ねて来ていただきたいと言っています。（誘い）
He insists on your coming to see him.
ぜひ来てください。
Be sure to come.
Come without fail.
ぜひ会いに来てください。
Do come and see me.
By all means, come and see me. (You're welcome to come.)
あの映画はぜひごらんになるといい。
You should definitely not miss that movie.
By all means go and see that movie.〔米〕
〈注〉 by all means の用法 →ぜったいに

せわ（世話）

1．面倒を見る

【世話をする】take care of
彼女は姉の子供の世話をしている。
She takes care of her sister's children.
あの人は月曜日と木曜日の午後，姉さんが学校に教えに行くのでその間子供の世話をしている。

She looks after her sister's children on Monday and Thursday afternoons when her sister goes out to teach at a school.

〈注〉 look after は一時的に短時間預かる感じである。

【世話になる】

私は15歳まで祖父母の世話になって育ちました。

I was brought up by my grandparents until I was fifteen.

私は父の友人の家で世話になっていた。

I lived with the family of / I stayed with an acquaintance of my father's.

私は今叔父の家で世話になっている。

I'm now staying at my uncle's.

〈注〉 stay at は短期間寝泊りしていること。

2. やっかい

【世話をかける】

あの頃はずいぶん先生方に世話をかけたものだ。

I remember I gave a lot of trouble to my teachers in those days.

時々かっとなっては問題を起してあの人たちには世話をかけた。

My fiery temper sometimes got them into trouble.

【世話が焼ける】

お前はまったく世話の焼ける子だ。

What a troublesome child you are!

あの人は時々本当に世話が焼ける。

He's really very troublesome sometimes.

He's a {great problem for / burden on} us.

She's such a nuisance sometimes.

【世話が焼けない】

あの子はちっとも世話が焼けない。

That child gives us little trouble.

【世話になりたくない】

私は姪の世話になりたくない。

I don't want to be a {burden on / nuisance for [to]} my nieces.

3. 仲立ち・斡旋(あっせん)

【世話をする】 give help [assistance〔*formal*〕]

私は彼が役所に入れるよう世話してやった。

I found him a position in a government office.

彼は私にパートの仕事を世話してくれた。

He helped me (to) find a part-time job.

彼女はとてもいい看護婦さんを世話してくれた。

She has found me a very good nurse.

【世話で】

彼の世話で私は今のポストにつくことができたのだ。

I got my present position {because of his recommendation. / through his help.}

〈注〉 through the good offices of (…の世話で) は形式ばった表現。

【世話になる】

彼にはずいぶん世話になった。

I owe him a lot [great deal].

He did a great deal for me.

4. 世話になったお礼

たいへんお世話になりました。

Thank you very much.

Thank you. I do appreciate it (a lot).

It was very kind of you.

Thank you for everything you did for me.

5. 慣用表現

世話役　a manager

世話女房　a good homemaker

世話好き　an obliging person

世話焼き　an officious; meddlesome person; a busybody

〈注〉 officious は世話好きが過ぎること。meddlesome, meddling, interfering は自分に関係のない

ことに口を出したがること。

余計なお世話だ。(失礼な言い方)

It's none of your business.

Mind your own business.

Don't poke your nose into [meddle in] other people's affairs.

せんきょ(選挙)

election

総選挙　general election
衆議院選挙
the House of Representatives election
the lower house election
参議院選挙
the House of Councilors election
the upper house election
知事選挙　election for (the) governor
市長選挙　election for (the) mayor
県議選挙　prefectural assembly election
cf. state legislative election〔米〕州議会議員選挙
市議選挙　city council election
選挙法　election law
選挙法改正　revision of the election system
選挙区　constituency(選挙区民の意味もある)
大選挙区制　large constituency system
小選挙区制　small constituency system
比例代表制
proportional representation system
選挙管理委員会　the board of elections; the elections board
選挙を公示する　announce
選挙は2月10日に行われる旨,昨日公示された。
It was announced yesterday that the election would be held on February 10.
選挙権　franchise; suffrage; right to vote
選挙人名簿　voter registration list〔米〕; electoral register [list]〔英〕
選挙人;有権者　voter
選挙民　electorate(集合的)
選挙運動　election campaign
選挙資金　campaign fund
後援会　campaign organization

【候補者】candidate
立候補する
run in an election
file《one's》candidacy(公式に届け出る)
候補者を立てる　field [endorse] a candidate
〈注〉 field は選挙戦に送り出すこと。endorse は公認候補名簿に載せること。
党公認候補　party-endorsed candidate
組合公認候補　union-endorsed candidate
遊説する
canvas; canvas《a district》for votes
stump; stump《a district》
政見　political view
票読みをする
project the vote count(事前に予想する)
【投票】vote; poll; ballot
投票する　vote for
私は土井氏に投票した。
I voted for Ms. Doi.
投票日　election day; polling [voting] day
不在者投票　absentee ballot(ing); absentee vote [voting]
棄権　abstention
棄権する　abstain from voting; not go to the polls
投票所　polling station; polls〔米〕
投票所は午前6時に開く。
The polls open at 6:00 a. m.
投票所のブース　voting [polling] booth
立会人　official observer
【開票】
投票は即日開票される。
The vote count starts right after the polls close.
開票結果　election returns
【当選する】win an election; be elected
彼は衆議院議員に当選した。
He was elected to the House.
He won a seat in the Diet.
【落選する】lose an election
彼は3000票の差で落選した。
He lost the election by three thousand votes.

せんこう（専攻）→ せんもん

1．学部学生

【専攻する】

〔米〕major in; specialize in《subject》

何を専攻しているんですか。

What's your major?〔米〕

What are you majoring in?〔米〕

What are you studying?〔英〕

大学での専攻は何でしたか。

What did you {major in / study} in [at] college?

うちの息子は大学で物理を専攻している。

My son is majoring in physics at the university.

彼は中央大学卒で専攻は法学だ。

He graduated from Chuo University with a degree in law.

【専攻科目】

a major〔米〕; a subject of study〔英〕

【専攻学生】

歴史学[化学]専攻の学生

a history [chemistry] major

〈注〉 a … major [majoring] は米国式。また，この表現は学部学生についてのみ使われる。英国の Oxford, Cambridge では独特な言い方で I'm reading English.（英語専攻）。他の大学では I'm studying English. と言う。

2．研究者（大学院生以上）（→せんもん）

【専攻分野】《one's》field

私の夫の専攻分野は流体力学です。

My husband's field is fluid dynamics.

中でも特に専門は「流れの可視化」です。

His {specialization is / specific area is} flow visualization.

He specializes in flow visualization.

せんし（戦死）→ しぬ

せんしゅつ（選出）→ えらぶ，せんきょ

an election; 選出する **elect;**（国会議員などに）**return**〔*formal*〕

【選出される】

彼は兵庫から選出された。

He was elected from Hyogo.

佐藤氏が議長に選出された。

Mr. Sato was elected chairman.

〈注〉 elected chairman, elected president などのように役職名は無冠詞。

【…県選出】愛知県選出国会議員

a Diet member from [for] Aichi Prefecture

センス

1．感覚的能力

彼はユーモアのセンスがある[ない]。

He has a [no] sense of humor.

He is a great one for jokes.

彼女は美的[色彩の]センスがない。

She has no sense of beauty [color].

She has no eye for beauty.

彼女は音楽的センスがない。

She has no ear for music.

彼女はすぐれた音楽[芸術]的センスを持っている。

She has a rare sensibility for music [art].

彼女は子供のときから美しいものに感応するセンスを持っていた。

From childhood she has {had a love / been keenly aware} of beauty.

2．趣味

彼女は服のセンスがいい。

Her dress shows good taste.（ある一着について）

She has good taste in clothes.（服一般について）

〈注〉◆「ハイセンス」は和製英語。また，good sense は単独で使えば common sense（常識，良識）の意味。

◆sensitive は(1)寒さ・熱などに敏感な，(2)デリケートな感覚を持った，(3)すぐ怒る，のような意味があり，近年の傾向として(3)の意味で使われることが多い。

She's a sensitive person. と言うと，あの人には口のきき方に注意しないと，すぐ泣きそうになったり気を悪くしたりするといった意味になる。

せんせい（先生）

教員 **a teacher;** 大学教授 **a professor;** 講師 **an instructor; a lecturer;** 博士，医師 **a doctor**

1. 職業・地位

先生をする　be a teacher; teach

【先生である】

父は東高校の先生をしている。

My father is a teacher at Higashi High School.

彼は音楽の先生をしている。

He teaches music.

He is a music teacher.

姉は高校の先生をしている。

My sister is a high school teacher.

〈注〉 an Énglish teacher　英語の先生
an Énglish téacher　英国人の先生
上のように強勢によって意味するところが違ってくるが，文に書くときなどあいまいになるのを防ぐには「英語の先生」を a teacher of English とする。

2. 敬称

〈注〉「先生」「教員」に当る英語は teacher であるが，呼びかけ，敬称での「先生」は teacher ではない。

【小中高の教員】

スミス先生

Mr. Smith, Mrs. Smith, Ms. Smith, Miss Smith

〈注〉 近年女性のみ既婚，未婚の別をつけるのは好ましくないとして Ms. [miz]を使う人が増えている。また，会話の中では sir, ma'am を敬語として差しはさむ。

【大学教授】

ジョンソン先生　Dr. Johnson（博士の学位のある場合）

【医師】

森先生　Dr. Mori

〈注〉 話の中で「ねえ先生」と語りかけるときは，単に doctor だけでよい。

ぜんぜん（全然）→ まったく・ぜんぜん

せんたく（選択）

a choice;（**a**）**selection**

選択する　**choose; make a choice**

（慎重に）**select;**（有形のものを）**pick**（**out**）

正しい選択をする

make a good choice

誤った選択をする

make ⌊a⌋ bad [the wrong] choice

【選択を誤る】

彼は職業の選択を誤った。

He chose the wrong occupation.

教職を選ぶとは，私は職業の選択を誤ってしまった。

I made a mistake when I chose to become a teacher.

I shouldn't have chosen [decided] to become a teacher.

【選択に気をつける】

友人の選択に気をつけなさい。

Be careful in your choice of friends.

Choose good friends.

【選択は自由】

好きなものは何でも選べる。

You can choose
{ whatever [whichever] you like.
{ any of these.

【選択の余地がない】

We have no choice.

There is nothing else.

There are no others.

【二者択一の選択】 an alternative

ほかに方法がない。

There's no alternative.

We have no alternative.

【選択科目】 an elective [optional] subject

cf. a required [compulsory] subject（必修科目）

【選択式テスト】multiple-choice questions
【授業科目を選択する】
私はフランス語を2科目選択した。
　I took two French classes [courses].
〈注〉 course は所定の期間（15週や30週など）で完結する教科目をいう。take a course [class] が普通の言い方。be enrolled in は「受講登録をする」。

せんぱい（先輩）・こうはい（後輩）

〈注〉 欧米人は先輩，後輩のように学年の上下または入社時期の前後により人間関係を分ける習慣がない。したがって先輩後輩の観念がなく，それを表す言葉もない。しかし日本の学校や社会について書くときに必要であれば次のようにすると意味は通じる。
【学校・大学】
彼女は学校で…年先輩だ。
　She was in the class above me at school.（1年先輩）
　She was in the third year when I was in the first year.（2年先輩）
　She was two years ahead of [in front of] me at school.（2年先輩）
　(cf. I was two years behind her.　2年後輩だった)
【大先輩】
　one of the oldest graduates（大学などの）
【クラブの先輩[後輩]】
　an older [a younger] club member [student]
クラブの先輩は新入りの私たちにたいへん親切だ。
　The older club members are very nice to us new ones.
先輩たちは私に…するように言いつけた。
　The older club members told me to ...
〈注〉◆be senior [junior] to ... は地位や年齢に関して時に使われることがあるが，学生間では用いない。
◆その他の表現
John F. Kennedy, Sr.　父ジョン・F・ケネディ
John F. Kennedy, Jr.　子ジョン・F・ケネディ
a meeting of the most senior army officers 陸軍最上級士官の会合
senior citizens 高齢者（特に65歳以上の年金生活者）

【社会】
彼は演劇界の大先輩です。
　He is { among the greatest of great actors. / eminent [foremost] in the theatrical world.（スピーチなどで）
彼はスタッフの中で一番の先輩だ。
　He is the oldest member of the staff.
　He has been on the staff the longest.

せんばつ（選抜）

選抜する　**choose; elect; select**

1．試験
【選抜試験】
大学の附属小学校では子供の選抜を抽選で決めるところと選抜試験を行うところとがある。
　Some elementary schools attached to universities select their pupils by lot and some by test.
【選抜される】
5000人の志願者の中からわずか70人が選抜された。
　Only 70 were selected from among 5000 applicants.
【選抜にもれる】
彼は選抜にもれた[されなかった]。
　He was not on [left off] the accepted list.
　He was not accepted.

2．スポーツ
【選抜された】
岐商チームは全国選抜に選抜された。
　The Gisho team won its way to the national level tournament.
中京高校は甲子園に選抜された。
　Chukyo High School has been selected to play in the Koshi-en baseball tournament.

せんもん（専門）→ せんこう

彼の専門は何ですか。

What is his specialty?（doctors, engineers, teachers, lawyers などに関して）

【専門は…だ】

彼の専門は日本史だ。

He's studying Japanese history.

彼は心臓が専門だ[の専門医だ]。

He's a heart specialist.

【専門用語】 a technical term

【専門技術者】 a technical expert

【専門技術をもっている】 be an expert at

彼は絵画修復技術をもっている。

He is an expert at restoring paintings.

【専門分野】 one's field（of specialization）

【専門ではない】

それは私の専門ではない。

That is outside my field [line〔*informal*〕].

経済は彼の専門外だ。

Economics is not in his line [field].

【専門家】 a specialist

税法の専門家　a tax law specialist

心臓病の専門医　a heart specialist

小児科医　a specialist in children's diseases

〈注〉 specialist, professional, expert の比較

specialist　上述のように専門教育を受けた人。

professional　「しろうと」(amateur)に対する「くろうと」，プロ。それを職業とする人であるから当然専門知識を持っていると考えられている。

expert　それを職業にしてもしなくても，ある道に熟達した人。

ex. I talked with specialists, but they turned out not to be experts and couldn't solve my problem.（専門家に相談したが専門家もたいしたことがなくて問題を解決してくれなかった）

そ

そう

1. そのように

そう思う。
Yes, I think so.
I believe so.

そうは思わない。
Well, I don't think so.
Umm, I don't agree with that.

もし君の手に負えないようなら(彼に)そう言いなさい。
If it's too difficult for you, ⌊say so [tell him so].

そう(です)か
Is that so? / (Oh,) Really? / Oh!

そうです[そのとおり]。(肯定)
Yes. / Right. / That's right. / True. / Certainly.〔強〕/ That's it.〔強〕/ Exactly. / Quite.〔英〕

そう聞いているが。 So I hear.

そうではない。(否定)
That can't be so.
Well, actually not.

そうとはかぎらない。
That is not always the case.
Not always.

【そうする】 do so

今すぐそうしなさい。
Do so [it] at once.

そうするより仕方がなかった。
I couldn't help it.
I couldn't have done otherwise.

二度とそうはさせない。
I won't let that happen again.

2. 条件・理由

【そうだから, そういうわけで】
and so; because of that

今日は早く来た。そういうわけで昼前に用事が終った。
We came early, (and) so we finished before noon.

〈注〉「そういうわけで」の such being the case は文語であるので普通の口語体の文では使わないこと。therefore もやや堅い語であるが書き言葉としてならば使える。

【もしそうなら】 If that's so, …

「明日は遠足に行くんだが, もし雨が降ったらどうする？」「そうなら来週にすればいい」。
"We're going on a picnic tomorrow. What if it rains?" "In that case [If that happens] we'll go next week."

【もしそうでなければ】
if that's not so; otherwise; or

今やってしまった方がいい。そうしないと今夜は遅くまでやらなければならなくなるから。
I'd better do this now, otherwise [or] I'll have to stay up late tonight.

〈注〉 命令文＋and (…しなさい, そうすれば…)
命令文＋or (…しなさい, そうしないと…)
次のようなぶっきらぼうな命令はけんか腰に聞えるから使わない方がよい。
△Leave now, or you'll miss the last train home.
○I'm afraid if you don't leave now, …〔*more polite*〕
(すぐ出発しないと終電に乗り遅れますよ)

3. 言葉のつなぎ, 応対

「彼に会いましたよ」「あらそう？」。
"I met him" "Oh, really? [Oh, did you?]"

【そう, それでよし】(肯定)

(子供に) テレビつけてよ, うんそう。
Turn on the TV. That's it [right]. / OK.

(子供に) ここに名前を書いて。そう［よろしい］。
Write your name here.
… That's the way [right]. / OK.

【(思い出して)そういえば】

ああ, そういえば 2, 3 日前, 通りでジムに会ったよ。

That reminds me that I ran into Jim on the street a few days ago.

(話題を持ち出すとき) それはそうと

by the way; incidentally; changing the subject; not to change the subject, but ...

〈注〉◆私たちは話している間「聞いている」「わかった」の意思表示として「ああそう」とか「はあ」「うん」などと何かしら相づちを打つが，英米人は日本人のようには相づちを打たない。

◆日本人はやたらと by the way を使うと言われる。by the way は「本筋からはずれているが」の意味で「ところで」とか「そう言えば」に当る。たとえば，会話の途中や，ある話題がまだ終っていないのに割り込むとき，または伝えたいことがあって言わないと忘れてしまうといけないので割り込むとき，忘れていたことに気がついて持ち出すときなどである。

［不自然になる例］

△「Hey, George! By the way, are you coming to the party tonight? (By the way は不要)」

また，もとの話題に戻すときは Getting back to what we were talking about ... などと言う。

【そうですね(考えながら)】

Well, let me see.

【ああそうだ(急に思い出して)】

I've got it!

Oh, I remember.

【そういえばそうだ(思い出して)】

あなたに言われて思い出した…

Now that you mention it, I remember ...

【そうかといって】

そうかといって私にいい考えがあるわけではないんだが。

Not that I have a better idea [suggestion].

…そう

1. 様子

【視覚的印象】

うれし[悲し]そう

look happy [sad, unhappy]

さびしそう　look lonely

さびしそうに

with wistful eyes; wistfully

彼女は人がよさそうだ。

She seems to be a good-natured woman.

彼は正直そうだった[に見えた]。

He seemed [appeared] to be honest.

〈注〉 look, seem, appear は「…そうに見える」の意味であるが，look はその原義が示すように目で見た印象を述べるもの。seem は「…らしい」「…と思われる」という判断を示す。appear は，「(本当のところどうかわからないが)…らしく見える」という表面的な印象を述べる。

【聴覚的印象】

(聞いて) 面白そうだ。

That sounds interesting.

2. 予想 (…しそうだ)

雨が降りそうだ。

It's likely to rain.

It looks like rain.

雨が降りそうもない。

It's not likely to rain.

It doesn't look like rain.

雨がやみそうもない。

There's no sign of the rain stopping.

It looks as though / The rain looks like } it will never stop.

〈注〉 like をこのように接続詞として使う表現は広まりつつあるが looks as if, looks as though とするのがオーソドックス。

彼女は今にも泣き出しそうだった。

She was about to cry.

彼はもう来てもよさそうなものだが。

It's about time for him to come.

彼はいっこうに来そうもない。

He's not likely to come.

あと1時間は終りそうにない。

It doesn't look as if we can get finished in another hour.

彼は勝ちそうもない。

I don't think he has a chance of winning.

私にもできそうだ。

I feel I can do it.

彼のやりそうなことだ。

That's just like him.

(札入れを紛失して)ありそうな場所は全部探

した。

I looked for my billfold everywhere I could think of.

3．当然だ

大学生ならこのくらいのことは知っていてよさそうなものだ。

A college student ought to know this sort of thing.

彼の年齢ならもう少しわかっていてもよさそうなものだ。

He ought to know better at his age.

彼も発つ前に「さよなら」ぐらい言いに来たらよさそうなものを。

He might have at least called me to say good-bye before he left.

4．伝聞

【…だそうだ】

I hear [I've heard] that ... / I'm told that ... / They say that ...

彼女はもうすぐパリに行くそうだ。

I hear that she's going to Paris pretty soon.

インドの人口問題は相当深刻だそうだ。

They say that the population problem in India is very serious.

〈注〉 日本人は断言を避ける習慣があるが，そのためか I hear や I've heard を使いすぎる。

そうい（相違）→ ちがう・ちがい

（a）**difference;** 不一致（a）**disagreement; a gap**

相違する（→ちがう）

be different from; differ from

【A と B の相違】

the difference between A and B

【意見の相違】

２人の間には意見の相違があった。

There was a difference of opinion between them.

彼らの間には最も基本的な点で意見の相違があった。

They disagreed on the most fundamental point.

【事実に相違する】

キング氏の言われたことは事実に相違する。

What Mr. King said is contrary to the facts.

今の話は事実と相違します。

That statement doesn't (seem to) fit the facts.

【相違を強調する】

英国英語と米国英語の相違をおおげさに言いすぎない方がよい。この両国の人はお互いに話が通じるのだから。

The difference between British English and American English should not be emphasized because people from the two countries can communicate with each other.

【案に相違して】

案に相違して広島カープが勝った。

Contrary to expectations, the Carps won.

【相違ありません】

上記の通り相違ありません。（公文書）

I hereby certify the above statement to be true and correct in every detail to the best of my knowledge.

I affirm the above statement to be true in every particular [respect].

【相違ない】

彼に何かあったに相違ない。（確信）

Something must have happened to him.

そうだん（相談）

1．助言を求める

相談する **consult**《a person》〔*formal*〕; **talk with**《a person》**over** [**about**]《something》（人と事はどちらを先にしてもよい）; **ask**《a person's》**advice**

法律的な問題に関しては弁護士に相談することが多い。

People often consult lawyers about legal problems.

弁護士に相談した方がよい。

You should talk to a lawyer about it.
そのことはご両親に相談しましたか。
Have you talked it over with your parents?
加藤先生に相談しなさい。
You had better go to Mr. Kato for advice.
【相談を受ける】
彼女からはよく相談を受けます。
She often comes to me for advice.
【相談に乗る】
いつでも相談に乗りますよ。
I'm always ready [willing] to
{ help you.
{ talk anything over with you.
【相談相手】
私には相談相手がいない。
I have no one to { advise me.
{ turn to for advice.

2. 話し合う
【相談する】
グループの長が集まってパーティーをいつどこでやるか相談した。
The group leaders discussed the date and place of the party.
【相談がまとまる】
うちのクラスは次の日曜日に北海道に出発と相談がまとまった。
It was agreed that our class would start for Hokkaido next Sunday.
【相談の上で】
ジムと相談の上で電話します。
I'll call you after talking it over with Jim.
〈注〉 Jim が lawyer などの専門職にある人であれば consulting を使ってもよいが，普通は talk over とか ask を使う。consult は非常に深刻な問題または公務やビジネスに関する相談の場合に用いる。

そくたつ（速達）→ ゆうびん

special delivery〔米〕, **express delivery**〔英〕
【速達で出す】
この手紙を速達にしてください。
Please send this letter (by) express [by special delivery].
(cf. air mail 航空便)
【速達郵便】 special delivery mail（集合的）
【速達の手紙】 a special delivery letter
【速達料金】 the special delivery charge

そくど（速度）

speed; velocity（物理学用語）
【速度を速める】 speed up
【速度を増す】［車主語］increase [gather] speed
列車は速度を増した。
The train gathered speed.
The train's speed increased.
この40年間に列車の速度はぐっと速くなった。
The speed of trains has increased greatly over the last 40 years.
【速度を落す】 slow down
雨の日は道路が滑りやすいので速度を落さなければいけない。
When it rains and the road is slippery
you should { slow down.
{ drive more slowly.
【全速力で走る】 run [go] at full [top] speed
【時速…キロ】
この列車は時速200キロで走る。
This train goes two hundred kilometers per hour.
【マッハ】 Mach /mɑ́:k, mǽk/
最高マッハ 2.4 の速度で
at a maximum speed of Mach 2.4.
【超音速】
SST は超音速ジェット機だ。
The SST is
{ a supersonic jet [plane].
{ faster than the speed of sound.
【高速[急行]列車】 an express train
【高速道路】
an expressway〔米〕; a motorway〔英〕
〈注〉 米国には有料高速自動車道 toll road がある。
【制限速度】 speed limit

制限速度時速20マイル（標識）

Speed Limit 20 M.P.H.（miles per hour）

【速度制限】

この辺は速度制限をした方がよい。

Speed limits should be set [posted] here.

【速度違反】

彼は速度違反で罰金をとられた。

He was fined for speeding.

そこ

1．空間

そこ[に，で] **there; over there; in [at] that place**

そこここ　here and there

【そこで】

彼の事務所にいたとき，そこで初めて彼女に会った。

I was in his office, and there I met her for the first time.

【そこから】

小道を行くと山の上にちょっと木を払った所があって，そこからはすばらしい眺めだった。

The lane led to a small clearing on the top of the hill, where there was a wonderful overlook.

【そこまで】

そこまでご一緒しましょう［お送りしましょう］。

Let me go part of the way with you.

2．時間

【そこへ】

悪者にあわや少年は殴り殺されるか，とそこへひゅっと飛んで来た石つぶてがたちまち悪者の頭に命中した。

The bad man was about to beat the poor boy to death, when suddenly a stone came whizzing through the air and hit the man on the head.

【そこで】

そこで君は何を[どう]した？

What did you do then?

3．その他

そこが問題だ。

That is the question.

そこまでは知っている。

I know that much.

〈注〉「そんなことは知っているよ」という失礼な言い方にならないようにやわらかに言うとよい。

…そこなう（…損なう）→ しっぱい

［人主語］ **fail（in）; be unsuccessful in; fail to do; miss**

［事主語］ **fail; be [prove, turn out] a failure; go（all）wrong**

1．失敗する

【もらいそこなう】

奨学金をもらいそこなった。

I missed winning [failed to win] the scholarship.

【食べそこなう】

夕飯を食べそこなった。

I missed supper.

【乗りそこなう】

終バスに乗りそこなった。

He missed the last bus home.

【行きそこなう】

旅行に行きそこなった。

I missed the chance of traveling.

I didn't get to travel.〔*informal*〕

【やりそこなう】

何もかもやりそこなった。

The whole scheme has gone wrong.

Everything's gone wrong.

2．危ない目にあいそうになる

彼はおぼれそこなったよ。

He came near (to) { being drowned. / drowning. }

He almost drowned.

〈注〉 drown は自動詞にも他動詞にもなるが,「おぼれる」は be drowned と受動態にするよりも自動詞 drown を使う方が普通である。

そだつ(育つ)・そだてる

1. 育つ

動 **grow**

彼は田舎で育った。

He grew up in the country.

彼女はきれいな娘に育った。

She grew into a very pretty girl.

2. 育てる

動他 **bring up;** (子供・動物を) **raise;** (植物を) **grow**

私の祖父母は10人以上の子供を育てた。

My grandparents brought up more than ten children.

人間は食用として穀物を育て,また動物を育てることを覚えた。

Humans learned to grow crops and also to raise animals for food.

あの人は母乳で育てているかしら。

Is she nursing [breast-feeding]?

彼は人工栄養で育てられた。

He was bottle-fed.

人工栄養で育った子供たち

bottle-fed children

〈注〉 on the bottle と言うと酒飲みのように聞える。

母乳で育った子供たち　breast-fed children

私は田舎で祖父母に育てられた。

I was brought up in the country by my grandparents.

3. 養成する

彼はその生涯で数多くの有名な音楽家を育てた。

He fostered [mentored] many renowned musicians in his lifetime.

〈注〉 実際に演奏技術を教えたのならば trained とする。foster は力を貸し,励まし,陰に日向に助けるという意味。mentor は賢い助言を与えること。

そつぎょう(卒業)

卒業 名 **graduation**

卒業する 動 **graduate from; finish**

エール大[ロンドン大]を卒業する

graduate from Yale [London University]

高校を卒業する　finish high school

〈注〉◆米国では graduate は大学以外の学校にも用いるが,英国では大学にのみ用い,それ以下の学校には finish, leave を使う。学制については「きょういく」の項参照。

graduate の他動詞用法(学位を与える)は,今はあまり使われない。×graduate the university は誤り。

◆Oxford や Cambridge では,入学する (come up),卒業する (go down) のような特殊な言い方もあるが,「私は○○大学を卒業した(学歴を言う場合)」の最も普通の言い方は I went to ○○ university. である。

彼は働きながら大学を卒業した。

He worked his way through university.

私たちの新しい英語の先生は大学を卒業したてだった。

Our new English teacher was fresh from [out of] university.

【優等で卒業する】 graduate with honors

【卒業後】 after graduation

【卒業論文】 a graduation [senior〔米〕] paper

cf. 修士論文　a master's [MA] thesis

博士論文　a doctoral [Ph. D] thesis

a dissertation

【卒業式】

a graduation ceremony

the commencement ceremony

Commencement Day (卒業の日)

【卒業証書】 a diploma

そっくり

1. 相似

そっくりである　**look [be] like; look alike**

あなたはお母さんの若いときにそっくりだ。

You {look exactly like / are the very picture of} your mother when she was young.

あの双生児の兄弟はそっくりだった。
　The twins looked exactly alike.
彼はお父さんに声がそっくりだった。
　His voice sounded just like his father's.
彼はおじいさんと性格がそっくりだ。
　He is just like his grandfather in personality [character].
〈注〉 前後関係で性格のことを言っていることが明らかであれば in personality [character] は省略する。
(その一族は)皆そっくりだ。
　They are { very like each other. / just alike. }
猿でも仲よくなってみると皆そっくりには見えなくなる。
　Monkeys don't look alike once you get familiar with them.
(その絵の)りんごは実物そっくりだ。
　Those apples (in the painting) look true to life.

2．全部

　all; そのまま just as it is
おばさんの家を家具ごとそっくり譲ってもらった。
　My aunt gave me her house with all its furniture.
留守中に衣類をそっくり盗まれた。
　All my clothes were stolen while I was away [gone].
〈注〉 I had all my clothes stolen. とも言えるが，こうすると「盗まれた」「盗ませた」の両方にとれるので前後関係から明らかな場合以外は前の文の方がよい。

【そっくり戻る】
なくしたお金がそっくりそのまま戻ってきた。
　The money I lost was { all returned. / completely returned. }

【そっくり移築】
その古い農家は明治村にそっくりそのまま移築されることになった。
　They decided to move the old farmhouse to Meiji Village and reconstruct it exactly [just] as it had been.

【そっくり保存】
壊れたドームは災害の記念碑としてそっくりそのまま残してある。
　The ruined dome has been kept [left] just as it was to commemorate the disaster.

そっと

1．やわらかく

【触覚】
そっとさわる[触れる]
　touch softly [lightly, gently]
彼はそっと私の腕にさわった。
　He touched me lightly on the arm.
彼はそっと私の肩をたたいた。
　He patted me gently on the shoulder.
〈注〉 He touched my arm …, He patted my shoulder … の形より上述の形の方が気持ちがこもる。偶然に触れたのではなく何かメッセージが伝わってくる。

2．音をたてないように，ひそかに

【音】
彼が目を覚まさないように彼女はそっと歩いた。
　She walked softly in order not to wake him.
猫が音もたてずそっとテーブルの上に飛び上がった。
　The cat jumped onto the table without a sound.
ドアはそっと開閉してください。
　Please open and shut the door quietly.

【人目を避けて】
彼女はドアをちょっと開け，そっと中をのぞいた。
　She opened the door slightly and peeped into the room.
彼女は部屋の中にそっと入って隅っこに座った。

She slipped into the room and sat in the farthest corner.

おばあさんは彼の耳元で何かささやき，彼を抱きしめると彼の手にそっと小さな包みを握らせた。

His grandmother whispered something into his ear, hugged him, and slipped a little package into his hands.

彼らは夜が明けぬうちにそっと家を抜け出した。

They stole [slipped] out of his house before dawn.

3. そのまま

彼のことはそっとしておいてやれ。

Leave him alone.

ぞっとする

動 ［人主語］ **shudder with horror**〔強〕; **be disgusted**

［事主語］ **make**《one》**shudder; give**《one》**the creeps**

形 こわい **horrible; hair-raising; scary;** いやな **disgusting; revolting; repulsive**

【見て】

事故現場の惨状にはぞっとした。

The sight of the damage sent a chill through me.

ヘビは見ただけでぞっとする。

The mere sight of a snake
{sends a shiver down my spine.
{gives me the creeps.

【考えて】

引っ越しをしなければならない。考えただけでもぞっとする。

I have to move, but the mere thought of it makes me shudder.

イナゴを食用にするなんてぞっとする。

Grasshoppers seem to me a really repulsive food.

皆その殺人犯のむごたらしさにぞっとした。

All the people were horrified at the cruelty of the murderer.

超大国の軍備競争にはまったくぞっとする。

The superpowers' arms race {is disgusting. / disgusts me.}

〈注〉 horrifiy は単に感情を表す語だが，disgust は感情的嫌悪感に加えて批判や非難を含む。

そと（外）

外側 **the outside**

戸外 **out-of-doors; the open air**

外はとても寒い。

It is awfully cold outside.

ビルの外が騒々しい。

It's noisy outside the building.

【外に出る】

go out; go outside; 出ている be out

母は今外へ出ています。（留守）

My mother is out just now.

【外を見る】

窓の外を見てごらん。もう春だよ。

Look out (of) the window. It's already spring.

〈注〉 英国英語では of が必要。米語では of なしでよい。

【外で】

子供は外で遊ぶのが好きだ。

Children like playing outdoors [outside].

彼は外で待っている。

He's waiting outside.

トムは外ではおとなしい。

Tom is as meek as a lamb among his companions.

彼はいつも外で食事をする。（外食）

He always eats out.

〈注〉 dine out はごく普通の人の毎日の外食にはぴったりしない。特別のごちそうの響きがある。

母は外に働きに出ている［外で働いている］。

My mother has a job (in the nearby town).

【外から】

そのドアは外からかぎがかかる。

The door locks from the outside.

私たちの様子は外から見える。

People can see us from outside.

私たちは外から人を頼まねばならない。

We need outside help.

外から見ると彼は健康そうに見える。

He looks just as healthy as anybody else.

〈注〉 look は外見のことであるからこの語を強調して発音すると「体の内部はいざ知らず外見は…」の意になる。

その → それ・これ・あれ

that; the same; the very

〈注〉 「あの」が that,「この」が this,「その」が the であると理解してはいけない。また its を「その」と同一視してもいけない。まして it's と書くのはまったくの誤りである。

「その」(this, that も同様)には，はっきりと「その日，その時，その人」など「そのもの」を指し示す意味がある。一方，the はすでに話題にのぼったり，相手にそれとわかる物につける符号で，特にとりたてて指示するほどの意味はない。its は it の所有格であるから，its name (犬や猫の名前) などのように，his や her などと同じ使い方をする。it's は it is の省略形で it の所有格ではないのは言うまでもない。

「その」は「この」と「あの」との中間であるが，this よりは that に近い。

最近夜ふかしがすぎるようになった。その影響が翌朝如実に現れている。

I've got into the habit of staying up until late these days, but that [this] naturally affects my mood the next morning.

【その日】

その日私はちょうどそこに居合せたのだ。

On that day I happened to be there.

【その時】

私がそこに到着したちょうどその時，入れ違いに彼はその地を去ったのだった。

I arrived there at the very moment he left.

【その人】

それはジョンソンその人であった。

It was Johnson himself.

そのうち

【近日中】

そのうちまた電話します。

I'll call you again (pretty) soon.

そのうち連れて行ってあげるよ。

I'll take you there { one of these days. / pretty soon.

【時が来れば】

警察が調べている。そのうち何もかもはっきりするだろう。

Police are investigating the case. Everything will become clear eventually [in the end].

あの人もそのうち落ち着く[わかる]でしょう。

She'll settle down [understand] by and by.

景気もそのうちよくなるだろう。

The economy will get better by and by.

〈注〉 by and by そのうち，little by little 少しずつ，day by day 日毎に。

《類義語》

【近未来】

shortly, before long あとで，のちほど。

soon すぐ，まもなく (before long と同義のときもあるが，もっと漠然と使うときもある。2, 3 時間ぐらいから数日後まで幅がある)。

【不確定未来】

one of these days そのうち (会話でよく使う)。

(1) pretty soon じきに

(2) very uncertain time 不確定，そのうち

(1)(2)のどちらにもなる。どちらになるかは声の調子や内容で決る。内容が愉快なことなら(1)，好ましくないことであれば(2)で，いつになるかわからない気のない言い方になる。

I'll take you there one of these days.
(そのうち連れていってあげるね)

I'll paint the kitchen one of these days.
(台所のぬり替えならそのうちやるさ)

日本語の「そのうち」もあやふやさがある点がよく似ている。

some day いつの日か (未来)

sometime いつか (未来または過去)

cf. one day
the other day } ともに過去の日を指す。
〈注〉 どれを使ったらよいか迷うときは，時間や日数をはっきり示すほうがよい。
ex. in a few minutes; in an hour; in three days; three days from now; in two weeks; in a few months

そのまま

1．前と変らない状態

彼の生れた家はそのまま保存されている。

The house he was born in has been left just as it was.

未亡人は彼の書斎に触るにしのびなく，すべてそのままにしておいた。

The widow didn't want to change things in his study, so everything remained as it had been [intact].

君が聞いたとおりそのまま僕に話してくれ。

Tell me the story as you heard it.

【服装】

そのままでいらしてください。(普段着のままで)

Come just as you are.

【人柄】

そのままのあなたが好き。

I like you just as you are.

【座ったまま】

どうぞそのまま（お立ちにならないでください)。

Please, don't get up [stay seated].

〈注〉 Please, keep seated. は非常のときなど「席を立たないでそのまま指示をお待ちください」の意味に使う。

【着たまま】

どうぞそのまま(コートを着ていてください)，中は寒いですから。

Please keep your coat on; it is cold inside.

【電話を切らないで】

そのままお待ち願います。

Please hold the line.

Hold on, please.

2．それきり

その悲劇的事件の後，彼は突然家を出てそのまま消息を絶ってしまった。

After the tragedy he suddenly left home and { has not been heard of since. / was never heard of again.

そば

1．近所 →きんじょ

家は駅のそばにある。

My house is near [by, close to] the station.

郵便局のそばに銀行がある。

There is a bank near the post office.

彼の家はすぐそばだ。

His house is close by [quite near].

2．身辺

彼女はどこへ行っても子供たちがそばに寄って来る。

Children gather round her wherever she goes.

よく見えるように，そばに寄ってごらん。

Come closer so you can see better.

私のそばにいなさいよ，迷子になるよ。

Keep close to [Stay near] me or you'll get lost.

3．横

ブラッドフォード家の晩餐会であの子のそばに座っていた背の高い人はだれ？

Who was the tall man who sat near her at Mr. Bradford's dinner party?

トムはやって来ると私のそばに腰を下ろした。

Tom came and sat by [beside] me.

曙のそばに並ぶと，どの力士も小さく見えた。

Any sumo wrestler looked small standing beside Akebono.

学校へ行く途中，私はいつも小さなおもちゃ屋のそばを通って行った。

On my way to school I used to pass by a

small toy shop.

かわいい女の子がそばを通りかかり，その子猫を拾い上げた。

A pretty girl happened to pass by and picked up the kitten.

それ・これ・あれ

1．英語との対応

【既出を示す定冠詞】 **the**

【既出の物を示す代名詞】 **it**

【既出の人物を示す代名詞】 **he, she**

【指示の意味をもつ代名詞】

これ(近くのものをさす) **this** (1)

それ(中間のものをさす)
あれ(遠くのものをさす) } **that** (2)

(1)	これ	この	こんな
	this	this	like this such
	ここ	これから	
	here	from now	
(2)	それ(まれに it)	その(まれに the)	そんな
	that	that	like that such
	あれ	あの	あんな
	そこ	それから	
	there over there	then, after that since then [that time]	
	あそこ	あれから	

2．それから，その時

〈注〉「それから」と「その時」は図示すれば次のように異なる。にもかかわらず，同じ then で表せるので誤りのもとになることがある。

それから → { after that; since then; and then

その時 ↑ { at that time; then; on that occasion

【それから】

それから後は彼に会うことはなかった。

I never met him after that.

私は買物に行って，それから友人を訪ねた。

I went shopping and then called on a friend.

【その時】

私が出かけようとしていたちょうどその時，彼が「ちょっと待って」と叫んだ。

I was about to start(,) when he shouted "Wait a minute."

母は肺結核で亡くなった。その時私はまだ5歳だった。

My mother died of tuberculosis. I was only five then.

そろい（揃い）・そろう・そろえる

1．同形

【服】

女子生徒はそろいの服[制服]を着ている。

The schoolgirls are wearing uniforms.

その双子の姉妹はいつもおそろいの服を着ていて，どっちがどっちかわからない。

The twin girls were always dressed just the same, and we couldn't tell which was which.

〈注〉 上の二つの例文を比べると，下の文の be dressed はだれかが dress する感じがある。制服の場合は他人に着せてもらうものではないから be wearing が適当である。

【背丈】

チアリーダーには背のそろった子がいい。

I think we should choose children of about the same height to be cheerleaders.

【切りそろえる】

前髪を(切り)そろえてください。

Trim [Cut] { the bangs.〔米〕 / the fringe.〔英〕

(生け垣やつつじなどを) そろえてください。

Trim the bushes even.

【整頓】

雑誌をナンバー順にそろえてください。

Put the magazines in numerical order.

氏名をアルファベット順にそろえてください。

Arrange the names in alphabetical order.

2．同質

【声】

少女たちは声をそろえて歌った。

The girls all sang in unison [chorus].

全員が口をそろえて試験よりレポート（を書く方）がいいと言った。

They all said they'd rather write reports than have an exam.

【外見】

あそこの娘さんたちはそろって器量よしだ。

Her daughters are all good-looking.

【能力】

ここは優秀な先生をそろえている。

The teaching staff here is exceptional.

この学校にはいい先生がそろっている。

The school has very good teachers.

生徒の学力のそろった組の方が教えやすい。

It's easier to teach a class in which students don't have much difference in ability.

3．品ぞろえ

ピーターソン宝石店は時計なら豊富に品をそろえている[品がそろっている]。

Peterson's Jewelry Store has a {large stock / big assortment} of watches.

あの店は大工道具をそろえている[がそろっている]。

They carry [stock] carpentry supplies at that store.

あそこは子供用衣類なら何でもそろえている。

They carry a complete stock of children's clothes.

私どもでは赤ちゃん用品を何でもそろえております。

Our shop has anything you might need for babies.

4．集める

カントの全集[ビートルズのアルバム]をそろえたい。

I want to get {a complete set of Kant's works. / all the Beatles' albums.}

もう１冊でシリーズ［セット］が全部そろう。

One more volume will complete the (whole) series [set].

〈注〉 series とは１冊ずつ次々に発行される刊行物・全集など。set は数巻でひとまとめになった選集・全集など。

ex. 2 sets of Encyclopedia Britannica
（２セットのブリタニカ百科事典）

お茶が出せるように(湯飲みその他を)そろえてください。

Please get the tea things ready.

明日までにキャンプに必要なものをそろえておいてくださいね。

Please get the camping things ready by tomorrow.

学校の道具はそろったかい？

Have you got everything ready for school?

野球をするだけの人数がそろえられるでしょうか。

Can you find [get together] enough people to play baseball?

5．集合する

皆そろったか。

Is everybody here?

皆そろって出発した。

They all started together.

おそろいでお出かけですか。

Are you going out together?

〈注〉 家族がそろって出かけるのを見て隣人が挨拶として上のように言う。同じ状況でアメリカ人は次のように声をかける。

Good-bye. Have a good time!
(行ってらっしゃい。楽しんでいらっしゃい)

そん（損）

1．金銭

【損をする】

彼は競馬で大損をした。

He has lost a lot of money betting on horses

[horse races].

宝くじを買って損をした。

I have wasted money buying [on] lottery cards.

ひょっとすると損をするかもしれない。

It would involve a big loss.

【取引】

5000円なら損はしない。

It's not bad for 5000 yen.

It's a good bargain at 5000 yen.

損をしてまで家を売る気はない。

I have no intention of selling my house at a loss.

2．努力・時間など

【骨折り損】

それは骨折り損だった。

It was a wasted effort.

それは骨折り損になるだろう。

It'll all be for nothing.

彼を説得しようと時間と精力を使ったが骨折り損だった。

I have wasted time and energy trying to persuade him.

私のアパート探しは骨折り損に終った。

I've wasted a lot of effort looking for an apartment.

心配して損をした。

I was worrying for nothing.

3．不利

君の損になる。(↔得になる)

It is to your disadvantage. (↔ It's to your advantage.)

社長の息子だということで損をすることがある。

It's sometimes a disadvantage to be the son of a company president.

残念ながら君は市街地から遠方に住んでいるために損をしている。

Unfortunately, it's a disadvantage that you live far from the city center.

〈注〉 cf. You have the disadvantage of living far from ... のような構文も使える。

背が小さいと損だ。

It's not an advantage to be small.

そんな → それ・これ・あれ

1．そんな＋名詞

【そんなもの】

そんなもの好きじゃない。

I don't like things like that.

【そんなこと】

そんなこと言ってません。

I didn't say that [so].

そう，そんなこと聞いたことがあるわ。

Yes, I've heard of something like that before.

そんなこと二度と言うな。

Don't ever say that [that sort of thing] again!

そんなことだろうと思った。

I thought so.

I thought as much.

Just as I thought!

【そんな人】

「スミスさんいますか」「いや，ここにはそんな人いませんよ」。

"Is Mr. Smith in?" "Sorry, there's no such person here."

【そんなふうに】

そんなふうに私を見つめないでください。

Don't stare at me that way.

【そんなわけで】

事故にあったんだ。そんなわけで遅れてしまった。

I had a car accident, and so I was late.

そんなはずはない。

That can't be.

すみません。そんなつもりではなかったんです。

I'm sorry. I didn't mean it.

2. そんなに

彼女の病気がそんなに悪いとは知りませんでした。

We didn't know she was so ill.

そんなに難しいのですか。

Is it so difficult?

〈注〉◆such a thing の誤用

「そんなこと」「そんなもの」の意味で such a thing がすぐ思いつくかもしれないが,「そんなもの」が「その種のもの」ではなくて, 下の例のように「ある特定のもの」を指す場合は such a thing とは言えない。that がぴったりする（下線部に注意）。

Husband comes home at 6:00 eager for dinner.
Wife : Oh ! Didn't you say you'd be home late tonight?
Hus : No, I didn't say <u>that</u>. It's <u>tomorrow</u> night (that) I'll be late.

夫が夕食のために6時に帰宅したところ,
妻「あら, 今夜は帰宅が遅いとおっしゃいませんでしたか」
夫「いや, そんなことは言わなかったよ。それは明日の晩のことだよ」

夫の言う「そんなこと」は I'll be late tonight（今日は遅くなる）という特定の言葉を指しているわけで, I didn't say that. がぴったりする。

◆強調するときは such a thing の形を使える。

Even a child knows that [such a simple thing].
（子供だってそんな（簡単な）こと知っているさ）

◆such の誤用例

そんな彼を見て腹が立った。
×I was angry to see such him.

「そんな」の内容によるが, 例えば次のように直す。
○ I was angry to see him behave like that.

×such one day（そんなある日）

「そんな」の説明は前にすんでいるので one day だけでよい。

た

…た

〈注〉・過去を意味しない「た」
曲った道。困ったこと。
おなかがすいた。疲れた。
みんな出かけた後で掃除をする。
・過去を意味する「た」
きのうは学校に行った。
上の2種類の「た」を混同しないように注意。

1．現在の状態

曲った道　a winding road

困ったこと

(a) trouble [difficulty]; a problem

ああ，おなかがすいた。

Oh, I'm starving [very hungry].

ああ，疲れた。

Oh, I'm tired.

2．完了を表す

【現在】

宿題は終った。

I've finished my homework.

【習慣】

母はみんな出かけた後で掃除をする。

After we {leave in the morning, / have gone off to school,} mother cleans the house.

子猫が食べた後，残ったものを親猫が食べる。

After kittens {have finished eating, / finish eating,} the mother cat eats what is left.

【未来】

旅行社に就職したい。私の立てた計画でお客さんが旅行すると思うとうれしいから。

I want to work in a travel bureau, because I'll get a lot of satisfaction (out of) thinking that people will be traveling according to the route I planned.

〈注〉「私の立てた計画」は次のようにも書ける。
the plan I {made / have made}
時制の問題を避けて次のように言ってもよい。
It will be satisfying to make travel plans for the customers.

3．条件

大人になったら世界旅行がしたい。

When I {am an adult, / grow up,} I will travel all over the world.

大人になったら選挙で投票ができる。

When I become an adult, I can vote.

試験が終ったらすぐ手術をすることになった。

It was arranged that I would have the operation soon after I finished the exams.

〈注〉これから試験がある。すなわちすべて未来の設定でも ×after I would … としない。finished と過去にするのは It was arranged が過去時制であるからで，これからのことを語るのなら，I'll have the operation soon after I finish all the exams. と finish でよい。または簡単に次のようにも言える。
The operation was planned after my exams.

…だ

1．断定

【…だ，…である，…です】

〈注〉日本語は省略が多く，論理的にルーズなところがあるので，「AはBだ[である]」を機械的に英語の“A is B.”と同一視してはいけない。
「彼は学生だ」は He is a student. でよいが，次のような場合はAとBが論理的にイコールで結べないので注意を要する。

彼は病気だ。

He is ill.（×He is an illness.)

明日は学校だ。

Tomorrow we'll have school.

Tomorrow there's school.

(×Tomorrow is school.)

中学は義務教育だ。

Junior high school (education) is compul-

sory.
(×Junior high school is compulsory education.)
彼女の髪は天然パーマだ。
Her hair is naturally wavy.
She has naturally wavy hair.
Her hair has natural wave (in it).
(×Her hair is natural wave.)

2. 過去の陳述
【…だった】
そのとき彼は5歳だった。
He was five then.
彼は小学校の3年生だった。
He was in the third grade at the time.
×He was the third grade at the time.
彼はたいへん元気だった。
He was in high spirits.

…たい → …したい・…したがる

だいいち（第一）→ はじめ

1. 順序
【第一に】
第一に健康でなければならない。
First of all, you must be healthy.
まず第一に率直に話し合おうじゃないか。
First [In the first place], let's be frank (with each other).
彼はロンドンから帰るとまず第一にマイクを病院に見舞った。
The first thing he did after coming back from London was to visit Mike in hospital.
【第1位】
彼のチームは県下で［リーグで］第1位である。
His team is { the best in this prefecture. / first in the league.

〈注〉◆第一に，第二に，第三に…と箇条書きのように並べるのは日本語ではごく普通である。英語の場合，公文書的なものなら箇条書きでよい。
(1) (number one)
(2) (number two)
(3) (number three)
論文・スピーチの類では，
First … Second … Last …
くだけた表現では別に規則はないが

はじめ	中間		終り
First	second / next then / also after that	など	last finally

◆「最後に」は last, finally 以外に in conclusion, to summarize（まとめると…）としてもよい。しかし，×at last, ×at the last は最後の締めくくりの言葉としてはおかしい。
最後に一言付け加えさせていただきます。
Let me add a few words in conclusion.
最後になりましたが（決して軽く見ているのではない）…
Last but not least, …（スピーチなどで）

2. 主要な
代表団の第一の目的は両国の親善を促進することである。
The delegation's primary objective is to cultivate [promote] friendly relations between the two countries.
健康が第一だ。
The most important thing is to be healthy.
Health is { the most important thing. / most important.
彼は実業界の第一人者だ。
He's a leading [prominent] figure in the business world.
彼はこの分野の第一人者だ。
He's the foremost expert in this field.

3. まず何よりも
第一，彼の名前も知らない。
I don't even know his name.
第一，僕には金がないよ。
To begin with, I don't have any [the, enough] money.

たいいん（退院）

退院する **leave（the）hospital**

〈注〉 米国では the をつける傾向があるが，英国では冠詞なしが普通。

彼女はこの前の日曜日に退院した。

She left（the）hospital last Sunday.

彼女は2か月ぶりにやっと退院を許された。

She was allowed to leave（the）hospital after two months.

2,3日のうちに退院できることになるだろう。

She will be released from（the）hospital in a few days.

彼女は明日退院する予定だ。

She is going to leave（the）hospital tomorrow.

彼女は退院したばかりだ。

She is just out of（the）hospital.

たいがい(大概)・たいてい(大抵) →ほとんど

1．一般に

generally; usually; in general

女の子ならたいがい着るものに関心を持っている。

{In general / Generally（speaking）} girls are interested in what they wear.

彼は日曜日はたいてい家にいる。

He {usually / generally} stays at home on Sunday.

2．ほとんど

almost all; most; mostly

近頃はたいがいの人は運転免許(証)を持っている。

{Almost everyone has / Most people have} a driver's license these days.

うちの大学の学生はたいてい近県から来ている。

The students of our college are {mostly / almost all} from neighboring prefectures.

3．たぶん

probably

たいていあすは雨になるだろう。

Probably it will rain tomorrow.

たいていそんなことだろうと思った。

I thought so.

4．慣用表現

働くのもたいがい[たいてい]にしておけ。

Don't work so hard.

Take it easy.

飲むのもたいがい[たいてい]にしておけ。

Don't drink so much.

Don't get so drunk.

You're drinking too much, aren't you?

〈注〉 「たいていにしておけ」はほとんどの場合親しい間柄で使う表現であり，英語でも友人や家族間で使われる。そうでなければ一番最後の例文を使うのが望ましい。

たいがく（退学）

退学する **leave college [school]; leave school halfway; quit college**〔*informal*〕

〈注〉 leave school は米語では退学の意味。英国英語では「中途で（half way）」と説明がなければ graduate（卒業する）の意味になる。文の前後関係ではっきりさせることが必要。なお大学も school でよい。

メアリーは働いて家計を助けるために退学した。

Mary left school to work and help（to）support her family.

あの子は学校を中途退学しなければならなかった。

She had to give up [quit]（going to）school halfway.

高校によっては生徒の10%がついていけなくなって退学していく。

In some high schools ten percent of the students drop out [quit].

彼は息子を退学させた。

He made his son leave school.

彼は退学させられた。

He was expelled from school.

〈注〉 school に冠詞はなくてよい。
「彼は1週間の停学になった」は
He was suspended from school for one week.

だいがく（大学）→ きょういく

1. 大学の種類と機構

総合大学 **a university;** 単科大学 **a college;** 国立大学 **a national university;** 公立大学 **a public university;** 県立大学 **a prefectural university [college];** 市立大学 **a city university [college];** 私立大学 **a private university [college];** 短期大学 **a junior college; a community college**

《関連語》
大学院
graduate school; postgraduate school〔英〕
修士課程 master's program
博士課程 doctoral program; Ph. D. program
学部 faculty (ex. 工学部 Faculty of Engineering)
系列 division (ex. 社会科学系 Division of Social Science)
学科 department (ex. 機械科 Department of Mechanical Engineering)
本部 central administration
事務局 office
庶務課 personnel office, general affairs office
教務厚生課 student affairs office
会計課 accounting office
総長，学長 President
学部長 Dean of the Faculty
学生部長 Dean of Student Affairs（米国の大きい大学では，このほかに academic dean（カリキュラムなど学業に関する事を取り扱う）がいる）
教授陣 faculty
教授 professor
准教授 associate professor〔米〕
助教授 assistant professor
講師 instructor〔米〕; lecturer〔英〕
専任教員 full-time staff member
非常勤教員 part-time staff member
助手 assistant（いろいろな身分の助手があり，仕事により呼称も異なる。欧米では大学院生が助手的仕事をする）
実験助手 lab assistant [technician]

2. 学生生活

学生 **a student;** 大学院生 **a graduate student**

【学部生】undergraduates

大学1年生
a fresher〔米〕; a first-year student

大学2年生
a sophomore〔米〕; a second-year student

大学3年生
a junior〔米〕; a third-year student

大学4年生
a senior〔米〕; a fourth-year student

【学生生活】
school life; college life; university life

〈注〉 学生生活に関する語彙中，次のものは別項目で解説してある。教育，クラブ，下宿，試験，就職，授業，成績，単位，入学，入試。

必修科目 a compulsory [required] course

選択科目
an elective course〔米〕; an optional course

単位登録 registration

単位登録をする register [enroll] in a class

専攻する
specialize in; major in〔米〕
study〔英〕

ベイカー先生の歴史をとる[の受講届を出す]
take [enroll in] Professor Baker's history class

近代哲学をとっている。
I'm taking Modern Philosophy.

アダムス先生の近代哲学をとっている。
I'm in Mr. Adams' modern philosophy class [course].

近代哲学は水曜日にある。

My modern philosophy class meets on Wednesday.

私は修士課程で勉強中だ。

I'm in the master's program.

この大学の博士課程は厳しい。

The Ph. D. program is very rigorous at this university.

教職課程　teacher education program

教育実習　student teaching; teaching practice [practicum]

【称号】 degrees

学士

（文系）　BA（Bachelor of Arts）

（理系）　BS, BSc（Bachelor of Science）

修士　MA（Master of Arts）

M. S., MSc（Master of Science）

博士　Ph. D.（Doctor of Philosophy; 文系・理系とも Ph. D. という）

【生協】 student union〔米〕

娯楽室　a recreation room; 食堂　a cafeteria

ラウンジ a lounge; 雑貨店　a sundries store

本屋　a book store

《関連語》

学問分野　area of study

人文科学　humanities

哲学　philosophy; 倫理学　ethics

文学　literature（ex. English, American, French, etc.）

比較文学　comparative literature

言語学　linguistics

外国語　foreign languages（ex. English, French, German, Chinese, etc.）

美術　fine arts; 音楽　music

演劇　theater and drama

宗教学　religious studies

法学　law

社会科学　social science

ジャーナリズム　journalism

考古学　arch(a)eology

人類学　anthropology; 民族学　ethnology

社会学　sociology; 心理学　psychology

教育学　education; 経済学　economics

政治学　politics; political science

歴史学　history; 地理学　geography

自然科学　natural science

物理学　physics; 数学　mathematics

統計学　statistics

情報科学　information science; informatics

化学　chemistry; 生化学　biochemistry

生物学　biology; 生態学　ecology

植物学　botany; 動物学　zoology

微生物学　microbiology; 地質学　geology

地球物理学　geophysics

天文学　astronomy; 気象学　meteorology

自然地理学　physical geography

海洋学　oceanography; marine science

学際的研究　interdisciplinary studies

地域研究　area studies

アジア研究　Asian studies

都会生活研究　urban studies

体育　physical education

〈注〉以上は大ざっぱな学問分野のリストで，この他に実学として工学 engineering, 商学 business, 農学　agriculture　などがある。また応用～学 applied ～や多くの専門科目があるが省略した。

たいくつ（退屈）→ つまらない

退屈する　**be bored with**《something》

退屈な人　a bore

彼のおしゃべりは退屈でうんざりした。

I was bored {to death / stiff / to tears〔*colloq.*〕} with his talk.

He bored me stiff [to death] with his talk.

彼は退職してから退屈で困っている。

After retiring from work, he found the boredom（of his days）oppressive.

ほんの退屈しのぎにデパートに入った。

I went into the department store just to pass the time.

退屈な一日も何とか過ぎていった。

The day {dragged on. / wore on.}

《類義語》

dull　つまらない。「退屈な」の最も一般的な語。

Life seemed dull and monotonous.
（人生が単調なつまらないものに思えた）

I fell asleep in class because his lecture was rather dull.（講義が退屈で眠ってしまった）

boring　つまらなくてうんざりする感じ。一般的な語。本文最初の例文のように be bored の形もよく使われる。

What a boring meeting! I could hardly stay awake.（何て退屈な会議だ。起きているのが精一杯だ）

That's a boring book.（面白くない[退屈な]本だ）

tedious　冗長な。つまらないうえに時間がかかる。主として行いについて言う。

Learning irregular verbs is awfully tedious.
（不規則動詞（の活用）を覚えるのにはうんざりする）

a tedious journey（長く退屈な旅）

Exciting in the beginning, this lab research has become really tedious; every day I do nothing but count bacteria that hardly vary.（はじめは面白かったが，この実習というやつは毎日代り映えのしないバクテリアの数ばかり数えさせられ，まったくうんざりしている）

irksome　つまらなくてやりがいがなく腹立たしい。不満の気持ちが強い。

tiresome　ひどく退屈でつまらなくてまったく疲れる。

What a tiresome person he is, always making jokes that aren't funny!
（面白くもない冗談ばかり言ってまったくあいつは疲れる）

wearisome　つまらなくて，おまけにのろくて心身ともに疲れる。tiresome よりさらに重苦しい感じ。

たいざい（滞在）

滞在する　**stay; make a long [short] stay in**《a place》

2, 3 日叔父の所に滞在する。

I'll stay with my uncle for a few days.

【宿に】

彼はいま長良館に滞在している。

He's now staying at the Nagarakan Hotel.

彼は海辺に 1 週間滞在していた。

He spent a week at the beach.

He stayed there for a week.（そこに）

【…日間】

スミス氏は 5 日間の日本滞在[訪問]のため東京に到着した。

Mr. Smith arrived in Tokyo on a five-day visit to Japan.

【滞在中】

私は東京滞在中のスミス氏を訪問した。

I went to see Mr. Smith during his stay in Tokyo.

〈注〉 stay は「滞在する」の意味では常に自動詞なので×I stayed Tokyo. は誤り。I stayed at a hotel in Tokyo. などとする。一方「…日間滞在した」の意味の spend は他動詞で，滞在日数を目的語とするので×I spent at the resort. は誤り。I spent a week [some time] at a resort. などとする。

だいじょうぶ（大丈夫）

1. 安心な状態

「大丈夫か」「大丈夫だ」。

"Are you all right?" "I'm ⌊all right [OK]."

病人はもう大丈夫だ。

The patient is now out of danger.

【安全】

こわがらなくても大丈夫。私がついています。

Don't be afraid. { I'll help you. / I'm with you. }

それは大丈夫か[安全か]。

Isn't it dangerous?

Is it safe?

【防水】

これは水にぬれても大丈夫だ。

This is waterproof.

【耐震】

このホテルは地震が来ても大丈夫だ。

This hotel is earthquakeproof.

2．確信
大丈夫，天気になる。
The weather [It] will surely be fine.
I'm sure it will be fine.
It will be fine; I assure you.（元気づけ）
彼女は「大丈夫」というように私を見てうなずきほほえみかけた。
She nodded and smiled at me reassuringly.（reassure＝restore to confidence 自信を回復させる）

たいせつ（大切）

1．重要な
important; valuable
この書類は大切なものだ。安全な場所にしまってください。
These papers are very important [valuable]. Keep them in a safe place.
健康は富より大切だ。
Health is more valuable than wealth.
彼は今や職場においてなくてはならぬ大切な人だ。
He is now indispensable in the office.〔強〕
【大切なこと】
あの子も何が大切で，何が大切でないかの区別ぐらいわかってよい年頃だ。
She is old enough to know what is important and what is not.
一番大切なことは率直に話し合うことだ。
The point / The most important thing } is to be frank.
そこが大切なところ[肝心な点]だ。
That is the point.

2．尊重
【大切にする】
（精神的に）**treasure; value;**（人を） **treat kindly; take good care of;**（物を） **handle with care**
彼女はアンティックドールを集めて大切にしている。
Her collection of antique dolls is her treasure.
彼は古いいろいろなコインを引き出しにしまって大切にしている。
He treasures various old coins in his drawer.
金より時間が大切だという人がたくさんいる。
There are many people who value time more than money.
私は子供のころのそれらの楽しかった思い出を大切に胸にしまっている。
I cherish those happy memories of my childhood.
両親が年をとったら大切に孝行しようと思っている。
We plan to take good care of our parents in their old age.
古い切手は大切に扱わないといけない。
Old stamps must be handled with care.

3．挨拶
どうぞお大切に。
Take（good）care of yourself.
Look after yourself.
〈注〉 英国では特に健康が気遣われるとき以外は，ただの挨拶としては言わないようである。アメリカ人はよく別れ際に "Take care." と言うが，これは「お元気で」と同じで，特に健康を気遣っているのではない。

だいたい（大体）→ たいがい・たいご

1．概して，おおよそ
roughly; on the whole; in general（一般に）**; for the most part**
名 だいたいのこと **gist**
だいたいのところそんなことだ。
That's the gist of it.
だいたいわかった。
I get [I've got] the general idea.
I think I understand the gist of it.
だいたいよろしい。
On the whole

{ you are right.（考え方が正しい）
 it has been done well.（よくできた）

君の意見にはだいたい賛成だ。

For the most part I agree with you.

だいたいでき上がった。

It is almost [practically] finished.

【概算】

被害額はだいたい5000万円と推定される。

The damage is roughly about [estimated at] fifty million yen.

2．もともと

だいたいお前(のやり方)が悪い。

Your policy was wrong to begin with.

You are wrong about it [that].

だいたい動機が間違っている。

The motive itself is wrong.

その計画はだいたい初めからうまく行かなかったのだ。

The plan was a failure from the very beginning.

だいち（大地）→ つち

たいてい → たいがい

たいへん（大変）

1．骨の折れる

たいへんな **tough**〔強〕; **hard;**（要求などが長くかかり難しい） **stiff**

たいへんな宿題

stiff homework [assignments]

たいへんな契約条件[給料]の要求

stiff demands { in contract terms / about wages }

広い庭の草取りはたいへんな仕事だ。

It's { tough〔*colloq.*〕/ no easy task } to weed a large garden.

Weeding a large garden is hard work.

たいへんですね。(ねぎらい)

You are really working hard, aren't you?

That's hard work, isn't it?

It's a tough job, isn't it?

〈注〉 日本語ではただ「ご苦労様」という気持ちを表す挨拶として「たいへんですね」と言うことがある。この習慣は欧米にはなく，本当に一生懸命働いている人には上のように言う。また，逆に怠けている人に皮肉っぽく "You're working hard."（精が出るね）と言うことがある。

これだけの手紙に返事を書くのは大変だ。

I'll have a hard [tough] time answering all those letters.

夫を失って母親だけの手で子供を育てるのはたいへんだ。

It's by no means easy for a widowed mother to bring up her children.

2．重大な

great; terrible; 致死の **fatal**

名神高速道路でたいへんな事故があった。

There was a terrible accident on the Meishin Highway.

私はたいへんな間違いをした。

I have made a terrible [great] mistake.

たいへんなことになった。

{ The situation has / Things have } become very difficult.

Things are in a mess!

What a mess!〔*colloq.*〕

あなたに何かあったらたいへんだ。

What if anything should happen to you!

失敗したらたいへんだ。(それで終りだ)

One mistake could be fatal.

One mistake and all is [would be] over.

【慰め】

お父様がご病気ですって。たいへんですね。

Your father's sick? It must be hard for you.

3．感嘆文

たいへんだ！（驚き）

Good gracious! / Good Heavens! / Goodness me! / Good grief! / Oh no! / Oh dear!〔弱〕

〈注〉 "Oh no!(—↘)"(ああたいへん，まあ気の毒に)
cf. Oh(↘) no(↘). (いや，そうじゃない)

4．大いに →おおいに，とても・とっても

たいへんお世話になりました。(別れの挨拶・今までのことに対するお礼)

Thanks for everything.

Thanks for all you've done (for me).

You've always been very kind, helpful and thoughtful.

I sincerely thank you.

I appreciate it very much.

たいへん悲しいお知らせですが，スミスさんが昨夜亡くなられました。

I have very sad news for you. Mr. Smith died last night.

たおす(倒す)・たおれる

倒す 動他 **bring [throw] down, knock down;** 負かす **defeat, beat;** (政権などを) **overthrow;** 殺す **kill**

倒れる 動自 **fall, collapse**(まれに 他); (病などで) **break down;** (政権・王朝などが) **be overthrown;** 死ぬ **die, perish** 〔*formal*〕

1．転倒・倒壊

【人】

少年が2人校庭の隅で取っ組み合いのけんかをしていて小さい方が大きい方を打ち倒した。倒された方は2, 3分間仰向けに倒れたまま動かなかった。

Two boys were fighting in one corner of the schoolground and the smaller one knocked down the bigger one, who lay still on his back for a few minutes.

【災害】

台風で取り入れ前の稲が倒された。

The typhoon {blew down / toppled} the rice just before it [the rice] was harvested.

大きな木が何本も台風で倒された。

Many big trees {fell (down) during the typhoon. / were blown down by the typhoon.}

10軒以上の家屋が地震で倒れた。

More than ten houses collapsed in the earthquake.

【物】

ウエイトレスがワイングラスを倒した。

The waitress tipped the wine glass over.

2．病気など

彼のお父さんが脳溢血で倒れた。

His father had a stroke.

彼は過労で倒れた。

He {had a physical breakdown / broke down} from overwork.

〈注〉 ただ breakdown と言うと，普通 nervous breakdown(精神的に参ってしまうこと)の意味になる。

おなかがすいて倒れそうだ。

I'm going to faint from hunger.

3．負かす，滅ぼす

【人】

光秀は主人の信長を倒したが，結局秀吉に倒された。

Mitsuhide killed his lord, Nobunaga, but in turn was killed by Hideyoshi.

【内閣】

田中内閣はロッキード事件のために倒れた。

The Tanaka Cabinet collapsed because of the Lockheed affair.

【銀行】

銀行が倒れた。

The bank has gone bankrupt.

【企業】

多くの中小企業が不景気で倒れた。

Many small and mid-sized businesses have failed because of the recession.

【政府】

暴動のために政府が倒れた。

The government was forced to resign because of the riot.

The government was overthrown [toppled] by the rioters.

The rioters brought down the government.

たがい → おたがいに

…だから

…である，だから　**... so; therefore**（並列）

…だから　**because; since; as**（従節）

〈注〉 日英の語順（word order）の違いが論理構造の違いをつくる。

(1)(a)病気だった。(b)だから会合に出られなかった。

(a)病気だった。(b)だけど会合に出た。

(2)(a)病気だったから，(b)会合に出られなかった。

(a)病気だったけど，(b)会合に出た。

(1)では(a)と(b)は並列。(2)では(b)が主で，(a)は説明的，従属的であるが，論理の進め方は(1)と(2)はほとんど同じである。

一方英語では(1)の並列型をとるか，(2)の主節・従節型をとるかは文の出だしから決めてかからなければならない。

【だから】

病気だった。だから会合に出られなかった。

(1) 並列

(a) I was ill (b) and so I couldn't attend the meeting.

(2) 主従 ((b) が主で (a) が従)

(a) As I was ill, (b) I couldn't attend the meeting.

【だけど】

病気だったけど会合に出た。

(1) 並列

(a) I was ill (b) but I still attended [yet I attended] the meeting.

(2) 主従　(b) が主で (a) が従

(a) Though I was ill, (b) I attended the meeting.

(b) I attended the meeting (a) even though I was ill.

《類義語》

理由・原因を表す英語としては because, since, as, for などがあるが，ニュアンスの違いは次の通りである。

because　理由の説明が主なポイントであるときに使う。理由の説明として一番強い。because 節は通常主節の後にくる。

I won't go because I don't like him.
（彼は好きではないから私は行かない）

because 節だけで独立文にはならないので注意。これは最も多い誤りのひとつである。

I don't want to marry quickly. ×Because I have things to do while I'm single.（早々と結婚なんかしたくない。ひとりのうちにやっておきたいことがたくさんあるから）

I don't ... quickly, because ... のように主節，従節で一文とする。

since; as　理由がすでに相手の知っている事柄であるか，それほど重要でない場合に使う。as 節，since 節は文頭にくる場合がある。英国では as の方を多く使う。米国では as は格式ばったかたい表現なので since の方を好む。また，since 節の前に間を置くと強調している感じになる。

Since you were so little [young], you don't remember him.

You can't possibly remember him, since [as] you were so little [young] .（as は軽く発音する）
（君は小さかったから彼をとても覚えてはいまい）

for　後から思いついて理由をつけ加えるような場合に使うので for 節は文頭にくることはない。また，文体上の理由で for を使うこともある。とにかく理由は重要でない。

I have to leave now, for I have a visitor in the aftenoon.（もうおいとましなきゃ，昼からお客があるの）

〈注〉 上のどの文にも because, since, as, for（文頭にこない時のみ）のいずれの接続詞も使えるが，理由の重要度などのニュアンスの違いが出ることになる。

たく（焚く，炊く）

1．火を燃やす

暖炉に火をたいてください。

Please make a fire in the fireplace.

森の中で暖をとるため，また，野獣を近づけないためにたき火をした。

They made a fire in the woods to warm themselves and also to keep wild animals away.

北海道では1年の半分はストーブをたかねばならない。

People in Hokkaido have to use a stove nearly half of the year.

彼らは私たちのために風呂をたいてくれた。

They ran [heated] the bath for us.

〈注〉 周知のように洋風バスはほとんどコックをひねれば湯が出る方式であるから「風呂をたく」にあたる作業はない。上の例文中コックをひねるのはran, 日本式のガス風呂ならば heated となる。

2．炊事する

近頃の若い者は，電気炊飯器を使わずにはごはんの炊き方も知らない。

Young people these days don't know how to cook rice without using an electric rice cooker.

だく（抱く）・だかれる

【状態】

赤ちゃんを抱く[抱いている]

hold [carry] a baby in one's arms

抱かれている　be in《one's》arms

【動作】

赤ちゃんを抱く[抱き上げる]

take a baby in《one's》arms

pick up a baby

【抱きしめる】

hug; give a hug; 強く抱きしめる embrace

〈注〉 embrace は主義主張を心に抱く意味にも使われる。

赤ちゃんを抱かせて。

Let me hold your baby.

赤ちゃんが泣いてもいちいち抱き上げたりしないで。

Don't pick her up every time she cries.

赤ちゃんを抱いているご夫人はどなたですか。

Who is the lady {with / carrying} the baby in her arms?

彼女はわが子をしっかり抱きしめて泣いていた。

She was crying, holding her boy tightly.

〈注〉 hug（しっかり抱きしめる）は愛情がこもっている。

【抱き合せ販売】 a tie-in sale

たくさん

［量］ **much; a great deal of**

［数］ **many; a great [large] number of**

［数・量とも］ **a lot of; lots of;（a）plenty of**

〈注〉 「たくさん」は量の場合にも数の場合にも使われるが，英語では量ではかる名詞（uncountable）と，数ではかる名詞（countable）の区別があるので要注意。たとえば日本語の「仕事」は英語の work（uncountable), job（countable）のどちらも含む概念であるが，「たくさんの仕事」は ×many works ではなく a lot of work となる。

1．多量・多数

宿題がたくさんある。

I have {many assignments. / lots of homework.}

今日はやることがたくさんある。

I have {a lot / many things} to do today.

最近は仕事がたくさんある。

Nowadays we have plenty of work to do.

この川には鮭がたくさんいる。

There are a lot of salmon in this river.

This river has lots of [abundant〔*literary*〕] salmon.

Salmon is abundant in this river.〔*literary*〕

2. 十分

enough; sufficient

もうたくさんです。(断る言い方)

No more, thank you.

I've had enough, thank you.

もうたくさん！(うんざり)

I've had it.

I'm fed up.

Enough!

That's the limit!

たいていの大人は7時間も眠ればたくさんだ。

Seven hours' sleep is sufficient for most grownups.

〈注〉 a lot of, lots of は同じように使われる。口語では肯定平叙文に a lot of, lots of が多く使われる。

3. たくさんは…ない

来る人はたくさんはいないでしょう。

There aren't many people coming.

タンクに石油がたくさんは残っていない。

There isn't much kerosene left in the tank.

だけ

1. 唯一，限定

ひとつだけ残っている。

There is only one left.

あの人には一度だけ会ったことがある。

I have seen her only once.

【人】

あの人だけが助かった。

He alone has survived.

He is the only person who (has) survived the disaster. (災害で)

あなただけが頼りです。

You are the only person I {can trust. / have to depend upon.}

I have no one {else / but you} to depend upon.

そんなばかげたこと信じるのはお前だけだ。

No one believes such nonsense but yourself.

【事】

それだけはごめんだ。

I will do anything but that.

これだけは確かだ。(ほかのことはまだ不明)

This much is certain.

今度だけは許してあげよう。

I will forgive you this once (but never again).

2. 強調

それを見る[考える]だけでうんざりする。

The mere sight [idea, thought] of it makes me sick.

あなたはいてくれるだけでいい。

Only stay with me. That's all. (恋人同士)

Your being here [there] will be enough to scare away the rogues. (用心棒)

彼の奥さんは美人だ。なるほど彼が自慢するだけのことはある。

His wife really is as pretty as he's boasting she is.

彼はその男を泊めてやっただけでなく仕事まで探してやろうとした。

He not only gave him a roof over his head but also tried to find him work.

3. 限度・範囲

【全部】

今日はこれだけ[おしまい]。

That's all for today. / So much for today.

やりたいのはそれだけだ。

That's all I want to do.

【最低】

彼は高校だけは出してやらねば。

He will have a high school education at least.

生活できるだけの年金を給付すべきだ。

One should be given {enough pension to live on. / a pension large enough to live on.}

ここに住所氏名を書くだけで結構です。

All you have to do is (to) write down your name and address here.

【範囲】

欲しいだけ取りなさい。

Take as much as you like.

彼はできるだけ速く走った。

He ran as fast as he could.

ぶどうを1000円分だけください。

Give me a thousand yen's worth of those grapes, please.

4. 過不足

5000円だけしかない。

I've got only 5,000 yen.

5000円だけ入金します。

I can put down 5,000 yen.

彼は私より３歳(だけ)年上だ。

He is three years older than I.

布が１メートルだけ足りない。

This cloth is one meter too short.

一つだけ余る。

There is one too many.

二つだけ余る。

There are two too many.

３個だけカップが足りない。

We need three more cups.

三つだけ見つからない。

Three are missing.

…だけど → …だから

たしか（確か）

1. 確かである →きっと，ぜったいに

【話者主語】

あの人は今度は確かに成功すると思う。

I'm sure [certain] (that) he will succeed this time.

このうわさが本当かどうか確かではない[私にははっきり言えない]。

I'm not {sure / certain} {if / whether} these rumors are true.

彼がいつ帰って来るか確かには知らない。

I don't know for {sure / certain} when he will come back.

【客観的】

彼は今度は確かに成功するだろう。

{He will surely [certainly] / He's sure to} succeed this time.

彼が成功するのは確かだ。

It is certain that he will succeed.

彼は生きている。それは確かだ。

He's still alive. There's no doubt about it.

〈注〉 sure と certain の違いについて

sure は話し言葉で個人的な話題に適し，certain は書き言葉で堅く，したがって社会的，知的分野の話題に適すが，ある程度同じように使える。ただし，It is certain that … は正しいが It is sure that … は正しい用法 ではないとする説もある。迷うときは certain を使うとよい。

【第三者の確信】

何もかもうまくいくことは確かだ[請け合う]と佐藤さんは言った。

Mr. Sato assured us that everything would turn out well.

【直接名詞を修飾】

それは確かな事実だ。

It's an undeniable fact.

〈注〉 △It's a sure fact. は文としておかしい。fact はもともと sure なものであるから意味が重複する。a certain fact は「ある事実」の意味で，「確かな」の意味にはならない。

【強い確信】(確実性がさらに強調される場合)

確かに本当だ[間違っている]。

That's definitely true [wrong].

cf. まったくむかつく。

That's absolutely [positively] disgusting.

確かあいつだ。

I'm positive that's the man.

That's the man, sure enough. 〔*colloq.*〕

2. 信頼し得る

reliable; trustworthy

【確かな人】a reliable [trustworthy] person

彼は確かな人ですか。

Can we trust him?

Can he be trusted?

【確かな情報】reliable information

【確かな出所】筋 a reliable source

〈注〉 情報について，確実な[信頼すべき]筋からのものであるが，出所を明らかにしたくないときには，A reliable source said that ... と言う。

ここにあるのは確かな筋からの情報である。

I have had this information on good authority.

【確かな証拠】

clear proof; compelling proof; clear evidence; compelling evidence

〈注〉 proof はすでにある推測が証明された場合の証拠。evidence はまだ完全に証明されるところまでいかないがデータとしての証拠。

Rising juvenile delinquency is {clear proof of / evidence for} the failure of modern education.（青少年非行の増加は現代教育の失敗の確かな証拠である）

3. 正気な，しっかりした

気は確かか。 Are you crazy [sane]?

〈注〉 気絶しかけている人に「しっかりしろ」「気を確かに」と抱き起すシーンは日本映画でおなじみであるが，英米ではその人の名前を呼ぶのが自然なことだという。

【足元が確か】

彼はそろそろ80歳なのに足元は確かだ。

He's nearly eighty,

but he {walks steadily. / doesn't totter.}

4. たぶん

君にこの前会ったのは，確か田中さんのところだったね。

It was at Mr. Tanaka's that I met you last, if I remember correctly.

それは確かこの次の日曜日だ。

It's next Sunday if I am correct.

君は確かオハイオから来られたんでしたね。

You're from Ohio, I believe.

確かにそう言ったかもしれないが，あのころは私も若かったもので。

I said so, it's true, but I was young then.

たしかめる（確かめる）

make sure; see if; ascertain 〔*formal*〕; （日付や予約を）**confirm**

まず事の真偽を確かめる方がよい[確かめなさい]。

You had better make sure of the truth first.

彼女は戸口の鍵をかけたかどうか確かめに戻って来た。

She came back to {make sure that / see if} she had locked the door.

答案を出す前にもう一度目を通して確かめなさい。

You should check your paper again before you hand it in.

列車がこのホームに着くかどうか，行って確かめて来てください。

Please go and see if the train is coming to this platform.

ホテルの予約を電話で確かめた[ホテルに予約の確認の電話を入れた]。

I phoned the hotel to confirm our reservations.

たす（足す）

add

1. 総計

２足す２は４。（２＋２＝４）

Two and two {is [makes] / are [make]} four.

Two plus two is [makes] four.

これら三つの数を足すと100になる。

These three numbers will add up to 100.

全部(の数を)足すといくらになりますか。

What do the numbers add up to?（先生が子供に）

What's the total?（店などで）

〈注〉 食堂などで食べた物の値段を「足し合せる（合計する）」は add up the bill と言う。「お勘定してください」は "Could I have the bill?"。

2. 補充

もう200円足して1000円にした。

I added two hundred yen to {make it / bring it (up) to} a thousand (yen).

ギターを買うには貯金では足りなかったので母さんがお金[差額]を足してくれた。

I didn't have quite enough savings to {buy / cover the cost of} a guitar, so my mother gave me the difference [the money to make up the difference].

だす（出す）→ でる

1. …から出す

窓から頭を出すのは危険だ。

It is dangerous to {stick / put / poke} your head out of the window.

ポケットから手を出しなさい。

Take your hand out of your pocket.

ここから出して。

Please let me out of here.

2. 差し出す，伸ばす

彼は親しげに手を差し出した。

He held out his hand in a friendly manner.

そんなふうに舌を出すのは失礼だ。

It's rude to stick out your tongue like that.

3. 提供する，提出する

【金】

彼は私の学費を出してくれた。

He paid my school expenses.

彼は新しい事業に金を出した。（投資）

He invested in a new business.

彼はその運動[企画]に多額の金を出した。

He contributed a large sum of money to the campaign.

He put up money for the project.（企画）

〈注〉 put up とは全費用の50～60%といった相当の額のお金を出すことを言う。

彼は銀行から金を引き出した。

He took [withdrew, got] some money from the bank.

【手紙】

私はあれからの出来事を綿々と書いた長い手紙を彼に出した。

I wrote [sent] a long letter telling him all that had happened.

私は行く[帰る]途中に手紙を出した。

I posted [mailed] the letter on my way.

【名刺】

私は名刺を出して用件を告げた。

I gave him my card and told him the purpose of my visit.

【書類・論文】

明日までにレポートを出さなければならない。

I must turn [hand] in my paper by tomorrow.

月末までに学位論文を出すことになっている。

He is to submit his Ph. D. thesis by the end of the month.

月末までに応募書類[願書]を出すことになっている。

Applicants are to {turn in（持参する）/ send in（郵送する）/ submit〔*formal*〕} their application forms by the end of the month.

【議案】

政府は新しい税制案を出すだろう。

The government will present a new tax bill.

【食べ物】

(ホテルなどで)朝食にバター付きトーストとコーヒーが出た。

They served buttered toast and (a cup of) coffee for breakfast.

サンセット・インではうまいものを出す。

They serve delicious food at the Sunset Inn.

4. 世に出す

【人材】

山口県は徳川末期以来多くの有名な指導者や政治家を世に出してきた。

Yamaguchi Prefecture has produced [supplied] many famous leaders and politicians since the last days of the Tokugawa Era.

【出版】

彼は2冊目の本を4月に出した。

He published his second book in April.

【掲載】

そのスキャンダルは新聞に出るだろう。

The scandal will be reported in the newspapers.

求人広告を新聞に出した。

We placed a want-ad in the paper.

5. 放出する

声[音]を出すな。

Don't utter a sound.

Don't say a word.

Don't make any noise.

蛍は青白い光を出す。

Fireflies {emit / give off} a pale light.

水道をひねってしばらく水を出してから飲みなさい。

Turn on the water and let it run for a while before you drink it.

彼は高熱を出している。

He has a high fever [temperature].

水は凍るときに熱を出す。

Water generates heat as it freezes.

彼はあがってしまって試験で実力を出せなかった。

Because he got nervous, he couldn't {do his best / perform up to his capacity} in the test.

【元気】

元気を出しなさいよ。

Cheer up!

6. 慣用表現

【手[口]を出す】

彼は何にでも手[口]を出す。

He {pokes his nose into / meddles in / has got his finger in} everything.

他人のことに口を出すな。

Don't interfere {in other people's affairs. / with other people.}

【足が出る】

(予算オーバーで) 足が出てしまった。

The money didn't cover (the) expenses.

【赤字を出す】

10万円の赤字が出た。

There was a shortfall [deficit 〔*formal*〕] of 100,000 yen.

今月は赤字が出た。

We went into the red this month.

【大学を出す】

彼女は苦労して息子二人とも,大学を出した。

She worked really hard to put her two sons through college.

彼らの夢は息子3人とも大学を出すことだ。

Their dream is to get their three sons educated in university.

たすける(助ける)・たすかる

1. 命を救う, 救われる

助ける㊍㊚ **save;** 助かる **be saved**

流れは深く速かったが私は若い人に助けられた[のでおかげで助かった]。

The water was deep and fast but I was saved by a young man.
ひとりの若者がおぼれかかっていた私を助けてくれた。
A young man saved me from drowning [being drowned].
火が出たとき彼は家にいたが助かった。
He was in his apartment when the fire started, but he escaped death.
消防士が子供を火の中から助け出した。
A fireman rescued the child from the fire.
命ばかりはお助けください。
Spare (me) my life.

2. 生き残る
survive; 治癒する **recover**
船は難破したが，私たち３人だけ助かった。
We three survived the shipwreck.
この病気で助かる人は少ない。
Few survive this disease.
【助かる見込み】
彼は助かる見込みがない。
There is no hope for his recovery.

3. 解放する
それで面倒が減ってうんと助かります。
That will save me a lot of trouble.
彼が交替に来てくれて助かった。
He came to relieve me of my duty.
試験が延期になって助かった。
We were relieved to know that the test was (to be) postponed.
ああ助かった。明日はテストなしだ。
What a relief! / Thank God! } There will be no test tomorrow!
お金を少し貸してもらえると助かるんだが。
If you can lend me some money I would be very grateful.
やれやれ助かった。彼は結局来ないことになった。
We can breathe a sigh of relief. He isn't coming after all.

4. 助力する
父が僕の宿題を助けてくれた。
Father helped me with my homework.
君の手助けがなかったら僕だけではとてもやり遂げられなかった。
Without your help I could never have finished it.
我々は発展途上国の手助けをしなければならない。
We should aid developing countries.
彼女は車の中に助け入れられた。
She was helped into the car.
運動は消化を助ける。
Exercise helps [aids] digestion.

たずねる（訪ねる，尋ねる）

1. 訪問する
come [go] to see 《a person》**; call on** 《a person》**; call at** 《a house》**; visit; pay a visit to**
ふと訪ねる **drop in on** 《a person》**; drop in** 《a place》
私は彼を事務所に訪ねた。
I { went to see / called on / visited } him at his office.
スミスさんという方が(あなたが)お留守の間に訪ねて来られました。
A Mr. Smith { called on / came to see } you while you were out.
彼女が思いがけず訪ねて来た。
She made a surprise visit to me.
彼女は時折ふらっと訪ねて来る。
She drops in (on me [to see me]) once in a while.
彼はまだ2,3軒訪ねなければならないところがあると言った。
He said he had a few more calls to make.

2．質問する

ask《a person》**a question; ask**《a person》**about**《something》

すみません。ちょっとお尋ねしますが，一番近い駅までどうやって行ったらいいでしょうか。

Excuse me, but could you tell me how to get to the nearest railway station?

3．探す

look for; search [**hunt**] **for**

私はその家を尋ねて歩きまわった。

I walked up and down looking for the house.

ただ（唯）→ だけ

1．もっぱら，わずかに

only; merely; simply; alone; nothing but

解決策はただひとつだけだ。

There's only one solution.

彼はホールにただひとり取り残された。

He was left all alone in the hall.

彼はその戦闘のただひとりの生き残りだった。

He was the only survivor of the battle.

彼はただ力になろうとしているだけだ。

He's only [merely, just] trying to help.

私はただ説明したかっただけだ。

I merely [just] wanted to explain.

子供はただ泣くだけだった。

The child did nothing but cry.

ただできる限りやってみるだけ[まで]だ。

I will do my best. That's all I can do.

彼にはただ1度会っただけだ。

I met him only once.

2．普通の

三つで天才，十で秀才，二十すぎればただの人。

A genius at three, a clever boy at ten and just an ordinary man after twenty.

彼はただ者ではない。

He's no ordinary person.

〈注〉 彼はとびぬけて優れている(extraordinary)の意。cf. He's not an ordinary person.（普通の人ではない）の場合は「とびぬけて」まではいかない。

ただのかぜだ。

It's [an ordinary [a common] cold.

【ただならぬ】unusual

これはただごとではない。

It's no trivial matter.

This is something serious.

ただならぬ気配を感じた。

I saw at once that there was something unusual.

3．無料の

ずばり当てればこの本がただでもらえます。

If you guess right, you'll get this book free.

ただで入れます。

Admission is free.

【標示】

入場無料

Admission Free / Free Admission

ただいま（只今）→ あいさつ

1．現在

now; just now

ただいま3時です。

It's three o'clock now.

時計はただいま3時を打ちました。

The clock struck three just now.

The clock has just struck three.

2．すぐに →すぐに

in a minute; soon

はい，ただいま(参ります)。

I'm coming.

I'll be right { there. / over〔米〕.

3．帰宅の挨拶

ただいま。

Hello!
Hullo, dear!〔英〕
Hi, Dad [Mom]!〔米〕
Hi, I'm home!
〈注〉 特に決った挨拶の言葉はない。

たたく（叩く）

1．軽打

knock; rap; tap; pat; 連打する **clap; beat**

だれかがドアをたたいている。

Someone is { knocking（コンコン） / rapping（トントン；ノックより弱い） } on [at] the door.

彼はテーブルをたたいて静粛を求めた。

He rapped on the table and called for silence.

【指で】

彼は私の肩をぽんとたたいて戸口に立っている女の子を指さした。

He tapped me on the shoulder and pointed to the girl at the door.

彼は指でたたいてリズムをとっている。

He was tapping out the rhythm.

〈注〉 tap は指１本または指先で，注意を引くために軽くたたくこと。

【平手で】

父は私の肩を優しくたたいて「忘れておしまい」と言った。

Father patted me on the shoulder and said "Forget it."

【パチパチ(手)】

子供たちは手をたたいて新入生を歓迎した。

The children clapped to welcome the new boy.

【ドンドン(連打)】

たいこをたたいている人はだれですか。

Who is the person { beating the drum?（祭りのたいこ） / playing the drum?（ドラム） }

2．ぶつ，殴る

slap; strike; spank

【パシッ】

彼女は彼の頬を平手でたたいた。

She slapped him on the cheek.

【コツン】

ジムが僕をたたいたからけんかになった。

Jim struck me and so we began to fight.

【ピシャン】

時には(罰として)子供のお尻をたたいてやることが必要だ。

Sometimes children need spanking.

〈注〉 strike, hit は１回だけ，beat, pound は繰り返し打つこと。

3．値切る

【値をたたく】

beat down the price

彼はいつも値をたたく。

He always tries to { beat down the price. / get the price lowered. }

4．批判する

【新聞・マスコミなどで】

彼の新しい政策は厳しくたたかれた。

He was severely { criticized / attacked } for his new policy.

ただしい（正しい）

1．道徳上

right

子供にはまず第一に何が正しいか，何が間違っているかを教えこまねばならない。

Children should be taught first of all and above all what is right and what is wrong.

正しいと思うことをしなさい。

Do what you think is right.

何が正しいかは時代によって変化する。

What is right varies with the time(s).

2. 礼にかなった

proper

称号・肩書のある人の正しい呼び方

proper way of addressing titled persons

正しい作法

good manners（しつけのよさ）

etiquette（公の場での作法）

正しい言葉づかいをする

use standard language

speak correctly (1)

speak politely (2)

〈注〉 (1)は文法的に正しく話すこと。(2)は礼儀正しく，感情を抑えて話すこと。

3. 正確な

correct; accurate

正しい答え

a correct answer（数学などのように答えが合っているか合っていないかの場合）

the right answer（正しい答えがはっきりしている場合）

a good answer（答えが適切か不適切かといった性格のとき）

君の時計は正しいですか。

Is your watch { correct? / accurate? }

【正しい知識】

thorough and accurate knowledge

中学生にはもっと正しい性の知識を与える必要がある。

Junior high students need to be given more accurate knowledge about sex.

つづりを正しく書きなさい。

Spell the words correctly.

4. 適切な

正しい研究法　proper research methods

正しい手順　proper [correct] procedures

ただちに（直ちに）→ すぐに

at once; immediately; right away; in a minute [moment]

ただちに出発しよう。

Let's go [leave].

ただちに参上します。

I'm coming right away [now].

軍隊に「ただちに出動」の命令が出た。

The troops were called out without delay.

彼は帰京後ただちに彼女に会いに行った。

When he returned to Tokyo he went directly [straight] to see her.

そのアイデアはただちに実行に移された。

The idea was immediately put into practice.

〈注〉 They { came up with the idea … / suggested that … , } のような説明の後

and it was immediately put into practice.

と言えば自然。

計画はただちに実行に移された。

The plan was carried out immediately [right away].

たちあがる（立ち上がる）→たつ（立つ）

たちば（立場）

a position; a place; 境遇 **situations;** 見地 **a standpoint [a point of view]**（ある問題についての個人・政府などの決意・信念など）

〈注〉 a point of view は standpoint（立場），perspective（考え方）の２つの意味がある。

1. 地位

…する立場にある[ない]

be (not) in a position to …

私は決断を下す立場にはない。

I am not in a position to give a decision.

彼は困った[難しい]立場にある。

He is in an awkward [a delicate] position.

2. 境遇

人の立場になってごらん。

Put yourself in other people's shoes.

僕が君の立場だったらそんなことは絶対しな

い。

If I were you, I would never do that.

WTO の勧告を受け入れなければ，日本の国際的立場はますます苦しくなるだろう。

Japan's international situation will become more difficult if we don't accept the WTO recommendation.

3．観点

立場を変えて考えてごらんなさい。

Consider it from a different point of view.

私は消費者の立場から発言している。

I'm speaking from the consumer's {standpoint. / point of view.}

彼は中立の立場をとった。

He had a neutral attitude.

He took a neutral stance.

〈注〉 neutral attitude とは反論もせず，両方の立場を認めること。無関心ではないが傍観者的である。He's a moderate [in the center].という言い方もある。

我々は彼らとは対等の立場だ。（商取引など）

We are on (an) equal footing with them.

たちよる（立ち寄る）→ たずねる

たつ（建つ，立つ）→ たてる

1．建っている，立っている

【建造物】

美しい町で東側の山の上にホテルが建っている。

The town is pretty. A hotel stands on a hill to the east.

〈注〉 上の文は町の描写である。"Is there a hotel around here ?"（この辺にホテルはあるでしょうか）に対する答えは "There's a hotel on the hill."（山の上にホテルがある）で，これは情報を提供する言い方である。

この辺はこの5年ばかりの間に家がたくさん建った。

This area has been built up over the last five years.

この辺は新しい家がどんどん建っている。

Many new houses are being built in this neighborhood.

〈注〉 「家がひどく建て込んでいる」は次のように言う。This area is very built up.

【人】

入口に人が大勢列を作って立っていた。

Many people lined up [queued] at the entrance.

東京までずっと立っていた［立ちんぼだった］。

We had to keep on standing all the way to Tokyo.

2．立ち上がる

立ってください。

Please stand up.

立たないで（どうぞそのまま）。

Please don't get up [rise].

男の子は手を貸して老人を立たせた。

The boy helped the old man to his feet.

彼女はぱっと立ち上がった。

She jumped [sprang] to her feet.

彼女はよろよろと立ち上がった。

She staggered to her feet.

その子は転んだが（ひとりで）立ち上がるとまたスキップをして行った。

The little boy tripped and fell but got to his feet [got up] and went on skipping.

3．物主語 →たてる

【碑】

犠牲者のために慰霊碑が建った。

A monument was set up to commemorate the victims.

【施設】

この病院は約100年も前に建ったものだ。

This hospital was founded about one century ago.

【煙】

積み重ねた草の山からうっすらと煙が立ちの

ぼっていた。

Thin smoke rose from the heap of grass.

【風】

風が立った[風立ちぬ]。

The [A] wind has {come up. / risen.}

4. その他

【気が立つ】

彼は今は気が立っているからうっかり刺激すると何をしでかすかわからない。

He is excited now and can easily be provoked into doing something wild.

【計画】→たてる

日時と行先を決めていただかなければ計画が立ちません。

We can't make plans unless you agree on when and where to go.

【立候補】

この選挙にはたくさんの候補者が立っている。

Many candidates are {running / up} for this election.

たつ（経つ）→ すぎる・すごす

【時間の経過】

東京を出て1時間たった。

We're an hour out of Tokyo.

母が亡くなって10年がたった。

{Ten years have passed / It's ten years / It's been ten years〔*most common*〕} since my mother died.

【未来】

1時間たったらまた電話します。

I'll call you again {in an hour. / an hour from now.}

ゼリーを冷蔵庫に入れて1時間たったらかき混ぜてください。

Put the jelly into the fridge [refrigerator].

{An hour later, / In [After] an hour,} stir it.

【過去】

彼の死は2,3日たってから知った［知らされた］。

I learned [was told] of his death a few days later.

時がたつにつれて彼の怒りも治まってきた。

His anger {gradually left him. / left him as time went by [on].}

彼は本を読みふけり，時のたつのも忘れていた。

He was so absorbed in reading (that) {he forgot about (the) time. / he was unconscious of the lapse of time.〔*formal*〕 / he didn't notice (the) time passing.}

たつ（断つ・絶つ・裁つ）

1. 切断する

cut

服地[型紙]を裁つ

cut out {a coat [a dress] / a pattern (型紙)}

2. 途絶する

【連絡】

その飛行機は離陸後1時間で無線連絡を絶った。

The airplane {disappeared from the radar / went out of radio contact} an hour after takeoff.

登山隊が連絡を絶って3日が過ぎた。

Three days have passed since we lost contact with the mountaineering group.

【関係】

人との関係を断つ

cut [break] (off) {contact(s) / relations} with 《a person》

国交を断つ
cut [break] (off) diplomatic relations with 《a country》

【酒・たばこなど】

彼は酒を断った。
He's given up drinking.

たっする（達する）

1. 到達する

reach; arrive at [in]; get to

〈注〉 reach は他動詞であるからreach to としない。arrive は自動詞なので at や in が続く。

車で走ること１時間にして探検隊は現地に達した[到着した]。
After an hour's drive the expedition {reached / arrived at} the site.

ついに我々は頂上に達した。
At last we {reached / got to} the summit.

2. 及ぶ

amount to; come up to

【金額】

その地方の地震による被害(額)は５億円にも達した。
The earthquake damage in those areas {amounted to / reached} 500 million yen.

〈注〉 amount to は被害額がいくらになるという事実を述べ，reach の方は地震被害の大きさに重点がある。

【積雪】

この前の冬は積雪が１メートルにも達した。
The snow lay a whole meter deep last winter.
There was a whole meter of snow last winter.

3. 達成する

attain（目的，念願などを）

彼女はその道でプロとして認められるという目的を達した。
She attained her goal of becoming a recognized professional.

彼は念願を果してついに家を買った。
He achieved his dream {when he bought a house. / of having a house of his own.}

…だった → …だ

たてる（立てる，建てる）→たつ(建つ，立つ)

〈注〉 「たつ」(自動詞)と「たてる」(他動詞) はペアである。「たつ」の英語例文で「たてる」の例文にもなるものがある。「たつ(建つ，立つ)」の項参照。

1. 垂直に置く，起す

旗[さお／看板]を立てる
put up a flagpole [post / sign (post)]

ほこりを立てる
raise dust（路上）

うわさを立てる
spread a rumor

声をたてるな。
Be quiet.

大きな音を立てるんじゃない。
Don't make [so much [a lot of] noise.

〈注〉 「音を立てた，声を立てた」について，さらにどんな音か，どんな声か述べるには「擬声語・擬態語」の項参照。「ドン」とひとつの大きな音ならば a big noise とも言える。

2. 突きさす

【とげなど】

のどに魚の骨をたてた。(骨が刺さった)
He got a (fish) bone stuck [caught] in his throat.

彼女はあっと声をあげた。親指にとげをたてた[とげがたった]のだ。
She cried out because a splinter had {got / gotten} {stuck / caught} in her thumb.

3. 建築する

家を建てる **build a house; have a house built** (注文建築); **establish, found** (公共施設)

今息子の家を建てています。

I'm now having a house built for my son.

彼の遺志によりその遺産で孤児院を建てた。

Using the property he left in his will, they founded an orphanage.

4. 樹立する

世界記録を立てる set a world record

規準を立てる

set a standard; set standards [criteria]

5. その他

誓いを立てる make a vow

夏休みの計画を立てる

make a plan for (the) summer vacation

家計費の予算を新たに立てなければならない。

I'll have to make a new household budget.

来年度の予算を立てなければならない。

We'll have to make a budget for next year.

彼はついに作家として身を立てることができた。

He has at last established himself as a writer.

彼女は近所の人の着物の仕立てをして暮しを立てていた。

She made her living by sewing kimonos for her neighbors.

〈注〉 kimono は英語に取り入れられ，単数は a kimono，複数は kimonos。

たとえ →ても・でも

たのしい(楽しい)・たのしむ・たのしみ

〈注〉 楽しい，または楽しかった経験を述べるのに，人間を主語にして表現することもできるし，経験を表す it を主語にして表現することもできる。

［人主語］ **have a good [great, wonderful] time; have fun; enjoy** 《oneself》; (娯楽) **amuse** 《oneself》; **find pleasure in**

［It 主語］ **be good [fun]; be great [wonderful]** (すごく楽しい)

【楽しい】

今日は楽しかった。

［人主語］

We had { a good time / fun } today.

We enjoyed ourselves very much today.

We enjoyed our day.

［It 主語］

It's been good [wonderful] being together today.

楽しかったね。

［人主語］

What a great time we had, didn't we!

(辞去のときなど)

We've had a good [great, marvelous] time. Thank you very much.

［It 主語］

It's been fun, hasn't it!

あなたがそばにいてくださるときが一番楽しい。

I am happiest when you're with me.

楽しい思い出 →おもいで

happy [good, wonderful] memories

彼女は楽しそうだ。

She looks happy.

女の子たちは楽しげに歌っている。

The girls are singing { merrily. (1) / happily. (2) }

〈注〉 (1)は生き生きと元気がよい面を強調。(2)は心楽しく満たされ平穏な状態を強調。

【楽しむ】

多くの若者が冬はスキーを楽しむ。

Many young people enjoy skiing in winter.

彼は日曜の朝はずっとベッドの中で漫画本を読んで楽しんでいる。

He amuses himself by reading comic books in bed all Sunday morning.

楽しんでおいで。

Have a good time.

Enjoy yourself.

【楽しみ，娯楽】

カラオケは僕の主な楽しみのひとつだ。

Karaoke is one of my chief amusements.

僕にとって人生最大の楽しみは食べることだ。

My greatest pleasure in life is eating.

庭いじりは父の楽しみだ。

Gardening is my father's hobby.

【(心の)喜び】

いい息子さんを持たれてお楽しみですね。

It is a comfort to have such a good son.

〈注〉 自分のことであれば「いい息子を持って楽しみだ」の意味になる。

【…を楽しみにする】 look forward to ～ing

次の日曜日にお目にかかるのを楽しみにしています。

I'm looking forward to seeing you next Sunday.

〈注〉◆enjoy は楽しむことであるから "How was the concert?" "Oh, I enjoyed it very much." (「コンサートどうだった」「ああとてもよかったよ」) のように使えるが，"What did you do last Sunday?" △"I enjoyed swimming." (「日曜日何してたの」「水泳を楽しんだよ」) のように使うのは不自然。次のように本当に「楽しんだ」場合に使うので，「…をした」の代りには使わないこと。

I went to a Tigers game and I really enjoyed it. (タイガースの試合を見にいって大いに楽しんで来た)

なお，He enjoys an excellent income from his trust fund. (信託資金から結構な収入がある) のように right (権利), benefit (利益), privilege (特権) などについて have の意味で enjoy を使うことができるが，have を使う方が普通。

◆楽しみの度合は左から右に強くなる。

amusements＜pleasures＜delights＜joys

たのむ（頼む）・たのみ

1．依頼する

ask; request; 強く頼む **plead**

彼に推薦書を(書いてくれと)頼んだ。

I asked him to write a letter of recommendation.

彼女は彼にどうか自分も連れていってくれと頼んだ。

She pleaded with him to take her along.

ちょっとお頼みしたいことがあるのですが。

I have a favor to ask of you.

彼女は私に頼みがあると言った。

She said she had a favor to ask of me.

彼の頼みは聞き入れられた［聞き入れられなかった］。

His request was granted [turned down].

2．任せる

隣の人に子供を頼んで用足しに出た。

I went on an errand, leaving my baby with my neighbor.

〈注〉 Could you look after the baby while I go out and buy something for dinner?「夕食の買物に行く間，子供をみていただけませんか」が直接頼む場合の言い方。

【一任】

彼は私に何もかも頼んでいった。

He left everything (up) to me.

そういうことは専門家に頼んだ方がいい。

You ought to
- leave that kind of thing to specialists.
- ask specialists to do that kind of thing.

3．頼り

それが頼みの綱だ。

That is my last resort.

君が頼みの綱だ。

You're my last resort [hope].

頼もしい人　a dependable [reliable] person

たび（旅）→ りょこう

a trip; travel; a tour; a journey; 船旅 **a voyage**

ヨーロッパひとり旅

a journey alone round Europe

空の旅　a trip by air

彼は旅先で病気になった。
He became sick on his journey.

(…する)たびに（度に）→ ごとに

たぶん（多分）→ おそらく

たべる(食べる) → しょくじ

eat; have

1．食事

私は7時に朝食を食べる。
I have [eat] breakfast at seven.
私は朝食にトーストと紅茶と何か果物を食べる。
I have [eat] bread and butter, a cup of tea and some fruit for breakfast.
昼食はごく軽く食べる[あまり食べない]。
I don't eat much for lunch.
もう昼食は食べましたか。
Have you had [eaten] your lunch yet?
私は忙しくて晩飯を食べるひまがなかった。
I was so busy that I missed [didn't have] dinner.
〈注〉 dinner は昼でも晩でも一番ごちそうが出る食事のこと。

2．食する

これ食べてごらん。
Try this one.
彼は一口食べてみて「おいしい」と言った。
He tasted it [took a bite] and said it was good.
何か食べるものをください。
Please give me something to eat.
日本人は魚を生で食べる。
Japanese people eat { raw fish. / fish raw. }

3．生活していく

食べるためには働かなければならない。
You have to work in order to live.
彼女は小さな店をやって家族を食べさせていた。
She ran [had, operated] a small shop to keep her family going.
【生活できる】
こんな安月給では食べられない。
We can't live on such a small income.
こんな給料では5人家族を食べさせられない。
My salary isn't (big, high) enough to support a family of five.
cf. I don't know { how we'll eat. / where the next meal will come from. }
（どうやって食べていったらいいかわからない）

4．食べられる

【食べる余裕がある】
食べようと思えばまだまだ食べられた。
I could have eaten much more.
おなかがいっぱいでもう食べられません。(食事を断るとき)
(Oh,) Thanks but I'm already quite full. I couldn't (possibly) eat any more.
Thanks (a lot) but I'm afraid I've had enough.
彼は食べられないくせに欲ばる。
His eyes are bigger than his stomach. (一種の諺)
【食用に適する】
これは食べられるよ。塩でもちょっとつけて。
{ This can be eaten. / You can eat this. } Just add a bit of salt.
桃はすっかり熟してすぐにも食べられそうに見えた。
The peaches seemed ripe and ready to

{ eat.
{ be eaten.

ベリーは美しくて食べられそうだった。（毒ではない not poisonous）

The berries were pretty and seemed edible.

たまる（溜まる，貯まる）・ためる

1．集積する，集める

collect; gather

【水】

夕立が降ると校庭に水がたまる［水たまりができる］。

Puddles form in the schoolyard after a shower.

あの大地震のあと風呂桶に水をためておく習慣がついてしまった。

I've gotten the habit of keeping the bathtub full of water ever since the great earthquake.

【ほこり】

床にほこりがたまっていた。その部屋は何年も使われていなかったのだ。

Dust lay thick on the floor. }
The floor was covered with dust. }
The room hadn't been used for years.

【不用品】

ガレージにがらくたがいっぱいたまっている。

The garage is { overflowing with / full of } junk.

こんなところに古新聞をためないでくれ。

Don't pile (up) old newspapers here.

Don't let old newspapers pile up here.

押入れにいっぱい古着がたまっている。

The closet is { filled (up) / crammed } with old clothes.

【涙】

彼女は目に涙をためて私を見た。

She looked at me with tears in her eyes.

2．貯金する

save; put [lay] aside

彼女は相当金をためているらしい。

She seems to have
{ saved a lot of money.
{ put away quite a bit of money.

彼女は給料の5パーセントをためている。

She is putting five percent of her salary aside.

最初はほんの少しの株式投資も，長い間にたまってかなりの額になる。

Even a small initial investment in stocks will come to a fairly big sum over time.

3．滞る

stay; stand; be overdue; つけがたまる **run up (a bill)**

【仕事】leave (work) undone

仕事がうんとたまっている。

I have a lot of work on my hands.

I have lots of work left.

出張で留守にしているうちに仕事がたまってしまった。

The work piled up while I was away on a business trip.

【借金】

彼には1000万円も借金がたまっていた。

His debt(s) { totalled / amounted to / came to } ten million yen.

〈注〉 もし借金の金額を問題にしているのならば He was ten million yen in debt. が普通。

酒屋につけがだいぶたまってしまった。

I've run up a big bill at the liquor shop.

彼は家賃を3か月分ためている。

He owes three months (worth of) rent.

家賃が3か月分たまっている。

He's three months behind in [with] his rent.

ため（為）

〈注〉 日本語の「ため」は英語でほとんど正反対と思われる「原因」「目的」と「結果」を包括するもの

である。これは語順に関する日英両語の違いによるもので日本語の論理構造に欠陥があるわけではないが，とにかく気をつけないと非論理的な英文をつくるもととなる。

He worked hard
{ × because of supporting his family.
  ○ (in order) to support his family.

1．利益

for 《one's》 **sake; for the sake of; on** 《one's》 **account; on behalf of** 〔*formal*〕; **in the cause of** 《social justice》

私のためにどうぞここにいてください。

Stay with us for my sake.

彼らは祖国のために勇敢に戦った。

They fought bravely for the sake of their country.

君のためなんだよ［これが君のためになるのだ］。

It is for your good.

この本は面白くてしかもためになる。

This book is interesting and instructive as well.

あの経験はたいへんためになりました。

That experience has
{ done me a great deal of good.
  taught me a great deal.

I have learned a great deal from that experience.

そんなことをしても君のためにならないよ。

That won't do you any good.

君のしていることは全然君のためになっていない［君の不利益になっている］。

You are acting { contrary to / against } your own interests.

2．目的

in order to; so that ... may; so as to; for; with a view to

彼は試験に合格するために一生懸命勉強した。

He studied hard in order to pass the exam.

学費を得るために学校が終ってからアルバイトをしている。

I work part-time after school to earn money for school expenses.

3．原因・理由

because; as; since; because of; owing to; due to; thanks to

病気のため，会に出席できなかった。

He couldn't attend the meeting ⌊because [as] he was ill.

He couldn't attend the meeting ⌊because of [due to, owing to] an illness.

彼はまだ独立していなかったために親の言う通りにしなければならなかった［親に逆らえなかった］。

He had to do as he was told, since he was not yet independent of his parents.

前の晩の大雨のため道路はぬかるみだった。

Owing to the heavy rain the night before, the road was muddy.

悪天候のため定刻に間に合わなかった。

Thanks to the bad weather we couldn't arrive on time.

〈注〉◆because of, owing to, due to, thanks to は意味はほぼ同じであるが文体レベルの相異がある。
because of 〔*common*〕; owing to 〔*more formal*〕; due to 〔*formal*〕
◆thanks to は thank の本来の意味が根底にあるので thanks to your help（助力のおかげで）のように肯定的な内容に使う。皮肉で thanks to bad weather のようにも言えるが，日本語でも「悪天候のおかげ」と「おかげ」を使うのとよく似ている。「…のために」は病気・悪天候など否定的な原因に使われることが多く，ありがたい場合は「…のおかげで」を使うことが多い。
◆because of ⌊an illness [the heavy snow] のように名詞が続くときはよいが，長い分詞形が続くような場合（ex. △because of his being unable to call on us）は because, as, since などの接続詞を用いて節にする方がよい（ex. because he was unable to call on us）。

なお，理由を表す because, since, as, for の区別については「…だから」の項参照。

4．結果

as a result; consequently

【そのため】

新幹線が遅れ，そのために式に遅れた。

The Shinkansen was delayed and consequently we were late for the ceremony.

母が急に病気になり，そのため京都への旅行を取りやめねばならなかった。

My mother suddenly got ill, and so I had to give up my trip to Kyoto.

〈注〉 子供を教育するために（目的）
子供が病気をしたために（原因・理由）
上の文でみるように日本語の「ため」は「現在形(〜する)＋ため」の場合は目的，「過去形・完了形(〜した)＋ため」の場合は原因・理由を表す。

だめ（駄目）

1．無益

useless; (of) no use; no good

だめな男　a good-for-nothing fellow

あいつはだめだ。

He's no good.

【無駄】

それはだめだ。

It is useless.

彼にもう一度やってみろと言ってもだめだよ。

There's no use telling him to try again.

2．不成功・絶望

hopeless; impossible

【事・物】

だめだ[望みなしだ]。

It's impossible [hopeless].

だめだった。

It was unsuccessful.

すっかりだめになってしまった。

It was all spoiled.

肉がだめになってしまった。

The meat has gone bad.

提案をしたがだめだった[断られた]。

My proposal was turned down [rejected].

彼が何もかもだめにしてしまった。

He spoiled it all.

【人】

僕はもうだめだ。

I'm done for.

It's all up with me.

あいつはすっかりだめになってしまった。

He was ruined.

彼は試験がだめだった。

He has failed the exam.

「彼は試験に通るだろうか」「たぶんだめだろう」。

"Will he pass the exam?" "Perhaps [Maybe] not, I'm afraid."

【病気】

「彼は持ち直すだろうか」「だめだと思う」。

"Will he live?" "I'm afraid not."

3．命令・禁止

すぐしなければだめだ。

You should do that at once.

たばこを吸ってはだめだ。

You mustn't smoke.

Don't smoke.

【激励】

投げちゃだめだ，がんばれ。

Don't give up!

Never say die!

【叱正】

だめだめ[間違っている]。

No, no, that won't do.

だめだめ，やり方が違う。それじゃだめだ。こっちに貸してごらん。

No, no, that's not the way to do it. That'll never work! Give it to me!

【拒絶】

「彼と一緒に行ってもいい？」「だめ」。

"May I go with him?" "No, you can't [may not, 〔強〕]."

絶対だめ！（強い拒絶）

Absolutely not!

Impossible! (It's) Out of the question! (問題にならない)

（何か止めるときに）だめだめ，やめろ！

No! No! / Stop it! / Don't do [say] that!

たよる（頼る）・たより

rely on; depend on; 信頼する **trust**

その老人は息子を頼りにしている［頼っている］。

The old man depends a lot on his son.

〈注〉 経済的に老後をゆだねている事実を言っている。気持ちの上で頼りに思っていることを言うのであれば，He expects his son to support him. とでも言う。

君だけが頼りだ。

You are the only one I can rely on.

他人を頼るな。

Don't depend [rely] on others.

兄弟を頼りにするな。

You shouldn't count on your brother for help.

【頼れる人】

私には頼れる人がいない。

I have no one to rely on.

あの人は頼れる人だ。（客観的に信頼がおける）

That man { can be trusted. / is trustworthy. / is dependable. }

そのドイツ語の書類はありったけの辞書や文法書を頼りにしてやっと翻訳した。

We could translate that German document only with the extensive help of dictionaries and grammar books.

…たら → だろう（に）

だらしない

1．外見・服装・態度

だらっとしている **sloppy;** きたない，ひどい **slovenly;** きちんとしていない **untidy**

だらしない服

sloppy slovenly clothes

だらしない人

（外見上）an untidy person

（姿勢が悪い）a slouch

2．精神的・道義的に

だらしない学生 a sloppy student

〈注〉 a lazy student は自分で承知で怠けている学生。a sloppy student はもともとだらしないこと。

彼は酒を飲むとだらしなくなる。

He gets sloppy when he's drunk.

〈注〉 酒飲みのタイプ

He's { a laughing drunk.（笑い上戸） / a crying drunk.（泣き上戸） / an aggressive [a violent] drunk.（怒り上戸） }〔米〕

【不甲斐ない】

あんな男にだまされるとはだらしない。

How silly you were to be taken in by such a man!

10対０で負けるとはだらしない。

How spineless they were to let themselves be beaten 10-0!

〈注〉 同じ気持ちを次のように言うこともできる。They were beaten 10-0. They didn't (even) put up a fight.

《類義語》

sloppy びしょびしょの，泥んこの，ずさんな，不注意な，だらしない。

slovenly （外見上）だらしない，うすぎたない，ひどい，ずさんな，ぞんざいな。

untidy （部屋などが）ちらかっている，きちんとしていない，（服装が）だらしない。

loose 解放された，束ねていない，ゆるんだ，たるんだ，しまりのない，だらしない，ふしだらな。

たりる（足りる）

1．十分である

5000円あれば足りる。

Five thousand yen will { do. / be enough [sufficient]. }

石油がポリ容器に３杯もあれば１か月は足りる。

Three containers of kerosene a month will {do. / be enough [sufficient].}

これだけお金があれば1か月は十分足りる。

This much money will {last me / be enough for} a whole month.

今のところ足りている。

We have enough for the present.

【足りない】

5000円では足代にも足りない。

Five thousand yen will not even cover the train fare.

いくら[いくつ]足りないのですか。

How much [many] more do you need [want]?

電車賃にもう10円足りない。

{We need another ten yen for / We are ten yen short of} train fare.

すみません。(代金に)10円足りません。

Another ten yen, please.

1000円に少々足りないということね。

It is just under a thousand yen.

1万ドルに100ドル足りないってとこだ。

I'm a hundred dollars short of ten thousand.

席が2つ足りない。

We need [We'd like] two more seats.

今月は金が足りなくて行かれないよ。

I'm short of money this month. I don't have enough (money) to go there.

彼は経験[常識]が足りない。

He lacks {experience. / common sense.}

彼にはいくらお礼を言っても言い足りない。

We cannot thank him enough.

【紛失】

2巻足りないね。(全集など)

Two volumes are missing.

2. 価値がある

彼は信頼するに足りる人物だ。

He can be trusted.

この本は読むに足る本だ。

This book is worth reading.

だろう → おそらく

【疑問】

いったいだれだろう。

Who is it, I wonder?

Who can that be?

彼女は来るだろうか。

Will she come?

雨が降るだろうか。

Is it going to rain?

君,あれ忘れてしまったんだろう。

You've forgotten that, haven't you?

君は来ないんだろう。

You aren't coming, are you?

【単なる推量】

彼女はじきに来るだろう。

She will come soon.

午後には雨になるだろう。

It will rain in the afternoon.

【主観】

本当だろう(と思う)。

{I think / I suppose / I guess} it is true.

【推量の確かさを加味する】→おそらく

〈注〉 下へ行くほど不確実になる。

おそらくまだ彼女は知らないだろう。

Probably she doesn't know it yet. (almost sure ほとんど確実)

彼女は遅れて来るだろう。

She may be a little late for the party. (likely きっとそう)

もしかしたら彼女は遅れて来るだろう。

Perhaps [Maybe] she'll be a little late for the party. (somewhat likely, そうかも知れない)

彼はひょっとしたら受かるかもね。

Possibly he'll pass the exam. (possible but

not likely あり得るがあやしい)

【感情的色合を加味する】

彼女はまだ知らないんだろう。(不吉な推量)

I'm afraid she doesn't know it yet.

今夜は嵐になるだろう。

I fear it's going to be stormy tonight.

〈注〉 … , I'm afraid. / … , I fear. と後につけてもよい。

朝までにはすっかり終ってしまうだろう。(希望)

It will all be over by morning, I hope.

〈注〉 希望・悪い予想の言い方

彼は受かるだろうか。

Will he pass the exam?

危ないんじゃないか。

I'm afraid not [Perhaps not].

受かればいいけどね。

I hope he will.

彼らは離婚するだろうか。

Will they divorce?

別れなければいいが。

I hope not. (別れるか否かについて予想はしていない)

残念だが別れるんじゃないか。

I'm afraid they will. (離婚を予想し残念な気持ちも述べている)

次の形も可能である。

They aren't going to divorce, I hope.

They're going to divorce, I'm afraid.

【控え目】

彼はおそらくもう70歳は越えているだろう。

He must be over 70.

He's over 70, I should [would] say [think].

〈注〉 I should [would] say [think] は標準的な会話体。should は〔英〕, would は〔米〕。この付け足し句は文頭, 文尾どちらにも用いられる。

だろう(に)

1. 現在・未来についての仮定

【不確定なこと】

もしも…なら, …だろう。

If … 現在形, … will …

一生懸命働けば成功するだろう。

If I work harder, I will succeed.

【あり得ないこと】

もし万一…なら, …だろう。

If … should … would [should, might] …

(飛込み練習で)もし万一なかなか浮き上がってこないようなことがあったらすぐに彼が助けに行くだろう。

(diving lesson) If you should be down too long, he would quickly come to your rescue.

2. 現在の事実に反する仮定

もし…だったら, …するだろうに。

If … were [did] (過去形) … , … would [should, might] …

僕が君だったらそんなことはしないだろうに。

If I were you, I would never do a thing like that.

3. 過去の事実に反する仮定

もし…だったら, …しただろうに。

If … had done … , … would [should, might] have done …

彼がパーティーに来ていたらもっと楽しかっただろうに。

If he had been at the party, we would have enjoyed it more.

たんい(単位)

1. 計量

a unit

ここでは味噌は(グラム単位で)計り売りしている。

Here miso is sold in grams.

毛糸はオンス単位で売っている。

Knitting yarn's sold by the ounce.

紅茶カップは普通6個単位で売っているが, 日本の緑茶の湯呑は5個単位だ。

Teacups are usually sold in sets [units] of six, but those for Japanese green tea come in sets [units] of five.

12をひとつの単位としたのは人間が10本の指

と２本の足があってそれで物を数えたからではなかろうか。

It may be that people chose twelve as a unit because they had ten fingers and two legs to count with [by].

2．金銭

【貨幣】

ドルとセントはアメリカのお金の基本単位である。

Dollars and cents are the basic units of American currency [money].

【…円単位】

この表の数字は1000円単位です。

The amount of money in this table is shown in thousands.

3．授業

単位　a credit

必修の　compulsory; required

選択の　selective; elective; optional

単位制度　the credit system; the unit system

63単位とる

get [have] 63 credits

英語を８単位とる

get [have] eight credits of English

卒業単位が不足する

do not have sufficient credits to graduate

彼は卒業資格に２単位足りない。

He needs two more credits / He is short of two credits } { to graduate. / for graduation.

数学の単位を落す

fail maths [the math exam]

〈注〉 math〔米〕, maths〔英〕

だんげん（断言）

断言する　**declare; assert**

【客観叙述】

彼はそれは絶対間違っていると断言した。

He declared it was definitely wrong.

彼はその件と自分は無関係だと断言した。

He { asserted / declared } that he had nothing to do with the case.

【直接的発言】

断言するよ，彼はきっとまた同じことをやる。

I assure you he'll do that again.

断言することはできないが，彼が間違っていると思う。

I cannot say definitely but I think he is in the wrong.

《類義語》

declare　確信と権威をもって発言する。反駁に応じ断言するような場合にも使う。

affirm　念を押すように，または問いや抗議に答えて断言する，肯定的答えをする。

cf. negate, deny　否定する

ex. The company affirmed its intention to promote women to responsible positions.（会社は女子を責任ある地位に登用する意図を確言した）

assert　反対されるのを覚悟で大胆に自己の所信を述べる，権利を主張する。

ex. He asserted that he was innocent.（彼は自分の無実を強く主張した）

protest　特に不服や異議を唱えてはっきり発言する。

ex. He protested that the newspaper account was misleading.（彼はその新聞記事は誤解を招くと抗議した）

たんしょ（短所）→ けってん

だんだん

gradually; little by little; bit by bit; more and more; less and less

彼はだんだん仕事が好きになってきた。

Little by little he came to like his job.

彼はだんだん興奮してきた。

He grew [became] more and more excited.

×More and more he was excited. (動詞および語順に注意)

だんだんに［徐々に］彼は健康を取り戻した。

Gradually he recovered his health.

だんだん暗くなってきた。

It is getting darker and darker.

だんだんに…なくなる →なる

彼はだんだん数学の授業についていけなくなっているのに気がついた。

Before long he found himself unable to follow what the teacher said in the mathematics class.

台風は峠を越したようだ。風も雨もだんだん治まってきていた。

The end of the typhoon was in sight; the wind was subsiding and the rain (was) lessening.

たんとう（担当）・たんにん（担任）

1. 担当

担当する　be in charge of

吉田氏がこの件の担当である。

Mr. Yoshida is in charge of the case.

だれが旅行の準備を担当しているんですか［旅行の係ですか］。

Who is in charge of the tour arrangements?

彼女は今，営業部全般を担当している［営業部長である］。

She's now in charge of / She supervises } the entire sales staff.

私は手話クラブの会報発行を担当している。

I'm in charge of issuing the bulletin of our sign language club.

【教師】

ヒックス先生は音楽を担当している。

Miss Hicks teaches music [is a music teacher].

【医師】

武田先生はこの病棟を担当している。

Dr. Takeda is { responsible for / in charge of } { this ward. / several patients in this ward. (患者数人を) }

私の担当は武田先生だ。

My doctor is Dr. Takeda.

2. 担任

クラス担任

a teacher in charge of a class; a class teacher; a homeroom teacher〔米〕

アダムス先生がうちのクラスの担任です。

Mr. Adams is { our class teacher. / our homeroom teacher. / in charge of our class. }

アダムス先生がこのクラスの担任です。

Mr. Adams is responsible for this class.

これがアダムス先生担任のクラスです。

This is Mr. Adams' class.

〈注〉◆be in charge of ～ は担当している状態を言う。一方 take charge of ～ は担当し，行動すること。

The local tax offices can take charge of tax collection from the single-shop owners in their respective areas. (地方の税務署は各管轄区域の商店経営者からの徴税を担当する)

◆take charge of と take on の比較

Mr. Kato takes charge of the summer swimming class. (加藤先生は夏の水泳教室の責任者である) (1)

I've taken on the summer swimming class. (私は夏の水泳教室の指導を引き受けた) (2)

(2)は(1)の文より自発的に「やってもいいよ」と引き受けたという含みがある。

ち

ち（地）→ つち

1．地面

the earth; land; place; ground

〈注〉 植物を育む「大地」the earth は，それが実は球形をしていることがわかり「地球」をも意味するようになったが，日本語の「大地」と「地球」は著しく違ったイメージをもつ。英文中に出てくる the earth を訳すとき前後関係に気をつけて訳し分けなければならない。

【陸地】 land（↔ sea）

地[陸]上でも海上でも　on land or at sea

【土地】

（まとまった）土地

a tract of land

土地を売る[買う]　sell [buy] land

〈注〉 土地も地図上での位置を意識すれば place, spot となる。position（位置）は土地としての広がりよりも位置が中心となる。

【地面】

ground（大地の表面，面積が感じられる）

2．土 →つち

soil; earth; ほこり **dirt;** 粘土 **clay;** 泥 **mud**

【土壌】 soil（農作物を育てる土）

肥沃な土　fertile soil

土を耕す　till the soil〔*poetic*〕

土を盛る[除去する]　heap up [remove] earth

3．国

【国】

父祖の地　one's native country [land]

一国民の領有地　the territory of a nation

【田舎】 country（都市ができると対立するものとして田舎の観念が生れた）

【故郷・故国】

生地，生国　the land of one's birth（生地を離れ都市生活をする者が現れると故郷の観念が生れた）

《関連語》

天と地　heaven and earth

地の果て　the ends of the earth [world]

遊園地　an amusement park

誕生の地　《one's》birthplace

地理　geography

地質学　geology

地学　earth science

耕地　a cultivated area; farm land; arable land（耕作に適する地）

ち（血）

1．血液

血　**blood;** 血が出る　**bleed**

傷口[切り傷]から血が出ている。

The cut is bleeding.

彼は鼻や口から血を出していた。

He was bleeding from the nose and mouth.

彼は鼻血を出している。

His nose is bleeding.

He has a nosebleed.

【血を止める】 stop（the）bleeding

〈注〉 一般的に「止血」というときは冠詞なし。具体的に今「血を止めろ」というような場合は the が必要。

【血が止まる】

血が止まった。

The bleeding stopped.

【血のついた】

血のついたナイフ　a blood-stained knife

2．血縁・血筋

徳川家の血を引いている[子孫である]

be descended from the Tokugawa family

同じ血筋[親戚，血縁]である

be related by blood; be blood relatives

左側の人たちは血縁の人たちです。

The people on the left are related to each other by blood.

（cf. related by marriage 姻戚である）

血は争えない。

Blood will tell.

Blood will out.〔*colloq.*〕

3．慣用表現

血の気のない　pale; white

血の気が引く　turn pale [white]

血の気の多い人　a hot-blooded person

〈注〉 日本語の「熱血漢」はよい意味だが，この英語は一般的によい意味ではない。

血の巡りのよい[悪い]
be quick [slow]-witted

血も涙もない人
a cold-hearted person
a bloodless [cruel] person

ちい（地位）

a position; a standing

1．社会的立場

彼は社会的に高い地位にある。
He has high social standing.
cf. He comes from a family with high social standing.（名門の出である）

人間の値打ちはその人の地位や権力とは何のかかわりもない。
A person's worth has nothing to do with his rank or power.

彼女は女性の地位向上に貢献した先達の一人だ。
She is one of those who have done a great deal to
{ achieve higher social status for women.
{ bring women higher social status.

日本の国際的地位は大いに向上したと考える人もある。
Some people think Japan's international
{ position has improved } a lot.
{ standing has risen }

2．職業上の役職

彼女は国(政府)で重要な地位にある。
She has an important post in the government.

〈注〉 post は重要な任命による地位で，政府・県庁や軍隊・企業などでも高い地位の役職について使う。委員会(committee)の委員の役職にも用いる。

彼の会社での地位(役職)は何ですか。
What is his job title?

ちいさい（小さい）

small (↔large); **little** (↔big); ちっちゃい **tiny**; 微小な **minute**

〈注〉 littleは small より小さいこともある。また「かわいい」を伴うことが多い。

1．形・サイズ

小さな車　a small [little] car

小さな家　a small [little] house

【比較上】

このシャツは小さすぎる。
This shirt is too small for me.

洗ったら小さくなった[縮んだ]。
This shirt shrank in the wash.

この衣類はみんな小さくなってしまった。(子供が成長した)
The child has outgrown these clothes.

子供たちの小さくなった衣類
children's outgrown clothes
cf. hand-me-downs　お下がり

2．幼い

小さな男の子
a little boy

彼なら小さい頃から知っている。
I've known him since
{ we were children.（私と彼は同年輩）
{ he was a child.（私がかなり年上）

3．音声

彼は小さい声で話した。
He talked in a low voice [an undertone].

4．ささいな

つまらない　**trivial**

そのけんかはほんの小さなことから始まった。

Their quarrel started over a very trivial [small] matter.

5．転義

【小さくなる】

私は有名な学者にまじって小さくなって座っていた。

I felt really small sitting among well-known scholars.

彼は部長が入ってくるといつも小さくなっていた。

He cowered whenever his boss came in.

ちえ（知恵）

《類義語》

wisdom（形 wise） 人生に処する叡智。

intelligence（形 intelligent） 知的能力。

wit（形 witty） 機知。

sense（形 sensible） 賢いこと。

common sense 常識・分別。

resources 事に対処する工夫の才。

〈注〉「知恵がある」を英訳する場合，一般的な言い方はしないで具体的にどんな能力を発揮しているのか述べるのが普通。

ex. She's exceptional at jigsaw puzzles [speaking] for her age.

（あの子は年のわりに知恵がある。ジグソーパズル[話のしかた]がすごく上手だ）

1．赤ん坊

【知恵づく】

〈注〉漠然と「赤ん坊が知恵づいてきた」と言うことがあるが，多くの場合，具体的に「あやすと笑うようになった」とか「人見知りを始めた」とか付け加えるのが普通である。英語でも具体的に話すのが普通で，「知恵づいた」に当る表現はないようだ。

単に He's developing. He's growing. と言っても前後関係から，体のことだけではない。「知恵づき」のことも含めているとわかる場合もある。しかし，はっきり具体的に述べる方がよい。

【知恵づきの具体例】

赤ちゃんはまわりの人がわかって反応するようになってきた。

The baby is beginning to respond consciously to those around him.

母親や他の人の顔がわかるようになる

begin to recognize its mother and other people

うれしいと笑う

smile when happy

変だと思うと真面目そうな顔をする

look serious when suspicious

珍しい物に何でも手を出して調べてみる

examine unfamiliar objects

この子は小さいなりに思考を始めた。

This child is beginning to reason.

2．慣用表現

知恵比べ　contest of wits

知恵者　a person of resources

知恵の輪　a ring puzzle

知恵のおそい子

a slow child; a backward child

知恵がない

be unwise; be foolish; be stupid; be silly

知恵のないやり方だよ。

That's a stupid [an unwise] way of doing it.

何かうまい考えはないかと知恵をしぼった。

I racked my brain for something better.

知恵を働かせなさい。

Use your brains.

Be more sensible.

知恵を貸す

suggest an idea to《a person》

give《a person》a suggestion

あなたのお知恵をお借りしたいんですが。

I want to ask you for advice.

彼にいい考えがあるかも知れない。彼は知恵があるからね。

He may have some good idea. He's very resourceful.

だれかが入れ知恵したに違いない。

Somebody must have planted [put] that idea in his head.

ちかい（近い）・ちかく

1．空間

近い　**near; close to; nearby; close by; near here [there]**

近づく　**approach; come up to; go near**

近づかない　**keep away from; not go near**

彼は我が家の近くに住んでいる。

He lives quite close to [near] us.

He lives close by [nearby].

His house is near ours.

この近くに本屋はありますか。

Is there a bookstore near here?

近くのおもちゃ屋ですてきな贈物を見つけた。

I found a nice gift in the { toy shop nearby. / nearby toy shop. }

郵便局は近くにある。

The post office is not far.

学校へはどちらが近道ですか。

Which is the shortest way to school?

水に近づきすぎないように。

Don't go too near the water.

悪い仲間に近づくな。

Keep [Stay] away from bad company.

2．時間

12時に近い。

It is nearly [almost] twelve.

〈注〉 almost の方が nearly よりさらに近い感じ。

終りが近い。

It's { drawing to a [its] close. / nearing its end. }

クリスマスが近い。

Christmas is { drawing near. / just around the corner. }

近いうちに桜も開くだろう。

The cherry blossoms will be out soon [before long].

彼の新著が近いうちに出版される。

His new book will be published in the near future.

近いうちにお訪ねしたいと思っています。

I'd like to call on you one of these days.

〈注〉 soon の方が before long より「すぐ」である。one of these days は漠然としていて「そのうち」の意。

3．関係

あの人達は血縁の近い人達だ。

They are all closely related.

〈注〉 近い親戚は叔父とかいとこと言うのが普通。
ex. 遠い親戚だ　be distantly related
He's one of my distant cousins.
（彼はまたいとこか何か遠い親戚だ）

4．ほとんど

彼がラテン語を始めたのはもう70歳近くになってからだった。

He was nearly [nearing, almost, close to] seventy when he began to study Latin.

1000人近い人が葬儀に参列した。

Nearly [Close to] 1000 people attended his funeral.

ちがう（違う）・ちがい → そうい

1．相違

【比較】

A と B は性格が違う　→せいしつ・せいかく

［A, B主格］ A and B are quite different in nature [character].

［A 主格］ A is quite different from B in nature [character].

［性格主格］ Their characters are completely opposite [different from each other].

〈注〉 nature, character については「せいしつ・せいかく」参照。

A 組と B 組は感じが違う。

There is some difference in the atmosphere of the A and B classes.

A class and B class are quite different in atmosphere.

トムとボブは全然違う。兄弟なのに。

Tom and Bob are most unlike each other though they are brothers.

彼は昔の彼とは違う。

He isn't what he used to be.

He's quite changed.

【趣味】

彼らは趣味が違う。

They have different tastes.

人の趣味は年齢や教育によっても違う。

People's tastes are different according to their age and education.

【意見】

我々は最も基本的な点で意見が違っていた。

We disagreed on the most fundamental point.

彼らの間に意見の違いがあった。

They had a difference of opinion.

二つの語の意味にほとんど違いはない。

There is little difference between the two words.

それらはたいして違わない。

They are much the same.

どっちにしてもたいして違わない。

That makes little difference.

兄は勉強家です。私と違って。

My brother is a hard worker, unlike me.

あの子とあの子の双子の妹はそっくりで違いがわからない。

I cannot tell her apart from her twin sister.

〈注〉 tell《something》apart from《something else》は二つのものを識別すること。

知っていることとそれを教えられることとは違う。

It is one thing to know something, and quite another to teach it.

【当てはずれ】

これは私のものと違う(私のものではない)。

This isn't mine.

これは私の思っていたのと違う。

This is not what I expected.

これでは約束と違う。

This isn't what you promised.

それでは契約と違う。

That's not
{ what the original agreement was [contract said].
{ according to the original agreement.

2. 間違い

【勘定書】

勘定書の計算が違っている。

The bill has been figured wrong.

このお勘定違っているんじゃないでしょうか。

I'm afraid there's some mistake in this bill.

【電話番号】

番号が違います[番号違いです]。

You've got the wrong number.

You are calling the wrong number.

【道】

道が違っていた。

I took the wrong road.

I went the wrong way.

違ったところへ行ってしまった。

I went to the wrong place.

【答え】

違っている。(正解でないときの言い方)

That's surely not so.

That can't be.

No, that's wrong.

〈注〉 上の No, that's wrong. は教室での質問で，特に解答がはっきり決っているときまたは討論などで使える。

違ってますか。

Am I mistaken?

ちかごろ(近頃) →さいきん

ちから(力)

1. 体力

力 **strength; might**

力がある **strong;** 力がない **weak**

筋肉の力　muscular strength
力持ち　a strong man
彼は大した力持ちだ。
He's as strong as an ox. (cf. as weak as a kitten)
力いっぱい（引っぱる）
(pull) as hard as《one》can
(pull) with all《one's》strength [might]
彼らは縄を力いっぱい引いた。
They pulled on the rope with all their strength.
力ずくで，力まかせに
by sheer force
彼らは力ずくで石を動かした。
They moved the stone by sheer force.
力に訴える
use violence [force]

【力が尽きる】
(力仕事がまだ終らないのに)彼は力尽きてへたばった。
His strength failed him.
彼は手を上げる力もなかった。(へたばりの程度を示す)
He had no strength even to lift his hand.
彼はへとへとだった。(何をする力もない状態)
He was spent.
He had absolutely no energy.

2. エネルギー

power; energy; 動かす力 **force**

【動力】
風車は風の力で，水車は水の力で回る。
A windmill is driven by the force of the wind, and a watermill by that of water.

〈注〉 水力発電所　a hydroelectric / 火力発電所　a thermal / 原子力発電所　a nuclear } power station

3. 意力

【気力】
力づける　encourage
力を落す
be disheartened; be discouraged; be dispirited

【努力】
この学校は語学教育にたいへん力を入れている。
This school is { putting a great deal of effort / really throwing itself〔*colloq.*〕} into language teaching.
力を合せる
cooperate in《something》

4. 助力

力になる[力を貸す，力添えをする]
help《a person》{ do《something》 / in《something》 / with《something》}
彼女は彼のアパート探し［研究／市長選］に力を貸した。
She helped him { find an apartment. / in his research. (研究に) / in his campaign to become a mayor. (市長選に) }
あなたのお力になれればうれしいです。
I'll be happy if I can { do anything for you. / help you. / be of help (to you). }

【…の力で】
あなたのお力で
because of you
親の力で
through the influence of one's parents
親の力で彼は今の職[地位]に就いた。
He got his present position through the influence of his parents.
彼女の力でこのコンサートを開くことができました。
It's thanks to her efforts that we were able to hold this concert.

5．権力

反乱を未然に防ぐために警察力を動員して警備に当った。

The police took crowd control action to prevent the riot.

警察の力をもってしても…はできない。

The authority of the police does not extend to ...

【金権】

金の力で動かしたという風評だ。

It is rumored that money changed hands.

彼は金の力[裏金]で大学に入った。

He entered the university on the strength of a little money passed under the table.

〈注〉 上記2文とも賄賂（bribery, payoffs）のことを言っている。

cf. to pay《someone》off（賄賂をつかう）

威光，権力の意味で次のようにも言える。

親の力(威光)　parental authority

学校の力　school authority

警察の力　police authority

6．その他

【科学】

科学の力でよりよき明日を！

A Better Tomorrow Through Science!〔*slogan*〕

科学の力で新しいエネルギー源が開発されるだろう。

New sources of energy will become available through { scientific research.（科学研究） / advances in science.（科学の進歩） }

【能力】

彼は人の上に立って指導する力がある［ない］。

He has excellent [no] leadership abilities [capabilities].

彼にはクラブを立て直す[組織する]力はない。

He isn't capable of reorganizing the club.

He has no ability to reorganize a club.

彼には募金を集める力はない。

He has no ability to gather funds.

〈注〉◆isn't able to ... とすると能力の有無にかかわらず，とにかくできないこと。internal reason(能力なし）か external reason（ほかの外的理由）かはわからない。

「能力なし」の意味で has no capability ... とするのはくどい言い方で，isn't capable ... とする方が好まれる。

◆ability と capability の比較

ability の有無とは有能な質か役に立たない質かその人の生れつきに関することであり，一方 capable, capability は具体的にある仕事を処理する能力があるかないか more practical（もっと実際的）な見方からの能力のことである。その差が上記例文で具体的な the club と一般に「クラブなど」の意味の a club に表れている。

【学力】

彼は英語[数学]の力がある。

He is good at [proficient in] English.

He is good at [well-grounded in] math.

〈注〉 be proficient は英語がよく話せるとか実技的な面の学力を指すのに対して，be well-grounded は基本がしっかりわかっていること。

彼は英語の力がついてきた[向上した]。

He has improved in English.

His English has improved a lot.

《類義語》

power, force, strength は物を動かす力というもとの意味を共有しているが，派生した意味にはそれぞれの語のニュアンスが見られる。

power　身体や物を動かす力，馬力；[転義] 権力，勢力，国力，大国。

force　肉体的力(ex. use of force 実力行使)。万有引力 (gravitation)，磁力，求心力などのように物に作用する力；［転義］政治的力，武力(ex. air force 空軍)。

strength　腕力，体力，精神力；耐久力，強度。

energy　行動のための潜在力，消費されるものとしてのエネルギー。

ちこく（遅刻）

【遅刻する】 be late for; come late to

学校に遅刻する

be late for school; come late to school
仕事に遅刻する
be late to [for] work
come late to the office [to work]
会合[デート]に遅刻する
be late for the meeting [a date]

ちしき（知識）→ しる・しらせる

knowledge; 情報 **information**
【…の知識がある[ない]】
have some [no] knowledge of《something》
彼はラテン語の知識がある[ない]。
He has some [no] knowledge of Latin.
【知識を得る】
get [gain, acquire] knowledge
get [obtain] information
知識を得る一番よい方法の一つは自分とは違った人たちと話すことだ。
One of the best ways to gain [acquire] knowledge is to talk with people different from ourselves.
知識なんてものは大学も結構だが，実人生や本からも得ることができるのだ。
One can gain knowledge from life and books as well as at university.
近頃は多くの人がコンピュータ[インターネット]を使って最新の音楽やミュージシャンについての知識を得ている。
Nowadays many people use their computers [the Internet] to get information about the latest music and musicians.
【知識階級】
the educated; intellectuals; the intelligentsia; the highbrows〔*derogatory*〕
〈注〉 highbrow（知識人・インテリ）には「知識人ぶっている」というような意味が含まれる。インテリでない人がインテリをけなす語。使わない方が無難（感情的色彩のある語）。
intellectual は客観的に知的精神活動を指す語。「知識人」を高く評価する人たちの間では intellectual と言われるのはほめ言葉である。

ちしつ（地質）

地質学；地質（的特徴） **geology**
地質学者 **geologist**

《関連語》
砂 sand / 小石 pebble / 石 stone / 岩石 rock / 大きな岩石 boulder / 土 →つち / 土(壌) soil; earth / 粘土 clay / ローム(沃土) loam / レス(黄土) loess / ラテライト(紅土) laterite / マール(泥灰土) marl / 微砂，沈泥 silt
【岩石】 rock
火成岩 igneous rock / 堆積[沈積]岩 sedimentary rock / 変成岩 metamorphic rock / 石灰石 limestone / 砂岩 sandstone / 粘板岩 slate / 泥板岩 shale / 石灰岩 limestone / 花こう岩 granite / 方解石 calcite / 雲母 mica / 石英 quartz / 石炭 coal (*cf.* 炭田 coal field)
【火山】 volcano
活火山 active volcano / 休火山 dormant volcano / 死火山 extinct volcano / 火山帯 volcanic zone / 噴火する erupt / 溶岩 lava / 火砕流 pyroclastic flow [blast] / 火山灰 volcanic ash / 軽石 pumice /pʌ́mis/ / 断層 dislocation, fault / 活断層 active fault

ちぢむ（縮む）・ちぢめる

1．幅・長さなど

【縮む，縮まる】 shrink
この布は洗っても縮みません。
This cloth won't shrink in the wash.
【縮める】 幅を縫いこんでつめる tuck; 折り返して短くする turn up; 短くする shorten
[物主語] be shortened
そでが長すぎるので縮めてもらった。
The sleeves were too long, so I had them shortened.
スカートが長すぎたので5センチ縮めた。
The skirt was too long, so I turned [hemmed] it up 5 cms.

2. 身体

彼は首を縮めてボールを避けた。

He ducked his head to avoid the ball.

彼は年をとって体が曲り縮んでしまった。

He is bowed and shrunk with age.

彼女はガラガラ蛇を見て縮み上がった。

When she saw the rattlesnake she shrank with fear [cowered].

3. 短縮・要約・省略

ストレスと過労が彼の命を5,6年縮めた。

Stress and overwork
{ took several years off his life.
{ shortened his life by several years.

この文章は長さを半分に縮めるといい。

You can condense this passage to half its length.

彼は世界記録を0.3秒縮めた。

He bettered the world record by 0.3 seconds.

ちっとも

ちっとも…ない **not at all; not a bit; not in the least**

1. 主観的表現と共に

私が行くのはちっともかまいませんよ。

I don't mind going myself.

ちっともわかりません。

I don't understand it at all.

彼なんかちっともこわくない。

I'm not in the least afraid of him.

あの映画はちっとも面白くない。

That movie's not a bit interesting.

彼は行くのはちっともかまわないと言っている。

He says he doesn't mind going himself.

彼はちっともわからないと言っている。

He says he doesn't understand it at all.

結婚したの！ おめでとう。ちっとも知らなかった。

You're [You've] married ! Congratulations. I didn't know that.

2. 変化を表す語と共に

会議がちっとも始まらない[終らない]。

The meeting doesn't seem to be beginning [ending].

【進歩】

彼はちっとも上手にならない。(習い事など)

He isn't making any progress.

彼は英語がちっともうまくならない。

His English hasn't improved a bit.

【変化】

あなたはちっとも変りませんね。

You haven't changed a bit.

ちゃくちゃく(着々)・ちゃくじつ(着実)

着々と[着実に] **steadily**

研究は着々と進行している。

The research is { well underway. / progressing steadily.

その子は着々と進歩している。(勉強・けいこごとの進歩)

The child is making steady progress.

〈注〉 ある計画の進行過程は次のように表現できる。
beginning（着手）→getting into it（調子が出る）→well-underway（かなり進行）→moving along, progressing steadily（着々と進行）→the end is in sight（完成見通しがつく）→be in the homestretch（もうすぐ終り）→the end（完成）

ちゃめ(茶目)

茶目っ気 playfulness

お茶目な人

a playful person

茶目をやる(罪のないいたずらをする)

play pranks; play a trick

あの子はお茶目だ。

The child is full of fun and mischief.

〈注〉 mischievous は playful(お茶目な)という意味もあるが，人の迷惑になる「悪さ」をする意味もあるので「お茶目な」と同義ではない。

チャンス → きかい，みこみ

a chance; an opportunity

絶好のチャンス

a golden opportunity

a chance in a million [thousand]

今がチャンスだ。

Now is our chance.

チャンスを逃がす

miss [lose] a chance

〈注〉◆「チャンス」はもちろん英語の chance からだが，上述の表現以外は chance の訳語として「機会」「見込み」などがふさわしい。

They wanted to give their children the chance to get a higher education, which they themselves had not had.

（子供には自分たちの受けられなかった高等教育を受ける機会を与えたいと思った）

There is hardly any chance for us to win.

（我々にはとても勝つ見込みはない）

◆chance を使う構文として(1) I have a chance 型と(2) There is a chance 型とがある。

(1) We have no chance of winning [to win].

（勝つ見込みはない）

He has little chance { of recovery [recovering]. / to recover.

（回復の見込みはほとんどない）

(2) There is little chance for him to recover [that he will recover].

(2)の文の chance は possibility で置き換え可能。

ちゃんと → きちんと

1．正しく，十分に，間違いなく

彼はちゃんと約束を守った。

He has kept his promise.

彼は学校で習ったことはちゃんとみな覚えている。

He remembers all he has learned at school.

彼は彼女が何をたくらんでいるかちゃんと知っている。

He knows exactly what she's up to.

彼は自分の欠点ぐらいちゃんとわかっている。

He's well aware of his own faults.

座席はちゃんと予約しておきました。

I have reserved our seats already.

【勘定】

勘定がちゃんと合っている。

The account is balanced [balances].

通帳と私の控えとはちゃんと合っている。

My personal record tallies with my bank book exactly.

〈注〉 tally とは A tallies with B.（A と Bはきちんと合う）のように agree（合う）の意。また keep tally [score], make a running tally [score] とは日本で正の字を書いて数えるように卌を書いて数を記録すること。最後の集計をすることを tally up と言う。

2．安全に，時をたがえず

金はちゃんと私のところにある。

I have the money here safe.

小包はちゃんと届いた。

The package { arrived as expected. / duly arrived. 〔*formal*〕

その子はちゃんと帰って来た。

The little boy came home safely.

ちゃんと時間に帰って来いよ。

Be sure to come back on time.

ちゃんと５時に起してよ。

Be sure to wake me at five.

彼は家賃をちゃんと支払っている。

He pays his rent regularly.

3．整然と，標準通り，立派な

【整頓】

自分の持ち物をちゃんとしなさい。

Put your things { in order. / where they belong.

【行動】

ちゃんとしなさい。（行儀よく）

Behave yourself.

ちゃんとやりなさい。（仕事などを）

Do it properly.

ちゃんとしたやり方

the proper way of doing things

ちゃんと座りなさい。

Sit up straight.

【服装】
ちゃんとした服装である
be dressed tidily
彼女はいつもちゃんとしている。
She always dresses neatly.
【人物】
ちゃんとした人　a decent person

チャンネル → テレビ

a channel
第3チャンネルで
on channel 3
3チャンネルで何をやっている？
What's on channel 3?
5チャンネルにまわす
turn on [get] channel 5
チャンネルを変える
change the channel
子供たちがチャンネル争いをした。
The children quarreled about which program [channel] to watch.

…ちゅう（…中）

1. …の範囲内で

【時間】
2,3日中　in a few days
彼は2,3日中に帰って来るだろう。
He'll be back in a few days.
今月中開いて[やって]います。
It will be open till the end of this month.
今月中に完成します。
It will be finished by the end of this month.
〈注〉 till と by の相違については「まで・までに」参照。
東京に滞在中に
during my stay in Tokyo
while I was in Tokyo
休み中　during the vacation
【割合】
十中八九
ten to one [10 to 1]; ninety percent, 90%
十中八九間違いないと思う。あの落ちた飛行機に隣の家の人が乗っていたんだ。
Nine chances out of ten [10 to 1] my neighbor was on the plane which crashed.
その知らせは十中八九間違いない。
The report is ninety percent true.
〈注〉◆「十中八九」は予想を表す。それと同じく 10 to 1 [ten to one] も予想・見込み(probability, chance)を表す。天気予報で次のように言う。
There's a 90% chance of rain tonight.（90%[十中八九]今夜は雨になります）
◆次の表現は予想ではなく事実についての記述。日本語では「たいてい」となる。
nine cases [times] out of ten = most of the time
ex. Nine times out of ten I miss the 6 p.m. news.（たいてい夕方6時のニュースは聞きそこなう）

2. 進行中

【日常的】
彼は今勉強中だ。
He's studying now.
彼は今仕事中だ。
He's working.
He's at work now.
彼は今会議中だ。
He's in conference now.
今試験の最中だ。
Examinations are now going on.
Now they are having tests.
社長は東京に出張中です。
Our president is now in Tokyo on business.
話し中です。
[電話が] The line is busy.〔米〕
The number is engaged.〔英〕
[人が] He's on the phone now.
【長期的】
彼は糖尿病の治療中だ。
He's {under treatment / being treated} for diabetes.
新しい橋が建築中だ。
The new bridge is {under construction. / now being built.}
新しいカリキュラムを検討中だ。

A new curriculum is now being planned.

今，夏休みの計画中です。

We are now planning our vacation.

新カリキュラムを試験的に実施中だ。

The new curriculum is in the process of being tested.

私たちはクラブの立て直し中です。

We're in the process of reorganizing our club.

〈注〉 in the process of ～ing はかなり長期にわたる複雑な仕事の場合に使う。

ちゅういする（注意する）

1. 心に留める

pay attention to; attend to; mind; be mindful of; be careful of; note

【注意して】

先生の言われることを注意して聞きなさい。

Pay attention to what your teacher is saying.

先生の注意を忘れないで。

Don't forget what your teacher said.

私の言うことを注意して聞きなさい。

Listen to me carefully.

A と B の相違に注意してください。

Note the difference between A and B.

2. 配慮する，用心する

気遣う **take care (of)**

配慮する **see that ...**

用心する **look out for; watch; be careful [watchful] of [about]; guard against**

【健康】

体[健康]に注意してください。

Please take care of yourself [your health].

【飲食物】

アルコール類を飲まないように注意してください。

Be careful not to drink any alcohol.

【病・けが】

かぜを引かないように注意して。

Take care [See] that you do not catch a cold.

子供にけがをさせないように注意して。

Take care that the child does not get hurt.

【危険物】

その道は蛇に注意してくださいよ。

Look out [Watch] for snakes when you walk on that path.

踏切を渡るときは列車に注意して。

Watch out for trains when you cross the railroad tracks.

道路を横断するときは(車に)注意して。

Be careful in crossing the street.

足元に注意して歩きなさい。

Watch your step.

【対人】

人の感情を害さないように注意せねばならない。

We should take care [be careful] not to hurt other people's feelings.

We should be mindful of other people's feelings.

パーティーでは全部のお客様にくつろいでいただけるように注意してください。

I'd like you to make sure [see] that everybody's comfortable at the party.

あいつには注意しろ[気をつけろ]。

Keep an eye on him.

【取扱い】

取扱い注意。

Handle With Care（荷物の貼り紙）

この箱は細心の注意を払って取り扱ってください。

The greatest care must be taken in handling this casket.

Be careful with this casket.

3. 忠告する・諭す

advise; suggest; criticize; warn; admonish

〈注〉 友人が注意するのは suggest, hint であり，先生が注意をするのなら「こうした方がよい」(advise),「だめじゃないか」(scold, admonish),「勉強しないと落第するぞ」(warn) と内容により異なった語を使う。

ジムが僕に，もっと勉強した方がいいと注意した。(友人の場合)

Jim suggested [recommended] that I study harder.

マクドナルド先生にもっとしっかり勉強しろと注意された。

Mr. Macdonald told me to study harder [that I should study harder].

マクドナルド先生に「怠けすぎだぞ」と注意された。

Mr. Macdonald criticized my laziness [me for being lazy].

〈注〉 この場合，声を荒らげてしかればscold, 口語でbawl me out for ... などという言い方もある。回想的，思索的な文中でならば，reprimand(叱責する)，admonish (説諭する)などもよい。

マクドナルド先生に「勉強しないと落第するぞ」と注意された。

Mr. Macdonald warned me that if I didn't study harder I would fail.

【とがめる】

その人があまり失礼な態度なので注意してやった。

She was so rude that I told her off.

4. 思い出させる

remind《a person》**of**《something》

傘を忘れないように私に注意してね。

Please remind me to take my umbrella.

彼は彼女に政治にかかわると危険だと注意した。

He reminded her of the danger of being involved in politics.

ちゅうがく (中学) → がっこう

a junior high school

長良中学校

Nagara Junior High School

〈注〉 固有名詞の時は上の例のように各語の1字目を大文字にする。

私は中学生である。

I'm a junior high school { student.〔米〕 / pupil.〔英〕 }

I go to junior high school.

〈注〉 米国では中学生でも student を使うが，英国では中学生，高校生には student を使わない。

私は中学2年生である。

I'm in the second year of junior high school.

I'm a second year student in junior high school.

〈注〉 「私は2年生だ」の直訳×I'm the second year ... はよくある誤り。I'm in the second year ... とするか，上の例文のように I'm a secend year student ... とする。

中学(生)時代

when I was in junior high school

〈注〉 in my (junior) high school days は誤りではないが，上の表現の方が普通。

中学校を卒業する

finish junior high school

〈注〉◆英米の学制の相違については「きょういく」を，成績などの言い方については「せいせき」参照。
◆以上の例にみるように junior high school が中学校の建物でなくその教育を意味するときは無冠詞でよい。

ちゅうこく (忠告) → ちゅういする

advice

忠告する　advise《a person》(**not**) **to do**《something》

忠告を求める

ask《a person's》advice

ask《a person》for advice

忠告に従う

follow [accept] a person's advice

忠告を聞かない

{ pay no attention to / disregard } 《one's》advice

ジムは僕にたばこをやめろと忠告した。

Jim advised me to stop smoking.

彼は僕の忠告を聞こうとしない。

He wouldn't listen to my advice.

〈注〉 名詞は advice, 動詞は advise。advice は×an advice でなく，a piece of advice のようにしなければならない。

ちゅうし（中止）

中止する **stop; give up**《doing》; **cancel**
call off（試合，ストなど）

【スト】

労組はストを中止した。

The union {canceled / called off} the strike.

【仕事】

彼は病気のため仕事半ばで中止せざるを得なかった。

He had to give up his project halfway through because of sickness.

【中止になる[される]】

be stopped; be called off; be canceled;

〈注〉 政府の仕事 government programs などの中止には cancel, be canceled を用い，be called off … は使わない。継続審議になったのは be pending と言う。

【会合】

その会合は中止になった[された]。

The meeting was canceled.

【試合】

試合は雨で中止になった。

The match was called off because of the rain.

〈注〉 cancel, call off はどちらも，試合が始まる前でも始まってからでも，最後のイニングでも中止する場合に使える。また，試合に限らずコンサートや講演などの催し物にも使える。また put a stop to は悪いことを止めさせる感じがある。

ex. The government is trying to put a stop to air pollution from motor vehicles.

（政府は車の排気ガスによる大気汚染を何とかしようとしている）

【工事】

建設工事は資金不足で一時中止になった。

The construction work has been suspended due to the shortage of funds.

【運行】

新幹線が2時間近く運行中止になっていた。

The Shinkansen has been stopped for nearly two hours.

〈注〉 この場合は suspended より stopped を使う。形のある「物」（列車の車体）については stop がよい。形のない「サービス」であれば suspend がぴったり。

{… train service / telephone service} has been suspended …

なお，suspend はやや堅い語。

ちゅうしゃ（駐車）

駐車する **park a car**

駐車場 **a parking lot**〔米〕; **a car park**〔英〕

（屋根つきの）駐車場 a parking garage (covered); 地下駐車場 an underground parking garage

（1台分の）駐車スペース

a parking space

1台[2台]用ガレージ

a one-car [two-car] garage

家の駐車場

a place for the car; a car port; a garage

〈注〉 garage は自動車修理工場の意味もある。

客待ちタクシーの駐車場 a cab stand

駐車禁止 No parking.（掲示）

駐車禁止区域 no parking zone [area]

駐車違反 a parking violation

駐車違反カード a parking ticket

駐車規制 restricted parking

駐車料金 parking fee

駐車許可証

parking permit; parking card [sticker]

駐車許可券

parking pass（駐車規制などがあるときに報道関係者に発行されるものなど）

ここは駐車禁止です。

Parking is prohibited here.

どこに駐車しようか。

Where shall we park?

Where can we park?

駐車場がない[路上駐車ができない]。

There's nowhere to park.

駐車する場所がない。（満車である）

The car park's full.

There're no parking places [spaces] (free).

新しいパチンコ屋は駐車場をたっぷりとっている。

The new pachinko parlor has
{ lots of parking spaces [places].
{ a lot of parking (space).

大きな駐車場が裏手にあります。

There is a big parking lot [car park] at the back.

そのスーパーには駐車場が3か所もある。

The supermarket has three parking lots.

駐車場が建物本体と同じくらい場所をとってしまった。

The car park [The parking area] took up as much space as the building itself.

ちゅうと（中途）

中途で **halfway; in the middle; unfinished**

彼は仕事を中途でやめてしまった。

He left his work unfinished.

何でも中途で投げ出すんじゃないぞ。

Don't leave things half done.

中途半端な仕事をするな。

Don't do things by halves.

〈注〉「半分終えた，半分まで来た」は I'm halfway done. あるいは We're halfway there. などとなる。悪い意味はない。

彼は家庭の事情で中途退学してしまった。

He quit [left] school halfway (through) for family reasons.

雨が降り出したので中途で引き返してしまった。

He turned back halfway because it began to rain.

ちょうこう（聴講）

【聴講する】 audit a course

今学期は歴史の講義を聴講している。

I'm auditing [sitting in on] a history class [course] this term.

〈注〉class は lecture, lab (laboratory), discussion, seminar などを含む1回1回の授業のこと。ただし次の course の意味にも使われる。course は半年または1年で完結する一連の授業のこと。

【聴講生】 an auditor

【聴講を許可される】

be enrolled as an auditor

彼はグラスゴー大学で2科目聴講を許された［することになった］。

He is enrolled as an auditor in two classes at Glasgow University.

ちょうさ（調査）

《類義語》

【調査】

survey 測量・統計などによる概観的調査。

investigation 事実関係や原因など，細かい徹底的調査。また警察の「捜査」。

examination 検査や実際の観察などに基づいた調査。

inquiry 主として質問に対する答えをもとにした調査。

research 学問的調査研究。

【調査する】 examine; investigate; make an investigation; research; do research; inquire [look] into; make inquiries into [about]（問い合せ照会により調査する意味もある）

〈注〉同語源の名詞・動詞の場合，動詞になると名詞形のときよりも意味範囲が広くなる。

調査団

an investigation committee

an inquiry commission

調査報告

an investigation report（口頭または書面）

調査研究

research; a research study

国勢調査

census; national census

世論調査

an opinion poll

世論調査を行う

take [conduct] an opinion poll

調査書（アンケート）

questionnaire

（中学・高校の）成績調査書
transcript of one's school record
その件は目下鋭意調査中である。
The matter is now under vigorous investigation.
極秘で調査進行中である。
A secret investigation is proceeding.

ちょうし（調子）

1．音調

【音楽】
調子が合う［はずれる］
be in [out of] tune
調子がよい（音楽的な）musical;（リズミカルな）rhythmical
このピアノは調子がはずれている。調律が必要だ。
This piano is out of tune. It needs tuning.

【口調】
怒ったような調子で
in an angry tone; angrily
命令するような調子で
in a commanding tone
非難する［哀れむ］ような調子で
as if to blame [pity] me
with censure [pity] in his tone [voice]
気に入らないような調子で
disapprovingly
with disapproval in his tone [voice]

2．具合

【体】
体の調子はどう？
How are you (feeling, doing)?
調子は上々だ。
I'm in the best of health [in good shape].
彼は体の調子がいい。
He's fit and well.〔英〕
右脚の調子が悪いんだ。
Something's wrong with my right leg.
今朝は調子がよくない。
I don't feel well this morning.
（運動選手など）彼は調子がよくない。
He's not in the best of shape.
〈注〉 be out of shape は一般人にも運動選手にも用いられる。

【仕事】
仕事の調子はどうだい？
How's business (going, doing)?
調子は上々だ。
It's brisk.（ここ1週間ばかり好調）
It's thriving.（ずっと長期にわたり好調）

【機械】
エンジンは一日中調子がよかった。
The engine worked beautifully all day.
今日はエンジンの調子が悪い。
The engine isn't working well today.

【やり方】
パーティー［会議］は調子よく進行した。
The party [conference] went beautifully.
その調子！
That's it!
That's the way to do it!
この調子ではこの仕事は期限に間に合わない。
At this rate this work won't be finished on time.

ちょうしょ（長所）

a strong point; a good point;
利点 **an advantage**
長所と短所
strong points and weak points; advantages and disadvantages（利点と不利な点）
（cf. merits and demerits 実際的に世の中のやり方，方式の「功罪」を述べるのに用いられるが，使用頻度は減る傾向にある）
彼の隠し立てのない率直さはビジネスマンとしては長所であると同時に短所にもなる。
His outspoken frankness is at once his strong point [strength] and his weak point [weakness] as a businessman.

この新しい布地の長所は摩擦に強い[いたみにくい]ことです。

The advantage of this new fabric is that it withstands wear and tear.

ちょうせい(調整)・ちょうせつ(調節)

《類義語》
adjust 調整して合せる。
control 統制・制御して基準に合せる。
modulate 音や声の調子などを変えて調節する。
tune in (**the radio**) 受信するよう調節する。
regulate 規制・調節して基準などに合せる。

物価の調整のために政府は新しい価格表によって原料費の規制を行った。

In order to control prices, the government regulated the cost of raw materials according to a new scale.

5か月後, 政府は価格表の調整［見直し］をせねばならなかった。しかし, その後は順調にいって物価は安定した。

After 5 months, the price scale had to be adjusted, but since then, the system has been working well [effective] and prices have stabilized.

テレビの色を調整してくださいませんか。ばかにオレンジ色がかっているんです。

Will you adjust the color on the television? It's too orange.

このエアコンは自動的に温度調節をいたします。(広告)

This air conditioner has automatic temperature control.

ちょうわ(調和)

調和する **harmonize with; agree with; go with; match**

彼はインテリア装飾家で, 思いがけない素材の組み合せから調和を創り出す才能をもっている。

He's an interior decorator who really knows how to harmonize unlikely materials.

【服】
彼女は新調のスーツと調和するバッグと靴を買った。

She bought a bag and shoes to go with her new suit.

【色】
色彩が調和しない。

The colors don't match [go together, go with each other].

オフィス内の色彩に調和があるかないかは社員の気分や仕事の能率にまで影響してくる。

The presence or absence of color harmony in offices affects employee moods and work efficiency.

カーテンや壁紙などあらゆる装飾が一つに調和して異国情緒を醸し出している。

The curtains, the wall paper and all the decorations work together to produce an exotic effect.

ちょきん(貯金)

［行為］**saving** (**money**); 金 **savings; a deposit**

貯金する **save money; put** [**deposit**]《one's》**money in a bank**

彼には250万円の銀行貯金がある。

He has 2,500,000 yen in the bank.

His account now totals [stands at] 2,500,000 yen.

貯金から10万円下ろした。

He drew 100,000 yen out of [from] his savings.

《関連語》
貯金通帳 a savings [deposit] book; a pass book; a bankbook (銀行預金)
〈注〉 欧米では小切手 check〔米〕[cheque〔英〕]が普及しているので買物には check [cheque] book が普通に使われる。
郵便貯金 postal savings

郵便貯金をしている。
I keep my savings in the post office.
積立貯金　installment savings
月掛け貯金　monthly savings
定期預金
fixed-term-deposit; time deposit
預金証書　CD（Certificate of Deposit）

ちょくせつ（直接）

㊎ **direct;**（時間的）**immediate**
㊗ **directly; straight; firsthand**

1. 自分で

私は直接この目で見た。
I saw it with my own eyes.
どうぞあなたが直接彼に尋ねてください。
Please ask him yourself.
あなたに直接お話ししたいのです。
I'd like to speak to you personally [in person].
その話はジョン自身から直接聞いたのです。
I heard the story firsthand from John himself.

2. ずばり，直に

為替レートの変動は我々の生活に直接影響は与えない。
The fluctuations in the exchange rate don't directly influence our lives.
生活は為替レートの変動には直接影響されない。
Our lives will not be directly affected by the fluctuations in the exchange rate.
成田に着くと私は直接病院に彼を見舞いに行った。
After arriving at Narita, I went straight to the hospital to see him.
彼の直接の死因は心不全だ。
The immediate cause of his death was heart failure.

ちょくつう（直通）

【列車】
東京行き直通列車
a through train to Tokyo
この列車は東京行き直通列車です。
This train goes direct(ly) to Tokyo.
【飛行機】
直行便
non-stop flight [through flight]
成田―ミラノ間の直行便が開かれた。
Direct air service has started between Narita and Milan.
【電話】
直通電話
direct dial telepbone
1990年代までに地球上のほとんどすべての国々が互いに直通電話でつながれた。
By 1990s, almost every country on earth was connected with every other by direct dial telephone.

ちょくめん（直面）

直面する　**face** (**up to**)**; confront; come face to face with**
直面している(状態)　**be faced with; be confronted with** [**by**]
死に直面する
be confronted by death
face [confront] death
危険に直面する
be in the face of danger; face danger
政府は自動車輸出制限の難題に直面，苦慮している。
The government is now confronted with the difficult problem of car export restrictions.
〈注〉「直面」は，死，危機，危険などに対することであるが，confront, face は人や事件との対決・遭遇などにも広く使われる。
He was suddenly faced [confronted] with the possibility that he would be transferred to Hong Kong.
（彼に突然寝耳に水のホンコン転勤話が持ち上が

った）
Everyday she confronts [faces] the veiled dislike of her classmates.
（毎日彼女は級友に白眼視されながら耐えねばならない）

ちらかす（散らかす）・ちらかる → きたない

1. 室内

部屋がひどく散らかっていた。

The room was in a great mess [very untidy, very messy].

あなたの部屋を散らかさないで。

Don't let your room get messed up.

〈注〉 "Don't mess up your room." と言うと「わざと散らかさないで」の意味になる。

おもちゃを散らかさないように。

Don't leave your toys lying about.

彼女の部屋は足の踏み場もない散らかりようだった。

Her room was extremely messy.

新聞，灰皿とたばこの吸いがら，よごれた衣類，ウイスキーの瓶などが雑然と床に横たわっていた。（散らかりようの描写例）

Newspapers, ashtrays filled with butts, dirty clothes and whisky bottles lay scattered all over the floor.

2. 公共の場所

ごみを散らかさないでください。（掲示）

Don't throw away trash here!
No litter please.
Don't be a litterbug!

公園にごみを散らかさないでください。どこを見ても空き缶がころがっています。

Don't litter in the park! Everywhere you see empty cans lying about.

景勝地にごみが散らかっているのはいかにも情けない。

What a pity { these scenic places are full of rubbish [trash]! / there's trash [rubbish] all over these scenic places! }

cf. ごみはごみ箱へ。

Put trash into the trash bin [can].

自分のごみは自分で持ち帰れ。

Take all trash with you.

ちる（散る）・ちらす・ちらばる

1. 散る

動自 **fall; be scattered**

【花・葉】

木の葉が散り始めた。

Leaves began to fall.

散り敷く

lie scattered about; be strewn on the ground

木の葉が散り敷いていた。

The leaves lay scattered about.

【気が散る】

今日はどうも気が散って仕方がない。

I can't concentrate today.

2. 散らす

動他 **scatter; disperse;**（人垣など）**break up**

【花】

さっと風が吹いて桜の花を散らせた。

A gust of wind scattered the cherry blossoms.

【群衆】

警官がやじ馬を散らした。

The police dispersed [broke up] the crowd.

【気】

気を散らせないで，集中しようとしているんだから。

Don't distract me; I'm trying to concentrate.

【排気】

車の排気ガス中の化学物質が都市やその周辺に広くまき散らされている。

Chemicals in car exhaust disperse quite widely over a city and its outskirts.

3. 散らばる →ちらかす・ちらかる

be scattered; lie scattered; be dispersed

広い湾内に七つの小島が散らばっている。

Seven islands are scattered [lie scattered] over a large area in the bay.

【群衆】（人垣など）break up; disperse

（事故を見に集まっていた）やじ馬は散（らば）ってゆき，渋滞していた車も動き出した。

The crowd dispersed and traffic started moving.

《類義語》
散らす　scatter
散らかす　mess up
散らばる　be scattered
散らかる　be messed up; become messy
散らばっている　lie scattered
散らかっている　be messy

ちんぎん（賃金）→ きゅうりょう

wages　日雇い労働者（day laborers）など主として肉体労働者に支払う報酬。時間給，日給，週給がある（pay base は hourly, daily or weekly calculation）; **pay** 報酬（くだけた語）

賃金格差　a wage differential
賃金水準　a wage level
賃金体系　a wage scale
賃金凍結　a [the] wage freeze

賃上げを要求した。

They demanded a raise.

労働者は賃上げストを敢行した。

The workers went on strike for higher wages.

つ

ついて

1. …に関して

about; on; over; as to; concerning; relating to

《類義語》

about もっとも一般的に広く使われる。

We talked about { our plans for the summer. / the problem of air pollution.

（夏休みの計画[大気汚染の問題]について話し合った）

on スピーチ，論文などの演題，題目を表す。

That group will talk on energy prospects in the 21st century.

（そのグループは21世紀のエネルギー(源)の見通しについて論ずる）

over いろいろな意見があり，よく話し合ったことを表す。

We talked over { where to go for vacation. / the family tension and emotional conflicts.

（休みにどこに行くかについて[家庭内の感情的対立について]よく話し合った）

concerning; regarding; as to〔英〕 限定的なことについて。

He said nothing as to whether he was for or against it.

（彼は賛否について何も言わなかった）

He said nothing concerning [regarding] his present occupation.

（彼は自分の現在の職業については何も言わなかった）

【情報】

その新しい実験については何も情報はありません。

We have no information about the new experiment.

この本を読んで貿易問題についていくつかのことがわかった。

I found several things in this book relating to trade problems.

〈注〉 about は直接的にそのものについて，relating to はそのものずばりではなく間接的に「関係がある」という程度。

2. …の指導の下に

山本先生について俳句の勉強をした。

We studied haiku under Mr. Yamamoto.

バートル先生について子供たちはみっちり仕込まれた。

The boys have been trained by Mr. Bartle.

〈注〉 train されるのは skills であり，前後関係からスポーツ，絵画，ダンス，演技などの何を仕込まれたかは通常わかっているので，上の英文中では言及していない。

3. …の割合で（値段）

このさじは１ダース（について）1000円です。

These spoons are (sold for) a thousand yen a dozen.

ついとつ（追突）→ しょうとつ

追突 **a rear-end collision**

追突する **strike from behind**

追突される **be struck from behind**

彼の車は追突されて大破し，彼自身もむち打ち症になった。

His car was struck from behind and was badly damaged, and he himself got [has (a case of)] whiplash.

ついに（遂に）

1. 完成・達成

at last; finally; in the end; eventually

新しいハイウェイは難航したがついに完成した。

The new highway was finally [at last] completed after many difficulties.

彼は数回受験に挑戦し，ついに合格した。

He tried several times to pass the exam, and eventually [finally, in the end, at last] he succeeded.

うれしいです。ついに合格しました。

I'm glad I { finally passed the exam. / passed the exam at last. }

ついに彼は山頂をきわめた。

He at last succeeded in attaining the summit.

《類義語》

at last 長い努力，曲折の後ようやく目的を遂げた強い感動がある。ただし，努力にもかかわらず不成功であったときは使えない。

finally ついにやり遂げた場合に使えるが，不成功に終った場合にも用いられる。単に「最後に」(last)の意味にも使われる。

in the end いろいろな困難や迷いがあったが，最後はここに落ちついたというぐらいで，感情的にはそれほど強くない。

eventually 長いことかかったが…という，時が過ぎ去った感じを含む。

cf. ついに雪になった。

Eventually it began to snow.

意味的にこの雪を待っていたのか恐れていたのかは前後関係による。

2. 挫折・失望

午前中ずっと待っていたのに彼はついに現れなかった。

I waited for him all morning, but he never turned up.

彼は新しい機械の発明に生涯をささげたが，ついに失敗に終った。

He tried in vain all his life to invent a new machine.

彼はさんざん考えたが，ついにその問題を解けなかった。

He tried very hard but couldn't solve the problem in the end.

事はスムーズには運んでいるように見えたが交渉はついに決裂した。

Things seemed to be going smoothly, but finally [in the end] our negotiations broke down after all.

〈注〉 after all は「ついに」よりむしろ「やはり，やっぱり」に近い。after all の使い方は次の(1)(2)に分けられる。

(1) We mustn't forget「この点を忘れてはいけない」の含意で次のような場合。

Bill forgave Jim; Jim is his son after all.（ビルはジムを許した。何といってもジムは彼の息子だもの）

(2) 「予期に反して，いろいろあったが結局」の意で次のような場合。

We didn't plan to go, but we went after all.（行く予定ではなかったが結局行った）

I'm sorry I can't come after all.（残念ながらやはり行かれません）

子供たちは迷子の子猫にミルクをやったけれども弱っていて飲む力もなく，ついに翌日死んでしまった。

Though the children gave the stray kitten milk, it was too weak to drink and died the next day.

その子はじっと我慢していたが，ついに泣き出してしまった。

The boy finally burst out crying [burst out crying in the end] though he tried ever so hard not to.

彼らは数か月も無給で残業を続けたが，ついにもう限界だと仕事をやめてしまった。

They worked overtime without pay for several months, but finally they got so tired of it that they quit the job.

【終りまで】

うちのおばあさんは一生家族のために働いて，ついにただの一度も泊りがけの旅行に行く暇もなかった。

Our grandmother spent all her life working for her family and never once had any time at all to go on an overnight trip anywhere.

つうがく（通学）

何で[どうやって]通学していますか。

How do you come [go] to school?

バスと電車で通学しています。

I come [go] to school by bus and train.

歩いて通学しています。

I walk to school.

通学の途中いつも古い教会のそばを通ったものだったが，その墓場がたいへん気味が悪かった。

On my way to and from school I used to pass by an old church that [which] had a very scary churchyard.

〈注〉◆go [come] to school は，家にいて「学校に行く」(go) と考えるか，学校にいて「学校に来る」(come) と考えるかの違いである。
◆commute は通学の意味に使われることもあるが本来は通勤することである。→つうきん

つうかん (痛感)

痛感する 動他 **strongly [keenly] feel; really feel**

社長は正式な委員会を設ける必要を痛感した。

The president strongly felt the necessity of setting up an official committee.

やっぱりもう年だと痛感しています。

I really feel my age catching up with me.

彼は自分の限界を痛感した。

He felt his limitations keenly.

He really felt his limitations.

〈注〉 feel keenly を用いて△ I felt keenly the importance of her existence. (あの人の存在の重さを痛感した) のように書く例をよく目にするが，動詞と目的語は結びつきが強く，間に副詞が入るのを嫌うので keenly felt と語順を逆にするか，目的語が長い語群でなければ felt《something》keenly のようにするとよい。また existence は presence とすべきである。
I fully realized her importance as a leader. (指導者としての彼女の存在の重さを痛感した) のようにも言える。

つうきん (通勤)

通勤する **go [come] to** 《one's office》; **commute** 《by train》; **go to work** 仕事に行く

通勤者 〔米〕a commuter

通勤手当 〔米〕a commuting allowance

通勤定期 〔米〕 a commuter ticket;〔英〕 a season ticket

通勤電車 a commuter train

〈注〉 a commuter line; a suburban line (都会と近郊を結ぶ通勤用の路線) を走るのが a commuter train, ただし日中も運行している。朝夕のラッシュ時に走るのが a rush-hour train [bus]。

通勤には電車で1時間半かかる。

It takes me an hour and a half [one and a half hours] by train to go to the office.

〈注〉 commuteは郊外の住宅から都心の勤務先に列車でかなり時間をかけて通勤すること。

彼は電車とバスで通勤している。

He commutes by train and bus.

彼は鎌倉の自宅から青山の会社に通勤している。

He commutes between his home in Kamakura and his office in Aoyama.

彼は通勤に千代田線と日比谷線を使っている。

He takes the Chiyoda Line and Hibiya Line to get to his office.

つうこう (通行) → こうつう

passing; passage; transit

通行する **pass through [along]**

1. 車の往来

street traffic

通行料金 a toll; a fee

通行料金所

a toll booth (個々の); a toll station (総称)

通行禁止区域 a no-passing zone

道路が通行止めになっている。

The street is closed. (通行止めの柵が置かれている)

The street is blocked. (通行止めの柵または落石などで道がふさがれている)

cf. 交通渋滞の場合は (The) traffic is held up [tied up].

交通麻痺状態は（The）traffic is completely tied up [at a standstill].

2．掲示

通行止め　No entry / Closed to traffic

通り抜けできません

No through road / No thoroughfare

左[右]側通行　Keep left [right]

（歩行者に）Walk left [right]

一方通行　One way

つうじる(通じる) → つづく・つづける

1．空間的

【道路】

この道路は羽島駅に通じています。

This road goes to Hashima Station.

〈注〉 This road leads to … は話し言葉ではまれだが，比喩的に使われたり，方向を示して This road leads south.（南の方に行く）のように使われることはある。

【部屋など】

そのドアは大ホールに通じていた。

The door opened into a large hall.

階段が下のホールに通じていた。

A flight of stairs led（down）to the hall.

【交通機関】

美濃太田と多治見の間に鉄道が通じている。

There are trains between Mino-Ota and Tajimi.

The railroad runs between Mino-Ota and Tajimi.

まもなく北海道から鹿児島まで新幹線が通じるだろう。

Shinkansen lines will reach all the way from Hokkaido to Kagoshima before long.

〈注〉 上の文は全体的にとらえた表現。細かく分ければ，(1)計画（planning）の段階，(2)工事（construction work）の段階，(3)工事が完成し運転開始（operation）の準備中の段階でそれぞれ次のように言い分けられる。

(1) 計画中

The Shinkansen will be extended to Kagoshima very soon.（まもなく新幹線が鹿児島までのびることになる）

(2) 工事中

Construction work on the（new）Shinkansen line to Kagoshima（鹿児島新幹線の建設工事は）

{ is well underway.（着々と進行中）
  will be completed before long.（まもなく完成）
  is almost finished.（ほとんど完了）}

(3) 運転開始直前

The（new）Shinkansen line to Kagoshima will { open / go into service } soon.（まもなく運転開始）

【電話】

電話が故障で通じない。

The line is dead.

The line is down.

電話が話し中で通じない。

The（phone）lines are all busy [tied up].

電話が混線してよく通じない。

There seems to be some interference on the line.

佐藤さんに電話が通じない。

I couldn't get Mr. Sato on the phone.

【電気】

この電線は(電気が)通じている。

This is a live wire.

彼のつくった丸太小屋には電気もちゃんと通じている。

The log hut he made for himself has electricity.

2．時間的

これらの島では1年を通じて気候温暖である。

In these islands it's warm all（the）year round [all through the year].

3．精通する

彼はヨーロッパの歴史に通じている。

He is an expert on European history.

彼は国際事情に通じている。

He is well-informed [well-versed] in international affairs.

〈注〉 well-versed（精通している）は knowledge（知識）に関する言い方で，skill（語学力）については言わない。スペイン語に通じている［よくできる］は ×He's well-versed in Spanish. とは言えない。He's good at Spanish. が正しい。ただし「スペイン文学」の場合は He's well-versed in Spanish literature. でよい。

4．相互理解

英語は世界中で通じる。

English is used [understood] all over the world.

私の英語は通じなかった。

I couldn't make myself understood in English.

People didn't understand my English.

あいつには冗談が通じない。

Jokes are lost upon him.

彼には私の冗談が通じなかった。

He didn't catch [get] my jokes.

彼には婉曲に言っても通じなかった。

He didn't catch my hint.

5．媒介

彼のことは文通を通じて知っていますが，直接会ったことはありません。

I know him through correspondence but not in person.

我々はテレビを通じて多くのことを知ることができる。

We can get a great deal of information from TV.

つうしん（通信）

［行為］**correspondence** 文通；（a）**communication**

［情報］**news; a report; information**

通信する　**correspond** [**communicate**] **with** 《a person》〔*formal*〕; **write to** 《a person》

商業通信

a correspondence with 《a company》

通信員　a correspondent (for the Asahi)（朝日新聞の）; a reporter

通信欄（新聞・雑誌）

the 'letters-to-the-editor' column

通信網　a communications network

通信衛星　a communications satellite

衛星による通信で　by satellite transmission

通信社　a news agency [association]

通信販売で　by mail order

通信販売会社　a mail-order company

通信販売部　a mail-order division

通信販売カタログ　a mail-order catalog

通信簿，通知票　one's school report

通信教育課程　a correspondence course

パソコン通信

computer mediated communication

【無線】

探険隊は無線で基地と通信し，連絡を保った。

The expedition kept in touch with the base by wireless.

【報道】

パリ特派員は反乱のニュース（の通信）を急ぎ送信してきた。

A correspondent in Paris dispatched the news of the revolt.

パリ発の通信によれば，今朝フランクフルトとパリの間でエールフランスのジェット機が乗っ取られた。

A Paris dispatch says that an Air France jetliner was hijacked between Frankfurt and Paris this morning.

【交信】 have [make] contact

山岳救助隊は行方不明の登山者と3時間前に無線で通信を行ったが，その後交信は途絶えている。

The mountain patrol made radio contact with the lost climbers three hours ago but they haven't heard from them since.

これらの地区との通信は全面的に途絶している。

All communication with these areas has been cut off.

（受信した）最後の通信は「エンジンの一つが

停止」というもので，それから2分後に航空機は墜落した。

The last communication [message] they got was “One engine stopped”, and two minutes later the plane crashed.

つうち（通知）→ しる・しらせる

通知 **notice**〔*formal*〕; **notification; information;** 報告 **a report**

通知する　**notify**〔*formal*〕(《a person》that [of]...); **inform** (《a person》that [of]...); **let**《a person》**know** (《something》[that...])

結果はわかりしだい，ご通知します。

I will let you know the result as soon as possible.

彼の到着日時に変更がある場合は通知いたします。

We will notify you [inform you, let you know] if there is any change in the date and time of his arrival.

裁判官は弁護士に次回審問は2週間以内と通知[通告]した。

The judge informed the lawyers that the next hearing would be in two weeks.

追って通知があるまで待機せよ。

Wait till further notice.

彼は北山大合格の正式通知を受けた。

He was officially notified / He received a formal notice } that he had been accepted into Kitayama University.

両親は法的に権利がある旨通知を受けた。

The parents were informed of their legal rights.

事前通知が必要だ。

It is necessary to give notice in advance.

We need prior notification.

《類義語》

let《a person》**know**　標準的だが正式な堅い文にはそぐわない。

notify　公式用語で堅い語。出廷の日時・場所を通知するようなときに使う。

inform　標準的な文から正式な文までかなり広く使われるが，口語ではまれ。

◆**report** と **inform** の比較

report は報道などのように伝える内容が大きく長く客観的・公的であるのに対し，inform は伝える内容が短く日時・場所などの個人的な情報が多い。個人的な場合のごく一般的な語は tell である。

つかう（使う）

［一般的］**use; spend**《money》; **keep** [**have**]《servants》; **speak**《a language》

〈注〉　人を使う以外はほとんど use で間に合うが，use 以外の語もあげておく。

【物】

この機械の使い方を教えてください。

Please tell me how to use [operate, run] this machine.

日本の家では居間が寝室にも使われる。

In Japanese houses living rooms are used [serve] also as bedrooms.

【金】

彼は本に結構金を使う。

He uses [spends] a lot of money on books.

僕はそんなくだらない物に使う金は持っていない。

I have no money to use for [spend on] such junk.

【人】

あなた方のおじい様の時代にはお手伝い3人とコック1人を使っていましたよ。

In your grandfather’s time we had three maids and a cook.

あの工場では300人の人を使っている。

Three hundred men are employed in that factory.

【言語】

英語は全世界で使われている。

English is used all over the world.

【慣用表現】

使い古しの　much used; (すり切れた) worn-out

使い古された決り文句　a cliché

【物主語】

使っている　be in use

毎日使っている

be in daily use

もう使っていない

be out of use; not be used any more

使い道のない

be useless; be good for nothing

【人主語】

使い果す

use something up

使い道に困る（捨てるわけにもいかず…）

not know what to do with《something》

使い方がわからない

not know how to use《something》

下宿のおばさんの洗濯機を使わせてもらっている。

I have the use of my landlady's washing machine.

つかむ・つかまえる・つかまる

1．つかむ

seize;（強く）**grasp;**（急に）**grab**

【握る，手に取る】

彼は私の肩をぐっとつかんで揺さぶった。感情がひどく高ぶっていたのだ。

He grasped me by the shoulders and shook me, so great was his feeling.

おぼれる者はわらをもつかむ。

A drowning man will grasp [grab, catch] at a straw.

彼はウナギをつかもうとした。

He tried to seize the eel.

【把握する，とらえる】

私はこの文の意味がつかめなかった。

I couldn't understand [get, grasp] the meaning of this sentence.

探偵は真実をすべてつかんだ。

The detective found out the whole truth.

2．つかまえる

catch; catch [take, get] hold of; hold;［状態］**keep hold of**

警官が泥棒をつかまえた。

The policeman caught the thief.

小さい頃よく捕虫網で蝶をつかまえたものだ。

We used to catch butterflies with a net when we were little.

おばあさんは私の手をぎゅっとつかまえて放そうとしなかった。

Grandmother took hold of my hand and wouldn't let it go.

エスカレーターの乗降にはお子様の手をつかまえていてください。

Please hold the hand of your child when you get on and off the escalator.

Please help your children on and off the escalator.（簡略な表現）

3．つかまる

be caught; すがる　**hold on**　(**to**《something》)

【逮捕】

泥棒はその場でつかまった。

The thief was caught [arrested] on the spot.

〈注〉　次の文は誤文である。

×The police was caught the thief.

スピードの出しすぎでパトカーにつかまった。

I was stopped by a police car for speeding.

【すがる】

吊り革につかまってください。

Hold on to the strap.

《類義語》

grab　急にぎゅっとつかむ。抽象物でなく「物」を対象とする。

grasp　強くしっかりつかむ。「意味をつかむ」など抽象物にも用いられる。

seize　上の2語，特に grasp に近いが，通常もっとアクションが大きい。悲しみが人を「襲う」など抽象物にも用いられる。

つかれる（疲れる）→ くたくた

疲れる　**get tired, get fatigued;**〔強〕**get dead-tired; get exhausted**

疲れさせる　動他　**tire; exhaust**〔強〕;

形　**tiring**　人を疲れさせるような; **exhausting**〔強〕

疲れている（状態）

〔弱〕**be tired out; be weary; be fatigued**

〔強〕（くたくたに）**be worn-out; be dead-tired; be exhausted**

学校への往復を歩くのではあの子は疲れすぎる。

Walking to and from school is too tiring for him.

彼はもう年なのですぐ疲れる。

He gets tired easily because of old age.

くたくたに疲れたよ。

I'm utterly ⌊worn out [exhausted].

I'm dead tired [beat].

彼は心身ともに疲れている。

He feels weary in body and mind.〔*rather poetic*〕

〈注〉「生きていることも面倒くさい」life-weary, world-weary, soul-weary のような詩的な言葉もある。俗語ではまったくくたくたの意味で all done in, fagged out などがある。

小さな活字を読むと目が疲れる。

Reading small print is hard on the eyes.

彼はまだ旅の疲れが抜けない。

He has not yet recovered from the trip.

He's still tired out from the trip.

つく（付く，着く，就く，点く）

1. 付着する

泥のついた靴

muddy boots

靴についた泥

mud stuck on one's boots

ポケットにウサギの刺繍（ししゅう）のついた子供用スカート

a child's skirt with a rabbit embroidered on the pocket

この膏薬（こうやく）[テープ]はよくつかない。

This plaster [tape] doesn't stick well.

ハンカチにインク[血]が付いていた。

Her handkerchief was stained with ink [blood].

男の子は口の端に卵をつけたままあわてて飛び出した。

The boy rushed out with egg at the corner of his mouth.

ペンキが指についたよ。

Paint got on my fingers.

2. 同伴・味方

【付き添い】

患者さんにはベテラン看護婦がついています。

The patient is being cared for by quite experienced nurses.

An experienced nurse is with the patient.（専属の付き添い）

【味方】

こわがらないで。私がついています。

Don't be afraid. I'm with you.

彼らはいつも強い方につく。

They always side with the stronger group.

【敵方】

彼は敵方についた。

He has gone over to the enemy.

【従う】

その子の行く所どこにでも犬がついていった。

The dog followed the boy wherever he went.

3. 席に，職に

どうぞ席に着いてください。

Please ⌊sit down [take your seats].

Be seated, please.

彼は教職に就いた。

He became a teacher.

彼女は実業に就いた。

She has gone into business.

彼の父は政府の要職に就いていた。

His father held important offices in the government.

4．到着する

この列車は何時に東京に着きますか。

When does this train get to [arrive in, arrive at] Tokyo?

列車は2時に着きます。

The train is due at two o'clock.

私たちは昨日着いたばかりです。

We got [came, arrived] here only yesterday.

〈注〉 arrive でもよいが get の方がずっと多く使われる。

やっとのことでホテルに着いたのはもう11時すぎだった。

When we finally got to the hotel it was past eleven.

さあ駅に着きましたよ。

Here we are at the station.

あなたの手紙は今朝着きました。

I received [got] your letter this morning.

5．その他

【点灯】

電灯もヒーターもついたままなのに家にはだれもいなかった。

The lights and the heater were on but there was nobody in the house.

【点火】

新聞紙もたきつけも皆ぬれてしまってなかなか火がつかない。

The newspaper and firewood are all wet and won't ⌊kindle [light].

わらに火がついて納屋は5分で完全に火に包まれてしまった。

The straw caught fire and the barn was completely ⌊on fire [ablaze] in five minutes.

【根づく】

桜の若木を植樹したが，その90パーセントが根づいた。

We transplanted young cherry trees and 90 percent of them took root.

【利子】

その債券は年利6パーセントの利子がつく。

The bond yields [bears] 6 percent (interest) a year.

〈注〉 利子 interest は話し言葉では省略し，文に書くときには入れる。This is a six percent bond. とも言える。

【食事】

食事付き宿(泊)

a boarding house; board and lodging

【学力】

あの子は英語の力がついてきた。

Her English ⌊is improving [has greatly improved (たいへんついた)].

【幸運】

ついている　lucky

つくる（作る，造る）

1．製作・産出

make;（大きいもの）**build**

〈注〉 形のある物を「つくる」の意味ではたいていの場合 make で間に合う。

子供たちが校庭に大きな雪だるまを作っている。

Children are ⌊making a big [building a huge] snowman in the schoolyard.

【材料】

今日では多くの分野で環境に配慮し，自然に還元できる材料でもの作りをすることが重視されている。

From the ecological point of view it is now considered important ⌊to use biodegradable materials for various products [to use non-polluting substances in the production of various goods].

〈注〉 「環境にやさしい」を eco-friendly〔*informal*〕という。

【原料】

酒は米から，ワインはぶどうからつくる。

Sake is made from rice and wine from grapes.

【建造】
政府は道路や橋をつくるのに多額の金を使った。
The government spent a great deal of money to build [construct] roads and bridges.
【書物・文学】
彼は余暇に詩を作っている。
He writes poems in his spare time.
〈注〉 make poems は口語では使われることもあるが，奇異に感じる人もあるので避ける方がよい。
私たちは高校の英語の教科書を作っている。
We are making English textbooks for high school.
【裁縫】
姉が私にドレスを作ってくれています。
My sister is making [sewing] a dress for me.
【料理】
晩ごはんに何をつくったらいいかしら。
What should we make [cook] for dinner?
私はお菓子作りが好きです。
I like making [baking] cakes.
〈注〉 火を使わない料理はcookと言わない。×She's cooking sandwiches. は誤り。making sandwiches とする。
【栽培】
彼女は裏庭で野菜[花]をつくっていた。
She grew some vegetables [flowers] in the backyard.
【生産】
あの工場ではエンジン部品をつくっている。
That factory manufactures [makes] engine parts.
【工面】
我々は国際会議に代表を送る金をやっとつくった。
We managed to raise money to send our delegates to the international conference.
【時間】
その件に関してお話をしたいので時間をつくっていただけないでしょうか。
Can you spare some time to talk over the matter?
【機会】
我々はビルをお茶に招いて娘と引き合せる機会をつくった。
We invited Bill to tea to provide a chance for our daughter to meet him.

2. 形成
【組織】
彼らは新会社をつくった。
They established [set up] a new company.
彼の指導のもとに労働者たちは労働組合をつくった。
Under his leadership the workers formed [organized] a labor union.
【列】
切符を買うために人々は列をつくっていた。
People were standing in line to buy the tickets.
バスに乗るために人々は列をつくっていた。
People queued (up) for the bus.〔英〕

つける(着ける, 付ける, 点ける) →つく

1. 身体に
［動作］つける **put on**
［状態］つけている **wear**
〈注〉 put on はつける動作，wear はつけている，または着ている状態を表す。「リボンをつけている(状態)」を She's putting on ... としないように。「つけている最中」の意味になる。
彼女は絹のドレスに真珠のネックレスをつけている。
She is wearing a silk dress and a string of pearls.
【飾り】
彼女は帽子に羽飾りをつけている。
She's put a feather on her hat. (1)
She's wearing a hat with a feather [a feathered hat]. (2)
She sports a feather on her hat. (3)
〈注〉 (2)は羽飾りのついた帽子の意。「つけている」は後から羽を自分でさした意味にもとれるが，それならば(1)にする。(3)は「羽などをつけて得意になっ

ている」の意。

【化粧】

彼女は口紅をつけない。

She never wears [uses] lipstick.

彼はいつも外出する前に香水[髪にポマード]をつける。

He puts on perfume } before going out.
He pomades his hair }

【薬】

切り傷に軟膏を少々つけてください。

Put [Apply] a bit of [little] ointment on the cut.

〈注〉 口語では put, 使用説明書などでは apply を使う。

2. 物に

彼女はトーストにマーマレードをつけるのが好きだ。

She likes marmalade on her toast.

〈注〉 パンにつける(ぬる)動作は spread を使う。spread ... on one's [the] toast

電話[新しいエアコン]を取り付ける

install a telephone [a new air conditioner]

家を離れて独り暮しなので，自分で食事の用意もボタンつけもしなければならない。

Now that he lives alone apart from his family, he has to cook and sew buttons on for himself.

【お代り】

もう一杯つけましょうか。

Would you like [Won't you have] another helping?

【貼る】

葉書に切手を貼りつける

put [stick] a stamp on the postcard

壊れたかけらを接着剤でつける

glue the broken pieces together

壁紙を貼りつける

hang wallpaper

〈注〉 「壁紙を貼る」という表現には hang がごく普通に使われるが，wallpaper a room という言い方もある。
ex. Yesterday, I was wallpapering the bathroom.
(きのう浴室の壁紙貼りをしていた)
I couldn't spread the glue on the wallpaper very well. (まんべんなくのりづけができなかった)

シーツをのりづけしてください。

Please starch the sheets.

3. 記入する

【名前】

自分の持ち物に名前をつけなさい。

Mark your belongings.

Put your name on your belongings.

名前を書きつけてください。

Write down your name, please.

彼はきちんと日記をつけている。

He regularly keeps a diary.

代金は私の分としてつけておいてくれ。

Charge it [Put it down] to [on] my account.

4. その他

彼は息子にウィリアムと名前をつけた。

He named his son William.

明りをつけてくれ。

Turn on the light.

私がお茶の用意をしている間にガスに火をつけてお湯をわかしてください。

Would you light the gas and heat the water while I'm getting the tea things ready?

〈注〉 「お湯をわかしてください」は次のようにも言える。Would you put the kettle on?

彼はたばこに火をつけた。

He lit his cigarette.

指に水をつける

wet one's finger

豆を一晩水につける

soak the beans overnight

アシの茎をかご作りのために水につける

steep reeds for basketweaving

彼の父親に連絡をつけなければならない。

We have to contact his father.

彼はだれかがあとをつけてきていると気がついていた。

He knew someone was following him secretly.

都合をつける →つごう

つごう（都合）

1．事情・理由

circumstances; reason →じじょう

彼は家庭の都合で退学した。

He left school because of family circumstances [for family reasons].

彼は何かの都合で予約を取り消した。

He canceled the reservation for some reason.

2．便宜

それなら都合がよい。

That suits me perfectly.

この次の月曜日はご都合いかがでしょうか。

Is next Monday convenient for you?

Will next Monday suit you?

〈注〉 次の文はよくある誤りの例である。(2.の最後の〈注〉参照)

×Are you convenient on next Monday?

もし都合がつきましたら出席させていただきたいと存じますが，今のところまだはっきりいたしません。

If circumstances permit I would like to attend the meeting, but I'm not yet sure if I will be able. 〔*rather formal*〕

都合がつきしだい会いに行きます。

I'll come to [and] see you as soon as I can.

次の月曜日はあなたの都合が悪くて，火曜日は私が一日家をあけてしまう。いつ会いましょうか。

Next Monday is not convenient for you, and Tuesday I'll be away all day. When shall we meet?

【都合が悪ければ】

もし会社までお金を取りに来られるのがご都合が悪ければそうおっしゃってください。お送りしますから。

If it is inconvenient for you to pick up the money at the office, please let us know. We can send it.

【都合のよいとき】

あなたのご都合のよいときに参ります。

I'll come { at your convenience. / at any time convenient for you. }

いつでもあなたのご都合のよいときに会いに来てください。

Come and see me at your convenience.

【都合に合せる】

ご都合が悪ければあなたに合せます[こちらの予定を変えてもいいのです]。

I'll / We can } change if

{ you like. (1)
it's more convenient some other time. (2)
it suits your convenience. (3) 〔*formal*〕 }

〈注〉 (2)の it は不定の it で，some other time に行うことを指す。(3)の it は to change を指す。

他人の都合を考えるべきだ。

You need to consider other people's schedules [plans, time].

〈注〉 「あなたのご都合がよければ[悪ければ]」は If it is convenient [inconvenient] to [for] you … となる。(人を主語にできない)

×If you are convenient [inconvenient] …
×I'm convenient … }

○《some date or arrangement》is convenient for someone（日時や手はずを主語にする）

ex. Saturday is convenient for me, but how about for you?

3．幸運

【都合よく】

luckily; fortunately

うまく well

都合よく(お金の)持ち合せがあった。

Fortunately I had enough money to pay for it.

都合よくすぐにタクシーが来た。

Luckily a taxi came by in a minute.

万事都合よく運んだ。

Everything has gone wonderfully well.

4. 繰り合せ

【都合する】

［時間］君と一緒に行かれるよう何とか都合をつけられるだろう。

I think I can somehow manage to go with you.

彼は時間の都合がつかないと言った。

He said { he had no time to spare. / he couldn't find [make] time.

彼は予定を組み替えて何とか都合して私たちの会に出席したいと言った。

He said he would try to rearrange his schedule and come to our meeting.

［部屋］彼の叔父さんが自分の持っているアパートの一つを都合して貸してくれた。

His uncle let him stay in one of his apartments.

〈注〉「都合をつける」accommodate は堅い語で，日常的な口語文にはそぐわない。

［金］彼が頭金を都合してくれる。

He will lend me the deposit money [down payment, initial payment].

お金を少し都合していただけませんか。

Could you lend me some money, please?

つたえる（伝える）・つたわる

1. 伝言

彼にたまには私のところへ来るよう伝えてください。

Please tell him to come and see me once in a while.

あの人に私に電話するようお伝え願えませんか。

Would you mind asking her to phone [call] me?

何かお伝えしておきましょうか。

Would you like to leave a message for them?

ご伝言をお伝えしておきます。

I will give them your message.

どうぞご両親によろしくお伝えください。

Please remember me [give my regards] to your parents.

cf. Say hello to your mother for me. 〔*colloq.*〕

2. 伝承

その伝統は代々受け継がれ伝えられてきたのだ。

The tradition has been handed down from generation to generation.

【伝来】

仏教は西暦538年に初めて日本に伝えられた。

Buddhism was first introduced into [brought to] Japan in 538 A.D.

3. 報道・うわさ

【報道】

彼の暗殺のニュースは全世界に伝えられた。

His assassination was reported all over the world.

【うわさ】

うわさによれば彼はアメリカに渡り現地でアメリカ人女性と結婚したと伝えられる。

Rumor says [According to rumor] he went over to America and married an American girl there.

悪いうわさはすぐに伝わる。

Scandals circulate [go round, get round] quickly.

cf. The rumor spread like wildfire. 〔*cliché*〕（そのうわさはたちまちに広まった）

4. 熱・電気・光

conduct; transmit

金属は木よりもよく熱を伝える。

Metal conducts heat better than wood.

光は音より速く伝わる。

Light travels faster than sound.

5. 水・涙

涙がほおを伝わった。

Tears ran down her cheeks.

つち（土）→ち（地），どろ

大地 **the earth; Mother Earth;** 土壌 **earth, soil;**（特にばらばらの）土 **dirt;** 地面 **the ground;** 泥，ぬかるみ **mud;** 粘土 **clay**

土を掘る　dig in the ground
土に埋める　bury in the ground
土をかける　cover with earth
土を盛る　heap up earth
土を耕す　cultivate the soil

【土に親しむ】

彼は生涯を土に親しんで生きた。
He lived the life of a farmer.
He lived close to the soil.〔*poetic*〕

彼は土に親しむ作家[農民作家]だ。
He was a writer and a farmer.
He was a farmer as well as a writer.

〈注〉 土の平らな表面，人間の足の下にある平面は the ground，頭上の天 heaven に対しては the earth（大地）と呼ぶ。それを掘り，ばらばらこぼれる土も earth。この earth は後に球形とわかり the Earth として地球の意味がつけ加えられた。soil は耕す土。
cf. 肥沃な土壌 fertile [rich] soil / やせた土壌 poor soil

つづく（続く）・つづける

1．時間的

continue; go on《with your work》**; keep on**
［事主語］**last; hold out**

【天候の継続】

雨が2週間降り続いた。
It was [kept (on)] raining for two weeks.
There were two whole weeks of almost nothing but rain.
There was a long spell of rainy weather.

晴天が1週間以上続いた。
The good weather lasted more than a week.

【状態】

こんな状態は長くは続かないだろう。
This will not go on forever.

【戦争】

戦争が10年近く続いた。
The war lasted [continued] for nearly ten years.

【辛抱】

あの人は何をやっても続かない。
He can stick to nothing.

【頻発】

悪いことが続いた。
One bad thing followed another.
Misfortunes happened [occurred] one after another.
A series of misfortunes followed.

【続き・次】

次号に続く
(to be) continued in the next issue

35ページに続く
continued on page 35

15ページから続く
continued from page 15

週刊誌サンの連載「病院生活物語」は3月10日号に続きが出ます。
The next episode of the serial "Story about Hospital Life" in the weekly magazine *The Sun* will appear in the March 10th issue.

この話の続きは明晩のテレビで。
The rest of the story will be shown on TV tomorrow night.

続きは明日の晩ね。
I will tell the rest of the story } tomorrow night.
You'll hear the rest of the story }

【順序】

まず大統領が，続いて大統領夫人が戸口に現れた。
First the president appeared in the doorway, then his wife.

【続行】

仕事を続けなさい。
Go on with [Continue (with)] your work.

彼は途中5分の休憩を入れただけで2時間歌い続けた。
He sang for two hours with only a five minute break [intermission].

2．空間的

【行列】

行列が１マイルも続いた。

The procession stretched for a mile.

【土地】

学校の敷地は山のふもとまでずっと続いている。

The campus extends to [reaches, stretches to, goes all the way to] the foot of the hill.

【道】

その道は長野まで続いている。

That road goes to Nagano.

この道はどこまで続いているの？

Where does this road end up [go]?

(この道は)何マイルも続いて最後に151号線に出ます。

It continues [goes (on)] for miles until it finally joins Route 151 [one fifty one].

〈注〉 米国では州と州にまたがる長い道路はナンバーで呼ばれるものが多い。英国でも M56; motorway fifty six のようにナンバーで呼ぶ。

【接続】

隣接する 形 adjacent; adjoining

ホールに続いて小さな書斎があった。

There was a small study {next to / adjacent to / adjoining} the hall.

つとめ（勤め，務め）・つとめる

1．勤務

勤め 名 **a job; work** →しごと，しゅうしょく

彼は勤め先を探しているところだ。

He's now looking for a job.

彼は銀行[会社]に勤めている。

He works at a bank [for a company].

〈注〉 「〜に勤めている」の言い方

〜会社〜支店に勤めている work at 〜 Office of 〜 Company

〜会社に勤めている work for 〜 Company

〜さんの所で働く work for Mr. 〜

彼は新聞社に勤めたいと思っている。

He wishes to get a job with the press.

彼女は勤めをやめて故郷に帰った。

She gave up her job and went back to her village.

彼は今のところ勤め口がない[失業中だ]。

He is now out of work [a job].

2．義務

すっかり片付くまで[終るまで]ここに残っているのが私たちの務めだ。

It's our duty [obligation] to stay here until everything is over.

3．努力

努めて野菜を食べるようになさい。

Try to eat more vegetables.

彼女は努めて明るく振舞おうとしている。ほんとうはまだ息子の死の痛手から立ち直っていないのだが。

She is making an effort to behave cheerfully although she hasn't yet got over the loss of her son.

つぶす（潰す）・つぶれる

《類義語》

crush 力をかけて押しつぶす。

smash 急激な力でつぶす。

mash 芋などをつぶして形をなくす。

squash ぺちゃんこにする。

break 硬い物がばらばら，粉々になる(つぶす行為よりも壊れた物のイメージ，すなわち結果に重きを置いた語)。

1．有形物

ぎゅうぎゅう詰めの満員電車でバッグの中のサンドイッチはぺちゃんこになるしクッキーの箱もつぶれてしまった。

In overcrowded train my sandwiches in the bag were squashed flat and the box of cookies (were) crushed.

卵はつぶれやすい[壊れやすい]。

Eggs are easily broken.

〈注〉 easy to break とすると「わけなくつぶせる」と「故意につぶす」の意になる。

【家屋】

地震で町の3分の1の家がつぶれた。

About one third of the houses in the town were destroyed [collapsed] in the earthquake.

地滑りで山麓の7軒の農家がつぶれた。

The landslide destroyed seven farmhouses at the foot of the mountain.

2. 抽象物

顔をつぶす

make《a person》lose face (cf. save face)

顔をつぶされる　be humiliated

この不景気が続けば店がつぶれてしまう。

The store will fail if the recession lasts.

私たちは時間つぶしにデパートに入った。

We went into the department store just to kill time.

またお決りの昔話を聞かされて彼に大事な時間をつぶされた。

He wasted my time (by) telling me
I lost a lot of time listening to him tell me
the same old story.

つまらない(詰まらない) →くだらない

1. 価値のない

ささいな　**trivial**

〈注〉 trifling と比べると trivial の方がよく使われる。

価値のない　**insignificant; worthless; unworthy;** 役に立たない　**useless;** ばかばかしい　**stupid**

つまらないこと　a trivial matter

無意味な事　nonsense

彼はつまらないことですぐ腹を立てる。

He easily take offense at trivial matters.

これはつまらない本だ。

This book's rubbish.

2. 面白くない

[物主語] 退屈な　**dull; monotonous; tiresome; boring**

[人主語] **be bored**

パーティーはつまらなかった。

The party was dull.

彼のスピーチは長くてつまらなかったから眠っている人が大勢いた。

His speech was so long and boring [tiresome] (that) many people fell asleep.

【興味を引かない】

その劇はつまらなかった。

The play wasn't good.

彼の小説はつまらない。登場人物が平凡だよ。

His novels aren't interesting. The characters are only commonplace.

その計画はつまらない，がっかりだ。

The project is unattractive, uninteresting and disappointing.

[人主語] I'm not keen on the project.

I'm unhappy with [about] the project.

【不機嫌な】

なぜそんなつまらなそうな顔をしているの？

Why do you look so glum?

ほかの子は皆ピクニックに行っているのに，彼女はじっと家にいなければならないなんてつまらなかった。

She was unhappy about having to stay home while other girls were going on a picnic.

日曜日にじっと家にいるなんてつまらない。

It's no fun staying home on Sunday.

彼のせいでつまらなくなった。

He has spoiled our fun.

プレゼントのないクリスマスなんて全然つまらない。

Christmas won't be Christmas without any presents!

【ばかばかしい】

張り切るのもほどほどにしなさい。けがをしたらつまらない。

It doesn't pay to be too brave. You can get

hurt.

つみ（罪）

刑法上の罪 (a) **crime;** 法律上・社会生活上の軽い違反 **an offense**
宗教・道徳上の罪 (a) **sin;** 悪徳 (a) **vice;** 落ち度 **a fault;** 有罪 **guilt**（道徳上・刑法上の罪）

【罪深い】（神に対し）be sinful; 裁判で有罪である be guilty; 罪悪感を感じる feel guilty

罪のない 形 innocent; 無害な harmless

罪を犯す（刑法上の）commit a crime;（宗教上の）sin, commit a sin

罪を告発される（刑法上の）be accused of a crime

罪を許す forgive an offense

〈注〉 sin を許せるのは神のみである。なお，「恩赦」は a pardon,「大赦」は an amnesty と言う。

死にたいなどと考えるのは罪(悪)だ。
It's a sin to want to die.

彼には…という罪の意識［やましい気持ち］がある。
He feels guilty about …

【罪を着せる】 lay the blame on《someone》

彼は金を盗んでおいてその罪を私に着せようとした。
He stole the money and then tried to lay [put] the blame on me.

つめる（詰める）・つめこむ・つまる

無理に入れる **cram;** 詰め物を押し込む **stuff;** 入れ物に詰める **pack;** 穴をふさぐ **stop up;** いっぱいにする **fill**

1．詰め込む

【食物】

その子は口にパンを詰め込み，学校の道具をひっつかむとスクールバスに遅れまいと飛び出して行った。
The boy crammed bread into his mouth, fetched his things and rushed out to catch the school bus.

【荷物】

最後のスーツケースを車のトランクに詰め込み，やっと出発した。
We finally crammed [stuffed] the last suitcase into the car trunk and drove off.

彼はトランクに衣類を詰めた。
He packed { his trunk with his clothes. / his clothes into his trunk. }

【詰め物】

クッションには羽毛が詰めてある。
The cushion is stuffed with feathers.

右下の臼歯に大きな穴がある。詰めてもらわないと。
You have a big cavity in your right lower molar. You'll have to have it filled.

【勉強】

彼は今，明日のテストのために詰め込み勉強中だ。
He's now cramming for the test tomorrow.

2．間を狭める

【座席】

すみません。もう少し詰めてこのご老人に席をつくってください。
Please sit a little closer and make room for this old man.

〈注〉 Can you make room for one more (person) on this bench? とも言える。

【乗物】

後ろ［前］へ詰めてください。
Move up to the rear [the front] please.

3．ふさぐ

【詰っている】

鼻が詰っているんだ。
My nose is stuffed up.（〔英〕口語で bunged up とも言う）

下水路［管］が詰っている。
The sewage system is plugged up.（広域の下水路が詰っている）

The drain pipe is stopped [bunged] up.（自分の家の下水管がつまっている）
道路が詰っていた。
The street was jammed [clogged] (up).
予定が詰っている。
I have a heavy [tight] schedule.
My schedule is tight [crammed].
〈注〉 heavy はする事が多いこと，tight は時間の余裕がないこと。

4．短縮する
【縮む】
スラックスを洗ったら丈が詰ってしまった。
My slacks shrank in the wash.
【縫い込む】
スラックスを体に合うように詰めてあげよう[丈を詰めてあげよう]。
I will take in [shorten] the slacks to fit you.
〈注〉 take in はヒップ，ウエスト，股下などを全体的に詰めること。shorten は丈を詰めること。

5．慣用表現
生活費を切り詰めねばならない。
You have to cut down (on) housekeeping expenses.
行き詰ってどうしたらよいかわからなかった。
I didn't know what to do.
言葉に詰った。
I didn't know what to say.
I couldn't find the right words.
〈注〉◆「言葉に詰った」は I was at a loss for words. とも言える。しかし be at a loss は使いすぎないように。
◆stuff（詰め込む）と結びついてよく使われる語
Stuffed toys are favorites of small kids.
（ぬいぐるみは小さな子の大好きなおもちゃだ）
Stuffed turkey is the typical Thanksgiving meal.
（詰め物をした七面鳥の丸焼きは感謝祭の代表的なごちそうだ）

つもり（積り）
1．予定・計画
【つもりである】
be going to（未来の単なる予定）
intend to; be planning to [plan to]（意志の表明）
明朝出発のつもりです。
We are starting tomorrow morning.
〈注〉 be going to＋go [come, start, leave, etc.]
上の[ ]内のような交通動詞や have, take などが続くときは簡略に上の例や次のように going を省くことができる。
I'm going to leave → I'm leaving ...
次の土曜日にパーティーをやるつもりです。
We are going to have a party next Saturday.
この次の夏にアリメカに行くつもり[計画]です。
I intend [plan] to go to America next summer.
卒業したら働く[就職する]つもりです。
I will [plan to] go to work after graduation.
どうするつもり？
What are you going to do?
What are you planning to do?
What are your plans?
彼女は親族に会うつもりで日本に来た。
She came to Japan hoping to see her relatives.
【意図】
私はあそこで一生働くつもりはない。
I have no intention of working [to work] there all my life.
【詰問】
これどういうつもり？
What do you mean by this?

2．意志に反して
あの人の気持ちを傷つけるつもりはなかった。
I didn't mean to hurt her feelings.
本当に申し訳ありません。でも決してそんなつもりではなかったのです。
I'm terribly sorry, but believe me I didn't mean to.
あなたが間違っているなんて言うつもりじゃ

ありません。

I don't mean to say that you're mistaken.

彼は日本文学を研究するつもりで日本に来たのだが，実際には英語の先生になってしまった。

He came (over) to Japan ⌊with the intention of studying [to study] Japanese literature, but actually he became an English teacher.

〈注〉 「つもりで」という表現は「実際にはその通りにいかなかった」ことを含むが，with the intention ... にもその含みがある。mean も後から振り返り，実際と意図の食い違いを述べるときによく使われる。

つらい（辛い）

1．肉体的＋心理的

hard; painful

朝早く起きるのはつらい。

It is hard [painful] to get up early in the morning.

貧乏はつらいものだ。

Poverty is ⌊hard to bear [painful].

飲まず食わずで何マイルも歩くのはまったくつらかった。

We had really a hard time of it walking for miles without eating or drinking.

彼もつらいよ，男手一つで3人の子供を育てるなんて。

He has a hard lot raising three children without any help.

つらい人生だ。日曜日まで働かなければならないとはね。

It's a hard life. I'll have to work on Sundays.

私にとって生きることはつらいことだ。

Life hangs heavy on me.〔*literary*〕

Time hangs heavy on my hands.〔*literary*〕

2．心理的

息子を手離すのは身を切るようにつらかった。

It almost broke my heart to part from my son.

おばあさんの宝石類を手離すのはつらかった。

It was painful to part with my grandmother's jewelry.

〈注〉 人との別れは from，物との別れは with を使う。

高校の3年間は彼にはつらい月日だった。

The three years spent in high school were a very trying time for him.

〈注〉 trying とは忍耐力を試されているようにフラストレーションのたまる「つらさ」。

I just can't seem to master the rhythm in this piano piece; it's very trying.（どうしてもうまくリズムがとれないの，いらいらしちゃう）

Children can be very trying.（子供はまったく腹にすえかねるようなことをするときがある）

彼はつらい立場にある。

He's in a difficult position.

私につらく当らないで。

Don't be hard on me.

彼は私につらく当る。

He's too hard on me.

He's always picking on me.

〈注〉 「つらく当る」は上のような言い方でよいが，「つらく当られる」側からの「何をしても気に入られないつらさ」の表現を挙げてみる。

Why does he always (seem to) disapprove of everything I do?

Why can't I ever please that person?

She's always expecting me to do the impossible.（彼女はいつも無理なことをしろと言う）

つれていく（連れて行く）・つれてくる

→もっていく・もってくる

take [**bring**]《a person》**with**《someone》

私は妹を連れて行った。

I took [brought] my little sister along with me.

父は犬を散歩に連れて行った。

My father took the dog for a walk.

母は私を医者に連れて行った。

My mother took me to see the doctor.

毎朝彼は子供たちを公園に連れて行き，2時間ほどして連れて帰った。

Every morning he took the children to the park and brought them back after [in] two hours.

できるだけ早く彼を連れて来なさい。

Bring him here as soon as possible.

犬を連れた婦人を見た。

I saw a lady walking a [her] dog.

ケイト(姉さん)，私も連れてって！

Let me go with you, Kate!

連れてってくださる？

Can I come with you?

て

…て[で]

1. 理由

お目にかかれてうれしいです。

I'm glad to see you.

パーティーに招待されてうれしかった。

I was glad to be [have been] invited to the party.

パーティーに行けてうれしかった［うれしい］。

I was [I'm] glad I could go to that party.

パーティーに呼んでもらえなくて気が滅入っていた。

I felt depressed because I wasn't invited to that party.

私たちは騒いでいてしかられた。

We were scolded
{ for being noisy.
because we made too much noise.

2. 手段

働いて金をつくった。

I made the money working.

彼はもっといいのを買ってあげようと言って私を慰めてくれた。

He comforted me (by) saying that he would buy me a better one.

〈注〉 最初に例文としてあげた「お目にかかれてうれしいです」I'm glad to see you. からの類推で，「…て」のつもりで，不定詞を誤用することがある。たとえば「…と言って慰めてくれた」を ×He comforted me to say he would buy me a better one.（正しくは下線部は by saying）とする類である。「…て」の意味で不定詞が使えるのは glad, happy, sorry, sad などの感情に関係のある形容詞のあとに続くときのみである。

彼は昼夜働いてその金をためた。

He saved the money (by) working day and night.

3. 並列

彼女は気立てがよくて働き者だ。

She is good-natured and hardworking.

その計画は金がかかって非実用的に思える。

The plan seems both expensive and impractical.

彼はスケートで滑って転んで右足の骨を折った。

While skating, he slipped, fell, and broke his right leg.

〈注〉 滑って，転んでのように動詞によって「て」「で」が使いわけられる。基本は「て」であるが「で」となる動詞は語根が g, b, m, n（有声音子音）で終る五段活用の動詞（騒ぐ，呼ぶ，読む，死ぬなど）で，その「連用形＋て」が音便で「～いで」「～んで」となるのである。

…で

1. 限定

【場所】in; on; at

ボートレースはテムズ川で行われる。

The boat race will be held on the Thames.

能面の展示会が仙台の文化会館で開かれる。

An exhibition of Noh masks will be held in Sendai at the Cultural Center.

〈注〉 at は一点を，in は入れ物またはスペースの中を指すのであるが，これは視点の問題で心理的である。日本地図の中で「仙台で」は点と感ずるから "at Sendi"，仙台地図の中で（in Sendai）「JR 駅で」は "at JR station" であり，さらに JR 駅の中で（in JR station），「改札口で」は "at the wicket" となる。

【時間】in; within

これは1時間で仕上げられる。

This will be finished in an hour.

【時限】

犬がいなくなって今日で1週間になる。

It is already a week since the dog disappeared.

私は次の誕生日で20歳になる。

I'll be twenty on my next birthday.

【年齢】

彼女は17歳で結婚した。

She got married when she was seventeen.
彼は40代でフランス語を習い始めた。
He began to study French in his forties.

2．手段

【原料・材料】

父の机は木製で，僕のはスチールでできている。
My father's desk is made of wood and mine (is) of steel.
ワインはふつうぶどうでつくる。
Wine is usually made from grapes.
私たちはレタス，ニンジン，グレープフルーツ，キウイフルーツとツナ缶でサラダをつくった。
We made a salad {of / with} lettuce, carrots, grapefruit, kiwi fruit, and tunafish.

〈注〉 **of＋材料**
材料が本質的に変化しない場合。
from [out of]＋原料
原材料が原形をとどめないときに使う。

【言語】

我々は英語で話した。
We talked in English.
我々は身振り手振りで何とか彼にわからせようとした。
We tried to make him understand using [by] gestures.

【交通機関】

私はバス[電車/自動車]で学校へ行く。
I go to school by bus [train / bicycle].

【電話】

あまり時間がない。電話で知らせよう。
We don't have much time. Let them know by telephone.

【道具】

彼はふたをくぎづけしていて２度も金づちで親指を打ってしまった。
He hit his thumb twice with the hammer while nailing the lid.
鉛筆で書きなさい。
Write in pencil.
油絵の具でかきなさい。
Paint in oil.
顕微鏡で物を見るのは初めての経験だった。
It was my first experience of seeing something through [under] a microscope.

【メディア】

私たちはテレビで試合を見た。
We watched the game on TV.
私たちはラジオでそのニュースを聞いた。
We heard the news on the radio.

【年金】

その人たちは年金で生活している。
They live on a pension.

【値段】

このバッグは１万5000円で買った。
I bought this bag for 15,000 yen.

【金】

働いてつくったお金で北海道旅行をした。
With the money I made working I traveled to Hokkaido.

3．原因・理由

【原因】

彼はがんで亡くなった。
He died of cancer.
彼は流感でのびている。
He is down with flu.
彼は空腹でふらふらだ。
He is faint with hunger.

【理由】

遠足は雨で延期になった。
The picnic is to be put off because of rain.
私はかぜで家にいた。
I stayed (at) home because of [with] a cold.
私は病気で寝ていた。
I was ill in bed.
生徒は皆クリスマス休暇で家に帰ってしまった。
All the students have gone home for the Christmas holidays.

4．基準

【時計】

私の時計でちょうど6時だが合っているかどうかわからない。

It's just six by my watch, but I'm not sure if it's correct.

【単位】

今日は農家の市がたって桃をダース単位で売っている。

They're selling peaches by the dozen today in the farmers' market.

【日給・時給】

彼らは日給[時給]で支払われている。

They get paid by the day [hour].

【スコア】

5点差で　by five points

我々は5対0で試合に勝った。

We won the match by a score of 5–0.

【判断】

我々は人をその行いで判断する。

We judge a person by his conduct.

であい（出会い）・であう

【出会い】　meeting《a person》

国内各地からの人々との出会いがこの夏の一番の思い出になるだろう［最大の出来事だった］。

Meeting people from many parts of the country
{ will be one of my best memories of this summer. (1)
{ was one of the highlights of this summer. (2)

〈注〉　日本語では「思い出」とよく言うが，英米人には(2)の方が自然。

2人は角を曲って出会いがしらにどんとぶつかった。

The two bumped into each other as they came round the corner.

〈注〉　「偶然の出会い」の意味でencounterがあるが，この語は敵味方がばったり出会ったような緊張感を伴っている。

【出会う】

私が夫のジョンと出会ったのは1975年軽井沢の夏期講習のときであった。

It was at the summer seminer at Karuizawa in 1975 that I met John, my husband.

ていあん（提案）

提案する　**propose; suggest; make a proposal** [**an offer**]

彼は新企画を提案した。

He proposed [suggested] a new plan.

彼女はみんなを自分の車で空港まで送ろうと提案した。

She suggested that she take them to the airport in her car.

彼女は皆で自分のベニスの別荘に来て休暇を過したらと提案した。

She suggested they (should) spend their holidays at her villa in Venice.

会社側は給料の5パーセントアップを提案した。

The company proposed a 5% increase in salary.

〈注〉　proposeは正式な言い方で，日常的な事についてはsuggestを用いる。

【会議用語】

…という動議を提案する

make [propose, introduce] a motion that …

move that …

動議を支持する

second the motion

提案説明をする

explain the proposal

give a rationale（理論的根拠をあげる）

give details about the implementation（実行についての具体的な案を説明する）

提案を支持する

support the proposal [proposition]

〈注〉　名 support（for the proposal）には(1)支持の裏づけになるデータ。(2)支持者，の二つの意味がある。

ex. "How much support do you have?"
"About half of the committee."
(「どのくらいの支持者がありますか」「委員会の約半数です」)

提案に反対である
be against a proposal
提案に反対する
speak against a proposal
提案を擁護する
defend the proposal
speak in support [favor] of the proposal
提案に賛成する →さんせいする
agree with [approve of] the proposal
agree to [approve] the proposal
〈注〉 agree with は賛成であるという態度を，agree to は賛成の行動をとることを思わせる積極的賛成を示す。

提案は満場一致で可決された。
The proposal
was approved [carried, passed]
{by a unanimous vote. / unanimously/juːnǽniməsli/.}

提案は反対多数で否決された。
The proposal was {rejected / voted down} by a large majority.

〈注〉◆proposal と proposition の比較
proposal 提案・申し出などに広く使われる。
proposition 正式な言葉で，委員会などで proposal を具体的に細部にわたり審議した結果到達した案としての提案を言う（国会に出される案は proposition)。論理学・数学の命題も proposition と言い，そのニュアンスがある語。
◆approve of と approveの比較
approve of 態度として「良いと思う」の意。
approve 「良しとする」の意もあるが，さらに賛成票を投じたり，書類に署名したりといった行動をとることをも意味する。
ex. His father was not happy about approving his son's marriage with the girl whose background he didn't approve of.
(彼の父は息子の結婚をしぶしぶ認めはしたが，相手の女の子の素性や育ちが気に入らなかった)

ていいん（定員）

1．収容人数

このバスの定員は50人だ[50席ある]。
This bus {seats / holds} 50 passengers.
The seating capacity of this bus is 50 persons.

このスタジアム[競技場／音楽会場／劇場／教室]の定員はX人だ。
This stadium [arena / concert hall / theater / classroom] has X seats.

その船は定員以上を乗せていた。
The boat was overloaded.
The boat was carrying more than [over] its capacity.

2．規定された人数

a quota; fixed number〔英〕

定員をきめる
set [decide on] a quota

各専攻の定員は50名である。
Each course is {restricted / limited} to 50 students.

志願者は定員の8倍だった。
The number of applicants was eight times {the number of openings [places]. / (more than) the quota.}

【定員に達する】 to reach [meet] a quota

志願者数が定員に達しなかった[ない]。
{The number of applicants fell short of / The applications have not yet reached} the quota [goal]. (達しない)

〈注〉 goal は「目標数」の意味で定員。また，the set [desired, expected] number とも言える。

ていがく（停学）→ たいがく

ていし（停止）

名 ［一般］ **a stop;** 一時停止 **suspension;** 禁止 **a ban;** 立ち止まり **a standstill;** 停滞

a deadlock

停止する　動自 **stop; come to a standstill; be suspended**

動他 **stop; suspend; put a ban on**

1．**物体**

【乗物】

車が停止した。

The car stopped.

【機械】

エンジンが停止した。

The engine {stopped. / gave out [failed].（故障で）}

2．**抽象物**

支払い停止

supension of payment

ストライキで会社は一時操業停止になった。

The company closed down temporarily because of a strike.

食中毒事件でそのホテルは1週間営業停止になった。

That hotel was ordered to close for a week because of a food poisoning case [incident].

取引が停止になっている。

Business is at a standstill.

5日間支払いが停止された。

Payment was suspended for five days.

新聞が発行停止になった[発行停止処分になった]。

The newspaper was placed under a suspension order.

停止処分が解除された。

The suspension order was lifted.

〈注〉 関連表現「禁止」

報道関係者による開廷中の写真撮影は禁止されている。

Reporters are banned from taking photos in the courtroom during a trial.

賃上げ交渉は目下停止している。

Salary negotiations are deadlocked at this point.

漁業権の話し合いは選挙が終るまで停止されている。

Fishing rights talks {have been {suspended / called off} / are at a standstill} until the upcoming elections are over.

3．**運転関係**

停止信号

a stop signal; a stop light; a signal light

停止線　a stop line

停止信号を無視する

ignore a stop light

彼は1か月の運転免許停止［免停］になった。

He had his driving license {revoked / suspended} for a month.

His license was suspended for a month.

ていしゅつ（提出）

1．**書類**

turn in; 手渡す **hand in;** 郵送する **send in; submit**〔*formal*〕

月末までに必要書類を提出のこと。

Submit the necessary forms by the end of the month.

【願書】

願書を提出する

submit a written application

土曜日までに入学係あてに願書を送ってください。

Send a written application (form) to the Admissions Office by Saturday.

〈注〉 上の文中の form は公式書類の場合はつけるが，口頭であれば不要。

【答案・レポート】

（宿題は）土曜日までに提出しなさい。

Turn it in [submit] by Saturday.

今すぐ答案用紙[マークシート／レポート／期末レポート]を提出してください。

Please {turn in / hand in} your {test paper / answer sheet / report / term paper} now.

【学位論文など】

彼は昨年修士論文を提出して2,3か月後に学位をもらった。

He submitted an [his] M.A. thesis last year and received his degree a few months later.

《類義語》

turn in 手渡しで提出すること。(宿題などについて) Turn it in by Saturday. のように使う。

hand in 教室で「さあ，出しなさい」と今すぐ提出する感じ。

send (in) 郵送する。

submit 審査の対象として提出すること。submit new plans (試案を提出する) のように使う。

〈注〉 答案やレポートの類には turn in, hand in, submit のどれでも使えるが，卒論 (senior thesis) や修論 (MA thesis) のような重みのあるものには正式な submit (審査の対象として提出する) の方を使う。

2．議案・法案

提出する **submit; present; introduce**

政府はその法案を議会に提出した。

The government {submitted / brought / presented} the bill to the Diet.

〈注〉 submit が最も一般的。present は plan (案)のほかに idea についても使える。

ていすう（定数）

委員会は定数を満たした[に達していた]。

The committee made [constituted 〔*formal*〕] *a quorum.*

委員会は定数に達しなかった。

The committee lacked a quorum.

〈注〉 *quorum* は会議成立のための必要最少人数のことで，通例過半数(*majority*)。

ていど（程度）

1．度合

度合 **a degree;** 限度 **an extent**

損害の程度

the degree of loss

ある程度まで

to some degree; to some [a certain] extent

あの人の言うことにもある程度の真実がある[一理ある]。

There is {a certain / some} {degree / measure} of truth in what he says.

What he says is to some extent true.

どの程度…なのか。

To what extent ...?

程度の問題だ。

It's a matter [question] of degree.

【限度】limit

何にでも程度というものがある。

There's a limit to everything.

2．基準

レベル **a level;** 規準 **standard**

知能程度

intellectual level

生活程度

standard of living; living standard

高校程度の学校だ。

These schools are the same level as regular high schools.

これは高校程度の講座だ。

This is a high-school level course.

程度の高い学校と言われている。

These are considered high level schools.

〈注〉 高卒程度の学力を認定する試験(大検)

a high school equivalency examination

彼の講義は程度が高すぎる。

The level of his lecture is too high for us to follow.

彼は話[講義]を聴衆の程度に合せなければならなかった。

He had to adapt his lecture to the level of the audience.

彼は生徒の程度に合せてやさしく話した。

He talked down to the pupils.

〈注〉 この言い方には「わからないだろうからやさしく話してやった」というようなニュアンスがある。

3. 約…, …くらい

【予算】

会の予算は1人5000円程度に抑えたい。

We'd like to keep the budget for the party to 5000 yen per person.

5000円程度であの人に何かちょっとしたプレゼントがしたい。

I'd like to get him a nice gift for about 5000 yen.

ていねん (定年)

age limit; retirement age

定年制

the retirement system

定年前に退職する

retire early

定年で退職する

retire (at the age limit)

彼は今年定年だ。

He will reach retirement age this year.

彼はもうじき定年だ。

He'll soon reach the age limit.

60歳がうちの会社の定年です。

Sixty is the retirement age in our company.

この会社では定年前[後]退職の制度がある。

This company offers early [late] retirement.

〈注〉 retire は普通年齢の規定でやめることである。定年前にやめるのが early retirement, 定年に達してさらに数年勤めてやめるのが late retirement である。定年に関係なくやめるのは resign。

a mandatory age limit 法規による定年

a tacit age limit 慣行による定年

てがみ (手紙)

a letter; (簡略なもの) **a note;** メモ **a memo;** [集合的] **mail;** やりとり **correspondence**

手紙を書く

write to 《a person》

write a (long) letter 《to a person》

手紙をもらう receive [get] a letter

手紙が着く[来る]

[人主語] get a letter (もらうと同じ)

[手紙主語] arrive; come

手紙を出す(投函する)

mail〔米〕[post〔英〕] a letter

私は月に1度両親に手紙を書きます。

I write to my parents once a month.

〈注〉 write だけで手紙を書く意味になる。特に「長い」とか「おかしい」とか形容詞をつけるのでなければ letter はいらない。

この手紙が着いたらすぐ返事をください。

Please write to me as soon as you get this letter.

彼の手紙は彼女が立ち去ったあとに届いた。

His letter arrived after she left.

もう1年以上も彼から手紙をもらっていない[便りがない]。

I haven't heard from him for more than a year.

私に手紙が来ていませんか。

Is there any mail for me?

この手紙の郵送料はいくらですか。

What's the postage on [for] this letter?

彼から…という手紙をもらう。

He says in his letter that …

His letter says that … (…と書いてある)

彼はもうすぐ帰るという手紙を私によこした。

He sent me a letter telling me [saying] that he would come back soon.

私は彼からもうすぐ帰るという手紙をもらった。

I got a letter from him saying [which said / in which he said] (that) he would come back soon.

〈注〉 the news that he will come back の類推で ×the letter that he will come back のように接続詞 that を使うのは誤りである。上記のように saying, which said などを入れる。

《手紙の形式》

住所 151-0053 東京都渋谷区代々木1-23
1-23 Yoyogi Shibuyaku,
Tokyo 151-0053
JAPAN
米国コロラド州80302
ボールダー，カスケード通り1990
1990 Cascade
Boulder, CO 80302
U. S. A.

日付 June 4, 2003　June 4, '03〔*informal*〕
4th June 2003
June 4th 2003; 4•6•03〔米〕
(1st, 2nd, 3rd, 4th … は主として〔英〕)

月名の省略

1月　2月　3月　4月　8月　9月　10月　11月　12月
Jan.　Feb.　Mar.　Apr.　Aug.　Sept.　Oct.　Nov.　Dec.
(May, June, July は略さない)

西暦年の省略　1998 → '98 / 2005 → '05

初めの挨拶[呼びかけ]

目上の人，初めての人には姓で呼びかけ
Dear Mr. Tanaka [Ms. Tanaka …],
親しい人には呼び名で
Dear Mary [John / Mariko …],
会社などにあてた手紙では
Dear Sir:/ Dear Sirs:
Dear Madam:/ Dear Madames:

〈注〉 手紙の相手として数人を考えるならば -s をつける。

終りの挨拶

〔*formal*，ビジネスレターなど〕
Yours sincerely, / Sincerely yours, (心からあなたのものである《発信人》の意)
〔casual〕
Best wishes, / Regards,
[親しい間柄のとき]
With love, / Love, (愛をこめて，女性間，家族間)
Yours always, / Yours as ever,
[ごくくだけた状況で]
So long,〔米〕/ Bye for now, (今日はこれだけ)

署名 (signature)　本文および肩書，名前をタイプしても必ず手書きで署名する。

正式

自分の住所
発信日付
相手の氏名
相手の住所

Dear ____,

終りの挨拶
署　名

略式

(自分の住所)←略してもよい
発信日付

Dear ____,

終りの挨拶
署　名

〈注〉 英文の手紙では日本の手紙のような時候の挨拶はなく，すぐ本題に入ってよい。知らない人に書くのであれば I am … と名乗り，自分の現在の状況，用件を述べ，何か依頼するのであれば I would like to ask you … と本題に入る。知っている人には日本語の手紙と同じで話をするように書けばよい。終りの挨拶についても決りの文句はない。「お体を大切に」と本当に思うなら書いてもよいが，決り文句として書くのではない。

てき（敵）

1．かたき

an enemy; a foe

敵国　a hostile country
敵意　ill feelings against a person
敵がい心　a hostile feeling
敵がい心をそそる[かき立てる]
　excite hostility
彼らは人類の敵だ。
　They are an enemy to humanity.
彼らは世界最強国のひとつを敵にして戦った。
　They fought against one of the most powerful countries in the world.
新聞(社)を敵にまわすのはまずいよ。
　It is unwise to set yourself against the press.

彼らは互いに敵味方になるように運命づけられていた。

They were destined to be enemies.

2. 試合・競争の相手

争いの相手 **an opponent;** 競争相手 **a rival**
敵方の選手 **an opposing player; a player on the opposite team;** 好敵手 **a match**

敵はA組の女の子だった。

Our opponents in the match were the girls of Class A.

We played (against) the girls of Class A.

彼はとてもジョージの敵ではない。

He is no match for George.

できごと（出来事）→ こと，じけん

（比較的小さい）**an incident;**（不慮の）**an accident;**（重要な）**an event;**（偶然の）**an occurrence; a happening**

日々の出来事

everyday happenings [occurrences]（毎日起るような普通のこと）

cf. daily happenings＝routine（毎日繰り返す決りきった日課）

世界の出来事

world events; what is going on in the world

その年の主要な出来事

chief events of the year

テレビをつけて今日の出来事でも見よう。

Let's turn on the TV and see what happened today.

夏休み中に二つの面白い[奇妙な]出来事があった。

There were two interesting [curious] incidents during the summer vacation.

Two interesting [curious] incidents occurred during the summer vacation.

このところうちの学校では奇妙な出来事がちょくちょく起る。

There are strange happenings in our school these days.

できる（出来る）

1. 可能

［人主語］ **can do; be able to do**
［事主語］ **be possible**

【技能】

彼女はテニスができる。

She can play tennis.

彼女はフランス語(で話すこと)ができる。

She can speak French.

【行動】

彼女はきっと夢を実現できるだろう。

She'll be able to realize her dreams.

〈注〉 can には未来形がないので will be able to を使う。

2,3 日で世界一周をすることもできる。

It's possible to [One can] go round the world in a few days.

【できるだけ[限り]】

as much [hard] as possible
as much [hard] as I can

〈注〉 ×as possible as I can はよくある誤り。

できるだけのことをします。

I will do { anything in my power. / everything [all] I can for you.

I will do my best.

2. 不可能

【できない】

もう我慢ができない。

I can't bear it any longer.

1週間でその仕事を終えることは到底できない。

It's impossible to finish the work in a week.

〈注〉◆「テニスができない」を ×I can't tennis. とするのは誤り(正しくは I can't play tennis.)。また，「私は行くことができない」を ×I'm impossible to come. としてはいけない。It's impossible (for me) to come. と事主語にしなければならない。

◆ could と「できた」

can が「できる」だから「できた」は could と考えて could を使いすぎる傾向がある。「入学できた，卒業できた，就職できた」などでよく「できた」と言うが，それは必ずしも困難を克服して

ということではなく，ただ「ありがたい気持ち」を表す慣用にすぎないことがあり，「おかげ様で」と同じ心情である。

I could pass ... や I could be in time ... としなくても Luckily [Fortunately] I passed the exam. あるいは Fortunately I was in time. でよいし，「できた」気持ちを強調したければ，I somehow managed to pass [I succeeded in passing] the exam. のように言える。また，was able to を使うこともできる。

could には（might, would の場合と同様）can の過去とは異なる丁寧表現（一種の仮定法）の用法があり，can の過去の could よりその用法の方が頻度が高い。

一方，否定形 couldn't は自由に使え，実際の文章の中に could よりはるかに多く出てくる。

3．完成

［物主語］ **be done; be completed; be finished**

［人主語］ **complete; finish**

【建物】

この建物は来月末までにできるだろう。

This building will be completed by the end of next month.

【課題】

宿題ができた。

I have finished my homework.

レポートができた。

The report [paper] is done.

【準備】

スピーチの原稿ができた。

The speech text is ready now.

朝食の用意ができた。

Breakfast is ready.

〈注〉 My mother is ready for breakfast. はお母さんがいつでも食事のできる状態であることで，「食事の用意をした」ことではない。→ようい（用意）

【開業・創設】

近所に大きなスーパーができた。

A big supermarket opened in this neighborhood.

この大学は50年前にできた。

This college was founded 50 years ago.

4．産出・発生

［物主語］ **be made; be manufactured; grow; yield**

【原材料】

パンは小麦粉からできている。（原料）

Bread is made from flour.

これらの机はスチールでできている。（材料）

These desks are made of steel.

大豆から醤油，豆腐，味噌などができる。

Soybeans are used to make shoyu, tofu, miso and many other products.

【農産物】

このあたりでは一等米ができる。

This part of the country produces [grows] first class rice.

米は気候温暖の地によくできる。

Rice grows best in hot weather.

【懐妊】

ケイトにまた子供ができた。

Kate is pregnant again.

Kate is expecting another baby.

Kate is going to have another baby.

cf. They had a baby last week.（先週生れた）

【形成】

表面に氷ができた［張った］。

Ice formed on the surface.

5．成績優秀

【英語】

彼は英語がよくできる［できない］。

He is [isn't] very good at English.（一般的）

He does well [poorly] in English class.（教室で）

【試験】

彼は今度の試験はよくできた。

He did well in this test.

【学校】

彼はよくできる。

He is bright [smart〔米〕].

彼はあまりできない。

He isn't so bright [smart〔米〕].

〈注〉◆He is dull.（鈍い）はあからさまでひどい言い方。

◆clever は実際的な事に器用な，または頭の回転が速いとか，話が上手であるといった，全体的というよりある一方面の能力がすぐれていること。bright は全体的にすぐれていること。brilliant は天才的に頭のよいこと。米国では smart students も頭のよい学生の意だが，英国では smart は外見についてのみ使われる。

でしょう → だろう

です → …だ

てつづき（手続き）

procedure;（法的な）**proceedings**

奨学金の申し込みにはどんな手続きがいるんですか。

What is the procedure [for applying [to apply] for the scholarship?

パスポートをとるにはややこしい手続きがいる。

You have to go through troublesome procedures to get a passport.

離婚手続きは長くかかることがある。

Divorce proceedings often take a long time.

【養子縁組の手続き】

adoption formalities（＝signing the papers and filing them）

彼らは養子縁組に必要な手続きをとった。

They've finished（all）the procedures（needed）to adopt the child.

【入学・入社手続き】

入籍[登録，入学]手続き

registration procedures

入学手続きは３月20日までです。

The deadline for school registration is the 20th of March.

入学[入社]の手続きは済みましたか。

Have you finished the entrance procedures for the school [firm]?

入会手続きはどうしたらいいか教えてください。

Can you tell me how to become a member?

【書類】

手続きの書類はそろった。

We finished getting the necessary documents.

旅行会社が僕のヨーロッパ旅行の手続きをしてくれている。

The travel agent is taking care of getting the documents I need for my trip to Europe.

空港で入国手続きを済ませなければなりません。

You have to go through entry [formalities [procedures] at the airport.

入国手続きが不完全で彼は入国を拒否された。（ビザやパスポートなど必要な書類をそろえていなかった）

He was denied entry because he
{ hadn't fulfilled the entry requirements.
{ didn't have the necessary documents.

てはい（手配）・てはず（手筈）→じゅんび

手配する　**arrange; prepare**

1．手配

準備 **preparations;** 手配 **arrangements**

会議の手配はすっかりできています。

Everything is ready for the conference.

できるだけ速く小包をあなたあてに発送するよう手配しましょう。

We will see（to it）that all these parcels are sent to you as soon as possible.

来週北海道に出張[旅行]するので手配を頼みます。

Please make arrangements for us to travel to Hokkaido next week.

車の手配をお願いします。

Could you order some taxis, please.

【警察】

警察は強盗犯人の手配をした。

The police began a search for the burglar.

2．手はず

a plan; arrangements

すべて手はずが調っている。

Everything is arranged.

手はず通りことが進んでいる。

Things are proceeding as scheduled.

これのおかげで手はずがすっかり狂ってしまった。

This upset all our plans.

〈注〉 **preparations** 準備を全体的にとらえた語。**arrangements** 何はだれに頼む，何はどこに注文する，会場の準備，当日のプログラム等々組織的に手配準備すること。

ても・でも

1．にもかかわらず

but; yet; still; though; although

彼は体は小さくても精力的だった。

He was small but full of energy.

彼は10時間眠ってもまだ眠かった。

He slept ten hours but was still sleepy.

Although he slept ten hours he was still sleepy.

〈注〉 though と although は互換できるが，くだけたスピーチや手紙では though の方が自然。また，though は however のように副詞として文尾につけ加える言い方ができるが，although はこの使い方はできない。

2．仮定・条件

どちらでも　no matter which; whichever

何でも　no matter what; whatever

だれでも　no matter who; whoever

いくら…でも　no matter how; however

君が何と言っても僕は計画を変えないからね。

No matter what [Whatever] you say, / I don't care what you say, } I won't change my plan.

いくら一生懸命がんばっても１年や２年で技術をマスターすることはできない。

No matter how [However] hard you try, you will never [can't] master the technique in only a year or two.

降っても照っても絶対行きます。

Rain or shine, I will go.

明るいうちに着いても着けなくても，別にかまわない。

It doesn't matter whether I can [can't] get there before dark.

I don't care if I get [don't get] there before dark.

〈注〉 can get there, can't get there どちらも言えるが，怒った調子のときは否定形になりやすい。

【無条件】

気が向いたらいつでも遊びにいらっしゃい。

Please drop in any time you feel like it [inclined to].

クラブに入りたい人はだれでも歓迎。

Whoever wants to join our club is welcome.

だれでもそんなことはできる。

Anyone can do that.

何でもお好きなものをあげます。

You can have whatever [anything] you like.

あなたの行く所ならどこでもついて行きます。

I'll follow you anywhere [wherever you go].

【…でさえも】

子供でもそんなことはできる。

Even a child can do that.

今でもそのシーンをありありと覚えている。

I remember the scene vividly { even now. / still yet. }

【…にでも】

次の日曜日にでも遊びにいらっしゃい。

Come and see me, say, next Sunday.

テレビでも見よう。

Maybe I'll watch TV.

でる（出る）

1．外へ出る

go [come] out (of); start (from); leave

【戸外に】

外の空気のよい所へ出よう。

Let's go out into the fresh air.
さあ出てきて仲間にお入りよ。
Do come out and join us.
彼女は大急ぎで部屋を出ていった。
She hurried out of the room.
彼女は日差しの中に飛び出して行って，一瞬まぶしさに立ち止まった。
She rushed into the sunlight and stopped short, dazed.

【出発】
彼は旅に出た。
He set out on a journey.
列車は9時に5番ホームから出ます。
The train {starts / leaves} at nine o'clock from track [platform] (number) five.

【卒業】
彼は3年前に大学を出た。
He graduated from university three years ago.
どこの大学を出られたのですか。
Which university did you go to?
早稲田大学を出ました。
I went to Waseda University.
彼はまだ大学出たてのほやほやです。
He's fresh {out of / from} university.

【道など】
この路地は海岸通り[大通り]へ出る。
This alley comes out {at the waterfront. / on(to) Main Road.}
我々は茂みをかき分けて30分ほど歩き，やっとあたりの開けた所へ出た。
We made our way through thickets and after half an hour came into an open space.

2. 現れる
appear; show up; emerge

【星・月】
夜になり星が出た。しかし，月はまだ出ていなかった。
Night fell and the stars were out but the moon had not risen yet.

【遺失物】
財布は出てきたかい？
Was the purse found?

【証拠】
何か証拠になるものは出ましたか。
Did any evidence ever emerge [appear]?

3. 応対する

【電話に】
(電話のベルが鳴っている) 私が出ます。
I'll take [get] it.
ビルのアパートに電話をしたがだれも出なかった。
I phoned Bill's apartment, but no one answered.

4. 出演する
彼は平日のテレビのニュース番組に出ている。
He's on a TV news program on weekdays.
彼女はその映画に出ている。
She's in that film.
彼女は舞台に出ている。
She's on stage.
彼女は5歳でもう映画[舞台]に出た。
She made her film [stage] debut when she was five.
彼は国立劇場に出たし，テレビの劇にもいくつか出た。
He appeared at the National Theater and did several TV plays.

5. 参加・出席・勤務
be present at; attend; take part in

【参会・参加】
彼は私にスタッフ会議にきちんと出るようにと言った。
He told me to attend staff meetings regularly.
私はこの競技会に出ることにしている。

I'm going to {take part / participate} in this contest.

【出馬】

彼は政界に打って出るつもりだ。

He's planning to go into politics.

彼はこの前の選挙に出たが落選した。

He ran for the Diet in the last election but failed.

He lost his bid for a Diet seat in the last election.

6．発生

早春には小さな黄金色の芽が吹いて出る。

Tiny golden leaves come out in early spring.

風が出た。→かぜ（風）

A wind is blowing [coming] up.

The wind has risen.

市の中心部から火が出た。

A fire broke out in the central part of the city.

【病気】

近所からコレラが出た。

Cholera has broken out in the neighborhood.

A case of cholera has been found [diagnosed].

寒くなってくるといつも喘息が出る。

He always has an asthma spell when the cold season sets in.

湿気の多い季節になると彼はリューマチが出る。

His rheumatism gets worse in damp weather.

He has some chronic disease which gets worse in damp weather.（持病が出る）

【来歴】

彼によれば彼の家は平家から出ているそうだ。

He says he is descended from the Heike clan.

彼はその地方の名家の出だ。

He {belongs to / comes from} a famous family in that district.

あなた方の祖先は皆ウェールズの出[出身者]ですか。

Are you all of Welsh ancestry?

【語源】

この言葉はラテン語から出たものだ。

This word is derived from Latin.

7．発行・課題

【出版】

彼の新著がもうじき出る。

His new book will be {out / published} soon.

学校新聞は月に１度出る。

The school paper is published once a month.

【掲載】

それは朝刊に出ている。

It is in the morning paper.

彼の書いたものが毎日新聞に出ている。

His article is in *The Mainichi*.

【議題】

その件[話題]は討論の場に持ち出された。

The subject was brought up for discussion.

この件は議事の中に出て[載って]いた。

This topic was on the agenda.

【宿題】

宿題がたくさん出た。

We had [were given] a lot of homework.

ロス先生は宿題をたくさん出す。

Mr. Ross gives us lots of homework.

【問題】

その数学の問題は奥田先生の期末試験に出た。

That math problem was on Mr. Okuda's final test.

どんな問題が試験に出るだろう。

What kind of problems will there be on the test?

8．産出・流通

【農産物】

秋田県は良質米を産出する。

Akita Prefecture produces high quality rice.

スイカの初物がもうじき店頭に出るだろう。

The first watermelons of the season will soon be { on the market. / in the shops. }

【鉱業】

日本は石油がほとんど出ない。

Japan produces { hardly any oil. / almost no oil. }

【商業】

新型車がまもなく出る[売り出される]。

The new-model cars will be available [in the showrooms] soon.

この型のテレビはよく出ます。

This type of TV sells well.

【料理など】

サンセットインはおいしい料理を出す。

The food at the Sunset Inn is very good.

They serve delicious food at the Sunset Inn.

そのパーティーではごちそうがたくさん出た。

We had a lot of good food at the party.

手をかけた凝った料理が次々と出た。

Many especially well-prepared dishes were served one after another.

〈注〉 凝った料理には dishes が使えるが，普通は food, dinner などを使う。→りょうり

【金】

きのう，ボーナスが出た。

We got our bonuses yesterday.

9．放出・流出

【生理現象】

彼の講演は長くて退屈で，皆あくびが出はじめた。

His lecture was so long and boring everyone began to yawn.

くしゃみが続けざまに出た。

I had a sneezing fit.

彼はひどいせきが出る。

He has a bad cough.

熱が出た。

I have a fever [a high temperature].

【流出】

子供が泣いて帰って来たが両膝から血が出ていた。

The child came home crying with his knees bleeding.

彼の話を聞いて涙が出た。

I was moved to tears by his story.

私たちはうれし涙が出た。

We cried for joy.

彼の額に玉の汗が出ていた。

Drops of sweat stood on his brow.

煙突から一筋の煙が出ていた。

A thin line of smoke rose from the chimney.

水道の栓から水がぽたぽた出ているよ。

The water is dripping from the tap.

水道から水が一滴も出ない。

There is not a drop of water left in this tap.

Not a drop of water will come from this tap.

(川が氾濫して)水が出た。

The river is { in flood. / flooding. }

隣の町に水が出た。

The [A] neighboring town is flooded.

【出力】

このモーターは100馬力だ。

This motor has 100 horsepower.

This is a 100-horsepower engine.

10．突き出る

額が出ている

have a prominent forehead

目が出ている

have protruding eyes

彼は腹が出てきた。

His stomach is beginning to { bulge. / stick out. / be noticeable. 〔*euphemism*〕 }

〈注〉 おなかの余分の脂肪を spare tire と言う。
気をつけてください，くぎが出ています。
Be careful. There are nails sticking out.

11．その他
君の出る幕じゃないよ[余計な口出しはしないでくれ]。
This is no business of yours.
It's none of your business.（かなり失礼な言い方）
【齢】
あの人はもうとうに50は出ている。(50歳以上)
She is well past [over] fifty.
【色】
それは洗っても色が出ません。(色が落ちない)
The color won't run in the wash.
【お茶】
このティーバッグはとてもよく出る。一つのバッグで3杯出せる。
The tea in these teabags is very strong. One bag makes three cups.
きっとお湯が十分熱くなかったんでしょう。お茶がよく出ません。
Maybe the water isn't hot enough. The tea isn't steeping well.

テレビ

television; TV
テレビ（受像機）
a television (set); TV (set); telly〔英〕
テレビをつける[消す]
turn on [off] the television
テレビを見る
watch television [TV]
11チャンネルをつける
switch on channel 11
テレビ局
a TV station; TV studio; broadcasting station
テレビで何をやってるの？
What's on TV?
子供たちはいつもテレビのチャンネル争いをやっている。
The children always quarrel over which television program they will watch.
サッカーのワールドカップを皆でテレビ観戦し，盛り上がった。
We were all excited watching the soccer World Cup on TV.
私たちはテレビを消して静かに話をしていた。
We were talking quietly with the television off.

《関連語》
【放送[放映]する】 broadcast; telecast
放送中　on the air
テレビ放送[映]される　be televised
ラジオ[テレビ]放送網
radio [television] network
実況放送　live report
生放送　a live TV show [performance]
衆議院本会議が生放送された。
The Diet Session was broadcast live.
衛星放送　satellite broadcasting
オリンピックが衛星放送で実況生中継された。
The Olympic Games were broadcast via [by] satellite (relay).
放送衛星　telecommunications satellite
UHF (ultra high frequency)
VHF (very high frequency)
【テレビ番組】 television program
ニュース　news
ニュース速報　spot news; news flash
ニュース解説　news commentary
天気予報　weather report
ドキュメンタリー　documentary
教育番組　educational program
娯楽番組　entertainment program
リクエスト番組　request program
深夜放送　midnight program
ショー番組　music [talk, variety] show
スポーツ番組　sports program

対談　TV interview
テレビドラマ　TV drama
再放送　rerun
コマーシャル　commercial
【番組制作者・出演者】
スポンサー　sponsor
プロデューサー(製作者)　producer
ディレクター(演出担当者)　director
テレビ俳優[女優]　TV actor [actress]
ミュージシャン　musician
歌手　singer
〈注〉 タレントは talent (才能) からきているが，和製英語。
アナウンサー　announcer
ニュースキャスター　newscaster
レポーター　reporter
司会者　master of ceremonies [㊥ MC]; emcee; (クイズの) quizmaster; (トークショーの) talk show host
インタビュアー　interviewer
【その他】
オーディション　audition
視聴者　audience (総称); viewer
視聴率　audience rating

てん（点）

1. しるし

a spot; a dot; a speck

汚点　a blot; a stain

汚点のある
spotted; speckled

小数点
a decimal point (4.6 は four point six と読む)

【点を打つ】 ㊐㊎ dot

'i' や 'j' に点を打つのを忘れないで。
Don't forget to dot the i's and j's.

空には一点の雲もなかった。
There wasn't a bit [a speck] of cloud in the sky.

点と点を番号順に線で結ぶと皆さんのよく知っている動物の絵ができます。
If you {connect the dots / draw lines from one dot to another} in the order in which they are numbered, you'll find (you have drawn) an animal quite familiar to you.

2. 評点 →せいせき

points (60 points); **score** (a score of 60); **grades** (A, B, C, D, & F)〔米〕
marks (full marks (満点) a mark of 60, または 60 marks〔英〕)

彼は数学でいい[悪い]点をとった。
He got {high [low] points / a good [bad, poor] score} in maths.

彼はかなりよい点をとっている。
His {grades〔米〕/ marks} are pretty good.

何点とりましたか。
How did you do?
What mark(s) did you get?
What was your score?

化学は何点とれると思いますか。
What score [mark(s)] do you expect on the chemistry test?

彼は物理で満点をとった。
He got {full marks〔英〕/ a perfect score} in physics.

彼はあの試験で80点をとった。
He made [got] {80% on that exam. / 80 points [marks〔英〕].}

50点に満たないと単位がとれない。
You cannot {pass / get credit} if {you get less than 50. / your marks are below 50.}

平均点以上[以下]をとる。
score higher [lower] than the average

レポートを期限内に出さないと点を減らされるよ。
Your mark(s) will be lowered, if you don't hand in the paper before the deadline.

あの先生は点が辛い[甘い]。

He's a strict [generous] {marker. / grader.}

〈注〉 米語では mark は名詞としてはあまり使われない。He's marking the papers.（彼は点つけをしている）のように動詞として使う。一方 grades は英国では使わない。

3. 競技の点

a point; a score; a run

【得点】

うちのチームは3点とった。

Our team gained three points.

得点は10対0だった。

The score was 10-0.

〈注〉 10-0 は ten nil〔英〕; ten to zero〔米〕と読む。

うちのチームは最終回の裏に3点入れた。

Our school's team scored three {points / runs} in the second half of the last inning.

巨人が5対3で勝っている。

The Giants are leading [ahead] (by) five to three.

【点差】

うちのチームは1点差で勝った[負けた]。

Our team won [lost] the game by one point.

4. 論点

a point; respect; a standpoint

私はその点で彼とは意見が合わなかった。

I couldn't agree with him on that point.

値段の点で折り合わない。

We can't agree on the price.

いろんな点であの人はお母さんにそっくりだ。

In many ways she's like her mother.

あらゆる点で新しい機械は古い機械に勝る。

The new machine is superior to the old one in every respect [point, way].

そこが難しい点だ。

That's where the difficulty lies.

そこが君が間違っている点だ。

That's where you are mistaken.

てんき（天気）→ てんこう

でんき（電気）

1. 電気

electricity

形 **electric; electrical**

この自動車は電気で動く。

This automobile runs on electricity.

ゴムは電気を通さない。

Rubber does not conduct electricity.

その山小屋にはまだ電気が通じていない。

That cottage hasn't got electricity (yet).

(不払いが続くと)電気は止められてしまう。

The power will be cut off.

【電気代】 the charge for electricity

お宅では1か月の電気代はいくらですか。

How much {do you pay for electricity / is your electricity bill} every month?

【家電製品】 electrical appliances

電気かみそり　an electric shaver

ドライヤー　a hair dryer

電気炊飯器　an electric rice cooker

洗濯機　an electric washing machine

掃除機　a vacuum cleaner

電気ストーブ

an electric heater〔米〕, an electric fire〔英〕

電気毛布　an electric blanket

【その他】

電気機関車　an electric locomotive

電気技師　an electrical engineer

電気工学　electrical engineering

電気自動車　an electric car

電気ショック療法　electric shock therapy

電気分解　electrolysis

静電気　static electricity

《関連語》

電力　electricity; electric power (cf. 電力不足

shortage of electric power) / 停電　blackout / 電圧　voltage / 電流　electric current / 回路　circuit / 集積回路　integrated circuit (㊧IC) / トランジスタ　transistor / コンセント(差し込み口)　(electric) outlet [socket]; (差し込み) (electric) plug / 電気コード　an electric cord〔米〕[flex〔英〕] / ブレーカー　circuit breaker / ヒューズ　fuse / 電池　battery

2. 電灯

an electric light; 街灯 **a street lamp [light]**

〈注〉 米国では light は灯火そのものを，lamp は照明用の器具全体を言う。

電気スタンド

a reading lamp; a table lamp; a floor lamp

懐中電灯　a flashlight; a torch〔英〕

部屋の電気をつけた[消した]。

I turned on [off] the room light.

彼の部屋の電気がついていた。

The light was on in his room.

《関連語》

蛍光灯　flourescent light(s) [tube(s)] / ネオン　neon light(s) / 照明(天井や壁面に取付けた)　light fixture / スタンドの笠　lamp shade / 車のヘッドライト　car headlight / 電球　light bulb

てんきん（転勤）・てんにん（転任）

転勤　㊔ **a transfer**

転勤させる　㊍㊎ **transfer**

転勤になる[させられる]

be transferred《to another office [school]》

転勤する　㊍㊉ **transfer; move**

〈注〉「転勤(転任)になる」は be transferred と受身が普通。自分から進んで会社を変えたようなときは自動詞の transfer も使え，move はどちらの場合でも使われる。

1. 転勤

彼のお父さんは最近名古屋支社に転勤になった。

His father has recently been transferred to the Nagoya branch office.

His father moved to the Nagoya (branch) office recently.

会社の転勤は家族には負担になる場合が多い。

Business transfers are frequently hard on the family.

会社によって転勤の方針もかなり異なる。

Companies differ considerably in their transfer policies.

2. 転任

織田先生は北方中学に転任なさった。

Mr. Oda was transferred to Kitagata Junior High School.

てんけん（点検）

1. 機械

check; 分解修理する **overhaul**

君の車は詳しく点検してもらう必要がある。

Your car needs a thorough check.

うちの掛け時計は点検分解修理が必要だ。

Our clock needs an overhaul.

燃料系統がおかしい。車を持って行って点検してもらわなければならない。

There's something wrong with the fuel system, so I have to take the car in and have it checked.

(車などの)燃料系統を完全に点検してもらった。

We had the fuel system thoroughly checked.

〈注〉 車，家屋，建築物などを点検，修理することを maintenance と言う。その内容としては
checking（点検）
repairing small things（簡単な修理）
replacing small things（部品取替え）などがある。

車検(2年に1度)

two-year inspection [check, safety check]

6か月点検　a six-month check

定期点検　routine maintenance

〈注〉 examine はふつう人について使い，機械には check を使う。ただし米国では健康診断を check

up, 名 a checkup という。

2. 人員

人員点検[点呼]をする

call (the) roll; take (the) roll

てんこう（天候）

climate and weather; 気候 **climate**

天気図

a weather [meteorological] map [chart]

天気予報

a weather [meteorological] forecast [report]

天気予報官

a meteorologist, a weather forecaster

天気はどうですか。

How's the weather?

いい天気よ。

It's a lovely day.

明日の朝の天気はどうだろう。

What will the weather be like tomorrow morning?

明日の天気予報はどうなっていますか。

What's the weather forecast for tomorrow?

雨が降っている。

It's raining.

雨が降り出した。

It's [It has] started to rain [raining].

雨は止みましたか。

Has it stopped raining yet?

午後3時から9時の降水確率は40%だ。

There is a 40 percent chance of rain between 3 and 9 p.m.

《関連語》

気象庁

Meteorological Agency; Weather Bureau

気象台　meteorological observatory

測候所　meteorological [weather] station

寒冷[温暖]前線　cold [warm] front

停滞前線 stationary front

梅雨前線　seasonal rain front

気圧　atmospheric pressure

高[低]気圧 high [low] pressure（テレビでは気圧を pressure を省略して high, low のみで示す。気温にも用いる表現なので混乱しないように）

天気　weather

晴れ　fair; sunny

だいたい晴れ　generally fair

晴れ時々曇り

fair, occasionally cloudy

fair with occasional clouds

曇り時々雨[雪]

cloudy with occasional rain [snow]

雨が降ったり止んだり

with intermittent rain [showers]

曇り時々晴れ

cloudy, occasionally sunny

cloudy with occasional sun

雨のち曇り　rain; later cloudy

晴れのち時々曇り

fair; later occasionally cloudy

曇り　cloudy; overcast

ところにより曇り　partly cloudy

雨　rain, 形 rainy

一日中雨　steady rain

大雨　heavy rain

どしゃぶり　torrential rain, downpour

洪水　flood

にわか雨　shower

〈注〉 スコール squall は突風でしばしば雨，雪を伴う。

小雨　light rain, drizzle

霧　fog; 形 foggy　霞　mist; 形 misty

霜　frost　ひどい霜　hard [severe] frost

みぞれ　sleet; あられ　hail

雪どけ，ぬかるみ　slush

雪　snow; 形 snowy

ふぶき　snowstorm; 猛ふぶき　blizzard

にわか雪　snow squall; snow shower

ふぶきの中を　in the driving snow

風　wind; そよ風 breeze

風が強い　windy; 突風 gust; blast

強風　gale

砂あらし　sandstorm; dust storm

竜巻　tornado; twister

海上の竜巻　waterspout
つむじ風　whirlwind; dust devil〔米〕
暴風，あらし　(electrical) storm(雷 thunder や稲光 lightning を伴う)
台風　typhoon; ハリケーン　hurricane
サイクロン　cyclone; 暴風雨　rain storm
津波　tidal wave, tsunami
日照り続き，干ばつ　drought; dry spell
雨続き　rainy spell
暑い　hot; 温かい　warm
涼しい　cool; 冷たい　cold
湿気のある　humid; 名 humidity
蒸し暑い
close; sultry; muggy; (肌がべたべた) sticky; (蒸し暑い部屋) a stuffy room
乾燥した　dry
気温　temperature
摂氏　°C (Celsius / Centigrade)
華氏　°F (Fahrenheit)
最高[低]気温　highest [lowest] temperature; maximum [minimum] temperature
20°C＝twenty degrees (Celsius)
〈注〉摂氏，華氏の温度は次のように対応
(沸点) 100°C — 212°F; (氷点) 0°C — 32°F

てんこう（転校）→ たいがく

転校する　**change** one's **school; transfer to another school**

僕は父の転任のため 5, 6 回も転校しなければならなかった。
I had to change my school several times because my father was transferred.

【転校生】
a transfer (student); a transfer from another school

彼は九州からの転校生だ。
He is from Kyushu.

9 月に北海道からの転校生が新たに加わった。
We added a new pupil from Hokkaido in September.

でんし（電子）

電子の　**electronic**
電子音楽　electronic music
電子顕微鏡　an electron microscope
電子工学　electronics
電子出版　electronic publishing
電子商取引　electronic commerce
電子図書館　an electronic library
電子マネー　electronic money
電子メール　electronic mail [e-mail]
電子レンジ　a microwave (oven)

電子商取引の扱い高は年々増えている。
Electronic commerce is increasing year by year.

電子出版の普及で，海外の情報を手軽に入手できるようになった。
As electronic publishing is becoming more common, we have easy access to more and more foreign sources.

でんしん（電信）→ つうしん

てんそう（転送）→ ゆうびん

転送する　**forward**

下記に転送してください。
Please forward this letter to the following address.

手紙は転居先，また次の転居先と数回転送され，2 か月遅れて着いた。
The letter reached him two months later, after having been forwarded many times.

メールで友人への伝言を言付かったので，転送しておいた。
I got an e-mail message asking me to forward a message to a mutual friend, which I did.

【転送先】　forwarding address

でんとう（伝統）

名 **tradition** (しばしば pl. traditions)

伝統を守る
keep up [maintain] traditions
伝統を重んじる
value tradition
100年の伝統をもつ学校
a school with a hundred {year tradition / years of tradition}
長い名誉ある伝統をもつ大学
a university with a long and honorable tradition
皇室に伝わる種々の儀礼は千年以上の伝統をもっている。
Various rites observed in the royal household go [date] back more than ten centuries.
…するのはわが校[社]の伝統である
It's a tradition in our school [company] to …
いつも伝統を破ろうとするのは若い世代だ。
It is usually the young generation that defies tradition(s).
茶道は15世紀から伝えられた日本の伝統的芸術のひとつだ。
Sado, or tea ceremony, dating from the 15th century, is one of the traditional Japanese arts.
本学は伝統的にバレーボールが強い。
Our college is traditionally strong in volleyball.

でんぽう（電報）

名 **a telegram**（個々の電報）; **a wire; a telegraph**（システム全体の呼称）
電報料金
a telegram fee [charge]
電報局　a telegraph office
その新婚カップルは100通近い祝電をもらった。
The young couple received nearly 100 congratulatory telegrams.

《電文例》
電文は簡潔にするために be 動詞，冠詞，and，前置詞などを省略。
未来表現は動＋〜ing形，will＋動で，特に強調する必要のないときは一人称主語を省略，また意味明瞭ならば you も省略。
【迎え頼む】
8 月15日15:30 日航300便で成田到着。迎え頼む。
ARRIVING NARITA 15:30 AUG 15 JAL-300. PLEASE MEET.
【祝電】
ご結婚おめでとう。お幸せを祈る。
CONGRATULATIONS ON YOUR WEDDING (DAY).
BEST WISHES FOR YOUR FUTURE HAPPINESS.
【弔電】
心よりお悔み申し上げます。
HEARTFELT CONDOLENCES.
心よりお悔み申し上げ，お力落しのないようお祈りいたします。
MY [OUR] CONDOLENCES. MAY YOU HAVE STRENGTH.
父上ご逝去の由，心よりお悔み申し上げます。
VERY SORRY TO HEAR OF YOUR FATHER'S DEATH.
クリスチャンであれば次のような文面を加えてもよい。
神のご加護がありますように。
GOD BE WITH YOU.
GOD GIVE YOU STRENGTH.

てんもん（天文）

天文学　**astronomy;** 形 **astronomical**
天文台　astronomical observatory
天体望遠鏡　telescope
天体観測　astronomical observation
天文学者　an astronomer
天文学的な　astronomical
コンピュータを使えば天文学的数字でも瞬時に計算できる。

Computers can calculate astronomical figures in an instant.
〈注〉 星の名称は「ほし」の項参照。

でんわ（電話）

電話機 **a telephone; a phone**
通話 **a call; a ring; a phone call**
〈注〉 日本語では「電話ですよ」のように **call** の意味も「でんわ」，電話機の意味も「でんわ」と言うが英語では **telephone** は電話機のことで通話の意味には使えない。
電話番号 telephone number
市外局番(地域の局番)
area code〔米〕; district number〔英〕
留守番電話 answering machine
携帯電話 cellular (mobile) phone
コードレス電話 a cordless phone
内線 extension
〈注〉 読み方 ex. 0582-31-5010 oh-five-eight-two, three-one, five-oh-one-oh
電話局 a telephone office
公衆電話 a public phone, a pay phone〔米〕; a coin phone〔英〕
電話案内係 an information operator
直通電話 direct phone [line]
長距離電話 a long-distance call
コレクトコール[料金受信人払い]
a collect call
国際電話 an overseas call
電話料金 telephone charges
基本料金 basic charge
通話料金 charges for calls
夜間割引 night discount rate
深夜割引 off-hours rate
電話帳 a telephone ⌊directory [book]
職業別電話番号簿 yellow pages〔米〕
彼の電話番号は電話帳に載っていない。
His number is not listed in the phonebook.
cf. an unlisted number (電話帳に載っていない番号)

【電話による申し込み】
電話による注文に応じます。
Telephone orders taken.
電話による予約注文受け付けます。
Telephone reservations accepted.
電話による申し込み受け付けます。
Telephone applications accepted.
電話による情報提供をします。
Telephone information available.

【電話に出る】
電話に出て[をとって]ください。
Will you answer [get] the phone?
受話器をとる
pick up [answer] the phone
やっと誰かが電話に出た。
The phone was eventually picked up.
どなた様ですか。
Who is this please?〔米〕
Who's calling, please?
(こちらは) 山田太郎です。
This is Taro Yamada speaking.

【取り次ぎ】
ウィリアムズさんはいますか。〔*informal*〕
Is Mrs. Williams there?
ウィリアムズさんを(電話口に)お願いしたいんですが。
May I speak to Mr. Williams, please?
I'd like to speak to Mr. Williams, please.
Could you get Mr. Williams, please?
マネージャーのジョーンズさんにつないでいただきたいんですが。
Please connect me with Mr. Jones, the manager.
内線25番をお願いします。
Extension 25, please.
そのまま(切らずに)お待ちください。
Please hold (the line) a moment.
あなたに電話ですよ。
It's for you.
山田さんから(電話)ですよ。
It's Mr. Yamada.
Mr. Yamada's on the phone.
明日電話を(かけて)ください。

Please phone [call, ring] me (up) / Please give me a ring [call] } tomorrow.

【電話に出られない】

すみませんジョーンズ(氏)は外出中です。

I'm sorry but Mr. Jones { is out / isn't in } now.

彼は今ちょっとほかの電話で話し中です。

He's now talking to someone else.

He's on the phone at the moment.

あとでこちらから電話します。

I'll call you back.

【居留守】

チャールズから(の電話)だったら，今外出中と言ってくれ。

If it is Charles, tell him { I'm not in. / I've gone out.

【伝言】

ご伝言をうかがっておきましょうか。

Is there any [May I take a] message?

(留守中) どこからか電話がありましたか。

(Were there) Any calls for me?

山田さんという方から電話がありました。

There was a phone call for you from a Mr. Yamada.

A Mr. Yamada called you (up) this afternoon.

彼から明晩着くという電話をもらいました。

I got a call [He called] saying that he would arrive tomorrow night.

彼は私がいつ発つかと電話で尋ねてきました。

I got a call from him [He called] asking me when I was leaving.

【電話を切る】 ring off; hang up

「じゃあね」と言ってルイーズは電話を切った。

"See you." said Louise, and rang off.

大事な電話がかかってくることになっているんだ。彼女にいいかげんに電話をやめるように頼んでくれないか。

Ask her to get off the phone because I'm expecting a very important call.

彼女はやっと電話を切った。

She finally hung up.

彼はガチャンと受話器を置いた。

He slammed down the phone.

〈注〉 電話を切るときはお礼を言って，次に会う予定などつけ加えることがよくある。
ex. Thank you for calling. See you next week [on Thursday / tomorrow]. Bye.

【故障・間違い】

なかなかジョーンズさんに電話が通じない。

I cannot { get through to Mr. Jones. / get [reach] Mr. Jones on the phone.

この電話は故障している。

This phone's out of order.

The phone is dead.

雪で電話線が切れた。

The telephone lines were down because of the snow.

話し中に電話が切れた。

We got cut off in the middle of the conversation.

混線している。(他人の声が聞こえる)

The connection isn't clear.

The lines are crossed.

電話が遠くて聞えないんです。大きい声で話してください。

I can't hear you. Speak a little louder, please.

番号が違います。

You've got the wrong number.

番号を間違えました。

Sorry, I had [called] the wrong number.

何番におかけですか。

What number are you calling, please?

【その他】

(交換手が)お話し中です。

The line's busy. 〔米〕

The number's engaged. 〔英〕

電話を借していただけませんか。

May I use the phone please?

〈注〉 ×May I borrow your phone? とは言わない。borrow とは借りてどこかへ持って行って使うことである。

緊急の場合は110番に電話しなさい。(警察を呼びなさい)

Call [Dial] Emergency at 110! (Call [Dial] the police station!)

私は到着を知らせる電話を家にかけた。

I called home to tell them of my arrival.

彼の机の上の電話が鳴り出した。

The phone on his desk began to ring.

あの子は友達と何時間でも長電話をしている。

She spends hours on the phone with her friends.

あの子は夕方からずっと電話器にかじりついている。

He has been on the phone practically all evening.

〈注〉 evening とは通常は日暮れから就寝時間まで。

電話をひとり占めしないで。

Don't monopolize the phone!

電話が鳴りっぱなしだ。

These phones never stop ringing.

電話がうるさい。

I have been bothered by a lot of phone calls.

いやがらせ電話

a dirty [an obscene] telephone call

いやがらせ電話をかける人

a nuisance caller; a harassing caller

電話料金を払うのを忘れたので，今電話が停められている。

My telephone service is suspended because I forgot to pay my bill.

と

…と

1. 並列・対立・比較

【並列】

A と B と C

A, B and C

私は弟と東京に行った。

I went to Tokyo with my brother.

私はビルとテニスをした。

I played tennis with Bill.

彼女は外国人と話をしていた。

She was speaking to [talking with] a foreigner.

【対立】

明治大と慶応大が今日の午後試合をする。

Meiji will fight Keio this afternoon.

人々は困難と戦った。

People struggled against hardships.

住民と侵入者の間で激しい戦いが行われた。

There was a fierce battle between the inhabitants and the invaders.

【比較】

［同じ］彼は私の妹と同い年です。

He is the same age as my sister.

［違う］あなたのバッグは私のと色違いです。

Your bag is a different color than mine but the same make.

〈注〉 論理的，文法的には of a different color, of the same make と考えられるが of はつけない。

［どちらが］これとあれとどちらが好きですか。

Which do you like better, this one or that one?

2. 時・条件

【時】

学校が終ると彼女はいつも走って帰ってお母さんの手伝いをする。

After school she always runs home to help her mother.

目が覚めるともう日は高く上っていた。

When I woke, it was already broad daylight.

ちょうど東京に出かけようとしていると，大地震があって鉄道が止まっているというニュースが入ってきた。

I was just about to leave for Tokyo when the news came that there'd been an earthquake and the railroads weren't running.

Just as I was about to leave for Tokyo, the news came that …

東京に着くとすぐ病院に彼を見舞った。

As soon as I reached Tokyo, I went to the hospital to see him.

彼は私の顔を見るといつでもこの前会ったときより若く見えると言う。

Every time he sees me he says I look younger than the last time he saw me.

【条件】

あまり食べると眠くなるよ。

If you eat too much, you'll get sleepy.

どんなことが起きようと僕は君の味方です。

Whatever happens [may happen], I'll always be with you.

3. 内容伝達

【…と言う】 →いう

［命令］彼はすぐ出かけなさいと言った。

"Start at once."

He told me to start at once.

［疑問］彼はそれはどんな(外観の)ものかと言った。

"What does it look like?"

He asked me what it looked like.

［提案］彼は彼女に会いに行ったらどうかと言った。

"How about going to see her?"

He suggested that we (should) go to see her.

［誘い］彼女は我々と一緒にやりませんかと

言った。

"Would you please join us?"

She invited us to join them.

〈注〉 上記の“　”内を伝達する文を作るとき，He said“　”としてあるのを小説などでよく見る。しかし普段の会話や手紙文の中で，この形を使うのは不自然である。ただし面白い発言であったり，特に声色でもつけてそのまま伝えるのが効果的な場合はもちろん“　”で発言を引用してよい。直接話法を間接話法に，またはその逆への転換が同じように使えるわけではないので注意。

【…と思う】 →おもう

［願望］私も一緒に行けたらと思う。

I wish I could go with them.

［疑念］彼，本気で言っているのかしらと思う。

I wonder if he really means it.

〈注〉「私に行けと言った」(He told me to go) からの類推であろう ×He said me to go は誤り。say と tell の用法に注意。

また「ハワイへ行こうと思っている」(I'm planning to go to Hawaii.) からの類推であろう △I'm thinking to go. … と書く人があるが，これはかなり口語的で避けるほうがよい。I'm thinking of going … とする。

どう → どの・どれ

1．安否・容態

【ご機嫌伺い】

どうですか。　How are you?

このところずっとどうでしたか。

How have you been?

How have you been doing?

先週どうしてた？

How have you been the last week?

どうしている？

How are you getting along?

ご家族［仕事］はどうですか。

How's your family [job, business]?

【事態】

（世の中）どうですか［どうだね］。

How are things? / How's everything? / How's life? / What's been happening? / How's it going?

【天候】

天気はどうですか。　How's the weather?

【容態】

今朝はどうですか。

How do you feel this morning?

どうかしたのですか。

Is anything the matter? / Is there something wrong? / What's the matter? / What's wrong? 〔*familiar*〕

〈注〉 最後の2例は親しい間柄の場合のみ。語調によっては失礼にひびく。

【故障】

このカメラはどうかしている。

Something's wrong with this camera.

2．何を，いかに

【何を】

私はどうしたらよいかわからなかった。

I didn't know what to do [I should do].

それ，どうするつもり？

What are you going to do with that?

彼はいったいどうなってしまったの？（消息不明）

What has become of him?

【いかに】

どうやってドアを開けたらよいのかわからなかった。

I didn't know how to open the door.

どうして［どうやって］お金をつくるつもり？

How are you going to make the money?

〈注〉「どう…」に対して what が当てはまるか，how が当てはまるかは，前後関係によって決る。what は何をしたらよいか，どう考えるかなど「すること」がわからないときに，how は「すること」はわかっているが「やり方」がわからないときに使う。

ex. どうしていますか。

What are you doing?（何をしているか）

How are you getting along?（いかに過しているか）

どう思いますか。

What do you think about it?（何を思うか）

How do you like it?
How do you feel about it? }（いかに感じるか）

×How do you think? は誤り。
How's this?（これはどう）はよい。

3．慣用表現

どうしても　→どうしても
どうみても　to all appearances
どうにか　somehow
cf. anyhow（ともかくも）
barely（やっとのことで）
どうにも　→どうしても
それ，どういうつもり？
What do you mean by that?
〈注〉 口調によっては挑戦的にひびく。
それがどうした？
So what?（挑戦的）

【勧誘】

ご一緒にお茶でもどうですか。
How about having tea with us?
どうです。一緒にいらっしゃいませんか。
Why don't you come with us?

【不確か】

どうでしょうか。（よくわからない）
Well, I'm not sure.
Well, I don't know.
どうでもよい。
It doesn't matter.（どちらでも構わない）
I don't care.（どうでも知ったことじゃない）
〈注〉 たとえば Tea, or coffee？と聞かれた場合，「どちらでも」の意味で I don't care. を使えるが，その場合は失礼にひびかぬようソフトに次のように言うとよい。Oh, I don't care. Either will do.
どうでもいいようにしてください。
You can do as you please [like].（ソフトに言う）

どうい（同意）→ さんせいする

同意する **agree with** [**to**]; 承諾する **consent to;** よしとする　**approve of**
〈注〉 君に同意する agree with you; 君に同じ意見である　agree with your view [opinion]; 企画[提案]に賛成する agree [consent] to a plan [proposal]
この点で私は君に同意する。
I agree with you on this point.
君の見解に同意する。
I agree with your view.
〈注〉「さんせいする」「ていあん」の項参照。

とうぎ（討議）→ ぎろん

討議 名　**discussion**
討議する 動 他　**discuss**《something》; **debate**《something》論争をする
我々は税金について長時間熱心に討議[討論]した。
We had a long and heated discussion about [on] taxes.
彼らはそのことについて徹底的に討議[討論]した。
They discussed [debated] the issue thoroughly.
その問題は討議中である。
The problem is under discussion.
次の討議事項[議題]は予算案です。
The next item on the agenda is the budget.
cf. bring up the foreign trade issue for discussion（外国貿易問題を議題にする）
〈注〉 discuss は他動詞であるから，×discuss about the matter は誤り。
○discuss the matter
○have a discussion about the matter
このほかの語彙については「ぎろん」参照。

どうきゅう（同級）

【同級生】　a classmate
彼らは同級(生)である。
They are in the same class.
They are classmates.
僕たちは岐阜高校で同級でした。
We were in the same class in Gifu High School.
私の兄が静岡高校で川崎氏と同級でした。
My brother was in the same class as Mr. Kawasaki in Shizuoka High School.
【同級会】　a class reunion

どうさ（動作）

【全身の動作】

仰向け［腹ばい / 横向き］に寝る
lie on one's back [stomach / side]
横になる，寝る　lie down
大の字になる，手足をのばして寝る　sprawl
起き上がる　get up
降りる　get down;（乗物から）get off
立ち上がる　stand up
脇によけて立つ　stand aside
離れて立つ　stand apart
上に［下に］立つ
stand above [below]
stand over [under]（覆うように）
…の間にまじって立つ　stand among ...
つま先立ちをする　stand on one's tiptoes
さっと［急いで］立ち上がる
leap [scramble] to one's feet
身を起す（ベッドの上など）　sit up
座る（椅子などに）　sit down
うずくまって座る　squat
身を曲げる　bend over
しゃがむ，うずくまる　crouch
前に［後ろに］曲げる
bend forward [backward]
おじぎをする　bow
前に［後ろに］よりかかる
lean forward [backward]
壁によりかかる　lean against a wall
もじもじする，身もだえする　squirm; wriggle
ふるえる（一般的，がたがた）shake;（感情的要因で，ぶるぶる）tremble, quiver;（寒さで）shiver

【足】

動く　move
中に入る
move into
come in（中に入って来る）
go in（外から中に入って行く）
歩いて行く［来る］　walk
すたすた歩く　stalk
大またで歩く　stride
いばって歩く　swagger
堂々と歩く　march
どしんどしんと歩く　lumber
すべるように歩く　slide, glide
するりと入る　slip in
軽やかに歩く　trip
急いで行く　hurry
走る　run
疾走する　dash
走りこむ［出る］　run into [out of]
スキップする　skip
小走りする　trot
よろよろ歩く，足をひきずって歩く
shuffle;（千鳥足）wobble, reel along
よろめく　stagger
とぼとぼ歩く　trudge; plod
足を引きずって歩く　limp
皆より遅れる　fall behind
追いつく overtake; catch up with
遅れずについて行く　keep up with
追い越す　pass（by）;（競走で）get ahead of, outstrip
先を行く　go ahead of
つまずく　stumble on [over]《something》
転ぶ　fall
手探りして進む　feel / grope [pick] } one's way
ひざまずく　kneel
踏む　step on
ける　kick
（溝などを）またぐ　step across
跳ぶ　leap; jump; hop →とぶ・とばす
踊る　dance
登る　climb; go up
はう　crawl; creep
足を組んで座る　sit cross-legged

【手・腕】

腕を組んで
（with one's）arms folded [crossed]
指を組む　cross one's fingers
指を組んで　with one's fingers crossed
つまみ上げる　pick up
つねる　pinch
ひねる，ぐいと引く　tweak; twitch
握る　clasp（ゆるく）; grip（強く）

つかむ　grasp; hold in one's hand →つかむ・つかまえる・つかまる
絞る　squeeze
包む　wrap
すくう　scoop (up)
指さす　point at
手をもむ　rub one's hands together
ひっかく　scratch
手を振る　wave one's hand; wave good-bye
手招きする　beckon
握手する　shake hands with《a person》
押す　push
引っぱる pull
押しつける press
押しつぶす　squash (ぺちゃんこに); crush (粉砕する)
すりつぶす　mash
手を伸ばす
reach for《the paper》(物を取ろうとして)
stretch [extend] one's arm(s) [hand(s)]
手を腰に当てて　with arms akimbo
投げる　throw; (強く) fling; トスする toss
たたく (手を) clap one's hands; (人・物を) hit, strike, (ぽんと) rap, tap; (バンと) thump《the table》
こぶしを振り上げる　shake one's fist
持ち上げる　lift
積み上げる heap (up)
下に置く[下ろす] put [set] down
手(足)をぶらぶらさせる
dangle; (大きく振る) swing

【ひじ】

ひじでつく
nudge《a person》(何かの合図として)
ひじで押しのける　elbow《a person》aside
机にひじをつく
rest one's elbows on the table
ひじをついて頭を支える
rest one's head in one's hands
頭をかかえる
chin in hand (考え込んで, 閉口して)

【頭・首】

うなずく　nod
首を横に振る　shake one's head
首をかしげる　put one's head on one side
横目で見る　look askance
首をまわす　turn one's head
首を突き出す　poke one's head out

【肩】

肩をすくめる　shrug (one's shoulders)
肩[背]をまるめる　hunch one's shoulders
肩ごしに見る　look over one's shoulder

【額・まゆ】

まゆを上げる　arch [raise] one's eyebrows
まゆをひそめる　knit one's brow; frown

【目】→ひょうじょう

前[後ろ / 横]を見る
look ahead [back / sideways]
じっと見る　watch (注意して); gaze at (喜んで, 興味をもって); stare at (じろじろ見る); look fixedly at
怒ってにらみつける　glare at; glower at
ちらっと見る　glance at
まぶしそうに細目で見る, 横目でちらっと見る
squint
まばたきをする　blink
ウインクする　wink
のぞく　peep
人なつこい[温かい / 冷たい / 意地の悪い]目
friendly [warm / cold / unfriendly] eyes
物問いたげな目　questioning eyes
あこがれをこめた目つき　longing look

【鼻】

くしゃみをする　sneeze
くんくんかぐ　sniff; sniffle
鼻声を出す　snuffle
いびきをかく　snore
鼻をかむ　blow one's nose
鼻くそをほじる　pick one's nose

【口】

口を開ける[閉じる]
open [shut] one's mouth
あくびをする　yawn
口をとがらす　pout
口をすぼめる　screw up one's mouth
つばを吐く　spit
つばを飲む　swallow
(おいしそうなので)つばが出る

one's mouth waters
赤ちゃんがよだれを垂らす　dribble; slobber
キスをする　kiss
舌を出す　stick out《one's》tongue
笑う　laugh; (にっこり) smile; (くすくす) giggle; (ひとり笑い，含み笑い) chuckle
【のど】
せきをする　cough
せき払いをする　clear one's throat
ぜいぜい息をする　wheeze
しゃがれ声を出す　croak
ささやく　whisper
叫ぶ　cry, shout
きんきん［金切り］声を出す　scream
静かな[低い]声で話す
speak in a quiet [low] voice
大きな声で話す　speak in a loud voice
声を上げて泣く　cry (泣く); sob (すすり泣く); weep (声を出さずに泣く)

どうして → どう

1．いかにして，どうやって

how; in what way [manner]

どうして吹雪の中をベースキャンプまで戻って来たの。
How did you get down to the base camp in the snow storm?
どうして法務省の許可を取ったの。
How did you get permission from the Ministry of Justice?
どうしてあなたが彼と知り合ったか話して。
Tell me how you've come to know him.
Tell me how you know him.

2．なぜ

【不思議】

どうして今年のブドウは小粒なのだろう。
Why are the grapes small this year?
どうして失業率が下がらないのだろう。
Why isn't the unemployment rate decreasing?

【文句】

どうして一緒にやらないの。
Why aren't you joining us?
〈注〉 上の例文は，他意のない質問なのか，文句を言っているのか，その口調によって決る。「一緒に来たら？」と誘うのは Why don't you join us?
どうしてもうちょっとましな運転ができないんだ。
Why aren't you a better driver?

【困惑】

どうしてお前はそうなんだ。よその子はみんな楽しそうにしているのに。
Why aren't you happy like other children?

どうしても

1．強い意志

私たちはどうしてもそれを手に入れなければならない。
We must definitely get it.
どうしても[絶対に]行く。
Whatever happens, I'll go.
彼はどうしても彼女に会いに行くと言っている。
He insists on going to see her.
〈注〉 「どうしても，絶対に」の意味で，at any cost, at all costs, by hook or by crook などが辞書に出ているが今ではあまり使われない。また by all means は英国では By all means come and visit me. (ぜひ訪ねて来てください) のような誘いに使うのみである。米国ではこの誘いのほかに強い意志を表すときに，By all means we must get it. (どうしても手に入れなければならない) のように使われることがあるが，今では古風で，かつまれである。使わない方が無難。

2．否定形との組み合せ

【どうしても…ない】

どうしてもその提案は受け入れられない。
We will never / By no means will we } accept that proposal.
彼はどこに行くのかどうしても話そうとしなかった。
He wouldn't tell me where he was going.

君のプランにはどうしても賛成できない。

I will on no account approve of your plan.

どうしてもいや。

No, I won't.

3. 不成功

【どうしても…できない】

彼はどうしても[どんなにがんばっても]一番になれなかった。

He couldn't come out on top ⌊no matter how [however] hard he tried.

〈注〉 米語では no matter how の方が普通。

いったいけんかのもとは何だったのかどうしても思い出せない。

I cannot for the life of me remember }
I simply can't remember }
what it was that caused our quarrel.

ふたが堅くはまってどうしてもとれなかった。

The lid was stuck tight and would not come off.

〈注〉 この表現 would not は「ふた」に意志があるかのように擬人化してある。

4. 必然

どんな分野でもその道の専門家になるにはどうしても10年はかかる。

It takes }
You have to work } at least ten years to be considered an expert in any field.

絶体絶命，どうしても5万円入り用なんだ。

I desperately need fifty thousand yen to keep me alive.

とうぜん（当選）→ せんきょ

1. 選挙

当選する **be elected; win the election**

当選者 **(the) one elected; a successful candidate**

彼は市長[知事／議長]に当選した。

He was elected Mayor [Governor / chairman].

〈注〉 Mayor, Governor, chairman などは通常無冠詞。

彼女は衆議院選挙で当選した。

She was elected to the House.

She won a seat in the Diet.

【得票】

当選確実である

be sure of ⌊success [being elected]

当選の見込みがある

have a fair chance of success

〈注〉 当選に限らず広く使われる表現。

最高点で当選する

come in ⌊first [on top]〔米〕

be returned at the head of the poll〔英〕

彼は70%の得票率で当選した。

He was returned with 70% of the votes.

2. 懸賞・受賞

当選する **win a prize**

彼は標語の懸賞に1等で当選した。

He has won the first prize in the slogan contest.

当選作は文藝春秋の新年号に掲載される。

The prize novel will appear in the New Year issue of *Bungei-Shunju*.

cf. 彼の最近作は直木賞を受賞した。

His latest novel won the Naoki Prize.

3. 抽選・当りくじ

当選番号 a winning number

彼はくじ引きで当選した。

He drew the winning number.

（宝くじなどで）当選した。

One of my numbers was a winner.

〈注〉 同じくじが当るのでも The lot fell on me. は何か不愉快な役が当る意味合いがある。

とうぜん（当然）→ あたりまえ

1. 論理的・法的

当然の帰結[結果]

a natural consequence;（論理的に）a logi-

cal conclusion;（避けられない） an inevitable result
当然の要求　a reasonable demand
それには私に当然の権利がある。
It's mine by right.（財産権など）
I have a right to it.
受賞は当然のことです。
You deserve the prize.
It's your due.（賞に重点）
You are worthy of the prize.（受賞者の功績に重点）
彼の報酬は当然だ。
He deserves the reward.

2．道義的
今日私があるのはあなたのおかげです。私にできることをさせていただくのは当然です。
I owe (to) you what I am now. It's only natural for me to try to do what I can to help you.
彼の罰は当然だ。
He deserves the punishment.
He had it coming.
It serves him right.（天罰てきめん）
【当然の処置・行動】
公害の元凶と判定されている会社の社長などは当然懲役にすべきだ。
It's justifiable and desirable to imprison presidents of companies found guilty of polluting the environment.
我々が老人や障害者を助けるのは当然だ。
We ought to [should] help the aged and people with disabilities.
君は当然我々の許可を取りに来るべきだった。
You ought to [should] have come to get our permission.
君がそう言うのは当然だが…。（当り前）
You may say so but ...
It's understandable that you say so but ...
〈注〉　この表現は「当然だが，しかし…」と否定する文が続くのが普通。

今日では言論の自由は当然のことと思われている。
Nowadays freedom of speech is taken for granted.

どうそう（同窓）

同窓会
［組織］an alumni association
［総会］an alumni association meeting
同窓会の事業
an alumni association project
クラス会
a class [an alumni] reunion
（同窓会）関西支部　(the) Kansai Chapter
同窓会役員　officer(s)
彼女と私は同窓です。
She and I went to the same school.
I graduated from [went to] the same college as [that] she did.
私たちは同窓です。
We are graduates of the same school.
正月休みに高校卒業20周年の同窓会に出ることにした。
I've decided to go to my twentieth year high school class reunion, which is during the New Year holiday(s).

とうちゃく（到着）

到着する　**come to; get to; reach; arrive at [in]**
到着駅（終着駅）　the train's destination
次の到着駅　the next station
到着ホーム　the arrival platform ※
到着の列車　the arriving train ※
〈注〉　※は駅のアナウンスには使われるが，それ以外ではあまり使われない。下記例文のような文の形にする方がよい。
ひかり315号は17番ホームに到着します。
Hikari 315 comes in at track [platform] 17.
cf. starts from ...（…から発車します）
次の到着列車　the next train in

到着時刻
the time of arrival; the arrival time
彼は暗くならないうちに町に到着した。
He {reached / arrived in [at]} the town before dark.
〈注〉 reach は他動詞であるから ×reach to としない。
救急車は5分で到着した。
The ambulance arrived [came] in five minutes.
彼は来月の12日に(ここに)到着する予定だ。
He is expected here on the 12th of next month.
彼は10時の列車で到着予定だ。
He {will come [arrive] / is arriving [coming]} on the 10 o'clock train.
列車は10時に到着予定だ。
The train is due here at 10 o'clock.
荷物は無事到着した。
The package arrived in good condition.
列車の到着がずっと遅れている。
The train is very late [far behind schedule].
ホノルル発101便の到着時刻を教えていただけませんでしょうか。
Could you tell me when flight 101 from Honolulu is coming in [is due]?
【申し込み】
到着順[先着]100名で締め切ります。
We will accept the first 100 entries.

とうとう → ついに

とうひょう (投票)

投票 名 (投票すること) **voting;** (個々の票) **a vote; a ballot**
…に投票する 動 **vote for [against]** 〔*most common*〕; **give** one's **vote to; cast a vote [a ballot] for**
投票に行く go to the polls
〈注〉 go to the polls はほとんど vote と同義。ただし「選挙のための投票をする」の意味。
投票で決める decide by vote
投票者 a voter
投票日
(the) voting [polling] day
(the) election day
投票数
total number of ballots cast
記名投票 an open vote
無記名投票 a secret vote; a secret ballot
無効票 an invalid vote
決戦投票 a final ballot
信任投票 a vote of confidence
不信任投票 a failed vote of confidence
私は鈴木氏に投票した。
I voted for Mr. Suzuki. 〔*common*〕
I gave my vote to Mr. Suzuki.
cf. 社民党に支持の票を入れた。
I voted for the Social Democratic Party.
投票結果は夜半前にはわかるだろう。
The results will be known before midnight.
投票結果は賛成27, 反対12, 白紙[棄権]1票だった。
The ballot results were 27 in favor and 12 opposed with one blank ballot [abstention].
〈注〉 the election results は選挙でだれが選ばれたかの結果のことで, 議案の賛否を投票する場合には使われない。the ballot results は選挙の場合でも議案の賛否の投票の場合でも使われる。

どうぶつ (動物)

animals

1. 哺乳類 **the mammals**
【ペット・家畜】 pets, domestic animals
イヌ dog; (子イヌ) puppy, pup / ウサギ rabbit / ウシ(雌) cow; (雄) bull, ox (pl. oxen); (子牛) calf; (総称) cattle / ウマ horse; (子ウマ) foal; (小形) pony; ロバ donkey; (小形) burro / ネコ cat; (子ネコ) kitten / ヒツジ sheep; (子ヒツジ) lamb / ブタ pig; (子ブタ) piglet / ヤギ goat; (子

ヤギ) kid
【野生動物】 wild animals
[食肉目] carnivores, meat eaters
(一部雑食も含む) アナグマ badger / アライグマ raccoon / イタチ weasel / イヌ dog / オオカミ wolf / キツネ fox / クマ bear / コヨーテ coyote / ジャガー jaguar / ジャッカル jackal / スカンク skunk / タヌキ raccoon dog / チーター cheetah / トラ tiger / ネコ cat / ハイエナ hyena / パンダ panda / ピューマ puma / ヒョウ leopard / ミンク mink / ライオン lion
[霊長目] primates
オランウータン orangutan / ゴリラ gorilla / サル monkey / チンパンジー chimpanzee
[有蹄類] the ungulates, hoofed animals (偶蹄目・奇蹄目)
(草食動物) herbivores, grass eaters
ウシ cow; bull / ウマ horse / イノシシ boar / カバ hippopotamus / カモシカ antelope / キリン giraffe / サイ rhinoceros / シカ deer / シマウマ zebra / スイギュウ water buffalo / トナカイ reindeer / バイソン bison, (バッファロー buffalo) / バク tapir / ヤク yak / ラクダ camel / ラマ mule
[有袋目]marsupials
オポッサム opossum / カンガルー kangaroo / コアラ koala / ワラビー wallaby
[齧歯目及び類似小動物] rodents and others
ウサギ rabbit; ノウサギ hare / ネズミ (大) rat; (小) mouse (*pl.* mice) / ハリネズミ hedgehog / ビーバー beaver / モグラ mole / ヤマアラシ porcupine / リス squirrel; シマリス chipmunk
[長鼻目] proboscidians
ゾウ elephant / マンモス mammoth
[その他]
アルマジロ armadillo / カモノハシ (duck-billed) platypus / コウモリ bat / ナマケモノ sloth
【海生哺乳動物】 marine mammals
アザラシ, オットセイ seal / アシカ sea lion; トド sea lion / イルカ dolphin / クジラ whale / シャチ(サカマタ) killer whale / ジュゴン dugong, sea cow / スナメリ porpoise / セイウチ walrus / マナティ manatee / ラッコ sea otter

2. 爬虫類 the reptiles
イグアナ iguana / ウミガメ turtle / カメ tortoise; ウミガメ turtle / 恐竜 dinosaur / トカゲ lizard / ヘビ snake(毒ヘビ adder; viper); ガラガラヘビ rattlesnake; コブラ cobra; ニシキヘビ python, boa constrictor; マムシ *mamushi*, pit viper / ヤモリ gecko / ワニ crocodile, alligator

3. 両生類 the amphibians
イモリ newt / カエル frog (オタマジャクシは tadpole) / ガマ toad / サンショウウオ salamander

どうめい (同盟)

名 **an alliance; a league; a confederation**

1. 国際的な同盟

同盟する ⌊enter into [form] an alliance with
同盟している be allied with
同盟国 an ally; an allied ⌊power [country]
非同盟国 a nonaligned nation

2. 民間の同盟

〈注〉 労働組合などの同盟にも alliance は使えるが, 次のような表現もできる。

水俣病被害者同盟
　Minamata victims' organization
同盟をつくる[結成する]
　form [set up] an organization
　organize (themselves) into an association
事故の被害者は同盟を結成した。
　The accident victims formed an organization.

どうろ（道路）→ みち

とうろん（討論）→ ぎろん，とうぎ

とうわく（当惑）→ こまる

1．きまりの悪さ

当惑する　**be embarrassed**

彼があまり優しくじっと見つめるので，彼女は当惑して目を伏せた。

He gazed at her so fondly she looked down embarrassed.

彼があまり立ち入って個人的なことを尋ねるので，彼女は当惑したように何も言わなかった。

He asked her very personal questions. She looked embarrassed and said nothing.

cf. He embarrassed me by shouting at the children from the car window.

（彼は車の窓から首を突き出して子供たちを怒鳴りつけたりするので，私は体裁が悪かった）

〈注〉「恥ずかしい」と「当惑」の比較

shyness（恥じらい）とembarrassment（当惑）は双生児。shame （恥）もembarrassmentにつながるが，shame からくる be ashamed（恥じいる）は自分の行為を恥じて「恥ずかしい」のである。遅刻して教室にあとから入って行くのは shy な人には very embarrassing，特に shy でなくてもばつが悪いことで，良識のある人なら be ashamed であるはずだ。しかし be in an awkward position（具合の悪い立場にある）といっては大げさ。

2．途方に暮れる

be perplexed; be bewildered; be puzzled

（be embarrassed と異なり，知的だが感情的ではなく，わからなくて困ること）

老婦人は人込みの中でどちらへ出たらよいものか当惑してあたりを見回した。

The old lady looked around her bewildered as she tried to find her way through the crowd.

その問題はどう考えてやったらよいか当惑しています。

That problem puzzles me.

（何と答えたらよいか）わからなくて当惑した。

I was perplexed, for I didn't know what to say.

〈注〉「当惑する」というと be at a loss を日本人は使いすぎる傾向がある。be at a loss for an answer [words] は使えるが，使いすぎないように。

とおす（通す）→ とおる

1．案内する

すみませんが通してくださいませんか。

Excuse me, but could you let me by?

お客様を客間にお通ししてください。

Please show the guests to the drawing room.〔*formal*〕

私たちは居間に通された。

We were shown into the living room.

2．開通させる

恵那山にもう一つトンネルを通す計画がある。

They are planning another tunnel through Mt. Ena.

3．一貫する

君の言っていることは筋が通らない。

What you are saying doesn't make sense.

彼は最後まで信念を通した。

He stuck to his convictions to the end.

生涯がんこ者で通す人がいる。

Some people remain stubborn to the end of their days.

彼女は生涯独身で通した。

She remained single all her life.

4．仲介する

ジムは僕の親友だが，アリスを通して僕らは知り合ったのだ。

Jim's now a great friend of mine.

{ I got to know [met] him through Alice.
{ Alice introduced us to each other.

このゴアテックスのスキーウェアのことを友人を通して知った。

I learned [found out] about Gore-Tex ski-wear from a friend.

とおり（通り）

道路 **a road; a street;** 交通 **traffic**

【道路】

市の主な役所，企業のほとんどがこの通りにある。

Most of the city offices and main businesses are on this street.

【人通り】

人通りがほとんどありませんね。

There are few people }
There aren't many people } { going by. / on this street.

この通りは夜はほとんど人通りがない。

Few people pass on this street at night.

cf. この通りは車が多い。

The traffic is heavy on this street.

…とおり（…通り）・…どおり

1．…のように

前 **like**（口語では接としても使う）; **as** 接

この[その]通り　like this [that]

次の通り　as follows

いつもの通り　as usual

【言う通り】

言われた通りにしなさい。

Do as you are told.

言う通りにしなさい。　Do as I tell you.

言われた通りにします。

I'll do exactly as you say.

言った通りでしょう。（それごらん）

Didn't I tell you so?

What did I say?

Just as I told you!

I was right, wasn't I?

あの人の言うことは言葉通りには取れない。

You cannot take him at his word.

【思う通り】

彼はいつも自分の思う通りにする。

He always has to have his own way.

何でも自分の思い通りというわけにはいきませんよ。

You can't have your own way in everything.

【予定[計画]通り】

彼らは予定通り今朝アメリカに出発した。

They left for the US this morning as scheduled.

すべて予想[計画]通りにいきました。

Everything went just as we (had) expected [planned].

校舎の建築は予定通りには進んでいなかった。

The construction work on the new school building was behind schedule.

【時間通り】　on time

お客様は時間通りにお着きになった。

The guests arrived on time.

会は時間通りに始めよう。

Let's start the meeting on time.

2．慣用表現

そのとおり！

That's right! / You're right! /〔米〕Right!

まったくその通り。

You're quite [absolutely] right.（やや厳しい口調になりやすい）

とおる（通る）

1．通行する

（人・車が）

go / **run** / **walk** } { **by**（そばを） / **along**（…に沿って） / **through**（…を貫いて）

pass by（そばを）

駅には川の堤防を通って行けばいい。

We can reach the station by going along the river bank.

学校への往復にいつも鍛冶屋の前を通ったものだが，それがえらく気に入っていた。

On my way to and from school I used to pass (by) a blacksmith's shop, which pleased me very much.

私は人込みをかき分けて通って何とかホテルに着いた。

I pushed my way through the crowd and managed to get to my hotel.

【通り…】

通りがかりの人

a passer-by (*pl.* passers-by)

私はちょうどそこを通りかかった。

I happened to be passing by the spot.

彼は私には気づかずに通り過ぎた。

He passed by without noticing me.

我々は暗い部屋をいくつも通り抜けた。

We went through many dark rooms.

通り抜けできません。

This is a dead end.

［標識］No Outlet / No Through Road

【道路】

今朝は人も車もあまり通っていない。

The road is not crowded this morning.

この道路は通れない。

This road is blocked.

【交通の便】

高崎と東京を結ぶ新しいハイウェイはうちの村を通っている。

The new highway connecting Takasaki and Tokyo runs through our village.

あの村にはバスが通っている。

There is bus service to that village.

鉄道が北濃まで通っている。

A rail line [The railroad] runs as far as Hokunō.

【経由】

彼はアメリカからヨーロッパを通って帰って来た。

He came back from America through [via / by way of] Europe.

2．合格する

pass

やっと試験に通ってうれしい。

I'm glad I eventually passed the exam.

公害規制が厳しくなってきている。旧式のエンジンは試験を通らないだろう。

The pollution regulations are becoming more severe; old-type engines won't pass the test.

3．通用する

【名前・外見】

彼はキムタクで通っている。

He goes under [by] the name of Kimutaku.

うちの社長，「おやじ」で通っていたのだが突如引退宣言をした。

The head of our company, better known among us as "Oyaji [Dad]," declared his decision to retire.

彼女はペンネームの方が通りがいい。

She is better known by her pen name.

彼女はうんと若く見えるから20歳といっても通るだろう。

She looks so young she could [would] pass for twenty.

【意見】

君の意見はたぶん通らないだろう。

They will probably not accept your opinion.

【言い訳・要求】

そんな言い訳[要求]は通らないよ。

Such an excuse will not do.

Such an excuse [a request] will not go down well with them. 〔*colloq.*〕

【意味・論旨】

この文章は意味が通らない。

This sentence doesn't make sense.

筋が通るように話をしてください。

Please try to talk logically.

この論説は筋が通っていない。

This essay is { inconsistent. (1) / not logical. (2)

〈注〉 (1)は言っていることが矛盾している，(2)は論理的に話が進められていない，という意味。

4．貫く

彼は声が通る[彼の声はよく通る]。

He has a sonorous voice.（素晴らしい声）

His voice carries very far.

この素材は水を通さないがあれはそうでない。

This material is waterproof but that one isn't.

この肉は中まで火が通っていない。

This meat is underdone [still rare] in the middle.

銃弾を通さない 形 bullet-proof

とき（時）

1．時間

time 時間（↔空間 space）

時（↔場所 place）

時と潮は人を待たない。（歳月人を待たず）

Time and tide wait [waits] for no man.

時は流れる。（立ち止まらない）

Time ⌊never stands [doesn't stand] still.

Time rolls on.

時は飛ぶように過ぎて行く。

Time flies.

2．おり（時点）

【瞬間】 when; at

戸を開けたとき…

when I opened the door …

目を覚したとき…

when I awoke …

【ある範囲にわたる時】

小さいとき…

when I was little

5歳のとき…

when I was five (years old);

at five; at the age of five

高校のときに良い友達をたくさんつくった。

I made many good friends (when I was) in high school.

【期間】 while; during

私がいないときにだれかが訪ねてきた。

While I was out / During [In] my absence } someone came to see me.

私がヨーロッパにいる時に戦争が勃発した。

While I was in Europe, the war broke out.

【動作進行中】 as; while＋進行形

勉強をするときラジオをつけておいた。

While I was studying I had the radio on.

通りを歩いているとき警察の車がスーパーの前に止まっているのに気づいた。

As [When, While] I was walking down the street I noticed a police car in front of the supermarket.

3．時期・場合

a time; an occasion; 場合 **a case**

緊急のときは110番を呼びなさい。

In (case of) an emergency, call 110.

【…のときがある[来る]】

自分の力以外には頼るものはない。そんなときがあるものだ。

There are some situations in which no one can help you but yourself.

沈黙が最上の策というとき[場合]がある。

There are occasions ⌊when [on which] silence is the best policy.

私は時々ぐっすり眠りこんで目覚しが聞えないときがある。

I am sometimes sleeping so deeply that I don't hear the alarm clock ringing.

〈注〉 ×There is the case that I don't hear the alarm clock …

このような単純で日常的な話題は There is … 構文にそぐわない。しかし There is 構文を使う場合は，There is a [the] case in which I don't … とすべきであり，×There is the case that … と同格接続詞 case that で結ぶのは誤り。

発展途上国が我々に追いつくときがやがて来

るであろう。

The time will come when the developing countries will overtake us.

〈注〉 The time will come when ... の形は普通によく使われる。

The time will come when you can have your own house.

(今に自分の家ぐらいもてるときがくるさ)

【好機】

今こそそのときだ。

Now is your chance.

彼はちょうどいいときに来た。

He came in just at the right moment.

そろそろ寝るとき[時間]だ。

It's about time we go [went] to bed.

(=It's about time for us to go to bed.)

そろそろ子供たちを寝かすとき[時間]だ。

It's about time we send [sent] the children to bed.

〈注〉 上の2文の went, sent は一種の仮定法過去で should go [send] 程度の気持ち。単純な過去ではない。米語では go, send を使うようになってきている。または It's ... for ... to do と不定詞構文を使う。

4. 慣用表現

【時がたてば[たって]】

in due time (=at the proper time; as time goes on)

時がたてば[そのうちには]結婚する気にもなるだろう。

In due time she will decide to get married.

時がたてば浜も海水に浸食されていくだろう。

In due time the ocean will erode the beach.

時のたつのも忘れて →たつ(経つ)

forgetting about { time passing away / the passing of time

【時を過す】

私たちは学生時代の思い出話をしてたいへん楽しい時を過した。

We had a very good time talking about our school days.

私たちは食っちゃ寝，食っちゃ寝で時を過した。

We did nothing but eat and sleep.

【時に】(話題を変えるとき)

by the way; changing the subject

《頻度表現の比較》

never 一度も…しない

rarely; seldom めったに…しない

once in a while ほんの時たま…する

sometimes; occasionally 時には…する

often; frequently しばしば…する

all the time いつも…する

constantly; continually しょっちゅう…する

always; continuously いつも…しづめである

ex. 彼はしょっちゅうお金をせびりに来る。

He's constantly asking for money. (口頭表現であれば憤懣をこめた言い方)

《時の表現》

A. 現在完了

【完了】

ちょうど朝食をすましたところだ。

I've just finished my breakfast.

【時の幅】

さっきまで降りそうだったのにすっかり晴れ上がりましたね。

It looked like rain a while ago, but it has cleared up.

〈注〉 この文は「完了」と考えてもよいし，「さっき」から「今」の時の幅と考えてもよい。 ... it cleared up とすると過去のことになってしまう。

中学に入って以来もう10年間も英語を勉強している。

I have been studying English more than ten years now, ever since I entered junior high school.

【経験】…したことがある(か) →こと

広島に行ったことがありますか。

Have you ever been to Hiroshima?

〈注〉 この答えとしては Yes であれば，Yes(, I have). I went there last summer. のように具体的に行ったのはいつかも述べるのが普通。×Yes, I have ever been to Hiroshima. とは言わない。No であれば No, I've never been there. は正しい文。

Did you ever go to Hiroshima?

〈注〉 米語ではこの形も Have you ever ...? と同じように使う。人によっては，Did you ... はこれから先もあまり行きそうにないと思いつつ尋ねる場合であるともいう。

英国で Did you ... は英国に帰国した人に日本滞在中のことを尋ねるなど，すべて過去のことになっているときに尋ねる形である。

【見たことがない】

パンダはテレビでしか見たことがない。

I have never seen a panda except on TV.

cf. 彼は自分の息子を見たことがなかった。

He never saw his own son.（彼が故人ですべて過去のことである場合）

【見たことがある】

×I have ever seen ... は誤り。（I have never seen の裏返しでこのように書く間違いが多い）

１回だけ見たのならば，どこでいつ，と具体的に過去形で言うのが普通。

I once saw that famous comedian Charlie Chaplin in Tokyo.

（かの有名なコメディアン，チャーリー・チャップリンを東京で（一度）見たことがあります）

現在までに何回か見たことがあるならば現在完了を使うが，「たびたび」や「ときどき」などと頻度も含めて言うのが普通。→とき《頻度表現の比較》

I have often seen him on TV.

（彼はテレビでたびたび見たことがある）

B.　過去完了

(1) (a)He said, "Joe had already left town when I phoned him."
(b)He said Joe had already left town when he (had) phoned him.

（彼が言うには，僕［彼］が電話したときジョーはもう町を出てしまっていたということだ）

日本語訳では(a)(b)はほとんど訳し分ける必要がない。話法の習慣の違いである。

(2) He asked me, "Had the computer been installed when you came back?"
He asked me if the computer had already been installed when I had come [came] back from Europe.

（君が［僕がヨーロッパから］帰ってきたとき，もうコンピュータが入っていたかと彼に聞かれた――［　］が間接話法の訳）

上の(1)(2)の英文で上段の文が直接話法で，それを間接話法にしたのが下段の文である。どちらも厳密に文法的には "when he had phoned" "when I had come back" と過去完了にするところであるが，時の前後関係について誤解を生じるおそれがないときは，煩雑になるのを避けて "when he phoned" "when I came back" と過去形にする方が一般的である。

C．その他

［季節］

this summer　４月から９月頃までは「この夏」と感じる。

last summer　12月になるともう「この前の夏」と感じる。

next summer　12月から３月頃まで「次の夏」は next summer という。

［先週・今週・来週］

last week　先週
this week　今週
next week　来週
これ以外は先々週とか，さ来週と言わず，何月何日と日付 (dates) を言うのが普通。

とくい（得意）

1．自慢

得意になる　**be proud, be elated**（悪い意味はない）; **be flattered**（おだてに乗っておめでたい感じ）

得意になって 副　**boastfully**（自慢げに）; **gloatingly**（得々と，気配りが欠ける。よくない意味）; **proudly**　誇らかに（悪い意味を含まない）; **triumphantly**　意気揚々と（上の３語よりはるかに強い語。鬼の首でもとったような調子。だいたいにおいてよい意味）

その子はクラブの部長に選ばれて得意であった。

The boy was very proud because he was chosen chairman.

彼らは成功して得意［意気揚々］であった。

They are elated with their success.

得意に[いい気に]なるんじゃない。君のような立場にあったらだれだってそのくらいできただろうよ。

Don't be flattered. Anyone in your position might have done it.

彼は大得意になってその話をした。

He told the story triumphantly.

2. 得手

歌うのは得意じゃありません。

Singing is not my forte [strong point].

【科目・学科】

得意の科目は？

What's your favorite subject?

彼は数学が得意[不得意]だ。

He is good [not good] at mathematics.

【得意わざ】

彼が得意なのはアップルパイだ。

His specialty is apple pie.

3. 顧客

彼はうちの古くからのお得意さんです。

He is one of our oldest and best customers.

彼は着々と得意先を広げている。

He is steadily gaining customers.

とくに（特に）・とくべつ（特別）

特に，特別に 副 **especially; specially; particularly; in particular;** ある目的のために **expressly;** 常になく **unusually;** 例外的に **exceptionally**

特別な 形 **special; particular;** 余分の **extra;** 例外の **exceptional**

〈注〉◆「特別な」を special,「特に」を especially と片づけてしまうことが多いが，special とはほかの普通のものと区別して特色のあるものを指す。また，全体に対して個を強調するのは particular である。なお particular には「詳細な，きちょうめんな，気むずかしい」の意もある。

It's nothing special.（これは特別なことではない；いつもどおりのことだ）

in this particular case（ほかの場合と区別して「特別この場合」）

a special case（普通にはない「例外的な場合」）

I did nothing in particular.（特にこれと取りたてて言うようなことはしなかった）

◆specially は「特に，わざわざ」，especially は「特別に他より卓越して」の意。ただし区別はさほどはっきりしているわけではなく，用法に地域差，個人差もあるようだ。

ex. ［その目的のために］He came all the way specially to meet you.

（遠くから特にあなたに会うためにわざわざ来てくださった）

［例年になく］The cherry blossoms are especially fine this year.

（今年の桜は特に見事です）

1. 普通以上

彼の健康には特に注意してあげてください。

You should pay special attention to his health.

その未熟児の保育に彼らは特別に注意を払った。

They took special care in feeding and handling the premature baby.

子供の頃，彼女はほかの子供たちと比べて知能がずばぬけていたので特別扱いを受けていた。

As a child she was given special treatment because she was much more intelligent than her classmates.

人々は彼を特別扱いしていた。

They made an exception for him [treated him as an exception].

彼女は特別だった。

She was an exception.

我々はあの人たちと特別な関係はない。

We have no special connection with them.

特上品　extra-fine [choice, luxury] goods

特別席　reserved seats

2. 例外

extra

特別号(雑誌など)

an extra number（定期刊行以外）

a special number（何かのトピックについて

の特集などを定期・非定期刊行物で扱う)
特別手当　a special [an extra] allowance
特別配当　an extra dividend
特別国会
an extraordinary [a special] session of the Diet
特別予算　a special budget

3. ことさら，わざわざ
先生は我々の会に出席されるため，特に仙台からおいでくださったのです。
He has come all the way from Sendai just [expressly] to attend our meeting.
この教科書は優秀な学生を対象として特別に作られたものです。
This textbook is designed specifically [expressly] for bright students.
高名な科学者，今井博士が特にうちの学校新聞のために随筆を寄稿された。
Dr. Imai, the famous scientist, has sent an essay specially written for our school paper.
私はこの夏はこれといって特に何もしなかった。
I have done nothing in particular [to speak of] this summer.
特に何も言うことはありません。
I have nothing in particular to say.

4. なかでも
今の若い人はたいてい音楽が，特にロックンロールが好きだ。
Most young people today love music, especially rock and roll.

どくりょく（独力）→ ひとり

ところ（所）

1. 場所
ここが私の生れたところです。
This is (the place) where I was born.
どこでも好きなところに行きなさい。
Go wherever you like.
私たちのいるところがなかった。
There was no room for us.
彼は駐車するところを探している。(→ちゅうしゃ)
He's looking for a place to park.

《「ところ」と関係節》
「ところ」を関係節で修飾するとき，先行詞が place や Tokyo, Osaka のような場所の名前だからといって where 節で修飾するとは限らない。先行詞を修飾する節の中で先行詞が文法的にどんな位置を占めるかによって，関係代名詞の which [that] 節にするか，または関係副詞の where 節にすべきかが決るのである。
(1)　I went to Osaka (先行詞)
{ ×where is the second biggest city in Japan.
{ ○which is the second biggest city in Japan.
↓
(Osaka) is the second biggest city in Japan.
Osaka　は主語であるから，関係代名詞 which を用いる。
(2)　I went to Osaka (先行詞)
{ ×which I stayed for two weeks.
{ ○where I stayed for two weeks.
↓
I stayed (in [at] Osaka) for two weeks.
in Osaka は場所を表す副詞句であるから，関係副詞 where を用いる。または in を加えて in which I stayed ... とする。

2. 住所
封筒にところ番地をはっきりと正確に書いてください。
Address an envelope clearly and correctly.
新しいおところがわかりしだいお知らせください。
Please give me your new address as soon as you have one.
今でも同じところに住んでおられますか[おところは変りませんか]。

Do you still { live in the same place? / have the same address? }

僕はしばらく叔父のところにいます。

I will stay with my uncle for some time.

彼はその夜は友達のところで過した。

He spent the night with a friend.

3. 部分

【性格】

よいところがある

have a good [strong] point

悪いところがある

have a bad [weak] point

彼の態度には冷たいところがある。

{ He has a bit of coldness / There is something cold } in his manner.

彼にはがんこ［ユーモラス］なところがある。

He has some obstinacy [humor] in him.

彼女には芸術家らしいところがある。

There is something of the artist

{ in her.（資質がある） / about her.（雰囲気をもっている） }

【健康・行為】

彼には何も悪いところはない。

There is nothing wrong with him.

【論点】

そこが君に賛成できないところだ。

That's where I can't agree with you.

4. 時・場面

今のところ　at present

今までのところ　so far

君はちょうどいいところに来てくれた。

You have come just at the right moment.

彼はちょうど悪いところに来合せた。

He came at an ill-chosen [a bad] moment.

私はおぼれるところを通行人に助けられた。

I was rescued from drowning by a passerby.

あの男の人が私がおぼれるところを助けてくれた。

That man rescued me from drowning.

私はもう少しでひかれるところだった。

I was nearly run over.

時計がちょうど12時を打ったところだ。

The clock has just struck twelve.

ちょうど仕事から帰ったところです。

I've just come home from work.

私がまさにドアを開けようとしたところ，だれかが外からドアを開けた。

I was just about to open the door when it was opened from outside.

5. 話題の転換

えー，ところで今日の午後はどうするつもり？

Well, by the way, what are you going to do this afternoon?

〈注〉 Changing the subject ...（話は変るけど…）という言い方もある。

とし（年）

1. 暦年

a year

毎年　every year

年月がたつにつれて

as the years go by [pass]

with the passage of time

年が明けると，年の初めに

［1月の初め］

early in the new year

at the beginning of the year

［元日の朝早く］

early on New Year's (Day)

〈注〉 元日は New Year's Day と大文字で書く。あくまでこの日1日のことで，英語には「正月」に当る呼称はない。

年の暮れ(近く)

toward the end of the year

その年のうちに，年内に

by the end of the year

before the year is out [up]

古い年を送り新しい年を迎える

see [send] the old year out and welcome the new year in [greet the new year]

〈注〉 the New Year と大文字で書くのは新年を指すときに限る。新しい年１年間を指すときは the new year とする。

2．年齢

age

彼女の年はいくつ？

How old is she?

(年は)13です。

She is thirteen (years old).

私たちは同い年です。

We are the same age.

君は年の割に若く見える。

You look young for your age.

彼はもう学校に上がる年だ。

He is old enough to go to school.

彼はこのぐらいのことはもうわかる年だと思う。

I think he is old enough to understand this.

彼はまだ学校に上がる年ではない。

He is still too young to go to school.

僕が君の年にはもう家族持ちだったよ。

When I was your age, I had a family to support.

年をとると忘れっぽくなる。

We become [get] forgetful when we get old.

近頃は男の人の方が女の人より早く年をとる［老ける］。

Men age quicker than women nowadays.

彼は年相応に見える［見えない］。

He looks [doesn't look] his age.

年のせいで眼［記憶／耳］が悪くなりました。

Age is telling on my eyesight [memory / hearing].

My eyesight [memory / hearing] isn't what it used to be.

この年になれば何を言ってもおかまいなし。

At my age anything I say will be all right.

とち（土地）

1．土地

land （海に対し）陸

a tract of land 広々とした土地

a piece of land １区画の土地（一般的）

a lot 家・アパートなどの敷地

a plot 大学・病院・工場などの大きな建物の敷地，また家庭菜園用の土地にも使う。

estate 地方の地主などの広い邸宅と周囲の地所

real estate 法的な不動産としての土地

cf. personal estate [property]（動産）

彼女は広い土地を持っている。

She has [owns] a lot of land.

祖母は広い土地を持っていた。

My grandmother had a large tract of land.

彼は300平方メートルの土地を買［売］った。

He bought [sold] { a 300 square meter lot. / a lot measuring 300 square meters. }

この土地は私の叔父のものだ。

This land belongs to my uncle.

土地つきの家

a house with a lot

土地家屋

land and buildings; real estate（不動産）

土地に投資する

invest in real estate

土地を売買する

deal in real estate

土地ブローカー

a real estate agent; an estate agent〔英〕

土地を借りる

lease [rent] land

家庭菜園用に［車庫用に］土地を貸す

rent a plot for a family vegetable garden [a garage]

2．地域

a locality; a region; a district; a place

土地の人

a native (of a place)

田舎の人 (the) local people

土地の習慣

a local custom

土地のなまり
a local accent
土地の名産
famous [well-known] local products
彼の家は土地の旧家だ。
His family goes back several generations here.
They're an old, old family here.
His family is of long standing here.
彼の親は土地の者ではない。(外から移り住んだ人)
His parents came from elsewhere.
私は土地の者ではありません。(旅行者)
I'm a stranger here.
あの人たちは土地に詳しい[明るい]。
They have a good knowledge of the neighborhood.
They know the neighborhood well.

3．耕地
soil →つち
肥えた土地　fertile [rich] soil [land]
やせた土地　poor soil [land]
不毛の土地　barren soil [land]
〈注〉 land は広大な土地の場合に使う。
天気がよければ土地を耕す。(晴耕雨読)
If the weather is good, he works in his vegetable plot.
ここの土地はジャガイモに適している。
This soil is good for potatoes.

どちら・どこ →どの・どれ

1．どなた
どちら様ですか。(取り次ぎ)
Who shall I say it is?
What is your name, please?
May I ask your name, please?

2．どれ →どの・どれ
どちらがいいですか。
Which do you like better?
Which do you prefer?
明日と明後日とどちらがご都合がいいでしょうか。
Which would be [do you think is] more convenient, tomorrow or the day after tomorrow?
どちらでも好きな方を取ってよろしい。
You may take whichever you like.
どちらの道を通っても明るいうちに(そこに)着きますよ。
Whichever route you take, you'll reach the place before dark.
どちらとも言えない。
I have divided [mixed] feelings about it.
I'm of two minds. (半々の気持ち)
I can't give a definite answer. (決めかねている)

3．どこ
この夏はどちらへお出かけになりますか。
Where are you going this summer?
どちらからいらっしゃったのですか。
Where are you from?
What part of the country do you come from?
(公共の)お手洗いはどちらですか。
Where is the rest room, please?
〈注〉 個人の家の手洗いは bathroom。

4．どちら，どっち
【二者択一】
(アルかボブか)どちらかが譲らなければならない。
Either Al or Bob has to give up.
One of them has to give up.
(ともに単数一致で has となる)
君か僕かどちらかが悪いのだ。
Either you or I am to blame. (動詞に近い主語に一致)
【両者】
どちらでもよい。
Either will do.

Either will be OK.
どちらも好き。
I like both of them.
どちらもいや。
I don't like either of them.
I like neither of them.
I like neither this one nor that one.
〈注〉 Which would you like to have, tea or coffee? のように聞かれ，どちらでもよいのであれば Either will be fine [OK]. のように答えてよいが，どちらか選択してはっきり言った方が先方は喜ぶ。他人に合せて同じものにすることもよくあるのは日本と同じ。
どちらでもたいして変らない(からどちらでもよい)。
It doesn't matter / It makes little difference } either way.
〈注〉 There were cherry trees on either side of the river. は「川の両側に桜の木が植えてあった」の意で「片側に」の意味ではない。しかし私たちが書くときは「両側に」ならば on both sides of the river とはっきり書く方がよい。
どちらにしても明日うかがいます。
I'll come tomorrow anyway.
どちらかと言えば家にいたい。
I'd rather stay home.
どちら[だれ]が部長に選ばれましたか。
Which of them [Who] was chosen president of the club?
〈注〉 上の例文のように対象が人であっても「どちらが…？」を Which of them ...? としてよい。

(…に)とって

1. …に（対象指示）

to

それは私にとってはたいへん重要なことだった。
To me it was very important.
それは彼らにとっては死活問題である。
It's a matter of life and death to them.
これは私にとっては忘れられない思い出です。
These are memories I shall [will] never forget.

2. …のために

for

それは君にとってよいことだ。
It's good for you.
それは彼にとってはよい教訓になる。
It will be a good lesson for him.
〈注〉 to, for の使い分けについて
good, bad（よい，悪い），difficult, easy（難しい，やさしい）などを述べるとき，次が「人」である場合，to よりも for を用いる。
△ This is difficult [easy] to me.
○ This is difficult [easy] / This is good [bad] } for me.
This is a good lesson for me.（＝to my benefit）
This is interesting to [for] me.
This sounds difficult to me
cf. This feels good to me. (for me とはしない）
服，靴，コートなどについて「よさそうだ」と思う，また車などに試乗して「これでいい」(This is what I want.) の意味でこの表現を使う。
温泉につかって，「いい気持ちだ」という場合は This feels good.

3. …に関しては

with; for

喫煙は彼らにとっては健康の問題になってしまった。
Smoking has become a health problem for [with] them.
何代も漁業にたずさわってきた沢田家にとって，漁業を生業とすることは当然のしきたりになっていた。
For generations they were fishermen. That has become a tradition for [with, in] the Sawada family.

とても・とっても

1. 大いに

quite; very　まあまあ，相当
really　ほんとに

awfully; terribly
utterly; absolutely } ものすごく
extremely

とても結構なごちそうだった。

It was quite a [a very] good dinner.

「お幸せですか」「とても幸せです」。

"Are you happy?" "(I'm) Very happy."

とってもおなかがすいた。

I'm awfully hungry. (1)

君，とってもすてきだよ。

You look absolutely stunning. (2)

音楽はすばらしかった。とってもよかったよ。

The music was heavenly. I enjoyed it immensely. (3)

〈注〉 (1)(2)(3)の3例の英文は強い表現。

2. どうしても…ない

certainly not; not at all; not possibly; hardly

とても我慢ができなかった。

I just couldn't stand it.

とても信じられない。

I cannot possibly believe it.

彼女はとても30代には見えない。

She hardly looks in her thirties.

彼はとても治る見込みはない。

There is no hope of his recovery.

His recovery is utterly hopeless.

僕はとても君には及ばない。

I'm certainly no match for you.

彼は事務能力でとても前任者の足元にも及ばない。

He is not { half so [at all as] / by any means as } efficient as his predecessor.

〈注〉 話し言葉としてはby any [no] means よりは肯定文なら certainly，否定文なら certainly not を使う方が安全。

となり（隣）

1. 隣・近所

隣の家 **a neighboring house; the house next door; adjacent houses;** 隣の人 **a (next-door) neighbor**

〈注〉 neighbor は隣の人のみならず，近所の人を指す。前後関係から明らかならば next-door は必要ない。

隣の子

the children (from) next door

the neighbor children

右隣の人

our right hand [side] neighbor

彼女は私の隣に住んでいる。

She lives next door (to me).

She lives next door on the right side.

私たちは隣同士です。

We live next door to each other.

彼は一軒おいて隣に住んでいる。

He lives { next door but one. / two doors away [up / down]. }

彼女は隣の家に入って行き，そこにいた婦人にスミスさんは引っ越されたのかと尋ねた。

She went next door and asked the woman there if Mr. Smith had moved out.

若い夫婦者が隣に越してきた。

A young couple moved into the next house [the house next door].

うわさ話が隣近所にぱっと広がった。

The rumor has gone all round my neighborhood.

2. 隣接

…の隣に[の] **next to; adjacent to; adjoining**

隣の建物[部屋] the next building [room]

隣の村 the neighboring village

私の家はバーチ通りの郵便局の隣です。

My house is next [next door] to the post office on Birch Street.

病院の隣に研究所が2棟あります。

There are two research institutes adjacent [next] to the hospital.

もうじき学校の隣に体育館ができます。

Soon a gym will be built adjoining the

school.
食堂の隣に居間があります。
Next to the dining room there is a living room.
うちの農場の隣の農場はグレッグさんの所有だ。
The farm next to ours is owned by Mr. Gregg.
彼は私の隣に座った。
He sat next to me.
私たちは隣り合せに[並んで]座った。
We sat next to each other [side by side].
夕食のとき，だれの隣に座った？
Who(m) did you sit next to at dinner?
隣に座ってもいいでしょうか。
May I sit down by you?

どなる（怒鳴る）・どなられる

cry loudly; shout; 大声でどやす **roar at; thunder at**
「だれだ！ そこにいるのは」。暗闇で男の声でどなりつけた。
"Who's there !" thundered a man's voice in the dark.
〈注〉 " "で人の発言を引用するとき，リズムの関係で上の例文のように主語と動詞の位置がしばしば逆になる。(cf. A man's voice thundered ...)
「僕だ，デイビッドだよ！」。僕がどなりかえした。
"It's me, David !" I shouted back.
「出て行け」。父が怒ってどなりつけた。
"Get out," roared my father in anger.
【どなられる】
いたずらをしては父にどなられたものだ。
My father used to scold me for doing mischief.
体育館で遊んでいたら「こんな所で遊んではいけない」とどなられた。
They shouted at us that we shouldn't be playing in the gym.
〈注〉 上の2例でわかるように，「どなられる」と日本語では受動態表現でも英語にすると能動態の文の方が普通。「しかる」の scold は他動詞であるから「しかられる」は I was scolded ... とすることはできるが，shout, roar, thunder は自動詞であるから受動態文がつくれない。
×I was shouted [roared, thundered]. は誤文。

どの・どれ → どちら・どこ，どんな

1．どの
〈注〉 「どれ」は代名詞であるが「どの」は形容詞であるから名詞と結合する。
どの人　which person; who
どの家　which house
どの辺
what part of the city（市の中のどのあたり）
どの程度　to what degree
どのように　how
どの点から見ても
from every point of view; in all respects
cf. to all appearances（どう見ても）
どの［どちらの］大学に行っておられますか。（この「どちら」は丁寧語）
Which [What] university do you go to?

2．どれ
which; what; who
どれでも
whichever; any; every
どれも…ない　none
〈注〉 日本語の指示語「こそあど」の「ど」と結合したもので「どれ，どの［どちら，どなた］」のように使う。それに対応する英語も前後関係により上に挙げたように多様である。which と what は前者が少数（2～4）の中からの選択，後者は多数の中からの選択という傾向であるが，かなりフレキシブルである。
どれ読んだの？（数冊の本を前にして）
Which book(s) did you read?
What book(s) did you read?
どれを取られてもきっとご満足いただけるでしょう。
No matter which you take / Whichever you (may) take } I'm sure you'll be satisfied.

〈注〉「…にしても」の「ても」の気持ちからか，次のような誤文を見かける。
×Even if which you will take …（“even if”は「たとえ…しても」でif節，仮定法であり，「もしA[B]をとったら，もしAもBもとったとしても」の場合に使われ，「AにしてもBにしても」という選択にはwhichever を使う。）

どれを取ってもいいですよ。
You may take any of them.
You may take whichever you like.

3．どのくらい

【距離】

どのくらい行かなければならないの？
How far do I have to go?

ロンドンからあなたの町までどのくらいありますか。
How far is it from London to your town?

【時間】

町までどのくらいかかりますか。
How long will it take to get to the town?

どのくらいしたら結果を知らせていただける？
How soon can you tell me the result?

【数】

本をどのくらい[何冊ぐらい]読んだ？
How many books have you read?

【量】

ケーキにはどのくらい粉がいるの？
How much flour do you need for the cake?

【金額】

お金はどのくらい入り用なのですか。
How much money do you need?

値段はどのくらいのところを考えているの？
What price range are you thinking of?

【程度・能力】

彼女はどのくらい英語が話せるのだろうか。
How well can she speak English?

【大きさ】

君んとこの犬はどのくらいの大きさ？
How big is your dog?

【背丈】

君の兄さんの身長はどのくらい？
How tall is your brother?

【重量】

荷物の重量はどのくらい？
How heavy is the luggage?

【深さ・長さ】

新トンネルの長さはどのくらい？
How long is the new tunnel?

この辺の湖の水深はどのくらい？
How deep is the lake here?

…とは・…なんて

1．定義・提題

【…とは】

〈注〉「人生とは…」「芸術とは…」などと主題を強調する言い方で，preaching tone（説教調）になる。

人生とはそんなものだ。
Such is life.
That’s life.

大学とはどんなものだと思いますか。
What do you think ‘university’ means?

大学時代とは勉学のための時であってアルバイトのためではないことぐらいよくわかっているはずだ。
You surely know that university time is a time for study and not for part-time jobs.

2．意外・驚き

【…とは，…なんて】

彼が亡くなったとはまだ思えない[なんて信じられない]。
I still can’t believe that he ⌊has died [is dead].

だれも彼が70歳とは思わないだろう。
No one would take him for seventy.

こんな所でお目にかかるとは思いませんでした。
I didn’t ⌊expect to [think I would] meet you here.

〈注〉I didn’t think to meet you here. は Hornby の『英語の型と正用法』に正用法として出ているが，think＋不定詞の使える例外的な例として出ているのであって，上記のような言い方の方が普通である。think のあとに不定詞は使えないと考える方がよい。

そんなことを信じるとはまったく愚かなことだ。

It's terribly foolish to believe a thing like that.

あなたが彼の息子さんだとは彼女が知るはずがないじゃないか。

How should she know that you are his son?

彼がこんなありがたい申し出を断るとは考えられない。

It's unlikely that he will refuse such a good offer.

彼女がすでにそのことを知っているとは不思議なことだ。

How strange that she knows [should know] it already.

〈注〉 It is strange [wonderful, unlikely] that ... の構文で should を使うのは英国でも古風とされ，米国ではすたれてしまったが，この How strange ... の文型ならば英国英語では should を使ってもよい。

まあ考えてみてくれよ，あいつが今度僕たちのボスになるなんて。

Just think of him being our new boss!

とぶ（飛ぶ，跳ぶ）・とばす

1. 空中，飛行，飛散

飛ぶ **fly; flutter;** うろうろ飛ぶ **hover;**（油や水しぶきが）**spatter**

飛ばす **fly;**（紙片などを）**scatter;**（水滴を）**splash**

高く[低く]飛ぶ fly high [low]

風が飛ばす

blow away《something》《somewhere》

風で紙が部屋中に飛ばされた[飛んだ]。

The wind was blowing papers all over the room.

Papers were being blown all over the room.

風で帽子が飛ばされた[飛んだ]。

The wind blew my hat away [off my head].

My hat was blown away by the wind.

窓が開いていたので紙片がそこらじゅうに飛ばされていた[飛び散っていた]。

The window was open and papers were scattered all over.

2. 地上，跳躍

jump（一般的）; **leap**（力をいれて）; **spring**（はねる）

《関連語》
スキップする，かすって飛ばす skip
片足でぴょんぴょん跳ぶ hop
はずむ，はずませる bounce
飛びつく pounce

彼女は跳び上がるように(さっと立って)電話をとった[食事の後片づけを手伝った]。

She jumped up to answer the phone [to help with the dishes].

水面をかすって石を飛ばすのは面白い。

It's fun to skip a stone across water.

3. 比喩的用法

急行する **hurry to, hasten to**（目的地へ向かって）; **drive very fast**

伝令を飛ばす

send a messenger

デマを飛ばす

start a false rumor（最初に言い出す）

spread a false rumor（皆に言いふらす）

【省略する】 skip; omit

飛ばし読みする

skim (through) a book（ほんのざっと目を通す）

flip through a book（ページをぱらぱらめくって目を通す）

第1章は飛ばして第2章から始めよう。

Let's skip [omit] the first chapter and begin with the second.

25ページから50ページまで飛ばします。

We'll skip from page 25 (over) to page 50.

4．種々の合成語

【跳び上がる】

うれしくて[痛くて]跳び上がった。

He jumped for joy [in pain].

【飛び立つ】

塔(の窓)から１羽の鳥が飛び立った。

A bird flew out of the turret.

飛行機が飛び立った[離陸した]。

The airplane [plane] has taken off.

【飛び起きる】

彼は飛び起きて窓を開けた。

He jumped [hopped] out of bed and opened the window.

彼はその音に飛び起きた［さっと立ち上がった］。

He sprang
He jumped
He started〔*literary*〕
} to his feet at the noise.

【飛び降りる】

泥棒は２階の窓[動いている列車]から飛び降りた。

The burglar leaped [jumped] out of a second story window [from a moving train].

その男の子は屋根から飛び降りたが骨折もしなかった。

The boy leaped down from the roof but did not break any bones.

〈注〉 leap は力を入れて「えいっ」と飛ぶこと。jump は一般的な語。

【飛びかかる】

警官は殺人犯に飛びかかった。

The policeman flung [threw] himself at the murderer.

けんかの仲裁に２人の間に割り込んでいったところ，突然そのうちの１人が彼に向かって飛びかかってきた。

He was trying to part the fighting boys when one of them turned on him.

【飛び越す】

女の子は流れを飛び越して走り続けた。

The girl leaped over the stream and ran on.

彼はネットを飛び越えて飛んできたボールを避けて後ろに跳びのいた。

He jumped aside to avoid the ball that came flying over the net.

【飛び出す，飛び出る】

run [rush, dash] out; jump [leap] out

小さな男の子がボールをとろうと，走って来た車の前に飛び出した。

A little boy ran out in front of an approaching car to get his ball.

その子の目はすごく大きくて，飛び出しているように見えた。

Her eyes were so large they seemed to protrude.

老人は木の根の飛び出た所につまずいた。

The old man stumbled on a projecting tree root.

【飛び散る】

つむじ風に木の葉が飛び散った。

The whirlwind sent the leaves flying.

事故現場にはガラスの破片が飛び散っていた。

There were fragments of broken glass
{ scattered about
all over [around]
everywhere }
at the scene of the accident.

【飛びつく】

私の犬は私が家に帰るといつも飛びついてくる。

My dog always jumps up on me when I come home.

魚がえさに飛びついた。

The fish snapped at the bait.

彼女はその提案に飛びついてきた。

She jumped [leaped] at the proposal.

【跳び乗る】

そのカウボーイは馬に跳び乗ると悪者の後を追いかけた。

The cowboy jumped on his horse and took off after the badman.

動き出した列車に跳び乗ろうとしてはいけません。

Don't try to jump onto [into] a moving

train.

【飛びはねる・跳びはねる】

私が料理すると油がすごく飛びはねる。

The oil spatters a lot when I cook.

車が通るたび歩道の人々に泥水が飛びはねた［車が…にはねをあげて走った］。

The cars ⌊sped by, splashing [splashed] muddy water on the people on the sidewalk.

子供たちは陽光を浴びて跳びはねて遊んだ。

Children romped about in the sun.

【飛びまわる・跳びまわる】

蜜蜂は花から花へ蜜を集めに飛びまわる。

Bees fly from flower to flower to gather nectar.

彼は今，金策に飛びまわっている。

He is now busy raising money.

子供たちはみんな運動場に出て跳びまわっている。

Children are out romping on the playground.

【その他】

学園祭には飛び入りの競技会がある。

There are free-for all contests at the school festival.

鳥は森の中に飛び去って行った。

The bird flew away into the forest.

その女の子はクラスで飛び抜けてよくできた［いい点をとった］。

That girl is a far better student than anyone else in her class.

That girl got by far the best marks in her class.

とまる（止まる）・とめる

1. 停止する

stop; hold up; draw up; pull up

驚いて彼は一瞬息を止めた。

He held his breath in astonishment.

私たちは暗がりでおしゃべりをしていた。停電していたので。

We were chatting in the dark because the power wasn't on.

地震のためガスも水道も止まってしまった。

The gas and water supply failed [stopped] because of the earthquake.

彼はガス代を払わなかったので止められてしまった。

His gas was {disconnected / turned off / cut off} because he didn't pay his bill.

料理中に電話が鳴ったら，まずガス（の栓）を止めてから電話に出るように。

If the telephone rings while you are cooking, switch [turn] off the gas before answering it.

眠る前にラジオをちゃんと止めなさいよ。

Be sure to switch [turn] off the radio before going to sleep.

【停車】

この列車は各駅に止まります。

This train stops at every station.

その車は玄関の前で止まった。

The car drew [pulled] up at the door.

【停滞】

名古屋・春日井間は事故のため2時間交通が止まっている。

The traffic between Nagoya and Kasugai has been ⌊tied up [stopped] for two hours because of an accident.

大雪のため新幹線が2時間近くも止まっている。

The Shinkansen has been stopped for nearly two hours because of the heavy snow.

【駐車・停車】

パトカーが銀行の前に止まっていた。

A patrol car was parked in front of the bank.

どこに車を止めたらいいだろう。

Where can I park?

Where shall we park?

車を止める場所がこのあたりにはない。

There's no parking place around here.
There's nowhere to park.
彼は(手を上げて)タクシーを止めた。
He hailed a taxi.
警官は手を上げてトラックを止めた。
The policeman raised his hand and stopped the truck.
その女の人は急にブレーキをかけて車を止めた。
The woman braked suddenly.
【流動物】
この流れを止めてダムを作る計画がある。
They are planning to dam this stream [make a dam].
大きな岩が川の中に転げ落ちて流れを止めてしまった。
A boulder rolled down into the stream and obstructed the current.
まず出血を止める。これが救急の第一歩。
To stop bleeding is the first rule of first aid.
出血が止まった。
It has stopped bleeding.
涙が止まらなかった。
I couldn't keep [hold] back my tears.

2. 固定する

彼は好きなスターの実物大写真を壁にピンで止めた。
He pinned up a life-size picture of his favorite star on the wall.
cf. a pinup (girl) ピンナップ(ガール)
そんな小さな背中のボタンをどうやって止められるのか，(私には)想像もつかない。
I can't imagine how you can fasten those tiny buttons in the back.
この服は背中でチャックで止めるの。
This dress zips (up) at the back.
This dress has a back zipper.
〈注〉 日本語ではチャックとかファスナーと呼ぶが，英語では zipper である。動詞は zip。
この釘は短すぎて打っても板が止まらない。
These nails are too short to hold the board in place [firmly].
【着地】
小鳥が１羽私の窓の真ん前の小枝に止まった。
A bird { settled / perched / alit [alighted] 〔*literary*〕 } on a twig right in front of my window.

3. 抑制する，制止する

男の子２人が道路でけんかをしていたので，僕は中に入って止めようとした。
Two boys were fighting on the road, and so I tried to part [stop] them.
レフェリーが試合を止めた。一方のボクサーがもう何回も頭を打たれていたので。
The referee stopped the match because one of the boxers had already been hit repeatedly on the head.
長いことお引き止めしてすみませんでした。
I'm sorry to have kept you so long.
【禁止する】 forbid; prohibit 〔*formal*〕
医者にたばこを止められている。
The doctor told me not to smoke.
彼は息子が回復するまで息子の外出を止めた。
He told his son not [forbade his son] to go out before he recovered.
私は止めようとしたのだが，彼女は家を出てしまった。結婚たった１か月で。
I tried to { stop her, / persuade her otherwise [not to], } but she left him one month after marrying him.
【留意】
考えてから物を言うべきでした。このことはこれからいつも心に留めておきます。
I should have thought before I spoke. I'll always remember this lesson.
【鎮静】
腰の痛みが止まった。

The pain in my back has [is] gone.
薬が効いてきて痛みが止まった。

The drug began to work and {stopped / took away / alleviated} the pain.

とまる（泊まる）・とめる

泊まる **stop; stay at** [**in**]《a place》**with**《a person》; **lodge**（**in** [**with**]）; **put up at**《an inn》; **stay overnight; pass** [**spend**] **the night**

私たちはグランドホテルに泊まっています。

We are staying at the Grand Hotel.

お客が3人泊まっています。

We have three guests staying with us.

そこはたぶん泊まるところがありません。

You probably can't find a place there to stay.

【泊める】put up《a person》《at a hotel》

ジョイスのアパートは狭すぎて君を泊められないが，ケイトがもしよければ泊めてあげてもよいと言っている。

Joyce's apartment is too small to put you up there, but Kate is willing to let you stay with her, if you like.

彼女はお客を大勢呼びすぎて数人は町の旅館に泊まってもらわなければならなかった。

She asked too many people to stay and had to lodge some in the town.

ともかせぎ（共稼ぎ）

〈注〉「共稼ぎ」にあたる特別の語はないので，その人の立場から状況を説明すればよい。（ ）内は発言者。

あの夫婦は共稼ぎだ。（第三者）

The couple are both working.

うちの親は共稼ぎだ。（子供）

Both my parents⌊are working [work].

うちは共稼ぎです。（当人）

My wife⌊works [has a job].（夫）

I⌊work [have a job].（妻）

ともだち（友達）

a friend

a pal〔*informal*〕; 文通友達 **a pen pal**

〈注〉友達とは，学校の同級生などでたいして親しくなかった者も含めるが，friend は友情で結ばれた仲，また「敵」に対して「味方」を意味することもある。友達と friend では 意味に多少のずれがある。pal は通常男同士の仲よし。

仲のよい友達

a close friend; a good friend

〈注〉an intimate friend は米国では肉体関係のある仲を思わせる。避ける方が無難。

クラスの友達　a classmate

幼なじみ

a childhood friend [playmate]

a friend of [from] my childhood〔*literary*〕

僕らは友達だ。

We are friends.

これは僕の友達のジョンです。

This is my friend John.

僕は図書館へ行って偶然高校（時代）の友達に会った。

I went to the library and there I happened to see {a friend I had / a person I knew} in high school.

佐藤と僕は高校のときの友達[同級生]だ。

Sato and I were {⌊in the same class [classmates] in high school. / high school classmates.}

「あの人知っているの？」「ええ，学校時代の友達[同級生]なんです」。

"Do you know her?" "Why, she and I were ⌊at school together [classmates]."

高校の友達から手紙をもらった。

I got a letter from a high school⌊friend [classmate].

〈注〉a friend of my high school days は正しいが，上の例文の言い方がより自然である。

【友達になる】

あの子たちと友達になりたい。

I'd like to make friends with those kids.

あのご夫婦とお友達になりたい。

I'd like to become friends with that couple.

〈注〉 make friends with は子供について使う。旅先で知り合いになってすぐ別れた程度であれば meet people でよい。

まず meet して気に入れば友達になりたいと思うようになる。例えば今夜パーティに行くが,「誰か友達になれそうな人に会えるかも」は Maybe I'll meet someone that I can become friends with.

旅をして各地から来たたくさんの人々と友達になれたことがこの夏の一番の思い出だ。

Meeting a lot of people from many parts of the country
{ is one of my best memories of the summer.
{ was the best thing about the summer.

《「私の友達」の言い方と意味》

(1) my friend

「ただ一人の友」の含み,または「私の味方」。

(2) a friend of mine

不特定の一友人。ほかにも友達がいる含み。

(3) one of my friends

ある一友人。ほかにも友達がいる含み。

(2)(3)は人によって使い分けが違うようだが,だいたい同じと考えてよい。

《友達・仲間のいろいろ》

Do you know Pat? (パットを知っているかい)に対する答えは,(1)から(7)にいくほど親密な関係を表している。

(1) No, I'm afraid I don't.
(いやあ,ちょっと知らないね)

(2) Well, I've heard the name.
(そうね,名前は聞いたことがあるね)

(3) Yes [Well], I recognize [know] his face.
I know him when I see him.
(うん,顔ぐらい知ってるよ。会えばわかるよ)

(4) Yes, I do. / Yes, we've met. / Yes, we're acquainted. / Yes, a bit.
(うん,知ってるよ。会ったことがある)

(5) Yes, we're on rather friendly terms.
(かなり親しい仲)
Yes, we get together sometimes.
Yes, pretty well.
} (時に会っている)

〈注〉 be on friendly terms は普通より親しい。たとえば親しそうに見えない,ライバル同士の2人が何となくウマが合っているなど。

(4)(5)は,たとえば Yes, we work in the same company. のような関係に適用できる。

(6) Why, yes, we're friends. / Why, yes, we're really good friends.
(いやあ,とても親しい友達さ)

たとえば Yes, we're jogging friends [cooking pals / colleagues]. (ジョギング友達[料理仲間/職場の同僚])

(7) Oh, we're close [best] friends.
(いやあ,親友なんだよ)

【その他の知人】

acquaintance; someone I know　知人
co-worker; officemate　職場仲間
colleague　同僚; 特に知的職業の同僚
my father's friend (特定)
one of my father's friends (不特定)
} 父の友人

〈注〉 be friendly は人の性格について「人なつっこい,親切な」の意味で,友達であることではない。

とり(鳥)

a bird; 家禽 **poultry;** ニワトリ **a chicken, a fowl;** めんどり **a hen;** おんどり **a cock; a rooster** 〔米〕

《関連語》

アヒル duck / ウグイス bush warbler / ウズラ quail / エミュー emu / オウム parrot / カササギ magpie / カッコウ cuckoo / カモ wild duck / カモメ sea-gull / カラス crow / カワセミ kingfisher / ガチョウ goose (*pl.* geese) / カナリア canary / キジ pheasant / キウイ kiwi (bird) / キツツキ woodpecker / キュウカンチョウ myna(h), mina(h), myna bird / コウノトリ stork / コマドリ robin / コンドル condor / サギ heron (シラサギは egret) / シギ snipe / シチメンチョウ turkey / スズメ sparrow / タカ hawk / ダチョウ ostrich / ツグミ thrush / ツバメ swallow / ツル crane / トビ kite /

ハクチョウ swan / ハゲタカ vulture / ハチドリ humming bird / ハト pigeon; (小形) dove / ヒバリ lark / ヒワ finch / フクロウ barn owl / フラミンゴ flamingo / ブンチョウ paddybird / ペリカン pelican / ペンギン penguin / ミミズク horned (eared) owl / ムクドリ starling / ヤマウズラ partridge / ヨルウグイス nightingale / ライチョウ grouse / ワシ eagle

とる(取る, 捕る, 採る, 摂る, 執る, 撮る)

1. 手に取る

take; seize; hold; take hold of; 手をのばして取る **reach;** 渡す **pass, hand;** 取ってくる **fetch;** 手に入れる **get**

彼はその写真を手に取ってしばらくじっと見ていた。

He took the picture in his hand and looked at it for some time.

彼女は私の手を取って泣いて喜んだ。

She {took [held] me by the hand / held my hand} and wept for joy.

テーブルの上の新聞を取ってくださいませんか。

Could you give [pass] me the newspaper on the table?

塩を取ってくださいませんか。

Pass me the salt, please.

その犬はボールを取ってくるよう飼い主に訓練されている。

The dog is trained to fetch balls for its master.

〈注〉 fetch は英国では人間にも使うが, 米国では主として犬に使う。

彼は駅に荷物を取りに行ってきたところだ。

He has been to the station to get his luggage.

2. 収穫する, 採取する

【収穫】

この地方では最高級の米がとれる。

The best quality rice is produced [grown] in this part of the country.

今年はたくさん米がとれた。

The rice harvest this year was very good.

この旅館ではこの湖でとれた魚を食べさせてくれる。

This inn serves fish caught in this lake.

この湖ではいろいろな種類の魚がとれる。

This lake yields various kinds of fish.

We can get various kinds of fish from this lake.

【採取】

ライチョウ[高山植物]をとることは法律で禁じられている。

It is prohibited by law to {catch snow grouse. / pick [take] alpine plants.}

子供たちはうんと早起きして森にカブトムシ[薬草]をとりに行った。

The children got up very early and went to {catch bugs / pick herbs} in the woods.

3. 得る, もらう

get; obtain

【賞】

歌唱コンテストで彼が1等賞を取った。

He got [won] (the) first prize in the singing contest.

彼は賞を取れなかった。

He couldn't win a prize.

〈注〉 作品を主語にしてもよい。
ex. His work didn't win a prize.

【点】

私は前学期はいい評点[ひどい点]を取った。

I got good [poor] grades [marks] last semester.

いくらがんばっても満点は取れない。

I can't get full marks no matter how [however 〔英〕] hard I try.

【学位】

彼は修士号を取るために勉強をしている。

He is studying [working] for an MA degree.

彼は去る５月に修士号を取った。

He got his MA degree last May.

【免許】

彼女は先週運転免許を取った。

She got [took] her driver's license last week.

やっと彼は税理士の免許が取れた。

He at last succeeded in getting a tax accountant's license.

He was licensed at last as a tax accountant.

【単位】

彼は１年生のとき46単位を取った。

He took more than 46 credits during his freshman year.

【給料】

新しい職場では彼は月給をいくら取っているんだ？

How much does he make [get] a month in this new job? (1)

彼は月給を30万円取っている。

He gets [draws] a salary of 300,000 yen.
He gets [makes] 300,000 a month.
His salary is 300,000. (2)

〈注〉 (2) が上の問い (1) の返答であれば，He gets も a month も不要。金額だけ言うのが普通。日本語でも英語でも会話の進め方は同じ。

【賄賂】

彼は賄賂を受け取った嫌疑をかけられた。

He was suspected of taking [accepting] a bribe.

4．採用する

take; admit; 雇用する **employ;**（方法を）**adopt;**（態度を）**assume**

【人員】

800人の応募者中たった40人しかとらなかった。

They accepted [admitted, took] only 40 out of 800 applicants.

今年は昨年よりも大卒を大勢とるだろう。

The companies will employ [take] more college graduates this year.

【方法】

彼らは新方式をとることに決定した。

They decided to adopt the new method.

我々はもっと強硬な手段をとらなければならない。

We must take stronger measures.

〈注〉 手段を「とる」の意味の resort to は「最後の手段」の含みのあるときに使われる。

【態度】

何か話そうとすると，私が何も言わないうちからお前はもう「いや」という態度をとる。

(Even) Before I tell you what it is, you take the attitude that you won't like it.

お金の話をしようとするといつもお前は聞きたくないという態度をとる。

Whenever I want to discuss money, you assume a hurt attitude.

5．選択する

take; choose

欲ばりばあさんは大きな箱を取った。

The greedy old woman took [chose] the bigger casket.

フランス語もドイツ語もスペイン語もみな選択科目です。どれを取りますか。

French, German, and Spanish are all elective subjects. Which are you going to choose [take]?

私は富よりも精神の自由をとる。

I would {take freedom of mind over / prefer freedom of mind to} wealth.

6．料金・罰金など

charge; ask

【月謝】

彼は１回のレッスンで１万円とる。

He charges 10,000 yen for each [one] lesson.

【料金・家賃】

駐車場使用料に１か月１万円とる。

They charge 10,000 yen a month for parking.

The parking charge [fee] is 10,000 yen a month.

アパート代に1か月8万円とられます。

I have to pay 80,000 yen a month for the apartment.

【罰金】

彼はスピード違反で4万円の罰金をとられた。

He was fined 40,000 yen for speeding.

7. 奪う

take away from《a person》

steal; rob [**deprive**]《a person》**of**《a thing》

ジムは子供(の手)からナイフを取り上げた。

Jim took the knife (away) from the little boy [out of the little boy's hands].

【盗難】

昨夜2人組の強盗が銀行に押し入り，1000万円を取った[強奪した]。

Last night two burglars broke into the bank and took [stole] 10,000,000 yen.

Ten million yen was stolen from the bank during the night.

彼はへそくりをだまし取られた。

He was cheated out of his private savings.

彼女は自転車に乗った少年にハンドバッグを取られた。

A boy on a bicycle snatched (away) her purse.

She got [had] her purse snatched by a boy.

【占領】

城をとる　take a castle

領土をとる　annex a territory

アレクサンダー大王は近隣の国を次々ととっていった[征服した]。

Alexander the Great conquered neighboring countries.

8. 除去する

remove; take away

彼女は庭の草を取って[草取りをして]います。

She is weeding (in) the garden.

彼は帽子を取って挨拶した。

He took off his hat in salute.

コートのボタンが一つ取れた。

A button has come off the coat.

あなたのコートのボタンが一つ取れていますよ。

A button on your coat is missing.

There's a button off your coat.

君は扁桃腺を取ってもらわ[取ら]なければならない。

You'll have to have your tonsils taken out [removed].

このしみは洗えば取れるかしら。

Will this stain wash out?

宿題をやっておしまい，あなたの分のお菓子はとってあるからね。

Finish your homework and then you can have the cake I've saved [put aside] for you.

この3語を取りなさい，くどいから。(文章の手直し)

Take out [Delete] these three words. It's too wordy.

〈注〉 校正の「トル」は dele (delete の略)を使う。

9. 食べる，摂取する

【食べる】

あの人たちはいつも8時に朝食をとる。

They always have [regularly take] breakfast at eight.

【栄養】

彼は野菜も十分とるよう気をつけている。

He is careful to eat [take] enough vegetables.

あの子は栄養のとりすぎだ。

The child is overfed.

cf. underfed; undernourished 栄養不良の。

10. 予約する，購読する，確保する

take; 予約購読する **subscribe;** 予約する **reserve, book**

【新聞】
うちは「朝日イブニング・ニュース」をとっています。

We take *The Asahi Evening News*.

我々は「ポエトリ」誌をとっている。

We subscribe to *Poetry*.

〈注〉 subscribe とは sub=under と scribe=write から成る語で，寄付をするとか雑誌購読の際に予約のサインをすることである。学会誌などは会費を払った会員に送ってくるので予約購読とは言わない。

【切符】
7時半の新幹線の座席を3つとりました。

I've reserved [booked] three seats for the 7:30 Shinkansen.

【ホテル】
次の月曜日と火曜日の分のシングルを2部屋(ずつ)とりたかった。

I wanted to reserve two single rooms for next Monday and Tuesday.

【注文】
うちではいつも初寿司からお寿司をとる。

We usually get [order] sushi from Hatsuzushi.

They had sushi delivered from Hatsuzushi.(寿司の出前を頼んだ)

They placed a take-out order at Hatsuzushi.(注文して受け取りに行く)

〈注〉 日本語で「とる」と言うのは「配達してもらう」(be delivered)の意味を含む。注文して受け取りに行くのは pick up という。英語の take out は「持ち帰り」のこと。なおホテルで食事を部屋に運んでもらうのは room service。パーティーなどの食事を請け負ってまかなうのは cater と言う。

今どき，じっと座って待っていても仕事は来やしない。彼は今注文取りにまわっているよ。

Nowadays you can't just sit and wait for business to come in. He's now out getting [taking, collecting] orders.

【車間距離】
必ず車間距離を十分とりなさい。

Be sure to keep [maintain] a proper distance between cars when driving.

11. 要する

【時間】
現金をおろすだけなら時間はとりません。

It won't take much time just to draw (out) some cash.

時間はとりません，すぐです。

I'll not be long.

正式の手続きをすますのに彼はさんざん時間と手間をとられた。

It took much time and labor on his part to get through the formalities.

【場所】
駐車場が家の建物本体と同じくらい場所をとった。

The parking lot took up [covered] as much space as the building itself.

今度の新しいコンピュータは場所をとりません。

Our new computer system won't require much space.

12. 執務する

【事務】
彼は8時に出勤し，机に向かい正午まで事務をとる。

He appears at 8, sits down at his desk, and works until noon.

彼は毎朝2時間事務をとり，そのあとはもっぱら研究に没頭する。

He attends to routine business every morning for two hours and then spends the rest of the day on his research.

〈注〉 attend to business は 執務すること。
cf. get down to business 仕事を始める

【労】
彼女はその恵まれない少女に食べさせ，着る物を与え，さらに適当な仕事をさがす労までもとった。

She gave the poor girl food and clothing and even took the trouble to find her a suitable job.

13. 写真・記録

【写真】

彼は自分の花嫁の写真を何枚も何枚も撮った。

He took many pictures of his bride.

この写真はよく撮れている。

This photograph { has come out fine. / is a good one. }

【テープ】

私はそのスピーチをテープ［ビデオ］にとった。

I recorded the speech on audio tape [video (tape)].

【記録を】

広津氏はその裁判について詳細な記録をとった。

Mr. Hirotsu kept a detailed record of the trial.

【コピー】

この書類のコピーをとってもいいでしょうか。

May I make copies of [xerox] these papers?

14. 理解する

take; understand

【解釈】

彼らの不平は非難ともとれる。

Their complaint could be taken as a reprimand.

この文章はいろいろな意味にとれる。

This passage can be interpreted in various ways.

彼女はだれの言うことでも善意にとる。

She takes everybody's words kindly.

彼女は彼に偏見をもっていて，彼の言うことは何でも悪くとる。

She is prejudiced against him, so anything he says she will take unkindly.

彼女は行間の意味をよく読み取る。

She understands what is written between the lines very well.

彼は裏の意味まですぐ感じ取る。

He is very sensitive to hidden meanings.

どれ → どの・どれ

どろ（泥）→ つち

mud; mire; 雪どけのどろどろ **slush**

トラックが泥をはねかけた。

A truck splashed mud on her.

橋の近くで車が泥にはまって1時間も動かなかった。

Our car was bogged down [mired] for an hour near the bridge.

車を泥から引きずり出すのに1時間もかかった。

It took an hour to dig our car out from the mud [mire].

地すべりで4軒の民家が1メートルもの泥［土砂］に埋まった。

The landslide left four houses engulfed [buried] in a meter of mire [mire a meter deep].

〈注〉「洪水で泥やごみがあたり一面に散らかった」様子は次のように言えばよい。
The flood left muck and debris everywhere.

【泥遊び】

play in the mud; play with clay （粘土細工をすること）

その子は泥んこ［泥だらけ］になって帰って来た。

The boy came home muddy all over [covered with mud].

泥まんじゅうをつくる　make mud pies

【泥を塗る】

お前はお父様の顔に泥を塗った。

You have disgraced your father.

お前は家名に泥を塗った。

You have brought disgrace to [upon] your family.

You have disgraced { your family. / your family name. }

（よほどの名家の場合は name をつけてよい）

どんな → どの・どれ

1. どのような

それはどんなところ？

What kind [sort] of place is it?

それはどんなもの？

What is it like?

彼女はどんな人？

［外見］ What does she look like?

［人柄］ What kind [sort] of person is she?

What is she like?

どんな人［こと］でも

anybody, anything

どんな人［こと］でも…ない

nobody, nothing

あなたのためならどんなことでもします。

I would do anything for you.

I will do everything in my power.

2. たとえ

どんな子供でもそんなことならできる。

Any child can do that.

どんな小さな子でもそれぐらい知っている。

The smallest child knows that.

どんなことがあっても取り乱さないように。

No matter what happens, / Whatever happens [may happen 〔英〕], don't be upset.

ついに結婚することができて二人はどんなに喜んでいることでしょうか。

How happy they must be to be married at last! / finally to be married!

孫の大学卒業を見ることができてどんなにうれしいことでしょう。

How happy they must be to see their grandchild graduate!

どんなに疲れていても宿題はちゃんとしなければだめだ。

However [No matter how] tired you are, you must do your homework.

あなたにはどんなにお礼を言っても言い足りません。

I can't thank you enough.

な

ない（無い）

1．打ち消し（…でない，…しない）

【動詞の打ち消し】

not; don't ...; isn't ...; never

彼女は私の妹ではない。

She isn't my sister.

私は彼女を知らない。

I don't know her.

私は彼女に会ったことがない。

I never met her.

【名詞・代名詞の打ち消し】

no ～; nobody; no one; nothing; nowhere

2．存在しない

水差しに水がなかった。

There was no water in the jug.

あとに何も残っていなかった。

Nothing was left behind.

この辺には学校がない。

There is no school around here.

この植物はこの地方にはない。

This plant {doesn't grow / isn't found} in this part of the country.

×There is not this plant in ...

彼の学校はこの近所ではない。

His school is not in this neighborhood.

3．所有しない

彼はお金がない。

He doesn't have any money.

He hasn't got any money.

He has no money {with him.（所持金がない） / for that.（それを買う金がない）}〔*rather formal*〕

He's poor.（一般の状況）

私はやることがない。

I have nothing to do.

心配事がない。

He has nothing to worry about.

4．欠乏

あの子は常識がない。

She has no [lacks] common sense.

あの子はユーモアのセンスがない。

She {has no sense of humor. / lacks a sense of humor.}

彼は熱意がない。

He isn't earnest [serious] enough.

〈注〉「欠けている」の意味の want, lack [be wanting, be lacking] は堅い表現なので，不自然な文になりやすいため注意が必要。

彼はカリキュラム改正に熱意がない。

He isn't enthusiastic about curriculum reform.

彼は本気でない［いいかげんにやっている］。

He's（only）half-hearted.

5．尽きる

ガソリンがない。

I've run out of gas〔米〕[petrol〔英〕].

金がない。

I'm broke. / I'm hard up for money.

新しいホテルはお金がなくて中途で建築中止になった。

The new hotel wasn't finished because they ran out of money.

〈注〉「資金不足で」for lack of money という言い方は堅いので，上のように because ... と節で説明を加える方がよい。

6．紛失

あれっ，財布がない！　どこを探してもない。

Oh no, my purse is gone! I cannot find it anywhere.

気がついたら包みがない。

I found that {I didn't have my parcel. / my parcel was missing.}

7. なくても，なしでも，なしでは
私はめがねなしで(も)新聞が読める。
I don't need glasses to read newspapers.
私はめがねなしでは新聞が読めない。
I can't read newspapers without glasses.
彼は地図がなくてもどこにでも間違わずに行ける。
He can find his way anywhere without a map.

8. …なくなる →なる 5. 否定形への変化

なおす（治す，直す）・なおる

1. 治療する，回復する
［治す動他］治療する **cure;**（人・傷を）**heal**
［治る動自］治癒する **be cured; heal;** 回復する **get well; recover**

【病気・けがを治す】
スミス先生が息子のぜんそくを治してくださった。
Doctor Smith cured {our son's asthma. / our son of his asthma.}
新学期が始まる前にかぜを治しておかなければならない。
I must get over my cold before the new term begins.
〈注〉 get over はちょっとした病気から「回復する」の意味に使える表現。
彼は結婚する前に歯を治しておきたいと思っている。
He wants to have [get] his teeth fixed before he gets married.

【病気・けがが治る】
今では息子は慢性のぜんそくが治った。
Now our son is cured of his chronic asthma.
切傷はすぐ治った。
The cut healed quickly.
頭痛が治りました。
The headache is gone.
彼女は手術をしたがもう治りました。
She has recovered from the surgery.
すぐ治ります。
It'll be better soon.（けがの場合）
You'll get well soon.（病気の場合）
〈注〉 「すぐ治る」という客観的判断にも使えるし，励ますような調子で言えば「元気づけ」になる。
私は一度かぜをひくと何週間も治らないんだ。
When I catch cold, it hangs on [lasts] for weeks.
骨は順調に治っています。
The bone is mending [healing] nicely.

《類義語》
be cured 医者の治療で病気が治る。
be healed （その人の）治癒力により，傷 wounds, 切傷 cuts, すり傷 bruises, ねんざ sprains, 骨折 broken bones が治る［治った状態］。heal自 も傷などが「治る」という場合に使われる。たとえば吹出物 rash, にきび pimples などが be cured（すっかり治る）は The skin healed.

2. 修理する
直す **repair; set [put] right; fix**〔米〕; **mend**（〔米〕布などを繕う，〔英〕修繕する）
昨夜はひどく雨もりがしたので，彼は今屋根を直しています。
He is repairing [fixing] the roof because it leaked badly last night.
僕の自転車を直してもらえますか。
Can you repair [fix] my bicycle?
この古い型のテレビはちょっと直りません。部品がもうないんです。
This old type of TV set can't be repaired because we don't have any spare parts any longer.
時計を直さなければならない。
I have to have [get] my watch repaired.
This [My] watch has to be repaired.
（時計屋で）This watch needs repairing.

3. 修正する，訂正する，矯正する

【服】

彼女は自分の古着を直して子供の遊び着を作る。

She makes playclothes for her children out of her old clothes.

〈注〉 古い服を縫い直すことを日本ではリフォームと言うが，英語の reform は criminals, sinners（犯罪者）や薬物・アルコール依存症患者などを立ち直らせることを意味する。また機構改革は structural reform。

【誤り】

誤りがあれば直しなさい。

Correct the errors if any.

私は2，3日でその答案(の誤り)を直さなければならない。

I have to correct those papers in a few days.

【癖】

悪い癖[習慣]を直すのは容易ではない。

It is hard to {break / get rid of} bad habits.

【性質】

人の性質は直らない。

One's nature cannot be helped.

One [You / We] cannot change one's [your / our] nature.

4. 翻訳する，変換する

【翻訳】

ここの部分をフランス語に直していただけませんか。

Will you translate [put] these paragraphs into French?

【換算】

１ポンドをグラムに直すとどれだけになりますか。

How many grams are there in a pound?

円をドルに直す

change [convert] yen to dollars

１マイルをキロに直すと約1.6キロメートルです。

One mile is about 1.6 kilometers.

5. 元へ戻す，調整する

【機嫌】

彼女はすぐ機嫌を直すだろう。

She'll soon be in a good mood again.

それで彼女は機嫌が直った。

That put her back into [in] a good mood.

【服装・身じたく】

服がしわになったり曲ったりしているのを直してきちんとしなさい。

Straighten up your clothes to make yourself look nice

コート[ドレス / カラー / ネクタイ]を直す

{straighten (out) / smooth（しわを伸ばす）} a coat [a dress / a collar / a tie]

ベルトを直す

tighten a belt

髪を直す

comb [brush] one's hair

化粧を直す

touch up one's makeup

〈注〉◆「身づくろいをする」tidy [clean]（oneself）up とは洗顔・歯みがき・調髪（wash one's face; brush one's teeth; fix one's hair）などすべてを含む意味で，着替え(change to nicer clothes)を含むこともある。

◆You straighten out.（＝Behave yourself.）は「(いい加減に)しゃんとしなさい[きちんとしなさい]」としかるときに使う。

なか（中）→ うち（内）

1. 内部・内側

in; inside

【家】

きのうは一日中家の中にいた。

Yesterday I stayed indoors all day.

家の中に入ったとき変なにおいに気づいた。

When I entered the house, I noticed a strange smell.

私は部屋の中を見回した。

I looked around the room.

家自体は古かったが中はすべてきちんときれいにしてあった。

The house itself was old but everything was neat and clean inside.

中に入れて。

Let me in, please.

【中身】

なにがこの瓶の中に入っているの？

What does this bottle contain?

What's in this box?（箱の中）

中はなに？

What's inside?

この包みの中身は危険物かもしれない。

The contents of this package may be dangerous.

2. 範囲

彼は大勢の応募者の中から選ばれた。

He was selected from among many applicants.

この中からどれでも三つ取りなさい。

Choose any three of [from among] these.

人込みの中に小さな子供がいた。

There was a small child in [amid] the crowd.

乗客の中には子供もまじっていた。

There were some children among the passengers.

〈注〉 among, in は間にまじって全体として一つのまとまり（unity, integrated group）と感じられ，amid〔*literary*〕はその中にあるものが孤立している感じが強い。また，amid は confusion のような抽象名詞とともに用いることができる。「3.最中」参照。

バスは森の中を通り抜けた。

The bus went through the woods.

3. 最中

in; amid

混乱[貧乏 / 喜び]の真っただ中

amid confusion [poverty / joy]

彼女は雨の中を出て行った。

She went out in the rain.

嵐の真っただ中にトラックが着いた。

The truck arrived in the middle of a storm.

4. 慣用表現

（対立する意見があり）我々はその中を取った。（折衷案で合意した）

We agreed upon a compromise.

We compromised.

ながす（流す）・ながれる

1. 水・液体が移動する

流す　㊍㊩ **let（water）flow [run] out; pour; drop;** 排水する **drain;** 涙[血]を流す **shed**《tears / blood》

流れる　㊍㊠　速く流れる　**stream; flow; run;** チョロチョロ流れる　**trickle**

【流す】

時には台所の排水管を水を流して洗いなさい。

Flush the kitchen drain once in a while.

下水がよく流れない[詰った]。

The drain { isn't draining. / is clogged. }

〈注〉「下水が流れる」と言うが，drains は「下水の溝」のこと。

【流れる】

テムズ川はロンドンの市中を流れている。

The Thames runs [flows] through the city of London.

水が流れている。水道の栓を止めて。

The water is running. Turn off the tap [faucet].

涙が頬を流れた。

Tears streamed [ran] down her cheeks.

【流される】

従兄と泳いでいるうちに私はずっと沖合まで潮に流された。

While I was swimming with my cousin, the current carried [pulled] me far from the shore.

【流れを止める】

流木が流れを止め，水がよどんでいた[よく流れない状態だった]。

Driftwood blocked the flow. The water

pooled behind it.

2. 浮遊する

float; drift

大きな桃が川に浮んで流れてきた。

A large peach came floating down the stream.

雲の流れが速いからきっと嵐がやって来る。

See how fast the clouds are moving. That means a storm is coming.

The swift movement of the clouds tells us that a storm is coming.

昔は木材を川に流して運んだものだ。

In former days they floated timber down the river.

3. 流失する

昨年，洪水で橋が流された。

The bridge was carried [washed] away by the flood last year.

洪水で多くの家屋や家畜が流された。

The flood washed away many houses and drowned a lot of cattle.

4. 汚れを水で落す

体を流しておいで。

Have [Take] a shower.

Have a wash.〔英 *colloq.*〕

《「洗い流す」の類義語》

wash up　皿洗いをする，または顔・手・足・腕・首などを洗う。

take a sponge bath; give oneself **a sponge bath**〔米〕スポンジに石鹼をつけて洗う。「赤ちゃんを洗ってやる」は give a sponge bath to a baby〔米〕。

wash off under a tap　(戸外で)水道の蛇口の下で洗い流す。

rinse off under the shower　プールや海水につかった後にシャワーで消毒剤・塩分を洗い落す。また米国ではプールから出る時に水虫 (athlete's foot) の予防のためきれいな水の foot bath を通って出る。

〈注〉 公衆浴場で他人と一緒に入浴する習慣が欧米にはないので「人の背中を流す」という英語はない。

5. 転義

【時】

時が流れる。

Time passes swiftly.

【音】

通りを歩いているとどこからともなくショパンのピアノ曲が流れてきた。

As I was walking down the street, the sound of Chopin's piano music came floating from somewhere.

【うわさ】

あの人たちはどうも別れるらしいといううわさが流れている。

There's a rumour / A rumour is circulating } that they're going to divorce.

大きな政策の変更があるらしいといううわさが流れている。

Rumors about a big policy change have been circulating.

だれが最初にうわさを流したのかだれも知らない。

Who first started the rumor no one knows.

【流し】

このあたりは流しのタクシーがたくさんいますからすぐつかまります。

Taxis cruise (the street) / There are a lot of taxis } in this area, so it's easy to get one.

その流しのバイオリン弾きは家から家へと流しながら遠く旅をし，ついにローマに流れついた。

The fiddler traveled far and wide singing and playing from door to door and finally drifted to Rome.

【流罪】

僧俊寛は鬼界ヶ島に流された。

The priest Shunkan was exiled to Kikaiga-shima.

【質流れ】forfeit; be forfeited

質屋の利息を払わないと質草が流れてしまう。

If you don't pay the pawnbroker's interest, the article in pawn will be forfeited [is forfeited].

【中止になる】be called off

今日の試合は雨で流れた。

Today's match was called off because of rain.

人々の協力を得られそうになかったので，その計画は流れてしまった。

We had to give up the plan because we realized few people would cooperate.

〈注〉 call off は上の文のように be called off として使われるが，give up の受身形 be given up はあまり使われない。

【流れ作業】assembly line

あの機械は流れ作業で生産している。

Those machines are produced on an assembly line.

【感情に流される】

一時的な感情に流されて結婚を決めてはいけないよ。

Don't decide to marry in a fit of passion.

【水に流す】

過ぎたことは水に流そう。

Let's let bygones be bygones.

なかま（仲間）

1. 集団・グループ

company; a group

【仲間に入る［なる・入れる］】

彼はやって来て僕らの仲間に入った。

He came in and joined us.

僕らは転校してきた男の子を呼んでゲームの仲間に入れてやった。

We invited the new boy to {join us / take part} in the game.

兄は僕を仲間に入れたくなかったのだが，ほかの年上の人たちが僕の肩を持ってくれて，ついに僕は「タイガース」の仲間に入れてもらえた。

Although my brother didn't want to let me into his group, the other big boys backed me up, and so finally I was able to become a member of the Tigers.

彼は夜はたいていひとりぼっちでほったらかされていた。さびしいのでつい外に出て行き，しまいに悪い仲間に入ってしまった。

He was left alone at home most nights, so in his loneliness he began to go out, and finally he got into bad company.

付き合っている仲間を見ればその人がわかる。

You can tell a person by the company he keeps.

私は政治活動家の仲間には近づきたくないと思った。

I wanted to stay {away from / out of} political action groups.

私は何のグループでも仲間に入りたくなかった。

I didn't want to belong to any [a] group.

【仲間はずれ】

その子はかわいそうにいつも仲間はずれだった。

The poor boy was always left out.

私はみんなに交じって座っていたが，仲間になじめずひとりぼっちであった。

I sat among them but I felt left out.

ジムはクラブで仲間はずれにされていた。

Jim was excluded from the club.

〈注〉 仲間はずれがひどくなると Jim was kicked out of the club.（クラブを追い出された）となる。

2. 個人的な関係

遊び仲間（幼児） **a playmate**

学校の仲間（10歳くらいまで） **a schoolmate**

クラスの仲間（中学・高校） **a classmate**

職場の仲間（同僚） **a colleague; a fellow**

worker

仕事の仲間(相手) **a partner; a co-worker**

ジョンとは仕事仲間である。

I'm working with John.(一時的な感じ)

John is my co-worker [colleague].

I work with John.(職場の仲間)

仲間うち[仲間同士]のけんかはやめよう。

Let's not quarrel with each other.

〈注〉◆「仲間」が相棒や相手1人なのかグループなのかを考えて語を選ばなければならない。

◆ company は集合的な概念で,また I enjoy your company.(一緒にいると楽しい)といった抽象的な意味もあるので,×He's my company. のような使い方はできない。He's a member of our group. や He's in my group. と言う。

◆circle が同好会(sewing, reading, concert going など)の性質のものを指す場合は She joined the tennis circle.(テニス同好会の仲間に入った)のように言える。しかし circle が仲良しグループ(a set or clique, my circle of friends)の意味のときは,circleのmembers が仲間の選択をすることになるので「仲間に入れる」は admit her into our circle(入会を許す)のように言う。

ながめ(眺め)→ けしき

a view

【いい眺め】

来てごらんなさい。すばらしい眺めですよ。

Come here, the view is wonderful [superb].

このあたりの田園が一望のもとに眺められます。

You can get a very good view of the countryside.

眺めのいい部屋がいい。

I want a room with a view.

【眺める】

私は一日中海を眺めて暮した。

I spent a whole day looking out over [at] the sea.

私たちは何時間もじっと座って古いアルバムを眺めていた。

We sat for hours looking through the old album.

なく(泣く)

cry; 声を出さずに泣く **weep;** すすり泣く **sob;** きんきん声で泣く **scream;** ワーワー泣く **howl**

1.いろいろな泣き方

彼女は子供の無事な姿を見てうれし泣きに泣いた。

She wept for joy when she saw her boy safe.

彼女は思いきり泣きたかった。

She wanted to have a good cry.

彼女は思いきり泣いてさっぱりした。

She had a good cry and then felt much better.

その子はお母さんにしかられてめそめそ泣いていた。

The girl was sobbing because she had been scolded by her mother.

彼女は泣きたい気持ちだった。

She felt like crying.

この子は毎朝保育園に連れて行って,おいて帰るときひと泣きする。

Every morning he cries when I leave him at the nursery school.

その子は泣きながら寝入ってしまった。

The child cried [sobbed] himself to sleep.

彼は泣き上戸だ。

He's a crying drunk.〔米〕

老婦人は私たちがどうしたのかと尋ねると,わっと泣き出した。

The old woman burst into tears when we asked her what was the matter with her.

婦人たちはみんなその哀れな物語に泣いた。

All women were moved to tears at her sad story.

2.泣かされる,泣かせる

家に帰る途中にいじめっ子がいて,彼にいつも泣かされていた。

There was a bully on my way home and he always made me cry.

泣かせる話だね。

It's a very moving story.

〈注〉　「泣かされた」は ×I was cried. とは言えない。It [He] made me cry. のようにするのが無難である。

なく（鳴く）→ 擬声語・擬態語

…なくてよい → …ならない

…なくなる → なる 5.

なつかしい（懐かしい）

1. 過ぎ去ったものへの思い

懐かしむ

long for; hold dear; miss

子供のころが懐かしい。

I miss my childhood.

I wish I were a child again.

これはとっても懐かしい写真なの。

This photo is very dear to me.

町に住むようになっても私たちはずっとその山並を懐かしんでいた。

After we moved away from the mountains, we missed them for a long time.

一緒に過したあの幸せな日々を今も懐かしく思い出しています。

I fondly remember the happy days we spent together.

2. 離れているものへの思い

懐かしむ　miss; feel homesick for; long for

故郷の父母が懐かしい。

I miss my parents back home.

30年前に出た故国が懐かしい。

I long for my homeland, which I left 30 years ago.

3. 久しぶりの再会の喜び

いやあ，ジャック，久しぶりだなあ。どうしていた。…まったく懐かしいな，会えてよかったよ。（…には近況報告などが入る）

Hello, Jack. It's been a long time. How have you been? ... It's been good to see you again!

昔の友人に会ってとても懐かしかった。

I met an old friend, and it certainly was good to see him again.

Meeting an old friend again brought back many memories.

久しぶりに母校を訪ねて，昔の先生に会ってまったく懐かしかった。

I visited my high school after a long time and met my old teacher, which
{ filled me with nostalgia.
{ made me miss those bygone days.

〈注〉　「会えて懐かしかった」のつもりで ×felt a yearning to see ... と書くのは誤り。また「懐かしかった」のつもりで felt dear はおかしい。felt nostalgic [nostalgia] とする。

《参考文》

「アルプスの少女」でハイジが，こがれて病気になったほどの懐かしいアルプスに帰り，家に着くところの英訳を引用する。随所に「懐かしさ」の表現がある。

... Heidi looked around her and began to tremble with excitement, for she knew every tree along the way, and there overhead were the high jagged peaks of the mountain looking down on her like old friends. And Heidi nodded back to them, and grew every moment more wild with her joy and longing, feeling as if she must jump down from the cart and run with all her might till she reached the top.

... and before Alm-Uncle had time to see who was coming Heidi had rushed up to him, thrown down her basket and flung her arms round his neck, unable in the excitement of seeing him again to say more than "Grandfather! Grandfather!" over and over again.

――Johanna Spyri, *Heidi*（The C. I. C. Series 13, J. M. DENT SONS LTD）

なめる（嘗める，舐める）

1. 舌で

ぺろぺろなめる **lick**

猫がお皿をきれいになめてしまった。

The cat licked the dish clean.

〈注〉 lap は舌でぺちゃぺちゃやることだが，「なめる」には当らない。The cat lapped up the milk. を訳せば「猫がミルクをぺちゃぺちゃ飲んだ」となる。

犬が私に飛びついてきて顔をなめた。

The dog jumped up on me and licked my face.

飴(あめ)はかまないでなめなさい。

Lick the sucker, don't bite it.

2. 経験する

have; experience

彼は辛酸をなめた[つらい経験をした]。

He had a lot of trouble.

彼は戦時中あらゆる辛酸をなめた。

He experienced [suffered] a lot of hardships during the war.

〈注〉 「辛酸をなめた」を had a lot of hardships とすると書き言葉と口語表現を組み合せたことになり，ちぐはぐになる。

3. 侮る

underestimate; trifle with

彼は若いけれどなめてかかれない相手だ。

Though young, he's not a man to be trifled with.

山はこわい。なめてはいけない。

Don't underestimate the danger of the mountains.

なやむ(悩む)・なやみ → こまる，しんぱい

《類義語》

【悩み】名

worry くよくよ思い悩むこと。気苦労・本人の気持ち中心の語。

trouble (1)(不可算名詞) difficulty と同義。大小の心配，苦労，悩み（気持ち中心）。

ex. I had some trouble with my neighbor last week.（先週隣人との間にトラブルがあった）

be in trouble（警察などとごたごたを起こしている）

I had trouble understanding the lecture.（講義がよくわからなくて困った）

(2) the trouble, troubles で problem(s) の意味。一般にちょっとした心配事(事中心)。

ex. People often talk about their troubles.（人はよくあれこれ自分の心配事の話をする[ぐちをこぼす]）

The trouble was I couldn't understand the lecture.（困ったことには私は講義の内容がわからなかった）

この trouble は problem で置き替え可能。a trouble とは普通言わないので迷うときは a problem とするとよい。

(1)(2)どちらの場合も some, any, a lot of, no など修飾語をつけることがある。

care（気苦労）; **concern ; anxiety**（心配）ともに本人の気持ち中心。

problem（問題） 心配の元になる「事」を指す。

【悩んでいる】

be worried くよくよ悩んでいる。

be concerned 対処しなければならない問題について考え心配している。

be troubled 心配事があって悩んでいる。

be distressed 大きな心配事でひどく悩む。

be annoyed いらいらさせられて悩む［悩まされる］。

suffer from 長期にわたる病苦などに悩まされる。

be anxious about 何か悪いことが起りはしないかと心配している。

1. 心配する，思い悩む

彼女は息子の行く末について悩んでいる。

She feels very (much) concerned about her son's future.（思慮）

The question of her son's future worries her.（感情）

何を悩んでいるんですか。

What are you worrying about?

What's on your mind?

Can you tell me what is troubling you?

何も悩みがないような顔をしている。

He looks as if he has no problems.

この世は悩みばかりなり。

There are many troubles in life [this world].

2．苦労する

彼は住宅がなかなか見つからずに悩んでいる。

He is very worried about finding a place to live.

〈注〉 the housing problem（住宅問題）と言うと，もっと広い自治体や国家レベルの住宅問題のことになる。

【悩みの種】

彼女は末の息子が悩みの種だ（いつも悩まされている）。

Her youngest son was the source of her annoyance [troubles].

〈注〉 annoyance は腹立たしさを，troubles は心配の気持ちを表す。

息子の成績がよくないのが悩みの種です。

I'm { anxious / worried / concerned } about my son because he isn't doing well at school.

彼の成績がよくないのが両親の悩みの種だ。

His poor school record is a (big) headache to his parents.（第三者から見て）

【被害】

彼女は年とった父親にあれこれせびられていつも悩まされていた。

Her old father used to trouble her with [by making] endless demands.※

She used to feel troubled by her old father's demands.

〈注〉 ※の例文は意図的に悩ました場合も含む。

私はいつも親戚に悩まされている。

I am constantly annoyed [pestered] by my relatives.

〈注〉 annoyed は腹が立つ気持ち，pestered は実際に何かされて困っていることを表す。

【虫】

昨夜は一晩中蚊に悩まされた。

We were annoyed by mosquitoes all last night.

はじめて温暖な土地に住んで，彼女はゴキブリに悩まされている。

Living in a warm climate for the first time, she is troubled by the presence of cockroaches.

【騒音】

このあたりの住人は絶えず飛行機の騒音に悩まされている。

People living in this neighborhood are constantly annoyed by the noise of planes.

【精神的被害】

彼は生涯，戦争の記憶に悩まされた。

Memories of the war disturbed him all his life.

〈注〉 disturb とは心の平静を破ることで，disturb the silence とは静けさを破ること。a disturbed child とは自閉的でときに乱暴したり，だまりこんだりして情緒に障害のある子。

She was very disturbed [upset] when she heard the news.（彼女はその知らせを聞いてたいへん動揺し，取り乱した）

3．病苦

彼女は難聴に悩んでいる。

She's troubled with poor hearing.

彼女はしつこいリューマチに悩んでいる［悩まされている］。

She { has / suffers from / is afflicted with } bad rheumatism.

彼は不眠症［頭痛］に悩んでいる［悩まされている］。

He's suffering from { insomnia. / headaches. }

〈注〉 「絶えず頭痛に悩んでいる」には suffer from headaches が使えるが，普通は I have a headache.

とする。

4．迷う

誕生日に兄さんに何をあげようか悩んでいる。（迷っている程度，ふざけておおげさに表現）

I'm troubled about what to give my brother for his birthday.

ならう（倣う，習う）→ べんきょう

1．まねる

imitate; follow; copy (from); ape

手本にならう　copy (from) a model

〈注〉 受動文では be copied from a model とする。

先例にならう　follow a precedent

欧米にならう

take on Western manners

adopt European ways

さるまねをする　ape（批判的な言い方）

2．学習する

learn; be taught

〈注〉 be taught, learn, study の違い

be taught 先生がいて習うこと。

learn 習い覚えることで，結果的に knowledge（知識），skill（技能）を身につけること。

study 系統的に努力して勉強すること。 try to learn すること。

僕は中学に入ってからずっと英語を習っている。

I have been learning [studying] English since I entered junior high school.

あの人は週に１度アメリカ人に英語を習っている。

She studies English with an American once a week.

She takes [has] an English lesson from an American once a week.

私はギターを習っている。

I take guitar lessons.

I'm learning guitar.

だれに英語を習いましたか。

（下にいくほど〔*formal*〕）

Who taught you English?

Who was your English teacher?

From whom did you learn English?

By whom were you taught English?

学校で柔道を習った。

I did [learned] judo at school.

ドイツ語は習ったことがない。

I was never taught German.（習っていないが分かるかもしれない）

I never took German.（ドイツ語の単位は取らなかった）

I never learned how to speak German.（ドイツ語は話せない）

彼女は水泳を習っている。

She is learning (how) to swim.

〈注〉 **learning to**《swim》と **learning how to**《swim》 単に事実として述べるとき，上の二つは同じように使われる。ただし，特にやり方に重点を置くときは learn how to ... が好まれ，習得したこと自体に重点が置かれるときは learn to ... である。次のような場合その差がよく分かる。

The child is learning to walk.（幼児が歩き出した）

She is learning how to walk.（けがをしてリハビリで歩行練習をしている）

…ならない

1．必要

…しなければならない　**must; have to**

…する必要がある **need**

【現在】

屋根を修理しなければならない。

The roof needs { repairing. / to be repaired. }

〈注〉 repairing, to be repaired の使用頻度は半々。

自分の生活費は自分で稼がなければならない。

I have to earn my own living.

行かなければならないでしょうか。

Do I have to go?

できるだけ早くこの仕事を終えなければならない。

I have to [must] finish this work as soon as possible.

【未来】

高校を卒業したらすぐ，自分の生活費は稼がなければならない。

I'll have to earn my own living once I finish [graduate from] high school.

【過去】

高校を卒業したらすぐ，自分の生活費を稼がねばならなかった。

I had to earn my own living once I finished high school.

〈注〉◆**must と have to**

must は話者の意向が前面に出るので，You must ..., He must ... などは強制[命令]になる。have to は話者以外の周囲の状況などにより，「やらなければならない」となるので調子が穏やかになる。

しかしこの区別は米語では薄れ, have to の方がくだけていてやわらかいが, must と同じように使われている。

◆**must と 時制**

must は未来形が作れず，また過去の意味には普通使われないので，未来・過去については have to で代用される。

ex. You must [You'll have to / You had to] work harder.

have to の疑問形は Do I have to go?，否定形は You don't have to go.（行かなくてよい）（＝need not go)。

cf. You must not go.（行ってはならない）

I've got to go.〔*colloq.*〕（＝I have to go.)

Have you got to go?（疑問）〔英〕

You haven't got to go.（否定）〔英〕

◆**need** は「…する必要がある」の意から「…せねばならない」の意味になるので，must, have to のような強制力はない。

This fax needs repairing.

（このファックスは修理しなければならない）

なお，need はneed not, don't need 〔米 *colloq.*〕のような否定形で使われる方が多い。→ひつよう

ex. You need not come.（来る必要はない）

You don't need to worry.（必配しなくてよい）

2．義務・道義

must; have to; ought to; should

核兵器廃絶のために我々はできるだけのことをしなければならない。

We must [have to] do what we can to abolish nuclear weapons.

我々は貧しい人，体の不自由な人を助けなければならない。

We ought to [should] help the poor and the disadvantaged.

我々はお互いに思いやりの心を持たねばならない。

We ought to [should] be considerate of each other.

〈注〉 **must, ought to, should の強制力**

must 100％すべきである（命令・義務）

ought to 70～90％すべきである（要求）

should 40～75％すべきである（説得）

修飾語や主語，トピックなどにより，強さにかなり幅がある。

3．禁止

…してはならない **must not; ought not to; should not**

【規則】

この湖で泳いではいけない。

It is forbidden to swim in this lake.

【強制】

信号が青にならないうちに道を横切ってはいけない。

You must not cross the road before the signal light turns green.

【忠告】

子供に寛大すぎてはならない。

You should not be too lenient with your children.

〈注〉 you must は非常に強くひびくので相手に失礼になるおそれがある。次のような慣用句では差し支えないが，［ ］内の方が無難である。

I must be going now [I have to go now].（もう失礼しなければなりません）

Must you go so soon [Do you have to go ...]? You must stay a little longer. [Can't you stay ...?]（もうお帰りになるの？ もう少しゆっくりなさいませんか）

ならぶ（並ぶ）・ならべる → となり

1．並ぶ

【隣り合せ】

あの人たちの家は並んでいる。

Their houses are [stand〔*literary*〕] {next to each other. / side by side.}

彼とは教室で並んでいた。

I sat next to him in class.

私たちは並んで席についた。

We found seats together.

We sat together.

【整列】

大通りの両側には大きな並木が並んでいた。

Big trees {line / stand on} both sides of the main street.

ダンサーたち全員がステージに並んだ。

The dancers (all) lined up on the stage.

いい席をとるには早くから並ばなければならない。

We must queue [line up] early to get a good seat.

〈注〉 この queue〔英〕は「順番待ちの列に並ぶ」意。

若者が大勢ホールの前に列をつくって並んでいた。

Many young people were lining up [queuing] in front of the hall.

子供たちが２列に並び，音楽に合せて行進した。

Children marched to the music in two lines.

机は５つずつ６列並んでいる。

The desks are lined up six across and five deep.

2．並べる

【配列】 put things in a row

机を５つずつ６列に並べてください。

Put [Arrange] the desks in six rows of five.

彼はいすを横に並べた。

He put the chairs side by side.

彼はいすを縦に並べた。

He put the chairs in a row {one behind the other. / from front to back.}

【順番】

(子供たちを)背の順に並ばせてください。

Line the children up according to their height.

Have the children line up in order of height.

彼女は答案を得点順に並べ始めた。

She started to put the papers in numerical order by test scores.

cf.「ＡＢＣ順に」は in alphabetical order。

【展示】 exhibit; display

そのショーではあらゆる分野で流行の先端を行くあらゆるインテリア製品が並べてある。

All sorts of fashionable interior goods are exhibited in the show.

【配膳】

彼女はテーブルに食器を並べた。(食卓の用意をした)

She {laid / set} the table.

〈注〉 西洋料理の正餐(せいさん)では皿・グラス・ナイフ・フォーク類がまず並べられ，客が食卓についてから料理が一品ずつ運び供される。しかし一般家庭の通常の食事の場合，温める必要のない料理が初めから食卓に置かれ，温かい料理は大皿に盛って食卓に出し，その家の父親か母親がそれを取り分けたり，各自が自分の皿に取る。

She set the cold food on the table [out] early.（彼女はオードブルやサラダなど温める必要のないものをあらかじめテーブルに並べた）

She brought the food.（料理を持って来た）

She set the food on the table.（料理をテーブルに出した）

【整頓】

本を全部本棚に戻してきちんと並べなさい。

Put all the books back on the bookshelf in order.

3．慣用表現

【文句を並べる】

make complaints; complain

【肩を並べる】

彼の名声[富]は武藤氏と肩を並べている。

His fame [wealth] equals Mr. Muto's.

現代作家のうち彼と肩を並べる者はいない。

He has no peer among contemporary writers. 〔*literary*〕

走ることでは彼と肩を並べる者はいない。

In running he has no equal. 〔*literary*〕

なる

1．身分・職業・地位

【身分・地位】

彼女はプロ野球セ・リーグのコミッショナーになった。

She became the commissioner of baseball's Central League.

彼は重役になるためなら手段を選ばない。

He'll do anything in order to become a director of the company.

私の祖父は人間国宝になることを辞退した。

My grandfather refused to be designated a living national treasure.

【職業】

大きくなったら何になるの？

What are you going to be when you grow up?

僕は先生[技術者 / 医者]になる。

I'll be a teacher [an engineer / a doctor].

I'll go into teaching [engineering / medicine].

彼の父は彼に医者になってほしいと思っている。

His father thinks (that) he would like him to become a doctor.

His father wants him to become a doctor.

【成長】

隣の家の男の子が立派な青年になった。

The neighbor's boy has grown into a fine young man.

彼女は今度大学３年生になる。

She'll be a third year college student.

〈注〉 She'll become a third year student. とも言えるが，be の方が口語的である。

×She'll become third year. はよくある誤り。

彼女はきっといい奥さんになる。

She'll make a good wife.

うちの娘も２児の母になりました。

My daughter is the mother of two children [has two children] now.

〈注〉 「なった」はこのように be 動詞を使って言うことが多い。「なる」(未来)はwill be soon,「なった」(完了)は be now で表せる。

2．年齢・時・季節

【年齢】

トムは12月で５歳になる。

Tom will be five (years old) in December.

彼女はもうじき17歳になる。

She's going on seventeen.

うちの末の息子はちょうど13歳になったところです。

My youngest son has just turned thirteen.

うちの長男が成人しました。

My oldest son has become an adult.

私は50代前半ですが，家内はまだ40になりません。

I'm in my early fifties but my wife is not yet forty.

【年月】

私は日本に来て５年になる。

It's / It's been } five years / Five years have passed } since I came to Japan.

今月の終りで日本に来てちょうど５年になります。

I will have been (here) in Japan for five years at the end of this month.

【季節】

春になるとすべての物に生命力がみなぎる。

In spring / When spring comes round } everything is full of life.

もう2，3週間で春になる。

Spring will be here in a few weeks.

春になった。

Spring has come.

It's spring now.

梅雨になった。

The rainy season has { come. / set in. / begun.

8月は過ぎ9月に，9月は10月になり…。

August passed into September and September into October …

【天候】

気候はずっと涼しく過しやすくなるでしょう。

The weather will get a good deal cooler and pleasanter.

だんだん寒く[暗く]なる。

It is getting cold [dark].

寒くなった。

It's cold these days.

雨になった。

It began [started] to rain.

It has started to rain.（今降り出したところ）

3．状態の変化

［get＋形容詞比較級］

変化して…になる **change into; turn into**

発展・発達　**develop**（ゆっくりとした感じ）

衰退・減少　**be reduced to**（ぎりぎりまでの含意）

【病状】

彼はずっとよくなった。

He's now a great deal better.

彼はいい調子でよくなってますよ。

He's coming along fine.

彼は悪くなっているのではないかと思う。

He's getting worse, I'm afraid.

病状が重くなった。

It grew more serious.

彼女はかぜから肺炎になった。

Her cold developed into pneumonia.

彼は過労から病気になった。

He overworked and
{ became sick [ill].
got himself sick. 〔*colloq.*〕
was taken ill.

彼ははしか[神経衰弱]になった。

He's got the measles.

He's got [become] neurotic.

〈注〉 ×He's become measles [neurosis].
×He's measles [neurosis].
become は同じ内容を結ぶ働きをする動詞であり，異質の名詞は原則として結べない。上の誤り文の場合は，人そのものが抽象的な病気に変化したかのような表現になってしまっている。

【気持ち】

彼女の彼に対する同情が知らず知らずのうちにいつしか愛情になっていった。

Her sympathy toward the man developed into love before she knew it.

その運動に対する共感は彼女をかりたて，やがてボランティア活動に打ち込むようになった。

Her sympathy for the cause developed into active volunteer work.

【変形】→かわる・かえる

水が氷になった。

The water has frozen.

氷が水になった。

The ice has melted.

オタマジャクシがみんなカエルになった。

All the tadpoles have turned into frogs.

城は焼け落ちて灰になってしまった。

The castle was
{ burned down.
reduced to ashes.〔*literary*〕.

【変色】

その知らせに彼は青くなった。

He turned pale at the news.

それから空が赤くなった。

Then the sky
{ became reddish.
took on a reddish hue〔*literary*〕.

【低下】

わが社のキャンディー生産高は平常の7割[半分]になった。

Candy production at our factories has been reduced by 30% [half].

【結果】turn out; end up; prove

その後どうなったの？（事態）

How did it { turn out? / end up?

思いのほかよくなった［望んだ通りになった］。

Things have { turned out unexpectedly well. / ended up as they hoped they would.

あの人はいったいどうなったのだろう。

I wonder { what has become of him. / where he is and what he's doing.

〈注〉 What has become of him? は消息が絶えている人について言う。2，3日前に会った人について言うのはおかしい。

こんなことになろうとは！

I had never thought it would come to this!

その人はしだいに金持ちになった。

The woman gradually became [grew] rich.

難しいことになった。

Things have become (very) difficult.

その計画は失敗に終った。

The project { turned out to be a failure. / failed.

その傷が致命傷となった。

The wound proved (to be) fatal.

夢が本当になった。

The dream has come true.

【回想】

いい経験になった。

It was a good experience.

いい思い出になった。

It is one of my best memories.

〈注〉「いい…になった」を，It became a good experience. と become を使って表すと，「初めは辛い経験」と思っていたが，その後になり「いい経験」に変ったという意味合いになる。普通に回想して「結局あれはいい経験だった」という場合は It was a good experience. でよい。

【利益】

英語なんか勉強して何になるの？

What's the use of studying English?

こんな古靴下をつくろって何になるの？

Is it worth the [your] effort [time] to mend all these old socks?

そんなことしても何にもならないよ。

That's { useless. / of no use.

That won't help { you. / your career.（出世の助けにならない） / the situation.（状況はよくならない）

4．…するようになる

come to; begin to

【習慣】

高校を出てまもなく彼はボランティア活動をするようになった。

He { started [began] to do / took to doing } volunteer work soon after he finished high school.

【疑問】

私はその仕事が自分に向いていないと思うようになった。

I came [began] to think the work didn't suit me.

【好きになる】

私は日本食が好きになった。

I've come to like Japanese food.

父がバイオリンが上手だったので，私は小さいときから音楽が好きになった。

As my father was a good violin player, I came to love music when quite young.

私はまた，大きなデパートの食品売場であれこれ買うのが好きになった。

I have also grown fond of shopping for food in big department stores.

〈注〉「好きになった」のつもりで，×I became to like her と書くのは誤り。become の後に不定詞は続けられない。came to like ... とすべきである。変化の始まりに関しては begin to も使える。

いつから彼女を好きになったの？
When did you begin to like her?
初めて会ったときから好きになった。
I liked her (from) the first time we met.（会った瞬間から）

【いやになる】→いやな

5．否定形への変化（…しなくなる）

かぎがなくなった。（紛失）
I've lost my key.
My key is {missing. / lost.}

車のガソリンがなくなった。（底をつく）
The car has run out of gas [petrol].

【動詞との組み合せ】

〈注〉「好きになる」は come to like だが，「好きでなくなる」は don't come to like とは言えない。これは「好きにならない」という意味。そこで「…しなくなる」は become や come to に固執せず，ここではほかの言い方でその内容を述べる例文を示す。

【見えなくなる】 disappear; vanish（さっと消える）; fade (away)（だんだん薄れる）; go [move] out of sight （視野から消える）; become invisible

男の子は角を曲って見えなくなった。
The boy vanished [disappeared] round the corner.

星は夜明けが近づくと見えなくなる。
The stars fade towards dawn.

ジェット機があっという間に見えなくなった。
The jet plane shot out of sight.

【聞えなくなる】 go out of hearing [earshot]

騒々しい楽隊の音が遠のきやがて聞えなくなり，再び静けさが戻った。
The noisy band {passed / moved} out of {hearing / earshot} and silence returned.

その音は弱くなり，ついに聞えなくなった。
The noise {died away. / faded.}

【動かなくなる】
stop moving; cease to move [moving]

【会えなくなる】
もう彼女に会えなくなるのではないかと心配だった。
I was afraid I might not be able [be unable] to see her again.

【わからなくなる】
彼がやっと学校にもどってきたときは英語の授業で何もわからなくなってしまっていた。
When he at last returned to school he found he was unable to understand anything in English class.

もう暗くなってきて，どの家も同じように見えた。私はすっかり迷ってしまい，叔父さんの家にはどちらに行ったらいいのかわからなくなってしまった。
It was getting dark and the houses all looked the same. I felt lost and didn't know which way I should go to get to my uncle's house.

〈注〉「わかるようになった」は They have come to understand it. でよいが，「わからなくなった」は，△They have come not to understand it. はそぐわない。そのため上記例文または，次の「ついていけなくなる」の例文のような工夫が必要になる。

【ついていけなくなる】
3か月して私は学校に戻ったが，数学やその他2，3の教科でほかの生徒についていけなくなっていた。
After three months I returned to school, but in math and a few other classes I found myself unable to catch up with the other pupils.〔*written*〕

【好きでなくなる】
どういうわけか数学が好きでなくなった。(興味を失った)
Somehow I lost interest in mathematics.

彼女がもう好きではなくなっていた。
I found I didn't like her any longer.

【食べたくなくなる】
なぜかとにかくもう食べたくなくなった。

Somehow
{ I've lost my appetite for that.
{ I don't want to eat that any longer.

【見たくなくなる】

あなたがあまり恐ろしい話をして脅かすからもう見たくなくなったわ。

Since you've frightened me by talking about all the horrid things in it, I don't think I'd like to see it any longer.

【行きたくなくなる】

博覧会に行きたいと特に思っていたわけではなかったが，そのニュースを聞いてますます行きたくなくなった。

I wasn't particularly keen to see the exhibition, but then what I heard about it made me feel even less inclined to.

6．数量

【計算】

6たす4は10になる。（6＋4＝10）

Six and [plus] four make(s) [is / are / equal(s)] ten.

〈注〉 計算で出た答えの数を一つのまとまりとして考えれば単数扱い，また1より大きな数と考えれば複数扱いとなるので上記のように単・複どちらに扱ってもよい。

10ひく6は4になる。（10－6＝4）

Six from ten leaves [is] four.

Ten minus six is [equal(s)] four.

4かける5はいくつになるか。（4×5＝？）

How much is five times four?

23割る4は5，余り3となる。

Twenty-three divided by four { is / equals } five with three remaining [left over].

【勘定】

いくらになりますか。

How much is that altogether?

How much will that be?

How much does that { come / add up } to?

（買物・見積り）

2万円以上になります。

It totals [comes to] more than 20,000 yen.

【回数】

もしこの夏アメリカに行けば5度目になる。

If I go to the States this summer, I will have been there five times.

It will be my fifth visit to the USA if I go there this summer.

7．その他

【成り立つ】

水は酸素と水素からなる。

Water { consists / is composed } of oxygen and hydrogen.

そのチームは男性20名と女性5名からなる。

The team consists of 20 men and 5 women.

〈注〉 consist (of)は自動詞であるから，×be consisted of と受身にしてはいけない。

【役を演じる】

彼がロメオ，私がジュリエットになります。

He { plays / acts } the part of Romeo and I Juliet.

木箱が食事時には食卓に，そうでないときは彼の書き物机になった。

A wooden box served as the dining table at meal times and as his writing desk at others.

【成り行き・決定】

私はみんなが帰って来るまでここで待つことになっている。（予定）

I am to wait here till they come back.

その2人は来年結婚することになった。（予定）

It was settled that they were to get married next year.

なるようになれ[ほっておけ]。（成り行き）

Leave it to take its own course.

数学となるとまったくお手上げだ。

I'm a total loss when it comes to mathematics.

その作品の美術的価値となると，いろいろな

意見があるだろう。(論点)

When it comes to its artistic value, opinions may differ.

なる (鳴る)・ならす

1. 鳴る

〈注〉 ring (リンリン鳴る), rumble (ゴロゴロ鳴る), creak (キーキー鳴る) のように英語では音自体が動詞になっている。 →擬声語・擬態語

摩擦で鳴る　creak (キーキー)

鳴り響く　resound (大きな音); echo (こだま)

【ベル】

リンリン鳴る ring

戸口[学校]のベルが鳴っている。

The doorbell [schoolbell] is ringing.

そら，ベルが鳴っている。

There goes the bell.

電話が鳴り出した。

The telephone began ringing.

目覚しが鳴った。

The alarm clock went off. (セットしたものが鳴り出した)

cf. 時計が3時を打ったところだ。

The clock has just struck three.

【サイレン】

昨夜サイレンが鳴っているのを聞いた。

I heard a siren last night.

【雷】

稲妻が光り，1，2秒後に雷が鳴った。

The lightning flashed and a second or two later the thunder clapped.

The thunder
- cracked. (ピシャッ)
- rumbled. (ゴロゴロ)
- rolled. (ゴロゴロ移動して聞える場合)

【風】

松林に風が鳴っていた。

The wind whistled among the pines.

2. 鳴らす

クラクションを鳴らす

blow [toot, honk] the horn

〈注〉 クラクション (klaxon) は自動車の horn (警笛) のことで昔の自動車の商標に由来する。

ベルを鳴らす　ring the bell

【いろいろな音】

たたいて鳴らす

clang; jingle (リンリンという金属音)

jangle (ジャンジャンという金属音)

rumble (低音)

吹いて鳴らす blow; whistle (笛など)

なんて (何て)・なんと →…とは・…なんて

1. 疑問文

【何て言う】

聞かれたらなんて言いましょうか。

What shall I say when they ask me?

英語ではこれをなんて言いますか。

What do you call this in English?

日本語の「人情」を英語ではなんと言いますか。

What is the English for (the) Japanese "ninjo"?

【聞き返し】

なんておっしゃったのですか。

What did you say?

〈注〉 口調とイントネーションに注意。文尾を上げてやわらかに言わないと詰問に聞える。丁寧に言うのならば I beg your pardon [Pardon, Sorry]. (◡)

2. 譲歩

【なんと言っても】

なんと言われても私の気持ちは変らない。

No matter what you say / Whatever you say [may say 〔英〕] } I won't change my mind.

3. 感嘆文

なんてばかだったのだろう！

What a fool I was!

How foolish I was!

〈注〉◆上記の感嘆文はたいへん強いので使いすぎないように。

◆「What 型の感嘆文」と「How 型の感嘆文」の混同がよく見られる。
×How pretty girl she is! は誤り。
次のように考えるとわかりやすい。

She is pretty. → How pretty (she is)!

She is a pretty girl. → What a pretty girl (she is)!

実際の会話では (she is) は省略されることが多い。

How pretty!

What a pretty girl!

と覚えておくとよい。

に

…に

〈注〉 日本語と英語は異なった統語体系をもつので「…に」(およびほかのいわゆる「てにをは」)に当る英語はないが，意味範囲を分類し，英語表現を当てはめてみる。

1．時間

【時刻】

7時に　at seven

8時頃に　(at) around [about] eight

【1日の区分】

朝[午後/夕方]に

in the morning [afternoon / evening]

夜に　at night

真夜中に　in the { dead of night / middle of the night }

〈注〉 midnight は真夜中，特に夜中の12時のこと。(cf. noon)

【曜日】

日曜日に　(on) Sunday

日曜の夕方に　(on) Sunday evening

【日付】

5月5日に　(on) the 5th of May [May 5, May 5th]

【年】

2003年に　in 2003

【期間】

1時間以内に　in an hour

約60分後に　after about 60 minutes

〈注〉 within an hour はもう少し幅があり，45分から60分以内。

1週間[1か月]以内に　in a week [month]

【年齢】

5歳の時に

at five

at the age of five

when I was five (years old)

高校の時に　when I was in high school

【刻限】

学校に[列車に]間に合う[遅れる]

be in time [be late] for school [the train]

〈注〉 日本語でも「昨日に，去年に」とは言わないが，英語でも tomorrow, yesterday, last year, last Sunday などは前置詞なしで副詞として使われる。

2．割合 (…につき)

【時】

5年に1度

(once) every five years (サイクルを表す)

once in five years (サイクルではなく，だいたいの頻度を表す)

2時間に1度　(once) every two hours

1日(に)3回　three times a day

1日おきに　every other day

【その他】

5人に1人　one out of five (people)

3．場所・方向

〈注〉 「…に」は必ずしも to ではない。「京都に着く」は ×reach to Kyoto と to をつけると誤りになる。間違えやすい動詞について以下にまとめる。to 以外の前置詞が必要な場合もあるので注意。

	他動詞	(目的語)	自動詞＋前置詞
(場所)に行く	reach	the place	arrive at [in] the place
			get to the place
	approach	the house	go up to the door
	visit	my aunt	go to see my aunt
		the museum	go to the museum
	enter	the room	go into the room
に似る	resemble	his brother	look like his brother

〈注〉 上の表の動詞はだいたい右欄がより口語的(arrive は例外)である。自動詞・他動詞の区別については辞書をまめに引いて確かめることが必要。

【場所】

岐阜に住む　live in Gifu

住吉通り35番地に住む

live at No. 35 Sumiyoshi Street

彼は今名古屋にいる。

He is in Nagoya now.

長良館に泊まる
　stay at [in] the Nagarakan Hotel
ホテルに泊まる　put up at [stay in] a hotel
　cf. spend a week at a hotel（1週間泊まる）
京都に行く
　go to Kyoto
　visit Kyoto（用事ではなく遊びに行く）
午前10時の新幹線で大阪に向かう
　leave for Osaka by the 10 a.m. Shinkansen
明日の午後ロンドンに向かって成田から発つ
　leave from Narita to go to London tomorrow afternoon
駅に近づく
　get near the station〔*informal*〕
　approach the station〔*formal*〕
…に着く
　get to the place; reach the place
　arrive { at《a building / an office》 / in《a country / a city》}
〈注〉 at か in か迷うようならば reach, get to を使うとよい。
プラットホーム[戸口]に立つ
　stand on the platform [at the door]
部屋に入る　go into a room; enter a room
物を箱に入れる　put a thing in [into] a box
手をポケットに突っ込む
　put [thrust] one's hand in [into] one's pocket
古い手紙を火に投げ込む
　throw old letters into [in] the fire

【方角】
太陽は西に沈む。
　The sun sets in the west.
私たちの学校は市の北部にある。
　Our school is (located) in the northern part of the city.
病院はうちから2キロばかり北にある。
　The hospital is about two kilometers (to the) north of our house.
風が南に吹いている。
　The wind is blowing southward [from the north].

【対人】
彼女はお母さんによく似ている。
　She { resembles / is just like / looks just like（外見が）} her mother.
お父さんに聞いてごらん。
　Ask your father about it.

4. 授与関係
(人)に《物》をあげる[買う / 貸す]
　{ give / buy / lend }《a thing》{ to / for / to }(a person)
　{ give / buy / lend }(a person)《a thing》
〈注〉 おみやげ，プレゼントなどを「…に」買ったりあげたりするときは，for the sake of の気持ちで for を使う。
　ex. I bought souvenirs for my family.
　　I gave my sister a pretty doll for her birthday.
　　cf. This is a present for my sister.

【対物[事]】
兄は本にたくさんお金を使う。
　My brother spends a lot of money on books.
彼は雑誌を読むのに何時間もかける。
　He spends many hours reading magazines.
適当な運動は健康にいい。
　Moderate exercise is good for health.

5. 受動態
その子はよくお母さんにしかられている。
　The child is often scolded by his mother.
〈注〉 上記のような習慣的なことについては受動態で落ちつくが，The mother scolded her child for telling a lie.（子供がうそをついたので母親がしかった）のように1回きりのことについては受動態にしないのが普通。
　habitual（いつものこと）になると状況（condition, state of affairs）と感じられるから受動態で落ちつく。しかし母親を中心に能動態で次のようにも言える。
The woman is always shouting at her little boy.（その婦人はいつも小さな息子を怒鳴っている）

にあう（似合う）

become; be becoming; suit; be suitable; be right for

1．服装など

【服】

そのドレスは君によく似合うよ。

That dress { suits [becomes] you. / is (just) right for you. / looks becoming on you. }

You look nice in that dress.

【髪形】

あの髪形があの人には一番似合う。

She looks best in [with] that hairdo.

あの髪形はあの人に似合わない。

That hair style does not suit her.

【色】

あの人はブルーが好きで，またそれがよく似合った。

Blue was her favorite color, and it suited her, too.

【宝石】

うちの母にはダイヤモンドよりもエメラルドが似合う。

Emeralds suit my mother more than diamonds.

【タイ】

このネクタイはあの背広には似合わない。

This tie doesn't go well with that suit.

2．ふさわしい

似合いの夫婦　a well-matched couple

２人はお似合いだと思いますよ。

{ They are well suited, / They make a fine pair, } I think.

彼は彼女にちょうどお似合いだ。

He's just right for her.

これはまったく君に似合わない[君らしくない]じゃないか。

This is most unlike you.

彼は年に似合わず賢明だ。

He is wise for his age.

におい（匂い，臭い）

《類義語》

smell　におい；におうを表す最も一般的な語。ただし good や nice といった形容詞がついていないときは普通「くさい」の意味になる。

stink　悪臭；悪臭を放つ。

stench　ひどい悪臭；ひどい悪臭を放つ。

scent　におい。英国では化学的合成品のにおいによく使う。cf.「無臭の」は unscented。

perfume　たいへん強いにおい；花や香水などのにおい；全体にたちこめる香り。

fragrance　花または花のような香り。

aroma　お茶，コーヒー，料理，スパイスなどの芳しいにおい；全体にたちこめるにおい。

bouquet　ワイン，ブランデーなどの香り。

odor　smell と同じだが，いいにおいには使わない。

においをつけたヘアスプレー

scented hairspray

ヘアスプレーのにおい

scent of hairspray

【いいにおい】

ああ，いいにおい。

What a good smell!

Oh, it smells good.

空気がいいにおい。

The air smelled sweet.

ローストビーフのようなにおいがする。

It smells like roast beef.

魚の焼けるにおいがしていた。

There was a smell of { cooking fish. / fish being cooked. }

花のにおい[香り]があたりに漂ってきた。

The fragrance of flowers came drifting in the air.

コーヒーのいいにおい[香り]

the aroma of coffee

朝食のにおいで目が覚めるのが大好きな人がいる。

Some people love to wake up to the aroma [smell] of breakfast.

【いやなにおい】

どぶがすごいにおいだ。

How the ditch stinks!

魚が悪臭を放っている。

The fish stinks.

ゴムの焦げるにおいがする。

I can smell rubber burning.

It smells like rubber's burning.

〈注〉「…が焼ける」を関係節にしてにおいと結びつけることはできない。上述例文のようにする。
There was a smell
×that fish was being cooked.
×which someone was cooking fish.
×that rubber was burning.

【においを消す】

deodorize (cf. deodorizer におい消し)

肌のにおい消し (personal) deodorant

においを取り去る remove a smell

においをごまかす mask [hide, cover] a smell

にげる(逃げる)・にがす

1. 逃げる

run away [**off**]**; flee; fly**

拘束から逃げる **escape; get free**

こそこそ逃げる **sneak** [**slip**] **away** (**from**)

身をかわす **dodge**

【危険から】

男の子は彼めがけて石を投げつけると一目散に逃げて行った。

The boy threw a stone at him and ran away as fast as he could.

ウサギは犬が追って来るのを見て命がけで逃げた。

The hare fled for its life when it saw dogs running after it.

銃声に驚いて鳥たちは飛んで逃げた。

Birds flew off at the sound of the gunfire.

【拘束から】

トラが1頭おりから逃げた。

One of the tigers broke loose from the cage.

昨夜囚人が1人逃げた[脱獄した]。

A prisoner escaped last night.

その子は教室の後ろのドアからこっそり逃げ出した。

The boy sneaked out [away] through the back door.

【避ける】

私は都会の喧騒から逃げ出したい。

I want to get away from the noise and bustle of the town.

彼は雪の玉から上手に逃げた[身をかわした]。

He dodged the snowballs.

彼は私の質問から逃げた[質問をかわした]。

He avoided my question.

2. 逃がす

故意に逃がす **let**《a person / a thing》**go; set**《a person / a thing》**free**

のがす **miss; lose**

【故意に】

浦島(太郎)は亀を哀れに思って逃がしてやりました。

Pitying the turtle, Urashima { set it free. / let it go.

【意に反し】

彼は泥棒を取り逃がした。

He failed to catch the thief.

〈注〉前後関係で明らかならば The thief escaped. とするのが一番自然である。He let the thief [allowed the thief to] escape. とすると自らの意志で「逃がしてやった」ことにも,偶然「取り逃がした」意味にもとれるので文脈で判断する。駅で「跡をつけたが見失った」のなら He followed the man to the station but lost track of him there. となる。

女房に逃げられた。

His wife left him.

〈注〉被害を表す受動態は英語に訳しにくく,無理にこじつけると不自然になる。能動態で述べる方が無難。

【チャンス】

僕はいいチャンスを逃した。

I missed [lost] a good chance.

このチャンスを逃さないようにしろよ。

Don't let this chance slip by.

にている（似ている）

(性質が) **be** ｝ **like**《a thing / a person》
(外見が) **look** ｝

resemble《a thing / a person》(全般的); **be alike;** 共通点がある **have something in common**

1．人と人

【外見】

彼はおじいさんが若かったころによく似ている。

He looks like his grandfather when he was young.

【性質】

彼はおじいさんに(性質が)似ている。

He { is just like / takes after / resembles } his grandfather.

【声】

妹の声は私(の声)とよく似ている。

My sister's voice is just like mine.

【生き写し】

彼女はお母さんに本当によく似ている[生き写しだ]。

She is the very picture of her mother.

【うり二つ】

あの子たちは本当によく似ている。まさにうり二つというところだ。

They are { very much alike. / like two peas in a pod.

【似ていない】

あの人たちは兄弟なのに見たところも性質もあまり似ていない。

Although they are brothers they aren't much alike either in appearance or character.

2人は全然似ていないと思う。

I see no likeness whatever between them.

彼はお父さんに似ていなくて無口だ。

Unlike his father, he is rather reticent.

2．物と物[人]

その二つの仏像には著しく似ている点[類似点]がある。

There is a marked resemblance between the two Buddhist images.

この肖像画は(本人に)よく似ている。

This portrait is a good one.〔*colloq.*〕

〈注〉 直訳すると This portrait is a good likeness of the person. となるが日常会話としてはぎこちない。

【共通点】

物理と化学には似ている点がある[共通する点がある]。

Physics and chemistry have some things in common with each other.

酒の愛好家と興奮剤常用者には性格的に似ているところがある。

Alcohol users and stimulant drug users have certain traits in common.

〈注〉◆resemble は他動詞であるから，×He resembles to his father. としない。また「似ている」のつもりで ×be resembling と進行形にしてはいけない。そのままで「似ている」の意である。

◆like と alikeの比較

○ A is like B.　　× A is alike B.

○ A and B are alike.　　× A and B are like.

○ A and B are like each other.

にゅういん（入院）

【入院する】

enter (a [the]) hospital; go to (the) hospital; be hospitalized; be in (the) hospital

〈注〉〔英〕では be in hospital, go to hospital のように定冠詞をつけないのが普通だが，〔米〕では be in [go to] the hospital と定冠詞をつけるのが普通。

彼は精密検査を受けるため昨日入院した。

He { was hospitalized / entered / was sent to } (the) hospital } yesterday for a thorough examination.

彼は入院しなければならない。

He must { go to (the) hospital.（文脈によっては通院の意味にもなる） / be hospitalized. / stay in the hospital. }

彼女はまだ入院している[入院中だ]。

She is still in (the) hospital.

彼女はもう１か月も入院している。

She has been in (the) hospital for a month.

彼女はもうあと１か月入院していなければなるまい。

She will have to stay in (the) hospital another month.

【入院見舞い】

私は入院している友だちを見舞いに行った。

I went to see my friend in the hospital.

【入院申し込み[待機中]】

先生[医師]が県立病院に私の入院を頼んでくださった。

The doctor requested admission to the Prefectural Hospital for me.

今入院の順番を待っているところです。

I'm waiting for admission to the hospital.

彼は市民病院に入院した[入れてもらえた]。

He was admitted to the City Hospital.

【入院患者】

an inpatient (↔ outpatient 外来患者)

【入院料】

hospital charges (cf. medical expenses 医療費)

〈注〉 日本の診断書には「○○(病名)のため１か月の入院加療を要す」のように書くが，米国でそれに当ると思われるのは，a signed statement from a doctor で，

《Name》 was under treatment from 《date》 to 《date》.

《Name》 needs hospitalization for medical treatment [from 《date》 to 《date》].

のような書式である。健康診断書は medical certificate と言う。

にゅうがく（入学）

入学する **enter a school [university / college]**

合格する **be accepted by; be admitted to;**

登録する **enroll [enrol〔英〕] in**

入学金 an entrance fee

入学手続き

enrollment procedures

入学式 an entrance ceremony

入学者 a new [newly enrolled] student

彼は日大に入った[入学を許可された]。

He was accepted by Nichidai.

今年は英語科に55人の学生が入学した[入学の登録をした]。

Fifty-five students enrolled [are enrolled] in the English department this year.

〈注〉 **be admitted to** は次のような場合に使える。

be admitted to { Kyodai（京大に） / the Prefectural Hospital（県立病院に） / the Honors Program（優秀者コースに） / the history seminar（歴史のゼミに：入りにくいゼミの場合） }

be accepted by も選考の上，入学を許されること。就職に関しても使える。しかし，be accepted by Toyota より be offered a job by Toyota の方が自然。「入社できたか」と尋ねるのは Has X Company offered you a job (yet)? でよい。

enroll は入学手続きをして名簿に載ることで，自動詞・他動詞の両用法がある。

enrolled は手続きをしたという行動を，be enrolled は名簿に載っているという状態を言っているという違いがある（上記例文参照）。

にゅうし（入試）

an entrance examination [exam]

あの学校の入試では英語，数学および社会科４教科の中から１科目を選択することになっている。

The entrance examination for that school includes [covers] English, mathematics and one of four social science subjects.

入試で私は化学を選択する。

I'll take the chemistry section of the entrance exam.

彼は5つの大学の入試を受けた。

He {took / sat for} the entrance examinations for five universities.

入学を志願する

apply for admission to a college [university]

入学願書を出す

send in an application (form) for admission 《to a school》

【定員】

各学科[専攻]の定員は50名だ。

Each course is {limited / restricted} to fifty students.

【合格・不合格】

彼は県立大学{に合格した[受かった]。/ は不合格だった。}

He {succeeded in [passed] / failed (不合格)} the entrance exam for the prefectural college.

市立大に受かりましたか。

Have you {been / gotten〔米〕} accepted by [into] City University?

【合格発表】

(合格)発表はいつですか。

When can we get the results?

(合格)発表は日曜日です。

The results will be announced on Sunday.

They will announce the results of the exam on Sunday.

【合格通知】

今朝合格通知をもらいました。

This morning I got notice [was informed] that I'd passed the examination.

《関連語》

志願票　application form

志願者　applicants; candidates

〈注〉 applicants は志願の手続きをした人のこと。candidates は出願に必要な条件を満たし選考の対象になる候補者のことで，大学院入試に使う。

合格者　successful applicants [candidates]; entrants; those who passed the examination

高校の成績　one's high school grades

人物証明書　character reference

推薦書　letter of recommendation

選抜方法　selection process

テスト形式　method of testing

客観テスト　objective test

○×式テスト　true-false tests

選択式テスト　multiple-choice questions

論文試験　essay exam

口頭試問　oral exam

面接　interview

合格点　cut-off point

にんげん（人間）→ ひと

a human being; a human; a person; 人類 **humankind**

〈注〉 man はかつては人間の意味に使われたが，今は男性の意味に使われることが多いため，代りに人の意に a person が使われるようになった。

1. 神との対比

人間は死すべきものだ。

Man is mortal.（決った言い方）

Humans are mortal.

天候を支配することは人間の力ではできない。

It's beyond human power to control the weather.

誤りを犯すは人間の性(さが)，許すは神の性。

To err is human, to forgive divine.

——Alexander Pope, *An Essay on Man*

2. 人間性中心

人間の　**human;** 人間性　**human nature; humanity**

彼だって我々と同じ人間だ。

He is human like the rest of us.

ひとり孤立して住むのは人間性に反する。

It is against human nature to live {isolated from others. / alone.}

人間性[人情]はいずこも同じだ。

Human nature is the same everywhere.

彼は人間味がある。

He is warm-hearted.

彼は人間味がやや乏しい。

He lacks humanity a bit.〔*informal*〕

He is lacking a bit in humanity.〔*written*〕

3．人柄

彼は人間ができている[人柄がよい]。

He has a good character.

He is a man of character.

cf. He's quite a character. 彼は変り者だ。

（＝He's unique and interesting [odd].）

彼女はそんなことをするような人間ではない。

She isn't a person to do a thing like that.

にんめい（任命）

任命する　**appoint a person**（**to**《a position [an office]》）

任命される　**be appointed** [**designated, placed**]《position》

佐藤氏は法務次官に任命された。

Mr. Sato was appointed Vice-Minister of Justice.

彼は言語学の教授に任命された。

He was appointed (a) Professor of Linguistics.

彼女は衆議院議長に任命された。

She was {designated / named} Speaker of the House of Representatives.

彼は後任として任命された。

He has been appointed to fill the vacancy.

〈注〉 be appointed (a) director 2人以上が就いている役職名には冠詞はつけてもつけなくてもよい。ただしポストが一つしかない役職の肩書であれば役職名を大文字にして冠詞は省く。

ぬ

ぬう（縫う）

sew; stitch

1．裁縫

手で縫う
　sew by hand
ミシンで縫う
　sew with a sewing machine
服を縫う　sew [make] a dress
(細かく)縫う
　sew a seam（with a fine stitch）
粗く縫う［しつけをする］　baste
ほころびを縫う　mend a rip
ジーンズのかぎ裂きを縫う
　mend a tear in the jeans
縫い合せる　sew together
縫い目をほどく
　open the seam
　take the hem out（すそかがりなどをほどく）
ボタンを縫いつける　sew a button on
丈を縮める
　shorten the hem（すそ）[the dress（服）/ the sleeves（そで）]
すそを3センチ上げる
　turn up the hem（by）three centimeters
丈をのばす［すそを出す］
　lengthen the dress（服）[the sleeves（そで）]
　turn down the hem（すそ）
ウエストを縫い込む［出す］
　take in [let out] the waist
ズボンに折返しをつける
　cuff trousers

2．その他

【傷】
傷を閉じるのに5針も縫った。
　The wound was closed with five stitches.
　Five stitches were needed / It took five stitches } to close the wound.
　The doctor had to put in five stitches to close the wound.

【群れ】
彼は人の群れの中を縫うようにして通った。
　He {threaded / wove} his way through the crowd.

【流れ・道】
流れは大平原を縫うように蛇行していた。
　The stream {threaded / meandered} across the big plain.
山の小道は山間を縫うようにたどっていた。
　The mountain path meandered up and down.
〈注〉 thread には平面上を蛇行するイメージがあるので，山道に thread はそぐわない。

《関連語》
sewing　一般的な語
　mending　繕い
　making garments out of cloth　布から服を作ること
needlework　針仕事，特に刺繡（embroidery），アップリケ(appliqué)など。きれいなもの。
stitch　いろいろな縫い方の縫い目
　running stitch　平縫い
　hemstitch　かがり
　backstitch　返し縫い
　buttonhole stitch　ボタン穴かがり
patch　小布を当てる
darn　布地の薄くなった所をなぞって糸で補強する。穴など糸を縦横に渡して繕う。
baste　しつけをかける
tack　糸で留める，しつけをかける（カフスやえりなど）
tuck　タックをとる（布の長さ・幅の調節，または飾りとして）
dart　ダーツ（ふくらみを持たせるために縫い目が表に表れないようひだを取る縫い方）

pleat　プリーツ
gather　ギャザー。gathered yoke（ギャザーをとったヨーク）。gathered skirt（ギャザースカート）。
fold　折りたたむ（プリーツなどを作るため）
button　ボタン
snap　スナップ
zipper　ジッパー，チャック，ファスナー
hook and eye　ホックとホックを引っ掛ける金具
velcro　マジックテープ

ぬく（抜く）

1．引き抜く

draw; pull; pluck; take out;（根こそぎ）**root up**

【草花など】

庭の雑草を抜かなければならない。

We have to weed the garden.

草むしりをするときここの花を抜かないように。

Don't pull up these flowers while weeding.

【歯】

僕はこの歯を抜かなければ[抜いてもらわなければ]ならないんだ。

I must have this tooth pulled (out).

親知らずを抜く

have a wisdom tooth pulled out [extracted]

〈注〉 日常の会話では堅い extract より pull out の方がよく使われる。

【釘】

このくぎを抜いてください。服を引っかけてかぎ裂きを作りますよ。

{Pull [Take] this nail out. / Remove this nail.} It will catch on clothes and tear them.

【銃弾】

ピストルから銃弾を抜く

unload a revolver

外科医がその男の足から銃弾を抜いた。

The surgeon {extracted [removed] the bullet from / took the bullet out of} the man's leg.

【栓】

（ワインの）栓を抜いてください。

{Open / Uncork} this bottle (of wine).

【刀】

（さんざんけしかけられ）ついに彼は刀を抜かざるをえなくなった。

At last he was provoked to draw his sword.

2．抜粋する →いんよう

（本の中から）「心象」という概念を例証していると思われる部分を数か所抜き書きした。

I picked out passages which illustrate the concept of imagery.

〈注〉 この場合の pick out は choose, select の意味。

3．省く

leave out; omit; ページを飛ばす **skip over a page**

【範囲から】

試験の範囲は教科書１冊全部。ただし，教室で飛ばした２章は抜かす[抜く]。

The examination will cover the whole textbook except for the two chapters we have skipped in class.

【食事】

私は普通昼飯は抜く。

I usually {skip / go without} lunch.

【手抜き】

屋根が材料は悪く，仕事も粗雑な手抜き工事なのでもう雨漏りがしだした。

Because the roof was built with inferior materials and workmanship, it's already leaking.

4．取り除く

remove; take out

このインクのしみは抜けるでしょうか。

Will this ink spot come out?

Can this ink spot be removed?

だれかがタイヤの空気を抜いたに違いない。

Someone must have let air out of the tire [tyre].

5. 追い抜く

outstrip; outrun; get a lead (**on** one's **rival**) (競技などで); **go** [**get, move, push**] **ahead of** one's **opponent** (競技などで)

【競走】

初めボブが先頭だったが，後半でアレックスが追いつき，ゴール前で彼を抜いた。

At first Bob was in front, but in the latter half of the race Alex caught up with him and near the (finish) line got ahead of him.

彼はたちまちほかの選手を抜いてトップになった。(the field 全競技者)

He quickly outstripped the rest of the field.

【順位】

セントラルリーグではジャイアンツがドラゴンズを抜いて首位となった。

The Giants moved into top place in the Central League, past the Dragons.

スーパーソニックとは音速を抜いているという意味です。

The word 'supersonic' means "moving faster than sound".

彼女は数学ではすぐに兄を追い抜いてしまった。

She soon {outstripped / surpassed} her brother in mathematics.

〈注〉 outstrip の方が大差を意味する。

6. 貫く

pierce; go through; penetrate

目下，山の西側を貫くトンネル工事をしているところだ。

They are now constructing a tunnel through the west side of the mountain.

7. やり通す

戦い抜く

fight it out; fight to the last [the end]

苦労し抜く →くろう

彼女は苦労し抜いた。

She had a terribly [an awfully] hard [unlucky] life.

She met many problems.

〈注〉 {have [go through] / experience [suffer]} {all sorts of / many} hardships とも言えるが，hardship は本当にひどい苦労のことで，多少センチメンタルで陳腐な (sentimental and clichéd) 感じを与える。

ぬける (抜ける)

1. 取れる

come [**fall, slip**] **out** [**off**]

乳歯が抜けると子供はそれを枕の下に入れて寝る。

When a milk tooth falls [comes] out, the child puts it under his pillow.

〈注〉 欧米では夜中に tooth fairy (歯の妖精) が来て，銀貨と替えてくれるという言い伝えがある。

僕が回したらドアの取っ手が引っこ抜けた。

The door knob came off when I turned it.

彼女は飲んでいる薬の副作用で髪がたくさん抜けてしまった。

She has lost a lot of hair as a side effect of the medicine she's taking.

彼のズボンの膝が抜けていた。

His trousers were out at the knee.

彼のズボンのお尻が抜けた。

He has worn out the seat of his pants.

〈注〉 ズボンは〔米〕では pants,〔英〕では trousers と言う。

くぎが抜けかかっている。

The nail is loose.

くぎが抜け(落ち)ている。

The nail is missing [has come out].

引き出しがかたくて抜けない。

The drawers are very tight; they won't come out [slide out].

〈注〉 「引っこ抜く」意味なら take out [remove] the

drawers を使う。

2．不足する

be left out; be omitted; be missing

【ページ】

この本は2,3ページ抜けている。

A few pages are missing in this book.

【内容】

一番大切な部分が抜けている［に触れていない］。

The most important part is left out.

【間抜け】

あいつは少々間が抜けている。

He is a bit soft in the head.

He has something / Something is } missing upstairs.

〈注〉 上の例文はちょっとばかにした言い方。He is stupid. は，はっきり言いすぎである。

3．なくなる

be gone

すっかり力が抜けてしまった。

All my strength has gone.

I feel completely worn out.

火事があり，おじいさんはこわくて腰が抜けてしまった。

There was a fire, and the old man was so terrified that he couldn't move.

〈注〉 He was scared stiff. とも言える。また，paralyzed with fear とも言えるが「へたへたと座りこむ」ところまで含む言い方はない。

どうもかぜが抜けません［治りません］。

I can't shake off my cold.

My cold is still hanging on.

一度ついた癖はなかなか抜けないものだ。

It is hard to { change / get rid of } one's habits.

このビールは気が抜けてしまった。

This beer has gone [become] flat.

ゴールデンウィークに帰省しても1時限(授業が)抜けるだけだ(ほかの先生は皆休講にしたから)。

I will miss only one class if I go home for Golden Week (because most teachers cancelled class that week).

4．通り抜ける

go through; pass through

【公園】

公園を抜けて行こう。

Let's go through the park.

【市街】

我々は市の中心を通り抜けて行った。

We passed through the center of the city.

5．逃れる

get out of; get away; go out; slip out

【仕事・雑事】

今朝はずっと忙しくてとても抜けられない。

I'll be too busy all morning to go out.

しばらくは仕事が忙しくてちょっと抜けられない［抜け出せない］。

I can't get away (from work) for the time being.

I can't get out of the office right now.(今)

今日の午後の会合はちょっと抜けられない。

I can't get out of the meeting this afternoon.

〈注〉 (1) get away from / (2) get out of } the meeting

(1)は leave the meeting for a while [early] と言い換えられ，ちょっと抜け出す（また戻るかも知れない），(2)は don't go at all, avoid [evade] the meeting で避ける，逃れるの意。(2)の方が完全に抜ける意である。抜け出すのが office のように場所であるときは(1)(2)どちらでも同じに使える。

I can't get out of the party, but maybe I can get away early.（パーティーは抜けるわけにいかないが早目に抜け出すことはできるだろう）

【抜け出す】

彼はコンサートの途中で抜け出して家に帰った。

He slipped out of the concert (early) and went home.

【サボる】

彼女は学校から抜け出した。

She sneaked out of school.

【脱退】

彼は1年もするとそのバンドを抜けてしまった。

He left [quit] the band after a year.

ぬすむ（盗む）・ぬすまれる

steal そっと盗む; **rob**（奪う意を含む）; **rob**《a person》**of**《something》; **run** [**walk**] **away with**《something》持ち逃げする

1. 泥棒

泥棒が独り住まいの老婦人の家に押し入り，ナイフを突きつけてお金を盗んだ。

A burglar broke into a house where an old lady lived alone and threatened her with a knife and stole her money.

【盗まれる】

繁華街を歩いていて財布を盗まれた。

My purse was stolen while I was walking downtown.

彼は人込みで財布を盗まれた。

His wallet was stolen in the crowd.

〈注〉◆×I was stolen my purse. はよくある誤り。I had my purse stolen. は正しい文だが,「盗まれた」「盗ませた」の両方の意にとれるので My purse was stolen. の方が自然な文である。

◆A が B から金を盗んだ。B は(A に)金を盗まれた。

A stole money from B.
Money was stolen from B (by A).
(×B was stolen money by A.)
A robbed B of money.
B was robbed of money (by A).
(×B was robbed money.)

その銀行員は自分の銀行の金を盗んだ。

The bank clerk {embezzled / stole / ran away with} money from his own bank.

〈注〉 embezzle は横領する，着服するの意。

2. 慣用表現

【人目を】

毎夜2人は神社の大木の下で人目を盗んで[忍んで]会っていた。

Every night they met secretly under the big tree at the shrine.

【暇を】

暇を盗んでひと眠りする[何かをする]

steal (a) few minutes' sleep [the time to do something]

彼は暇を盗んでコンピュータ・プログラミングの講習を受けている。

He steals the time to take a computer programming course.

〈注〉 steal the time とは忙しい人がほかの仕事の時間を削ってやりたいことをする意。

ね

…ね

【念を押す言い方】

〔強〕I'm sure

〔弱〕I suppose; you know

彼女はきっとうまくやりますよね。

She'll do fine, I'm sure.

これ，あなたのですね。

This is yours, I suppose.

彼は悪いやつじゃないよね。

He isn't a bad fellow, you know.

〈注〉 **付加疑問文の作り方**

本文が肯定文なら付加疑問文は否定文，本文が否定文なら付加疑問文は肯定文になる。

He is … , isn't he? / He isn't … , is he?

She does(一般動詞) … , doesn't she?

She doesn't … , does she?

「…ね」のつもりで何でも isn't it? ですまそうとするのは誤り。文頭の主語と動詞によって形が決まる。動詞が be(〔英〕では haveも)以外の一般動詞のときは付加疑問の部分には do(またはその変形)が使われる。なお，返事を期待しない疑問文なのでイントネーションは下降調になる。

それじゃ君は僕らに賛成というわけだね。

So, you agree with us, don't you?

それが起ったとき彼女はいなかったというわけね。

She wasn't there when it happened, was she?

僕たちは友達だよね。

We are friends, aren't we?

〈注〉 話の間に念を押すようにやたらに you know を連発する人がいるが，無意味な言葉は避ける方がよい。

ねえ

【呼びかけ】→あの

Excuse me.（最も一般的で無難にいつでも使える表現）

ねえ［もしもし］，財布が落ちましたよ。

Excuse me, you dropped your wallet.

おい，ジム，財布が落ちたよ。

Hey, Jim, you dropped your wallet

〈注〉 Hey は音がよく通るので，このように相手の注意を引くときにはよいが，荒っぽい言葉であるからごく親しい間柄に限る方がよい。

ねがう（願う）・ねがい → がんぼう

1. 願う

（心に）**desire; want; wish; hope**

神に **pray（for）**

【希望する】

すべての人が世界平和を願っている。

Everybody wants [desires, wishes for, hopes for] world peace.

〈注〉 desire は want より堅い表現。wish は実現しそうにないと思いつつ願う。hope は実現できるだろうと思いつつ願う。hope は be hoping の形も可能。

人々がこれ以上の自然破壊をしないように何とか阻止したいと願っている。

We wish [hope] to stop people from destroying nature more.

われわれはきれいな空気がほしい。市が新型で強力な焼却炉を設置してくれることを願う。少なくともすべての小型焼却炉は廃棄してほしい。

We want to have clean air, so we wish the city would build new and efficient incinerators. At least we hope to get all the small incinerators torn down.

人々は元旦には初参りをして昔から家族の幸せを神様にお願いする。

On New Year's Day people visit shrines, traditionally to pray for the happiness of their families.

2. 頼む

ask for; request

何かひと言(感想を)お願いできますでしょうか。

May I ask you for (your) comments?

ドラッグストアまで行って来る間，子供たちをお願いできますかしら。
Can [May] I leave the children with you while I go to [I'm at] the drugstore?

【切り出し】
お願いがあるのですが。
Can I ask you a favor?
Will you do me a favor?
I'd like to ask you to do something.
There is something I'd like to ask you to do for me.
May I ask a favor of you?〔*rather formal*〕

【電話】
中村さんを(電話口に)お願いします。
Could I speak to Mr. Nakamura?
I'd like to speak to Mr. Nakamura.
人事課をお願いします。
Could you {put me through to / give me} the personnel section, please?

3．願い →がんぼう
彼の長い間の願いがやっとかなった。
What he had wished for so long finally came true.
法務省は市長たちからの指紋押捺廃止の要望を長い間退けてきた。
For a long time the Justice Dept. refused to accede to the city mayors' petition that fingerprinting be abolished.
願いを聞く
grant a request〔*formal*〕
do what is asked / say OK
願いを退ける
refuse [turn down] a request
〈注〉「願いを聞く，要望を入れる」には次のような語もある。
agree（提案などに)同意する，賛成する。
ex. He agreed to buy me a car [lend me the money for a car].（彼は私の願いを入れて車を買ってくれる［車を買うお金を貸してくれる］ことになった）
comply（**with**）要求に応じる，命令に従う。
ex. Some of the students refused to comply with the order to take part in the parade.（生徒の中にはパレード参加命令に従わない者もいた）

4．届け出
休暇願　leave of absence
休暇願を出す
request {sick [medical] leave（病欠願） / maternity leave（産休願） / academic leave（離席研修願）}
〈注〉欠席届は notification of absence。欧米では小・中学生などは sick note を親から担任に出すか親が電話をかける。
彼は退職願を出した。
He {sent in his resignation.（郵送した） / submitted his resignation. / tendered [offered] his resignation.〔*formal*〕}
〈注〉閣僚が交替するときなどに形式的に辞表を出すことは欧米でもあり，そのような場合は tender または offer one's resignation と言う。

ねだん（値段）・ねあげ・ねさげ

1．値段
売値　a price
生産にかかった値段
the cost（原料・労賃など）
適正な値段
a reasonable price
値段が高い
be expensive; be high in price; be high-priced
値段が安い
be inexpensive; be low in price; be low-priced
安い[高い]値段で買う
buy at a low [high] price
この時計の値段はいくらですか。
How much is this watch?
How much does this watch cost?
1000円(の値段)で買う
buy《a thing》for 1,000 yen

2. 値上げ・値下げ
【値上げする】 raise the price of a thing
このところ物の値が上がっている。
Prices have been going up recently.
市場の品物を買い占めてはその品物の値上がりを待つけしからん業者がいる。
There are some dishonest dealers who buy up [corner] goods in the market and then wait for their prices to go up.
【値下げする】 lower the price of 《a thing》; 名 a reduction
2500円から1300円に値下げする
lower the price from 2,500 yen to 1,300 yen
2割の値下げをする
lower [reduce] the price by 20 percent
海外からの直輸入が可能になったのでスーパーの中にはビールの値下げを行ったところがある。
Some supermarkets have reduced the price of their beer because they can now buy directly from abroad.
(バーゲンなどで) 2割値引きをする
give a 20 percent discount
discount (by) 20%
明日から3日間全商品2割の値下げをするそうだ。
There'll be a 20% discount on all goods for three days starting tomorrow.

ねつい (熱意)・ねっしん (熱心)
1. 熱意・熱心・熱中
熱心である **be eager**
彼は車の運転を早く覚えようと熱心だ。
He is eager to learn how to drive.
He's enthusiastic about learning how to drive.
彼は熱心な学生だ。
He is a hardworking student.
彼は熱心に英語を勉強している。
He is bent on learning English.
彼はいつも本に熱中している。→むちゅう
He's always got his head (stuck) in a book.
彼は音楽[スポーツ]に熱中している。
He has a passion for music.
He's keen on sports. 〔英〕
十代の女の子たちはそのロックシンガーに熱を上げた[熱狂した]。
The teenage girls went crazy over the rock singer.
あの人は事業に熱中している。
She devotes all her energy to her business.
うちの十代の娘はファッションに熱中している。
My teenager is heavily into fashion these days. 〔*colloq.*〕
彼は熱心なクリスチャンだ。
He's a devout Christian.
君は熱意が(足り)ない。
You lack enthusiasm.

2. 没頭する，余念がない
彼女は論文[コンピュータゲーム]に熱中している。
She is intent on getting her paper written.
She is absorbed in a computer game.

ねまわし (根まわし)
〈注〉 政治などにつきものの「根まわし」は，日本だけの専売特許ではなく欧米においても行われる。その証拠には次のような表現があるが，これらは皆いわゆる「根まわし」をすることである。必ずしも悪い意味ではなく，紛争国の和平のための裏工作など必要なときもある。
予備的な工作をする
do the [some] spadework
mobilize [gather] support beforehand
地ならしをする
lay the groundwork
政治的取引をする
do some politicking
裏取引をする
talk behind the scenes 〔*often negative*〕

打診する

sound out the opposition

税制改革を成立させる[阻止する]ための根まわしをしている。

They are lobbying for [against] tax reform.

〈注〉「闇取り引きをする」は make a backroom deal, 裏工作は behind-the-scenes negotiations と言う。

ねむる（眠る）・ねる → すいみん

〈注〉「寝る」は「眠る」意味と「寝床に入る」意味の両方に使われる。また，体を横にすることも「寝る」と言う。それぞれ sleep, go to bed, lie down であり別のことである。

ex. I went to bed quite early but couldn't sleep for a while.（私は早く寝たのだが，しばらく眠れなかった）

また「眠る」に関しても sleep は一般的に眠る，go to sleep, fall asleep は目覚めていた状態から眠りにつくことを，be sleeping, be asleep は眠っている状態を指す。

be in bed は寝床に入っていることで，目覚めているか眠っているかは関係ない。昼間なら「病気」の意味になることが多い。lie in bed は目を覚していても眠っていてもとにかくベッドに横になっていること。on the bed はいる場所を示す。

1．眠る

sleep

眠っている　be sleeping; be asleep

眠りにつく

go to sleep;（知らぬ間に）fall asleep;（やっと寝つく）get to sleep

【よく眠った[眠れなかった]】

昨夜はよく眠りました[眠れませんでした]。

I slept [didn't sleep] well last night.

彼はぐっすり眠った。

He slept like a log [top].

一晩ぐっすり眠ったら頭痛が治るでしょう。

A good night's sleep will cure (you of) your headache.

【寝つく】

薬を飲まないと眠れません。

I cannot sleep without taking a pill.

(昨夜)は遅くまで眠れなかった[寝つきが悪かった]。

I wasn't able to get to sleep for a long time.

私は寝床に入るとあっと言う間に眠ってしまった。

I fell asleep the moment { I got into bed. / my head hit the pillow. }

【睡眠中】

赤ちゃんが眠っています。

The baby is sleeping [asleep].

【眠れぬ夜】

彼は息子のことが心配でいく晩も眠れぬ夜を過した。

He had a series of sleepless nights worrying about his son.

2．寝床につく

寝に行く　**go to bed;** ベッドに入っている **be in bed; lie in bed**

【寝る時間】

子供たちはもう寝る時間です。

It's time for the children to go to bed.

It's time the children go [went] to bed.

〈注〉It's time ... children go [went] to bed. の go も went も一種の仮定法で went といっても過去のことではない。英国でよく使われる。米国では for the children to go ... の形が一番一般的な言い方。

3．病気で寝込む

be sick [ill] in bed

インフルエンザで寝込んでいる

be laid up with flue

お医者様から起きてもよいというお許しが出るまで寝ていなければなりませんよ。

You should stay in bed until you get your doctor's permission to get up.

4．寝そべる

lie down

私は草の上に寝て白い雲が流れてゆくのを見つめていた。

I lay down on the grass and watched the

white clouds floating by.
猫が暖炉の敷物の上に長々と寝そべっていた。
A cat was lying stretched out on the hearth rug.

5. 寝坊する

get up late; sleep late; oversleep

眠たがり　a sleepyhead
今朝は寝坊をして授業に遅れた。
This morning I overslept and was late for my lesson.
この2, 3週間はねむくてねむくてたまらなかった。
I've been such a sleepyhead the past few weeks.

6. 慣用表現

寝た子を起すな。
Let sleeping dogs lie!
そのニュースはまさに寝耳に水だった。
The news hit me like a bolt from the blue.
寝ても覚めても彼女は金もうけのことを考えていた。
Asleep or awake, she thought of making money.

ねんちゅうぎょうじ(年中行事)

Annual Events, Festivals, and National Holidays

1. 日本の年中行事・祝日

【伝統的行事】 Traditional Annual Events

1月 January

1日　元日　New Year's Day
神社参拝　visiting shrines
〈注〉 英米の正月は大晦日の夜（New Year's Eve）から元旦にかけて祝うだけで，職場は2日から平常に戻る。日本のように3日間，または1週間の松の内のような習慣はない。

2月 February

3日または4日　節分　*Setsubun* (the last day of winter by the old Japanese calendar)
節分には「鬼は外，福は内」と叫びながら豆をまく。
People scatter beans crying "Devils, get out! Good luck, come in!"

3月 March

3日　ひな祭り　*Hinamatsuri* (Doll Festival; *Momo-no-Sekku*)
古代宮廷の様子をかたどった内裏様，女官，廷臣の人形を飾り女の子の成長を祝う。
People display a set of dolls representing an ancient emperor, empress, and courtiers to celebrate the growth of their little girls.
21日頃　春のお彼岸　*Ohigan*（春分の日 Vernal Equinox Day を中心とする7日間）
ご先祖のお墓参りをする。
People visit their ancestral tombs.

4月 April

3～10日　各地の神社の春祭り　Spring Festival (of Shinto shrines)
もとは五穀豊饒を祈る農耕儀礼
originally agricultural rites to pray for good crops

5月 May

5日　端午の節句　*Tango-no-Sekku* (Boys' Day)
鯉のぼりを立てて男の子の成長を祈る。
People set up bamboo poles to which are attached colorful cloth streamers in the shape of carp to celebrate the growth of their little boys.

7月 July

7日　七夕　*Tanabata* (Star Festival)
子供たちが短冊に思い思いに願いを書いて竹の枝に飾る。
Children decorate bamboo branches with strips of colored paper with their wishes written on them.

8月 August

13, 14, 15日　お盆　*Bon* Festival
仏教ではお盆の法要をする。お盆には先祖，近親者の霊が家に帰ると考えられており，都会に暮す人々も故郷に帰り，親族が一堂に会するときとなっている。
Buddhists observe the Bon Festival. They believe the spirits of the dead return to visit their families on earth. People living in cities return to their ancestral homes or birth places to join the festival. It is now a family reunion time.

9月 September

23日頃　秋のお彼岸　*Ohigan*　(秋分の日 Autumnal Equinox Day を中心とする7日間)
ご先祖のお墓参りをする。
People visit their ancestral tombs.

10月 October

10〜20日　各地神社の秋祭り　Autumn Festival (of Shinto shrines)
収穫感謝の儀礼　thanksgiving rites

12月 December

20〜30日　年末大掃除　end-of-the-year [thorough] cleaning of one's house and office
31日　大晦日　*Omisoka*, the last day of the year
正月の飾り，おせちをつくり，年越しそばを食べる。
People make New Year's decorations, prepare New Year's food and eat end-of-the-year soba noodles.

【国民の祝日】National Holidays (newly established festivals and events)
1月1日　元日　New Year's Holiday
第2月曜日　成人の日　Coming of Age Day, Adults' Day
2月11日　建国記念日　National Foundation Day
3月21日頃　春分の日　Vernal Equinox Day
4月29日　みどりの日　Greenery Day
5月3日　憲法記念日　Constitution Memorial Day
4日　国民の祝日　National People's Day
5日　こどもの日　Children's Day
7月第3月曜日　海の日　Marine Day
9月第3月曜日　敬老の日　Respect for the Aged Day
23日頃　秋分の日　Autumnal Equinox Day
10月第2月曜日　体育の日　Sports Day
11月3日　文化の日　Culture Day
23日　勤労感謝の日　Labor Thanksgiving Day
12月23日　天皇誕生日　the Emperor's Birthday

2. 米国の年中行事・祝日・休日

National Holidays, Annual Events in the US

(◎国で定めた休日，○多くの州で休日，△休日にならない，S日曜日・安息日)

January

◎ 1日　New Year's Day　元日
○ 16日前後　Martin Luther King, Junior Day　マーティン・ルーサー・キング記念日

February

△ 14日　Valentine's Day　バレンタインデー
○ 15日に近い月曜日　President's Day　ワシントン・リンカーン記念日

February
March　} Lent—Easter　復活祭を中心とする行事
April

△ Shrove Tuesday (Lent に入る前日の「ざんげ火曜日」であるが，Pancake Tuesday「パンケーキの火曜日」とも呼ばれ，楽しみ収めの日でもある)
△ Lent 四旬節(Ash Wednesday 聖灰水曜日

に始まり復活祭までの日曜を除いた40日間；節食と改悛の期間）

△ Good Friday　聖金曜日，キリスト受難日（復活祭直前の金曜日）

S Easter Sunday　復活祭（春分後の最初の満月の日の次の日曜日に行われる。3月末から4月半ばまでの日曜日で毎年変る。Lent その他も復活祭から逆算して定まるので毎年変る）

April

△ 22日　Earth Day　地球の日

May

S 第2日曜日　Mother's Day　母の日

○ 最後の月曜日　Memorial Day　戦没将兵追悼の記念日（多くの州で休日）

June

△ 14日　Flag Day　国旗制定記念日

S 第3日曜日　Father's Day　父の日

July

◎ 4日　Independence Day ((the) 4th of July)　独立記念日（この日が土曜日に当れば金曜日が，日曜日に当れば月曜日が休日となる）

September

◎ 第1月曜日　Labor Day　労働の日（勤労をたたえる日）

October

○ 第2月曜日　Columbus Day　コロンブスの日（コロンブスのアメリカ大陸発見の記念日; Discovery Day ともいう）

△ 31日　Halloween　ハロウィーン（All Saints' Day の前夜祭；元の宗教的な意味は薄れ，今は子供の楽しむお祭り）

November

○（隔年）第1月曜の次の火曜日　Election Day (the Presidential election をはじめ原則としてすべての選挙はこの日に行われる）

◎ 11日　Veterans' Day　復員軍人の日

◎ 第4木曜日　Thanksgiving Day　感謝祭

December

◎ 25日　Christmas Day　クリスマス（学校は (the) Christmas holidays (12/25〜1/1) に入る）

3．英国の年中行事・祝日・休日

National Holidays, Annual Events in Britain

（◎休日，○地方により休日，△休日にならない）

January

◎ 1日　New Year's Day　元日

February
March
April
} Lent—Easter
復活祭を中心とする行事

△ Shrove Tuesday　（米国の年中行事参照）

△ Lent　四旬節（Ash Wednesday　聖灰水曜日に始まり復活祭までの日曜日を除いた40日間；節食と改悛の期間）

◎ Good Friday　聖金曜日，キリスト受難日（復活祭直前の金曜日）

S Easter Sunday　復活祭（春分後の最初の満月の日の次の日曜日に行われる）

○ Easter Monday　復活祭の翌日の月曜日

May

△ 1日　May Day　メーデー（昔からの春祭り。今は労働者の祭りでもある）

◎ 第1月曜日　Early May Holiday　5月はじめの休日

◎ 最後の月曜日　Spring (Bank) Holiday　銀行法定休業日

August

◎ 最後の月曜日　(Late) Summer (Bank) Holiday　銀行法定休業日

October

△ 31日　Halloween　ハロウィーン（All Saints' Day の前夜祭；今は子供の楽しむ祭り）

November

△ 5日　Guy Fawkes Day　ガイ＝フォークスの日（火薬陰謀事件の首謀者ガイ＝フォークスの逮捕を祝って行う記念日）

5日の夜は Bonfire Night といって大きなかがり火をたく。

December

◎ 25日　Christmas Day　クリスマス

◎ 26日　Boxing Day　クリスマスの贈り物の日（かつて使用人・郵便配達人・お巡りさんなどに祝儀や贈り物をした）

◎ 31日　New Year's Eve　元日前夜

〈注〉 米国，英国の年中行事としてキリスト教の行事のみを述べたが，世界全体の流れとして両国とも今日では他の宗教を信じる人々も多く移り住み，古くからのユダヤ教のほかイスラム教，ヒンズー教，仏教などを信じる人々はそれぞれの宗教行事を守っている。

の

…の

1．所有・所属

【人の】

私の家　my house

私の弟の子

my brother's child（＝my niece [nephew]）

彼の父の名前　his father's name

私の友人の１人　one of my friends

ビルがロブの頭をたたいた。

Bill hit Rob on the head.(1)

ボールがとんできてロブの頭にあたった。

A ball came flying and hit Rob's head.(2)

〈注〉(1)の形は故意にたたいた場合，(2)の形は主語が人ならば故意とも偶然ともとれる。look me in the eye（私の目をじっと見る）という言い方もある。

【ものの】

クラブの部員

a club member; a member of a club

家の一部が地震で壊れた。

Part of the house was damaged by the earthquake.

【同格】

弟のジョン　my brother John

これは妹の春子です。

This is my sister, Haruko.

〈注〉×This is Haruko of my sister.

【…に関する，…に対する】

〈注〉「の」の用法は多様であるため「A の B」は必ずしも A's B または B of A と置き換えられない。

音楽の先生　a music teacher

胃の薬　stomach medicine

英文学の本

a book on English literature

１万円の小切手

a check for 10,000 yen

a 10,000 yen check [cheque〔英〕]

裏口のかぎ

the key to the back door; the backdoor key

社長[学長]の秘書

the secretary to the president

家の恥

a disgrace to the family; a family disgrace

【…による，…という性質の】

漱石の作品

the works of Soseki（全作品）; a novel by Soseki（一つの小説）; Soseki's novels（漱石の小説）

啄木の詩　a poem by Takuboku

ブロンズの胸像　a bronze statue

女の先生　a woman teacher

各種サイズのドレス　dresses in all sizes

流行のドレス　a fashionable dress

【場所・時間】

本郷の学校　a school at [in] Hongo

長良川の橋　bridges over the Nagara River

木曽川の橋の一つ

one of the Kiso River bridges

１時間の休み時間　an hour's break

今日の新聞　today's paper

数千年前の人

people who lived thousands of years ago

古代の人

people in ancient times; ancient people

〈注〉**of か at か**

◆「この学校の先生」は a teacher at this school と言う。of が使えるのは a teacher of English（英語の先生）のような場合で，普通は前後関係から「この学校の」の意味とわかるので，a teacher here [there] で十分と思われる。

ex. My father {teaches / is a teacher of} English at ○○ High School.

（私の父は○○高校の英語の先生です）

The library at my high school is excellent.

（うちの高校の図書館は大変すばらしい）

◆of は既出の「所属」の例のように全体の一部 a part of the whole や計量などを表す場合に使うのが自然。

ex. one of them; a member of a club; a piece of chalk; a loaf of bread; a pound of cheese, etc.

2. 従節中の主体・対象を表す「の」

【主体】

雨の降る日　a rainy day

桜の咲くころ　cherry blossom time [season]

父のお気に入り　my father's favorite

【対象】

川の見える部屋

a room with a view of the river

a room overlooking the river

校舎の建築

the construction of the school house

3. もの・名詞化の「の」

【もの】

大きい方の　the bigger one

もっと安いのを見せてください。

Can you show me {something cheaper, / a cheaper one,} please?

【こと】

私の知りたいのはそんなことではない。

That's not what I want to know.

の（野）

1. 原野

field　野原; **fields**　畑（farmland）

《類義語》

grassland　草地

plain　平原・原野など一般的な地勢（topology）に関する言い方

prairie　プレーリー（米国からカナダにかけての大草原）

plateau　高原

steppe　ステップ（砂漠よりやや湿潤な地域の大草原）

swamp; marsh　湿地

riverbed　河川敷

wilderness　人手の入らない土地

2. 慣用表現

野の花　a wild flower

野遊び　a picnic

野に出て働く　work in the fields

彼は90歳近いが天気がよければ野に出て働いている。

He's nearly ninety years old but he works in the field when [whenever] the weather is good.

のうか（農家）

農家 **a farmhouse;** 農場 **a farm;**（農業従事者）**a farmer**

【職業】

うちは農家です。

We are farmers.

私は農家出身です。

I come from farming stock [people].

【場所】

私たちは農家で育ちました。

We were brought up on the farm.

〈注〉◆映画などで見る通り米国の農場は日本の農家と広さと規模が違う。次の例のように北海道の農場なら farm がぴったりする。

I spent the summer vacation working on a farm in Hokkaido.（北海道の農家でバイトをして夏休みを過ごした）

◆△work in [at] a farmhouse とすると，農業ではなく，家の中で事務の仕事や炊事の手伝いなどをしたことになる。

【人々】

今は農家の忙しいときだ。

This is the busiest season for farmers.

近頃は農家を取り巻く環境が厳しくなってきた。

Things are getting harder for farmers these days.

のうりょく（能力）

《類義語》

ability　一般的な能力（何かをしたり考えたり作ったりする力，技能）

faculty　知的能力

capacity　やればできる潜在能力，容量・収容能

力，生産能力から出た語
capability 実務的能力，特に複雑で困難な仕事をこなす能力
competence（**competency**） 適性

【能力】
能力がある，できる can do《something》
能力別クラス編成
homogeneous [ability] grouping; streaming
生徒の能力を伸ばす
help students to develop their abilities
年をとると体温調節の能力が低下する。
As people get older the ability of their body to regulate (body) temperature decreases.
私の息子は有能な運転手だ。
My son's very capable as a driver.

【知的能力】
彼にはその問題を解く能力があると確信している。
I'm sure he is able to solve the problem.
彼には人を統率する能力がある。
He is capable of organizing people.
彼は仕事の上で[部内で]抜群の能力を買われている。
He is considered (to be)
{ very competent in his business.
{ one of the most competent in his section.
彼の計算能力はすごい。
He's very good at calculation.
新しいコンピュータはその計算をほんの2，3秒でやる能力がある。
The new computer can do the calculation in a few seconds.

【支払い能力】 名 solvency（法律用語）
彼にはそんな金を支払う能力がない。
He cannot pay that much.
彼には借金の返済能力[ローンの支払い能力]がなかった。
He wasn't able to
{ pay his debts.
{ repay [pay off] the loan.

【収容能力】
このホールは約1500人の収容能力がある。
This hall can seat about 1,500 people.
The seating capacity of this hall is about 1,500.

【生産能力】
production capacity（1か月何万台の生産能力がある，などについて使う語）
productivity（1人当り1時間の生産高によってはかる能率）

【能力を活かす】
だれもが自分の能力をフルに活かせる職業につけるというものではない。
Not everyone can expect to find a job that makes the best of their ability.
サラは研究所の仕事ならよいと思った。彼女の分析能力を活かせるからだ。
Sarah felt that a job at a research institute would be good, because it would allow her to use her analytical ability [abilities].
佐藤氏は彼の説得能力をフルに活用した。
Mr. Sato made full use of his persuasive abilities.
彼はいつも自己の能力をフル回転して働いている。
He always works to the best of his abilities.

【能力主義】
彼らは能力に応じて昇進することになっている。
They are promoted according to ability.

【能力以上】 beyond one's ability
あなたはあの人に能力以上のことを要求している。
You're asking something beyond her ability.

のこる（残る）・のこす

〈注〉「残る」（動自 remain）と「残す」（動他 leave）を混同しないように。

1．残る

㊍㊀ **remain; stay;** 残される **be left;** 生き残る **survive**

【人】
皆は急いで立ち去ったが我々２人は残った。
They hurried away, but we two remained.
cf. ×We were remained.

【仕事】
僕はもうちょっと仕事が残っています。
I have [I've got] some more work to do.

【お金】
いくらかお金が残った。
There is some money left.

【心に】
(そのことは)生涯人々の心に残るでしょう。
It will stay [remain, live] in people's memory as long as they live.
They'll remember this as long as they live.

【雪】
遠くの山にはまだ雪が残っていた。
There was still (some) snow (lying [left]) on the distant mountains.

【生き残る】
その飛行機事故では10歳の男の子が奇跡的に生き残った。
A ten-year-old boy miraculously survived the plane crash.
だれが経済戦争で生き残るだろうか。
Who can survive the economic war?

【霊魂】
私は死後に霊魂が残るとは考えない。
I don't believe in life after death.

【計算】
10から７を引くと３残る。(10 − 7 = 3)
7 from 10 / 10 minus 7 } { is [equals] / leaves } 3.
10割る３は３，残り１。(10÷３＝３…１)
10 divided by 3 equals 3 with 1 remaining [a remainder of 1].

2．残す，遺す

㊍㊉ **leave**

【置き去り】
病気の子を１人残して皆仕事に出かけた。
They all went (off) to work leaving the sick child alone.

【居残り】
僕は罰として放課後学校に残された。
As punishment I was made [had] to stay after school.
２人とも放課後残っていなさい。
You will both stay in after school.

【やりかけ】
仕事をやりかけで残してはいけない。
Don't leave your work half done.
彼は宿題をやらずに残したまま遊びに行ってしまった。
He went out to play leaving his homework undone.
あまりたくさんごちそうがあるのでほとんどのお客は食べきれずに残してしまった。
There was so much to eat that most of the guests left some of the food on their plates.

【死んで遺す】
彼は若い妻と生れたばかりの子供を遺して死んだ。
He died leaving his young wife with a new born baby.
彼は莫大な財産を遺した。
He left a large fortune behind.
彼が死んで遺したのは借金だけだ。
When he died
{ nothing remained but debts.
{ he left nothing but debts behind.※

〈注〉 ※の文では腹立たしさが感じられる。

3．残り

残り物を集めて箱に詰めてください。
Gather up what's left and pack it in that box.
残り物を冷蔵庫にしまってください。
Put (away) the leftovers in the refrigerator.
残りのお金はどう使うつもりですか。
How are you going to use the rest of your

money?

〈注〉 rest とは何かほかに目的があって使った残りのこと。

のぞく（除く）→ いがい(以外)，ほか

のびのび（延び延び，伸び伸び）

1．延引

延び延びになる

be put off day after day

be delayed a long time

その決定は延び延びになっている。

The decision has long been delayed.

借金の返済が延び延びになっている。

The debt repayment is long overdue.

2．自由

卒論が終ったのでのびのびした気分だ。

I feel greatly relieved, now that the thesis is finished.

あの人の子供たちは皆できるだけ自由に育てられたのでのびのびしている。

All her children are being brought up with as little restraint as possible, so they act quite freely.

のびる（伸びる，延びる）・のばす

1．長くなる，長くする

stretch; extend

【伸びる，延びる】

ここにはゴムが使ってある。ゴムは伸びるからね。

Rubber is used here because it's elastic.

（ソックスの）ゴムの部分が伸びてしまった。

The elastic { has stretched out. / has lost its stretch. / is worn out. }

輪ゴムが伸びるだけ伸びている。

This rubber band is stretched as far as it'll go.

枝は太陽に向かって伸びる。

Boughs reach out toward the sun.

君の髪はずいぶん伸びたね。

Your hair has grown a lot.

道路は島の北端まで延びている。

The road now goes [extends] to the northern end of the island.

【伸ばす，延ばす】

彼は新聞を取ろうと手を伸ばした。

He stretched out his hand [reached] for the newspaper.

朝顔が隣の軒までつるを伸ばした。

The morning glories stretched (all the way) to the neighbor's eaves.

服のすそを伸ばしていただけませんか。

Would you let down the hem?

〈注〉 「ダーツの分を出して肩幅を広げる」は let out the darts to make the shoulders fuller と言う。

あの子は髪を伸ばしている。

She wears her hair long.

鉄道を青森市まで延ばすことに決定した。

It was decided to extend the railroad as far as Aomori City.

コードをつないで延ばさないと届かない。

The cord is too short. We need an extension cord.

2．まっすぐにする

伸ばす **stretch; straighten;** （しわを） **smooth out**

伸びる **be straightened;** （しわが） **become smooth**

〈注〉 stretch はその材質の限界まで引っぱり伸ばすこと。straighten は真っすぐにする，きちんとなおす。extend はさらに付け足して長くすること。

彼は体を伸ばしてあくびをした。

He stretched himself and yawned.

どうぞ足を伸ばして楽になさってください。

Please stretch out your legs and relax.

彼は針金を伸ばして一方を水道の蛇口につないだ。

He straightened the wire and fastened one

end to the water tap.

彼女はしわくちゃになったお札を1枚1枚丹念に伸ばした。

She laboriously {smoothed out / straightened} the crumpled bills one by one.

彼はコートのえりの折り返しのしわを手で伸ばした。

He smoothed down [out] his coat flap.

彼女はスカートのしわをアイロンで伸ばした。

She ironed [pressed] out the creases in her skirt.

3．時間延長

【延ばす】

先送りする　put off [postpone]

遅延する　delay (one's answer)

延長する　extend [prolong] (one's stay)

【延びる】

be put off [postponed]; be delayed; be extended

【延長】

夏に向かうにつれて日が延びてゆく。

The days become longer toward summer.

平均寿命が年々延びている。

The average life span is lengthening every year.

会議が(予定時間を越えて)延びた。

The conference was extended.

The meeting continued longer than scheduled [was prolonged].

我々は会議を延ばして討論を続けた。

We extended [prolonged] the meeting and contiuned the discussion.

国会の会期は1か月延ばされるだろう。

The Diet session will be extended for a month.

【予定先送り】

レポートの締切が1週間延びた。

The deadline for the report was extended one week.

締切を延ばすわけにはいかない。

We can't extend the deadline.

遠足は1週間延びた。

The picnic was put off for a week.

彼は体調をこわして出発が延びている。

His departure is being delayed because of his ill health.

今日できることを明日に延ばすな。

Don't put off until tomorrow what you can do today.

私はまだ決心がつかないので返答を延ばしています。

I haven't answered yet, because I haven't made up my mind.

4．進歩する，増進する

伸びる **make progress; advance;** 伸びる［伸ばす］**develop**

【人】

彼はきっと伸びることだろう。

He has a great future before him.

小学校で秀才と思われている子がその後伸び悩んでしまうこともよくある。

Some children who were regarded as very bright in elementary school don't amount to much intellectually later.

〈注〉 He won't amount to much. はほとんど He's no good.(あいつはだめだ)であり，「どうせたいした者にはならない」といったひどい言い方である。上の文では intellectually (知的に) と限定しているので救われる。

私は彼の持っている音楽の才能を伸ばしてやりたいと思う。

I'd like to help him (to) develop his musical abilities.

【事業】

彼の事業が着実に伸びてきていたときにあのオイルショックが起った。

His business was growing steadily, when suddenly the oil shock occurred.

それらの国に対する日本の貿易はまだ伸びる可能性がある。

Japan's trade with those countries is capable of further growth.

5．ぐったりする

のびている **be exhausted; be dead tired; be down with**《illness》

のびる **collapse; get knocked out**

【病気で】

彼はインフルエンザでのびている。

He's down with the flu.

【お酒で】

彼は酔いつぶれてのびてしまった。

He drank until he passed out.

【ボクシング】

第3ラウンドでチャンピオンは挑戦者をノックアウトでのばしてしまった。

The champion knocked his challenger out in the third round.

…のほか → いがい(以外)，ほか

のみもの（飲み物）

drinks; beverages

《関連語》

1．ノンアルコール飲料

non-alcoholic drinks [beverages]

ミルク milk / ミルクセーキ milkshake / ココア cocoa / お茶 tea (紅茶 black tea, 緑茶 green tea, 麦茶 barley tea, ウーロン茶 oolong tea) / コーヒー coffee / カフェオーレ café au lait / ミネラルウォーター mineral water

【清涼飲料】 soft drinks

ジュース fruit juice / レモネード lemonade / ソーダ sodas (non-alcoholic, carbonated beverage) / コカコーラ Coca-Cola / ファンタ Fanta

2．酒

alcoholic drinks [beverages]

酒 sake / ビール beer / ワイン wine / シャンパン champagne / ウイスキー whisk(e)y / ブランデー brandy / リキュール liqueur / ウオッカ vodka / シェリー酒 sherry / ジン gin / ラム酒 rum / バーボン bourbon / カクテル cocktail

のむ（飲む，呑む）

1．飲む

drink; have; take

【水】

彼は水差し1杯の水を一気に飲み干した。

He drank a jugful of water in one long swig.

【茶】

仕事をひと休みしてお茶でも飲もう。

Let's stop work and have some tea.

コーヒー[お茶]でも飲んでひと休みしよう。

Let's have a coffee [tea] break.

How about a coffee [tea] break?

〈注〉 a coffee [tea] break は15分程度の小休憩。

私たちはコーヒーを飲みながらおしゃべりをした。

We chatted over a cup of coffee.

【スープ】

スープを飲むときは音を立てないように。

Don't { make noises [any noise] / slurp } when you eat soup.

〈注〉 スープが深皿に入っていてスプーンで飲むときは eat と言い，カップに入っていてカップを持ち上げて飲むときは drink と言う。

【酒】

君，酒は飲みますか。（習慣）

Do you drink?

昨夜は飲みすぎた。

I drank too much last night.

そんなに飲むなよ。

Don't drink so much.

君は飲むと[酔うと]前後の見境がつかなくなる[わけがわからなくなる]。

You always { lose control / act crazy } when you're drunk.

【薬を】
毎食後薬を飲むのを忘れないように。
Don't forget to take your medicine after every meal.
〈注〉「薬を飲む」は drink とは言わない。

【哺乳】
赤ちゃんはお乳を飲んでいる。
The baby is nursing.
〈注〉母乳でも粉ミルクでも nurse でよい。

【ストローで】
子供はレモネードをストローで飲んだ。
The child drank his lemonade through a straw.

【少しだけ】
彼女はソーダ水をほんの少し飲んだだけで何も言わなかった。
She only sipped at her soda and said nothing.

【丸ごと】
ヘビはカエルや鳥の卵を丸ごと飲むことができる。
Snakes can swallow frogs and birds' eggs whole.

【飲み込む】
おもちを飲み込むのに苦労することがある。
Sometimes it's hard to swallow *mochi*.

2. 比喩的用法

【受諾】
条件をのむ　accept the terms

【忍耐】
涙をのむ　keep back [swallow] one's tears
〈注〉「涙をのむ」には口語で grin and bear it という言い方がある。(屈辱などを受けて)恨みをのむは swallow an insult。

【真に受ける】
あの人は何でもうのみにする。
She will swallow any story.

のる（乗る・載る）・のせる

1. 乗物

ride《a horse》; **have [take] a ride in [on]; take**《a train, bus, ship》
（乗せてもらう） **ride in**《a car》
（自分で運転する） **drive**《a car》
（バス / 電車） **go by**《bus / train, tramcar, subway》
（航空） **go by air; fly to**
（航海） **sail to**
〈注〉ride はもともと馬に乗るように上にまたがる感じであるから，ride a bicycle はぴったりする。箱型の乗物に乗るのも ride と言うが，get on, get in がよく使われる。その交通機関を「利用する」意であれば take the bus [train / ship, etc.] とする。自動車であれば drive, take a drive to ... , 飛行機であれば fly (to Hawaii) でよい。交通機関を副詞句でつけ加えるには，go by bus のようにする。

【乗る】
あの人の新しい車に乗ってみたい。
I'd like to take a ride in that new car of his.
今日は駅まで迎えに行けないのでタクシーに乗って帰って来てください。
I can't meet [get] you at the station today, so please take a taxi home.
飛行機に乗るのは今回が初めてです。
This is the first time I've ever been on an airplane [a plane].
国際線543便はただ今25番ゲートより搭乗中です。お乗りのお客様はゲートにお進みください。
International Airways Flight five-four-three is now boarding at Gate 25. All passengers (will) please proceed to the gate.

【乗せる】
僕が学校まで乗せて行こう。
I'll { give you a ride [lift] to school. / take you to school. }
バス停［地下鉄の駅］まで乗せてくださらない？
Can you give me a ride as far as the bus stop [subway station]?
スクールバスが回って子供達を乗せて行く。
The schoolbus { goes round picking / picks } up the children.

彼に助けてもらってトラックに乗り込んだ。

He helped me get {in / up into} the truck.

彼はひどく酔っていて私の車に乗せるのがひと苦労だった。

He was so drunk I had a hard time dragging him into my car.

【ヒッチハイク】

私はヒッチハイクで軽井沢まで乗せてもらった。

I {hitchhiked / thumbed a ride} to Karuizawa.

〈注〉 この thumb は親指を立てて「車に乗せてくれ」と合図すること。

【荷物を】

トラックに載せる

load a truck (with《something》)

load《something》onto [into] a truck

トラックから降ろす

unload《something》from a truck

【乗り降り】

お客が乗り降りしているバスのわきを通り抜けるとき,車の運転者は十分な注意が必要だ。

The driver of a car passing a bus {which is loading or unloading / with people getting on and off} should be very careful.

〈注〉 loading or unloading はバスの終点か,観光バスのように大勢の人々の乗降を連想させる。

2. 物・台の上

今日の新聞はテーブルの上に載っているし,きのうのはあそこにある。

Today's paper is on the table and yesterday's (is) over there.

その踏み台の上には乗らないように。危ないからね。

Don't get [stand] on that stool. It's dangerous.

ちょっと手伝って。この箱を上の棚に載せたいの。

Please come and help me put this box on the top shelf.

女の人が水がめを頭に載せて運ぶ習慣のある国があります。

In some countries women carry water jars on their heads.

3. 記事・記録

載る,載っている **be recorded (in**《some record》**); be mentioned; be put in a book**

【ギネス】

彼の記録[業績]はギネスブックに載った。

His achievement is [was] (recorded) in the *Guiness Book of Records*.

〈注〉 この場合 is, was どちらでもよい。is recorded は「載っている」状態を表し,was recorded / was put in は「載った」という動作を表す。

【新聞】

あなたの書いた文が学校新聞の第1面に載りましたよ。

Your essay appeared on the first page of the school paper.

〈注〉 essay は小論文・随筆などを含む。

【連載】

毎日新聞に彼の随筆が毎週載ることになった。

The Mainichi agreed to publish an essay of his weekly.

彼は三つの有名雑誌に小説を載せている。

He is writing novels for three famous magazines.

彼の本が新刊書欄に載っている。

His book is mentioned in the "New Books" column.

【記事】

あのスキャンダルは今日の新聞に出ていて,おまけにあの人の写真まで載っている。

That scandal is in today's paper, and they even have a picture of her.

新聞にあの人の名前まで載せるなんてひどいじゃない。

It isn't fair to mention her name in the paper, is it?

【広告】

この会社は数社の新聞に広告を載せている。

This company {advertises / puts ads} in several papers.

【歴史】

この事件はわが校の歴史に載せるべきものだ。

This incident should be recorded in our school history.

【地図】

この村はどの地図にも載っていない小さな村だ。

This is such a small village that it's not shown on any map.

4. 手に乗る, 波に乗る

わなにはまる **fall into a trap**

えさに食いつく **bite**

私はその手には乗らないよ。

I'm not to be taken in by such a trick.

I won't {fall into that trap. / bite on that.}

That trick won't work with me.

【サラ金】

彼はサラ金業者の口車に乗って無一文になってしまった。

He was taken in by a loan shark and lost everything.

【軌道に乗る】

日本の気象衛星「ひまわり」は地球を回る軌道に乗った。

Japan's weather satellite *Himawari* has gone into orbit around the earth.

君の新しい事業が軌道に乗ってよかったね。

I'm glad your new business {has got(ten) into gear. / is well-launched.}

【調子に乗る】

新大関は好調の波に乗って大関２人と横綱１人を負かした。

Spurred on by his success, the new *ozeki* defeated two other *ozekis* and one *yokozuna*.

ビデオ産業は好調の波に乗っていた。

The video industry was riding {on a boom. / the crest of the wave.}

パソコンブームに乗ってあの会社は巨額の利益をあげた。

That company made huge profits because of the PC [personal computer] boom.

のんき

1. 性格

【屈託がない】

彼女はのんきだ。

She is {cheerful [happy] and carefree. / happy-go-lucky.}

【気楽な】

彼はのんきだ。

He's easygoing.

〈注〉 easygoing に批判的な意味はない。「いいかげんすぎる」と非難するときは too easygoing とする。

2. 人生観

私はのんきだ。

I'm optimistic by nature.（取り越し苦労をしない）

I don't take things too seriously.（深刻に考えない）

のんきにしていなさいよ。

Take it easy and relax.

〈注〉 一般的に「物事を気楽に考えることにしている」は I don't take things seriously. であるが，ある特定の問題について「楽観している」は I don't take it seriously. である。Take it easy.（気楽にやれ）は慣用的表現。

3. 暮し

彼はいかにものんきそうに見える。

He looks perfectly carefree.

私ものんきな暮しをしてみたい[のんびり暮したい]。

I'd like to live a quiet and untroubled life.

引退したらもう少しのんきな暮しができるといいが。

I hope I can live a more relaxed and carefree life after I retire.

この休暇中に君はあちこち旅行をしたいと思っているようだが，僕はただのんびりしたいね。

You want to visit lots of places, but I'd like just to relax and take it easy this vacation.

学生時代はほんとにのんきだった。

How easy things used to be when I was at school!

〈注〉◆スーパーにお使いに行ってくれと頼まれたら，用件も聞かずにさっさと出かけ，「何を買うんだっけ」と電話して来るような人のことはscatter-brained, feather-brained, rattle-brained, hare-brained と言う。

◆自分がいつも神経質で，のんきになれる人をうらやましく思う，という人から見ると，心の余裕のある人を次のように言うこともできる。

She can let {things / worries / problems / cares} go for a while and relax.

She's basically optimistic.

◆水がめに水が半分入っているのを，The bottle is half full. と思うのが optimistic（楽観的），The bottle is half empty. と感ずるのが pessimistic（悲観的）と言われる。

◆She has a sense of fun. は何を見ても面白い面を見られるということ。

は

ばあい（場合）

1．時

an occasion; a case

非常の場合はこのボタンを押してガードマンを呼んでください。

In case of (an) emergency push this button and call the guard.

〈注〉 an emergency の方が一般的。

JR が運休の場合は休講となる。

Classes are cancelled when JR stops running.(1)

Classes will be cancelled if JR stops running.(2)

〈注〉 (1)は一般的な記述。ゼネスト・台風などとにかく JR が運休の場合。(2)はたとえば「豪雪が予想される」というような具体的，特定の場合の指示であり，そのようなときは will be, if の形をとる。

(今夜)私が遅刻した場合は待たずに行ってください。

Don't wait for me if I am late (this evening).

〈注〉 JR 運休の例文と同じく上の文は特定の場合の条件であり，「私はよく遅れるので，そんなときは…」と一般的叙述であれば，Don't wait for me when I am late. のようにする。

そういう場合は，それが大いに役に立つでしょう。

{In such cases / If that should happen} it might prove {very useful. / of great help.}

今はそんなくだらないことでけんかをしている場合ではない。

This is {not the time / no time} for quarreling over [about] such trivial matters.

2．事情

circumstances

場合によっては，私が(自分で)彼に会いに行きます。

Depending on the circumstances, I may go to see him myself.

〈注〉 上の例の場合 If it is necessary, … とするのがもっとも普通な言い方。

時と場合によりけりだ。

It depends.

3．事例

case

【…の場合もある】

この規則が適用できない場合もある。

There are times when [some cases in which] this rule doesn't apply.

〈注〉 ×There are some cases which [that] this rule doesn't apply. は誤り。

教師自身が校内暴力にどう対応したらよいかわからない場合もある。

Sometimes teachers themselves don't know how to deal with those who use violence at school.

【私の場合は】

私の場合は何もかもうまくいきました。

In my case, everything went quite smoothly.

君の場合は例外ということにしよう。

We will make an exception in your case.

パーセント

1．率

給料の10パーセントは税金にとられてしまう。

Ten percent of my wages {goes for / is taken in} taxes.

中学卒業者の90パーセントは高校に進学する。

Ninety percent of junior high graduates go on to senior high school.

〈注〉 この場合，動詞は go, goes の両方が考えられるが，多くの文法書では「... percent of に続く名詞が可算名詞で，したがって複数ならば動詞は複数一致，不可算名詞（beef, milk など）であれば単数一致」と説明している。

... percent of the beef consumed in Japan is from Australia（日本で消費される牛肉の…パーセントはオーストラリアから入って来る）

Ten percent of the children are absent.（児童の10パーセントが学校を休んでいる）

売出期間中は40パーセントの値引きをいたします。

Sale goods are discounted (by) 40 percent.

We give a 40 percent discount during the sale.

現内閣の支持率が5パーセント上がった。

The percentage of those who support the present Cabinet went up 5 points.

100パーセントの[完全な]成功だ。

It's really a one-hundred percent success.

高卒者の何パーセントが就職しますか。

What percentage of high school graduates go into business?

〈注〉「何パーセント？」とたずねるときに口語では What percent も使われるが percentage が優勢である。×How many percent とは言わない。

2．高[低]率

住民のかなりのパーセンテージを占める者が農業に従事している。

A large percentage of the inhabitants are engaged in farming.

昨年会合に来た人は全体のほんの数パーセントにすぎなかった。

Only a small percentage of our members came to meetings last year.

今や国会議員にも女性がまじっている。しかしそのパーセンテージはまだ低い。

Now some of the Diet members are women, but the percentage is still small.

〈注〉percent と percentage の使い分け

percent は10%，15%のように具体的な数字がつくときに用いる。percentage は数を明示しない場合に使い，通常 small, large, fair などの形容詞を伴う。

はい

1．問いに対する答え

【依頼・誘いに対して】

「電話をお借りしていいですか」「はい，どうぞ」。

"May I use the telephone?" "Certainly [Of course]."

「一緒にいらっしゃいませんか」「はい，喜んで／はい，ありがとう」。

"Won't you come with me?" "Yes, certainly. / Yes, thanks."

【否定的な問いに対して】

「あなたは来られないんでしたね」「はい，その日は東京に行かなければならないので」。

"You can't come, can you?" "No, I'm afraid I have to go to Tokyo that day."

「ホラー映画はお好きじゃないでしょう」「はい，私には恐ろしすぎます」。

"You don't like horror films, do you?" "No, I feel they're too creepy."

〈注〉問いが「否定」を含む場合，日本語では問いの内容に同意すれば「はい」であるが，英語では答えの内容が否定の語（not, never など）を含めば no，肯定的内容であれば yes である。

"Don't you know him?" "Oh, yes, of course I do."

「彼を知らない？」「いえ，知ってますとも」。

「テレビをつけてもいいでしょうか」「はい，どうぞ」。

"Would you mind my turning [if I turn] on the TV?" "No, certainly not. [No, not at all. / No, go ahead.]"

〈注〉mind は「いやだ」と思うことであるから，答え方に注意を要する。

cf. 同じ内容を May I turn on ...? とたずねられたら，Oh yes. とか Certainly と答えることになる。ちなみに，テレビをつけてほしくない場合は，Well, I'd rather you wouldn't. のように断る。

2．気軽な応答

はい，はい[よし，よし]。

Sure. / OK. / All right.

3．呼ばれたときの応答

【点呼】

はーい。

Here, sir [ma'am].

Present.

Yes, sir [ma'am].

〈注〉 sir, ma'am はつけないこともある。

【呼ばれて】

はい［ええ］。

Yes.

〈注〉 生徒が先生に対して，また軍人やウエイターなどは sir, ma'am をつけて丁寧な感じを出す。

4．注意を喚起する呼びかけ

【物を渡すとき】

はい，これ。

Here you are.

Here it is.

〈注〉 Would you pass me the salt, please?（すみません塩をまわしてください）のような問いに対する答えは Certainly. または Sure. でよい。

【子供・生徒に】

はい，静かにしなさい。

Hey, shut your mouths all of you.

Ssh. Be quiet.

Hey, shut up.（乱暴な言い方）

ばい（倍）

1．…倍

～ times as many [much / long / large / heavy] as

～ times more [longer / heavier] than

今年の入学志願者数は昨年の1.5倍だ。

This year there are one and a half times {more applicants than / as many applicants as} last year.

彼は私の２倍もお金を稼ぐ。

He earns twice as much money as I do.

物価は５年前に比べると２倍になった。

Prices are twice as high as they were five years ago [have doubled in the last five years].

日本の人口はオーストラリアの約９倍である。

The population of Japan is about nine times that of Australia.

Japan has about nine times as many people as Australia.

国土面積はオーストラリアの方が日本の約20倍もある。

Australia is about twenty times larger than Japan.

Australia has about twenty times more land than Japan.

2．掛け算

15の２倍は30。15×２＝30

Two times [Twice] 15 is [equal(s)] 30.

125の４倍はいくつ？

What is four times one hundred (and) twenty-five?

ハイキング

hiking

私たちは嵐山にハイキングに行った。

We went {to Arashiyama for a hike. / {on a hike / hiking} in Arashiyama.}

〈注〉◆「…にハイキングに行った」の「に」につられて went hiking to と考えやすいが，in とするのが慣用。

◆ hiking とはかなりの長距離を歩くことで，きちんとハイキング用の服装・装備をととのえ，弁当を持って，１日がかりで出かけるものである。

歩くのを楽しむのにもいろいろな段階がある。

take a stroll [a walk] 散歩する。

walk, hike 体を鍛えるつもりで歩く。

ex. We hiked〔米〕[walked] more than ten kilometers.（私たちは10キロ以上歩いた）

cf. picnic ピクニック（野外で弁当を食べる楽しみを主としている）

【ハイカー】

そこにはハイカーが大勢来ていた。

The place was crowded with hikers〔米〕[walkers].

【ハイキングコース】
そこは1日がかりのいいハイキングコースだ。
It's a good day's hiking course.

はいし（廃止）→ やめる

【法律】
市川女史は彼女の支持者と共に生涯かけて男女差別の法律廃止[撤廃]のために尽力した。
Miss Ichikawa, along with her followers, did her best as long as she lived to abolish laws discriminating against women.

【慣行】
もとの意味を(とうに)失い形骸化した慣行は廃止すべきだ。
We should do away with customs that have (long ago [since]) lost their original meaning.

【鉄道】
JR は赤字ローカル線をいくつか廃止する決議をした。
Japan Railways decided to discontinue service on some of the unprofitable local lines.

はいたつ（配達）→ ゆうびん

配達する **deliver**
配達される **be delivered**

配達人 a delivery man
新聞配達(人) a newspaper carrier
郵便配達(人) a mail [letter] carrier
牛乳配達(人) a milk deliverer
宅配便(会社／トラック)
a small-parcel delivery (company / truck)
配達業 delivery service
配達料金 a delivery charge

この辺では郵便は午後に配達される。
Mail is delivered every afternoon here.
それを配達していただけますか。
Can I have it delivered?
ストライキで郵便の配達が遅れている。
Mail delivery has been delayed because of the strike.
手紙が間違った住所に配達された。
The letter was delivered to the wrong address.
市内は配達無料。市外は1個につき300円いただきます。
Goods are delivered free within the city limits but you have to pay 300 yen per piece [an item] outside them.

はいる（入る）→ いれる

1．場所[建物]に
enter; go [come] in; get into

【部屋】
私たちは皆部屋に入った。
We all went into [entered] the room.
人々は部屋に入って来た。
They all came into the room.
「お入り」と声がした。私たちはそっとドアを開けた。
"Come in," said a voice. Slowly we opened the door.
声がして私たちに入るようにと言った。
A voice told us to come in.
彼は私たちに中に入るように言った。
He told us to come in.
彼はドアを開け私たちを中に入らせた［入れた］。
He opened the door and let us into the room.
ドアは全部かぎがかかっていたので我々は窓を壊して入った。
The doors were all locked, so we broke a window and got in.

〈注〉 enter は普通，建物などに「入る」。また，学校や大学に「入る」意味のときは他動詞である。ただし，enter by the window ［at the back door］（窓から[裏口から]入る）のように「入り方・入る場所」を述べるとき，enter は「部屋[家]に入る」の意味になり，自動詞として使われる。
enter into conversation [discussion]（談話[討論]

を始める）のように抽象的無形のものに入る場合も自動詞で使われる。

【押し入る】

昨夜彼の家に泥棒が入った。

A burglar broke into his house last night.

【いろいろな入り方】

すたすた歩いて入る　walk in

無理に押し入る　break in

こっそり入る　steal in

音もなくすべり込む　slip in

(やっと)入る　get into [in]

彼は拍手喝采の中をホールに入って来た。

He walked into the hall amid applause.

私は先生が出席をとっている最中にやっと教室に入って間に合った。

I slipped into the classroom just in time to answer the roll call.

店の前は長い行列だったが何とか中に入った。

I got into the store although the line was very long.

〈注〉 普通の入り方なら I went in [into] the store.

【空気】

窓を少し開けてください。いい空気が入るように。

Please open the window a bit to let in the fresh air.

【位置】

列車は５時に駅に入ります。

The train gets in [into] the station at five.

彼の事務所は大通りからちょっと入った所の赤レンガの建物の中にある。

His office is in a red brick building just off the main street.

【寝床】

彼はいつもより早く寝床に入った。

He went to bed earlier than usual.

僕はレポートを書き終えたのが12時過ぎで，それからちょっと食べて，シャワーを浴びて，やっと寝床に入ったのは２時半だった。

I finished my report after midnight, ate a bit, then had a shower and at last got into bed at half past two.

【風呂】

彼は今風呂に入っています。

He is now taking a bath.

【写真】

いらっしゃい，一緒に写真に入りましょう。

Come, we can both be in the picture.

【施設】

彼のお母さんはきのう病院に入った。

His mother entered hospital yesterday.

〈注〉 入学する，入院するの意味のとき school, hospital は無冠詞で使われる。

ビルは今，刑務所に入っている。

Bill is now in jail [gaol /dʒéil/〔英〕].

cf. go to jail（刑務所行きになる）

2．容器・容量・収容

このカメラは小さくてポケットに入る。

This camera is so small you can carry it in your pocket.

この瓶は１リットル入る。

This bottle holds [can hold] one liter.

このかばんには2,3日程度の旅行に必要なものなら何でも入ってしまう。

This bag { can hold everything you need / is big enough (to hold everything you need) } for a few days trip.

このホールには約500人入る。

This hall can hold [holds, is large enough for] about 500 people.

〈注〉 「収容力がある」に当る英語は accommodate (500 people)〔*formal*〕であり，広告文などで時々見られる。

もう2,3人入りますよ。

There is room for a few more people.

3．団体[会社]の一員になる，仲間に加わる

私たちはコンピュータの講座に入った。

We've enrolled in a computer course.

【就学】

子供は６歳で小学校に入ります。

Children enter elementary school at the age of six.

【就職】

彼はあの会社に入った[就職した]。

He {got a job in / was employed by} that company.

彼は市役所[県庁，町役場]に入った。

He entered the civil service.

【政党】

彼は社民党に入った。

He became a member of [joined] the Social Democratic Party.

【クラブ】

今度は気分を変えてコーラスクラブに入ってみたい。高校では ESS に入っていたから。

I want to join the Chorus Club to do something new, because I belonged to the ESS Club in high school.

〈注〉 join は新たに「加わる」という行為であり，belong to ... は「…に属している」という状態を表す。join は他動詞だから直接目的語をとり，belong は自動詞であるから to が必要である。

×I joined to the ESS. (to は不要)

×I'm wondering which club I should belong. (文末に to を補う)

4. 入賞する

彼が3着以内に入るといいが。

I hope he will finish in one of the first three places.

彼の出品作品は賞には入らなかったが選外佳作に入った。

His entry [painting] didn't win a prize but it did receive honorable mention.

彼の作品[彼]は上位に入っていた。

His novel was short-listed.

He was on the short list.

5. 時間

【時代】

我々は今や核の時代に入った。

We've entered the nuclear age.

【季節】

梅雨に入った。

The rainy season has started [begun, set in].

イチゴが最盛期[旬]に入った。

Strawberries are now in season.

6. 入手する

【金】

思いがけないお金が入った。

I've had [gotten] some unexpected income.

【情報】

何か新しい情報が入ったら教えてください。

If you get [have] new information, please let us know.

今入った報道によれば，エジプトでハイジャック事件があった。(報道文)

According to the latest news, there was a hijacking in Egypt.

【文化】

仏教は6世紀の中頃に日本に入ってきた。そしてそれとともに多くの文物・文化財・美術・物の考え方などが入ってきた。

Buddhism was first introduced into Japan in the middle of the sixth century, and with it came many new things—cultural artifacts, arts and attitudes.

7. 含む

この飲み物にはアルコールは入っていません。

This drink contains no alcohol.

This is a non-alcohol drink.

このクッキーには保存料は入っていません。

These cookies don't contain preservatives.

紅茶にはミルクと砂糖を入れます。

I drink tea with milk and sugar.

8. 慣用表現

お茶が入りましたよ。

The tea is ready.

cf. 彼女は私たちにお茶を入れてくれた。

She made tea for us.

ばか（馬鹿）

名 **a fool; an idiot**

ばかな 形 **foolish; stupid; silly; ridiculous; absurd**

《類義語》

foolish 判断力・知力が欠けている。（ほかの語より意味が弱い）

stupid 考える力，知力がない。（foolish より強い）

silly 判断力も想像力もない。（foolish の最も強い意味を表す）

idiotic ばかな。（強い語）

以上の4語は多少のニュアンスと強さの相違があるが，多くの場合互換性がある。ideas, plans, remarks, explanations, regulations などは上のどの形容詞でも修飾できる。

これらの語は個人的，かつ感情的なもので，区別のはっきりしない部分があり，人により地方により使い方に差がある。

ridiculous, absurd ばかばかしい。

preposterous 最高にばかばかしい。

以上の3語は知的・論理的見地からおかしい，ばかばかしいの意で，第一にあげたグループと区別される。説明などが筋が通らずおかしい場合，3つの形容詞のどれでも使える。

1．ののしり言葉

ばか！（人に対して）

（You）Stupid!

（You）Fool!

Dummy!（たいへん強くひびく言い方）

（親が子に） Silly kid!

（兄弟などに） Stupid kid! / Dumb kid!

ばかな！ Nonsense!（発言，考えなど）

2．愚かな

【愚かな】

あんなことするなんて私もほんとにばかだった。

I really was a fool to do that.

How stupid [foolish, silly] I was to do that.

彼女も本当にばかだ。まる1か月分の給料をはたいて贈り物を買って，そのあと部屋代も払えないなんて。

It was very silly of her to go and spend her whole month's salary on gifts and then not have enough money for rent.

〈注〉 You are such a fool. はひどい言い方で，It's foolish of you ... とすればずっと軽くなる。be a fool とはばかそのものであることであり，be foolish はその人の「たち（性質）」またはその時の行為がばかげていることを意味する。

だれも守れない規則を作るなんてばかげている。

It's stupid to make regulations no one can observe.

そんなことを信じるなんてほんとにばかげている。

It's terribly foolish to believe a thing like that.

ばかなことを言うな。

Don't talk nonsense!

Don't be so foolish!

〈注〉 「ばかな」と決めつけるだけでなく，そのあと「こうしたらよいのではないか」Maybe it would be better ... / It would have been better ... / They should have ... のように建設的な意見を続けるのが一般的である。

3．慣用表現

皆で僕をばかにした。

They made a fool of me.

ばかを見たよ。わざわざ銀行まで出かけて行ったら今日は休みだった。（時間と精力のむだ遣い）

What a waste of time and energy! I went all the way to the bank and found it closed.

野菜の値段もばかにならない。（家計の上で）

Vegetable prices are nothing to sneeze at. 〔*colloq.*〕

交通費もまったくばかにならない。

Transportation expenses
{ (do) add up.
{ are certainly not negligible.

4. 強意

awfully; terribly

彼はばかに遅いな。

He's awfully [terribly] late.

〈注〉 awfully は米国ではあまり使われない。またこのような強意語は時代により変るものである。

…ばかり

1. およそ，だいたい

about; ... or so; some →ほど

1か月ばかり家をあけていました。

I have been away { about a month. / for a month or so.

30年ばかり前になります。

It was some thirty years ago.

小麦粉大さじ2杯に牛乳コップ半杯ばかり加えてください。

Put two spoonfuls of flour in a cup and add half a cup of milk.

2. 唯一，もっぱら →だけ

【唯一】

ひろみばかりが女の子じゃないよ。

Hiromi isn't the only girl in the world, you know.

【もっぱら】

あの子は泣いてばかりいた。

She kept on crying.（客観的な事実）

She did nothing but cry all the while.（あきれた気持ち，いら立ちなど感情的な要素の入った言い方）

She cried all the while.（上記の中間）

テレビばかり見てないで！　宿題まだ終っていないんでしょう？

You shouldn't be watching TV. You haven't finished your homework, have you?

テレビばっかり見てるんじゃない。宿題やっといで！

Stop watching TV. Go do your homework!

【厄介・心配】

ご厄介ばかりかけました。

I have given you so much trouble.

I've always been a pain in the neck for you.〔*colloq.*〕

親には心配ばかりかけてきた。

I've always been a problem to my parents.

My parents have always had to worry [be worried] about me.

【悪化】

できるだけの手は尽したが，彼は悪くなるばかりだった。

Although they did everything they could (do), he got worse and worse.

物価は上がるばかりだ。

Prices keep [go] on rising.

3. …するところ，まさに…

私たちは用意ができていつでも出かけるばかりだった。

We were ready to leave at any moment.

あの子はまさに泣かんばかりだった。

She { was nearly crying. / nearly cried. / was on the verge of tears.

はく(穿く，履く)・はいている → きる

1. はく（動作）

put on; get in(to)

【スカート・ズボン】

私は古いだぶだぶのズボンをはいていたので，それを脱いでスカートをはいた[にはきかえた]。

Since I was wearing old, baggy trousers, I took them off and got into [put on] a skirt.

〈注〉 日本語では「はく，着る，かぶる，はめる」など身体の部位により分類が細かいが，英語では身につける（動作）put on，身につけている（状態）wear, have ... on ですまされる。

【靴・靴下】

外出するときは清潔なソックスをはいて行きなさい。

Put on clean socks before you go out.

Wear clean socks when you go out.

この長いブーツははいたり脱いだりがたいへんだ。

It is not easy to get into and out of these long boots.

【はいてみる】

この靴をはいてみてごらんなさい。

Try these shoes on.

【はける，はけない】

このズボンはまだはける。

These trousers [pants] { are still good enough to wear. / can still be worn. }

この靴は(すりへって)もうはけない。

These shoes are worn out.

この靴は小さくなってもうはけない。

These shoes don't fit any more.

2．はいている（状態）

have on; wear

彼は古くて汚いジーパンをはいていた。

He wore dirty old jeans.

He had dirty old jeans on.

はこぶ（運ぶ）

carry; take; bring

1．運搬する

ある国では女の人が頭に水がめを乗せて水を運ぶ。

In some countries women carry water bottles on their heads.

スクールバスが子供たちを学校の行き帰り運んでくれる。

The school bus takes the children to and from school.

お客様を新幹線の駅からホテルに，またホテルから駅に運ぶバスをチャーターしなければならない。

We have to charter a bus to take guests from the Shinkansen station to the hotel and back to the station again.

朝食を部屋まで運んでください。

Bring my breakfast to my room, please.

このケースを下に運んでください。

Take this case downstairs, will you?

〈注〉 carry は重い物，持ちにくい物を運ぶ。take は go と同じく，ほかへ持って行くこと。bring は come と同じく，ほかから自分のいる場所へ持って来ること。take it there, bring it here と覚えておくとよい。

ただし，たとえばパーティーに関し主催者にものをたずねるような場合，相手の立場に立って言うので次のように言うことができる。

Can I bring a friend with me?（友達を連れて行っていいですか）

Shall I bring something?（何か持って行きましょうか）

2．はかどる

事はスムーズに[何事もなく]運んでいる。

Things are going well [smoothly].

まあ，うまく運んでいる。

Things are going satisfactorily.

建設事業[会議]は滞りなく運んでいる。

The construction [The conference] is proceeding without a hitch.〔*colloq.*〕

はさむ（挟む）・はさまる

1．間に入れる

【挟む】

私は本の間に紙片を挟んで，後でコピーしたい所がわかるようにしておいた。

I put slips of paper in the book to mark the pages I wanted to copy [zerox] afterwards.

彼は学校を去ってから僕のところに本を送り返してきたが，その中の1冊の間に手紙が挟んであった。

After leaving the school he sent back some books he had borrowed, and in one of them he had put a letter to me.

彼らはテーブルを挟んで向き合って座っていた。

They sat facing each other with a table

between them [across a table].
寄宿舎は，道を挟んで校門の向かい側にあった。
The dormitory was just across the street from the school gate.
【挟まる】
彼の指がドアに挟まった。
He got his finger pinched [caught, jammed] in the door.
彼は母親とおばの間に挟まって何ともぎこちなく座っていた。
He sat uncomfortably sandwiched between his mother and his aunt.
ベナンとトーゴはガーナとナイジェリアの間に挟まれている。
Benin and Togo lie between Ghana and Nigeria.

2. つまむ
書類をクリップで挟んでおいてください。
Clip the papers together.
彼はすぐにはしの使い方を覚え，豆を挟んでみせて皆をおもしろがらせた。
He soon learned to use chopsticks and would amuse people by picking up beans with them.

3. 慣用表現
彼があまり熱弁を振るうのでだれも言葉を挟もうとしなかった。
He talked on so vehemently that no one dared to interrupt.
私は双方の板挟みになってしまった。
I found myself [felt] caught in the middle.
彼は板挟みになってしまった[ジレンマに陥った]。
He was on the horns of [put into] a dilemma.

はじまる（始まる）・はじめる

1. 始まる
【活動】
学校は8時半に始まる。
School begins at 8:30.
「彼の仕事はいつから始まるの？」「来週の月曜日からです」。
"When does he start his job?" "He starts on Monday next week."
食事はスープで始まった。
The meal started with soup.
劇は城にある王の接見室から始まる。
The play opens [begins] in the reception room in the castle.
【災禍】
その2国の間に戦いが始まった。
War began [broke out] between the two countries.
【起源】
この祭りは鎌倉時代に始まったと言われる。
This festival is said to {date from / date back to / go back to} the Kamakura Period.
【悪癖】
そら，また始まった。
There you go again!
You're starting that again!

2. 始める
【仕事】
彼は仕事を始めた。
He started [began, set about] his work.
〈注〉 set about にはいよいよ取りかかるという決意がある。
彼らは新しい事業を始めた。
They started (on) a new project.
〈注〉 動詞 start は start thinking, start a new business のように目的語として動名詞・名詞のどちらもとれる。start on では start on a new topic [a new project] のように on のあとは名詞をとり，その名詞も終り (end) のあるものをとる傾向がある。

新しいお店は朝9時半に始めて午後7時半に閉める。

The new store opens at 9:30 a.m. and closes at 7:30 p.m.

彼は名古屋でレストランを始めた。

He opened a new restaurant in Nagoya.

〈注〉 begin a new business（新しい会社を始める）は時々使われるが，△ begin a new restaurant は使わない。

【日常的動作など】

55ページ[第1章]から始めましょう。

Let's start [begin] from [at, with, on] page fifty-five [the first chapter].

昼すぎには雨が降り始めた。

It started [began] to rain in the afternoon.

彼らはしゃべり始めた。

They started talking.

彼はさっきまでいったい何を考えていたのだったかと考え始めた。

He started [began] wondering what he was thinking about before.

はじめ（初め，始め）→ だいいち

1．初め

名 **the beginning;** 起源 **the origin**

その文を初めから読んでください。

Read the passage from the beginning.

私は初めから新しい仕事が気に入った。

I liked my new work from the beginning [outset].

初めから終りまで

throughout; from beginning to end

初めよければ終りよし。

Well-begun is half done.

初めからやり直しましょう。

Let's do it (all) over again.

2．初めて（新しい経験）

私たちが初めて会ったのは東京駅だった。

We first met at Tokyo Station.

It was at Tokyo Station that we first met.（場所を強調）

子を持って初めて親の恩を知る。

We don't realize how much we owe our parents till we have our own children.

歌舞伎についてはずいぶん聞いていたが今日初めて実際に役者が舞台で演じるのを見た。

I had heard a great deal about Kabuki drama but today I saw real actors acting on a stage for the first time.

3．初めに

初めに[まず第一に]貴君のご助力に対しお礼を申し上げたいと思います。

First, I'd like to thank you for your help.

初めに[まず]宿題をしてしまって，それから遊びに行きなさい。

Finish your homework first (of all) and then you can go out to play.

4．初めは

初めは彼の言ったことが信じられなかった。

At first I couldn't believe what he had told me.

初めはあの子はすごくはにかんでいた。

At first she was very shy.

〈注〉 first, at first, for the first time は混同されやすい。first は「第一に，初めに」と順序を述べる。at first は「初めは」の意であるから，後から変化が起る含みがある。for the first time は「初めての経験」を述べるときの言い方。

はじる（恥じる）→ はずかしい

《類義語》

be put to shame 他人から行為または言葉で恥をかかされる。

be disgraced 不道徳または反社会的行為のために名誉を失うこと。

be humiliated 屈辱感，劣等感に打ちのめされ，卑屈になりいやになること。

以上の3語句はすべて「恥をかいた［かかされた］」ことであり，互いにオーバーラップしているが，他人のかかわる度合は上にいくほど強い。

1．良心に恥じる

彼は自らを恥じている。

He is ashamed of himself.

彼は母親の気持ちをあのように傷つけてしまったことを恥じた。

He is ashamed of having hurt his mother that way.

〈注〉 内気で「恥じらう」意味の「恥ずかしがる」は be shy であって be ashamed とは言わない。be ashamed は自分の良心に照らして，または世間に対して恥じることである。

2．社会的な恥

彼は家名を辱めた。

He is a disgrace to his family.

He has disgraced his family name.

恥を知れ。

You ought to be ashamed!

Shame on you!

彼は恥知らずだ。

He has no sense of shame [honor].

He is shameless [brazen].

〈注〉 「恥をかく」は主として他人に対しての気持ち，世間体。一方，「恥ずかしく思う」be ashamed は自分自身についての感情に重点がある。他人に何か言われたりしてもしなくても自分自身の心の中で「恥じる」ことを意味する。

彼女は恥をかかされた。

She was disgraced [humiliated, put to shame].

満座の武将たちの前で恥をかかされた[辱めを受けた]ために光秀は復讐を決意したのであった。

Having been put to shame in the presence of other lords, Mitsuhide was determined to avenge himself.

3．慣用表現

彼は会社の女性たちを恥も外聞もなく追いかけた。

He had no inhibitions about chasing after the office women.

はず → とうぜん

1．予定

be due; be to《do》

式は明日行われるはずだ。

The ceremony is to {be held / take place} tomorrow.

列車は5時到着のはずだ。

The train is due at 5 o'clock.

【不確実】

彼は昨夜出発のはずだったが本当に出発したかどうかは知らない。

He was to {start / have started} last night, but I don't know if he really did.

【成就せず】

もしストライキがなかったら彼は昨夜出発するはずだった。

He would [could] have started last night if it hadn't been for the strike.

彼は昨夜出発するはずだったが，ストライキがあったので出かけられなかった。

He should [would, could] have started last night, but there was a strike and so he couldn't.

2．当然

should; ought to

彼はもう(ここに)着くはずだ。

He should be here by now.

彼は朝の列車に乗ったのだから，もうこの時間なら着いているはずだ。

He took the morning train, so he should [ought to] have arrived by now.

キーが見つからないの？　その引き出しに入っているはずなんだが。

Can't you find the key ? It should be in that drawer.

彼が腹を立てるはずだよ。

It's no wonder that he's offended.

大学卒ならだれでも少しは英語が話せていい

はずだ。

Every university graduate ought to be able to speak some English.

君はそんなことは当然知っているはずだ。

You ought to know that.

〈注〉 ought to の方が should より意味が強い。

君は「知らない」なんて言えないはずだよね。

You surely can't say you don't know, can you?

あなたに頼んだはずだが。(念を押す)

I told you to, I'm sure.

【はずがない】

そんなこと本当のはずがない[うそに決っている]。

It can't [cannot] be true.

彼がそんなこと言うはずがない[言わなかったに決っている]。

He can't [cannot] have said that.

3. 予期

すべて周到に準備をしたのだから今度はうまくいくはずだ。

Everything's been carefully prepared, so {it should succeed / it'll surely succeed / it'll go smoothly} this time.

もっとうまくいくはずだった。

I expected something better.

こんなはずではなかった。

That's not what I expected.

That wasn't what I (had) expected. (過去のことについて)

はずかしい (恥ずかしい) → はじる

1. 恥と思う

be ashamed of 《one's conduct》

そら，また妹をいじめている。恥ずかしいと思わないのか。

Here you are—bullying your little sister again! Aren't you ashamed of yourself?

彼のおかげで家族は恥ずかしい思いをしている[彼は家の恥だ]。

He is a disgrace to his family.

〈注〉 自ら省みて，または社会的に恥ずかしいと思う意味(上の1.)と内気で恥じらう意味(次の2.)とは英語では別の表現になる。1.と2.に共通するのは embarrassment (当惑)であるが，1.は自らの道徳観に照らし世間の目を意識して be embarrassed (当惑する)，2.は生れつきの shyness (内気)のゆえに be embarrassed という違いである。

2. 内気な，きまりが悪い

shy 内気な，はにかんで(生れつきの性質)

恥ずかしがる

be abashed (状況に対する反応)

恥ずかしそうにする

look shy; look abashed

【恥ずかしくて当惑する】 be embarrassed

私は5,6歳の頃，お客様があって皆で食事をするようなとき，恥ずかしくて皆のところに出て行くことができなかった。

When I was five or six, I was (far) too shy to join my family at the dinner table whenever we had guests.

恥ずかしそうにあの子はそっと私たちの方を見た。

Shyly she stole a glance at us.

教授が彼の研究をほかの学生の前でほめたので彼は恥ずかしそうにしていた。

He was [looked] abashed as his professor praised his research before the other students.

皆が私たちをじっと見ているので恥ずかしくて赤くなった。

I blushed knowing that everyone was staring at us.

〈注〉◆blush とは恥ずかしくて赤くなることであるから blushed with embarrassment とする必要はない。なお，embarrassment と shyness は後者が原因で前者がしばしばその結果であり，2語を同一視してはいけない。

◆目の前で自分がほめられたとき

(1) 照れ笑い(giggling)，また Oh, don't say that. などと言う。

(2) もっと落ちついた大人らしい反応

Thank you.
How nice of you to say that!

決った言い方はないがこのような言い方でよい。

また Thank you, but .... と「たいしたことではない」と謙遜することもあるので，そのときの気持ちを素直に述べればよい。

◆ばかなことをしたエピソードなど持ち出されたとき

Oh, don't tell that story.（やめてください）
How embarrassing!（恥ずかしい）

次の2文は腹を立ててつっかかるような語調になる。

How dare you embarrass me!（よくもそんな恥ずかしいことを）
Do you want [Are you trying] to embarrass me?（私を困らせるつもり？）

◆見られたくないもの(日記・手紙など)をとられて「いやあ」と言って取り返すとき

Oh, no you don't!

はたけ（畑・畠）

1．農地・耕地

a field,（pl.）**fields; a farm** 農場

a cultivated field
cultivated land } 農地

a plowed field
plowed land } 耕地

両親は一日中外で畑仕事をしています。

My parents are working out in the fields all day long.

この辺は昔は畑だった。

In former days there was farmland here.

学校の周りは畑ばかりです。

The school is surrounded by fields.

その人たちの家の裏には野菜畑[イチゴ畑]があった。

They had { a vegetable [kitchen] garden / a strawberry patch } in the backyard.

2．専門分野

彼は長く教育畑で暮してきた。

He has had a long teaching career.

彼には英語は畑違いだ。

English is not his field.

ばつ（罰）・ばち

㊔ **punishment** 一般的な語。道徳的悪に対する罰。

penalty 規則違反に対する罰。ゲームの決りや法規についての違反で，道徳違反に対するものではない。具体的には通常罰金，または特典の剝奪のような形をとる。

罰する ㊖ punish

罰せられる，罰を受ける be punished

カンニングをしたら罰は免れないよ。

You cannot escape punishment for cheating.

【罰金】

制限速度を10キロから20キロの間でオーバーすると罰金4万円で2点の減点となる。

The penalty for going between ten and twenty kilometers over the speed limit is a 40,000 yen fine and two points off the driver's license.

彼はスピード違反で罰金4万円をとられた。

He was fined 40,000 yen for speeding.

〈注〉 penalty は違約金とか延滞金，加算金などの意味にも使われる。税金を期限までに納めないと penalty interest（延滞利子）と penalty fee（延滞金）が加算される。自動車保険では事故を起すと penalty（罰）としてランクが落ちて掛金が増える。

【慣用表現】

ほら，罰が当った。

It serves you right.
You had it coming.

罰が当るぞ。

You'll pay dearly for it.〔*cliché*〕（＝There'll be a lot of trouble in the end.）

ばっすい（抜粋）→ いんよう

はっぴょう（発表）

㊔ **announcement; publication; declaration; release**（情報の公開，映画の封切り）

発表する **announce; make public; publish; make**《something》**known**

1. 公表

結果は1週間以内に発表される。

The result will be announced in a week.

世論調査の結果は新聞に発表された。

The results of the public opinion poll were published in the newspaper.

2. 口頭発表

今夜6時30分よりテレビで立候補者の政見発表がある。

The candidates will give their political views on TV from 6:30 this evening.

彼は日本物理学会の年次総会で研究発表をする。

He will present the results of his study at the annual meeting of the Japan Physics Society.

彼は日本英文学会で研究発表をする。

He will give [read, present] his paper at the annual meeting of the English Literary Society of Japan.

はな（花）

a flower;（主として果樹の）**a blossom**

花が咲く 動 **flower; bloom; come out;**（咲いている）**be out**

桜の花が咲いた。

The cherry blossoms are out.

花屋（人） a florist

（店） a flower shop; a florist's

花売り娘 a flower girl

花時計 a floral clock

造花 an artificial flower

花言葉 the code for flowers

花を育てる grow flowers

花を摘む（一つ） pick a flower

（たくさん） gather [pick] flowers

花を飾る decorate with flowers

花を生ける arrange flowers

生け花 flower arrangement

生け花を習う

take lessons in flower arrangement

【花ざかり】

桜が花ざかりだ。

（The）Cherry blossoms are {at their best / in full bloom} now.

【花が終る】

花が終った。

The blossoms have finished.

The flowers are gone.

【花を供える［手向ける］】

彼は彼女の墓に花を供えた。

He offered flowers at her tomb.

【比喩的】

花道 a runway

両手に花である

be（sitting, standing）between two pretty women

【人生の花ざかり】

彼女はまさに青春，人生の花ざかりだ。

She's now in the bloom of（her）youth.

【花を持たせる】

彼らはその成功は彼のおかげだと彼に花を持たせた。

They let him take the credit for their success.

《関連語》

アサガオ morning glory / アマリリス amaryllis / アヤメ iris / カーネーション carnation / キク chrysanthemum / キズイセン jonquil / キンギョソウ snapdragon / キンセンカ nasturtium / キンポウゲ buttercup / グラジオラス gladiolus / クロッカス crocus / ケシ poppy / サクラ cherry blossom / サクラソウ primrose / シクラメン cyclamen / シャクナゲ rhododendron / シャクヤク peony / ジャスミン jasmine / ジンチョウゲ fragrant daphne / スイセン narcissus / スイートピー sweet pea / スイレン water lily / スズラン lily of the valley / スミレ violet / ゼ

ラニウム geranium / タチアオイ hollyhock / ダリア dahlia / タンポポ dandelion / チューリップ tulip / ツキミソウ evening primrose / ツツジ azalea / ツバキ camellia / テッセン clematis / ナノハナ rape blossoms / バラ rose / パンジー pansy / ヒナギク daisy / ヒマワリ sunflower / ヒャクニチソウ zinnia / ヒヤシンス hyacinth / フジ wistaria, wisteria / フリージア freesia / ベゴニア begonia / ペチュニア petunia / ポインセチア poinsettia / マーガレット marguerite / マリーゴールド marigold / モクレン magnolia / ラッパズイセン daffodil / ラン orchid / ワスレナグサ forget-me-not

〈注〉 ここでは花の名をすべて単数で示してあるが普通英文の中で花は複数(ex. lilies, violets)で語られることに注意。

はなし（話）

1．発言

【発言】

彼の話が聞えない。

I can't hear him.

彼の話は信じられない。(彼はうそつきだ)

I can't believe what he says.

彼のいまの話は信じられない。(ショッキングな話だ)

I can't believe what he said just now.

彼の話に賛成だ。

I agree with him [what he said].

彼の話は筋が通っていてよくわかる。

What he says makes sense.

〈注〉 what 構文を活用しよう。
上の例のように「言っていること」「言ったこと」の意味での「はなし」が動詞(believe, agree with, say)の目的語となるとき，what に導かれる名詞節を使うと自然な文になる。
ex. 彼の話はわからない。
×I don't understand his saying.
○I don't understand what he says.

【談話・雑談】

私たちは夜遅くまで話をしていた。

We chatted [talked] far into the night.

私たちはしばらく楽しく話をした[さんざん長話をした]。

We had a nice little talk [a long talk].

〈注〉 have a talk の形では上の例文のように通常修飾語がつく。次の例文のように have a talk だけのときは何かお説教か小言をいただくときである。

【ひと言】

ちょっとひと言お話がしたくてお寄りしました。

I stopped by just to have a word with you.

〈注〉◆「ひと言話をしたい」は次のようにも言う。
I'd like (to have) a word with you.
cf. I'd like to have a chat with you. (親しい人との間で)
◆「言葉」には「別れの言葉」のようにメッセージの意味があるが，word(s)は個々の言葉の意味でメッセージの意味はない。上の例 have a word は例外的である。
I don't understand these words. (これらは難しい言葉なのでわからない)
His words are well-chosen. ((談話や文章で) 彼の使う言葉が適切で語の選択がすぐれている)

彼はひと言話して立ち去った。

After making a brief remark he walked away.

2．はなし

【大事な話】

授業の後でちょっと話があります。

We'll have a talk after class.

ここに来てお座り。大事な話があります。

Come and sit down. I'd like [We have] to have a serious talk.

お父様にお話ししなければなりません。

I'll have { to speak [talk] to / a talk with } your father.

ちょっとあなたに話があります。

I have something to tell [say to] you.

〈注〉 この表現はよいことにせよそうでないにせよ，大切なことを切り出すときに使う。

【相談】

まず両親に話をした方がいい。

I think you should talk to your parents

about it.
弁護士に話をしたらどうですか。
How about seeing [consulting〔*formal*〕] a lawyer?

【合意】
話がつく agree; come to an agreement
話がわかる
understand; come to an understanding

【交渉・折衝】
話し合い negotiations
話し合いをする，交渉する negotiate

【物語・実話】
おばあちゃん，お話をして。
Tell me a story, Granny.
どんなお話？
What's the plot?（映画・テレビ・小説について，また，雑談・出来事など）
What happened?（何があったの？）
What's the story?〔*informal*〕（事のいきさつを尋ねる）
How did it happen?（全体の話・事のてんまつ）

【…の話】
初恋[モンブラン登山]の話をして。
Tell me the story of your … first love [climbing Mont Blanc].

【講演】
彼は PTA の会合で話をすることになっている。
He's going to give a speech at the PTA meeting.

3．問題・話題

【話題】 topic; subject
何の話？ What's the topic?
その話はやめよう。
Let's drop the subject.
【問題】 どうすべきか迷う問題 a question; 困っている問題 a problem
それは別の話だ。
That's another matter [question].
そりゃひどい話だ。
That's a problem.

【その件】
例の話はそれからどうなった？
So what's next (in the story)?
What happened in the end?
〈注〉 ×What has become of the story? とは言わない。
例の話は結局どうなったか聞いていない。
I never heard the end of that story.
引っ越しの話はどうなった？
You were talking about moving. Have you done it yet?
家主との部屋代の話はどうなった？
You were negotiating with the landlord about the rent. What happened [How did it go]?

4．その他

【談話の流れ】
話が途切れた。 They became silent.

【電話】
お話し中です。
The line is busy.
The number is [It's] engaged.〔英〕

【伝聞】
彼の話によればあの子は裕福な家の出だ。
According to him, the girl is from a wealthy family.
それはよくある話だ。
It is the same old story.
彼女のことは話に聞いている。
I have heard a lot about her.

【結論】
それで話がつくだろう。
That would settle the matter.
話がついた。
They've agreed [settled] on what to do.
They've reached an agreement [an understanding].〔*formal*〕
我々は彼に話を決めてくれと頼んだ。
We asked him to decide.
それでは話が違う。

That's not our understanding.

それなら話は違う。

That alters ⌊things [the case].

That puts a new light on the situation.

《類義語》

1. 内容にまとまりのある発言

【フィクション】

story　首尾一貫した筋のある物語。

tale　story に近いが「作り話」の意もある。

【ノンフィクション】

talk　談話，講演。

speech　演説，スピーチ。

lecture　講義，講演。

sermon　説教。

statement　陳述，申し立て，声明。

story　事のてんまつ，来歴など。

report　報道。

account　事件の説明など。

give an account（事のてんまつを話す）

〈注〉 report, account は内容が雑談的であれば次にあげる「雑談的くだけた発言」の分類に入る。

2. 雑談的なくだけた発言

talk　雑談。

I had a long talk with Mary.（メアリーと長話をした）

chat　おしゃべり。

conversation　話のやりとり。

remark　一言二言の感想。

comment　一言二言の短評。

Well, it's a good idea.（そりゃ，いい考えだ）のような短評。

make ⌊a remark [a comment] の形でよく使う。

He made several comments [remarks] at the PTA meeting.（彼はPTA で何回か発言した）

cf. He spoke ... とすればもっと長く，内容のある発言をしたことになる。

また，remark は批判的な面をもち，intelligent [scathing / silly] remarks（聡明な［痛烈な / ばかばかしい］発言）のように形容詞と共に用いられることが多い。

story〔*informal*〕 話。What's the story?（どんな話さ？）のように聞き手にとって面白そうな内容の場合に使う。

rumor　うわさ話，真偽不明な話。

3. 公式発言

statement　声明。

comment　公式発言でも短いもの。

はなす（話す）→ はなし，いう

1. ものを言う

彼女は一言も話さなかった。

She didn't say a word.

僕は彼と話すチャンスがない。

I never have a chance to talk to him.

マコがいろんなことを話すようになった。

Mako has started to talk a lot.

【話し方】

もっとゆっくり話してくださいませんか。

Would you speak [talk] a little more slowly, please?

2. 相談・伝達・説明

君はそのことをお母さんに話すべきだ。

You should talk to your mother about that.

だれにも話さないで。これは私たちの間の秘密だから。

Please don't tell anyone. It's a secret between us.

決心がついたら話してください。

Please let us know ⌊when [once] you've decided.

この前会ったときのメアリーの様子を詳しく話してくださいませんか。

Could you describe [tell me, say] exactly how Mary looked when you saw her last?

どうやってお金を手に入れたか話してくれませんか。

Would you explain [describe, tell me] how you got the money?

【…と話す】

彼は空港でビルを見たと話していた。

He said he'd seen Bill at the airport.

母は亡くなる前に私の父がまだ生きていて神戸にいると話してくれた。

My mother told me before she died that my father was still alive and lived somewhere in Kobe.

3．外国語を話す

彼は５か国語を話す。

He can speak five languages.

私はフランス語は読めるが話すのは苦手だ。

I read French but cannot speak it well.

4．慣用

ほんの二言三言お話ししたくてお寄りしました。

I dropped in just to have a few words with you.

彼は立去る前に彼の心のうちを話した。

He spoke his mind before he left.

わけのわからないことを話すな。

Don't talk nonsense.

《類義語》

【say, tell, talk, speak の使い方】

say　言った言葉をそのまま伝え，または，間接話法にして伝える。伝える言葉，内容が重要。他動詞である。

〈注〉「彼は一日中外出していたと言った」は He said he was out all day. とするのが普通。He said, "I was out all day." とするのは不自然。その発言が特にユニークなときにのみ直接引用する（直接話法・間接話法については「いう」の項参照）。またただれかの発言を紹介するのに次のように書くのは不自然である。内容が長ければ要約して伝えるのが普通。

△Mr. Takahashi said the following at the conference; "Rain forest conservation should be ...."

次のように書くのが普通である。

At the conference Mr. Takahashi said that rain forest conservation should be the primary concern of the next ten years.（会議の席上高橋氏は熱帯雨林の保護こそこれからの10年間第一の問題とすべきだと話した）

tell　言った内容を要約して伝える。伝達内容と聞き手を要す。他動詞。

He told me that she was ill [how she got ill].

He told me about her illness.

He told me to go to see her.（軽い命令）

talk　話をした内容は雑談的なもので，それほど重要ではない。語り合う動作が浮かぶ。talk nonsense のようなイディオム以外は自動詞。

He talked with me for some time about Jane and her illness.

speak　話をする動作が第一で，speak in a loud [low] voice（大声で話す，低い声で話す）と発話に重点が置かれる。speak English のように言語を話す，speak one's mind, speak nonsense のような数種のイディオム以外は自動詞。

Please speak a little more slowly. I cannot follow you.

〈注〉上の例文では talk も使える。talk, speak どちらも使える場合がある。

【その他】

おしゃべりする　**have** { **a（little / long）talk** / **a chat** }

ふれる　**mention; refer to; touch upon**

説明する　**explain**

（時事問題などについて）短評[論評]する　**comment; make comments**

（短評・所見を）述べる　**observe**〔*formal*〕

（一言二言）感想を述べる　**remark; make a remark**

"Take care what you say" he remarked.（言葉に気をつけなさいと彼が言った）

「いう」の項参照。

はなす（放す）

放す　**let go**（行かせてやる）; **turn loose; release**（おりや鎖から放す）

放してーっ！　Let me go!

手を放せ！　Let go!

【放してやる】

set《an animal》free; 動 free; let《it》go

やめなさい，犬に妹の服着せようなんて！放してやりなさい。

Stop trying to dress the dog in your sister's clothes. Let it go.

男が動物園に忍び込んで猿をおりから放して

しまった。

A man crept into the zoo and set the monkeys free.

我々は稚魚を川に放った[放流した]。

We put the fingerlings [young fish] into the river.

散歩させるとき犬を放さないでください。

Don't let the dog run loose when you take it for a walk.

〈注〉 let the dog loose とすると「うっかりして逃がした」ことになる。また上の例文を「犬をつないでおいてください」として訳すと次のようになる。
Please leash your dog ...

ハンドルから手を放すな。

Don't let go of the steering wheel.

はなす（離す）・はなれる

1. 行動

【分かつ】 separate; divide

彼はけんかをしている子供たちを離そうとした。

He tried to separate the quarrelling children.

【近づけない】 keep away; keep apart; isolate

病気の子はほかの子供たちから離された[隔離された]。

The sick child was isolated [kept away] from her playmates.

【手放す】

若い未亡人は子供を手放さなければならなかった。

The young widow had to give up the child.

【去る】 leave

アダムズさんは来月日本を離れる。

Mr. Adams is leaving Japan next month.

船は岸を離れた。

The ship left the shore.

【離れる】 be away from

家を離れて暮した経験のある者はごく少数で，多くの者がホームシックにかかった。

Few of them had (had) much experience of living away from home and many got homesick.

斉藤さんは気の毒にも名古屋支局に転勤となり家族から離れての独り暮しだ。

Poor Mr. Saito was transferred to the Nagoya branch office and now he has to live alone apart from his family.

通りを歩くときは私から離れないように。

Keep close to me when you walk in the street.

【分かれる】

列を離れないで。

Stay in line.（一般的な注意）

Stay in the line.（列からとび出ている子への注意）

Don't fall out of (the) line.

Don't lose your place in (the) line.

群れを離れた羊　a stray sheep

【独立】

子供たちは皆大人になりました。一番下の子が先月家を離れました。

All our children are grown up now. The youngest one just moved out last month.

３人の子は皆親元を離れています。

The three children have left home now.

Our children don't live at home any more.

ニックもボブもケイトも親元を離れていった。

Nick, Bob and Kate have moved out.

【目を離す】

その子から目を離さないでください。

Don't take your eyes off the child.（ちょこちょこして危いから）

彼から目を離すな。

Keep an eye on him.（危険人物だから）

2. 状態

彼の家はここからだいぶ離れた所です。

His house is far from here.

あの人たちは互いに遠く離れて暮している。

They live far apart (from each other).

あの人たちの家は互いに何マイルも離れている。

Their houses are many miles away [apart] from each other's.

弁天島は岸から１キロ離れた所にある。

Benten Island is one kilometer from [off] (the) shore.

人里離れた所　a place far from town; an out-of-the-way place

〈注〉 remote country と言えばまったくの荒野のことなので，a place somewhat remote くらいに和らげればよい。

3．慣用表現

２人はずいぶん年が離れている。

They are very different in age.

Their ages are very different.

There is a big difference in their ages.

私には姉[妹]が１人おりますが年はずっと離れています。

I have only one sister, who is many years older [younger] than I.

利害を離れた[無私，無欲な]愛

disinterested love

はやい（早い，速い）

1．時期・時刻

early（１日のうちの早い時間，人の一生の早い時期）（↔ late）; soon（間もなく）

【時間】

彼女は朝早く着くだろう。

She will arrive early in the morning.

早寝早起きは健康と富と知恵をもたらす。

Early to bed, early to rise makes a man healthy, wealthy and wise.

彼は５分早めに到着した。

He arrived five minutes early.

早く帰って来てね，お母さん。

Come back soon, Mother.

できるだけ早く来てください。

Please come as soon as possible.

結果が早く知りたいわ。

I'm anxious to know the result.

【時期】

決定的なことを言うのはまだ少し早すぎる。

It's a bit too early to say anything decisive about it.

お正月が早く来るといいなあ。

I wish the New Year's holidays would come soon.

早くあなたの赤ちゃんが見たい。

I'm eager to see your baby.

I do want to see your baby.

【年齢】

将来の職業を決めるのはまだ彼には早すぎる。

It's too early for him to decide on his career.

彼女はまだ結婚するのは早すぎる。

She's too young to get married.

2．速度

（連続的動作）**fast; swift**

彼が(クラスで)一番走るのが速い。

He runs the fastest (in his class).

He is the fastest runner.

何と月日は速く過ぎ去るのだろう。

How fast time flies!

Time flies!

《類義語》

fast, swift　動作が速いこと。swift は fast, quick より堅い語。

rapid　運動動作が速いこと。

quick　瞬時的動作の速さ。応答，反応の速さ。ただし次のようにも使える。

How quickly time passed!

このあたりは流れが速いが下流にいくと緩やかになる。

The stream runs fast here but it runs more slowly downstream.

早く早く。皆が待っています。（催促）

(Be) Quick. / Hurry up. } They are all waiting.

3．敏捷

brisk; quick

【動作・仕事】
彼女は何でもすばやい。
　She is quick in everything.
彼女は仕事が早い。
　She does her work very fast.
　She gets her work done very quickly.
【記憶】
彼は外国語の覚えが早い［語学の才がある］。
　He is quick at learning languages.
【耳が早い】
彼は耳が早い。
　He has a nose [an ear] for news [rumor(s), scandal(s)].
彼は早合点でいつも問題を起す。
　His hasty judgments always create problems.
早合点するな。
　Don't jump to conclusions.

はらう（払う）

1．金
　pay《a person》《money》**for**《something》
ベビーシッターに1万円払った。
　I paid the babysitter 10,000 yen.
子守りの分5000円のほかに洗濯してもらった分として3000円を余分に彼女に払った。
　I paid her 5,000 yen for babysitting and an extra 3,000 yen for doing the wash.
庭の草取りに3000円払います。
　I'll pay you 3,000 yen to weed the garden.
このバイクに10万円払ったよ。
　I paid 100,000 yen for this motorbike.
それに1万5000円払ったよ。
　It cost (me) 15,000 yen.
このスーツはまだお金を払ってない。
　This suit is not yet paid for.
借金を払い終える
　pay (off) [clear (up)]《one's》debts

2．ほこり・物など
コートのほこりをよく払っておきなさい。
　Brush your coat well.
彼女は（家の）中に入る前に戸口で足を止め，コートの雪を払った。
　She paused and brushed the snow off her coat before coming in.

3．気持ちを向ける，費やす
君は私の言うことに注意を払っていない。
　You don't pay attention to what I say.
勝利の陰では大きな犠牲を払っているのだ。
　The victory was ⌊dearly bought [achieved at great sacrifice [cost]].
親は自分たちの欲望を抑え子供のためには犠牲を払うものだ。
　Parents often ⌊deny themselves [sacrifice their own desires] for the sake of their children.

はらをたてる（腹を立てる）→おこる

はりきる（張り切る）

1．元気
　be full of energy [vitality, vigor]; be full of pep〔*colloq.*〕**; be in high spirits**（何か特別のことのために）
明日から修学旅行なので私たちは皆張り切っていた。
　We were all in high spirits, with the school trip starting tomorrow.
子供たちは張り切っている［元気はつらつとしている］。
　The children are full of pep.

2．熱心
　be eager to《do something》**; be enthusiastic about**《something》
彼女は早く働きたいと張り切っている。
　She's eager to start working.
彼女は新しい仕事に張り切っている。
　She's enthusiastic about her new job.
皆新しい計画で張り切っている。

They are enthusiastic about the new plan.

はる（張る）

1．たるみをなくす

stretch; pull

【ロープ】

警察は危険箇所にロープを張って仕切った。

The police roped off the dangerous spot.

ロープを引っ張りすぎると切れますよ。

If you {put too much strain on the rope / pull the rope too hard} it will snap.

このロープはもう少し引っ張ると向うの柱まで届くだろう。

If this rope is stretched a little further, it will reach (to) the other pole.

【テント・ネット】

彼らは流れのほとりにテントを張った。

They pitched their tent by the stream.

テニスコートはまだぬれていたが，僕たちはネットを張ってテニスを始めた。

The tennis court was still wet but we put up the net and began playing.

部屋中クモの巣が張っていた。

There were spider webs all over the room.

2．一面に覆う

【氷】

夜のうちに氷が張った。

Ice formed during the night.

湖面にすっかり氷が張った。

The lake is frozen over.

【根】

土砂崩れを防ぐために根をしっかり地中に張って土を保持する木を植えるといい。

One can plant the kind of trees that spread their roots and thus anchor [hold, bind] the soil in order to prevent landslides.

【水】

私たちは寝る前に水がめに水を張っておくように言われた。

We were told to fill the basin with water before going to bed.

3．その他

胸を張って

with pride and confidence

私はお偉方と一緒に座っていて気が張った。

I was very tense sitting with the VIPS.

これは値が張りすぎる。

This is too expensive.

意地を張りなさんな。

Don't be stubborn.

彼は欲の皮が張っている。(次から次と欲しがる)

His desires have no end [are endless].

He's avaricious.（金銭欲がたいへん強い）

彼は見栄を張る［見栄っ張りだ］。

He shows off a lot.（行動）

He's vain.（状態）

【腹】

おなかが張っている。

My stomach is full.

【肩】

肩［首筋］が張っている。（凝っている）

My shoulders are stiff.

I've got stiff shoulders [a stiff neck].

【平手で打つ】

彼は息子の頬を張った［ビンタを食わせた］。

He slapped his son on the cheek.

はる（貼る）

絆創膏(ばんそうこう)を貼る　put on [apply] a plaster

ポスターを貼る　stick [put] up a poster

壁にポスターを貼る

stick a poster (up) on the wall（のりで）

tape a poster to the wall（テープで）

〈注〉「壁にポスターを貼る」のように場所を示す副詞句があるときは up は省略可能，ないときは up が必要。

封筒に切手を貼る

put a stamp on the envelope

stamp an envelope

この葉書は切手が貼ってない。
This postcard is not stamped.
台所の壁にはタイル，寝室の壁には壁紙が貼ってあった。
The kitchen walls were tiled and the bedroom walls were papered.
伝言がドアに貼ってあった。
There was a message on the door.
写真をここに貼ること。
Attach your photograph here.

ばん（番）

1．番号
number
あなたの番号は何番ですか。
What number do you have?
私の座席番号は17番の A です。
My seat number is 17A.
あなたの電話番号は何番でしょうか。
What is your telephone number?
何番におかけでしょうか。
What number are you calling?
当選番号は何番ですか。（くじ）
What are the winning [lucky] numbers?
5番の問題が一番難しかった。
The fifth problem was the most difficult.

2．順位
ranking; standing
彼はクラスで何番ですか。（席次）
What is his rank [standing, position] in his class?
What is his class standing?
彼はクラスで3番だ。
He's third in his class.
この前の試験で彼は何番だった？
Where did he rank in the previous exam?
彼は1番でした。
He was the first in the class.
He had the highest marks.
（スポーツで）彼女は結局何番［何等］だった？
Where did she finish?
富士山が一番高い山だが，二番目に高い山は知っていますか。
Mt. Fuji is the highest mountain, but do you know which is the next [second] highest?

3．順序・順番
order;《one's》**turn**
だれの番ですか。（順番）
Whose turn is it? / Who's next?
まだ私の番ではない。
It's not my turn yet.
私の番になった［が来た］。
It was my turn.
My turn came.
〈注〉 直訳して×It became my turn.は誤り。△It came to be my turn. は可能だがまれ。
今週は早［遅］番だ。
This week I am on the early [late] shift.
〈注〉 午前2時からならば 2 a.m. shift とか，朝番ならば morning shift のように言える。
ページの順番が狂っている。
The pages are in the wrong order.

4．見張り番
番をする **watch**
すみません，切符を買ってくる間，荷物の番をしてくださいませんか。
Would you mind watching my suitcase while I'm buying the tickets?
明日は両親が一日中留守をするので店番をしなければなりません。
Tomorrow I'll have to take care of [handle, manage] the shop because my parents will be out all day.
〈注〉 tend the shop（店番をする）は英国では使われるようだが米国では上記のように言う。

はんかん（反感）・はんぱつ（反発）

1．反感
(an) antipathy; hostility; an antagonistic

feeling

〈注〉 **antipathy** 内面に深く根ざした嫌悪感, 反感。
hostility 反感, 敵意, 敵愾心。行動として外にほとばしり出るような感情。
antagonism 反目, 敵意で積極的な感情。
下の例文でも上の三語を使いわけることにより, 文のニュアンスが変る。

社長の金もうけ主義は人々の反感を買うだろう。
The company president's money-first policy will arouse people's hostility [antipathy].

イスラム世界と反イスラム世界の間の反感は長年にわたる深刻な問題で, 1年や2年で解決できるものではない。
Hostility [Antagonism] between the Islamic world and the non-Islamic world is a problem too long-standing and too serious to be solved in a year or two.

この地域では原子炉反対の気運が高まっている。
In this area antipathy to nuclear reactors is growing.

2. 反発

反発する **repel; be repelled by**

磁石の同じ極は互いに反発する。
The same-charge poles of magnets repel each other.

彼はその学校の規律の厳しさに反発して1年で退学した。
He was repelled by the stoicism of that school and left it after a year.

〈注〉 Her untidy appearance repelled him. (彼女は不潔なので彼はそばに寄りたくなかった)

3. 反抗

反抗する 動 **oppose; resist; rebel** (行動的)

そんなに心配なさることはありません。あの子は今反抗期なのです。そのうち卒業しますよ。
Don't worry too much. She is now at a rebellious age. She will soon grow out of it.

思春期の子たちは精力を持て余し精神的に不安定で, 大人の世界の慣習に反抗的になりやすいのだ。
Adolescents, full of energy and uneasiness, are likely to reject [resist, rebel against] the conventions of the world of grownups.

統治者は10年以上にわたり重税を課し続け, ついに民衆が反抗して立ち上がった。
The ruler imposed such heavy taxes for more than ten years that people at last revolted [rebelled].

ばんごう (番号) → ばん

ハンドバッグ → さいふ

ハンドル → じどうしゃ

自動車のハンドル **a (steering) wheel;** 自転車のハンドル **a handlebar;** ドアのハンドル **a door-knob** (丸いもの), **a door-handle** [**latch**] (棒状のもの)

【車】

ハンドルを右にまわす
turn the wheel (to the) right

右ハンドルの車
a right-hand drive car
a car with a right-hand drive

【ハンドルを切る】

小さな男の子が左側から突然飛び出してきたので, 私は子供を避けようと力いっぱいハンドルを右に切った。
A little boy suddenly ran out from the left, so I swerved [turned] right as hard as I could to avoid him.

〈注〉 ハンドルを夢中で右にまわす動作は jerk(ed) the wheel とも言える。

【機械など】

ハンドルを右にまわす
turn the lever (to the) right

ひ

ひ（火，灯）

1．火

fire

【火を使う】

人間だけが火を使うことを知っている。

Only human beings know how to use fire.

【火をおこす】make [build] a fire

火をおこすには，新聞紙を丸めて，その上に小枝や落ち葉をのせて火をつける。

To start a fire, crumple a piece of newspaper, put twigs and dry leaves on it and light it.

【火をつける】

ガスの火をつける（点火する）

turn on the gas

〈注〉 火をつけるのはガスレンジか，ガス湯沸かし器かは前後関係から分かるはずなので，どちらも turn on the gas でよい。

彼はたばこに火をつけた。

He lit his cigarette.

【放火】

自暴自棄になって，彼は自分の家に火をつけた。

In desperation he set fire to his own house.

【火がつく】

不注意なたばこの投げ捨てで枯れ草に火がついた。

The dry grass caught fire from a carelessly thrown cigarette [butt [end].

ガソリンは引火しやすい。

Gasoline is highly inflammable.

〈注〉 化粧品・殺虫剤などの缶によく書いてある注意書き。

Do not use near flammable [inflammable] things.（燃えやすい物の近くでは使用しないでください）

【火が出る，火元】

火は台所から出て一瞬にして家中に広がった。

The fire started in the kitchen and spread almost instantly through the whole house.

昨夜火事があった。火元はラーメン屋で，火は私の家のかなり近くまで来た。

There was a fire last night. It started from a ramen shop and came pretty near my house.

【火が消える】

山火事は大事に至らずに火が消えた[燃えつきて消えた]。

The forest fire burned itself out before any serious damage occurred.

火が消えないうちにもっと石炭をくべておきなさい。

Put more coal on the fire before it goes out.

【火を消す】

子供たちは一生懸命火を消そうとした。

The boys tried to put out the fire.

【料理】

火にかける[火を通す] cook

【慣用表現】

彼になぐられて目から火が出た。

He hit me, and I saw stars.

それでは火に油を注ぐようなものだ。

It's just like throwing fat on the fire.

火のない所に煙は立たぬ。

There's no smoke without fire.

2．灯

a light

灯をつける turn on the light

灯を消す

turn off the light; put the light out

【灯が見える】

はるか彼方に目的地の町の灯が見えてきた。

We saw the lights of our destination far ahead.

ひあい（悲哀）

悲哀 **sorrow; sadness;** 幻滅の悲哀 **disillusionment**

その劇は下っ端サラリーマンの悲哀をユーモラスに描いている。

The play humorously depicts the misery of minor salaried men.

彼女の後ろ姿には人生の悲哀がにじみ出ていた。

As I watched her walk away I felt something like the sorrow of life.

ひがいしゃ（被害者）

a victim（犠牲者）

〈注〉 戦争(war)，病気(disease)，自然災害(natural disaster)，航空機事故(airplane crash)，台風(typhoon)，なだれ(avalanche)，地すべり(landslide) などのために死んだ人や被害をうけた人。

(在日)韓国人は差別意識の被害者だ。

Koreans are victims of discrimination.

水俣病患者が被害者同盟を結成した。

Minamata victims formed a union.

〈注〉 人災（human-caused accidents），交通事故（car accidents），戦争による死者を統計的に扱うときは casualty と言う。また，時がたって客観的に見られるようになると victim という感じが薄れて，casualty と言う傾向がある。

ひかく（比較）→ くらべる

比較 名 **comparison**

比較する 動 **compare**《something》**with [to]**《something》

A と B とを[A を B と]比較すると…

When you compare A and B [A with B] …

A … in comparison with B

比較的 副 **comparatively; relatively**

本館はたいへん古いが，その後ろの建物は比較的新しい。

The main building is very old, but the one behind it is comparatively new.

1. 最上級

【一番…である】

それが世界で一番大きな都市だ。

That's the largest city in the world.

これは大きい方から二番目だ。

This is the second largest.

その子はクラスで一番きれいな子だ。

She is the prettiest (girl) in her class.

彼女はベネット姉妹の中で一番頭がいい。

She is the smartest of (all) the Bennett sisters.

四季の中で春が一番好きだ。

Of all seasons I like spring best.

春はピクニックには一番いい季節だ。

Spring is the best season for picnics.

走るのは彼が一番速い。

He runs (the) fastest. (1)

He is the fastest runner. (2)

〈注〉 上の(1)(2)の英文は同じ意味だが，(1)の fastest は副詞の最上級，(2)の fastest は形容詞の最上級である。副詞の最上級には the をつけないと言われるが，諸文法家の例文にも the のつくもの，つかないもの両方あり，結論としてどちらでもよいことになる。次の文はアメリカの中学校の教科書に載っていたもので，アメリカ英語の方が the をつける傾向が強いようである。

He does his work the most carefully of all the students.（生徒たち皆の中で彼が一番正確な仕事をする）

彼女は目下一番の人気歌手の一人だ。

She is one of the most popular singers now.

【…ほどのものはない】

こんな美しい音楽は聞いたことがない[今まで聞いた中で一番美しい音楽だ]。

I have never heard such beautiful music (as this).

This is the most beautiful music (that) I have ever heard.

コンピュータにかけてダイアナほどの達人を私は知らない[ダイアナこそ一番の達人だ]。

I know of no one better at computers than Diana.

Diana is the best person at computers I know.

軽いやけどには無塩バターが一番だ。

Nothing is better for minor burns than unsalted butter.

2．比較級

僕の方が君より年上だ。

I am older than you.

私は妹より3つ年上だ。

I am three years older than my sister.

私たちは思ったより早く着いた。

We arrived earlier than we (had) expected.

この次はもっと良い点をとるように。

I hope you will get better marks next time.

お前は我々3人(の使う)分を合せたよりもっとお金を使う。

You spend more money than we three put together [all together].

【どちら】

青いのと赤いのとどちらがいい？

Which do you like better, the blue one or the red one?

青いのがいい。

I like the blue one better.

I prefer the blue one.

The blue one. [common]

3．同等　→おなじ

the same as; be similar; be like; be alike; look like

【the same (as)】

私たちは年も生れた日もいっしょです。

We are the same age to the day.

私たちはたった1か月違いの同い年です。

There's only one month's difference in our ages.

【as ... as】

あなたは彼女に劣らず英語が上手ですね。

You speak English just as well as she does.

彼は昔とちっとも変らず，元気がよくて親切だ。

He is just as kind and energetic as he used to be.

【not so [as] ... as】

彼には昔の元気はない。

He isn't so [as] energetic as he used to be.

もう私はそんなに若くない，君が考えているほど若くはないんだ。

I'm not so young, not as young as you think.

【be like, look like, look alike】

その双生児の姉妹はそっくりだ。

The twin sisters look just alike.

坊主くぎは普通のくぎと変らない，ちょっと短くて頭がないだけだ。

Brads are like ordinary nails except that they're usually shorter and have no head.

私たちはよく似ている。2人とも雷雨のゴロゴロザーザーが好きだ。

We're just alike; we both like thunderstorms.

漬物はピクルスと似たようなものだ。

Tsukemono is similar in some ways to pickles.

Tsukemono is like pickles in some ways.

彼は私の妹と音楽の好みがよく似ている。

He's similar to my sister in his music(al) tastes.

My sister and he have similar music(al) tastes.

〈注〉 英語では何と何を比較するのかを日本語よりも几帳面に明示する。

ex. 学生時代のように長い休暇はとれない。

× I cannot have a long vacation like school life.（学生時代はすべて vacation なのかと思われる）

○ I cannot have such a long vacation as I had during my school days [while (I was) at school].

自分の高校時代と比べて生徒たちはおとなしい。

× They are obedient boys compared with my high school days.

○ The boys are docile compared with those I knew in my high school days.

彼らは道化師のような服装だ。

× Their clothes are like a clown.

○ Their clothes are clownish.

ひがし（東）→ ほうがく

ひかん（悲観）

悲観する **be disappointed**（がっかりしている）; **be discouraged, lose heart**（もうだめだと先を悲観する）; 悲観的である **be pessimistic**（**about**）

私は試験結果を見て悲観してしまった。

I'm utterly disappointed at my exam result.

自動車学校のこの前のテストに失敗してまったくがっかりした。先行き悲観的になったよ。

I'm so disappointed about failing the last test at driving school that I'm losing heart.

失敗したからといって悲観するんじゃないよ。

Don't be [feel] discouraged at your failure.

そんな悲観した顔をするんじゃない。まだもう一度チャンスがあるじゃないか。

Don't look so gloomy. You'll have another chance.

彼はこの事業の先行きには少々悲観的だ。

He is rather pessimistic about the future of this project.

ひきおこす（引き起す）→ おきる・おこす

ひく（引く）

1. 引っ張る

ぐっと引く **draw; pull;** 引きずる **drag**

日差しが暑い。カーテンを引いてくださいませんか。

The sun is too hot. Could you please close [draw] the curtains?

〈注〉 draw the curtain は open の意味と close [shut] の意味と両方に使われる。前後関係から分かるはずであるが draw it open [closed] とすればはっきりする。

真っ白な子馬が2頭立てで馬車を引いた。

Two white ponies pulled [drew] the cart.

この文章は重複している。赤インクで線を引いて消しなさい。

This sentence is redundant. Cross it out in red ink.

作業員が道路に線を引いている。

Workmen are putting [painting] the lines onto the road.

我々は試合のためにコートの線引きをした。

We redid the white lines on the court for the matches.

〈注〉 コートの白線をはっきりさせるために引き直したのであるから redid（redo の過去形）がふさわしい。

2. 引きつける

attract; 注意を引く **draw attention;** 同情を引く **win sympathy**

その男の子は皆が(彼の妹の)赤ちゃんを可愛い可愛いと言うので焼きもちを焼いて，わざと音をたてたりして皆の注意を引こうとした。

The little boy was jealous and made noises to attract people's attention because everybody was busy fussing over his baby sister.

3. 引き入れる

新しいアパートには水道・ガス・電気が引いてある。

Water, gas and electricity have been installed [put in] in the new apartments.

4. 引用する

他人の文章を引く[引用する]ときは引用符で囲まなければならない。

When you quote a passage from (the writings of) someone else, you have to put it in quotation marks.

〈注〉 シェイクスピア[ハムレット]から引用する
quote (from) Shakespeare [Hamlet]
シェイクスピアから2,3行引用する
quote a few lines from Shakespeare
quote とは原典の言葉をそのまま引用すること。cite は quote と同義にも用いるが，さらに，引き合いに出す，言及するの意味もある。この場合は言葉をそのまま (exact words) 引用するのではない。

5．辞書を引く

look up; see

その単語は辞書で引きましたか。

Did you look up the word in the dictionary?

何と書いてあるか辞書を引いてみましょう。

Let's see what the dictionary says.

6．引き算

【引き算】subtraction

【引く】subtract

10引く6は4。10－6＝4

Six from ten is [leaves] four.

Ten minus six is [equals] four.

【値を引く】

値は引けませんか[値引きはできませんか]。

Can you reduce the price [take something off the price]?

1000円ほど引けませんか。

Can you lower the price [discount it] (by) 1,000 yen?

【天引き】

普通，税金・保険料は給料から天引きされている。

Generally taxes and insurance are deducted from the salaries.

7．その他

【かぜをひく】→かぜ(風邪)

かぜをひいた。

I've caught (a) cold [a chill〔英〕].

【くじ】

だれが行くかくじを引いて決めた。

They drew lots to decide who should go.

ピクニック → えんそく

ひげ（髭）

口ひげ　**a mustache; a moustache**〔英〕

あごひげ　**a beard**

ほおひげ　**full sideburns**（もみあげからほおを覆うひげ); **whiskers**（耳から下を覆うひげ；猫のひげも whiskers）

もみあげ　**short sideburns; side whiskers**

ひげをそる　動 } shave

ひげそり(そること)　名 } shave

(ひげがだいぶ伸びたから)そらなきゃならない。

I really need a shave.

(ひげを)そりたての　形 clean-shaven

かみそり　razor

電気かみそり　electric shaver

ひさしぶり（久し振り）→あいさつ

【挨拶】

久しぶりですね

It's [It's been] a long time since I saw you last [we last met].

I haven't seen you for a long time.

Hello, long time no see.（ごくくだけた表現だがよく聞かれる）

【久しぶりに】

久しぶりに家に帰った。

I went home after a long time.

〈注〉「久しぶり」の気持ちを表すのに次のような言い方が一般的である。

I hadn't been home for a long time.（ずっと家に帰らなかったなあ）

The last time I went [I'd been] home was five years ago.（この前帰ったのはもう5年も前のことだ）

彼は久しぶりに日本に帰国した。

He came back to Japan after many years.

父と息子は久しぶりに再会した。

The father and (the) son met after many years (of separation).

彼が久しぶりに手紙をくれた。

He wrote (to) me after a long time.

彼女から久しぶりに電話があった。

She phoned me after a long time.

〈注〉「久しぶりに」の英訳として，表現に変化をつけるためか after a long absence とか after a long silence などが辞書に出ているが，absence は留守にしていたことで，その意味にぴったりの状況(久しぶりの帰国とか帰郷など)で堅い文章中であれば使える。しかし「久しぶりに手紙をもらった」ときに after a long absence はおかしい。after a long silence は silence が沈黙のことであるから，手紙の場合に使える理屈だが，けんかでもしてわざと便りをよこさなかったの意にとられそうだ。after a long time や after many years はどんな場合でも使えるので無難である。

ひじょう (非常)

非常の際[場合]

in an emergency; in case of emergency

非常口　an emergency exit [door]

非常階段　an emergency stairway

(旅館・ホテルの注意書き) 非常口を確認してください。

Check the location of the fire escapes. 〔*written*〕

Check where the fire escapes are. 〔*spoken*〕

非常ブレーキ　the emergency brake

非常手段をとる

take [adopt] emergency measures

非常手段が必要である

require emergency measures

非常報知器　an alarm

cf. 火災報知器　a fire alarm

盗難報知器　a burglar alarm

ガスもれ報知器　a gas alarm

ひじょうしき (非常識) → じょうしき

ひじょうに (非常に) → おおいに，とても

very much; awfully; terribly; greatly; extremely; remarkably 〔*rather formal*〕

私は結果を見て非常に失望した。

I was very much [awfully, terribly] disappointed at the result.

〈注〉日本人は「非常に」の意味の強意語を文末にもっていく傾向があるが，次のように書くのは不自然である。

△I was disappointed at the result very much.

非常に多忙で歯医者の予約を忘れてしまった。

I was so busy (that) I forgot my appointment with the dentist.

彼は非常に急いでいたので別れの挨拶に来る暇もなかった。

He was in such a hurry (that) he couldn't come to say good-by.

〈注〉強意の so, such は as や that などそれを受ける説明部分のあるときに使うべきである。

びっくり → おどろく

びっくりする　**be surprised** (不意のこと，一般的な語); **be astonished** (強い驚き); **be startled** (はっとする); **be frightened** (ぎょっとする)

〈注〉人が「びっくりする」は be ～ed の受身形。予期しないことまたは人が「びっくりさせる」のであれば能動態となる。

彼が急に帰って来たのでびっくりした。

His sudden return surprised us.

We were surprised (because) he came back so suddenly.

He returned so suddenly we were surprised.

1. 強い驚き

【びっくりして】

彼は彼女にコーヒーショップを開く資金を貸してやろうと申し出た。あまり突然のことで彼女はびっくりして何と言ったらいいか分からなかった。

He offered to loan her the money to open a coffee shop of her own, but the offer came so abruptly that she was taken aback [flabbergasted 〔*colloq.*〕] and didn't know what to say.

〈注〉「びっくりして口もきけない」には次の言い方もある。

be struck dumb [dumbfounded, speechless]

昨夜地震があったとき，僕はびっくりして目を覚したが彼は平気で眠っていた。

When the earthquake hit last night I woke up with a start, but he slept right through it.

赤ちゃんが窓から落ちて火がついたように泣き出した。しかしたいしたけがはなくびっくりした方が大きかった。

The baby fell from the window and began to scream, but he was more frightened than hurt.

2．感嘆文

びっくりするじゃないか［ああびっくりした］。

What a start you gave me!

You scared the life [living daylights] out of me!

ひっこし(引っ越し)・ひっこす → かわる・かえる

引っ越し 名 **moving;** 引っ越す 動 **move**《one's place of residence》

引っ越しの費用　moving expenses

古いアパートから［新居へは］いつ引っ越すの？

When are you going to move out of the old [into the new] apartment?

私たちは引っ越して来たばかりです。

We have just moved here.

父が亡くなってから一家をあげて九州から東京に引っ越しました。

Our family moved from Kyushu to Tokyo after our father's death.

私たちは父の転勤のため何度も引っ越しをしなければならなかった。

We had to move often because our father was transfered many times.

ひつよう（必要）

名 **need**

必要である

［人主語］**need**

［事主語］**be necessary; be needful; be needed; be required;** 欠くべからざる **be indispensable; be essential**

【…が必要である】 need; be necessary →いる（要る）・いらない

彼には君の助力が必要だ。

He needs your help.

彼の助力が必要だ。

His help is necessary [needed].

このカメラは修理が必要だ。

This camera needs mending.

〈注〉 be necessary を使うならば事物を主語に，need を使うならば主体となる人間を主語にする（上の「カメラ」のような例外的表現もある）。

×He is necessary your help.（君の助力が必要だ）

【…は必要ではない】

彼は君の助力を必要としていない。

He doesn't need your help.

これ以上車を買う必要はない。

It's not necessary to buy another car.

必要以上のお金を持っていかないように。

Don't take more money than you need.

【…する義務はない】

彼はそんなことをする必要はない［なかった］。

He { doesn't have [need] to do so. / need not do so. }

He didn't have [need] to do so.

〈注〉 上の用例は疑問文および否定文で need を助動詞として扱うか本動詞として扱うかの問題があるが，アメリカ口語では do not need の形が普通(cf. need not)。特に過去形では did not need が無難である（cf. need not have done)。

自分でやる必要はありませんよ。

You don't have to do [don't need to do, need not do] it yourself.

There is no need to do it yourself.

【辞退】
私のことを心配する必要はありません。
  You don't have to [needn't] worry about me.
私のことをご心配くださる必要はありませんでしたのに。
  You needn't have worried [didn't have to worry] about me.
断ったら悪いなどと心配する必要はありません。
  You needn't [don't have to] feel obliged to accept.
【欠くべからざる】be essential; be indispensable
この仕事には英語の知識がぜひ必要だ。
  For this job knowledge of English is essential [necessary].
英語を必要とする仕事がしたい。
  I want to get a job in which English is necessary [needed].
〈注〉 次の例は誤文である。
  ×I want to get a job which is necessary English.
会社にはどうしても強力な社長が必要だ。
  A strong president is essential to a company.
彼女は会社にとって必要不可欠な人間になってしまった。
  She has become quite indispensable to the company.

ひと（人）→ にんげん

1．人間一般

man (1) 人間(↔神)。人間性まで含む抽象概念のときは無冠詞。
  Man is mortal.（人は死すべき者である）
(2) 男(↔女)。a man は普通名詞で，人・男を表し，その複数が men。
〈注〉 ただし，近年「人」の意味では man の代りに person を使う傾向が強くなっている。男の意味の man で人間を代表させるのは男女差別につながるとの考え方からである。
mankind (1) 人類(human race)。集合的。神に対して人類と聖書を思わせる言葉。日本人は「人類」の意味でこの語を使いすぎるようだ。
(2) 男性(↔女性)。集合的。
a human (being) 神や他の動物と区別した「人間」。感情を持ち，過失を犯す人間性を思わせる。
a person 個々の人。個々の人の複数が persons。男女の区別なしに使われる person が近年広く用いられるようになってきた。
people 個々の人を考慮しない不特定多数の人々。集合的。
〈注〉 a peopleと単数扱いできるのは「国民」の意味のときである。
すべてのヒトがただ一つの種に属することを我々が真に理解したときはじめて人種差別は終るだろう。
  When we finally understand that all human beings [all persons] are truly one species discrimination should end.
人[人間]は皆音楽を愛するようだ。
  It seems that (whole) human race loves music of one kind or other.

2．三人称

【あの人】she, he, that lady, that person
あの人はだれですか。（初めて出会ったとき）
  Who is that man [woman, lady]?
〈注〉 Who is that lady? はよいが Who is that gentleman? はかなり社交的に聞える。gentleman は改まった場合（演説の初めの Ladies and Gentlemen）や社交的な場において，または客に対して営業上用いる以外は，立派な人の意味で He is a gentleman.（彼は紳士だ）のような言い方に用いられるだけである。
あの人はいつも遅く来る。
  She [He] is always late.
あの人は技師です。
  He is an engineer.
〈注〉 日本語の「あの人」に当る英語は，前出の例文のように「あそこにいる人」の意味で，初めての出会いの場合は that man [woman] であるが，それ以外は he, she である。

3．不特定の人

【人は皆…】 everyone; everybody

人は皆それを知っている。

Everyone knows that.

【どんな人でも…】 anyone; anybody

どんな人でもそんなことはできる。

Anyone can do that.

4．だれか

someone; somebody

手伝ってくれる人が欲しい。

I want somebody to help me.

人が来ます。

Someone's coming.

【…な人はない】 no one; nobody

行きたい人はだれもいなかった。

No one wanted to go.

【人(集合的)】

若い人　young people

年とった人　old people

これは若い人のための場所だ。

This is a place for young people.

【人手】

人手が足りない。

We are short of workers now.

【訪問者】

今日の午後は人が来ることになっている。

We are expecting a visitor this afternoon.

5．性格・人柄 →せいしつ・せいかく

人がいい

good-natured; kind-hearted

人が悪い　mean

あの人はいい人だ。

She is ⌊a nice person [very nice].

〈注〉 a nice woman といういい方は失礼に聞える。「女」が失礼なのと同じ。

He is a ⌊gentleman [nice person].

あの人はすっかり人が変ってしまった。

He is quite another ⌊man [person] now.

He isn't what he used to be.

6．他人

人に親切にしなさい。

Be kind to others.

人の身になって考えなさい。

Be considerate.

Be thoughtful of others.

人の都合を考えなさい。

Consider ⌊other people's convenience [others].

彼はいつも酔っぱらっては人に迷惑をかけている。

He's always getting drunk and disturbing people.

人に迷惑をかけるな[ちゃんとしなさい]。

Try not to give other people trouble.（＝Behave yourself.）

人の言うことなど気にしなさんな。

Never mind what people say.

〈注〉 日本語の「人の言うことを少し聞いたらどうだ」「人をばかにしている」の「人」はしばしば自分（語り手）のことを指す。自分が相手の立場に立って物を見ている発言である。 Listen to ⌊what I'm saying [me]. や You are making a fool of me. にあたる。

人の噂だとあの人たちは離婚するそうだ。

People say they are going to divorce.

人のせいにするな。

Don't blame other people.

世のため人のために尽くす

be dedicated to《some cause》

〈注〉 英語では何に尽くすのか対象について具体的に述べるのが普通。

ex. work for world peace [the poor / the under-privileged]（世界平和[貧しい人々/恵まれない人々]のために尽くす）

Do your part [Be active] in the wider world.（何か世のため人のためになることをしなさい）

強い表現としては次のようにも言える。

Dedicate yourself to something.

人ごとだと思っているようだが，そうではないよ[君の問題だよ]。

You think that concerns others only, but it doesn't.

人ごとだと思っているようだが，君の責任で

もあるんだよ。

That's not only someone else's responsibility; it's yours too.

ひどい

1. むごい，意地が悪い

《類義語》

severe 心身ともに強じんでなければ耐えられないような厳しさ，荒々しく厳しい（look 目つき，rules 規則，tasks 任務などについて）。

cruel 過酷な，冷酷な（最も強い語；person（人），punishment（罰），requirements（要求）などについて）。

inhuman 非人間的な
merciless 無慈悲な
unfair 不当な
}（treatment（取扱い）などについて）。

harsh 荒々しく，手厳しい。

hard 堅く手ごわい，厳しい（必ずしも意地悪くない）。

mean けちな，卑劣な，汚い，意地悪な。

nasty 汚い，意地の悪い。

（それは）あまりにひどい！（命令・要求などに）

That's too much.

Don't be hard on me!（「勘弁してくれ」との抗議）

そんなことを言うなんて彼もひどい。

It's really mean [nasty] of him to say so.

ひどい目にあったよ。

I had a bad experience.

うっかりサインしてひどい目にあったよ。

I signed, and paid dearly for it.

〈注〉何かばかなことをして，おかげでひどい目にあったときの言い方。その上の a bad experience の例文は自分のせいでなくて運が悪かったこと。

2. 粗悪な

terrible; dreadful; bad

【施設】

ひどい道路　a bad road

当時の孤児院なんてひどいものだった。

Orphanages in those days were really dreadful (places).

【食事】

その頃の寮の食事はひどかった。

The food at the dormitory was terrible in those days.

【言語】

ひどい誤り　a bad mistake

彼の英語にはひどいなまりがある。

His English has a terrible accent.

知らない男の人がひどい英語でこの近くに銀行があるかと尋ねた。

A man asked me in terribly broken English if there was a bank nearby.

3. 強度の

ひどい風　a violent [harsh] wind; biting wind（凍てつく風）

ひどい雨　a heavy rain

ひどい天気　terrible weather

ひどい寒さ　severe cold

ひどい暑さ　terribly hot weather

ひどい痛み　severe pain

彼は事故でひどいけがをした。

He was badly hurt in the accident.

ひどいかぜをひいてしまった。

I've caught a bad cold.

チリでひどい地震があった。

There was a big earthquake in Chile.

平和通りはひどい渋滞です。

Heiwa-dori is heavily congested.（報道文）

ひどい渋滞だ。

This congestion is terrible.（車に乗っている人の感想）

The traffic is terribly heavy today.（客観的）

4. ひどく

【感情】→たいへん，とても・とっても，ひじょうに

very 一般的でどの形容詞にも合う。

awfully
terribly
}口語で広く使われる。

greatly 一般的または文語。

deeply　一般的。幸，不幸にかかわらず真情を表す。

下の表は強意語と形容詞の結びつきを調べたもので，４人の米国人インフォーマントが可とするものを選んでもらい，その人数を書き込んだものである。

ひどく	very	terribly	awfully	greatly	deeply	extremely	
幸せ	4	3	3			3	happy
喜ぶ	4	3	4			4	glad
喜ぶ	4	4	4	3	3	3	pleased
興奮	4	3	3	2	1	4	excited
怒る	4	3	4		1	4	angry
失望する	4	4	4	4	3	4	disappointed
すまない 残念 同情	4	4	4		1	3	sorry
気を悪くする	3	4	2	2	3	3	hurt (feeling)
感動	3	1	2	3	4	3	touched
感動	3	2	1	4	4	3	moved

【体・感覚】

ひどく疲れる　be awfully [terribly] tired

ひどくなる（病気など）

get [become] worse

ひどく痛い。

It's very painful.

足がひどく痛む。

My feet hurt terribly.

【行動】

ひどくしかる　scold severely

ひどくこきおろす　criticize severely

ひどくほめる　praise greatly [highly]

彼はつえで私をひどく打った。

He struck me hard with his cane.

ひとがら（人柄）→ せいしつ・せいかく

ひとり（一人，独り）

1．一人

私には弟が一人いる。

I have one brother.

【一人っ子】

彼は一人っ子だ。

He is an only child.

彼はあの夫婦の一人っ子だ。

He is their only child.

【一人だけ】

彼一人だけ試験に受かった。

He was the only one that passed the exam.

彼が事務所を開いて最初の週はお客がたった一人来ただけだった。

During [In] the first week after opening his office he had only one client.

【一人も…ない】

困ったときに頼れる人は一人もいない。

There is no one I can turn to for help.

時間通りに来た人は一人もいない。

None of them arrived on time.

通りには人っ子一人いない。

Not a soul was to be seen on the street.

【一人につき】

子供たちはオレンジを一人２個ずつもらった。

The children were
{ given two oranges each [apiece].
{ each given two oranges.

【一人ひとり】

その人は子供たちを一人ひとり抱きしめた。

She hugged the children one by one.

我々一人ひとりが皆核兵器廃絶に向かって努力しなければならない。

Each and every one of us should try to have nuclear weapons abolished.

【孤独】

かわいそうにその子は独りぼっちで家に残されていたのだ。

The poor child was left alone in the house.

彼はまだ独り者だ。

He's still single.

お願いだから独りにしておいてください。

Leave me alone, please.

彼を独りにしておこう［放っておけ］。

Let [leave] him alone.

その老人はアパートで独り暮しをしている。

The old man lives (all) ⌊alone [by himself] in an apartment.

2. 独力で，自然に

by oneself

【ひとりで】

その坊やはひとりでパジャマが着られて得意になっていた。

The little boy was proud that he had put on his pajamas [pyjamas] all by himself.

彼女はあの豪華なウエディングドレスを自分ひとりで縫い上げた。

She made that gorgeous wedding dress by herself.

そんなことはひとりでやりなさい。

Do that by [for] yourself.

ひとりで[自力で]考えなさい。

Think for yourself.

〈注〉 by oneself＝without help from others; for oneself＝in order to benefit oneself であるが，上の例文「ひとりでやれ」「ひとりで考えろ」は特別で for oneself を使う。

【ひとりでに】

by [of] itself; (自動的に) automatically; of its own accord

何もしないのにガス警報器がひとりでに鳴り出した。

My gas alarm went off of its own accord.

ドアがひとりでに開いた。

The door opened by itself.

ドアの前に立つとひとりでにドアが開くので，その老人はびっくりしてしまった。

The old man was surprised that the door opened automatically when he stood in front of it.

ひとりでに泣けてくる

tears ⌊run down one's face [come to one's eyes]

〈注〉 涙は意志にかかわらず自然に出てくるものであるから，特に involuntarily としなくてよい。しかし意に反して涙が出れば，それは involuntarily である。

びょういん（病院）→ いりょう

病院 **hospital;** 総合病院 **general hospital;** 診療所 **clinic**(外来患者専門で数人の専門医をかかえている)

かかりつけの医師 family doctor; G. P. (general practitioner の略)

【診察】 medical examination

診察を受ける see a doctor

診断 diagnosis; 動 diagnose《病名》

健康診断

a (health) checkup; a physical examination

初診です。

This is my first visit.

再診です。

I'm on a follow-up visit.

【診療科目/専門医】

内科 internal medicine / an internist

循環器系 circulatory system

呼吸器系 respiratory system

消化器系 digestive system

外科 surgery / a surgeon

脳外科 brain surgery / a brain surgeon

整形外科

orthopedics / an orthopedic surgeon

腫瘍学 oncology / an oncologist

産婦人科 obsterics-gynecology, ob-gyn / an obsterician, a gynecologist

助産婦 a midwife

精神科・神経科 psychiatry / a psychiatrist

耳鼻咽喉科

otolaryngology / an otolaryngologist

ear-nose-throat department / an ear-nose-throat specialist

眼科 ophthalmology / an ophthalmologist, an eye dochor

皮膚科 dermatology / a dermatologist, a skin specialist

泌尿器科 urology / a urologist

肛門科 proctology / a proctologist

放射線科 radiology / a radiologist

小児科 pediatrics / a pediatrician

歯科　dentistry / a dentist
【検査・治療】tests; treatments →いりょう
【病棟】ward
ex. 内科病棟　internal medicine ward
看護婦詰所　nurses' station
【薬局】（病院内の）dispensary; （一般の）a drugstore〔米〕; a pharmacy; a chemist's (shop)〔英〕

びょうき（病気）

【病気】illness; sickness; disease
かぜ　cold
流感　flu [influenza]
百日咳　whooping cough
水ぼうそう　chicken pox
はしか　measles
おたふくかぜ　mumps
花粉症　pollinosis; hay fever
アレルギー性鼻炎　nasal allergy
アトピー性皮膚炎　atopic dermatitis
水虫　athlete's foot
喉頭炎　laryngitis
気管支炎　bronchitis
喘息　asthma
肺結核　tuberculosis [TB]
肺気腫　emphysema
肺炎　pneumonia
心臓病　heart disease
心臓発作　heart attack
狭心症　angina pectoris
心筋梗塞　myocardial infarction
動脈硬化　arteriosclerosis
高血圧症　hypertension
脳卒中　stroke
脳溢血　cerebral hemorrhage
脳梗塞　cerebral infarction
白血病　leukemia
貧血　anemia
血友病　hemophilia
梅毒　syphilis
淋疾　gonorrhea
エイズ　AIDS /éidz/
癌　cancer
盲腸炎　appendicitis
痔疾　hemorrhoids; piles
糖尿病　diabetes
肝炎　hepatitis
肝硬変　cirrhosis of the liver
腎炎　nephritis
ネフローゼ　nephrosis
腎臓結石　kidney stone
膀胱炎　cystitis
ヘルニア　hernia
赤痢　dysentery
コレラ　cholera
マラリア　malaria
熱射病　heatstroke
日射病　sunstroke
痛風　gout
神経痛　neuralgia
リューマチ　rheumatism
リューマチ性関節炎　arthritis
ヘルペス　herpes
神経衰弱　nervous breakdown
ノイローゼ　neurosis
パーキンソン病　Parkinson's disease
アルツハイマー病　Alzheimer's disease
自律神経失調症
autonomic nervous system disorder
自閉症　autism
統合失調(精神分裂)症　schizophrenia
躁鬱病　manic-depression
心身症　psychosomatic disorder
てんかん　epilepsy
不眠症　insomnia
緑内障　glaucoma
白内障　cataract
結膜炎　conjunctivitis; pink eye
網膜剥離　detached retina
筋ジストロフィー　muscular dystrophy
原爆病　radiation sickness
公害病　pollution disease
水俣病　Minamata disease

じん肺　black lung disease
【症状】 symptoms and conditions
熱　fever; temperature
不整脈　irregular heartbeat　(cf. 脈 pulse)
高血圧　high blood pressure
低血圧　low blood pressure
咳　cough
鼻水　runny nose
痛み　ache (鈍い); pain
頭痛　headache
のど痛　sore throat
発疹　rash
じんましん　hives
湿疹　eczema
アレルギー　allergy
アレルギー性湿疹　allergy rash
できもの　boil
浮腫，水腫　edema
潰瘍　ulcer
腫瘍　tumor　(cf.　良性の　benign; 悪性の malignant)
膿瘍　abscess
化膿する　fester
妊娠　pregnancy
不妊　infertility
栄養不良　malnutrition
消化不良　indigestion
胸やけ　heartburn
下痢　diarrhea
便秘　constipation
吐き気　nausea; vomiting; 動 to vomit
黄疸　jaundice
外傷性ショック　shock; trauma　(cf. ショック症を起す go into shock; suffer trauma)
昏睡　coma
麻痺　paralysis　(cf. 麻痺させる paralyze)
炎症　inflammation
感染　infection
【身体の損傷】 bodily damage
骨折　a fracture
脚を骨折する
break《one's》leg; have a broken leg
捻挫　a sprain
足首を捻挫する　sprain [twist]《one's》ankle
やけど　burn　(cf.　やけどをする　be [get] burned)
凍傷　frostbite　(cf.　凍傷にかかった　frost-bitten《toes》)

ひょうじょう（表情）

1．客観的な印象

look ～; have a ～ look

彼女はうれしそうな表情をしている。
She looks happy.
彼はいらいらした表情をしている。
He looks irritated.
上の例文のように，次にあげる形容詞を She [He] looks ～ 形 にあてはめてみる。

【She [He] looks ＋ 形】
とてもきれい　beautiful; lovely
うれしそう　delighted; happy; pleased
元気そう　cheerful (陽気な); lively (活発な)
熱心そう　eager; enthusiastic; passionate
満足そう　content; satisfied
誇らしげ　proud
優しく　kind; affectionate; friendly; gentle (声や表情がもの静かな)
ほっとした
relieved; comforted (慰められた)
冷静な　calm
きちんととりすました　prim
まじめな　serious; sober
厳しい　stern
こわい　grim
決心した　determined
一途な，集中した　intent
思慮深い　thoughtful
思いにふけった　meditative
悲しそう　sad; sorrowful
寂しげ
forlorn; helpless; alone and unhappy
怒った　angry; annoyed; vexed
むっとした　offended

いらいらした　irritated
待ちきれない　impatient
苦々しい　disgusted
不機嫌な　cross
悪い　guilty
すまない　remorseful; sorry
憂鬱な　depressed
がっかりした　disappointed; discouraged
絶望した　despaired
必死な　desperate
当惑した　puzzled
はにかんだ　shy
困った　embarrassed
いばった　arrogant; haughty
欲深い　greedy
びっくりした　surprised; astonished; amazed
ぎょっとした　frightened; scared; terrified
興奮した　thrilled; excited
心配そうな　nervous; anxious; worried
居心地の良さそうな　comfortable
居心地の悪そうな　uncomfortable
くたびれた　tired; weary
退屈した　bored
くたくたになった　exhausted
やつれた　worn out

【その他】

かわいそうにといった目つきで
　with a pitying look
憧れの眼差しをする　have a longing look; look nostalgic; look at《a thing》wistfully
ばかにした表情をする
　have [give] a sneering look
ぼうっとした目つきをする
　have a far away look; look abstracted

2. 具体的な表現

にこにこして　smiling; with a smile
笑って　laughing
にっと笑って　grinning
泣いて　crying
泣き出す　burst into tears
目に涙をためて　with《one's》eyes full of tears; with tears in one's eyes; in tears
目を伏せて　with downcast eyes
じっと見つめる　gaze at
じろじろ見る　stare at
ちらっと見る　glance at
のぞき見をする　peek / peep (through a hole)
横目[白目]で見る　look askance
目をそらす　look away; avert《one's》eyes
顔を赤らめる　blush
顔をしかめる
　grimace; screw up《one's》face; frown
眉をひそめる　knit《one's》brow
つまらない顔をする
　put on a long face（＝look unhappy）
不機嫌な顔をする，すねる　pout; sulk
　be in a snit; look sulky [cross]

ひらく（開く）

1. 開ける

【包み】

早く箱を開けてください。
　Please unpack the box quickly.

【本】

13ページを開いてください。
　Open the book at [to] page 13.

【戸】

風がさっと吹きつけドアがひとりでに開いた。
　There was a gust of wind and the door opened by itself.

〈注〉 of itself（ひとりでに）は英国では使うが，米語では使わない。

2. 開催する

【パーティーを開く】

　have [give, hold] a party

〈注〉 give は主格になる人が費用を持つとき，hold は公式の大きな会のとき。have は広く使われ，だれがお金を出すかにはふれない。

もし天気がよければ，ガーデンパーティーを開きます。

We are going to have a garden party if the weather is good.

【会議を開く】

課の会議が月曜日に開かれる。

There will be a department meeting on Monday.

We will have a department meeting on Monday.

英語科の会議は月曜日午前10時から開かれる。

The English department will have a meeting on Monday at 10 a. m.

今週会議はあるの？

Will we meet this week?〔*informal*〕

3．始める

【営業】

銀行は９時に開きます。

The bank opens at nine.

スミスさんはニューヨークに店を開いている。

Mr. Smith has [owns, runs, keeps] a store in New York.

〈注〉 own は店の持ち主であること。keep〔英〕，run は自分で店をやっていること。have はどちらでもよい。

4．咲く

桜の花がもうすぐ開くだろう。

The cherry blossoms will soon be out.

月見草は日が暮れてから開く。

Evening primroses open after sunset.

ひる（昼）

1．昼間

day; the daytime

その小説家は夜仕事をして昼寝るのだそうだ。

They say that the novelist works at night and sleeps in the daytime.

道路工事の労働者たちは道路を仕上げるために夜も昼も働かねばならなかった。

The road crew had to work day and night to finish the road.

もう夏至も過ぎたので，これからは昼が短くなっていく。

It's past the (summer) solstice now and the days are becoming shorter.

昼が一番長いのが夏至で，一番短いのが冬至だ。

Daylight is [lasts] longest at the summer solstice and shortest at the winter solstice.

2．正午

noon; 真昼 **midday**

【昼飯時】 lunchtime

昼に会おう。

See you at lunchtime.

【昼前，昼から】

昼前[午前中] 4 時間，昼から[午後] 2 時間授業があります。

We have four classes in the morning and two (classes) in the afternoon.

昼から買物に行きます。

We'll go shopping in the afternoon.

【昼まで】

今日は学校は昼まで[午前中だけ]です。

Today we have no class in the afternoon.

We have only morning classes today.

School will close at noon today.

ひろい（広い）

1．幅

wide (↔ narrow); 広々した **broad**

ヨーロッパの都市には広い大通りのあるところがある。

Some European cities have broad boulevards.

古い都市では新しくできた都市のように通りが広くない。

In old cities the streets are not as wide as in newly-built cities.

2．面積

広大な　**large**（↔　small）; ゆったりした **roomy**（↔ 狭苦しい　cramped）

川の土手の向こうは野原で，その先は広い荒野になっていた。

Beyond the river bank are open fields and then large moors.

ビルの裏手に広い駐車場があります。

There is a large parking lot at the back of the building.

彼の新しい事務所は前のより広い。

His new office is larger than the [his] former one.

部屋は広々としていて趣味のいい家具がしつらえてあった。

The rooms were spacious and tastefully furnished.

《類義語》

spacious　広くゆったりとした意で，かつ優雅で上品な意味合いがある。広告のコピーなどによく使われる。やや文語的。家や部屋の「広い」ことは wide とは言わない。the wide world とか the wide ocean のような言い方があるが，wide のもとの意味は幅の広いことである。

roomy（↔ cramped）　広くゆったりとした部屋には roomy も使える。roomy には広く居心地のよいイメージがあり，houses, rooms, cars, clothes にも用いられる。

big（↔ small）　広い部屋は a big room とも言える。反対に狭い部屋は a small room, a cramped roomであり，a narrow room は幅の狭い部屋（うなぎの寝床）のことである。

3．転義

広い意味で　in the broad sense of the word

広く使われている言語

the most widely spoken language

【広い知識】

彼は植物学に関して広い知識をもっている。

He has extensive [wide, broad] knowledge of botany.

【顔が広い】

彼は顔が広い[知人が多い]。

He has a wide [large] circle of acquaintances.

〈注〉 a wide circle とすると各方面に知人があること。a large circle とすると知人の数が多い含みになる。

彼女は芸術家[芸術家と実業家]仲間に顔が広い。

She knows many people in the art world [the worlds of business and art].

【心が広い】

彼は心の広い人だ。そんなことを根にもったりはしないだろう。

He is a broad-minded man. He won't hold it against you.

〈注〉 a broad-minded man とは視野が広く寛大で，くだらないことに腹を立てたりしない人のこと。

ひろがる（広がる）・ひろげる

1．広がる

㊐㊂ **spread**

【田】

水田が山のふもとまでずっと広がっている。

Ricefields stretch [extend] as far as the foot of the hills.

【道】

両市を結ぶ道路は2,3年中には広がるだろう。

The road between the two cities will be widened in a few years.

【火】

火は台所から出て2,3分で家中に広がった。

The fire started in the kitchen, and in a few minutes spread all over the house.

【戦火】

第一次世界大戦は1914年に中欧の列強の間に起ったが，ほとんどヨーロッパ全域に広がった。

World War I started in the Central Powers in 1914, but it spread through most of Europe.

2. 広げる

【新聞紙】

新聞を広げる

open the paper（読むために）

spread the newspaper(s)（壁を塗るときなどに床の上に新聞紙を広げて敷くこと）

put down newspaper（靴を磨くためなどに新聞紙を敷くこと）

【地図】

テーブルの上に地図を広げる

unfold [spread] the map on the table

【翼】

ワシが翼を広げた。

The eagle spread its wings.

【事業】

ヤマハはピアノの製造で出発したが，ほかの楽器にも手を広げ，やがてオートバイや家具の製造まで事業を広げた。

Yamaha first started manufacturing pianos, but they expanded to other musical instruments, and then motor bikes and even furniture.

〈注〉 一般的に widen は幅を広げること，spread は平面的に広げることを意味する。

3. 広まる

【うわさ】

あっという間にうわさが広まった［広がった］。

The rumor spread [ran] like wildfire.

【教え】

キリストの教えは半世紀のうちに，ギリシャ・ローマ文化圏に広まった。

The teachings of Christ spread across [disseminated throughout] the Greco-Roman world within half a century.

宣教師たちはその地方の人々にキリスト教を広めた。

Missionaries spread Christianity among the people of the area.

弘法大師は広く仏法を広めた。

Kobo-daishi taught Buddhism far and wide.

〈注〉 far and wide は古風で上述のような文ならばよいが，日常的に使ってはおかしい。

ふ

ふあん（不安）→ しんぱい

不安である **be uneasy; be nervous**

何か悪いことが起りそうで不安だ。

I fear something unlucky will happen.

(就職したが)仕事のことが不安だ。

I feel uneasy about my job.

(レストランで)料理は上等だったが，勘定のことを考えると不安になった。

The food was excellent but I became uneasy [nervous] about the bill.

行方不明の飛行機についてのニュースを人々は不安げに待っていた。

People waited nervously for news about the missing plane.

ラジオは台風の接近を報じ，人々は不安な一夜を過した。

The radio reported that a tyhoon was approaching and the people passed an anxious night.

風がひどくなるにつれて人々の不安は募った。

Their anxiety increased as the wind rose.

当時は生活に不安があった。

Living conditions were precarious in those days.

インフレは社会不安を引き起す。

Inflation causes social unrest.

ふい（不意）→ おどろく

1．思いがけないこと

【不意打ち】

彼らは彼に不意打ちを食らわした。

They have taken him by surprise.

〈注〉 take him by surprise そのものには「不意打ちを食らわす」のような悪い意味はない。良くも悪くもびっくりさせることを指す。

【不意を食う】

不意を食ってとっさに何と言ったらよいかわからなかった。

Taken by surprise, I didn't know what to say.

【不意の来客】

不意の来客があった。

We had an unexpected guest.

彼女は不意に訪ねて来た。

She paid me a surprise visit.

2．突然

不意に **suddenly**

彼は不意に振り向いた[立ち止まった／駆け出した]。

He suddenly turned round [stopped/began to run].

彼女は不意に立ち止まった。

She stopped short.

ふうけい（風景）→ けしき

ふうしゅう（風習）→ しゅうかん

manners and customs

今でも葬式から帰って来ると塩をまいて清める風習がある。

Many people still keep [observe] the old custom of sprinkling salt to purify themselves after coming back from a funeral.

大きな川で隔てられているので，二つの村の風習はまったく異なっている。

Because a wide river separates the two villages, their customs and ways of life are quite different.

ふえる（増える）・ふやす

1．増える

㊍㊐ **increase; multiply**

【数】

(この市では)事故が増えている。

There are more and more traffic accidents in this city.

The number of traffic accidents is increasing [on the increase].

年ごとに事故が増えている。

Every year there are more traffic accidents.

ネズミはどんどん[ねずみ算式に]増える。

Mice multiply quickly [in geometric progression].

世界の人口がこれ以上増えないようにせねばならない。

We should try to check any further increase in world population.

1個の癌細胞が増え続けてやがて病気を起す。

One cancer cell keeps multiplying until illness results.

あそこは家族が増えて家が手狭になった。

Their house became too small as
{ the family grew larger.
{ the number of children increased.

あそこはまた1人増えた[生れた]。

They had another child.

彼の仕事がどんどん増えてゆく。

The duties of his job keep (on) multiplying [increasing].

【量】

彼女はものすごく食べるのにちっとも体重が増えない。

She eats huge amounts and yet never puts on [gains] an ounce.

昨夜来の雨で川の水が増えた。

The river is swollen from the overnight rain.

2. 増やす

㊍㊗ **increase**

【数】

名古屋・京都間を走る列車を増やしてほしい。

I wish they would increase the number of trains (running) between Nagoya and Kyoto.

あの大学では学生の定員を増やした。

The university increased the number of students.

友だちを増やしたくてそのクラブに入りました。

I joined the club because I wanted to get to know more people.

【量】

お金を増やすことには興味がない。

I'm not interested in making money.

モルヒネは習慣性になると量を増やさなければ効かなくなる。

Morphine won't work once you become addicted to it unless you increase the quantity.

ふく（服）→ いふく

clothes; 上下一揃い **a suit;** 婦人用ワンピース **a dress**

［集合的に「衣服」を指す語］

clothing; attire〔*formal*〕; 服装一式 **outfit** (ex. ski outfit, school outfit); **apparel**〔米 *formal*〕; **～wear** (ex. sportswear, skiwear)

【服を着る】

put on《one's》clothes; get dressed

服を着て今すぐ降りておいで。

Put on your clothes [Get dressed] and come down immediately.

【服を着ている】wear; be dressed in; be in

あの人はすてきなローズ色の服を着ている。

She is wearing a nice rose-colored dress.

彼は焦げ茶色の服[背広]を着ていた。

He was in a dark brown suit.

黒い服[スーツ]を着た人が3人店に入っていった。

Three people wearing black suits went into the shop.

【服の好み[趣味]】

彼女は服の好みがよい。

She always dresses in good taste.

She always has good clothes sense.

【適当な服(ある場に適した)】

着ていくのに適当な服がない。

I don't have anything (good enough) to wear.

【服を脱ぐ】

子供にはひとりで着たり脱いだり楽にできる服を与えるのがよい。

Give children simple clothes which they can put on and take off easily by themselves.

【服がきつい】

この服は私にはきつい。

This dress is too tight for me.

【服装】

人を服装で判断してはいけない。

We shouldn't judge people by their clothes [appearance].

あの人は服装には無頓着だ。

She is indifferent about what she wears.

彼はTシャツにジーンズで結婚式に来た。あんな服装は花嫁の兄としてはどうかと思う。

He wore a T-shirt and jeans to the wedding. Such {dress is / clothes are} {inappropriate / unsuitable} for the brother of the bride.

〈注〉「服装」にあたる英語を示すために Such clothes ... のようにしたが，前後関係から明らかなので，実際には That is inappropriate ... で十分である。

ふくし（福祉）

社会福祉　**social welfare**

福祉制度　**welfare; the welfare system**

福祉事務所　**a welfare office**

福祉国家　**a welfare state**

福祉事業　**welfare work**

《関連語》

社会厚生施設　welfare facilities

社会保障　social security

生活保護　welfare; social aid

生活保護で生活する　live on welfare

老人ホーム　old people's home; nursing home

乳児院　children's home

託児所　nursery; day-care center

精神発達遅滞児収容施設　home for mentally-challenged

身体障害者　physically-challenged persons; the physically-challenged

職業訓練所　vocational training center

民生委員　social worker

ケースワーカー　case worker

介護　nursing; care

介護福祉士　(licensed) caregiver

介護保険　extended care insurance

ふくしゅう（復習）→ べんきょう

復習する **review** 《one's》 **lesson; go over** 《one's》 **lesson**

きのうやったところを復習しましょう。

Let's go over yesterday's lesson.

私は今日学校でやったところを復習していると言った。

I said I was reviewing today's lessons.

友だちが英語の復習はやったかと私にたずねた。

My friend asked me if I had reviewed today's English lesson.

ふくむ（含む）

1．含有する

contain; have; include

【含有】

この飲料は着色料・保存料を何ら含んでいません。

This drink has [contains] no artificial coloring or preservatives.

イチゴはビタミンCをたくさん含んでいる。

Strawberries have [contain] a lot of vitamin C.

2．一緒に入っている

【加入】

派遣団には数人の学者も含まれている。

The delegation includes some scholars.

【勘定の内訳】

勘定は税金・サービス料を含んで19,820円になります。

The bill comes [amounts] to 19,820 yen, with [including] the tax and service charge [tip].

3．了解する

keep in mind; remember; understand

来週監査があることを含んでおいてください。

Please keep in mind
Please remember
Don't forget
} that we're having inspection next week.

〈注〉 keep in mind は話者が相手に何かしておくことを言外に期待し，聞き手にもそれがわかっているときに用いる。

この事業には反対者もいることを含んでおいてください。

I hope you understand that there are some people who aren't very happy about this project.

ふけつ（不潔）→ きたない

不潔な **dirty;** ひどく不潔な **filthy**

【不衛生】

台所はひどく不潔だった。

The kitchen was really dirty [filthy].

地震のあとに建てられたバラックは超満員で不潔であった。

The camps built after the earthquake were overcrowded, dirty and unsanitary.

難民キャンプは不潔な状態におかれ，赤痢が流行した。

Unsanitary conditions at the refugee camp led to a severe dysentery epidemic.

【嫌らしい】

不潔なじいさん！　Dirty old man!

ふごうかく（不合格）→ にゅうし

1．学校，会社の試験

彼は3科目で不合格だった。

He failed (in) [flunked〔米俗〕] three subjects.

彼は早稲田大学が不合格だった。

He failed (in) the entrance examination for Waseda University.

彼は身体検査で不合格になった。

He did not pass the physical (examination).

不合格者　an unsuccessful candidate [applicant]（応募して選にもれた者）

cf. 失格者　a disqualified person（必要条件を満たしていないため失格した者）

2．製品検査など

不合格となる

be rejected; fail to stand the test

不合格品　a rejected item（規格に合わず検査を通らなかった物）

cf. seconds 傷物

新型車に欠陥があることが判明し，不合格となった。

The new model has been found defective and been rejected.

ふざい（不在）→ るす

ふさわしい

【仕事】

彼にふさわしい仕事を見つけてやろう。

I'll try to find him a suitable job.

これは彼にちょうどふさわしい仕事だ。

It's just the right kind of work for him.

【人物】

彼こそその地位にふさわしい人物だ。

He is the right man for the position [post].

彼女のことなど忘れてしまいなさい。彼女だけが女の子じゃない。君にふさわしい子を紹介してあげるから。

Forget her. She isn't the only girl in the world. I'll introduce you to someone just right for you.

【能力がある】

彼ならその仕事にふさわしい。

He is equal to the task.

君は賞をもらうにふさわしい。

You deserve the prize.

【(慣習に照らして)その場に】

彼女はその場にふさわしい服装をしていた。

She wore a dress appropriate [proper] for the occasion.

【行為】

そのような振舞は若い女性にはふさわしくない。

It { isn't appropriate for / doesn't become } a young girl to behave like that.

ふしぎ（不思議）

wonders　驚きの気持ちが中心。

a mystery　なぜかと思う知的探求心に焦点がある。

a miracle　ありそうもないこと(奇跡)に焦点がある。

【奇妙な】 strange; odd

昨夜は不思議な夢を見た。

I had a strange dream last night.

彼女がそのことを何も知らなかったなんて不思議だ。

{ It's strange [odd] (that) / I wonder why } she didn't know anything about it.

【えも言われぬ】 wonderful; wondrous

えも言われぬ不思議な楽の音

wonderfully beautiful music

【神秘的な】 mysterious

彼は不思議な体験をして，それからすっかり人が変った。

He had a mysterious experience, which utterly changed him.

この薬草は私には不思議に効きます。

This herb has a miraculous effect on me.

【奇跡的な】 miraculous

高名な弘法大師は日本全国を行脚(あんぎゃ)して不思議を行ったと信じられている。

It is believed that the famous Buddhist saint Kobodaishi did miraculous deeds all over Japan.

あの事故にあって脚の骨折だけで済んだとはまったく不思議というものだ。

It's a miracle that he got only a broken leg from [in] the accident.

【魔法のような】

まったく不思議だ。信じられない。

It's like magic. I can't believe it.

どうやって昨夜猫が中に入ったかまったく不思議だ。ドアも窓もたしかにかぎをかけておいたのに。

How the cat got in last night, since I'd certainly locked all the doors and windows, is a mystery.

【信じられない】 incredible

なくした財布が冷蔵庫の裏から出てくるなんてまったく不思議だ。

It's quite incredible [amazing] that my lost purse was found behind the refrigerator.

彼女が「うん」と言ったとはまったく不思議だ。

It's incredible that she (should have) said "Yes".

【理屈に合わない】

彼が職にありつけたら不思議だ。見るからにだらしないんだから。

It'll be a wonder [miracle] if he ever gets a job, he's so slovenly in appearance.

【不思議なことに】 strangely enough

なくした指輪が不思議なことに私の机の上にあった。

My lost ring was found, strangely enough, on my desk.

ふしょう（負傷）→ けが

負傷する **be wounded**

彼は負傷者の中にいた[負傷していた]。

He was found among the wounded.

ふせぐ（防ぐ）→ まもる

1．防御する

defend《oneself [one's country]》**against**《the enemy》

protect《oneself [one's country]》**from** [**against**]《the enemy》

日本は外国の侵略を防ぐために自衛隊を持っている。

Japan has Self-Defense Forces to defend itself against possible invaders.

2．寄せつけない，食い止める

keep off [**away, out, back**]

【寒さを防ぐ】keep out the cold; protect oneself from the cold

寒さを防ぐためにドアは厚手でがっしりと造られていた。

The doors were made heavy and thick to keep out the cold.

【腐るのを防ぐ】preserve《things》from decay

塩は食物が腐るのを防ぐ。

Salt preserves food from decay.

【伝染[感染]を防ぐ】prevent infection

家族にかぜひきがいるときは熱い湯で衣類を洗うと感染を防ぐ効果がある。

Washing clothes in very hot water helps prevent infection when someone has a cold in the family.

以前は上流に深い森林があり下流での洪水を防いでいた。

Formerly there were deep forests upstream which prevented floods [flooding] downstream.

そのホテルは災害を防ぐために何ら[十分な]方策を講じていなかったことが明らかになった。

It became clear that the hotel hadn't taken any [sufficient] disaster prevention measures.

現在のところ値上がりを防ぐのは難しい。

At present, it is difficult to prevent prices from rising [going up].

ふそく（不足）→ たりる

不足している 形 **insufficient; short;** 不十分な **not enough;** 動 **want; lack; be short**

【金銭】

買物は総計２万5000円ほどになり，私の手持ちでは6000円不足で正直あわてた。

My purchases totaled nearly 25,000 yen, and to my horror I found I was 6,000 yen short.

僕の貯金は目標額にはほど遠かったが，ジムが不足分を貸してくれると言った。

My savings were far short of the target, but Jim offered to lend me the difference.

〈注〉「不足分」は少額のときは difference と言う。「不足している」の意味の deficient は堅い語で，その名詞形 deficit（不足分，赤字）は会社の会計のような高額な不足の場合に使う。

【切手】

この手紙は切手が不足している。

There aren't enough stamps on this letter.

この小包は切手が不足している。

This package is too heavy for the postage (that's) on it.

【水】

今年は雨の降る季節にあまり降らなかったので水不足が起るかも知れない。

This year we didn't have much rain during the rainy season, so there will be a shortage of water [water will be short].

【食糧など】

食糧[燃料]が不足してきた。

We are running short [out] of food [fuel].

【睡眠】

彼は睡眠不足のため間違ってばかりいた。

He made several mistakes
- because he hadn't slept well.
- due to lack of sleep.〔*formal*〕

【経験】

彼は経験不足だ。

He lacks experience.

【人手】

彼らは人手不足で困っている。

They are short of hands.

〈注〉 日本語の「人手」と同じく hands と言う。手や体を使う単純な仕事（manual, unskilled labor）やボランティアの仕事（volunteer work）などに用いる。

僻地の医師不足は深刻な問題になっている。

The shortage [lack] of doctors in remote districts is a serious problem.

【住宅】

住宅不足はおいそれと解消しないだろう。

The housing shortage will not be solved easily.

【不満，不平】

不足を言う　complain

彼はいつも何やかやと不足を言っている。

He is always complaining about something.

不足を言い出せばきりがない。満足することを知らねばならない。

There is nothing perfect in this world. You should learn how to be contented.

なぜいつも不満げな顔をしているのだ。

Why do you always look dissatisfied?

【何不足ない暮し】

彼らは今何不足ない暮しをしている。

They now live an easy life [quite comfortably].

They are now quite well-off.

〈注〉 on Easy Street〔*colloq.*〕という言い方もある。

ぶちょう（部長）→ かいしゃ

vice / president / head	of	sales	営業部長
		finance	財務部長
		personnel	人事部長

〈注〉 head は課長でも係長でも使える。正式な肩書ではない。vice president は部長，また時には課長にも用いることがあるので「副社長」を英訳するには executive [senior] vice president とする。

上記の営業部長は vice president of sales でよいが，department または division をつけるならば，vice president of the sales department のように冠詞 the が必要。

ふつう（不通）

1．交通 →こうつう

土砂崩れのために鉄道が不通になっている。

Rail traffic has been stopped [blocked] because of a landslide.

（高山線は）下呂と萩原の間が不通になっている。

Railway service has been suspended between Gero and Hagiwara.

豪雪で155号線が不通になっている。

Heavy snow is blocking Rte 155.

〈注〉 Rte は route /rúːt, ráut/ の略。155 は one-fifty-five と読む。

2．通信 →でんわ

通信衛星が故障して丸1日通信が不通になった。

Telephone communications were disrupted for a whole day after the satellite failure.

電話が不通になった。

Telephone communication was cut off.

台風の後3つの村との交信が丸2日間不能になった。

Communications with three villages were out for two days after the typhoon.

〈注〉 disrupted はテレビ，電信などに広く使われる。ex. Television transmission is often disrupted during a thunderstorm.（雷雨でテレビ放送が妨害されることがよくある）

ふつう（普通）

《類義語》

形 **normal**（正常な）↔ abnormal

ordinary（通常の）↔ extraordinary

common（普通の）↔ uncommon

〈注〉 common は時として「平凡な」の意味になるので，人についてはこの語の使用は避けるのがよい。

usual（いつもの）↔ unusual

average（平均的な）

副 普通，たいてい

normally / ordinarily } 普通は…だが…
commonly「よく…する」から「ほとんどいつも…する」までを含む。
usually / generally } 広く使われ，一番無難である。

次々と新車に買い替えたりせず，自分の車は何回でも修理して使うのが普通なようだ。
Having one's car repaired rather than frequently getting a new one seems a normal thing to do.
四輪駆動車はこのところごく普通に見かける。
Four-wheel drive vehicles are common these days.
学校にいた頃，彼はごく普通の元気な若者だった。
When he was at school he was just an ordinary, cheerful youngster.
彼には普通以上の芸術的才能があった。
He had more { than average artistic talent. / artistic talent than average.
彼は数学では普通[平均]以下だった。
He was below average in mathematics.
【普通(に)】 normally; ordinarily; commonly; usually; generally
この頃は郊外でも新しい道路は普通片側2車線だ。
New roads even in suburban areas these days generally [usually, ordinarily] have two lanes in each direction.
日本では大掃除は普通正月前に行う。
Major housecleaning in Japan is usually [commonly, ordinarily, generally] done just before the New Year.
彼は普通8時に朝食をとる。
He ordinarily [usually, normally] has breakfast at eight.
成功した政治家は普通お金に困っていない。
Successful politicians are generally [usually, ordinarily] not poor.
長距離通勤は日本では普通必要悪[やむを得ない]と考えられている。
Commuting long distances is generally [usually, commonly] considered a necessary evil in Japan.
選挙運動では普通選挙カーを使う。
Election campaigners commonly use sound trucks.
【普通…ない】
英国人は普通腹を立てていながらにこにこしたりすることはない，日本人にはよく見られるが。
English people do not usually smile when they feel offended as Japanese often do.
彼の沈みようは普通ではない。
He looks unusually depressed.
彼の様子はこの2，3週間どうも普通ではなかった。
His behavior has been somewhat abnormal these last few weeks.
〈注〉 これまでに挙げた語の否定形と反意語では反意語の方が意味が強い。

normal / not normal / abnormal	ordinary / out of the ordinary / not ordinary / extraordinary
usual / not usual / unusual	common / not common / uncommon

ぶつかる

1. 人と物，物と物

hit; bump into; run into

【人】
男の子が(向こうとこちらから)走ってきてぶつかった。
Two boys ran into each other.
〈注〉 ran against とすると競争(compete)したことになる。
階段を駆け降りて来たら，こともあろうに私のサボった授業の担当教授とぶつかりそうになった。
As I was running down the stairs I nearly bumped into the very professor whose class

I had cut.

【物】

トラックが車に後ろからぶつかった。

A truck
- hit the car from behind.
- bumped into the car.(弱いぶつかり方)
- crashed into the car.(ひどいぶつかり方)

ボールが彼の頭にぶつかった。

The ball {hit [struck(強くぶつかる)] / bumped (弱くぶつかる)} him on the head.

【波】

波が岩にぶつかっては砕けていた。

The waves were breaking [hitting, crashing] against the rocks.

2. 出会う

問題[困難]にぶつかる

face《problems》

run up against《difficulties》

君もときどき，こういう問題にぶつかることがあるだろう。

You will sometimes run up against [come across, meet, have] this kind of problem.

3. 対立する

【意見】

彼らの意見は真っ向からぶつかった。

Their opinions clashed head on.

車をだれが使うかということで，僕はよく家族とぶつかる。

I {often have conflicts / am often in conflict} with my family {over / about} the use of the car.

4. 重なる

【会合】

出なければならない会が二つ同じ時間帯にぶつかった。

I have two meetings to attend at the same time.

【クラス】

この心理学のゼミは，私がとりたいと思っている美術の授業とぶつかる。

This psychology seminar conflicts with an art class I'd also like to take.

【祝日】

国の祝日が日曜日とぶつかるときは代りに次の月曜日が休日となる。

If a national holiday falls on Sunday, we have a substitute holiday on the following Monday.

【行事】

私の友だちの結婚式が兄の結婚式とぶつかってしまう。

My friend's wedding will fall on the same day as my brother's wedding.

ぶつける

1. 打ち当てる

hit; bump; 打ちつける **knock;** 投げつける **throw**

彼は犬に石をぶつけた[犬をめがけて石を投げた]。

He threw [hurled〔*literary*〕] a stone at the dog.

彼は柱に頭をぶつけてけがをした。

He bumped [hit, knocked] his head against the pole and was hurt.

〈注〉 knock も hit もわざとぶつけたようにもとれる。

彼は新車を電柱にぶつけた。

He hit a lamppost with his new car.

〈注〉 He ran his new car into a lamppost. とすると，わざとぶつけたように聞える。

彼は前のトラックに車をぶつけた。

His car bumped the truck ahead of him.

私は車にぶつけられた。

I was hit by a car.

2. 比喩的な表現

彼らは互いに悪口雑言をぶつけ合った。

They hurled insults at each other.

彼は鬱憤がたまると，かわいそうにいつも子供たちにそれをぶつけていた［八つ当りした］。

He used to vent his dissatisfaction on his poor children.

〈注〉 vent は不満など negative feeling のはけ口を求めること。

I vented my indignation by doing club activities.
（私は憤懣のはけ口をクラブ活動に求めた）

情熱をぶつける

throw oneself into《something》

give a lot of energy to《something》

彼は大学時代ハンググライダーに情熱をぶつけた。

He threw himself into〔*informal*〕
He became totally involved in
} hang gliding while he was in college.

君の若いエネルギーと情熱をこの仕事にぶつけてくれたまえ。

Devote your youthful energy and enthusiasm to this work.

ぶつり（物理）

physics

1．一般語彙

物質　matter

物質の（３つの）状態　(three) states of matter

気体　gas; 液体　liquid; 固体　solid

（気体・液体）流体　fluid

長さ　length（略 L); 時間　time（略 T); 質量　mass（略 M); 面積　area; 体積　volume

2．力学関係

力学　mechanics（静力学　statics; 動力学　dynamics; 運動力学　kinematics）

変位　displacement

速度　velocity; 加速度　acceleration

力　force; 作用　action; 反作用　reaction

仕事　work; 仕事率　power（略 P)

摩擦力　frictional force

斜面　inclined surface

圧力　pressure

大気圧　atmospheric pressure

渦　vortex; 流線　stream line

浮力　buoyancy

超音速　supersonic speed [velocity]

衝撃波　shock wave

マッハ　Mach /mάːk/（略 M)

密度　density; 比重　specific gravity

重量　weight; 重力　gravitational force

重心　center of gravity

万有引力　universal gravitation

慣性　inertia; 遠心力　centrifugal force

向心力［求心力］　centripetal force

円運動　circular motion; 振り子　pendulum

振動　vibration; oscillation

振動数　frequency

波長　wavelength; 周期　cycle

振幅　amplitude

位相　phase

位置エネルギー　potential energy

運動エネルギー　kinetic energy

3．熱関係

熱　heat; 熱力学　thermodynamics

カロリー　calorie

温度　temperature

摂氏　Celsius [Centigrade]（略 C))

華氏　Fahrenheit（略 F)

対流　convection

熱輻射　thermal radiation

熱伝達　heat transfer

エントロピー　entropy

融解　melting [fusion]; 融点　melting point

沸騰　boiling; 沸点　boiling point

気化　vaporization

蒸発　evaporation; 昇華　sublimation

凝縮　condensation

熱機関　heat engine

蒸気機関　steam engine

内燃機関　internal combustion engine

点火　ignition; 燃焼　combustion

火炎　flame; 爆発　explosion

4．音関係

音　sound; 音響学　acoustics
音波　sound wave
超音波　ultrasonic wave
音速　velocity [speed] of sound
音の高さ　(sound) pitch
音の強さ　(sound) intensity
音の大きさ　loudness; ホン　phon
音色　tone (color), timber
反射　reflection; 共鳴　resonance
うなり　beat; 騒音　noise
反響[こだま]　echo
音叉(おんさ)　tuning fork

5．光関係

光　light; 光学　optics
レンズ　lens; 凸レンズ　convex lens; 凹レンズ　concave lens
虫眼鏡　magnifying glass; 顕微鏡　microscope; 望遠鏡　telescope
焦点　focus; 入射角　angle of incidence
反射　reflection
屈折　refraction; 屈折率　index of refraction
干渉　interference; 干渉縞　interference fringe
回折　diffraction; 回折格子　diffraction grating
プリズム　prism; 散乱　scattering
光量子　photon
光速度　light velocity
可視光線　visible light
偏光　polarized light
赤外線　infrared ray; 紫外線　ultraviolet ray
明るさ　brightness; ルクス　lux

6．電気・磁気関係

電気　electricity
陽電気　positive electricity; 陰電気　negative electricity
電場　electric field; 電位　electric potential
導体　conductor; 不導体　non-conductor
半導体　semi-conductor
超電導　superconductivity
放電　electric discharge; 電離　electric dissociation
電気分解　electrolysis; 電極　electrode; イオン　ion
電池　battery; 乾電池　drycell
蓄電池　storage battery
電圧　electric voltage; 電圧計　voltmeter
ボルト　volt (略 V)
電流　electric current; 電流計　ammeter
アンペア　ampere (略 A)
電気抵抗　electric resistance; オーム　ohm
直流　direct current (略 DC)
交流　alternating current (略 AC)
コンデンサー　condenser
真空管　vacuum tube
ブラウン管　Braun tube
直列の　serial; 並列の　parallel
電力　electric power; ワット　watt
電力計　wattmeter
キロワット/時　kilowatt-hour (略 kWh)
変圧器　transformer; 発電機　generator
ダイナモ　dynamo
感電　electric shock
漏電　leakage of electricity
安全器　circuit breaker
ヒューズ　fuse
スイッチ　switch
差し込み，プラグ　plug
差し込み口，コンセント　outlet〔米〕; socket〔英〕
磁気　magnetism
磁気学　magnetics
電磁気学　electromagnetics
磁石　magnet; 電磁石　electromagnet
磁極　magnetic pole; 磁場　magnetic field
磁位　magnetic potential
電磁波　electromagnetic wave
磁気嵐　magnetic storm
電磁誘導　electromagnetic induction

磁気テープ　magnetic tape
磁気録音　magnetic recording
周波数変調　frequency modulation（略 FM）
振幅変調　amplitude modulation（略 AM）

7．分子・原子関係

分子　molecule; 原子　atom; 電子　electron
原子核　atomic nucleus; 陽子　proton
中性子　neutron
電子顕微鏡　electron microscope
気体分子運動論　kinetic theory of gases
分子量　molecular weight
分子式　molecular formula
分子構造　molecular structure
分子間力　intermolecular force
高分子　macromolecule; 高分子化学　macromolecular chemistry
原子量　atomic weight; 原子番号　atomic number; 原子価　valence
原子爆弾　atomic bomb; 水素爆弾　hydrogen bomb
原子エネルギー　atomic energy
原子力　atomic power
原子力工学　nuclear（power）engineering
原子核工学　nucleonics
原子炉　nuclear reactor; 原子炉の安全性　nuclear reactor safety
核分裂　nuclear fission; 核融合　nuclear fusion
核爆発探知　detection of nuclear explosion
放射能　radioactivity
連鎖反応　chain reaction
放射線障害　radiation hazard
ラジウム　radium
ウラン　uranium
プルトニウム　plutonium
量子力学　quantum mechanics
不確定性原理　uncertainty principle
相対性理論　Theory of Relativity
　特殊相対性理論
　　Special Theory of Relativity
　一般相対性理論
　　General Theory of Relativity

ふと

〈注〉「ふと」というと，とってつけたように unintentionally, unawares, by chance などをつけ加えるのではなく，次にあげる例文を参考にして場面により表現を使い分けること。

1．動作

私は横断歩道を急ぎ足で渡っていたが，ふと見ると雪子が舗道に立っていた。
　I was hurrying across the zebra crossing when I happened to look up and see Yukiko standing on the sidewalk.

2．心の動き

彼女はもう二度と帰って来ないのではないかと，私はふと思った。
　{It just occurred to me / The thought crossed my mind} that she might never come back again.
川べりを歩いているとき，ふとそのアイデアが心に浮かんだ。
　I was（just）walking along the river when the idea ⌊popped into my mind [came to me].
真夜中にふと何かうめき声のような物音を聞いたように思って目を覚した。
　I woke up at midnight hearing {as I thought〔*formal*〕/ what I thought was} a strange moaning sound.
彼女はふと故郷が恋しくなった。
　She had a sudden ⌊fit of [attack of] homesickness.
ときどきふと過ぎ去った日々が懐かしくなることがある。
　Sometimes {a vague longing for things past / a wave of nostalgia} comes over me.

3．偶然
ふとしたことから彼女は彼を知ることになった。
She came to know him accidentally.
It was quite by accident [chance] that she came [got] to know him.

ふとる（太る）

㊀ **get [become] fat;** 体重が増える **put on [gain] weight**
太っている ㊁ **fat;** 丸々としている **plump;** (婉曲語法) **stout**
太った赤ちゃん
a plump baby
a roly-poly baby（ころころに太った）
僕はこのところ太ってきた。
I'm getting fat.
彼は退院してから太った。
He has {grown stouter [fatter] / put on weight} since he left the hospital.
〈注〉 put on flesh は，病後などに衰弱してがりがりにやせてしまったのが正常に戻りつつあるときの言い方。また His weight is back up.（体重が戻った）という言い方もある。
この3か月で彼は3キロ太った。
He has gained 3 kilograms in the last three months.
ルイーズはいつだって，すごく食べるのにちっとも太らないの。私もそうなんだけど。(いくら食べても太らない)
Louise always eats an enormous amount and never puts on an ounce. So do I and neither do I.
——M. Drabble, *Summer Bird Cage*
私は10キロばかり太りすぎだ。
I'm about 10 kilograms overweight.
〈注〉 「やせすぎ」は underweight。
兄のところの赤ん坊は順調に太ってきている[体重が増えている]。
My brother's baby is gaining weight right on schedule.

ふとん（布団）→ しんぐ

ふべん（不便）→ べんり

㊔ **inconvenience**
不便をかける ㊀ **inconvenience**《a person》; **cause**《a person》**inconvenience**
ゼネストは多くの人にたいへんな不便をかけた。
The general strike caused great inconvenience to many people.
火曜日の9時から10時まで断水いたします。ご不便をおかけしますがよろしくお願いいたします。(お知らせ)
The water will be turned off (on) Tuesday from 9 to 10 a.m. We apologize for the inconvenience.
不便を忍ぶ[我慢する]
put up with the inconvenience of《something》
以前はまったく不便で，村の共同井戸から水を汲んで来るという始末だった。
We used to have to put up with (the inconvenience of) getting water from the village well.
〈注〉 inconvenience a person（人に不便をかける），およびその受身形 be inconvenienced などは堅い表現で，改まった場合以外，日常ではあまり使わない。

【不便である】
細身のロングドレスは働くには不便である。
Long narrow dresses are inconvenient to work in.
このスーツケースは大きすぎて(持ち運びに)不便だ。
This suitcase is unwieldy (to carry about).
台所(の配置)が不便にできている［使いにくい]。
This kitchen is {badly laid out [planned] / inconvenient} to work in.

その学校は不便なところにある。

The school isn't in a convenient place [conveniently located].

ここは乗り物が不便だ。

There's no convenient bus or train service near this place.

今度の所は買物が不便だ。

My new place is inconvenient for shopping.

バスの乗り換えが２度もあって不便だ。

It's troublesome [inconvenient] to have to change buses twice.

〈注〉◆ convenient, inconvenient は日時・スケジュールなどに関しても使われる。

出発が早すぎて（都合が）悪いんですが，これだと乗り換えなしで行かれます。

Leaving so early is an inconvenience, but this way you can have a direct flight.

金曜日ではご都合いかがでしょうか。

Will Friday be convenient for you?

◆ be convenient [inconvenient] は人間を主語にできない。「うちが遠いので［田舎なので］学校に行くのが不便です」は

×I am inconvenient to go to school. は誤り。

I live so far away, }
My house is so far out in the country, }
it's difficult for me to get to school.

とする。

ふる（振る）・ふりまわす

1．揺り動かす

wag《a tail》; **shake**《a head》; **wave**《a hand》; **swing**《a club》

〈注〉 揺れ方は語の音にかなり表れている。shake ガタガタ；wag 尾をぴんぴん；wave 波のうねりを思わせるゆらゆら；swing はぶらんこや時計の振り子，野球のバットのように大きな弧を描く揺れ方。ぶらんぶらん; quake や tremble は揺れ方が細かくぶるぶる。

【振る，振り回す】

部屋の中でバットを振る［振り回す］な。

Don't swing your bat in your room.

男の子が傘を振り回しながら歩いていた。

A boy was walking along swinging his umbrella.

彼はデッキの上に立ちハンカチを振っていた。

He stood on the deck waving his handkerchief.

彼女は「さよなら」と手を振って行ってしまった。

She waved goodbye and was gone.

彼女は首を縦に振って「よろしい，心配いりません」と言った。

She nodded saying, "O. K. Don't worry."

彼女は悲しげに首を横に振った。

She shook her head sadly.

犬はうれしいときしっぽを振る。

Dogs wag their tails when they are happy.

【振りかける】

魚に塩を振っておいてください。

Sprinkle salt on the fish [the fish with salt].

肉は焼く前に塩・胡椒を振っておいてください。

Season the meat with salt and pepper before you broil it.

イチゴには砂糖を少々振りかけてください。

Sprinkle a bit of sugar on the strawberries.

2．はねつける

【男女関係】

ジムはあの子をふってほかの女性に乗り換えた。

Jim threw her over for another woman.

彼女はふられた。

She was turned down [rejected, jilted].

〈注〉 仕事・就職などに関し次のような言い方もある。

彼はくびになった。

He was given his walking papers [a pink slip].

ふるえる（震える）

《類義語》

shake 一般的な語。

tremble 恐怖・予感・喜び・寒さなどで体や手がぶるぶる震えること。次の shiver より大きな震え。

shiver 瞬間的にぶるっと震える。寒さで震えるときに多く使う。tremble より小さな動作。

quiver　かすかな震え。
shudder　恐怖•嫌悪などにより突然激しく身を震わす。
quake　恐怖や驚きのため身体が大きく震える。cf. heart-quaking（心臓がどきどきするような），quaking in one's boots（(こわくて)がたがた震える）
earthquake は地面の「揺れ」を言う。
vibrate　細かい規則的な振動でしばしば音を伴う。物理的な動きであり，比喩的な言い方を除いては特に感情的色彩はない。

彼の名前を聞いただけでぞっとして震えがくる。
The mere mention of his name makes me shudder.
I shudder at his name.
彼らは寒さと恐怖に震えながら身を寄せ合って座っていた。
They sat together shaking [trembling, shivering] with cold and fear.
哀れな子供達は家もなく寒さに震えていた。
Poor children were shivering with cold in the street.

【細かい震え】
子供は震え声でお母さんに会いに行ってもよいかとたずねた。
The child asked in a tremulous [shaking] voice if she could go to see her mama.
声が震えていたので，あの人が心の中で泣いているのがわかった。
There was a quiver in her voice, and I knew she was crying inside.

【かすかな震え】
ポプラの葉がかすかに震え，風のそよぎを見せていた。ポーチの我々にまでは届かないかすかな風の震え。
The aspen leaves quivered a little, the sign of a breath of air which we didn't feel at all sitting on the porch.

【振動】
電線が震えてブンブン鳴った。
There was a buzzing sound as the electric wires vibrated.
嵐で窓ガラスがガタガタ鳴った。
The windowpane vibrated [shook] from the gale.
〈注〉　vibrate は vibrate in memory のような比喩的用法もある。
It's the natural, almost overlooked pat on the back that vibrates in memory.（ふと何気なく背中をたたく，見過してしまいそうな小さな励ましのしぐさだが，いつまでも心にしみる）

ふるさと（故郷, 古里）→きょうり•こきょう

one's **old home**（郷里の家）
one's **hometown**（生れ育った町・市・村）
one's **birthplace**（生れた所）
だれでも年をとるとふるさとが恋しいものだ。
Everyone longs for their old home in their old age.
ここは私の心のふるさとだ。
This place is like my old home.

ブレーキ → じどうしゃ

名 **brake**
ブレーキをかける　動 **brake; put on the brakes**
子供の姿を見て彼はブレーキをかけた。
At the sight of the child he { put on the brakes. / braked the car. }
ブレーキがきかなかった。
The brakes failed.
ハンドブレーキ
hand brake; parking brake〔米〕

ふれる（触れる）

1．接触する
【指で】
彼は指先で亀の甲羅に触れた。
He touched the turtle's shell with his finger tip.

【手に】
(彼は)ポケットの中の何か丸くて堅い物に手が触れた。
He felt something round and hard in his pocket.
展示品に手を触れないでください。
Don't touch the exhibits.
Hands off! (掲示)

2. 精神的接触
be [come, get] in touch with
彼女は自分でも自分自身の心の奥底にあるものにほとんど触れることがなかった。(気づかなかった)
She wasn't much in touch with her inner soul.
〈注〉 米語では be [get] in touch with は本当の自分自身などに目を開く[触れる]意で使うが，英国では be [get] in touch with《a person》として，人と連絡をとる意味に使うだけで米語のような用法はない。
【自然】
都会に住んでいる人の多くは時には自然に触れたいと思う。
Many city people want to
{ get in touch with nature〔米〕 / get out into the countryside } now and then.
【人情】
私は彼の心の温かさに触れた。
I felt his warm-heartedness.
I was impressed by his humanity [kindness].
I was touched by his kindness.
I now realize how good and kind he was.
私は知らぬ土地に来て人情の温かさに触れた。
Although I was a stranger there, everyone I met was very kind and good to me.
〈注〉 「心に触れた」のつもりで ×I touched human heart. とか ×I felt his heart. と直訳しないで上記のように具体的にやさしい言葉で述べた方が自然である。

3. 言及する
refer to; touch upon
彼は話の中で西欧文明に深く根差したキリスト教の影響にも触れた。
In his speech he referred to the deep-rooted influence of Christianity on European culture.
我々の会合では財政問題に関してはほんのちょっと触れただけであった。
We only touched on financial problems in our meeting.
その論文は関連する論題にもいくつか触れている。
The essay touched on several related topics.
〈注〉 「触れる」は簡潔に言及することであるが touch on; refer to も軽く触れることを言う。

4. 抵触する
go against《the law》
【法に】
法に触れるようなことをするな。
Don't do anything against the law.
再軍備は現行法に触れる。
Rearmament would violate the present constitution.
【怒りに】
あの人は家業を継ぐのを拒んで父親の怒りに触れた。
He angered his father by refusing to inherit his family business.
〈注〉 「痛いところに触れる[を突く]」に近い英語に touch a raw nerve; hit a sore spot〔*colloq.*〕(痛いところに触れて怒らす)がある。

ふろ (風呂) → ゆ

ぶん (分)

1. 分け前・持ち分
【分け前】
これがあなたの分です。
This is for you.

彼は人の分まで欲しがる。

He insists on taking more than his share.

彼の分を取っておこう[取り分けておこう]。

We'll save [keep, leave] some for him.

【分割分】

5月分の家賃をまだ払ってない。

I haven't yet paid the rent for May.

【持ち分】

自分の分は自分で払うことにしよう。

You pay your bill and I'll pay mine.

cf. Let's split the bill.（割り勘にしよう）

君の分の切符も買っておいたよ。

I have bought a ticket for you, too.

2. 分量

【…人分】

10人分の食事を用意した。

We prepared dinner for ten persons.

彼は2人分食べる。

He eats enough for two.

彼は実際2人分の仕事をする。

He does practically two people's work.

【…円分】

私はすき焼きのために5000円分の牛肉を買った。

I bought 5,000 yen worth of beef for sukiyaki.

【…(期間)分】

医者は1週間分の薬をくれた。

The doctor gave me enough medicine for a week. ※

The doctor gave me 7 days' worth of medicine.

〈注〉 上の※印の文は「たくさん薬をくれて1週間ももちそうだ」の意にもとれるが，前後関係でわかる。日本語の「1週間分の薬」の意にもなる。

うちにはひと冬分の灯油がある。

We have enough kerosene for the whole winter.

数か月分の石炭

several months' supply of coal

3. 分数

a fraction

【…分の…】

$\frac{1}{3}$ one-third

$\frac{3}{4}$ three-fourths; three-quarters

$\frac{2}{3}$ two-thirds　$\frac{4}{5}$ four-fifths

[3けた以上の数(three-digit numbers)の読み方]

$\frac{1}{100}$ { one hundredth / one one-hundredth

$\frac{1}{160}$ { one one-sixtieth / one one-hundred-sixtieth

$\frac{1}{165}$ { one one-sixty-fifth / one over one-sixty-five

$\frac{22}{130}$ twenty-two over { one-thirty / one-hundred-thirty

$\frac{150}{165}$ { one-fifty over one-sixty-five / one-hundred-fifty over one-hundred-sixty-five

4. 調子

【この分なら[では]】

この分なら1年で終るだろう。

If things go on at this rate it will be finished in a year.

この分では1年はかかるだろう。

If things go on at this rate it won't be finished for a year.

5. 身分

one's **status;** one's **social rank**

【分相応[不相応]】

分相応の貢献　→ぶんたん

彼女は分相応[不相応]の暮しをしている。

She lives { within her means. / beyond her means.(不相応)

【分をわきまえる】

彼は分をわきまえている。

He knows his place.

ぶん（文）

1. 文法単位としての文

sentence

文の最初は大文字で始まる。

A sentence begins with a capital letter.

文とは語の集合で，通常，主語と動詞を含んでいる。

A sentence is a group of words that usually contains a subject and a verb.

ヘンリー・ジェイムズの文は長いので通常たった 2, 3 の文で 1 つの段落を成している。

Henry James' sentences are quite long, so there are usually only a few of them in one paragraph.

2. 文章

日本語では字で書かれたものすべて「文」というが英語では文の種類により次のような語を用いる。

paragraph 段落。通常いくつかの文より成り，まとまった考えや論点を表すかたまりだが，文章全体の一部。

composition 作文。学校で教える作文，文を作ること。

essay エッセー。ある一つの題目について作者の個人的考えや感想をまとめたもの。

article 新聞・雑誌などの記事。

report 報道記事

survey 概説

review 短評（ex. book review 書評）

news item ニュース

account 事実・事件のレポート（文も口頭の話も含む）。give an account（経緯を述べる）の形でよく使われる。

writing; writings 集合名詞として「書いたもの全体」を指すときは不可算名詞，「書いたもの個々」を指すときは可算名詞。

ヘーゲルの書いたものは難しくてわかりにくい。

Hegel's writings are very difficult to understand.

Hegel's writing is very difficult to understand.

〈注〉 上の 2 つの文はどちらも可能。writing(s) は彼の文体の意味にも思想の意味にもとれる。また Hegel's writings はまとめて Hegel's works（作品）としてもよい。

【例文】

次の文を読んで 1 から 5 の問いに答えよ。

Read the following paragraph(s) [article / piece/excerpt from *Newsweek* for 3/25/99] and answer questions 1-5.

〈注〉 長文読解問題の場合，その「文」が 1 段落か 2, 3 の段落か，または記事のような文，まとまった小文，ニューズウィークからの抜粋，などのいずれであるかにより，それに当る英語を選ばねばならない。

次の文の空所を埋めなさい。

Fill in the blanks in the following sentences (1) [paragraph (2)].

〈注〉◆(1)は one sentence の問題が 1, 2, 3 と数題続く場合。(2)は問題が 1 段落だけで空所が数か所作ってある場合。

◆「ある文に感銘を受けた」を英訳する場合，「文」というとすぐ sentence を思い浮かべる傾向があるが，その文の内容により下に示すように言葉を使い分けねばならない。

×I was impressed by the sentence.

I was impressed by
- *Gone With The Wind.*（作品名）
- her article on love.（雑誌などに書いたもの）
- her work(s).（作品(群)）
- her ideas.（思想・内容）
- her style.（文体）

【新聞・雑誌の文】

［…氏が…に文を書いている］

辻氏が『新潮』に文を書いている。

Mr. Tsuji is writing an essay [an article] for *The Shincho*.

［…氏の文が…に載っている］

根岸氏の文がきのうの新聞に載っていた。

There was an article [an essay] by Mr.

Negishi. (1)

Mr. Negishi's article [essay] appeared in yesterday's newspaper. (2)

〈注〉 (1)は初めて話題にする時の表現。
(2)は前にも話題になった根岸氏の文を話題にする場合。

[…に…についての文が載っている]

今日の新聞に人間の脳についての面白い文が載っている。

There is an interesting article about the human brain in today's paper.

【引用】

彼はベーコン(の書いた文)から数行[一部]を引用した。

He quoted a few lines [a passage, a paragraph] from Bacon.

3. 文体

style

【文がうまい】

彼は文がうまい。

He is a good writer.

【文が明快】

芥川の文は明快である。

Akutagawa's writing is very clear.

Akutagawa writes in a very clear style.

【文が口語調】

近代作家は口語調の文を書く傾向がある。

Modern writers tend to write in a colloquial style.

今日では口語調の文が多い。

Much writing today is colloquial (in style).

〈注〉 ×Many writings とは言わない。

【…の文が好き】

私は太宰の文(文章)が好きだ。

I like Dazai's writing [style].

〈注〉◆I like Dazai's works [Dazai〔*colloq.*〕]. は内容も文章もひっくるめて太宰文学が好きだの意。その意味で ×I like Dazai's sentence. とは言わない。
◆This sentence is terrible. と言う場合は，文法的誤りや綴りの誤りがあること，文が下手という意味で，内容がひどいということではない。次のようにすれば内容がひどいという意味にできる。

The ideas in this work are terrible.

ぶんか（文化）

culture

文化生活　a civilized life

文化交流　cultural exchange(s)

文化財　cultural heritage; cultural assets

〈注〉 cultural assets とは properties (建造物など)，tradition(s) (祭りなど)，handicraft(s) (伝統工芸品など)を指す。

文化勲章

the Order of Cultural Merit (勲章に伴う名誉も含む)

a Medal of Cultural Merit (勲章そのものを指す)

文化の日　Culture Day

文化祭(学校などの)

an annual school festival; a university [college] festival

〈注〉 欧米でも school [college] festival のようなものはあるが，内容はその土地や学校の事情により異なる。運動会は an athletic meet，陸上大会は a track meet と言い，football 大会を中心にして同窓生が集まる a homecoming day [week] という行事もある。

外国文化を取り入れる

adopt foreign culture

日本人は外国文化を摂取するのが得意である。

Japan is very good at adopting various aspects of foreign culture.

〈注〉 adopt とは日常生活に取り入れて実践すること。

日本には文化財として保存されている建物がたくさんある。

Japan has many buildings preserved as part of its cultural heritage.

この寺は重要文化財に指定されている。

This temple is (designated (as)) a cultural treasure.

This temple is an important cultural property.

政府は文化財を保護するためにもっと予算を使わなければいけない。

The government should use more money to protect cultural assets.

ぶんたん（分担）

1．役割分担

分担する **divide the work among**《people》

私たち皆で仕事を分担しましょう。

Let's divide the work among ourselves.

皆で分担すれば１人の負担が軽くなる。

If we divide up the work, it won't be too much trouble to any one person.

年齢[専門]によって仕事を分担した。

The work was divided by age [the field of expertise].

【…の分担をする】

be in charge of [take charge of, be responsible for]《a job, a task》

私たち２人が宣伝広報[照明]の係を分担する。

Two of us are responsible for [in charge of] publicity [lighting].

私は衣装の係を分担している。

I am responsible for making costumes.

だれかプログラムの係を分担する人が必要だ。

We need someone to be in charge of [take charge of] the program.

〈注〉「分担」とは仕事を分割して各部分を担当することであるから「担当」と同じ言い方になる。I, you が主語になる場合に be in charge of よりも take charge of の方が，主体性・意欲が感じられるので，進んで担当する気持ちを強調するならば後者を使う。主語が三人称（he, she）のときはほとんど同じように使われる。

私の分担は？

What's my job?

What am I supposed to do?

What should I do?

私の分担は切符売りだ。

My job [task] is to sell [selling] tickets.

〈注〉ビジネス，ボランティア，警察の仕事などでは「分担」は次のようにも言える。

This is my assignment.（これは私の仕事[分担]です）

リーダーが分担を決めた。

The group leader assigned work [jobs] to each of us.

劇上演に向けて皆が仕事を分担している。

We each have a job [something to do; something we are supposed to do] for the drama performance.

2．費用の分担

【費用を分担する】

share expenses with《someone》

私たちは旅行費用を分担した。

We shared the traveling expenses.

We split the traveling expenses (among us).

私にも費用[欠損の埋め合せ]を分担させてください。

Let me share the expense(s) [loss].

君の分担は3500円だ。

Your share (of the expenses) is 3,500 yen.

〈注〉share について

(1) 金銭に関して，(a)分担金
(b)もらい分，取り分

(2) 自分の当然なすべき分や具体的な個々の仕事を指すときは，share は使わず job, task と言う。

He's not doing his job.（具体的に「分担の仕事をやっていない」）

He's not doing his share.（抽象的に「ちっとも真面目にやらない」の意。He never does his share. とも言う。He's not contributing enough. と同義）

「私の分担は…だ」は △My share is ... ではなく，My job is ... である。

I want to do my share.（私なりに自分の分を果たしたい；＝I'd like to do my part.）は，世界平和とか，日本の教育のためとか大きな目的に関しても使える言い方である。

へ

…へ →…に

へいき(平気)・へいせい・へいぜん

1．無頓着な

don't care; don't mind

形 **indifferent;**

nonchalant /nànʃəlɑ́ːnt〔米〕, nɔ́nʃələnt〔英〕/

【平気】

私は他人が何と言っても平気だ。

I don't care (気にしない)
I'm not affected by (動じない)
what other people say.

人は彼のおかしなアクセントを笑うが，彼は一向に平気だ。

People laugh at his queer accent, but he doesn't mind [care] a bit.

私は北海道育ちだから寒いのは平気だ。

I don't mind the cold weather because I was brought up in Hokkaido.

彼は失敗しても平気だった。

He thought nothing of his failure.

He took his failure nonchalantly.

His failure didn't bother him.

彼は平気でうそをつく。

He has [feels] no sense of shame at telling lies.

He tells lies shamelessly.

He makes no bones about telling lies. 〔*colloq.*〕

2．体力的に

【平気】

彼は毎日10キロ歩いても[徹夜をしても]平気だ。

He thinks [makes] nothing of
walking ten kilometers every day.
sitting up all night.

彼は昔は徹夜をしても翌日平気だった。

He used to be able to sit up all night and feel all right the next morning.

彼はウイスキーの瓶を半分も空けて平気な顔をしている。

He drinks half a bottle of whisky without getting too drunk.

3．冷静な

calm; composed; 冷淡な **cool**

【平然】

どんなことが起ろうと彼は平然としている[平気である]。

He always {stays cool / keeps his head} in {a crisis. / an emergency.}

彼はストレスがあっても平然としている。

He stays cool under stress.

彼はその知らせを聞いても平然としていた。

He didn't turn a hair at the news. 〔*colloq.*〕

He heard the news with no change in (his) expression.

【平静を失う】

その知らせに彼女は(平静を失い)泣きくずれた。

She broke down {at the news. / when she heard that.}

火事が出たとき彼女は平静を失った。

She lost her head when the fire broke out.

彼は議論になっても平静さを失わなかった。

He didn't lose his presence of mind in the argument.

【平静を取り戻す】

しばらくして彼は平静を取り戻した。

He regained his composure after a while.

へいきん（平均）

an average;（数学） **the** （**arithmetical**） **mean**

平均して　on（the, an）average

彼は１日平均８時間勉強する。

He studies
8 hours a day on（the, an）average.
an average of 8 hours a day.

都会では平均的家族の子供の数は1.５人だ。

The average family size in cities is 1.5 children.

１家族の人数は平均３.５人というところだ。

There are 3.5 people per family on（the）average.

アメリカでは自家用車は年間平均１万2000マイル走る。

The average American car owner drives 12,000 miles per year.

彼らのかせぎは週給平均５万円といったところだ。

They earn an average of 50,000 yen a week.

〈注〉◆「平均して」というと on（the, an）average がまず頭に浮かぶが，上の例のように average は名詞を修飾する形容詞として用いられることが多い。

◆ average は名詞として an average of ... としてもよく使われる（上の例文参照）。

◆ on（the, an）average について
数に関しては on（an）average;〔米〕on（the）average が使われ，また commonly true（ふつう）の意味で使われるときは on average と冠詞なしで用いる。しかし区別は厳密なものではない。迷ったときは冠詞をつける方がよい。

【平均的，平均以上，平均以下】

私の収入は（ちょうど）平均的［平均以上／平均以下］だ。

My income is（just）[above / below] average.

今回の英語のテストの平均点は63.5点だ。

The average mark for [on, in] this English test is 63.5.

彼はＡもいくつかあるしＣも少しあるので，成績は平均Ｂというところだった。

He had some As and a few Cs, so his grade average was B.

【平均値】

平均値　the mean [average]（value）

平均気温　the average [mean] temperature

平均年齢　the average age

うちの学校の６年生の平均身長は150㎝です。

The sixth grade [year] boys in our school average 150 centimeters in height.

Their average height is 150 cm.

過去４か月間の売り上げの平均をとり，来年の売り上げを予想しなさい。

Take the average sales [the sales average] of the last four months and estimate next year's sales.

７と９と14の平均はこれらの数を足して３で割れば出せる。

The mean of 7, 9 and 14 is found by adding them together and dividing by 3.

【平均寿命】

the average life span; life expectancy

彼は平均寿命まで生きた。

He lived the average life span.

私は少なくとも平均寿命までは生きたい。

I'd like to reach [live] at least the average life span.

日本では平均寿命がまだ伸びつつある。

Life expectancy is still rising in Japan.

日本の女性の平均寿命は今や84歳だ。

The life expectancy of Japanese women is now 84 years.

へいこう（平衡）

名 **balance**

平衡を保つ　balance

平衡を失う　lose one's balance

彼女は平衡を失って平均台から落ちた。

She lost her balance and fell from the beam.

へいこうする（閉口する）

1．不快

まったく暑くて閉口だ［参っている］。

The heat is unbearable, isn't it?
It's intolerably hot, isn't it?
I can't bear [stand] this hot weather.

音がやかましくて[蚊がうるさくて／押し売りにねばられて］閉口した[参った]。

I was annoyed by the noise [the mosquitoes / an aggressive salesman].

彼の自慢話にはほとほと閉口した。

I was bored to death by his boasting.

〈注〉「閉口する」といっても，つまらなくてうんざりするのが be bored to death。うるさくて悩まされるのが be annoyed である。

2．迷惑・当惑（人に対して）

酔っぱらいには閉口する[参る]。

Drunken people embarrass and annoy me a lot.

彼の不作法なのには閉口した[参った,困ってしまった]。

I was embarrassed by his bad manners and became very annoyed at him.

あいつには参る[閉口する]。

He's a terrible nuisance.

あの子にはいったいどうしたらいいか参っている[困っている，閉口している]。

I don't know what to do with that boy.

彼がしつこくて閉口しています。

He's too persistent; I can't stand [take] it any more.

彼の強引なのには参って[閉口して]いる。

I'm fed up with his being pushy.

〈注〉 be fed up with はうんざりして閉口していること。

3．難問・難事業

最後の問題には閉口した[参った]。

The last problem beat me [had me beat].

〈注〉 beat me は俗語で I don't know. I haven't the faintest idea.（全然わからない）の意。

雨の中を車で走ってまったく閉口した。

I had a hard time driving in the rain.

…べき → とうぜん

1．当然

…すべきである **should; ought to**

我々は世界平和を守るために各自できるかぎりのことをすべきである。

We should do everything in our power to keep world peace.

我々は互いに助け合うべきだ。

We ought to help each other.

そんなことはもう何年も前から知っているべきことだ。

You should have known that years ago.

【…すべきではない】

年老いた親につらく当るべきではない。

You shouldn't be harsh to your aged parents.

彼女はあの人たちにそんなことを言うべきではなかった。

She shouldn't have said such things to them.

〈注〉「当然…すべき」の must, ought to, should の強さの順は次の通り。（上から強い順）
① must　絶対に…すべきである
② ought to　当然…すべきである
③ should　当然…するものだ
上記の各例文は obligation（義務感）の強さにより①②③どれでも入れ替えられる。ただし，否定形は ought not, oughtn't よりも should not, shouldn't の方が普通である。

【すべきこと】

遊びに行く前にすべきことをしてしまいなさい。

Do what you should do before going out to play.

この夏休み中にすべきことがたくさんある。

There are a lot of things I have to [must] do during this summer.

2．可能

【…するための】

彼には住むべき家もない。

He has no house to live in.

【…することのできる】

彼は頼るべき友もない。

He has nobody [no friend] to turn to.

You will lose again if you aren't careful.

へた（下手）

下手な　**poor; not good**

これは下手な[まずい]絵だね。

This is not a good painting [picture].

【下手だ】

あの人は運転[料理]が下手だ。

He's a poor driver [cook].

She isn't a good driver [cook].

私たちの音楽の先生はピアノは上手だったが，歌は下手だった。

Our music teacher was good at playing the piano but was poor at singing.

彼は話をするのは下手だ。

He isn't good at telling stories.

彼は絵は下手だ。

He is poor at painting.

彼は英語をしゃべるのは下手だ。

He is poor at speaking English.

彼は野球は下手だ。

He's a poor baseball player.

あの子は裁縫は下手だ。

She's not handy at sewing clothes.

〈注〉 上記例文の handy は skillful（上手な）の意であるが，have [keep]《something》handy では「手元におく」の意になる。

【下手になる】

練習をしないでいると下手になるよ。

You'll fall back [regress, backslide] if you get out of practice.

日本に帰って来てから英語が下手になってしまった。

My English has {been slipping away / gotten worse / deteriorated} since I came back to Japan.

【慣用表現】

下手をすると[気をつけないと]また負けるよ。

べつ（別）

1. …の別 →くべつ

【善悪】

子供にはまず第一に善悪の別を教えなければならない。

Children should be taught first of all {the distinction between right and wrong. / what is right and what is wrong. / to distinguish right from wrong.}

【公私】

公私の別をはっきりさせることを覚えなければならない。

You should learn {to separate between public and private life. / not to mix public and private matters.}

【男女，年齢】

料理に興味のある方ならば男女や年齢の別なくどなたでも会員になれます。

Anyone interested in cooking can be a member (of the club) regardless of age or sex.

2. ほかの

【別の物[事]，別の人】 something else;（人）someone else; some other person

何か別のを見せていただけませんか。

Please show me something else.

今日はとても忙しいのでまた別の日に来ていただけませんか。

Today I am very busy. Can you come some other [another] day?

【問題】

それは別の問題だ。

That's another question.

知っていることと教えることは別だ。

To know is one thing, to teach another.

3．取りのける

【別にする】

１ダースばかり私の分を別にしておいていただけませんか。

Set aside [Save] a dozen of them for me, will you?

彼は車を買うお金は別に(口座をつくって)貯金している。

He has been saving money in a separate account to buy a car.

悪い品はいいのと別にしておいてください。

Separate the bad ones [Set the bad ones apart] from the good ones.

4．除外・追加 →ほか

【除外】

…は別にして　apart from …

悪いけど今お金がないんです。それに費用の問題は別にしても旅行に行く暇がないんですよ。

I'm sorry, but I'm hard up now, and apart from the question of expenses, I have no time to spare for the trip.

考えてみれば今回の問題を別にすれば，彼はまあまあいいやつじゃないか。

After all, apart from this business, isn't he rather a nice fellow?

サービス料は別にして7800円です。

It will be 7,800 yen, not including the service charge.

cf. The cost for the trip is [will be] 10,000 yen (all) inclusive. (旅行費用は何もかも含めて１万円です)

【追加】…とは別に　in addition to …

国の所得税とは別に私たちは高額の市民税を払わねばならない。

In addition to national income tax, we must pay a large city tax.

請求書にはホテル代とは別に税金とサービス料も入っていた。

In addition to the hotel charge, there was tax and a service charge on the bill.

私は別に10万円の(余分の)収入があった。

I had (an) additional income of 100,000 yen.

5．特別に

別に[特に]あなたに話すことはありません。

I have nothing ⌊in particular [special] to tell you.

別に[特に]面白いことは何もなかった。

There was nothing particularly [especially] interesting.

6．個々に

【個別に】

彼らは別々に部屋をとった。

They took separate rooms.

おじいさんとおばあさんは私の家族とは別々に住んでいる。

My grandparents live apart from my family.

〈注〉　自分の家の「離れの隠居所」に住んでいるならば They live in ⌊a separate section of [separate quarters in] our house. とでもする。

もう私たちは皆大人になったので，別々に暮しています。

Now that we have all grown up we live separately.

子供たちがめいめい別々に宝を探しにかかった。

The children went off separately to find the treasure.

志願者はグループ面接ではなしに１人ずつ別々に面接を受けた。

The applicants were interviewed ⌊singly [one by one], not in a group.

彼らはめいめい別々の道を行った。

Each of them went his own way.

They went (their) seperate ways.

【分別する】

ぬれた物と乾いた物を別々にしておいてください。

Keep wet things and dry things separate [apart].

へる（減る）・へらす

1．減る 動自

decrease; diminish; dwindle; fall

【数】

交通安全キャンペーンをやったがいっこうに事故は減らない。

Despite the (traffic) safety campaign, accidents haven't decreased.

【量】

ガソリン[お金]が減ってきた。（不足）

I'm running short of gas [money].

Gas [My money] is running low.

（瓶の）ウイスキーが半分に減ってしまった。いったいだれが飲んだのだろう。

Half a bottle of whisky has disappeared [is gone]. Whoever drank it?

タンクの水が減った。

The water in the tank is running low.

貯水池の水が平常の水位より減ってしまった。

The (water in the) reservoir has sunk below its usual level.

川の水が減った。

The river has gone down.

洪水の水が減った[引いた]。

The flood waters have decreased.

森林の減少により最近10年間に水の供給量が減った。

The water supply has decreased [diminished] over the last ten years because the forest area is dwindling.

今年は去年より収穫が減った。

Crop yields are lower this year than (they were) last year.

Crop yields have decreased this year compared to last year's.

今年の米の収量は雨不足のために10%減った。

The rice crop decreased by 10 percent this year because of [due to] the lack of rainfall.

【消耗】

過労で彼は体重が(10キロ)減った。

He has lost weight [ten kilograms] because of overwork.

靴のかかとが少し減っている。

The heels are a bit worn out.

【売り上げ】

車[テレビ]の売り上げがこの半年間減ってきている。

Car sales [Sales of TV sets] have been falling off for the last half year.

【需要】

米の需要が減ってきている。

The demand for rice is { on the decrease. / decreasing. / falling off.

【注文】

住宅の注文が減ってきている。

Housing starts are on the decrease [decreasing, falling off].

《類義語》

decrease　一般的な語。語の選択に迷ったときは decrease を使うのが無難。

diminish　〔*formal*〕

dwindle　徐々に減って消滅していく。

wane　月の欠けること。比喩的に，力・影響力などが衰えることも意味する。

2．減らす 動他

会社は従業員を30人まで減らす計画だ。

Their plan was to reduce [decrease] the number of employees to 30.

労働者は仕事を減らし給料を上げるように要求した。

The workers demanded less work and more pay [higher wages].

高コレステロールの食品を減らしなさい。

Reduce your intake of high cholesterol foods.

〈注〉　コレステロールを「減らす」には次の動詞が使える。lower [reduce, decrease] cholesterol

食事中の脂肪(の量)を減らしなさい。

Cut down on the amount of fat in your diet.

【体重】

私は今食事を減らして体重を減らそうとしている。

I am now dieting.

もし体重を減らしたければ，アイスクリームとケーキをやめなさい。

If you want to lose weight, stop eating ice cream and cake.

【予算，お金】

来年の予算は5パーセント減らされるだろう。

Next year's budget will be cut [reduced] (by) 5 percent.

食費を切り詰めるわけにもいかないので，衣類に使うお金を減らさなければならなかった。

We had to cut down on our clothes budget [spend less on clothes] because we couldn't change the amount we spend on food.

へん（辺）

1．地域，場所

【場所】

この辺にホテルはありますか。

Is there a hotel around [near] here?

彼女はどこかこの辺に住んでいます。

She lives somewhere around here.

私はこの辺のことはよくわかりません。

I am a stranger in this part of (the) town [neighborhood].

この辺は静かです。

This is a quiet neighborhood.

この辺は秋の紅葉が有名です[紅葉の名所です]。

This area [part of the country] is famous for maple leaves in the fall.

【部分】

「どの辺が痛みますか」「ここのところです」。

"Where do you feel pain?" "Right here."

2．程度，範囲

今日はこの辺までにしておきます。

That's all for today.

So much for today.〔米〕

まあその辺だ。(当らずとも遠からず)

That's about it [all].

3．図形などの辺

三角形の一辺　a side of a triangle

底辺　the base

べんきょう（勉強）

〈注〉「勉強する」「習う」に当る study と learn の区別がはっきりわかっていないことが多い。learn は習い覚えることであり，study はこつこつ努力して try to learn (習得しようとする)ことである。

I've studied English long enough; you'd think I would have learned it by now. (私はもうずいぶん長いこと英語を勉強しています。ですからもう英語はすっかり身についてペラペラになっていると思われるでしょうね)

1．学業・勉学

学校の勉強　one's **lessons; school work**

勉強をする　**do**《one's》**lessons; study**《something》

〈注〉one's studies は大学レベル以上について使われる。

勉強したことを覚える

learn what is taught at school

勉強をしている　be studying

勉強をさせる　get《a child》to study

勉強を見てやる

help《a child》with his lessons

英語の勉強をする

study English; learn English

中学[高校]では英語を勉強する[習う]。

They learn English in junior high school [study English at high school].

専門の勉強をする

major in《chemistry》〔米〕; study《chemistry》

勉強家

a hard worker; a hardworking boy [girl]

勉強家の 形 hardworking

〈注〉 diligent（勤勉な）という語をよく使うが，特に目立った勉強家に使う語で，使いすぎない方がよい。同じく industrious は体を使う仕事や毎日の決った仕事に精を出すことで，これも使いすぎない方がよい。

兄さんが私の算数の勉強を見てくれた。

My brother helped me with (my) arithmetic.

【猛勉強する】

［一夜漬け］

cram; swot 動他 swot《something》(up)

動自 swot at《something》

［一夜漬けでも常時でも］

grind (away) at《something》**for**《an exam》

彼は歴史の試験のために年代や事実を詰めこんで［猛勉強して］いる。

He's cramming dates and facts for his history exam.

2．成績 →せいせき

【勉強ができる［できない］】

彼女は勉強が（よく）できる［できない］。

She does [doesn't do] well at school.

Her grades [marks] are [aren't] good.

Her school record is [isn't] good.

3．教訓

【人生勉強になる】

あの経験は彼にはいい人生勉強になった。

That (experience) taught him a good lesson.

4．値引き

勉強する **sell cheap; reduce [cut] the price; take**《something》**off**

ご希望に沿うようにできるだけ勉強します。

We will do our best to meet your requirements.

もう少し勉強できませんかね。

Could you mark it down a little more?

全商品20%引き大勉強！

All goods marked down 20 percent.

［広告］20% OFF!

〈注〉 mark down は値下げ札を書くことから値下げの意味になる。

あのお店は勉強する。

Things are cheaper at that store.

へんな（変な）

1．奇妙な

strange; odd; 興味をそそる **curious;** たいへんおかしい **queer**

《類義語》

odd 標準からはずれていること。

strange 見なれないので変に見える。ほとんど odd と同じ。

curious 変っていて興味をそそり，面白いことを強調。

queer その現象が普通の常識では理解できないことを強調。

〈注〉 queer は「ゲイ（の）」の意味に使われることがある。また口語で頭が変だ（loony, a bit insane）の意にも使われる。

変な話だ。 It's a strange story.

彼がそんなことを言うなんて［それを知らなかったなんて］変だ。

It is strange [odd] that
{ he should say such things.
{ he didn't know that.

彼は変な老人だ。

He is a strange old man.

あの子はどこか変だ。

There is something strange about that child.

変だな。確かにここに財布を置いたんだがないんだ。

That's odd [strange]. I'm sure I put my purse here, but it's gone.

2．怪しい

suspicious; suspicious-looking

【変な目】

人々は私たちを変な目で見た。

People eyed us suspiciously.
People are biased against us.(偏見を持っている)

【変な男】
変な男が町をうろうろしている。
There is a suspicious-looking fellow hanging about the town.

3. 気が変な
彼は少し頭が変だ。
He is a bit odd [queer] in the head.
彼は気が変になった。
He has gone crazy [mad, round the bend 〔*colloq.*〕, loony].

4. いつもと違った
君[あの子]は今日は変だ。
You aren't your usual self / She doesn't seem herself } today.

べんり（便利）→ ふべん, つごう

1. 好都合
【交通関係】
その場所は買物に[バスが]便利だ。
The place is convenient for shopping [the bus].
自家用車があると便利だ。
It is convenient to have a car.
列車よりもバスの方が通学に便利だ。
It's { more convenient / easier } for us to go to school by bus than train.
バスの新路線が運転を始めたので駅に行くのがずっと便利になった。
It's much easier to get to the station now that the new bus service has started [begun].
私たちの学校はあまり便利な所にない。
Our school is not { in a very convenient place [location]. / very conveniently located. }
今は交通の便があります[交通は便利です]。
There is transportation now.
Transportation is available now.

2. 役立つ
【道具・設備など】
当社のアパートは最新の設備すべて完備。(広告)
The apartments have all the latest conveniences.
新しいアパートの台所には便利な設備が何もかも備わっている。
The new apartments have fully equipped, modern kitchens.
【手頃】
こういうノートはとても便利だ。
This kind of notebook is very handy.
この辞書は大きすぎて持ち歩くには便利でない。
This dictionary is too big and unwieldy to carry about.
【役立つ】
とても便利なバッグを持っているの。
I have a very handy purse.
このバッグは入れる所がいろいろと工夫されていてとても便利なの。
This purse is very handy for me — the arrangement of the sections is really convenient.
〈注〉 上の文の handy は convenient, useful の意だが次のような言い方もある。
Keep it handy [near you]. (手元におきなさい)
前後関係から handy が「手頃で便利である」か「手元にある」のどちらの意味かわかる。
この道路地図はとても便利だ。
This road map is very useful.
旅行をするならトラベラーズチェックが便利ですよ。
Travelers cheques may come in handy [be useful] when you travel.
〈注〉「私の所は買物には便利です」のつもりで ×I am convenient to go shopping. のような言い方はできない。

○My new place is convenient for shopping. とする。
convenient は「便利な」(空間的)のほかに「都合がよい」(時間的)の意もある。

It's convenient for me to go shopping this afternoon.（今日の午後は買物に行かれる［都合がいい］）

ほ

ほう（方）→ ひかく

ほうがく（方角）→ ほうこう

a direction

火事はどちらの方角ですか。
Where [Which way] is the fire?

郵便局はどっちの方角ですか。
Which way is the post office?

こっちです。私もその方角に行きますからご一緒しましょう。
This way, but I'll go with you because I'm going in the same direction.

うちの学校はここからそっちの方角に2kmのところにあります。
Our school is located 2 kilometers in that direction from here.

暗がりで方角がわからなくて道を間違えてしまった。
In the dark I lost my sense of direction and took the wrong way.

山の中で自分のいる位置がわからなくなり，どちらの方角に行ったらよいかわからなかった。
In the mountains I lost my bearings while hiking and didn't know which way to go.

【方角の呼び方】

北　north; 北方の　northern
北東　northeast; 北東の　northeastern
北西　northwest; 北西の　northwestern
南　south; 南方の　southern
南東　southeast; 南東の　southeastern
南西　southwest; 南西の　southwestern
東　east; 東方の　eastern
西　west; 西方の　western
東[西]方に　to the east [west]
東寄りの方角に　a bit to the east

市の東部に
in the east(ern) part of the city

〈注〉 in the east part (of the city) 市の東部 (1)
to the east (of the city) 市の東方 (2)

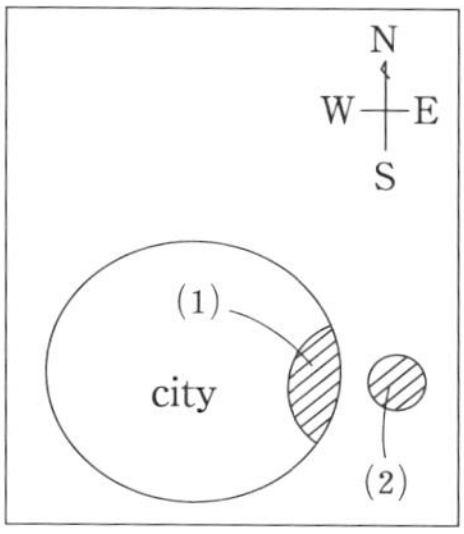

ほうこう（方向）

1. 方角 →ほうがく

あの人たちはどの方向に行きましたか。
Which way [direction] did they go?

我々は反対の方向に行った。
We went in opposite directions.

彼は別の方向に向かった。
He went in a different direction.

船は方向を変えながら港に入っていく。
Ships change direction(s) on their way to the port.

方向を間違える
take the wrong direction
go (in) the wrong direction
go the wrong way

私は方向音痴です。
I have no sense of direction.

2. 方針

【方向を決める】

君の将来の方向を決めた方がいい。
You should decide on your career [future course of life].
You should plan your future.
Consider your future.

大学に進学するかどうか決める前に将来の方向について考えなさいよ。
Think of your future life before you decide whether to enter university or not.

【方向を誤る】
就職に際して方向を間違える
make an error in choosing one's / choose the wrong job [occupation, profession, company]
法律は私には方向違いだった。(専攻したのは誤りだった)
Law was the wrong career [field] to take up.
討論が変な方向に行ってしまった。
Discussion went the wrong way.
【方向転換】
2,3年会社勤めをしてから，彼はまた大学に入り直し(人生の)方向転換をはかった。
After working a few years at an office, he quit the job and entered university again in order to change his career.
君[あれ]が私の人生の方向をすっかり変えてしまった。
You [That] changed my course of life completely.

3. 風の吹く方向の呼称

北風とは北から南に吹く風のことである。
A north wind is a wind blowing southward. / from the north (to the south).
南風は南から北に向かって吹く。
A south wind blows from the south to the north.
南風が吹いている。
The wind is blowing from the south.
There is a south wind.
A south wind is blowing.

ほうこく（報告）

報告　名 **a report**
報告する　**give [make] a report**
動 他 **report;** 動 自 **report on; submit a report**〔*formal*〕(口頭・書類どちらでもよい)
報告書　a report
委員会報告　committee reports
中間報告　an interim report
最終報告　the final report
報告書を提出する
hand in (手渡し) [send in (送付)] a report
彼は簡単[詳細]に報告した。
He made a brief [full] report.
He reported briefly [fully].
彼は事故を警察に報告した。
He reported the accident to the police.
彼はその事故で2名の死者があったと報告した。
He reported that two people had been killed in the accident.
彼は地震の被害を報告した。
He reported on the damage caused by the earthquake.

ほうじ（法事）→ ねんちゅうぎょうじ

ほうせき（宝石）

gem
ダイヤモンド　diamond
ルビー　ruby
サファイア　sapphire
ベリル(緑柱石)　beryl
アクアマリン　aquamarine
エメラルド　emerald
スピネル　spinel
アレキサンドライト(金緑石)　alexandrite
ジルコン　zircon
トパーズ(黄玉)　topaz
ガーネット(ざくろ石)　garnet
オパール　opal
トルコ石　turquoise
キャッツ・アイ(猫目石)　cat's eye
メノウ　agate
ヒスイ　jade
【準宝石】
コハク　amber
真珠　pearl

サンゴ　coral

【誕生石】 birthstones

1月	Jan.	ガーネット	garnet
2月	Feb.	アメシスト	amethyst
3月	Mar.	ブラッドストーン	bloodstone
		アクアマリン	aquamarine
4月	April	ダイヤモンド	diamond
5月	May	エメラルド	emerald
6月	June	真珠	pearl
		ムーンストーン	moonstone
7月	July	ルビー	ruby
8月	Aug.	サードニックス	sardonyx
9月	Sept.	サファイア	sapphire
10月	Oct.	オパール	opal
		トルマリン	tourmaline
11月	Nov.	トパーズ	topaz
12月	Dec.	トルコ石	turquoise
		ジルコン	zircon

ほうっておく（放っておく）→ そのまま

そのままにしておく　**put** [**lay**] **aside;** 構わずにおく　**leave** [**let**]《a thing, a person》**alone;** 怠ける　**neglect**《one's work》

彼は仕事を(やりかけで)放っておいた。

He left his work half-done.

彼は放っといた方がいい[彼の邪魔をしない方がいい]。今忙しそうだから。

Let him alone [Don't bother him]. He's busy now.

(世話を焼かずに)放っておきなさい。彼女はもう自分で判断できる年なんだから。

Leave her alone. She's old enough to judge for herself.

放っといたらいい。時が解決してくれる。

Leave things alone. Time will take care of it.(them).

放っといたらいい。自然の成り行きにまかせよう。

Leave it as it is. Let it take its own course.

ずっと庭を放っておいたので雑草に埋もれてしまった。

I've neglected the garden {for so long / so badly} the weeds have overrun it.

校内暴力は放っておけない。

We can't ignore [neglect] (the) violence in (the) schools.

〈注〉 neglect (放置する，怠る) と ignore (無視する) はニュアンスが違うが，どちらも何もしないことである。また上の文を肯定文で言うと次のようになる。

We must do something about (the) violence in (the) schools.

ほうふ（豊富）

豊富な　**abundant; plentiful; rich**

1．具体的な物について

【資源】

大陸のこの地方は天然資源が豊富だ。

This part of the continent is rich in [has an abundance of] natural resources.

この国は豊富なエネルギー資源を持っている。

This country is rich in energy resources.

この国は石油を豊富に産出する。

This country produces a lot of oil.

【魚類】

この湖は魚が豊富だ。

This lake has a large quantity of fish.

【食糧】

うちのあたりでは戦争中でも食糧は豊富でした。

{There was plenty of food / Food was abundant} in our area even during the war.

【滋養】

チーズや卵は滋養豊富である。

Cheese and eggs are nutritious [nourishing].

【在庫】

私どもの店は(商品の)在庫が豊富にあります。

Our store has a large stock of merchandise.

角の小さな洋装店はものすごく品数が豊富だ。

The little clothing shop around the corner has an amazingly large variety of things.

うちの近所のスポーツ用品店はスキーウエアを豊富に取りそろえている。

Our local sports shop has a big selection of skiwear.

〈注〉 この local は in the neighborhood（近所の）の意。

マルエスストアは，かばん類の色も形も種類が豊富である。

There's a big range of colors and styles of luggage at Maru S Store.

Maru S Store has luggage in a large variety of colors and styles.

【広告】

各種在庫豊富!!

BIG VARIETY!!

2. 抽象的なものについて

【経験】

彼はその方面の経験は豊富だ。

He has a lot of experience in that area.

【知識】

彼は知識が豊富だ。

He has a great store of knowledge.

彼は種々の分野にわたり豊富な知識を持っている。

He's knowledgeable in various [a number of] fields.

我々は化学にも事業経営にも専門知識の豊富な人物を必要としている。

We need a person with expertise in both chemistry and business management.

〈注〉 He is very learned /lə́ːrnid/. は豊富な深い知識を持ち，賢明であることを言い，最高の賛辞である。He is widely read. は読書から広い知識を持っていること。

【語彙】

あの人は語彙が豊富だ。

She has a rich vocabulary.

君はもう少し読書をして語彙を豊富にしなければいけない。

You have to read more to enrich your vocabulary.

【内容】

この本は内容が豊富だ。

This book contains a lot of information on the subject.

I learned a lot from this book.

彼女はものすごくアイデアが豊富だ。

She's amazingly rich in ideas.

ほうほう（方法）

《類義語》

way 一般的な語だが，「ユニークな，その人独自のやり方」の意味をもつことがある。
ex. in my own way（私のやり方で）

method 科学的・論理的に組織立った方法。

system method に近い，一つの体系をなしたやり方。

means スケールの大きいものについて言う。何かをするための手段。

どんな方法で見つけ出したのですか。

How did you find out?

皆どんな方法で問題を解いたらよいかわからなかった。

They didn't know how to solve the problem.

彼を救助する方法を何とか考えなければならない。

We must find some way to rescue him.

彼らは算数を教えるのに新しい教授方法を採択した。

They adopted a new method for teachng arithmetic.

彼は彼独自の勉強方法を工夫した。

He has devised his own system of studying.

彼と連絡をとる方法がない。

There's no way to communicate with him.

日本の教育方法は丸暗記に基づいているよう

に見える。

The Japanese system of education seems based on rote learning.

20世紀の通信方法は通信衛星の導入で大幅に広がった。

Twentieth-century means of communication expanded with the introduction of satellites.

先進的工業にとっては効率のよい輸送方法が不可欠だ。

An efficient system of transportation is necessary for an advanced industrial economy.

ほうりつ（法律）

a law; legislation

法律の **legal; juridical**〔*formal*〕

法律家 a lawyer

法律事務所 a lawyer's office

法の精神 the spirit of the law

法の抜け穴 a loophole

この法律は4月1日より施行される。

This law shall come into force on [take effect from] April 1.

《関連語》

憲法 constitution

日本国憲法 The Constitution of Japan; the Japanese Constitution

基本的人権 fundamental human rights

戦争放棄 the renunciation of war

戦争放棄の憲法 a war-renouncing constitution

表現の自由 freedom of expression

言論の自由 freedom of speech

第2章9条 Chapter II, Article 9

憲法擁護論者 defender of the Constitution

改憲論者 advocate of constitutional amendment

民法 civil law; civil code

刑法 criminal law

行政法 administrative law

選挙法 election law

著作権法 the Copyright Act

少年法 the Juvenile Act

破壊活動防止法 the Subversive Activities Prevention Act

労働基準法 the Labor Standards Law

独占禁止法 the Anti-monopoly Law; Anti-trust Law

道路交通法 Road and Traffic Law

軽犯罪法 Minor Offences Law

情報公開法 Disclosure of Official Information Law; Public Information Act

個人情報保護条例 Personal Privacy Law

法令 ordinance

条例，規則 regulations; laws

財産権 property rights

団結権 the right to organize

施行する（人主語） enforce;（法主語） come into force; take effect

有効な valid

無効な null and void; not valid; invalid

合法の legal

非合法の illegal

ほか（他）→ いがい（以外），べつ

1．それ以外に

ほかに質問はありませんか。

Are there any other questions?

Have you any other questions?

ほかにもお聞きしたいことがあります。

I have some other questions.

There is something else I'd like to ask you.

《**any** の用法》

any には次の2通りの用法がある。

1．some との対比で不定数量を表す。

some / **any**	量	some / any	《water》単数(不可算)
	数	some / any	《questions》複数(可算)

［肯定文 some］

There's some water left in the bottle.

I have some other questions.

［疑問文 any］

Is there any water left in the bottle?
Are there any girls who want to join the trip?
[否定文 not any; no]
There isn't any water left. (=There's no water left.)
We don't have any other questions. (=We have no other questions.)
We don't use any weapons in 'judo'. (=We use no weapons ...)
2.「何でも，どれでも」の意の **any**。通常は単数名詞が続く。この場合の any は every に近い。
She's as beautiful as any other girl in her class.
Any book about driving will tell you how to ...
Anybody can show you the way.

だれかほかの人に聞いていただけませんか。
Could you ask someone else [some other person]?
何かほかの(品)を見せていただけませんか。
Could you show me
{ some others [other ones]?
{ another (one)?
私たちはほかにもう1軒寄らなければならない[1件電話しなければならない]のです。
We have another call to make.

2. 除外
ジョージのほかは皆，会合に出た。
Everybody went to the meeting except George.
「日本料理は食べられますか」「ええ，納豆のほかは何でも」。
"Can you eat Japanese food?" "Yes, anything [everything] except *natto*."
隅の棚の商品のほかは店内全品2割値引きいたします。
We give a 20% discount on everything in the store except (for) those on the corner shelf.
時たま頭痛があるほかは，この数年間彼女はずっと健康だった。
Except for occasional headaches she has been healthy all these years.
ちょっと疲れているだけで，そのほかは何ともありません。
There's nothing the matter with me except that I am a bit tired.
〈注〉 except と except for は多くの場合，ことに口語では同じように使われる。ただし，その違いについては「以外」の項の〈注〉参照。
眼下は雲の海で，ほかには何も見えなかった。
Nothing but [except] a sea of clouds could be seen underneath.

3. 追加
【そのほか】
キャロルのほかアンとベティも来ていた。
Besides Carol, Ann and Betty were there.
アンにベティにキャロル，そのほか何人かがパーティーに来ていた。
Ann, Betty, Carol and some others were at the party.
【私のほか】
私のほかにもホームシックになった女の子がいた。
I was not the only girl who got homesick.
【ほかに】
彼は事業に失敗し，ほかにも夫婦の不和という心配事があった。
He was a failure as a businessman, and in addition he had marriage problems to worry about.
ホテル代のほかに税とサービス料を請求書につけてきた。
They put tax and a service charge on the bill in addition to the room fee.
「おはようございます」と「こんにちは」とそのほかには何を知っていますか。
"Ohayo-gozaimasu," "Kon-nichiwa," and what else do you know?
そのほかは何も知りません。
I know nothing more [beyond that].
彼は英語のほかフランス語もドイツ語も話せ

る。

He speaks not only English but also French and German.

ほがらか（朗らか）

朗らかな　**cheerful; cheery; sunny**

朗らかな人

a person with a bright [happy, sunny, cheerful] disposition〔*rather formal*〕

彼女は朗らかな子だ。

She is a cheerful girl [a happy kind of girl].

私は朗らかな人が好きだ。

I like people with [who have] a bright temperament [disposition].

彼女は朗らかだ。

She has a cheerful disposition [personality].

私は朗らかな性質だと皆に言われます。

Everyone says I have a cheerful disposition.

〈注〉 △She has a cheerful character. とは言わない。character は strong（強い), weak（弱い), angelic（天使のような), twisted（ひねくれた）などの形容詞と結びつく。character は道徳的資質である善悪・正直・不正直などの見地から見た人格のことで，temperament（明るい，暗いなどの気質）のように生れつきではなく，教育で身につけるものを指す。

ほけつ（補欠）

【補欠入学】

彼女は補欠で大学に入った。

She was admitted to the college on the second round.

彼女の名前が補欠合格者の中にあった。

Her name was on the second list of {successful candidates. / people to be admitted.}

彼は補欠で入学できた。

He was admitted later to fill a vacancy.

【授業】

佐藤先生が服部先生の補欠で1時間［2,3日］授業をされた。

Mr. Sato substituted for Mr. Hattori [took over Mr. Hattori's class] for one hour [a few days].

〈注〉 substitute は短期間の場合。take over は短期間でも長期間でもどちらでも用いられる。学年末まででもよい。

【補欠選手】

a substitute player（↔a regular player)；（野球）a player on the bench; a reserve; a sub〔*colloq.*〕

【補欠選挙】

a special election; a by-election

谷氏死去に伴う補欠選挙で森氏が当選した。

Mori was elected in the by-election to fill the vacancy left by Tani's death.

ほけん（保険）

insurance

【種類】

健康保険　health insurance

養老保険　annuity

生命保険　life insurance; life assurance〔英〕

総合生命保険　life plus medical insurance（life 生命および medical treatment 医療についての保険）

傷害保険　accident insurance

労災保険　worker's compensation insurance

自動車保険　car insurance

強制(加入)　compulsory

任意(加入)　voluntary

火災保険　fire insurance

海上保険　marine insurance

【保険会社】　insurance company

保険勧誘員　insurance salesman [agent]

保険代理店　insurance agency

保険に加入する　take out [buy] insurance

保険を解約する　cancel an insurance policy

保険契約(証書)　insurance contract

〈注〉 保険契約証書と約款を引っくるめて an insurance policy と言う。

掛金　premium

満期　maturity

満期になる　動 mature; reach maturity

満期配当金　maturity dividend
保険金　insurance money（広い意味の語）; compensation（労災保険などの保険金）
【保険をかける】
彼は生命保険をたくさんかけてある。
He has a lot of life insurance.
彼は1000万円の生命保険に入っている。
He carries life insurance for 10,000,000 yen.
He carries 10,000,000 yen in life insurance.
この家には500万円の火災保険がかけてある。
This house is insured against fire for 5,000,000 yen.
私の車は200万円の保険がかけてある。
My car is insured for two million yen.
約款を調べてごらん。地震の場合が保険に含まれているかどうか。
Check the policy to see if earthquake damage is covered [you are covered in the case of earthquakes].
私は家と家財に火災・洪水・地震保険をかけている。
I have combined fire, flood, and earthquake insurance on my house and personal property.
車の保険が来週切れるから店に電話して更新しなければならない。
My car insurance expires next week, so I have to call the agent and get it renewed.
車の総合保険は掛金が高い。
The premium for (the) liability coverage in my auto insurance is very high.

ぼこう（母校）→ どうそう

one's **alma mater;** one's **old school; the school** [**college, university**] one **graduated from**

ほし（星）

a star; 星印 **an asterisk**
［隠語］犯人 **a criminal;** 容疑者 **a suspect**
星に願いをかける
make a wish upon a star
幸運な星の下に生れる
be born under a lucky star
３つ星のホテル
a three-star hotel
星印を付ける
mark ... with an asterisk

《関連語》
星座　constellation; 恒星　star
惑星　planet; 彗(すい)星　comet
星雲　nebula (*pl.* nebulae, nebulas)
新星　nova; 銀河　galaxy
銀河，天の川 the Milky Way, Galaxy
小惑星　asteroid; 衛星　moon; satellite
流れ星　shooting star; meteor
隕石　meteorite; 宇宙　the universe
太陽系外の空間　outer space
星間空間　interstellar space
【太陽系】 solar system
地球　Earth
火星　Mars; 水星　Mercury
木星　Jupiter; 金星　Venus
土星　Saturn; 天王星　Uranus
海王星　Neptune; 冥王星　Pluto
太陽　the sun; 太陽黒点　sunspot
日食　solar eclipse; 月　the moon
クレーター　crater; 月食　lunar eclipse
【身近な星と星座】
familiar stars and constellations
北極星　the Pole Star
南十字星　the Southern Cross
北斗七星　the Big Dipper（大ぐま座 the Great Bear の７星）
小北斗七星　the Little Dipper（子ぐま座 the Little Bear の７星）
はくちょう座　the Swan; オリオン座　Orion
プレヤデス，すばる　the Pleiades
織姫星　Vega（こと座 the Lyre のヴェガ）
彦星　Altair（わし座 Aquila のアルタイル）
カシオペア座　Cassiopeia
シリウス　Sirius, the Dog Star
アークトゥルス　Arcturus
アンタレス　Antares

ほしい(欲しい)・ほしがる →いる(要る)・いらない

1．欲しい（ほとんど一人称主語で使われる）

【欲求】

もっとお金が欲しい。

I want more money.

パーティーに着ていく新しい服が欲しい。

I'd like a new dress for the party.

私は名声なんか欲しくない。

I don't care for fame.

【入用】

私たちは助手が１人欲しい。

We want an assistant.

彼女は新しいメイドが欲しいと言っている。

She says she needs a new maid.

【苦言】

君にはもう少し気をつけてほしい。

I want you to be more careful.

〈注〉 日本語でも「もっとお金が欲しい，服が欲しい」は親しい人たちに言う言葉であるが，英語でも家族・友人間であればI want ... と言う。しかし「…していただきたい」の意味であれば want はぶしつけで失礼になる。I'd like ... または Could you ...? の形を使う方がよい。

【依頼】

この手紙を速達で出してほしいのですが[出していただけますか]。

Could you send this letter by express?

【希望】

できるだけ早くあなたの新しい住所を知らせてほしいのです。

I'd like you to let me know your new address as soon as possible.

あなたに私の力になってほしいのです。

I hope you will help me.

【後悔】

もっと早く来てほしかった。

I wish you had come earlier.

〈注〉 wish の後に過去形・過去完了形が続くときは，実現しなかったことを嘆く，すなわち「…すればよかった，したらよかった」「…してほしかった」などの意味になることに注意。この場合 want は使えない。

×I want you were there.

【欲しいのか】

（子供や友人などに向かって）オレンジジュースが欲しいのか。

Do you want orange juice?

オレンジジュース欲しくないのか。（出されたオレンジジュースがいらないのか）

Don't you want the orange juice?

2．欲しがる（第三者が述べる形）

彼女は息子に欲しがるものは何でも与えた。

She gave her boy anything he wanted.

赤ちゃんがお乳を欲しがって（泣いて）いた。

The baby was crying for [wanted] milk.

そんなに欲しがるんじゃない。

Don't be greedy.

〈注〉 hope, want, wish について →したい

hope 可能性のある希望に使う。

want 「…したい」というあからさまな気持ちの表明。失礼にならないよう使い方に注意。

wish とても実現の難しいと思われる希望に使う。

ぼしゅう（募集）

1．学校

【募集人員】

法学部の募集人員は100名です。

One hundred students are to be admitted to the Law Department.

【募集開始［締切］】

募集は２月１日に開始する[締め切る]。

Registration will start [end] on Feb. 1st.

【募集中】

あの学校は今生徒募集中だ。

That school is now taking applications.

春期生徒募集中。

Applications for the spring term are now being received.

【広告】

新入生募集中。

Applications invited.

Apply now.

2. 会社

その会社は今新入社員を募集している。

The company is now looking for new employees.

そこは今年は新入社員を募集しない。

They will not take on any new employees this year.

2, 3人だが募集をしている。

A few positions are open [available].

〈注〉 few positions と a がなければ「ほとんど空席はない」の意味になる。

3. その他

寄付を募集する[募金する]

collect contributions [donations, money]

raise funds; do fund raising（基金づくりの募金）

【懸賞募集】 hold [sponsor] a (prize) contest

トヨタは新車の名前を懸賞募集している。

Toyota is sponsoring [holding] a car-naming contest.

朝日新聞は毎月俳句の懸賞募集をしている。

The Asahi holds [sponsors] a haiku competition [contest] every month.

〈注〉 募集要項はおおむね次のように書かれている。

Please send your idea [proposal] / Send manuscripts / Haiku are to be submitted } { to 《address》 / by 《date》

【会員を募集する】

get [seek, recruit] new members

バレーボール部は部員募集中である。

The volleyball club is recruiting new members.

ほす（干す）

1. 乾燥させる

1週間も雨が続いたので子供の衣類を家の中で干さなければならなかった。

It had been raining for a week and so we had to dry the children's clothes inside the house.

翌日は晴れ上がったので，我々はぬれた物を皆持ち出し綱に引っ掛けて日に干した。

The next day it cleared up and we hung all the wet things out in the sun.

【虫干し】

1年に1度はしまってある衣類を虫干ししなければならない。

We must air unused clothes at least once a year.

2. 液体をなくす

【池の水を干す】

dry out the pond（一時的）

drain the pond

〈注〉 dry out は「酒飲みに酒を与えない」の意味もある。

【飲み干す】

彼はコップのビールを一気に飲み干した。

He drank (up) the whole glass of beer [emptied his glass] at a gulp.

ほそい（細い）

1. 細長い

【糸】

細い糸　a fine thread（↔thick thread）

細い針金[ひも]　a thin wire [string]

【体】

細い子（やせっぽち）　a thin child

細い腕[首]　a slender arm [neck]

細い指[手足]　slender fingers [limbs]

cf. 太く短い指　pudgy [〔英〕podgy] fingers

〈注〉 slender, slim はすらりとしているの意味であるが，thin はやせすぎの意で，否定的に使われる。

【鉛筆・ペンなど】

細書き用ペン[マーカー]　a fine-point pen [marker]

cf. ボールペン a ball-point pen

〈注〉 細書き　fine point [tip]
中細書き　medium point [tip]
太書き　broad tip

しんの細い[とがった]鉛筆　a sharp pencil

(↔ a dull [blunt] pencil「先の丸くなった，とがっていない」の意)

〈注〉 いわゆるシャープペンシルは a mechanical pencil〔米〕; a propelling pencil〔英〕という。

細くする[とがらす] sharpen

2．幅が狭い

細い道 a narrow path (↔ a wide path)

細い目 narrow eyes

(目を)細くする 動 narrow

彼女は火のそばに座り，目を細めていた。

She sat by the fire, her eyes narrowed to slits.

3．声

細い声 a weak voice (↔ a strong voice)

cf. 弱い声 a thin voice (↔ a loud voice)

低い声 a low [deep] voice (↔ a high voice)

抑えた声 a low [quiet] voice

きつい声 a sharp voice

4．繊細な

彼女は食が細い。

She eats very little.

She is a light eater.

彼女は神経が細い。(線の細い人だ)

She is delicate.

ほっとする

be [feel] relieved; 安堵のため息をつく **give [heave] a sigh of relief**

1．くつろぐ

試験が終ってほっとしました。

I feel greatly relieved now (that) the examination is over.

彼らは10時間も一生懸命働いて，やっと家に帰ってふろに入りほっと一息ついた。

After 10 hours of hard work, they went home, took a bath, and relaxed.

2．安堵する

彼の名前が事故の負傷者の中になくて本当にほっとしました。

It was a great relief to me to find out that his name was not among the names of those injured in the accident.

赤ちゃんがやっと生れたと聞いて，皆ほっと安堵のため息をついた。

We all breathed a sigh of relief when we heard the baby was born at last.

ほど(程)

1．程度

それほど **so**

…するほど～ **so《形容詞》that …**

…できないほど～ **too《形容詞》to …**

どれほど

How much …?; To what extent …?

私は夕食後すぐ寝床に入った。それほど疲れていたのだ。

I went to bed right after dinner because I was so tired.

〈注〉 cf. I was so tired (that) I went to bed right after dinner.

上の文と同じことを述べているのだが焦点が違ってくる。上の文は「すぐ寝た」ことに，下の文は「疲れた」ことに焦点をおいている。

【それほど…ない】

それほどおなかがすいていない。

I am not so hungry.

【死ぬほど】

ああ死ぬほど疲れた[退屈した]。

I was tired [bored] to death.

あなたを死ぬほど愛しています。一緒にいられなかったら死んでしまいます。

I love you so much. I'll die if I can't be with you.

【涙が出るほど】

彼女は涙が出るほど喜んだ。

She nearly cried for joy.

She was so happy (that) she nearly cried.

【…できないほど】
私は口もきけないほど疲れていた。
I was too tired to speak.
言葉ではうまく言えないほどすてきだ。
It's too wonderful for words.
【…と言うほどの】
私には趣味と言うほどのものは何もない。
I have no hobby [to speak of [worth mentioning].
この辺には取り立ててあげるほどの景色のよい所はない。
There are no scenic places worth mentioning hereabouts.

2．約
about
それを修理してもらうのに5か月ほどかかりました。
It took some five months to get it repaired.
ここから名古屋までは500kmほどです。
It's about 500 kilometers from here to Nagoya.

3．比較
【～ほど…ない】 not as … as ～
彼女は姉さんほどきれいではない。
She isn't as beautiful as her sister.
私はあなたが考えているほど利口ではない。
I am not as clever as you think I am.
その仕事は思っていたほど難しくなかった。
The work turned out to be easier than we expected.
【～ほど…なものはない】
[nothing＋比較級＋than ～]
健康ほど大切なものはない。
Nothing is more important than health.
There's nothing as [so] important as health.
【…すれば…するほど】→ますます
早ければ早いほどよい。
The sooner the better.
先に行けば行くほど道が狭くなっていった。
The road got narrower the farther they went.

4．その他
ほど近い(所)
not far off from; a little way from
のちほど
later on
それじゃ，のちほど。
See you later (on).
冗談にもほどがある。
You carry your jokes too far.
It's going beyond a joke.

ほとんど

1．肯定
almost; nearly（「もう少しで…になる」と程度を表す）
most of《them》 **…**（「大部分は…」と全体に占める割合を表す）
cf. mostly（主として，たいてい）
ほとんどの生徒は出席していた。
Almost all the students were present.
ほとんどが女の子だった。
They were mostly girls.
Most [Almost all] of them were girls.
〈注〉 most と almost の混同に注意。
almost は副詞なので，主語にはできない。
×Almost of them were …
○Most of them were …
また，形容詞のように名詞を直接修飾できない。
×Almost students were …
○Most students were …
almost は nearly と同じく「もう少しで…になる」程度を表す。「ほとんどが女の子だった」は ×They were almost girls. でなく，上の例文のように Most [Almost all] of them were girls. とする。
ex. These peaches are almost ripe.（もう少しで完熟するが，やや早い）
Most of them are ripe.（大部分は熟しているが熟していないものも少しある）
仕事はほとんど終った。
The work is almost finished.
The work is finished for the most part.

その子はうちの男の子とほとんど同い年だ。
The child is about [almost] the same age as my boy.
彼はほとんど毎日曜日私をドライブに連れていってくれる。
He takes me for a drive practically (almost) every Sunday.
そこにはほとんど30人近い外国人留学生がいる。
There are nearly thirty foreign students.
その人たちのほとんどがアジア諸国からの留学生だ。
They are mostly [Most of them are] from Asian countries.

2. 否定

【ほとんど…ない】
little; few; hardly; scarcely〔*literary*〕;（回数の少ないこと） seldom; めったに…ない rarely
霧のためほとんど何も見えなかった。
I could hardly [scarcely] see anything in the mist.
その頃は100歳まで生きる人はほとんどいなかった。
Hardly [Scarcely] any people / Very few people / People seldom } lived to be a hundred years old in those days.
そのことは私はほとんど知らない。
I know very little about it.
I know scarcely [hardly] anything about it.
私たちは同じ町に住んでいるというのにほとんど[めったに]会わない。
Although we live in the same town we seldom [rarely, hardly ever] see each other.
〈注〉 little, hardly, rarely ... などはそれ自身の中にすでに否定の意味を含んでいるので，否定の not をつけ加えてはいけない。
×I couldn't hardly see anything.
×They hardly never see each other.
seldom を使えるときは，hardly ever も使える。

ほんき（本気）

1. そのつもり

【本気か？】
それ[今言っていること]本気？
Do you really mean it?
さっきのは[さっき言ったこと]本気？
Did you mean that?
Were you serious?
【本気だ】
僕は本気だ[本気で言っているのだ]。
I mean what I say.
I really mean that.
I'm not joking.
This is not a joke.
I'm serious.
【本気ではない】
くたばってしまえなんて彼が言ったけど，本気で言ったわけではないよ。
He didn't mean it [wasn't being serious] when he told you to go to hell.
彼は君のことを本気で批判するつもりではない。
He didn't really mean to criticize you.

2. まじめ

【本気になる】
たまには本気になりなさい。
You have to be serious once in a while.
本気になりなさいよ。そうすれば勝つから。
Put your heart in it; then you'll win.
彼は何をやるにも本気にはならない。
He does everything half-heartedly.
【本気で】
私はまた大学で勉強し直そうかと本気で考えている。
I am seriously thinking of going to college again.
彼も本気で勉強を始めた。
He began to study in earnest.

3. 信じる

【本気にする】

彼は私の言うことは何でも本気にする。

He believes whatever I say.

彼は何でも本気にする。

He takes everything seriously.

彼女は冗談半分に言ったのに，彼はそれを本気にした。

She said so half jokingly, but he took it ⌊in earnest [seriously].

ほんとう（本当）

1. 真実

本当の　**true; real**

【真実】

「本当ですか」「ええ本当です」。

"Is it true?" "Yes, it's true."

「彼が来月日本に来る」「本当？」。

"He'll come to Japan next month." "Really?"

【事実】

その小説は本当にあったことをもとにしている。

The novel is based on fact.

【実の，実は】

彼女の本当の名前は「はな」という。

Her real name is 'Hana'.

私は彼女が本当はいくつか知らない。

I don't know how old she really is.

彼の本当の意図はいったい何だろう。

I wonder what his real [true] ⌊intention is [intentions are].

〈注〉 上記の例は，口語では下のようにも言える。ただし驚きを表す言い方で，必ずしも skepticism (疑念)を表さない。口調や前後関係で決るのである。

Whatever does he want to do that for?

【本当の意味の】

彼こそ本当の意味の紳士だ。

He is a gentleman in the real [true] sense of the word.

He is a real [true, genuine] gentleman.

【本物の】

本当の金の鎖だ。

The chain is real [genuine] gold.

〈注〉 この場合 true は使えない。

【本当のやり方】

これは本当のやり方じゃないかも知れないけれど，私はいつもパイはこうやって作る。

It may not be the right [proper] way, but I always make my pies (in) this way.

【本当のところ】

本当のところ私はその新しい計画にあまり興味はないのだが，反対もしなかった。

It's true I am not much interested in the new plan, but I never objected to it.

本当は彼をあまり好きじゃない。

I don't like him so much actually [really].

〈注〉 frankly; to be frank with you; to tell the truth; in fact など「本当のところ，本当は」は「率直に言えば，ざっくばらんに言えば」とほとんど同義だが，frankly や to be frank with you は大げさになるので使いすぎない方がよい。また to tell the truth は秘密を明かすとか思いがけないことを切り出すときに使われる言い方であるからやたらに使うとおかしい。Why secret? との印象を与える。in fact は単なる強意語の場合と to tell the truth (実のところ)の意味のときがある。

There was a big storm last night. It snowed and snowed. In fact, there were two and a half meters of it.［強意］(ひどい吹雪で，降りに降ってとうとう2.5mも積った)

He doesn't mind. In fact, he's very pleased.［本当は］(彼はいやがっていない。それどころか本当は喜んでいる)

2. 実際に

【本当に】

彼は午後遅く雨になると言ったが，本当に降り出した。

He said it would rain late in the afternoon, and sure enough it actually ⌊did start [started] to rain.

本当にその考えはいいと思いますか。

Do you really like the idea?

彼がパーティーに来ても本当にいいですか。

Are you sure you'd like him to come to the

party?

3. 強意語

【とても】

本当にすてき。

It's really [truly] wonderful.

本当に寒い。

It's really [awfully] cold.

本当にご親切で。

You are very kind indeed.

本当にありがとう。

Thank you very much.

【間投詞的】

本当？

Really? （驚いて，または不信）

Are you sure? （信じられない）

「ロバートが来るって」「へえ本当？いいじゃない」。

"Robert is coming." "Oh is he? That's nice."

4. 信じる

【本当にする[しない]】→ほんき

彼女は彼の言うことなら何でも本当と思う。

She believes anything he says.

彼が試験に合格したと私が言っても彼は本当にしなかった。

He didn't believe me when I said he had passed the exam.

《類義語》

true, real, actual について基本的概念の違いは反意語を考えるとわかりやすい。もちろん重なり合う部分もあるが，だいたい次のように分けられる。

true ↔false

主張・命題などについて，真偽の判断をすること。

It's true.

It's not true.

（なおこの文型で real, actual は使えない。×It's real [actual] that …）

The truth is that …

real ↔imaginary

「現実に存在する」の意。存在に関する判断。

the real＝that which exists

real は things, actions, phenomena（物事，行為，現象）について存在するかしないかに関して使われる。

People say his fears are not real, (There's no reason for his fears) but to him his fears are real. (He feels them.)（人は彼の恐怖は根拠がないと言うが，彼は実際に恐怖で血の凍る思いをしている）

〈注〉 real の名詞形 reality はしばしば truth のように現象の奥の本質を意味する。

actual ↔imaginary

現実に行動・事実の形で存在する。

There was an actual case of treason.

（だれそれがどこそこで実際に謀反を起した）

前出の2語とくらべ事実に一番近い意味の語。その副詞形 actually は「現実に，実際に」の意。

The city needs a new concert hall, but actually [in fact] there will not be enough money for several years.（市には新しい音楽堂が必要なのだが，実際にはここ数年間は建設費がまかなえないだろう）

一般的に考えられているのと違って「実は…」といった意味で actually は使われる。

He seems cold, but actually he's just shy.（彼は冷たく見えるが，実は照れ屋なだけだ）

genuine ↔fake

「偽物」に対して本物。

ぼんやり

1. 放心して

blankly; vacantly; absent-mindedly

彼はぼんやり窓の外を見ていた。

He was looking out of the window vacantly [blankly].

2. 不注意

不注意である **be careless**

私はぼんやりしていて危うく帰りの列車に乗り遅れるところだった。

I was so careless I was about to miss my

train home.

その辺にはさみを出しっぱなしにしておくなんて私もまったくぼんやりしていた。

How careless [thoughtless] I was to have left the scissors lying about.

〈注〉 **be careless** 不注意である。

be thoughtless 思慮浅薄である; 他人の気持ちに気がつかない。

上例の careless と thoughtless は, その「ぼんやり」の結果が重大であれば thoughtless, たいしたことがなければ careless と, 話し手の主観的気持ちの差でどちらでも可。

まああなたを門の所に立ちんぼさせておくなんて私もまったくぼんやりしておりました。

How thoughtless of me to have left you standing at the gate.

【気のゆるみ】

列車の中でついぼんやりしていて財布を盗まれた。

My purse was stolen in the train when I was off guard.

3. 無為

ぼんやり過す 動 他 **idle; be idle**

ぼんやりと 副 **idly**

私はぼんやりと時を過した。

I idled my time away.

青年時代をぼんやり過したのを後悔している。

I regret (that)
{ I passed my youth idly.
  I idled away my youth [my young days].

ばかみたいにぼんやり突っ立っていないで何か手伝ってくれよ。

Don't just stand there like a fool. Do something to help.

4. 不明瞭

ぼんやりと **vaguely** (主として思考); **dimly**

【見える】

船の輪郭がぼんやりと霧の中から現れた。

The dim shape [outline] of a ship emerged from [out of] the mist.

やぶ[夕やみ]の中にぼんやり猫の姿が見えた。

I saw a cat dimly [faintly] in the bushes [twilight].

何もかもが私にはぼんやりかすんで見えた。

Everything looked blurred (to me).

【はっきりわからない】

彼は早口なので講義の内容はぼんやりわかっただけだ。

He spoke too fast for me, so I could get only a vague idea of his lecture.

私はぼんやりわかっただけだ。

I understood only vaguely [a little].

【ぼんやりした記憶】

私はおじいさんのことはぼんやりした記憶しかない。

I have but a misty recollection of my grandfather.

【頭がぼんやりしている】

I'm muddleheaded [fuzzyheaded] today.

My mind is fuzzy [foggy].

I can't think straight.

My brain's not working properly.

ま

まあ → ああ

まい（毎）

毎日　every day; daily
毎日曜日　every Sunday
毎時[分]　副 every hour [minute]; hourly
毎年[月]
　副 every year [month]; yearly [monthly]
彼は毎日曜日教会に行く。
　He goes to church every Sunday.

【毎日の生活】
電子レンジは今では毎日の生活に欠くことができないものとなった。
　Microwave ovens are indispensable for daily life these days.
うちでは毎日の生活で[ふだん]は牛肉を食べません。
　In everyday life / Ordinarily } my family doesn't eat beef.

〈注〉 副 every day = daily　毎日，日々（daily は形副両用あり）
形 everyday = ordinary　ふだんの
上の例で daily life は毎日のきまった日課（routine）を指し，everyday life は特別の場合と対立する表現。したがって in everyday life は「ふだん」（ordinarily 副）の意味である。意味領域の重なる部分もあるが，daily と everyday は同一の意味ではない。
daily は副詞として使う方が多いが，形容詞としては次のような語句で使われる。
daily use（日常使用），daily occurrences（日々の出来事），daily necessities（日常必需品）

…まい → ない，だろう

1．否定推量
おそらくそれは真実ではあるまい。
　Very probably it's not true.
おそらく彼は自分が悪かったとは言うまい[自分の非を認めまい]。
　Most likely he won't admit { it was his fault. / he made a mistake.
彼が計画をあきらめることはあるまい。
　I don't think he will give up his plan.
彼にはもう２度と会えまい。
　I shall never see him again.
「彼は試験に受かるだろうか」「まず受かるまいね」。
　"Will he pass the exam?" "Probably not, I'm afraid."

2．否定意志
２度とあのようなことはすまい。
　I'll never do that again.
彼女が多少でも感謝の気持ちを見せないのなら，もう絶対彼女に何もしてやるまいと彼は心に誓った。
　He was determined not to help her at all unless she started showing some gratitude.

まいる（参る）→へいこうする，こまる，まける

まえ（前）

1．空間・場所

【物の】
あのホテルの前で止めてください。
　Please stop in front of that hotel.
何か黒っぽいものが突然車の前に飛び出した。
　Something shadowy suddenly leaped out in front of the car.

【列の】
小学生が並んで向うから行進して来た。列の一番前にうちの娘がいた。
　The schoolchildren came marching down the street, and (there) right at the head [in the front] of the line was my daughter.

〈注〉 先頭 first in line; at the front of a line
先頭の次 the next [second] in line

【席】

私の席は前から[後ろから] 3 番目です。

My seat is in the third row from the front [back].

彼女は私の真ん前[真後ろ]に座った。

She sat just in front of [behind] me.

彼女は一番前[後ろ]に座った。

She sat in the first [last] row.

She sat in the front [back] row.

車の後ろの座席より前の座席の方が座り心地が良い。

It's more comfortable to sit in the front (seat) of a car than (in) the back.

【前部】

車はがけから落ちて前の部分がひどく壊れていたが，運転していた人は奇跡的に助かった。

The car fell off the precipice and was found with the front (part) badly damaged, but the driver miraculously escaped death.

〈注〉

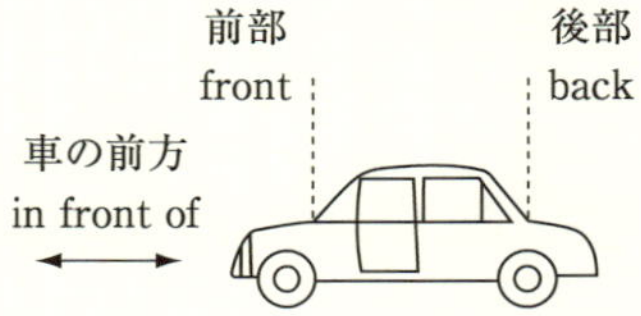

in front of は「…の前」を表す前置詞句で front に冠詞がつかないが，「車の前の部分」 the front (part) of a car，「部屋の正面部分」 the front of the room は冠詞が必要。

【その他】

前に出て詩の暗唱をしませんか。

Wouldn't you like to come up now to the front (of the room) and recite the poem?

How about coming up now and reciting the poem?

彼女は私の前を歩いていた。

She walked ahead of me.

一歩前[後ろ]に出なさい。

Take a step { forward. (1) / back. (2) / backward. (1)′ }

〈注〉 (1)(1)′は実際に「一歩出る[退く]」ことにも，比喩的に「一歩前進[後退]する」ことにもなる。

子供はまさに私の目の前で車にはねられた。

The child was hit by a car right in front of my eyes.

子供たちはお客さんの前では静かにするようにしつけられていた。

Children were trained to be very quiet { in the presence of guests. / when guests were present. }

2. 時間

【時刻】

5 時10分前です。

It is ten minutes to five.

【…時間[日]前】

ジムは 1 時間[3 日]前に帰った。

Jim left an hour [three days] ago.

ジムは 3 日前に帰ったとその人が言った。

The man told me Jim had left three days before [earlier].

〈注〉 上の文の three days ago は今から 3 日前。three days before [earlier] は the man (その人)が私に話している時点(過去)から数えて 3 日前のことである。

【以前】

前は静かな漁村だった。

It used to be a quiet fishing village.

あなたに前にもお会いしたように思います。

I think I've met you before.

あのパブには以前はいつも仲間と行っていた。

I used to go to that pub with my pals.

応募するには前に教職についた経験が必要である。

Applicants must have previous teaching experience.

君はもうずっと前にここに着いていなければいけなかった[着いていていいはずだ]。

You should have arrived here much earlier.

〈注〉 「来るのが遅かった」ことを言っているのであるが，正当な理由があって遅れたのであれば別に非難は含まれない。すべて前後関係による。

【前もって】

君は前もって準備を整えておくべきだった。

You should have made arrangements beforehand.

【…の前に】

我々は日の出前に[暗くなる前に]頂上に到着した。

We reached the top before sunrise [dark].

遊びに行く前に宿題をやってしまいなさい。

Finish your homework before
- going out to play.（一般的注意）
- you go out to play.（今やってしまいなさいという命令）

【前から】

どのくらい前からここにご滞在ですか。

How long have you been staying here?

半年も前からこの旅行を楽しみにしておりました。

I've been looking forward to this trip for six months.

〈注〉「半年」は half a year より six months とするほうが一般的。

【ずっと前から】

私はずっと前からそれを知っていた。

I've known that
- for a long time.
- for months [years, ages].
- from way back.〔*colloq.*〕

I knew that all along.

【前回】

この前お会いしたときは2人とも大学生でしたね。

The last time we met we were both in college.

遠足は前の日がひどい雨だったので1日延期された。

The school picnic was postponed for a day because it had rained severely the previous day.

この前の日曜日，僕はガールフレンドとドライブに行った。

Last Sunday I went for a drive with my girlfriend.

この前の台風ではたいへんな被害があったが，そのまた前の台風ほどではなかった。

The last typhoon did great damage, but not as much as the previous one had.

根岸氏はうちの大学の前の学長です。

Mr. Negishi is the former president of our college.

〈注〉◆「3年前」は three years ago で×before three years とは言わない。「3年前から」は「3年間続いている」と考え for three years でよい。since three years ago は理屈から言うとよさそうだが認められないとする人もあり，要注意。2003年時点で3年前を暦年で示せば since 2000 でよい。

I haven't heard from him for the past three years.（彼とは3年前から音信不通だ）

Since the letter (which) I got three years ago, I haven't heard from him.（3年前に手紙をもらって以来彼とは音信不通だ）

◆「前から」は×since before とは言わない。「子供のときから」とか「長年の間」のように言い換えて次の文のように書けばよい。

I have wanted to go abroad since my childhood [for many years].

この場合 for some time now も使える。

I've been taking harp lessons for some time now.（前からハープを習っている）

《類義語》

		[基準時]
former	last	present 現在
	previous preceding	past 過去
…… before ……		いつでもよい

former 以前。多少遠い過去。

last この前。現在のすぐ前。

preceding
previous } 話題の時間(過去)のすぐ前。

（この二つはだいたい同じだが，previous の方が preceding より多少前を指すこともある）

before 前に。もっとも一般的，包括的な語。

3. 能力・分量

【…人前】

彼は2人前働く。

He does two men's work.

彼は２人前食べる。
He eats enough for two.
彼は食事を３人前注文した。
He ordered dinner for three.
これだけあれば５人前にはなる。
This is enough (food) for five people.
(料理記事) ５人前
for five people; Serves five.

まかせる（任せる）

1. 委任する

leave 《something》 **to** 《a person》
entrust 《something》 **to** 《a person》

当時の父親は生活のために働き，家事と子供の教育は母親に任せるのが普通だった。
In those days fathers usually worked to earn a living and left household affairs and the children's education to mothers.
医師はよく税金の申告を専門の税理士に任せてやってもらう。
Doctors often have a certified tax accountant { do their tax returns. / make out their tax returns. }
我々は万事弁護士に任せている。
We've left it all [everything] to our lawyer (to take care of).
ごく小さい子供を託児所に任せるのをためらう向きもある。
People often hesitate to { entrust very young children to / leave very young children at } day care (facilities)〔米〕[nurseries〔英〕].
夏休みで家をあけている間，家のことは隣の人に任せておいた。
We had our neighbors look after our house while we were gone for the summer.
彼は息子に仕事を任せて１か月のヨーロッパ旅行に出かける。
He is going on a month's trip through Europe, leaving his son in charge of the business.

〈注〉 正式に委任することは delegate 《authority, a power》 または ask [appoint] 《someone》 to take care of 《something》 と言う。

2. 慣用表現

運を天に任せるより仕方がない。
We cannot but resign ourselves to our fate.
昔はよく足に任せて山を歩き回った。
I used to wander in the hills as far as my legs could take me.
彼らは豪華な庭園を金に任せて造りあげた。
They built luxurious gardens regardless of expense.
この世には思うに任せぬことが多々あるものだ。
There are many things in this world (which) you cannot do anything about.
You cannot always do what you want.
There may be many things in your life which do not go as you wish [the way you want].

〈注〉 ことわざに次のようなものがある。The world goes its own way. (この世はままならぬ)

まがり（間借り）→ げしゅく，かす

まがる（曲る）・まげる

1. 湾曲する

曲がる **be bent;** 曲げる **bend**

【腰】
彼女は年をとって腰が曲ってしまった。
She is { bowed / bent } with age.

【棒など】
サーカスのあの男の人は鉄棒を曲げた。
That man at the circus bent an iron bar.
鉄棒でも真っ赤に熱すると曲る［曲げられる］。
Iron bars can be bent if heated red hot.

【道】
道路は丘陵地帯にかかると，うねうねと曲っ

てくる。

The road {twists and turns / has many curves [bends]} as it gets into the hilly area.

道はこの先ゆるやかに左に曲る。

The road gradually curves left.

cf. hairpin turn〔米〕[bend〔英〕]（ヘアピンカーブ）

2. 方向を変える

turn

次の角で左[右]に曲ってください。

Turn left [right] at the next corner.

郵便局は角を曲った所です。

The post office is just round the corner.

私の家は角を曲って３軒目です。

My house is the third one round the corner.

【ネクタイ】

ネクタイがちょっと曲っていますよ。

Your tie is a little {crooked. / off to the left [right].（左[右]に）}

3. 性質・考え

曲ったことは大嫌いだ。

I hate dishonesty.

彼女には曲ったところがない。

There is nothing at all distorted in her character.

Her character isn't warped [twisted].

4. 歪曲する

事実を曲げる　falsify [misrepresent] a fact

意志を曲げる　act against one's will

主義を曲げる　do《something》against one's principles; compromise one's principles

彼は主義を曲げない。

He never compromises.

〈注〉 攻撃に対して主義を「守る」

uphold　主義を支持し，守る。

defend　攻撃に対し，主義の正当性を大いに弁じる。

彼女は自説を曲げない。

She stands by her personal views.（性格が強い）

She sticks to her own views.〔*rather colloq.*〕（頑固である）

君はわざと私の言ったことを曲げてとっている。

You deliberately misread [misjudged] what I said.

You are twisting my words.

まく（巻く）

くるくるたたむ　**roll;** 巻きつける　**wind**（過去形は wound）

【時計】

おばあさんはいつも土曜日の晩に大時計のねじを巻いていた。

Grandmother used to wind the big clock on Saturday night.

【毛糸】

おばあさんが毛糸を玉[糸を糸巻き]に巻くのを手伝ったものだ。

I used to help my grandmother wind {wool into a ball. / thread onto a reel.}

【スカーフ】

あの子は赤いスカーフを首に巻いていた。

She had a red scarf around her neck.

【包帯】

彼は頭に包帯を巻いていた。

His head was bandaged.

彼は手首に包帯を巻きつけた。

He bandaged his wrist.

【カーペット】

カーペットを巻き上げてください。

Roll up the carpet.

【縄】

彼は木の周りに縄を巻きつけた。

He wound a rope around the tree.

まける（負ける）→ かつ

1. 勝負・競争に敗れる

負かす 動他 **defeat;** 動他 **beat**

負ける **be defeated; be beaten; lose** 《a battle》**; be outdone**

【競技】

今日の試合で阪神が巨人を負かした。

Hanshin defeated Kyojin in today's game.

函館は6対3で負けた。

Hakodate {was defeated [beaten] / lost the game} (by) six to three [6-3].

彼らは3点負けている。

They are three {runs [goals] / points} behind.

あいつはだれにも負けないぞ。

He is not to be outdone by anybody.

彼は負け越してしまった。

He lost more matches than he won.

【戦争】

紀元前146年，カルタゴはついにローマに負けた。

Carthage was eventually defeated by the Romans in 146 BC.

【技能】

彼女は英語ではだれにも負けない。

She is second to none in English.

【議論】

彼は議論になるといつも負けてしまう。

He always {loses / gets the worst of} an argument.

【選挙】

彼は選挙に負けた。

He was defeated in the election.

2. 比喩的用法

【感情】

感情に負けてはいけない。

You shouldn't give way to your feelings.

【誘惑】

彼は誘惑に負けたりしない。

He wouldn't {give in / yield} to temptation.

【暑さ】

彼女はこの暑さに {夏負けもせず健在だ。/ 夏負けして参っている。}

She {is unaffected by this hot weather. / is affected by [suffering from] this terrible heat.}

【譲歩】

議論で声の大きな者に負けてしまう者が多い。

Many people {give way / yield} to the one who argues the loudest.

彼はあまり気乗りがしなかったが，じきに妻に負けてしまった。

He didn't like it but soon {gave in / gave way〔英〕} to his wife.

〈注〉 英国では gave in, gave way どちらも使う。米国ではこの意味では way は使わない。

【敏感肌】

私は虫に刺されるとすぐ負ける［かぶれる］。

I'm very sensitive to insect bites.

ウルシ負けする get lacquer poisoning

かみそり負けする get razor rash

3. 値引きする

負ける **reduce [cut, lower]** 《the price》

少し負けられませんか。

Could you lower the price a bit?

Could [Would] you give a discount?

1500円に負けられませんか。

Can you lower it to 1,500 yen?

（売り手）1700円がギリギリだ。

1,700 yen is the limit.

それ以上は負けられん。

That's the rock bottom price.

I can go absolutely no lower.

彼はこの古いつぼを2万円に負けさせた。

He beat the price of this old pot down to 20,000 yen.

10個買ってくれるなら1個お負けしますよ。

(If you) Buy ten of them, you get one [for free [extra].

まごつく → あわてる，こまる

1．当惑する

彼が突然結婚を申し込んできたので，私も私の家族もすっかりまごついてしまった。

His abrupt proposal quite upset me and my family.

ボブがいきなり「赤ちゃんはどこから来たの？」と聞いたので，まごついてしまった。

I was embarrassed because Bob abruptly asked me where his baby sister came from.

2．うろうろする

地下鉄の駅にはいくつも出口があるので，とてもまごついてしまった。

There were so many exits from the underground that I became quite confused.

彼の家はまるで迷路のようなところにあったが，あまりまごつかずに行かれた。

It seemed as if his house was [were] in a maze, but I found my way there without much difficulty.

暗闇でもまごつかずに探せるように，物は決った所にしまっておきなさい。

Put things where they belong so that you can find them {without difficulty / easily} even in the dark.

まさか

1．予期せぬ事態に対する反応

【予想外】

まさかそんなことができるとは思わなかった。

I never thought it possible.

まさかあのようなことになるとは夢にも思わなかった。

I never expected things would turn out that way.

まさか勝つとは思わなかった。

I never dreamed that I would win.

まさか彼にお金を貸してくれなんて頼めない。

How can [could] I ask him for a loan?

まさか車をぶつけた[壊した]なんて彼に言えない。

I can't possibly tell him (that) I crashed the car.

だれもまさかこんなひどい災害が自分自身にも起るなんて思わない。

No one thinks this kind of terrible disaster {will [would] / can [could]} happen to themselves.

【驚きの叫び】

まさか(そんなことはあり得ない)。

It [That] can't be true!

It's not at all likely!

「新さんは本当は将軍吉宗だって」「まさか」。

"Shin-san is actually Shogun Yoshimune."

{"No kidding!" / "I don't believe it!" / "You don't say!"}

「彼女は彼の求婚を受けると思うかい？」「まさかね」。

"Do you think she will accept his offer?"

{"Impossible!" / "Never!" / "Not on your life!"}

2．あり得ないことに関する確認

【過去のこと】

まさかそんなことしなかっただろうね。

Surely you didn't do that, did you?

Don't tell me you did that!

【未来のこと】

まさかひとりで行くんじゃないだろうね。

You certainly aren't going alone, are you?

3．まさかの時 →ひじょう

まさかの時は呼んでくれ。
　If { anything happens, / things get worse, } call me.

まず → だいいち，はじめ

まずい

1．味が悪い

[動] **taste bad**

まずそうな
　unappetizing; uninviting
このチーズはまずい。
　This cheese { doesn't taste good. / tastes bad. }
あそこの料理はまずい。
　The cooking there is unappetizing.

2．下手な

【話】
彼は話がまずい。
　He is poor at giving speeches.
【字】
彼の字はまずい。
　His handwriting is { very poor. / illegible. }
【文章】
彼の文章はまずい。
　His writing is very poor.
　He is a poor writer.
【運転】
彼は運転がまずい。
　He is a poor driver.

3．具合が悪い

【感情的に】　awkward; embarrassing
2人一緒にいるところを奥さんに見られたらまずいわ。
　It would be awkward if your wife should see us together.

彼を正面切って非難するのはまずい。
　It is inadvisable to accuse him outright.
それをあの人に言ったのはまずかった。
　That was the wrong person to say that to.
〈注〉　You said that to the wrong person. とも言えるが，you を主語にすると口調がたいへん強く，怒って責めているようにとられるので注意。

【理性的に】　unwise; inadvisable
君が暴力を振るったのはまずかった。
　It was unwise of you to have resorted to violence, so now we are both in an awkward situation.
今それをやるのはまずいよ。
　It's bad tactics to do that now.

【まずいことに】
まずいことにボスを怒らせてしまった。
　Unfortunately we offended the boss.
まずいことになった。
　Things { are taking / have taken } a bad turn.
　　　　　　　　　　　　　　　（成り行き）
　What a fix we are in!（結果）

ますます

1．…すればするほど…となる

the more [〜er] …, the more [〜er]

高く登れば登るほど，ますます空気は希薄になってきた。
　The higher we climbed the thinner the air grew.
コンピュータでうまくいかずにいらいらすれば，それだけ今にきっと上手に使いこなしてやるぞという気がますます起る。
　The more frustrated I get with my computer, the more determined I am to master it.
〈注〉　「…すればするほど，ますます…」の意味で比較級を重ねる表現法はよく知られているが，機械的に The more …, the more … を使う誤りがよくあるので注意。
　× The more she works hard, the more she gets rich.
　○ The harder she works, the richer she gets.

2. 程度の変化

more and more; less and less; increasingly; all the more

高齢者の就職はますます難しくなってきている。

It's becoming more and more difficult for older people to get a job.

市の税収はますます減少してきている。

The city's revenues from taxes are becoming less and less.

〈注〉 上の文の less and less の逆で，ますます増収しているのであれば greater and greater とする。more and more はここでは使えない。more and more は more and more difficult, more and more excited のように形容詞または副詞を修飾するときに使われる。

皆が慰めようとしたが，彼女はそれでますますみじめな気持ちになった。

They tried to comfort her, which made her all the more miserable.

私はとりたてて博覧会を見に行きたいと思っていたわけではなかったが，それを聞いてますます行きたくなくなった。

I wasn't particularly keen to see the exhibition anyway, and [but] hearing about it made me feel even less inclined (to go).

事態はますます悪化した。

Things have gone from bad to worse.

また・または

1. 再び

again

また来てください。

Come to see me again.

そのうちまた来ます。

I'll call you again { one of these days. / some other time. }

またいつかお目にかかりたいですね。

I hope I can see you some day.

じゃ，またね。(別れの挨拶)

See you.

So long.

〈注〉 See you. はまた会う人に言う。See you later. (またあとでね)はその日のうちにまた会う人に言う。
See you tomorrow [on Monday ...], のように次に会う日を言って別れる言い方もある。
So long. はくだけた感じで広く使われる。

また伊豆半島で地震があった。

There was another earthquake in the Izu Peninsula.

またいつもの痛みが始まった。

The same old pain started again.

彼はまたもとどおりに健康になった。

He has regained his health.

He is now as healthy as he used to be [(he was) before].

2. 同じく，やはり →も

too; also

彼もまた同意見だ。

He thinks so too.

彼はばかだがお前もまた同様だ。

He is a fool { and you are another. / but so are you. }

3. そのうえ

and; besides; moreover

彼は学者であり，また偉大な教育者でもあった。

He was a scholar and { moreover, a great teacher. / a great teacher besides. } (1)

He was both a scholar and a great teacher. (2)

He was a great teacher as well as a scholar. (3)

〈注〉 上の(1)(2)の文は学者・教育者両方を強調。(3)の文は a great teacher であったことの方を強調。

【否定】neither ... nor

彼は金持ちでも貧乏でもなかった。

He was neither rich nor poor.

彼もまた彼の息子も町の発展に大いに貢献したが，2人ともあまり世に知られていなかった。

Neither he nor his son were well known,

although they contributed a great deal to the development of the town.

私は金持ちではないし，またなりたいとも思わない。

I am not rich,
- nor [neither〔強〕] do I wish to be.
- and I don't wish to be, either.

4．一方では

while; but

ジョンは分析能力がある。また一方，弟のビルは芸術家肌だ。

John is analytical, while his brother Bill has
- an artistic bent.
- something of the artist in him.

彼は攻撃的なところがあるが，また一方ではたいへん優しいところもある。

He is aggressive but [and] (at the same time) very tender-hearted.

〈注〉「また一方では」の意味の on the other hand は討論・議論の中で使うか，もしくは意外性を強調するときに使われる。その他の場合は but を使えばよい。

ex. He doesn't like American rock music at all; on the other hand, he loves British rock.（彼はアメリカのロックは好きじゃないのに不思議に英国のロックは大好きなんだ）

5．あるいは

彼は今60歳かまたは61歳です。

He is sixty or sixty-one now.

私かまたはあなたが行かなければならない。

One of us has to go.

ジョンかまたはビルが私たちと残らなければならない。

Either John or Bill has to stay with us.

まだ

1．まだ…ない

（否定文で）**not yet**

私はまだ終っていない。

I haven't finished yet.

「終りましたか」「いやまだです」。

"Have you finished?" "Not yet."

私はまだ小さくて死の意味もわからなかった。

I was {still too young / too young yet} to understand what death meant.

私はまだ飛行機に乗ったことがない。

I have never been in an airplane.

(警察は)有罪に結びつく証拠は今のところまだつかんでいない。

They haven't found any negative evidence so far [yet].

2．まだ…ある

（肯定文で）**still; yet**

【時】

まだ少し時間がある。

There is still (some) time (left).

There's (some) time left yet.

【金】

(財布に) まだ1ドルある。

I've still got one dollar (in my purse).

【道のり】

町に着くまでまだ10マイルはあった。

There were still ten miles to go before we would reach the town.

彼はまだソファで眠っている。

He's still asleep on the sofa.

【ほかに】

ほかにまだ何か言うことがありますか。

Have you got anything else [more] to say?

まだひとつだけ言いたいことがあります。

I've got just one more thing to say.

まだちょっとすることがある。

I've still got something to do.

I've got something to do yet.

3．わずか

母が亡くなったとき，私はまだ4歳でした。

I was only four years old when my mother died.

彼がアメリカに発ってからまだほんの１か月です。

It's [been] only one month since he left for America.

【比較】

これはまだあれほどひどくはない。

This one is not as bad as that one.

まち（町，街）

a city; a town

1．都会

【町】（↔田舎）

彼は町に野菜を売り［仕入れ］に行った。

He went to town to sell vegetables [to get supplies].

〈注〉 日本語の「仕入れ」は商売用の品物についての表現だが，get supplies は前後関係により日用品の補給の意にも商品の仕入れの意味にもなる。

彼は山の中で生れたが，今は町に住んでいる。

He was born in the mountains but now lives in town.

〈注〉 上の文のように「山の中，田舎」に対する町を指す場合には town に冠詞はなくてよい。

【町の人】

町の人にとって田舎に住みつくのは容易なことではない。生活慣習が違っているからである。

It is not easy for city dwellers to settle in the country, where social conventions are different.

〈注〉 日本でいう「市」と city の概念にはずれがあり，市制の敷かれた市でも場合によっては city と呼ぶより，むしろ town と呼ぶ方がふさわしいこともある。また日本では市の中に○○町の地名があるが city の中の地名を town とは呼ばない。「私は北町に住んでいますが私の町が好きです」の私の町は，my town ではなく次のように言うのが好ましい。

I live in Kitamachi, and I like this part [area] of the city.

2．繁華街

町に買物に行きましょう。

Let's go downtown and shop.

私たちは人込みの町を，泊まることになっているホテルを探し歩いた。

We walked along the crowded street looking for the hotel where we were to stay.

3．区画としての町

【町】（↔村）

彼は東京を少しはずれた小さな町に生れた。

He was born in a small town just outside of Tokyo.

町中がサーカスのうわさでもちきりだった。

The whole town was full of talk about the circus.

私たちの町は安全である。

Our streets are safe.

【町はずれ】

町はずれに新設の病院があり，この町とほかの二つの町の町民が利用している。

There is a new hospital on the outskirts of town that serves this and two other towns.

まちがえる（間違える）・まちがう

間違い 名 **a mistake; an error**（mistake と同様に使われるが，error の方が非難の気持ちが強く含まれる）; 大失敗 **a blunder**

間違える［間違う］ **make a mistake [mistakes]; make an error [errors]**

【誤り】

彼はいつも数学の問題［計算］を間違えてばかりいた。

He always { made mistakes in his math problems. / did his sums wrong.〔英〕 }

私はよく計算を間違える。

I often make numerical mistakes [errors].

I don't handle numbers accurately.

スペリングの間違いをしないように。

Don't { make spelling mistakes. / misspell words. }

日本人学生の英語の間違いは日英２か国語の

論理構造の相違が原因となっていることが多い。

Japanese students' errors in English are often due to (the) differences between the two languages in logical structure [framework].

子供だけでなく大人もよく漢字を間違える。

Not only children but also grownups use the wrong [incorrect] kanji very often.

私たちは道を間違えてしまった。

We have { taken the wrong road. / gone the wrong way. }

私は電話番号を間違えた。

I called the wrong number.

手紙のあて名を間違えた。

The letter was addressed wrong.

〈注〉 上例のように日本語で「間違える」と動詞を使うところを英語では have [take] the wrong ... と wrong（または not right）で表現することが多い。

バスを間違えないように気をつけてください。

Be sure [careful] to take the right bus.

〈注〉 See that you take the right bus. とも言えるが，これはぞんざいなので子供に注意するようなときでなければ使わない方がよい。

もし記憶に間違いがなければ，あれはちょうど20年前のことです。

If my memory is correct, it was just [exactly] twenty years ago.

それが間違いのもとだ。

That was the cause of the trouble.

〈注〉 酒癖の悪い人を招いたとか，いいかげんな人を信用して金を貸したなど。

【男女間の間違い】

妻がたった1度，それも何年も前に間違いを犯したことを彼はどうしても許すことができなかった。

He could never forgive his wife's infidelity, although it happened only once and many years ago.

【取り違える】

私はよく彼女を彼女のお姉さんと間違える。2人はそっくりなので。

I often take her for her sister. They look just alike.

彼はよく自分の双子の息子を間違える。

He often gets his twin sons confused.

「質量」と「重量」を間違える人が多い。

Many people confuse mass and weight.

間違えて彼女の傘を持って来てしまった。

I took her umbrella by mistake.

〈注〉 どれがどれかわからなくて間違えるのは get (something) mixed up を使う。

The twins got their clothes mixed up.（その双子はどっちがどっちの服かわからなくなった）

【反省】

彼を解雇したのは間違いであった。

I made a mistake in firing him.

It was a mistake to { fire him. / have fired him 〔*formal*〕. }

Firing him was a mistake.

〈注〉 I've done wrong ... も「…は間違いであった」と反省する言い方だが，これは道徳的に悪かったということ。

【確かである】

今度は成功すること絶対間違いない。

{ I'm absolutely sure [certain] / It's an absolute certainty } that it will succeed this time.

どちらの国も当分行動に出ることはあるまいと見て間違いなかろう。

It's safe to say that neither country will make a move at present.

まちどおしい（待ち遠しい）

［人主語］ **look forward to; wait eagerly [anxiously] for; be impatient for**

［待つ対象が主語］ **be long in coming**

【行事など】

クリスマスが待ち遠しい。

{ I'm so impatient / I can hardly wait / I just can't wait } for Christmas to come.

Christmas seems [is] long in coming.

〈注〉 ×I am long in coming Christmas. のような文を書かないように。

子供たちは本当に遠足が待ち遠しい。

The children are really [certainly, eagerly] looking forward to the picnic.

【人に対して】

ああ，待ち遠しい！（彼女はいったいいつまで私たちを待たせるの？）

How long is she going to keep us waiting?

まっくろ（真っ黒）

1．色

deep black; jet [coal] black; inky black

2．日焼け

(a) tan

真っ黒に日焼けする

get (a) tan; be tanned

夏休みが終ると子供たちは真っ黒に日焼けして登校した。

After the summer vacation the children came to school all tan(ned).

〈注〉 sunburned（または sunburnt）と tanned は別のことである。sunburned は急に強い日に焼かれて赤くなり，熱をもってひりひりしている状態。

3．汚れ

まあ，真っ黒な手。食事の前に洗っておいで。

What dirty hands! Wash them before you sit down at the table.

炭鉱夫は地下で，炭じんで顔も手も真っ黒になって働いている。

Coal miners work under ground, their faces all dark with coal dust. 〔*literary*〕

4．焦げ

あれ，まあ！ ホットケーキが真っ黒焦げになっちゃった。

Oh no [dear]! My hotcakes are
- all burned.
- all black.
- burnt to a frazzle.

《焦げる，焦がすの関連語》

scorch アイロンなどが布を焦がす，焦げる。

parch 表面をからからに乾かす。豆などを炒る，焦がす。

char （木・肉などについて）表面が黒く炭化するほど焦がす。

cf. brown 食物などをきつね色に焼く

まっさお（真っ青）

1．色

真っ青な **deep blue**

イタリアの空は真っ青であった。また地中海も真っ青であった。

The sky in Italy was deep blue, and so was the Mediterranean Sea.

2．顔色

真っ青な **deathly [ghostly] pale; as white as a sheet**

あの子は真っ青になった。私たちは皆あの子が失神するのではないかと思った。

She went so pale [white] we all thought she was going to faint.

彼はその知らせを聞いて真っ青になった。

He became [turned] very pale at the news.

〈注〉 blue や white を使うと次のような意味になる。

He became
- blue.（寒くて青くなった）
- white.（恐怖で，または気分が悪くなって血の気が引いた）

恐怖や寒さで血の気が引くと色の白い人は本当に white や pale になるが，色の白くない人には上の表現は的確ではない。

まったく（全く）

1．本当に（肯定強調）

truly; really; indeed

【相づち】

まったくその通り。

Quite (so). / That's true. / Yes, indeed. / That's right. / Exactly.

【落胆・絶望】

まったく，ばかなんだから！

What a fool!
まったく，へまなんだから！
What a blunder!
【強め】
まったく暑いですねえ。
It's terribly hot, isn't it?
まったくばかだ。
How stupid!
まったくおかしい。
How strange!
びっくりさせるじゃないか，まったく！
What a surprise you've given me!
まったくのところ恥ずかしくて死にそうだった[穴があったら入りたかった]。
Honestly, { I felt I could have died [crawled under the rug] for shame. / I wanted the ground to swallow me up. }

2. 肯定形（否定概念）
まったくの失敗だった。
It completely failed.
It was { an utter [a total] / a complele } failure. / a complete flop [washout].〔*colloq.*〕
It bombed.〔米・豪〕(演芸，ショーなどについて)
〈注〉 It bombed. は〔英〕では It was a success.(成功だった)と反対の意味になるので注意。
まったくだめだった。
It didn't work at all.
まったくのうそだ。
It's a downright lie.
まったくのナンセンスだ。
It's downright nonsense.
まったく時間の無駄だ。
It's a sheer waste of time.
彼のスピーチにはまったく参ったよ，退屈で。
His speech bored me to death.
この問題にはまったく参った。(解決できない)
This question { utterly baffles me. / baffles me altogether. }
彼はまったく参ってしまった。
He was completely done in.
〈注〉 perfectly は良い意味の形容詞のみと結びつき，completely は良い意味，悪い意味両方と結びつくことが可能。ただし，例外的に He's a perfect fool. のような言い方もある。

3. 全然（否定強調）
not at all; not a bit; not in the least; never; utterly [quite, completely] ＋ 形
まったく[全然]知らない。
He knows nothing about it.
He doesn't know anything about it.
He is utterly ignorant (of it [that]).
私は彼がだれかもまったく知らない。
I don't even know who he is.
The man is a total [an utter] stranger to me.
私は彼とはまったく関係がない。
I have no connection with him.
〈注〉 I have nothing to do with him [it]. は「何かよくないことに自分は無関係だ」との意味合い。
あなたがその件にまったく[全然]無関係だなんて言わせない。
Don't tell me you have nothing to do with that business.
まったくわからない。
I don't understand it at all.
君の言っていることはまったく[全然]わからない。
I haven't the faintest [slightest, foggiest, haziest] idea (of) what you mean.
まったく覚えていない。
I've forgotten all about it.
まったく関心がない。
{ I'm not in the least interested / I have no interest whatever } in that.

4. 部分否定
彼の言うことはまったくうそでもない。
What he says is not altogether a lie.

まったくの悪人なんてそういるものではない。

Few men are wholly [thoroughly] bad.

〈注〉 not quite, not altogether のように強調の副詞に not を加えると部分的否定になる。
「まったく知らなかった」は I didn't know it at all. で ×I didn't know it completely. とは言わない。

まつり（祭り）→ ねんちゅうぎょうじ

まで・までに

1. 時間

till; until; up [down] to

【…から…まで】

ショーは1時から5時まで上演します。

The show will run from 1:00 to 5:00.

彼らは朝から晩まで一生懸命働いた。

They worked hard from morning till night.

【…まで】

彼は高校を終えるまで伯父さんの家にいた。

He lived at his uncle's till he finished high school.

あの部屋はついこの間までふさがっていた[入居者がいた]。

That apartment has been [was] occupied until quite recently.

彼の父は85歳まで生きた。

His father lived to be eighty-five.

【今まで】

今までのところ彼の仕事はかなりうまくいっている。

Up till [Until] now / Up to the present } his business has been fairly prosperous.

今までいったいどこにいたんだ。

Where have you been all this while?

今までのところ別に問題はない。

So far there's no problem.

今までのところわかっているのはそれだけです。

That's all we know { as yet. / so far.

【終りまで】

彼は最後まで武士の品位を持ち続けた。

He kept the dignity of a samurai to the end.

パーティーが終るまでいなければならないと思いますか。

Do you think we should stay till [to] the end of the party?

【期限】

試験までもう2週間しかない。

We have only two weeks before the examination.

月曜日まで休業[閉館]いたします。（掲示）

Closed till Monday.

〈注〉 cf. Open from [on] Monday.（月曜日から始めます[に開店致します]）
店の改装などで臨時に休むときの言い方。

この切符は9月30日まで有効だ。

This ticket is valid { until / up to / through } September 30.

This ticket is no longer valid after September 30.

次の列車まで1時間半待たなければならなかった。

We had to wait one and a half hours for the next train.

〈注〉「1時間半」は次のどちらでもよい。
an hour and a half / one and a half hours

【…までには】

日曜日までには帰って来る。

I'll be back { by Sunday. / on Sunday or before.

あなたもそのころまでには新しい生活に慣れるでしょう。

You'll get used to your new life by that time.

あなたが帰って来るころまでには仕事を終えてしまっているでしょう。

I'll have finished my work by the time you come back.

〈注〉「まで」と「までに」，**till** と **by**

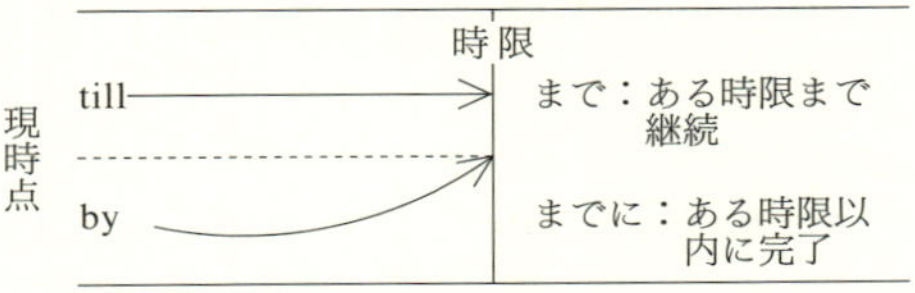

月末まで授業がある。(継続)

We have classes {○till / ×by} the end of the month.

日曜までにレポートをまとめねばならない。(完了)

I have to finish my paper {×till / ○by} next Sunday.

2. 空間

「どちらまで行くのですか」「名古屋まで」。

“Where are you going?” “To Nagoya.”

彼は今日はどこまで行くんだろう。

How far {is he going / will he get} today?

彼は福岡まで車で行った。

He drove as far as Fukuoka.

途中まで行ってから昼食にしよう。

We'll go part of the way and stop for lunch.

途中までご一緒しましょう。

I'll go part of the way with you.

〈注〉 道などをたずねられて，「そこまでご一緒に」と言うとき使う。「橋まで」のようにはっきりしていれば to the bridge のように具体的に言えばよい。
ex. 駅まで迎えに来ていただけませんか。
Could you come and get me at the station [to the station to get me]?

3. その他

【範囲】

私はこの本を終りまで読んだ。

I read this book to the end.

この本は終りまでは読まなかった。

I didn't finish it [this book].

今日はここまで。(教室などで)

That's all [it] for today.

【貸付限度】

個人の借りられるのは最高100万円までだ。

One million yen is the maximum amount that a person can borrow.

The maximum amount one can borrow is one million yen.

〈注〉 貸付額は the amount to be advanced と言えるが，これは銀行員の用いる語であり，一般には上記例文のように言う。
数は 1, 2 語で，また時には 3 語で書けるものは数字でなく spelling で書くのが普通。統計資料，日付などは例外。

【程度】

彼はついにカンニングまでしてしまった。

He went so far as to cheat on an exam.

家族までが彼の言うことを信じなかった。

Even his own family didn't believe him.

そこまでやらなくていいだろう。

There's no need to go that far.

〈注〉 ただし，このような場合もっと具体的に述べるのが普通。
ex. They don't have to give him financial help. (彼に資金援助まですることはない)
cf. それは行きすぎだ。
He's gone too far. / That's going too far.

まとめる(纏める)・まとまる

1. 一括する

put [bring] together; gather

そこの物をまとめてあのトランクに入れなさい。

Pack [Put] those things in that trunk.

荷物をまとめなさい，できるだけ早く出発できるように。

{Get your things together / Gather up your belongings} so that we can leave as soon as possible.

【集大成】

彼は雑誌に連載していた随筆を1巻にまとめて出版した。(彼が主導する場合)

He {had a collection of his essays published. / collected his essays and had them published in one volume. / had his essays collected and published.}

彼が連載した随筆はまとまって1冊の本になった。(他の人が主導)

His magazine essays were collected and published in one volume.

A collection of his essays was published.

【まとめ買い】

このごろは１週間分の食料品をまとめて買い込む家が多い。

Many families these days buy a whole week's worth of groceries at a time.

【一括払い】

市民税をまとめて１年分前払いすると割引がある。

There's a reduction in the city tax if
{the whole sum is paid / it's paid in a lump sum} in advance.

私は彼の借金をまとめて払ってやった。

I paid all his debts at the same time.

【一致】

税制改革について党の意見をまとめる

consolidate party opinion about tax reform

自民党の党首は党員の意見をひとつにまとめることができなかった。

The president of the LDP was unable to get his party members to agree among themselves.

2．整理する

【資料】

膨大な資料を分類してまとめるのはたいへんな仕事だ。

It's a laborious task to classify and organize a vast amount of material.

彼は論文のために実験資料をまとめているところだ。

He is compiling his experimental data for his thesis.

【意見】

委員長は各委員の意見をまとめて整理した。

The chairman summarized the opinions of the committee members.

【内容】

この論文の内容を500語以内にまとめてください。

Summarize the contents of this essay within 500 words.

【考え】

考えがまとまらなくていつまでも寝つけなかった。

I tossed in bed for a long time unable to give shape to my idea.

3．解決する

【話をまとめる】

（論争を） settle《a dispute》; bring《something》to a conclusion

（交渉を） conclude a negotiation

（紛争を） mediate in a disagreement

（縁談を） arrange a marriage

（仕事を） complete [finish] one's work

〈注〉 fix も「まとめる」に近いが，fix は日時，人数などに関することなどを相談し，調整して決めること。

私はやっている辞書の仕事を今年中にまとめるつもりだ。

I intend to complete my dictionary work this year [by the end of this year].

4．まとまる

【荷物】

荷物がまとまったらすぐ電話してください。

Phone me as soon as you have finished packing your things.

【話】

その運動に各自1000円ずつ寄付することに話がまとまった。

It has been agreed that each member will donate 1,000 yen for the campaign.

【気持ち】

このクラスはまとまっている。

There's unity in this class.

【考え】

そのことについてはまだ考え［意見］がまとまっていない。

I haven't any [have no] definite opinion about it (as) yet.

考えがはっきりまとまってきた。
My idea began to take definite shape.
【内容】
君の論文はよくまとまっている。
Your report is {compact and well-organized. / well-written.}
このストーリーはよくまとまっている。
This is a well-knit story.
【交渉】
組合と会社の賃上げ交渉はまだまとまっていない[妥結していない]。
The union has not yet come to terms with the company about a wage increase.
私たちの家の売却価格についてはまだ話がまとまっていない。
We have not yet {come to terms about / agreed on} a selling price for our house.

まなぶ（学ぶ）→ べんきょう，ならう

1．学問をする

…の指導で学ぶ
study under [with] a teacher
彼は慶應義塾で福沢のもとで学んだ生徒の1人だ。
He was one of {those who studied in Keio-gijuku under Fukuzawa. / Fukuzawa's first students at Keio-gijuku.}
よく学び，よく遊べ。（ことわざ）
All work and no play makes Jack a dull boy.

2．教わる

私はフランス人の女性からフランス語を学びました。
I learned French from a French lady.
【けいこする】
彼はシルバースタイン先生についてピアノを学んだ。
He took piano lessons from Mr. Silverstein.
【教訓を得る】
私はこの経験から多くを学んだ。
I learned a great deal from this experience.
私は彼の恋愛事件からいろいろ学んだ。
His love affair taught me a lesson.

まにあう（間に合う）

1．時間に

急いだら7時の列車に間に合いますよ。
If you hurry, you'll be {in time for / able to catch} the 7:00 train.
昨夜は終バスに間に合わなかった。
I missed the last bus home last night.
私は独奏会の開演に間に合わなかった。
I was late for the recital.
〈注〉「間に合わなかった」の be late for は遅れて参加することであるから，×be late for a train とは言えない。miss a train である。
ドレスは次の日曜日に間に合いますか。（その日の）パーティーに着て行きたいんですが。
Will the dress be ready by next Sunday? I'd like to wear it to a party then [that day].

2．役立つ

「これで間に合うかしら」「ええ上等ですよ」。
"Will this do?" "Oh yes, (that's) fine [excellent]."
5000円あれば当分間に合う。
Five thousand yen will be enough for the time being.
このハンドブックがあれば当座は間に合う。
These handbooks will {do / be fine / be good enough} for {the present. / the time being.}
〈注〉「間に合う」の意味の will serve our purpose は使い古された決り文句である。

3. 足りている

今のところウエイトレスは間に合っています。

We don't need any waitresses at the moment.

We have { no vacancies [openings] for waitresses. / enough waitresses. }

洗濯機なしでも間に合います。近くにコインランドリーがありますから。

I can do without a washing machine. I live near a coin laundry now.

【注文】

そうね，今日は間に合っているわ，ありがとう。

Well [No], { I don't need anything / I've nothing to order } today, thank you.

4. 間に合せる

【代用】

腕時計の修理ができるまでこの古い方で間に合せよう。

I will make do with this old watch till mine is repaired.

【間に合せ】

間に合せに屋根にビニールシートをかぶせた。

We covered the roof temporarily with plastic.

ほんの間に合せに割れた窓ガラスにボール紙をあてておいた。

We stuck [put] a piece of cardboard over the broken window (as a stopgap solution).

この間に合せの本箱は意外にしっかりしている。もうこれでいいことにするか。

This makeshift bookcase is more sturdy than we expected; maybe I won't build one (after all).

【時間内に】

明晩までに絶対にこの服を間に合せよう。

I'll definitely get [have] this dress ready by tomorrow evening.

まぬがれる（免れる）

1. 助かる・逃れる

escape; escape from; be saved from; be relieved from; be released from

【事故など】

彼の家の近所で火事があったが，彼の家は類焼を免れた。

There was a fire in his neighborhood but his house { escaped damage. / was not damaged. }

団体旅行の観光バスが1台事故を起した。しかし彼の乗ったバスは難を免れた。

One of the tourist buses in [of] his group had an accident, but his was safe.

地すべりで3戸が倒壊した。住民3名は危うく難を免れたが7名の死者が出た。

The landslide crushed three houses; three people narrowly escaped but seven were killed.

生あるものはすべて死を免れることはできない。

Everything has to die.

Every living thing dies.

【罰】

連中は初犯だったので罰金を免れた。

They were excused from the fine because that [it] was their first offense.

彼は処罰を免れない。

He cannot { escape punishment. / go unpunished. }

彼は減給は免れないと知っている。

He knows he can't be exempt from a salary cut.

彼は放校は免れない。

He can't avoid expulsion from school.

2. 避ける

avoid; escape from

彼女は責任を免れようとあがいたりしなかっ

た。

She didn't try to {evade / avoid} her responsibility.

われわれの必死の努力で会社は倒産を免れた。

Because of our desperate efforts the company was saved from bankruptcy.

まま

1. 状態の維持

【姿勢】

どうぞ立たないでそのまま，と彼はその人を手で制した。

He motioned the man {to remain seated. / not to rise.}

どうぞそのまま，はい，チーズ。(写真撮影)

Please keep still and say cheese.

【放任】

彼女はそっとそのままにしておいた方がいい。

We'd better leave her alone.

【保存】

警察が来るまでは何にも触らずそのままにしておきなさい。

Leave everything as it is until the police come.

〈注〉 the police は複数扱いなので comes としない。

【人柄】

僕はそのままの君が好きだ。

I love you just as you are.

【服装】

どうぞそのまま[普段着]でいらしてください。まったくの気楽なパーティーですから。

Please come as you are. It's a very informal party.

オーバーはどうぞそのままで，ここはとても寒いですから。

Please keep your overcoat on, for it's very cold here.

【電話】

どうぞそのまま(切らずに)お待ちください。

Hold the line, please.

【行動＋まま】

京都からずっと立ったままだった。

{I was standing / I had to stand} all the way from Kyoto.

〈注〉 まだその列車に乗っているならば I've been standing all the way … . (…ずっと立ったままだ)となる。

明りをつけたまま眠ってしまわないように。

Don't leave your light on when you go to sleep.

ドアが開けたままになっている。

The door has been left open.

だれなの，またドアが開けたままになっている。

Who's left the door open again?

彼は5年前にアメリカに行ったまま住みついている。

He went to America five years ago, and he's still there.

【不変の状態】

だれも全然変らずそのままでいられる者はいない。

Nobody {stays / remains} the same.

何もかも20年前の昔そのままに見える。

Things look just as they {used to (look) / did} twenty years ago.

2. …の通り

何が起ったのかあなたの見たままを話してください。

Tell me what happened just as you saw it.

Describe exactly what {you saw. / happened.}

(詳しく)

【思うまま】

何もかも私の望むまま[望み通り]になった。

Everything turned out as I wished.

何でも自分の思うまま[思い通り]にできるものじゃないよ。

You can't have your own way in everything.

【言われるまま】

私はただ言われるままにしただけだ。

I only did what I was told.

請われるままに彼女はショパンの曲をもう1曲弾いた。

At their request she played another ⌊of Chopin's pieces [Chopin piece].

まもる（守る）

1．保護する

保護する **protect;** 防御する **defend;** 警護する **guard**

犬はよく子供を守ることがある。

Dogs often protect children.

土の壁は住人を夏の暑さから守るために分厚く造られている。

The clay walls were made thick to protect the inhabitants from the heat of summer.

インディアンが襲って来たとき，砦(とりで)を守る兵隊はあまりいなかった。

There were few soldiers to defend the fortress when the Indians attacked.

昼も夜も城の入口を2人の兵士が守っていた。

Day and night two soldiers guarded the entrance to the castle.

自分の利益を守るためにはどんなことでもやる人間がいる。

Some people would do anything to protect their own interest.

嫌疑から身を守るため，彼は知事に長い手紙を書いた。

To defend himself against suspicion, he wrote a long letter to the governor.

昨夜のゲームではゴールキーパーがよく守った。

The goalkeeper defended very well in last night's game.

ゴールキーパーはちょうどそのとき左側からのシュートに備えて守っていなかった。

The goalkeeper was not guarding the cage at the moment against a shot from the left.

神様があなたをお守りくださいますように。

God be with you.

2．遵守する

observe; keep; obey

【規則】

ゲームをするときはルールを守らなければならない。

You should {observe / keep} the rules when you play a game.

〈注〉 observe はやや文語的。

【法】

悪法でも法は守らねばならない。

We must obey a law even if it's a poor one.

【制限速度】

彼は制限速度を守らなかったので罰金をとられた。

He was fined because he didn't observe [keep] the speed limit.

【時間】

母さんが10時までに帰って来るようにと言ったので，時間を守ると約束した。

My mother told me to be home by ten o'clock, {and I promised I would. / which I promised to be.}

【慣習】

古くから伝わるお盆の慣習はたいていの地方で守られている。

In most areas people still observe the old customs of the *Bon* Festival.

【約束】

彼は約束を守って美しい誕生祝いのカードを送ってくれた。

He kept his promise and sent me a beautiful birthday card.

【秘密】
君は秘密を守れるか。
Can you keep a secret?
僕は面白いことを知っているんだが，秘密を守ると約束するかい？
I know something interesting, but will you promise to keep it secret?
【言いつけ】
お父さんの言いつけを守りなさい。
Do as your father tells you.
先生の指示を守りなさい。
Follow your teacher's instructions.

まやく（麻薬）

drugs; dope〔*slang*〕
麻薬常用者[患者]
a drug addict; a junkie〔*slang*〕
麻薬密売
drug traffic [trade, business]
麻薬密売者　a (drug) trafficker; a (drug) peddler [dealer]（末端の売人）
〈注〉 trafficking は麻薬を原料のまま，または処理された形で取り扱い売ること。peddling は流通の末端で直接麻薬使用者に売ること。
麻薬取締法　Narcotics Control Act
ヘロインは麻(酔)薬だ。
Heroin is a narcotic (drug).
先週東京でマリファナ所持で7人が検挙された。
Seven people were arrested in Tokyo last week for possession of marijuana.

《関連語》
narcotics　通常アヘンから得た麻酔薬を指す。
heroin　ヘロイン
morphine　モルヒネ
marijuana　マリファナ，大麻
hemp, hashish　大麻
cocaine　コカイン
crack　純度の高いコカイン。
【覚醒剤】stimulant drug(s)
amphetamine(s)　アンフェタミン

まよう（迷う）

1．道を見失う

lose one's **way; be lost**
彼は森の中で道に迷った。
He had lost his way in the wood.
子供は人込みで迷子になってしまった。
The child got lost in the crowd.
〈注〉◆「道を見失う」のつもりで ×miss one's way とは言わない。miss は曲り角，交差点，信号などに気づかないこと。その結果，道に迷うのである。
ex. He missed the turning, so he got lost.（曲り角に気づかず通り過ぎて道に迷った）
◆「迷子になった」を子供の立場で言うと，I got lost in a department store when I was five.（5歳の時デパートで迷子になった）となる。be lost とは心細い寂しい状態であるから迷子の心情を描くのに適する。親の立場で言うと，My child is missing [has disappeared]. または I've lost my child. となる。

2．思い惑う

ためらう **hesitate**（Yes か No かを決めかねる）
彼女はしばらく迷っていたが，結局彼の申し出を受けた。
She hesitated a while but eventually accepted his proposal.
【決断がつかない】
彼はどちらにしようか迷っている。
He cannot {make up his mind / choose} which to take.
He is wavering between the two.
彼は行こうかどうしようか迷っている。
He is in [of] two minds whether he should go or not.
He can't decide whether to go or not.
【困惑】
彼はどうしたらよいか迷っていた。
He didn't know what to do.
He was puzzled [perplexed] about what to do.

3．魅惑におぼれる

女に迷う　lose one's head over a woman

欲に迷う　be blinded by love of gain [money, power]

まる（丸）

円　**a circle**

丸い **round; circular;** 球の **spherical** 〔*formal*〕

丸をかく　draw a circle

番号を丸で囲む　circle the number

先生は正しい答えには丸をつける。

Teachers mark correct answers by circling them.

この書類はマル秘だよ。

This document is strictly confidential.

【全部】

丸暗記する　learn by heart

彼は関西弁丸出しだ。

He speaks in full Kansai dialect.

面目丸つぶれだ。

It's a complete and utter disgrace.

まわす（回す）・まわる

1．回転させる［する］

㊍㊐ **turn round; revolve; go round; spin**

㊍㊌ **turn round; revolve; set** 《a thing》 **going; spin**

ハンドルを時計回りに回してごらん。

Turn the handle clockwise.

車は駅の方向に角を回って行った。

The car turned the corner and went towards the station.

このスイッチを押すとプロペラが回ります。

If you turn on the switch the propeller rotates [revolves].

地球は（地軸を中心に回りながら）太陽のまわりを回る。

The earth rotates on its axis as it revolves around the sun.

The earth goes round the sun.

パパ，このこま回せる？

Can you spin this top, Dad?

見てごらん。こまはよく回っているときはまるでじっとしているように見えるんだ。

Look. When the top spins very fast it looks like it's standing still.

2．巡回する

make a round; go one's rounds; patrol

彼は今世界中を回って旅をしている。昨年は日本中を回ったのだ。

He is now on his round-the-world trip. Last year he traveled all over Japan.

泥棒が押し入ろうとしているところにちょうど警察官が回って来た。

A policeman happened to be patrolling there as the thief was breaking into the house.

【寄り道・迂回】

家に帰る途中ちょっと病院に回って病気の友人を見舞って来た。

On my way home I went around [round] to the hospital to see my sick friend.

どうぞ裏口の方に回ってください。

Please come round to the back door.

3．送り渡す

その書類を係の人に回さなければならない。

We have to send the papers round [over] to the man in charge.

手紙を私の新しい住所に回してください。

Please forward [send] the letters to my new address.

すいません，新聞を読み終ったら私に回してください。

Please give me the newspaper when you're finished.

【上告】

その事件は最高裁に回された。

The case was transferred to the Supreme Court.

【手渡し】
すいません，塩を回してください。
Please pass me the salt.
雑誌をこちらに回していただけませんか。
Could you hand me the magazine?
あの子たちのハネムーンの写真がテーブルについたお客さんの手から手に回り，人それぞれに種々の反応を見せていた。
Their honeymoon photos were passed round the table, creating various reactions among the dinner guests.

4. 差し向ける

【転勤】
彼は高山支店に回された。
He was transferred to the Takayama (branch) office.
【転科】
患者を外科に回す
refer a patient to a surgeon

5. 行き渡る

【酒・毒】
自分でも知らない間にかなりお酒が回ってしまった。
Before I knew it I had got pretty drunk.
毒が回ってきた。
The poison is taking effect.
【知恵】
彼は知恵が回らない。
He is slow and dull.

6. 慣用表現

【気を回す】
君は何でもすぐ気を回す。
You are too suspicious about everything.
気を回さないでくれよ，僕があいつらと裏取引をしたなんて。
Stop suspecting me of having backdoor dealings with them.
【気が回る】
そこまで気が回らなかった。
I didn't get [take] the hints.
彼女が…しに来たなんて，そこまで気が回らなかった。
I didn't {imagine / guess / catch on 〔*colloq.*〕 / realize} (at the time) that she had come to ....
【切り回す】
あの人は家事をうまく切り回している。
She handles [manages] the household well [with skill].
彼がこの式に関することすべてを切り回している。
He is handling everything concerning the ceremony.
実際に会社を切り回しているのは社長の秘書だ。
It's the president's secretary who actually controls [runs] the company.
【手回し】
手回しをよくするには早くからとりかかる方がよい。
We need to begin early enough to do the preparations well.
事前の手回しがよくなかった。
Preparations were not made enough in advance.
社内に不正行為の疑いがあり，会社は手を回して[探偵を雇って]調査した。
A detective was hired to investigate possible fraud in the company.
彼女は手を回して夫の行動を監視しようとした。
She hired a detective to {track / check out} the movements of her husband.
手を回してもみ消す　cover [hush] up
【根回し】
根回しをする
{do spade work / lay the ground work} (悪い意味はない)

do some politicking（良い意味と悪い意味のどちらでも使われる）
cf. dealing under the table（裏取引き）

み

み（実）

1. 果実

果実 **fruit;** 小粒でやわらかいもの **a berry [berries];** 堅果 **a nut;** 種子 **a seed**

うちの庭のリンゴの木はよく実がなる[たくさん実をつける]。

The apple trees in my garden
{ have a lot of fruit.
{ bear well.

その木は実がならない。

Those trees don't bear fruit.

子供たちは木の実拾い[イチゴ摘み]に森に行った。

The children went
{ nut collecting
{ berry-picking [berrying] }
in the woods.

〈注〉◆「木の実拾いに森へ行った」を英語にするとき to the woods としたくなるが，in the woods が正しい。同様に「川へ泳ぎに行く」も go swimming in the river である。go to school, hurry to the station などのように「動きを表す動詞」に直接続くときに to を使う。

◆ fruit は果物一般を意味するときは集合名詞，食品として考えるときは物質名詞なので，ともに 'a' はつけず，複数形にしない。米語では，いろいろな種類を念頭におく場合は普通名詞として 'a' をつけるか複数形にする。例文については→くだもの

《関連語》

berries

イチゴ strawberry / 桑の実 mulberry / ブラックベリー blackberry / コーヒーの実 coffee berry / ラズベリー raspberry

nuts

クリ chestnut / アーモンド almond / ギンナン gingko nut / カシューナッツ cashew / ピーナッツ peanut / ココナツ coconut / クルミ walnut / ペカン pecan / ハシバミ hazelnut

fruit →くだもの

〈注〉 berries, nutsの類はふつう複数形で表わされる。

2. 成果

彼の努力が実を結んだ。

His efforts proved fruitful.

私の夢が実を結んだ。

My dream has come true.

みあげる（見上げる）・みおろす（見下ろす）

【見上げる】

look up at; raise [lift] one's eyes to

子供は目に涙をためて父親を見上げた。

The child looked up at his father with tears in his eyes.

彼女の見上げた顔が夕闇の中に白く浮き出して見えた。

Her upturned face showed white in the dusk.

【見下ろす】look down on

その大木は何百年もの間，人間の不幸をじっと見下ろしてきたのだ。

That big tree has looked [gazed] down upon human misery for centuries.

子供ははしごのてっぺんまで登り，誇らしげに私たちを見下ろした。

The child climbed to the top of the ladder and looked down on us proudly.

〈注〉 look down on は文脈により scorn（見下す，軽蔑する）の意にもなるので注意。

Because he always gets good marks he looks down on us.（彼はいつもいい点をとるので，僕たちをばかにしている）

みえる（見える）

1. 視力がある

ネコは暗がりでも目が見える。

Cats can see in the dark.

私はめがねがないとよく見えない。

I can't see well without glasses.

彼はもうすぐ80になるのに目がよく見える。

He has good eyesight though he is nearly 80.

2. 目に映る

山の上にお城が見えると，ああ岐阜に帰って来たなと思ったものだ。

I used to feel that I'd come back to Gifu when I could see [saw] the castle on the mountain top.

通りには人っ子ひとり見えなかった。

Not a soul was to be seen on the street.

ここから富士山は見えません。

You can't see Mt. Fuji / Mt. Fuji can't be seen } from here.

窓からは町全体の景色が見える。

From the window we can { see / get a good view of } the whole town.

〈注〉 The window commands a fine view. は辞書に出ているが堅すぎる表現である。
The window overlooks the whole town. は口語ではないが，物語調でならば使える。

角を曲ると海が見えてきた。

Turning the corner, we came in sight of the sea.

バスが角を曲ると海が見えてきた。

The sea came in sight when the bus turned the corner.

【見えなくなる】

彼は船の姿が水平線の彼方に見えなくなるまでじっと立ちつくしていた。

He stood watching the ship till it disappeared beyond the horizon.

ジェット機があっと言う間に見えなくなった。

The jet flew out of sight.

【見えない】

オリオン座には星雲があるが，肉眼では見えない。

There's a nebula in Orion though it is invisible to the naked eye.

【のぞく】

下着のシャツが首[袖口]のところから見えていた。

His undershirt was { showing at the neck. / sticking out from his shirt sleeves.

スリップがスカートの裾から見えていますよ。

Your slip is showing [hanging down].

3. 見受けられる

彼は年より若く見える。

He looks younger than { he really is. / his age.

この前会ったときは，あの人たちは幸せそうに見えた。

They seemed happy the last time I met them.

〈注〉 look は外観からそう見えること。seem は話者・筆者の主観が入って，そう思われること。

コアラは小型の熊のように見えるが，カンガルーと同じ有袋類に属す。

The koala looks like a small bear but it belongs, together with the kangaroo, to the marsupials.

彼はまだ元気だと見える。

He seems to be getting along very well yet. 〔*common*〕

It seems he's still getting along very well.

彼も結局あきらめたと見える。

He seems to have given up after all.

It seems he has given up after all.

彼は奥さんがこわいと見える。

He seems to be afraid of his wife.

4. 来訪する

市長さんが明日の朝，地震の被害状況を視察に見える。

The mayor will come here tomorrow morning to inspect the earthquake damage.

議長さんがまだ見えない。

The chairman hasn't come yet.

みおくる（見送る）

1．送別する

see《a person》**off**

友人を見送りに成田に行って来たところです。

I have been to Narita to see my friend off.

いとこが私をバス停まで見送ってくれて，そこで互いに手を振って別れた。

My cousin came along with me as far as the bus stop, where we waved goodbye to each other.

弟は私についてバス停まで来ては，そこで私を見送って帰らなければならなかった。

My little brother used to follow me to the bus stop, and then he had to go back home.

私は父を戸口で見送った。

I saw my father to the door.

〈注〉◆ 送る（＝見送る）を間違えて send としないように。◆ follow は後からついて行くこと。accompany は一緒に行くことである。She accompanies him. というときは彼が主で彼女は「彼と同行する」のである。しかし二人は対等の立場で，escort のように彼に「付き添って行く」の意ではない。

2．目で追う

彼女はじっと立ったまま母を乗せた列車がトンネルの中に姿を消すまで見送っていた。

She stood gazing at the train that was bearing her mother away until it disappeared into the tunnel.

3．取りやめる

列車がひどく込んでいたので，一列車見送って次の便を待つことにした。

The train was so awfully crowded he decided to give up and wait for the next one.

国会の会期が終ったので政府は選挙法の改正案を見送らざるを得なかった。

The government had to table [shelve] the bill amending the election law because the (legislative) session ended.

決定は見送るべきだ。

The decision should be postponed.

彼は昇進の機会を見送ってしまった。転勤を断ったのだ。

He passed up the chance of promotion by refusing to be transferred.

彼女はチャンスを見送ってしまった。

She let the chance { pass. / go (by). }

みこみ（見込み）

1．可能性

（a）**chance; possibility;** 見通し**prospect**（s）

【見込みのある】

彼は見込みのある若者だ。

He is a promising youth.

これは見込みのある事業だ。

This is a promising enterprise.

【見込みがある［ない］】

彼は勝つ見込みが { ある。 / あまりない。 / 全然ない。 }

He has { some / little / no } chance of winning.

There's { some / little / no } { chance / possibility } that he will win.

彼女には赤ちゃんができる見込み［望み］がない。

There's no { hope [chance] / possibility } { of her having a baby. / that she will ever have a baby. }

〈注〉　「彼女には見込みがない，残念ながら」には次の２通りの言い方がある。

(1)She is a hopeless case, I must admit.

その人の内面的なもの，性格，しつけなどについて今さらどうしようもない。

(2)Her case is hopeless.

外部のことについて，病気が治る，職業につけるなどの見込みがない。

以上の区別は絶対的なものではないが，だいたいこのようである。

見込みはどうだろう。

What are the prospects?（How likely is it? の意味で重要なことについて使う）

彼には昇進の見込みがかなりある。

He has some prospect of promotion.

十中八九見込みがない。

There is one chance out of ten.

彼の見込みは五分五分だ。

He has an even chance.

2．予想

東海道線は午後には全線通常運転に復旧する見込みだ。

All trains on the Tokaido Line will resume normal service in the afternoon.

線路の破損箇所の修復には1か月を要する見込みである。

It will take a month to repair the damaged section of the line.

台風11号による被害額は100億円を上回る見込みだ。

The damage caused by typhoon No.11 is expected to exceed ten billion yen.

彼女は来春卒業の見込みです。

We expect that she will graduate next spring.

〈注〉「卒業見込み証明書」では Graduation expected, March 2003 のように書く。

《類義語》

probability

確率（単数形が普通）

科学的・統計上の予想に用いられる。high, great, low などの形容詞で修飾できる。

ex. What is the probability?

The probability of rain this evening is 90%.（今夜の降水確率は90%です）

prospect(s)〔*formal*〕

予想・見通し（単複両形使用）

日常生活レベルのことではなく，ビジネス・就職・重大な決断・状況変化・政治上などの予想に使用。

ex. What are the prospects for economic recovery?（経済回復の見通しは？）

possibility

可能性（単数）

much, good, slim, little, slight などの形容詞で修飾される。

ex. Do you think there's a good possibility that she'll find a publisher?（出版社を見つけられる可能性はありそうか）

There's little possibility of rain.（降水確率は低い）

選択の余地（複数）

many [few] possibilities（選択肢の数が多い［少ない］）

ex. You need a new hobby, and there are [you have] many possibilities.（何か新しい趣味でも始めたらいい。それにいろいろ君にやれそうなのがあるじゃないか）

◆（chance, possibility, possibilitiesの用法例）

Is there any possibility of getting [to get] your novel published?（君の小説は出版できる見込みはあるのか）

I'm afraid the chances are low. There aren't many possibilities; most publishers are decreasing their fiction budgets this year.（どうにも見込み薄だ。やってくれそうなところがあまりない。たいていの出版社は小説部門の予算を縮小してきているんだ）

みじめ（惨め）

みじめな **miserable;**〔強〕**wretched**

雨のなか来ないバスを待ちあぐね，まったくみじめな気持ちだった。

I felt miserable standing in the rain, waiting for a bus that never arrived.

彼女は夫の死後はずっとみじめな暮しだった。

She led a wretched life after her husband died.

彼女はひとり寂しくみじめな死に方をした。

She died alone and forsaken.

当時は小作農民はまったくみじめな暮しをし

ていた。

In those days tenant farmers lived really miserable lives.

モーツァルトの葬儀は生前の彼の偉業にふさわしからぬみじめなものであった。

Mozart suffered a burial far below what he deserved.

【惨敗】

彼のチームはみじめな負け方をした。

His team was soundly beaten.

〈注〉 suffered a crushing defeat という言い方があるが，使い古された決り文句である。

みせ（店）

a store; a shop; 露店 a stall; a booth

〈注〉 概して米国は store を，英国では shop を使う傾向があるが，米国でも小規模な店は shop と呼び，英国でも大きな店は store と呼ぶ。

【開店・閉店】

デパートは通常10時開店，7時閉店だ。

Department stores usually open at ten and close at seven.

当店は6時に閉店いたします。

We close [The shop closes] at six.

【店を持つ，店に出る】

私の父はニューヨークに店を持っています。

My father owns [has, runs] a store in New York

〈注〉 run と言えるのは大規模な仕事の場合に限る。

私は仕事の見習い中なのです，それで店に出てお客様の応対をしています。

I'm learning the ropes, so now I'm working at the counter serving customers.

【店番をする】

両親が用事で留守になるときは私が店番をしなければならない。

I have to {mind / tend} the shop while my parents are away on some other business.

【店を広げる】

元旦には神社の参道に飲食物や玩具の露店がぎっしり立ち並び，皆お店を広げて通りがかりの人々に呼びかけたりする。

On New Year's Day the approach to [road into] the shrine is lined with stalls selling food and drink and toys. They display their wares and call out to the persons passing by.

《関連語》

【食品】

果物屋　fruit shop [stand]（stand は露店）

菓子屋　candy store〔米〕; confectionery; sweet-shop〔英〕

総菜屋　delicatessen; 略 deli

八百屋　vegetable store; greengrocer's〔英〕; greengrocery

乾物屋　grocery store [shop];

自然［健康］食品店　natural [health] food store

パン屋　baker's; bakery; bake shop

肉　屋　butcher's (shop); butcher shop

牛乳屋　dairy

魚　屋　fishmonger's; fresh fish shop

お茶屋　tea dealer's shop

コーヒー屋　retail coffee shop; coffee bean store [shop]（コーヒー豆などを売る専門店）

酒　屋　liquor store

【食堂・バーなど】

食　堂　restaurant

料　亭　high-class Japanese-style restaurant

喫茶店　tearoom; coffee shop

バー［飲み屋］　bar; pub; tavern; saloon; (cocktail) lounge

ナイトクラブ　night club

ディスコ　disco

カラオケ　karaoke bar [spot]

【衣類】

衣料品店　clothing store

呉服店　kimono shop

洋品店　sewing goods shop; dry goods store〔米〕(布地，糸などのほか衣類も扱う)

ブティック　boutique

紳士服店　tailor's

帽子店　hat shop; milliner's

靴　屋　shoe store; shoemaker's（製造・修理）

毛皮店　furrier's; fur salon

皮革製品店　leather goods store
宝石店　jewelry store
クリーニング屋　laundry (水洗い); dry cleaner's (ドライ専門)
【理容・美容・薬】
理髪店　barbershop; barber's (shop)〔英〕
美容院
beauty |shop [parlor, salon]; hair stylist's
化粧品店　cosmetic(s) shop
薬　屋　drugstore〔米〕(元来薬屋だったが，ほかの品物も売るようになった); pharmacy; chemist's〔英〕
【家具・日用品】
家具屋　furniture store
金物屋　hardware store (金物・刃物・大工道具)
文具店　stationery store; stationer's; office supply store (事務用品店)
日用品店　housewares store; home supplies [furnishings] store [shop]; cutlery shop (ナイフ・フォーク類)
電気屋　electric appliance store [shop〔英〕]
瀬戸物屋　china shop
雑貨店　general store [shop〔英〕]
【娯楽・教養・その他】
本　屋　bookstore; bookshop
古本屋　used-book store
美術材料店　art supplies shop [store]
毛糸屋　yarn shop
花　屋　flower shop; florist's
おもちゃ屋　toy shop
みやげ物店　gift shop; souvenir shop (観光客相手のみやげ物屋)
民芸品店　handicraft shop (handmade items)
大人のおもちゃの店　novelty shop; joke shop
骨董屋，古美術店
curiosity shop; antique shop
ペットショップ　pet shop
スポーツ用品店　sporting goods shop [store]; sportswear shop [store]
カメラ屋　camera store [shop]
写真屋　photo studio
ビデオ店　video store [shop]
オーディオ店　audio shop
コンピュータ販売店　computer store
ホームセンター
home supplies store, do-it-yourself store
新聞屋　newsstand (路上販売)
たばこ屋　tobacco shop
印刷屋　print shop (名刺・挨拶状などの簡易印刷，コピーサービス)
自動車販売店 car dealer's (showroom)
中古自動車販売店　used car dealer's
自動車用品店
automobile |supply [parts] shop [store]
自動車修理工場
garage; auto(mobile) repair shop
ガソリンスタンド　filling [service, gas] station
中古品店　resale shop [store]; thrift shop
質　屋　pawnshop; pawnbroker's
【大規模小売店舗】
デパート　department store
スーパー　supermarket
ディスカウントストア　discount store
コンビニエンスストア　convenience store
100円ショップ　98¢ (cent) store

みせる (見せる)

show; let one **see;** 展示する **exhibit; display**

1. 示す

あなたに見せる物がある。
I have something to show you.
朝刊を見せてください。
Let me see the morning paper.
あなたの新しい家を見せていただけますか。
Could {I have a look at / you show me} your new house?
何かほかの(品物)を見せてくださいませんか。これは少し大きすぎるので。
Could you show me [Let me see] some others, please? This is a bit too big.
彼は金庫の錠の開け方を見せてくれた。
He showed me how to unlock the safe.

2．診察してもらう

お医者さんには見せたのか。

Did you see the doctor?

赤ちゃん，お医者さんに見せたの？

Have you taken your baby to the doctor?

3．慣用表現

彼はまだ顔を見せない。

He hasn't {appeared. / shown up.〔*colloq.*〕}

あの子はお客様の前ではいつも得意になっていいところを見せようとする。

The child always shows off in front of company.

…みたい → らしい

1．例示

それは氷みたいに冷たかった。

It was cold like ice.

猫みたいに見えた。

It looked like a cat.

魚みたいな味だった。

It tasted like fish.

太鼓みたいに聞えた[な音がした]。

It sounded like a drum.

魚みたいなにおいがする。

It smells like fish.

絹みたいな手ざわりだった。

It felt like silk.

彼女は夢を見ているみたいな気がした。

She felt as if she were in a dream.

彼のすることなすことばかみたいだ。

He acts like an idiot.

2．類似

【そっくり】

犬みたいにくんくんかいだりするんじゃない。

Don't sniff like a dog.

目の前を通り過ぎて行った車の後部座席にいた女の子が洋子みたいだった。

The girl in the back seat of the car going past looked like Yoko.

それは何か鳥みたいなものだった。

It looked something like a bird.

【同様に】

もう私も若くないから今までみたいには働けない。

I'm not as young as I used to be. I can't work {the way / as} I used to.

彼は彼女にまるで初めて会ったみたいなそぶりをした。

He {acted [behaved] as if / pretended} he had never met her before.

私はまるでただみたいな値段でそれを買った。

I bought it for next to nothing.

3．推量

彼，今日はご機嫌がいいみたい。

It seems he's in a good mood today.

彼まだ怒っているみたい。私の顔を見ようとしないのよ。

He seems (to be) angry yet. He won't look at me.

みだす（乱す）・みだれる

1．乱す

throw into disorder [**confusion**]

disrupt《meeting / plan / trip》

disturb《peace / order》

【列・髪を】

列を乱さないで。

Don't fall out of line.

彼女は髪をふり乱して現れた。

She appeared with her hair disheveled.

〈注〉 disheveled はやや詩的な表現で，自分のなりふりを構わぬ状態について言う。unkempt は髪・服装すべて不潔なこと。風に吹かれて乱れているならば windblown,「くしゃくしゃ」ならば all messed up と言う。

【平静を】

別荘で静養中は訪問客に生活を乱されたくない。

I don't like to be disturbed by visitors while staying in my villa.

彼はその家族の平穏な生活を乱すには忍びなかった。

He couldn't bear to disturb the peace of the family.

【心を】

彼の厳しい言葉に彼女はひどく心を乱されたようだった。

His harsh words seemed to have disturbed [upset] her a great deal.

She seemed greatly disturbed [upset] by what he had said.

〈注〉 disturb は内面的に深い動揺を与えること。

【秩序を】disturb order

私たちは学生の制服ボイコット運動をあおって学校生活の秩序を乱したと非難された。

We were accused of disturbing school life by urging students not to wear school uniforms.

クーデターで国中がかき乱された［混乱に陥った］。

The coup d'état put the whole country into confusion.

〈注〉 「秩序を乱す」は秩序を作っている側の見方で権威主義的なニュアンスがある。be against public good を使うと「公共の福祉に反する」と国民の側から見た感じになる。

ex. Lobbyists often act against the public good.（ロビイストたちはしばしば公共の利益に反する行動をとることがある）

【足を乱す】

台風が地域住民の足を乱した。

Transportation in the region was disrupted by the typhoon.

2. 乱れる

be thrown [put] into disorder [confusion]
be disturbed [disrupted]

ただ窓が１枚破られていただけで家の中は何ひとつ乱されていなかった。

Except for one broken window, nothing in the house was disturbed.

当時は国中が乱れていた。

The country was in {chaos [a chaotic state] / a lawless state} in those days.

〈注〉 in chaos, in a chaotic state とは，秩序がまったくなく，人々がどうしたらよいかわからない状態。in a lawless state とは 犯罪の横行という chaotic state の一面を言ったもの。

その乱れた世では農民や下層階級が一番辛苦をなめることになった。

During those wild [stormy] times, peasants and people of the lower classes suffered most.

彼は世の中が道徳的に乱れていることを嘆いた。

He lamented that the world was morally corrupt.

〈注〉 morally corrupt とはかなりひどい道徳の腐敗，堕落を意味する。

彼は学校で落ちこぼれになってからはまったく乱れた生活をしている。

He's been leading a life of complete dissolution since he dropped out of school.

〈注〉 completely dissolute life とは，若者ならば仕事にも行かず悪い仲間に入り，親の金を盗み出して遊ぶような乱れた生活。disordered life は生活のパターンがくずれ，ぶらぶらといい加減な生活をすることを指す。

【髪・服など】be disheveled; be messed up

服は破れ，髪は乱れ，彼女はまったく取り乱した様子であった。

With her garments torn, her hair {unkempt, / disheveled, / messy,} she looked utterly distracted.

みち（道）

1. 道路

道路 **a road;** 通り **a highway; an avenue;**

a street; a thoroughfare; 小路 **a lane; a path, a track;** 通路 **a passage;** 峠道 **a mountain pass**

雨が降ると道がぬかるみになる。

The road gets muddy if it rains.

〈注〉「道が悪い」とは road (道路)がでこぼこなことで, way ではない。実際地面に作られた道路の路面を考える場合は road, それがどこに通じるかを主にした考え方であれば way, passage となる。

原っぱに斜めに人が歩いてできた小道がある。

There's a well-worn path across the field.

私は彼が博物館の方に向かって道を歩いているのを見た。

I saw him walking along the street toward the museum.

私は道を間違えて迷ってしまった。

I {took the wrong road / went the wrong way} and got lost.

〈注〉国道155号線は Route 155 /ruːt wʌn fifti faiv/ と呼ぶ。

2. 道筋

way

国会議事堂に行く道を教えていただけませんか。

{Could you tell [show] me the way / Can you tell me how to get} to the Diet Building?

群衆は救急車に道をあけて通した。

The crowd made way for the ambulance to get through.

警官がその車に向かってどいて道をあけろと合図した。

The policeman signaled the car to get out of the way.

3. 方面

２人は卒業後はそれぞれ別の道に進んだが生涯よい友だちであった。

They went their separate ways after graduation but remained good friends all their lives.

彼は今やその道の大家だ。

He is now an authority in that field [area].

〈注〉 cf. Ask him. That's his field [area, line].
（彼に聞いてごらん。彼の専門だから）

4. 方法

そうするより道がない。

We have no other choice.

この世で私たちが生き残る道はこれだけだ。

This is the only way for us to survive in this world.

みつける（見つける）・みつかる

〈注〉「見つける・見つかる」はそれぞれ他動詞, 自動詞でペアをなす動詞だが, 英語では see, be seen; find, be found; discover, be discovered のように能動・受動の対応で表される。

【求職】

やっと仕事が見つかった。

I've got a job at last.

彼はやっといい仕事が見つかったと言っていた。

He said he had found a good job at last.

どうも私に合う仕事が見つからない。

I can't find a job that suits me.

【探しもの】

(その家は)すぐ見つかりますよ。

You'll find it [the house] easily.

You can't miss it.

なくした指輪は見つかりましたか。

Did you find the ring you lost?

あの人の財布が見つからない。どこを探しても見つからない。

Her purse {is lost. We can't find it anywhere. / hasn't been found yet; it's still missing.}

〈注〉「見つける」は「探す」の意に転用されることがあり(「コンタクトを落したの。見つけてよ」など), その場合は look for で try to find (見つけようとする)である。また,「見つかる」は「見つける」ことができる (can find) の意をもつこともある。混同しないように。

【突き止める】
私は人込みの中で彼を見つけた。
I spotted him in the crowd.
彼はタイヤの空気の漏れる所を見つけた。
He found the leak in the tire.
我々は地図の中でグリーンランドを見つけた。
We located Greenland on the map.〔*formal*〕
【発覚】
彼はだれにも見つからずに裏口から抜け出した。
He slipped out of the back door {unnoticed. / without being seen.}
田中先生が彼のカンニングを見つけた。
Mr. Tanaka {caught / saw} him cheating.
警備員が彼の万引を見つけた。
A guard caught him shoplifting.
水中に微量の青酸化合物が見つかった[検出された]。
A small amount of cyanide was detected in the water.
陰謀は事前に見つかった。
The conspiracy was {uncovered / discovered / detected} beforehand.

みとめる（認める）

1．目にとめる

see; notice; find; catch sight of
島影のようなものを遠くに認めた。
We saw something like land in the distance.
濃霧で島影ひとつ認められなかった。
We could hardly make out anything in the dense fog.
そのときはまだアルツハイマー病の兆候が認められなかった。
At the time there were no symptoms of Alzheimer's disease.

2．認識する

recognize; appreciate
【値打ち】
彼の才能が認められるまでには何年もかかった。
Many years passed before his genius was recognized.
彼女の業績は広く世に認められた。
Her achievements {received / met with} world-wide recognition.
彼は生前は世に認められなかった。
He remained obscure in his lifetime.
彼らの作品の真価を認められるのは彼らと同じ高度の美的センスの持ち主だけである。
Only those gifted with the same sense of beauty can appreciate the true worth of their works.
【必要】
多くの人が大学教育の必要性を認めている。
Many people regard college education as necessary.

3．承認する

admit《a fact》**; accept**《a resignation》**;** 非を認める **confess**《one's error》**; acknowledge**《one's fault》**; own**《oneself guilty》
【過ち】
彼は自分の過ちを認めた。
He admitted that he had been wrong.
【許可する】approve of (the match)
父はその計画を認めていない。
Father does not approve of the plan.
私がみんなと一緒に行くことを彼はやっと認めた。
He at last gave me leave to go with them.
He at last let me go with them.
君の要求を認めるわけにはいかない。
I cannot grant your request.
I'm afraid I can't do that.

みなみ（南）→ ほうがく

みはらし（見晴らし）・みはらす → みえる

見晴らし　名　**a view; an extensive view; a landscape**

【見晴らす】

その部屋からはあたり一面の田園が見晴らせた。

From that room we {have / can get} a wonderful view of the countryside.

山頂からは周囲の畑や山々を見晴らすことができた。

From the hilltop we {can see / have a full view of} the surrounding fields and mountains.

【見晴らしがきく】

窓からは湾の見晴らしがきいた。

The window opens out upon the bay.

〈注〉「見晴らせる」の意味で command a view という表現があるが，堅すぎる表現である。

みまう（見舞う）・みまい

【病気】

私は病院にビルを見舞いに行った［見舞った］。

I {visited / went to see} Bill in hospital.

スミスさんがこの花を見舞いにくださった。

Miss Smith gave [sent] me these flowers to cheer me up.

彼が見舞いのカードをくれた。

He sent me a get-well greeting [card].

〈注〉「見舞う」の意で pay a sympathy visit という表現もあるが，堅いので親しい間では使わない。見舞いの品，花，カードなど，前後関係から見舞いとわかるのであれば，「見舞い」にあたる英語をつける必要はない。

【暑中見舞い】

私は彼に暑中見舞いを出した。

I wrote to him asking how he was doing in this hot season.

〈注〉欧米には暑中見舞いを出す習慣はない。

【火事見舞い】

あの人の家の近所に昨夜火事があったので，今朝見舞いの電話をした。

There was a fire in her neighborhood last night, so I phoned her this morning and asked if she and her family were all right.

〈注〉見舞いの習慣について
普通，欧米で病院に見舞いに行くのは親族や友人である。政界の人間同士，会社の上司への見舞いなど形式的なものもあるが，それらは主として見舞いのカードを送る。日本の場合のように他人に遅れまいと駆けつけるといったことは少ない。また，親しい人たちの間では留守を預かる家族に食事や手作りパイなどを運んだり，実際役に立つことをする。

【襲う】

昨夜青森は豪雨に見舞われた。

A heavy rain hit Aomori last night.

みる（見る）→ みえる

1. いろいろな見方

see　一般的な語。見える，見る（目に入る）

沖に漁船が 2,3 隻見えた。

I saw two or three fishing boats in the offing.

涙で目が曇り，彼女の顔がはっきり見えなかった。

Tears blinded my eyes, and I couldn't see her face clearly.

きのうトムを見た［に会った］。

I saw Tom yesterday.

彼女が私に向かってにっこりした（のを見た）。

I saw her smiling at me.

look at　静止したものを注視する（意識的に見る；see と look at の関係は hear（聞こえてくる）と listen to（意識的に聞く）の関係に対応する）

彼は足を止めて私を見た。

He stopped and looked at me.

have a look　よく見る

きれいなかばんですね。ちょっと見せてくださいませんか。

What a beautiful bag! Would you mind if I have a look at it?

give a look ちらりと見る

彼女は怒った顔で私を見た。

She gave me an angry look.

watch じっと注視する(特に動きを)

彼は庭に来る小鳥たちを見(てい)るのが好きだ。

He likes watching the birds that come to his garden.

keep an eye on 目を離さない(見張る; watch の一種)

彼から目を離さないように(警戒しなさい)。彼は危険人物だ。

We should keep an eye on him. He's dangerous.

子供から目を離さないで。迷子になるといけないから(警戒の意味はない)

Don't take your eyes off the child. She'll get lost.

glance ちらっと見る

彼は彼女をちらっと見ただけで，また仕事を続けた。

He only glanced at her and continued with his work.

steal a glance 気づかれないようにちらっと見る

彼女は彼をちらっと盗み見た。

She stole a glance at him.

gaze じっと見つめる

彼は彼女をじっとやさしく見つめた。

He gazed at her kindly.

stare あきれたようにじっと見つめる(不快な見方)

彼女は感心しないという面持ちで彼をじっと見た。

She stared at him disapprovingly.

find ... (形容詞)行ってみたら…していた

彼女が行ってみたら彼はよく眠っていた。

She found him sound asleep.

regard 見なす(＝look on《something》as)

彼女は日本で屈指のピアニストの1人と見られている。

She is regarded as one of the best pianists in Japan.

examine 詳しく見る，調べる

医師は彼をていねいに診て別にどこも悪くないと言った。

The doctor examined him thoroughly and said there was nothing wrong with him.

observe 観察する

その研究所の研究者はハツカネズミの習性を続けて見て[観察して]いる。

The researchers of that institute are observing the behavior of mice.

inspect 視察する(＝check out)

政府の役人が工場を見に[視察に]来る。

The government people are coming to inspect the factory.

view 眺める

遠くから見る[眺める]と私の家など山腹の赤い1点にすぎない。

Viewed from a distance, my house is only a red spot on the mountainside.

at the sight of ... …を見て

やぶからヘビがはい出て来るのを見て，彼女はきゃあっと叫んだ。

She screamed at the sight of a snake coming out of the bush.

to all appearances どう見ても

彼女はどこから見ても非の打ちどころのない女性だ。

She is to all appearances a perfect lady.

2. 慣用表現

彼は人を見る目がある。

He's a good judge of character.

あの人は絵[焼き物]を見る目がある。

She has an eye for paintings [pottery].

今に見ていろ。

See what I'll do.

それ見たことか[言わんこっちゃない]。

There, I told you so!

みわける（見分ける）

1．区別する

distinguish; tell A **from** B**; distinguish** A **from** B [**between** A **and** B]

双子の女の子がそっくりでどっちがどっちか見分けられない。

The twin sisters look so alike I can't tell { which is which. / one from the other. }

あなたは本真珠と人工真珠とを見分けられますか。

Can you tell a real pearl from an artificial one?

Can you distinguish { between a real pearl and / a real pearl from } an artificial one?

2．識別する

recognize

彼はすっかりとぼけて自分の息子も見分けられない［わからない］。

He's too senile to recognize his own son.

男の子たちはみんな制服を着ていたので，私は自分の息子も見分けられなかった。

Because the boys were all in uniforms I couldn't { recognize my son. / spot my son. }

〈注〉 recognize はある人や物をそのものであるとわかること。特に探している場合のことではない。spot は探していて多くのものの中から見つけること。次の２つの例文のニュアンスの違いを参考にしてほしい。

I can always { recognize (1) / spot (2) } my daughter in a crowd because she's very tall.

(1) どれが娘かわかる。

(2) 娘を探せる，娘を見つけられる。

みんしゅしゅぎ（民主主義）

democracy

【民主主義者】

a person with democratic ideas, democrat

【民主主義国家】 a democratic country

民主主義国家においては主権在民である。

In a democratic country sovereignty resides in the people.

cf.［米国］民主党　the Democratic Party; the Democrats; 民主党員　a Democrat

共和党　the Republican Party; the Republicans; 共和党員　a Republican

［日本］自由民主党　the Liberal Democratic Party; 略 the LDP; 自民党員　a member of the LDP, an LDP member

民主党　the Democratic Party of Japan

みんな（皆）・みな → すべて

1．みんな…である［する］（全部・肯定）

形 **all; every**

彼女は火事でみんななくしてしまった。

She lost all [everything] she had in the fire.

みんな楽しそうに見えた。

Everybody looked happy.

みんな出ていらっしゃい。踊りましょうよ。

Come on, everybody [all of you]. Let's dance.

【一括】

みんなで彼に会いに行こう。

Let's go to see him together.

【勘定】

みんなで［全部で］いくらになりますか。

How much do they come to in all [all together, altogether]?

〈注〉 上の例では áll togéther と altogéther は強勢が違うだけでここでは同じように使えるが，次のような文では all together と altogether の違いがわかる。

The choir couldn't quite manage to sing all together. 合唱はうまく声が合わなかった（全体がひとつにならなかった）

There were six of us altogether. 全員で（総計）6人であった（altogether＝all told）

みんなで女の子は10人でした。

There were ten girls { all told. / in all. / altogether. }

2. みんな[だれも]…しない（全否定）
みんな[全員，だれも]土地を売りたくなかった。
None of them wanted to sell the land.
10年前の今日あの人たちは出発したが，みんな[全員，だれも]戻って来なかった。
They started out ten years ago today, and nobody [none of them] returned.
〈注〉「みんな［だれも］…しない」と全員について否定するときは，上の例のように none や nobody を使い，次のように書いてはいけない。
×All of them [Everybody] didn't …
文法書には not all は部分否定になると書いてあるが，日本語で「みんなが…とは限らない」を逆から見て「…しない人もいる」が普通に使われる。英語でも部分否定は次の 3.のような形が多く使われる。

3. みんな…とはかぎらない（部分否定）
（…でない人もいる）
〈注〉「一部が…ない」と部分否定をする場合にその程度により下のような語を使い分ける。
彼のための募金に（みんな）賛成であった［なかった］。
All [All of them]
（みんな賛成であった）
Most of them
（大部分の人が賛成であった）
Some [Some of them]
（賛成する人もあった）
A few [A few of them]
（少数の人が賛成であった）
Few [Few of them]
（ほとんどの人が賛成しなかった）
None [None of them]
（だれも賛成しなかった）
agreed to raise money for him.
金持ちがみんな幸福とは限らない。
The rich are not always happy.

む

むかう（向かう）・むかって

1．正対する

【向かって右[左]】 on the right [left]

向かって右の人　the person on the right

向かって左から　(from) left to right

〈注〉 右・左は話者ないし見ている人の立場で言うので，特に断らなくても普通は「向かって右[左]」のことである。ただし on Mrs. Smith's right と言えば Smith 夫人から見た右側となる。

次のような写真の配置を説明するには

ⓐⓑⓒⓓ
ⓔⓕⓖⓗⓘⓙ

from the back left a, b, c, d は後列左から…。
from the front left e, f, g, h, … は前列左から…。
the girl on g's left（g の左の女の子）は h を指す。
ただし the girl to the left of g (as we are looking at them) は f を指す。

2．対立関係（物・人に向かって）

【風に】

少年は風に向かって走っていた。

The boy was running into [against] the wind.

【人に】

牧羊犬は泥棒に向かって猛然と襲いかかった。

The sheepdog attacked the thief furiously.

犬が突如私に向かって来た。

The dog suddenly turned upon me.

〈注〉 turn upon は「思いがけず向かってきた」の意。

ギャングは警官に向かって発砲した。

The gangster fired at the policeman.

【物に】

彼はもう3時間以上も机に向かっている。

He's been at his desk for more than three hours.

【向き合う】

私は小さなテーブルをはさんで，彼女と向き合って座った。

I sat opposite her
{ across a small table.
{ with a small table between us.

3．方向（…を目指して）

…に向かって出発する　start [leave] for …

…に向かって行く　make for …

(cf. …行きである　be bound for …)

彼は明日ニューヨークに向かって発つ。

He will leave for New York tomorrow.

〈注〉 「成田からニューヨーク行きに乗る」と言うつもりで，He will leave Narita for N. Y. とすると成田に住んでいるように聞える。出発地点として特に「成田から」と言いたいのならば leave [fly] from Narita のように言えばよい。

船はシンガポールに向かっていた。

The ship was making for Singapore.

汽船は南に向かって航行中だった。

The steamer was sailing { (to the) south. / southward.

台風はこちらに向かっている。

The typhoon is heading { straight for us. / this way.

暴れ馬は私の方に向かって直進してきた。

The wild horse ran straight for [at] me.

〈注〉 at と for の使い分け

【生物が主語の場合】

The child ran straight { at me. (1) / for me. (2)

（子供は私の方に向かってまっすぐ走って来た）

(1) run straight at《a person》とすると攻撃的な感じになる。前出の暴れ馬の文ならば，わざと突っ込んで来る感じになる。

(2) 一般に，run straight for《a person》は「人に助けを求めて来る」の意になる。

【無生物が主語の場合】

at も for も同じ。

ex. The hurricane is coming straight at [for] us.（ハリケーンが向かって来る）

目的語が場所のときは come straight for《a place》。

むかえる（迎える）

1. 人を

【出迎え】

加藤さんは家族を連れて，空港まで私を迎えに来てくださった。

Mr. Kato came to meet me at the airport with his family.

到着の時間を知らせてくだされば，空港まで迎えに行きます。

If you let me know { when you'll be arriving, / the time your plane gets in, } I'll { meet you at the airport. / be at the airport to meet you.

【応接】

皆さんは私を温かく迎えてくださった。

They welcomed me { warmly. / with open arms.

They gave me a warm welcome.

【呼んで来る】

御高名な田辺先生を講師にお迎えできましたことは私どもの誇りとするところであります。

It's our privilege to welcome Mr. Tanabe, the well-known lecturer.

彼らは佐藤夫妻を来賓として迎えた。

They invited Mr. and Mrs. Sato as honored guests.

【迎えに行く】

彼女はたった今，子供を迎えに保育園に行ったところです。

She's just gone to the nursery school to pick up her child.

【迎えにやる】

お医者さまを迎えにやりましょうか。

Shall I send for the doctor?

2. 時を

彼女は88歳の誕生日［米寿］を迎えようとしています。

She's going to celebrate her eighty-eighth birthday soon.

She will be eighty-eighth soon.

人々は皆，正月を迎える準備に忙しかった。

People were busy { making New Year preparations. / getting ready for the New Year's celebrations.

〈注〉 正月のための飾りやごちそうなどの用意という意味で for the New Year's celebrations とした。元日のためなら for New Year's Day である。

むく（向く）・むき・むける → ほうこう

1. 方向・方面

上［下］を向く　look up [down] (at)

前を向く　look ahead

後ろを向く　turn around

振り向く　look back

私の部屋は南向きです。

My room faces (the) south.

彼はまっすぐ前を向いたまま何も言わなかった。

He looked straight ahead and said nothing.

後ろを向いてごらん。背中に虫がついているようだ。

Turn around. I think there's a bug on your back.

彼は川の方に向いて歩いて行った。

He was walking toward the river.

汽船はブラジルに向けて出港した。

The steamer left for Brazil.

彼の皮肉たっぷりな言葉は私に向けられたものだった。

His cynical remarks were intended for me.

2. 適合する

彼はビジネスマンには向いていない。

He's not { { suited / cut out } to be a businessman. / cut out for business.

彼は学問に向いている。

He has { a natural bent / an aptitude } for study.

このタイプ(の商品)は万人向きだ。

This type suits all tastes.

ここの本は一般向きだ［専門家向きではない］。

These books are { for general readers. / not for specialists. }

3．比喩的表現

彼女は内心感心したが，そぶりに見せまいとそっぽを向いた。

She looked away [aside], pretending she wasn't impressed.

どうしたら子供たちの興味をもっと授業に向けることができるでしょうか。

How can we get the children more interested in classwork?

むく（剥く）

1．果物の皮

peel　指またはナイフではがすようにむく(タマネギ・ミカン・バナナなど)。

pare　ナイフでむく。

猿でも食べる前にバナナの皮をむく。

Even monkeys peel bananas before eating them.

私はリンゴの皮をあなたのように上手にむけない。

I can't pare apples as well as you (do).

2．堅い皮

樹皮をむく

debark a tree; strip (the) bark off a tree

穀物[豆]をむく　husk corn [peas]

〈注〉「クルミの殻を取り除く」は shell nuts と言う。

3．包み紙

キャンディの紙をむく

unwrap a candy

むくち（無口）

名 **reticence;** 形 **reticent**

彼は無口だ。

He { talks little. / doesn't talk much. }

彼女は無口な性格だ。

She is reticent (by nature).

She's the silent type.

むこう（向う）

1．反対側

【通りの】

通りの向う側のあの高いビルに部屋を借りて事務所にしています。

I rent an office in that tall building just across the street.

【川の】

彼は川の向う岸に(立って)いる人に大声で叫んでいた。

He was yelling to a man (standing) on the opposite side of the river.

【対向車線】

彼は前を走っていたバンを追い越そうとして向う側から来た車と衝突した。

He tried to pass the van ahead of him and collided with a car coming in the opposite direction.

【あちら】

向うへ行け！　Go away!

向うに見えるあの大きな煙突は何ですか。

What is that big chimney you see over there?

彼が向うへ着く頃までには雨は上がっているだろう。

By the time he gets there it will have stopped raining.

山の向う(の地域)は福井県だ。

The area beyond the mountains is { in Fukui prefecture. / part of Fukui prefecture. }

2．相手，先方

〈注〉日本語では方向で相手方を意味する「向う・こ

ちら・あなた・そなた」の類がある。これらは they, he, she, I, we, you などの人称代名詞で表現できる。

向うからけんかをしかけてきたんだ。

They [He, She] started the quarrel.

私もうちの者も結婚式はあまり型どおりの派手なのはやりたくないのだが，向うの家はやりたいようだ。

My family and I don't want to have a big, formal wedding, but my fiancé's family does.

僕たちは議論を始め，僕は自分が正しいと主張するし，向うは向うで自分が正しいと言い張った。

We began to argue and I insisted that I was right and he [she] insisted he [she] was right.

〈注〉 聞き手が「相手方」をよく知らない場合に the other party という言い方があるが，これは冷たくよそよそしい感じがするので，知り合いに関しては使わない方がよい。名前を言うか he, she, they を使う。

むし（虫）

insects（広義にはクモ，ダニなども含まれる）

虫の音　singing of crickets

虫食いの　moth-eaten

虫に食われた毛布　a moth-eaten blanket

虫の害を受けた　形 insect-infested

今年の稲作は虫害を受けている。

This year's rice plants are [crop is] infested with [by] insects.

〈注〉 虫害にやられたことを言うならば by, やられた状態に重点があれば with を用いる。

【虫刺され】

ハチに刺された。

A bee stung me.

I was stung by a bee.

昨夜眠っているうちに何か虫に刺された［食われた］。

{Some kind of bug / Something} bit me last night while I was sleeping.

【比喩的表現】

泣き虫　a crybaby

弱虫　a weakling

虫が知らせた。

I had a {premonition / foreboding} that it was coming.

君が寄付を頼みに行ったとき，彼はちょうど虫の居所が悪かったんだ。それでどなられたんだよ。

He happened to be in a bad mood when you asked him for a donation, so he yelled at you.

彼は虫の息だった。

He was {almost lifeless. / dying.}

なぜかあの人は虫が好かない。

I don't know why, but somehow I don't like her.

そりゃ虫がよすぎる。お菓子は食べたらなくなるもの。

That's asking too much. You cannot have your cake and eat it too.

彼はまったく虫がいいんだから。

He has a lot of {cheek / nerve} to ask that much.

〈注〉 cheek とは生意気，厚かましさの意。

《関連語》

変態　metamorphosis（*pl.* -ses）

幼虫　larva（*pl.* -vae）

さなぎ　pupa（*pl.* -ae, -s），chrysalis（*pl.* -lises）

（カイコなどの）繭　cocoon

羽化する　emerge

イモムシ　worm; 毛虫　caterpillar; カイコ　silkworm; ミミズ　earthworm, angleworm（釣りのえさ）

甲虫　bug

カブトムシ，クワガタムシなど　beetle

ゴキブリ（アブラムシ）　cockroach

テントウムシ　ladybird, ladybug

ゲンゴロウ，タガメなど　waterbug

ホタル　firefly, glowworm
チョウ　butterfly (*pl.* -lies); ガ　moth (*pl.* -s)
ブヨ　gnat, midge; アブ　horsefly
アリ　ant; シロアリ　termite
ミツバチ　bee; スズメバチ　wasp; (大型の)スズメバチ　hornet
バッタ，キリギリス　grasshopper; コオロギ　cricket; スズムシ　(bell) cricket; カマキリ　(praying) mantis; イナゴ　locust;
セミ　locust〔米〕, cicada
クモ　spider
ムカデ　centipede
【害虫】 harmful insects
(不潔な虫) ハエ　fly; ハエのウジ　maggot
ゴキブリ[アブラムシ]　cockroach
(吸血虫) カ　mosquito; ノミ　flea; シラミ　louse (*pl.* -lice); 南京虫　bedbug; ヒル　leech
(ダニ科総称) mite, マダニ　tick
(穀類を食べる害虫) ウジ　mealworm; 甲虫　mealbug; コクゾウムシ　weevil
(植物につく虫) アリマキ，アブラムシ　aphid; plant louse (*pl.* -lice); イナゴ　locust
(衣類・本につく虫) ガ　moth; シミ　silverfish
(家につく虫) シロアリ　termite
(人体に寄生する虫) 回虫　roundworm; サナダムシ　tapeworm
(病気を媒介する虫) disease-carrying insects
(毒虫) poisonous insects
(毒グモ) poisonous spider; タランチュラ　tarantula
【昆虫採集】 insect collecting; bug hunting
【虫よけ】 (体に塗るタイプ) insect repellent; (衣類の) a mothball
【殺虫剤】 an insecticide, a pesticide; (スプレー) insect spray

むし (無視)

【無視する】

知らんふりをする **ignore;** 軽視する **disregard;** …に注意を払わない **pay no attention to ...**

彼女は私がショックを受けた様子を見ても無視して話を続けた。

She {ignored / took no notice of} my shocked look and continued her story.

彼は医者の注意を無視して出張に行ってしまった。

He {ignored / disregarded} his doctor's advice and went on his business trip.

老人の意見は非常に賢明なこともあるのだから，無視するものではない。

We ought not to {disregard / ignore} old people's opinions, since they are sometimes very wise.

彼は無視できない人物だ。(ひとかどの人物だ)

He is a person to be reckoned with.

〈注〉 日本語の「ないがしろにする」にあたる英語は neglect である。
She felt she was being neglected by her husband.
(彼女は夫にないがしろにされている[妻らしい扱いを受けていない]と感じていた)

講演者と感謝の握手をしてコーヒーを１杯出してしまうと彼らは皆自分たちの問題を論じ始め，講演の先生の存在など完全に無視されてしまった。

After giving the speaker a handshake and a cup of coffee, they turned to discussing their affairs and completely neglected him.

【信号無視】

彼は停止信号を無視した。

He ignored the stop light.

彼は信号無視で罰金をとられた。

He was fined
{for going through the red light. (運転者の場合)
for crossing the street against the red light. (歩行者の場合)}

むじょう (無常)

この世はすべて無常である［移ろうものである］。

Everything in this world is transient.
Nothing stays unchanged in this world.
人生は無常だ。
Life is but an empty dream.
——Longfellow, *Psalm of Life*
〈注〉 transient=coming and going, not lasting（やがて過ぎ行く，一時的な）
ex. a transient sorrow（一時の悲しみ）

むずかしい（難しい）

1．困難な

暗くならないうちにそこに到着するのは難しい。

It'll be {hard / difficult} (for you) to / Maybe {you'll not be able to / you can't} get there before dark.

〈注〉 ×You are difficult [hard] to get there … とは言えない。

この段階から逆転するのは非常に難しい。
It's nearly impossible at this stage to turn the tables on the foe [enemy].

【やっかいな】

話が難しくなってしまった。
The discussion has become difficult.
〈注〉 a ticklish problem（難しい問題）のような言い方もあるが，これはたいして深刻な問題ではない。

【微妙な】

これは難しい問題だ。
This is a delicate question.
〈注〉 人間関係の問題などに使う。

2．不機嫌な

あの人は気難しい人だ。
He is a difficult person.
He is hard to please.
あの人は難しい人だが，付き合うコツを覚えてしまえばうまくやっていける。
He is hard to please, but once you find out what his sore spots are you can get along with him pretty easily.
私がボーイフレンドを家に連れて来たとき父は難しい顔をした。
My father looked sullen when I brought my boyfriend home.
私の結婚具体化という段階になったら父はさぞ気難しくなることだろう。
I could see he would be difficult when it came time to make marriage plans.
あのおじいさんはいつも難しい顔をしているから，あの人が孫をあやしてるところなんて想像できない。
The old man always looks so grave I cannot imagine him coaxing his grandchild to smile.
彼女は食べる物がたいへん難しい[食べ物の好みがうるさい]。
She is very particular about what she eats.
〈注〉 「…の難しさ」と難しさの内容をつけ加えるのに接続詞 that で文をつなぐのは無理。
×I knew the difficulty that we get on well with each other.（私たち２人がうまく折り合っていくのはとても難しいということがわかった）
○I found that it was difficult for us to get on well with each other.

むすぶ（結ぶ）・むすび

1．結わえる

（ひもなどを） **bind; tie; knot**

彼女はおさげに赤いリボンを結んだ。
She tied her braids with red ribbons.
その包みは（丈夫な）青いひもで結んであった。
The package {had blue string around it. / was bound with strong blue cord.}
日本の正式のお祝い用のし袋は紅白のちょう結びの水引きをかけたものだ。
A formal Japanese congratulation envelope has around it red and white strings gathered together and tied in a kind of bow.
彼はロープを結んで結び目を作った。
He {knotted / tied a knot in} the rope.

【口を結ぶ】
彼はずっと口を結んだままであった。

He kept his mouth shut all the while.

He didn't { once open his mouth. / say a word. }

2．連結する

link; connect

この道路は米原と福井を結んでいる。

This highway { links / connects } Maibara and Fukui.

点と点を番号順に結んでごらん。

Connect the dots in the order in which they are numbered.

Draw a line from one dot to another in the order they are numbered.

3．締結する

conclude

【条約】
これらの２国はいまだに平和条約を結んでいない。

These two countries haven't { concluded / signed } a peace treaty yet.

【同盟】
日本は1902年に英国と同盟を結んだ。

Japan { allied itself (1) / entered into an alliance (2) } with Britain in 1902.

〈注〉 (1) 広く使われる。
(2) 公式表現である〔*formal*〕。

【国交】
日本はまだ北朝鮮と正式な国交を結んでいない。

Japan hasn't yet established formal diplomatic relations with North Korea.

【契約】
彼はその会社と売買契約を結んだ。

He { made / signed / concluded〔*formal*〕 } a sales contract with that company.

4．結実する

bear fruit

彼女の努力が実を結んだ。

Her efforts { were rewarded. / bore fruit. }

彼の年来の夢のいくつかがようやく実を結ぶというところで彼は突然死んだ。

Some of his dreams { were nearly realized, / had almost come true, } when he suddenly died.

5．締めくくる

conclude

彼はスピーチの最後をジョークで結んだ。

He concluded his speech with a joke.

むだ（無駄）

1．無益

無駄である　**be useless; be no good; be in vain**

無駄になる　**come to nothing**

これ以上がんばっても無駄だ。

It's { no use making / useless to make } any more efforts.

彼を説き伏せようなんて無駄なことだ。

It's no good trying to persuade him. 〔*colloq.*〕

彼の努力はすべて無駄になった。

All his efforts { came to nothing. / were in vain. / proved fruitless. }

2．浪費

【時・金】
それは時間とお金の無駄だ。

It's a waste of time and money.

あの人は服に凝ってお金を全部無駄遣いしてしまう。まるでどぶにお金を捨てるようなものだ。

She wastes all her money on clothes. It's like throwing money (away) in the gutter [down the drain].

無駄な出費を省けば，収入の範囲内でやっていける。

If you cut down on unnecessary expenses, you could live within your means.

3．無駄口

無駄口ばかりきく[たたく]んじゃない。

Quit talking [chatting].

無駄話をやめて。

Be quiet.

Shut up.（静粛に）

無駄なことを言わない人

a person of few words (1)

佐藤氏は無駄なことを言わない。

Mr. Sato is concise. (2)

彼女は発言に無駄がない。

What she has to say is always relevant and succinct. (2)

〈注〉 (1)は発言回数が少ないこと。(2)は発言が簡潔で要点をついて無駄な部分がないこと。

だれかの言ったことがずばり的を射ているとき That hits the nail on the head. と言う。

また，Say what you mean and mean what you say.（よくわかるように言いなさい）は親が子供などによく言う言葉。

むちゅう（夢中）

1．忘我・熱中

【有頂天】

彼はうれしくて夢中だった。

He was beside himself with joy.

【熱中】

ジグソーパズル[小説]に夢中になっている

be absorbed in / be engrossed in〔強〕 / be caught up in / be wrapped up in〔informal〕 — a jigsaw puzzle / some novel

(be absorbed in, be engrossed in〔強〕; be caught up in, be wrapped up in 〔*informal*〕 + { a jigsaw puzzle / some novel })

〈注〉 be involved in は「（事件などに）かかわり合いになる」の意味だが「夢中になる」の意にも使われる。

He's deeply involved in the chess game right now.（彼は今チェスに夢中だ）

まさにその時夢中で対戦中である場合，または熱中状態が当分続く場合のどちらにも用いられる。

【熱愛】

彼女はあの映画スターに夢中だ。

She's mad [crazy] about that movie star.

あいつは会社の同僚に夢中だ。

He's lost his head over a coworker in his office.〔*informal*〕

【恍惚】

聴衆は彼の音楽に何もかも忘れて夢中で聴いた。

The audience was completely carried away by his music.

【集中】

彼は金もうけに夢中だ。

He is bent [intent] on making money.

〈注〉 He's committed to making money. とも言えるが，commit は意図を持って意識的に目的に向かって邁(まい)進することである。またこの語は主として社会的倫理的な目的や主義主張のために夢中になることを意味する。

ex. He committed himself to the cause of peace.（彼は平和運動に身をささげた）

be bent on, be intent on も目的に向かって夢中であることを意味する。

2．必死

彼は夢中で走った。

He ran for his life.

彼は夢中に泳いで岸まで泳ぎ着いた。

He swam desperately [frantically] to (the) shore.

〈注〉 desperately は「最後の力を振りしぼって，恐怖にかられて必死で」を意味し，frantically は「死にものぐるいで無茶苦茶に，パニック状態で」を意味する。

むなしい(空しい,虚しい)→むじょう,むだ

1. 甲斐がない

すべてはむなしい努力であった。

All our efforts { came to nothing.
were wasted [useless].

2. はかない

あの生か死かという経験をしてからは俗世の名誉欲，金銭欲などが皆むなしく見えるようになった。

After that life-and-death experience, all worldly desire for fame and money seemed vain to me.

人生はむなしい夢にすぎない。

Life's but a dream.

すべてむなしい。

All is vanity.

むね（胸）

1. 胸部

chest; breast; 女性の胸囲 **bust;** 乳房 **breasts**

胸焼け heartburn

彼女は立派な胸をしている。

She's full-busted.

胸のレントゲン写真を撮ってもらった。

I had a chest X-ray taken.

2. 心臓

heart

(興奮で)胸がどきどきした。

My heart beat fast with excitement.

3. 肺

彼は胸が悪い[肺結核だ]。

He has tuberculosis [TB].

4. 心

胸が躍った。

I was thrilled.

胸がいっぱいで何も言えなかった。

My heart was too full to say anything.

それは人の胸を打つ物語だ。

That is a moving story.

私は胸をなで下ろした。

I felt relieved.

I breathed a sigh of relief.〔*cliché*〕

私は彼の胸のうちを察することができる。

I can imagine how he must be feeling.

そのことが何か月も私の胸につかえていたのです。あなたに何もかもお話ししてすっきりしました。

That has bothered me for months. I feel good after talking to you all.

そんなもの見るだけで胸が悪くなる。

The mere sight of it makes me sick.

もっと胸を張って生きていけ。

Hold { up your head.（プライドを持て）
your head high.

Have more self-confidence.（自信を持て）

〈注〉 よく似た表現の Keep your chin up. は，Don't be so sad and discouraged.（悲しそうな顔をするな，元気を出せ）の意。場合によっては上の Hold up your head. と同義に使われる。

むり（無理）

1. 過度の

over-; excessive; too ～

彼女は無理をして病気になってしまった。

She overworked and became ill.

どうぞご無理をなさらないように。

Take care } not to { overwork〔米〕.
Try } overwork yourself〔英〕.

〈注〉 Take it easy.（気楽にやってください）も同じことを逆から言っていることになる。

(神経の細い)彼女には無理だった。

It put a great strain on her nerves.

過度の緊張で無理がたたり彼女は早世した。

Stress caused her ⌊to die young [an early death].

2. 不可能な

impossible; beyond one's **power**

彼の(高校の)成績ではあの大学は無理だ。

His high school grades are not good enough for that university.

彼にあの仕事は無理だ。

He is not equal to the task.

そんな大金をつくるのは無理だ。

I can't possibly make ｝
It's impossible for me to make ｝ such a large amount of money.

〈注〉 同じ趣旨のことを次のようにも言える。

Making such a large amount of money! That's beyond my wildest dreams.

皆の気に入るようにするのはどだい無理だ。

It's impossible to satisfy everyone.

そんな夢の実現は(彼には)とても無理だ。

[夢の性質上]

It's impossible to realize this dream.

This dream cannot be realized.

[能力不足]

It's impossible for him to realize his dream.

He'll never be able to do it.

3. 理に合わない

unreasonable

それは無理な要求だ。そんなお金はない。

That's asking [expecting] too much. We can't afford it.

「私一人の部屋が欲しい」「無理を言うな」。

"I'd like to have a room of my own." "You ask too much."

無理を言うんじゃない。

Don't be unreasonable.

彼は無理なことを要求した。

He made an unreasonable request [demand].

彼が拒否するのも無理もない。

He has good reason to refuse.

彼が腹を立てるのも無理もない。

It's {no wonder / natural} (that) {he should get / he got} angry.

4. 強制

無理に…させる **force**

無理に **by force; against** one's **will**

彼は無理にドアを押し開けた。

He forced the door open.

彼は無理に人をかき分けて通った。

He forced his way through the crowd.

彼女はいやがる子供を無理に学校に連れて行った。

She took her child {to school {by force. / against the child's will.} / bodily to school.}

彼は無理にやめさせられた。

He was forced to resign.

無理に酒を勧めるのはばかげている。

It's absurd to force people to drink sake against their will.

彼女はにっこりしたが，無理な笑いだった。

She smiled but it was a forced smile.

め

め（目，眼）

eye; eyes; an eye

1．目

あの子はきれいな青い目をしている。

She has beautiful blue eyes.

東洋人風の目の男の子

a boy with Asian eyes

〈注〉◆ slanted eyes（つり目）はアジア人の特徴（Asian features）と考えられている。目の描写としてはOK だが，米国では人種差別につながるおそれがある。アーモンド型の目 almond-shaped eyes とも言われる。

◆いわゆる「一重まぶた，二重まぶた」は英語にならない。欧米人の眼にはその区別がないので表す言葉もない。強いて言えば single fold [double fold] eyelids とでも言う。

その子は目に涙をためてじっと彼を見た。

She stared at him with tears in her eyes.

彼は目を開け[閉じ]たままベッドに寝ていた。

He lay in bed with his eyes open [closed].

【視線・まなざし】

女の子は縫いものの手元から目を上げた。

The girl looked up from her sewing.

彼は当惑して目をそらした。

He {looked aside / averted his eyes} out of embarrassment.

女の子は目を伏せたまま立っていた。

The girl stood with her eyes cast down.

女の子はまっすぐに彼の目を見た。

The girl looked straight into his eyes.

【目が合う】

2人の目が合ったので，彼はにっこりした。

He smiled, his eyes meeting hers.

【目のやり場】

私は目のやり場に困った。

I didn't know where to look.

【目を離す】

ちょっとの間も子供からは目が離せない。(危くて)

You can't take your eyes off a child for a minute.

彼はスクリーンから目を離すことができなかった。

He couldn't take his eyes from the screen.

彼から目を離さないようにする方がよい。(危険人物だから)

We'd better keep an eye on him.

【疑いの目】

人々は私を疑いの目で見た。

They eyed me with suspicion.

2．視力

【目が見える[見えない]】

猫は暗がりでも目が見える。

Cats can see in the dark.

彼は5歳のとき目が見えなくなった。

He {lost his eyesight / became blind} when he was five.

彼は右目が見えない。

He is blind in his right eye.

【目がくらむ】

対向車のライトで目がくらみ，ドライバーはどこで曲るのか見えなかった。

The lights of the oncoming cars were so bright that the driver couldn't see where to turn.

映画館から日の当る通りに一歩出た途端，目がくらんだ。

I was dazzled the moment I stepped into the sunny street from the theater.

【目を凝らす】

彼女は暗がりで目を凝らしそれがテッドだとわかった。

She strained to see in the dark and found out it was Ted.

3．慣用表現

布の織り目　texture

編み物の目　a stitch

【見る目】

ものを見る目

an expert eye; a critical eye; an unerring eye

彼は美術品を見る目がある。

He has an eye for works of art.

彼は人を見る目がある。

He is { a good judge of character. / always right in his judgments about people. }

【見た目】

これは見た目にはたいへん美しいがあまり役に立たない。

This thing is very beautiful to look at but not very useful.

【ひどい目にあう】

私はひどい目にあった。

I had a bitter experience.

【…に目がない】

彼女はアイスクリームには目がない。

She has a weakness for ice cream.

【目を覚ます】

彼女は今朝は早く目を覚ました。

She woke early this morning.

牛乳配達が来たとき彼はもう目が覚めていた。

He was awake when the milkman came.

【目を通す】

編集長は原稿にさっと目を通した。

The editor-in-chief { took a look at / glanced over } the draft.

〈注〉 glance over はどんな出来かさっと目を通すこと。

スミス先生に論文に不自然な表現がない[のまとめ方が適切]かどうか，目を通してくださるようお願いした。

I asked Mr. Smith to { take a look at / check (over) } my paper for { unnatural expressions. / organization. }

うちの父は朝食をとりながら，朝刊にざっと目を通す。

My father scans the morning paper at the breakfast table.

〈注〉 scan とはこの場合ごく軽くざっと目を通すこと。よく似た表現に look over があるが，この方がもう少し注意をして見ること。

米語では morning paper に the が必要。

【目の前で】

その子供はまさに私の目の前で車にはねられた。

The child was hit by a car right in front of my eyes.

大きな猫が私の目の前にでんと座って毛づくろいをしていた。

A big cat sat preening right in front of me.

めいめい（銘銘）

どの子もめいめい[思い思い]のちょっとしたプレゼントをビルに持って行った。

Each { child / of the children } took some small present for Bill.

もしめいめいが好き勝手なことをしたら，秩序なんてなくなってしまう。

If everybody { does as they please, / tries to have their own way, } there will be no order.

〈注〉 every～ は単数扱いであるが，he / she の男女差別を避けるため they, their で受けるのが普通になってきている。次の表現は慣用句。

人にはめいめい好き嫌いがある。

Everyone has his own likes and dislikes.

Each to his own.

To each his own.

〈注〉 Each person has his own likes ... とすると一般論にも，また今話題になっている数人についてのことにもなる。

めいめい番号札を１枚取って席に着いてください。

Each of you take one number and then sit down, please.

この箱にキャンディーが入っています。めいめい５個ずつです。

Here's a box of candies. There are five pieces {each. / for each child.}

〈注〉「５個ずつ取って回してください」は Take five and hand them on.

私はめいめいに意見を聞いて回った。

I asked their opinions individually.

めいろう（明朗）→ ほがらか

1．朗らかな

cheerful

明朗な人

a cheerful [bright, sunny] person

a person of sunny disposition〔*literary*〕

明朗な人がまわりにいるのは愉快なことだ。

A person of bright temperament is a delight to be around.

2．不正のない

明朗な政治　clean [honest] politics

組織を改革し，すべてをオープンで明朗にしよう。

Reform the organization so that everything will be open and aboveboard.

〈注〉everything とは具体的には選挙や会計などを指す。

めいわく（迷惑）

1．迷惑をかける

（面倒を）**cause** [**give**]《a person》**trouble**

（不便・負担を）動 **bother; disturb**

彼はいつも酔っ払って人に迷惑をかけている。

He's always getting drunk and disturbing people.

【陳謝】

ご迷惑をおかけして申し訳ございません。

I'm sorry I've {put you to / given [caused] you} so much trouble.

〈注〉謝るときは相手に直接言うのであるから目的語は you である。もし him が目的語であれば「彼に迷惑をかけて悪かったと思っている」と反省している文になり陳謝はではなくなる。

I'm sorry to trouble you. は謝るというより何かを頼むときに使う表現。

【負担・不便】

私はだれにも迷惑をかけたくない。

I don't want to {trouble anyone. / make myself a nuisance. / make a nuisance of myself.}

何をするにしても人に迷惑をかけないようにしなさい。

Whatever you do, try not to {give anyone trouble. / inconvenience other people.}

まったく迷惑千万だ。

What a nuisance!

How annoying!

近所の猫には迷惑している。

We are {annoyed / irked} by the neighbor's cats.

The neighbor's cats bother us.

騒音でたいへん迷惑している。

The noise annoys us a great deal.

2．丁寧な表現

もしご迷惑でなければ，拝借したご本をご自宅に送らせていただきたいと存じます。

If it isn't inconvenient for you, I'd like to send the books I borrowed to your house.

〈注〉「ご迷惑でなければ」という日本語は丁寧で形式ばった言い方なので上の英文とほぼ釣り合う。しかし普通に都合を尋ねるには次のように言う。

Would it be convenient for you to …?

→つごう

めでたい

1. 喜ばしい

desirable; satisfactory; worthy to be congratulated

めでたい知らせ　good news

彼が間もなく90歳の誕生日を迎えることになるとは，(まったく)めでたいことだ。

It's { (really) { great / wonderful } / a matter for congratulation〔*formal*〕} that he will soon celebrate his ninetieth birthday.

2. 祝いの言葉

おめでとう　Congratulations!

お誕生日おめでとう(ございます)。

Happy Birthday!

Many happy returns of the day.〔*formal*〕

新年おめでとう。

(A) Happy New Year!

〈注〉 口頭で言うときは a をつけない。

【物語の結末 (a happy ending)】

そこで王子様と王女様は結婚しましたとさ。めでたし，めでたし。

And so the prince and the princess married, and they lived happily ever after.

めんきょ (免許)

a license〔米〕**; a licence**〔英〕

弁護士の免許　a lawyer's license

医師免許　a medical license

不動産業者の免許

a broker's [real estate (agent's)] license

【運転免許】

彼はまだ先週運転免許を取ったばかりだ。

He got (obtained) his { driver's license〔米〕/ driving licence〔英〕} only last week.

【教員免許】

彼女は教員免許を取るためにもう1年勉強しなければならない。

She has to study another year to get her teaching certificate.

【免許停止[取り消し]】

彼は1か月の免許停止[免停]を食らった。

His license was suspended for a month.

彼は免許取り消しになった。

He had his license revoked.

彼女は無免許運転[免許証不携帯]で罰金を取られた。

She was fined for driving without a license [not having her license with her].

〈注〉 license は「免許」「免許証」両方の意味に用いられる。

めんどう(面倒) → こまる，やっかい

1. 手間・骨折り

自炊なんて面倒だ。

It's troublesome to have to cook for myself.

【面倒をかける】

ご面倒をおかけしてすみませんが…していただけませんか。

I'm sorry to { trouble [bother] you, / put you to the trouble, / cause you so much trouble, } but could you ...?

ご面倒をおかけしてすみませんでした。

I'm sorry to have caused [given] you so much trouble.

【面倒を省く】

それでずいぶん面倒が省ける。

That would save us a great deal of trouble.

2. 困難・いざこざ

《類義語》

「面倒なこと」の同義語としては次のような語がある。

difficulty　やっかいだが比較的小さい問題。

trouble [名]　困った気持ちを強調。いくつかの決り文句に使われる。次のような決り文句以外では trouble を名詞として使用するのは避ける方がよい。[動] trouble は悩ます，困らせる。

be in trouble（面倒を起して困っている）
get into trouble（面倒なことになる）
cause [give] a person trouble（人に面倒をかける，a trouble とはしない）
There's [I see] trouble ahead.（面倒なことになるぞ）
He is having some trouble with math. [Math is giving him trouble.]（彼は数学で困っている）
Leave your troubles at home.（個人的な問題を持ち込むな）
trouble と **troublesome** の比較
Small jobs are often troublesome.（細々した仕事は面倒くさいものだ）
troublesome は細々としたことについて使われ，trouble は大きなことについて使われる。
problem　面倒のもとである状況に重点。
Pollution is a big problem in a city.（都会では公害が面倒な問題だ）
problem は可算名詞であり，具体的である。
delicate matter　感情的な面倒さ。

こいつは面倒な仕事だ。
This is a difficult job.
事が面倒になってきた。
Things are becoming complicated.
彼はいつも事を面倒にする。
He always complicates things.
連中のことは放っておけよ。面倒に巻き込まれるだけだから。
Leave them alone. You'll only get involved in their problems.
〈注〉 problem は具体的だが，trouble は抽象的であり，英語では具体的に面倒の内容を述べるのが普通である。

3．世話
彼女は夫の年老いた両親の面倒を見ている。
She {takes care of / looks after} her husband's aged parents.

めんどうくさい(面倒臭い)→ めんどう

面倒くさい　**troublesome**（面倒で腹立たしく，苦になる）
面倒くさい仕事だよ。
It's a troublesome task.
I found it {very troublesome. / a great bother.}
(毎日のおきまりの仕事が）面倒くさくなった。
I'm tired of doing chores.
ああ，雨が降り出した。出かけるのが面倒くさくなった。
It has started raining; what a {bother / nuisance} (that) I have to go out!
ああ面倒くさーい！
It's too much bother!
Oh, what a bother!
面倒くさい，いやだよ！
Don't bother me!
面倒くさいな。
(It's) troublesome.
面倒くさい，今は動きたくないよ。
I'm feeling lazy now.
I don't feel like it. I'm lazy now.
〈注〉 頼まれたがやりたくないとき
Surely you don't really mean that, do you?（それ本気なの）
You must be kidding.（冗談でしょ）
などと言うこともある。

も

も

1. 並列

「ああ，おなかがへった」「私も」。

"I'm hungry." { "So am I." / "Me, too."

「おなかはすいていない」「私も」。

"I'm not hungry." { "Neither am I." / "Nor am I." 〔*literary*〕 / "I'm not, either."

君が行くなら，僕も行く。

I go if you go.

君が行かないなら，僕も行かない。

I won't go unless you go.

昨夜はジョーが来ていた。君もいたの，リディア？

Joe was there last night. Were you { also there, / there, too, } Lydia?

ジョーもリディアも来ていた。

Both Joe and Lydia were there.

ジョーもリディアも来ていなかった。

Neither Joe nor Lydia was there.

彼はフランス語もドイツ語も話せる。

He can speak both French and German.

私はフランス語もドイツ語も話せない。

I can't speak { French or German. / either French or German.

I can speak neither French nor German.

〈注〉 not either ... or ... の方が一般的。Can you ...? と聞かれて can ... neither ... nor ... の形で答えることはよくあるが，自分でただ述べる形としてはは多少形式ばった感じになる。

買うのは別に今日でも明日でも構わない。

I can buy that either today or tomorrow.

私はここにじっとしていることも，行ってしまうこともできない。

I can't stay here, but I can't leave either.

〈注〉 上の文は堅い言い方であるが，特に強調するためにこの形を話しことばで使うこともある。「並列」の too を使った，次のような諺がある。

You can't have your cake and eat it, too.

（お菓子は食べたらなくなるもの。食べたいし，なくなるのはいや，というのは無理である）

彼は子供たちの先生であり，友だちでもあった。

He was a friend as well as a teacher to the children. (1)

He was not only a teacher but also a friend to the children. (2)

He was a teacher and a friend to the children. (3)

〈注〉 上記 (1) (2) (3) の異同について

(1) a friend as well as a teacher（友だちであったことを強調）

(2) not only a teacher but also a friend （(1)より弱いが友だちの方に重点）

(3) a teacher and a friend（先生と友だち共に同じ重み）

【…する人もあり…する人もあり】

ステーキが中までよく焼けている方が好きな人も，中くらいが好きな人も，生が好きな人もいる。

Some like their steak well-done, some medium, and others rare.

【…も連れて行く】

僕も行きたい。連れて行って。

I want to go, too.

Let me go, too.

Take me with you.

弟が僕も連れて行ってとせがんだ。

My little brother { wanted us to let him go with us. / insisted that we let him go with us. / pleaded with us to let him go too.

母さんが私に弟も連れて行ってやりなさいと言った。

My mother told me to take my brother with me.

2. 強調

〈注〉 通常イントネーションと強勢で気持ちを表す。

この真珠のネックレスは50万円もした。

This pearl necklace cost 500,000 [a whole 500,000] yen.

彼には子供が７人もいる。

He has seven children in all [all together].

彼女は彼が帰るまで５年間も待った。

She had to wait for five long years before he came back.

彼は「さよなら」も言わずに行ってしまった。

He went away without { even saying good-by. / so much as a good-by. }

私はまだ１ページも読んでいない。

I haven't { even read a page of it. / read even a page. }

2,3か月もすれば何もかも忘れてしまうでしょう。

She will forget all about it in a few months.

そのことは何も覚えていません。

I don't remember anything about it.

あの人たちは新築の家に１億円も金をかけたとか。

Believe it or not, they spent no less than 100 million yen on their new house.

cf. 結婚式をたった10万円ですませた。

Believe it or not, they spent no more than 100,000 yen on their wedding.

〈注〉「…も」の意味で as much [many] as を使うよりも，むしろ音調で驚きを表す方が自然である。as much [many] as は上限を，no less than は下限を表し，文脈によっては「…も」と驚きを表す（上の例参照）。しかし表現そのものには，驚きを表す含みはない。

新居にかけたお金は…円を下らない。

They spent no less than … yen on their new house.

彼には兄弟が10人はいる。（11人かもしれない）

He has no fewer than ten brothers.

もう

1．まもなく

もうすぐ春です。

It will be spring before long.

バスはもう来るでしょう。

The bus will come soon.

2．もはや，すでに

もう帰らなくちゃ。

We must be going home now.

これらの服はもう流行遅れだ。

These dresses are out of fashion now.

もう暗くなりかかっている。

It's getting dark already.

宿題はもう終ったの？

Have you finished your homework yet? (1)

Have you finished your homework already? (2)

〈注〉(2)は「もう終ってしまったの」と驚いている場合，(1)は含意なくただ尋ねる場合である。

もう宿題はやってしまった。

I've already finished it.

お客様はもうずっと前に着かれて応接室で待っておられます。

He arrived a good while ago and is waiting for you in the reception room.

もう子供たちは寝る時間だ。

It's time { the children go [went] to bed. / for the children to go to bed. }

〈注〉It's time … の構文では次に仮定法過去（went）を使った文がくるのが慣用的な言い方であったが，現在では go の形も聞かれる。for … to 不定詞の形を使うのが無難である。

もう子供じゃないんだからこのくらいのことはわかるはずだ。

You are old enough to understand this.

You aren't a child any more [longer].

私たちも若くて元気だったが，それももうずっと昔の話だ。

We were young and happy, but it was such a long time ago.

彼女はもう今ごろは家に着いているだろう。

She may be home by now.

明日の今ごろはもうパリに着いてます。

I will have arrived in Paris by this time tomorrow.

【もう…ない】
彼の彼女への愛情はもう冷めていた。
He didn't love her any longer.
〈注〉◆×He didn't already love her. は誤り。
◆私はもう我慢ができなかった。
I couldn't bear [stand] it any longer. (1)
I could bear [stand] it no longer. 〔*literary*〕(2)
一般的に言って(1)のように動詞を打ち消す方が話し言葉では普通。(2)のように副詞を打ち消すのは文語である。

3. さらに，それ以上
お茶をもう１杯いかがですか。
Would you like another cup of tea?
もう少しお金がいる。
I need a little more money.
君はもう10分早く起きなきゃだめだ。
You must get up ten minutes earlier.
もうあと10ページばかり読まなければならない。
I have to read ten more pages.
彼はあともう１週間留守になります。
He'll be away another week.
ああ，もう10年若かったらなあ。
I wish I were ten years younger.
もう一度言ってみてください。
Say that {once more, / again,} please.
彼には息子が２人あって，１人は大学生，もう１人は彼の事務所で働いている。
He has two sons, one a college student and the other working in his office.
何か別のをもうひとつ見せてください。
Show me another, please.
私はチョコレートを３つ買ったの。ひとつはアンナに，ひとつはメグに，もうひとつは私の分。
I bought three packages of chocolate, one for Anna, one for Meg and one for myself.
〈注〉「もうひとつ」と言っても，たくさんの中のもうひとつは another, ふたつの中の「もうひとつ」は the other である。

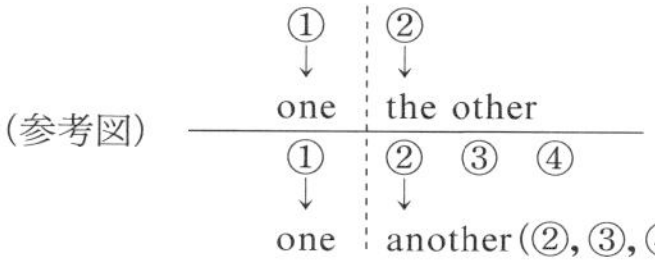

②③④まとめて the others
①～④それぞれについては次のように言える。
the first one, the second one, the third one, the fourth [last] one
不特定多数の中の「あるもの」は some,「その他」は the others または the rest と言う。

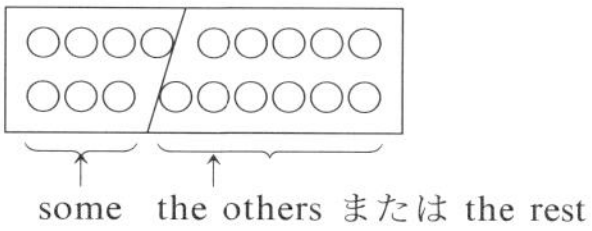

もうける(儲ける)・もうかる・もうけ

1. 利益を得る
profit (by); make a profit (from); make [earn] money
大もうけする
make a large [huge] profit
彼は町にある自分の店を売ってうんともうけた。
He has made {a lot of / good} money by selling his store in town.
戦後の2,3年間は闇商売でひともうけした。
For a few years after the war he earned a lot of money on the black market.
彼は大売り出しでひともうけした。
The sale netted him a lot of money.
連中は5000万円もうけた。
They made fifty million yen.
【もうからない】
こんなに飼料が値上がりしては酪農は全然もうからない。
Dairy farming doesn't {pay / bring much profit} now that the cost of feed has risen so much.
その種の仕事はもうからない。
There's no money in that kind of business.

この値段じゃもうけはゼロですよ。(お客が値切ろうとしているのに対し店主が答えて)

This price leaves me no profit (margin). I'll make no profit.

もともともうけはわずかなものだ。

The mark-up is already very small.

この商品のもうけはいくらだ？

{How much profit do you make / What's the mark-up} on this item?

〈注〉 mark-up とは retail price (小売値) から wholesale price (卸値) を引いたもので，日本で言うマージンのこと。profit とは人件費，家賃・運送費などの諸経費をさらに引いたあとの純益のこと。

【もうけが薄い】

もうけの薄い商売　a low-profit business

鉄鋼業のもうけは年々薄くなってきている。

Profit margins have been shrinking in the steel industry.

あの会社ではここ 2, 3 年，もうけを薄く抑えて薄利多売をねらっている。

That company has kept the profit margin low for a few years to attract customers.

2. 得をする

この買物はもうけものだった。

It's a bargain.

このウールのコートで 1 万円もうかった。(得な買物だった)

I've saved 10,000 yen on this wool coat.

〈注〉 bargain とは 40～50% off 以上，ときに 70% off もあるたいへんお買い得の値段の場合である。

もうける (設ける)

1. 用意する (臨時)

湯茶の接待所を設ける (学会・研究会など)

have [provide] a hospitality area

喫煙所を設ける　provide a smoking room

救護所を設ける (競技会・マラソンなどで)

set up a tent for first-aid [medical aid]

スミス氏のために一席設けた。

They held [gave] a banquet in honor of Mr. Smith.

2. 設置する (恒久的)

細則を設ける

establish bylaws 〔*official*〕

set up bylaws 〔*informal*〕

あの病院では慢性疾患で就学できない児童のために特別学級を設けている。

Special classes have been {set up / started} in that hospital for the children who cannot attend school because of chronic diseases.

資金集めのための委員会を設けることになった。

It was decided to {form / establish} a committee to manage a fund-raising campaign.

会社は長崎に事務所[支店]を設けることにした。

That company is going to {set up / establish} an office [a branch] in Nagasaki.

もうしこむ (申し込む)・もうしこみ

1. 申し出る

我々はその決定について県に抗議を申し込んだ。

We protested to the prefectural government about the decision.

多くの人々がその子供のために献血を申し込んできた。

Many people offered to donate blood for the child.

彼女は彼の結婚の申し込みをその場で受け入れた[断った]。

She accepted [declined] his marriage proposal on the spot.

コロラド大学が我々に親善試合を申し込んできた。

The University of Colorado challenged us to a friendly match.

2. 応募する

申し込み期限

the time limit [deadline] (for an application)

申し込み[購読・寄付の予約]を受付ける

accept [receive] an application [a subscription]

申し込み受付は2月1日からです。

Applications will be accepted starting February 1st.

〈注〉 accept と receive の比較
receive は単に受け取ること。受け取ってどうするかには触れない。accept は積極的に同意して受け取る，受け入れること。

本人が来社して申し込んでください。

Apply in person.

手紙(文書)か電話で申し込んでください。

Apply by letter or telephone.

申し込みは手紙にかぎる。

Application by letter only.

会報は申し込み順に先着5000名様に送付します。

The bulletin will be sent to the first 5,000 applicants.

【講座】

セミナー参加希望者は今月末までに申し込んでください。

Those who wish [desire] to take part in the seminar should register their names by the end of this month.

シンポジウム開催の新聞広告を出したが申し込みが少なくて中止になった。

Although it was advertised in newspapers, there weren't enough applicants to hold the symposium.

【求職】

たった1人の求人に30名もの申し込みがあった。

Nearly thirty people applied for one position.

【助成金】

我々は市の助成金を申し込んだ。

We applied to the municipal authorities for financial help.

〈注〉 apply は職業，免許，試験(jobs, licenses, important tests) などに申し込む場合に使われる。何らかの申し込み用紙に書き込んで，申し込むという含みがある。
ex. apply for a job at Sony (ソニーに求職の申し込みをする)

【依頼】

パンフレットはお申し込みがあれば無料で送ります。

Pamphlets will be sent free on request.

詳細資料は…に直接[手紙で/電話で]申し込んでください。

For further information,
please {contact / write to / telephone} ....

【懸賞】

「ハワイへの夢の旅」が当ります！　さあ今すぐ葉書にあなたの住所・氏名・年齢・性別・職業をご記入の上，コロラド州デンバーのXYZテレビまで申し込みましょう。

To win a dream trip to Hawaii, send a postcard now with your name and address, age, sex and your job to channel XYZ TV, Denver, Colorado.

【注文】

(テレビ・雑誌を通じての通信販売)

このすばらしいスーツがあなたのものに。お申し込みは電話 052-12-3456 または葉書で名古屋市中村区問屋町1-11山田屋までどうぞ。

You can order this fine suit by calling 052-12-3456 or sending a postcard to Yamadaya, 1-11 Tonyamachi, Nakamuraku, Nagoya.

【購読】

ジャパン・タイムズの購読申し込みをしたいのですが。

I'd like to subscribe to *The Japan Times*.

【寄付】 →きふ

同窓会の基金募集に申し込んでください。

Please subscribe [donate] to the alumni fund.

【予約】
次の日曜日に予約を申し込みたいのですが。
I'd like to make a reservation for next Sunday.

もうしでる（申し出る）

ボランティア **offer; volunteer;** 提案する **propose**
たくさんの人が独り暮しの老人の援助を申し出た。
Many people volunteered to help the old people living alone.
【届け出る】
遺失物にお心当りの方は受付まで申し出てください。
Those who believe they have a claim on the lost article should report to the desk.
税金について疑義のある方は税務所に申し出てください。
If you have any question about your tax, please contact the tax office.
異議があれば申し出てください。
Inform [Tell] us if you have any objections.
学年末試験に欠席した者は，欠席理由を添えて教務課に申し出ること。
Those who were absent from the final examination must report to the office, giving the reason for their absence.

もし → ねえ

もじ（文字）

文字 **a letter;** 一体系としての文字 **a character;** 筆跡 **a hand, handwriting**
ギリシア文字
the Greek alphabet; Greek letters
ローマ文字
the Roman alphabet cf. ローマ字 *romaji*
音声記号 phonetic alphabet
アラビア数字 Arabic numbers
漢字 Chinese characters; Chinese ideograms（表意文字）
（古代エジプトの）象形文字 hieroglyphics
表音文字 phonograms
カナ *kana,* a phonetic syllabary（表音式音節文字表）
カタカナ *katakana*（the squarish form of the written Japanese syllabary）
ひらがな *hiragana*（the cursive [rounded] form of the written Japanese syllabary）
アルファベットは26字である。
There are 26 letters in the English alphabet.
〈注〉 英語の letter とは alphabet のこと，それを組み合せて word（語）ができる。日本語の場合は漢字なら１字で１語を表すこともあり（ex. 私，愛），「かな」であれば１字１音節を表す。日英の表記の相違からしばしば「字」と「語」の混同があるので注意。
Summarize the essay above in less than 200 words.（上文の要旨を200語以内にまとめなさい）
She can input more than 40 words a minute.（彼女は１分間に40語以上入力できる。（和文なら…字となるところ））
【字を書く】write
〈注〉 write a letter というと手紙を書くこと。
彼は３歳で字を書くことを覚えた。
He learned how to write at the age of three.
彼は字が上手だ。
His handwriting [penmanship〔米〕] is good.
彼は字がきれいだ。
He writes neatly.
字をもっときれいに書きなさい。
Write more neatly.
字が読みやすい[読みにくい]
be legible [illegible]
字が小さくて読みにくい。
（手書き）His handwriting is too small and hard to read.
（印刷）This print is too small for me to read.
This is in such small print that it is hard to read.

もしも → だろう

もつ（持つ）

1. 手に

hold; carry（手に持って運ぶ）

彼は右手に葉巻を持っていた。

He had a cigar in his right hand.

彼は両手に大きなスーツケースを持っていた。

He was carrying a big suitcase in each hand.

傘を持って行った方がいいですよ。

You'd better take your umbrella with you.

2. 所持する

have; have got

ライターを持っていますか。

Have you got a lighter?

お金はいくら持っているの？

How much money do you have with you?

3. 所有する

have; own

あの人はパソコン関連のものなら何から何まで持っている。

She has all kinds of personal computer peripherals.

彼はこのあたり一帯に広大な地所を持っている。

He owns a large tract of land hereabout.

〈注〉 ひと続きの広い土地であれば a large tract of land, あそこにも, ここにもと散らばっているのであれば a great deal of (the) land とする。

4. 心に抱く

恨みを持つ

bear [have, have got] a grudge

犯人は殺された人物に恨みを持っていた者にちがいない。

The culprit must be someone who bore a grudge against the murdered man.

私は民俗学に興味を持っている。

I'm interested in folklore.

私は彼女の将来に希望を持っている。

I'm hopeful about her future.

5. 引き受ける

assume《the cost》; **cover**《the expenses》; **take care of**《the expenses》

だれが勘定を持つのですか。

Who will pay [foot] the bill?

〈注〉 foot the bill は口語の決り文句。

今日の食事は僕が持つからね。

This meal is on me.

社員の社会保険の保険料の半額は通常会社が持つことになっている。

Usually companies assume half the cost of the premium for ⌊Social Security [the pension fund] for the employees.

会社が調査研究費を持つだろう。

The company will pay for the investigation.

【担任】

池野先生が2年B組を持っている。

Mr. Ikeno is in charge of the second-year B class.

私は2年生全員の英語を持っている。

I teach English to all the second-year students.

6. 長続きする

keep; last

【病人】

あの病人は夏まではもたないだろう。

The patient will not live till summer.

【体】

君, そんな物を食べていては体がもたないよ。

You cannot ⌊keep yourself in [maintain] good health on such a diet.

【食品】

この陽気では魚は明日まではもたないだろう。

The fish won't keep until tomorrow in this weather.

【金】
僕は３万円持っていた。それだけあれば月末までもつだろうと思っていた。

I had 30,000 yen. I thought it would last me for the rest of the month.

【会社】
彼でこのお店がもっているんだ。

Without him, the store would fail.

He is propping up the store.

もったいない

1．無駄な

そんな高価な服をたくさん買ってもったいない。

Buying all those expensive dresses is {a sheer waste of money. / just throwing money away.}

時間がもったいないよ。

It's an utter waste of time.

まったくもったいない！

What a waste!

〈注〉◆上の表現は energy, time, talent, potential, intelligence, ability, resources などについて広く使える。その点日本語の「もったいない」と同じである。
I was not much used to happiness. But it was very nice, too nice to waste in sleep.
——M. Drabble, *The Millstone*
(子供を出産した後の主人公の感慨一私は幸福には慣れていなかった。しかし幸福とはよいものだった。眠ってしまったりするのはもったいないくらいよいものだった)
◆アイスクリームを道端に落としたときなどの「ああもったいない」は，What a shame! または What a pity! でよい。

2．分不相応な

［対象主語］**be too good for**
［人主語］**be unworthy of; do not deserve**

まあなんてきれいな。ふだん使うのはもったいないわ。

How beautiful! It's too good {for daily use. / to use every day.}

彼からもらった贈物は私にはもったいない。

His gift is too good for me.

そんなに親切にし［ほめ］ていただいてはもったいない。

I don't deserve such kindness [praise].

〈注〉 上の文の気持ちは It's very kind of you.でも表せる。I'm unworthy of your kindness. という言い方もあるが，形式ばって堅すぎる。

3．不敬な

sacrilegious; profane; blasphemous

信者にとってイエズスの絵姿を踏むなどもったいない冒瀆の行為だった。

To the believers it was sheer sacrilege to tread on the image of Jesus.

〈注〉 冗談めかして冒瀆（sacrilege）が軽い意味で使われることがある。
It's sacrilege to add water to fine whisky like this.（こんな上等のウイスキーを水で割るなんてもったいない（冒瀆だよ））

神様の名を口にするなんてもったいない。

Don't swear. It's profane.

Don't use profane language.（＝Don't swear or curse.）

〈注〉 swearing とは「神にかけて…を誓う」ことから転じて「やたらに神の名を口にすること」。cursing は「呪うこと」。たとえば Go to hell!（くたばりやがれ）の類。

神様を恨むなんてもったいないことだ。

Blaming God for evil is blasphemous [blasphemy].

〈注〉 **sacrilegious,** 名 **sacrilege** は神聖を冒瀆することで，意図的で重大な冒瀆，最も基本的な主義や価値を侵すこと。
profane　多くは言葉遣いに関して言う。
blasphemous　神の名を汚す。
以上あげた形容詞のほか言葉遣いについて用いる disrespectful（尊敬の念を欠いた），vulgar（下品な）などもある。

もっていく(持って行く)・もってくる → はこぶ

〈注〉◆「持って行く・持って来る」（take, bring）の方向性は「行く・来る」（go, come）の方向性と一致する。
(中心の人)→take there（持って行く）

←bring here（持って来る）
⊃fetch（取って来る）

◆fetch は米国では犬がボールを追ってくわえて来るような場合にしか使わないが，英国では犬に限らず，人についても使う。

cf. carry（運ぶ）は方向に関係なく使える。

1．持って行く

(出がけに親が子に)傘を持って行きなさいよ。

Take your umbrella with you.

これを私の手紙に添えてジムの所へ持って行ってください。

Please take this to Jim with my letter.

彼女は家の中のものを根こそぎ持って行ってしまった。

She carried [took] away everything in the house.

(パーティーには)お花を持って行きましょうか。(電話で，これから訪れる先方に)

Shall I bring flowers (to the party)?

〈注〉 電話などで相手の立場を中心に考え，Can I come?（行ってもいいですか）と言うのと同じく，上の文は先方を中心に考えて bring（持って行く）を使っている。

2．持って来る

お茶を1杯持って来てくださいませんか。

Could you bring me a cup of tea, please?

彼は大きな包みを持って(入って)来た。

He came in carrying a big parcel [package].

トム，朝刊を持って来てくれないか。

Tom, can you {get me / go and get me / bring me} the morning paper?

お茶が冷えてしまったでしょう。入れたてを持って来ましょうか。

The tea is getting cold. Shall I get [bring] you some fresh (tea)?

もと（元，本，基，素）

1．起源・基本

【起源】

この祭りは16世紀に農民の行った豊穣祈願の農耕儀礼にもとを発する。

This festival originated in a fertility rite observed by farmers in the 16th century.

彼の家柄はもとは源氏の出である[15世紀までさかのぼれる]。

His family can trace their origins back to the Genji clan [the fifteenth century].

【始め】

失敗は成功のもと。

Failure is but a stepping stone to success.

【基本】

教育こそ一国のもとである。

Education is the foundation [root] of a nation.

2．原因

かぜはこじらすと万病のもとになる。

{Colds, if prolonged, / Prolonged colds} may lead to many other diseases.

子供ってものは家族がもめるもとだ。

Children are the source of trouble in the family.

いったい何がけんかのもとだったかしら。

What was the cause of the quarrel?

What caused the quarrel?

3．素材・材料

スープの素 (soup) stock

プディングの素 an instant pudding mix

ホットケーキの素 a hotcake mix

味噌は大豆をもとに作る。

Miso is made from soy beans.

彼女の小説はほとんどが自分の経験をもとにしたものだ。

Most of her novels are based on her own experiences.

4．資本

capital; 元金 **the principal;** 原価 **cost;**

卸値　**wholesale price**

元をかける

put money into《something》

元値を切って売る

sell at a loss

元が取れない

can't recoup the original costs

cannot return the original investment

彼の事業は失敗して元も子もなくなった。

His business failed and he lost everything.

5．以前

formerly; once; before

元の　**former; past; ex-; one-time;** 退官［退役］した **retired**（略 ret.）

高名な学者であり，元岐阜大学学長の今西氏

Mr. Imanishi, (a) noted scholar and former president of Gifu University

元京大教授佐藤博士

Dr. Sato, a retired professor of Kyoto University

あの人は加藤氏のもとの奥さんだ。

She's Mr. Kato's ex-wife.

【場所】

もとの所にちゃんと返しておいてくださいね。

Be sure to put them back in their places.

彼女は戻って来るとひと言も言わずにもとの席に座った。

She came back and resumed her seat without saying a word.

道は迷路のように入り組んでいて，30分も歩き回って気がついたら，もとの所に戻っていた。

The roads ran [were] like a maze, and after walking half an hour I found myself in the (same) place where I had started.

【もとのまま】

何もかも10年前の通り，もとのままであった。

Everything { looked as it used to look / was as it used to be } ten years ago.

【もとは】

酒田はもとはその地方の商業の中心地として栄えた町であった。

Sakata was once a prosperous commercial center of the district.

【元通り】

あのことがあってから２人の友情はもう元通りには戻らなかった。

After that incident their friendship was never { on the same footing again. / quite what it had been before.

一度起ったことは元通りにはならない。（覆水盆に返らず）

What's done cannot be undone.

傷んだ絵は完全に元通りにすることはできない。

It's impossible to restore the damaged picture completely.

もどす（戻す）

1．もとに

return; put back; give back; send back

おもちゃをおもちゃ箱に［もとの棚に］戻しなさい。

Put the toys back in the toy box [on the shelf].

子猫を見つけた場所に戻しておいで。

Take the kitten back where you found it.

【状態】

話題をもとに戻そう。

Let's get back to the point at issue.

【差し戻す】

最高裁はその事件を高等裁判所に差し戻すことを決定した。

The Supreme Court decided to send the case back to the High Court.

【払い戻す】

新幹線が２時間以上も遅れたので特急料金が払い戻しになった。

The Shinkansen was delayed more than two hours, so the express fare was

{ returned.
paid back.
refunded.

2. 後ろに

車をほんの１メートルほど後ろに戻して[バックして]彼の車を通らせてください。

Back your car just one meter, please, to let his car pass.

その時計は進んでいる。5分戻してください。

That clock is too fast. Please turn it back five minutes.

3. 吐く

throw up; vomit

彼は夕食に食べたものを全部戻してしまった。

He threw up everything he had eaten at dinner.

その患者は何を食べても戻してしまう。

The patient cannot { hold down any food. / keep food down. }

〈注〉 reject any food を使って次のように言うこともできる。

He rejects any food. (何も食べようとしない)

His stomach rejects any food. (胃が食物を受けつけない)

また，吐くところまでいかないが胃がむかむかするのは be sick to [at] the stomach。

ex. 列車で気分が悪くなったので途中下車し，冷たい空気を吸ってひと休みした。

I felt sick to my stomach in the train and so I got off at a station and sat in the cool air for a while.

もどる（戻る）

1. 帰る

【帰宅】

彼は1時間もしたら戻って来るだろう。

He'll be back in an hour.

ちょうど仕事から戻ったところです。

I've just come home from work.

村山さんがお戻りになったら，私にお電話くださるように伝えていただけませんでしょうか。

Could you ask Mr. Murayama to call me when he { returns? / comes back? }

【引き返す】

もうあきらめて戻った方がいいと思うよ。暗くなってきたし。

I think we'd better give up and turn [go] back; it's getting dark.

【席に】

席に戻ってもよろしい。

You may go back to your seat.

2. 以前の状態に返る

彼はタクシーにブリーフケースを置き忘れたが無事に戻って来た。

He left his briefcase in a taxi, but it was returned to him [he got it back].

【金】

今年は税金が戻って来た。

I got a tax refund this year.

【血色】

あの人が真っ青になって，私は本気で心配しました。でもちょっとしたら顔色がだんだんもとに戻って来ました。

She went so pale I was really worried, but after a while her color gradually returned.

この前彼に会ったときは顔色もよく元気にしていましたが，それからまた病状が後戻りしてしまったのです。

Last time I saw him his color was good and he was cheerful, but then he had a relapse.

【記憶】

彼は記憶が戻って来た[を取り戻した]。

His memory returned.

He recovered his memory.

【話題】

さあ，もとの問題に戻ろう[話題をもとに戻そう]。

Let's { get back / return } to the point (at issue).

もの（物）

1.物品・物体

a thing

うちのおばあさんの所には戸棚があってね，あめだのチョコレートだの子供たちが好きないい物がいっぱい入っていたの。

There was a cupboard at my grandmother's where she kept lollipops, chocolates and all sorts of nice things for us children.

UFO は "unidentified flying object"（未確認飛行物体）を省略した呼称です。

UFO is short for (an) "unidentified flying object".

その瓶の中の黒っぽい物は何ですか。

What's that dark stuff in the bottle?

〈注〉 stuff は，口語でしばしば things と同じように使われる。次のような用法がある。

ex. 掃除用品 cleaning { stuff 〔*colloq.*〕 / things 〔*colloq.*〕 }

教材 teaching { stuff 〔*colloq.*〕 / material(s) }

みんな長すぎたり短すぎたりで，私にちょうど合うものはひとつもない。

Some are too short and others are too long. There's nothing that fits me.

何か食べるものをいただけますか。

Could [Can] I have something to eat, please?

「どんなものがいいですか[食べたいですか]」「何か柔らかくて温かいもの」。

"What would you like to eat?" "Something soft and hot."

2. 品質

あの店の商品はものがいい。

They sell high quality goods at that store.

3. 材質

「これはものは何ですか」「綿100パーセントです」。

{ "What is the material?" / "What kind of material is this?" }

"It's 100 percent cotton."

ものはプラスチックです。

This is plastic.

It's made of plastic.

4. 資質

彼はほんものの学者の資質をもっている。

He has the right stuff to be a scholar.

英雄を英雄たらしめているもの(資質)

the stuff heroes are made of

5. 所有物

私[君 / あの人 / 私たち / あの人たち]の物

mine [yours / his / hers / ours / theirs]

人の物には触るな。

Don't touch what { isn't yours. / doesn't belong to you. }

それは私のではない，妹のものです。

It's not mine; it's my sister's.

6. 慣用表現

ものになる succeed

物事 things

【物言い】

物言いには気をつけなければいけない。

You should be careful about what you say and how you say it.

【ものを言う】

お金がたちまちにものを言った。

The money { had / produced } an immediate effect.

チェスでは一手がものを言う。(一手たりともおろそかにできない)

In a game of chess,

{ every move tells. / no move is unimportant. }

血筋[家柄]がものを言う。

Blood [Family] will tell.

〈注〉 この形には experience(経験)，education(教養)なども使える。

人としての成熟度がものを言う。

Maturity is what counts.

もやす(燃やす)・もえる → やく・やける

1．燃やす

私は引っ越しの前に古い手紙を燃やした。

I burned my old letters before I moved.

小枝を集めて火を燃やしなさい。

Gather twigs and make a fire.

私たちはたき火を燃やしてその周りを囲み歌いながら踊った。

We lit the bonfire and danced round it singing.

2．燃える

その火事で家が3軒燃えた。

Three houses (were) burnt down in the fire.

暖炉ではたきぎがパチパチと勢いよく燃えていた。

In the hearth firewood was {burning / crackling} briskly.

3．高揚させる

【闘志】

わがチームは来るべき決勝戦に向けて闘志を燃やしている。

Our team is full of fight for the coming final game.

【情熱】

その当時彼は社会制度の改革に情熱を燃やしていた。

In those days he was {passionately in favor of reforming / burning with the desire to reform} the social system.

〈注〉 be in favor of はそれを(知的に)支持することで，感情的に燃えているという意味ではない。

彼女は障害児の福祉に情熱を燃やした。

She was committed to the welfare of handicapped children.

〈注〉 「夢中になる，情熱を燃やす，心血を注ぐ」などに当る英語表現を比較する。

be committed to 意志の固さを強調。

ex. 日本の母親のほとんどが子供の教育に打ち込んでいる。

Most Japanese mothers are committed to their children's education.

be devoted to 温かい心がこもっている。燃える心ではなく，もっと深い思いである。

なお，一般的に「情熱」は日本文化で評価されているほどには英米の文化では重んじられない。

ex. 極端な情熱を抱く者に対しては批判的な人も多い。

People tend to be critical of those people who have extreme feeling for or against something.

もよう（模様）

1．図案

全体的な柄 **design;** 繰り返し模様 **pattern**

【水玉模様】polka dot

青に白の水玉模様のネクタイ

a blue and white polka dot tie

a blue tie with white polka dots

〈注〉 polka dot は大きめで形のそろった水玉。

【縞模様】

青と白の縞模様のカーテン

a blue-and-white striped curtain

白地に赤い縞模様が入っている。

It's white with red stripes.

It has red stripes on a white background.

cf. It has red and white stripes.（赤白の縞）

【花模様】

緋色の地に大きな白い花模様が入った絨毯。

a bright red carpet with large white flowers.

【チェックの模様】

赤のチェックのスカート

a red checked skirt〔米〕

a red check skirt〔英〕

【デザイン】

緑色系の地の上に騎馬の人物が青と黄で織り出されたタペストリー

a tapestry with several men on horseback woven in shades of blue and yellow on a greenish background

白い大きな輪の模様のある緋色のじゅうたん
a bright red carpet with a pattern of large white rings

2. 様子
会議の模様を報道するため，NHK の特派員が現地に派遣されていた。
An NHK reporter was there to report on the conference.
【天候】
彼は空模様を見た。
He checked on
{ the sky.
{ snow conditions.（雪が降っている様子）
空模様はどうですか。
What's the weather like?
How does the sky look?
【予想】
2, 3 日は晴天が続く模様だ。
It seems the good weather'll continue for a few days.
円がまた値上がりしそうな模様だ。
There are indications that the yen will rise again.

もよおす（催す）

1. 開催する
（会を）**hold a meeting;**（晩餐会を）**give a dinner;**（ショーを）**put on a show**
来る金曜日から大学祭を催します。
Our college festival will begin next Friday.
〈注〉 公的発表の場合は We are having ... のように人称代名詞を使うのは避ける。
被服学科はファッションショーを催します。
The Clothing Department girls will give a fashion show.
今度の国体は静岡県で催される。
The next National Athletic Meeting will be held in Shizuoka prefecture.
天皇陛下はイタリア大統領を迎え晩餐会を催された。
The Emperor { held a reception / gave an official dinner } in honor of the President of Italy.

2. 感じる
【眠気】
本を読んでいたら，突如眠気を催した。
I suddenly felt sleepy while I was reading.
【寒気・吐き気】
彼は学校で寒気を催したと思ったら，翌日はひどいかぜで寝込んでしまった。
He felt chilly at school and the next day he was in bed with a bad cold.
私は吐き気を催した。（気分が悪くなった）
I felt sick.
それを考えただけで吐き気[寒気]を催す。
The mere thought [idea] of it makes me sick [shiver].

もらう（貰う）

1. 受け取る，得る
get; have; take; receive; accept; be given; be awarded; be presented with
今日彼から手紙をもらった。
I { got / had / received } a letter from him today.
このネックレスは私の17歳の誕生日に母からもらったものです。
This necklace was a present from my mother on my seventeenth birthday.
This is the necklace my mother gave me for my seventeenth birthday.
【賞】
今年はだれが１等賞をもらいましたか。
Who { took / got } the first prize this year?
私のおばが文化勲章をもらいました。
My aunt was awarded the Order of Cultural Merit.
【嫁】

長男が先月嫁をもらいました。

My oldest son got married last month.

2. …してもらう

どこへ行ったら靴を直してもらえるでしょうか。

Where can I {get / have} my shoes repaired?

私の手紙をフランス語に翻訳してもらいました。

I {had / got} my letter translated into French.

君は一度医者に行ってよく診てもらわなければならないよ。

You have to see a doctor and get checked over.

【依頼】

彼に入ってもらってください。

Have him come in.

〈注〉 Let him come in now. と let を使うと，何か入れない理由があるが，「入れてやってくれ」の意になる。

いつでも遊びに来てもらうよう彼に言っておいてください。

Please tell him {he's welcome / he can come} anytime.

この手紙を投函してもらえるかしら[いただけますか]。

{Would / Could} you post this letter for me, please?

【希望】

君にはきちんと時間通りに来てもらいたかった。

I expected you'd be here on time.

静かにしてもらいたい。

I wish you'd be quiet.

彼に会いに来てもらいたい。

I'd like him to come and see me.

もんだい（問題）

1. テスト

数学の最後の問題がとても難しかった。

The last problem in mathematics was very difficult.

〈注〉 problem は作図，計算などを必要とする問題。

社会科学の問題は案外やさしかった。

The questions in social science were easier than I expected.

小川先生の問題はいつも難しいね。

Mr. Ogawa's tests are always difficult.

2. 課題

【主題】

私はその問題には大いに興味があります。

I'm very much interested in the subject.

その問題に関してはすでに数冊の本が出版されている。

Several books have already been published on that subject.

【社会的問題】

緊急の問題

a pressing question; an urgent problem

我々は人口問題について何時間も論じ続けた。

We discussed the population problem for hours on end.

〈注〉 discuss は他動詞であるから，×discuss about … とはしない。

当面の最大の問題は国家経済の立て直しだ。

The greatest issue is how to reconstruct the national economy.

【問題点・問題の核心】

いまだに合意に達しない…つまり問題点はここなのだ。すなわち失業とインフレとどちらがまだましかということだ。

No agreement has been reached because the point at issue is this: which is more tolerable [worse], unemployment or inflation?

妊娠中絶の可否をめぐる論争の本当の問題点は胎児が受胎直後から人間であるかどうかという点だ。

{The real issue / What's at issue} in the abortion debate is whether the embryo is human from the very beginning.

〈注〉 issue とは問題点やその核心が重大かつ複雑で，種々の見解・意見が錯綜しているような問題を言う。

この計画には多くの問題(点)がある。

There are many { controversial points in / possible drawbacks in / problems with } this plan.

【問題意識】

彼らはだいたいにおいて現在の生活に満足しているので社会問題についてはほとんど問題意識がない。

Because they are mostly content with their lives, they have little awareness of social problems.

人々はもっと世界的な問題について問題意識を持つべきだ。

People should be more aware of world problems.

〈注〉 「問題意識がない」は次の表現でも表せる。

indifferent 無関心，考えようとしない(批判的ニュアンスを持つ語)。

be not aware of 見えていない(批判的な語ではない)。

3．トラブル

彼はいつも問題を起す。(いざこざ)

He's a trouble maker.

The boy often causes trouble.（よく問題を起す)

彼はしょっちゅう学校で問題を起している。

He's always in trouble at school.

彼女は問題児だ。

She's a problem child.

彼は人妻と問題を起した。(男女間の問題)

He had an affair with a married woman.

住宅問題 the [a] housing problem

〈注〉 個人の問題として「彼は住宅問題で困っている」は別の表現になる。家が見つからないのならば，He is very worried about finding a place to live. と言う。近所がやかましいとか不便だとか現在の家に不満で困っているのならば，his housing problem, problem with the house [housing] を使えるが，あいまいな言い方であるから具体的に説明する方がよい。

4．「問題」＋動詞表現

【問題になる】

教科書検定問題は深刻な問題になった。

The textbook censorship problem became a serious issue.

総理大臣の靖国神社参拝がたいへんな問題になった。

The Prime Minister's visit to Yasukuni Shrine { caused / elicited } much criticism.

There was much criticism of the Prime Minister's visit to Yasukuni Shrine.

【問題を起す】

それは新たに問題を引き起した。

It raised a new question.

彼の演説が教育界に問題を引き起した。

His speech has { given rise to / caused } a controversy in the educational world.

【問題にぶつかる】

彼はまったく偶然にその問題にぶつかったのだ。

He ran up against the problem quite accidentally.

【問題を解決する】

環境ホルモンの問題を解決するには人知を集めても数十年はかかるだろう。

It will take decades of human effort(s) to solve problems involving environmental hormones.

【問題に対処する】

現在の経済問題にどう対処すべきかいまだに意見の一致を見ない。

No agreement has been reached about how to { deal with / handle } the present economic problems.

【問題を大きくする】

それは問題を大きくした[悪化させた]だけだ

った。

It only { aggravated the problem. / made it worse. }

【問題を放置する】

この問題を黙って放置するわけにはいかない。

We cannot pass over this question in silence.

5．慣用表現

【疑わしい】

彼にお金がつくれるかどうかは問題だ。

It's doubtful whether [if] he can make the money.

問題の人　the person in question

【困る点】

だれが猫の首に鈴をつけるのかが問題だ。

The question is who will bell the cat.

問題はお金がかかりすぎることだ。

The trouble is that it will cost too much money.

【重要な点】

値段ではなくて品質が問題なのだ。

It's the quality that matters, not the price.

【判断基準】

君はこれが好きで，彼はあれが好き。これは好みの問題さ。

You like this one and he likes that one. It's a matter of taste.

それはたいへんいい考えだ。しかし金の問題はどうする。

Well that's a very good idea, but there's the question of money.

【問題にならない】

問題なく

beyond question; undoubtedly

それは問題にはならない［ではない］。

That doesn't matter.

It makes no difference.

彼は問題なく合格するだろう。

There's no doubt he'll pass the exam.

すべて問題なし。大成功だった。

Everything went smoothly. It was a great success.

問題がない。（OKである）

There's no problem.

It's no problem.

問題外である

out of the question; impossible; unthinkable

彼はとても問題にならん。（だめである）

He's no good.

彼は私が何か言ってもほとんど問題にしなかった。

He { paid little [no] attention to / slighted [made light of] } what I said.

〈注〉「問題にしない」「注意を払わないと」という意味では，次のような表現もある。

don't take me seriously　私のことを真面目に考えてくれない。

be indifferent to me　私に無関心だ。

ignore me　私を全然無視している。

や

や（屋） → みせ，しょくぎょう

〈注〉 日本語の「肉屋」「魚屋」などは店のことでもあり，その店の人のことでもある。「角の魚屋さん」は店，「おーい魚屋さん」と呼び止めるのは魚を商う人を指す。英語では「人」を表す言葉が発達し，パン屋のおじさんは baker，それを売っている店は bakery，肉屋のおじさんは butcher，その店は butcher's（shop）である。以下に店の人と店を対比して示す。

【…屋，…屋の人 / …屋の店】

八百屋　vegetable man / vegetable shop
　greengrocer〔英〕 / greengrocery〔英〕
魚屋　fishmonger / fishmonger's; fish store
肉屋　butcher / butcher's（shop）
パン屋　baker / bakery
米屋　rice seller / rice shop
酒屋　sake seller / liquor store
　wine seller / package store〔米〕
　off-licence〔英〕
菓子屋　candy maker / candy store
豆腐屋　tofu seller / tofu shop
乾物屋　grocer / grocery
荒物屋　/ household supply store
花屋　florist / flower shop; florist's
本屋　book seller / bookstore [shop]
文房具屋　stationer / stationer's; stationery store
おもちゃ屋　/ toy shop
たばこ屋　tobacconist / tobacco shop
呉服屋（仕立を含む）/ kimono shop
紳士服屋　tailor / tailor's
婦人服屋　dressmaker / dressmaker's
クリーニング屋　launderer / laundry
　（ドライ～）　dry cleaner / dry cleaner's
薬屋　pharmacist / pharmacy
　druggist〔米〕 / drugstore〔米〕
　chemist〔英〕 / chemist's（shop）〔英〕
家具屋　furniture seller / furniture store
電気屋（店員） / electric appliance store
新聞屋　news dealer〔米〕/ news agency
　news agent〔英〕
　（配達人）　news boy [girl]
風呂屋（店番）　attendant / public bath
床屋　barber / barber's; barber shop
美容院　beautician / beauty parlor [salon]
　（美容師）　hair stylist / hair stylist's
料理屋　/ restaurant
　（料理人）　cook
ラーメン屋　/ ramen shop
寿司屋　/ sushi shop
　（職人）　sushi chef
コンビニ　/ covenience store
雑貨屋（田舎などの） / corner shop
　general store
不動産屋　real estate agent / real estate agency
宿屋　innkeeper / inn
下宿屋　landlord of / private dormitory
　/ student hostel

〈注〉◆例えば寿司屋［風呂屋］の主人というときは the owner of a sushi shop [public bath] のようにすればよい。
◆「何でも屋」（物知り）は know-it-all という。
◆店員はsalespersonでよい。

【職業の表し方】

うちは八百屋です。

My family has a vegetable shop.

兄は渋谷で電気屋をやっている。

My brother has an electric appliance store [shop] in Shibuya.

〈注〉◆ … run a ～ store と run を使うのはかなり大きな商売でないとおかしい。また店は owner（店主）と manager（店長）が別の人であることもあるので own a store（店の所有者である）とmanage a store（店の経営を任されている）の意味を知った上で使い分けねばならない。
◆「商品を取り扱う」の意味で deal in を使えるのは
(1) 大手の商社
Cargill deals in chemicals.
（カーギル社は化学製品を扱っている）
(2) 小規模な，様々な商品の仲介販売をする会社の場合
Daiko deals in [handles] office equipment and supplies, including furniture, computers, etc.
（ダイコーは事務機器，事務用品からコンピュー

タまで扱っている)

【慣用表現】

彼はがんばり屋だ。

He always works hard at everything.

He's a hard worker.

彼は皮肉屋だ。

He's very sarcastic.

彼女は締り屋だ。

She's very tight-fisted.

やかましい → うるさい

1. 音がうるさい

ジェット機がやかましくてお互いの話し声も聞えなかった。

Jets made so much noise we couldn't hear each other.

おい，やかましいぞ。(何て騒ぎだ)

What a noise you're making!

What's all the noise!

cf. 静かにしろ。 Be quiet!

Shut up! (おだまり)

2. 厳しい

【厳格な】strict (with)

彼女は子供たちに行儀をやかましくしつけている。

She is strict with her children about manners.

【高級嗜好】critical

これならワインにやかましい人でもきっと満足するだろう。

This wine will please the most critical person [palate〔*formal*〕].

【好みが難しい】particular

彼は食べ物にやかましい。

He's particular about food [what he eats].

〈注〉 strict about what he eats と strict を使えば，たとえば健康のために塩分を厳しく制限しているとか，食事の分量を計量していることなどを指す。particular は好みが難しいことである。

【口うるさい】

彼は口やかましい母親のもとからできるだけ早く逃げ出したいと言っていた。

He said he'd like to get away from his nagging mother as soon as possible.

3. 言い立てる

【世評】

日本の再軍備問題がやかましく論議されている。

Japan's rearmament problem is causing a lot of controversy.

消費税問題が新聞紙上でやかましく取り上げられている。

The consumption tax issue is being given a lot of coverage in the papers.

【やかましく言う】

din《something》into a person's head [ears]

じいさんが「倹約，倹約」とあまりやかましく言うので彼女はまったくうんざりした。

The old man dinned "economy" into her head until she could hardly stand it.

ジムはビルに借金返済をやかましく催促した。

Jim pressed Bill hard to repay his debts to him.

《類義語》

strict 規則ややり方をきちんと守ることを要求する。

severe 厳しくて譲らない。性格的なものであり，にこりともしないイメージ。a strict person は普通に使うが a severe person のように直接人を形容する用法はまれである。

particular 好みに関してうるさいこと。

やきゅう (野球)

baseball; プロ野球 **pro(fessional) baseball**

「どことどこの試合ですか」「巨人と中日です」。

"Who's playing?" "The Giants are playing the Dragons."

「今何回ですか」「６回裏です」。
“What inning is it?” “The second half of the 6th (inning).”
横浜のピッチャーはだれですか。
Who's the Bay Stars' pitcher?
「中日はだれが登板ですか」「川上です。彼は今調子がいい[悪い]ようだ」。
“Who's pitching for the Dragons?” “Kawakami is. He seems [He doesn't seem] to be in good shape today.”

《関連語》
球場 ballpark, stadium
スタンド stands / スコアボード scoreboard / バックネット backstop / ダッグアウト dugout, bench
試合 game
デーゲーム day game / ナイター night game / イニング，回 inning / 表 first half / 裏 second half / 得点 score
内野 infield
内野手 infielder / ホームベース home (base) / １[２/３]塁 first [second / third] base / バッターボックス batter's box / 投手[ピッチャー] pitcher / 救援投手[リリーフピッチャー] relief pitcher / 捕手[キャッチャー] catcher / １[２/３]塁手 first [second / third] baseman / 遊撃手 [ショート] shortstop / マウンド pitcher's mound / 審判員[アンパイア] umpire
外野 outfield
右翼[中堅/左翼]手 right [center / left] fielder
投球 pitching
直球 straight ball / 速球 fast ball / カーブ curve(ball) / フォークボール fork ball / スライダー slider / ストライク strike / ボール ball / 四球 [フォアボール] base on balls, walk / 死球 [デッドボール] hit by a pitch / 三振をとる strike out (a batter)
打者 [バッター] batter
ピンチヒッター pinch hitter / ウエイティングサークル on-deckcircle; batter's circle / 打順 batting order / 打率 batting average / バント bunt / スクイズ squeeze / 空振り swing wide / 三振する swing out / 見送る let a pitch go by
打球 batting
安打 hit / ゴロ grounder / フライ fly / ライナー liner, line drive / ファウル foul (ball) / 単打 [シングルヒット] single (hit) / 二塁打 double / 三塁打 triple / ホームラン home run, homer / ランニングホーマー inside-the-park homer /
走者 runner
すべり込む slide / 盗塁 steal
守備 fielding
ダブルプレー double play / エラー error / タッチ touch, tag〔米〕/ セーフ safe / アウト out

やく（焼く）・やける

1．燃やす，焼失する

彼女は身の回り品の荷造りをすませると，古い手紙を集めて裏庭で焼いた。
After she'd packed her things she gathered up some old letters and burned them in the backyard.
この辺の家屋は戦争中全部焼けてしまった。
All the houses in this area burned (down) during the war.
母の写真はこの１枚を残してほかは全部火事で焼けてしまいました。
All the photographs of my mother were destroyed [were burnt up] in the fire except this one.

【火葬】
火葬にする cremate
焼き場，火葬場
crematory〔米〕, crematorium〔英〕

2．日焼け

人々は砂浜で体を焼いている。
People were sunbathing on the beach.
みんな沖縄から少々日焼けして帰ってきた。

They came back from Okinawa
{ slightly tanned.
{ with some tan.

〈注〉 日焼けして黒くなったのは have a tan, be tanned と言う。sunburnt は赤くなってひりひりする状態を指す。

【変色】

空色や浅緑は日に焼けやすい。

Light blue and light green easily fade in the sun.

3. 熱する

【陶磁器】

土のつぼは窯で20時間かけて焼き上げる。

The clay pots are placed in a kiln and baked for 20 hours.

【真っ赤に焼く】

彫刻家は鉄が真っ赤に焼けているうちにハンマーで打って形をつける。

While the iron is red hot the engraver beats it into shape with a hammer.

4. 料理 →りょうり

【焼く】

直火で焼く

grill（ガス・炭火で）; broil（grill と同様，または網焼き）

フライパンで焼く　saute, pan fry

オーブンで焼く

（肉などを）roast;（パン・菓子を）bake

トーストにする

toast（表面をこんがり焼く）

〈注〉 ごまを炒るのも toast または parch。

【焼き加減】

焼き上がる［焼ける］

be roasted [baked, toasted]

パン（焼きすぎ） overbaked
（上出来） baked; baked just right; baked perfectly
（生焼け） not baked enough; underbaked

ステーキ（十分火を通したもの） well-done
（中位焼き） medium
（生焼き） rare

こんがりきつね色に焼き上がる

be roasted [toasted, done] to a golden brown

5. 写真の焼き付け

この写真を焼いてください。

Please print these pictures.

〈注〉 写真屋の D. P. E. は developing（現像），printing（焼き付け），enlarging（引伸ばし）の略。

6. 慣用表現

【嫉妬(しっと)する】

ちょっと妬ける。 I'm a bit jealous.

まったく妬ける。

I'm full of envy.

How I envy her!

彼のガールフレンドのことでひどく妬ける。

I'm burning with envy over his girlfriend.

【胸焼け】

食べすぎるといつも後で胸が焼ける。

I always have heartburn if I eat too much.

【手を焼く】

あの子の両親はあの子には手を焼いた。

His parents { didn't know what to do with / couldn't handle } the boy.

【世話を焼く】

世話焼き　a busybody（おせっかいをする人）

休暇で息子が帰省したので彼女はうれしそうに世話を焼いている。

She looks happy taking care of her son who's come back on vacation.

うちの息子は全く世話が焼ける。

Our son gives us a lot of trouble.

It's really frustrating to deal [cope] with our teenager.

やくそく（約束）

名 動 **promise**

約束事　a convention; a rule;（しきたり，慣例） tradition; cultural patterns

彼はきっと帰って来ると約束した。

He promised { that he would come back. / to come back. }

もう二度とやりません。約束します。

I'll never do it again, I promise.

二度とこんなことにならないようにします。

I promise you it shall not [won't] happen again.

君は約束を守らなければならない。

You should keep your word.

もし約束を破ったら「針千本」だよ。

If you break your promise, "needles through your tongue".

〈注〉◆子供たちがかたい約束を誓うときに唱える「うそついたら針千本の一ます」にたいへん似た上の表現は Saroyan の短篇 *Sunday Zeppelin* の中にあるものである。「指切りげんまん」に相当する言葉としては Cross my heart and hope to die ... が一般的。

◆「約束をする」は make a promise とするよりは動詞形 promise to を使う方が現代的である。

残念ですが伺えません。ほかに約束がございまして。

I'm sorry, I can't come. I have another engagement.〔*formal*〕

〈注〉 招待を断る言い方としては I'm sorry, のように「,」(コンマ)が必要である。I'm sorry I can't come. とコンマを入れずに続けると行かれなくて残念だとの感想になる(口で言うときはもちろんコンマは休止(pause)になる)。単に「ほかの約束」と言うだけでなく，その内容を言う方が普通。

I'm sorry, I can't go with you. I've made an appointment with a dentist Monday morning.(残念ですが一緒に行けません。月曜日の午前は歯医者に予約を入れてしまったので)

なお，appointment は病院，弁護士，美容院の予約,子供の担任の先生との面談の約束などを言う。

今日はスミスさんと昼食のお約束がございます。(秘書が社長などに言う)

You have a luncheon appointment with Mr. Smith.

僕は彼と昼食をする約束をしたんだ。

I promised to meet him for lunch.

【条件】

約束はこうだった。彼は下宿の息子の家庭教師をする代りに，部屋代は払わなくてよい。

The agreement was that he would tutor the landlord's son in exchange for a rent-free apartment.

彼は下宿の息子に教える約束で部屋代なしでやっている。

He lives there rent-free in exchange for tutoring his landlord's son.

やくにん（役人）

1．集合的

【官僚】 bureaucracy

【高位の役人】

政府の役人

a government official

a public official（市・州の衛生課の検査官や警官など）

【一般公務員】 a civil servant

地方公務員

prefectural [city, town, village] { officials / workers / employees }

a civil service worker〔米〕(事務員その他を含み，教員は除く)

彼は外務省の役人だ。

He works in the Ministry of Foreign Affairs.

2．その他

役人根性　traits [frame of mind] common in bureaucrats

官僚主義　bureaucratic way; red tape

〈注〉 公文書を縛るのに赤テープを用いたことから書類・届けが複雑で非能率的な役所のやり方を指すようになった。

役人根性まる出しの人

typical bureaucrat [official]

まったく官僚主義だ！

Typical bureaucratic way [attitude]!

官僚主義［お役所仕事］だから建築許可をとるにも手間がかかる。

You have to go through a lot of red tape to

get a building permit.

There's a lot of red tape in getting a building permit.

官僚主義［役所の手続き］がますますひどくなってきている。

The amount of red tape is increasing year by year.

やさい（野菜）→ くだもの

vegetables; 青物 **greens**

生野菜　a fresh vegetable

野菜サラダ　vegetable salad

野菜ジュース　vegetable juice

野菜スープ　vegetable soup

野菜炒め　stir-fried vegetables

野菜が煮えたら塩を少々入れてください。

Add a pinch of salt when the vegetables are tender.

《関連語》

〈注〉 可算名詞には冠詞 a, an または複数の s をつけた。また，冠詞をつけなかったもの（ex. eggplant, pumpkin など）は状況により可算になることもある。

【葉菜】

キャベツ　a cabbage / レタス　lettuce / セロリ　celery / パセリ　parsley / ホウレンソウ　spinach / 長ネギ　leek

【芽・花】

アスパラガス　asparagus / カリフラワー　cauliflower / ブロッコリー　broccoli / 竹の子　a bamboo shoot / ワラビ　ferns

【果菜】

キュウリ　a cucumber / ナス　eggplant〔米〕, aubergine〔英〕 / トマト　a tomato / カボチャ　squash / クリカボチャ　pumpkin / ピーマン　a green pepper [bell pepper] / トウモロコシ　corn〔米〕, maize〔英〕 / クリ　a chestnut

【豆】

サヤインゲン　string beans / インゲン豆　haricot beans, kidney beans / エンドウ豆　peas / 大豆　soy beans / 小豆　azuki beans

【根菜】

ダイコン　a Japanese radish / ハツカダイコン　a red radish / カブ　a turnip / ニンジン　a carrot / ゴボウ　burdock / タマネギ　onion / ジャガイモ　a potato / サツマイモ　a sweet potato / サトイモ　taro / レンコン　lotus roots

【香草野菜】

ショウガ　ginger / ミョウガ　Japanese ginger bud / ニンニク　garlic / トウガラシ　red pepper / カラシ　mustard / ワサビ　Japanese horseradish [wasabi]

【その他】

キノコ　mushroom

やさしい（優しい，易しい）

1．人柄

柔和な **gentle, tender, mild, tenderhearted;** 愛情深い **affectionate, sweet, loving(-hearted);** 親切な **kind, kindhearted**

ジェーンは心の優しい子だ。

Jane is a tenderhearted girl.

彼は見たところ荒っぽくぶっきらぼうだが根は優しい。

He looks rough and surly but he is actually affectionate.

私たちの今度の先生は優しい（若い女の）先生だ。

Our new teacher
- is a mild [gentle] young woman.
- is gentle with [to] her pupils.
- treats us in a gentle way [gently].

赤ん坊は虚弱児でね，2日で死んでしまったの。そりゃすごく…わかるでしょう。でも周りの人が皆とても優しくてね，ありがたかったわ。

My baby was born weak and lived only two days. You can imagine how I felt. But all the people around me were very kind, which helped me.

2. 容易な

数学の問題は思ったよりやさしかった。

The math problems were easier than I expected.

この本はやさしい英語で書かれている。

This book is written in simple [easy] English.

〈注〉 上の例文は simple [easy] English が正しい。plain English と表現する「やさしい英語」とは意味に相違がある。plain English とは簡単な言葉で書かれていること。すなわち，まわりくどく言葉を飾ったりせずにはっきり言い，また難しい専門用語を避けることを意味する。
cf. plain ↔ obscure　　easy ↔ hard

やすい（安い）

cheap, inexpensive; 安く **cheaply, at a low price**

安く値踏みする　underestimate the cost

ディスカウント店では何でも安く売っている。

They sell things cheaply at discount supermarkets.

このかばんは安かった。

This bag was cheap.

This bag didn't cost much.

I didn't pay much for this bag.

もう少し安いのを見せてくださいませんか。

Can you show me something cheaper [less expensive]?

この頃はかなり安く携帯電話が買える。

You can buy a cellular phone at a pretty low price nowadays.

自動化で製造コストを安くすることに成功した。

By automation they succeeded in lowering production costs [the cost of production].

もう少し安くできませんか。

Could you make it a bit cheaper?

【物価】

このあたりは物価が安い。

Prices are lower in these parts.

安物　cheap things

安物をつかまされた。

I got taken [ripped off〔*slang*〕].

I was cheated [swindled].

近頃は安かろう悪かろうとはかぎらない。

These days low prices do not necessarily mean low quality.

〈注〉◆low price と言うが，×cheap price とは言わない。値引きした値は reduced prices と言う。
◆安くて品のよいものを「掘り出し物」と言うが，「これは掘り出し物だった」「上手な買い物をした」に当たる英語は
I made a great buy. または I got the only real bargain.
しかし，これはかなり高価なものを半値以下で買ったような，非常に得な買物の場合に使う。

【大安売り】

セール　sale

歳末売り尽くしセール　end-of-season sale

「値下げ，お値打ちセール」（看板など）

"Prices reduced, great values"

〈注〉◆「バーゲンセール」は和製英語。
◆「傷物」は seconds,「はんぱ物市」は odd-lot sales という言い方があるが，一般的ではない。

《類義語》

cheap　値が安い。時に質も安っぽいことを意味する。

low-priced　ただ単に値が安いことを示す。

inexpensive　品の割に値が安い，高くない。

reasonable; moderate　妥当な値段，まあまあの。品物ではなく，値段を形容する形容詞。

modest　ほどよい，穏当な〔*old fashioned*〕

【慣用表現】

彼をお安く見るんじゃない。（見くびるな）

Don't underestimate what he can do.

He's a person to be reckoned with.

お安いご用　an easy request

【依頼に対する応答】

行きがけにこの手紙を出していただけませんか。

Could you mail this letter for me on your way to the office?

お安いご用です。

Sure, { I'll do that. / I can do that.（やや難しいことを頼まれた場合）/ I'll be happy [glad] to. }

No problem. 〔*colloq.*〕

〈注〉 I'm afraid it's troublesome but … / I'm sorry to bother you but … 「ご面倒でしょうが…」のように頼まれたのならば次のように答えてもよい。

It's no trouble at all.（ちっとも面倒じゃありません。すなわち「お安いご用です」）

Don't mention it. / Not at all.（お礼を言われて）「いいえお安いご用です」

…やすい（…易い）

1．物

気をつけて，これは壊れやすいんです。

Be careful. This ⌊breaks easily [is easily broken].

これは燃えやすい。

This ⌊can catch [catches] fire easily.

暑いときは食べ物が腐りやすい。

Food easily goes ⌊bad [off] in hot weather.

〈注〉×Food is easy to go bad … とは言えない。

【人にとって】

うちの電話番号は覚えやすい。

My phone number is easy to remember.

はきやすい靴　comfortable shoes

〈注〉「…やすい」は [S is easy to V] の形

This is easy to break. は「壊しやすい」（人為的）。

This ⌊is easily broken [breaks easily 〔*far more common*〕]. は「壊れやすい」。

2．人

【敏感】

この子はかぜをひきやすい。

This child { is susceptible [prone] to colds. / catches cold easily. }

〈注〉 よく似た表現だが，The child is liable to catch colds.は，風が冷たい，雨にぬれたなどで「かぜをひきそうだ」の意によく使われる。口語では I feel a cold coming on. とも言う。

彼女は感じやすい子だから傷つきやすい。

She is very sensitive and easily hurt.

彼女は人を信じやすい。

She's { too ready to believe people. / too trusting. / naive. }

【傾向】

我々は安易な道を選びやすい。

We are apt [liable] to take the easier course.

我々は近視眼的になりやすい。

We are liable [apt, likely] { to think only of the short-term benefits. / not to think of long-range consequences. }

やすむ（休む）・やすみ → きゅうか

1．休息する

rest; take [have] a rest

あの木の下でひと休みしましょう。

Let's { rest / take [have] a rest } under that tree.

30分間休みましょう。

Let's take a half hour break.

彼女は朝から休まずずっと働いている。

She's been working without a break since this morning.

雪[雨]が休まず降り続いている。

It has been { snowing ⌊without letup [non-stop]. / raining steadily. }

〈注〉 「休みなく」の意味の副詞に ceaselessly, incessantly があるが，これは騒音・波・要求などに絶えず悩まされるような被害の含意がある。

【休み時間】

私たちは，昼に1時間と午後に15分間の休み時間があります。

We have an hour('s) lunch break and a fifteen minute('s) coffee break in the afternoon.

僕は1時間の休み時間をもらって駅まで彼に会いに行った。

I took an hour's break and went to meet him at the station.

〈注〉 recess も休み時間であるが小学校の休み時間である。

午前の休み時間　morning recess
昼の休み時間　lunchtime
午後の休み時間　afternoon recess

2．欠席する

トムは今日休んでいる。
Tom is absent today.

トムはひどいかぜで学校を休んだ。
Tom { didn't come [go] to school because of a bad cold. / was absent from school all last week. （先週ずっと）}

〈注〉 School was off. は学校全体が休みだったこと。

僕は来週は授業を休みます。
I won't be able to come to class next week.

〈注〉 be absent は英国では小学生の場合に使い，米国では学校の欠席であれば小学校に限らず使える。「欠勤する」には absent は使わない。He won't be in tomorrow. のように言う。

【休講】

野田先生はめったに授業を休まれない。
Mr. Noda seldom cancels (his) classes.

3．休暇をとる →きゅうか

【有給休暇】

今日は休みをとりたい。
I want to take off work today [the day off; today off].

彼は1週間休みをとって北海道に行った。
He took a week's vacation [holiday] / He took a week off } and went to Hokkaido.

僕は明日休みをとる。
I'll be off tomorrow [have tomorrow off].

【休業】

この国では土曜日は学校が休みです。
There's no school on Saturdays in this country.

あの店は一年中休みなしでやっている。
That store is open every day of the year.

〈注〉 ×That store takes no days off ... とは言えない。take [have] days off の主語は人間に限る。

ヨーロッパでは8月いっぱい休業する工場が多い。
Many factories in Europe shut down for the whole month of August.

【非番】

今日は僕は休み[非番]だ。
I'm off duty today.
cf. I was on duty last night. （昨夜は当直だった）

4．寝る

さあ，もう休みましょう。
Let's go to bed now.

昨夜はよくお休みになりましたか。
Did you sleep well last night?

やせる（痩せる）

㊀ **lose weight; become thin**
やせた ㊁ **thin; lean** （生れつきやせた）; **slender, slim** （すらりとして美しい）
やせている（生れつき） **lean build** （↔ stocky build）

〈注〉 lean は生れつきであるから be lean はよいが「やせる」という「変化」を表す場合には使えない。

だいぶおやせになりましたね。（健康を心配しての発言）
You've become [got] much thinner.

ずいぶんやせてスマートになったね。（ダイエットでやせた場合）
You've { become much slimmer. / lost a lot of weight. }

彼女は以前はがっちりして元気のいい人だったが，すっかりがりがりにやせてしまった。
She used to be a stout and vigorous woman but she has worn away to [become] a skeleton.

私は夏の間に8キロもやせた[減量した]。
I have lost [taken off] 8 kilograms during this summer.

〈注〉 「10キロやせる」
reduce one's weight (by) ten kilograms / take off ten kilograms }（ダイエットでやせる場合）

lose ten kilograms （ダイエットでも自然にでも，どちらの場合でも使える）

私，今ダイエットしているの。

I'm on a diet. / I'm dieting.

（これから） I'll go on a diet.

〈注〉 いろいろなダイエット

低塩分の食事　a low-salt diet

低コレステロール食　a low-cholesterol diet

無糖食　a sugar-free diet

【心労】

彼女はきっとたいへんな気苦労だったんでしょう。１か月に10キロもやせたんだから。

She must have been terribly worried; she'd lost ten kilograms in a month.

〈注〉 「心配でやつれた」に当る careworn は，やつれてしわが増えた顔を連想させる。極端なやせ方を表す形容詞に gaunt, haggard（がりがりの），emaciated（やせ細った）がある。

【不毛の】

やせた土地　infertile soil; poor soil (↔ rich soil); impoverished soil（やや詩的情感のこもった表現）

地味がやせていて植物が育たない。

The soil is too poor to grow any plants [for plants to grow].

やっかい（厄介） → めんどう，せわ

1．面倒

そいつは厄介な問題だね。

That's a troublesome question, isn't it?

厄介なことになった。

Now I'm really in a mess.

Now it really is a mess.

彼はスピード違反で捕まって，また厄介なことにお巡りさんの顔を殴ってしまったのだ。

He was caught for speeding, and to make it [matters] worse, then he hit the policeman in the face.

ご厄介をおかけしてすみませんでした。

I'm sorry to have put you to [have given you] so much trouble.

cf. I'm sorry to trouble you.（事前に，「お手間をかけてすみませんが…」と用事を頼むときの言い方）

私はだれにも厄介をかけたくない。

I don't want to bother anyone.

【厄介者】 a nuisance; a burden

私は子供たちの厄介者にはなりたくない。

I don't want to make myself a nuisance [to be a nuisance] to my children.

【厄介払い】

これで彼を厄介払いできたんじゃないかな。

I hope I've gotten rid of him.

厄病神め，これで厄介払いさ！

Good riddance to a troublemaker!

2．世話

【親類・友】

私は両親が外国生活をしている間の２，３年間，おばの厄介になっていた。

I lived with my aunt for a few years while my parents were abroad.

僕は京都では友達の所で厄介になっていた。

I stayed with a friend [at a friend's] while I was in Kyoto.

【警察】

彼はしょっちゅう警察の厄介になっている。

He's constantly in trouble [He's been in constant trouble] with the police.

《類義語》

troublesome　難しいというより面倒くさい。

difficult　労力も技術も知恵も必要で難しい。

awkward　やりにくくてすっきりいかず，当惑するような。

やっと → ついに，ようやく

1．ついに

finally; at last

【到着】

やっと着いた。

（ここに） Here we are at last. / We're finally here.
（家に） We're home at last.
（やれやれとほっとした気持ち）

We're finally home.（本当にどうなることか

と思ったが…)

【時】

長い冬だったがやっと終った。

It's been a long winter, but it's over at last [finally over].

赤ん坊はしばらく母親を求めてむずかったがやっと眠った。

The baby fretted for its mother but finally fell asleep.

【理解】

今，自分の子供を持って，やっと母の私に対する気持ちがわかったように思う。

Now that I have my own children I can imagine [see] how my mother must have felt toward me.

〈注〉 I finally understood how ... としてもよい。

2. かろうじて

【刻限】

やっとのことで列車に間に合った。

I was just in time for the train.

I only just caught the train.

I caught the train with not a moment to spare.

彼女が赤ちゃんを生んだのはやっと17歳になったばかりの頃だった。

She was only [barely] seventeen years old when she had the baby.

〈注〉 only seventeen (17歳の年のうち)
barely seventeen (17歳になったばかりのとき)

【合格】

やっとのことで試験にパスした。

I barely passed the exam.

I managed to score just above passing. (合格点ぎりぎりにこぎつけた)

【脱出】

火が出たときみんな2階にいたので[いたのだが]やっとの思いで脱出した。

They were upstairs when the fire started
{ and they just (barely) managed to escape.
{ but somehow they managed to escape.

〈注〉 上の例文で and ... の方は「2階にいたので逃げ出すのがやっとだった」，but ... の方は「2階にいたのだが何とか逃げられた」というニュアンスの違いがある。

彼はやっと逃げのびた。

He narrowly escaped getting caught.

【解決】

「問題解けた?」「ああ，やっとね」。

"Have you solved the problem?" "Yes, but I had a lot of trouble."

〈注〉 Yes, but with difficulty. とも言えるが，堅苦しい表現で，もっと形式ばった内容にふさわしい。

やど(宿)・やどや → とまる(泊まる)

an inn; a small hotel

民宿

a family-run hotel

宿賃，宿泊料，ホテル代

hotel charges; room rates

宿をとる(予約する)

make reservations

宿に泊まる

stay at《a hotel》; put up at《an inn》

宿の主人

an innkeeper (小旅館の主人)

a hotel owner [proprietor, proprietress(女)] (小規模ホテルの主人でもホテルオーナーである)

宿[泊まる所]は見つかった？

Have you found a place to stay?

駅の近くのホテル[宿屋]にその晩泊まった。

We put up for the night at a hotel near the station.

彼女は小さな旅館をやっている。

She operates a small hotel.

ホテルの主人[おかみさん]が特別にコーヒーをいれてくれた。

The hotel owner made coffee specially for me.

やはり・やっぱり → も

1. 同様に

too; also

私もやはりそう思う。

I think so, too.

I also think so.

俊夫もやはり九州出身だ。

Toshio's also from Kyushu.

「僕は彼の意見に賛成できない」「僕もやっぱりできない」。

"I can't agree with him." "No, I can't either."

2. 依然として

君は今もやはりあそこで働いているのですか。

You still work there, don't you?

彼は今でもやはりがんばって働いている。

He works as hard as ever.

3. 思った通り

君はきっと成功すると思っていたが，やっぱりそうなった。

I thought [believed] you would succeed, and indeed you did.

やっぱり期待通り彼はすばらしい演技を見せてくれた。

He put on a wonderful performance just as I expected.

4. 結局は

残念ですがやはり行かれません。

I'm sorry I can't come after all.

あの子を勘当なんて彼女にどうしてできるだろうか。やっぱりあの人にとっては自分の息子だもの。

How can she disown the boy? He's her son after all.

〈注〉 after all には次の２つの使い方がある。

(1) in spite of what was said before …（前にああ言ったけれど）

contrary to what was expected …（予期に反して）

(2) We mustn't forget that …（やはりこのことは忘れるわけにいかない）

5. 選択変更

「コーヒーですか，お茶ですか」「そう，お茶にして…ああ，やっぱりコーヒーいただける？」。

"Coffee or tea?" "Well, tea please … Oh, I've changed my mind. How about coffee instead?"

やぶる（破る）・やぶれる

1. 裂く

tear; rip

【紙】

彼は彼女に手紙を書いたが，自分で破り捨ててしまった。

He wrote a letter to her and then tore it up.

彼は自分のノートを１枚破いて私に渡してくれた。

He took [tore] a page out of his notebook and handed it to me.

【布】

くぎにひっかけてこんなに破れてしまった。

A nail made this tear.

彼のジャケットのそでがくぎに引っかかってひどく破れた。

His jacket sleeve was badly torn when it caught on a nail.

彼のジャケットのそではひじのところが破れそうに薄くなっている。

His jacket sleeves were (worn) out at the elbow.

2. 壊す

【静寂】

突然夜の静けさを破って犬がほえ始めた。

Suddenly the dog began to bark, breaking the silence of the night.

【平和】

彼らの幸福は彼女の前夫が戻って来たことで

破られてしまった。

Their happiness was disturbed by the return of her former husband.

【夢】

彼女の夢は結局破れてしまった。

Her dreams ⌊weren't realized after all [were shattered〔強〕(粉々に砕かれた)].

【伝統】

彼は伝統を破ったというより伝統に新しいものをつけ加えたというのが正しい。

He didn't actually break with tradition so much as he added something new to it.

3. 違反する

【規則】

規則を破る者には罰則を適用する。

There are penalties for those who ⌊break [violate〔*formal*〕] the rules.

【約束】

今度約束を破ったらもう二度と君を信用しないからね。

If you break your promise this time, I'll never believe you again.

4. 負かす

beat; defeat →かつ

私のチームは彼のチームを 2 対 0 で破った。

My team defeated [beat] his team 2–0.

〈注〉 2–0 のスコアは two-[to-]zero〔米〕; two nil〔英〕と読む。

やめる(止める, 辞める, 罷める)

1. 終りにする

stop (行動)

【授業】

ここでやめておきましょう。

Let's stop [quit, leave off] here.

So much for today.

先週はどこでやめましたか[どこまでやりましたか]。

Where did we leave off last week?

【けんか・私語】

音をたてるの[けんか / おしゃべり]をやめなさい。

Stop ⌊making noise [quarreling / chatting].

cf. stop a quarrel (けんかをとめる)

【やむ】

音がやんだ。

The noise stopped.

雨がやっとやんだ。

The rain has finally stopped.

風がやんだ。

The wind has died down.

【生活習慣】

彼はたばこ[酒]をやめた。

He quit [stopped, gave up] smoking [drinking].

【けいこ事】

彼はピアノのけいこをやめてしまった。

He stopped [gave up] taking (his) piano lessons.

【やり方】

こんなばかばかしいことは早くやめればいいのに。

I wish this absurd business would come to a quick end.

成績を厳格な相対(カーブ)評価でつけるのはやめるべきだ。

The practice of grading students on a rigorous curve should be ⌊stopped [brought to an end].

2. 断念する

彼は計画を取りやめにした。

He gave up [abandoned] his plan.

その事業計画は財政的な理由でやめになった。

The project was abandoned for financial reasons.

台風が来ているので旅行は取りやめにした。

We decided not to go on a trip because a typhoon was coming.

バーベキューパーティーは子供たちがはしかになってしまったので取りやめにした。

We gave up having a barbecue party because the children came down with the measles.

仲間が２人もひどい頭痛だったのでパーティーはやめにした。

We canceled the party because two of us had a bad headache.

〈注〉 give up は十分に案がまとまらないうちに投げ出すので敗北感がある。cancel はすべてきちんと決定し実行間近のものが急な障害でだめになる含みがある。

彼女はやめておけばよかったと思った。

She wished she hadn't done that.

やめとこうよ。今日は，皆くたくただもの。

Let's not go today; we are too tired.

〈注〉 Let's go の否定形は Let's not go.

彼はレースの途中でやめてしまった。

He dropped out of the race.

3．退学する，退職する

leave; quit; 退職する **resign, retire**

彼女は２年のとき大学をやめてしまった。

She left [quit, dropped out of] college in her second year.

彼は学校をやめて就職した。

He left [quit] school and went to work.

彼女は家庭の事情で仕事をやめた。

She left [quit, gave up] her job for family reasons.

彼は会社をやめて家業を継いだ。

He left the company and took over the family business.

【引退】

彼女は女優としての舞台生活をやめた。

She abandoned her stage career.

彼は大学をやめてからも研究を続けた。

He continued with his studies after retiring from the university.

ブラウン先生はこの３月でやめられる。

Prof. Brown is going to resign [retire] next March.

〈注〉 resign は定年以外の理由でやめること。retire は定年退職。

田辺氏は議長をやめた。

Mr. Tanabe resigned as chairman.

市長は任期満了前にやめるだろう。

The mayor will leave office before the end of his term.

〈注〉「市長などが自分の意志でやめる」は，wishes to [intends to, promises to] resign。

「やめさせられる」は will be forced to resign [recalled〔*formal*〕]。

cf. 米国大統領やその他選挙による役職者については be impeached とも言う。

議員などが辞職を迫られるのは be pressed to resign，それにまけてやめるのは be forced to resign，辞表を提出するのはtender one's resignation (from the Diet)

【解職】

be dismissed〔英〕〔*formal*〕; discharged〔*very formal*〕(軍隊など); be fired〔*colloq.*〕; be let go; be laid off

〈注〉 be laid off は操業縮小などで一時的に解雇されること。

彼は会社をやめさせられた［くびになった］。

He was dismissed from the company [fired〔*colloq.*〕].

【退学】

彼女は学校をやめさせられた。

She was expelled from school.

cf. be suspended from school（停学処分を受ける）

やりかた（やり方） → かた（方）

私にはやり方がわかりません。

I don't know how to do that.

それにはそれが一番いいやり方だ。

That's the best way of doing it.

彼女には彼女のやり方がある。

She has her own way of doing it.

どこの家にもその家のやり方がある。

Each family has its own way of doing things.

彼は数学の勉強のやり方がわかっていない。

He doesn't know how to study mathematics.

しみの種類によってしみ抜きにもいろいろなやり方がある。

There are different ways to take out different sorts of stains.

これを開けるにはやり方がある［技術が必要だ］。

It requires technique to open this.

You need technique to open this.

Technique is needed [required] to open this.

なに，これで掃除をしたと言うのか。(やり方が悪いという叱責)

What! { You call this sweeping your room [this room swept]! / You said you swept your room! }

掃除のやり方がなっていないよ。

This room hasn't been cleaned properly.

私はこのあたりの人々のやり方を知らない。

I don't know { how / the way } { you do things here. / things are done here. }

I don't know the way to do things here.

《類義語》

how to ... やり方。

way やり方，方法。一般的な語。

method 確立した体系的方法。

ex. teaching methods (教授法)

methods of cooking (料理法)

procedure 何かを具体的にやる手順。

ex. procedure for making a pair of jeans (ジーンズの作り方)

rough procedure (大筋のやり方)

get the cloth and pattern (型紙), cut the cloth (裁断), sew the pieces together (縫合), and iron (アイロンかけ)

detailed procedure (詳細なやり方)

どのような順序で布切れ(pieces)を縫い合わせるかまでを指示。

technique 技術。

〈注〉 way が最も一般的な語。どの語にしようか迷うなら way を使うとよい。

やりとり(遣り取り) → やる

【手紙】

私たちはお互いに時には手紙のやりとりをしている。

We write (to) each other [exchange letters] occasionally.

〈注〉 ×exchange letters each other とは言えない。

【言葉】

あの人たちはしばらくの間，激しくやりとりしていたが，結局仲直りした。

They bandied words for some time but eventually made peace with each other.

〈注〉 bandy は口語で，議論を戦わせる場合に使うが，冗談に言葉を投げつけ合って楽しむ場合もある。それを verbal tennis match と言う。

やる

1. 与える

give →あげる

僕のおもちゃはみんな甥(おい)にやってしまった。

I've given all my toys to my little nephew.

私は息子に小遣いとして月3000円やっている。

I give my son 3,000 yen a month as pocket [spending] money.

毎朝仕事に出かける前に花に水をやります。

I water my flowers every morning before going to work.

彼が大学に入ったとき独英辞典を買ってやった。

I bought him a German-English dictionary when he entered university.

彼が眠っていたので私のショールをかけてやりました。

As he was asleep I put my shawl over him.

2. 行かせる，移す

【送り出す】

彼は自分の卒業した学校に息子をやった。

He sent his son to the same school he graduated from.

私の薬を取りにだれか医院に使いをやってくれ。

Send someone to the doctor's to get my medicine.

彼は空港まで車をやった。

He drove to the airport.

【紛失】

ボールペンをどこかにやってしまった。

I've left my ball-point pen somewhere.

私のスリッパをどこにやったんだ。

Where did you put my slippers?

3. する，実行する

【実行】

まず宿題をやりなさい。

Do your homework first.

僕はもうやってしまった。

I've already finished it.

計画通りやってごらんなさい。

Try to carry out your plan [put your plan into action].

僕はやる気だぞ。

I've a good mind to do that.

(成功の叫び) やった! 僕の名前が (合格者名簿に) 載っている。

I made it! [Made it!] My name's on the list! Made it onto the list!

【専門職】

彼は医者[歯医者 / 弁護士]をやっている。

He is a medical doctor [a dentist / a lawyer].

He practices medicine [dentistry / law].

【店を】

彼は公園の近くで食堂をやっている。

He runs a restaurant near the park.

彼は駅のそばでみやげ物店をやっている。

He has a souvenir shop near the station.

【専攻】

彼は文学をやっている。

He's in literature.

彼はジェームズ・ジョイスをやっている。

He specializes in James Joyce.

彼は生命科学をやろうとしている。

He's going to study life science.

【趣味】

彼女は水彩画をやろうとしている。

She's taking up watercolor painting.

She goes in for watercolor painting. (やっている)

〈注〉 go in for ... はただ「やる」のではなく，たいへん熱心にやっていること。

日本では今テニスをやる人が多い。

In Japan many people play tennis nowadays.

4. 上演[上映]する，演ずる

御園座では今何をやっていますか。

What is on at the Misonoza?

勧進帳をやっています。

They are doing [giving, performing] Kanjincho.

【役】

幸四郎がハムレットをやっています。

Koshiro acts [plays] the role [part] of Hamlet.

やわらかい (柔らかい)

ジャージは(手ざわりが)柔らかい。

Jersey material feels soft.

この肉は柔らかくておいしい。

This meat is tender and good.

私は柿は熟して柔らかいのが好きだ。

I like persimmons ripe and juicy.

〈注〉 桃などの柔らかいものを ripe，未熟でかたいのは not ripe (enough)，完熟は perfect ripeness (名詞形) と言う。soft の反対語は firm。hard には好ましくないという含みがある。「柔らかすぎる」のは unpleasantly soft。粥(かゆ)のような柔らかさは mushy。

私は春のやわらかい日差しを浴びて坐っていた。

I sat basking in the gentle [warm] spring sunshine.

彼女は人当りのやわらかい人だ。

She's a mild person.

やわらぐ（和らぐ）・やわらげる

【和らぐ】

風が和らいだ。

The wind has died [gone] down.

寒さが和らいだ。

It's not as cold as it was.

It's [It has] become warmer.

コデイン（鎮痛剤）で痛みが和らいだ。

The pain was eased a bit by codeine.

彼は初めはかちかちだったが，だんだん緊張が和らいできた。

He was tense at first but gradually grew calm and relaxed.

赤ん坊が生れてから彼の態度が和らいできた。

His attitude softened after the baby was born.

彼の怒りは徐々に和らいだ。

His anger gradually left him.

彼女の誠意で彼の怒りは和らいだ。

Her sincerity melted his anger.

【和らげる】

規則を和らげる［緩める］

make the regulations less severe

我々は彼の痛み［心配／怒り］を和らげようと努力した。

We tried to	ease / relieve	his	pain.（痛み） / anxiety.（心配）

We tried to	mitigate his anger.（怒り） / to calm him (down).（怒り）

彼はいつも厳しい顔をしているが，小さな子供たちには表情を和らげる。

He usually looks stern but he's very gentle with small children.

ゆ

ゆ（湯）

温水　**hot water;** 熱湯　**boiling water; boiling hot water**（強調）; 風呂　**a bath**

湯に入る　take [have] a bath

〈注〉 風呂は熱いものと決っているので，特に「熱い」を強調するのでなければ hot は不要。
ex. Uh, it's cold outside. A hot bath would be very nice ...（ああ外は寒い。熱い風呂で温まりたい）

【飲料】

湯を沸かす　boil water

お湯を沸かして[やかんを火にかけて]ください。

Please put the kettle on.

待っているとお湯はなかなか沸かない。(待つ身は長い)

A watched pot never boils.（ことわざ）

お茶を入れるにはお湯がぬるかった。

The water was not hot enough for tea.

【給湯設備】

ガス湯沸かし器　a gas water-heater

全館給湯設備　central hot water system

これを回すとお湯が出て，これを回すと水が出ます。

Here's the hot water tap and here's the cold.

いつでもお湯が出る。

We have running hot water.

ボイラーが壊れて台所も風呂場もお湯が出ない。

The boiler's broken. We can't get hot water in either the kitchen or the bath.

ゆう（言う） → いう

ゆういぎ（有意義）

【休暇】

この夏は有意義に過したい。

I hope { to do a lot of things this summer. / to spend the vacation productively.

I'm determined to have a productive summer this year.（絶対に）

〈注〉 productive とは大いに成果の上がること。

両親は私が夏休みを有意義に過すことをいつも望んでいる。

My parents always hope I'll make good use of my summer vacations.

【学生生活・人生】

私は有意義な学生生活を送りたい。

I'd like to lead a worthwhile school life.

有意義な人生

a worthwhile life; a life worth living

【余生】

余生は何か有意義なことをして暮したい。

I'd like to do something useful with the rest of my life.

【小遣い】

有意義に使いなさいよ。(臨時の小遣いなど)

Use it wisely.

ゆううつ（憂鬱）

（主観）　**sad; unhappy; down; down in the dumps**〔*colloq.*〕; **miserable**〔強〕; **dejected; depressed**

（客観）　**gloomy; cheerless; melancholy**〔*literary; a bit formal*〕

【気分】

彼は憂鬱そうだ。

He looks unhappy [down, down in the dumps].

彼女は憂鬱だった。

She felt sad [melancholy].

(来週から)試験が始まるかと思うと憂鬱だ。

I feel depressed thinking of the exams starting next week.

The idea of the tests depresses me [has me down].

ああ憂鬱！　来週から学年末試験！

Oh, no! The finals will start next week.

The finals will start next week, unfortunately [worse luck〔英 *colloq.*〕]!

【天候】

憂鬱な雨の日　a cheerless rainy day

何とも憂鬱な天気だった。雲は垂れこめ，ずっと雨が降ったりやんだりしていた。

We had terribly gloomy weather. The clouds were low and half the time it was raining.

雲が垂れこめ憂鬱な天気だった。

The weather was gloomy with overcast skies.

〈注〉 melancholy は文語。また人についての out of spirits は形式ばった古風な表現である。

ゆうしゅう（優秀）

【人】

彼は優秀な学生だ。

He is one of the best students.

彼はテストで優秀な成績だった。

He got very high marks [excellent results] in [on] the test.

彼女は優秀な成績で試験に合格した。

She passed the examination with flying colors.

彼は優秀な技術者だ。

He is {an excellent / a superior} technician.

〈注〉 superior は最優秀の意。

最優秀選手

the most valuable player (略 MVP)

【物】

私どもの商品は優秀な品質で定評がございます。

Our goods are known for their excellence [excellent quality].

ゆうじん（友人）→ ともだち

ゆうとう（優等）→ ゆうしゅう

彼女は優等で大学を卒業した。

She graduated from university with honors.

彼はその年度の最優等生として銀時計をもらった。

He was awarded a silver watch for being the best student of the year.

cf. 彼は「年間最優秀学生賞」をもらった。

He was given the Best Student of the Year Award.

〈注〉◆米国では高校などで最優等生は卒業式にスピーチをする。それを valedictory (speech) と言う。
◆「賞」は award 名,「賞を与える」も award 動を使う。prize はコンテストの勝者に与える賞。ただしノーベル賞は Nobel prize と言う。

この「露のしずく」というお菓子は昨年の品評会で最優等賞をとった。

This cake, "Dew Drop", was awarded the prize for best cake last year.

【優等生】

彼は高校で優等生だった。

He was an honor(s) student in high school.

彼女は優等生だ。

She's an honor student [a very good student, one of the best students].

〈注〉 an honor student とは学業成績優秀な生徒を指す。

優等生でもちっとも優等生タイプでない人もいる。

Sometimes honor students are not the honor student type at all.

〈注〉◆「彼女は優等生タイプ…」は優等生タイプを好まない者が皮肉な口調で言うこともあり，英語でも次の表現は批判的意味をもつ。
She's one of those honor-student types.
She's too much the honor-student type.
◆優等生はエリートコースをすいすい行って一般人の苦しみや気持ちがわからない，といったイメージがあるが，英語では次のような表現がだいたいそれに当る。
She is in another world [belongs to a different world; is out of touch with reality].

模範生(必ずしも学生でなくてもよい)

a model of good behavior

a model worker

彼女[あの人たち]は優等生だ。

She is a model [They are models] of good

behavior.

ゆうびん（郵便）

mail〔米〕**; post**〔英〕

【郵便制度[業務]】 mail [postal] service

国内郵便　domestic mail

外国郵便　foreign [overseas] mail

郵便屋さん　a letter carrier

郵便局　a post office

郵便局長　a postmaster

郵便局員　a post office clerk

郵便ポスト　a mailbox〔米〕; a postbox〔英〕

郵便受け　a mailbox〔米〕; a letterbox〔英〕

私書箱　P. O. Box（＝Post Office Box）

郵便番号　zip code; postal code

郵便料金　charges

小包料金　(parcel post) rates

この郵便料金は？

What's the postage?

How much is it?

【郵便貯金】 postal savings; a postal deposit

郵便貯金の口座　a post office account

郵便貯金をする

deposit in the post office

郵便貯金が50万円ある

have 500,000 yen in a post office account

《関連語》
はがき　postcard／絵はがき　picture postcard／封書　letter／切手　stamp／速達　special [express] delivery／速達を出す　send a letter by express delivery／書留　registered mail／書留にする　have [send] it registered／現金書留　cash remittance／現金書留封筒　cash remittance envelope／小包　package〔米〕, parcel〔英〕／為替　money order, postal order〔英〕(英米では小切手(check)を使うことが多く，checking accounts(当座預金口座)を持たない人が為替を利用する)／為替で5000円送る　send 5,000 yen by money order／為替を現金に替える　have a money order cashed／代金引換え払い　collect〔米〕[cash〔英〕] on delivery（㊙略 COD)／為替振替　postal transfer／振替用紙　postal transfer form／配達する　deliver／転送する　forward／(この郵便を)下記住所にご転送ください。 Please forward this letter to the following address.

ゆうゆう（悠々）

1. 落ち着いているさま

【沈着】

何が起っても彼はゆうゆうと落ち着いている。

No matter what happens he remains calm and collected.

雷鳴がとどろき稲妻が走ったが，彼はゆうゆうとたばこをくゆらしていた。

Thunder rolled and lightning flashed, but he calmly continued smoking.

【自適】

彼は悠々自適の生活を楽しんでいる。

He lives comfortably, free from worldly cares.〔*cliché*〕

He's been enjoying a free life.

【ゆっくり】

彼は草の上に寝そべり白雲がゆうゆうと行くさまを眺めた。

He stretched out on the grass and watched the white clouds go by.

彼は悠々たる足取りで歩いていた。

He was walking in a leisurely way.

2. 余裕

【能力】

彼はゆうゆうと優勝した。

He won the first prize easily.

【時間】

今すぐ出発すればゆうゆうと間に合いますよ。

If you start now, you'll be there in good time [ahead of time].

【空間】

5人はゆうゆうと乗れます。

There is enough room for five people.

This car seats five persons comfortably.（広告文など）

〈注〉「私の車には…人乗れる」は次のようにも言える。

I can take four people.

My car will hold [take] five.

Well, my car can take five.（詰め込んで５人が乗れるということかも知れない）

ゆかい（愉快）→ たのしい・たのしむ・たのしみ

cheerful（外面的）; **happy**（内面的）

1. 楽しい

愉快でした。ありがとう。

We've had a wonderful time, thank you.

愉快にやろうぜ。

Let's have a good time.

たいへん愉快にやりました。食べたり，しゃべったり，笑ったり。

We had a very good time, eating, talking and laughing.

彼女は新しい仕事を愉快にやっています。

She's happy with her new job.

みんな愉快そうだった。

They all looked happy [cheerful(陽気)].

2. 面白い

彼は実に愉快な話をした。

He told us a hilarious story.

彼は愉快なやつだ。

He's a cheerful fellow.

さあスキーをしてごらん。実に愉快だよ。

Come and try to ski. It's a lot of fun.

《類義語》

pleasant　a pleasant person は，一緒にいて楽しい人。pleasant とは胸がわくわくする愉快さではない。物静かに快いこと。

happy　a happy person は，満ち足り，他と争うこともない幸福な状態の人。happy は人の心の状態を示す語。

cheerful　a cheerful person は，にこにこ愉快そうに見えて，陽気なタイプの人。cheerful は人や人の表情・外見などのほかに部屋の感じや雰囲気などについても使える。

ゆきすぎ（行き過ぎ）→ きょくたん

ゆく（行く）→ こうつう

go（**to**）; **come**

訪れる　**visit**《a place / a person》; **call on**《a person》

〈注〉電話などで「すぐに行きます」は自分中心に考えれば I'll go ... だが，相手を中心に考えて次のように言う。

I'm coming.（略してComing.）

I'll come right away [in a minute].

「来られるか」に対して

"I'll come."「行きます」

"I won't be able to come."「行かれません」

さあ行こう。

Let's go.

どこに行くの？

Whrere are you going?

彼は姪の結婚式で東京に行った。

He went to Tokyo to attend his niece's wedding.

私はロンドンにいる彼女に会いに行きました。

I went to see [visited, called on] her in London.

桜の花が咲く頃までにはそこに行きます。

I'll be there by the time the cherry blossoms are out.

行ってしまえ！（消え失せろ）

Get [Go] away!

Get lost!

Scram!〔*slang*〕

Out!（部屋の外へ）

「どこへ行くの？」「ちょっと街まで買い物に」。

"Where are you going?" "I'm going to town to do some shopping."

財布はどこへ行ったんだろう？（探し物）

Where is my purse?

Where has it gone?

今までいったいどこに行っていたの？

Where have you been all this time [while]?

町までお祭りを見に行っていた。

I've been to town to see the festival.

バスが行ってしまった。

The bus has gone.

彼は朝の列車で九州に行ってしまった。

He left for Kyushu on the morning train.

駅までは5分で行けます。

You can get to the station in five minutes.

It takes only five minutes to get to the station.

駅まで5分で行けた。

I made it to the station in five minutes.

【旅行に行く】 go; make a trip to; travel →りょこう

毎年夏には鎌倉に泳ぎに行きます。

Every summer we go swimming at Kamakura.

この夏は北海道に行きます。

I'll go to Hokkaido this summer.

この週末には京都に行こうと思っています。

We are planning to visit Kyoto this weekend.

ちょっと信州に行ってこようと思う。

I'm going to make a trip to Shinshu.

いつか外国に行ってみたいと思う。

I'd like to travel abroad some day.

【旅行経験】

〜に行ったことがあるか。

Did you go to 〜?

Have you been to 〜?

Have you gone to 〜?

Have you ever been to 〜?

(昨年)旅行したときにパリにも行ったか。

Did you go to Paris when you went to Europe last year?

Did you go to Paris (on your trip)?

今までにパリに行ったことがあるか。

Have you ever been to Paris?

パリに行ってきたか。

Have you gone / Did you go } to Paris yet?〔米〕

(You said you were going to Paris, but have [did] you ...? パリに行くと言っていたが行ってきたかのような状況で使う)

何回ぐらいアメリカに行かれましたか。

How often {
have you been to America?(1)
have you gone to America?〔米〕(2)
did you go to America?(3)

〈注〉 (1)have been, (2)have gone は米語ではどちらも使えるが改まった文では have been を使う方がよい。(3)も使われることがあるが did には「すべて過去のこと」の感じがある。外国旅行などから帰った人に旅行中のことを尋ねる場合には did をよく使う。

修学旅行で広島に行った。(過去のこと)

I went to Hiroshima on my school excursion.

長崎には前に行ったことがある。(経験)

I've been to Nagasaki before.

近くに住んでいるのに金沢には行ったことがない。(未経験)

I haven't been [I've never been] to Kanazawa although I live quite near.

【行った，行っている，行ってしまった】

went to; have gone to

彼は南米に行った。

He went to South America. (その後のことには触れない)

He has gone to South America.

〈注〉 has gone の文は2通りの解釈が可能。前後の文で(1)か(2)かがわかる。

(1) 南米に行っている。(旅行などで)

(on a trip) He went to S. A. and he is now in S. A. (He'll be back in September.)

(2) 南米に行ってしまった。(移住した)

He went to S. A. to stay.

He moved to South America.

バスが行ってしまった。

The bus has gone.

【行ってきた】 have been to; went to

おばさんを空港まで見送りに行ってきた。

I've been to the airport to see my aunt off.

I went to the airport to see my aunt off and just returned a few minutes ago. (2, 3分前帰着)

【方向・道順】

まっすぐ行く　go straight on

まっすぐ行きなさい。

Go [Keep] straight (on).

～の方へ行く　make for [toward] ～

右[左]へ行く　turn (to the) right [left]

～まで行く　go as far as ～

交差点までまっすぐ行く

go straight (on) [go, continue] till you come to a crossing

【道順の説明】

建物を出たら右に行ってください。

Go out of the building and turn right.

5分ばかり歩いて行くと交差点に出ます。

Walk straight along the road for about 5 minutes until you come to a junction.

そこを左に曲って100メートルほど行くと右手にバス停があります。

Turn left, and the bus stop is about 100 meters along the road [ahead] on the right hand side.

1番のバスに乗って市民会館まで行ってください。

Take the number 1 bus to Shimin Kaikan.

バスを降りたら左手に行ってください。

Then turn [go] left as you get off the bus.

道路を渡って左に曲り，ジョークという喫茶店のところまで行きます。

Cross the road and turn left. Walk to the Joke cafe.

喫茶店の前の路地を曲りまっすぐ行くと交差点に出ます。

Take the turning immediately in front of the cafe and walk straight (along) until you come to a crossroads.

そのまままっすぐ行ってください。私の家は道の右側で幼稚園の隣にあります。すぐわかりますよ。

Keep [Go〔米〕] straight on. My house is on [at〔米〕] the right hand side next to a kindergarten. You can't miss it.

〈注〉　道順を説明する語彙にも米・英で多少の差がある。〔米〕としてあるのはアメリカで使われることを示すが，特に表示のない言い方は英米ともに使われる。

右手に

to your right〔米〕; on the right

交差点で

at the crossroads [junction, intersection]

信号で

at the stop [signal] lights〔米〕; at the traffic lights

横断歩道で

at the (pedestrian) crosswalk〔米〕

on the zebra crossing

角の

at the corner〔米〕; on the corner

【出勤する，登校する】

go to one's [the] office (通勤); go to school (通学); commute〔米〕(遠距離の通勤・通学)

彼は鎌倉から横浜の会社に行っている。

He goes from Kamakura to his office in Yokohama.

彼はバスと電車で学校へ行っている。

He goes to school by bus and train.

私は歩いて学校へ行く。

I walk to school.

(今日) 何時に学校へ行きますか [出かけますか]。

What time are you leaving [going to leave]?

8時半までに行かなければならないので，遅くとも7時半には出なければなりません。

I have to be there [arrive] by 8:30, so I'll start [leave] by 7:30 at the latest.

弟は高校に行っています[高校生です]。

My brother goes to high school.

My brother is a high school student.

【用件】

買物[水泳 / スキー / 釣り]に行く

go shopping [swimming / skiing / fishing]

〈注〉　湖へ魚釣りに行く。

I went fishing at the lake. (1)

×I went fishing to the lake. (2)

湖へ行く went to the lake の連想で (2) の文のよう

にしがちだが fish at the lake と考えるか，または他の構文にする。
ex. I went to the lake to fish.
ほかの go ～ing 形についても同じ注意が必要。

【道】
この道は松本に行く。
This road goes to Matsumoto.

【乗物】
列車[バス / 飛行機 / 船 / 自転車]で行く
go by train [bus / air / ship / bicycle]

【成り行き】
うまくゆく →うまい・うまく
［仕事］go well; work well; be successful
［協調］get along fine
試験はうまくいった。
I did well in the exam.
彼は何とかうまくいっている[やっている]。
He's getting along.
すべてうまくいった。
Everything went well [wonderfully, beautifully].
あのやり方は今回はうまくいかなかった。
That didn't work this time.
彼の事業はだいたいにおいてうまくいっている。
His business is successful on the whole.
うまくいった［やった］！ 僕の名前が出ている。
I made it! / Made it! } My name's on the list!

【行方】 one's whereabouts
行方を探す
look for《a person》

【行方不明の】 lost; missing
５名が死亡，さらに５名がいまだに行方不明である。
Five persons were found dead and five (more) are still missing.
長く行方不明であった彼の兄が中国で生きているとのことである。
His long lost brother is reported to be alive in China.

【行く末】
彼は息子の行く末を案じている。
He feels anxious about his son's future.
彼は息子の行く末を見届けたいと思っている。
He wants to see his son settled in life.

【過ぎ行く】
行く年[逝く年] the old year
行く春[逝く春] the departing spring

ゆだん（油断）→ ようじん

【油断をする】
be off one's guard
lower one's guard
let one's attention lapse〔*formal*〕
（軽い意味） be careless; be inattentive; slack off
油断をすると試験に受からないぞ。
If you don't keep at it〔*colloq*〕, you won't pass the exam.
(cf. I kept at it and in the end I passed. がんばってついにパスした)
私はつい油断をしては牛乳をふきこぼしてしまう。
I'm so careless I let the milk boil over.

【油断するな】
あいつは危険だ，油断するな。
He is dangerous. Don't take your eyes off him.
この世は油断禁物。
You must be alert [on your guard] in this world.

ゆめ（夢）

1. 睡眠中の夢
a dream
夢を見る　動 **dream; have a dream**
昨夜は父の夢を見た。
Last night I saw my father in a dream.
遅刻する夢を見た。
I had a dream about being late.

どこかの大学の入学試験を受けている夢を見た。

I dreamed I was taking an entrance exam for some college (or other).

私はおかしな夢を見た。どこかの洞穴で小人たちとトランプをしているのだ。

I had a funny dream in which I was playing cards with some dwarfs in a cave.

〈注〉 私に2人も子供がいる夢を見た。

I dreamed that (1) / I had a dream in which (2) } I had two children.

(1) dream を動詞として使うのが普通。

(2) その夢の中では (in which) ...

次の用法は正用法とは認められない。

△I had a dream that I found a wonderful job.（すてきな仕事にありついた夢を見た）

I dreamed that ... とすればよい。同格接続詞that節で修飾できるのは fact, belief, idea など限られた名詞だけで，dream がその仲間に入るかどうかは意見の分かれるところである。上の例のように dream を動詞として使うのがよい。または「夢の中で…」と考えて in which ... とする。in を落さないように。

× I had a dream last night which you were still a child ...

○ I had a dream last night in which you were still a child and ...（昨夜の夢ではあなたがまだ子供でそして…）

2. 将来の希望

a dream

【実現】

彼女の夢が本当になった。夢の王子様を見つけたのだ。

Her dream has come true. She has found her prince.

【宿願】

自分のボートに乗って世界一周をすることが私の長い間の夢だった。

It has been my dream to go sailing round the world in my own boat.

【幻滅】

若いときにはいろんな夢を持っていたが，年を重ねるにつれ，朝日に露が乾くように夢も次々と消えていった。

I had many dreams when I was young, but my dreams grew fewer [evaporated] as I grew older, just as dew dries in the morning sun.

未来は宇宙へ移り住むのだと夢見る人もいる。

One vision of the future portrays the colonization of space.

3. 比喩的慣用句

夢見るまなざし dreamy eyes

私は夢でも見ているようだった。

I felt as if I were in a dream.

彼女は夢の世界に生きている。

She lives in a dream world.

こんな賞をいただくなんて夢にも思いませんでした。

I never dreamed that I should be awarded such a prize.

君のプランはまるで夢だね[実際的でない]。

Your plan is quite unrealistic.

講義の間中夢うつつだった。

I was half asleep during the lecture.

《類義語》

dream あこがれを強調。夢はやがて覚めるもの，また実現が難しいこと。

vision 目の当りに見ているように視覚化された夢，こうあってほしいと想像して思い描いた大きな夢，将来についてのはっきりした見通し。

ambition 原義は大きな夢のことであったが，後に世俗的権力や名声などに対する野心すなわち人を攻撃的・自己中心的にする欲望を連想させる危険な感じを持つ語となった。ただし ambitious for justice (= committed to justice)（正義の達成にかける）のような用法もある。

〈注〉 このほか，考え方が「現実ばなれ」しているという意味の表現に次のようなものがある。

He's in an ivory tower.（象牙の塔にこもっている）

He's in cloud-cuckoo land.（雲の上に住んでいる）

His head's in the clouds.（頭を雲につっこんでいる）

ゆるす（許す，赦す）

1．許可する

そんな薬を売ることが法律で許されているなんて驚いています。

I'm surprised that the law allows [permits] the sale of such drugs.

医者はまだあなたに外出を許さないだろう。

The doctor won't let you go [allow you to go] out yet.

政府は航空会社間のもっと自由な競争を許すことになるだろう。

The government will permit more free competition among airlines.

〈注〉 委員会は…を許すことに賛成した。
The committee approved more free ....

彼女の両親は彼女とあの人の結婚を許していない。

Her parents haven't approved [consented to 〔*formal*〕] her marrying that man.

〈注〉 **approve** 動の意味
(1) approve 正式に…することを許可する。
(2) approve of 何かを「なるほど結構だ」と考える。肯定的態度をとる。
approval は上の approve 動の名詞形である。正式な許可の言葉や，よろしい，よかろうと是認する気持ちも表す。
cf. consent は実行してもよいか否かに関する言葉。単によいと思うのではなく，実行に同意することである。

そんなわがままはここでは許されない。

Such willfulness is not allowed here.

そこでは喫煙は許されていない。

They do not allow smoking.
Smoking is not allowed here.
Smoking is prohibited here.
No smoking.

〈注〉「許す」のつもりで admit が誤用されることがある。admit は「その通り」と認めること。
cf. approve of＝agree that something is good.
admit が「許す」の意味に使われるのは，「入学［入室］を許す」の場合である。
×We shouldn't *admit* abortion.（妊娠中絶を許すべきではない）は誤り。ここでは allow としなければならない。

【余裕】

事情が許せば

if possible; if I can

時間が許せば

if I have time

そんな高いアパートに住むなんて経済が許さない。

I cannot afford to live in such an expensive flat.

〈注〉 as far as circumstances permit（事情の許す限り），if circumstances allow（事情が許せば）は formal な文にのみ使われる。

2．容赦する

【許す】 forgive; pardon; excuse

彼女は私がうわさを流したのだと思い込んで，真相がわかるまで何か月も許してくれなかった。

She believed I had started the rumor and wouldn't forgive me for months, until she found out the truth.

cf. Once she knew the truth she forgave me.（いったん真相がわかったら私を許してくれた）

私たちは彼女の気ままを許してはおけない。

We can't excuse her waywardness.

彼女はその子に二度とあんなことはしないと約束させてから許してやった。

She made him promise he would never do that again and then let him go.

3．信用する

心を許せる人 a confidant

彼には彼女だけが心の許せる相手だった。

She was the only one (whom) he trusted [could open himself up to; could confide in].

彼に気を許すな。 →ゆだん

We must guard against him.

ゆれる（揺れる）

1．揺れ動く

shake

【振り子など】 swing（弧を描くような揺れ）

【ガタガタ】

昨夜は家がガタガタとひどく揺れた。

I felt the house shake violently last night.

新幹線が通ると家がガタガタ［ビリビリ］揺れる。

The house shakes [vibrates] when the Shinkansen passes.

〈注〉 You can see and feel it when things shake.
You can only feel it when things vibrate.
shake は目で見える揺れ，vibrate は目に見えにくく感じるだけの振幅の小さい揺れ。

【ごとごと】

老朽列車はゴトゴトと揺れながら１時間走り続けた。

The old train rattled on for an hour.

【ガタン】

突然大きくガタンと揺れて列車は止まった。

There was suddenly a big jolt and the train stopped.

〈注〉 rattle はゴトゴト揺れ続けることであり，jolt はガタンと揺れる１回の大きな動きである。

【風に】

木々は北風に揺れている。

The trees are swaying in the north wind.

ロープに干した洗濯物が風に揺れている。

The clothes on the clothesline are blowing in the wind.

窓に干した服がそよ風に揺れていた。

The dress hanging in the window to dry was swinging in the breeze.

わずかに枝に残った2,3枚の木の葉が風にひらひら揺れている。

The few leaves still clinging to the bare branches are fluttering in the wind.

【水の揺れ】

バケツにくんだ水がテントに運ぶまでにピシャピシャ揺れてこぼれ，着いたときには半分になっていた。

The water slopped around [about] as he was carrying the buckets up to the tent, and there was only half of it left by the time he got there.

【船】

船が上下左右に揺れるのが面白くて好きです。

I love it when the boat pitches and rolls.

【揺りかご】

ネンネ赤ちゃん木のてっぺん，風吹きゃ揺りかごゆーらゆら

Hush-a-bye, baby, on the tree top,
When the wind blows, the cradle will rock,
Mother Goose

2．動揺する

【心】

「ジョーは男らしいし，ジムはやさしいし」。彼女の心は揺れ動いた。

“Joe is manly, Jim is nice.” She was wavering.

【政界】

汚職事件で政界は大揺れに揺れた。

Government circles were shaken by the bribery scandals.

〈注〉 揺さぶる，揺れるの意の動詞のうち，
・受動態にできる動詞
shake→be shaken　joggle, jiggle→be joggled, be jiggled　jolt→be jolted
・受動態にできない動詞　quake, sway, tremble

よ

よい（良い）→ いい・よい

〈注〉「よい」の口語的な言い方は「いい」であるので「いい」の項に詳述。ここには「よい」と発音する場合のみ記す。

1. よくなる

【快方】

すぐよくなりますよ。

You'll get well soon.

【正常】

2, 3 年すれば何もかもよくなるだろう。

Everything will be all right in a few years.

【進歩】

君の発音はたいへんよくなった。

Your pronunciation improved a great deal.

2. よかった

【うれしい】

こんないいアパートが見つかってよかったね。

You were lucky to find a good apartment like this.

仕事が終ってよかった。

I'm glad I've finished the work.

仕事が終っていたらよかったのに。

I wish I had finished the work.

コンサートよかった？

Was the concert good?

Did you enjoy the concert?

お気に召せばよいのですが。

I hope you'll like this.

【差し支えない】

よかったら一緒にいらっしゃい。

Come with us if you want [wish].

よかったらいらっしゃいませんか。

Would you like to come with us [join us]?

【よしよし】

よしよし，泣くんじゃない。

There, there. Don't cry.

よしよし。（赤ちゃんに）

Hush! Hush! / Shhh!

3. よくない

【道徳的に】

子供にお金を与えすぎるのはよくない。

It's not good to give children too much money.

責任を逃れようとするのはよくない。

It's wrong to try to evade responsibility.

彼をそんなふうに扱うのはよくない。

It's not fair to treat him like that.

【気分】

今日は気分がよくない。

I'm not feeling well today.

4. その他

【許可】

君はもう家に帰ってもよろしい。

You can go home now.

君はお金を払わなくてもよい。

You need not pay.

You don't have to pay.

【助言】

…した方がよい

It would be better to …

…しない方がよい

It would be better not to …

〈注〉◆「…した方がよい」「…しない方がよい」と勧めるとき，△you had better … は子供に対してでもなければ使ってはいけない。you had better … はたいへん強い言い方で，ほとんど命令のようにひびく。We had better … は自分のことに関してであるから差し支えない。He, She のような第三者に関して言うときは He [She] ought to … が普通である。

◆意見を求められた場合

ex. 早い列車で行かれる方がいいでしょう。

It would be better to / It might be good to / Maybe you should { take / go by } an early train.

Why not go [How about going] by an early train?
I suggest you go / I recommend you (to) go } by an early train.
旅行会社の人が客に言うような場合，どのレベルの表現を使うかはもちろん状況による。すなわち話し相手との親しさや，話題が気楽なことか深刻なことかなどを考慮する必要がある。

よう（用）・ようじ（用事）

1. 何の用

何かご用ですか[何のご用ですか]。
What would you like?
〈注〉 先生が生徒に，親が子に言うときの言い方。近所の人などとは，ちょっと世間話でもしてからこのように切り出す。またお店の人がお客になどにも使える。
おや，どうした，何か用かい？
Well, what brings you here?
〈注〉 気軽に驚きや喜びを表すが，言い方によっては（you を強調して言うと）不快を表す。

【不快を表す言い方】
いったい私に何の用だ。
What do you want with me?
何の用事でこんな所まで来たんだ。
What have you come here for?

【店員など】
どんなご用でしょうか。
Can [May] I help you?
What can I do for you?
〈注〉 上の表現はサービス業の人が顧客に，医師が患者になど，だれでも同じように使える。

2. 用[用事]がある

今日は用事があるの。
I'm afraid I'm busy today.
〈注〉 「用事がある」の意味の I'm engaged. は堅い表現であり，また「婚約している」の意味にもとれる。
ちょっと君に用事があるので，授業が終ったら私の部屋まで来てくれませんか。
I have something to ask you, so could you come to my office after school?
用があったら電話をください。
Call me if you need me.

【断り】
本当に残念ですが，ちょっと用事[先約]がありまして伺えません。（招待を断るとき）
I'm sorry, but I already have a prior engagement.
伺いたいんですけど今日はちょっと用事があって…。
I'd like to, but { there's something else / there are some other things } that I have to do today.

3. 用事がない

今日は特に[緊急な]用事がない。
I have no work that has to be done [no pressing work] today.
I've got nothing special [urgent] to do today.
今日の午後は特に用事はありません。
I'm free this afternoon.
〈注〉 「なにもすることがない[退屈だ]」は I have nothing to do today. 労働者が「仕事がない」の意味ならば I have no work today. が可能だが，ただ「用事がない」の意味であれば，上の例文のように no pressing work とか nothing urgent のように特定するのが普通である。

【不用】
お前なんかに用はない[出て行ってくれ]。
Go away!
You have no business being here.
子供に用はない。忙しいんだ。あっちへ行った行った。
Run along now. I'm busy.

【不用品】
ここにある参考書はもう不用になった。
I don't need these reference books any more.

4. 用を足す

父は用事で大阪に行った。
My father went to Osaka on business.
彼は町まで用足しに行った。
He's gone to town.
彼はちょっと用足しに出かけている。
He's gone on an errand.

私はフランス語で用を足せなかった。

I couldn't make myself understood in French.

僕は中国で漢字を書いて用を足すことができた。

In China I could communicate by writing kanji.

僕はやっと用が足せる程度しか知らない。

I know just enough to get around [by].

〈注〉 やっと用が足せる程度の英語，日本語を survival English, survival Japanese と言う。

【用便】

すみません，ちょっと用を足してきたいんですが。

Excuse me. Could you tell me where is the
- bathroom?（個人の家）
- rest room?〔米〕（公共の場所）
- washroom?（公共の場所）
- ladies' room?（公共の場所）
- men's room?（公共の場所）
- the gents'〔英〕（公共の場所）

5. …向けの

婦人用　… for women; women's …; lady's …; ladies' …

婦人用自転車　a women's bicycle [bike]

子供用　… for children; children's …（ex. the children's bicycle [bike]）

寒冷地用の車　cars for cold regions

…よう

1. …様

どのように how　→どう

あなたのお名前はどう[どのように]綴りますか。

How do you spell your name?

どのような　what　→どんな

彼女はどんな[どのような]人ですか。

What kind of person is she?

このように　(in) this way; like this

このような　so …; such …

そのように　(in) that way; so … like that　→そう

そのような　so …; such …　→そんな

あのような　→あんな

まずお砂糖を入れて軽く泡立てるように混ぜます…このように。

First put some sugar in and then whip it lightly … like this.

女の子は皆同じ髪形なので同じように見えた。

All the girls had the same haircut and so looked just the same [alike].

僕はガレージを洗えと言われたのでそのようにした。

I was told to clean the garage and I did.

僕は言われたよう[通り]にガレージを洗った。

I cleaned the garage the way I was told.

2. 比喩・比較

養父母は私を実の娘のように扱ってくれた。

My foster parents treated me just like their own daughter.

雪のように白い。

It's as white as snow.

氷のように冷たい。

It's icy cold.

凍てつくように寒い。

It's freezing cold.

我が家のような所はない。

There's no place like home.

彼は何も知らないようなふりをした。

He pretended he didn't know anything about it.

彼はそこに行って見て来たような話をした。

He talked as if he had been there and seen it.

泣きたいような気持だった。

I felt like crying.

【比較】

彼はいつものように7時に帰宅した。

He came home at seven as usual.

彼は相変らず[いつものように]若々しく精力的に見えた。

He looked as young and vigorous as ever [always].

彼は以前のように精力的ではなかった。

He wasn't as vigorous as he used to be [before].

〈注〉 as he used to be は今の状態が前ほど元気ではない場合に使われる。今も変らない場合は used to be を使わない傾向がある。

ex. He's as vigorous today as he was twenty years ago.（彼は20年前と同じように元気だ）

He still cleans the garage every Saturday as he always did.（彼は以前のように毎土曜車庫の掃除をしている）

【種類】

彼はそんなことをする[言う]ような人ではない。

He isn't the kind [sort] of man to do [say] things like that [such things].

〈注〉 日本人は such a thing を使いすぎる，またはその誤用が多いと指摘される。such と言うときには何らかのカテゴリーを指すわけで，上の例文では法にふれる行為や反社会的言動を念頭においている。「ああもう生きているのがいやになった」に対して「そんなこと言うな」は Don't say that. である。このような特定の発言を指さして such a thing と言うのは誤りである。

だいたい「…のような」「そんな，こんな」は断言を好まない日本人の心情の表出で英語に直訳しない方が無難である。また，such a thing よりも a thing [things] like that を使うとよい。

暗がりで何か犬のようなものがかさこそ逃げていった。

In the dark something [an animal] like a dog scurried away.

あそこのスタンドではパンに牛乳，ジュースのようなものを売っている。

At that stand they sell simple lunch things such as buns, milk and juice.

〈注〉 前記〈注〉で述べたように英語ではカテゴリーが先で次に例がくる。simple lunch things (such as) buns, milk, juice の順である。ただし例は2，3にとどめるのが普通であり，最後に etc., and so on などをつけない方がよい。

私は野球やバレーボールのような団体競技が好きだ。

I like team sports such as baseball and volleyball.

〈注〉 I like sports such as baseball and tennis. この文では baseball と tennis ではカテゴリーがはっきりしない。hit balls の点がいいのか，played out-of-doors の点が好きなのか，team sports だからいいのか，あいまいなのでこれはよい文ではない。

そんな[そのような]言い方しないで。

Don't talk like that.

〈注〉 上の表現は，語調がいやである，きたない言葉を使うな，また内容に関してそんなこと言うな，などの場合にも使える。

3．…よう（意向）

【客に】

どうぞ気楽になさって，何でもお入り用のものがあればお好きなようにお使いください。

Please make yourself at home and help yourself to anything you need.

【許容】

好きなようになさいな。(ほしかったらとっておいで / やりたかったらやったらいい)

If you like it, go ahead (and get [do] it).

好きなようにして[好きな方にして]いいですよ。

Whichever you like is fine (with me).

【怒り】

好きなようにするがいい。(怒って)

Do as you like [please].

【目標】

今月中には終るようにしてください。

See that everything is finished by the end of this month.

スペリングの間違いなどしないように注意してレポートを書いた。

I wrote the paper carefully
{so that I wouldn't make / so as not to make} spelling mistakes.

塗りたてのペンキに触らないように気をつけて。

Be careful not to touch the wet paint.
私は間に合うようにタクシーで行った。
I took a taxi in order [so as] to get there in time.
〈注〉 in order to, so as to は formal である。to … の意味が目的であることが明らかで誤解のおそれがなければ I took a taxi to get there … とすればよい。

【願望】
早くよくなられますように。
I hope you'll get well soon.
〈注〉 I wish … ではじめると you would と続けなければならず，実現しそうもないことを願う言い方になるので見舞いの言葉にならない。
君が試験に受かります[無事に帰ってくる]ように。
I hope you'll pass the exam [come back safely].

【推量】
彼らはうまくやっているようだ。
It seems they are getting along quite well.
天気予報によれば明日は晴れのようだ。
According to the weather forecast it will be fine tomorrow.

ようい(用意) → じゅんび, したく

用意ができている（状態） **be ready; be prepared**
用意をする（行動） **make [get] ready for; fix; prepare for; make preparations for; prepare**《a thing》**for;** 準備をする **make arrangements for**

1．準備，支度，手配

【用意できている】
「用意はできているの？」「できています」。(外出などの)
"Are you ready?" "I'm [We're] ready."
お食事の用意ができました。
Dinner is ready.
珍しいことに，最初のお客が来る１時間も前にすっかり(会の)用意ができ上がったのだ。
Amazingly, everything was ready an hour before the first guest arrived.
この報告書は会合の１日か２日前に用意できないと困る。秘書がコピーをつくる時間がいるからだ。
This report has to be ready a day or two before the meeting so that the secretary has time to make copies.

【用意をする[した]】
私たちは旅行の[東京を発つ]用意をした。
We got ready for the trip [to leave Tokyo].
彼女は今昼食の用意をしています。
She is preparing lunch [fixing lunch, getting lunch ready].
彼女は栄養たっぷりの昼食を私たちのために用意してくれた。
She fixed [made] us a hearty lunch.
もう帰らないと。夕飯の用意があるので。
I have to go now. I have to fix supper.
彼はグリーンホテルでのパーティーの用意万端の手配をした。
He made arrangements for the party [arranged for the party to be held] at the Green Hotel.
明日の英語の用意[予習]をしなければ。
I must prepare (for) tomorrow's English class.
〈注〉 この発言が，先生が教材などをそろえる意味で授業の準備をすることであれば for はなくてもよい。

【用意をさせる】
いやがる子に学校に行く用意[したく]をさせるのはたいへんだ。
It's a pretty hard job to get a reluctant child ready for school.

2．持参

お弁当を用意すること。(指示)
Bring your own lunch.
傘を用意して行きなさいよ。
You should take your umbrella with you.

3. 心の用意 →じゅんび

常に非常の場合のために心の用意ができていなければならない。

We must be prepared for any emergency.

私は何が起ってもあわてない心の用意ができています。

I'm prepared for anything to happen.

彼らは彼の妻に悲報を聞く心の用意をさせた。

They prepared his wife for the fatal news.

《類義語》

ready be ready (準備 OK), get《something》ready((何かを)準備する)の形で使う。Dinner is ready. (夕食の仕度 OK)

cf. Mother is ready for dinner. は母さんが食事に出かける身じたくが OK のこと。

×Mother readied dinner.

prepare 使えるように準備すること。get ready より堅い古風な語。また prepare 動他 と prepare for 動自 と両用の用法あり。

prepare a meal 食事をつくる

prepare for a trip 旅行のための準備をする

prepare for tomorrow's classes [lessons] 学校の予習をする

be prepared for 心の準備のできていること。

He prepared himself (for ...). はあまり使われない。He was prepared (for) ... が普通。

〈注〉「母さんが食事の用意をした」は次のように言える。

Mother { cooked [prepared, fixed] dinner. / got dinner ready.

make arrangements 準備・手配, 外部との交渉をすること。

ようい (容易) → やさしい

容易な 形 easy

これだけの論文に目を通すのは容易ではない。

It's no easy task to read through all these papers.

外国語を習得するのは容易ではない。

It's not easy to learn a foreign language.

航空機の出現が外国旅行を容易にした。

Airplanes have made travel abroad easier.

ようきゅう (要求)

名 **a requirement; a demand**

(権利に基づく)要求 **a claim**

(職権に基づく)要求 **a demand**

要求する **ask for; require**

会社側は労働者側の賃上げ要求を受理[拒否]した。

The company accepted [rejected] its employees' demand for higher wages.

債権者は債務の支払いを要求した。

The creditors demanded payment.

彼は私に1か月以内に金を返すよう要求した。

He demanded that I pay back the money in a month.

彼らは病院を相手に損害賠償を要求した。

They claimed damages against the hospital.

cf. 彼らは車の損傷に対し保険金の請求をした。

They made an insurance claim for the damage to their car.

ようじん (用心) → きをつける, ちゅういする

【忠告】

インフルエンザがはやっている。かからないよう用心しなさい。

There's a lot of flu about. Take care not to catch it.

地下鉄ではすりにご用心。

Look out for pickpockets in subways.

足元にご用心。

Watch your step.

【指示】

あの人には用心した方がいい。危険人物だ。

Keep an eye on him; he's dangerous.

用心のためもう1日寝ていなさい。

Stay in bed for another day just as a precaution.

泥棒に用心しなさい。
　Guard against burglars.
火の用心。
　Be careful about fire.
火の用心たのむよ。たばこの吸い殻は灰皿に。
　Watch out for fire. Put cigarette butts in ashtrays.
【警戒】
彼を怒らせないよう用心してしゃべった。(言葉遣いに注意した)
　I chose my words carefully in order not to provoke him.
彼女はたいへん用心深い人だ。
　She's very cautious.

ようす（様子）

1．状態
　a (general) state
【変化・動き】
町の様子はどうだ？
　How is it in town?
名古屋の様子はどうだ？
　What's it like in Nagoya?
　How are things going in Nagoya?
彼は学校の様子を話してくれた。
　He told us how things were going at school.
彼らは試合の様子を見守っていた。
　They were watching how the game was going.
だれかが部屋の中の様子をうかがっていた。
　Someone was looking into the room to see what was going on there.
彼らは敵の様子[動き]をうかがっていた。
　They were watching the enemy's movements.
2,3年の間に通りの様子がすっかり変ってしまった。
　The streets have changed completely in a few years.
　The streets have been completely changed in a few years.(人為的)
〈注〉 町ゆく人が変ったことを強調するなら People changed ... としてもよい。2番目の受動態の文は人為的に変えられたことを強調。
2,3年のうちに何もかもすっかり様子が変ってしまっていて驚いた。
　I was surprised to see that [how] everything had changed in a few years.
【事情】
彼は事故が起ったときの様子を詳細に話してくれた。
　He { described the circumstances of the accident in detail. / explained in detail how it happened. }
彼は一目で様子を飲み込んだ。
　He took in the situation at a glance.
警察は有力容疑者の身辺の様子を探っている。
　The police have been making a thorough investigation of the potential suspect.
〈注〉 「身辺の様子」をもっと具体的に言えば，例えば次のようになる。
... of the potential suspect's { acquaintances.（知人） / movements.（動き） / business activities.（事業） / bank accounts.（銀行預金） }
【様子に明るい】
彼は土地の様子に明るい。(地理)
　He is { familiar with the place [city]. / well acquainted with the place. }
彼は土地の様子に明るい。(風習)
　He is completely familiar with life in this area. (1)
　He knows the ways of the place. (2)
〈注〉 (1)は風習・土地勘。(2)は風習を知っていること。
犯人は土地の様子に明るいものと思われる。
　The culprit must have known the area very well.
　The culprit is thought to be extremely familiar with the area.

2．姿，外見

どんな様子の人？

What does he look like?

〈注〉 cf. What is he like?（どんな人？）
人柄・仕事ぶりなどをたずねるときの表現で，外見のことではない。
cf. What does he like?（彼は何が好き？）

様子のよい人だ。

［男性］He looks [is] handsome.

［女性］She's nice-looking.

【模様（…らしい）】

彼は結果に満足の様子だった。

He looked [seemed] satisfied with the result.

この様子では雨になりそうだ。

It looks like rain.

彼女は振り返り，驚いた様子で立ち上がった。

She turned round,
{ seemed surprised and rose to her feet.
{ and rose to her feet surprised [with an air of surprise 〔*literary*〕].

3．具合・兆候

【ありさま】

私は鳥たちがていねいに巣造りしていく様子をじっと見ていた。

I watched the birds carefully building their nest.

【具合】

どんな具合にいくか様子を見よう。

Let's see how it works.

Let's try it out.

しばらく様子を見よう。

Let's see how things（will）go.

病人の様子がおかしいのです。

There are some alarming changes in the condition of the patient.

彼はこのところ少々様子がおかしい。（奇行）

He's been acting a bit [rather] strange(ly) nowadays.

この頃彼の様子がいつもと違う。

He isn't his usual self [quite himself] these days.

【兆候】

病人はいっこうによくなる様子がない。（病状）

The patient shows no sign of getting better.

【気配】

泥棒が寝室を荒らした様子はない。

There is no evidence of the robber having searched the bedroom.

彼女は2週間前に家出して，帰って来る様子はない。

She { walked out of her house / abandoned her family } two weeks ago, and there is no sign that she will come back.

ようやく → ついに，やっと

1．待ちに待った末に

【夜明け】

長い夜だったがようやく夜が明け始めた。

The night seemed so long, but finally [at last] day began to break [dawn came].

【目覚め】

お母さんに10回も起されてようやく目を覚ました。

My mother called me ten times before I（really）woke up.

【到着】

我々はようやく村にたどり着いた。

We reached the village at last.

【決心】

さんざん考えてようやく決心がついた。

I thought and thought and I finally made up my mind.

【わかる】

ない知恵をしぼってさんざん考えてようやく答えがわかった。

After racking my brain I finally found an answer.

2．かろうじて

ようやくのことで何とか間に合った。

I barely managed to arrive in time [be on time].

よきん（預金）→ ちょきん

名 **a deposit;** 動 **deposit**

預金通帳　a bankbook

【残高】

彼は銀行預金が100万円ある。

He has one million yen in the bank.

【預け入れ】

私は持ち金全部を預金した。

I put all the money in my account.

私はいつも月末に残った分を預金することにしている。

I usually deposit what is left over at the end of a month.

【引き出し】

今月は母の病気のため２か月分の預金を引き出さねばならなかった。

This month I had to withdraw two months' savings because of my mother's illness.

よこ（横）

1. 水平の方向

【サイズ】

横の[水平の]　horizontal（↔ vertical）

横３センチ縦５センチの写真

a 3 by 5 centimeter photo

a 3 by 5 [3 × 5] photo（この表記では centimeter をつけないのが普通）

縦横５センチ四方の布

a piece of cloth 5 centimeters square

横幅1.5メートル，高さ１メートルの机

a desk 1.5 meters wide and 1 meter high

標準的な便せんのサイズは横18センチ縦25センチだ。

Standard letter paper is 18 centimeters wide and 25 centimeters long [18 by 25 centimeters].

縦50センチ横30センチの板が必要だ。

I need a board 50 by 30 centimeters [a board (which is) 50 centimeters long and 30 centimeters wide; a 30 by 50 (centimeter) board].

【線】

20センチの横線を引きなさい。

Draw a 20-centimeter horizontal line.

【切る】

紙を横半分に切りなさい。

Cut the paper in half (horizontally).

〈注〉 horizontally はあえて「横」と言う必要があるとき。「縦半分に切る」は次のように言う。

Cut the paper in half lengthwise [from top to bottom].

【並ぶ】

横１列に並びなさい。（教壇の前に）

Stand across the front of the room.

Stand [Line up] side by side.

Line up in a row.

いすを横１列に並べた。

We placed the chairs sideways in one row.

〈注〉 row は縦の列，横の列どちらにも使えるがどちらかと言えば横の列。また縦に長い列を column と呼ぶことがあるが，少なくとも15人以上の長い列を言う。縦列は次のように言う。

Line up (in) single file.（通常縦１列）

Line up [Stand] double file [two by two].（縦２列，２人ずつ）

【傾斜】

塔が横に傾いている。

The tower is leaning to one side.

【寝る】

私はソファに横になった。

I lay down on the sofa.

I stretched myself out on the sofa.

この弁当箱は横に傾けないで。液体が入っているから。

Don't tip this lunch box because it contains liquid.

〈注〉 be slanting は斜めに傾いている状態を指す。ベッドに通常寝る方向に対して直角に横向きに寝るのは stretch crosswise on the bed。

2. 側面

side（↔ front, back）

【状態】
彼女の横に子供が1人，後ろに1人いた。
There was one child at her side and one on her back.
トムはメアリーの横に座っていた。
Tom was sitting beside [next to] Mary.
【動き】
彼女は横にどいて[よけて]その人たちをやりすごした。
She stepped aside and let them go.
彼女は不機嫌に横[そっぽ]を向いて私の問いに答えようとしなかった。
She looked aside, sulking, and wouldn't answer my questions.
彼は読みかけの本を横に置いて私たちの話に加わった。
He laid aside [put down] the book he was reading and joined our conversation.
〈注〉 lay aside は 横に押しやるように置いて，当分取り上げないという含みがある。 put down は単に下に置くだけ。
正面から見るとそのホテルは豪華だが，横にまわって見ると無格好だ。
From the front, the hotel is gorgeous, but from the side it's ugly.
私は体を横向きにしてひじで人込みをかき分けて進んだ。
I edged through the crowd.
子供たちは横に並んで歩いていた。
The children were walking side by side.
【曲る，それる】
体を横に曲げて！（体操）
Bend sideways!
彼女はエイモスの頭をたたこうとしたが(むちは)横にそれて頭をかすっただけだった。
She tried to hit Amos on the head with it, but the blow was only a glancing one.
She gave him only a glancing blow.
銃弾は的の横にそれた。(的をはずれた)
The bullet [He] missed the target.
〈注〉 射撃コンテストなどであれば人が主語。

3．比喩的な表現
横から口を出すな。
Don't interfere [meddle].
Don't tell us what to do.
Don't poke your nose into other people's business [affairs].
彼の話が横道にそれた。
He got off the subject [digressed].
縦の物を横にもしない。
He's a complete lazybones.
He is the sort of person who never lifts a finger to help.
〈注〉 上の表現は常に非難の意味で言われる。口語では ... who never pitches in. も使われる。

よごす（汚す）・よごれる → きたない

汚す **make dirty**（一般的な表現）; **make filthy**（ひどく汚す）; **smudge**（こすったような汚れをつける）; **stain**（しみをつける）; **litter**（ごみを捨てて公共の場を汚す）; **pollute**（公害，化学物質により汚染する）
汚れる **become dirty [filthy]; get dirty [filthy]**
汚れている **be dirty [filthy]; be smudged**（こすれて黒くなっている）; **be stained**（しみがついている）
〈注〉◆「汚す」「汚れる」に対し，「汚れている(状態)」が英語では受動態になっていることがわかる。この種の動詞では受動態は状態を表す。
◆get dirty（汚れる）は get《something》dirty として他動詞にできる。
動自 My shirt got dirty when I leaned against the car.（車によりかかったときシャツが汚れてしまった）
動他 Don't get your shirt dirty; you have to wear it again tomorrow.（シャツを汚さないでよ，明日も着ていかなきゃならないんだから）

1．きたなくすること全般
子供はすぐ服を汚してしまう。
Children get their clothes dirty very fast.

白いセーターは汚れやすい。

White sweaters get dirty easily.

彼女のシャツは本当に汚れていた。

Her shirt was actually dirty.

外で遊んでよそ行きを汚さないでね。

Don't spoil your Sunday best by playing outdoors.

スカートが汚れているよ[にしみがついているよ]。

Your skirt has some spots [stains, dirt] on it.

〈注〉 通常 at the back とか，しみのある場所も述べる。stains は取れないしみ，spots は落ちる汚れ。

パンくずでテーブルを汚さないように上手に食べなさい。

Eat so you don't leave crumbs on the table.

Don't mess up the table with crumbs.

午前中手袋もはめないで庭いじりをしていたら爪が真っ黒に汚れてしまった。

After working in the garden all morning without gloves, I found my fingernails were really dirty.

2．公害・ごみなどできたなくする

…のごみがちらかっている

be littered with …

汚染されている　be polluted

そこは空き缶や紙くずで汚れていた。

The place was littered with tins [cans] and paper.

大気は常に車やトラックの排気ガスで汚されている。

The air is constantly being polluted by cars and trucks.

cf. The main air pollutants in big cities come from vehicle exhaust fumes and power plant smoke.（大都市の大気の主たる汚染源は車の排気ガスや発電所の排煙である）

3．比喩的な表現

あいつは家の面汚しだ[家名を傷つけた]。

He is a disgrace to our family.

He has disgraced our family name.

よさん（予算）

1．公的

a budget;（見積り）**an estimate**

【…年度予算】

本年度の予算　the budget for this year

来年度の予算

the budget for the coming year

2002-03会計年度の予算

the budget for the 2002-03 fiscal year

〈注〉 the two thousand two to two thousand three fiscal year と読む。

【審議】

［立案］政府は予算案を立案し議会に提出する。

The government makes [compiles] a budget and presents it to the Diet.

［可決・否決］議会が予算案を可決[否決]すれば…

If the Diet approves [rejects] the budget …

［通過］予算案が議会を通過した。

The budget passed the Diet.

議会の会期は明後日終るので，政府はそれまでに予算案を通してしまおうとしている。

The Diet session will end the day after tomorrow and the government is trying to get the budget approved [passed] by then.

［修正］予算の大幅な修正を提案する。

propose a drastic revision of the budget

【執行】

予算執行　spend money; follow a budget（予算の範囲内で）

【超過】

予算を超過する　exceed the original budget

【節減】

予算を引締める

allot less（money）to a budget request than the projected expenses

〈注〉 予算の費目「備品・消耗品」の英訳について

備品　equipment and furniture

消耗品　expendable supplies（分類法が違うた

め，消耗品に当る費目は英語にはないがこれでわかる。具体的に，事務用品の補給，新聞，テープなどと説明するとよい）

【再編成】

予算を見直す　revise a budget

《関連語》

本年は歳入・歳出[収支]がぴったり合った。(赤字にも黒字にもならなかった)

Revenue(s) and expense(s) balanced this year.

会計報告　financial report

2．家計　→かけい

予算を立てる　make [draw up] an estimate

建築費の予算は5000万円である。

The cost of the building is estimated at 50 million yen.

家計予算の範囲内で暮すのがますます難しくなってきている。

It's becoming more and more difficult for us to live within (the limits of) our family budget.

旅行費用が予算を超過してしまった。

(The) Travel expenses have gone over (the) budget.

ご予算はどのくらいで？（店員が客に）

How much would you like to spend?

May I ask what price range you (have) had in mind?

よしゅう（予習）

彼はいつもちゃんと翌日の授業の予習をする。

He always prepares for the next day's lessons [classes].

明日の予習はしたの？

Have you prepared [got ready] for tomorrow's classes?

〈注〉 他動詞 prepare は教材・食事などをつくる意味に使われ，自動詞 prepare は何かに備えて準備することである。

ドイツ語[化学]の予習した？

Are you ready for German (class) [chemistry (class)]?

予習をしなければいけないね。

You should prepare in advance.

よてい（予定）

名 **a plan; a program**

a timetable; a schedule; an itinerary（旅程）

予定を立てる　動 **plan; make a plan**

旅行の予定を立てようよ。

Let's plan our trip.

Let's make a plan [an itinerary] for our trip.

〈注〉 この文の plan の位置に program, schedule はなじまない。itinerary はどこにいつ行くという旅程のこと。

私は予定を変更して，１日早く帰って来た。

I changed my plan [my schedule] and came back a day earlier.

〈注〉 schedule は出張などの場合には使える。私的旅行ならば plan を使う方がよい。

赤ちゃんの出産予定日はクリスマスの頃だ。

The baby is due about Christmas time.

列車は５時到着の予定だ。

The train is due (to arrive) at five.

結婚式は次の春挙行の予定だ。

The wedding ceremony is to be held next spring.

知事がその会で話をする予定になっている。

The governor is scheduled to give a speech at the meeting.

私たちはニューヨークに息子を訪ねて行く予定にしている。

We are planning to visit our son in New York.

すべて予定通りに運んだ。

Everything went
{ as { arranged. / scheduled. } / on schedule. }（事務的）

飛行機は予定より30分遅れて離陸した。

The plane took off half an hour late

[behind schedule].

〈注〉◆ behind schedule の反対「予定より早く」は ahead of schedule。

◆「…したい」と希望をもってから，心に決め，手はずを整え，用意がいよいよできるまでの各段階の表現を比べてみる。

したい	I wish I could go.(but I can't) I wish to go. I hope I'll be able to go. I want to go.	(気持)
つもり	I intend to go. (意志)	
予　定	I'll go. I'm going (to go).	
計画中	I'm planning to go.	
手はずが整う	I've made arrangements to go.	
行くばかりとなる	I'm ready to go.	

《類義語》

a plan　一般的な語。広義の計画。

a program　こまごまとしたところまで論じた計画。

a schedule　きちんと時間を割り当てた時間表，公式の計画。次の(1)(2)に分けられる。

(1) routine　いつも決った行事について言う語。何曜日は何をする，何曜日は何がある，は … my weekly schedule。列車時刻表，学校の時間割も schedule。

(2) それぞれの行動ごとに何時から何時と時間を割りつけた予定。

ex. 今日の予定は？

What are your plans for today?(大まか)

What's your schedule for today? (旅行日程でも学生の学校の予定でも使える)

cf. What's your plan for this vacation? (休暇の計画は毎年違う。繰り返しではないから plan とする)

よぶ (呼ぶ)

1. 声をかける

call; call to; call out [after]

彼は通りの向こう側から私を呼んだ。

He called to me from across the street.

だれかが私の名前を呼んだのでびっくりした。

I was surprised that someone called me by name.

「ジャケットを忘れましたよ」と後ろから呼びかけられた。

They called after me that I'd forgotten my jacket.

お店に買い物に行くときミルクを買って来てと彼女が私に呼びかけた。

She called out to me to get some milk when I went to the store.

母が私に夕食には帰るかと呼びかけた。

My mother called out (to me) to ask if I'd be back for supper.

明日の朝 9 時頃に呼びに来るね。

I'll come for you around nine tomorrow morning.

2. 呼び寄せる

call; go for; go and get; fetch〔英〕

send for; summon (役所・警察・裁判所などが呼び出す，出頭を命ずる)

彼は緊急な用事で呼び戻された。

He was called back on urgent business.

医者を呼んで診てもらわなくてはいけないよ。

You should
- call [ring up] the doctor to come and see you.
- send for the doctor.

〈注〉 send for … はもともと人を使いに出して呼んで来ることであったが，今は電話で呼ぶことが多いのでその意味にも使える。上の 2 文はともに電話で呼ぶこと。なお，send for … は「…を注文する」の意味にも使える

ex. I sent for a recipe book. (料理のつくり方の本を注文した)

彼はひとまず落ち着いたところで家族を呼び寄せた。(単身赴任者)

He sent for his family when he was settled.

校長先生がお呼びです。

The principal wants to see you.

彼は校則を破ったので，校長室に呼ばれた。

He was called [summoned] to the principal's room for violating school regulations.

もう帰らなければならない。子供たちを呼んでおいで。

We have to leave now. Go and get [fetch〔英〕] the children.

タクシーを呼んでくださいませんか。

Will you call [get] a taxi for me?

すみません，彼を電話口に呼んでくださいませんか。

Please call him to the phone.

今度は前より大きなアパートに移ったので(故郷から)母親を呼び寄せて一緒に暮したいと思っています。

Now (that) we've moved to a bigger apartment, we'd like to have my mother come ⌊to [and] live with us.

3. 招く

invite; ask

今晩はマクドナルドさん一家を夕食にお呼びしてあります。

We've invited [asked] the MacDonalds to dinner this evening.

私たちはベティーの誕生パーティーに呼ばれています。

We've been invited [asked] to Betty's birthday party.

4. 引き起す

このニュースはセンセーションを巻き起すだろう。

This news will cause a sensation.

この発明はたいへんな反響を呼んだ。

This invention drew [attracted] a lot of attention.

5. 名付ける

【命名】

生れた子はウィリアムと呼ばれることになった。

The baby was named William.

【呼称】

人は彼をビリー=ザ=キッドと呼んだ。

People called him Billy the Kid.

どうぞ，ジョーと呼んでください。

Please call me Joe.

よむ（読む）

1. 文字・書物を読む

【字を読む】㊐㊎

学齢前に字が読めるようになる子が多い。

Many children learn to read before school age.

【～を読む】㊐㊍

彼はよその子と遊ばないで家の中でお話の本ばかり読んでいた。

He didn't play with other children but stayed indoors reading storybooks.

彼女はときどき子供たちにグリムのおとぎ話を読んでやったものだ。

Sometimes she read
{ her children Grimm's fairy tales.
{ Grimm's fairy tales to her children.

朝刊を読んだら，名神の一宮のインターチェンジ付近で事故があったようだ。

I read in the morning paper that there was a car accident on the Meishin near the Ichinomiya Interchange.

君が読んでしまったら彼の手紙を僕にも見せてくれませんか。

Please let me have a look at his letter
when { you're done with it.
{ you're finished.

【言語】

彼はラテン語もギリシア語も読める。

He can read Latin and Greek.

【作品】

彼は学生とシェイクスピアを読んでいる。

He's reading Shakespeare with his students.

【音読】

英語の教科書を家で声を出して読みなさい。

Read your English text books aloud at home.

【…と読める】
看板は「古着売買します」と読めた[書いてあった]。
The sign read "Secondhand Clothes Bought and Sold".
それは次のように読める[書いてある]。
It reads as follows: …
その古い石碑の碑文は私には読めなかった。
I couldn't make out the inscription on the old stone monument.

2. 理解する
行間の意味を読みとる
read between the lines
著者の意図しない意味までを読み込む
read too much into; misread
【心を読む】
彼は私の思っていることを読んでしまった。
He read my thoughts.
お前の考えていることなんか簡単に読める。
I read you loud and clear.〔*colloq.*〕

よゆう（余裕）

1. 時間
家まで車で帰るのに所要時間に10分ばかり余裕を見ておいた。
I gave myself ten minutes more for driving home than I needed [I would need].
ツアーの庭園見学に15分間の余裕をとった。
They had [allowed themselves] 15 minutes' leeway on the garden tour.
私の火曜日の予定は詰っていてほとんど余裕がない。
I have almost no leeway in my schedule on Tuesday.
列車が出るまでにまだ10分ほどお買い物なさる余裕があります。
We have ten more minutes for shopping before the train leaves.
買い物に行く[買い物をする]時間ならまだ十分余裕がある。
There is enough time to go shopping [to do some shopping].
今は彼の所に寄る時間的余裕がない。
There is no time to drop in on him just now.
あの人たちは時間的余裕がない。
They are pressed for time.

2. 空間
私の車にはまだ２人分の余裕があります[２人は十分乗れる]。
There is still enough room for two more in my car.
駐車場には私の車を駐車する余裕がなかった。
There weren't any spaces left in the parking lot.
〈注〉 The lot was full. とも言える。駐車場の表示は「満車」Full,「余裕あり」Spaces Available。motelの表示は Vacancies（空室あり), No Vacancy（空室なし)が多い。

3. 金銭
彼はお金の余裕がある。
He has more than enough money [plenty of money].
〈注〉 enoughは「ちょうど足りるだけ」, plentyは「余裕がある」。
マンションなんか買うお金の余裕はない。
I can't afford to buy an apartment.
１円たりとも使う余裕はない。
I can't really spend a penny.
I haven't a penny to spare [spend].
私は余裕のないその日暮しだ。
I live a hand-to-mouth existence [from hand-to-mouth; from day to day].
彼らは余裕のある暮しをしている。
They are comfortably off.（楽な暮しである）
They live in comfort.（裕福である）

4. 精神
彼女は自分のことで頭がいっぱいでほかのことを考える余裕がない。

She is too wrapped up in [busy with; involved in] her own affairs to think of other things.
彼はいつも落ち着いて気持ちに余裕がある。
He's always calm and composed.

よる（寄る）

1．近づく
もう少し近くに寄って。
Come close to me.
火のそばに寄って体を温めてください。
Come near the fire and make [get] yourself warm.
男の人がそっと近寄って来てあの人に手紙を渡した。
A man stole up to her and handed her a note.
黒の覆面をした男がそっと寄って来ていきなり彼女のハンドバッグをひったくった。
A man in a black mask stole up on her and grabbed her purse.
〈注〉 steal up to はそっと近づき驚かすとか何かをささやいたりすること。steal up on はそっと近づいて物をとる，傷つけるなど，何か起こりそうな場合に用いる。to と on の語感の違いに注意する。

2．立ち寄る
もし時間があれば彼のところに寄ろう。
If we have time, let's
{ visit [drop in on; call on] him.
{ go to his house.
ほんのちょっとだけ寄っていらっしゃいませんか。
Won't you come in just for a minute?
今度の旅行では時間がなくてギリシアには寄って行かれなかった。
We had no time to go to Greece on this trip.
〈注〉 英国では visit《a person》として使い，visit《a place》とは言わない。英米とも日常の言い方では go to《a place》, go (to) see《a person》が普通。

3．わきに寄る
私たちはわきに寄ってその人たちを通した。
We stepped aside and let them pass.
少し寄って[詰めて]このご婦人に席をつくってあげてください。
Please sit a little closer and make room for this lady.
〈注〉 親しい人には次のように言ってもよい。
ex. Excuse me. Can you make some room for me?
（すみません。詰めていただけますか）

4．集まる
ガやハムシは明りに寄ってくる。
Moths and flies are drawn toward light.
どこに行っても彼のまわりには子供たちが寄って来た。
Wherever he went, children gathered round him.
三人寄れば文珠の知恵。
Two heads are better than one.

よる（因る・依る・由る）

1．基づく
万事古式[規則]により執り行われた。
Everything was done according to tradition [regulations].
万事ご指示により執り行いました。
Everything was carried out according to your instructions.
【伝聞】
彼によるとあの2人は絶対うまくやっていかれないとのことだ。
According to him, those two men will never get on together.
【記事】
今日の新聞によれば，あの実験は大成功だったそうだ。
Today's paper says that }
According to today's paper }
the experiment was a great success.

2. 起因する →ため

彼は一身上の都合によって退学した。

He left school for personal reasons.

〈注〉 personal reasons のほか，いくつか例を挙げる。

for {economic / health / legitimate} reasons　経済上の理由によって／健康上の理由によって／正当な理由によって

事故はしばしば不注意によって起る。

Accidents are frequently caused by carelessness.

コンピュータチップ業界の不況で，先月はまた失業率が上がった。

The national unemployment rate rose again last month due to [because of] the depression in the computer chip industry.

彼の時宜を得た警告により，我々は洪水から逃れられた。

We escaped the flood thanks to his timely warning.

3. …次第

それは事と次第によりけりだ。

That depends.

君があの大学に入れるかどうかは君の努力によって決る。

Whether (or not) you're accepted by that college depends entirely on how much effort you make.

〈注〉 **be due to** と **depend upon**

- be due to 「…のせい」(事実についての原因)
  Your success is due to your effort. (君が成功したのは君が努力したからだ)
- depend upon …次第 (これからの見込みについて)
  Success depends upon your own effort. (君の成功は君の努力次第なのだ)

4. 方法

力によって事を解決しようとしてはいけない。

Don't try to settle the problem by force.

率直に話し合うことによって解決すべきだ。

You should settle the matter by talking it over frankly.

よろこび（喜び）・よろこぶ

喜び **joy; pleasure; delight**

彼は天にも昇る［手放しの］喜びようであった。

He couldn't contain himself for joy.

His joy knew no bounds.

彼は跳び上がって喜んだ。

He jumped for joy.

加藤先生をご紹介いたしますことは私の喜びと致すところでございます。

It's my pleasure to introduce to you Mr. Kato.〔*formal*〕

【喜んでいる，喜んだ】

《類義語》

be glad happy よりも心の中の深い静かな喜び。

be happy glad や pleased よりも外面的笑いやうれしそうなしぐさを思わせる表現。

be pleased 心の満足感を強調。

be delighted 強い喜び。

彼の母は彼の成功をたいへん喜んだ。

His mother was very happy with his success.

彼は帰って来てよかったと喜んでいる。

He's glad he's back.

ベスはあなたが元気なので喜んでいる。

Beth is happy to see you so well.

私たちはそれがたいしたことでなかったので喜んでいます。

We are glad [pleased] it was nothing serious after all.

〈注〉 delighted は強い語で，次のような決り文句以外 I, we を主語としてはあまり使われない。

I'm delighted to see you. (お目にかかれてうれしいです)

We are delighted to have you here tonight. (今夜ここにあなたをお迎えできてうれしく思います；テレビのショーなどで司会者がゲストを迎える挨拶)

国中どこに行っても人々は戦争終結の喜びにわきたっていた。

Everywhere in the country people were rejoicing at the end of the war.

〈注〉 rejoice は個人的でなく社会的広がりのある場面に使われる。

【喜んで…する】 be willing to; be ready to

いいですとも，喜んで。

Sure, I'll be glad to.

あの方たちは喜んで手伝ってくださいます。

They are willing to help us.

〈注〉 I'm always ready to help you.（私はいつだって喜んであなたのお力になります）は決り文句で，やたらに言うとおおげさに聞える。同じ意で ready の代りに glad や pleased を使ってもよい。

よわい（弱い）

形 **weak**

1．体質

【身体】

彼は子供のとき体が弱かった。

He was weak when he was a child.

He was a weak child.

彼女は体が弱い。

She has delicate health.

私は胃腸が弱い。

I have poor digestion.

彼は心臓が弱い[悪い]。

He has a weak heart.

彼女は脚が弱い。

She has weak legs.

彼はかぜに弱い[すぐかかる]。

He has no resistance to colds.

〈注〉 She is delicately built.
（華奢である；骨格が細く，ひ弱に見えること）

【乗物】

私は車[飛行機 / 船]に弱い。

I easily get car [air / sea] sick.

【酒】

私はお酒に弱い。

I can't drink.

2．気質

彼女は気が弱い。

She's timid.

彼は意志が弱い。

He's not strong-willed [weak-willed].

私は意志が弱い。

I have a weak will.

I'm weak-willed.

3．対人関係

弱い立場の人々　the weak

私はあなたには弱い。（かなわない）

I'm no match for you.

You beat me.

彼は弱い立場にある。

He's in a disadvantageous position.

彼はご婦人[チョコレート]に弱い[目がない]。

He has a weakness for ladies [chocolates].

彼は孫に弱い[甘い]。

He has a soft spot for his grandchildren.

〈注〉 He can't { resist. / stay away from《a person / a thing》.
いやと言えない，ついつい引かれてしまうこと。男女関係，金，地位に関する場合は批判的な意味になる。be liable to be too indulgent（甘い）はやわらかな言い方で批判的含みは少ない。

4．能力

私は数学が弱い。

I'm weak in [poor at] mathematics.

彼はトランプは上手なのにチェスは弱い。

He's poor at chess, though he's a good card-player.

5．自然現象

昨夜は弱い地震があった。

There was a slight earthquake last night.

もやがかかっていて日の光は弱かった。

It was hazy and the sunlight was weak.

光が弱くて壁に書かれた字はたいへん読みづらかった。

It was hard to read the words on the wall in

the faint light.

ガスの火を弱めて，約2時間弱火でことことと煮ます。

Turn down the gas and simmer for about two hours.

6. 材質

ナイロンは火に弱い。

Nylon isn't heat-resistant [can't take heat].

〈注〉「火に強い」は heat-resistant,「水濡れに強い」は water-resistant, waterproof (完全防水の)。

ら

らいきゃく（来客）→ きゃく

a caller; a visitor; a guest

残念ですが，ちょっと伺えないのです。来客がありますので。

I'm sorry, I can't go, because we're expecting guests.

今日の午後に来客があります。

I'm going to have a visitor this afternoon.

cf. 昼から人が来るんだ。

Someone's coming this afternoon.

今日は来客が多かった。

A lot of people came over today.

今日は来客が１人もなかった。

Nobody came over [by] today.

〈注〉「訪問する」の意味の call は古くさい。来客も個人的な客については上の表現がごく普通。

open house 自宅開放パーティー（通常夕食をすませてから集まり，何時から何時と決められた時間内に自由に出かけ，自由に帰ることができる）の来客やグループで来る客，また博物館，展覧会などの客の出入りについては次の表現が適切。

We've had a good many [no] visitors today.

ああ，来客中ですね。

You have company, I see.

少々お待ちください。ただいま来客中ですので。

Could you wait a minute, please?　He has a visitor now.

来客お断り。

I'll see no visitors today.〔*stiff*〕

cf. 電話がかかって来ても私は留守ということにしてくれ。

If anybody phones, I'm not in [here].

らく（楽）

1．余裕

【生活】

楽に暮す

be comfortably off; live in comfort; live an easy life

あの人たちも以前よりは楽な暮しをしている。

They are better off than before.

私たちは楽な暮しに慣れっこになってしまった。

We are used to an easy life.

末息子が小学校に上がったので彼女も少し楽になった。（自分の時間ができた）

Now that her youngest son is in primary school, she has some time for herself.

あの人たちも息子が独り立ちしてお金がかからなくなり少しは生活が楽になった。

Now that they aren't supporting their son any more, they can live better.

〈注〉 they are relieved とすると精神的にほっとして they are glad [happy] の意味になる。

【精神的】→ほっとする

その知らせでやっと気が楽になった。

I was relieved to hear the news.

【空間的】

この教室は80人は楽に入れる。

This classroom
{ can hold
  can accommodate〔*formal*〕} eighty students or more.
  has enough room for eighty students. }

【容易に】

easily; without difficulty

楽な仕事　an easy job

そんな問題なら１時間に10問は楽に解ける。

We can solve ten such problems in an hour without difficulty [quite easily].

町には１時間もあれば楽に行ける。（１時間とかからない）

It won't take an hour to reach town.

2．鎮痛

この新しい鎮痛剤は慢性の痛みをずっと楽にしてくれる。

This new painkiller is much more effective against [in relieving; in easing] chronic pain.

「頭痛はどうですか」「ずっと楽になりました。おかげ様で」。

"How's your headache?" "I feel much better, thank you."

アスピリンを飲んだら楽になった。

Aspirin brought me some relief.

Aspirin helped (me).

らくだい（落第）→ おちる・おとす

落第する　**fail** 《an exam》; **flunk** 〔米 *colloq.*〕

【試験】

彼は数学・法学・フランス語の試験に落第した[を落した]。

He failed math, law and French.

小田先生は採点が辛い。この前のテストでは40人中20人も落第だった。

Prof. Oda is a strict marker. He failed [flunked] twenty students out of forty in the last test. [Twenty students flunked.]

彼は３科目不合格で落第した[留年した]。

Because he failed three subjects,

he has to { stay { back a year. / in the 1st (2nd ...) year. } / repeat the year. }

落第点　a failing grade

〈注〉 成績評価の段階は grades A, B, C, D, F (fail 落第)の５つ。「落第点をとる」は fail the exam。

【生産物など】

生産物の10パーセントが規格に合わず落第[不合格]となった。

Ten percent of the products have been rejected as substandard.

【比喩的用法】

彼は父親[芸術家 / 人間]として落第だ。

He's a failure as a father [an artist / a person].

〈注〉 failure は次のようにも使える。

He's a failure. (彼は人生の敗者だ)

He's a failure in math. (彼は数学はからっきしだめだ)

らしい

1. 推測

㊐ **look like; seem; appear**

㊊ **probably; presumably**

【…のようだ】

午後は雨になるらしい。

It looks like rain in the afternoon.

名神(高速道路)は渋滞しているらしい。

The traffic seems { congested / backed up } along the Meishin Expressway.

このあたりの電話が不通になったのは落雷のせいらしい。

Presumably it's the lightning that knocked out telephone service in this area.

【…のように思われる】

彼はビルをよく知っているらしい。

He seems to know Bill well.

It seems that he knows Bill well.

彼は新しい車に満足しているらしい。

He seems [looks] happy with his new car.

It seems that he is happy with his new car.

〈注〉 He seems ... の形と It seems that ... の形では前者は話者のその場(on the spot)での感想，後者は後からの報告 (reporting) である場合が多い。

彼は友人が多いらしくみえる。

He appears to have a lot of friends.

It appears that he has a lot of friends.

ジョーはパーティーに来るらしい。

Joe will probably be coming to the party.

It seems [appears] that Joe will be coming to the party.

〈注〉◆×Joe seems to come to the party.

seem to の次に来る動詞は状態を表す動詞に限られる。

ex. seem to be ... / seem to know [like]

上の文も Joe seems to be coming ... とすれば可。

◆seem, appear はほとんど同じ意味だが seem の方がずっと多く使われる。

2. 似ている，ふさわしい

紳士[淑女 / 子供]らしい

　形 gentlemanly [ladylike / childlike]

男[女]らしい

　形 masculine [feminine]

彼は紳士らしく見える。

　He looks like a gentleman.

それは本当らしく聞えない。

　That doesn't sound true.

それではフランス語らしく聞えない。

　That doesn't sound like French.

彼には学者らしいところがない。

　There's nothing of the scholar about him.

彼には芸術家らしいところがある。

　He has something of the artist in [about] him.

〈注〉 in him とすると資質のあること。about him とすると芸術家的雰囲気のあること。

彼は教師らしく振る舞わない。

　He doesn't act like a teacher.

観光名所らしいものが何もない。

　There are no sightseeing spots to speak of.

　There are no special sightseeing spots.

彼にはこれといって才能らしいものがない。

　He has no special talents.

私には何も特技らしいものはない。

　I don't have any particular specialty.

【その人らしい】

あなたらしいよ。

　That's just like you.

遅れて来るなんてあの子らしい。

　It's just like her to come late.

忘れるなんてあなたらしくもない。

　How unlike you to forget it!

君らしくもない。どうしたんですか。

　You don't usually do this [make this kind of mistake; act this way]. What got into you!

それは彼女らしいやり方ではない。

　That's not her style.

ラジオ

radio

【ラジオで放送される】

　be broadcast; be carried on the radio

NBC 放送は開会・閉会の挨拶を，ABC 放送は開会から閉会までの全体を放送する予定です。

　The opening and closing addresses will be carried on NBC, while ABC will offer complete coverage.

台風関係の新しい情報は 5 分ごとにラジオを通じて入手できる。

　Updated typhoon news will be available on the radio every five minutes.

【ラジオで聞く】

ラジオの天気予報をいつも聞きますか。

　Do you listen to the weather forecast on the radio?

彼はラジオのニュースを聞いていた。

　He was listening to the radio news.

【ラジオをつける[消す]】

　turn [switch] on [off] the radio

まったくいらいらした。隣の人が夜遅くまでラジオを大きな音でつけっぱなしにしているんだもの。

　I was annoyed because our neighbor {kept the radio on very loud / played the radio loudly} far into the night.

【ラジオを合せる】

私は JOAK にダイヤルを合せた。

　I tuned in to JOAK.

ラジオ(の音)をもう少し大きく[小さく]してください。

　Turn up [down] the radio a bit.

【受信する】

このラジオはよく音がはいる。

　This radio has good reception.

BBC がよくはいる。

　We can hear (the) BBC very clearly.

外国放送がよくはいる。

Foreign stations come in well.

【ラジオでやっている】

ラジオで今ビートルズをやっている。

The Beatles are now on the radio.

They're playing the Beatles now on the radio.

〈注〉［生演奏でも録音放送でも］
Beatles music is being played on the radio.
曲目として Beatles songs をやっているのでも，本物の Beatles によるレコード・CD を放送しているのでもどちらでもこの表現でよい。

《関連語》
放送局　radio station
番組　radio program [programme〔英〕]
深夜放送　midnight broadcasting
深夜番組　midnight broadcast [program]
アナウンサー　radio announcer
ラジオ解説者　radio commentator
聴取者　radio listeners
ディスクジョッキー　disc jockey; DJ
放送音楽会　radio concert
放送劇　radio drama [play]
インタビュー　radio interview
トークショー　talk show; call-in show
ラジオ体操　radio gymnastics [calisthenics]
FM (frequency modulation)
AM (amplitude modulation)
短波放送をする　broadcast [transmit] a program by shortwave
短波放送受信機　shortwave receiver
生放送　live show [concert, interview, presentation] (↔ taped)
放送大学　the University of the Air

られる → れる

らんぼう（乱暴）

1．暴力

名 **violence;** 乱暴な 形 **violent**

とにかく乱暴だけは絶対にしないように。

Don't use violence whatever you do.

彼は飲むと乱暴をする［暴れる］。

He gets violent when (he's) drunk.

2．荒々しい，無作法な

【取り扱い】

ステレオを乱暴に扱わないで。

Don't be rough with the stereo.

これを乱暴にしないでください。(丁寧に扱ってください)

Please be careful with this.

〈注〉（あちこちぶつけたりして）手荷物を乱暴に扱うなよ。Don't bang that baggage〔米〕[luggage]. は荒っぽい言い方なので，直接注意を与えるときは Don't の形を避けて Be careful. のように言う方がよい。「取扱注意」の掲示は Handle with Care.

【人】

彼は荒々しく乱暴そうに見えるが，よく知り合ってみると心のやさしい人だとわかる。

He looks rough and aggressive, but when you know him better you'll see he's actually gentle-hearted [tender at heart].

【言葉】

乱暴な言葉　rough language

〈注〉rough language とは (1) vulgar language (社会的禁句・罵言・ばかやろうの類), (2) rude remarks (失礼な言葉), (3) harsh words (相手を傷つけるようなひどい非難の言葉) を指す。

乱暴なしゃべり方をやめて，きちんと品よく話しなさい。

Don't speak roughly. Speak like a gentleman [lady].

〈注〉「言葉遣いに気をつけよ」Watch your tongue. という表現もある。

3．思慮の欠ける

【運転】

彼の運転がすごく乱暴で本当にこわかった。

He drove so recklessly I was really scared.

【無茶】

こんな天候を押して山に登るなんて乱暴ですよ。

It's reckless of you to climb the mountain in such weather.

乱暴なこと言うんじゃない。

Don't be unreasonable.

そりゃ乱暴だ。（ばかげているよ）

That's absurd.

〈注〉 **reckless** 思慮も判断力もないこと。
unreasonable 理性的にじっくり考えてみていないこと。

4．女性に

女性に対する乱暴

sexual harassment

〈注〉 家庭内での乱暴は domestic violence と言う。

女性に乱暴をする

molest《someone》sexually

〈注〉 sexually molest《someone》としてもよい。「女性に乱暴する」はときに rape（女性を犯す）も意味する。

り

りこう（利口）

【幼児】

お利口だね。

You're a good boy [girl].

さあ静かにしてね，お利口だから。

Please don't make any noise, there's a good boy [girl].

あなたはお利口だから知らない人とお話をしたりしないわね。

You know better than to talk to strangers, don't you?

【子供】

利口な子

bright children （よくできる子）

smart children〔米〕（頭の回転の速い子。〔英〕で smart は外見のことのみ）

intelligent children （知力のすぐれた子）

clever children （よくできる子。〔米〕では創意に富む子の意，〔英〕では clever は bright と同じ）

あの子は利口だ。

He's pretty smart.〔米〕

年の割に利口な子だ。

He's sensible for his age.

〈注〉 sensible は foolish, silly の反意語。7, 8 歳の子で迷子になってもあわてないで交番に行って事情を説明した，というような物事を冷静に処理できる賢い子について言う。

利口そうな子 an intelligent-looking child

お利口さん

a good student

a goody-goody（ゴマすりのお利口さん）

【大人】

彼は利口な人だ。

He's quick to grasp things [intelligent, smart〔米〕].

〈注〉「あいつは利口だ」は，しばしば「抜け目ない」の意味に使われる。英語でも，次の表現はよくない意味。

あいつは利口だ。

He's a smart aleck.

He's a wise guy.

He's too clever [shrewd].

彼は利口に立ち回るので皆に嫌われている。

He always tries to look good, so people dislike him.

彼は利口に立ち回っている。

He's manipulating things to make himself look good.

He's shrewdly manipulative.（自己に有利に操作する）

【利口な手】 a wise [shrewd] move（チェスの手，政治家の使う手などに用いる）

〈注〉◆ shrewd は分析能力があり，実際的で自分に有利なように動くことである。shrewd と言われる人はしばしば世の中をうまく立ち回っていくところがあるが，ほかの人に関係なく shrewd ということもあり得る。

ex. a shrewd investor（頭の切れる投資家）

◆ 悪い意味の「利口な」は「ずるい」に通じる。「ずるい」に対応する英語 crafty, foxy, wily は要領よくすり抜ける才のあること。

【利口ぶる】（衒学的な）pedantic；（利口ぶって）knowingly

彼はいろいろと利口ぶった(何でも知っているような)口振りで話した。

He made all kinds of knowing remarks.

〈注〉 to play one-upmanship（人の上をゆく術をつかう）もある。

りせい（理性）

reason; reasoning power; 良識 **good sense**

人間は理性をもっている[理性的生物である]。

Humans are rational beings.

諸君の理性[良識]に訴える。経済的危機に際して些細な賃上げ額を争ってはいられないはずだ。

I appeal to your reason [good sense]. A time of economic hardship is not the time for us to be quarreling over the size of the wage increase.

〈注〉 reason は次の(1)(2)(3)の意味をもつ。

(1) faculties of the mind (心の働き)の中の１つとしての「理性」

⇩

reason, imagination, will 理性・想像力・意志
intuition, memory 直観・記憶

(2) good judgement and sound sense 適正な判断と良識

(3) cause of an event 理由

【理性的】

彼女は理性的に見える。

She looks cool and intelligent.

〈注〉 listen to reason は「物の道理を聞き分ける」である。「理性に従う」というほど堅い言い方ではなく，日常的な状況，たとえば重い荷物を旅行に持って行こうという子に言い聞かせるときなどにも用いられる。

Listen to reason. Who's going to carry it?
(考えてもごらん，だれがそれを持ち運ぶの？)

りつ（率）→ パーセント

a rate; a ratio; a percentage

【出生率】

この国の出生率は年々低下している。

The birth rate in this country is going down every year.

【死亡率】

伝染性疾患による死亡率はこの50年間でめざましい減少を見せた。

The death rate [The number of deaths] from infectious diseases has diminished remarkably in fifty years.

【競争率，成功率】

競争率は５倍だ[成功率は５分の１だ]。

The odds are only 5 to 1 that you'll win [succeed].

この大学の入試は本年は競争率５倍だった。

Only one out of every five candidates passed the entrance exam for this university this year.

「成功率はどのくらいだろう」「５パーセントといったところだ」。

"What's the success rate?" "It's five percent."

【見込み】

君の成功する率はどれくらいか[あるのか]。

What are your chances (of success)?

Do you have much chance of success?

〈注〉 success rate と言うのは実際の数字に基づく場合。chances はそれほど厳密ではなく，成功率のデータがあれば，それについての主観的判断を加味したもの。

【合格率】

今年も去年と同じなら(志願者の)合格率[競争率]はざっと10人に１人だ[10倍だ]。

If this year is like last year, applicants have one chance in ten (of succeeding).

【生存率】

生存率は４人に１人だ。

One in four will survive.

The chances of survival are four to one [one in four].

〈注〉 4：1 と書いて four to one と読む（常に大きい数を先にする)。

【投票率】

今回の投票率は過去10年間で最低だった。

The voting rate this time was the lowest [worst] in the last ten years.

【関税率】

高い関税率 a high tariff

【効率】

熱効率がよい。

The thermal efficiency is very high.

新しいヒーターはとても効率がいい。

The new heater's very efficient.

りっこうほ（立候補）

名 **candidacy; candidature**〔英〕

立候補する **stand for election; run in an election**

立候補届を出す

announce [file] one's candidacy [candidature] for ...

だれが知事選に立候補していますか。

Who's running for governor?
Who are the candidates for governor?
彼は会長に立候補するつもりである。
He intends to run
{ in the presidential election.
  for president.
〈注〉上の2文の for governor, for president は，地位の意味であるから冠詞なしでよい。
【立候補者】 a candidate
山田氏は民主党の立候補者だ。
Mr. Yamada is a Democratic candidate.
【…党推薦の立候補者】
青木氏は自民党推薦で市長に立候補しているが，牧野氏は無所属で立候補している。
Mr. Aoki is running for mayor supported by the LDP, but Mr. Makino is running as an independent [without any party's support].

りっぱ（立派）

1．外見

立派な **fine; splendid; superb; magnificent**
【建造物・家具調度】
あの辺にいくつか立派なビルがあるのが見えますか。
Can you see those magnificent buildings over there?
あの時代にどうやってあんな立派な宮殿を建てたんでしょう。
How did people build such magnificent palaces in those days?
彼女の家は立派な家具調度がそろえてあった。
Her house furnishings were superb.
【人】
彼は立派な紳士といった風采だった。
He looked like a fine gentleman.
彼は立派な体格で，また立派な服装をしていた。
He was well-built and very well-dressed.
彼は立派な顔立ちの若者だ。
He is a handsome young man with clear-cut features.
彼女の態度は立派だった，高ぶらず卑下せず。
She took a wonderful attitude, not imposing but not too humble.
彼も立派な若者になった。
He's become a fine young man.
He's really grown up.
〈注〉「立派に成長した」には「ずいぶん心配したが」とか「苦労したが」といった感慨があることが多い。そんな気持ちは次の口語表現にこもっている。
He's going to make it.〔*colloq.*〕
（＝grow up properly; he'll succeed 何とかうまくやっていくだろう）

2．社会的に

【家柄】
彼はその地方の立派な家柄の出である。
He's from some well-known family in the district.
【教育】
彼は子供たち皆に立派な教育を受けさせた。
He gave all his children a good [fine] education.
【学者】
立派な学者 a distinguished scholar
cf. すぐれたミュージシャン a fine musician
【一人前】
蚊だって立派な生態系の一員だ。
Even mosquitoes have their place in the ecosystem.

3．道徳的に

【人・人生・行為】
立派に生きる live a worthwhile life
彼の生涯は立派な生涯だった。（追悼文など）
He lived { a commendable [virtuous] life.
  honestly and actively.
彼は立派な人物だと思っています。
I have a high opinion of him.
〈注〉◆He was an honorable [a respectable] man. は堅すぎる。honorable や praiseworthy は人について

よりも行為について使われる。

ex. That's an honorable [praiseworthy] thing to do.（それは立派な行いだ）

◆「立派な人である」を別の視点から見て次のように言うこともできる。

He isn't that type of person. I don't believe it.（彼はそんな人ではありません[立派な人です]。そんなこと信じません）

また，「立派な息子さんを持たれましたね」は次のようにも言える。

You may well be proud of your son.（息子さんを誇りに思われるのは当然です）

4．十分な，堂々たる

君には彼に腹を立てる立派な理由があるよ。

You have good reason to get angry at him.

彼女は短距離で立派な記録をつくった。

She made a good time in the sprint race [dash].

彼は立派に仕事をやっている。

He's doing good business.

20万円あればあの人たちは立派に（生活を）やっていける。

Two hundred thousand yen will be enough for them to live on.

りゆう（理由）

（a）**reason;** 動機 **a motive;** 根拠 **grounds, why ...;** 口実 **a pretext, an excuse**

【理由がある［ない］】

彼女がそう信じる立派な理由がある[理由はない]。

She has every [no] reason to believe it.

There's every [no] reason for her to believe it.

There's good [no] reason for that.

【理由がわかる［わからない］】

君が腹を立てている理由はわかる。

I see why you are angry.

彼女が躊躇（ちゅうちょ）する理由がわからない。

I see no reason why she should hesitate.

なぜ君が反対するのか理由がわからない。

I don't see [know] why
I can't see any reason [why]
- you should object.
- you object [are objecting].

彼は彼女がどうして会社をやめたのか理由を知っている。

He knows why she left the company.

【何かの理由で】→つごう

彼女は何かの理由で（理由もわからず）解雇された。

She was fired for some unknown reason.

She was fired for no conceivable reason.

She was fired, and no one knows why.

健康上の理由で彼女は退学した。

She gave up school
- because she became ill.
- because of ill-health.

私たちの提案は実行しにくいとの理由でだめになった。

Our proposal was turned down on the grounds that it was impractical.

【どんな理由があっても】

盗みは盗みだ。たとえどんな理由があっても。

Theft is theft, whatever the reason [whatever reason he might have].

【理由をこじつける】

何だかんだと理由をこじつけて彼は税金を払わなかった。

On some pretext or other he evaded paying (his) taxes.

彼女は何だかんだと理由をこじつけてデートを断った。

She turned down dates with all kinds of excuses.

【どんな理由で】

どんな理由できのう欠席したのだ。

Why didn't you come to class yesterday?

どんな理由で反対するのだ。

On what grounds do you object?

〈注〉 理由を説明する場合の because と why が混同されることがあるが因果関係は逆である。→ため

因 is why 果

- 因 果 She stole his money and so she was fired.
  (お金を盗んだ)ので(くびになった)
- 因 果 She stole his money.
  ↓
  This is {the reason / why} she was fired.

果 is because 因

- 果 因 She was fired because she stole his money.
- 果 因 She was fired.
  ↓
  This is because she stole his money.

cf. 日本語の「ため」の使い方が混同のもとである。
彼の金を盗んだ。そのためくびになった。
金を盗んだ。くびになったのはそのためだ。
くびになった。彼の金を盗んだためだ。

He lost his wallet. He couldn't buy the ticket.
He lost his wallet. That was ((1)) he couldn't buy the ticket.
He couldn't buy the ticket. That was ((2)) he lost his wallet.
正解 (1) why; the reason (2) because

りゅうこう(流行)

1. ファッション

fashion; the vogue; 一時的流行 **a fad**

【流行する】
ミニスカートがまた流行しだした。
Miniskirts are coming into vogue [fashion] again.
ロングスカートは今は流行遅れだ。
Long skirts are now out of fashion.
このスタイルのコートが今年の流行です。
This style of coat [coat style] is fashionable [in fashion] this year.
〈注〉「流行している」は be in fashion [vogue]。「流行していない」は be out of fashion。ただし, ×out of vogue とは言わない。

【流行に敏感[無関心]】
彼女はたいへん流行に敏感だ。
She's very keen on fashion.
彼女は全然流行に無関心だ。
She's indifferent to fashion.

【流行の先端】
彼女のコートは流行の先端だ[流行遅れだ]。
Her coat is very fashionable [old-fashioned].

2. 趣味・スポーツ

ゴルフは中流階級の人の間に流行しはじめている。
Golf is becoming more and more popular among middle-class people.
プリクラは大流行している。
Print clubs are all the rage.
国中でカラオケが大流行している。
There's a karaoke craze throughout the country.

3. 病気

関西方面でインフルエンザが流行している。
{There's a flu epidemic / (The) Flu is rampant} in the Kansai area.
cf. インフルエンザがはやっている。
Flu is going around now. 〔*colloq.*〕

りゅうつう(流通) → けいざい

(商品の) **distribution;** (通貨などの) **circulation;** (手形などの) **negotiation**
流通する[させる] **circulate; negotiate; float**

流通革命 a revolution in the distribution system
流通機構 the distribution system
流通経路 a distribution channel
流通資本 floating capital

《関連語》
市場 market / 市場独占 monopoly / 販売網 sales network [channels] / 出荷 shipment / 卸売 wholesale / 小売(店) retail (store) / チェーン店 chain store / スーパー supermarket / レジ check-out counter / 百貨店・デパート department store / 大売出し sale; 開

店大売出し opening sale; 目玉商品 loss leader / 仕入れ値 wholesale price / 小売値 retail price / 純益 net profit / 消費税 sales tax; value added tax (略 VAT); consumption tax

りょう（寮）→ げしゅく

りょうきん（料金）

《類義語》
charge 公共料金やサービスに対する料金，請求金額。請求書は bill。
ex. telephone charges [bill]（電話料金）
rate 単位あたりの規定料金。
ex. electricity [gas / water] rate（電気[ガス / 水道]料金）
postal rate（郵便料金）
group rate [fee]（団体割引）
雑誌・新聞の購読料も rate。
fare 交通機関の運賃，料金。
ex. train [taxi / bus / air] fares 鉄道[タクシー / バス / 航空]料金
fee 専門職や学校などの団体に払う料金。
ex. doctor's fee（診察代）; tuition fee（授業料）; entrance fee（入学金）; license and certification fee（諸免許下付のための料金）
toll 道路通行料金，長距離電話料金。
cf. 料金所 tollgate

【料金を請求する】
料金1000円を請求する
charge 1,000 yen

【料金を支払う】
謝礼[運賃 / 電話料金 / クレジットカードの請求額 / ガス料金]を支払う
pay fees [fares / a telephone bill / a credit card bill / a gas bill]

【料金を集金する】 collect fees [fares]

【料金の値上げ】
鉄道・バス料金の値上げがあるそうだとみんなが言っている。
There's a lot of talk about raising train and bus fares.
〈注〉 上の文によく似た文だが次の文は意味が異なる。
There's a lot of talk about the rise in train and bus fares.（鉄道・バス料金の値上げでみんなぶつぶつ言っている）

【料金の値下げ】
電気料金が近頃少々値下げになった。
Electricity charges have recently been reduced a bit.

【均一料金】
バス料金は市内均一210円です。
The fare on all buses is 210 yen within the city.

【１回の料金】
銭湯の料金は400円です。
The public bath charge is 400 yen.

【料金が高い[安い]】
ここらのホテルは(料金が)高い。
These hotels are expensive.
こっちのビジネスホテルの方が(料金が)安い。
These business hotels are less expensive.
〈注〉「ホテルの料金」は hotel rate(s), room rate(s)。

【料金を尋ねる】
この小包を速達にしたいのですが，料金はおいくらですか。
I want to send this parcel by express. What's the charge? [How much does it cost [will it be]?]

【料金は半額】
子供の入場料は半額です。
Children are allowed (entry) at half price.
子供の乗車賃は半額です。
Children ride [travel, go] at half fare.
〈注〉 at half price はさまざまに使える。
子供は半額 Half price for children（広告）

【料金投入口】
100円を料金投入口に入れてボタンを押してください。
Put a 100 yen coin into the slot and push the button.

【料金表】
a tariff 鉄道・バス・電信の料金表; ホテ

ル・レストランの料金表〔英〕
a rate schedule　単位ごとの価格や料金を示したもの

りょうしょう（了承）→ しょうち

りょうほう（両方）・りょうがわ（両側）

【両方に】
彼女は両方に［双方に］本当に教会で結婚したいのかと尋ねた。
　She asked both of them if they really wanted to get married in a church.

【両方とも】
両方ともいただきます。
　I'll take [have] both.
彼は耳が両方ともよく聞えない。
　He is hard of hearing in both ears.
彼は事故で両方の脚が不自由になった。
　He lost the use of both his legs in the accident.

【両側】
通りの両側には新築のビルが立ち並んでいる。
　The street is lined with newly built buildings on both sides.
大通りの両側の街路樹はちょうど花盛りであった。
　The trees on both sides of the avenue were in full bloom.
通りを横断するときは両方［両側］をよく見てからにしなさい。
　Look carefully both ways [in both directions] before crossing the street.
雨は同時に両側から［四方から］たたきつけてくるように見えた。
　The rain seemed to come from both [all] directions at once.

【両方とも…ない】
両方とも私のではない。
　Neither of them is [are 〔*colloq.*〕] mine.

〈注〉◆上の英文の場合，is と単数一致が原則である。
　◆×Both of them aren't mine.「両方とも私のではなくて一つだけ私のもの」（部分否定）なのか「どちらもちがう」のか不明瞭であり不自然な文である。「どちらもちがう」ならば上の例文のようにする。
　「一つだけが私のもの」の場合
　One of these is mine, but the other one isn't [belongs to somebody else].
　Only one of them is mine.
　One of them isn't mine.
　◆both, either, neither の使い方については「どちら・どこ」参照。
　There were trees on either side of the street.
　（通りの両側に木が植えられていた。）
　英・米どちらでも使われる表現だが，文語的で堅苦しい印象を与える。紛らわしさを避けるため，each side, both sides を使う方がよい。

りょうり（料理）→ あじ

1．料理すること
cooking; 料理する　【動】**cook**
料理教室　a cooking class
彼女は料理は好きだが裁縫は嫌いだ。
　She likes cooking but doesn't like sewing.
彼女は料理が上手だ。
　She is good at cooking.
　She is a good cook.
彼は彼女の好きなメキシコ料理を誕生日のお祝いにつくっている。
　He's cooking her Mexican food—her favorite kind of food—for her birthday.
母は台所であなたに何か温かいものを料理しています。
　My mother's in the kitchen making you a hot dinner.
私は魚の料理の仕方がわからない。
　I don't know how to cook fish.
〈注〉　He's making hot potato salad for the Boy Scout picnic. この文は二つの意味に解釈できる。
　(1) He's going to provide it.（ボーイスカウトのピクニックのため温かいポテトサラダをつくることにしている）
　(2) He's actually cooking it now.（今料理しているところ）

おばさんが私に料理の本をくださった。
　My aunt gave me a cookbook [cookery-book / cookery-book about breadmaking (パンの本)].

2. 料理されたもの
food, dish; （美食）**cuisine**

西洋[中華／日本]料理
　Western [Chinese / Japanese] food
これは上出来な料理だ。
　These are nicely cooked.
ここの料理はうまい。（レストランなど）
　They serve good food here.
　The food [cooking] is good here.
私たちは料理がくるのを待っていた。
　We were waiting for the food to be served.
中華料理とフランス料理が世界でトップの美味と考えられている。
　Chinese and French cuisines [cooking] are considered two top cuisines in the world.
〈注〉◆日本人は dish, dishes を「料理」の意味で使いすぎである。また,「おいしい」をいつも delicious と言うが, これも使いすぎである。
(1) dish, dishes の使われる場面
　　手をかけた料理や, メインになる料理によく使われる。
　There were as many vegetable dishes as main dishes, and we had all kinds of desserts.
　（メインの肉料理と同じくらいたくさんの野菜料理があったし, いろいろなデザートもそろっていた）
　main dish (肉・魚・卵・チーズなどを主とした料理)
　vegetable dish (コーン・豆などの肉の付け合せになる料理 side dish。サラダは別)
　meat dish, beef [pork] dish などのように言えるが, 要するに念入りに調理した料理や大皿に見事に盛りつけたものを念頭に dish と言うのである。
(2) エスニック料理についてもしばしば dish を使う。
　He can cook four or five Burmese dishes. (彼はビルマ料理を4,5種類つくれる)
　このような場合,「4,5種類」のような数字がともに使われることが多い。
　◆普通に料理というときは food を使うのが無難である。
　Have you tried Japanese food?
　（日本料理を食べてみたことがありますか）
　My favorite food is chawan-mushi.
　（私の好きな料理は茶わん蒸しです）
　a full-course French dinner [meal]
　（フルコースのフランス料理）
　I bought a new cookbook full of wonderful salad recipes. (すてきなサラダのいっぱい載った料理本を買った)
◆delicious を使う場面
　ごちそうになっているとき, 料理をほめて delicious と言うのはよい。しかし普通に「おいしい」は Good., It's good. でよい。tasty はスパイスがきいておいしいこと。

《関連語》
【下ごしらえ】
切る　cut (総称)
　大切りにする　chop; 角切りにする　chop into cubes; サイコロ切りにする　dice; 小さく切る　cut into tiny pieces; きざむ　mince; 線切りにする　shred (cabbage); 八つに切る　cut into eight parts
おろす　grate; grater (おろし器); grated cheese (おろしチーズ)
皮をむく　[動] peel; pare
　ジャガイモなどの皮　skin
　丸焼きジャガイモの皮　jacket
　リンゴの皮　skin
　バナナ・オレンジの皮　peel
豆を一晩水につける　soak beans overnight
【材料】　ingredients
材料の量は好みに応じて加減してよい。
　The amount of any of the ingredients can be varied to suit individual taste.
【調味】
調味する　[動] season (塩, コショウ, スパイスで)
調味料
　塩　salt; 砂糖　sugar; しょう油　shoyu, soy-sauce; 酢　vinegar; ソース　Worcestershire sauce; ケチャップ　ketchup; マヨネーズ　mayonnaise
油　cooking oil; サラダオイル　salad oil; バター　butter; マーガリン　margarine
スパイス, 香辛料　spice
　コショウ　pepper; シナモン　cinnamon; パプリカ　paprika; ガーリック[ニンニク]　garlic;

ナツメグ nutmeg; カラシ mustard
ハーブ herb
ローズマリー rosemary; タイム thyme; パセリ parsley; ミント mint; セージ sage; 月桂樹［ベイリーフ，ローレル］bay leaves, laurel
香りつけ flavoring
バニラ vanilla
【焼く】
bake《bread, pie, cookies》
roast《meat, chicken, fish, some vegetables》
オーブン oven
トースター toaster; toast（こんがり焼く）
フライパン frying pan
焼く } pan-broil
いためる } fry [saute]《potatoes in butter》
（きつね色に）brown《onions, beef》
焼き網 grill; 鉄板 metal plate
直火焼きする grill
【揚げる】 fry;（たっぷりの油で）deep fry
【煮る】
鍋 saucepan, pot; 煮る boil; ことこと煮る simmer; 弱[強]火で煮る cook over low [high] heat
ふかす steam
【計量】
重さ ～kg, ～g; 量 ～cc
カップ ～cup
大さじ（tablespoon）～tbs
小さじ（teaspoon）～tsp
（塩）少々 a pinch of《salt》
【定番料理名】
カレーライス curry
ビーフシチュー beef stew
ハンバーグ hamburger; beefburger
ステーキ steak
焼き加減 I'd like it（生焼き）rare [（中焼き）medium-rare,（並み焼き）medium,（かなりよく焼く）medium well-done,（よく焼く）well-done].
卵料理
かき卵 scrambled egg
ゆで卵 {（固ゆで）hard / （半熟）soft} boiled egg
オムレツ omelet; ポーチドエッグ poached egg
目玉焼き fried egg;〔米〕sunny side up;（両面焼き） easy over
天ぷら
えび天 batter-fried shrimp（batter は粉を水でといたもの）
なすの天ぷら tempura-style eggplant〔米〕[aubergine〔英〕]
とんカツ a breaded pork cutlet
【味の表現】
おいしい good
まずい not good
薄い味 {（悪い）tasteless; weak《drink》 / （良い）light《dipping sauce, dressing》}
〈注〉 スープが水っぽい thin と言えばけなしていることになるが，さっぱりしている light は悪い含意はない。
濃い味（悪い）overdone, heavy
（良い）hearty, robust
概して九州の人は濃い味を好む。
Generally speaking, people in Kyushu like {things with strong [heavy] flavoring. / to use {lots of shoyu. / heavy [strong] shoyu.}}
甘い sweet
塩辛い too salty; heavy on the salt
塩分を控える go light on the salt
こってりした rich; filling
しつこい heavy; too rich
油っこい oily
さっぱりした light（軽い食事，白身の魚などについて言う）
酢のきいた vinegary; sour
苦い bitter
ひりひり辛い hot

りょこう（旅行）→ えんそく

名 **travel(ing); a trip; a tour; a journey**
動 **travel; go on [take, make] a trip; make a tour**
バス旅行 a bus tour [trip]
周遊旅行 a round trip
団体旅行 a guided [conducted] tour

観光旅行 a sightseeing trip [tour];（休日の）行楽旅行 a holiday [vacation] trip
出張旅行 a business trip
修学旅行 a school excursion
彼女は旅行好きだ。
She likes traveling.
退職したら世界中を旅行してみたい。
I'd like to {travel all over the world / make a tour of the world / make a round-the-world tour} after I retire.
彼女は今北海道を旅行中だ。
She's now on a trip to Hokkaido.
彼は休暇でベニスに旅行してきた。
He took a holiday trip to Venice.
あの人たちは昨年オーストラリア旅行をしてきた。
They made a trip to Australia last year.
父は今年は3回も出張でヨーロッパ旅行をした。
My father went to Europe three times this year on business.
タイへの長旅はしんどかった。
The long journey to Thailand was fatiguing [tiring].

《類義語》

travel フランス語の travail（＝work, suffer）と同語源であることからも察せられるが，旅といっても行く先が問題ではなく，旅行をする動作に重点がある。主に動詞として使う。
travel by air（空の旅をする）
travel thousands of miles（何千マイルも旅をする）
travel in space（宇宙旅行をする）
名詞としては普通，無冠詞で使い，space travel（宇宙旅行），air travel（空の旅）のような複合語で使われる。

trip 動詞としては足どり軽く歩く，また足をすべらすことで，旅行をする意味には使えない。名詞では陸上の小旅行，観光保養旅行，遠足の意味になる。行く先に重点があり，かつ出発地点にまた戻って来るのが普通である。
a round trip（往復旅行）
trip は使用範囲が広く，月旅行でも隣町までの旅行でもあらゆる旅行に使われ，今や travel をしのいで主流。
旅行中である be on a trip
旅行をする take [make] a trip to

tour 視察，巡遊，観光の一周旅行。
a sightseeing tour（観光旅行）

journey 行く先に重点があり，trip より長い旅行，出発点に戻る含みはない。
It's a whole day's journey from here by train.（ここから列車でまる1日かかる）
のように「行程」を念頭に浮かべた語。また，reach one's journey's end（旅を終える）など journey は象徴的に人生を指すこともあり詩的な語である。かつてのつらい旅を思わせる語で古風。

excursion 団体旅行，小旅行，修学旅行。
pleasure trip, bus trip（観光バス旅行）も excursion と言える。

expedition 多くは組織された団体によって特定の目的遂行のために行われるものを指す。学術的，科学的目的のものが多い。
an archaeological expedition（考古学調査隊現地調査）

outing 遠足，2,3時間の「お出かけ」，楽しむためのもの。

pilgrimage 信仰上の巡礼。比喩的に人生の意義を求めての心の旅を指すこともある。

《関連語》

旅行社 travel bureau
旅行代理店 travel agent
旅行案内所 tourist information office; visitors' center
ガイドブック travel handbook; guide book; travel guide
列車時刻表 train [railroad] timetable [schedule]
予約する reserve《a seat / a hotel / a flight》
取り消す cancel
周遊切符，往復切符 round-trip ticket〔米〕; return ticket〔英〕
片道切符 one-way ticket

る

るす（留守）

留守である　**be away from home; be out; be not in**

あなたがお電話をくださったとき，留守にしていてすみませんでした。

I'm sorry I was out when you called.

１週間ばかり出張で留守にします。

I'll be away [gone] on business for a week.

彼女は今留守です。

She's not in at the moment.

彼は休暇で出かけて留守です。

He's away on vacation〔米〕[holiday〔英〕].

彼は出張で１年の半分は留守だ。

He's away on business half the year.

〈注〉「留守です」と言うとき，親しい人には
She's shopping just now.（買い物に出かけた）
He's away on business.（出張です）
He's gone on a trip.（旅行している）
のように留守の理由を言うのが普通。他人には She's not in., He's out. のように言えばよい。

【居留守】

今日はだれが来ても私は留守だからね。

Today I'm not at home to anyone.

電話がかかってきたら，私は留守だと言ってくれ。

If anyone calls, say that I'm out.

【留守中】 while one is away [out]; in one's absence〔*formal*〕

昨日息子が車の事故を起してね。困ってうちに電話してきたがちょうど僕は留守中で誰も出なかったんだ。

My son had a car accident yesterday. It happened when I wasn't home [while I was out], so nobody answered when he called to ask what to do.

【留守番】

きのうは１日中１人で留守番だった。

Yesterday nobody but me was at home all day.

皆で結婚式に出かけるので，その日はスミスさんにお店の留守番[店番]を頼んだ。

We were all going to the wedding, so we asked Mrs. Smith to come over and to {take care of / mind} the shop for the day.

私は一番上の子に留守番を頼んで外出した。

I went out, leaving the oldest child in charge.

私は休暇で旅行に出かけ留守番を兄に頼んだ。

I asked my brother to look after the house while I'm on vacation.

〈注〉◆look after the house とはごく普通の毎日の仕事をすること。たとえば窓を開けて風を通したり，郵便物を取り入れたりなど。leave《someone》in charge というとそれ以上に責任をもたせ何かあったらその裁量に任せること。
◆「いない」の意味に日本人はよく absent を使うが，学校や会合に出席していないのが absent で，「家にいない」のは be out, be not (at) home, be not in である。「留守中に」には in my absence があるが，かなり堅い表現であるから普通は while I was out [away from home] のように節にするとよい。

【おろそかになる】

テレビなんか見ていると宿題をやる手がお留守になるよ。

You can't concentrate on your homework and watch TV at the same time.

れ

れい（例）

1. 実例・類例

an example; an instance; 場合 **a case**

例を挙げると…[例えば…]　for instance ...

これはほんの１例にすぎない。

This is only one instance [example] out of many.

彼は論点をはっきりさせるためにいくつかの例を挙げた。

He gave some examples to make his point clear.

彼は彼女の場合を例にとって，愛情のない結婚がどんな結末になるのかを話した。

He used [took] her case to illustrate the consequences of loveless marriages.

これはまさに「まかぬ種は生えぬ」のよい例だ。

This is a fine example of "no pain, no gain."

〈注〉 ×This is a fine example that "...." とは言えない。

これこそ遺伝的継承というものの立派な例であります。

Here's a wonderful example of inherited tradition.

彼女の例でよくわかる。人は不遇の時を考えて備えねばならない。

Her case clearly shows that we should provide for rainy days.

これは政治の腐敗の典型的な例だ。

This is a typical case of political corruption.

〈注〉 example, instance は，その背後にある大きな真理の例証のための具体例であり，背後の真理が重要である。case は具体的事実がまずあり，それが普遍的真理を示すことで，example の場合よりも実例に重点がある。ただし，互いに重なり合う部分(あいまいな部分)があることは example, instance, case のどの語でも当てはまる類例のあることで明らかである。

2. 先例・慣例

【先例】a precedent

そんな先例はない。

There has been no precedent.

There hasn't been a case of this sort before.

それが先例にならないようにと思う。

I don't want it to become a precedent.

【先例にならう】

follow a《someone's》example

私たちは皆彼の例にならってやった。

We all did as he had done.

【例のごとく】

彼は例のごとく朝食前に軽い運動をした。

He took [did] some light exercise before breakfast as usual.

【例の場所】

５時に例の場所で会いましょう。

Let's meet at five at the usual spot.

【問題の】

あれが例の加藤氏か。

Is that the Mr. Kato (whom) we were talking about?　(1)

Is that the Mr. Kato?　(2)

〈注〉 (1)は否定的な含みはない。前後関係による。(2)は the に重点を置き，[ði] と発音，口調で否定的になる。

3. 例外

an exception

生あるものすべて死す。例外なし。

Every living thing has to die. There's no exception.

彼は例外的に知力がすぐれている。

He is exceptionally intelligent.

4. 例文

an example (sentence)

例文を作っていただけませんか。どうもその言葉の使い方がいまひとつわからないのです。

Could you give me an example sentence? I don't quite understand how that word should be used.

【例題，練習問題】

宿題として例題を与える[出す]

give an exercise as homework

れい（礼）

1．お辞儀

bowing

神社では人々は賽銭を投げ，礼をし，柏手を打って祈る。

At a shrine people throw coins as an offering, bow, clap their hands, and pray.

2．礼儀

礼儀は社会生活をスムーズにする。

Etiquette oils the social machinery.

【礼儀を失する】

話しかけられたとき返事をしないのでは礼を失する[失礼である]。

It's rude not to respond when you are spoken to.

3．感謝の表現

【言葉】

私が娘さんを車で送ってあげたことに彼女は礼を言った。

She thanked me for driving her daughter home.

何とお礼を言っていいかわかりません。

I don't know how to thank you (enough).

【贈り物】

先生が学校を去られるにあたり，子供たちはお礼の贈り物をした。

The children gave their teacher a farewell present [a present at his retirement].

同窓会は彼の功績をたたえお礼の贈り物をした。

The alumni association gave him a gift in acknowledgement of his services.

〈注〉 引退する人に贈る贈り物は retirement gifts と言う。

【お礼のしるし】

これはほんのお礼のしるし[気持ち]です。

This is only a token of my thanks.

〈注〉 贈り物の上に in token of my thanks と書いたカードなどをのせる。

【謝金】

〈注〉 謝金には次の 2 つがある。(1)お礼の気持ちをあらわす少額のもの。(2)一般にお礼と言うが双方合意の月謝など，相当の額のもの。

(1) **token gift** 世話になった分をお金にして贈るもの。

honorarium (*pl*. -ia) 講演者などにお礼の気持ちとして渡すもの。

(2) **education fee; tuition** 塾，家庭教師の月謝など。

いくらお礼を差し上げたらいいのですか。

How much is the tuition?

【礼金】

お金のいっぱい入った財布を君が拾ったとしよう。もし落し主が現れたなら，慣例では落し主は拾得した君にお礼として 1 割贈ることになっている。

Suppose you find a wallet full of money on the road. If its owner turns up, it's customary for him to give you, the finder, ten percent of the money as a reward.

れいせい（冷静）→ へいき

れつ（列）→ ぎょうれつ

a line; a queue

（動く行列）**a procession; a parade**

（縦の列）**a file;**（主として横列）**a row;**

（横列）**a rank**

私は最前列のジムの隣に座った。

I sat in the front row next to Jim.

机を 7 列に並べてください。

Arrange the desks in seven rows.

〈注〉 line, queue とも縦の列の場合が多いが，横列でもよい。それに対して row は横列が主だが縦列も可。縦列で長めのものは column という言い方もある。

Children lined up
in (a) single file. 1列
in twos [double file]. 2列
in threes. 3列
in fours. 4列
five across. 5列
(子供たちは1[2/3/4/5]列に並んだ)

【行列】

私が到着するまでにもう出札口の前に長い行列ができていた。

By the time I arrived there was already a long line [queue] of people in front of the ticket window.

タクシーが1列に並んで客待ちをしている。

Taxis are standing in a line [rank].

【動く列】

オリンピック開会式の選手の行列は色とりどりで壮観である。

The Olympic opening procession is a colorful spectacle.

私は行列[パレード]を見に行った。まずバトンガールがやってきた，横6列に並んで。

I went to see the parade. First came baton girls six abreast.

偉い人たちの列が何ブロックにもわたって続いた。

The procession of dignitaries went on for blocks.

【列に割り込む】

(子供に) 列に割り込んではいけません。

Don't ˌbreak into a line [jump a queue].

(割り込もうとした人に)割り込まないで。列の後ろにつきなさいよ。

Don't push in. Go to the end of the queue.

れる

〈注〉 日本語では「…は…に…を〜ら[さ]れた」は自由に言える。ついそのつもりで英語の動詞が二重目的語をとり得る動詞であろうとなかろうとおかまいなく，次のような受身文を作る誤りが非常に多い。

×He was hurt his pride. (プライドを傷つけられた)
×He was praised his son. (息子をほめられた)
×I was deeply hurt my feelings. (気持ちを傷つけられた)
×She was broken her dream. (夢をこわされた)

正しくは次のようにしなければならない。

His pride was hurt.
His son was praised.
I was deeply hurt. / My feelings were hurt.
Her dream was destroyed.

以下，日本語と英語の受身表現を例を挙げて比較しながら見てゆく。

1. 英語で能動・受動両構文が可能な場合

山がはっきり見える。

We can see the mountains clearly.
The mountains can be seen clearly.
The mountains are clear.

市長は彼の市に対する功績をたたえた。

The mayor praised him highly [He was highly praised] for his services to the city.

芽は塩をつけて食べられる。

You can eat sprouts [Sprouts can be eaten] with a bit of salt.

2. 英語では受動が普通

英語は世界中で話されている。

English is spoken all over the world.

クリントン氏は1992年に大統領に選ばれた。

Mr. Clinton was elected president in 1992.

彼は人事部長に任命された。

He was appointed head of the personnel section.

彼は裁判所に呼び出された。

He was summoned by the court.

彼は山形で1943年に生れた。

He was born in Yamagata in 1943.

3. 日本語では「(ら)れる」でも英語では能動が普通

私は10時だよと母に起されるまでぐっすり寝た。

I slept well till my mother woke me and told me that it was already ten o'clock. (受動態もあるが能動態が一般的)

彼は弟をぶって父親に怒られた。

His father scolded him for hitting his brother.

〈注〉 He was scolded by his father ….
は正しい文だが，1回限りの行為については能動の方が普通。

先生に怒られた[先生によく怒られた]。

My teacher scolded me. [I was often scolded by my teacher.]

cf. 先生を怒らせた[先生が怒った]。

My teacher got angry at me.

〈注〉 「怒る」とは「腹を立てる」と「しかる」と両方の意味がある。「怒られた[しかられた]」のつもりで，次のような誤文を書かないように。
×I was got angry by my teacher. (正解は上掲)

【ほめられる】

先生に絵をほめられた。

My teacher praised my picture.

×I was praised my picture.

○I was praised for my picture.

○My picture was praised.

〈注〉 ひとつの具体的な出来事を(何に重点を置くということなく)報道する文では通常，受動態は使われない。しかし，習慣的なこと，すなわち「よく怒られた」のような場合には受動態を用いることがある。

4. 日本語独特の受動表現

【被害の受動】

子供に泣かれて困った。

The child wouldn't stop crying and I didn't know what to do.

×I was cried by my child.

彼は奥さんに死なれて落ち込んでいる。

He was very depressed after his wife's death.

His wife's death deeply depressed him.

〈注〉 His wife died …. と depressed の部分を2つの文に分けてもよい。
×He was died by his wife.

【断言の緩和】

新方式の[その]方が効果的と思われる。

The new method is presumably more effective.

It will probably be more effective.

〈注〉 perhaps, probably, presumably などの副詞や，It seems to me …. は断言を避ける場合に用いられる。

【自発】

息子のことが案じられてならない。

I can't help feeling anxious about my son.

あの子の目に涙をいっぱいためた顔が思い出されてならない。

Her tearful look haunts me.

I'm haunted by her tearful look.

戦災孤児の[その]悲しい話に皆泣かされた。

People couldn't help weeping at the sad story of the war orphans.

The sad story made them cry.

5.「漢熟語＋する」の受動

その政策は来月実施されるだろう。

The policy will be put into practice from next month.

展覧会は三越ホールで開催される。

The exhibition will be held at Mitsukoshi Hall.

炭坑労働者の一部は救出された。

Some of the miners were rescued.

6. 日本語では受動でないが英語で受動

【感情表現(be＋～ed の形)】

〈注〉 この受動形はこの形で定着し，受動形であるとほとんど意識されていない。

彼女は新しい仕事が気に入っている。

She is pleased with her new job.

彼は結果に満足している。

He is satisfied with the result.

ドアが顔のすぐそばで突然開いたときはびっくりした。

I was surprised when the door opened in my face.

【日本語では自動詞で英語ではしばしば受動】

彼は助かった。

He was saved.

財布が見つかった。

The purse was found.

〈注〉 彼は就職が決った[決らない]。

△His job {has been decided / hasn't been decided yet.

○He has(n't) decided where {he's going to work. / he'll work.

日本語では普通「決った」と言うが，欧米の考え方では本人の選択・決断で主体的に「決める」という考え方である。そのため，His job を主語にした受動文は文としては正しくても奇妙にうつる。

問題はまだ解決していない。

The problem hasn't been solved yet.

〈注〉 英語では行為者がはっきりしているときは能動文が普通である。上の例では行為者にはふれていない。聞き手に光景が見えるように話したければ能動態を使う方がよい。

7．使役 →させる・させられる

【される】

私はあの子にいじめられて泣かされた。

That boy bullied me and so I cried [made me cry].

×I was cried by that boy.

（彼女に）いつも同じ話を聞かされた。

I had to hear the same old story every time.

She always told me the same old story.

×I was heard the same old story.

先生がシェイクスピアをやっているとかで，高校でハムレットを読まされた。

I read *Hamlet* during high school because our teacher was a sort of Shakespearean scholar.

ジョーンズ先生に（夏休みに）『ヴェニスの商人』を読まされた。

Mr. Jones's summer assignment was to read *The Merchant of Venice*.

Mr. Jones assigned us *The Merchant of Venice*.

（どちらの文も宿題を出されたが，それをやったかどうかにはふれていない）

〈注〉◆「ハムレットを読まされた」は I was made to read *Hamlet*. とも言えるが，「無理やりに読まされた」と，いやであったことを強調する文になる。×I was read *Hamlet*.

◆「…される」を単純に他動詞の受動と思ってはならない。しかし「される」が使役の受動でも，be made to ... はしばしばぎこちないので避けて前後関係から意味を補う方がよい。たとえば「心配させられる」も be made to worry は使わないで次のようにするとよい。

あの子には心配させられた。

That boy always made me worry.

He was quite a cause [source] of worry.

また，もっと単純に次のようにしてもよい。

I always worried about that boy.

◆日本語の「受動」と「可能」が同じ「(ら)れる」の形であるので，その混同と思われる誤りがある。

彼は全部食べられると言った。

×He said he could be eaten them all.

○He said he could eat them all.

大きくて赤いおいしそうな実は食べられそうに見えた。

×The big, red luscious berries seemed to be able to eat.

○The big, red luscious berries seemed (to be) edible [ready for eating].

◆(柔道で) あの男は君には投げられまい。

You won't be able to throw him down. (可能)

He won't be thrown by you. (受動)

れんしゅう（練習）

名 **practice, practise**〔英〕; **training; a drill; an exercise**

練習する 動 **practice, practise**〔英〕; **exercise**

(劇の練習)名 **rehearsal;** (本番前の総練習) **dress rehearsal; practice run** (dress rehearsal も含めて通し稽古のこと)

【練習中】

彼女は今ピアノの練習中です。

She's practicing the piano now.

チームは目下，大学対抗フットボール試合に向けて猛練習中だ。

The team is training for the intercollegiate football game.

【練習不足】

私は休暇でしばらく遊びに行っていたので練習不足だ。

I've been away on vacation and now I'm out

of practice.

【練習すれば】

練習すれば上手になりますよ。

You'll improve { with practice. / by practicing.

Practice makes perfect.

【…の練習】

仲間には今では有名な俳優になった人もいますが，その頃は毎晩古いガレージで練習したものです。

Some of them are famous actors now, but in those days they rehearsed every night in an old garage.

学生はもっと英語の聞き取り練習が必要だ。

The students need more { practice in listening to English. / listening practice.

〈注〉 発音練習は drills in English pronunciation と言う。

【練習問題】

先生が英文法の練習問題を出した。

Our teacher gave us English grammar exercises [drills].

【練習曲】 étude

練習のための曲　a practice piece

〈注〉 試験の練習は模擬試験 sham-testと言う。

【運転】

彼は今車の運転を練習中だ。

He's practising driving.

実地練習　a practice run [test run]

(車のみならず比喩的に広く使われる)

【練習車】

「練習車」「教習車」の表示

"Student Driver"

【練習試合】 a practice game [match]

れんらく (連絡)

1．交通

連絡する **connect with;** 合流する **join**

連絡している **be connected with**

連絡点［駅］ a transfer point; a junction point

連絡切符　a through [transfer, combination] ticket

【連絡の便】

この列車はフェリーに連絡していますか。

Does this train connect with the ferry?

この列車は福島で本線と連絡します。

This train connects with the main line at Fukushima.

ここは列車とバスの連絡が悪い。

This place has poor train and bus connections.

【連絡地点】

名鉄津島線は一宮で名鉄本線と連絡している。

The Meitetsu Tsushima Line meets the Meitetsu Main Line at Ichinomiya.

塩尻は名古屋発の中央線下り列車と新宿行き上り列車の連絡駅だ。

Shiojiri is the transfer point on the Chuô Line between down-trains from Nagoya and up-trains for Shinjuku.

【支線】

名鉄本線は愛知県内を走る数本の支線と連絡している。

The Meitetsu Main Line has several junctions with branch lines within Aichi Prefecture.

2．通信

【連絡を断つ】

その町には連絡のしようがない。

The town is completely out of contact with the outside world.

地震の被害により，その町には電話連絡も無線連絡もできない。

Because of the damage caused by the earthquake the town has neither telephone nor radio communication.

その飛行機は離陸後１時間で管制塔との連絡を絶った。

The plane lost contact with air controllers an hour after takeoff.

登山隊は昨夜無線連絡を絶った。
The mountaineering team lost radio contact last night.

【警察に】

(けんか中) 警察に連絡しろ[を呼べ]!
Call (for) the police!

警察に連絡しよう。これは我々の手に余る事件だ。
Contact the police. This is more than we can handle by ourselves.

【一般の人と】

もし電話で連絡がとれないようなら手紙を書かなければならない。
We'll have to write to him if we can't contact him by phone.

あの子の先生やお医者さんと連絡をとってやっていかねばならないね。
We should keep in touch with her teacher and her doctor.

〈注〉 get in touch は日常的なことについて連絡，相談する。keep in touch は連絡を絶やさないこと。初めて「問題を持ち出す」のは bring it up, 「話し合う」のは talk it over。

到着しだい連絡します。
I'll {let you know / get in touch} as soon as I arrive.

今朝8時からずっと電話連絡しようとしていたんだよ。
I've been trying to phone you since eight this morning.

ろ

ろう → だろう

ろうどう（労働）

名 **labor; labour**〔英〕

《関連語》
【労働者】 worker; laborer
肉体労働　manual labor
熟練労働　skilled labor
肉体労働者　blue-collar worker
職人　workman
サラリーマン　office worker; white-collar worker（役職者も含む）
〈注〉 広い意味の「労働者」は CEO（chief executive officer, 企業の最高経営責任者）まで含み，CEO は white-collar workers にはいる。
労働人口　the working population
労働力　manpower; labor force
労働市場　labor market
【労使】 labor and management
雇い主　employer
雇用者，使用人　employee
労働組合　union
労働組合運動　labor movement
労働争議　labor dispute
春闘　spring labor offensive
団体交渉　collective bargaining
ストライキ　strike; walkout
ストライキをやる　go on strike; walk out
ロックアウト　lockout
サボタージュをする　go slow
座り込み　sit-in
賃上げ　pay increase; pay raise
調停　mediation
和解　reconciliation
解雇する　dismiss; fire〔*colloq.*〕; lay off
失業する　lose one's job
失業中である　be unemployed
【労働条件】 working conditions
初任給　starting salary
昇進　promotion
昇進する　be promoted
年功序列制　seniority system
終身雇用制度　lifetime employment system
配置転換　job rotation
出向(社)員　visiting employee
パートタイム労働　part-time labor
パートタイマー　part-timer
労働時間　working hours
週休２日制　five-day workweek
有給休暇　paid leave
有給休暇をとる　take a leave
産休　maternity leave; 忌引　compassionate leave
超過勤務手当　overtime pay
定年　retirement age
退職する　leave;（定年で）retire
退職金　retirement allowance; retirement money
年金　pension
年金生活をする　retire on a pension
【労働法制】
労働基準法　Labor Standards Law
雇用機会均等法　Equal Employment Opportunity Law

ろうひ（浪費）→ むだ

名 （a）**waste**
浪費する　**waste; squander**《money》
それは時間と金の浪費だ。
It's a waste of time and money.
彼は父の遺した金をすべて浪費して無一文になった。
He squandered what his father left him and became penniless.
浪費家　a spendthrift

ろこつ（露骨）

彼は露骨に敵意を示した。
He showed hatred outright.

彼女は露骨にいやな顔をした。

She didn't even try to hide her disgust.

その小説は露骨な性描写がやたらに出てくる。

That novel is too full of sexual descriptions.

〈注〉 露骨とは隠すべきものを敢えて示す意味があるので frankly, openly では表現できない。

ろんじる（論じる）→ ぎろん

1. 議論する

その当時若者たちは，この居酒屋に集まっては酒を飲んで天下国家を論じ，宗教や人生について論じたものだった。

In those days young people used to gather at this inn, drink sake and discuss politics, religion and life.

最後のパネルディスカッションでは航空力学の将来が論じられた。

The final panel discussed the future of aerodynamics.

2. 問題にする，取り上げる

この論文で著者は性差別について論じている。

This essay is about [deals with] sexual discrimination.

In this essay the writer treats sexual discrimination.

彼は今日の日本が直面する様々な問題について論じている。

He comments on various problems {facing Japan. / Japan is facing now.}

ろんそう（論争）→ ぎろん

名 (a) **dispute;** (a) **controversy;** (an) **argument**

論争する **dispute; have a dispute about** 《something》

新空港建設については論争がやかましい。

There is a great deal of controversy [argument] about the construction of a new airport.

論争には健康的なこともあるし破壊的なこともある。

Controversy is sometimes healthy, sometimes destructive.

ろんぶん（論文）

1. 卒業論文・学位論文

4年制大学学部学生（undergraduate）の卒業論文

a graduation paper; a senior thesis〔米〕

大学院修士論文

a MA thesis; a master's thesis

大学院博士論文

a PhD thesis; a dissertation

〈注〉 学位論文も PhD のみ dissertation と呼ぶ。

《類義語》

articles 一般的な語。新聞・雑誌の記事に至るまで多くのタイプをひっくるめて articles と呼べる。随筆・新聞報道・記事・書評・劇評・音楽評・学術的小論文など。

papers 学術論文。research papers は主として自然科学・社会科学の論文に用いられる語。

essays articles のひとつ。次のような種類がある。

(1) academic essays 学術的小論文。paper よりも気楽なもの。学術雑誌に載っている2, 3ページの論文は article とも essay とも呼べる。

(2) informative essays 解説的論文，評論。exposition とも呼ばれる。

(3) personal essays ある題目についての個人的考え，感慨などを述べたもの。随筆，雑誌などへ寄稿した文をまとめて essays（随筆集）として出版することがある。

writings 種々のジャンルにわたる著作の場合 writings of Ernest Hemingway, Hemingway's writings（ヘミングウェイ著作集）のように呼ぶ。小説・劇・評論といった場合である。

thesis 学位論文。修士，博士どちらにも使える。

dissertation (1) 博士号の学位論文。

(2) かなり長文の形式の整った学術論文。
treatise 何々論，本質的な問題を広い視野で深く考察，総合した長論文。ただし，これは堅い格式ばった語で学術，法律用語以外では使われない。

2. 関連表現

【提出】

彼は先月博士論文を提出した。

He submitted his PhD thesis last month.

〈注〉 submit, present は形式的で堅い語。普通にレポートなどを「出す」のは hand in, 郵送で出すのは send in。

【執筆】

彼はいま大学の研究紀要に出す論文を執筆中だ。

He's now writing a paper for the faculty research bulletin.

〈注〉 欧米では大学で出版する学術雑誌はほかの大学の学者にも公開されており，審査委員が採否を検討して載せる。日本の大学の紀要のようなものはない。また bulletin は，大学に関しては専門コースの何でもわかる大学要覧を指す。大学要覧は英国では Graduate Catalog (コースの説明をする大部の印刷物) と言う。bulletin を簡略にして学校の宣伝を兼ねたものが brochure (パンフレット)。

彼が訪ねて来たのは冬のことで私はちょうど修士論文を書いていた。

When he called me it was winter and I was doing my MA thesis.

こうして夏が過ぎ秋が来て私はまだ論文が仕上がっていなかった。

So summer wore away, the autumn set in and I still hadn't finished my thesis yet.

【発表】

彼は次の日曜日に京都大学で開かれる大会で論文を発表する。

He will give [read] a paper at the conference which is to be held at Kyoto University next Sunday.

〈注〉 論文の口頭発表は名詞では presentation という。

彼の論文読んだ？

Did you see {the article on / what he wrote about} 《the topic》 in 《magazine》?

〈注〉 気楽な会話では上述のように，論文も書評も what he wrote でよい。

わ

わがまま

《類義語》

selfish 利己主義な。自分のことしか考えない。わがままな人についても行為についても使う。

self-centered 自己中心の。普通「人」について言う。自分のことに没頭し，他人のことに考えが及ばない。

egoistic; egotistic 自己中心的で，利己主義でうぬぼれが強いこと。性格について言う。行為に関しては使われない。egotistic は egoistic に輪をかけた自己中心的厚かましさを意味する。

self-indulgent したい放題すること。これもよくない意味であるが，自分では好きなようにしても他人の迷惑にならなければよいわけで，たまには後の〈注〉にあるような意味に使われることもある。

【わがままな子】

a spoiled [spoilt] child（甘やかされた子）

a willful child（わがままで強情な子）

a disobedient child（言うことを聞かない子）

【わがままに育てる】 spoil [pamper]《one's》child

私は乳母に育てられたので，すっかりわがままになってしまった。

Because I was brought up by my nanny, I got quite spoilt.

【わがままだ】

彼はわがままでいつでも［何でも］自分の思う通りにしたがる。

He's willful and wants his own way all the time.

He wants everything his own way.

He thinks [is aware] only of himself.（自分のことしか考えない）

【独占】

おもちゃを一人占めにするのはわがままよ。

It's selfish of you to keep all the toys for yourself.

いつも自分の好きな番組を見るってがんばるのはわがままよ。ほかの人は別の番組を見たいのに。

It's selfish of you to insist on always seeing your program when another person wants to see another program at the same time.

【食事】

彼は食べ物についてわがままだ。

He's self-centered in his eating habits.

あれが嫌いこれが嫌いと食べ物でわがままばかり言うんじゃないの。

Don't complain all the time about food you (personally) don't like.

〈注〉◆ self-indulgent は「わがまま」というよりむしろ「ぜいたく」の意味に使われることがある。

I'm awfully self-indulgent about clothes; I buy a pair of shoes once a month.（私は身につけるものにはとてもぜいたくをしていて月に1足は靴を買う）

◆ egoistic, egoism を使った例文

Some people believe that humans are egoistic by nature.（人間は生来自己中心的なものだと信じている人もいる）

Egoism often leads to selfishness.（自己中心は利己主義になりやすい）

わかる（分かる）

1. 識別できる

know; recognize

彼は私が(だれか)すぐわかった。

He knew [recognized] me at once.

私がわかりますか。

Do you recognize [remember] me?

双子の兄弟はまったくそっくりだ。どちらがどちらかわからない。

The twin brothers look exactly alike. I can't tell which is which [them apart].

私はどれが天然真珠でどれが養殖真珠かわか

らない。

I cannot tell natural pearls from cultured ones.

〈注〉 know は「知っている，わかっている」という状態を表す動詞だが recognize（それとわかる）の意味もあり，「わかる」に近い意味の広い動詞であると言える。

2．内容を理解する

understand; see; get

わかった！

I see. / I get it. / I've got it.

〈注〉 考えていた問題が急に解けたときの「ああ，わかった」に当るのは，Ah! / Ah I see. / I've got it.（この場合 I've は非常に軽く速く発音され，got it の部分が強く聞える）

君の言いたいことはよくわかるよ。

I know what you mean.

彼の言っていることがわかりますか。

Do you understand what he's saying?

彼の言いたい[かった]ことはよくわかった。

I understood what he meant.

彼が言おうとしていたことはよくわかった。

I knew [understood] what he was trying to say.

君の言っていることがわからない。

I don't understand what you are saying.

私は自分の思っていることをわかってもらえなかった。

I couldn't ⌊make myself understood [get my meaning across].

最後にやっとあの人たちの言っていることの意味がわかった。

I finally realized what they meant.

彼女の考えていることはわかりにくい。

Her ideas are incomprehensible.

あの先生の講義はとてもわかりやすかった。

Her lecture was very understandable.

彼はラテン語もギリシア語もわかる。

He knows both Latin and Greek.

【真価がわかる】

彼は音楽のよくわかる人だ。

He has ⌊a great appreciation [an ear] for music.

彼は詩がわからない。

He has no appreciation for poetry.

He cannot appreciate poetry.

He has no sense of the beauty of poetry.

He doesn't understand poetry. *

私は絵はわかりません。

I'm no judge of pictures.

彼はジョークのわからない人だ。

He doesn't understand jokes. *

He has no sense of humor.

〈注〉◆Jokes are lost upon him. は，彼にはジョークを言っても全部無駄になる，全然わからないことを面白く言ったもの。

◆上の＊印の文はそれぞれ「詩やジョークの意味がわからない」のほかに「詩やジョークの存在価値がわからない」の意にとられることもあり得る。

3．知識・情報を得る →しる・しらせる

［人主語］**come to know; find (out); learn;**

後からわかる **realize;** 知っている **know**

［事主語］**prove; turn out**

【知識・情報】

中古コンピュータのいいのはどこで買ったらいいかわかったよ。

I found out where I could buy a good used computer.

歴史の面白さがわかったよ。

I found [realized] that history is interesting.

その人はまだ意識を回復していなくて身元がわからないままだ。

The man is still unconscious and hasn't been identified yet.

私が投票するのはおかしい。だって，候補者のことが何もわかっていないし判断のしようがないもの。

It's not fair for me to vote, because I don't know anything about them and have no basis for judgment.

【了解】

ああわかった，わかった。（聞こえてるよ）

Yes, yes, I hear you.

「まただめだったんだ。それで彼落ちこんでい

るんだ」「わかってる」。

"He failed again. He's depressed." "I know."

「夜，一人で歩いて帰ったりするなよ」「もちろんよ。わかってるわ」。

"Don't walk home alone at night." "I know better."

〈注〉 I know better. は I know better than to walk alone at night. の意味。So I won't do that.（だからやらない）を含意する。

【原因】

火事の原因はわからなかった。

The cause of the fire was unknown.

【方法】

よしわかった。（方法を思いついた）

I know what to do.

I know what.〔*spoken*〕

「あれあれ，またカーペットの角がほぐれている！」「わかった，こうすりゃいい。両面テープで角をおさえるんだ」。

"Oh, dear, the carpet is raveling at the corner again!" "I know what. Let's use 2-sided tape to make the corner stay."

【理由】

私にはなぜか（理由が）わかる［わからない］。

I can see { the reason. / why〔*more common*〕.

I can't see why.

I can't see why not.（なぜだめなの）

【真相】

彼の人物証明書はたいへんよさそうに見えたのだが，いんちきだったとわかった。

His credentials looked excellent, but they proved to be false.

〈注〉 proved to be ... は形式的で堅い表現であるから日常的なことには使えない。

The predictions proved false.（予言は結局うそだとわかった）

上記の文は二様に解釈可能である。

(1) うその予言をした。

(2) うそのつもりはなくとも予言が当らなかった。

The rumor proved false.（うわさはうそとわかった）

「うそだった」は次のように言ってもよい。

The politician said (so and so), but it wasn't true.（その政治家は…と言ったが，本当ではなかった）

【結果の判明】

選挙の結果はいつわかりますか。

When will [shall] we find out the full election results?

When will the full election results be announced [in]?

夜の12時頃まではわかるでしょう。

We will have them all by midnight. (them＝election results)

だれが当選したかわかるでしょう。

We will find out who has been elected.

明日にはわかるかもしれないが，たぶん水曜日まではわからないだろう。

We might know tomorrow but probably we won't know till Wednesday.

【伝聞】

あの人が亡くなったことは2,3日後になってわかった［知った］。

I { learned [was told] of / found out about } his death a few days later.

【事情がわかってきた】

彼女も（すぐに）事情がわかってきた。

She { has come / soon began } to understand the situation.

【知らない】

彼の住所がわからない。

I don't know his address [where he lives].

それについては（聞いたことがないから）何もわからない。

I haven't heard anything about it.

彼が今どこにいるか（覚えていないから）わからない。

I don't remember where he is now.

〈注〉「わからない」について

「わかる」の意味が広いので，その否定形「わからない」も意味が広く，英語に直すにはよく考えなければならない。1. 識別できる，2. 内容を理解するの項ではそれぞれ「わからない」の例文もあげた。3. 知識・情報を得るの項でも「わからない」

の例をあげている。何か英語で尋ねられてよくわからない時，何でも I don't know. ですませるわけにはいかない。各項にあげてあるような，内容にふさわしい表現をしなくてはならない。

4. その他

わかりやすいんですよ[すぐわかります]。
　It's quite easy [simple].
　You can't miss it. (場所探しなどで)
彼の手紙はたいへんわかりやすい[読みやすい]字で書かれていた。
　His handwriting in the letter was easy to read.
　His letter was easily readable.
彼の字はとてもわかりにくい[読みづらい]。
　His handwriting is hardly legible.
お酒に酔っているときの彼女の言ってることはちっともわからない。
　Her speech is incomprehensible when she's drunk.

【物わかり】
彼は物わかりがよい[話のわかる人だ]。
　He's a sensible person.
彼はときどき恐ろしく物わかりの悪いときがある。
　He's sometimes very unreasonable.

わかれる（別れる，分かれる）

1. 離別

その女の子は古いお人形さんと別れるのはいやだと言った。
　The little girl refused to part with [be separated from] her old doll.
〈注〉 refuse to part with [give away; give up] は，捨てない，手放さないということ。また part with はしばしば permanent separation（永久の別離）を意味する。refuse to be separated from ... の方は，いつも手元に置きたいということ。
その子は小さいのに母親と別れて暮している。
　The little girl lives apart [separated] from her mother.
その若夫婦は別れて暮している[別居している]。
　The young couple live(s) separated from each other.
〈注〉 2人がうまくいっていない含みがある。ただ別々に暮していることを言うのは live in different towns [cities / places]
彼は早く親に別れた。(死別)
　He lost his parents early in life.
あの人たちが別れたなんて驚いたよ。(離婚)
　I was surprised to hear that they had divorced.
〈注〉 They had separated. は別居中のこと。一定期間別居の後，法的に離婚の手続をとると They had divorced. となる。

【さよなら】
私たちは仲直りして[憎しみ合いながら / 黙って]別れた。
　We parted friends [enemies / in silence].
私たちはお互いに手を振って別れた。
　We waved good-by to each other.

【離散】
その一家は戦争中に別れ別れになってしまった。
　The family was broken up [separated] during the war.
パーティーの後みんなそれぞれに別れていった。
　After the party they went their own ways.

2. 分岐

branch off (**from**); **split** (**into**); **diverge** 〔*literary*〕
2キロほど先で道は二つに分かれる[小道が本道から分れている]。
　Two kilometers ahead
　{ the road splits [divides] (into two).
　{ a narrow road branches off from the main road.

3. 区分

be divided
2年生は45人ずつ2組に分かれている。

Second-year pupils are divided into two classes, forty-five children in each.
2年生は3クラスに分かれている。
There are three classes of second graders.
市政は21の部に分かれて行われている。
City administration is taken care of by twenty-one departments.
県の庁舎は二つの建物に分かれている。
The government offices are in two different buildings.
その本は10章に分かれている。
The book is divided into ten chapters.
レースが始まって15分後には，走者は大ざっぱに言って3つのグループに分かれてしまった。先頭集団，中間の集団としんがりの集団である。
Fifteen minutes into the race, the runners were split into roughly three groups, the leading, the middle and the trailing groups.

4．対立
この問題に関しては意見が分かれてしまった。
Opinions are [Opinion is] divided [split] on this issue.
They have different [differing] opinions about this issue.
委員会の意見が分かれてしまった。
The committee didn't agree.
The committee members were split [differed] in their opinions.
〈注〉 differ（自動詞）には対立の感じがある。

わく（沸く）

1．飲用の湯
沸かした湯（滅菌のため） sterilized water
沸きましたよ。
The water's boiled.（火を止めなさいの含みがある）
沸いていますよ。
The water is boiling.
The kettle is boiling.
The water is hot.（沸騰はしていない）
The kettle is singing.（沸いてシュンシュンいっている）
この水は一度沸かしたものです。
This water has been boiled.

2．風呂
（和式）風呂を沸かしてください。
Please heat the bath.
風呂が沸きました。
The bath is ready [hot].
〈注〉 西洋式バスで The bath is ready. と言えば，きれいにバスタブを洗っていつでも使えるようにしてあることか，または子供相手ならば，お湯が入れてあることになるだろう。

3．興奮で
スタジアム全体が彼のファインプレイで興奮にわいた。
The whole stadium rang [exploded] with excitement over his outstanding play.

わけ（訳）

1．意味
【わけがわからない】
君は何を言いたいのかわけがわからない。
I don't understand what you mean.
彼はときどきわけのわからないことをぶつぶつ言っている。
He sometimes mutters something unintelligible.
わけのわからないことを言うんじゃないよ。
Don't talk nonsense.

2．理由・原因・事情
【わけがある】
それにはわけがあるに違いない。
There must be a reason for it.
ときどき私はわけもなく落ち込むことがある。

Sometimes I feel depressed for no reason.

〈注〉「わけがあって」と for a certain reason

時代劇などで「わけあって…」などとよく使われるが，英語で for a certain reason などと言えば，知っているのにわざともったいぶって教えてやらない感じとなる。もし人の名誉に関することであれば何も触れないのが普通。

また，今はまだ明らかにできないが，やがて発表されるという含みで次のように言うこともできる。

For reasons that cannot be revealed [made known] yet …

… there is a reason but it cannot be revealed yet.

わけを話せばわかってくれますよ。

He will understand if you explain.

〈注〉説明が先にあればこれでわかる。事情説明が必要であれば次のように続けてもよい。

He will understand if you explain
{ why ….
what happened.
how it all came about. }

【どういうわけ(理由・事情)】

どういうわけで学校を退学したのですか。

Why did you quit school?

What's your reason for quitting school?

〈注〉２番目の例文は面接のような公式の場合（formal circumstances）ならよい。それ以外では堅すぎる。

学校が嫌いなわけは？

Why don't you like school?

いったいどんなわけがあって学校がいやなの？

Whyever can it be that you don't like school?

どういうわけで私の兄と知り合われたのですか。

How did you come to know my brother?

いったいどんなわけ[根拠]があって私が自分の仕事を十分果していないなんて言われるのですか。

On what grounds do you insist that I'm not doing my job?

あの人はどういうわけか，パーティーに来なかった。

She didn't come to the party for some reason or other.

私たちはどういうわけか最初から気が合ってしまった。

Somehow we { liked each other / got on excellently [well] } from the first.

〈注〉for some reason はなぜかわからないけれど…という puzzled feeling（当惑した気持）を表す。

【そんなわけ】

(説明が先行して)そんなわけでここにたった１人で住みつくことになりました。

That's why I came to live here alone.

そんなわけで私は故郷を出る方がよいと考えたのだ。

Under those circumstances I thought it better to leave my home town.

〈注〉such being the case（そんなわけで）は堅い表現であるから，公式文書で「上記の理由により…」のように改まった場合に適している。given those circumstances も同様で，日常の表現ではない。

【わけ(事情)がわかる】

(説明が先行し）それでわけがわかった。

That accounts for it.

Now I know what it's all about.

Now I understand the situation.

【わけ(事由・事情)がわからない】

なぜ彼女があんなに怒っているのかわけがわからない。

I don't see [I've no idea] why she's so angry.

何が何だかわけがわからない。

I don't understand anything at all.

It is all a mystery.

彼女のことはわけがわからない。ずいぶん長い間の付き合いなのにまだ彼女のことはわからない。

She's still a mystery to me. After all these years I still don't understand her.

3. 道理・成行き

わけのわかった人　a sensible person

あの子が怒るわけだよ。

She has good reason to be angry.

It's natural that she is angry.

【…である[する]わけがない】

彼女がそんなに忙しいわけがない。

She can't be so busy.

彼女がだれにだってそんなことを言うわけがない。

She can't have said such things to anyone.

【…というわけ】

君に腹を立てているというわけではないんだよ。ただ心配でたまらないんだ。

Not that I'm angry with you, but I feel very concerned about you.

君のことを心配しないわけにはいかないんだ。

I cannot help feeling anxious about you.

それでは北海道行きは1日3便しかないというわけですね。

Do you mean to say that there are only three flights a day to Hokkaido?

〈注〉 上の文は「念を押す」言い方で Did you say …? と同じような意味。

…というわけだ。(経過を述べて現在の状況を説明し，しめくくる言葉)

That's the present situation.

That's where things are [stand] now.

That's the way it is now [at this point].

わける（分ける）

1．引き離す

【引き分け】

彼はけんかしている子供たちを引き分けた。

He separated the fighting children.

【隔離】

医師たちは彼の病気をコレラと診断し，ただちにほかの患者から分けた[隔離した]。

The doctors diagnosed his illness as cholera and at once put him in quarantine [isolation].

【分離】

今日ではある特定遺伝子を分け[分離し]て取り出す新しい技術が開発されている。

There are some new techniques now for isolating specific genes.

2．分割する

先生はクラスを6つのグループに分けた。

The teacher divided the class into six groups.

【財産分け】

彼は財産を分けて子供たちに与えた。

He divided his property among his children.

【切り分け】

彼女はケーキを6つに切り分けた。

She cut [divided] the cake into six pieces.

主人は焼いた肉の塊を切り，客の皿に取り分けた。

The host carved the roast and served it.

サラダをこの小さいお皿に盛り分けてください。

Please put the salad onto these small plates.

【髪】

彼女は髪を頭の真ん中から分けて三つ編みにしていた。

She wore her hair in braids, parting it in the middle.

【山分け】

彼らは利益を山分けにした。

They split the profits half and half [fifty-fifty].

【頒布】

その人たちは市民全員に聖書を1冊ずつ分けることを企てている。

They are planning to distribute a copy of the *Bible* to everyone in the city.

【分け合う】

その頃は友だち同士でよく食べ物を分け合ったものだ。

Friends often shared their food in those days.

物をたくさん持っている人が他人に分けたがらないことがよくある。

Those who have a lot often do not wish to share (with others).

【かき分け】
私はその男を人込みの中で見つけ，人をかき分けて彼に近づいた。

I spotted the man in the crowd and pushed [elbowed] my way through to him.

【分配】
彼女はオレンジの箱を開けてみんなに３つずつ分けた。

She opened the boxes of oranges and gave
{ each of them three.
{ three to each of them.

〈注〉 distribute は分配の意だが堅い語なので，上のような普通の家庭の場合には使わない。
Queen Elizabeth distributed presents to children.
(エリザベス女王が（孤児院の）子供たちにプレゼントをくださった)のような場合ならば使える。

【割当て】
１万円が月々の衣料費として取り分けてあった。

Ten thousand yen per month was allotted for clothing.

皆で仕事をそれぞれに分けた。→わりあて

Different people are assigned different jobs.

3．分類する

［人主語］**classify**
［事主語］**be classified**

誤答はざっと３つの種類に分けられる。

The errors can be roughly classified into three categories [groups].

彼は宝石を色と重さによって分けた。

He classified the gems according to color and weight.

わざわざ

【わざわざ行く[来る]】
go [come] all the way to
go out of《one's》way to(寄り道をして)

遠い所をわざわざ[はるばる]いらしてくださってありがとうございます。

Thank you for coming all the way to see us.

彼はミネソタから君に会うためにわざわざ出て来るというのか。

Is he coming all the way from Minnesota just to see you?

【特にそのため】expressly; specially
彼は私の母の若い頃の写真を見せようと昔のアルバムをわざわざ取り出してきた。

He brought out his old album specially to show me pictures of my mother when she was young.

【労をとる】bother to; take the trouble to
本当にわざわざおいでになるには及びませんから。お電話でうかがえればよろしいのですから。

Don't bother [take the trouble] to come over. We can talk on the phone.

わすれる（忘れる）

1．忘却する

［人主語］**forget; think no more of**
［事物主語］**slip [escape]**《one's》**mind [memory]**

【忘却】
その事件のことはすっかり忘れてしまった。

The incident slipped out of my memory completely.

彼はどうしてもその事件を忘れることができなかった。

He just couldn't get the incident out of his head [mind].

あれは忘れられない日だ。

That was ⌊an unforgettable [a memorable, a never-to-be-forgotten] day.

【忘失】
彼の名前を忘れてしまった。

I've forgotten his name.

私は約束を忘れてしまった。

I forgot my promise.

手紙を出すのを忘れた。

I forgot to mail [post] the letter.

彼が（私に）会いに来るということを忘れた。

I forgot that he was coming to see me.

It just slipped my mind that he was coming to see me.

彼は息子におみやげを買ってやると約束したことを忘れてしまった。

He forgot that he had promised to bring his son a souvenir.

【失念】

今日がトミーの誕生日だということを忘れていた。

I forgot [I've forgotten] that today is Tommy's birthday!

〈注〉 過去形，完了形どちらでもよい。過去形にした場合は today was でも，today is でもよい。今日の夜遅くの発言なら was も可。

やかんを火にかけっぱなしにして忘れていた。

I forgot the kettle was boiling on the stove!

〈注〉 何かを忘れてそれに気づいたとき,「ああ忘れていた」は理屈から言えば現在完了のはずであるが,実際にはI forgot ...！と言う。この使い方は土地や人により異なるかもしれないが，たとえば「やかんを火にかけっぱなし」に気がついたというような前後関係では I forgot！の形が普通。

20年ぶりの再会で話しが尽きず，私たちは時のたつのも忘れて夜中まで話し続けた。

We met after twenty years. There was so much to talk about in fact, that we talked far into the night, forgetting the time.

【忘れ物】

これで練習帳を忘れたのは２度目ですよ。もうこれっきり忘れないように。

This is the second time you've forgotten [you forgot] (to bring) your exercise book. Don't let it happen again.

私は財布を忘れてしまった。

I forgot my purse.

【きっと】

忘れずに５時に声をかけてよ。

Don't forget [Be sure, Remember] to call me at five.

【忘れろ(苦にするな)】

あれはちとまずかったが，そんなこと忘れてしまいなさい。

That was a mistake,
but { think no more of it. / forget it.

cf. Don't let it bother you.（苦にするな）

過ぎたことは忘れてしまえ。

Let bygones be bygones.

【物忘れ】

私は何でもすぐ忘れてしまう。

I have a poor [bad] memory.

このところ物忘れがひどくなった。

I've become very forgetful these days.

2．置き忘れる

leave; leave behind; forget

傘を列車の中に置き忘れた。

I've left [forgotten] / I left [forgot] } my umbrella in [on] the train.

めがねをどこに(置き)忘れたのかしら。

Where have I left my glasses?

Where did I leave my glasses?

わたす（渡す）→ わたる

1．横断させる

溝の上に板を渡して歩きやすくした。

They laid a plank across the ditch to walk on.

渡しの船頭さんはもう20年間も村人を川の岸から岸に渡してきた。

The ferryman has taken the villagers across the river for twenty years.

今，海峡に橋を渡す工事をしている。(海峡横断橋を建設中だ)

Now they are building a bridge across [over] the strait.

2．手渡す

この手紙をお父様に渡してください。

Please hand this note to your father.

この紙をテーブルの向う端に座っている人に渡し[まわし]てくださいませんか。

Will you give [pass] this paper to the man sitting at the end of the table?

駅で母がそっと私に封筒を渡した。

At the station my mother slipped an envelope into my hand.

〈注〉 slipped は「そっと」の意味を含む。

【引き渡す】

酔っ払いは警察に引き渡された。

The drunkard was handed over to the police.

【引き換え】

このクーポンと引き換えに…をお渡しします。

This coupon can be redeemed [is redeemable; is good] for ….

You can get … (in exchange) for this coupon.

【支給】

私たちの給料は現金で渡される。

Our wages are paid in cash.

【委任】

彼にお金は渡せない[任せられない]。

He cannot be trusted with money.

【手放す】

伝来の土地[家宝]を人手に渡す

hand over [transfer] the hereditary lands [family treasures] to outsiders

どんなことがあっても君をだれにも渡さないよ。

I'll never leave you [part from you] whatever happens.

わたる(渡る, 亘る)

1. 越える, 横切る

go over; go [walk / run] across; cross over

【橋】

駅に行くまでに橋を3つも渡らなければならない。

I had to go over three bridges to reach the station.

年とった人には歩道橋を渡るのはひと仕事だ。

It's hard work for old people to walk over pedestrian bridges.

【道路】

道路を渡るときは必ず横断歩道を渡りなさい。

When you cross a street, be sure to walk in {a zebra zone. / a pedestrian crossing.}

【川】

橋ができるまでは, 川を渡るには渡し舟を使ったものだ。

Before the bridge was built people used ferryboats to cross [go across] the river.

【海峡】

あの(女の)人が去年の夏英仏海峡を泳いで渡ったんだ。

That woman swam (across) the English Channel last summer.

2. 移住する, 所有が移る, 暮していく

【渡り歩く】

彼は生涯町から町へ渡り歩いて暮した。

He wandered from place to place all through his life.

【世渡り】

お前は自己中心すぎる。そんな風では世の中は渡れない。

You are too self-centered. You can't get along in life like that.

【伝来】

仏教はその学問・美術とともに朝鮮を経て6世紀に日本に渡って来た。

Buddhism with all its learning and art came to Japan via Korea in the sixth century.

【人手に渡る】

彼の父の家は彼が借りた金を返済できなかったため銀行の手に渡ってしまった。

His father's house was foreclosed on [taken] by the bank because he had failed to make mortgage payments.

【行き渡る】
ワインが少なくてみんなに行き渡らなかった。
There wasn't enough wine to go round.
小冊子は皆さんに渡りましたでしょうか。
Has everyone got the booklet?
【渡り鳥】a migratory bird
ツバメは秋になると[涼しくなると]暖かい国に渡って行く。
Swallows migrate to warmer countries when autumn begins [the weather becomes cooler].

3. 及ぶ，続く
（空間）**extend; cover**
（時間）**continue; last**
【範囲】
汚染された地域は数マイルにわたった。
The polluted area extended over [for] many miles.
彼の知識は広範囲にわたっている。
His knowledge covers [extends over] a wide area.
【時間】
委員会は延々５時間にわたった。
The committee meeting continued [lasted] for five hours.
徳川将軍の治世は300年にわたった。
The Tokugawa shogunate lasted for three hundred years.
彼の長年にわたる遺伝学の研究に対して文化勲章が贈られた。
He was awarded the Order of Cultural Merit for his long years of research in genetics.
その事業は２世代に渡る大事業になるだろう。
The project will extend over two generations.

わびしい（侘しい）

【わびしい光景】 a desolate [dreary, cheerless, lonesome]《scene》
寒々とした冬の夕暮時，静かに絶えず吹きつづける風に鳴る松籟（しょうらい），それに耳を傾ける人一人というわびしい風景であった。
It was a dreary scene with a lone man listening to the wind blowing softly but insistently through a few pines on a cold winter evening.
せまり来る夕闇の中で古い教会と苔むした墓地はいかにもわびしげであった。
The old church and its moss-covered graveyard looked really lonesome and desolate in the gathering dusk.
【わびしい暮し】 lonely [sad, poor, forlorn]《life》
宴会のあと皆は家族の待つ家に，独り者のおれはわびしいからっぽの部屋に帰る。
We parted after the party, they to their families but I to my cold empty room.
彼らは一杯のお茶と一切のパンというわびしい食卓についていた。
They sat at table having their frugal supper of a cup of tea and a piece of bread.
その老夫婦は世間との交渉もなく貧しくわびしい暮しをしていた。
The old man and his wife lived in poverty, cut off from the world.
〈注〉「わびしい」は雰囲気であるから，風景や状況を付け加える必要がある。

わらう（笑う）

1. 楽しくて，おかしくて
【大笑い】laugh（ハハハと笑う）
彼が笑った。
He laughed.
彼が大笑いした。
He laughed heartily.
彼が笑いころげた。
He roared with laughter.
みんな笑いころげた。
They were convulsed with laughter.

みんなおなかが痛くなるほど笑った。

They all held [split] their sides with laughter.

みんなプッと吹き出した。

They burst out laughing.

They burst into laughter [a roar of laughter].

彼は私の心配を笑いとばした。

He laughed away my fears.

【にっこり笑う】 smile

彼女は通りすがりに私の方を見てにっこり笑った。

She smiled at me as she went by.

She greeted me with a smile in passing.

僕がケイトと一緒なのを見ると彼は皮肉っぽくにやりと笑ってさっさと行ってしまった。

Seeing me and Kate together, he smiled ironically and walked away.

【くすくす笑う】 giggle

若い女の子は何でもないことですぐくすくす笑う。

Young girls often giggle over nothing.

神道の祝詞（のりと）がおかしくて私たち子供は式の間中笑いをこらえるのがたいへんだった。

The Shinto Norito (prayer) sounded so funny we children could hardly smother our laughter during the ceremony.

〈注〉 smothered laughter は「こらえ笑い」で giggle とは区別される。

【くっくっと笑う】 chuckle（含み笑い）

老人はあの事件のこと[何かおかしいこと]を思い出して，ひとりでくっくっと笑っていた。

The old man chuckled
{ as he remembered that incident.
{ remembering something funny.

〈注〉 chuckle は愉快または満足で静かに笑うこと，またはひとりで喉の奥でくっくっと笑うこと。意地の悪い笑いではない。また，鶏の「コッコッ」も chuckle という。

【にっと笑う】

名 a broad [big] smile; a grin

動 smile broadly; grin（歯を見せて笑う）

男の子は歯を見せていたずらっぽくにっと笑った。

The boy grinned at me mischievously.

〈注〉 grin は happiness, pleasure, amusement を示すもので悪い意味はない。grin ironically（皮肉に笑う）grin maliciously（悪意のある笑い方をする）のような副詞を加えると悪い意味になる。

2. 嘲笑する

ばかにして笑う laugh at

人は笑うだろうが，私はあきらめない。

People will laugh at me but I'll never give up.

〈注〉 類義語としては次のようなものがある。

jeer at 人をばかにした声を出したり，やじる。

sneer at 人を見下げた表情でせせら笑う。

ridicule 軽蔑的な言葉を浴びせて相手を笑いものにする（言った本人も品を下げることになる）。

3. 慣用表現

そんなことをすると人に笑われるよ。

You'll make a fool of yourself }
Everybody will laugh at you } if you do that.
You'll be laughed at }

そのコメディアンは病院のベッドの上でもまだ冗談を言って人を笑わせていた。

The comedian, even on his hospital bed, was joking and making people laugh.

それは笑ってすませることではない。

This is no [not a] laughing matter.

This can't be laughed away.

わり（割）・わりあい（割合）

1. 割合

この症例はまれと言えます。この病気を持っているのは新生児1万人に1人の割ですから。

This is rather a rare case; only one out of 10,000 new-born babies has this disease.

交通事故では10分に1人の割で死者が出ている。

One person is killed every ten minutes in

traffic accidents.

【頭割り】

私たちはクリスマスパーティーのために1人3000円の割でお金を集めた。

We collected 3,000 yen {per person / a head} for our Christmas party.

【比率】

もち米3にうるち米1の割合で混ぜます。

Mix 3 parts (of) mochi-rice with [to] 1 part (of) uruchi-rice. (1)

Mix mochi-rice and uruchi-rice (in a ratio of) 3 to 1. (2)

〈注〉 (1)は料理の本に多く使われ，(2)は科学書などに使われる。

支持者の数は4対1の割で反対派を上回った。

The supporters outnumbered the opponents (by) four to one.

得票数の割合は20対5であった。

The vote was twenty to five.

〈注〉 この the vote は 最終得票数の意味であるから単数でよい。

賛成票対反対票の割合は4対1であった。

The ratio of yes to no votes was four to one.

新規の市債発行(の議案)はほぼ4対1の割合で市議会を通過した。

A new city bond issue was passed (by a ratio of) nearly four to one.

2. ～割 →パーセント

ここにおいでの主婦の何割の方が職業を持っておられるでしょうか。

What percentage of the housewives here have jobs?

ほんの2,3割がフルタイムの職業についているだけですが，全体的には8割の人が何らかの仕事をもっています。

Only twenty to thirty percent of them work full-time, but altogether eighty percent of them have some kind of job. (1)

cf. Only twenty to thirty percent of them work full-time, although eighty percent of them have some kind of job. (2)

〈注〉 (1), (2)は同じ事実を述べたものだが，焦点の当て方が異なる。(1)は働いている人が多いことを強調し，(2)は正式に職についている人が少ないことを強調している。はじめにかかげた日本文の英訳としては(1)がぴったりする。

【利率】

彼は銀行から年利率4分の割で金を借りた。

He borrowed money from the bank at four percent interest (per annum) [4% p. a.].

〈注〉 日本語の「ローンを借りる」から考えて He loaned ... とすると，英語では彼が「貸した」ことになる。

cf. The interest rate will be raised. (利率が引き上げられるだろう)

3. 比較

【割に】

彼女は年の割に若く見える。

She looks young for her age.

【比較的】 rather; comparatively

テストは割にやさしかった。

The test was {comparatively easy. / easier than I (had) expected.}

僕たちは割にうまくやってます。

We are getting on rather well.

【割に合う】 pay; be worth

その仕事は割に合わない。

That business doesn't pay.

(面倒な割に)割が合わない。

It's not worth the trouble.

わりあてる（割り当てる）

【仕事】

彼はクラブ員それぞれに仕事を分配して割り当てた[分担させた]。

He allotted different parts of the job to each club member.

私は本の最後の章の翻訳を割り当てられた。

I was assigned to translate the last chapter of the book.

慈善バザーでは各自役割を割り当てられた。

Each person has a role in the charity bazaar.

【予算】
我々の部署への予算割り当ては要求額を下回った。

Our budget allotment is less than we requested [asked for].

〈注〉× … less than we { demanded. (強すぎる) / required. (主語が人は誤り) }
正しくは less than the project requires (事業が必要とする金額を下まわった)のように使う。

【時間】
仕事を今月末で終えるためには，時間を上手に割り当てなければならない。

We have to budget time well in order to { finish the work / get the work done } by the end of this month.

わりびき（割引）

1．値引き

discount; give [allow] a discount; take off

割引価格　a discount price

【まとめ買い】
まとめて買えば割引してくれますか。

Do you give a discount for bulk purchases [if we buy in bulk]?

【現金払い】
現金払いの場合は10パーセント割引します。

We'll give you a ten percent discount for cash.

〈注〉　この割引を a cash discount と言う。

【メンバー割引】
もし会員証を持って行けば，定価から10パーセントを割引してくれます。

If you have [bring] a membership card, they'll take ten percent off the price.

【団体割引】
団体には割引があります。

You can get reduced rates for a group.

(広告など) 団体割引あり

Group Rates Available

【割引切符】

a discount ticket

【その他の割引】
障害者割引[学生割引 / 高齢者割引]

a reduced fare for the handicapped [students / the elderly]

周遊割引切符　an excursion ticket

昼間割引切符　a reduced-price ticket for off-peak hours [times]

2．内輪の評価

彼女の言うことは割引して聞かなければ。

We can't believe everything she says.

We'd better not take her story at face value.

Discount her story.

Take what she says with a pinch [grain] of salt.

cf. We can discount the effects of unemployment at present. 〔*formal*〕

(＝We don't have to pay attention to …)

(今のところ失業問題の影響はそれほど気にしなくてよい)

わる（割る）・われる

割れる(自動詞) { { **break** 動自 / **be broken** } { **crack** 動自 / **be cracked** } { **split** 動自 / **be split** } }

割る(他動詞) { **break** 動他 / **crack** 動他 }

1．壊す

【陶器・ガラス・殻】

[割れた]

皿が手からすべりコンクリートの床に落ちて割れてしまった。

The plates slipped out of my hand and broke on the concrete floor.

[割れていた]

警察が来てみるとガラスの食器類がみんな床に落ちて割れていた。

The police came and found all the glassware broken on the floor.

［割る］

卵を３個ボールに割り入れてください。

Break [Crack] three eggs into a bowl. (1)

テレビで男の人が５枚の瓦を積み上げて空手チョップで割るのを見た。

On TV I saw a man break a pile of five roof-tiles by a karate-chop. (2)

彼の投げた石が的をはずれて隣家の窓ガラスを割ってしまった。

The stone he hurled missed the target and broke his neighbor's windowpane. (3)

〈注〉 上記３つの「割る」の例文中，(1)(2)は割るつもりで割ったのであるが，(3)はそのつもりがなくて割ったのである。

【氷】

今年は例年になく氷が薄いので，ほんの少しの重さでも割れる［ひびが入る］だろう。

The ice is unusually thin this year. It will break [crack] under [with] only the slightest weight.

【地面】

私は阪神大地震で道路が割れてぽっかり口を開いている写真を見た。

I saw a picture of a road in the Hanshin area which had { opened up / cracked open } during the earthquake.

【大木・岩】

神社のそばのイチョウの木に雷が落ちて根元まで真っ二つに割れてしまった。

The old gingko tree by the shrine was struck by lightning and split in two down to the roots.

〈注〉 thunderstruck は「雷に打たれた」ではなく「びっくり仰天した」の意味なので，ここでは使えない。

【割れやすい】

この頃の卵はすぐ割れてしまう。

Eggs break easily these days.

この瀬戸物のカップは割れやすいので，ていねいに取り扱ってください。

These china cups are fragile, so please handle them with care.

〈注〉◆「壊れ物・取扱注意」（ラベル）
Fragile——Please handle with care.
◆fragile, brittle ともに割れやすいことである。
fragile 軽くてきゃしゃなつくりであること。薄手のデリケートなカップなどを思わせる。
brittle 生地がもろく，弾性がなく，くだけやすい。比喩的に人の性格についても brittle personality（気難しい，怒りっぽい性格）のように使う。

2．薄める

ウイスキーの水割りをください。

I'd like a whisky and water.

「どうやって飲まれます？」「水で割って飲みます」。

"How do you drink it?" "I drink it [mine] with water."

あのバーはだめだよ。出す酒がどうも水で割ってある。

That bar's no good; it always ⌊waters down drinks [serves watered down drinks].

3．割算

50÷２＝25

Fifty divided by two equals [is] twenty-five.

10個のキャンディーは３人では割り切れないからだれか１人にはおまけがつく。

Ten candies cannot be divided by three equally, so someone gets extra.

4．比喩的表現

【分かれる】

その問題では自民党員の意見が２つに割れた［３つに割れた／今までになくいくつかに割れた］。

The LDP were
{ split ⌊on the issue. / split in three ways on the issue. / divided more than they have ever been.

この問題で意見が割れた。→わかれる

Opinions are [Opinion is] split on this issue.

They have differing [different] opinions about this issue.

委員会の意見が割れた。

The committee didn't agree.

The commitee members were divided on the issue.

【下回る】

選挙の投票率は60%を割った。

The election turnout fell below 60 percent.

【割れるような】

割れるような頭痛がする。(ひどい)

I have a splitting headache.

割れるような拍手であった。(すごい)

There was thunderous applause.

わるい(悪い)

1. 不良・粗悪

bad; inferior; poor; coarse

【品質】

品質の悪い品物

inferior goods; low quality goods

あのスーパーは時として品質の悪い品物を売っていることがある。

That supermarket sometimes sells inferior products.

こんなに安いということはきっと物が悪いんだろう。

These are so cheap they must be poor in quality [inferior goods].

この品は安物で品質が悪い。

These are cheap and poor in quality.

このブランドの米は君がいつも買っているのより品質が悪い[落ちる]。

This brand of rice is {not as good as / a lower grade than} the brand you usually buy.

味が悪い。

It doesn't taste good.

今年は作柄が悪い。

We've had a poor crop this year.

暑いのでポテトサラダが悪くなった[腐った]。

The potato salad has gone bad [off] in the hot weather.

【人について】

彼は頭が悪い。

He's not very bright.

〈注〉 He's dull. は小学生などでは clever の反対で頭の悪いこと。大人についは人間に面白味のないこと。

have a weak head [mind] for figures [chemistry] は stupid で算数[化学]に弱いこと。しかし, weak-minded は「優柔不断な」の意である。

私は記憶が悪い。

I have a poor memory.

彼は顔色が悪い。

He looks pale.

彼女は器量が悪い。

She isn't good-looking.

私は太って背が低くてスタイルが悪いから,その手の服は着られない。

I'm too short and fat to wear that style.

〈注〉 自分以外の人についてこう言っては失礼である。

このところ視力が悪くなってきた。

My eyesight is getting worse these days.

2. 不健康

ill; sick

【不快】

今朝は気分が悪い。

I don't feel well this morning.

どうしたの? どこか悪いの?

What's the matter? What's wrong?

〈注〉 きつい調子で What's the matter with you? は「どうかしているんじゃないか」となじるときに使われる。また語調にかかわらず よくない意味なので注意。

【病気】

どこが悪いんですか。

What's the problem? (病気を含め「どうしたのか」を尋ねる言い方)

彼はいつから悪いんですか。

How long has he been ill?

私は胃が悪い。

I have a weak stomach.

私は心臓[腎臓]が悪い。

I have heart [kidney] trouble.

彼女の容態が急に悪くなった。

Her condition has taken a sudden turn for the worse.

彼女はたいへん悪い[危篤だ]。

She is seriously ill.

3. 有害な，悪性の

悪いかぜがはやっている。

There's a bad cold going around.

喫煙は健康に悪い。

Smoking is ⌊bad for health [harmful (to health)].

人工保存料の中には人体[健康]に悪いものもある。

Some artificial preservatives are harmful.

〈注〉 この文の前後関係によって harmful to health に決っている場合には to health は不要。また injurious も「有害な」の意であるが，たいへん堅い語。

【食あたり】

今朝食べた魚が悪かったんだ。

The fish I ate this morning didn't agree with me.

4. 故障・不都合

【機械】

テレビの調子が悪くなった。

My TV set has gone out of order.

時計の調子が悪い。

Something's wrong with my watch.

このカメラは調子が悪い。

This camera doesn't work.

【道・天候】

雨のあとで道が悪かった。

The road was in bad condition after the rain.

私たちが出発した日は天気が悪かった。

The weather was bad on the day we left.

【誤り】

私の論文に目を通して悪いところを指摘していただけませんか。

Will you read through my paper and point out anything that you think ⌊should be changed [needs changing]?

5. 正しくない，不正な

wrong

テストで不正行為をするのは悪いことだ。

It's wrong to cheat on a test.

君は自分のしたことを悪いとは思わないのか。(恥ずかしくないのか)

Aren't you ashamed of what you've done?

私は悪いことをいたしました。(反省・告白)

I have done wrong.

【罪】

私のおじいさんは生きものの命をとるのは悪いことだと思って野菜しか食べない。

My grandfather feels it is sinful to take life, so he eats only vegetables.

〈注〉 sin は宗教的な悪で，神に対して犯す罪である。
→つみ

【邪悪な】evil; wicked

彼の頭に悪い考えがふと浮かんだ。もし仲間の2人を亡き者にしたら，彼は財宝を独り占めできるのだ。

An evil thought crept into his mind, that if the other two were killed, he'd be able to have the treasure all to himself.

【責め】

私が悪かったのです。あなたが悪いのではありません。

It was my fault, not yours.

I was (in the) wrong, not you.

The blame is on me.

6. 社会的・人間関係上よくない

【性質】

彼女は性格が悪いとみんな言っている。

People say she's ill-natured.

【申し訳ない】
長いことお待たせして悪かったですね。
　I'm sorry I've kept you waiting so long.
もし彼を傷つけるようなことをしたのなら本当に悪かった。
　I'm very [so awfully] sorry if I've done something to hurt him.
〈注〉 so awfully は女性語。
本当に悪いんですけど 4 時に歯医者の予約があるので，この辺でお開きにさせていただきたいのです。
　I'm terribly sorry but I have an appointment to see a dentist at four, so I'm afraid we'll have to stop.
たいへん悪いんですが，どうぞお引き取りください。
　I'm really terribly sorry, but I'll have to ask you to leave.
〈注〉 会社やレストランなどで酔っ払いや迷惑な客に言う言い方。
【悪く言う，悪く思う[思わない]】
彼のこと悪く思わないでね。善意でやったことなのだから。
　Don't think ill of him. He meant well.
　Please don't have any hard feelings. He meant well.
こんなことで私たちの間が悪くなったりしませんように。
　I hope this will not cause any hard feelings [stand between us].
だれでもほめられて悪い気はしない。
　Everybody likes to be praised.
　No one is displeased when they are praised.
彼の言葉で彼女はひどく気を悪くした。
　She was terribly hurt by his words.
　His words hurt her terribly.
【悪いことは言わない】
(「…したらどうですか」という助言に対し，あまり気のない顔をしている人に)悪いことは言わないから私の言うことを聞きなさい。
　Listen to me. I know what I'm talking about.
悪いことは言わない。こう言うのもみんなお前のためなんだ。
　Listen. I'm saying this for your own good [benefit].
【口が悪い】
彼は少々口が悪い。
　He's rather sarcastic.

《関連語》
sarcastic　辛辣なこと。
too outspoken　ずばり，ずばりと言いすぎること。
loud-mouthed　大声で饒舌で自信過剰なこと。
foul-mouthed　下品な言葉を使うこと。

【悪い習慣】
悪い習慣がいったんつくとなかなか直せない。
　It's hard to get out of bad habits.
【評判が悪い】
彼は学生の間で評判が悪い。
　He isn't very well-liked by [popular among] his students.
彼は評判が悪い。
　They don't like him very much.
　People don't speak well of him.
あの店は評判が悪い。
　That store has a bad reputation.
悪い人[やつ]だ。
　You rascal! (いたずらな人に冗談で)
　You monster! (「人間じゃない」の意だから強い言い方だが，もちろん冗談)
【いたずら】
彼が小さな男の子を 2 人つれて来たんだが，すごく悪いんだ。
　He brought his two little boys, who were very very naughty.
【悪口を言う】
　speak ill of; slander (誹謗(ひぼう)・中傷する)
陰で人の悪口を言うのはよくない。
　It's not good
　　{ to speak ill of others behind their back.
　　{ to say bad things about others.

彼は酔っ払って上司に向かって悪口の数々を浴びせた。

He got drunk and called his boss all sorts of names.

〈注〉 call《someone》names とは「ばか野郎，とんちき…」の類を叫ぶこと。

立候補者たちは互いにほかの候補者の悪口を言い合った。

The candidates were slandering each other.

〈注〉◆「中傷する」には smear the candidate のほかに mudsling (原義は「泥を投げる」) の表現があり，まさに日本語の「泥仕合」に当る。

◆「悪口を言い合う」の類義語

criticize each other harshly

speak ill of each other

rake each other over the coals

◆「けなす」の類義語

belittle　軽視する，見くびる，けなす。

Don't belittle me. (見くびるな［ばかにするな］)

deride　あざける，ばかにする。

discredit　信用を落とさせる。

They tried to discredit the candidate by disclosing scandalous behavior with women. (対立候補者を女性問題を持ち出しておとしめようとした)

【人聞きが悪い】

そんなこと言わないで。人聞きが悪い！

Don't say that. / What a thing to say! } What would people think if they heard you?

【不都合，悪いところ】

悪いところに来たね。

You came at [an unlucky [the wrong] moment.

彼はちょうど悪いところに来た。

His visit was ill-timed.

彼は悪くするとだめかも知れない。

He'll fail, I'm afraid [I fear].

悪いことに道がぬかるみだった。

Unfortunately, [What was bad was (that)] the road was muddy.

悪いことに彼はひどいかぜまでひいてしまった。(何かよくないことがあったが「おまけに」)

What was worse [To make things worse], he caught a bad cold.

【悪くないね】

(何か提案がありそれを受ける場合)

That's not bad.

That wouldn't be bad.

ノルウェーに行くのも悪くないね。(いくつかの案があり，A もよいがB (ノルウェーへ行くこと) も悪くないとき)

Going to Norway wouldn't be bad.

やってみるだけなら悪くないんじゃない？

There's no harm in trying.

(辛辣(しんらつ)に) もう少ししっかり働いても悪くないんじゃないか。

It wouldn't hurt you to work a little harder.

［付録］ 不定詞および同格 that 節で修飾できる名詞

(1) 子供が波とたわむれる光景
(2) 頼まれたらいやと言えない性格
(3) 今にも泣き出しそうな顔つき
(4) 正しい者が勝つという信念
(5) 誰にも言わない約束
(6) 夏休みにアメリカに行く計画
(7) 一生独身を通す決意
(8) 高校に合格した喜び
(9) 魚を焼く匂い
(10) 子供たちが母を呼ぶ声

日本語における動詞の連体形は，自由に名詞を修飾できる機能をもつ。このような名詞修飾の形を英訳する際，何のためらいもなく関係代名詞（ことに which）を使って直訳を試みる誤りが非常に多い。上記のような例は，関係代名詞では処理できないものである。名詞の内容を規定する機能をもつ文法形式には，関係節以外にも，前置詞＋名詞，前置詞＋動名詞（～ing)，分詞，不定詞(to ～)，同格 that 節などがある。このなかの不定詞および同格 that 節は，被修飾語になり得る名詞が一部の特殊なものに限られている。それらの名詞群をリスト 1, 2 に示す。

1. 「to-リスト」について

名詞を不定詞で修飾する形には 2 種類がある。

第一は，

- someone to help me（誰か私を助けてくれる人）のように被修飾語―ここでは someone―が不定詞の主語にあたる場合
- something to eat（何か食べるもの）のように被修飾語―ここでは something―が不定詞の目的語にあたる場合

などで，このように被修飾名詞と不定詞の関係が上記の文法的関係になる時は被修飾語になる名詞について特に制限はない。

第二は，courage to say what one thinks right（正しいと思うことを言う勇気）や time to start（出発する時間）のように，不定詞部分が被修飾名詞の内容規定もしくは副詞的関係にある場合である。この不定詞修飾では，修飾される名詞は特殊なものに限られる。

代表的な例を挙げると，

- 「時・所・方法」に関する語（time, place, measures, ...）
- 「志向・傾向」に関する語（hope, intention, tendency, wish, ...）
- 「不定詞と連結しやすい形容詞」の名詞形（ability, curiosity, strength, possibility, ...）
- 「不定詞と連動する動詞」の名詞形（agreement, decision, invitation, temptation, ...）

などである。最初に挙げた例文(1)～(10)のうち，不定詞で表現できるのは(5)(6)(7)である。(5)(6)(7)には不定詞がぴったりする。それは，約束・計画・決意がすべて「未来」，すなわちこれからのことに関する思考を表す語であるためだ。「to-リスト」には，この第二の不定詞修飾の対象となる観念名詞を挙げている。

2. 「that-リスト」について

名詞のなかで同格 that 節(関係節ではなく)で修飾できるのは，どのような性質の名詞であろうか。

- 「事実・報道」に関する語（fact, information, news, ...）
- 「思考・陳述」に関する語（belief, idea, statement, ...）
- 「感情・判断」に関する語(feeling, realization, supposition, ...)

などである。詳しくは『英語語法大辞典』（大修館書店）p.1137を参照されたい。

冒頭の例文(1)～(10)のうち，同格 that 節で表現できるのは(4)である。同格 that 節の守備範囲は事実に関する分野であり，“the fact that ...”がこの文法形式の代表である。「that-リスト」には that 節で修飾できる名詞を挙げている。

［英訳についての注意］

これらのリストの内容は，日常的に使うと思われる語に限って選び出したもので，リストにない語でこの文法形式に当てはまる語ももちろんある。リストに見当たらない場合は辞書で用法を確かめていただきたい。

なお(1)(2)(3)(8)(9)(10)に関しては，英訳にあたっては名詞形に固執せず，むしろ動詞を上手に使い，文全体として同じ意味を表現することが望ましいだろう。(4)(5)(6)(7)はもとの日本文の形を直訳することができるが，これらでは修飾される名詞がみな動詞形をもとにしているので，それぞれ(　)内に示したように動詞を使う方が自然な文になる。英語では**動詞を活用**するのが普通である。

英訳例

(1)　……光景をじっと見ていた。
I watched children playing in the waves.

(2)　あの人は生れつき親切で，……性格だ。
She is by nature too kind to refuse anyone anything when she is asked.

(3)　今にも……な顔をしていた。
He looked {as if he {was / were} going / ready} to cry at any moment.

(4)　my belief that the just will win in the end (I believe that ...)

(5)　our promise not to tell anyone about it (We promised not to ...)

(6)　her plan to go to the States this summer (She's planning to ...)

(7)　her determination to remain single all her life (She determined to ...)

(8)　……の喜びでいっぱいだった。
She was very happy that she passed the entrance examination to high school.

(9)　……匂いがした。
I smelled fish being grilled.

(10)　……声が聞こえた。
I heard children calling their mother.

1. to-リスト（不定詞で修飾できる観念名詞）

ability	everywhere	obligation
aim	freedom	occasion
agreement	heart (have no heart to)	offer
ambition	hurry (be in a hurry to)	opportunity
anxiety	impulse	order
anywhere	inclination	permission
arrangement	intention	place
attempt	invitation	plan
care (take care to/not to)	kindness	position (be in a position to)
cause	law	possibility
chance	leave	power
condition (in a condition to)	leisure	promise
confidence	liberty	proposal
courage	licence	readiness
curiosity	longing	reason
decision	means	refusal
demand	measures	request
desire	mind	resolution
determination	money	right
direction	necessity	room
duty	need	somewhere
effort (make efforts to)	notice	strength
enough	nowhere	temptation

tendency threat time	way will willingness	wish

〈注〉 to-リストに挙げた名詞の中で不定詞修飾以外に「of＋動名詞」(また名詞によっては for, in＋動名詞) で修飾できるものがある。

ex. chance

海外にゆくチャンス　her chance to go abroad [of going abroad]

本表中このような用法が可能なのは次の名詞である。

aim, chance, freedom, intention, need, necessity, obligation, plan, possibility, power

2. that-リスト（同格 that 節で修飾できる名詞）

agreement ＊ assurance belief care (take care that) ＊ claim conclusion condition (on condition that) ＊ confidence ＊ decision ＊ demand ＊ doubt evidence fact fear feeling hope	idea impression knowledge law ＊ message news notice (give [take] notice that) ＊ notion opinion order ＊ point possibility ＊ principle probability promise ＊ proposal ＊	report request ＊ rumour statement suggestion supposition suspicion theory thought truth understanding view wish ＊ word

〈注〉 ＊印の付けてある語は to-リスト，that-リスト両方に挙げてある語である。どちらの形を使うかは文脈の中できまる。また promise, wish など未来に向けての内容を表す that 節では will, would, should など未来の助動詞を使うとよい。

ex. the promise that we will [would] never tell anyone about it

関連語索引

左側の語義は，右側の見出しの中に含まれている。

運搬する → はこぶ
映写 → うつる・うつす
得手 → とくい
エネルギー → ちから
得る → うける，おさめる・おさまる，とる・とれる，もらう
延引 → のびのび
援助 → おうえん
演ずる → やる
延長する → のびる・のばす
追い抜く → ぬく
お祝い → あいさつ
横断させる → わたす
応対する → せっする，でる
応募する → もうしこむ・もうしこみ
大いに → たいへん，とても・とっても
大まか → あらい
おおよそ → だいたい
お気に入り → きにいる
置き忘れる → わすれる
お悔やみ → あいさつ，くい・くやむ
贈る → あげる
起す → たてる
おごる → ごちそう
幼い → ちいさい
お辞儀 → れい
おしまい → いじょう
襲う → みまう・みまい
教わる → まなぶ
穏やかな → しずかな・しずめる
おぼれる → まよう
おまけに → うえ
思い出させる → ちゅういする
思い悩む → なやむ・なやみ
思い惑う → まよう
面白い → ゆかい
面白くない → つまらない
思ったとおり → やはり・やっぱり
およそ → …ばかり
及ぶ → たっする，わたる
折 → とき
お礼 → あいさつ
愚かな → ばか
終り → あがる
終りにする → やめる
恩師 → おん
恩人 → おん
音調 → ちょうし

〈か〉

快 → かんじょう
甲斐がない → むなしい
快感 → いいきもち
解決する → すます・すむ，まとめる・まとまる
会合 → かいぎ
開催する → ひらく，もよおす
概して → だいたい
会社 → きぎょう
解析 → すうがく
開通させる → とおす
回転する → まわす・まわる
回復する → なおす・なおる
解放する → たすける・たすかる
帰る → もどる
顔色 → かお，まっさお
学業 → べんきょう
確実 → きめる
学習する → ならう
確信 → だいじょうぶ
確保する → とる・とれる
家系 → いえ，かぞく
重なる → ぶつかる
果実 → み
数 → いくつ，すうがく
家族 → いえ
課題 → もんだい
かたき → てき
形 → かた，すがた
価値ある → たりる
価値のない → つまらない
勝ち目 → かつ
活用する → いかす
活力 → げんき
家庭 → うち
過度 → …すぎ，すぎる・すごす，むり

軍事 → せいじ
刑 → さいばん
警戒 → ようじん
警戒する → きをつける
計画 → つもり
経験する → なめる
警告 → あぶない
形成 → つくる
傾聴する → きく
激励 → がんばる
血液 → ち
血縁 → ち
結局は → やはり・やっぱり
結実する → むすぶ・むすび
決心 → かくご
欠席する → やすむ・やすみ
決断 → いし，きめる
決定 → きめる
欠点 → きず
欠乏 → ない
結末 → あと
けばけばしい → しつこい
懸案 → しゅくだい
原因 → せい，もと，わけ
けんか → あらそい・あらそう
厳格な → こわい・こわがる
嫌疑 → うたがう・うたがい
元気 → はりきる
言及する → ふれる
言語 → ことば
健康 → げんき
現在 → ただいま
建築する → たてる
倹約する → かけい
権力 → ちから
合意 → いっち
幸運 → つごう
効果 → かんじ
合格する → とおる
豪語 → いばる
口座 → ぎんこう
交差させる → くむ
行進 → 行列
豪勢な → ぜいたく
耕地 → とち
好都合 → べんり
購読する → とる・とれる
効能 → きく
公表 → はっぴょう
興奮 → しげき
高揚させる → もやす・もえる
考慮する → くむ
越える → わたる
五感 → かんかく
顧客 → とくい
故郷 → いなか
国連 → こくさいれんごう
焦げ → まっくろ
個々に → べつ
心地 → きもち
心 → むね
心配り → き
快い → いい・よい
故障 → わるい
応える → こたえ・こたえる
答える → おうじる
こだわる → くよくよする
滑稽 → おかしい
固定する → とまる・とめる
ことさら → とくに・とくべつ
このところ → さいきん
好み → かんじょう，しゅみ
好む → えらぶ
拒む → ことわる
雇用 → さいよう
怖い → すごい
壊す → やぶる・やぶれる，わる・われる
混同 → いっしょに
困難 → こまる，めんどう
困難な → むずかしい
困惑する → こまる

〈さ〉

材質 → もの
採取する → とる・とれる
最上級 → いちばん

十分 → たくさん，たりる
十分な → りっぱ
十分に → ちゃんと
充満 → いっぱい
収容人数 → ていいん
重要な → たいせつ
修理する → なおす・なおる
終了 → おえる・おわる
受諾 → うける
主張 → ぎろん
出演する → でる
出現 → すがた
出席 → でる
出版する → だす
首尾よく → うまい・うまく
趣味 → このみ，せんす
主要な → だいいち
樹立する → たてる
順位 → ばん
巡回する → まわす・まわる
遵守する → まもる
順序 → しだい，ばん
順番 → ばん
準備 → ようい
上演する → やる
紹介 → あいさつ
正気な → たしか
上記の → いじょう
正午 → ひる
上質 → いい・よい
焼失する → やく・やける
上昇 → あげる
上手 → うまい・うまく
状態 → ようす
招待客 → きゃく
承認 → きょか
承認する → みとめる
将来 → さき
除外 → いがい，べつ，ほか
除去する → とる・とれる
職業 → しごと
食事 → たべる
食する → たべる
助言 → そうだん
所在 → ある
所持 → ある
所持する → もつ
所有しない → ない
所有する → もつ
所有物 → もの
助力 → ちから
助力する → たすける・たすかる
調べる → あらう
視力 → め
思慮に欠ける → らんぼう
知る → わかる
しるし → てん
事例 → ばあい
審議 → かいぎ
診察してもらう → みせる
真実 → じじつ，ほんとう
信じる → ほんき，ほんとう
親切にも → せっかく
心臓 → むね
心配する → なやむ・なやみ
身辺 → そば
進歩 → よい
進歩する → のびる・のばす
信用する → しんじる・しんこう，ゆるす
信頼できる → かくじつ
心労 → き
図案 → もよう
炊事する → たく
吸い取る → すう
姿 → かげ，ようす
好き嫌い → き，すき
すくい取る → くむ
すぐに → ただいま
優れた → すばらしい
図形 → すうがく
スコア → しあい
ずっと長く → いつまでも
ずばり → ちょくせつ
する → やる
成果 → み
性格 → いし

直ちに　→　しだい
立ち上がる　→　たつ
立ち寄る　→　よる
達する　→　およぶ
達成する　→　たっする
たとえ　→　どんな
他人　→　ひと
楽しい　→　ゆかい
頼む　→　ねがう・ねがい
たぶん　→　たしか
ためらう　→　えんりょ
頼り　→　たのむ・たのみ
頼る　→　うったえる
堕落　→　くさる
足りている　→　まにあう
多量　→　たくさん
短縮　→　ちぢむ・ちぢめる
短縮する　→　つめる・つめこむ・つまる
担当　→　うけもち
担任　→　うけもち
断念する　→　あきらめる，やめる
地位　→　たちば
地域　→　とち，へん
違い　→　さ
近頃　→　さいきん
近づく　→　よる
血筋　→　ち
仲介する　→　とおす
忠告　→　いい・よい，ようじん
忠告する　→　ちゅういする
中断　→　じゃま
中途　→　かてい
中毒　→　あたる
兆候　→　ようす
調子　→　ぶん
嘲笑する　→　わらう
調整する　→　なおす・なおる
跳躍　→　とぶ・とばす
貯金する　→　たまる・ためる
散らかる　→　きたない
治療する　→　なおす・なおる
鎮静する　→　おさめる・おさまる
沈着　→　ゆうゆう
鎮痛　→　らく
追加　→　べつ，ほか
費やす　→　はらう
通過　→　すぎる・すごす
通学　→　かよう
通勤　→　かよう
通信　→　れんらく
通行する　→　とおる
通行止め　→　こうつう
通用する　→　とおる
突きさす　→　たてる
突き出る　→　でる
突き止める　→　みつける・みつかる
尽きる　→　きる・きれる，ない
土　→　ち
続く　→　わたる
つまむ　→　はさむ・はさまる
積み上げる　→　かさなる・かさねる
貫く　→　とおる，ぬく
出会う　→　ぶつかる
提案　→　あいさつ
低下する　→　おちる・おとす
提供する　→　だす
締結する　→　むすぶ・むすび
停止する　→　とまる・とめる
提出する　→　だす
抵触する　→　ふれる
訂正する　→　なおす・なおる
程度　→　へん，ほど
適合　→　あわせる
適合する　→　あう，かなう，むく・むき・むける
出来事　→　じけん
適切　→　いい・よい
適切な　→　ただしい
的中　→　あたる，あてる
テスト　→　しけん
デザート　→　おやつ
手配　→　ようい
手放す　→　わたす
手間　→　めんどう
手回し　→　まわす・まわる
出迎え　→　むかえる

入手する → はいる
入賞する → はいる
人間関係 → かんけい
認識する → みとめる
値切る → たたく
寝込む → ねむる・ねる
寝そべる → ねむる・ねる
値段 → いくら
熱心 → はりきる
熱する → やく・やける
熱中 → ねつい・ねっしん，むちゅう
値引き → べんきょう，わりびき
値引きする → まける
寝坊する → ねむる・ねる
根回し → まわす・まわる
寝る → やすむ・やすみ
年齢 → いくつ，とし
農地 → はたけ
能力 → しかく
逃れる → ぬける，まぬがれる
遺す → のこる・のこす
残り → あと，のこる・のこす
のために → （…に）とって

〈は〉
場合 → とき
肺 → むね
輩出する → だす
配慮 → しんぱい
配慮する → きをつける，ちゅういする
はかどる → はこぶ
はかない → むなしい
吐く → もどす
励み → しげき
初めて → はじめ
始める → ひらく
場所 → ところ，へん
働きかける → うったえる
発覚 → みつける・みつかる
発言 → はなし
抜粋する → ぬく
発生 → できる，でる
話し合う → そうだん
はねつける → ふる・ふりまわす
省く → ぬく
場面 → ところ
払い戻す → もどす
範囲 → なか，へん
反映 → うつる・うつす
繁華街 → まち
判決 → さいばん
反抗 → はんかん・はんぱつ
番号 → ばん
犯罪 → けいさつ
反省 → まちがえる・まちがう
反対側 → むこう
販売する → うる
被害 → こまる
控えめ → えんりょ
日陰 → かげ
引き入れる → ひく
引き受ける → もつ
引き起す → よぶ
引き返す → もどる
引き算 → ひく
引きつける → ひく
引き抜く → ぬく
引き離す → わける
引き渡す → わたす
飛行 → とぶ・とばす
被災者 → さいがい
日差し → かんかん
飛散 → とぶ・とばす
非常手段 → きょくたん
ひそかに → そっと
引っ越す → うつる・うつす
必死 → むちゅう
筆写 → うつる・うつす
必然 → どうしても
引っ張る → ひく
必要 → いる・いらない
ひどい → すごい
人柄 → ひと
ひどく → ひどい
非難 → いけない
非番 → やすむ・やすみ

本当に → まったく
翻訳する → なおす・なおる

〈ま〉
埋没 → うめる・うまる・うもれる
負かす → たおす・たおれる，やぶる・やぶれる
任せる → あずかる・あずける，たのむ・たのみ
まさに → …ばかり
まじめ → ほんき
間違い → ちがう・ちがい
まっすぐにする → のびる・のばす
まなざし → め
間に合わせる → すます・すむ
招く → よぶ
まねる → ならう
まもなく → もう
迷う → なやむ・なやみ
見合う → おうじる
見受けられる → みえる
見失う → まよう
見送り → おくる
味方 → つく
店番 → みせ
道筋 → かてい，みち
身にしみる → こたえ・こたえる
見張り → ばん
身分 → ぶん
身分不相応な → ぜいたく
耳にする → きく
無為 → ぼんやり
ムード → きぶん
無益 → しかたない・しかたなく，だめ，むだ
向け → よう・ようじ
むごい → ひどい
無駄な → もったいない
夢中 → あこがれる，いっしょうけんめい
無頓着な → へいき・へいせい・へいぜん
無料の → ただ
命令 → だめ
迷惑 → こまる，へいこうする
目にとめる → みとめる
免許 → きょか
面倒を見る → せわ
持ち分 → ぶん
もっぱら → ただ，…ばかり
元へ戻す → なおす・なおる
基づく → よる
もともと → だいたい
物陰 → かげ
物足りない → さびしい
もはや → もう
燃やす → たく，やく・やける
模様 → ようす
もらう → とる・とれる
問題 → はなし

〈や〉
約 → ほど
役立つ → べんり，まにあう
安売り → うる
やっかい → じゃま，せわ
やはり → また・または
敗れる → まける
やり通す → ぬく
やわらかく → そっと
唯一 → …ばかり
有害な → わるい
有給休暇 → きゅうか
優先 → さき
郵便為替 → かわせ
夢 → きぼう
揺り動かす → ふる・ふりまわす
許す → かんべんする
揺れ動く → ゆれる
結わえる → むすぶ・むすび
よい → けっこう
用意する → もうける
容易な → やさしい
容易に → すぐに
要件 → しかく
容赦する → ゆるす
用心 → いけない
用心する → きをつける，ちゅういする

［著者略歴］

松井恵美（まつい　えみ）

1923年生れ。東京府立第五高女を経て津田塾大学（当時専門学校）を卒業。現在は岐阜に在住。岐阜市立女子短期大学英文科で42年，岐阜聖徳学園大学で7年間英語教育に従事。現在，岐阜市立女子短期大学名誉教授，岐阜聖徳学園大学名誉教授。著書に『英作文における日本人的誤り』（大修館書店）がある。

Margaret Lynne Roecklein（マーガレット・リン・レックライン）

1944年米国生れ。シカゴ大学で英語学英文学修士号，コロラド大学で理論言語学修士号を取得。1975年に来日以来，岐阜大学で教鞭をとる。20年以上にわたる日本での英語教育を通し，言語と認識，言語の変化，統語論と意味論の狭間の問題等に興味を持つようになり，目下鋭意これらの問題に取り組んでいる。

和英表現辞典（わえいひょうげんじてん）

NDC 837　866p　22cm

初版第1刷――2003年6月10日
第2刷――2004年9月1日

著者――松井恵美（まついえみ）／M・リン・レックライン
発行者――鈴木一行
発行所――株式会社大修館書店
〒101-8466 東京都千代田区神田錦町3-24
電話03-3295-6231販売部／03-3294-2357編集部
振替00190-7-40504
［出版情報］http://www.taishukan.co.jp

装丁者――川畑博昭／イラスト(函) 白川三雄
印刷所――文唱堂印刷
製本所――難波製本

ISBN4-469-04164-5　Printed in Japan